A
GUIDE
TO THE
SOURCES
OF
BRITISH
MILITARY
HISTORY

Edited by ROBIN HIGHAM

ources of
History

There are at least two ways in which this book is unique: it provides a single unified introduction to bibliographical sources of British military history, and it suggests topics which are as yet untouched, and are therefore likely candidates for future research. Moreover, it includes guidance in a number of fields in which no similar source is available at all, gives information on how to obtain access to special collections and private archives, and links military history, especially during peacetime, with the development of science and technology.

It is the purpose of each contributor to lead the interested researcher (for this is a book to be used, not simply to be read) along paths both familiar and unfamiliar, and in the process to point

s and weaknesses of the
discussion.
intention that this work
ustive; it is designed in-
overlooked gap in the
British history and thus
pringboard from which
histories can be written.
British history, of war-
nd technology will find
ference tool.

Professor of Modern
and of Technology and
State University. He is
urnals *Military Affairs*
space Historian* and the
r of several books and
history of warfare.

A Guide to the Sources of British Military History

EDITED BY
ROBIN HIGHAM

SPONSORED BY THE
Conference on British Studies

UNIVERSITY OF CALIFORNIA PRESS
BERKELEY AND LOS ANGELES, 1971

University of California Press
Berkeley and Los Angeles, California

International Standard Book Number 0-520-01674-2
Library of Congress Catalog Card Number 74-104108
Printed in the United States of America

Dedicated to
J. JEAN HECHT,
—one of the founders of the
Conference on British Studies—
whose idea this volume was.

EDITORIAL NOTE

The task of an Editor is never easy. In this case he had to work with people whom he has never met. While each author was sent a style guide, instructions and a tentative table of contents for the whole book, together with a draft of the Introductory chapter—for which amending suggestions were asked—each was allowed a certain leeway. Some problems of style, notably numbering, did not appear until the volume was well along. Thus some authors solved the difficulty of adding new items by an alphabetical numbering while others simply placed the item at the end of the list. Moreover, it must be remembered that the deadline for chapters was October 1967 and that some essays were, therefore, in the Editor's hands for much longer than others which appeared up to fourteen months later. In many cases the Editor and his Adviser were allowed to see drafts, and in fact urged authors to submit them, so that major misinterpretations of the approach could be corrected. Nevertheless, authors were given on the whole a free hand as to what they included. Each chapter reflects, therefore, individual approaches to the problem. Readers will notice that in some cases jointly written chapters flow as one all the way through and others are split into sections, each with its own bibliography. General information applicable to many chapters is to be found in the Introduction.

There are some problems which users will note. Most authors have done relatively little with foreign materials, partly because the subject has more often than not best been covered in English, since it is British; partly because relatively little work has yet been done in the foreign archives; and partly because being limited in space, authors have chosen to mention that foreign work which gives the best bibliographical introduction to the other side of the story. Much material, however, on the Second World War is coming to light in the works published by the French Comité d'Histoire de la 2ème guerre mondiale and the new International Committee, whose American newsletter put out by Professor Arthur Funk of the University of Florida contains a bibliography of research done since 1945 together with a list of libraries holding special World War II collections. Similarly, some authors have not had access to manuscript sources and other collections of papers, but have nevertheless described these briefly to point researchers towards what may be rewarding materials for their particular topic. In many cases it is hard to know what exists because of the paucity of guides to library collections. Moreover, as an exploration of the London Library catalogues will reveal, these lists are by no means infallible bibliographic guides, especially to items which appeared in series. Another problem has to do with the vision of his task on the part of each author. Add to this the problem of what is considered military, or diplomatic, or scholarly.

Some items are listed which are not referred to in the text, either because their value is self-evident or because they appeared after the chapter was completed.

Many other special problems could be mentioned, such as the fact that major military historical articles have often appeared not in the "best" journals, but in other publications, and indexers have often neglected these items, especially if their titles were obscure. Let us repeat, then, that what we have attempted to provide is a guide to what exists, not by any means a complete bibliography.

Military history is a vast field in which very few have been trained. At the risk of falling between two stools, the Introduction attempts to provide a basic background and guide for the novice as well as a handy reference for the more experienced scholar. Thus on the one hand it points to used-book catalogues and on the other to the more precise and sophisticated chapters which follow. At the same time, it was the logical place in which to list a number of general works which cover in a broad way the material in several subsequent chapters. Thus we have aimed in part for breadth as well as depth.

The Editor wishes to take this opportunity to thank all the authors for their co-operative spirit, even when faced with a demand for a complete revision. Most of us owe a debt of gratitude to the Bureau of General Research at Kansas State University which supported this project and to Mrs. Pauline Norby who did the retypings required.

We are most grateful to Professor Peter Paret of Stanford University for his comments and help.

ACKNOWLEDGEMENT

The Editor wishes to make special note of his indebtedness to Professor Arthur Marder of the University of California, Irvine, who in the midst of all his other activities and the work on his monumental study of the Royal Navy was good enough to serve as the Editor's unpaid advisor, reading each chapter and making useful comments and suggestions, as well as by his cheeriness and many letters keeping the Editor's spirits up and his nose to the grindstone during the long months of this project. In our book he deserves more than the RUSI's Chesney Memorial Gold Medal conferred upon him in 1968 for other services.

CONTENTS

AUTHORS

W. H. G. ARMYTAGE was born in South Africa in 1915 and educated in Cornwall and at Cambridge. He left schoolmastering to join the army where he served from 1939–1945 in the Orkneys, North Africa, and Italy and was mentioned in Dispatches. Since then he has been successively Lecturer, Senior Lecturer, Professor, and Pro-Vice-Chancellor in the University of Sheffield. He has also lectured at universities in Germany, U. S. A., and Australia. His Ballard Matthews lectures in the University of Wales have been published as *The Rise of the Technocrats* (1965). He has contributed to the *Biographical Dictionary of Scientists* (1969) and is the author of *A Social History of Engineering* (3rd ed. 1969), together with some eleven other books. One of these, *Yesterday's Tomorrows,* is a study of predictive fantasies, which themselves owed much to medieval wars.

DR. CHRISTOPHER BARTLETT was born near Wimborne, Dorset, in 1931. He was educated at the local grammar school, at University College, Exeter, where he gained a first class honours degree in history, and at the London School of Economics. He has taught in the Universities of Edinburgh and the West Indies, and is now lecturer in modern history in the University of Dundee. His published work includes two books, *Great Britain and Sea Power, 1815–53,* and a biography of *Castlereagh,* together with a number of articles on diplomatic and naval history.

DANIEL A. BAUGH is an Associate Professor of History at Cornell University and a Councillor of the Navy Records Society. He was born in Philadelphia, July 10, 1931. After graduating from the University of Pennsylvania he was commissioned in the U. S. Navy and spent three years in destroyers. He left the navy in 1957 and went abroad to study at Cambridge University, where he received the Ph.D. degree in 1961. The same year he began teaching at Princeton. His *British Naval Administration in the Age of Walpole* was published by the Princeton University Press in 1965. He is preparing a volume of naval administrative documents from 1714 to 1748 for the Navy Records Society, but is also working on other subjects within his broad field of interest—the social, economic, and administrative history of England from the seventeenth to early nineteenth century.

JOHN BEELER, currently Professor of History, University of North Carolina at Greensboro, was born 1 August 1916 at Franklin, Ohio. He received the A.B. and M.A. degrees from The Ohio University, the Ph.D. degree from Cornell University. He is a member of Phi Beta Kappa, a Fellow of the

Royal Historical Society, and is a member of other professional organizations. A veteran of both World War II and the Korean Conflict, the latter service including a tour in the Office of the Chief of Military History, he now holds the retired rank of Captain, CA, AUS. He revised and edited C. W. C. Oman's original essay, *The Art of War in the Middle Ages, 378–1515 A.D.* (Cornell University Press, 1953), and is the author of *Warfare in England, 1066–1189* (Cornell University Press, 1966), as well as of several articles on Anglo-Norman military history.

RONALD CLARK was born in London in 1916. During the last war he was attached to Canadian and British forces as a War Correspondent, landed in Normandy on D-Day and subsequently covered the campaign in North-West Europe. He remained in Germany for some two years after the armistice, attended many of the War Crimes Trials—including that at Nuremburg—and began as a freelance author in the early 1950's. He has since written on many aspects of science and society and his books include *The Birth of the Bomb,* which deals with early European work on nuclear fission; *The Rise of the Boffins* on British science in the last war; and *Tizard,* the life of the late Sir Henry Tizard. He is also the author of *The Huxleys,* a study of the family since the time of T. H. Huxley, and a life of the late Professor J. B. S. Haldane (both published in 1968). He is completing a life of Sir Edward Appleton, the pioneer of ionospheric research, and has recently been commissioned to write a full-scale account of Einstein and his times.

DR. C. G. CRUICKSHANK was born in Aberdeenshire in 1914, and was educated at Aberdeen, Oxford, and Edinburgh Universities. He entered the British Civil Service in 1940, and served as British Trade Commissioner in Ceylon, Canada, and New Zealand between 1951 and 1962. His Oxford D.Phil. thesis was published in the Oxford Historical Series as *Elizabeth's Army.* A revised edition which appeared in 1966 was reprinted as an Oxford Paperback in 1968. He is also author of *Army Royal: Henry VIII's Invasion of France, 1513* (1969) and has contributed to *The English Historical Review, History Today, Army Quarterly,* and *Punch.*

F. H. DEAN was born in Manchester in 1909. After he had taken his degree at Manchester University, a period of research into the international law of partnership was followed by call to the bar and a short spell of teaching. He was then in general practice on the Northern Circuit until the war, during which he was on active service with the Royal Air Force in the Middle East and East Africa. Although he returned to practice at the end of 1945, he had by that time developed a taste for life in contact with the Services and for travel, and doubtless this influenced him in 1950 to accept an appointment as an Assistant Judge Advocate General. Since then he has served in almost every part of the world in which British forces are to be found, from the United Kingdom to Mauritius, and from Korea to New Zealand. He has officiated at a number of important trials, including the case of Sergeant Page, in which the court had to consider whether the medieval doctrine that a victim of murder must be "under the King's peace" protects a British soldier who in a foreign country kills a local citizen from being tried by a British court-martial. Mr. Dean has recently become Vice Judge Advocate General, and although as he looks out over Trafalgar Square he says that he feels some nostalgia for the years of sitting in court and travelling the world, he also looks forward to being continuously within reach of the libraries and theatres of London and of the hills and downs of Surrey and the Cotswolds.

MARTIN EDMONDS was born at Nottingham, England, in 1939. He graduated from Keele University in 1962 in International Relations, and was a post graduate student at Manchester University. In 1965 he was appointed onto the Staff at Manchester, and in 1966 became lecturer in Strategic Studies at Lancaster University. His Masters thesis was a study of the Doenitz Government, in the context of the politico-military-strategic situation at the end of the Second World War, and his Doctoral thesis (in progress) is a study of weapons procurement in Britain between 1945 and 1957, with reference to the procurement of military aircraft. He has published articles in *International Affairs,* and has a chapter in *The Military Technical Revolution* (ed.) John Erickson, Praeger, 1966. His academic interests are in Military Sociology, Civil-Military Relations, and Strategic Studies, especially the technical, economic, psychological and social constraints upon the use of force in pursuit of political objectives in the International context. He is married, with two children.

LT. COL. WILLIAM A. FOOTE, JR. was born at Kansas City, Missouri. Dr. Foote attended college at Kansas City and at the Kansas State College of Emporia. He began his military service in the 110th Engineers (Missouri National Guard) in 1928, accepted a reserve commission in 1931, and entered active military service in the fall of 1940.

Returning to college while still in the service, he received the B.S. degree from the University of Maryland in 1954 while in Germany, and the M.A. degree from the University of Texas at El Paso in 1949. He retired there with the rank of lieutenant colonel in July of 1949. His doctoral degree was received from UCLA in 1966.

He became interested in the Anglo-American British army while doing graduate research at Texas Western, and wrote both his thesis and later his dissertation on it. He has taught at Texas A & I University, Kingsville, and is now living in San Diego, California.

DONALD C. GORDON was born in Melbourne, Australia, in 1911. He received his B.A. from the College of William and Mary in 1934, where he was Phi Beta Kappa, and his M.A. and Ph.D. (1947) from Columbia University. Since 1946 he has been a member of the faculty of the University of Maryland, where he is currently a professor of history. In 1957–58 he was a Fulbright Senior Research Scholar at the Australian National University in Canberra. One of the authors of Gewehr, Gordon, Sparks and Stromberg, *The United States: History of a Democracy,* he is better known for his two books, *The Australian Frontier in New Guinea, 1870–1885* (1951) and *The Dominion Partnership in Imperial Defence, 1870–1914* (1965). He also published *The Moment of Power* in 1969.

MARGARET GOWING is a graduate of The London School of Economics. She was a wartime civil servant and in 1945 joined the Cabinet Office to work with Professor Sir Keith Hancock on the civil war histories. She was joint author of two volumes in this series, *British War Economy* (with Sir Keith Hancock) and *Civil Industry and Trade* (with E. L. Hargreaves). She also helped with the editorial work on the series. In 1959 she became Historian and Archivist of the United Kingdom Atomic Energy Authority and in 1964 published *Britain and Atomic Energy, 1939–1945*. She is engaged on a second volume of atomic energy history but her main post since 1966 has been as Reader in Contemporary History in the University of Kent at Canterbury.

A. J. R. GROOM was born at Lincoln, England, in 1938. He has studied and taught at University College, London, Lehigh University, Pennsylvania, and the Institut Universitaire de Hautes Etudes Internationales, Geneva. He is at present Lecturer in International Relations at University College, London. He is currently terminating a study of *British Thinking About Nuclear Weapons* and has published articles on Strategic Studies, International Relations Theory, and International Institutions, in *World Politics, Political Studies*, the *Yearbook of World Affairs, International Affairs*, and *Revue Militaire Suisse*. His interests are Strategic Studies, International Relations theory and International Institutions.

PAUL GUINN was born at the Hague, the Netherlands, in 1928 of American parents and educated in schools in Europe and the United States. He received his B.A. from Swarthmore College and Ph.D. in Modern European History from Harvard University in 1962, and in between served in the United States Air Force. His *British Strategy and Politics, 1914–1918* (Oxford: Clarendon Press, 1965) was awarded the George Louis Beer Prize by the American Historical Association. He is currently an associate professor of history at the State University of New York at Buffalo.

ROBIN HIGHAM was born in Britain in 1925. Educated there and in the United States, he served as a pilot in the Royal Air Force, 1943–1947. He graduated *cum laude* from Harvard in 1950, obtained an M.A. at the Claremont Graduate School (1953) and his Ph.D. from Harvard in 1957. He has taught at the Universities of Massachusetts and North Carolina (Chapel Hill) and is currently Professor of Modern British History and of Technology and War at Kansas State University. In 1968 he became Editor of *Military Affairs* and in 1970 of *Aerospace Historian*. His books include *The British Rigid Airship, 1908–1931: a study in weapons policy* (1961), *Armed Forces in Peacetime: Britain 1918–1940* (1963), *The Military Intellectuals in Britain, 1918–1939* (1966), and the edited *Bayonets in the Streets* (1969) and *A History of Air Power* (1972). He co-authored with the late David H. Zook, Jr., *A Short History of Warfare* (1966). Higham has also published, in 1970, an edited work, *Official Histories: essays and bibliographies.*

J. MACKAY HITSMAN was born on April 19, 1917, in Kingston, Ontario, Canada, where he attended school and Queen's University. After receiving an M.A. in History in 1940, and being commissioned in the Canadian Officers Training Corps, he spent six and a half years in the Canadian Army. Retired on medical grounds in the rank of captain, he became a civilian archivist with the Historical Section, Army Headquarters, Ottawa (now the Directorate of History, Canadian Forces Headquarters, Ottawa). He received his Ph.D. from the University of Ottawa. He was a Fellow of the Royal Historical Society and the author of *Military Inspection Services in Canada 1855–1950; The Incredible War of 1812: A Military History;* and *Safeguarding Canada 1763–1871.* Dr. Hitsman, having been hospitalized for three years with a spinal disorder, died on 10 February 1970.

JOHN KEEGAN is Senior Lecturer in Military History at The Royal Military Academy, Sandhurst. He was born in 1934 and educated at King's College, Taunton, Wimbledon College, and Balliol College, Oxford, where he read modern and specialised in military history and the theory of war. After coming down from Oxford, in 1957 he visited the United States on a Balliol travelling scholarship. He has written many articles on strategy and modern military history.

P. K. KEMP entered the Royal Navy in 1904 and served in submarines until in an accident in 1928 he lost a leg. He spent the whole of the Second World War in the Naval Intelligence Division (U-boat tracking room). In 1950 he became Head of the Naval Historical Branch, Admiralty Archivist and Librarian, and from 1948 was also assistant editor and then from 1955 to 1968 Editor of the *Journal of the Royal United Service Institution.* He is the author of books on sailing as well as of a string of naval histories including *Nine Vanguards* (1951), *The Fleet Air Arm* (1954), *H. M. Submarines* (1952), *H. M. Destroyers* (1956), *Prize Money* (1946), and the official one-volume popular account *Victory at Sea 1939–1945* (1957). He also edited the Admiral Boscowen and Admiral Fisher papers for the Navy Records Society. Kemp is now retired, but recently edited a new history of the Royal Navy (1969).

CHRISTOPHER LLOYD was born in 1906 and was educated at Marlborough and Lincoln College, Oxford. From 1930 to 1934 he was a lecturer at Bishop's College, Quebec, moving from there to the Royal Naval College at Dartmouth. At the end of the Second World War he went to the Royal Naval College at Greenwich, becoming Professor of History in 1962 five years before his retirement. He has written a large number of books including *The Navy and the Slave Trade* (1949), *The Nation and the Navy* (1961), *William Dampier* (1966), *The British Seaman* (1968) and with J. L. S. Coulter, *Medicine and the Navy* (4 vols., 1961).

RUDDOCK F. MACKAY was born in 1922. Mr. Mackay was initiated into naval life through serving as a rating in the Royal New Zealand Navy from 1942 to 1946. During that time he graduated B.A. (N.S.) in history. After the War, he graduated (in subjects other than history) at the Universities of Oxford and London. Having taught as a schoolmaster in England and New Zealand, he served as a lecturer at the R. N. College, Dartmouth, from 1954 to 1965. In the latter year his biography *Admiral Hawke* was published at the Clarendon Press and he also took up his present appointment as Lecturer in Modern History at the University of St. Andrews, Scotland. He is currently working on a life of Admiral of the Fleet Lord Fisher.

ARTHUR MARDER was educated at Harvard (B.A., 1931, M.A., 1934, Ph.D., 1936). He has been Professor of History, University of California, Irvine, since 1964; George Eastman Visiting Professor, Oxford, 1969–1970; and Chesney Memorial Gold Medalist of the Royal United Service Institution, 1968. He is author of *The Anatomy of British Sea Power: a History of British Naval Policy in the Pre-Dreadnought Era, 1880–1905* (1940; winner of the George Louis Beer Prize of the American Historical Association, 1941); *Portrait of an Admiral: the Life and Papers of Sir Herbert Richmond* (1952); *Fear God and Dread Nought: the Correspondence of Admiral of the Fleet Lord Fisher of Kilverstone* (3 vols., 1952–1959); and *From the Dreadnought to Scapa Flow: the Royal Navy in the Fisher Era, 1904–1919* (5 vols., 1961–1970).

COMMANDANT NEIL ORPEN is South African-born and was educated in South Africa and at Cambridge, England, where he obtained an M.A. Honours degree in English Literature and Modern History, before returning to South Africa in 1935, where he was a journalist and an officer in the Coast Garrison Force when war broke out in 1939. He served in the S. A. Forces throughout the war, seeing active fighting in North Africa. Continuing in the Active Citizen Force after the war, he went on the Reserve in 1955, while commanding the 1st. Field Regiment, Cape Field Artillery, with the rank of Commandant (Lieut-Colonel). Having written the history of his own regiment as a labour of love, from 1964 onwards he has been employed full-time writing military histories for South African regiments and for the S. A. Ex-Services National Council, and the *Encyclopedia of Southern Africa*. He has just published a new official South African volume on the East African and Abyssinian campaigns (1968).

F. N. L. POYNTER (born in London in 1908) is Director of the Wellcome Institute of the History of Medicine and has an international reputation as a medical historian. He is an honorary member of many international and national societies and academies and has received honorary doctorates from the University of California and the Christiaan-Albrechts Universität at Kiel in Germany. He is the editor of a quarterly journal and an extensive monograph series and has written several books and many articles on his subject.

A. H. K. SLATER is a graduate of the Universities of Aberdeen and Oxford, and after service in the British Army in the Second World War in the Royal Artillery and on the General Staff, he joined the Home Civil Service in the United Kingdom in 1947. His service has included a period with the Public Record Office, and for the past 15 years has been concerned with various aspects of Government civil science policy. He is at present (October 1967) serving in the Department of Trade and Industry.

ALBERT TUCKER was born in 1923 in Toronto, Canada. After serving with the Royal Canadian Air Force during the Second World War, he attended the University of Toronto, where he received his B.A. in 1951 and M.A. in 1952. From 1954 to 1958 he was a resident tutor at Dunster House, Harvard University, where he completed the Ph.D. in 1958. After one year as Lecturer in History at the University of Illinois he returned to Canada, spending seven years at the University of Western Ontario and moving from there to York University, Toronto, in 1966, where he is now Professor of History. He has published a number of articles on English Conservative thought in the late nineteenth century and on the problems of reforming the British army between 1870 and 1914. His present research focuses on a social study of the nineteenth-century army.

DR. M. J. WILLIAMS was born in 1934, in Newport, Monmouthshire. He was educated at Newport High School and Jesus College, Oxford, where he read History, taking his B.A. in 1955, M.A. in 1961, D.Phil. in 1962. He then worked as a Research Assistant in the History of Parliament Trust, 1962–1964. He is now History Lecturer at Norwood Technical College (Inner London Education Authority).

His publications include: "Thirty Percent: A Study in Casualty Statistics," J.R.U.S.I., February, 1964; "The Treatment of the German Losses on the Somme in the British Official History," J.R.U.S.I., February, 1966; and "The Egyptian Campaign of 1882" in *Victorian Military Campaigns,* edited by Brian Bond, 1967.

I

INTRODUCTION

Robin Higham

In relatively pacific nineteenth-century Britain there was a considerable interest in military history. But as part of the reaction to the horrors of the First World War, in the first decades of the militant twentieth century the subject has been generally ignored. Since the Second World War, however, two new generations have become increasingly interested in it.

The long history of Britain has contained a steady core of military affairs. As Professor Armytage once pointed out, by 1815 the English had been involved in nine wars against Scotland, 13 in Ireland, and innumerable minor wars with Wales; in addition, they had fought 24 with France, seven with Spain, four with Holland, two with the Americans, and one each with the Danish and the Algerians. The influence of war is one which has been neglected in too many studies, thus making them unbalanced.

Research in British, and indeed world, history cannot be undertaken without a knowledge and understanding of military affairs. In the twentieth century the pendulum has swung too far to the left, and too much of the writing of the history not only of Britain but also of the United States has concentrated on domestic politics and on the influence of Labour, of depressions, and of other socio-economic factors. Too little attention has been paid to the role which defence and the armed forces have played in the evolution of the State in peace as well as in war. We have only to look at some of the newer writings in British history to realize that now a reinterpretation is taking place (101). The Roman Conquest is now being seen in the light of the small population which the legions had to conquer. The role and place of the Anglo-Saxons has been soundly reevaluated to their immense credit by C. Warren Hollister, who has shown how sophisticated was the Anglo-Saxon military organization and how it influenced the Norman (172). Moreover, our whole interpretation of the Norman victory at Hastings has had to be revised because Hollister has shown that no other army in Europe in the Middle Ages had to face the ordeal which Harold's experienced in fighting two major battles within a few weeks. During much of medieval time, the State was organized for defence and security from internal and external enemies whose eruptions had to be met by a loyal force. Taxation during the period was primarily, therefore, for

1

maintenance of the armed forces. In fact, it would not be stretching the truth to say that much of early British constitutional history involved problems of security and must, therefore, be seen in relation to a changing military picture. That canvas was coloured by the personality of the monarch, by internal politics, by strategic considerations, and by developments in military techniques and tactics. All of these are topics with which John Beeler, who has devoted much study to the problems of location of castles, covers in his chapter.

Though in the Renaissance Britain was largely concerned with internal problems, her armed forces developed in several notable ways. The Navy, as Daniel Baugh, an historian of the Admiralty, indicates became a permanent part of the forces of the Crown and consolidated the technological innovations in armament, sailing and navigational techniques which had begun to appear, even if so very slowly, in the late Middle Ages. The relationship of these developments to others in the State has only rarely been touched upon, and generally only in particular aspects, as did Robert Greenhalgh Albion in his classic study, *Forests and Sea Power* (5). The Tudor-Stuart period is also a most important one where land forces were concerned. C. G. Cruickshank, an expert on Elizabethan military science, deals not only with the relatively obscure developments of the Henrician and Elizabethan ages, but with the very important rise of Cromwell and developments to the end of the seventeenth century, an age in which the military were intimately involved in constitutional crises, but a military understanding of which has often been evaded by historians of the period. Even Sir Charles Harding Firth, who wrote of Cromwell's Army (92), admitted in his Preface that he really knew nothing about armies. And J. F. C. Fuller, who might have devoted a volume to Cromwell, never got farther than a chapter (100).

The studies of the eighteenth century should serve to emphasize the main theme of the work—a nation at war. One of the great truths of British history has been the usual unpreparedness of the armed forces for the wars which they were called upon to fight. Military history cannot be confined simply to battles and campaigns, but has inevitably to deal also with the country and its manipulation of its resources in wartime as well as, and increasingly more importantly, with its attitude and actions towards its armed forces in peacetime. These are themes which both Christopher Lloyd, Professor emeritus of the Royal Naval College, and William Foote, a student of the British Army in America, cover. They are dealt with in a different way by W. H. G. Armytage of Sheffield, an historian of technology, in his long chapter on the relationship of science, technology, and national developments to the armed forces, a topic which he continues in his nineteenth century chapter. In the Victorian age the impact of technology becomes much more pronounced and the stimulus of military demand begins once more to affect national development, for good and ill. The transition from the rather stable ways of the eighteenth is leisurely for the Army until late in the nineteenth century. The exception is the medical field. As Albert Tucker, Professor of History at York University in Ontario and a specialist on the Cardwell reforms, notes, the Crimean

War made hospital care a matter of high politics and introduced certain other changes which gave the middle class a better position in the Army. The impact of new technology came faster in the Navy despite the amount of resistance. The changes are to be seen in warship development and in the social evolution in the Navy, though economically the pay scale remained stable from 1840 to the First World War. C. J. Bartlett, noted for his study of the Navy in the first half of the Victorian age (18), and Ruddock Mackay, currently working on a life of Admiral of the Fleet Lord Fisher, share the naval century between them since their interests divide rather neatly at 1853/54.

The first ten chapters cover the period to the twentieth century. The remaining chapters are divided between those which carry the bibliographical story of the Services to the present and those which deal with some specialized theme, such as law or medicine, for the whole period of British history.

Three chapters are devoted to the First World War. The Navy is covered by Arthur Marder, the pre-eminent authority on the Royal Navy of the day (208); the Army, by M. J. Williams, a student of casualty figures; and the nation at war, by Paul Guinn, author of the recent volume (147) on British strategy and politics, 1914–1918. The Editor deals with the history of the R.A.F. to 1945. There follows a chapter on the interwar years by John Keegan of the Department of Military History at Sandhurst; the Second World War on land is the province of M. J. Williams, who also did the First; the war at sea is handled by no less an authority than Lt/Cdr. P. K. Kemp, until recently the Naval Librarian and Head of the Naval Historical Branch of the Ministry of Defence and an author in his own right; and the nation at war by Mrs. M. M. Gowing, one of the official historians of the war and now of the Atomic Energy Authority, and A. H. K. Slater, of the Ministry of Technology. Equally important is the chapter devoted to the development of science and technology whose author, Ronald W. Clark, already has a high reputation for his studies of "boffins" (48) and his biography of Sir Henry Tizard (49). And this group of bibliographical guides is concluded with some words of advice on the sources for studies of British defence since 1945 by A. J. R. Groom of London and Martin Edmonds of Lancaster, both specialists in modern British defence problems.

A special chapter on sources of British military history in the Commonwealth was originally intended to have but one author. But in the end, in a happy Anglo-Saxon-style compromise, it was possible to acquire the services of two official historians outside the United States, each of whom contributed part of a chapter: J. MacKay Hitsman of Canada, an authority on the War of 1812 and on Canadian defence in general, and Commandant Neil Orpen, the author of several volumes in the Union of South Africa's official and unofficial histories. Our biggest disappointment has been that we have been unable to get either an Australian or a New Zealander to contribute; the solution finally adopted, after the book was due at the Press, was for the Editor to provide a short section on each.

The remaining sections of the book are topical in a wider sense. Donald

Gordon, a scholar of imperial defence (104) at the University of Maryland, discusses colonial warfare from 1815 to the present, a period in which it has had a military significance much out of proportion to the recognition it has had both historically and even politically in its own time. Then come two chapters dealing with medicine. The naval side is the handiwork of Professor Lloyd, one of the authors of the multi-volume history of naval medicine (183). The military account is by Dr. F. N. L. Poynter, Director of the Wellcome Historical Medical Museum and Library. And lastly, there is the chapter on legal history by F. H. Dean, Deputy Judge Advocate-General of the Forces.

The reader should be aware from the foregoing that this is not just a random group of scholars from a particular clique, but a wide-ranging group of experts who are specialists primarily in the military aspects of British history and who have devoted a considerable part of their scholarly or working lives to military history in its broadest aspects.

Probably the most important things to be said about this volume are not, however, what it covers and who are its authors, but why it was conceived, what it tries to do, and what is unique about it.

It was decided to undertake this project because there is no bibliography of British *military* history in the widest sense of that word. Only three volumes of the Oxford *Bibliography of British History* (239) have appeared. The *Oxford History of England* (240) deals with this aspect of British history, but the entries are limited. Moreover, most of these volumes have been in print for long enough that they have not been able to take much note of recent scholarship. Even recent essays in a number of cases still reflect the old biases. This leaves a considerable gap to be filled in the knowledge of most historians and writers. It was part of the conception of this volume, moreover, that it would provide not only a useable single-volume bibliography, together with a general introduction to the problems of research in British military history, but that equally usefully it would suggest topics which still need to be explored. Thus there are at least two ways in which it is unique: that it provides a single unified introduction to bibliographical sources of British military history and that it points up areas yet untouched.

But more than this, for the first time it provides guidance in a number of fields in which no similar source is available at all. And beyond this, it ties in military history, especially during peacetime, with the development of science and technology, something which almost no other bibliographical work in the field has attempted to do. There is an old truism that says that British history provides an advanced look at American. If this holds true, then insight into many problems faced today by the United States may be gained by studying those the British have already tackled.

It is the purpose of each author, then, to lead the interested researcher, for this is not a book to be read *but to be used,* along both familiar and unfamiliar paths to virgin material. In the course of this journey he attempts to point out the strengths and weaknesses of the materials. Thus in the modern period, the researcher will find comments upon official histories, parliamentary papers, journals, and other printed matter. While in the earlier chapters he will be directed to observe both manuscript collections, often involving linguistic problems, and groundbreaking works some of whose points are now no longer valid.

Another unique feature is that each author provides information on how to obtain access to special collections and private archives.

It is not the intention that this work should be exhaustive. Printing costs and probably market alone preclude that. But it is intended that the work should fill a very much overlooked gap in the whole field of British history and thus provide a springboard from which more balanced histories can be written which will remind students everywhere that many of Britain's greatest achievements were due to her military prowess and to the security which her armed forces gave the island.

GENERAL BIBLIOGRAPHICAL GUIDANCE. The Appendix to this chapter contains basic works of reference, lists of journals, libraries, and other information which pertain in general to more than one chapter. What follows is an introduction to that material. The appendix here, however, differs slightly from that in other chapters in that not all the items in it are in the text, and in that journals have been segregated from books. Otherwise the arrangement is, as in all the other chapters, alphabetical to make it easier for librarians and others to check the items mentioned against their card catalogues or bibliographical files.

Following an initial overview of bibliographies listed by Besterman (21), the investigator will need some basic reference books. The Royal Historical Society has been endeavouring to supply these. Cheney (44), and Powicke, Johnson and Harte (253) are essential for chronology, and N. P. Ker (184) lists the surviving books from medieval libraries. Bibliographies of Romano-British, Anglo-Saxon and Celtic England have been compiled by W. Bonser (27).

An enormous amount of labour can be circumvented by examining the five volumes of A. T. Milne, published from 1900 to 1933. These contain names of books and articles on Great Britain from the year 400 A.D. So far this project has got down to the year 1914 (213ff). His earlier volumes, giving an annual coverage of writings on British history, began in 1934 and are models of their kind, divided as they are most conveniently into sections illustrating various aspects of the period (220).

Specialist bibliographies by Conyers Read (257), Godfrey Davies (67) and Pargellis and Medley (242) are most helpful, indexed as they are under various heads. To supplement them the regular bibliographies in the *English Historical Review,* even more the *American Historical Review* and the *Economic History Review* are essential. Local historical journals and periodicals—some 300 in all—are listed in Boehm and Adolphus (24), and the list of the societies is in Sara E. Harcup (155). The most recent guide to the historical and archaeological publications of the English and Welsh societies is by Mullins (228). Those of the Scottish societies have been listed by Terry (291) and continued by Matheson (210). Supplementing the *Dictionary of National Biography* other biographical dictionaries have been compiled for Scotland by Chambers (42), for Wales by the Honorable Society of Cymroddorion (64), for Ireland by Crone (410) and for Jersey by Batteine (13). In addition, in the modern period not only *Who's Who* and *Who Was Who* but also the alumni lists for various universities and public schools and the annual *Graduation Army Lists* will be found to be useful. English and Welsh newspapers, magazines and reviews from 1622 onwards for both London and the provinces, were listed by the *Times* in 1920 (293). Further information as to which of these are now microfilmed can be obtained from Schwegmann's list (270).

Invaluable is the *Guide to the Contents of the Public Record Office.* Originally written by Giuseppi in 1923–1924, it has been extensively revised by H. N. Blakiston, J. R. Ede and L. C. Hector and reissued in 1963, and is essential for any original study of the period under review (146). In 1969 a third volume, *Documents Transferred 1960–1966,* described both additional records and whole new classes of documents made available by the reduction of the Fifty-Year Rule to one of thirty years.

A most useful bibliographical pamphlet on the older official series of published papers is H.M.S.O.'s Sectional List No. 24, *British National Archives.*

Texts and Calendars of resources in British archival repositories and societies have been admirably listed by E. L. C. Mullins (228), who gives a good list of texts and calendars of the materials preserved, not only in the P.R.O. in London (pp. 16–36) but also in the Scottish Record Office (pp. 37–40), and in the Irish Record Office (p. 41). It has an excellent index.

The Record Commissioners have also published texts and calendars over the years 1802–1837, as did the Irish Record Commissioners from 1826 to 1901. Moreover, under the direction of the Master of the Rolls, some 99 volumes of *Chronicles* and *Memorials of Great Britain and Ireland during the Middle Ages* have been published over the years 1858 to 1896. The last of these is the well-known *Red Book of the Exchequer* dated by Hubert Hall which contains information on scutages and barons' charters. The Rolls Series should not be confused with that of the Pipe Roll Society, which has been, since 1884, publishing the various pipe rolls for Henry I, II, Richard I and King John. These pipe rolls contain the accounts of sheriffs and other ministers of the Crown as sent in and enrolled at the Exchequer. Before embarking on their study, the Society's *Introduction to the Study of the Pipe Rolls* (1884) is indispensable. Subsequent volumes edited and annotated by such scholars as Hubert Hall, Bishop Stubbs, F. W. Maitland and especially J. H. Round and Doris M. Stenton, are indeed models of their kind.

Of the twenty-one national societies whose publications should be consulted, the most rewarding is the Navy Records Society. Founded in 1894, its publications consist of many volumes of source materials covering important topics from the sixteenth century onwards. Similarly, the three series issued by the Hakluyt Society, First Series 1847–1899, Second Series from 1899 onwards and the Extra Series from 1903 onwards are very rewarding. Further source material on the Court of Admiralty, forest inquisitions, and charters of trading companies can be found amongst the volume published since 1888 by the Selden Society. Further records of the social and economic history of England and Wales are offered by the British Academy from 1914 to 1935 and information on others by the Index Library of the British Record Society Limited from 1888 onwards.

Miss Norton's guide to all the national and provincial directories of England and Wales published before 1856 is also invaluable (233).

Puzzling points of protocol and those having to do with medals are answered by Dorling (74), Campbell (36), Edwards (80) and Hering (157). Statistics are to be found in Mitchell (221) and Devons (68), not to mention official publications (111–119, 142).

SOURCES: GENERAL INFORMATION. Some general points about sources must be made.

(1) INDICES. Space makes it quite impossible to give lists of the many thousands of more recondite or specialist or personal books. For these it is essential to consult the quiquennial British Museum (BM) *Subject Index of Modern Books* (30), which indexes the Second World War as "European War, 1939–1945," with some bibliographies listed under the General History subheading. The entries are a mine of careful classification covering, apart from the military side, the political, economic and social history of the war, including under the headings trade, finance, supplies, food production and control, munitions, propaganda, and postwar reconstruction. Under the social heading are listed, e.g., arts and literature, education, religion and pacifism. The scope and cover of the entries can be seen in the fact that the Index for 1946–50 contains 23 entries (under Trade) for histories of the war effort of individual firms. And, though properly classified on the military side as "War memorials, rolls of honour," much information on civic and educational life in wartime may be tapped by consulting the entries cited there. Political and military memoirs covering or including the war must be sought elsewhere in the *Index,* usually under England, History; or under the appropriate more detailed heading if the author was a professional man (e.g., civil engineering, aviation, medicine).

Since it began in 1950, the *British National Bibliography* (31) has appeared in annual volumes, and should likewise be consulted, particularly for the years not yet covered by the *Subject Index.* "World War 2," as it is there called, is classified under 940.53, but the index should also be consulted for specialist entries (e.g., timber in wartime).

The other major subject-index is that of the Imperial War Museum (IWM). At the time of writing, the classification system of the library was being reorganised so that the index needs to be used with care. Whilst the IWM index has not the scope of the BM index for printed books, it does include reference to many privately printed or cyclostyled works, off-prints and copies of journal articles, and Government papers and circulars; and so is a very valuable key.

(2) GOVERNMENT PUBLICATIONS. There is always a vast outpouring of Government paper in modern wars. Some of it is in the form of statutory

documents and these can be tracked down in bound form. Some of it is in the form of Parliamentary papers which can also be found easily (see below). Some of it is in printed book form and can be traced through the British Museum Library. But a great deal is in the form of pamphlets, circulars, handbooks, leaflets and publicity material. Sometimes complete sets of all such papers are preserved intact in departmental libraries—this is true for example of the Ministry of Agriculture, Fisheries and Food. But in four notable cases of importance to World War II, for instance, the IWM is the depository, i.e., the wartime Ministry of Information, War Office, Admiralty and Air Ministry. The IWM also has many Ministry of Home Security instructions and leaflets. We fear that for some departments complete sets of wartime papers may be difficult to trace. Her Majesty's Stationery Office puts out some seventy Sectional Lists, miniature bibliographies of current Government publications. List No. 60, *Histories of the First and Second World War,* lists most of the volumes published, but not the date of publication. The latter can be found in Higham's work on official histories (160).

(3) FILMS: All the documentary films of the 1939–1945 war period are listed in *The British Film and Television Year Book* for 1949. The best way to check feature films is to go through the bound volumes of *The Monthly Film Bulletin* published by the British Film Institute (BFI). The National Film Archive (same address as BFI, 81 Dean Street, London, W.1.) selects films worthy of preservation and has reviewed films of the war years. Lists are not published but are available at the Archive. The Archive also has a card index of Sound News Films. No films can be borrowed from the Archive. The IWM has a large listed collection of wartime films and of those with a war background.

(4) PHOTOGRAPHS: The IWM has huge collections, including official, press and agency materials, noted in its *Handbook.* The other main source is the *Radio Times* Picture Library, which acquired the Hulton Library containing all the photographs of *Picture Post,* a weekly magazine in its heyday in the Second World War. This is a commercial library selling pictures, many in colour (at £1.10.0 to £4.10.0) for reproduction. The Library includes drawings and engravings. An author should write to the Library (35 Marylebone High Street, London, W.1.) saying which subjects interest him. There are various illustrated books about the War. *The Illustrated London News* photo archives were destroyed in 1941.

(5) RECORDINGS AND BROADCASTING MATERIAL: The chief source is, of course, the British Broadcasting Corporation (BBC). The resources of the BBC are not at present open to members of the general public, but urgent consideration is being given to making selective classes of documentary and other records generally available. In the meantime scholars and research workers should observe the following procedure (addressing correspondence to BBC, Broadcasting House, London, W.1.):

TEXTS OF PAST BROADCASTS. Apply in writing to the Head of the Programme Correspondence Section.

RECORDINGS OF PAST BROADCASTS. Apply in writing to the Head of Central Programme Operations for permission to hear recordings. No copies of these are available. There was no television in the Second World War, but facilities are not in any case available for viewing past programs (contact however, BBC Television Enterprises, Villiers House, Haven Green, London, W.1.).

HISTORY OF BROADCASTING. Apply in writing to the Reference Librarian.

MONITORING SUMMARIES OF WORLD BROADCASTS. It is hoped that these will shortly be available on microfilm. A public announcement will be made in due course.

In general, illustrations can be obtained from the appropriate Service Public Relations section of the Ministry of Defence upon the payment of a reproduction fee. Since these works are Crown Copyright items, a royalty fee must be paid for their use in a printed work. This is a matter upon which the Public Relations section concerned can provide advice in writing. Others also offer similar services and make the same reservations. Microfilm is more difficult to obtain. Some departments, such as the Public Record Office and the Naval Library, can supply the names of microfilmers who have already been cleared to use official materials, and for students and scholars from overseas these may prove cheaper than staying in Britain and working under the rather restricted, by American standards, hours at which archives are open.

For those preparing to write military history, there are two guides worth noting. The eminent American naval historian, Samuel Eliot Morison, published an article in *The American Neptune* in 1949, "Notes on Writing Naval [*not Navy*] English" and the U. S. Department of the Army's Office of the Chief of Military History put out in 1956 *The Writing of American Military History: a guide,* a part of which was originally printed in *Military Affairs* in 1950. Both of these works are helpful on points connected with style, rank, and technical terminology. There is no British equivalent, but a study of official histories can provide a basic guide as to the terminology and abbreviations commonly used. In general, the ranks from captain in the Navy, colonel in the Army and group captain in the R.A.F. are written in full. It is also normal practice to give a man's rank as it was at the time of the incident, with a qualifying clause if he later achieved higher rank or fame in another way.

While there are one-volume histories of the British Army by E. C. Shepperd and Brigadier Peter Young and two single volumes on the Navy by Michael Lewis, there are so far neither a one-volume history of the Royal Air Force and its antecedents nor a single tome on the military history of Britain in its broadest sense. Even the number of multivolume sets can be counted on the fingers of one hand: Fortescue for the Army and Clowes for the Navy, both out of date, and the incomplete Marcus' naval history. Apart from these, official histories exist only from the mid-nineteenth century.

There are two libraries which publish regular accessions lists: the Ministry of Defence (formerly the War Office) Library and the Imperial War Museum. These may be obtained free upon request. The need to keep them, together with H.M.S.O. Monthly and Consolidated indexes, must be firmly impressed upon your Librarian. In addition to these, the Ministry of Defense Library has over 1600 special reading lists which are constantly revised. An Index to these is available on request from the Librarian, D. W. King, OBE, FLA, who deserves our thanks for starting the accession lists project. All of the above cover all three Services and a wide range of subjects. Unfortunately, until 1964 the War Office lists did not cover accessions at the Admiralty and Air Ministry Libraries.

The Imperial War Museum holdings are being computerized and it will be possible by the time this volume appears for researchers to obtain a print-out of the Library's holdings in particular fields. In addition, the Library has a fair collection of papers, mainly from the twentieth century, a list of which is available on request.

Other libraries with valuable holdings in military history are listed in the Appendix to this chapter.

The acquisition of special papers by American libraries, a number of which bear on British history, can be followed on a current basis in the *AHA Newsletter*.

One of the major problems facing researchers is locating material already in existence. Various cataloguing schemes are in use at different libraries from the relatively simple case-and-shelf system employed in the Royal Aeronautical Society Library to the complex Library of Congress arrangement found in an increasing number of American libraries. In 1942 the Library of Congress (LC) reorganized its classes and a guide to these, *Outline of the Library of Congress Classification,* is available from LC in pamphlet form. It is useful in enabling the student to see how the subject is likely to be broken down. However, the major problem with military materials is that their actual location in the system depends upon the whim of a particular cataloguer. The Library of Congress now provides call numbers for most books before they are published. But older works may have to be located through the printed catalogues and their supplements, a useful way of checking bibliography. There are however some pitfalls which are described below.

Other useful bibliographical sources are the catalogues of booksellers who specialize in military books such as Francis Edwards, G. W. Walford, A. A. Johnston, Graham K. Scott, W. E. Hersant, and the Bohemia Bookshop, and to a lesser extent Blackwells, Heffer and Thin, whose addresses are given in the appendix to this chapter.

Some museums also publish occasional militaria. Apart from the National Maritime Museum at Greenwich, the Imperial War Museum in London, and the National Army Museum at Sandhurst, researchers should explore those listed in *Repertory of Museums of Arms and Military History* (Copenhagen, 1960). Then, too, provincial museums such as the Glasgow Art Gallery and Museum, the City of Birmingham Museum, and the Liverpool Public Museum have made their special contributions.

In recent years a great deal of material has become available in photo-reproduction. Major houses now dealing in this besides the Library of Congress are Microcard Editions of the National Cash Register Company, Johnson Reprints, Kraus Reprint Corporation, and University Microfilms, all of whose lists should be perused when seeking to locate special materials ranging from government documents to runs of periodicals. The Irish University Press has started a major reprinting of Parliamentary materials.

G. K. Hall & Co. have specialized in reprinting the catalogues of various libraries, and these in themselves are often major bibliographic sources and include, for instance, the author and subject catalogue of the Naval Library of the Ministry of Defence as well as of the collections of the Mariners Museum of Newport News, Virginia, and of the London School of Hygiene and Tropical Medicine, the School of Oriental and African Studies and the Colonial Office, the subject catalogue of the World War I collection at the New York Public Library and the corrections and additions to the *Dictionary of National Biography* printed in the *Bulletin* of the Institute of Historical Research of the University of London.

Out of print books may be located on the lists of University Microfilms in Ann Arbor, Michigan, or can be obtained from Blackwells of Oxford. In addition, most libraries will now make, under the generally accepted fair-use code, one copy of any item for scholarly research by a single individual. To obtain any of these out-of-print items, it is wise to consult with your librarian.

Research in progress is always a problem. Various organizations keep a registry of topics. The London Library can be queried as can the Institute of Historical Research and the American Historical Association. The latter two publish periodic lists. In addition, for a number of years the U. S. State Department's Office of External Research published lists of current research by private scholars and academic centers which listed by author, title, and estimated completion date, work being done in the social sciences. However, with the 27th issue in 1968 this came to an end. Its major weakness was that authors were only given an institutional and not a departmental affiliation, and mail inquiries were as often as not returned as "unknown" owing to the author not being in a particular department or being a graduate student. American researchers can often be located through *The Directory of American Scholars—History.* (There are other volumes for other fields.)

Much raw material for historical research is to be found in journals. These are, of course, of two sorts. First there are those which cater to scholars and contain monographic articles, notes, and book reviews, such as the *English Historical Review, History, Past and Present, Journal of British Studies, Victorian Studies, Military Affairs,* and the like. Second, there are those such as *Flight,* the *Naval Review,* and the journals of the various branches of the Services, which are basic sources in themselves. Some of the broader journals are listed at the end of this chapter and others are noted in the individual essays.

One of the problems in military history is the paucity of cumulative indices. To some extent this has been solved by *The Journal of the Royal United Service Institution, 1858–1963* (paperback) (372), the American *Military Review* (paperback) (383), the American *Military Affairs, 1937–1968* (380), the *Mariner's Mirror, 1911–1949* (378), and the *United States Naval Institute Proceedings* (microfilm) (418), while *The Journal of the Royal Aeronautical Society* does have quarter-century printed indices available from the Society (361). A recent addition is an index to volumes I–XL of the *Journal of the Society for Army Historical Research* (373). Like all such, these generally do no more than list authors and subjects. Many of them do not cover book reviews, quite understandably, but some of the special Service organizations, such as the Royal Artillery Institution (266), have partially filled the gaps by providing catalogues of their libraries. More of both indices and catalogues are needed, and it was hoped that the new U. S. National Foundation for the Humanities would see fit to grant money for making them, as this was one of its expressed aims. A committee of the American Historical Association has also been studying the problem. In this connection the USAF Air University made a considerable contribution some years ago in microfilming a number of periodicals (duplicates of these master films can be obtained under certain conditions) as well as in publishing a guide. However, there are still a number of important British military journals and publications which have not as yet received this treatment. *The Union List of Periodicals* gives the location of most of these in the United States, but in many cases no library holds a complete run. Outside of the strictly military field, there are a number of important technical serial publications which are mines of information. These are best approached through *Engineering Index* (87), which conveniently gives a summary of the articles noted, but it is only really useful for the twentieth century. One recent index of note is that to *The Engineer, 1856–1959* (86). For the nineteenth century there are a number of popular magazines and newspapers. But here again, indices are either unavailable or unreliable, though the *Wellesley Index of Victorian Periodicals* will help. Older indices and guides are not always reliable; for instance, *The Nineteenth Century and After* is supposed to be covered by the *Periodical Guide,* but a check revealed that most military articles in the interwar years were not mentioned, as military affairs were in disrepute.

A far larger source is the whole conglomeration of official records. These range widely from the well-known Parliamentary journals, debates, and reports, to the far less used special sessional papers (112–121), Estimates, special reports of medical officers, inspecting bodies, *Reports on the Health of the Army,* and the like. Many offices, such as that of the Royal Corps of Naval Constructors, have scarcely begun to have their papers collected by the Public Record Office. However, the latest *Guide to the Contents of the Public Record Office* does provide extensive information upon what the P.R.O. holds together with very useful short histories of particular departments. Fuller histories of a number of ministries are contained in the New Whitehall Series, a complete list of which is given in the bibliography in Chapter XX.

Before researchers actually go to the Public Record Office, they may be able to carry their knowledge of the requisite document-references a stage further than is possible by study of the *Guide* only. A number of P.R.O. Lists were published by H.M.S.O. before World War II. Latterly, the publication of Lists has been carried further by the Kraus Reprint Corporation; for example, the *List of Admiralty Records,* Vol. I, and the *List of War Office Records,* Vol. I, were both published by Kraus in 1963. Meanwhile, since 1954 H.M.S.O. has been publishing a series of Public Record Office Handbooks, some of which are particularly relevant to our purposes, e.g., the *List of Cabinet Papers 1915 and 1916* (1966). Finally, the List and Index Society—formed in 1966—plans to distribute to members photographic copies of such Lists as are not to be reprinted by Kraus. (Further information and subscription forms may be obtained from the Secretary, List and Index Society, c/o Swift Ltd., 5–9 Dyers Buildings, Holborn, London, E.C.1.)

A useful series of guides to official papers are to be found in the following Stationery Office pamphlets: *Published by H.M.S.O.; a brief guide to official publication;* H. M. Treasury, *Official Publications; Government Publications: official indexes, lists, guides, catalogues.* For official statistics see the series of which *Cmd. 6232* (1940) *Statistical Abstract for the United Kingdom for each of the fifteen years 1924 to 1938,* is the eighty-third annual volume. Then there are the *General Indexes to the Bills, Reports and Papers printed by Order of the House of Commons and to the Reports and Papers presented by Command.* In addition see the first two House of Commons Library Documents, *Acts of Parliament; some distinctions in their nature and numbering,* (1955), *A Bibliography of Parliamentary Debates of Great Britain* (1956), and No. 5, *Access to Subordinate Legislation,* as well as H.M.S.O. pamphlet *Looking up the Laws.* An official *Members' Handbook* is a guide to procedure in the Commons. Many American libraries have acquired the *Official Reports* of the Parliamentary debates (which, by the way, may be cited as: *310 H.C.Deb.5s, 1021,* for column 1021 in volume 310 of the fifth series of House of Commons Reports; for the Lords substitute *H.L.* for *H.C.* It is customary to give the date of the citation as well). However, these libraries have generally neglected to acquire the Sessional Papers, though these are available from both the Irish University Press and from Readex Microprint for the Nineteenth Century. While questions and their answers are useful, much of the meat for any research is to be found in the papers which include the Estimates, reports of committees, appropriations accounts, and papers by command. All of these for the period 1900–1949 are indexed in the *General Index* mentioned above.

The reports of the Historical Manuscripts Commission form the most wide-ranging body of printed source materials on British history before the early nineteenth century. Since the reports now run to more than 250 volumes they are not easy for the uninitiated student to use, unless he can link his topic to particular persons or places. The *Index of Persons* (163) (164) now covers all reports issued down to 1957; the *Topographical Guide* (162) thus far covers only publications down to 1911, but its extension is now in preparation. Unfortunately, in approaching military and naval topics such guides are often not very helpful, and there exists no comprehensive guide to the contents of each series of reports. The most recent official list of HMC publications (161) does indicate the periods covered by most volumes, but gives no clue as to the nature of the material in each series. For guidance here one should consult the pamphlet that R. A. Roberts produced back in 1920 for the "Helps for Students of History" series (167). Admittedly this pamphlet is sketchy and out-of-date, but it provides what the beginner needs, and it contains, in addition, special listings on the English civil war (pp. 66–67) and the Navy (pp. 68–70).

Guides to many current official publications are to be found in the more than 60 Sectional Lists published by the Stationery Office. These may be obtained free from either H.M.S.O. or from the British Information Service (845 Third Avenue, New York, N. Y., 10022). Librarians should be warned not to throw away the older issues as these mention items now out-of-print. Nos. 24 and 60 covering the National Archives and Official Histories are particularly useful.

Another very large and useful body of material is contained in the many volumes of official histories. At present these are only partially obtainable through H.M.S.O. Sectional List No. 60, for it does not cover all those volumes that are out-of-print and does not provide full bibliographical information. Some facets of the World War II problem were explored in the Australian journal *Stand-To* and reprinted in *Library Quarterly* (159) several years ago. A complete list and history of British official histories now appears in Higham's *Official Histories* (160). Attempting to trace various volumes through the Library of Congress printed catalogue is not always feasible, since LC did not always catalogue more than the first volume of a series, and in the case of the Second World War the series entry is under "History of," not under "Great Britain" or "United Kingdom." To counter these problems recourse can be had to the British Museum printed catalogue and to the catalogue of the London Library and since 1950 to the *British National Bibliography*. A letter to the Reference Librarian at the Library of Congress will sometimes produce a complete list as will the same sort of appeal to the Cabinet Historical Office in London. Researchers are well advised to consult not only the campaign but also the medical volumes both of official histories and of reports on various campaigns. These often give much needed background.

Many official papers were still covered by the Fifty-Year Rule in 1966. This has meant generally that high-level papers were not made available to other than official historians and to privileged ministers whose memoirs provide some access to confidential information. However, most bona fide historians with a letter of introduction from their Dean or from someone well-known in Britain, were able to see lesser records. This was particularly true of military materials of a non-confidential nature relating to campaigns, to the design and development of weapons, and to medical matters. The Fifty-Year Rule fell most heavily on documents affecting national security, international relations, individual compensation, and matters where libel might be involved.

The new Public Records Act of 1967 provides for a Thirty-Year Rule. Strictly applied, it would mean that Naval papers of 1939 vintage would be made available for public inspection in the Public Record Office at the beginning of 1970, those of 1940 at the beginning of 1971, and so on. But it is worth noting that in the case of World War I the whole corpus of war records was treated as a single release, and that official records from 1914 to 1922, the year of the signature of the peace treaty, were opened to the public in 1965. This does not mean to say, of course, that the same procedure will automatically be adopted in relation to the official papers of World War II, but at least a precedent for such enlightened treatment of war records does now exist. [They have now been opened—Ed.]

An additional complication is connected with the very longevity in and out of office of many prominent British personalities. Additionally, material on service records is not available to researchers without the written permission of the person concerned, or if he is deceased, of his next of kin. This prohibition extends even to material, such as dates of promotion and duties, which have been published in other form. Thus the material is sometimes available in Navy, Army or Air Force Lists or from public relations offices, but not easily and conveniently. The one other way around the difficulty, is to arrange for it to be required for official purposes. The National Register of Archives is useful in locating manuscript materials.

Despite these restrictions, there are many subjects which can be imaginatively and soundly attacked with the materials available. One reason for this is that besides ground-breaking works, there is a considerable need for analytical studies on such diverse topics as the number of sieges that were actually successful, the technical aspects of the design and construction of warships, especially in the transition to steel and the Royal Corps of Naval Constructors, and upon the evolution of airfields in relation to aircraft development, to cite just a few. Another much neglected subject, is the history of the women's forces: the Women's Royal Naval Service (the Wrens), the Auxiliary Territorial Service (the ATS, changed in 1949 to the Women's Royal Army Corps), and the Women's Auxiliary Air Force (the WAAF's), and the various nursing services, not to mention their forebears.

We can also point to the need of modern synthesizing studies of fortifications in the political, economic, technological and social aspects, and even of barracks design as related to medical and social improvements. Siege practices and effects might also merit further study particularly from an operational research angle. Another large and important subject is the whole area of armament exports, British developments, procurement, and industrial capacity, and the influence of disarmament upon both technology and the British economy. Then there is the matter of fuels and imperial policy. Yet another subject which is by no means dried up is the role and place of military correspondents of the major newspapers and the influence, if any, of retired officers in Parliament and company board rooms.

Much more could be done to study the development of tactical doctrine in the Services and of equipment with which to implement it. The subject of officer selection and career patterns is still largely untouched, though there has been a recent doctoral dissertation at Hull on it (237). Histories of recruiting and the interrelationship with medical standards and dental services might be rewarding. Perhaps even the study of War Pensioner annual reports and of old soldiers' homes would be of significance for a social historian. Field Marshal Montgomery's recent *History of Warfare* (222) revives an interest in the influence of G. A. Henty and other writers on potential officers and in the matter of military education in general on the lower as well as on the higher levels. Here histories of the Staff and War Colleges, of schools, and of training programs would be a real contribution. Even the story of that peculiarly English institution, the crammer, would be of interest. In addition to these, each author has provided some specific suggestions in his chapter about what else needs to be done.

Perhaps even more seminal would be works that parallel some of the studies being done in American history, such as a recent symposium entitled "Perspectives on the South: Agenda for Research" (292), Richard S. Kirkendall's *The Truman Period as a Research Field* (187) and Baldwin on the Defence Market (12). Students might here look at the various Lees-Knowles lectures published by Cambridge University Press.

BIBLIOGRAPHY

NOTE. The catalogues and lists of reprint services which handle books, library and other catalogues, as well as documents may be rewarding bibliographically. More and more they are making valuable collections available. Your librarian will be familiar with G. K. Hall, Readex Microprint, Microcard Editions, and University Microfilms. Both the last named and Blackwells in Oxford have reprint services through which copies of out-of-print (OP) books may be obtained, often at considerable savings over used book prices. A number of libraries and museums also publish both guides to their collections and pamphlets and books. Some attempt to note these may be found from 1968 onwards in "Museum Perspective" in *Military Affairs*.

BOOKS

1. Adam, F. *The Clans, Septs and Regiments of the Scottish Highlands*. Edinburgh: W. and A. K. Johnston and G. W. Bacon, 1965.
2. Admiralty (now Ministry of Defence—Navy Dept.). Hydrographic Dept. [Various volumes known as] *Pilots*.
3. *Air Force and Club Ties*. See No. 28.
4. *Air University Library Index to Military Periodicals*. Maxwell Field, Ala.: USAF Air University, 1949–   . This covers the period

since 1949 with greatest emphasis on the present. For details on the microfilm program consult the Librarian, the USAF Air University, Maxwell Field, Ala., and also *Union List of Military Periodicals.* Maxwell AFB, Ala.: Air University Library, 1960.

5. Albion, Robert Greenhalgh. *Forests and Sea Power: the timber problem of the Royal Navy, 1652–1862.* Cambridge, Mass.: Harvard University Press, 1926. Now reprinted: Hamden, Conn.: Archon Books, 1965.

6. Albion, Robert Greenhalgh. *Naval and Maritime History; an annotated bibliography.* Mystic, Conn.: The Marine Historical Association, revised and expanded edition 1963 and supplement 1966, is the only comprehensive bibliographical guide to works in English.

7. Anonymous. *A Dictionary of Military Biography: the British and their enemies, 1537–1956.* London: Leo Cooper, 1972.

8. Anonymous. *The Indian State Forces: their lineage and insignia.* London: Leo Cooper, 1969.

9. Archibald, E. H. H. *The Wooden Fighting Ship in the Royal Navy A.D. 897–1860.* London: Blandford Press, 1968.

10. *Army Annual Act.*

11. Baker, E. C. *Guide to Records in the Windward Islands.* Oxford: Oxford University Press, 1968.

12. Baldwin, W. L. *The Structure of the Defense Market, 1955–1964.* Durham, N. C.: Duke University Press, 1968.

13. Balleine, G. R. *A Biographical Dictionary of Jersey.* London: Staples Press, 1948.

14. Ballot, H. H., *et al.*, eds. *Writings on British History, 1901–1933.* New York, 1968, for the Royal Historical Society. 5 vols. Vol. III. *The Tudor and Stuart Periods, 1485–1714.* Vol. IV. *The 18th Century, 1714–1815.*

15. Barnaby, Kenneth Cloves. *The Institution of Naval Architects, 1860–1960.* London: Royal Institution of Naval Architects in Association with Allen and Unwin, 1960.

16. Barnes, Major Robert Money. *Military Uniforms of Britain and the Empire. 1742 to the present time.* London: Seeley Service, 1960.

17. Barnett, Correlli. *Britain and her Army.* London: Allen Lane, 1970.

18. Bartlett, C. J. *Great Britain and Sea Power, 1815–1853.* Oxford: Clarendon Press, 1963.

19. Baynes, John [C. M.]. *Morale: a study of men and courage; the Second Scottish Rifles at the Battle of Neuve Chapelle, 1915.* New York: Frederick A. Praeger, 1967.

20. Ben Hirsch, J. *Jewish General Officers: a biographical dictionary.* Vol. I. East Bentleigh, Victoria Branch: Military Historical Society of Australia, 1967.

21. Besterman, Theodore. *A World Bibliography of Bibliographies.* 4th ed., revised and enlarged. Lausanne: Societas Bibliographica, 1965–1966.

22. Bethell, Colonel H. A. *Modern Artillery in the Field: a description*

of the artillery of the field Army, and the principles and methods of its employment. London: Macmillan, 1911.

23. Bidwell, Brigadier Shelford. *Gunners at War: a tactical study of the Royal Artillery in the twentieth century.* London: Arms and Armour Press, 1970.

24. Boehm, Eric and Lalit Adolphus, eds. *Historical Periodicals: an annotated world list of historical and related serial publications.* Santa Barbara, Calif.: Clio Press, 1961.

25. Bond, Brian, ed. *19th Century Military Campaigns.* London: Leo Cooper, 1969–   . Series.

26. Bond, Maurice F. *A Short Guide to the Records of Parliament.* London:House of Lords Record Office, 1963.

27. Bonser, W., ed. *A Romano-British Bibliography 55 B.C.–A.D. 449.* Oxford: B. Blackwell, 1964.

28. *The Book of Public School Old Boys, University, Navy, Army, Air Force and Club Ties.* Introduction by James Laver. London: Seeley Service, 1968.

29. *Brassey's Annual: the armed forces yearbook.* (See 332 following.)

30. British Museum Department of Printed Books. *Subject Index of Modern Books Acquired.* London: The Trustees, 1881–1890 and quinquennial thereafter.

31. *British National Bibliography.* London: Council of the British National Bibliography, annual since 1950.

32. Brodie, Bernard. *Guide to Naval Strategy.* 5th ed. New York: Praeger, 1965.

33. Bugler, Arthur R. *H.M.S. Victory; building, restoration and repair.* London: H.M.S.O. (Ministry of Defense, Navy Dept.), 1966. 2 vols.

34. Butler, David E. and Jennie Freeman. *British Political Facts 1900–1960.* London: Macmillan, 1963.

35. Cambridge University Press: Bibliographical Handbooks. Conference on British Studies. No. 1. *Tudor England* by Mortimer Levine, 1968.

36. Campbell, Cdr. A. C., R.N. *Customs and Traditions of the Royal Navy.* Aldershot: Gale and Polden, 1956.

37. Canada. Parliament. House of Commons. Reports of the Special *Committee of the House of Commons on Matters relating to Defence.* Ottawa: Queen's Printer, 1965.

38. Carew, Tim. *How the Regiments Got Their Nicknames.* London: Leo Cooper, 1969.

39. Carman, W. Y. *British Military Uniforms from Contemporary Pictures; Henry VII to the Present Day.* New York: Arco, 1968 (reprint). London: L. Hill, 1957.

40. Carman, W. Y., ed. *Dress Regulations for the Army, 1900.* London: Arms and Armour Press, 1969. Part of facsimile reprint series.

41. Case, Margaret H. *South Asian History, 1750–1950: a guide to periodicals, dissertations and newspapers.* Princeton, N. J.: Princeton University Press, 1968.

42. Chambers, Robert, ed. *Biographical Dictionary of Eminent Scotsmen*. Edinburgh: Blackie, 1855.
43. Chandler, David, ed. *A Guide to the Battlefields of Europe*. Philadelphia: Chilton, 1965.
44. Cheney, Christopher R. *A Handbook of Dates for Students of English History*. London: Royal Historical Society, 1955.
45. Chichester, Henry Manners, and George Burges [*sic*] Short. *Records and Badges of the British Army*. Reprint of 1902 edition. London: Muller, 1969.
46. Churchill, Randolph and Martin Gilbert. *Winston Churchill*. London: Heinemann, 1966–   . In late 1968 Martin Gilbert took on the task started by Churchill's son of producing the life and companion documentary volumes.
47. Clark, Sir George, ed. *The Oxford History of England*. Oxford: Oxford University Press, 1936–1965. Fifteen volumes, with revised editions starting in 1937. See under *Oxford History of England* below.
48. Clark, Ronald W. *The Rise of the Boffins*. London: Phoenix House, 1962.
49. Clark, Ronald W. *Tizard*. London: Methuen & Co., 1965.
50. Clabby, Brigadier J. *The History of the Royal Army Veterinary Corps, 1919–1961*. London: J. A. Allen, 1961.
51. Clode, C. M., *Military Forces of the Crown*. London: John Murray, 1869.
52. Close, Colonel Sir C. *The Early Years of the Ordnance Survey*. Newton Abbott: David & Charles reprint 1969 (1926).
53. Clowes, Sir William Laird. *The Royal Navy: a history from the earliest times to the present*. London: Low, Marston, 1897–1903. 7 vols.
54. Cobbett, William. *Cobbett's Parliamentary History of England*. London: Longman, 1806–1822. 12 vols.
55. Cockle, M[aurice] J. D. *Bibliography of English Military Books up to 1642 and of contemporary foreign works*. London: Simpkin, Marshall, Hamilton, Kent & Co., 1900.
56. Collier, Basil. *The War in the Far East, 1941–1945*. London: Heinemann, 1969.
57. Comparato, Frank E. *Age of Great Guns: cannon kings and cannoneers who forged the firepower of artillery*. Harrisburg, Pa.: Stackpole, 1965.
58. Cook, Blanche Wiesen, ed. *Bibliography on Peace Research in History*. Santa Barbara, California: American Bibliographical Center, Clio Press, 1969.
59. Cousins, Geoffrey. *The Defenders*. London: Frederick Muller, Ltd., 1968.
60. Craig, Hardin, Jr. *A Bibliography of Encyclopedias and Dictionaries dealing with military, naval and maritime affairs, 1626–1961*. 2nd rev. ed. Houston, Texas: Fondern Library, Rice University, 1962.

61. Crone, John Smyth. *A Concise Dictionary of Irish Biography*. Dublin: Talbott Press, 1928.
62. *Current Research in British Studies*. Published spasmodically by the Conference on British Studies, 1960, 1964, 1969.
63. Curzon, Leslie Basil. *English Legal History*. (The M + E Handbook Series.) London: Macdonald, 1968.
64. Cymrodorion, Honorable Society of. *Y bywgraffiadur Cymreig Hyd 1940*. Llundain: 1953 (English translation 1959).
65. Damon, Albert, Howard W. Stoudt, and Ross A. McFarland. *The Human Body in Equipment Design*. Cambridge, Mass.: Harvard University Press, 1965.
66. Darvall, F. O. *Popular Disturbances and Public Order in Regency England*. London: Oxford University Press, 1934.
67. Davies, Godfrey. *Bibliography of British History, Stuart Period 1603–1714*. Oxford: Clarendon Press, 1928.
68. Devons, Ely. *An Introduction to British Economic Statistics*. London: Cambridge University Press, 1956 and later.
69. *Dictionary of National Biography.*
    The Main Dictionary to 1900 edited by Sir Leslie Stephen and Sir Sidney Lee and published 1885–1900.
    1900–1950. Oxford University Press, 1912–1959. 5 vols: *1901–1911*; 1912–1930, 2 vols.; 1931–1940; 1941–1950.
    The Concise D.N.B. Part I from the Beginnings to 1900. Being an *Epitome* of the Main Work and its supplement. (1903.) Part II: *1901–1950*. (1961.)
70. *Dictionary of National Biography, Corrections and Additions, cumulated from the Bulletin of the Institute of Historical Research, University of London,* is available in one volume from G. K. Hall & Co., Boston, Mass.
71. *Dissertation Abstracts; the Humanities and Social Sciences*. Ann Arbor, Michigan: University Microfilms. (Bimonthly).
72. *Doctoral Dissertations on Transportation 1961–1967 and Addendum December 1967–July 1968. A Bibliography*. The Library of the Transportation Center at Northwestern University, Evanston, Illinois. September 28, 1968.
73. *Dod's Parliamentary Companion,* 1832– . London: Business Dictionaries, annually since 1832.
74. Dorling, Captain Henry Taprell ["Taffrail"], R.N. *Ribbons and Medals; naval, military, air force and civil*. 2nd rev. ed. London: G. Philip and Son, 1963.
75. Dornbusch, C[harles] E. *Australian Military Bibliography*. Cornwallville, N. Y.: Hope Farm Press, 1963.
76. Dornbusch, C. E. *Canadian Army, 1855–1965; lineages, regimental histories*. Cornwallville, N. Y.: Hope Farm Press, 1966.
77. Drew, Lieutenant-General Sir Robert, ed. *Roll of Commissioned Officers in the Medical Services of the British Army, 1660–1960,*

London: Wellcome Institute of the History of Medicine, 1969. The second volume begins with the formation of the RAMC.

78. Dunlap, G. D. "Commercial Almanacs and Pilots." *United States Naval Institute Proceedings,* July 1969, 121–127.

79. Dunlap, G. D. and Captain H. H. Shufeldt. *Dutton's Piloting and Navigating.* 12th edition. Annapolis, Maryland: United States Naval Institute, 1969.

80. Edwards, Major T[homas] J. *Military Customs.* 5th rev. and enlarged ed. Aldershot: Gale and Polden, 1961.

81. Edwards, Major T[homas] J. *Regimental Badges.* Aldershot: Gale & Polden, 1951 and 1966.

82. Eggenberger, David. *A Dictionary of Battles.* London: Allen & Unwin, 1968.

83. Einaudi, L., and H. Goldhammer. *An Annotated Bibliography of Latin American Military Journals.* Santa Monica, Calif.: Rand Corp. Research Memo, 1965.

84. Elton, G. R. *England: 1200–1640.* Ithaca, New York: Cornell University Press, 1969. A guide to the records.

85. Emmison, F[rederick] G. and Irvine Gray. *County Records (Quarter Sessions, Petty Sessions, Clerk of the Peace and Lieutenancy).* London: Historical Association, 1948.

86. The Engineer: *The Engineer Index 1856–1959.* Prockter, C. E., compiler. London: Morgan Bros., 1964.

87. *Engineering Index, 1884–   .* Chicago: Association of Engineering Societies 1891–   . The usefulness of this index is that it provides precis of the articles it indexes. Certain problems do arise in using it, however, owing to changing nomenclature and indexing concepts. Only use will indicate the particular problems in any subject field.

88. Farnie, D. A. *East and West of Suez: the Suez Canal in history, 1854–1956.* London: Oxford University Press, 1969.

89. Fedden, Robin [Henry Romilly Fedden], and John Thomson. *Crusader Castles.* London: John Murray, 1957.

90. Fernyhough, A. H. *History of the Royal Army Ordnance Corps, 1920–1945.* London: the R.A.O.C., 1967.

91. Finberg, H. P. R., general editor. *The Agrarian History of England and Wales.* Cambridge: Cambridge University Press, 1968 [in process].

92. Firth, Sir Charles Harding. *Cromwell's Army.* London: Methuen, 1902. Reprinted: New York: Barnes & Noble, 1962.

93. Ford, Percy and Grace. *Breviates of Parliamentary Papers.* Oxford: Blackwells, *1696–1834,* 1953, *1833–1899,* 1953, *1917–1939,* 1951, and *1940–1954,* 1962. Their *A Guide to Parliamentary Papers and How to Use Them.* Oxford: Blackwells, 1955.

94. Ford, Percy and Grace. *A Breviate of Parliamentary Papers 1900–1916. The Foundation of the Welfare State.* Oxford: Basil Blackwell, 1957.

95. Fortescue, Sir John. *History of the British Army.* London: Macmillan, 1910–1935. 13 vols.
96. ffoulkes, Charles. *The Armourer and His Craft from the XIth to the XVIth Century.* London: Methuen, 1967.
97. ffoulkes, Charles. *The Gun-Founders of England.* Reprint of 1936 edition. London: Arms and Armour Press, 1969.
98. Fraccaroli, A. *Italian Warships of World War II.* London: Ian Allan, 1968.
99. Frederick, J. B. M. *Lineage Book of the British Army: mounted corps and infantry, 1660–1968.* Cornwallville, New York: Hope Farm Press, 1969.
100. Fuller, Major-General J[ohn] F. C. *The Military History of the Western World.* New York: Funk and Wagnalls, 1954–1956.
101. Furber, Elizabeth Chapin, ed. *Changing Views on British History: essays on historical writing since 1939.* Cambridge, Mass.: Harvard University Press, 1966.
102. Gardiner, Leslie. *The British Admiralty.* London: Blackwood, 1968.
103. Glubb, Sir John Bagot. *A Soldier with the Arabs.* New York: Harper & Brothers, 1957.
104. Gordon, Donald C. *Dominion Partnership in Imperial Defence, 1870–1914.* Baltimore: Johns Hopkins Press, 1965.
105. Gordon, Donald C. *The Moment of Power.* Englewood Cliffs, New Jersey: Prentice-Hall, 1969.
106. Gordon, L[awrence] L. *British Orders and Awards.* Stafford: W. H. Smith & Son, 1959.
107. Gray, Archibald. *Debates of the House of Commons, 1667–1694.* London, 1763. 10 vols. (Reprinted on Microcards, 1968).
108. Great Britain. Department of Education and Science and the British Council. *Scientific Research in British Colleges and Universities, 1968–1969. III, Social Sciences* (including Government Departments and Other Institutions). London: H.M.S.O., 1969.
109. Great Britain. Foreign Office. *Index to British Foreign Office Correspondence, 1920–1938.* Liechtenstein: Kraus-Thomson, 1969.
110. Great Britain. Ministry of Defence (Central and Army) Library. *Book Lists.* Originally known as the *War Office Library Book Lists.*
111. Great Britain. Ministry of Health. *On the State of the Public Health.* Annual Report of the Chief Medical Officer of the Ministry of Health. London, 1920–   .
112. *Great Britain. Ministry of Transport. Railway Accidents. Report to the Minister of Transport on the Safety Record of the Railways in Great Britain during the year 1967.* London: H.M.S.O., 1968.
113. Great Britain. Parliament. House of Commons. *General Index to the Reports of Select Committees, Printed by Order of the House of Commons 1801–1852.* London: 1853, Reprinted H.M.S.O., 1938.
114. Great Britain. Parliament. House of Commons. *General Index to the Bills, Reports, Estimates, Accounts and Papers Printed by Order of the House of Commons and to the Papers Presented by Command 1852/3–1869/70.* London: 1870. 2 vols.

115. Great Britain. Parliament. House of Commons. *General Index to the Bills, Reports, Estimates, Accounts and Papers Printed by Order of the House of Commons and to the Papers Presented by Command 1870–1878/79.* London: 1880.
116. Great Britain. Parliament. House of Commons. *General Index to the Bills, Reports, Estimates, Accounts and Papers Printed by Order of the House of Commons and to the Papers Presented by Command 1880–1889.* London: H.M.S.O., 1889.
117. Great Britain. Parliament. House of Commons. *General Index to the Bills, Reports, Estimates, Accounts and Papers Printed by Order of the House of Commons and to the Papers Presented by Command from 1890–1899.* London: H.M.S.O., 1904.
118. Great Britain. Parliament. House of Commons. *General Index to the Bills, Reports, Estimates, Accounts and Papers Printed by Order of the House of Commons and to the Papers Presented by Command 1900–1909.* London: H.M.S.O., 1912.
119. Great Britain. Parliament. House of Commons. *General Index to the Bills, Reports and Papers, Printed by Order of the House of Commons and to the Reports and Papers Presented by Command 1900–1948/49.* London: H.M.S.O., 1960.
120. Great Britain. Parliament. House of Commons. *Journals and Sessional Papers of the House of Commons.* London: All available on Readex Microprint, or soon will be.
121. Great Britain. Parliament. House of Lords. *Journal and Sessional Papers of the House of Lords.* London.
122. Great Britain. Post Office. *Post Offices in the United Kingdom.* Annual.
123. Great Britain. Public Record Office. *Acts of the Privy Council of England, Colonial Series* (1613–1782). W. L. Grant and J. Munro, eds. London: H.M.S.O., 1908–1912. 6 vols.
124. Great Britain. Public Record Office. *Calendar of the Home Office Papers, George III* (1760–1775). J. Redington and R. A. Roberts, eds. London: H.M.S.O., 1878–1839. (Calendar of S. P. 37). 4 vols.
125. Great Britain. Public Record Office. *Calendar of State Papers, Colonial Series* (1574–1737). W. N. Sainsbury and others, eds. London: H.M.S.O., 1860–19 .
126. Great Britain. Public Record Office. *Calendar of State Papers, Domestic, Anne* (1702–1704; 1705–1714 in preparation). R. P. Mahaffy, ed. London: H.M.S.O., 1916–1925. (Partial calendar of S. P. 34). 2 vols.
127. Great Britain. Public Record Office. *Calendar of State Papers, Domestic, William III* (1689–1702). W. J. Hardy and E. Bateson, eds. London: H.M.S.O., 1896–1937. (Calendar of S. P. 32 and 33). 11 vols.
128. Great Britain. Public Record Office. *Calendar of Treasury Books* (1660–17 ; projected to 1728). W. A. Shaw, ed. London: H.M.S.O., 1904– . 32 vols.
129. Great Britain. Public Record Office. *Calendar of Treasury Books*

and Papers (1729–1745). W. A. Shaw, ed. London: H.M.S.O., 1898–1903. 5 vols.

130. Great Britain. Public Record Office. *Calendar of Treasury Papers* (1557–1728). J. Redington. London: H.M.S.O., 1868–1889. 6 vols.

131. Great Britain. Public Record Office. *Journals of the Board of Trade and Plantations* (1704–1782). London: H.M.S.O., 1920–1938. 14 vols. (Before 1704, the Journals are included in the *Calendar of State Papers, Colonial*).

132. Great Britain. Public Record Office. List LIII. *Alphabetical Guide to War Office and Other Military Records Preserved in the Public Record Office* (1931).

133. Great Britain. Public Record Office. List LVIII. *List of Admiralty Records* (1904).

134. Great Britain. Public Records Office. List XXXVI. *List of Colonial Office Records* (1911).

135. Great Britain. Public Record Office. List II. *List and Index of Declared Accounts from the Pipe Office and the Audit Office, Henry VIII–1827* (1893).

136. Great Britain. Public Record Office. List XLIII. *List of State Papers, Domestic, 1547–1792, and Home Office Records, 1782–1837* (1914).

137. Great Britain. Public Record Office. List XLVI. *List of Records of the Treasury, Paymaster-General's Office, Exchecquer and Audit Department, and Board of Trade prior to 1837* (1922).

138. Great Britain. Public Record Office. List XXVIII. *List of War Office Records* (1908).

139. Great Britain. Public Record Office. *Maps and Plans in the Public Record Office.* London: H.M.S.O., 1967– .

140. Great Britain. Public Record Office. *The Records of the Foreign Office, 1782–1939.* London: H.M.S.O., 1969.

141. Great Britain. War Office. *Field Service Regulations.*

142. Great Britain. War Office. *Reports of the Health of the Army.*

143. Great Britain. War Office. *War Office Selected Papers.*

144. Gretton, Vice Admiral Sir Peter. *Former Naval Person: a study of Winston Churchill and the Royal Navy.* London: Cassell, 1968.

145. Griffiths, Sir Percival. *The British Impact on India.* Hamden, Conn.: Archon Books, 1965.

146. *Guide to the Contents of the Public Record Office.* London: H.M.S.O., 1963. Volume I covers *Legal Records,* including the High Court of Admiralty, and Volume II, *State Papers and Departmental Records* including the Service ministries and the records on which official histories were based. This work used to be known as *Guiseppi's Guide,* which appeared in 1922 but is now completely superseded by this new edition.

147. Guinn, Paul. *British Strategy and Politics, 1914 to 1918.* Oxford: Clarendon Press, 1965.

148. Guiseppi, M. G. *A Guide to Manuscripts in the Public Record*

Office. Vol. I, 1928, Vol. II, 1924. London: H.M.S.O., Reprinted 1963.

149. Haigh, Kenneth Richardson. *Cableships and Submarine Cables*. London: Coles, 1968.

150. Hall, H[essel] Duncan. *Commonwealth: a history of the British Commonwealth of Nations, 1900–1957*. Princeton: Van Nostrand, 1971.

151. Hamer, W. S. *The British Army: civil-military relations, 1885–1905*. (1970.)

152. Hamilton, E. *Colours of the Regular Army Infantry of the Line, 1st July 1881 to 1958; augmented with the post 1958 list of the amalgamated regiments, with dates of presentation of new Colours*. Special issue No. 1 of the *Bulletin of the Military Historical Society*. London: 1968.

153. Hamilton, J. A. B. *British Railway Accidents of the Twentieth Century*. London: Allen & Unwin, 1967.

154. Handover, P[hyllis] M. *A History of the London Gazette, 1665–1965*. London: H.M.S.O., 1965.

155. Harcup, Sara E. *Historical Archaeological and Kindred Societies in the British Isles*. London: University of London Institute of Historical Research, 1965.

156. Hayes-McCoy, G. A. *Irish Battles: a military history of Ireland*. London: Longmans, 1969.

157. Hering, S/Ldr. P[eter] G. *Customs and Traditions of the Royal Air Force*. Aldershot: Gale and Polden, 1961.

158. Higham, Robin, ed., with Karen Cox Wing. *The Consolidated Author and Subject Index to The Journal of the Royal United Service Institution, 1857–1963*. Ann Arbor, Michigan: University Microfilms, 1964 (1965 paperback).

159. Higham, Robin. "The History of the Second World War," *Library Quarterly*, July 1964, pp. 240–248.

160. Higham, Robin. *Official Histories: essays and bibliographies from all over the world*. Manhattan, Kansas: Kansas State University Library, 1970.

161. Historical Manuscripts Commission. Government Publications. *Publications of the Royal Commission on Historical Manuscripts*. Sectional List No. 17. London: H.M.S.O., 1967.

162. Historical Manuscripts Commission. *Guide to the Reports of the Historical Manuscripts Commission. Part I. Topographical Guide, 1870–1911. Part II. Index to Persons, 1870–1911, (2 vols.). Index of Persons 1911–1957* (3 vols.). London: H.M.S.O., 1914–1966.

163. Historical Manuscripts Commission. *Guide to the Reports of the Royal Commission on Historical Manuscripts 1870–1911. Part II. Index of Persons*. Francis Bickley, ed. London: H.M.S.O.

164. Historical Manuscripts Commission. *Guide to the Reports of the Royal Commission on Historical Manuscripts 1911–1957. Part II. Index of Persons*. A. C. S. Hall, ed. London: H.M.S.O., 1966. 3 vols.

165. Historical Manuscripts Commission. *A Guide to the Reports on Collections of Manuscripts of Private Families, Corporations and Institutions in Great Britain and Ireland Issued by the Royal Commissioners for Historical Manuscripts.* Part I. *Topographical.* R. A. Roberts, ed. London: H.M.S.O., 1914.

166. Historical Manuscripts Commission. *The Prime Ministers' Papers, 1801–1902.* John Brooke, ed. London: H.M.S.O.

167. *The Reports of the Historical MSS. Commission.* Roberts, Richard A., ed. Helps for Students of History. No. 22. London: S.P.C.K., 1920.

168. Hogg, Brigadier O[liver] F. G. *Castles in England.* New York: Arco, 1970.

169. Hogg, Brigadier O. F. G. *Clubs to Cannon: warfare before the introduction of gunpowder.* London: Duckworth, 1968.

170. Hogg, Brigadier O. F. G. *The Royal Arsenal: its background, origin, and subsequent history.* London: Oxford University Press, 1963.

171. Hollingsworth, T. H. *Historical Demography.* Ithaca, New York: Cornell University Press, 1969.

172. Hollister, C. Warren. *Anglo-Saxon Military Institutions on the Eve of the Norman Conquest.* Oxford: Clarendon Press, 1962; Hollister, *The Military Organization of Norman England.* Oxford: Clarendon Press, 1965.

173. Horrocks, Lt. General Sir Brian. Famous Regiments Series from Hamish Hamilton, 1967–
    The Royal Fusiliers by Michael Foss
    The Royal Norfolk Regiment by Tim Carew
    The King's Royal Rifle Corps by Herbert Fairlie Wood
    The Queen's Royal Regiment (West Surrey) by C. J. D. Haswell.
    And others.

174. Hughes, Major-General B. P. *British Smoothe-Bore Artillery: the muzzle-loading artillery of the 18th and 19th centuries.* London: Arms and Armour Press, 1969.

175. Hutchinson Library of Ships and Shipping, The.

176. Illinois, University of. Graduate School of Library Sciences. Occasional Papers Number 82. *A Guide to British Parliamentary Papers.* Urbana: University of Illinois Press, April, 1967.

177. Institute of Historical Research Bulletin. London.

178. The Institution of Mechanical Engineers. *The Reliability of Service Equipment.* London: The Institution, 1969.

179. International Association of Museums of Arms and Military History. *Repertory of Museums of Arms and Military History.* Copenhagen, Denmark: Töjhusmuseum, 1960.

180. Ireland, National Library of. *Sources for the History of Irish Civilization: articles in Irish periodicals.* Boston: G. K. Hall & Co., 1970.

181. Irish University Press (Shannon) Series of British Parliamentary papers. Military and Naval, 15 vols., so far. (All volumes classified separately.)

182. Kahn, David. *The Codebreakers: the story of secret writing.* New York: Macmillan, 1967.
183. Keevil, J[ohn] J., Christopher Lloyd, and J. L. S. Coulter. *Medicine and the Navy, 1200–1900.* Edinburgh: E. and S. Livingstone, 1957–1963.
184. Ker, N. P. *Medieval Libraries of Great Britain: a list of surviving books.* London: Royal Historical Society, 1941.
185. Kinross, John. *Discovering Battlefields in Southern England.* Tring: Shire Publications, 1968.
186. Kinross, John. *Guide to Military Museums.* London: Leo Cooper, 1970.
187. Kirkendall, Richard S., ed. *The Truman Period as a Research Field.* Columbia, Missouri: University of Missouri Press, 1968.
188. Kitchen, M. *The German Officer Corps, 1890–1914.* London: Oxford University Press, 1968.
189. Kubicek, Robert V. *The Administration of Imperialism: Joseph Chamberlain at the Colonial Office.* Durham, North Carolina: Duke University Press, 1969.
190. Kuhlicke, F. W. and F. G. Emmison. *English Local History Hand-lists.* London: The Historical Association, 1965.
191. Laffont, Robert. *The Ancient Art of Warfare.* New York: Time-Life Books, 1968. 2 vols. (The title is mistranslated from the French—*ancien* means former, not *ancient*.)
192. Lancaster, Joan C. and William Kellaway, comp. *Bibliography of Historical Works Issued in the United Kingdom, 1946–* .
 Works issued 1946–1956. London: University of London. Institute of Historical Research.
 Works issued 1957–1960. London: University of London. Institute of Historical Research.
 Works issued 1960–1965. London: University of London. Institute of Historical Research.
193. Langdon, Robert M. "Notable Naval Books of 19 ." USNI *Proceedings.* December issue since 1950.
194. Laws, Lt/Col. M. E. S. *Battery Records of the Royal Artillery, 1716–1859.* Woolwich: Royal Artillery Institution, 1952.
195. Le Fleming, H. M. *ABC Warships of World War I.* London: Ian Allen, 1962.
196. Lenton, H. T. and J. J. Colledge. *Warships of World War II.* London: Ian Allen, 1963.
197. Leslie, N. B., comp. *The Battle Honours of the British and Indian Armies, 1695–1914.* London: Leo Cooper, 1969.
198. Leslie, N. B., comp. *The Succession of Colonels.* London: Leo Cooper, 1970.
199. Lewis, Michael. *The Navy of Britain, an historical portrait.* London: Allen and Unwin, 1948.
200. Lewis, Michael. *A Short History of the Royal Navy.* Harmondsworth, Mddx.; Penguin, 1957.

201. Lloyd, Christopher. *The British Seaman, 1200–1860: a social survey*. London: Collins, 1968.

202. Lloyd, E. W. and A. G. Hadcock. *Artillery: its progress and present position*. Portsmouth: J. Griffin & Co., 1893.

203. London Library. *Catalogue of the London Library*. London: 1913–1953.

204. Macintyre, Donald. *The Man-of-War*. New York: McGraw-Hill, 1968.

205. Macksey, Kenneth. *The History of Armoured Vehicles and Tanks*. London: Macdonald, 1970.

206. Manning, Captain T[homas] D. and Cdr. C. F. Walker. *British Warships Names*. London: Putnam, 1959.

207. Manwaring, G. E. *A Bibliography of British Naval History. A Bibliographical Guide to Printed and Manuscript Sources*. London: Routledge, 1930. Part I—Authors. Part II—Subjects.

208. Marder, Arthur J. *From the Dreadnought to Scapa Flow; the Royal Navy in the Fisher Era, 1904–1919*. London: Oxford University Press, 1961– .

209. Marwick, Arthur. *Britain in the Century of Total War: war, peace and social change, 1900–1967*. London: The Bodley Head, 1968.

210. Matheson, Cyril. *A Catalogue of the Publications of Scottish Historical and Kindred Clubs and Societies and of the Papers Relative to Scottish History Issued by H. M. Stationery Office, including the Reports of the Royal Commission on Historical MSS 1908–1927 With a Subject Index*. Aberdeen: Milne & Hutchinson, 1928.

211. Matthews, William. *British Autobiographies: an annotated bibliography of British autobiographies published or written before 1951*. (1955) Hamden, Conn.: Archon Books (reprint, 1968).

212. Matthews, William, comp. *British Diaries: an annotated bibliography of British diaries written between 1442 and 1942*. Berkeley: University of California Press, 1951.

213. Milne, A[lexander] T., comp. *Writings on British History 1934. A Bibliography of Books and Articles on the History of Great Britain from about 450 A.D. to 1914 Published during the year 1934*. London: Jonathan Cape, 1937.

214. Milne, A[lexander] T., comp. *Writings on British History 1935. A Bibliography of Books and Articles on the History of Great Britain from about 450 A.D. to 1914 Published during the year 1935*. London: Jonathan Cape, 1939.

215. Milne, A[lexander] T., comp. *Writings on British History 1936. A Bibliography of Books and Articles on the History of Great Britain from about 450 A.D. to 1914 Published during the year 1936*. London: Jonathan Cape, 1940.

216. Milne, A[lexander] T., comp. *Writings on British History 1937. A Bibliography of Books and Articles on the History of Great Britain from about 450 A.D. ot 1914 Published during the year 1937*. London: Jonathan Cape, 1949.

217. Milne, A[lexander] T., comp. *Writings on British History 1938. A Bibliography of Books and Articles on the History of Great Britain from about 450 A.D. to 1914 Published during the year 1938.* London: Jonathan Cape, 1951.

218. Milne, A[lexander] T., comp. *Writings on British History 1939. A Bibliography of Books and Articles on the History of Great Britain from about 450 A.D. to 1914 Published during the year 1939.* London: Jonathan Cape, 1953.

219. Milne, A[lexander] T., comp. *Writings on British History 1940–1945. A Bibliography of Books and Articles on the History of Great Britain from about 400 A.D. to 1914 Published during the years 1940–1945, inclusive.* London: Jonathan Cape, 1960–   . 2 vols.

220. Milne, A[lexander] T., comp. *Writings on British History 1901–1933. A Bibliography of Books and Articles on the History of Great Britain from about 400 A.D. to 1914 Published during the years 1901–1933, inclusive.* Vol. I Auxiliary Sciences and General Works, Vol. II The Middle Ages 450–1485, Vol. III The Tudor and Stuart Periods 1485–1714. London: Jonathan Cape, 1968.

221. Mitchell, B. R. with . . . Phyllis Dean. *Abstract of British Historical Statistics.* London: Cambridge University Press, 1962, but where possible it is wiser to use the official volumes.

222. Montgomery of Alamein, Bernard Law Montgomery, 1st Viscount. *A History of Warfare.* Cleveland: World Publishing Co., 1968.

223. Morley, W. F. E. *Canadian Local Histories to 1950: a bibliography.* Vol. I, *The Atlantic Provinces.* Toronto: University of Toronto Press, 1967.

224. Morris, James. *Pax Britannica: the climax of an empire.* London: Faber, 1968.

225. Morris, J. E. *The Welsh Wars of Edward I; a contribution to medieval military history.* Oxford: Clarendon Press, 1901.

226. Moulton, Major General J[ames] L. *The Norwegian Campaign of 1940: a study of warfare in three dimensions.* London: Eyre and Spottiswoode, 1966.

227. Mowat, C. L., ed. *The New Cambridge Modern History.* Cambridge: Cambridge University Press, 1968–   . 12 vols.

228. Mullins, E. L. C. *A Guide to the Historical and Archaeological Publications of Societies in England and Wales, 1901–1933.* London: Oxford University Press, 1968.

229. Mullins, E. L. C. *Texts and Calendars: an analytical guide to serial publications.* London: Royal Historical Society, 1958.

230. *National Maritime Museum Library Catalogue: Voyages and Travel.* Vol. I. London. H.M.S.O., 1968.

231. Navy Records Society. *Publications of the Navy Records Society.* London: 1894–   .

232. Nelson, R. R. *The Home Office, 1782–1801.* Durham, North Carolina: Duke University Press, 1969.

233. Norton, Jane E. *Guide to the National and Provincial Directories of England and Wales excluding London, published before 1856.* London: Royal Historical Society, 1950.
234. Ogorkiewicz, Richard M. *Design and Development of Fighting Vehicles.* London: Macdonald, 1968.
235. Olson, M. *The Economics of Wartime Shortage: a history of British food supplies in the Napoleonic War and in World Wars I and II.* Durham, N.C.: Duke University Press, 1963.
236. O'Neill, T. P. *British Parliamentary Papers: a monograph on Blue Books.* Shannon, Ireland: Irish University Press, 1968.
237. Otley, Christopher Blackwood. *The Origins and Recruitment of the British Army Elite, 1870–1959; being a thesis submitted for degree of Doctor of Philosophy in the University of Hull.* Hull: 1965 (unpublished).
238. Ottley, George. *A Bibliography of British Railway History.* London: Allen and Unwin, 1965.
239. *Oxford Bibliography of British History.*
    Davies, Godfrey. *The Early Stuarts 1603–1660.* 2nd ed., Oxford: Clarendon Press, 1959.
    Pargellis, S. and D. J. Medley, eds. *Bibliography of British History, the Eighteenth Century 1714–1789.* Oxford: Clarendon Press, 1951.
    Reade, Conyers. *Bibliography of British History, Tudor Period, 1485–1603.* 2nd. ed. Oxford: Clarendon Press, 1959.
240. *The Oxford History of England.* Sir George Clark, general editor. From the Roman occupation to 1945. 15 vols.
    1. *Roman Britain and the English Settlements.* By R. G. Collingwood and J. N. L. Myres. 2nd ed., 1937.
    2. *Anglo-Saxon England.* By Sir Frank Stenton. 2nd ed., 1947.
    3. *From Domesday Book to Magna Carta, 1087–1216.* By A. L. Poole. 2nd ed., 1955.
    4. *The Thirteenth Century 1216–1307.* By Sir [Frederick] Maurice Powicke. 2nd ed., 1962.
    5. *The Fourteenth Century 1307–1399.* By M. McKisack. 1959.
    6. *The Fifteenth Century 1399–1485.* By E. F. Jacob. 1961.
    7. *The Earlier Tudors 1485–1558.* By J. D. Mackie. 1952.
    8. *The Reign of Elizabeth 1558–1603.* By J. B. Black. 2nd ed., 1959.
    9. *The Early Stuarts 1603–1660.* By Godfrey Davies. 2nd ed., 1959.
    10. *The Later Stuarts 1660–1714.* By Sir George Clark. 2nd ed., 1955.
    11. *The Whig Supremacy 1714–1760.* By Basil Williams. Revised by C. H. Stuart. 2nd rev. ed., 1962.
    12. *The Reign of George III 1760–1815.* By J. Steven Watson. 1960.
    13. *The Age of Reform 1815–1870.* By Sir [Ernest] Llewellyn Woodward. 2nd ed., 1962.
    14. *England 1870–1914.* By R. C. K. Ensor. 1936.

15. *English History 1914–1945.* By A. J. P. Taylor. 1965.

241. Pakenham-Walsh, Major-General R. P. *The Second World War 1939–45: Army Military Engineering (Field).* London: War Office, 1952.

242. Pargellis, S. and D. J. Medley. *Bibliography of British History, the Eighteenth Century 1714–1789.* Oxford: Clarendon Press, 1951.

243. Parry, Ann. *The Admirals Fremantle: a selection from the Fremantle family papers (1765–1958).* (1970)

244. Parsons, K. A. C. *A Checklist of British Parliamentary Papers (Bound Set) 1801–1950.* Cambridge: Cambridge University Press, 1958.

245. Partridge, Eric. *A Dictionary of Forces Slang, 1939–1945.* London: Secker & Warburg, 1948.

246. Partridge, Eric and John Brophy, eds. *Songs and Slang of the British Soldier: 1914–1918.* 2nd rev. ed. London: Eric Partridge Ltd., 1930.

247. Pendill, G. R. *Survey on the Use of Periodicals in Some British Medical Libraries.* Sheffield, 1967.

248. Poe, Richard. "Marine Museums of the World." *Popular Boating.* January, 1966.

249. Polmar, Norman. *Aircraft Carriers.* London: Macdonald, 1969.

250. Pope, Dudley. *Guns; from the invention of gunpowder to the twentieth century.* London: Weidenfeld and Nicolson, 1965.

251. Postal History Society, The. As, for instance, Colonel D. R. Martin's *The Postal History of the First Afghan War, 1838–1842.* Bath: Postal History Society, 1964. Special series No. 18.

252. Powell, W. R. *Local History from Blue Books: a select list of the Sessional Papers of the House of Commons.* London: For the Historical Association by Routledge and Kegan Paul, 1962.

253. Powicke, F. M., Charles Johnson and W. J. Harte. *Handbook of British Chronology.* London: Royal Historical Society, 1939.

254. *Rand Corporation, Papers.* Santa Monica, Calif.

255. *Rand Corporation, Research Memoranda.* Santa Monica, Calif.

256. Rawlings, John D. R. *Fighter Squadrons of the RAF.* London: Macdonald, 1969.

257. Read, Conyers. *Bibliography of British History Tudor Period, 1485–1603.* 2nd ed.

258. Reynolds, Major E. G. B. *The Lee-Enfield Rifle.* New York: Arco, 1969.

259. Rider, K. J. *A History of Science and Technology.* Special Subject List No. 48. London: Library Association, 1967.

260. Ritcheson, Charles R. and O. T. Hargrave. *Current Research in British Studies by American and Canadian Scholars.* Dallas: Southern Methodist University Press, 1969. Other editions from other presses; see Preface.

261. Roach, John, ed. *A Bibliography of Modern History.* Cambridge: Cambridge University Press, 1969.

262. Roberts, Richard A. *The Reports of the Historical Manuscripts*

Commission. Helps for Students of History. No. 22. London: S.P.C.K., 1920.

263. Rogers, Colonel H. C. B. *Weapons of the British Soldier.* London: Seeley, Service Co., 1960.

264. Rowney, Don Karl and James Q. Graham, Jr., eds. *Quantitative History: selected readings in the quantitative analysis of historical data.* Homewood, Illinois: The Dorsey Press, 1969.

265. Royal Aeronautical Society. *Centenary Journal 1866–1966.* London: Royal Aeronautical Society, 1968.

266. The Royal Artillery Institution. *Catalogue of the Royal Artillery Institution Library (Military Section).* Woolwich: The Royal Artillery Institution, 1913. The bound volume is supplemented by two accession lists: *since 1913* and *1921–1940.*

267. Royal Commonwealth Society. *Royal Commonwealth Society Centenary Souvenir, 1868–1968.* London: 1968.

268. Royal Society for the Prevention of Accidents. Publications.

269. Schmeckebeir, Laurence and Roy B. Eastin. *Government Publications and their Use.* Rev. ed. Washington, D. C.: The Brookings Institution, 1961.

270. Schwegmann, George A., Jr. *Newspapers on Microfilm.* 6th edition. Washington: Library of Congress, 1967.

271. Seth, Ronald. *The Truth Benders: psychological warfare in the Second World War.* London: Frewin, 1969.

272. Shaw, Henry I., Jr. "The Historian of the British Army" [Sir John Fortescue] *Military Affairs,* XVIII, No. 3., Fall, 1954, 113–117.

273. Sheppard E. W. *A Short History of the British Army.* New ed. rev. and enlarged. London: Constable, 1950.

274. Simpson, Brigadier I. *Singapore: Too Little, Too Late.* London: Leo Cooper, 1970. Simpson was on the staff from 1939 to 1942.

275. Skentelberry, Brigadier N. *A History of the Ordnance Board.* London: Ordnance Board, 1968.

276. Sigwart, Captain E. E. *The Royal Fleet Auxiliary: its ancestry and affiliations, 1600–1908.* London: Adlard Coles, 1969.

277. Silverstone, Paul H. *U. S. Warships of World War II.* Garden City, N. Y.: Doubleday, [1966].

278. Smitherman, P. H. *Uniforms of the Royal Artillery, 1716–1966.* London: Hugh Evelyn, 1966.

279. Smitherman, P. H. *Uniforms of the Scottish Regiments.* London: Hugh Evelyn, 1963.

280. Smitherman, P. H. *Uniforms of the Yeomanry Regiments.* London: Hugh Evelyn, 1967.

281. Smyth, Sir John. *In this Sign Conquer: the story of the Army chaplains.* London: Mowbray, 1968.

282. Smyth, Brigadier the Rt. Hon. Sir J. G. *The Story of the George Cross.* London: Arthur Backer, 1968.

283. Stanford University. Hoover Institution of War, Revolution and Peace. *Catalogs of the Collections.* Boston, Massachusetts: G. K. Hall, 1969–   . Several vols.

284. Stewart, James et al., ed. *British Union Catalogue of Periodicals and Supplement.* Reissue. Hamden, Conn.: Archon, 1968.
285. Sutherland, Douglas. *The Border Regiment.* London: Leo Cooper, 1971.
286. Sutton, S. C. *A Guide to the India Office Library* (Commonwealth Office). H.M.S.O., 1967.
287. *Tank Data.* London: Ian Allen, 1968.
288. Taylor, John Charles. *German Warships of World War II.* Garden City: Doubleday, 1966.
289. Taylor, John W. R. *Combat Aircraft of the World, 1909–1968.* London: Michael Joseph/Ebury Press, 1969.
290. Taylor, John W. R. and P. J. R. Moyes. *Pictorial History of the RAF.* London: Ian Allan, 1968–1969. 3 vols.
291. Terry, Charles Stanford. *A Catalogue of the Publications of Scottish Historical and Kindred Clubs and Societies and of the Volumes Relative to Scottish History issued by His Majesty's Stationary Office 1780–1908 with a subject index.* Glasgow: J. MacLehose & Sons, 1909.
292. Thompson, Edgar T., ed. *Perspectives on the South: agenda for research.* Durham, N. C.: Duke University Press, 1967.
293. *The Times. Tercentenary Handlist of English and Welsh Newspapers, Magazines and Reviews.* London: The Times, 1920.
294. Tylden, Major G. *Horses and Saddlery: an account of the animals used by the British and Commonwealth Armies from the seventeenth century to the present day with a description of their equipment.* London: J. A. Allen, 1965.
295. Uden, Grant. *A Dictionary of Chivalry.* London: Longmans, 1968.
296. Uhlaner, J. E. *The Research Psychologist in the Army, 1917–1967.* Washington: U. S. Department of the Army, Office of the Chief of Research and Development, Army Personnel Research Office, Army Behavioural Science Research Laboratory, TRR 1155, 1968.
297. U. S. Department of the Army. Army Library. *Checklist of Periodicals currently received in the Army library.* Washington, D. C.: January, 1963– .
298. U. S. Department of the Army. *The Subject and Author Index to Military Review.* Wing, Mark and Karen Cox under the direction of Robin Higham. Fort Leavenworth, Kansas: U. S. Army Command and General Staff College and *Military Review,* 1967. A personnel index is available at the USAC & GSC.
299. U. S. Department of the Army. *Technology and Armament.* Translation J-1667. Springfield, Virginia: Clearinghouse for Federal Scientific and Technical Information, 1966.
300. U. S. Department of the Army, Office of Military History. *Bibliography of American Military History.* ROTC Manual 145-20 (1968 mimeographed, to be published in 1969).
301. U. S. Department of State. *Major Publications of the Department of State; An Annotated Bibliography.* Rev. ed. Washington, D. C.: Historical Office Bureau of Public Affairs, June 1966.

302. U. S. Department of State. External Research Staff. ER 3.22-1964. *Western Europe, Great Britain, and Canada. Replaces ER List 9.17 (1961) Great Britain and Canada.*

303. U. S. Government. *How to Find U. S. Statutes and U. S. Code Citations.* Rev. ed. Washington, D. C.: U. S. Government Printing Office, 1965.

304. U. S. Military Academy, West Point, New York, Library. *Subject Catalogue with selected author and added entries of the military art and science collection and a preliminary guide to the manuscript collection.* Westport, Connecticut: Greenwood Publishing Corporation, 1970. 4 vols. with 66,000 entries.

305. U. S. Military Academy. The West Point Military Library. An open-ended reprint series by the Greenwood Press of Westport, Conn.

306. U. S. Military History Research Collection, U. S. Army, Carlisle Barracks, Pennsylvania. *Catalogue.* Westport, Connecticut: Greenwood Publishing Corp., 1970. 4 vols. with 80,000 entries covering all the books pulled out of the major American Army collections and centered for inter-library loan at Carlisle Barracks.

307. U. S. National Archives. *National Archives Accessions,* No. 1. Jan.–Mar., 1940–   . Washington.

308. U. S. National Science Foundation. *Current Projects on Economic and Social Implications of Science and Technology.* Annual.

309. U. S. Naval Institute. *Author, Subject, and Title Index to the United States Naval Institute Proceedings, 1878–1957.* C. W. Evans, ed. Washington: Library of Congress, 1957.

310. U. S. Naval Institute. *The Naval Review, 1962–1963,* and then annual.

311. van Doorn, J., ed. *Armed Forces and Society: sociological essays.* London: Christopher Hurst, 1968.

312. Veale, F. J. P. *Advance to Barbarism: the development of total warfare from Sarajevo to Hiroshima.* London: Mitre Press, 1968.

313. Wagner, Sir Anthony. *Heralds of England.* London: H.M.S.O., 1968.

314. Walton, Colonel Clinton Eliot Clifford. *History of the Standing Army of Great Britain.* London: Harrison and Sons, 1894.

315. Warner, Philip. *Sieges of the Middle Ages.* London: Bell, 1968.

316. Watkins, T. F. *Chemical Warfare, Pyrotechnics, and the Fireworks Industry.* Oxford: Pergamon Press, Commonwealth and International Library, 1968.

317. Watts, Anthony J. *Japanese Warships of World War II.* London: Ian Allan, 1966.

318. Webb, R. K. *English History, 1815–1914,* Service Center for Teachers of History. Publication No. 64. Washington, D. C.: Service Center for Teachers of History, 1967.

319. Westrate, J. Lee. *European Military Museums: a study.* The President's Committee on the American Armed Forces Museum. [Washington, D. C., 1959]. Smithsonian Institution, 1961.

320. White, A. S. *Bibliography of Regimental Histories of the British Army*. London: Society for Army Historical Research, 1965.
321. Wilkinson, F. J. *Badges of the British Army, 1820–1960*. London: Arms and Armour Press, 1969.
322. Williams, Colonel G. *Citizen Soldiers of the Royal Engineers Transportation and Movements and of the RASC, 1859–1965*. Aldershot: Institution of the Royal Corps of Transport, 1969.
323. Williams, Judith Blow. *A Guide to the Printed Materials for English Social and Economic History, 1750–1850*. New York: Octagon Books, 1966. 2 vols.
324. Winchell, Constance M. *A Guide to Reference Books*. Chicago: the American Library Association. 8th ed. 1967. Supplements biennially.
325. Winks, Robin, ed. *The Historiography of the British Empire-Commonwealth*. Durham, N. C.: Duke University Press, 1966.
326. Winstock, Lewis. *Songs and Music of the Redcoats, 1642–1902*. London: Leo Cooper, 1969.
327. Wise, T. *A Guide to Military Museums*. Bracknell, Berks.: Bellona Publications, 1959.
328. Woods, Frederick. *Churchill: a bibliography of the works of Winston Churchill*. Toronto: University of Toronto Press, 1969. rev. ed.
329. *Writings on American History, 1902–1919*. Published by the American Historical Association and by the National Commission on Historical Publications since 1902.
330. Young, Brigadier Peter. *The British Army 1642–1970*. London: Kimber, 1967.
331. Young, Brigadier Peter, ed. *Military Memoirs Series*. Hamden, Conn.: Archon Books, 1968–   .
332. Young, Brigadier Peter, ed. *Sandhurst Series on the History of War*. London: Weidenfeld & Nicholson, 1969–   .

PROFESSIONAL JOURNALS

This list is by no means complete and should be supplemented with the items given in the alphabetical lists at the end of each chapter. The journals here are ones which apply to more than one chapter. (See also Boehm & Adolphus in list of books above.)

Additional guides to journals may be found in:

333. Spence, Paul A. and Helen Hopewell. *Union List of Foreign Military Periodicals*. Maxwell AFB, Ala.: Air University Library, 1957. This locates holdings in the United States.
334. For a pure listing of current aeronautical periodicals see: *The Journal of the American Aviation Historical Society*, VI, No. 1, pp. 64ff, No. 2, p. 138, No. 3, p. 213 and VII, No. 2, pp. 136–139 and No. 3, 220.
335. Sayers, Lt. (j.g.) Ken. "Professional Periodicals for Naval Officers,"

United States Naval Institute Proceedings, November 1969, 118–124.

336. For a listing of American-University-Press-published journals consult the quarterly *Scholarly Books in America,* which lists journals by presses, but does not include those published independently of the academic community, such as *Military Affairs.*

337. *Admiralty and House Guards Gazette,* 1 November 1884–19 January 1901. Illustrated.

338. *An Cosantoir/The Irish Defence Journal.* Published by the Department of Defence, Dublin, since 1940. Monthly.

339. *Archeologia: or miscellaneous tracts relating to antiquity.* Journal of the Society of Antiquaries of London. London: 1770–   .

340. *Archaeologia Aeliana: or miscellaneous tracts relating to antiquity.* Publication of the Society of Antiquaries of Newcastle-upon-Tyne. Newcastle-upon-Tyne: 1st Ser., 1822–1855; 2nd Ser., 1857–1904; 3rd Ser., 1904–1924; 4th Ser., 1925–   .

341. *Army and Navy Gazette* 1860–1921. Became *Army, Navy and Air Force Gazette,* 1922–36 (Nov.) and *United Services Review,* 1936 (Suspended October 1939–1941).

342. *Army Quarterly* (incorporating the *United Service Magazine*). London: 1920–   . Index of *Articles, 1920–1970.*

343. *[Australian] Army Journal.* Melbourne: 1948–   .

344. *Brassey's Annual: The Armed Forces Year-Book* 1886–   .
   Various title changes: *The Naval Annual,* 1886–1914;
   Brassey's Naval Annual, 1915–16; *The Naval Annual,* 1919;
   Brassey's Naval and Shipping Annual, 1920/21–1935;
   Brassey's Naval Annual, 1936–49; present title since 1950.

345. *British Legion Journal.* London, July 1921–   .

346. *Broad Arrow* 1868–1917. Merged with *Army and Navy Gazette* in April, 1917.

347. *Bulletin of the Military Historical Society, The.* London: 1950.

348. *Cadet Journal and Gazette.* Army Cadet Force Association. London, 1920–   .

349. *The Canadian Military Journal,* Toronto, Ontario, since 1934. Quarterly.

350. *Cavalry Journal* (now *The Royal Armoured Corps Journal*). London: 1906–1942 (suspended 1914–1918, 1942–1946).

351. *Economist, The.* London: 1843–   .

352. *English Historical Review.* London: 1886–   .

353. *History, a quarterly magazine and review for the teacher, the student, and the expert.* Historical Association. London: 1912–1915; New Ser., 1916–   .

354. *Globe and Laurel: journal of the Royal Marines, The.* Southsea, Hants., 1892–   .

355. *Gunner: official organ of the Royal Artillery Association, The.* Woolwich, 1919–   .

356. *The Irish Sword.* Published by the Military Historical Society of Ireland, University College, Dublin, since 1949. Quarterly.

357. *Jane's Fighting Ships* 1898–   . Title varies: *All the World's Fighting Ships,* 1898–1904; *Fighting Ships,* 1905–15; present title since 1916.

358. *Journal of Administration Overseas.* London: (Colonial Office) 1962–   . Succeeds *Journal of African Administration* 1949–1961.

359. *Journal of British Studies.* Conference on British Studies. Hartford, Conn.: 1961–   .

360. *Journal of the Royal Aeronautical Society.* (1923–1966) Now *The Aeronautical Journal.* London: 1866–1893 as annual report; journal from 1897.

361. *Indices to the Journal of the Royal Aeronautical Society.* London: The Royal Aeronautical Society, 1926, 1951, 1970 [?].

362. *Journal of the Royal Army Chaplains' Department,* 1922–   .

363. *Journal of the Royal Army Medical Corps.* London: 1903–   .

364. *Journal of the Royal Army Veterinary Corps.* Aldershot: 1929–.

365. *Journal of the Royal Artillery.* Woolwich, 1858–   .

366. *Journal of the Royal Artillery Short Index of Subjects and Authors 1950–1959, Vols. 77 to 86.* Woolwich: R. A. Institution, 1967.

367. *Journal of the Royal Central Asian Society.* London: 1914–   .

368. *Journal of the Royal Electrical and Mechanical Engineers,* 1951–.

369. *Journal of the Royal Military College of Science,* 1947–   .

370. *Journal of the Royal Naval Scientific Service,* 1946–   .
     Restricted. May be consulted in such libraries as the Naval Library (Ministry of Defence) and the National Maritime Museum Library.

371. *Journal of the Royal Signals Institution.* 1954–   .

372. *Journal of the Royal United Service Institution, The.* The Royal United Service Institution, Whitehall, London, S.W.1. Indexed. See R. Higham and Karen Cox Wing, *The Consolidated Author and Subject Index to the J.R.U.S.I.* Ann Arbor, Michigan: University Microfilms, 1964. (♯TB 00002)

373. *Journal of the Society for Army Historical Research.* Begun in 1921, monthly thereafter, with an annual volume.

374. *Journal of the United Service Institution of India, The.* New Delhi, 1871–   .

375. *Lancet, The.* London: 1823–   .

376. *Land and Water.* London: 1862–1920. A sportsman's weekly until the outbreak of war in 1914; it then devoted itself entirely to the war.

377. *Listener, The.* London: 1929–   .

378. *Mariner's Mirror.* London: 1911–   . Volumes 1–35 have an Index.

379. *Marine-Rundschau* (Berlin) 1890–   (Suspended Aug. 1914–1920).

380. *Military Affairs.* Washington, 1937–1968. Manhattan, Kansas, 1968–   . Index *1937–1968.*

381. *Military Collector and Historian.* Washington, D. C. since 1951.

382. *Military Historical Society Bulletin.* London, since 1951. Quarterly.
383. *Military Review.* U. S. Army Command and General Staff College, Fort Leavenworth, Kansas, 1922– . Index *1922–1965.*
384. *Naval Chronicle.* 40 volumes: 2 a year. Vol. I, 1799, to Vol. XL, 1818. Contents: naval news—*London Gazettes*; historical narratives of naval actions, including extracts from authentic private letters, etc.; biographical memoirs of (mostly) deceased naval officers; reports of courts-martial; inventions and other subjects of naval interest; accounts of shipwrecks, etc.; hydrographical articles; correspondence, births, marriages and deaths.
385. *Naval and Military Record.* London: 1886–1936 (Nov.) Then merged with *Army, Navy and Air Force Gazette* to become *United Services Review.*
386. *Naval Review.* London: 1913– . Circulates only among the members, but its files may be consulted in the Naval Library (Ministry of Defence), National Maritime Museum Library, R.U.S.I., and elsewhere. See *Union List of Serials* for Canadian holdings. There is an almost complete run in the University of California (Irvine) Library.
387. *Navy, The.* London: 1895– . 1895–1908 as *Navy League Journal.*
388. *O.R.—Operational Research Quarterly.* London: March 1950– . After 1952 simply as *Operational Research Quarterly.*
389. *Past and Present; a journal of scientific history* (changed to: *Studies in the history of civilization*). London: 1952.
390. *Proceedings of the British Academy for the promotion of historical, philosophical and philological studies.* London: 1903– .
391. *Public Administration.* London: 1923– .
392. *Quarterly Transactions of the Royal Institution of Naval Architects.* London: 1860– . Index 1860–1938.
393. *Queen Alexandra's Royal Army Nursing Corps Association Gazette, The.*
394. *Railway Magazine, The.* London: 1897– .
395. *Review of the Royal Corps of Transport, The.* (See 401)
396. *Globe and the Laurel, The.* 1892– .
397. *Royal Air Force Quarterly, The.* London: 1920– .
398. *Royal Air Force Review, The.* London: 1946– .
399. *Royal Army Pay Corps Journal.* Winchester, 1931– .
400. *Royal Army Service Corps Journal, The.* (Now *The Waggoner; journal of the Royal Army Service Corps.*) Aldershot, 1891– .
401. *Royal Corps of Transport Review, The.* (See 395)
402. *Royal Engineers Journal, The.* Chatham, 1870– .
403. *Royal Military Police Journal.* Chichester, 1950– .
404. *Royal Signals Quarterly Journal, The.* London: 1933–1940.
405. *Royal United Service Institution Journal* 1857– . 1857–59 as *United Service Institution Journal.* (See also 360)
406. *Soldier; the British Army Magazine.* London: 1945– .
407. *Tank: the journal of the Royal Tank Regiment.* London: 1919– .

408. *Technology and Culture.* Detroit, 1959–1967, Chicago, 1967– .
409. *Territorial Magazine.* London: 1938– .
410. *Transactions of the Institute of Marine Engineers.* London: 1889– .
411. *Transactions of the Institution of Naval Architects.* London: 1860– .
412. *Transactions of the Royal Historical Society.* London: Old Ser., 1872–1882; New Ser., 1884–1906; 3rd Ser., 1907–1917; 4th Ser., 1918–1950; 5th Ser., 1951– .
413. *U. S. I. Journal.* New Delhi, 1871– .
414. *United Service Magazine,* was begun in 1829 as the *United Service Journal and Naval and Military Magazine.* In the 1840's the title was changed to *United Service Magazine and Naval and Military Journal.* In 1865 it was referred to as Colburn's *United Service Magazine and Naval and Military Journal.* (In the nineties J. F. Maurice failed to turn it into a staff journal.)
415. *United Services and Home Defence Review.* Croydon, 1860– .
416. *United Services Review.* See under *Army and Navy Gazette.*
417. *United States Armed Forces Medical Journal,* I, No. 1, January 1950– .
418. *United States Naval Institute Proceedings.* Annapolis, Md., 1874– . Indexed 1874–1956.
419. *Victorian Studies.* Bloomington, Indiana, 1957– .
420. *Wellesley Index to Victorian Periodical Literature,* Walter Houghton, ed. London: Routledge, 1966.
421. *The Wire.* London: The Royal Corps of Signals, 1924– .

SOME USEFUL BRITISH LIBRARIES:
(OTHERS ARE LISTED IN INDIVIDUAL CHAPTERS)

In all cases, write to the Librarian well ahead of time saying what you wish to use, why, and asking if there are any restrictions as to hours, seating, use of equipment, or upon the materials themselves; if permissions are needed, how can they be obtained? Make at least one carbon of your letter and take it with you if you have heard nothing in spite of making several requests.

Some libraries and archives require that they vet the notes taken there, others must see either the pages upon which the material used appears (the Cabinet Historical Office, for instance), others require the whole manuscript be submitted (the Air Department).

Air Historical Branch, Air Department, Ministry of Defence, Queen Anne's Chambers, 41 Tothill Street, London, S.W.1. Apply to S/Ldr. L. A. Jackets, ABH1.
Air Department Library, Ministry of Defence, Whitehall, London, S.W.1. Apply as above.
Army Library, now the Central and Army Library, Ministry of Defence,

Old War Office Building, Whitehall, London, S.W.1. Write to Mr. D. W. King, OBE, FLA, Librarian.

The British Museum, London, W.C.1. To obain Readers' Tickets, write to the Director asking for the necessary form and for any available information leaflets. There are separate Tickets for the Reading Room and the Department of Manuscripts.

In the Reading Room it normally takes at least an hour for a book to be produced. Conditions are becoming overcrowded but general amenities compare well with those at the P. R. O.

The Students' Room in the Department of Manuscripts remains an agreeable place in which to work, though there have been times this summer (1967) when no seat has been immediately available. The Department holds the personal collections of papers of many leading politicians, officers of the fighting services, and other public servants.

Imperial War Museum, Lambeth Road, London, S.E.1. Public libraries open daily, 10–6; Sunday, 2–6. Reference Libraries open Monday–Friday, 10–5. Write ahead of a visit to the Director, Dr. Noble Frankland, to ensure best results. Documentary films shown daily, 12–2. Tremendous photographic resources (write Mr. J. Golding, Photographic Librarian).

National Maritime Museum. Hours 10–5, Monday through Friday. Charing Cross: train to Maze Hill.

National Register of Archives, Quality Court, Chancery Lane, London, W.C.2.

Naval Library, Ministry of Defence, Empress State Building, Earls Court, London, S.W.7.

The Public Record Office, Chancery Lane, London, W.C.2. To obtain a Reader's Ticket, write to the Keeper of Public Records asking for the necessary form and for the latest information leaflet.

Researchers should know that the overcrowding at the P. R. O. has latterly become worse, especially during 1966–1968. Under present conditions it is necessary to arrive at the Office *before 9:30 a.m.* and stand in a queue in order to be sure of a seat. This is especially true of the summer months. There are plans to provide more accommodation; write to the P. R. O. well ahead, as alternate arrangements can be made.

The Royal Artillery Institution, Woolwich, S.E.10.

The Royal Engineers Institution, Chatham.

The Library of the Secretary of the Army Museums Ogilby Trust, Northumberland Avenue, London, S.W.1. This contains a small, but growing collection of manuscripts as well as a useful number of books.

British Military Booksellers

Blackwell's, Broad Street, Oxford.

The Bohemia Book Shop, 116 Bohemia Road, St. Leonards-on-the-Sea, Hastings, Sussex.

Francis Edwards, 83 Marylebone High Street, London, W.1.

Gale & Polden, Wellington Square, Aldershot, Surrey.
Heffer's, 3–4 Petty Curry, Cambridge, England.
W. E. Hersant, Ltd., The Cholmeley Bookshop, 228 Archway Road, Highgate, London N.6.
A. A. Johnston, Pitney, Langport, Somerset, England.
Graham K. Scott, 2 The Broadway, Friern Barnet, London, N.11.
James Thin, 53–59 South Bridge, Edinburgh.
G. W. Walford, 186 Upper Street, London, N.1.

SOME OTHER SOCIETIES' PUBLICATIONS

Other societies include the Alcuin Club Collections from 1899 onwards, the British Society of Franciscan Studies from 1908 to 1937, with its Extra Series 1912 to 1932; the Canterbury and York Society from 1909 onwards; the Catholic Record Society Publications from 1905 onwards; the Caxton Society from 1844 to 1854; the English Historical Society from 1838 to 1856; the English Place-name Society from 1924 onwards; the Hansard Knollys Society from 1846 to 1854; the Harleian Society Publication from 1869 onwards (particularly valuable for its visitations to the various countries and its sample of pedigree information as well as its Register Section from 1877 onwards, publishing the registers of various London churches); the Henry Bradshaw Society from 1891 onwards, mainly containing arcane information about abbeys and monasteries; the Huguenot Society of London from 1887 onwards (which as its name implies covers the contribution of French emigres in Britain); the Jewish Historical Society of England from 1901 onwards; the Parker Society from 1841 to 1855; and lastly the Camden Society Old Series from 1838 to 1872, New Series 1891 to 1901 and Third Series from 1900 onwards. To the printed material made available by these national societies should be added the modest but valuable local material made accessible by the local historical societies publishing original material—the Bedfordshire Historical Record Society from 1913 onwards; the Buckinghamshire Record Society from 1938 onwards; the Cumberland and Westmorland Antiquarian and Archaeological Society 1877 to 1937, this also was a Record or Chartulary Society 1897 to 1932 and has Tract Series from 1882 onwards; the Devon and Cornwall Record Society 1906 to 1954, New Series from 1955 onwards; the Surtees Society from 1835 onwards with some 165 volumes; the Bristol Record Society from 1930 onwards; the Hampshire Record Society from 1899 onwards; the Southampton Record Society from 1905 onwards, together with the Southampton Record Series from 1951 onwards; the Cantilupe Society 1908 to 1925 (concerned with Hereford); the Kent Archaeological Society Records Branch from 1912 onwards; the Lancashire and Cheshire Record Society, Series I 1844 to 1886 with two general indices, Vols. 1–30 (1836) and Vols. 31–114 (1893), New Series 1883 to 1947 and a Third Series from 1949 onwards; the Lincoln Record Society Publications from 1911 onwards; the Middlesex County Record Society 1886 to 1892; the Norfolk Record Society from 1931 onwards; the Newcastle-upon-Tyne Records Committee Publications 1920 to 1933; the Thoroton Society from 1903 onwards; the Oxford Record Society from 1919 onwards, Oxford Historical Society 1885 to 1936, New Series from 1939 onwards; the Somerset Record Society from 1887 onwards; the Staffordshire Record Society (before 1936 the William Salt Archaeological Society) from 1880 onwards (the subject index is contained in the 1950 to 1951 (1954) (Volume); the Surrey Record Society 1916 to 1931; the Sussex Record Society from 1902 onwards; the Dovedale Society from 1931 onwards; the Wiltshire Record Society 1896 to 1902; the Wiltshire Archaeological and Historical Society 1882 to 1930; the Wiltshire Archaeological and Historical Society Records Branch from 1939 onwards; the Worcestershire Historical Record Society from 1893 onwards; the Yorkshire Archaeological Society Record Series from 1885 onwards, together with its Extra Series 1888 to 1926 and its Record Extra Series from 1914 onwards; the Bradford Historical and Antiquarian Society Local Record Series from 1929 onwards; the North Riding Record Society 1884 to 1892, New Series 1894 to 1897; the Thoresby Society Publications from 1891 onwards; the Manx Society 1859 to 1882; the Société Jersiaise Publications 1876 to 1924.

II

MILITARY DEVELOPMENTS FROM PREHISTORIC TIMES TO 1485

John Beeler

An essay which encompasses the historiography of more than sixteen centuries of fighting can do little more than indicate what has been done in the field of military studies and suggest the numerous areas in which rewarding investigations may be undertaken. It should be evident that each of the three major periods included in this survey—Roman, Anglo-Saxon, and post-Conquest—is deserving of separate treatment, and only the exigencies of space preclude such an arrangement.

The military historian who would concentrate on pre-Tudor developments must be prepared for a frustrating experience from the very outset. No general bibliography in the field has ever been assembled, and the standard work on the historiography of medieval England, Gross (61), is now more than half a century old. A long-awaited new edition, sponsored in part by the Medieval Academy of America, has been delayed for lack of funds. More recent is the *Bibliography of the History of Wales* (133), which is indispensable for any study of Wales and the Marches. It is necessary, then, to supplement Gross with other and less satisfactory material. Such compilations as Bonser's *Anglo-Saxon and Celtic Bibliography* (14), Frewer (56), and Farrer and Evans' *English Translations* (52) are useful only if the researcher knows what he is looking for, or if he has the time for a page-by-page hunt. The second volume of *Writings on British History, 1901–1933* (11) contains a brief but useful section on military, naval, and maritime history, and *The International Medieval Bibliography* (76), inaugurated in 1967, will provide a continuing and up-to-date listing of current literature in all fields. For periodical material the problem is even stickier. The more eminent journals such as *Speculum* (125), the *English Historical Review* (49), and *Archaeologia* (3) are regularly indexed, but not all the significant articles appear in such prestigious publications. As examples, Canon William Bazeley's account of the Battle of Tewkesbury, long the most reliable, appeared in the *Proceedings of the Bristol and Gloucester Archaeological Society* (8), and King's excellent interpretation of the fight at Coleshill was published in the *Welsh History Review* (80).

Many articles of importance are to be found in the journals of local and relatively obscure societies. Complete runs of these periodicals are to be found only in major libraries. With modern means of reproducing the printed page, it is a simple matter to have an article copied, if the researcher knows what he wants copied and can locate the original. For the period prior to 1900, Gomme (60) and the *Index to Archaeological Papers, 1891–1900* (75) provide valuable assistance to the student of military architecture, but purely historical papers are not included. Mullins, *A Guide to the Historical and Archaeological Publications of Societies in England and Wales 1901–1933* (151) is indispensable, and it is to be hoped that a subsequent compilation will put this index on a more nearly current basis.

Something must now be said about the character of the narrative sources for the Middle Ages. A factor of significance which must be constantly kept in mind is that from the end of the Roman administration to the beginning of the fifteenth century at the earliest, virtually all the narrative history was written by non-combatants; that all of them were clerics— chiefly monks—and that while many of them had access to good sources of information, often eye-witnesses to the events they describe, few of them had much of an appreciation for, or knowledge of strategy and tactics. Frequently victory or defeat was ascribed to divine intervention, or to the judgment of God on some deserving or particularly sinful commanding officer. However edifying such conclusions might have been to contemporary readers, they are not very helpful to the student who is trying to find out exactly what happened in a specific campaign or engagement, and why. A notable exception to this general stricture is to be found in the writings of the Anglo-Welshman, Giraldus Cambrensis who, from his acute observations of military operations on the Welsh March and in Ireland, seems definitely miscast as a cleric. His *Descriptio Kambriae* (59) and *Expugnatio Hibernica* (58) are first-rate commentaries, and in the former he laid down the basic strategy for the conquest of Wales which Edward I was to follow a century later with such notable success.

In general, the narrative sources have to be used with a great deal of caution. Numbers, in those rare cases in which they are used, are completely unreliable, as Delbrück (41) and Ramsey (111) have demonstrated. Only when it is possible to check the figures of the chroniclers against some kind of official document can they be used, and this is seldom possible before the last quarter of the thirteenth century.

Fortunately for the investigator, the source materials, such as they are, are readily available. Most of the narrative sources have been published in definitive editions, many of them in the well-known *Rolls Series* (113) which includes, in addition, the cartularies of some of the more important monastic houses. Calendars of such useful documents as the *Charter Rolls* (25), various Inquisitions (26–27), the *Patent Rolls* (28), and others have all been published. The *Pipe Rolls* (107) and numerous ancient charters have appeared over the imprint of the Pipe Roll Society; and much of the *Guide to the Reports of the Historical Manuscripts Commission* (63) is now in print. The university presses have been active in publishing such useful materials as the *Regesta Regum Anglo-Normannorum* (112), and it would be impossible to list here the societies and publishers who have and are contributing to the constantly growing amount of source material available to medievalists.

There remains, however, a considerable body of manuscript material which has not been published. The principal repositories for these documents are the British Museum and the Public Record Office, although there are important collections in such hands as universities, cathedral chapters, municipal corporations, and private individuals. Access to this material is usually not difficult for qualified scholars to obtain, although it should be noted that there is a certain amount of red tape involved in getting permission to use the documents in the Public Record Office. The *Guide to the Public Records* (62) is invaluable in determining which of the many categories of unpublished documents might be worth investigating, and Davis' *Medieval Cartularies* (39) is useful in locating material in that special category.

Military developments in prehistoric England are, of necessity, a matter of conjecture. The landscape abounds with earthworks, many attributed to the early Britons, but their exact function is a matter of dispute. The short, but excellent exposition in Clark (31) is perhaps the best introduction to the subject. The classification of British earthworks was long clouded due to the absence of any clear notion as to which of the literally thousands of such constructions should be assigned to what periods. A system of classification was worked out jointly in 1903 by the Congress of Archaeological Societies and the Society of Antiquaries (121) which has generally been followed in Allcroft's still useful *Ancient Earthworks* (1), and in the pertinent sections of the *Victoria County Histories* (132) and the *Inventories* of the Ancient Monuments Commissions (116).

In the field of prehistory, the archaeologist's spade is the most significant contributor to the increasing store of information from which inferences may be drawn. Eventually some conclusions may be reached as to the purposes for which these earthworks were constructed, and about the military system which provided for their defense. Knowledge of the weapons used by the prehistoric Britons also derives from archaeological finds although it may be inferred, due to an inherent military conservatism, that weapons and armor used by the natives of Caesar's day were not of recent development. It should not be assumed, however, that the military organization of southeast Britain, the area most exposed to continental influence, was general throughout the island. Among the many questions remaining to be answered are those dealing with the military organization of pre-Roman Britain. It has been possible to determine the degree of military efficiency attained by the Britons at the time of the Claudian conquest, but much more evidence will have to be accumulated before it can be concluded even tentatively that these institutions antedate the first century A.D.

THE ROMAN PERIOD. The historic period is reached in the middle of the first century B.C. But until the fourteenth century it is virtually impossible to speak of "a nation at war." Until the ninth century at the very earliest there was not even a kingdom of the English, and it was even later that a true English nation emerged. For most of the period under consideration the sources are at once so scanty and so diverse that it is impossible to describe accurately the impact of warfare on the general population. It is frequently possible to outline invasions, campaigns, and battles; to report that on some occasions the countryside was ravaged; to note that in some cases the people rose in revolt, or again that civil war raged; but until the fuller documentation of the fourteenth century is reached, the evidence, except in very rare instances, is not available to record the activities of "a nation at war."

Caesar's *Commentaries* (24) provides the first literary evidence for the military capabilities of the Britons. The Roman general made two brief forays across the Channel from Gaul in 55 and 54 B.C. and with these reconnaissances, the military history of Britain begins. The Roman occupation of much of the island a century later is recorded in such contemporary sources as Tacitus (127), and on numerous inscriptions which have fortunately been preserved. As early as the eighteenth century John Horsley (74) compiled a list of such inscriptions which is still useful to the military historian. More recent and fuller are the archaeological surveys published by Collingwood (33) and Collingwood and Wright (34), the first volume of whose *The Roman Inscriptions of Britain* is particularly valuable for the military information included.

The operations involved in the reduction of Britain have been developed admirably in two volumes by D. R. Dudley and G. Webster (46–47), and by Colonel George P. Welch (135). The collected papers of Eric Birley (12), Salway's *Frontier People* (117), Grace Simpson's *Britons and the Roman Army* (124), and White's *Litus Saxonicum* (136) concentrate on specific problems of the conquest and subsequent occupation, while the military highways have been thoroughly treated by I. G. Margary (88–89). Dr. Simpson in particular brings a new approach to the distribution of Roman garrisons, challenging much of the accepted chronology of the occupation. All of the works noted above contain useful bibliographies, and Birley has carefully listed the literary and epigraphic sources. These should provide an adequate foundation for further investigation. Additional information, however, is likely to be derived from archaeological research designed to establish the sites of Roman military roads and installations, the dates of their construction and occupation, and the identification of the units furnishing the garrisons.

With the departure of the legions in the fifth century and the invasion of the island by the Angles, Saxons, and Jutes, a true "fog of war" descends. Only dimly can the military operations of the next four centuries be traced. Recently Vera Evison (50) has attempted, using archaeological evidence, to challenge the long-accepted thesis that the invaders of southeastern England were natives of the Jutish peninsula, but her assertion that they came from Frankish Gaul, or were at least subject to Frankish influence has not been widely accepted. Thus the whole problem of the Germanic invasions of Britain remains open and, in the absence of reliable literary sources, it again seems likely that even tentative conclusions as to the time, place, and rate of the barbarian advance will have to await the accumulation of additional archaeological evidence.

THE ANGLO-SAXON PERIOD. Little information exists about the military organization of the invaders, and there is still less about the unsuccessful measures taken by the semi-Romanized inhabitants to halt the barbarian advance. All of the general surveys of medieval warfare include English developments in greater or less detail. Although some of his premises are rather wide of the mark, Oman (103) is the most reliable of these, and certainly the most readable. Delbrück (42), Lot (84), and the most recent, Verbruggen (131), contain important information, and are of value in relating English practices and institutions to those on the continent. Verbruggen suffers the disadvantage of being written in Flemish, a language not widely used by scholars.

For the early centuries of the Germanic conquest, Colonel A. R. Burne's (20–21) reconstructions of some of the recorded battles, although done with considerable ingenuity and insight, are not based upon sufficient evidence to warant confidence in their accuracy. Indeed, until fuller and more accurate sources appear in the last half of the ninth century it is possible, at present, to only guess at much of the military history of Britain. One must also say, however regretfully, that until the very twilight of the old English state is reached, there is little modern literature that is worthy of consideration. There are exceptions, of course. For the period generally designated the Middle Ages, there is but a single work which attempts to survey the entire history of English warfare from any point of view. Michael Powicke (108) has made a thoughful and valuable study of the obligation of Englishmen to perform military service. Altogether, it covers the period from the late Anglo-Saxon *fyrd* to the contract armies of the fifteenth century. But as Powicke emphasises, the obligation to serve was frequently a theoretical one, as the crown often experienced difficulties in enforcing its claim. The author is not concerned with what commanders did with their troops once they were mustered, a limitation which also applies to C. Warren Hollister's (71) significant and well-documented study of the military institutions of the old English state. From the operational standpoint, virtually everything that is known prior to the eleventh century can be found in Sir Frank Stenton's admirable *Anglo-Saxon England* (126).

At first sight it would seem that this gap of half a millennium would provide ample scope for the military scholar. Bede (9) and the *Anglo-Saxon Chronicle* (120) abound with wars, for the period between the departure of the legions and the final subjugation of the Danelaw by the kings of Wessex in the tenth century was one of almost continuous strife. The opportunity is, unfortunately, more apparent than real; the narrative sources, virtually the only ones for these centuries, simply do not provide the material from which any significant conclusions can be reached concerning the military organization and institutions of the Anglo-Saxon conquerors.

1066 ONWARDS. Modern study of the post-Conquest military institutions of Britain began some seventy years ago with the appearance of

Round's (114) classic essay on the introduction of knight service into England. It is still the point of departure, and a most acrimoniously debated one, for any serious consideration of the Norman military structure. But Round failed to give due consideration to the other elements—the old English *fyrd* and the mercenaries—that were frequently utilized by the first Norman kings. These sources of military manpower have been given their proper emphasis by Hollister (72), Prestwich (110), Boussard (15), and Beeler (10). Hollister and Prestwich are concerned primarily with the institutions and procedures which produced the troops used by the Norman kings. Beeler is more interested in what was done with the soldiers after they had been collected. His *Warfare in England, 1066–1189* is the first general military history of the Norman and early Plantagenet periods. Accounts of individual battles are more numerous, but generally they have contributed little to existing knowledge. The reconstructions of Colonel Burne (20–21), previously noted, are usually a cut or two above the average, for he exhibits a better knowledge of the sources than most writers with a military background; even so, his account of the Battle of the Standard (1138) is not a model of its kind.

Not surprisingly, the military operations of 1066, including the battles of Fulford and Stamford Bridge and culminating in the decisive action at Hastings, have attracted wide attention and have produced an extensive literature. Most of this is of little value, being written primarily for popular consumption rather than for the advancement of scholarship. Stamford Bridge is best treated in a slim pamphlet by F. W. Brooks (17), and the most convincing account of the Battle of Hastings continues to be that of Colonel Charles H. Lemmon (83), whose familiarity with the terrain and the sources is unrivalled. William's operations subsequent to the victory at Hastings are thoroughly examined by Baring (6), and for the movements of the Norman army north of the Thames, a little-known article by G. H. Fowler (54) makes a notable contribution.

The latter two scholars illustrate rather vividly the sort of work military historians must do in order to piece out the story. No contemporary annalist saw fit to set down the exact line of William's march from Hastings to Canterbury to Wallingford to Berkhamstead. But Baring and Fowler, noting that the Norman army had reputedly devastated the countryside on its line of march, turned to *Domesday Book* (44), and by comparing the values of estates at the time they were awarded to Norman recipients with the value at the time of King Edward the Confessor, were able to trace, with what must be regarded as acceptable accuracy, the march of William's army around London.

For the period of unrest which followed the Conqueror's coronation—a period which can be characterized as one of thinly disguised military government—the recent biographies of William by Douglas (45) and Barlow (7) are important. The narrative sources, now fuller than ever before, are supplemented by the surviving royal enactments contained in the first volume of the *Regesta Regum Anglo-Normannorum* (112), plus such cartularies of religious houses as have been preserved.

Perhaps even more significant than the introduction of knight service was the importation of the Norman castle, which differed from the earlier English *burh* in being a royal or private fortress instead of a communal defense. The chronicles are useful in their frequent references to castles built by the Norman conquerors throughout England; other names are found in monastic compilations, such as those assembled in the *Monasticon* (94); still others are casually referred to in writs and charters, or mentioned in *Domesday Book* (44). It may be noted that the dry statistics of Domesday sometimes throw some light on the impact of the conquest on the civil population: "Of the aforesaid waste, 166 houses were destroyed because of the castle" at Lincoln; at Norwich 113 houses were demolished to make room for the castle.

But many castles had no written history and, being simple structures of earth and timber, they vanished, leaving behind only the earthworks. Here again the historian is dependent on the work of the archaeologist for approximate dating of these remains. The chapters on ancient earthworks in the *Victoria County Histories* (132), the *Inventories* of the Commissions on Ancient Monuments (116), and the annual summaries published in *Medieval Archaeology* (91) are of first-rate importance to the student of military architecture. Significant articles are, unfortunately, frequently tucked away in the journals and proceedings of local and county societies which, as noted previously, are not usually indexed and often hard to find.

Throughout the Middle Ages the castle continued to figure prominently in the military annals of England. Until long after the introduction of artillery, the defenders of fortified places, whether towns or castles, had a tremendous advantage over the attacker. The evolution of the English castle from the motte-and-bailey constructions of the eleventh century to refinements of the Edwardian concentric fortresses of the thirteenth can be traced in the works of Armitage (4), Braun (16), Brown (18), Cruden (36), Edwards (48), Mackenzie (85), Neaverson (97), Thompson (128), and Toy (129). Additional information is to be found in the *Victoria County Histories* (132), King and Hogg (69), and the *Inventories of the* Commissions on Ancient Monuments for England and Wales (116). Also to be consulted are the publications of the Ministry of Works (93), and the monumental volumes in the *History of the King's Works* (35). Clarke's *Mediaeval Military Architecture* (32), while outdated in many respects, is still useful for its descriptions and plans. And should a definitive history of an individual castle be planned, W. H. St. John Hope's exhaustive treatment of Windsor Castle (73) provides an excellent example.

The principal military events of the Norman era are the periodic baronial revolts, which culminated in the wholesale disorders of Stephen's reign (1135–1154), and the beginning of the Norman conquest of Ireland. It was in Stephen's reign also that the Saxon Chronicler at Peterborough (120) penned his vivid lines describing the impact of war on the countryside and its people, but it is doubtful that such misery and devastation was widespread. These wars are treated in some detail by Beeler (10), by Round in *Geoffrey de Mandeville* (115), and in R. W. C. Davis' recent biography of King Stephen (40). The principal events of the Irish adventure are discussed in Hayes-McCoy's *Irish Battles* (150), which covers the military history of the island from the early eleventh century to the end of the eighteenth.

The long reign of Henry II (1154–1189) is notable for the growing military strength of the crown in relation to that of the great tenants, and for the increasing amount of evidence on which this conclusion rests. The increasing financial resources of the crown may be seen in the *Pipe Rolls* (107), and in the heavy disbursements for military purposes. Both Brown (19) and Beeler (10) have attempted to assess the significance of what appears to have been a tendency for the crown to assume a greater share of the defense responsibility at the expense of the feudal classes, but it is doubtful if the last word has been said on this subject.

An area much in need of investigation is that extending from the death of Henry II to the reign of Edward I, a span of more than eighty years. While the *History of the King's Works* (35) give an excellent account of royal expenditures on fortifications and throws much light on the military interests of the crown during the thirteenth century, there is no adequate history of the numerous wars, both foreign and domestic, which mark the reigns of Richard I (1189–1199), John (1199–1216), and Henry III (1216–1272). Such studies as those of John T. Appleby (2), Sidney Painter (105), and W. L. Warren (134) deal frequently with the military concerns of Richard I and John, but only incidentally, and in connection with the broader problems of policy and statecraft.

It might be noted in passing that English participation in the crusades has been generally overlooked by military writers. While Englishmen in the crusading armies were never very numerous, it is recognized that improvements in the science of fortification date from this period and there is, of course, a considerable literature on the Third Crusade and the exploits of Richard I in Palestine. The account in Oman (103) is usually accepted, and the sources and secondary authorities are listed in Mayer's (90) valuable bibliography. But Englishmen participated in other crusades as well. Numbers of the Anglo-Norman baronage participated in the crusade of 1147, and a contingent of English and Flemish seamen, coasting around to the Mediterranean, contributed significantly to the capture of Lisbon from the Moors. This episode, commemorated in the *Expugnatione Lyxbonensi* (51), marked the beginning of the long friendship between England and Portugal. And even as late as the second half of the thirteenth century men of considerable rank, such as Simon de Montfort, Earl of Leicester, and Prince Edward, the future Edward I, are found campaigning in the Holy Land. A good deal of research remains to be done in this field of English military history.

For the reign of Henry III, military historiography is almost blank. Even for the Baron's War, so significant in the history of the military art, there is no thorough and complete study. Oman (103) and Burne (20–21) have dealt with the engagements at Lewes and Evesham, but these were only the climactic points in campaigns which deserve more searching inquiry. For the continental wars of John and Henry III there is no significant literature, although adequate sources exist on both sides of the Channel for a study of these conflicts. Sanders' *Feudal Military Service* (118) and *English Bar-*

onies (119) throw considerable light on the service due from the lay tenants-in-chief during the thirteenth century, and a similar survey for the ecclesiastical tenants has been made by Helena Chew (30).

With the reign of Edward I (1272–1307) the documentation becomes fuller, and it is possible to reconstruct the military history of the time in greater detail and with greater accuracy than hitherto. J. E. Morris' *Welsh Wars of King Edward the First* (95), although more than half a century old, still remains an outstanding example of the meticulous scholarship and attention to detail that must go into the investigation of military affairs. It was Morris who first utilized the unpublished documents in the Public Record Office in the writing of military history—not simply for a chronicling of campaigns and battles, but to determine the composition of armies and all the multiple activities that can be lumped into the modern science of logistics. For Edward's important campaigns against the Scots, the researches of A. Z. Freeman (55) seem about to bear fruit.

The reign of Edward II (1307–1327) is largely a gap, although the Bannockburn campaign is dealt with at some length by Oman (103), and the battle itself has been described in detail by Morros (96) and Mackenzie (86). While Edward II was no soldier, the reign saw a continuation of the military developments set in motion during the reign of his father, and they merit greater attention than they have hitherto received. Occasional articles, such as those by Keeney (77) and Powicke (109) indicate profitable lines for investigation.

When the long reign of Edward III (1327–1377) is reached, an increased interest is immediately detectable. This is due largely to the drama of the Hundred Years' War and the great English victories at Crecy and Poitiers. Colonel Burne's *Crecy War* (22) is by far the best description of the first phase of the struggle, and it illustrates what can be done when the sources are adequate and the author is an expert with a gifted imagination—and let no one be mistaken: imagination is vital in the writing of military history. It should be remembered, however, that Edward inherited a Scottish war from his predecessor, and that it was in the North that he served his military apprenticeship. Nicholson's (100) recent study of this all-but-forgotten conflict, while disappointing in some respects, is a useful addition to the literature of the reign. Important details on the strength and composition of Edwardian armies are also to be found in the studies of A. E. Prince (144). Kenneth Fowler's *The King's Lieutenant* (147), dealing with the career of Duke Henry of Lancaster, adds depth to the early phases of the war, too often overshadowed by the exploits of Edward II and the Black Prince.

Of greater importance is Hewitt's *Black Prince's Expedition* (64), an exhaustive study of the English operations in Aquitaine culminating in the Battle of Poitiers. This is a model of intensive research combined with crisp, concise writing, and it will long remain the final word on the campaigns of 1355–1357. But of yet more significance is the same author's *The Organization of War under Edward III* (65); indeed this is perhaps the finest analysis of medieval warfare yet to appear. Here for the first time it is possible to discern "the nation at war." Hewitt has carefully examined the

surviving records which, by the fourteenth century, have become sufficiently numerous to provide a valid picture. The impact of war on a civilian population which, for the most part, was not subject to hostilities is discussed at length. Not only has Hewitt made a notable contribution to the military literature of medieval England, he has suggested so many new approaches to "the practice of war" that military historians will be a long time in following through on all of them. It may be observed that while the sources for the fourteenth century are much fuller than those for earlier times, a closer look at the existing records might enable the student of warfare to relate his topic more closely to the life of the people.

The more than thirty years beginning with the Treaty of Bretigny in 1360 and ending with the truce of 1396 have been almost completely neglected, although it should be of considerable interest to the student of small-scale actions. During this time the English holdings were reduced to little more than the Bordelais and the bridgehead at Calais. These losses had been due in part to English mismanagement, but even more they were due to the genius and ingenuity of the French Constable, Bertrand du Guesclin. Several biographies of du Guesclin have been written, but none meet contemporary standards of scholarship. Here is surely a gap in English military history that needs to be filled.

The fifteenth century is, in a number of respects, the most interesting of all the medieval centuries from a military viewpoint—and the least understood. The opening years are notable for the disturbances that marked the accession of the House of Lancaster, including the rebellion of the Percies, the Shrewsbury campaign, and the repeated operations in the North where Henry IV (1399–1413) blasted his enemies out of their castles with artillery, the first recorded triumphs for the new weapons on English soil. Henry's reign was also marked by the successful Welsh rising of Owain Glyn Dwr, which the English were never able to suppress. It is surprising that none of these incidents has been studied seriously. Glyn Dwr's operations in particular should be of interest to the modern student, for the Welsh chieftain, like du Guesclin in the previous century, conducted a generally successful guerrilla campaign against the vastly more numerous and better armed English.

But the fifteenth century was also an age of transition. It witnessed the second phase of the Hundred Years' War which opened so brilliantly with the last great triumphs of the longbow and ended in disaster at Formigny and Castillon with artillery playing an important if not decisive role. Thereafter the English retired behind the Channel, and for the next thirty years their energies were devoted to the intermittent and bloody Wars of the Roses.

Modern commentary on this fascinating century is strangely uneven, with most of the emphasis on the Hundred Years' War. The general course of the conflict is admirably delineated by Colonel Burne in *The Agincourt War* (23), without doubt his best historical work. The Battle of Agincourt is vividly recreated by Christopher Hibbert (67), but the equally interesting engagement at Verneuil has yet to find a modern chronicler. The administrative and personnel problems that beset English commanders operating in France are thoroughly examined by Newhall (98–99) whose studies, unfortunately, do not extend beyond 1440. This phase of the long struggle between France and England is of significance for the first appearance of eye-witness accounts by participants in the action. These narratives suffer from the usual weaknesses of firsthand testimony, but they are probably much closer to the truth than are the vague and garbled tales of the monkish annalists of earlier centuries. Strangely enough, French scholarship has produced nothing to compare with Burne's (23) account. Ferdinand Lot (84) seems mainly concerned with attempts—not very convincing—to prove that in every general engagement of the war the French were outnumbered; Perroy (106) is not much interested in the military aspects of the struggle— he dismisses Agincourt in eight lines!

While a good deal has been written about the second half of the Hundred Years' War, most of it deals with the operation and administration of the armies maintained beyond the Narrow Seas. Little research has been undertaken on the impact of the war on the English people, other than their complaints about the cost and their charges of maladministration when English armies began to lose. It can be certain, however, that the drain of men, money, and supplies over a period of nearly forty years must have had an effect on English society beyond the political. Here is a field for investigation which should yield important results.

It is often said that the dynastic struggle known as the Wars of the Roses produced little of military significance saving only the career of Edward IV and the appearance of the first professional account of a military campaign in English, the anonymous *Arrivall of Edward IV* (68). Edward has been referred to as the "first modern general," and it is certainly true that his appreciation of the value of time distinguishes him from his more plodding contemporaries. But the numerous engagements, while lacking in tactical or technical innovations, are not without interest; the use of artillery becomes more frequent; hand-guns are mentioned at St. Albans II and during Edward's 1471 campaign. And certainly a war which was conducted with such savage bitterness and which resulted in the extinction of so many aristocratic families is not without social implications. It is regrettable that the contemporary narrative sources are so meager and unsatisfactory—the *Arrivall* (68) is the only really good account of any campaign—and that the histories published during the following Tudor age are so biased as to be inherently suspect. The documentary materials have never been fully exploited, and a definitive study of the Wars of the Roses has yet to be undertaken. Paul Murray Kendall's *Richard III* (78) and *Warwick the Kingmaker* (79) are useful, but Lander's *Wars of the Roses* (82) consists of little more than lengthy excerpts from contemporary accounts and contributes nothing in the way of analysis or interpretation. Simons' *Edward IV* (123) contains little that is new, and although the major emphasis is on Edward's military career, there is considerable confusion and ambiguity in the handling of military details. The system by which the tumultuary armies of the late fifteenth century were raised is described in the important studies of Dunham (145) and McFarlane (146), but the serious student should have the patience to tackle Scofield's massive *Life and Reign of Edward the Fourth* (122).

The study of the armor and weapons of the Middle Ages is a highly specialized one, and despite a considerable literature on these subjects— perhaps it should be said because of the extensive literature—a good deal of confusion continues to prevail, especially with regard to terminology. For the earlier periods, until the introduction of plate armor in the thirteenth century, surviving examples of armor are extremely rare, and considerable reliance must be placed on the pictorial representations found in manuscript miniatures, on tomb effigies, grave brasses and, of course, the unique Bayeux Tapestry. These representations have been variously interpreted with results that can be confusing, even to the knowledgeable. The most recent and best discussion of eleventh century arms and armor is Sir James Mann's article in *The Bayeux Tapestry* (87). Also useful for the period are Blair's *European Armour* (13), Davidson's *The Sword in Anglo-Saxon England* (38), and Oakeshott's *The Archaeology of Weapons* (101) and *The Sword in the Age of Chivalry* (102). Older works, such as those of Ashdown (5), Ffoulkes (53), Gardner (57), Hewitt (66), and Meyrick (92) are still of value, particularly for their illustrations, but the terminology is often confusing, and sometimes contradictory. It should be noted that most of these works are European in scope, but their application to developments in England, where actual remains are few, can be attested by reference to sepulchral monuments and the numerous surviving brasses.

Gunpowder, which was eventually to render armor obsolete, was employed in England as early as 1327 according to the evidence of the famous Milemete miniature (130), but to date no comprehensive survey of its effects on English military developments has been attempted. B. H. St. John O'Neil's *Castles and Cannon* (104) proves beyond doubt that artillery was soon utilized for the defense of fortified places; that older structures were modified to accommodate the new weapons, while new fortifications incorporated gun-ports into the defensive scheme. Such general surveys as Carman's *History of Firearms* (29) and Hogg's *English Artillery* (70) are helpful starting points, but a great deal remains to be learned about the employment of artillery in field armies, and about the introduction and use of individual weapons or hand-guns. Contemporary accounts frequently mention the use of such ordnance on the battlefield and in siege warfare from the middle of the fourteenth century. The Public Records contain numerous references to royal expenditures on guns and ammunition, but a definitive study has yet to be made.

While it is probable that "the nation at war" can never be clearly discerned in the centuries preceding the Tudors, much remains to be done in exploiting the existing sources. Eventually a picture will emerge much clearer than anything available at present.

BIBLIOGRAPHY

1. Allcroft, A. Hadrain. *Earthwork of England.* London: Macmillan and Co., 1908.
2. Appleby, John T. *England without Richard, 1189–1199.* Ithaca, N. Y.: Cornell University Press, 1965.
3. *Archaeologia: or miscellaneous tracts relating to antiquity.* Journal of the Society of Antiquaries of London. London: 1770– .
4. Armitage, Ella S. *The Early Norman Castles of the British Isles.* London: John Murray, 1912.
5. Ashdown, Charles Henry. *British and Foreign Arms and Armour.* London: T. C. and E. C. Jack, 1909.
6. Baring, Francis Henry. *Domesday Tables for the Counties of Surrey, Berkshire, Middlesex, Hertford, Buckingham, and Bedford, and for the New Forest.* London: St. Catherine Press, 1909.
7. Barlow, Frank. *William I and the Norman Conquest.* London: The English Universities Press, 1965.
8. Bazeley, Canon William. "Tewkesbury." *Proceedings of the Bristol and Gloucester Archaeological Society,* XXVI (1903), 173–193.
9. Beda Venerabilis. *Historia Ecclesiasticae Gentis Anglorum,* in *Opera Historica Bedae.* Charles Plummer, ed. Oxford: Oxford University Press, 1896. 2 vols.
10. Beeler, John. *Warfare in England, 1066–1189.* Ithaca, N. Y.: Cornell University Press, 1966.
11. Bellot, H. Hale, ed. *Writings on British History, 1901–1933.* 5 vols. Volume II, *The Middle Ages, 450–1485.* New York: Barnes and Noble, 1968.
12. Birley, Eric. *Roman Britain and the Roman Army.* Kendall: Titus Wilson and Son, 1953.
13. Blair, Claude. *European Armour, circa 1066 to circa 1700.* New York: The Macmillan Co., 1959.
14. Bonser, Wilfred. *An Anglo-Saxon and Celtic Bibliography (450–1087),* Berkeley: University of California Press, 1957. 2 vols.
15. Boussard, J. *Les Mercenaries au XIIe siècle: Henri Plantagenet et les origines de l'armée de metier.* Paris: Bibliothèque de l'École des Chartes, 1947.
16. Braun, Hugh. *The English Castle.* 2nd ed., rev. London: B. T. Batsford, 1943.
17. Brooks, F. W. *The Battle of Stamford Bridge* (East Yorkshire Local History Series: No. 6). York: East Yorkshire Local History Society, 1956.
18. Brown, R. Allen. *English Medieval Castles.* London: B. T. Batsford, 1954.
19. ———. "Royal Castle-Building in England 1154–1216." *English Historical Review,* LXX (1955), 353–398.

20. Burne, Lieutenant-Colonel Alfred H. *The Battlefields of England,* with a Foreward by G. M. Trevelyan. London: Methuen and Co., 1951.

21. ————. *More Battlefields of England.* London: Methuen and Co., 1952.

22. ————. *The Crecy War: a military history of the Hundred Years War from 1337 to the Peace of Bretigny, 1360.* London: Eyre and Spottiswoode, 1955.

23. ————. *The Agincourt War: a military history of the latter part of the Hundred Years War from 1369 to 1453.* London: Eyre and Spottiswoode, 1956.

24. Caesar, Caius Julius. *The Gallic War.* H. J. Edwards, tr. (the Loeb Classical Library). London: W. Heinemann, and New York: G. P. Putnam's Sons, 1917.

25. *Calendar of Charter Rolls.* London: H.M.S.O., 1903–1927. 6 vols.

26. *Calendar of Inquisitions Post Mortem and other analogous Documents.* London: H.M.S.O., 1904–   . 18 vols.

27. *Calendar of Miscellaneous Inquisitions.* London: H.M.S.O., 1916–   . 5 vols.

28. *Calendar of Patent Rolls.* London: H.M.S.O., 1891–   . 68 vols.

29. Carman W. Y. *A History of Firearms from Earliest Times to 1914.* London: Routledge and Kegan Paul, 1955.

30. Chew, Helena M. *The English Ecclesiastical Tenants-in-Chief and Knight Service, especially in the thirteenth and fourteenth centuries.* Oxford: Oxford University Press, 1932.

31. Clark, Grahame. *Prehistoric England.* Rev. ed. London: B. T. Batsford, and New York: W. W. Norton, 1962.

32. Clarke, George T. *Mediaeval Military Architecture in England.* London: Wyman and Sons, 1884. 2 vols.

33. Collingwood, R. G. *The Archaeology of Roman Britain.* London: Methuen and Co., 1930.

34. Collingwood, R. G., and R. P. Wright. *The Roman Inscriptions of Britain.* Vol. I, *Inscriptions on Stone.* Oxford: The Clarendon Press, 1965.

35. Colvin, H. M., gen. ed. *The History of the King's Works.* R. Allen Brown, H. M. Colvin, and A. J. Taylor, *The Middle Ages,* 2 vols. and case of plans. London: H.M.S.O., 1963. Subsequent volumes will carry the history of royal building activities to 1851.

36. Cruden, Stewart. *The Scottish Castle.* London: Thomas Nelson and Sons, 1960.

37. *Curia Regis Rolls.* London: H.M.S.O., 1923–   . 14 vols.

38. Davidson, H. R. Ellis. *The Sword in Anglo-Saxon England; its archaeology and literature.* Oxford: The Clarendon Press, 1962.

39. Davis, G. R. C. *Medieval Cartularies of Great Britain: a short catalogue.* London: Longmans, Green and Co., 1958.

40. Davis, R. H. C. *King Stephen, 1135–1154.* Berkeley: University of California Press, 1967.

41. Delbrück, Hans. *Numbers in History*. London: London University Press, 1913.

42. ———. *Geschichte der Kriegskunst im Rahmen des Politischen Geschichte*, 6 vols. Vol. III: *Das Mittelalter*. Berlin: Georg Stilke, 1920–1932.

43. *Descriptive Catalogue of Ancient Deeds*. London: H.M.S.O., 1890–1915. 6 vols.

44. *Domesday Book: Liber Censualis Willelmi Primi*. Abraham Furley and Henry Ellis, eds. London: Record Commission, 1783–1816. 4 vols.

45A. Douglas, David C. *William the Conqueror: the Norman impact upon England*. Berkeley: University of California Press, 1964.

45B. ———. *The Norman Achievement*. Berkeley: University of California Press, 1969.

46. Dudley, D. R., and G. Webster. *The Rebellion of Boudicca*. New York: Barnes and Noble, 1962.

47. ———. *The Roman Conquest of Britain A.D. 43–57*. London: Batsford, 1965.

48. Edwards, (Sir) J. Goronwy. "Edward I's Castle-Building in Wales." *Proceedings of the British Academy*, XXXII (1944), 15–81.

49. *English Historical Review*. London: 1896– .

50. Evison, Vera. *The Fifth Century Invasions South of the Thames*. London: The Athlone Press, 1965.

51. *De Expugnatione Lyxbonensi, The Conquest of Lisbon, from the unique manuscript in Corpus Christi College, Cambridge*. Charles Wendell David, ed. and tr. New York: Columbia University Press, 1936.

52. Farrar, C. P., and A. P. Evans. *Bibliography of English Translations from Mediaeval Sources*. New York: Columbia University Press, 1946.

53. Ffoulkes, Charles. *Armour and Weapons*. Oxford: The Clarendon Press, 1909.

54. Fowler, G. H. "The Devastation of Bedfordshire and the Neighboring Counties in 1065 and 1066." *Archaeologia*, LXXII (1922), 41–50.

55. Freeman, A. Z. "The King's Penny: The Headquarters Paymasters under Edward I, 1295–1307." *Journal of British Studies*, VI (1966), 1–22; "A Moat Defensive: the Coast Defense Scheme of 1295." *Speculum*, XLII (1967), 442–462. For a summary of the warfare between England and Scotland, see Edward Miller, *War in the North: the Anglo-Scottish wars of the Middle Ages*. Hull: University of Hull Press, 1960.

56. Frewer, Louis B. *Bibliography of Historical Writings Published in Great Britain and the Empire, 1940–1945*. Oxford: Oxford University Press, 1947. See also Joan C. Lancaster, *Bibliography of Historical Works issued in the United Kingdom, 1946–1956*. London: University of London Institute of Historical Research, 1957.

57. Gardner, J. Starkie. *Armour in England from the Earliest Times to the Reign of James the First.* London: Seeley and Co., and New York: The Macmillan Co., 1897.

58. Giraldus Cambrensis. *Expugnatio Hibernica.* In Vol. V, *Giraldi Cambrensis Opera,* James F. Dimock, J. S. Brewer, and G. F. Warner, eds. (Rolls Series). London: H.M.S.O., 1867.

59. ———, *Descriptio Kambriae.* In Vol. VI, *Giraldi Cambrensis Opera,* James F. Dimock, J. S. Brewer, and G. F. Warner, eds. (Rolls Series). London: H.M.S.O., 1868.

60. Gomme, George Laurence. *Index of Archaeological Papers, 1665–1890.* London: Archibald Constable and Co., 1907.

61. Gross, Charles. *The Sources and Literature of English History from the Earliest Times to about 1485.* London: Longmans Green and Co., 1915.

62. *Guide to the Contents of the Public Record Office.* Rev. ed. London: H.M.S.O., 1963. 2 vols.

63. *Guide to the Reports of the Historical Manuscripts Commission: Part I—Topographical Guide, 1870–1911; Part II—Index to Persons 1870–1911* (2 vols.); *Index of Persons 1911–1957* (3 vols.). London: H.M.S.O., 1914–1966.

64. Hewitt, H. J. *The Black Prince's Expedition of 1355–1357.* Manchester: Manchester University Press, 1958.

65. ———. *The Organization of War under Edward III, 1338–62.* Manchester: Manchester University Press, and New York: Barnes and Noble, 1966.

66. Hewitt, John. *Ancient Armour and Weapons in Europe: from the Iron Period of the Northern Nations to the end of the (seventeenth) century.* Oxford and London: J. Henry and J. Parker, 1855–1860. 3 vols.

67. Hibbert, Christopher. *Agincourt.* London: B. T. Batsford, 1964.

68. *Historie of the Arivall of Edward IV in England and the Finall Recoverye of His Kingdomes from Henry VI, A.D. MCCCCLXXI.* John Bruce, ed. London: Camden Society. Old Ser. I, 1838.

69. Hogg, A. H. A., and D. J. C. King. "Early Castles in Wales and the Marches." *Archaeologia Cambrensis,* CXVII (1963), 77–124.

70. Hogg, O. F. G. *English Artillery, 1326–1716; being the history of artillery in this country prior to the formation of the Royal Regiment of Artillery.* London: Royal Artillery Institution, 1963.

71. Hollister, C. Waren. *Anglo-Saxon Military Institutions on the Eve of the Norman Conquest.* Oxford: The Clarendon Press, 1962.

72. ———. *The Military Organization of Norman England.* Oxford: The Clarendon Press, 1965.

73. Hope, W. H. St. John. *Windsor Castle: an architectural history.* London: Country Life, 1913. 2 vols. and portfolio of plans.

74. Horsley, John. *Britannia Romana: or the Roman Antiquities of Britain.* London: John Osborn and Thomas Longman, 1732. Useful for materials discovered in the eighteenth century following the publication of Horsley's work is Rev. Thomas Reynolds' *Iter Britan-*

niarum; or that part of the itinerary of Antoninus which relates to Britain. Cambridge: J. Burges, 1799.

75. *Index of Archaeological Papers, 1891–1900.* London: Congress of Archaeological Societies in union with the Society of Antiquaries, 1892–1914.

76. *International Medieval Bibliography.* Robert S. Hoyt and Peter H. Sawyer, eds. Department of History, University of Minnesota, Minneapolis, Minnesota, 55, 455.

77. Keeney, B. C. "Military Service and the Development of Nationalism in England, 1272–1327." *Speculum,* XXII (1947), 534–549.

78. Kendall, Paul Murray. *Richard the Third.* New York: W. W. Norton, 1956.

79. ———. *Warwick the Kingmaker.* London: George Allen and Unwin, 1957.

80. King, D. J. Cathcart. "Henry II and the Fight at Coleshill." *The Welsh History Review,* II (1965), 367–373.

81. Laking, Sir Guy Francis, bart. *A Record of European Armour and Arms through Seven Centuries.* London: G. Bell and Sons, 1920–1922. 5 vols. This is still valuable for its illustrations, but subsequent research has outdated much of the text.

82. Lander, J. R. *The Wars of the Roses.* London: Secker and Warburg, 1965.

83. Lemmon, Lieutenant-Colonel Charles H. *The Field of Hastings.* St. Leonards-on-Sea: Budd and Gillatt, 1956. See also the same author's essay "The Campaign of 1066," in *The Norman Conquest, its Setting and Impact.* New York: Charles Scribner's Sons, 1966.

84. Lot, Ferdinand. *L'Art militaire et les armées au moyen age en Europe et dans le Proche Orient.* Paris: Payot, 1946. 2 vols.

85. Mackenzie, W. Mackay. *The Battle of Bannockburn: a study in mediaeval warfare.* Glasgow: James MacLehose and Sons, 1913.

86. ———. *The Mediaeval Castle in Scotland.* London: Methuen and Co., 1927.

87. Mann, Sir James. "Arms and Armour," in *The Bayeux Tapestry: a comprehensive survey.* Sir Frank Stenton, gen. ed. London: Phaidon Press, 1957. Good summaries of the development of armor in England are Sir James's chapter, "Arms and Armour," in Vol. I of *Medieval England,* new ed., Austin Lane Poole, ed. Oxford: the Clarendon Press, 1958; and his *An Outline of Arms and Armour in England from the Early Middle Ages to the Civil War.* London: H.M.S.O., 1960.

88. Margery, Ivan D. *Roman Roads in Britain.* London: Phoenix House, 1955–1957. 2 vols.

89. ———. *Roman Ways in the Weald.* 3rd ed., Foreward by O. G. S. Crawford. London: Phoenix House, 1965.

90. Mayer, Hans Eberhard. *Bibliographie zur Geschichte der Kreuzzüge.* Hannover: Hahnsche Buchhandlung, 1960.

91. *Medieval Archaeology.* Journal of the Society for Medieval Archaeology. London: 1957– .

92. Meyrick, Samuel Rush. *A Critical Inquiry into Antient Armour as it existed in Europe, particularly in Great Britain, from the Norman Conquest to the reign of King Charles II.* 2nd ed. London: H. G. Bohn, 1842, 3 vols.

93. Ministry of Public Buildings and Works. H.M.S.O. publishes a series of *Regional Guides to Ancient Monuments* under the ownership or guardianship of the Ministry of Works, as well as *Official Guide-Books* to individual structures now in the Ministry's care. A complete list of titles and prices may be had upon application for Sectional List No. 27.

94. *Monasticon Anglicanum.* John Caley, Henry Ellis, and Bulkeley Bandinel, eds. New ed., 6 vols. in 8. London: Longman, Hurst, Ress, Orme, Brown, *et multiis aliis,* 1817–1830.

95. Morris, John E. *The Welsh Wars of King Edward the First: a contribution to mediaeval military history, based on original documents.* Oxford: The Clarendon Press, 1901 reprinted 1968.

96. ———. *Bannockburn.* Cambridge: Cambridge University Press, 1914.

97. Neaverson, Ernest. *Mediaeval Castles in North Wales.* Liverpool: Liverpool University Press, 1947.

98. Newhall, Richard Ager. *The English Conquest of Normandy, 1416–1424.* New Haven: Yale University Press, 1924.

99. ———. *Muster and Review; Problems of English Military Administration, 1420–1440.* Cambridge, Mass.: Harvard University Press, 1940.

100. Nicholson, Ranald. *Edward III and the Scots: the formative years of a military career 1327–1335.* Oxford: Oxford University Press, 1964.

101. Oakeshott, R. E. *The Archaeology of Weapons; Arms and Armour from Prehistory to the Age of Chivalry.* London: Lutterworth Pess, 1960.

102. ———. *The Sword in the Age of Chivalry.* New York: Praeger, 1965.

103. Oman (Sir) Charles W. C. *A History of the Art of War in the Middle Ages.* 2nd ed., rev. and enl. London: Methen and Co., 1924. 2 vols.

104. O'Neil, B. H. St. John. *Castles and Cannon: a study of early artillery fortifications in England.* Oxford: The Clarendon Press, 1960. See also T. F. Tout. "Firearms in England in the 14th Century," in Vol. II, *Collected Papers.* Manchester: Manchester University Press, 1932–1934; and C. J. Ffoulkes. *The Gunfounders of England, with a list of English and Continental gun-founders from the XIV to the XIX Centuries.* Cambridge: Cambridge University Press, 1937.

105. Painter, Sidney. *The Reign of King John.* Baltimore: The Johns Hopkins Press, 1949.

106. Perroy, Edouard. *The Hundred Years War.* W. B. Wells, tr., with an introduction to the English edition by David C. Douglas. London: Eyre and Spottiswoode, 1951. An excellent and superbly illustrated

account of military organization during the Hundred Years' War is found in Chapter 3 of Kenneth Fowler's *The Age of Plantagenet and Valois: the struggle for supremacy, 1328–1498.* New York: G. P. Putnam's Sons, 1967. A useful bibliography is appended.

107. *Pipe Rolls.* The Record Commission originally published the *Pipe Roll for the Thirty-first Year of the Reign of King Henry the First* (London: 1833), and the *Pipe Rolls for 2, 3 and 4 Henry II,* and for *1 Richard I* (London: 1844) under the editorship of the Rev. Joseph Hunter. The first two of these volumes were reissued in facsimile editions by H.M.S.O. in 1929. Publication of the *Pipe Rolls* was undertaken in 1884 by the Pipe Roll Society. Beginning with the *Pipe Roll of 5 Henry II* (London: 1884), the series now extends well into the reign of King Henry III.

108. Powicke, Michael. *Military Obligation in Medieval England: a study in liberty and duty.* Oxford: The Clarendon Press, 1962. See also R. C. Smail. "Art of War," in Vol. I of *Medieval England.* New ed. Austin Lane Poole, ed. Oxford: The Clarendon Press, 1958.

109. ———. "Edward II and Military Obligation." *Speculum,* XXXI 1956), 83–119.

110. Prestwich, J. C. "War and Finance in the Anglo-Norman State." *Transactions of the Royal Historical Society,* 5th Ser., IV (1954), 19–43. See also Schlight, John. *Monarchs and Mercenaries.* New York: New York University Press, 1968. A closely related development, that of the money fief or *fief-rente,* is admirably treated by Bryce Lyon. *From Fief to Indenture: the transition from feudal to non-feudal contract in Western Europe.* Cambridge, Mass.: Harvard University Press, 1957.

111. Ramsey, Sir James H., bart. "The Strength of English Armies in the Middle Ages." *English Historical Review,* XXIX (1914), 221–227.

112. *Regesta Regum Anglo-Normannorum (1066–1154).* H. W. C. Davis, Charles Johnson, H. A. Cronne, and R. H. C. Davis, eds. Oxford: The Clarendon Press, 1913–1969. 4 vols.

113. *Rerum Britannicarum Medii Aevi Scriptores, or Chronicles and Memorials of Great Britain and Ireland during the Middle Ages.* London: H.M.S.O., 1858–1911. 254 vols. This is the *Rolls Series,* so named because it was published under the direction of the Master of the Rolls.

114. Round, J. H. "The Introduction of Knight Service into England," in *Feudal England: historical studies on the XIth and XIIth centuries.* London: Swan Sonnenschein and Co., 1909. No aspect of the Norman Conquest has been debated so acrimoniously as this one. In general, it can be said that Round's thesis, somewhat modified, still holds the field against all comers. The most eloquent and convincing support is found in Sir Frank Stenton. *The First Century of English Feudalism.* 2nd ed. Oxford: The Clarendon Press, 1961. The views of a raucous minority find expression in Eric John. *Land Tenure in Early England: a discussion of some problems.* Leicester: Leicester University Press, 1960; H. G. Richardson and G. O. Sayles. *The*

Governance of Mediaeval England from the Conquest to Magna Carta. Edinburgh: Edinburgh University Press, 1963; and D. J. A. Matthew. *The Norman Conquest.* New York: Schocken Books, 1966.

115. Round, J. H. *Geoffrey de Mandeville: a study of the anarchy.* London: Longmans, Green and Co., 1892.

116. Royal Commissions. These *Inventories* include: The Royal Commission on Ancient and Historical Monuments and Constructions in Wales and Monmouthshire. *An Inventory of the Ancient Monuments in Wales and Monmouthshire.* London: H.M.S.O., 1911–1925. 7 vols; The Royal Commission on Historical Monuments— England. *Inventories of the Historical Monuments in Buckinghamshire, Dorset, Essex, Herefordshire, Hertfordshire, Huntingdonshire, Middlesex, and Westmoreland.* London: H.M.S.O., 1911–1952. 14 vols; The Royal Commission on Ancient and Historical Monuments in Wales and Monmouthshire. *Inventories of the Historical Monuments in Anglesey and Caernarvonshire.* London: H.S.M.O., 1937–1956. 2 vols.

117. Salway, Peter. *The Frontier People of Roman Britain.* Cambridge: University Press, 1965.

118. Sanders, I. J. *Feudal Military Service in England: a study of the constitutional and military Powers of the Barons in Medieval England.* Oxford: Oxford University Press, 1956.

119. ———, *English Baronies: a study of their origin and descent, 1086–1327.* Oxford: The Clarendon Press, 1960.

120. *(Saxon Chronicle) Two of the Saxon Chronicles Parallel with Supplementary Extracts from the Others.* J. Earle and C. Plummer, eds. Oxford: Oxford University Press, 1892–1899. 2 vols.

121. *Scheme for Recording Ancient Defensive Earthworks and Fortified Enclosures.* London: Congress of Archaeological Societies, and the Society of Antiquaries of London, 1903. Recently, however, the thesis that the castle in England was a purely Norman importation has been challenged. While the contention that the least some of the medieval earthworks were of Saxon origin has so far failed to draw wide support, the existence of a "revisionist" point of view should be noted. See in particular: Davison, Brian K., "The Origins of the Castle in England," *Archaeological Journal,* cxxiv (1967), 203–211.

122. Scofield, Cora Louise. *The Life and Reign of Edwards the Fourth, King of England and of France and Lord of Ireland.* London and New York: Longmans, Green and Co., 1923. 2 vols.

123. Simons, E. N. The Reign of Edward IV. New York: Barnes and Noble, 1966.

124. Simpson, Grace. *Britons and the Roman Army.* London: Gregg Press, 1964.

125. *Speculum.* The Journal of the Mediaeval Academy of America. Cambridge, Mass., 1926– .

126. Stenton, (Sir) F. M. *Anglo-Saxon England (The Oxford History of England).* 2nd ed. Oxford: The Clarendon Press, 1947.

127. Tacitus, Cornelius. *Dialogus, Agricola, Germania.* William Peterson and Maurcie Hutton, trs. (Loeb Classical Library). London: W. Heinemann, and New York: The Macmillan Co., 1914. And *The Histories* (including *The Annals*). Clifford H. Moore and John Jackson, trs. (Loeb Classical Library). London: W. Heinemann, and New York: G. P. Putnam's Sons, 1925–1937. 4 vols.

128. Thompson, A. H. *Military Architecture in England during the Middle Ages.* Oxford: Oxford University Press, 1912. See also A. C. Taylor. "Military Architecture," in Vol. I, *Medieval England*. New ed. Austin Lane Poole, ed. Oxford: The Clarendon Press, 1958.

129. Toy, Sidney. *The Castles of Great Britain.* London: William Heinemann, 1953.

130. *Treatise of Walter de Milemete, De nobilitatibus sapientiis et prudentiis regum.* Reproduced in facsimile from the . . . manuscript . . . at Christ Church, Oxford . . . with an introduction by Montague Rhodes James. London: Roxburghe Club, 1913.

131. Verbruggen, J. F. *De Krijgskunst in West-Europa in de Middleeuwen (IXe tot begin XIVe Eeuw)* (avec un resumé français). Brussel: Verhandelingen van de Kononklijke Vlaamse Academic voor Wetenschappen, Letteren en Schone Kunste van België, 1954.

132. *The Victoria History of the Counties of England.* H. Doubleday, W. Page, *et aliis,* eds. Westminster: A Constable, 1900–1945, and Oxford: Oxford University Press for the Institute of Historical Research, University of London, 1953–   . *ca.* 110 vols.

133. (Wales) *A Bibliography of the History of Wales.* Prepared by the History and Law Committee of the Board of Celtic Studies of the University of Wales. 2nd ed. Cardiff: University of Wales Press, 1962.

134. Warren, W. L. *King John.* London: Eyre and Spottiswoode, 1961.

135. Welch, Colonel George Patrick. *Britannia: the Roman conquest and occupation of Britain.* Middleton, Conn.: Wesleyan University Press, 1963.

136. White, Donald A. *Litus Saxonicum; the British Saxon Shore in Scholarship and History.* Leiden: E. J. Brill, 1961.

SUPPLEMENT TO BIBLIOGRAPHY

137. Hogg, O. F. G. *The Royal Arsenal: its background, origins, and subsequent history.* New York: Oxford University Press, 1963. 2 vols.

138. Featherstone, D. *The Bowmen of England: the story of the English longbow.* London: Jarrolds, 1967.

139. O'Neil, B. H. St. J. *Castles and Cannon: a study of early artillery fortifications in England.* London: Oxford University Press, 1960.

140. Smail, R. C. *Crusading Warfare, 1097–1193: a contribution to medieval military history.* Cambridge: Cambridge University Press, 1956.

141. Renn, D. F. *Norman Castles in Britain*. London: John Baker, 1968.
142. Warner, P. *Sieges in the Middle Ages*. London: Bell, 1968.
143. Wilson, D. R. *Roman Frontiers of Britain*. Regional Archeologies Series. London: Heinemann, 1967.
144. Prince, A. E. "The Strength of English Armies under Edward III." *English Historical Review,* xlvi (1931), 353–371; "The Indenture System under Edward III," in *Historical Essays in Honour of James Tait.* J. G. Edwards, V. R. Galbraith, and E. F. Jacobs, eds. Manchester: Manchester University Press, 1933, 283–297; "The Army and Navy," in *The English Government at Work, 1327–1336.* 3 vols. W. A. Morris, J. R. Strayer, J. F. Willard, and W. H. Dunham, eds. Cambridge, Mass.: Harvard University Press, 1940–1950, I, 332–393.
145. Dunham, William Huse. "Lord Hastings' indentured retainers, 1461–1483; the lawfulness of livery and retaining under the Yorkists and Tudors." *Transactions of the Connecticut Academy of Arts and Sciences,* v(1955), 1–175.
146. McFarlane, K. B. "Bastard Feudalism." *Bulletin of the Institute for Historical Research,* xx(1943–1945), 161–180. These significant studies have appeared since the chapter was completed, and should be consulted for the appropriate period.
147. Fowler, Kenneth. *The King's Lieutenant: Henry of Grosmont, First Duke of Lancaster, 1310–1361.* New York: Barnes and Noble, 1969. This is an invaluable study of the early phases of the Hundred Years' War, and does much to put into proper perspective the operations of commanders whose achievements have long been obscured by the more dramatic exploits of Edward III and the Black Prince.
148. A comprehensive survey of the use of mercenary troops by the Anglo-Norman kings is to be found in John Schlight's *Monarchs and Mercenaries* (Bridgeport, Conn.: Conference on British Studies, 1968).
149. A thorough study of medieval siege warfare has yet to be made, but an excellent introduction to English sieges in the middle ages is *Sieges of the Middle Ages* by Philip Warner (London: G. Bell and Sons, 1968).
150. Hayes-McCoy, G. A., *Irish Battles*. London: Longmans, Green, 1969.
151. Mullins, E. L. C., *A Guide to the Historical and Archaeological Publications of Societies in England and Wales 1901–1933.* New York: Oxford University Press, 1969.

III

MILITARY DEVELOPMENTS OF
THE RENAISSANCE

C. G. Cruickshank

In 1485 the English army was recruited, weaponed, and organized very much on the medieval pattern. The influence of high chivalry was still evident. By 1714, the "art" of war had been for some time a "science." The bill and the longbow, with which the earlier English armies had won their great victories in France, had disappeared. The pike had come and gone. Fire-arms had progressed from the crude hand-gun and arquebus to the relatively efficient musket with bayonet. Gunpowder had been greatly improved. The enlistment of retainers through their overloads, a relic of the feudal army proper, had given way to the county militia system, and finally to a standing army, which none of the Tudors had dared countenance. In the field the army was no longer divided into three huge "battles" (fore-ward, middle-ward, and rear-ward) which were difficult to control and manoeuvre and impossible to weapon scientifically, but was organized in regiments and companies which could be manipulated with precision through an effective chain of command, and in which the proportions of weapons could be readily adjusted in the light of the theories of the day. At the beginning of the period, the commander-in-chief was still expected to rely heavily on the advice of a council of war: at the end he was virtually sole commander. At the beginning he and his subordinate leaders inevitably had to be of noble blood: at the end it was no longer inconceivable that a common man could achieve high rank. Above all the attitude to warfare had changed. In 1500 it was still sometimes the sport of kings. By 1700 it was no longer in any sense a game, but an instrument of policy.

The process of change was spread fairly through the whole period, but scholars have tended to concentrate more on the seventeenth century, partly because it saw the Civil War, and partly because the natural starting-point for any general survey of the English army is the foundation of a standing army in 1660. Sir John Fortescue in his monumental *History of the British Army* (48) devotes no more than fifty pages to the whole of the Tudor era; and Sir Charles Oman's wide-ranging *Art of War in the Sixteenth Century* (82) is largely concerned with continental armies. Cole and Priestly's *Out-*

line History of the British Army (25) begins in 1660. Other general historians of the British army, for example, Sir Sibbald Scott (102), and Clode (23) have tended to pass quickly over the Tudors. E. W. Sheppard's *A Short History of the British Army* (105) is very short indeed before the Civil War, covering the period 55 B.C. to 1642 A.D. in four pages.

In the sixteenth century the English army was rarely involved in spectacular action which demanded the attention of posterity; and until recently there have been few scholarly attempts to carry out basic studies of military oganization and administration. In the last twenty-five years, however, much has been done by scholars on both sides of the Atlantic to fill the gaps; and were Oman and Fortescue to embark on their mammoth tasks today they would have the advantage of building on much surer foundations, so far as the sixteenth century is concerned.

THE TUDORS. The Oxford Tudor bibliography (91) is a sound guide to contemporary books on the art of war, to later studies, and to the more important contributions to learned journals up to 1955, in spite of some deficiencies. That it occasionally nods is witnessed by the fact that Matthew Sutcliffe's *The Practice, Proceedings and Lawes of Armes* (112) (which is one of the ablest sixteenth-century books on the art of war) is recorded not as a military book but under "Special Fields of Law" and is said to deal with justifiable causes of war and the way it must be waged. Moreover, since the second edition of the Oxford bibliography went to press, there have been a number of important new works. Cockle (24), who lists English military books up to 1642 and notes where copies may be found, can be supplemented by Spaulding and Karpinski's *Early Military Books in the University of Michigan Libraries* (109), which includes an index of military books by mathematicians and of mathematical works with sections on military science, Spaulding's *Elizabethan Military Books* (108) and *"Early Military Books in the Folger Library"* (107).

The foregoing deal only with printed books, but some recent works list sources ranging from collections of manuscripts in private hands at one end of the spectrum to articles in learned journals at the other. Among the more notable is Dr. Lindsay Boynton's *The Elizabethan Militia* (16) which, in spite of its title, is largely devoted to the Stuart period. This book has a scholarly note on sources in general and lists more than one hundred and thirty printed books, and more than one hundred and sixty secondary authorities.

Some of the more important new groundwork on the earlier Tudor army has not been published. Military obligation in the first half of the sixteenth century as seen from the center of government has been admirably dealt with by Dr. Jeremy Goring (51), who examines in detail the final disappearance of the feudal obligation and the full restoration of the militia system, which had played second fiddle to the feudal array for over four hundred years. Obligation as it affected a local authority (in fact, the city of York) has been described by N. J. Longbone (69). The earlier Tudor supply services have been examined by Dr. C. S. L. Davies (31). These three unpublished studies explore interesting new ground and have very extensive bibliographical appendixes.

There is available an almost embarrassing richness of official papers for the sixteenth century army. Many of these have been printed. The calendars of state papers—*Foreign and Domestic* (1509–1547) (138); *Foreign* (1547–1590) (132); *Domestic* (1547–1603) (130); *Ireland* (1509–1654) (133); and *Scotland* (1547–1597) (135) alone account for nearly a hundred volumes. Some of the earlier volumes are merely an index that does little more than guide the student to the original material; and sometimes even a fairly full transcription misses the real point in a document. It is possible, however, to develop very quickly a sixth sense which detects when the calendar version must be checked against the original. Other important calendars are the *Venetian* (137), *Milan* (134), and *Spanish* (136), which between them add another thirty volumes containing much on the sixteenth-century English army.

The latest volume in the Foreign series is not a calendar in the accepted sense, but a *List and Analysis* (139) of the papers between August 1589 and June 1590. It represents an interesting experiment in the art of providing the student with a printed reflection of a manuscript collection, listing the documents under brief titles and later grouping them under various headings. The reader is thus presented with subject collections of the papers arranged logically, at least as the editor sees them. This development, which has been forced on the authorities by the rising costs of book production, may be deprecated by scholars who are unable to spend much time in the Public Record Office, and who have found the calendars a satisfactory source; but it is likely to be the shape of things to come—at least until such time as the manuscripts themselves are punch-coded and fed through a computer to answer questions posed by the scholar, who need never soil his hands with spade-work among the documents. The remaining Elizabethan state papers will, however, be "listed and analysed." They are expected to occupy a further seven or eight volumes.

The calendars provide a key to the vast treasure chambers of the Public Record Office. It is impossible to give anything like a comprehensive account of the manuscripts of particular interest to the military historian, but the Records of the Exchequer, The King's Remembrancer, may be singled out. They include Army, Navy and Ordnance papers (John to George III) which are rich in musters certificates for the time of Henry VIII and Elizabeth I. These provide a basis not only for an examination of the militia but also for population studies. The accounts of the garrison towns in France, especially Calais, are also valuable, while the accounts of the Clerk of the King's Works throw light on fortifications. The Declared Accounts (Pipe Office) covering the period 1500–1810 include accounts of the treasurers-at-war and purveyors for the early years of Henry VIII's reign; ordnance accounts from 1546; material on the Tower of London and the accounts of the Armoury 1551–1670; and accounts of military works and fortifications from 1542.

The manuscript collections in the British Museum which are most relevant for the sixteenth-century army are the Cottonian, Harleian, Lansdowne, Stowe, and the Sloane and the Additional Manuscripts. The individual catalogue entries relating to military subjects have been cut up and assembled in the four volumes of the *Class Catalogue of Manuscripts* (Military) (147) on the open shelves of the Students' Room in the British Museum. The entries are arranged according to subject under countries and lead the student quickly to the most rewarding sources.

Printed collections which are often complementary to the calendars of state papers are *The Acts of the Privy Council (New Series)* (140), the *Calendar* of the Carew manuscripts in Lambeth Palace Library (143) covering the period 1515–1624 (for the English army in Ireland), and *Tudor Royal Proclamations* (66). The *Proclamations,* particularly when read in conjunction with the *Statutes of the Realm* (71), throw light on many aspects of military affairs in the Tudor period. Of the numerous volumes of the *Historical Manuscripts Commission Reports* dealing with collections of manuscripts in private hands listed in H.M.S.O. *Sectional List No. 17* (146), the most important so far as the army is concerned is the *Hatfield* series (146d) but there is something to be found in many of the other volumes, for example, the *Ancaster* (146a) *Foljambe* (146c) and *More Molyneux* collections (146g). There is no subject index to the *Reports,* but there is an *Index of Persons* (144) and a *Topographical Index* (145), both of which can provide useful pointers.

It was not until the time of Elizabeth I that military books began to come off the printing presses in any great numbers. Even in the earlier part of her reign the conservative approach to the practice of warfare was paralleled by a conservative approach to writing, and no doubt thinking, about the subject. The few men who put pen to paper (for example, John Sadler in *The foure bookes of Flavius Vegetius* (100) contented themselves with translations, or with philosophising about the feats of armies in biblical and classical times. But in the second half of the sixteenth century there was an outburst of activity in which vigorous controversy based on practical experience of the wars largely replaced the academic approach based on the precedents or supposed precedents of many centuries ago. The more important contemporary books are discussed in the last two sections of this essay; but the contemporary chronicles must not be overlooked. Camden (19), Hall (58), Turpyn's *Chronicle of Calais* (117), Gruffudd (53), du Bellay (11), Fleurange (74), Bayard (10), Polydore Vergil (118), and Robert Macquereau's *Histoire générale* (72) all contain a good deal that is relevant to the Tudor army. Some must, of course, be treated with caution, but taken as a group these works provide a useful cross-bearing on, and occasional pointers to, the manuscript sources.

It has already been suggested that until comparatively recently there has been little attempt to specialize in the Tudor period. The student has often had to rely on references to the army in the general histories, which as a rule have been written from a political standpoint and have therefore been concerned mainly with the conduct of campaigns and their political results rather than with how they were mounted. Froude (49) is a good example. One of the rare exceptions is Grose's *Military Antiquities* (52), a collection of papers on organization and administration. It is uncritical in its approach, but contains a wealth of material on such subjects as discipline, castrametation, fortification, equipment, and so on, some of which needs to be checked against the original documents. Grose's two volumes, nevertheless, came a long way ahead of their time.

The new approach to the study of sixteenth-century military history really began with the appearance of Oman's *Art of War in the Sixteenth Century* (82). It is still primarily concerned with the conduct of campaigns, but it does pay more attention to the administrative side than was usual in earlier works. Firth's *Cromwell's Army* (46), however, had already provided a fresh dimension for the military history of the seventeenth century and pointed the way to the new approach adopted by Oman and the others who came after him. Miss Scott Thomson's *Lords Lieutenants in the Sixteenth Century* (114) is still valuable for the militia. Among the more important recent books is Professor Henry J. Webb's *Elizabethan Military Science* (121), which has a valuable chapter on English military writers and another chapter on "The Books and the Practice." The preface also contains some bibliographical material, and there is a very full bibliography of military books printed before 1640. Captain Cyril Falls's *Elizabeth's Irish Wars* (39) is an admirable narrative account that does not overlook organizational and administrative matters; and the same author's *Mountjoy: Elizabethan General* (40) is also important. A. L. Rowse has an interesting and well-documented chapter entitled "War on Land: Military Organization" in his *Expansion of Elizabethan England* (98). Perhaps the most comprehensive work on the Elizabethan army is the second edition of C. G. Cruickshank's *Elizabeth's Army* (27), which covers the administration and organization of the army both at home and abroad and provides a detailed narrative account of three typical campaigns. There is as yet no comparable single work on the earlier Tudor army, but in *Army Royal: Henry VIII's Invasion of France, 1513* (28), a detailed study of a single campaign which also examines administrative and organizational topics, and in *The English Occupation of Tournai 1513–1519* (149), which describes sixteenth century garrison life, C. G. Cruikshank has gone a little way towards filling this important gap. There is still need for an examination of Henry VII's forces.

THE STUARTS. The Oxford Stuart bibliography (34) is still a good starting-point, although it is nearly forty years since it was published. (A new edition is, however, in course of preparation.) It records some two hundred books in the military section, about half of which are regimental histories, biographies, and personal narratives; but until such time as the second edition appears it must be supplemented from a variety of sources for works which have appeared since 1928. Among the more important of these are the Ministry of Defence accession lists and classified book lists. About two dozen of the latter are relevant to the period. There has been a comparative dearth of bibliographical material for the years between the death of Elizabeth I and the beginning of the Civil War, but Boynton (16) now admirably covers the militia in those years. There is a good bibliographical note in *Battles of the Civil War* (128) by Professor Woolrych which, although it is devoted mainly to the battles of Turnham Green, Marston Moor, Naseby and Preston, also covers general sources and biographies. Earlier works with useful bibliographies include C. T. Atkinson's *The Wars of the Spanish Succession,* in Volume 5 of the *Cambridge Modern History* (5), and Parnell's volume on the same subject (84). The bibliographical notes in the two relevant volumes of the Oxford *History of England—The Early Stuarts 1603–1660* by Godfrey Davies (35) and *The Later Stuarts 1660–1714* by Sir George Clark (22)—provide one or two pointers, but in both cases even the second editions have been overtaken by events. Sir George Clark observed in *The Later Stuarts* that "a book on military organ-ization in the period of Queen Anne is badly needed," and more than thirty years later the need has been admirably filled by R. E. Scouller's *The Armies of Queen Anne* (103), although this work is not concerned with such matters as drill, tactics, and training. It is, however, an able study in its chosen field and has a comprehensive and scholarly bibliography and note on manuscript sources.

The basic manuscript collections for the seventeenth century are broadly the same as for the sixteenth, although there is inevitably some change in emphasis. The most important calendar is the *Calendar of State Papers, domestic* (131), of which nearly a hundred volumes are devoted to the period under review. They vary in usefulness and are seldom to be regarded as an adequate substitute for the original papers. This is especially true of the earlier volumes. There is also the *Acts of the Privy Council* (141), fourteen volumes running from 1613 to 1631 and still in progress; and the *Acts of the Privy Council: Colonial Series* (142) in two volumes covering the years 1613 to 1720. For collections of manuscripts in private hands the *Reports of the Historical Manuscripts Commission* are again important. They are examined in detail in the Oxford Stuart bibliography (34), but worth special mention are the *Foljambe* (146c), *Montagu* (146f), and *Somerset* (146j) for the earlier part of the century; the *Portland* (146i), *Verney* (146k), and *Coke* (146b) for the Civil War; and the *Ormonde* (146h) and *Marlborough* (146e) for the army in the reign of Queen Anne.

County records become more important in the seventeenth century, and the many volumes of the county record societies are a fruitful source. It is difficult to particularize about them; as a rule the student's best course is to study the indexes, where they exist, and where they do not, simply to go through the volumes covering the period in which he is interested. This process will often suggest that an examination of the original papers may be worth while. Some material is also to be found in *The Victoria County Histories* series.

The domestic state papers in the Public Record Office are of course con-cerned with all aspects of government. Of more direct relevance to the history of the army are the Commonwealth Exchequer Papers, which deal with military affairs from 1642 to 1660 and are not included in the *Domes-tic Calendar* (131). There is a vast quantity of papers relating to the Ordnance Office in-letters, out-letters, the journals of the proceedings of the Board of Ordnance, the summarized accounts of the treasurers and pay-masters of the ordnance, and so on. Once again the papers in the British

Museum are complementary to those in the Public Record Office, but for the seventeenth century there is relatively more material in the latter repository. Nevertheless, the British Museum collections, in particular the Landsdowne, Cottonian, Harleian and Additional Manuscripts, are important.

There are numerous standard works for the Civil War which are required reading for the military historian who seeks to specialize in the seventeenth century: Gardiner's classic *History* (50); Miss Wedgwood's equally classic *The King's War* (122); and Firth's *Cromwell's Army* (46)—yet another classic. The last has no formal bibliographical appendix, but in the prefaces to the first three editions the author provides some useful notes, and Professor P. H. Hardacre contributes a very full bibliographical introduction to the 1962 edition, which is available in paperback. Firth writes in the preface to the first edition that "a civilian who undertakes to write the history of an army courts many perils, and cannot hope to escape them all." It is, however, arguable that it is simply because of his academic "civilian" approach that the book is so well-balanced, and that the apology would be no less appropriate were "soldier" to be substituted for "civilian." The greater part of Fortescue's first volume (48) is devoted to the seventeenth century, and it does more justice to the period than his few pages on the Tudors. To these works of scholarship may be added a number of standard sources: for example, Rushworth's *Historical Collections* (99); Vicars' *Chronicle* (119); and Whitelocke's *Memorials of English Affairs* (123). Then there are Abbott's *The Writings and Speeches of Oliver Cromwell* (2) and *Bibliography of Oliver Cromwell* (1).

There is a wealth of contemporary books that carry on the tradition of the pioneer Elizabethan military writers: such works as Francis Markham's *Five Decades* (75); Gervase Markham's *The Soldier's Exercise* (76); Norton's *The Gunner* (81); Bariffe's *Militarie Discipline* (7); Elton's *compleat body of the Art Military* (37); and Binning's *Light to the Art of Gunnery* (12). Most of these are referred to in the Oxford Stuart bibliography (34).

The earlier part of the seventeenth century has been comparatively untouched, but now Boynton's *The Elizabethan Militia* (16) deals competently with the militia to 1638. Thereafter the volume of later scholarship greatly increases, and it is possible here to mention only a handful of works. For the Civil War there is Firth's *Oliver Cromwell* (45) and, with Davies, his *Regimental History of Cromwell's Army* (47), Ashley's *Cromwell's Generals* (3) and Phillips' *Cromwell's Captains* (89); and Burne and Young's *The Great Civil War* (18) and the latter author's *Edgehill 1642* (129), which has a good bibliography. This book is in two parts of which the first is devoted to the English soldier in 1642 and the second to the campaign. It succeeds in making the best of both the administrative and tactical worlds. Also worth noting is Edgar's *Sir Ralph Hopton* (148). Useful general studies for the second half of the seventeenth century are Scott's scholarly *The British Army* (Volume 3, *From the Restoration to the Revolution*) (102) and Walton's *History of the British Standing Army* (120). The former has a bibliography surveying a far wider period than the forty years covered by the book.

The individual campaigns of the Stuart period have been the subject of a good deal of examination. There are several recent works on Monmouth's rebellion: for example, Emerson's *Monmouth's Rebellion* (38) and Little's *The Monmouth Episode* (68). For the years between the Restoration and the Revolution there are Davis' *The History of the Second, Queen's Royal Regiment* (36) (Volume 1, 1660–1684), Dalton's *The Scots Army 1661– 1688* (30) and *English Army Lists and Commission Registers* (29). For the Revolution there is Ashley's *The Glorious Revolution of 1688* (4) and Trevelyan's *The English Revolution 1688–1689* (116). A good deal has been written about the Irish war of 1688–1691, much of it in the learned journals. Books on this subject include Boulger's *The Battle of the Boyne* (15), Milligan's *History of the Siege of Londonderry* (78), and Witherow's *Derry and Enniskillen in the Year 1689* (126). For the Scottish campaign there is Petrie's *The Jacobite Movement* (87), and Crichton's *Life and Diary of Lieutenant-Colonel John Blackader* (14). There are a good many books on Claverhouse, including Terry's *John Graham of Claverhouse* (113) and Barrington's *Graham of Claverhouse* (8).

Parnell's volume on the war of the Spanish succession has already been mentioned (84). There is also Prestage's *Portugal and the War of the Spanish Succession: a bibliography with some diplomatic documents* (90), Petrie's *The Marshal Duke of Berwick: the picture of an age* (88); Stebbing's *Peterborough* (111) and Earl Stanhope's *History of the War of the Succession in Spain* (110). Reference must again be made to Scouller's *The Armies of Queen Anne* (103). Its very full bibliography lists contemporary tracts and also provides detailed references to the manuscript material in the Public Record Office, a large number of secondary works, including nine biographies of Marlborough, and relevant articles in the learned journals. Finally, one work that straddles the Tudor and Stuart periods must be mentioned. It is J. R. Hale's *The Art of War in Renaissance England,* a tiny bibliographical gem of the first water (56).

TECHNICAL DEVELOPMENTS. The more general use of firearms at the beginning of the sixteenth century was accepted without protest by the military experts of the day. By the second half of the century it had become clear that they were likely to replace the longbow, and there was a storm of objection. The turning-point, however, came in 1595, when the Privy Council finally accepted that firearms were the weapon of the future and ruled that men equipped only with bows were no longer to be counted as trained men. Sir John Smythe, one of the more colourful minor Elizabethans, argued passionately in favour of the longbow in his *Certain Discourses* (106), while those in favour of replacing the bow with firearms were led by Sir Roger Williams in *A briefe discourse of Warre* (124) and *The actions of the Lowe Countries* (125) and Humfrey Barwick in *A Briefe Discourse concerning the force and effect of all manuall weapons of fire* (9). The Folger Library editions of Smythe's book (57) and of Williams' *The Actions of the Lowe Countries* (33) by Professor J. R. Hale and D. W. Davies, respectively, throw light on this subject in their admirable introductions. The most recent book on Williams is an annotated edition of his works by John X. Evans (150). The first four chapters of H. C. B. Rogers'

Weapons of the British Soldier (97) provide a well-illustrated, scholarly but inadequately documented (if the contradiction is permissible) account of developments in the two centuries under review. Ffoulkes's *Arms and Armament* (44) covers technical development in hand weapons and also deals with artillery.

Much has been written on arms and armour, sometimes more from the point of view of the art connoisseur than the military historian, and more for Europe as a whole than for England in isolation. Ffoulkes's studies, however, are concerned with the technical function and historical aspect of arms and armour. They include, in addition to that mentioned above, *Armour and Weapons* (41) and *Inventory and Survey of the Armouries of the Tower of London* (42). Other books of value to the military historian pure and simple are *Arms and Armour in England* by Sir James Mann (73) and Holmes's *Arms and Armour in Tudor and Stuart London* (64). Two recent studies by William Reid are important to the student of the administrative side of the Ordnance Office. They are "Commonwealth Supply Departments within the Tower, and the Committee of London Merchants" (93), which deals with the administration of the Tower during the Interregnum; and "Balkes, Balls and Bandaliers" (92), dealing with the issue and receipt of equipment in the Tower in the years 1672–1675. These essays serve as reminders that, although arms and equipment have been the subject of much study, the administrative matters surrounding them have been comparatively untouched. This is not surprising. Great quantities of "hardware" have survived, and perhaps it has been simpler for the metal historian than for his paper brother to reconstruct the past. Much paper is available to the student, however, although it is perhaps less easily worked than the "hardware"; and much remains to be done in the field of administration, including the manufacture, storage and issue of weapons.

The heavier forms of hardware—cannon—have had an even better chance of surviving than lighter military guns, of which virtually none have come down from the sixteenth century. Recent works on heavy guns include Hogg's *English Artillery 1327–1716* (62), which deals with the "origins and development of English artillery before the formation of the Royal Regiment of Artillery," *The Royal Arsenal* (63), "The Board of Ordnance" (60), and "The Dawn of Ordnance Administration" (61). Then there are Ffoulkes's *Gunfounders of England* (43) and Schubert's "The first cast-iron cannon made in England" (101). For the development of firearms Blackmore's *British Military Firearms 1660–1850* (13) is a standard work, which may be supplemented by Carman's *A History of Firearms* (20). Partington's *A History of Greek Fire and Gunpowder* (85) deals in scholarly fashion with the material on which both the heavy cannon and the hand firearm depended.

The subject of uniform is one that becomes progressively more difficult as the period examined becomes more remote, and indeed the word is something of a misnomer at the beginning of the sixteenth century. The student is entirely dependent on surviving records for the study of soldiers' clothing in the days before it became uniform in the modern sense; and while a good deal has been written about uniforms after 1660 there is room for a deeper study of earlier "uniform" than already exists. The main works are Luard's *History of the Uniforms of the British Army* (70), Lawson's *History of the Uniforms of the British Army* (67), and Carman's *British Military Uniforms* (21).

Much has been written in one place and another on fortification. A recent scholarly work is O'Neil's *Castles and Cannon* (83), which goes to the end of the seventeenth century and is therefore useful for the Civil War. *The History of Coast Artillery in the British Army* (77), by K. W. Maurice-Jones, is mainly concerned with later developments, but the first three chapters are devoted to the years 1540–1716. A recent work of scholarship in this field is Professor Shelby's *John Rogers: Tudor military engineer* (104). This is concerned with the second quarter of the sixteenth century and has a full bibliography.

The provision of rations is a subject that still needs to be studied in depth. J. R. Hooker's "Notes on the Organization and Supply of the Tudor Military" (65) throws light on the position in the reign of Henry VII. Miss Allegra Woodworth's "Purveyance for the Royal Household in the Reign of Queen Elizabeth" (127) is a scholarly essay which is of value for the military historian; and it can be followed up by Aylmer's "The Last Years of Purveyance 1610–1669" (6). Brian Pearce's "Elizabethan Food Policy and the Armed Forces" (86) and Dr. C. S. L. Davies' *Supply Services of the English Armed Forces 1509–1560* (31) and also his "Provisions for Armies 1509–1550" (32) are examples of the new scholarly approach to the problems of military administration; but there is still room for further study of developing techniques on the supply side of the army.

A broad survey of early technical development is provided by J. R. Hale's "International Relations in the West: diplomacy and war" (54) and his "Armies, Navies and The Art of War" (55) in the *New Cambridge Modern History*.

MILITARY THEORY AND LITERATURE. Professor Webb's comprehensive list of Elizabethan military books (121) has already been mentioned; and for the handful of English military books before Elizabeth I there is Cockle (24). There are, however, a number of manuscript treatises in the Public Record Office, British Museum, Cambridge University Library, and Bodleian Library which treat war as a science and shun the biblical and classical theory so beloved by some uncritical contemporary writers. It is, of course, occasionally possible to find the germ of a new scientific idea even in the most traditional work [perhaps in the preface where even the pure translator is required to think for himself, if not in the main text—Richard Morison's translation of Frontinus is an example. (79)]. As the period under review progresses this scientific element increases and finally predominates. The manuscript treatises mentioned above reflect the beginning of this process, and indeed part of them turn up again verbatim in some of the Elizabethan books. Some of the earlier manuscripts can be attributed to Thomas Audley, who was commissioned to write a book on warfare for the instruction of the young King Edward VI, but when they are taken as a whole it is not easy to sort out who wrote what; and it may be that a detailed study of the manuscript treatises of the earlier part of the century and the military books of Elizabeth I's reign would reveal that some of them have so much in common that they could readily be conflated into a single "Great Tudor Military Book."

There are, of course, many books that clearly stand on their own feet, and in which the personality of the writer is unmistakably revealed. The works of Sir Roger Williams and Sir John Smythe fall into this category, and to them can be added the numerous works of Barnaby Rich, in particular his *Allarme to England* (94), *A Pathway to Military Practice* (96), and *The Fruites of Long Experience* (95). By the second quarter of the seventeenth century the scientific approach is firmly established. For example, Robert Norton's *The Gunner* (81) is a beautifully illustrated scientific textbook, although admittedly it owes a good deal, including the plates, to the continent; and William Barriffe's *Militarie Discipline* (7) includes instructions for manoeuvring the troops, drill, and complicated field exercises spread over a period of six days which have a distinctly modern flavour. (It must be confessed that at one point Barriffe provides for "the beneficial use of the bow and pike" and it may therefore be argued that his line, although modern and scientific, is less enlightened than it might be.)

Barriffe's work was first published in 1635, and its sixth edition coincided with the establishment of the standing army at the beginning of Charles II's reign, which makes it something of a textbook for the seventeenth century. Although the appearance of the standing army is often taken as the starting-point for comprehensive studies of the English military forces, it is also a culminating point. There had been many proposals in the preceding hundred and fifty years for the introduction of a permanent element into the forces of the Crown, in spite of the powerful arguments against it. Some have seen in Henry VII's yeomen of the guard [which are dealt with by Hennell in *The History of the King's Body Guard of the Yeomen of the Guard* (59)] the germ of a permanent force; and indeed the guard has proved to be permanent, although it lost its military function in 1760. Henry VIII also came near to providing the germ of a standing army with his "gentlemen of the guard," whose history is traced by Brackenbury [*The Honourable Corps of Gentlemen-at-arms* (17)]. This experimental body is also studied by Goring (51).

Even at the end of the seventeenth century, when the English standing army proper had been in existence for a number of years, it was still possible for Trenchard (115) to suggest that a standing army meant "slavery, popery, mahometism, paganism, atheism." He considers that in peace a standing army must grow effeminate by living dissolutely in quarters: whereas in war a militia soon becomes a disciplined army. Trenchard's objections were shared by many from the middle of the sixteenth century. An examination in depth of the successive attempts to move towards a permanent force, and the considerations militating against this, is something that has yet to be done.

FURTHER RESEARCH. Two possible fields of study in addition to those already touched upon—that is to say, the military aspects of Henry

VII's reign generally, some aspects of Henry VIII's armies, the supply services of the armed forces during the greater part of the two centuries under review, and in particular the supply of victuals and uniform before 1660, the writings of the pre-Elizabethan military experts, and the early attempts to introduce an element of permanency into the English army—are perhaps worthy of mention.

They are, first, the financing of the military forces and the machinery for paying the troops; and second, the part played by the English and Scottish regiments in the Low Countries in the seventeenth century. A certain amount of work has been done on the latter subject, but it is on the whole out-of-date, and there is room for fresh studies in the light of newly-available evidence.

Relatively little has been done on the pay and financing of forces in the Tudor and Stuart periods. Sir John Neale's "Elizabeth and the Netherlands, 1586–7" (80) in the *English Historical Review* looks at this subject mainly from the standpoint of the government. C. G. Cruickshank's "Dead-pays in the Elizabethan Army" (26) in the same journal is concerned more with the mechanics of payment. But there remains much to be tackled in this field, for which there is an ample supply of documents.

Mentioned earlier have been such topics as obligation and recruitment in relation to the size of the population during the Tudor and Stuart periods; the Tudor army as a whole and that of Henry VIII in particular; drill, tactics and training; the army in the whole of the early seventeenth century outside of the role and place of the militia; garrisons, barracks, and billeting; the provision of rations and the supply of armies, not to mention a study of the military intellectuals of these two centuries and the development of military science. Much of this might be summed up in the idea of a study which might be entitled *Towards a Regular Army*.

In addition research into the sociological profiles of officers and men and economic and social studies of the development of uniforms, equipment, and field shelters might be rewarding. Lastly, not only is the evolution of military cartography worth some study, but it behooves English military historians to point out that Vauban's work was not nearly so original as has been suggested. This could well be approached through a study of fortifications in theory and practice using Hale's little work (56) as a starting point.

BIBLIOGRAPHY

1. Abbott, W. C. *A Bibliography of Oliver Cromwell.* Cambridge: Harvard University Press, 1929.
2. Abbot, W. C. *The Writings and Speeches of Oliver Cromwell.* Cambridge: Harvard University Press, 1937–1947. 4 vols.
3. Ashley, M. *Cromwell's Generals.* London: Cape, 1954.
4. Ashley, M. *The Glorious Revolution of 1688.* London: Hodder, 1966.

5. Atkinson, C. T. "The War of the Spanish Succession." *The Cambrige Modern History,* 1908, V, pp. 401–436.
6. Aylmer, G. E. "The Last Years of Purveyance 1610–1699," *Economic History Review,* X, 1957–8, pp. 81–93.
7. Barriffe, William. *Militarie Discipline, or the Young Artillery-man, wherein is discoursed and shown the postures both of musket and pike.* London: R.O. for Ralph Mab, 1639.
8. Barrington, M. J. *Graham of Claverhouse, Viscount of Dundee.* London: Secker, 1911.
9. Barwick, Humfrey. *A Briefe Discourse concerning the force and effect of all manuall weapons of fire and the disability of the long bowe or archery.* London: 1594?
10. Bayard, Pierre Terrail, Seigneur de. *Memoires du Chevalier Bayard dit le Chevalier sans peur et sans reproche. Collection universelle des memoires particuliers,* Volumes 14 and 15. London and Paris, 1786.
11. Bellay, Martin du. *Memoires de messire Martin du Bellay, Seigneur de Langey. Collection universelle des memoires particuliers,* Volumes 17–21, London and Paris, 1786.
12. Binning, Thomas. *A Light to the Art of Gunnery.* London: John Darby for the Author, 1676.
13. Blackmore, H. L. *British Military Firearms 1660–1850.* London: Jenkins. 1961.
14. Blakader, J. *The Life and Diary of Lieutenant-Colonel John Blakader.* A. Crichton, ed. Edinburgh: Baynes, 1824.
15. Boulger, D. C. *The Battle of the Boyne, together with an account based on French and other unpublished records of the war in Ireland 1688–1691.* London: Secker, 1911.
16. Boynton, Lindsay. *The Elizabethan Militia.* London: Routledge & Kegan Paul, 1967.
17. Brackenbury, H. *The Nearest Guard: a history of Her Majesty's body of the honourable corps of gentlemen-at-arms.* London: Harrison, 1892.
18. Burne, A. H., and Young, P. *The Great Civil War: a military history of the First Civil War 1642–1646.* London: Eyre & Spottiswoode, 1959.
19. Camden, W. *Annales.* London, 1615.
20. Carman, W. Y. *A History of Firearms.* London: Routledge & Kegan Paul, 1955.
21. Carman, W. Y. *British Military Uniforms from contemporary pictures, Henry VII to the present day.* London: Hill, 1957.
22. Clark, Sir George. *The Later Stuarts 1660–1714.* 2nd ed. Oxford: Clarendon Press, 1955.
23. Clode, C. M. *The Military Forces of the Crown.* London: Murray, 1896. 2 vols.
24. Cockle, M. J. D. *A Bibliography of English military books up to 1642 and of contemporary foreign books.* 2nd ed. London: Holland, 1957.

25. Cole, D. H. and Priestly, E. C. *An Outline History of the British Army 1660–1937.* London: Sifton Praed, 1937.
26. Cruickshank, C. G. "Dead-pays in the Elizabethan army." *English Historical Review,* LIII, 1938, pp. 93–97.
27. Cruickshank, C. G. *Elizabeth's Army.* 2nd ed. Oxford: Clarendon Press, 1966.
28. Cruickshank, C. G. *Army Royal: Henry VIII's Invasion of France, 1513.* Oxford: Clarendon Press, 1968.
29. Dalton, C. *English Army Lists and Commission Registers.* London: Eyre & Spottiswoode, 1892–1902. 6 vols.
30. Dalton, C. *The Scots Army 1661–1688.* London: Eyre & Spottiswoode; Edinburgh: Brown, 1909.
31. Davies, C. S. L. *Supply Services of English Armed Forces, 1509–1550.* Unpublished Oxford D. Phil. thesis, 1963.
32. Davies, C. S. L. "Provisions for Armies 1509–1560." *Economic History Review,* XVII, 1964–5, pp. 234–248.
33. Davies, D. W., ed. *The Actions of the Low Countries* by Sir Roger Williams. Ithaca: Cornell University Press, 1964.
34. Davies, G. *Bibliography of British History, Stuart Period, 1603–1714.* Oxford: Clarendon Press, 1928.
35. Davies, G. *The Early Stuarts 1603–1660.* Oxford: Clarendon Press, 1937. 2nd ed., 1959.
36. Davis, J. *The History of the Second, Queen's Royal Regiment 1660–1905.* London: Bentley, 1887–1906.
37. Elton, Richard. *The Compleat body of the Art Military.* London, 1650.
38. Emerson, W. R. *Monmouth's Rebellion.* Yale: Yale University Press, 1951.
39. Falls, Cyril. *Elizabeth's Irish Wars.* London: Methuen, 1950.
40. Falls, Cyril, *Mountjoy: Elizabethan General.* London: Odhams Press, 1955.
41. Ffoulkes, C. J. *Armour and Weapons.* Oxford: Clarendon Press, 1909.
42. Ffoulkes, C. J. *Inventory and Survey of the Armouries of the Tower of London.* London: H.M.S.O., 1916. 2 vols.
43. Ffoulkes, C. J. *Gunfounders of England.* Cambridge: Cambridge University Press, 1937.
44. Ffoulkes, C. J. *Arms and Armament: an historical survey of the weapon of the British army.* London: Harrap, 1945.
45. Firth, Sir Charles. *Oliver Cromwell.* Oxford: Clarendon Press, 1900.
46. Firth, Sir Charles. *Cromwell's Army.* London: Methuen, 1902. 4th ed., 1961.
47. Firth, Sir Charles and Davies, G. *The Regimental History of Cromwell's Army.* Oxford: Clarendon Press, 1940. 2 vols.
48. Fortescue, Sir John. *A History of the British Army.* London: Macmillan, 1899–1930. 13 vols.
49. Froude, J. A. *A History of England from the fall of Wolsey to the*

defeat of the Spanish Armada. London: Longmans, 1856–1870. 12 vols.

50. Gardiner, S. R. *History of the Great Civil War 1642–1649.* London: Longmans, 1886–1891. 3 vols.

51. Goring, Jeremy. *The Military Obligations of the English People, 1511–1558.* Unpublished London Ph.D. thesis, 1955.

52. Grose, Francis. *Military antiquities respecting a history of the English army from the Conquest to the present time.* London, 1786–1788. 2 vols.

53. Gruffudd, Elis. *Chronicle.* M. B. Davies, ed. and tr. *Bulletin of the Faculty of Arts, Fouad I University,* Volume 7, 1944; Volume 9, 1949; Volume 12, 1950. Cairo: Fouad I University Press.

54. Hale, J. R. "International Relations in the West: diplomacy and war." *New Cambridge Modern History,* I, 1957, pp. 259–291.

55. Hale, J. R. "Armies, Navies and the Art of War." *New Cambridge Modern History,* II, 1958, pp. 481–509.

56. Hale, J. R. *The Art of War in Renaissance England.* Washington: The Folger Shakespeare Library, 1961.

57. Hale, J. R., ed. *Certain Discourses Military.* Ithaca: Cornell University Press, 1964.

58. Hall, Edward. *The union of the two noble and illustre famelies York and Lancaster.* London, 1542.

59. Hennell, Sir R. *The History of the King's Body Guard of the Yeomen of the Guard.* London: Constable, 1904.

60. Hogg, O. F. G. "The Board of Ordnance." *The Journal of the Royal Artillery,* LVII, 1930–1, pp. 190–207.

61. Hogg, O. F. G. "The Dawn of Ordnance Administration." *The Journal of the Royal Artillery,* LIX, 1932–33, pp. 427–447.

62. Hogg, O. F. G. *English Artillery 1327–1716.* London: Royal Artillery Institution, 1963.

63. Hogg, O. F. G. *The Royal Arsenal: its background, origin, and subsequent history.* London: Oxford University Press, 1963.

64. Holmes, M. J. R. *Arms and Armour in Tudor and Stuart London.* London: H.M.S.O., 1957.

65. Hooker, J. R. "Notes on the Organization and Supply of the Tudor Military under Henry VII." *Huntingdon Library Quarterly,* XXIII, 1959–60, pp. 19–31.

66. Hughes, P. L. and Larkin, J. F. *Tudor Royal Proclamations,* New Haven and London: Yale, 1964, 1969. 3 vols.

67. Lawson, C. C. P. *A History of the Uniforms of the British Army,* Volume 1, *From the Beginnings to 1760.* London: Davies, 1940.

68. Little, B. D. G. *The Monmouth Episode.* London: Werner Laurie, 1956.

69. Longbone, N. J. *The Military Obligations of York Citizens in Tudor Times.* Unpublished Leeds M.A. thesis, 1953.

70. Luard, John. *A History of the Dress of the British Soldier from the earliest period to the present time.* London: Clowes, 1852.

71. Luders, A. etc. *Statutes of the Realm.* London, 1810–1828. 11 vols.
72. Macquereau, Robert. *Histoire générale de l'Europe.* Louvain, 1765.
73. Mann, Sir James. *An Outline of Arms and Armour in England: from the Early Middle Ages to the Civil War.* London: H.M.S.O., 1960.
74. Marck, Robert de la, Seigneur de Fleurange. *Memories mise en escrit par Robert de la Marck. Collection universelle des memoires particuliers,* volume 16. London and Paris: 1780.
75. Markham, Francis. *Five Decades of Epistles of War.* London: A. Matthewes, 1622.
76. Markham, Gervase. *The Souldier's Exercise in three bookes containing most necessary and curious rules for the exact mustering both of horse troopes and foote bandes.* London: printed by John Dawson, sold by Lawrence Blaiklocke, 1643.
77. Maurice-Jones, K. W. *The History of Coast Artillery in the British Army.* London: Royal Artillery Institution, 1959.
78. Milligan, C. D. *History of the Siege of Londonderry, 1689.* Belfast: Londonderry Corporation, 1951.
79. Morison, Richard. *The Stratagemes, Sleyghtes and Policies of Warre gathered together by S. Julius Frontinus.* London, 1539.
80. Neale, Sir John. "Elizabeth and the Netherlands 1586–7." *English Historical Review,* XLV, 1930, pp. 373–96.
81. Norton, Robert. *The Gunner, showing the whole practise of artillery.* London: A. M. for Humfrey Robinson, 1628.
82. Oman, Sir Charles. *A History of the Art of War in the Sixteenth Cenutry.* London: Methuen, 1937.
83. O'Neil, B. H. St. J. *Castles and Cannon.* Oxford: Clarendon Press, 1960.
84. Parnell, A. *The War of the Spanish Succession in Spain 1702–1711.* London: Bell, 1888.
85. Partington, J. R. *A History of Greek Fire and Gunpowder.* Cambridge:Heffer, 1960.
86. Pearce, Brian. "Elizabethan Food Policy and the Armed Forces." *Economic History Review,* XII, 1942, pp. 39–49.
87. Petrie, Sir Charles. *The Jacobite Movement: the first phase 1688–1716.* London: Eyre & Spottiswoode, 1948.
88. Petrie, Sir Charles. *The Marshal Duke of Berwick: the picture of an age.* London: Eyre & Spottiswoode, 1953.
89. Phillips, C. E. L. *Cromwell's Captains.* London: Heinemann, 1938.
90. Prestage, E. *Portugal and the War of the Spanish Succession: a bibliography with some diplomatic documents.* Cambridge: Cambridge University Press, 1938.
91. Read, Conyers. *Bibliography of British History, Tudor Period 1485–1603.* 2nd ed. Oxford: Clarendon Press, 1959.
92. Reid, William. "Balkes, Balls, and Bandaliers." *Journal of the Society of Archivists,* II, 1964, pp. 403–410.
93. Reid, William. "Commonwealth Supply Departments Within the Tower" and "The Committee of London Merchants." *The Guildhall Miscellany,* II, 1966, pp. 319–352.

94. Rich, Barnaby. *Allarme to England, fore-shewing what perilles are procured where the people live without regard to martiall lawe.* London: C. Barker, 1578.

95. Rich, Barnaby. *The Fruites of Long Experience.* London: J. Chorlton, 1581.

96. Rich, Barnaby. *A Pathway to Military Practice, containing Offices, Lawes, Disciplines and Orders to be observed in an Army.* London: J. Charlewood for R. Walby, 1587.

97. Rogers, H. C. B. *Weapons of the British Soldier.* London: Seeley, 1960.

98. Rowse, A. L. *The Expansion of Elizabethan England.* London: Macmillan, 1955.

99. Rushworth, J. *Historical Collections 1618–1649.* London: T. Newcomb for G. Thomason, 1659–1701. 7 vols.

100. Sadler, John. *The foure bookes of Flavius Vegetius.* London, 1572.

101. Schubert, H. R. "The first cast-iron cannon made in England." *Journal of the Iron and Steel Institute,* CXLVI, 1942, pp. 131–40.

102. Scott, Sir Sibbald. *The British Army: its origin, progress, and equipment.* London: Cassell, Petter and Galpin, 1868–1880. 3 vols.

103. Scouller, R. E. *The Armies of Queen Anne.* Oxford: Clarendon Press, 1967.

104. Shelby, L. R. *John Rogers: Tudor military engineer.* Oxford: Clarendon Press, 1967.

105. Sheppard. E. W. *A Short History of the British Army.* London: Constable, 1926; 4th ed., 1950.

106. Smythe, Sir John. *Certain Discourses concerning the formes and effects of divers sorts of weapons.* London: Richard Johnes, 1590.

107. Spaulding, T. M. "Early Military Books in the Folger Library." *American Military History Foundation Journal,* I, 1937, pp. 91–100.

108. Spauding, T. M. *Elizabethan Military Books, John Quincy Adams Memorial Studies.* Washington: Folger, 1948.

109. Spaulding, T. M. and Karpinski, L. C. *Early Military Books in the University of Michigan Libraries.* Ann Arbour: University of Michigan, 1941

110. Stanhope, Philip, 5th Earl of. *History of the War of the Succession in Spain.* London: Murray, 1832.

111. Stebbing, W. *Peterborough.* London: Macmillan, 1890.

112. Sutcliffe, Matthew. *The Practice, Proceedings and Lawes of Armes.* London: The Deputies of Christopher Barker, 1593.

113. Terry, C. S. *John Graham of Claverhouse, Viscount of Dundee, 1648–1689.* London: Constable, 1905.

114. Thomson, Miss G. Scott. *Lords Lieutenants in the Sixteenth Century.* London: Longmans, 1923.

115. Trenchard, T. *A Short History of Standing Armies in England.* London, 1689.

116. Trevelyan, G. M. *The English Revolution 1688–1689.* London: Butterworth, 1939.

117. Turpyn, R. *The Chronicle of Calais in the Reigns of Henry VII and*

Henry VIII to the year 1540. Camden Society: Volume 25, 1846.

118. Vergil, Polydore. *Historiae Anglicae.* Denys Hay, tr. and ed. Camden Society, 3rd series, volume 74, 1950.

119. Vicars, John. *England's Parliamentarie Chronicle.* London: For J. Rothwell and T. Underhill, 1643–1646. 3 vols.

120. Walton, C. *History of the British Standing Army 1600–1700.* London: Harrison, 1894.

121. Webb, Henry J. *Elizabethan Military Science: the books and the practice.* Madison, Milwaukee and London: University of Wisconsin Press, 1965.

122. Wedgwood, Miss C. V. *The Great Rebellion: The King's War 1641–1647.* London: Collins, 1958.

123. Whitelocke, B. *Memorials of the English Affairs.* London, 1709.

124. Williams, Sir Roger. *A briefe discourse of warre.* London, 1590.

125. Williams, Sir Roger. *The actions of the Lowe Countries.* London: Printed by Humfrey Lownes for Matthew Lownes, 1618.

126. Witherow, T. *Derry and Enniskillen in the year 1689.* Belfast: Mullan, 1873.

127. Woodworth, Allegra. "Purveyance for the Royal Household in the reign of Queen Elizabeth." *Transactions of the American Philosophical Society,* New Series, XXXV, 1945.

128. Woolrych, A. H. *Battles of the English Civil War.* London: Batsford, 1961.

129. Young, Peter. *Edgehill 1642: the campaign and the battle.* Kineton: Roundwood Press, 1967.

Calendars of State Papers, etc.

130. *Calendar of state papers, domestic, 1547–1603.* London, 1856–1872.

131. *Calendar of state papers, domestic, 1603–1704.* London. 1857–1924.

132. *Calendar of state papers, foreign, 1547–1590.* London, 1864–1964.

133. *Calendar of state papers, Ireland, 1509–1654.* London, 1860–1912.

134. *Calendar of state papers, Milan, 1385–1618.* London, 1912.

135. *Calendar of state papers relating to Scotland, 1547–1597.* Edinburgh and Glasgow, 1898–1952.

136. *Calendar of state papers, Spanish, 1485–1558.* London, 1862–1954.

137. *Calendar of state papers, Venetian 1202–1603.* London, 1864–1898.

138. *Letters and papers, foreign and domestic, of the reign of Henry VIII, 1509–1547.* London, 1862–1932.

139. *List and Analysis of state papers, Foreign Series, Elizabeth I.* Volume I, August 1589–June 1590. R. B. Wernham, ed. London, 1964.

140. *Acts of the Privy Council of England: New Series 1542–1604.* London, 1890–1907. 32 vols.

141. *Acts of the Privy Council of England 1613–1641.* London, 1921–1964. 14 vols.

142. *Acts of the Privy Council of England: Colonial Series.* London, 1908 and 1910. 2 vols.

143. *Calendar of the Carew Manuscripts in the Lambeth Palace Library 1515–1624.* London, 1867–1873. 6 vols.

144. *Guide to the Reports of the Royal Commission on Historical Manuscripts. Part II. Index of Persons.* London, 1966. 3 vols.

145. *A Guide to the Reports on Collections of Manuscripts of private families, corporations, and institutions in Great Britain and Ireland issued by the Royal Commission for Historical Manuscripts. Part I. Topographical.* London, 1914.

146. *Sectional List No. 17. Publications of the Royal Commission on Historical Manuscripts.* London: H.M.S.O., 1966.

146a. *Ancaster MSS.* London, 1907.

146b. *Coke (Earl Cowper) MSS.* London, 1888–1889. 3 vols.

146c. *Foljambe MSS.* London, 1897.

146d. *Hatfield MSS.* London, 1883–1942. (Microfilm available in British Museum and Folger Libraries). 18 vols.

146e. *Marlborough MSS.* London, 1881.

146f. *Montagu of Beaulieu MSS.* London, 1900.

146g. *More Molyneux MSS.* London, 1879.

146h. *Ormonde MSS.* London, 1902–1920. 8 vols.

146i. *Portland MSS.* London, 1891–1931. 10 vols.

146j. *Somerset MSS.* London, 1898.

146k. *Verney MSS.* London, 1879.

147. *Class Catalogues of Manuscripts* (Military). Volume 50 on open shelves of British Museum Students' Room.

148. Edgar, F. T. R. *Sir Ralph Hopton, the King's Man in the West.* Oxford: Clarendon Press, 1968.

149. Cruickshank, C. G. *The English Occupation of Tournai 1513–1519.* Oxford: Clarendon Press, 1971.

150. Evans, John X. *The Works of Sir Roger Williams.* Oxford: Clarendon Press, 1971.

IV

THE NAVY TO 1714

Daniel A. Baugh

Naval history has been predominantly the history of the naval service, with its accent on fleet engagements and the conduct of the great commanders. Until the late nineteenth century it was virtually this and nothing else. As such it seemed of no consequence to general historical studies, which were then becoming more scholarly and purposeful. In 1875 an instructor in meteorology at the Greenwich Naval College, John K. Laughton, observed that even naval officers considered the subject irrelevant. At a meeting of the Royal United Service Institution he pleaded for "The Scientific Study of Naval History" (129); he urged that it be rid of folk-lore, grounded on scholarship, and made to reveal not only the reasons for success or failure of campaigns, but also the "influences which . . . at different periods, rendered different countries powerful by sea."

The recasting of naval history began with Laughton. He got permission to lecture on naval history at Greenwich in 1876 and fought his way into the hitherto secret Admiralty records at the Public Record Office in 1879. Until 1885 only Laughton, by special permission, could consult these records, but after 1885 they were opened to everyone. He organized the Navy Records Society (N.R.S.) in the early '90s. To the end of his days he launched salvoes at those old-style naval histories in which we are given "the fighting and nothing else" with the result that "their descriptions— even of the fighting—are, for the most part, unintelligible." A typical case, he said, was James's famous *Naval History,* wherein "ships roam the ocean without any why or wherefore, like a black retriever on the rampage" (130).

Laughton's lecture of 1875 was eventually read by Captain A. T. Mahan, U.S.N. and helped open his eyes to the usefulness of scholarly and intelligible naval history. The staggering impact of Mahan's *The Influence of Sea Power upon History* (142) and *The Influence of Sea Power upon the French Revolution and Empire* (143) on world politics is well known. These books had an equally powerful impact on naval history. Mahan's high standard of scholarship, perceptive analysis of tactics, and recognition of the role of naval power in international politics became the model for naval historians. His concept of "sea power" triumphed. Sir William

Laird Clowes (in his massive *The Royal Navy* (61) to which Mahan contributed), Sir Julian Corbett (66) (67) (71), and Sir Herbert Richmond all followed in Mahan's wake. Richmond, especially in his later works (221) (222), traced the role of sea power in government policy by viewing the navy as an instrument of that policy.

In this manner naval history came into the mainstream of history, which, a half-century ago, was usually defined as the history of the struggle between the great powers. But as it did so, it became isolated from maritime history. For Mahan, sea power was naval power. Although the opening chapters of *The Influence of Sea Power upon History* recognized both the importance of basic maritime resources and the role of privateering, the book's message was clear: it was the naval manifestation of maritime resources that counted. The resulting isolation of naval from maritime history can only be regretted today, because the general interest of historians has changed. The struggle among the powers is now viewed as an aspect of historical study rather than its dominant concern, but to this aspect the bulk of naval history remains attached.

The farther back into the past one goes, the more necessary the integration of naval and maritime history becomes, because of the diminishing congruity of sea power and naval power. In the period before 1714 sea power was always a function of commerce, privateering, and piracy, as well as of royal fleets. The whole maritime sector of the nation was at war whenever war broke out. In the earliest days the navy itself was mainly drawn from private sources. Ships and seamen were commandeered for royal needs, and many of the best captains were men who lived by piracy in peacetime. By the end of the seventeenth century a sizeable force of royal fighting ships and something like a corps of regular officers had been built up. And yet, even then, privateering remained a crucial factor in war at sea, and within the navy itself the continued influence of the plundering spirit had significant operational consequences; British naval officers viewed prize money as their most important source of pay right down to the nineteenth century. The history of sea power during the centuries spanned by this essay is, in the largest sense, the history of the growth and eventual rationalization of violence on the high seas. It is a fascinating chapter in the history of mankind, and one in which England played a leading role.

GENERAL HISTORIES. At first glance it appears that this chapter has already been written. In respect to the main events it has. One thinks of James A. Williamson's numerous writings on English maritime history, C. R. Boxer's writings on the Dutch and Portuguese, and J. H. Parry's comprehensive *The Age of Reconnaissance* (186). Among naval historians, Michael Lewis, in his *History of the British Navy* (136), fully understood the mixed character of "the Old Navy," as did Laughton (129, 130), Hannay (106), Clowes (61), and Oppenheim (181) a half-century ago. Nevertheless, the chief intent of naval studies has been to trace the naval heritage and emphasize the role of sea power rather than to understand maritime developments. The hold of the traditional approach is compelling and sometimes deadening. The most recent general *Naval History of England* (148), by G. J. Marcus, aimlessly mixes the best of the sea-power school with material on administration, life at sea, and navigational techniques. Many readers will find the *Short History* (106) that David Hannay published fifty years ago sufficiently trustworthy and more rewarding.

Whatever its limitations, the work of naval historians during the past century has laid essential groundwork for a broader understanding of the phenomenon of sea power. Such work cannot be ignored. However, since it is our aim here to reveal anew the general significance of naval history, we shall pay special attention to two kinds of work; the one considers the private as well as the public aspects of sea power; the other studies the shift from private to public, that is, the way the navy developed.

GENERAL BIBLIOGRAPHIES. The select bibliography in Marcus (148) is well arranged and easy to use. R. G. Albion's *Naval & Maritime History* (3) is the best bibliography in the field; comprehensive and up-to-date, it includes books and unpublished theses (this essay will ignore the latter), but omits articles in journals. The Admiralty Library *Subject Catalogue of Printed Books* by W. J. Perrin (190), though published in 1912, is a wide-ranging guide to older works, while the *General Index to Volumes 1–35* of *The Mariner's Mirror* (151) provides an entry to many specialized older articles that this essay cannot mention for want of space. G. E. Manwaring's *A Bibliography of British Naval History* (145), though compiled in 1930, complements Albion's; it omits books and theses, but lists almost everything else, including essays in books. The reader will find a good introduction to the source materials for a particular period under the appropriate monarch's name. Some of the short titles in the "Subjects" section may be mystifying until checked against the full entries in the "Authors" section.

SPECIAL SUBJECTS. Aside from the general naval histories already mentioned, there are works treating particular aspects of naval history with which we must deal before turning to the three chronological divisions of the essay.

The best general study of the navy's organization, procedures, equipment, and personnel is Michael Lewis' *The Navy of Britain: a historical portrait* (137). An older but still useful book covering similar matters is C. N. Robinson's *The British Fleet* (225). Lewis has traced the changing situation of the naval officer in *England's Sea-Officers* (135). Both officers and seamen are colorfully sketched from literary sources by Robinson in *The British Tar in Fact and Fiction* (226); the book also serves as a guide to naval matter in English fiction before 1900. The major work on naval administration down to 1660 is Michael Oppenheim's *A History of the Administration of the Royal Navy* (181). The history of the Admiralty is briefly traced in articles by Perrin (193) and Sir Oswyn Murray (176), and that of the Navy Board in an article by A. H. Johns (117).

Douglas Browne's *The Floating Bulwark* (41) is a rather incoherent assemblage of what others have found out about ship design and armament;

it includes a bibliography. One may also consult the Andersons' (15) and G. S. L. Clowes's (62) histories of sailing ships, and R. C. Anderson's work on galleys (13). Serious students should go through the volumes of *The Mariner's Mirror* and note, in particular, articles by Anderson, R. M. Nance, L. G. Carr Laughton, W. Salisbury, and T. Glasgow, Jr., F. L. Robertson's *The Evolution of Naval Armament* (223) remains important. Surprisingly, there is still need for an interpretive study of the evolution of naval tactics. The best introduction is in Lewis' *Navy of Britain* (137). The Robinsons have studied the *History of Naval Tactics* (227) since 1530 in some detail, but without much analysis. Corbett's comments and documents in *Fighting Instructions, 1530–1816* (68) and also his revised views in the addenda to *Signals and Instructions, 1776–1794* (70) are essential foundations of further research. On all these subjects, works concerning particular periods will be mentioned in their places below.

NAVIGATION. Navigation is treated from ancient times to the eighteenth century in Eva Taylor's *The Haven-Finding Art* (262). Her books on Tudor and early Stuart geographical thought (263) (264) add a new dimension to our understanding of maritime expansion. On navigational techniques one should consult the articles of F. C. Lane (126) and G. J. Marcus (149) (150) touching the middle ages, and David Waters' rich study of *The Art of Navigation in England in Elizabethan and Early Stuart Times* (280). Chart-making is well analyzed in A. H. W. Robinson's *Marine Cartography in Britain* (224), which considers developments down to 1855; Mary Blewitt's *Surveys of the Seas* (24) is a briefer study annexed to a representative selection of charts.

ADMIRALTY LAW. The history of Admiralty law has been largely written by R. G. Marsden and published in various locations. His *Documents Relating to Law and Custom of the Sea* (154) provides a rich survey down to the eighteenth century, and his detailed introductions to *Select Pleas in the Court of Admiralty* (158) are a good history of Admiralty courts in England before 1600. He has treated the Vice-Admiralty in articles (160). For the seventeenth century there are also Helen Crump's *Colonial Admiralty Jurisdiction* (73), which considers more than the colonial courts, and Harold Hulme's *Sir John Eliot and the Vice-Admiralty of Devon* (113). Marsden's three articles on "Early Prize Jurisdiction and Prize Law in England" (156) bring the history of prize law down to the late seventeenth century where Richard Pares' *Colonial Blockade and Neutral Rights* (185) takes it up. Also useful are E. S. Roscoe's *A History of the English Prize Court* (230) and W. Senior's *Naval History in the Law Courts* (244).

International maritime law is too vast a field to consider properly here. Jessup and Deák's *Neutrality* (116) offers a sound introduction and good bibliography; it is on the whole more useful than Kulsrud's *Maritime Neutrality to 1780* (125). Especially valuable is T. W. Fulton's *The Sovereignty of the Sea* (92); based on original sources, it considers the legal history of the British seas—jurisdiction, rights, territorial waters—

and lays considerable stress on the role of the navy in the seventeenth century. No one working in the field should be unaware of J. M. Pardessus's comprehensive *Collection de lois maritimes antérieures au XVIIIe siècle* (184), recently reprinted.

I. THE NAVY BEFORE 1485

GENERAL HISTORIES. Medieval navies were normally assembled only for specific missions, usually the transporting of troops and supplies, and rarely remained mobilized for long; consequently fleet encounters were few, and tactics scarcely existed. Hence we are unlikely to learn much that is new and significant about medieval naval operations, and nearly all that we know has been known for a long time. The details are in Nicolas' *History of the Royal Navy, from the Earliest Times to the Wars of the French Revolution* (178) and Clowes's first volume (61). Nicolas was an indefatigable worker. He consulted not only the chronicles but also a vast number of then unpublished and uncalendared rolls in the Public Record Office; it is no surprise that he only reached 1422 before he died. Clowes, who drew heavily on Nicolas's work up to 1422, carried on the story, and until quite recently our knowledge of medieval naval activities has remained pretty much as he left it.

Recent work has taken a larger view of the subject. It studies the relationship between naval strategy, maritime resources, and administrative means. As C. F. Richmond has observed, "Sea power was a matter not of a struggle but of filling a vacuum; . . . ability to organize naval forces with speed and economy was at the centre of the efficient exercise of that power." This insight underlies Richmond's two important articles: "The Keeping of the Seas during the Hundred Years' War: 1422–1440" (219) and "English Naval Power in the Fifteenth Century" (220). Also of interest is Mrs. Stanford Reid's "Sea Power in the Anglo-Scottish War, 1296–1328" (218), which deals chiefly with the problem of maintaining military supply lines.

It appears then that the decisive measures were not those of disposition, but of mobilization—and hence administration. If historians of the medieval navy have been chiefly concerned with its administrative aspects, it is not merely because this is the field in which their main sources, the public records, are most informative, but also because the subject demands it.

ADMINISTRATION AND MERCHANT SHIPPING. Both Nicolas and Clowes deal with medieval naval administration, but the reader searching for a brief and well considered account of its development should turn to Oppenheim's first chapter (181). The Oxford History of England is also useful, particularly A. L. Poole's volume on the eleventh and twelfth centuries (196). For the thirteenth century F. W. Brooks, *The English Naval Forces, 1199–1272* (39) remains the standard work; the reprint edition of 1962 contains a new introduction which notes more recently published records and research. Although the role of the Cinque Ports in naval affairs has sometimes been exaggerated, Miss K. M. E. Murray's *Constitutional History of the Cinque Ports* (175) is a fine work. There is a detailed study of naval affairs by Albert E. Prince in the first volume of *The English Gov-*

ernment at Work, 1327–1336 (205) and a useful chapter entitled "Shipping and the Movement of Troops" in H. J. Hewitt, *The Organization of War under Edward III, 1338–62* (110). The means by which Edward III obtained shipping and manpower for naval purposes are analyzed by J. W. Sherborne (247). For the fifteenth century there are C. F. Richmond's articles (219) (220) and an essay by Mrs. W. J. Carpenter Turner entitled "Southampton as a Naval Centre 1414–1458" (273).

Although the king usually had some fighting ships of his own, the private shipping on which the medieval navy was largely based cannot be ignored. For information on the king's own ships, material in Clowes (61) may be supplemented by R. C. Anderson's articles in the earlier volumes of *The Mariner's Mirror*—see the *Index* (151)—the more recent articles by Mrs. Carpenter Turner (271) (272), and occasional articles in local history society journals, for example, the article on galley building under Edward I in *Archaeologia Aeliana* (286). Material on English trade and shipping in the middle ages is plentiful. Of particular interest to naval studies are: Geoffrey Scammell's article, "Ship-owning in England c. 1450–1550" (241), which notes some relationships between trade, piracy, and royal fleets; his "English Merchant Shipping at the End of the Middle Ages" (240), interesting on trends in ship size; Dorothy Burwash's *English Merchant Shipping 1460–1540* (48), which deals not only with ships, but also with seamen and navigation; and Charles L. Kingsford's *Prejudice & Promise in XVth Century England* (124), which has an illuminating chapter on West Country piracy and its relation to the royal navy.

SOURCES AND FURTHER STUDY. Although the extant chronicles—and it would be unwise to hope for many more—may possibly be used for new purposes, it is the official records, the municipal and royal archives, that will reveal most of what remains to be known about the medieval navy. Hence new discoveries are likely to be concerned with administration and finance rather than activities at sea. The medievalist of today is fortunate in that many of his sources are printed and calendared. (The 1963 edition of the official P.R.O. *Guide* (206) tells what records were in print at that date.) A sense of the kinds of printed materials available may be got from Hewitt's bibliography (110). Some of the most useful public records for naval studies, however, remain unprinted, particularly the Pipe Rolls (printed down to the reign of John by the Pipe Roll Society (194)) and the Exchequer Accounts. Another P.R.O. series of special interest is Early Chancery Proceedings, which contain occasional maritime cases similar to those which came under High Court of Admiralty jurisdiction in the sixteenth century. Kingsford (124) printed some of these documents in an appendix. Of course, those who would use medieval manuscript materials must first acquire special skills.

Where can further research in the field lead? The study of medieval naval and transport services is relevant to economic history, as has been suggested by recent articles in *Past & Present* (163) (197) dealing with the costs of the Hundred Years' War. Studies in medieval naval administration may also enrich constitutional history, although they can never be as important in this respect as military studies. But the most important task ahead is one of integration. There can be no doubt that future progress in this period depends on abandoning the idea of naval history in favor of that of maritime history.

II. THE TUDOR PERIOD, 1485–1603

BIBLIOGRAPHIES. By the end of the Tudor period the material on naval history becomes substantial. The most comprehensive guide to books and sources is Conyers Read's *Bibliography of British History: Tudor Period* (215), the most relevant sections being: "Naval History"; "Commerce"; and "Discovery, Exploration, and Colonization." An up-to-date and extensive bibliography of maritime activity in the Elizabethan period is available in T. K. Rabb's *Enterprise & Empire* (213).

SOURCES. An extraordinary effort has gone into discovering and printing the historical sources of Tudor England's maritime enterprise. Chiefly responsible for this is the Hakluyt Society; most of its relevant titles are listed in Rabb (213) and a full list up to 1956 was published in a Society *Prospectus* (105). Recently the Society published a reprint of the 1589 edition of Hakluyt's *Principal Navigations* (104) with a good modern index. In the more strictly naval sphere the Navy Records Society has produced volumes on administration in Henry VII's reign (180), the French War of 1512–13 (249), the Spanish war of 1585–87 (69), and the Armada campaign (128); it has also assembled *Monson's Naval Tracts* (182). A great many pertinent documents were published by E. M. Tenison in her thirteen-volume collection, *Elizabethan England* (267). Among the printed public records, the *Letters and Papers of Henry VIII* (133) the *Acts of the Privy Council* (205a), and the *Calendars of State Papers, Domestic* (50), *Spanish* (51) and *Venetian* (52) are of prime importance. But much remains unpublished. The *Calendars* omit a good deal, and the State Papers themselves represent only a portion of the extant public papers of Tudor England. The rest must be sought in the British Museum and private collections. For example, many of Lord Burghley's official papers are in the British Museum's Lansdowne MSS. Some family papers have been published, particularly by the Historical Manuscripts Commission (see Introduction for guidance). A representative selection of manuscripts for the Elizabethan period may be found in Rabb's bibliography (213). An important and still largely unexploited archive for the naval historian is the High Court of Admiralty collection in the Public Record Office (see below). These remarks on sources must necessarily be inadequate. The serious student is urged to read J. A. Williamson's Preface to *Sir John Hawkins* (290), consider the printed sources described in Read's *Bibliography* (215), and follow the advice given at the outset of each of its subdivisions.

STRATEGY AND OPERATIONS. The last chapter of J. A. Williamson's *Maritime Enterprise, 1485–1558* (292) offers a brief history of the pre-Elizabethan era. To this must be added Geoffrey Scammell's two articles on "War at Sea under the Early Tudors" (242), which, by scrutinizing activities on the northeast coast, show how both strategic thinking and administrative practice were moving from medieval to Elizabethan modes.

Gordon Connell-Smith's *Forerunners of Drake* (65) argues that the roots of Elizabethan maritime policy are to be found in the reign of Henry VIII, when those entrepreneurs who had been trading legitimately with Spain and her empire experienced a reversal of fortunes as the politico-religious issue heated up, took highhanded measures of reprisal, and found their actions supported at the English Court. His book should be read alongside R. B. Wernham's *Before the Armada: the growth of English foreign policy 1485–1588* (283).

A good introductory essay on the Elizabethan navy by D. B. Quinn may be found in *Shakespeare in His Own Age* (211). For the most part, however, the naval history of the Elizabethan period has been dominated by the great commanders, and much of the best work is biographically oriented. Sir Julian Corbett's *Drake and the Tudor Navy* (66) remains the standard history of naval operations and contains a useful chapter entitled "The Naval Art in the Middle of the Sixteenth Century." Other biographies of Drake, and they are legion, largely derive from Corbett's. Of particular interest, however, is a recent book by K. R. Andrews, *Drake's Voyages* (16); refreshingly realistic and shaped by broad understanding it is the best brief account of Elizabethan maritime history. J. A. Williamson has written two books on Hawkins; the second, *Hawkins of Plymouth* (291), contains new material and modified conclusions, but the first, *Sir John Hawkins* (290), supplies most of the references. Rayner Unwin's recent account of Hawkins' third slaving voyage (274) offers a detailed account of the man in action plus a useful bibliography. There is less that can be considered naval in A. L. Rowse's *Sir Richard Grenville* (235), since Grenville's naval fame owes more to the "manner of his death" than anything else, but Rowse, like Corbett and Williamson, displays his scholarship on a broad canvas and conveys a sense of the conditions and ambitions that lured men like Grenville to sea.

The Spanish War and the defeat of the Armada has spawned a vast literature. The most judicious work, placing the men and the struggle in a European perspective, is Garrett Mattingly's *The Armada* (162). For a more detailed study of the sea battle one should turn to Michael Lewis' *The Spanish Armada* (138), his *Armada Guns* (134), and D. W. Waters' article, with excellent illustrations, "The Elizabethan Navy and the Armada Campaign" (281). A recent book by Evelyn Hardy (107) studies the Armada's shipwreck on the Irish coast. The standard work on the navy between 1588 and 1603 is Corbett's *Successors of Drake* (71), but Oppenheim's introductions to the early volumes of *The Naval Tracts of Sir William Monson* (182) should not be overlooked. Nor should E. P. Cheyney's *History of England from the Defeat of the Armada to the Death of Elizabeth* (56); its recognition of the interrelation of commercial, diplomatic, naval, and privateering activities is not what one would expect from a work published fifty years ago.

ADMINISTRATION. Michael Oppenheim's book (181), which places great emphasis on the Tudor period, remains the most important work on naval administration. His work on Henry VII's reign, the introduction to *Naval Accounts and Inventories* (180), has not been superseded; C. S.

Goldingham's article, "The Navy under Henry VII" (98), is based almost entirely on the documents edited by Oppenheim (180). C. S. L. Davies' recent article dealing with the administrative innovations of Henry VIII (75) adds considerable detail to Oppenheim's survey and offers a good bibliographical guide. Davies also has a brief note on victualling in *Annales* (76). For naval administration in Elizabeth's reign Williamson's books on Hawkins (290) (291) are important. Questions concerning ships— their number, design, and weapons—have received considerable attention since Oppenheim, Corbett, and Sir John Laughton wrote on them. There is a *List of English Men-of-War, 1509–1649* (11) prepared by R. C. Anderson, and there are Tom Glasgow's recent articles on the navy under Mary and Elizabeth (95) (96) (298). The most important research into ship design is reported in R. C. Anderson's articles in *The Mariner's Mirror* (see the *Index* (151)). Anderson also wrote a chapter on Henry VIII's galleys in his *Oared Fighting Ships* (13). Characteristics of the ships that fought the Armada are described in an article by Tom Glasgow (97). On weapons, Lewis' *Armada Guns* (134) is the most important work; it suggests some interesting tactical implications. For the earlier period see L. G. Carr Laughton's posthumously published article, "Early Tudor Ship-Guns" (131). Carlo M. Cipolla's *Guns and Sails in the Early Phase of European Expansion 1400–1700* (57) is readable and suggestive, but has been raked fore and aft by the specialists.

NAVAL AND MARITIME. Tudor naval history is incomprehensible if confined to royal fleets and a handful of famous commanders. Oppenheim (181) understood the relevance of merchant shipping, and Cheyney (56) that of privateering, but notwithstanding this, the general maritime histories of the period have seldom delved below the level of great events. Williamson's *Short History of British Expansion* (293) contains, in Part II of the first volume, the best introduction to the subject and includes a useful commentary on sources. His narrative, *The Age of Drake* (289), is skillfully written and rich in naval matter, but fails to recognize the importance of privateering at the end of the period. A. L. Rowse's *The Expansion of Elizabethan England* (234), though it lacks unity, contains some interesting and readable chapters. Rabb's *Enterprise & Empire* (213) employs statistical analysis to discover the financial thrust behind English overseas expansion in late Tudor and early Stuart times. Anyone contemplating the large canvas on which maritime history might be sketched ought to read Eva Taylor's books on Tudor and Stuart geography (263) (264), and Fernand Braudel's *La Méditerranée et le monde méditerranéen à l'époque de Philippe II* (33).

We can only mention as starting points a few of the studies in various fields that bear on naval and maritime history, while recommending the bibliographies of Read (215) and Rabb (213). On foreign policy: Wernham's book (283); his articles on the Portuguese expedition of 1589 (285); his essay, "Elizabethan War Aims and Strategy" (284); Sir John Neale's essay, "Elizabeth and the Netherlands, 1586–7" (177); and Read's well-stocked biographies of Walsingham (217) and Burghley (216). On colonization: Rowse's *The Elizabethans and America* (233); Quinn's introductions to his Hakluyt Society volumes on Gilbert (210) and *The Roanoke Voyages* (209), and his essay, "Some Spanish Reactions to Elizabethan Colonial Enterprises" (212). On Raleigh, Quinn's short volume (208) is a good introduction, and W. M. Wallace's more detailed work (276) has a good bibliography. On shipping and commerce: G. D. Ramsay's *English Overseas Trade during the Centuries of Emergence* (214) is the best introduction and contains bibliographical commentary. Ralph Davis' "England and the Mediterranean, 1570–1670" (78) reveals the interaction of economic change, commercial activity, and naval power. One might also consult the work of Stone (253) and Willan (287) (288). The latter, in his study of the Moroccan trade (288), avoided privateering on the ground that it formed "a subject in itself." Whatever its relation to trade, it was "the characteristic form of Elizabethan maritime warfare" (16, p. 185), and we must say more about it.

"I myself am firmly convinced that there is not a sailor of that nation [England] but is a pirate." It is a Venetian view (quoted by Cheyney (56), I, 464), and distorted, but understandably so; the theme is developed by Alberto Tenenti in *Piracy and the Decline of Venice, 1580–1615* (266). The phenomenon of Tudor privateering has not of course gone unnoticed by historians—all the famous seamen of the period were involved—but until recently it has not of itself been the subject of much serious study. Aside from Cheyney's chapters, there has been J. W. Damer Powell's *Bristol Privateers and Ships of War* (202), Rowse's *Tudor Cornwall* (236), and a few articles: David Mathew's on Cornish and Welsh pirates (161); Florence Dyer's on reprisals (85); C. L'Estrange Ewen's on English coastal pirates (89); and Marsden's on Frobisher (155) and Cobham (159). M. Stanford's "The Raleghs Take to the Sea" (250) deals with the family's privateering investments. Investment is also touched on by Stone in a section of his *Crisis of the Aristocracy* (252) on shipping and is the focus of Rabb's book (213). Of the recent work on privateering—Scammell's articles (242), Connell-Smith's *Forerunners of Drake* (65), and Andrews' *Elizabethan Privateering* (17)—Andrews' is the most important. A scholarly and analytical study, it delves deeply into a segment of Elizabeth's reign and convincingly demonstrates the importance of its subject to naval history.

FURTHER STUDY. Our understanding of Tudor naval history is most likely to improve through detailed research into administration and finance, and the integration of naval, maritime, and political history. Our knowledge of administration, aside from Williamson's work on Hawkins (290) (291) and Davies' article (75), has advanced very little since Oppenheim wrote. Yet Stone's article on the Armada campaign (251) shows what may be gleaned even from readily accessible sources. Analytical studies on administration do not exist, and on naval finance we have only the scraps in Oppenheim (181) and Dietz (82) (83).

Before naval, maritime, and political history can be successfully integrated, more needs to be done on privateering. Richmond (221) and Wernham (283) have studied naval policy, but a clear and detailed picture of the clashing interests at court still remains to be drawn. On what occasions and in what ways did "the predatory proclivities of the Renaissance aristocracy and court gentry"—as Andrews puts it (16, p. 182)—shape policy? Who supported the buccaneers in their plunder of Spanish shipping? How did they stand to gain? What were the interests of those who opposed them? Perhaps by blending the themes taken up by Andrews (16) (17), Connell-Smith (65), and Rabb (213) historians may add a new dimension to their view of Tudor politics.

In respect to activities at sea the records of overwhelming importance are those of the High Court of Admiralty. Although some ports, like Newcastle and Hull, had Admiralty jurisdiction in Trinity Houses—the Hull records have been explored by F. W. Brooks, who has edited some *Early Judgements of Trinity House, Hull* (40)—the main body of Admirality legal records lies in the P.R.O. Selections from these High Court records have been published, chiefly by R. G. Marsden in two Selden Society (158) and two N. R. S. (154) volumes, and also by Andrews in his Hakluyt Society volume (18). But the records are vast and remain largely unprinted. For guides one may consult Marsden's and Andrews' introductions, and Alwyn Ruddock's article, "The Earliest Records of the High Court of Admiralty, 1515–1558" (237). Marsden pointed out the value of these records in 1902 (157). Their impact on our understanding of Tudor maritime history is at last being felt.

III. THE STUART PERIOD, 1603–1714

BIBLIOGRAPHIES. There is no recent comprehensive bibliography of naval history in the Stuart period. Until the long-awaited revised edition of Davies' *Bibliography of British History: Stuart Period* (77) appears, the section that W. G. Perrin did for the 1928 edition must be used. For political and economic background the more up-to-date bibliographies in Clark (59), Furber (93), and Charles Wilson's *England's Apprenticeship* (294) may be added. Maritime history is best served by listings in Rabb (213) and Wilson's *Profit and Power* (295), and an essay in the second edition of Ashley's *Financial and Commercial Policy under the Cromwellian Protectorate* (19). A. W. Tedder's bibliography in *The Navy of the Restoration* (265) is more useful than the scope of the book (1658–1667) would suggest. John Ehrman's *The Navy in the War of William III* (87) provides an unusually thorough list of sources and authorities. Finally, no student of Queen Anne's reign can overlook the exhaustive five-volume work of William T. Morgan, *A Bibliography of British History (1700–1715)* (172).

SOURCES. Generally speaking, while the sources of eighteenth-century naval history are rich, largely unprinted, and concentrated in the Public Record Office and the National Maritime Museum and those of the sixteenth-century navy are thin and scattered but often printed, those for the seventeenth century are both rich and scattered. Although many are printed, they are to be found in some very unlikely places. The reason is that the navy's mushroom growth in the seventeenth century was not simultaneously accompanied by the development of permanent administrative offices. Until the century neared its close the most important records that survived did so mainly in private hands.

Students dealing with Queen Anne's navy may, after checking obvious printed sources such as the *Calendars of State Papers* (49) (50) and the *MSS of the House of Lords* (112), reasonably go to the Public Record Office for the bulk of what remains to be seen. For example, the important Admiralty series of letters from captains dates from 1698. Admiralty archives become increasingly valuable from the Restoration onwards. (The Kraus reprint edition of the P.R.O. *List of Admiralty Records* (207) should be used because it supplies the new class numbers in the Table of Contents and includes some additional items important for the seventeenth century.) The Admiralty letters received from Secretaries of State, the Treasury, and the War Office date from 1689; Admiralty orders, from 1660; Admiralty out-letters, from 1689; Admiralty minutes, from 1657 (with gaps); instructions to officials, from 1660; list books of ships, stations, and officers, from 1673; letters from Admiralty to Navy Board, from 1660; Deptford yard out-letters, from 1688; Plymouth yard out-letters, from 1695; Victualling out-letters, for 1683–89 and from 1702 onwards; Victualling minutes, from 1701. There are many others. However, many naval developments, such as the formulation of strategic and mobilization plans, cannot be adequately traced in the Admiralty papers. For William III's reign the Finch MSS, now published up to 1693 by the Historical Manuscripts Commission (111), and William Blathwayt's correspondence in the British Museum, stand alongside the State Papers as a major source. Ehrman's bibliography (87) is an essential guide to sources for the 1690's.

The records of the Restoration navy are to be found in three main locations: the Public Record Office; the National Maritime Museum; and the Pepys Library at Magdalene College, Cambridge. For the first, the guide is the P.R.O. *List* (207); for the second, Lindsay-MacDougall's *Guide to the Manuscripts* (139); for the third, Part I of J. R. Tanner's *Bibliotheca Pepysiana* (254) and his brief commentary in *Samuel Pepys and the Royal Navy* (260). Ehrman's article on the papers transferred by Pepys to the Admiralty (88) is indispensable to anyone tracking down the records of the Restoration navy. Tanner calendared the Admiralty Secretary's letters in the Pepys Library for the period 1673–77 in the *Descriptive Catalogue,* published by the Navy Records Society (255), but the letters from 1684 to 1688 remain uncalendared. Policy-making must be studied in the State Papers and in various private collections. The bibliography in A. P. Thornton's *West-India Policy under the Restoration* (268) provides a good sampling of relevant private collections as well as those in the P.R.O.

Among P.R.O. collections other than Admiralty records, the Domestic series of State Papers is important for naval matters throughout the seventeenth century; it is calendared (50) down to 1703, the only gap being the year 1688. The *Colonial: America and the West Indies* (49) series, which becomes increasingly rich after 1660, is calendared for the entire Stuart period. The *Calendar of State Papers, Venetian* (52) is also useful and extends down to 1675. Naturally the *Calendars* omit a good deal. The Acts of the Privy Council (205a) are an important source for the first half of the century; the published volumes print the original registers in full down to 1631. The privy council registers after 1631 are reproduced in facsimile: on microcard to 1637 (205b), and in xerox form into the 1640's (205c). These facsimile reproductions, which the beginner will not have an easy time reading, include the indices that were made in Victorian times.

Familiarity with the numerous and varied archives outside the P.R.O. is the stock-in-trade of seventeenth-century specialists, and the farther back one goes, the more important such sources become. There is no short-cut to their mastery. All we can do here is suggest some useful guides. The naval manuscripts in the Bodleian Library, mostly seventeenth-century, were discussed in an article by Sir Charles Firth (90). Thornton's bibliography (268) has already been mentioned. Tedder's (265) is helpful on the 1650s and 1660s. For the 1640s and before, there is a good short list on pp. xi–xii of the N.R.S. volume on the civil war, edited by Powell and Timings (201). The *Reports of the Historical Manuscripts Commission* are valuable, but difficult to use; fortunately there is a handy guide for the period 1603–1660 by Eleanor Upton (275), but the user must realize that its subject index does not cover some of the most important collections. A partial list of Hakluyt Society volumes relevant to the period may be found on pp. 65–66 of Albion's *Naval & Maritime Bibliography* (3). The indispensable N.R.S. volumes touching the Stuart period will be mentioned in their proper place.

Finally, there is an extensive pamphlet literature of naval interest. The British Museum's Thomason collection, now being microfilmed by University Microfilms, is the most important gathering of such pamphlets for the period 1640 to 1661, and the printed *Catalogue* (267a) has a valuable, though not infallible, subject index. For the later Stuart period, one should consult the pamphlet listing in Ehrman (87) and Morgan (172).

GENERAL HISTORIES. Unlike the naval history of the eighteenth century which is unified by the long struggle with France, that of the seventeenth has four major aspects: the growing influence in the Mediterranean, the developing struggle with France in the North Atlantic, the contest with the Dutch, and the confrontation of Louis XIV. Three of these have received general treatment: on the first there is Sir Julian Corbett's *England in the Mediterranean, 1603–1713* (67), a perceptive narrative in the old tradition; on the second, the opening chapters of Gerald Graham's *Empire of the North Atlantic* (101); on the Dutch Charles Wilson's *Profit and Power* (295), a study of the origins and results of the first two Dutch wars.

1603–1650. Basically English naval history in this period bears a strong resemblance to that of Elizabethan times, the main differences being increasing penetration of the Mediterranean and diminished open hostility to Spain. Chiefly because of the latter, there was not much naval activity between 1603 and 1640. What there was is treated by C. D. Penn in *The Navy under the Early Stuarts* (187). The book, based on the State Papers, Domestic and Venetian, and French printed works, is really about naval policy; its treatment of administration does not go much beyond whether things were getting "better" or "worse." A more authentic introduction to this early period is G. E. Manwaring's *Life and Work of Sir Henry Mainwaring* (147). Unlike most Navy Records Society volumes this is really a biography of the nineteenth-century type, interlarded with letters, and finished off with appended documents. Mainwaring's career epitomizes the naval history of the period; after taking a degree at Brasenose, he sought his fortune abroad, took to piracy in 1612, acquired both wealth and a reputation for expertise and daring, had his services sought by the king of Spain and others, accepted instead the offer of James I (which included full pardon), was sent out to advise the Venetians on naval matters, sat on a Naval Commission of Inquiry, served in the "ship money fleets" and the Isle of Rhé expedition—indeed, took part in almost everything that happened except Mansell's expedition to Algiers and Cecil's to Cadiz. For insights into early seventeenth-century naval thought, one should consult Oppenheim's edition of *Monson's Naval Tracts* (182). Two *Journals* of naval expeditions in 1625 and 1627–29 were published by the Camden Society (43) (103).

J. R. Powell, *The Navy in the English Civil War* (200) traces the naval operations of the 1640's. It draws on the varied sources as well as articles which R. C. Anderson contributed to *The Mariner's Mirror* (151) over the years. However, for a view of the struggle which embraces not only operational but also political and administrative matters the best book is Powell and Timing's N.R.S. volume (201). Useful materials may also be found in Warburton's *Memoirs of Prince Rupert* (277) and Granville Penn's *Memorials of Sir William Penn* (188); the latter is important for both operational and administrative history in the period 1644–1670. The effects of revolutionary politics on the navy are discussed by D. E. Kennedy in three articles: "Naval Captains at the Outbreak of the English Civil War" (121), "The Establishment and Settlement of Parliament's Admiralty" (122), and "The English Naval Revolt of 1648" (123).

THE DUTCH WARS. Wilson's *Profit and Power* (295) and David Ogg's *England in the Reign of Charles II* (179) offer an introduction to the Dutch Wars; a fine collection of documents—French, Dutch, German, and English—was assembled by Colenbrander (64). The First Dutch War is studied in a Dutch monograph by Ballhausen (21), and by Tanner in the old *Cambridge Modern History* (257), but the riches in the six N.R.S. volumes edited by Gardiner and Atkinson (94) should not be overlooked; their introductions—Atkinson's are especially good—amount to a history of the war's naval operations. In addition there are R. C. Anderson's recent articles (5) (6) (7), and the biographies of Robert Blake, notably those by Beadon (23) and Curtis (74). J. R. Powell's edition of Blake's letters (199) is important for Blake's exploits at sea from 1648 to 1656. Powell has also written an article entitled "The Expedition of Blake and Montagu in 1655" (198), and C. R. Boxer, one based on Portuguese sources, "Blake and the Brazil Fleets in 1650" (28). Montagu's career is significant for the period between the first two Dutch Wars. F. R. Harris, *The Life of Edward Montagu* (108), is detailed and quotes extensively from the Sandwich manuscripts; Montagu's journals of the 1659–1665 period were edited for the N.R.S. by R. C. Anderson (8). Richard Ollard's recent biography of Admiral Sir Robert Holmes (297) offers some excellent insights into the character of the Interregnum and Restoration navy.

Mahan opened the historical portion of *The Influence of Sea Power* (142) with a study of the Second Dutch War. Tedder's study (265) is scholarly and provides some administrative background. A recent article by P. M. Bosscher on the Four Days' Battle (26) draws on de Ruyter's unpublished journal and corrects some errors in Mahan that arose from his dependence on French sources. R. J. A. Shelley's article, "The Division of the English Fleet in 1666" (246), gives an interesting view of the confusion and ill-preparedness of the English high command prior to the Four Days' Battle. Source material for naval operations in both the Second and Third Dutch Wars may be found in Anderson's edition of *The Journals of Sir Thomas Allin* (9) and in James, Duke of York's printed letters (166). The most detailed treatments of the Third Dutch War are contained in Florence E. Dyer's *Life of Admiral Sir John Narbrough* (84), Anderson's introductions to *Allin's Journals* (9), and *Journals and Narratives of the Third Dutch War* (10), the latter being chiefly devoted to Narbrough's journals. A recent article by C. R. Boxer (29) supplements Wilson's *Profit and Power* by investigating English public opinion and political maneuvering down through the Third Dutch War.

Students of these wars ought to know Dutch. In a recent edition of Dutch sea journals for 1673, which includes de Ruyter's, J. R. Bruijn (44) offers an up-to-date guide to Dutch sources and scholarship. Warssinck's work on de Ruyter (279) is important. Although there is an abridged translation of Blok's *Life of Admiral de Ruyter* (25) [a narrative based on G. Brandt's seventeenth-century biography (32)], de Jonge's massive survey of Dutch naval history (80), which is based on records that have been destroyed by fire, remains untranslated. C. R. Boxer has, however, given us a brief introduction to the lives of the great Dutch admirals in "M. A. de Ruyter, 1607–1676" (30) and "The Tromps and the Anglo-Dutch Wars, 1652–1674" (31).

Naval events in the revolution of 1688 are described in a book by E. B. Powley (203); his work may be supplemented by Ehrman's (87), which treats more fully the administrative aspects.

1689–1714. The important studies of the navy in the great wars with Louis XIV's France are Ehrman, *The Navy in the War of William III* (87), and J. H. Owen, *War at Sea under Queen Anne* (183). Both are written from the national viewpoint. For the maritime struggle in its European context see Corbett (67), Richmond (221), Trevelyan (269). Owen's work on the 1702–1708 period is a reliable study of operations and the main outlines of administration. Ehrman's book on the war of 1689–1697 breaks new ground. It studies how the sudden growth of English naval power—one of the momentous developments of modern European history—was accomplished, tracing how much was owed to pre-revolutionary inheritance, how much to post-revolutionary improvisation. Hence the accent is financial and administrative; the pitch of naval effort is understood in terms of the problem of mobilizing resources. Since Ehrman's work does not focus on naval operations, it should be supplemented by Clowes (61), Hannay (106), the old histories of Burchett (46) (47) and Lediard (132), and A. N. Ryan's recent article, "William III and the Brest Fleet in the Nine Years' War" (238), which is an important study of strategy formulation. H. Kamen has used P.R.O. and Spanish sources to re-assess the impact of the Vigo expedition of 1702 (119). The North Atlantic struggle and the Walker expedition are treated by Graham (101) (102). On the West Indies there are articles by Morgan (173) and Moses (174) touching the 1689–97 war, and Ruth Bourne's rather annalistic *Queen Anne's Navy in the West Indies* (27); Crouse's *The French Struggle for the West Indies, 1665–1713* (72) is a useful narrative. A comprehensive view of French operations, including privateering, is offered by the sixth volume of Charles de la Roncière's *Histoire de la marine française* (229).

There is some interesting biographical material on this period. The unknown eighteenth-century author of *Memoirs Relating to the Lord Torrington,* printed by the Camden Society (127), gave us some fascinating details of Sir George Byng's career down to 1705. Two other eighteenth-century biographies, spanning the whole 1689–1714 period and apparently based on original records, have been printed by the Navy Records Society: *The Life of Captain Stephen Martin* (153) and *The Life of Sir John Leake* (53), which were written by the son of the former and the nephew of the latter. C. R. Markham's *Life of Robert Fairfax* (152) also spans the whole period. Brian Tunstall's three-volume edition, with good introductions, of *The Byng Papers* (270) is a rich source for the history of naval operations from 1702 to 1717. The N.R.S. also published Sir George Rooke's journals of his expeditions to the Sound in 1700 and to Cadiz and Vigo in 1702 (42). As already mentioned, the *Reports of the Historical Manuscripts Commission* should be consulted by any serious student; for this period the *Finch MSS* (111) and the *MSS of the House of Lords* (112) are particularly rich in naval material. Also valuable is W. A. Aiken's edition of contemporary writings bearing on Nottingham's direction of naval strategy from 1688 to 1694 (2).

ADMINISTRATION. There exists no general history of the growth and development of naval administration during the Stuart period. Up to 1660 Oppenheim's book (181) remains the important work. Additional studies, extending past 1660, may be found in contributions to the *Victoria County Histories* of most of the southern maritime counties, and Oppenheim's contribution to the history of Devon, which never got included, has recently been brought to publication by W. E. Minchinton (296). (Minchinton's recent memoir of Oppenheim (170) offers an interesting side light on his contributions to the *Victoria County Histories.*) One aspect of administration is traced through the whole period in G. F. James and J. J. Sutherland Shaw, "Admiralty Administration and Personnel, 1619–1714" (115). As for the early period, some scraps of information may be found in the works of G. E. Aylmer (20) and M. Prestwich (204), but for the most part our knowledge stands as Oppenheim left it. The summary of A. P. McGowan's Corbett Prize Essay, "The Administration of the Navy under the First Duke of Buckingham" (164), suggests that some remedy for our ignorance of the period is being prepared. Two important printed sources are *The Autobiography of Phineas Pett* (191) and Hollond's *Two Discourses of the Navy, 1638 and 1659* (256). Tanner's introduction to the *Discourses* is, next to Oppenheim, the most valuable work on early Stuart naval administration. Hollond's second discourse is a highly informative tract on the Interregnum, perhaps the most important thing to read. There are also D. E. Kennedy's articles on the impact of the revolution and civil war on the navy (121) (122) (123) and A. C. Dewar's "Naval Administration of the Interregnum, 1641–59" (81).

The most important work on Restoration naval administration is Tanner's 250-page introduction to his *Descriptive Catalogue of Pepysian Manuscripts* (255); the treatment is structural, and developments in each aspect are clearly presented. Tanner's *Samuel Pepys and the Royal Navy* (260) tells the story more concisely. For the beginning of the period Tedder (265) is interesting. An essay by W. A. Aiken (1) sketches the feuds and intrigues that troubled the Admiralty Board between 1679 and 1684. Ehrman's (87) lengthy analysis of the state of the navy in 1688— Part I of his book—is an essential complement to Tanner's work. Sir Arthur Bryant's three-volume life of *Samuel Pepys* (45) is naturally more about the man than the navy, but the navy figures largely in it, and the work conveys a lively sense of the period and the perplexing problems the Admiralty's most famous Secretary faced. Thanks to Pepys's fame and the efforts of Tanner, we are well supplied with printed sources for the period. Most important are the four-volume *Descriptive Catalogue* (255) and *Samuel Pepys' Naval Minutes* (261). A collection of Pepys' jottings similar to the minutes is printed in *Tangier Papers* (55). In addition, there are *Pepys's Private Correspondence* (258) and *Further Correspondence* (259)—the former contains much less naval material than the latter, which deals with the period before 1679—and Helen T. Heath's *Letters of Samuel Pepys and his Family Circle* (109). Finally there is a modern printing of Pepys's own *Memoires of the Royal Navy* (189). The massive growth of naval administration immediately after 1689 is fully treated in Ehrman (87). This may be supplemented by D. C. Coleman's article on the dockyards (63). For sources see R. D. Merriman's edition of *The Sergison Papers* (168) and his article publishing "Gilbert Wardlaw's Allegations" (169). The only important work on naval administration in the 1702–1714 period since Burchett's (47) is R. D. Merriman's *Queen Anne's Navy* (167), a well ordered collection of administrative documents with useful introductory essays. Some perspective on Queen Anne's reign, may be got from Baugh's *British Naval Administration in the Age of Walpole* (22). Naval finance in the entire 1660–1714 period may be explored in the introductions and documents of W. A. Shaw's massive *Calendar of Treasury Books* (245). On the timber problem there is R. G. Albion's penetrating study, *Forests and Sea Power* (4), and on the New England naval stores, J. J. Malone's *Pine Trees and Politics* (144). The best account of naval purchasing in the later Stuart period is Bernard Pool's *Navy Board Contracts 1660–1832* (195).

SHIPS AND SAILORS. Aspects of seventeenth-century ship design are treated in various articles by R. C. Anderson, W. Salisbury, and L. G. Carr Laughton in *The Mariner's Mirror*. Of interest to the period is Anderson's *The Rigging of Ships in the Days of the Spritsail Topmast, 1600–1720* (14). Gunnar Schoerner's *Regalskeppet* (243) is an interesting essay on naval ship design; it has a bibliography and a summary in English. *The Autobiography of Phineas Pett* (191) throws light on the manner in which the great ship of the line developed in early seventeenth-century England. The building and rigging of ships in the same period is the subject of two treatises recently reprinted by the Society for Nautical Research (239). The same society has published Anderson's *List of Men-of-War* (11) (12), which cover the entire century. Other useful ship lists may be found in many of the Navy Records Society volumes mentioned. For nautical terminology in the early seventeenth century see Mainwaring's "The Seaman's Dictionary" (147) and *Boteler's Dialogues* (192).

The century is rich in published documents illustrating life at sea. *Boteler's Dialogues* (192) relate to the 1620's and 1630's. Ingram's edition of *Three Sea Journals* (114) contains two by naval captains (one dated 1625, the other 1659–91) and a third by a merchant on an East India voyage in 1702–1703. Baltharpe's *Straights Voyage* (34) offers a good view of the lower deck in Charles II's reign, and *The Diary of Henry Teonge: chaplain on board H. M.'s Ships Assistance, Bristol, and Royal Oak 1675–1679* (146) is informative and well edited by Manwaring. In *The Wooden World* (278) the navy of Queen Anne is cheerfully libelled by Ned Ward, a writer of the chamber-pot school who must have heard plenty of seamen talk. *Barlow's Journal of his Life at Sea in King's Ships, East and West Indiamen & other Merchantmen from 1659 to 1703* (141) is *inter alia* the best record of lower-deck life in the Restoration navy that exists.

FURTHER STUDY. Almost every aspect of seventeenth-century naval history could benefit from further research. Our knowledge of the development of naval administration and tactical practices is very incomplete. As to strategy and its relation to diplomacy and domestic politics, we are better informed, but a recent and stimulating essay by J. R. Jones, *Britain and Europe in the Seventeenth Century* (118), suggests that many important questions about the role of English sea power remain unanswered. And it is indisputable that we know too little about the commercial side of war at sea, the influence of commercial interests on naval warfare, and the impact of privateering on shipping.

WAR AND COMMERCE. Most of what has been done on this subject does not have a quantitative accent. There is nothing first-rate on piracy, although Philip Gosse's *History of Piracy* (99) and *The Pirates' Who's Who* (100) are useful. Chapin's work on American colonial privateering (54) is a chronicle, but a well-stocked one. The pirates of the West Indies and South Seas are described by Kemp and Lloyd in *The Brethren of the Coast* (120). Capt. Woodes Rogers' story (228) is one of the best accounts we have of a privateering voyage, and Bryan Little's study of him, *Crusoe's Captain* (140), is both scholarly and readable. Alberto Tenenti's *Piracy and the Decline of Venice, 1580–1615* (266) has a chapter on the appearance of the English in the Mediterranean and argues, without convincing evidence, that they and the Dutch gave the *coup de grace* to Venetian shipping. Sir Godfrey Fisher's *Barbary Legend: War, Trade and Piracy in North Africa 1415–1830* (91) is a somewhat incoherent book, but contains interesting material on Algiers and a useful bibliography; those who read Dutch will consult Weber's *De Beveiliging van de zee tegen Europeesche en Barbarijsche zeeroovers 1609–1621* (282). Mainwaring's "Discourse on Pirates," written in 1617 (147), is an interesting source. For the Restoration period J. S. Bromley's introduction to Baltharpe's *Straights Voyage* (34) is studded with bibliographical leads; there are also Enid Routh's authoritative *Tangier* (231), Edwin Chappell's edition of *The Tangier Papers of Samuel Pepys* (55), and W. B. Rowbotham's three articles on "The Algerine War in the Time of Charles II" (232). A. P. Thornton has written a good chapter on the defense of the West Indian possessions and their trade in *West-India Policy under the Restoration* (268), but no study of the seventeenth century comes close to doing what Richard Pares did for the eighteenth.

For the period up to 1689 there is no systematic study pursuing a quantitative approach to English shipping losses. After 1689 there is G. N. Clark's pioneering work, *The Dutch Alliance and the War Against French Trade 1688–1697* (58), and his article, "War Trade and Trade War, 1701–1713" (60); even these are chiefly concerned with seizure as a matter of war policy rather than quantitative analysis of results. The subject really requires research in "the enemy's" records as well. Bromley's article, "The French Privateering War, 1702–13" (37) is an important statistical study, which also provides some words of wisdom on the historical problem involved and a brief introduction to the considerable, but mostly non-statistical, French literature on the subject. Bromley has studied the Channel Island privateers of this period in considerable detail and with some statistical indications (35); he has also written on the policies of the predatory Zeelanders (36) (38). The above works, plus Ralph Davis' chapter on war's effects in his *Rise of the English Shipping Industry* (79), contain about all we have of statistical significance. Sources for the kind of research needed exist; they are no doubt incomplete, but perhaps sufficient. Patrick McGrath's *Merchants and Merchandise in Seventeenth-Century Bristol* (165) indicates the value of local records. Aside from such papers, and shipping registers, probably the most important source in Britain is the body of High Court of Admiralty papers (see above). A sampling of the latter may be seen in Marsden's *Law and Custom of the Sea* (154) and the printed volume of *High Court of Admiralty Examinations 1637–1638* (248).

In considering possible lines of inquiry for the entire period before 1714 we should bear in mind that, down to the eighteenth century, sea power was more commonly concerned with plundering or securing of trade than with the supporting of military operations. Alongside the development of organized, far-ranging trading and colonizing adventures in the sixteenth and seventeenth centuries went the expansion and systematizing of plunder and the growth of navies. Much remains mysterious about this process. The medieval antecedents of English maritime enterprise and naval power —technological, commercial, political—have not yet been clearly defined. Although the great Elizabethan adventurers have been repeatedly studied, the backgrounds, objectives, and exploits of other important Tudor commanders remain obscure. The impact of English privateering and piracy on other European countries has not been assessed; nor is the impact on English trade and shipping understood. To what extent, for example, did privateering direct the course of maritime expansion, or influence trends in English ship design? Problems similar to these have increasingly governed the outlook and approach of European scholars, most notably the French historians associated with the VIe Section of the École Pratique des Hautes Études. Anyone with a serious interest in the maritime history of this period should look at the published material, edited by Michel Mollat, of every Colloque International d'Histoire Maritime; of particular research interest is the fourth conference on *Les Sources de l'histoire maritime en Europe, du moyen age au XVIIIe siècle* (171). Also important are the titles published in the "Ports—Routes—Trafics" series of the VIe Section (86).

Naval growth hinged of course on maritime growth. The British navy was, in a sense, born of privateering. That circumstance influenced both administrative development and naval policy, yet naval historians have been slow to recognize it. An integrated naval administrative history of the period has yet to be written. As for policy, we may compare Corbett's *England in the Mediterranean* (67) and Ralph Davis' essay (78) on the same theme; Corbett's is a meritorious work, but Davis touches on important problems not considered in Corbett. Another example may be seen in Kamen's article (119) on the Vigo expedition of 1702—which was surely a prime instance of the influence of the plundering spirit on naval policy. Why did not naval historians heretofore discover that the Spanish crown became the chief beneficiary of the raid? The growth of systematic plunder was in these centuries a dominating force in maritime affairs, one which navies might advance, but could not stem. Until we take its measure we cannot properly assess the influence of sea power upon history before the eighteenth century.

BIBLIOGRAPHY

1. Aiken, William A. "The Admiralty in Conflict and Commission, 1679–1684," in *Conflict in Stuart England: essays in honour of Wallace Notestein*. W. A. Aiken and Basil D. Henning, ed. London: Cape, 1960.

2. ———, ed. *The Conduct of the Earl of Nottingham*. New Haven: Yale, 1941.

3. Albion, Robert G. *Naval & Maritime History: an annotated bibliography.* 3rd ed. Mystic, Conn.: The Marine Historical Assoc., 1963. *First Supplement, 1963–65.* Mystic, Conn., 1966.

4. ———. *Forests and Sea Power: the timber problem of the Royal Navy 1652–1862.* Cambridge: Harvard, 1926.

5. Anderson, R. C. "The English Fleet at the Battle of Portland." *Mariner's Mirror,* vol. 39 (1953), pp. 171–77.

6. ———. "The First Dutch War in the Mediterranean." *Mariner's Mirror,* vol. 49 (1963), pp. 241–65.

7. ———. "Denmark and the First Anglo-Dutch War." *Mariner's Mirror,* vol. 53 (1967), pp. 55–62.

8. ———, ed. *The Journal of Edward Mountagu First Earl of Sandwich, Admiral and General at Sea 1659–1665.* London: Navy Records Soc., 1929.

9. ———, ed. *The Journals of Sir Thomas Allin 1660–1678.* London: Navy Records Soc., 1939–40. 2 vols.

10. ———, ed. *Journals and Narratives of the Third Dutch War.* London: Navy Records Soc., 1946.

11. ———. *List of English Men-of-War, 1509–1649.* London: Society for Nautical Research (Occasional Publication no. 7), 1959.

12. ———. *Lists of Men-of-War, 1650–1700. Part I. English Ships.* 2nd. ed. London: Society for Nautical Research (Occasional Publication no. 5), 1966.

13. ———. *Oared Fighting Ships from Classical Times to the Coming of Steam.* London: P. Marshall, 1962.

14. ———. *The Rigging of Ships in the Days of the Spritsail Topmast, 1600–1720.* Salem, Mass.: Marine Research Soc., 1927.

15. Anderson, Romola and R. C. *The Sailing-ship: six thousand years of history.* London: Harrap, 1926. Reprinted, New York: Bonanza Books, 1963.

16. Andrews, Kenneth R. *Drake's Voyages: a re-assessment of their place in Elizabethan maritime expansion.* London: Weidenfeld & Nicolson and New York: Scribner's, 1967.

17. ———. *Elizabethan Privateering: English privateering during the Spanish War 1585–1603.* Cambridge: University Press, 1964.

18. ———, ed. *English Privateering Voyages to the West Indies 1588–1595.* Cambridge University Press for the Hakluyt Society, 1959.

19. Ashley, Maurice. *Financial and Commercial Policy under the Cromwellian Protectorate.* Oxford: Clarendon Press, 1934. Repr. London: Cass, 1962.

20. Aylmer, G. E. *The King's Servants: the civil service of Charles I, 1625–1642.* London: Routledge & Kegan Paul, 1961.

21. Ballhausen, P. Carl. *Der Erste Englisch-Holländische Seekrieg, 1652–1654.* 's-Gravenhage: Nijhoff, 1923.

22. Baugh, Daniel A. *British Naval Administration in the Age of Walpole.* Princeton University Press, 1965.

23. Beadon, Roger. *Robert Blake.* London: Edward Arnold, 1935.

24. Blewitt, Mary. *Surveys of the Seas: a brief history of British hydrography.* London: Macgibbon & Kee, 1957.

25. Blok, Petrus Johannes. *Michiel Adriaanszoon de Ruyter.* 's-Gravenhage: Nijhoff, 1928. Abridged translation, *The Life of Admiral de Ruyter,* by G. Renier. London: Benn, 1933.

26. Bosscher, Lieutenant Philippus M. "The Four Days' Battle—Some Remarks and Reflections." *Journal of the Royal United Service Institution,* vol. 112 (1967), pp. 56–65.

27. Bourne, Ruth. *Queen Anne's Navy in the West Indies.* New Haven: Yale, 1939.

28. Boxer, Charles R. "Blake and the Brazil Fleets in 1650." *Mariner's Mirror,* vol. 36 (1950), pp. 212–28.

29. ————. "Second Thoughts on the Third Anglo-Dutch War, 1672–74." *Trans. Royal Hist. Soc.,* 5th ser. vol. 19 (1969), pp. 67–94.

30. ————. "M. A. de Ruyter, 1607–1676." *Mariner's Mirror,* vol. 44 (1958), pp. 3–17.

31. ————. "The Tromps and the Anglo-Dutch Wars, 1652–1674." *History Today,* vol. 3 (1953), pp. 836–45.

32. Brandt, Geeraert. *Het leven en bedryf van den heere Michiel de Ruiter.* Amsterdam, 1686.

33. Braudel, Fernand. *La Méditerranée et le monde méditerranéen à l'époque de Philippe II.* 2nd ed. Paris: A. Colin, 1966. 2 vols.

34. Bromley, J. S., ed. *John Baltharpe, The Straights Voyage or St. Davids Poem.* Oxford: Basil Blackwell for the Luttrell Soc., 1959.

35. ————. "The Channel Island Privateers in the War of the Spanish Succession." *Transactions for the Year 1949 of La Société Guernesiaise,* vol. 14, pt. iv (1950), pp. 444–78.

36. ————. "Les Corsaires zélandais et la navigation scandinave pendant la Guerre de Succession d'Espagne," in *Le Navire et l'économie maritime du nord de l'Europe.* Michel Mollat, ed. Paris: S.E.V.P.E.N., 1960.

37. ————. "The French Privateering War, 1702–13," in *Historical Essays 1600–1750 Presented to David Ogg.* H. C. Bell and R. L. Ollard, ed. London: A. and C. Black, 1963.

38. ————. "Some Zeeland Privateering Instructions: Jacob Sautijn to Captain Salomon Reynders, 1707," in *William III and Louis XIV: essays 1680–1720 by and for Mark A. Thomson.* Ragnhild Hatton and J. S. Bromley, ed. Liverpool: University Press, 1968.

39. Brooks, F. W. *The English Naval Forces, 1199–1272.* London: A. Brown & Sons, 1933. Repr. London: H. Pordes, 1962, with a new introduction.

40. ————, ed. "A Calendar of the Early Judgments of the Hull Trinity House," and other documents of Hull Trinity House. *Yorkshire Archaeological Soc.: Record Series,* CXVI. *Miscellanea,* V (1951).

41. Browne, Douglas G. *The Floating Bulwark: the story of the fighting ship, 1514–1942.* London: Cassell, 1963.

42. Browning, Oscar, ed. *The Journal of Sir George Rooke, Admiral of the Fleet 1700–1702.* London: Navy Records Soc., 1897.

43. Bruce, John, ed. *Journal of a Voyage into the Mediterranean by Sir Kenelm Digby A.D. 1628*. London: Camden Soc., vol. 96 (1868).

44. Bruijn, J. R., ed. *De Oorlogvoering ter zee in 1673 in journalen en andere stukken*. Werken uitgegeven door het Historisch Genootschap (Gevestigd te Utrecht). Groningen: Wolters, 1966.

45. Bryant, Sir Arthur. *Samuel Pepys: I. The Man in the Making. II. The Years of Peril. III. The Saviour of the Navy*. London: W. Collins, 1933–38.

46. Burchett, Josiah. *Memoirs of Transactions at Sea during the War with France; Beginning in 1688, and Ending in 1697*. London, 1703.

47. ———. *A Complete History of the most Remarkable Transactions at Sea, from the Earliest Accounts of Time to the Conclusion of the Last War with France*. London, 1720.

48. Burwash, Dorothy. *English Merchant Shipping 1460–1540*. Toronto: University of Toronto Press, 1947.

49. *Calendar of State Papers, Colonial Series, America and West Indies, 1574–(1737)*. London: H.M.S.O., 1860–(1963)–in prog.

50. *Calendar of State Papers, Domestic Series*. London: H.M.S.O., 1856–(1964)–in prog.

51. *Calendar of Letters, Despatches, and State Papers, Relating to the Negotiations between England and Spain, 1485–(1558)*. London: H.M.S.O., 1862–(1954)–in prog.

52. *Calendar of State Papers and Manuscripts, Relating to English Affairs Existing in the Archives and Collections of Venice, and in Other Libraries of Northern Italy, 1202–1675*. London: H.M.S.O., 1864–1940.

53. Callendar, Geoffrey, ed. *The Life of Sir John Leake, Rear Admiral of Great Britain by Stephen Martin-Leake*. London: Navy Records Soc., 1920.

54. Chapin, Howard M. *Privateer Ships and Sailors: the first century of American Colonial Privateering, 1625–1725*. Toulon: G. Mouton, 1926.

55. Chappell, Edwin, ed. *The Tangier Papers of Samuel Pepys*. London: Navy Records Soc., 1935.

56. Cheyney, Edward P. *A History of England from the Defeat of the Armada to the Death of Elizabeth*. New York: Longmans, 1914–26. 2 vols.

57. Cipolla, Carlo M. *Guns and Sails in the Early Phase of European Expansion 1400–1700*. London: Collins, 1965.

58. Clark, Sir George N. *The Dutch Alliance and the War against French Trade 1688–1697*. Manchester University Press, 1923.

59. ———. *The Later Stuarts 1660–1714*. 2nd ed. Oxford: Clarendon Press, 1955.

60. ———. "War Trade and Trade War, 1701–1713." *Econ. Hist. Rev., I* (1927–28), pp. 262–80.

61. Clowes, Sir William Laird. *The Royal Navy, a History from the*

Earliest Times to the Present. London: Low, Marston, 1897–1903. 7 vols.

62. Clowes, Geoffrey S. Laird. *Sailing Ships: their history and development as illustrated by the collection of ship-models in the Science Museum.* 2nd ed. London: H.M.S.O., 1931–32. 4th edition 1951–52. 2 vols.

63. Coleman, D. C. "Naval Dockyards under the Later Stuarts." *Econ. Hist. Rev.,* 2nd ser. vol. 6 (1953–54), pp. 134–55.

64. Colenbrander, H. T., ed. *Bescheiden uit vreemde archieven omtrent de groote Nederlandsche zeeoorlogen 1652–1676.* The Hague: Rijks Geschiedkundige Publicatiën, Nijhoff, 1919. 2 vols.

65. Connell-Smith, Gordon. *Forerunners of Drake: a study of English trade with Spain in the Early Tudor Period.* London: Longmans, 1954.

66. Corbett, Sir Julian S. *Drake and the Tudor Navy.* 2nd ed. London: Longmans, 1898. 2 vols.

67. ———. *England in the Mediterranean: a study of the rise and influence of British power within the Straits 1603–1713.* 2nd ed. London: Longmans, 1904. (1st ed., 1904). 2 vols.

68. ———, ed. *Fighting Instructions, 1530–1816.* London: Navy Records Soc., 1905.

69. ———, ed. *Papers Relating to the Navy during the Spanish War 1585–1587.* London: Navy Records Soc., 1898.

70. ———, ed. *Signals and Instructions, 1776–1794, with Addenda to Vol. XXIX.* London: Navy Records Soc., 1908.

71. ———. *The Successors of Drake.* London: Longmans, 1900.

72. Crouse, Nellis M. *The French Struggle for the West Indies, 1665–1713.* New York: Columbia, 1943.

73. Crump, Helen J. *Colonial Admiralty Jurisdiction in the Seventeenth Century.* London: Longmans, 1931.

74. Curtis, C. D. *Blake, General at Sea.* Taunton: Barnicott & Pearce, 1934.

75. Davies, C. S. L. "The Administration of the Royal Navy under Henry VIII: the origins of the Navy Board." *English Hist. Rev.,* vol. 80 (1965), pp. 268–86.

76. ———. "Les rations alimentaires de l'armée et de la marine anglaise au XVIᵉ siècle." *Annales,* vol. 18 (1963), pp. 139–41.

77. Davies, Godfrey, ed. *Bibliography of British History: Stuart Period, 1603–1714.* Oxford: Clarendon Press, 1928.

78. Davis, Ralph. "England and the Mediterranean, 1560–1670," in *Essays in the Economic and Social History of Tudor and Stuart England.* F. J. Fisher, ed. Cambridge University Press, 1961.

79. ———. *The Rise of the English Shipping Industry in the Seventeenth and Eighteenth Centuries.* London: Macmillan, 1962.

80. De Jonge, Johannes C. *Geschiedenis van het Nederlandsche zeewezen.* 2nd ed. Haarlem: Kruseman, 1858–69. 5 vols.

81. Dewar, Captain A. C. "The Naval Administration of the Interregnum, 1641–59." *Mariner's Mirror,* vol. 12 (1926), pp. 406–30.

82. Dietz, F. C. *English Public Finance 1485–1558*. Urbana, Ill.: Univ. of Illinois Press, 1921. Repr. London: Cass, 1964.

83. ———. *English Public Finance 1558–1641*. New York: The Century Co., 1932. Repr. London: Cass, 1964.

84. Dyer, Florence E. *The Life of Admiral Sir John Narbrough*. London: P. Allan, 1931.

85. ———. "Reprisals in the Sixteenth Century." *Mariner's Mirror*, vol. 21 (1935), pp. 187–97.

86. École des Hautes Études—VIᵉ Section: Centre de Recherches Historiques, "Ports—Routes—Trafics" series of publications. Paris: S.E.V.P.E.N.

87. Ehrman, John P. W. *The Navy in the War of William III, 1689–1697: its state and direction*. Cambridge University Press, 1953.

88. ———. "The Official Papers Transferred by Pepys to the Admiralty by 12 July 1689." *Mariner's Mirror*, vol. 34 (1948), pp. 255–70.

89. Ewen, C. L'Estrange. "Organized Piracy Round England in the Sixteenth Century." *Mariner's Mirror*, vol. 35 (1949), pp. 29–42.

90. Firth, Sir Charles. "Papers Relating to the Navy in the Bodleian Library." *Mariner's Mirror*, vol. 3 (1913), pp. 225–229.

91. Fisher, Sir Godfrey. *Barbary Legend: war, trade and piracy in North Africa 1415–1830*. Oxford: Clarendon Press, 1957.

92. Fulton, Thomas Wemyss. *The Sovereignty of the Sea*. Edinburgh and London: Blackwood, 1911.

93. Furber, Elizabeth Chapin, ed. *Changing Views on British History: essays on historical writing since 1939*. Cambridge, Mass.: Harvard, 1966.

94. Gardiner, Samuel R. and C. T. Atkinson. eds. *Letters and Papers Relating to the First Dutch War, 1652–1654*. London: Navy Records Soc., 1899–1930. 6 vols.

95. Glasgow, Tom, Jr. "The Navy in Philip and Mary's War, 1557–1558." *Mariner's Mirror*, vol. 53 (1967), pp. 321–42.

96. ———. "The Royal Navy at the Start of the Reign of Elizabeth I." *Mariner's Mirror*, vol. 51 (1965), pp. 73–76.

97. ———. "The Shape of the Ships that Defeated the Spanish Armada." *Mariner's Mirror*, vol. 50 (1964), pp. 177–87.

98. Goldingham, Captain C. S. "The Navy under Henry VII." *English Hist. Rev.*, vol. 33 (1918), pp. 472–88.

99. Gosse, Philip. *The History of Piracy*. London: Longmans, 1932.

100. ———. *The Pirates' Who's Who*. London: Dulau & Co., 1924.

101. Graham, Gerald S. *Empire of the North Atlantic: the maritime struggle for North America*. 2nd ed. London: Oxford University Press and Toronto: University of Toronto Press, 1958.

102. ———, ed. *The Walker Expedition to Quebec, 1711*. London: Navy Records Soc., 1953.

103. Grosart, Alexander B., ed. *The Voyage to Cadiz in 1625. Being a Journal written by John Glanville*. London: Camden Soc., 1883.

104. Hakluyt, Richard. *The Principall Navigations Voiages and Dis-*

coveries of the English Nation. Facsimile edition with introduction
by D. B. Quinn and R. A. Skelton and a new index by Alison Quinn.
Cambridge University Press for the Hakluyt Soc., 1965. 2 vols.

105. The Hakluyt Society. *Prospectus with a List of Publications and
Maps.* London: Hakluyt Soc., 1956.

106. Hannay, David. *A Short History of the Royal Navy. Vol. I: 1217–
1688. Vol. II: 1689–1815.* London: Methuen, 1898–1909.

107. Hardy, Evelyn. *Survivors of the Armada.* London: Constable, 1966.

108. Harris, F. R. *The Life of Edward Mountagu, K.G. First Earl of
Sandwich (1625–1672).* London: Murray, 1912. 2 vols.

109. Heath, Helen T., ed. *The Letters of Samuel Pepys and his Family
Circle.* Oxford: Clarendon Press, 1955.

110. Hewitt, H. J. *The Organization of War under Edward III, 1338–
62.* Manchester: University Press, 1966.

111. Historical Manuscripts Commission. *Report on the Manuscripts of
the late Allan George Finch.* London: H.M.S.O., 1913–(1965)–in
prog.

112. ———. *The Manuscripts of the House of Lords, 1678–1693.* London: H.M.S.O., 1887–94. 4 vols. New series, continued by House
of Lords, *1693–1714.* London: H.M.S.O., 1900–1962. 11 vols.

113. Hulme, Harold. *Sir John Eliot and the Vice-Admiralty of Devon.*
Camden Miscellany, XVII. London: Camden Soc., 1940.

114. Ingram, Bruce S., ed. *Three Journals of Stuart Times: diary of
Dawtrey Cooper, 1625; journal of Jeremy Roch, 1659–91; diary
of Francis Rogers, 1703–4.* London: Constable, 1936.

115. James, G. F. and J. J. Sutherland Shaw. "Admiralty Administration and Personnel, 1619–1714." *Bulletin of the Institute of Historical Research,* vol. 14 (1936–37), pp. 10–24, 166–83.

116. Jessup, Philip C. and Francis Deak. *Neutrality: its history, economics and law.* New York: Columbia, 1935–36. 4 vols. *Vol. I: The
Origins,* 1935.

117. Johns, A. W. "The Principal Officers of the Navy." *Mariner's Mirror,* vol. 14 (1928), pp. 32–54.

118. Jones, J. R. *Britain and Europe in the Seventeenth Century.* London: Edward Arnold, 1966.

119. Kamen, Henry. "The Destruction of the Spanish Silver Fleet at
Vigo in 1702." *Bulletin of the Institute of Historical Research,* vol.
39 (1966), pp. 165–73.

120. Kemp, P. K. and Christopher Lloyd. *The Brethren of the Coast.*
London: Heinemann, 1960.

121. Kennedy, D. E. "Naval Captains at the Outbreak of the English
Civil War." *Mariner's Mirror,* vol. 46 (1960), pp. 181–98.

122. ———. "The Establishment and Settlement of Parliament's Admiralty, 1642–1648." *Mariner's Mirror,* vol. 48 (1962), pp. 276–
91.

123. ———. "The English Naval Revolt of 1648." *English Hist. Rev.,*
vol. 77 (1962), pp. 247–56.

124. Kingsford, Charles L. *Prejudice & Promise in XVth Century Eng-*

land. Oxford: Clarendon Press, 1925. Repr. London: Cass, 1962.

125. Kulsrud, Carl J. *Maritime Neutrality to 1780.* Boston: Little, Brown, 1936.

126. Lane, Frederic C. "The Economic Meaning of the Invention of the Compass." *Amer. Hist. Rev.,* vol. 68 (1963), pp. 605–17. Also in *Venice and History: the collected papers of Frederic C. Lane.* Baltimore: Johns Hopkins, 1966.

127. Laughton, Sir John K., ed. *Memoirs Relating to the Lord Torrington.* London: Camden Soc., 1889.

128. ———, ed. *State Papers Relating to the Defeat of the Spanish Armada, Anno 1588.* London: Navy Records Soc., 1895. 2 vols.

129. ———. "The Scientific Study of Naval History." *Journal of the Royal United Service Institution,* vol. 18 (1875), pp. 508–27.

130. ———. "The Study of Naval History." *Journal of the Royal United Service Institution,* vol. 40 (1896), pp. 795–820.

131. Laughton, L. G. Carr. "Early Tudor Ship-Guns." Posthumously publ. and ed. by M. Lewis. *Mariner's Mirror,* vol. 46 (1960), pp. 242–85.

132. Lediard, Thomas. *The Naval History of England, in all its Branches; from the Norman Conquest in the Year 1066 to the Conclusion of 1734.* London, 1735.

133. *Letters and Papers, Foreign and Domestic, of the Reign of Henry VIII.* (1509–47) J. S. Brewer, J. Gairdner, and R. H. Brodie, eds. London: H.M.S.O., 1862–1932. 21 vols. and addenda.

134. Lewis, Michael A. *Armada Guns: a comparative study of English and Spanish armaments.* London: Allen & Unwin, 1961. Originally appeared as articles in *The Mariner's Mirror* (1942–43).

135. ———. *England's Sea-Officers: the story of the naval profession.* London: Allen & Unwin, 1939.

136. ———. *The History of the British Navy.* Harmondsworth, Mddx.: Penguin, 1957.

137. ———. *The Navy of Britain: a historical portrait.* London: Allen & Unwin, 1948.

138. ———. *The Spanish Armada.* London: Batsford, 1960.

139. Lindsay-MacDougall, K. F. *A Guide to the Manuscripts at the National Maritime Museum.* London: National Maritime Museum, Greenwich, 1960.

140. Little, Bryan. *Crusoe's Captain: being the life of Woodes Rogers, seaman, trader, colonial governor.* London: Odhams Press, 1960.

141. Lubbock, Basil, ed. *Barlow's Journal of his Life at Sea in King's Ships, East and West Indiamen & other Merchantmen from 1659 to 1703.* London: Hurst & Blackett, 1934. 2 vols.

142. Mahan, Admiral Alfred T. *The Influence of Sea Power upon History, 1660–1783.* Boston: Little, Brown, 1890. Repr. New York: Sagamore Press, 1957.

143. ———. *The Influence of Sea Power upon the French Revolution and Empire, 1793–1812.* Boston: Little, Brown, 1892. 2 vols.

144. Malone, Joseph J. *Pine Trees and Politics: the naval stores and*

forest policy in Colonial New England 1691–1775. London: Longmans and Seattle: University of Washington, 1964.

145. Manwaring, G. E. *A Bibliography of British Naval History*. London: Routledge, 1930.

146. ———, ed. *The Diary of Henry Teonge: chaplain on board H. M.'s Ships Assistance, Bristol, and Royal Oak 1675–1679*. London: Routledge, 1927.

147. ———, ed. *The Life and Works of Sir Henry Mainwaring*. London: Navy Records Soc., vol. I, 1920. Vol. II, G. E. Manwaring and W. G. Perrin, eds., 1922.

148. Marcus, G. J. *A Naval History of England: I. The Formative Centuries*. London: Longmans, 1961.

149. ——— and Sölver, C. V. "Dead Reckoning and the Ocean Voyages of the Past." *Mariner's Mirror*, vol. 44 (1958), pp. 18–34.

150. ———. "The Navigation of the Norsemen." *Mariner's Mirror*, vol. 39 (1953), pp. 112–31.

151. *The Mariner's Mirror: The Journal of the Society for Nautical Research. General Index to Volumes 1–35*. R. C. Anderson, Comp. Cambridge University Press, 1955. Through 1949.

152. Markham, Sir Clements R. *Life of Robert Fairfax of Steeton, Vice-Admiral, Alderman, and Member for York, A.D. 1666–1725*. London: Macmillan, 1885.

153. ———, ed. *Life of Captain Stephen Martin 1666–1740*. London: Navy Records Soc., 1895.

154. Marsden, Reginald G., ed. *Documents Relating to Law and Custom of the Sea*. London: Navy Records Soc., 1915–16. (Vol. I: 1205–1648. Vol. II: 1649–1767.) 2 vols.

155. ———. "The Early Career of Sir Martin Frobisher." *English Hist. Rev.*, vol. 21 (1906), pp. 538–44.

156. ———. "Early Prize Jurisdiction and Prize Law in England." In Three parts. *English Hist. Rev.* Part I: to 1603, vol. 24 (1909), pp. 675–97. Part II: 1603–40, vol. 25 (1910), pp. 243–63. Part III: 1640–ca.1685, vol. 26 (1911), pp. 34–56.

157. ———. "The High Court of Admiralty in Relation to National History, Commerce and the Colonisation of America—A.D. 1550–1650." *Trans. Royal Hist. Soc.*, n. s. vol. 16 (1902), pp. 69–96.

158. ———, ed. *Select Pleas in the Court of Admiralty. I: 1527–1545. II: 1547–1602*. London: Quaritch for the Seldon Soc., 1894–97.

159. ———. "Thomas Cobham and the Capture of the 'St. Katharine'." *English Hist. Rev.*, vol. 23 (1908), pp. 290–1.

160. ———. "The Vice-Admirals of the Coast." *English Hist. Rev.*, vol. 22 (1907), pp. 468–77; vol. 23 (1908), pp. 736–57.

161. Mathew, David. "The Cornish and Welsh Pirates in the Reign of Elizabeth." *English Hist. Rev.*, vol. 39 (1924), pp. 337–48.

162. Mattingly, Garrett. *The Armada*. Boston: Houghton, Mifflin, 1959. Published in England as *The Defeat of the Spanish Armada*. London: Cape, 1959.

163. McFarlane, K. B. "War, the Economy and Social Change: England

and the Hundred Years' War." *Past & Present,* no. 22 (July, 1962), pp. 3–18.

164. McGowan, A. P. "The Administration of the Navy under the First Duke of Buckingham, Lord High Admiral of England, 1618–1628." Summary of Julian Corbett Prize Essay. *Bull. of the Institute of Hist. Research,* vol. 40 (1967), pp. 225–27.

165. McGrath, Patrick V., ed. *Merchants and Merchandise in Seventeenth-Century Bristol.* Bristol: Bristol Record Soc., 1955.

166. *Memoirs of the English Affairs, Chiefly Naval, from the Year 1660 to 1673. Written by His Royal Highness James Duke of York, under his Administration of Lord High Admiral.* London, 1729.

167. Merriman, Commander R. D., ed. *Queen Anne's Navy: documents concerning the administration of the Navy of Queen Anne 1702–1714.* London: Navy Records Soc., 1961.

168. ———, ed. *The Sergison Papers.* London: Navy Record Soc., 1950.

169. ———. "Gilbert Wardlaw's Allegations." *Mariner's Mirror,* vol. 38 (1952), pp. 106–31.

170. Minchinton, W. E. "Michael Oppenheim, 1853–1927, A Memoir." *Mariner's Mirror,* vol. 54 (1968), pp. 85–93.

171. Mollat, Michel, ed. *Les Sources de l'histoire maritime en Europe, du moyen age au XVIIIe siècle.* Actes du Quatrième Colloque International d'Histoire Maritime. Paris: S.E.V.P.E.N., 1962.

172. Morgan, William T. *A Bibliography of British History (1700–1715).* Bloomington, Indiana: Indiana University Studies, 1934–1942. 5 vols.

173. Morgan, William T. "The British West Indies during King William's War (1689–97)." *Journal of Modern History,* volume 2 (1930), pp. 378–409.

174. Moses, Norton H. "The British Navy and the Caribbean, 1689–1697." *Mariner's Mirror,* vol. 52 (1966), pp. 13–40.

175. Murray, K. M. E. *The Constitutional History of the Cinque Ports.* Manchester University Press, 1935.

176. Murray, Sir Oswyn A. R. "The Admiralty." *Mariner's Mirror,* in ten parts, vols. 23–25 (1937–39).

177. Neale, Sir John E. "Elizabeth and the Netherlands, 1586–7." *English Hist. Rev.,* vol. 45 (1930), pp. 373–96. Repr. in *Essays in Elizabethan History.* London: Macmillan, 1958.

178. Nicolas, Sir Nicholas Harris. *A History of the Royal Navy, from the Earliest Times to the Wars of the French Revolution.* London: R. Bentley, 1847. 2 vols.

179. Ogg, David. *England in the Reign of Charles II.* 2nd ed. Oxford: Clarendon Press, 1955. 2 vols.

180. Oppenheim, Michael, ed. *Naval Accounts and Inventories of the Reign of Henry VII, 1485–8 and 1495–7.* London: Navy Records Soc., 1896.

181. ———. *A History of the Administration of the Royal Navy and of Merchant Shipping in Relation to the Navy: from MDIX to MDCLX with an introduction treating of the preceding period.*

London: J. Lane, 1896. Repr. Hamden, Conn.: Archon Books, 1961.

182. ———, ed. *The Naval Tracts of Sir William Monson*. London: Navy Records Soc., 1902–14. 5 vols.

183. Owen, Commander John H. *War at Sea under Queen Anne 1702–1708*. Cambridge: University Press, 1938.

184. Pardessus, Jean Marie. *Collection de lois maritimes antérieures au XVIIIe siècle*. Paris: L'Imprimerie Royale, 1828–45. 6 vols.

185. Pares, Richard. *Colonial Blockade and Neutral Rights, 1739–1763*. Oxford: Clarendon Press, 1938.

186. Parry, John H. *The Age of Reconnaissance: discovery, exploration and settlement*. London: Weidenfeld and Nicolson, 1963. New York: Mentor, 1964.

187. Penn, Christopher D. *The Navy under the Early Stuarts and its Influence on English History*. Leighton Buzzard and Manchester: The Faith Press, 1913.

188. Penn, Granville. *Memorials of the Professional Life and Times of Sir William Penn (1644–1670)*. London: James Duncan, 1833. 2 vols.

189. Pepys, Samuel. *Memoires Relating to the State of the Royal Navy of England for Ten Years, Determin'd December 1688*. 1690. Facsimile repr. Oslo, 1965.

190. Perrin, William G. *Admiralty Library. Subject Catalogue of Printed Books. Part I: Historical Section*. London: H.M.S.O., 1912.

191. ———, ed. *The Autobiography of Phineas Pett*. London: Navy Records Soc., 1918.

192. ———, ed. *Boteler's Dialogues*. London: Navy Records Soc., 1929.

193. ———. "The Lord High Admiral and the Board of Admiralty." *Mariner's Mirror*, vol. 12 (1926), pp. 117–44.

194. Pipe Roll Society. *The Publications of the Pipe Roll Society*. London, 1884-in prog. 75 vols. to date.

195. Pool, Bernard. *Navy Board Contracts 1660–1832*. London: Longmans, 1966.

196. Poole, Austin Lane. *From Domesday Book to Magna Carta, 1087–1216*. 2nd ed. Oxford: Clarendon Press, 1955.

197. Postan, M. M. "The Costs of the Hundred Years' War." *Past & Present*, no. 27 (April, 1964), pp. 34–53.

198. Powell, John R. "The Expedition of Blake and Montagu in 1655." *Mariner's Mirror*, vol. 52 (1966), pp. 341–69.

199. ———, ed. *The Letters of Robert Blake*. London: Navy Records Soc., 1937.

200. ———. *The Navy in the English Civil War*. Hamden, Conn.: Archon Books, 1962.

201. Powell, John R. and E. Kenneth Timings, eds. *Documents Relating to the Civil War*. London: Navy Records Soc., 1963.

202. Powell, Commander John W. Damer. *Bristol Privateers and Ships of War*. Bristol: J. W. Arrowsmith, 1930.

203.   Powley, Edward B. *The English Navy in the Revolution of 1688*. Cambridge University Press, 1928.

204.   Prestwich, Menna. *Cranfield: politics and profits under the early Stuarts: The career of Lionel Cranfield Earl of Middlesex*. Oxford: Clarendon Press, 1966.

205.   Prince, Albert E. "The Army and Navy." Chapter VIII, Vol. I of *The English Government at Work, 1327–1336*. James F. Willard, William A. Morris, Joseph R. Strayer, and William H. Dunham, Jr., eds. Cambridge, Mass: The Medieval Academy of America, 1940–50. 3 vols.

205a.   Privy Council. *Acts of the Privy Council of England*. 1542–1631. London: H.M.S.O., 1890–1964. 46 vols.

205b.   ———. *Privy Council Registers. 1631–1637*. Microcard edition. London: H.M.S.O., n.d.

205c.   ———. *Privy Council Registers preserved in the Public Record Office*. 1637–   . Facsimile edition. London: H.M.S.O., 1967-in prog.

206.   Public Record Office, London. *Guide to the Contents of the Public Record Office*. Rev. ed. London: H.M.S.O., 1963. 2 vols.

207.   ———. *List of Admiralty Records Preserved in the Public Record Office. Vol. I*. Lists and Indexes, No. XVIII. London, 1904. New York: Kraus Reprint Corp., 1963.

208.   Quinn, David B. *Raleigh and the British Empire*. London: English Universities Press, 1947.

209.   ———, ed. *The Roanoke Voyages, 1584–1590: documents to illustrate the English voyages to North America under the patent granted to Walter Raleigh in 1584*. London: Hakluyt Soc., 1955. 2 vols.

210.   ———, ed. *The Voyages and Colonising Enterprises of Sir Humphrey Gilbert*. London: Hakluyt Soc., 1940. 2 vols.

211.   ———. "Sailors and the Sea," in *Shakespeare in His Own Age*. Allardyce Nicoll, ed. Shakespeare Survey Series, vol. 17. Cambridge University Press, 1964.

212.   ———. "Some Spanish Reactions to Elizabethan Colonial Enterprises." *Trans. Royal Hist. Soc.*, 5th ser., vol. 1 (1951), pp. 1–23.

213.   Rabb, Theodore K. *Enterprise & Empire: merchant and gentry investment in the expansion of England, 1575–1630*. Cambridge, Mass.: Harvard, 1967.

214.   Ramsay, G. D. *English Overseas Trade during the Centuries of Emergence: studies in some modern origins of the English-speaking world*. London: Macmillan, 1957.

215.   Read, Conyers, ed. *Bibliography of British History: Tudor Period, 1485–1603*. 2nd ed. Oxford: Clarendon Press, 1959.

216.   ———. *Mr. Secretary Cecil and Queen Elizabeth*. New York: Knopf and London: Cape, 1955. *Lord Burghley and Queen Elizabeth*, 1960.

217.   ———. *Mr. Secretary Walsingham and the Policy of Queen Elizabeth*. Cambridge, Mass.: Harvard and Oxford: Clarendon Press, 1925. 3 vols.

218. Reid, Mrs. Stanford. "Sea Power in the Anglo-Scottish War, 1296–1328." *Mariner's Mirror,* vol. 46 (1960), pp. 7–23.
219. Richmond, C. F. "The Keeping of the Seas during the Hundred Years' War: 1422–1440." *History,* vol. 49 (1964), pp. 283–98.
220. ———. "English Naval Power in the Fifteenth Century." *History,* vol. 52 (1967), pp. 1–15.
221. Richmond, Admiral Sir Herbert W. *The Navy as an Instrument of Policy 1585–1727.* Posthumously publ. and ed. by E. A. Hughes. Cambridge: University Press, 1953.
222. ———. *Statesmen and Sea Power: based on the Ford Lectures, 1943.* Oxford: Clarendon Press, 1946.
223. Robertson, Frederick L. *The Evolution of Naval Armament.* London: Constable, 1921.
224. Robinson, A. H. W. *Marine Cartography in Britain: a history of the sea chart to 1855.* Leicester University Press, 1962.
225. Robinson, Commander Charles N. *The British Fleet: the growth, achievements and duties of the navy of the Empire.* London: Bell, 1894.
226. ———. *The British Tar in Fact and Fiction: the poetry, pathos, and humour of the sailor's life.* London and New York: Harpers, 1911.
227. Robison, Rear Admiral Samuel S. and Mary L. *A History of Naval Tactics from 1530 to 1930: the evolution of tactical maxims.* Annapolis: United States Naval Institute, 1942.
228. Rogers, Captain Woodes. *A Cruising Voyage Round the World.* London, 1712. Repr. and ed. G. E. Manwaring. London: Cassell, 1928.
229. Roncière, Charles de la. *Histoire de la marine française.* Paris: Plon, 1899–1932. 6 vols.
230. Roscoe, Edward S. *A History of the English Prize Court.* London: Lloyd's, 1924.
231. Routh, Enid M. G. *Tangier, England's Lost Atlantic Outpost 1661–1684.* London: Murray, 1912.
232. Rowbotham, Commander W. B. "The Algerine War in the Time of Charles II." *Journal of the Royal United Service Institution,* vol. 109 (1964), pp. 160–68, 253–62, 350–56.
233. Rowse, A[lfred] L. *The Elizabethans and America.* London: Macmillan and New York: Harper, 1959.
234. ———. *The Expansion of Elizabethan England.* London: Macmillan, 1955.
235. ———. *Sir Richard Grenville of the Revenge: an Elizabethan hero.* London: Cape, 1937.
236. ———. *Tudor Cornwall: portrait of a society.* London: Cape, 1941.
237. Ruddock, Alwyn A. "The Earliest Records of the High Court of Admiralty (1515–1558)." *Bull. of the Institute of Hist. Research,* vol. 22 (1949), pp. 131–51.
238. Ryan, Anthony N. "William III and the Brest Fleet in the Nine Years' War," in *William III and Louis XIV: essays 1680–1720 by*

and for Mark A. Thomson. Ragnhild Hatton and J. S. Bromley, eds. Liverpool University Press, 1968.

239. Salisbury, W. and R. C. Anderson, eds. *A Treatise on Shipbuilding and a Treatise on Rigging written about 1620–1625.* London: Society for Nautical Research (Occasional Publication no. 6), 1958.

240. Scammell, Geoffrey V. "English Merchant Shipping at the End of the Middle Ages: some East Coast evidence." *Econ. Hist. Rev.* 2nd ser. vol. 13 (1961), pp. 327–41.

241. ———. "Shipowning in England c. 1450–1550." *Trans. of the Royal Hist. Soc.* 5th ser. vol. 12 (1962), pp. 105–22.

242. ———. "War at Sea under the Early Tudors: some Newcastle-upon-Tyne evidence." In two parts. *Archaeologia Aeliana,* 4th ser. vol. 28 (1960), pp. 73–97; vol. 29 (1961), pp. 179–205.

243. Schoerner, Gunnar. *Regalskeppet: A Study of the Seventeenth-Century Shipwrightry, with an English Summary.* Stockholm: Norstedt & Söners, 1964.

244. Senior, William. *Naval History in the Law Courts: a selection of old maritime cases.* London: Longmans, 1927.

245. Shaw, William A., ed. *Calendar of Treasury Books 1660–1718.* London: H.M.S.O., 1904–57.

246. Shelley, Roland J. A. "The Division of the English Fleet in 1666." *Mariner's Mirror,* vol. 25 (1939), pp. 178–96.

247. Sherborne, J. W. "The Hundred Years' War. The English Navy: shipping and manpower 1369–1389." *Past & Present,* no. 37 (July, 1967), pp. 163–75.

248. Shilton, Dorothy O. and Richard Holworthy, eds. *High Court of Admiralty Examinations (MS Volume 53) 1637–1638.* New York: Anglo-American Records Foundation, 1932.

249. Spont, Alfred, ed. *Letters and Papers Relating to the War with France 1512–1513.* London: Navy Records Soc., 1897.

250. Stanford, Michael J. G. "The Raleghs Take to the Sea." *Mariner's Mirror,* vol. 48 (1962), pp. 18–35.

251. Stone, Lawrence. "The Armada Campaign of 1588." *History,* vol. 29 (1944), pp. 120–43.

252. ———. *The Crisis of the Aristocracy 1558–1641.* Oxford: Clarendon Press, 1965.

253. ———. "Elizabethan Overseas Trade." *Econ. Hist. Rev.,* 2nd ser. vol. 2 (1949), pp. 30–58

254. Tanner, Joseph R. *Bibliotheca Pepysiana: a descriptive catalogue of the library of Samuel Pepys.* London: Sidgwick & Jackson, 1914.

255. ———, ed. *A Descriptive Catalogue of the Naval Manuscripts in the Pepysian Library at Magdalene College, Cambridge.* London: Navy Records Soc., 1903–23. 4 vols.

256. ———, ed. *Two Discourses of the Navy, 1638 and 1659, by John Hollond: Also a Discourse of the Navy, 1660, by Sir Robert Slyngesbie.* London: Navy Records Soc., 1896.

257. ———. "The Navy of the Commonwealth and the First Dutch War," in *Vol. IV. The Thirty Years' War* in *The Cambridge Modern*

History. A. W. Ward, G. W. Prothero, and Stanley Leathes, eds. Cambridge University Press, 1902–11. 13 vols.

258. ――――, ed. *Private Correspondence and Miscellaneous Papers of Samuel Pepys, 1679–1703.* London: Bell, 1926. 2 vols.

259. ――――, ed. *Further Correspondence of Samuel Pepys, 1662–1679.* London: Bell, 1929.

260. ――――. *Samuel Pepys and the Royal Navy.* Cambridge University Press, 1920.

261. ――――, ed. *Samuel Pepys' Naval Minutes.* London: Navy Records Soc., 1926.

262. Taylor, Eva G. R. *The Haven-Finding Art: a history of navigation from Odysseus to Captain Cook.* London: Hollis and Carter, 1956.

263. ――――. *Tudor Geography, 1485–1583.* London: Methuen, 1930.

264. ――――. *Late Tudor and Early Stuart Geography, 1583–1650.* London: Methuen, 1934.

265. Tedder, Arthur W., Lord, Marshal of the R.A.F. *The Navy of the Restoration from the Death of Cromwell to the Treaty of Breda; its work, growth and influence.* Cambridge University Press, 1916.

266. Tenenti, Alberto. *Piracy and the Decline of Venice 1580–1615.* Trans. from *Venezia e i corsari* (Bari, 1961) by Janet and Brian Pullan. London: Longmans and Berkeley: University of California, 1967.

267. Tenison, E. M. *Elizabethan England: being the history of this country "in relation to all foreign princes."* Limited ed. Leamington Spa, Warwicks., 1933–61. 13 vols.

267a. Thomason Tracts. *Catalogue of the Pamphlets, Books, Newspapers, and Manuscripts Relating to the Civil War, the Commonwealth, and Restoration, Collected by George Thomason, 1640–1661.* London: British Museum, 1908. 2 vols.

268. Thornton, A. P. *West-India Policy under the Restoration.* Oxford: Clarendon Press, 1956.

269. Trevelyan, George M. *England under Queen Anne.* London: Longmans, 1930–34. 3 vols.

270. Tunstall, W. C. Brian, ed. *The Byng Papers, Selected from the Letters and Papers of Admiral Sir George Byng, First Viscount Torrington, and of his Son, Admiral the Hon. John Byng.* London: Navy Records Soc., 1930–32. 3 vols.

271. Turner, W. J. Carpenter. "The Building of the *Gracedieu, Valentine* and *Falconer* at Southampton, 1416–1420." *Mariner's Mirror,* vol. 40 (1954), pp. 55–72.

272. ――――. "The Building of the *Holy Ghost of the Tower,* 1414–1416, and her Subsequent History." *Mariner's Mirror,* vol. 40 (1954), pp. 270–81.

273. ――――. "Southampton as a Naval Centre, 1414–1458," in *Collected Essays on Southampton.* J. B. Morgan and P. Pebedy, eds. Southampton: Southampton County Borough Council, 1958.

274. Unwin, Rayner. *The Defeat of John Hawkins: a biography of his third slaving voyage.* London: Allen & Unwin, 1960.

275. Upton, Eleanor S. *Guide to Sources of English History from 1603 to 1660 in Reports of the Royal Commission on Historical Manuscripts.* 2nd ed. New York and London: The Scarecrow Press, 1964.
276. Wallace, Willard M. *Sir Walter Raleigh.* Princeton University Press, 1959.
277. Warburton, Eliot. *Memoirs of Prince Rupert and the Cavaliers.* London: Bentley, 1849. 3 vols.
278. Ward, Edward. *The Wooden World.* London, 1707. Repr. from the edition of 1751, with a foreward by Geoffrey Callender. London: Society for Nautical Research (Occasional Publication no. 2), 1929.
279. Warnsinck, Johan C. M. *Admiral de Ruyter: De Zeeslag op Schooneveld, Juni 1673.* 's-Gravenhage: Nijhoff, 1930.
280. Waters, Commander David W. *The Art of Navigation in England in Elizabethan and Early Stuart Times.* London: Hollis and Carter, 1958.
281. ———. "The Elizabethan Navy and the Armada Campaign." *Mariner's Mirror,* vol. 35 (1949), pp. 90–138.
282. Weber, R. E. J. *De Beveiliging van de zee tegen Europeesche en Barbarijsche zeeroovers 1609–1621.* Amsterdam: Koninklijke Akademie van Wetenschappen, 1936.
283. Wernham, Reginald B. *Before the Armada: the growth of English foreign policy 1485–1588.* London: Cape, 1966.
284. ———. "Elizabethan War Aims and Strategy," in *Elizabethan Government and Society: essays presented to Sir John Neale.* London: Athlone Press, 1961.
285. ———. "Queen Elizabeth and the Portugal Expedition of 1589." *English Hist. Rev.,* vol. 66 (1951), pp. 1–26, 194–218.
286. Whitwell, Robert J. and Charles Johnson. "The 'Newcastle' Galley, A.D. 1294." *Archaeologia Aeliana,* 4th ser. vol. 2 (1926), pp. 142–93.
287. Willan, Thomas S. *The Early History of the Russia Company 1553–1603.* Manchester University Press, 1956.
288. ———. *Studies in Elizabethan Foreign Trade.* Manchester University Press, 1959.
289. Williamson, James A. *The Age of Drake.* London: A. & C. Black, 1938.
290. ———. *Sir John Hawkins: the time and the man.* Oxford: Clarendon Press, 1927.
291. ———. *Hawkins of Plymouth: a new history of Sir John Hawkins and of the other members of his family prominent in Tudor England.* London: A. & C. Black, 1949.
292. ———. *Maritime Enterprise, 1485–1558.* Oxford: Clarendon Press, 1913.
293. ———. *A Short History of British Expansion: I. The Old Colonial Empire.* 3rd ed. London: Macmillan, 1945.
294. Wilson, Charles. *England's Apprenticeship, 1603–1763.* London: Longmans, 1965.

295.   ————. *Profit and Power: a study of England and the Dutch Wars.*
        London: Longmans, 1957.
296.   Oppenheim, Michael. *The Maritime History of Devon.* Ed. by W. E.
        Minchinton. Exeter: Univ. of Exeter Press, 1968.
297.   Ollard, Richard. *Man of War: Sir Robert Holmes and the Restora-
        tion Navy.* London: Hodder and Stoughton, 1969.
298.   Glasgow, Tom Jr. "Maturing of Naval Administration 1556–1564."
        Mariner's Mirror, vol. 56 (1970), pp. 3–26.

Acknowledgement: In surveying so broad a field as this a scholar needs
help. I wish to thank Professors J. S. Bromley and David B. Quinn as well as
Theodore K. Rabb, Anthony N. Ryan, and Geoffrey Scammell for their
generous assistance. Responsibility for inclusion, omission, and commentary
is of course entirely mine.

V

THE ARMY IN THE
EIGHTEENTH CENTURY

William A. Foote

The eighteenth century is a curious one. Though it was filled with wars throughout its length from 1689 to 1815 and though the British fought on an average of every other year, few if any scholars regard themselves as competent to tackle the whole period. Thus there are experts on the wars of William and of Anne, on the period 1740–1763, on the American Revolution, and on the Napoleonic Wars. One of the first things needed is, in fact, a sound one-volume history of the British forces, both army and navy, and of grand strategy for the whole of this period.

OLDER SCHOLARSHIP. The older scholarship tended to be chronological or laudatory in nature. Certain of England's military heroes have been written up extensively. Wellington's life and writings appeared to have been worked to the ultimate, to cite one example (though Elizabeth Longford has now just brought out a new biography), while other competent soldiers have been completely neglected. Regimental histories written in the period before 1930 have tended to be more traditional than factual in the pre-Waterloo period, quite possibly because of a failure to use the ample factual materials for the earlier periods. The real story can be traced in most cases, by utilizing the documents in the Audit Office Series 1, which have valuable details contained in the reports of the Auditors of Army Accounts.

MODERN SCHOLARSHIP. Modern works tend to be analytical and to deal with battles, campaigns, generals, and conditions from a multi-angled approach. The central subject is taken in its international aspects rather than being treated from a distinctly British viewpoint, which has made the works the more valuable since they thus serve to broaden the history of nations and the study of warfare.

GENERAL BIBLIOGRAPHY MATERIALS. These are covered in the Introduction, but special attention should be given to the two volumes by

Godfrey Davies and Pargellis and Medley in the *Oxford Bibliography of British History* series. White's *Bibliography of Regimental Histories of the British Army* (276) is so complete and exhaustive that no listing of regimental histories is made here. The researcher will find these units classified by component.

The British government has done much to make the task of researchers using its materials easier with tools such as the *Guide to the Public Record Office* and *H.M.S.O. Sectional List No. 24* (See Introduction). Invaluable for the location of specific items are the *Public Record Office Lists and Indexes* (See Introduction). The Public Record Office *Guide* and the *Lists* must be used together, since not all materials in the one will necessarily be shown in the other. Generally the *Guide* gives an overview. The *Lists* pinpoint the location of documents by series and volume.

JOURNALS. There are no journals specializing in eighteenth-century military topics. Readers should, therefore, consult the Introduction to this work.

REPRINTS. The recent increased interest in Military History as a serious area of study has prompted the reprinting of books which have been unavailable for those who did not have access to a large university library. For the eighteenth-century period, the offerings of the Museum Restoration Service of Ottawa, Ontario, are of particular interest. In their Historical Arms Series and the Limited Edition Military Series, fourteen important books of the period are available. Five of the most important are: Muller's *Treatise of Artillery* (197) and *Treatise of Fortifications* (198), Wolfe's *Instruction to Young Officers* (283), Windham's *Discipline for the Norfolk Militia* (282), and Smith's *Universal Military Dictionary* (245). More such books will probably be forthcoming.

The announced West Point Library, published by the Greenwood Press, promises further reissues of rare books.

Francis Edwards, Ltd., has already brought out Dalton's *English Army Lists* (82), and Oman's *Wellington's Army* (205).

A further extremely valuable reprint is Vauban's *Mémoires,* published in translation by the University of Michigan Press under the title, *A Manual of Siegecraft and Fortification* (258). More reprints are to be anticipated.

MILITARY BIOGRAPHY. The number of distinguished British soldiers so studied has not been too large. William Augustus, Duke of Cumberland, has had only a single good biography, by Evan Charteris (62–63), which is perhaps too sympathetic. Another conspicuous figure who has had no biography is Sir Jeffrey Amherst, 1st Baron Amherst. The material is available in the multi-volume War Office Series 34 which contains his correspondence and his diary, a portion of which pertaining to his service as Commander-in-Chief in America was edited by Webster (272).

As might be expected, there is much on the first Duke of Marlborough. Of particular interest are three studies: the four volumes by his descendant Sir Winston Churchill (67), the five-volume work of letters and dispatches edited by Sir George Murray (66), and the six-volume *Memoirs* by his agent William Cox (76). Cox, founder of Barclay's Bank, had access to all of his papers and correspondence as well as being his financial confidant. Other biographies of Marlborough listed include Lediard's three-volume work (169) and single volumes by Banks (37) and Atkinson (34).

For the middle period of the century, we find a biography of Oglethorpe by Ettinger (107), the *Journals* of the Marquis of Townshend (255), and two biographies of Wolfe. Of these, the work by Willson (280) contains edited correspondence; that by Waugh (271) is directed toward his personality. General Whitworth's biography of Lord Ligonier (277) gives a valuable insight into the workings of the British inner War Cabinet during the Seven Years' War.

The biographies of the latter period of the century, taken chronologically, begin with that of the Duke of York by Burne (58), of Sir John Moore by Browning (53) and Oman (203), and Moore's diary edited by General Maurice (192). There are biographies of General Baird by Hook (147), and of Wellington by the Rev. Gleig (127), a two-volume work by Maxwell (183), one by Morris (193) which parallels the Atkinson biography of Marlborough, by Ward (302), by Petrie (214), and by Countess Longford (301).

Biographies for officers serving in India are not too numerous. Clive is represented in works by Forrest (114) and Minney (187). There is a biography of Coote by Shepard (236), one of Munro by Rev. Gleig (126), as well as an important biography of Stringer Lawrence by Biddulph (43). A useful work by Kaye (159) contains biographies of officers serving in India.

There is a volume on Wellington's officers by Bell (41) and two works which roughly parallel one another by Fortescue (118) and Wilkinson (278). Both begin with Cromwell and end with Wellington, comparing the subjects professionally.

This section has necessarily been selective due to limitations of space and balance; there are many other excellent biographies.

GENERAL WORKS. Of them all, nothing can rival Sir John Fortescue's *History of the British Army* (117), which deals principally with operations. It discusses the army chronologically, by area, with summaries at the end of wars or when there were considerable changes in administration. It is, regretably, sparsely footnoted. Details are difficult to find on occasion, and the index chapter summaries are often more useful for the location of specific information than is the volume index. There are three older works which cover the British Army as it entered the eighteenth century: *Records and Badges of . . . the British Army* by Chichester and Burges-Short (64), the two-volume *Military Forces of the Crown* by Clode (69), and Walton's *History of the British Standing Army* (262). Walton is particularly important, since while it covers only the period from the Restoration to 1700, it shows the evolution and development of the army, and explains (citing sources) the why of changes in administration, discipline, and arms. Clode is similarly valuable, while Chichester is primarily concerned with units and unit histories. Two more recent works are extremely valuable, since they show the British Army as it existed and operated under Marlborough at the beginning of the century and as the army was taken in hand by the Duke of York in its last few years. Major R. E. Scouller's *The Armies of Queen Anne* (235) discusses the structure of the army and its administration both in Britain and on the continent as well as in America, though in the latter there are some errors. S. G. P. Ward's *Faithful: the story of the Durham Light Infantry* (303) gives an excellent analysis of the organization and policies of an English regiment of the eighteenth and early nineteenth centuries. Richard Glover in *Peninsula Preparation, The Reform of the British Army, 1795–1809* (128), starkly states the situation on the eve of the War of the French Revolution. He explores thoroughly the weaknesses of Britain's military force. Comparing Scouller and Glover, one finds little change during the ninety years which had passed. Valuable for its views of the British Army in America as the overseas administration had developed during and just after the Seven Years' War is John Shy's *Toward Lexington* (237). Of particular interest here is the Constitutional question which arose by reason of the suspension of the clauses in the instructions of the various colonial governors which had made them Captain-General of all troops within the respective Colonies.

GENERAL BACKGROUND. British military history in the eighteenth century is divided roughly into four major areas: Europe, America, India, and Home. Each of these can be subdivided by topic. On the whole, the century from Marlborough to Wellington has been well covered. Almost every campaign and every commander has a volume, though some of them are narrow and others are out-of-date.

The general military environment of Europe in the eighteeth century is best analyzed in the fourth volume of Hans Delbrück's *Geshichte der Kriegskunst im Rahmen der politischen Geschichte* (308), which is currently being translated into English. The third volume of Max Jähn's *Geschichte der Kriegswissenschaften vornehmlich in Deutschland* (309) includes numerous English works and gives a good indication of the place that British writings on military affairs occupied in the European military literature. French military theory, to which English soldiers reacted as well as from which they borrowed (or was it vice-versa?), is best analyzed in the classic studies of Jean Colin, *L'Education militaire de Napoléon* (310); *La Tactique et la discipline dans les armées de la Révolution* (311); and *L'Infanterie au XVIIIᵉ siècle: la tactique* (312). A comparative analysis of British and continental military thought and practice is contained in the second and sixth chapters of Peter Paret's *Yorck and the Era of Prussian Reform* (306).

CAMPAIGNS. The earliest campaigns of the century are those of Marlborough in the Low Countries and of Peterborough in Spain. Of the works on Marlborough, the five-column compilation of *Letters and Dispatches* (66) of the Duke and the two-volume work by Kearsley (160) are among the best. Other volumes relating to Marlborough include those by Alison (7), Bredrick (49), Millner (185) and Taylor (251). A general overview of the wars between 1689 and 1712, which includes Marlborough's battles, is given in Kane's *Campaigns* (158). The events in the Netherlands after the disgrace and recall of Marlborough are to be found in the anonymous *Impartial Enquiery* (23). The involvement of Britain in the Spanish Peninsula is covered by Francis in the *Methuens and Portugal* (119), with a further work on the Earl of Peterborough by Freind (121).

The War of the Austrian Succession, though well handled by the Charteris biography of Cumberland (62–63) as well as by an anonymous "eyewitness" account (27), is also the province of Biggs (44), Brindley (50) and Skrine (243). Brindley includes a military dictionary explaining the "technical terms in the science of war."

The campaigns of the Seven Years' War include amphibious operations described in the anonymous *Journal* (24) and those in Germany under Ferdinand of Brunswick (26).

CAMPAIGNS (FAR EAST). The best overall work on campaigns in India is Fortescue's *History of the British Army* (117). Fortescue does not particularize on either Sepoy or European units in many cases, but for tracing regimental histories it is essential to remember that many of these Indian Army European regiments went on the British Army List with the amalgamation after the Indian Mutiny of 1857; further, most information on these units is not in the Public Record Office but rather in the records of the East India Company at India House. Selected published information from this source will be found in the bibliography (96–102). Contemporary works on these campaigns by Moodie (190), Diron (89), and Thorn (253–254) are useful, as are the modern works by Gopal (129), Edwards (103) and Parkinson (212). Among those by older scholars are Malleson's *Decisive Battles* (178), Broome's *Bengal Army* (51), Downing's *Indian Wars* (93), and Rennell's *Marches . . . 1790 and 1791* (220). Very few regular regiments of the British army actually served in India during the eighteenth century, and these were wartime reinforcements sent to balance French European forces during the Seven Years' War and in the later part of the century.

Of special interest is Colonel Walsh's *Military Reminiscences* (274) of forty years of East Indian service. These two volumes were extracted from his personal journals. Of the three-volume *Correspondence* of Charles Cornwallis (74), one volume pertains to India, as do the biographies of Clive and others mentioned previously in the section on Military Biography.

CAMPAIGNS (AMERICAN). Fortescue is not as solid on American campaigns as on those elsewhere, particularly for those at the beginning of the century, since he worked primarily with War Office records, and most of the operations during the reigns of William III and Anne were by fleets carrying an expeditionary force of troops who were actually serving as marines. Most of the little published in the area is found in the *Journal of the Society for Army Historical Research* (see Introduction). The War of the Austrian Succession is covered by Fortescue, who also does well by the Seven Years' War. Of importance in contemporary material is Knox's *Campaigns* (161), Mante's *History* (179), and Beatson's *Naval and Military*

Memoirs (39). Lord Loudoun's command has been extensively explored by Pargellis (210–211), and Webster's *Journal of Sir Jeffrey Amherst* (272) carries the theme further. Of special interest in this area are the *Bouquet Papers* (48) and Smith's account of Bouquet's 1764 Indian campaign in Ohio (246); this last, with its appendix on methods of Indian fighting may well have been studied by Anthony Wayne before his campaign there in 1793.

For the period of the American Revolution, Belcher (40), Mackesy (176), and Rankin (218)—all modern works—are best, supplemented by Curtis' *The Organization of the British Army in the American Revolution* (80), and of course Fortescue. For the War of 1812, Hitsman's *Incredible War of 1812* (144) is the best recent assessment from the British side.

One publication more must be mentioned—Carmichael-Smyth's *Precis of the Wars in Canada* (61), which covers the period 1755 to 1814. This was an official report prepared for the Duke of Wellington when he was Master-General of the Ordnance, and is actually a recommendation for fortifications to repel an American invasion.

Manuscript sources are centered largely at the William L. Clements Library (300), and at the Henry E. Huntington Library (299), and in the Canadian Archives (297) for the period between 1750 and 1815.

ARMY LISTS AND REGISTERS. The first comprehensive record of officers is the *Manuscript Army List for 1737* (293). From this, an Army List was compiled and printed in 1740; recently it has been reprinted by the Society for Army Historical Research with an added alphabetical list of officers. The 1737 List was corrected in manuscript to 1744, when the *Manuscript Army List for 1744* was made up. This list was kept posted until the preparation of the *Manuscript Army List of 1752,* which in turn was corrected until 1759.

Beginning in 1759, a series of Commission Registers by unit was commenced—*The Succession Books* of WO Series 25 (292). Printed *Army Lists* began with the previously mentioned *List of 1740,* the next list being that for 1754. These lists were issued regularly from 1756 but must be used with caution. None of the lists before 1759 are complete, not even the P.R.O. annoted copies (293)—particularly for units serving in America. The *Army List for 1763* and the *Army List for 1764* do not show commissions for the period between April 1 and December 31, 1763; but these commissions can be found with no difficulty in the *Succession Registers.*

Shirley's 50th Foot and Pepperrill's 51st Foot do not appear in any printed list; other officers were appointed, promoted, and killed without ever appearing by name in one of the printed lists. Although the *P.R.O. Guides* show the Army Lists to be in WO 64 and WO 65, these have been transferred to the classification of INDEXES. Earlier lists of officers were utilized by Charles Dalton in compiling *English Army Lists and Commission Registers, 1661–1714* (82), and *George the First's Army, 1714–1727* (83). These volumes are valuable not only for the lists of officers, but also for the biographical information and details on the military history of units involved.

TACTICS. The determining factor of eighteenth century tactics was the flintlock musket. *Blackmore's British Military Firearms, 1650–1850* (45) illustrates this development in the British army over a period of 150 years.

British drill and formations were approaching standardization under James II, when an abridgement (10) of the 1680 *English Military Discipline* (18) was ordered printed "by Special Command" for the use of the royal forces. A 1690 leaflet, *Commands for the Exercise of Foot Arm'd with Firelock Muskets and Pikes* (14) was followed amongst others in 1701 by a Dublin publication, the *Exercise of the Foot* (21), which included in a supplement the drill for horse, horse grenadiers, and dragoons. The earliest indication of the changes incorporated by the Duke of Marlborough which made the British infantry so formidable appears in the *Duke of Marlborough's New Exercise of Firelocks and Bayonets* (16) to which a 1712 date is attributed. Since this was "appointed by His Grace to be used by all the British forces and the Militia," an earlier date should most probably be assigned, since in 1712 Marlborough was no longer head of the army.

The publication which survived throughout the century was Bland's *Treatise of Military Discipline* (46), which was reprinted in many editions, two of them by Americans during the American Revolution. (The plates for the 1775 New York edition were engraved by Paul Revere.) The periodic revisions, as well as the original, were made official training doctrine by Royal Warrants. Eventually, as the staff of the army developed, Bland's *Manual Exercise* was made official by the Adjutant General's Office (1775) and in 1807 an edition (269) was distributed by the War Office. Official doctrine throughout the century directed that the infantry be formed in three ranks; in practice most units were formed only two deep in order to present a broader front. Some works, such as Lieutenant John Russell's *Remarks on the Inutility of the Third Rank of Firelocks* (229), questioned the official doctrine and advocated arming the third rank (when there was such) with pikes.

Close support of the infantry by artillery was provided for by the "Battalion Guns," which were only nominally under the control of the Ordnance in the field. In theory these guns were manned by a subaltern's detachment of an officer, one or two NCO's, and ten matrosses; in practice men of the battalion were trained to operate the light field pieces, and were carried on the roll of the Grenadier Company. In battle these field pieces were normally positioned between battalions, gunner casualties being replaced during action from the battalion's companies. This practice is not mentioned in official training doctrine, since it was forced upon all armies of the day by the paucity of trained artillerymen, but it can be traced in the contemporary accounts by Mante (179), Knox (161), and others. By accident the eighteenth century armies developed the "Infantry-Artillery team" which is today accepted military doctrine.

Light infantry became a popular subject in the second half of the century. DeJenny's *The Partisan* (152), Emmerich's *The Partisan in War* (104) and Fawcett's translation of the Prussian *Regulations for the Exercise of Riflemen and Light Infantry* (108) all antedate Sir John Moore's famous light infantry experiments which are discussed in detail by Fuller (123). Knox's

Campaigns in North America (161) details the practice of the Seven Years' War, in which elite infantry units were improvised by brigading the light companies from all of the battalions in the army, using these to stiffen the colonial Rangers—which were subject to all of the ills of irregular troops. Mante's *Late War in North America* (179), and Beatson's *Naval and Military Memoirs* (39) also show the utilization and accomplishments of these provisional units organized from regular troops. Lawson's *Uniforms of the British Army* (166), in addition to illustrating typical uniforms, gives considerable information on the raising of the various corps.

TACTICS (CAVALRY). The latter half of the eighteenth century saw an increasing formal distinction between the cavalry functions of reconnaissance and raiding on the one hand and shock on the other. Light Dragoon regiments were raised during the Seven Years' War, one by John Burgoyne of American Revolutionary fame. Lawson's *Uniforms* (166) is again useful in regard to uniforms and brief histories of the units. Dalrymple's *Military Essay* (81), Hinde's *Discipline of the Light Horse* (143), and Lord Beresford's *Peninsula Cavalry Journal* (42) show the direction and development of this separation of function—shock and reconnaissance. Major Tylden's *Horses and Saddlery* (257) is extremely useful in describing equipment.

TACTICS (ARTILLERY AND ENGINEERS). Throughout the eighteenth century, the artillery remained outside the Land Forces to the extent that the right of General William Phillips to command line troops was questioned during the American Revolution. The Board of Ordnance continued the practice of "loaning" the guns from its stores only for the duration of a war or an expedition, and until the Seven Years' War the number of trained artillerymen was inadequate, civilian gunners being used in fortresses. Demands always outran the supply and the artillery company remained an *administrative* unit until the middle of the nineteenth century. The formation of the units and assignments to expeditions and stations can be followed in detail from Lieutenant-Colonel Law's *Battery Records* (165).

Literature of the period indicates enormous interest in both weaponry and engineering. John Muller, a civilian employed by the Board of Ordnance at the Royal Artillery School (Woolwich) wrote extensively on both gunnery and engineering. His *Treatise on Artillery* (197) was read with interest by foreign experts and was the textbook for the American artillerymen of the Revolutionary period. Benjamin Robin's *New Principles of Gunnery* (221) advocated extensive changes in technology as did Muller's writings.

Muller's *Attack and Defence of Fortified Places* (195) remained a textbook through the remainder of this period, the original 1747 edition being revised and enlarged in 1756. In the preface to the third edition (1756) of the *Treatise of Fortifications* (198) Muller points out that both Vauban and Coehorn had written their books before undertaking their most noted engineering works; further, he notes that Vauban borrowed extensively from Dilichius' *Hiperbologia* (1640), and that Coehorn had likewise followed the work Daniel Specle published at Frankfurt a. m., in 1587. Muller proposed to fill in the gap between the writings and the actual practices of the master engineers, particularly with regard to the cases where the terrain did not permit the construction of "regular" works. All of Muller's writings were for use as texts at the Royal Military Academy, Woolwich. At the beginning of the century, Baron Coehorn's *New System of Fortifications for Low and Wet Terrain* (70) appeared in English translation the year before the Hague edition of 1706 was issued. Vauban had been translated in 1693, and other continental works followed periodically. For particular studies of the British artillery, Browne's *England's Artillerymen* (52), has been supplemented by Brigadier Hogg's *English Artillery, 1326–1716* (145) and Hogg's *The Royal Arsenal* (146). Brigadier Smyth's *History of the Royal Military Academy* describes that institution. Various histories of the Royal Artillery are listed in White's *Bibliography* (276), as are those of the Corps of Royal Engineers; in addition there is one in preparation by Brigadier Heniker. Again details are given in Lawson's *Uniforms of the British Army* (166) that are not to be found elsewhere.

MILITARY ART. Throughout the century there was considerable interest in foreign military writings such as Marshal de Saxe's *Reveries* (232) published in translation in 1757, a two-volume *Essay on the Art of War* (78) by Count Turpin de Crisse in 1761, Count John O'Rourke's *Treatise on the Art of War* (207) of 1778. At the same time theoretical treatises also appeared in Britain with *The Rudiments of War* (29) in 1799. In 1815 a synthesis of the methods of Marlborough, the Duke of Cumberland, George II, and Wellington appeared under the title *The Principles of War* (28), contemporary with Jomini's work. Other works worth noting are *The Compleat Gentleman Soldier* (13) of 1702, *The Elements of Military Arrangement* (17) of 1780, and Kane's *System of Camp Discipline* (31). Sir David Dundas's *Principles of Military Movements* (95) was a semi-official work of 1788 which attempted to tie theory to practice. So far the English contribution to European military thought has not been sufficiently analysed in the way that Luvaas has tackled the next century (see Chapter VIII).

MILITARY JUSTICE. Standardization of court procedures seems to have been one objective of Captain Stephen Adye's *Treatise on Courts Martial* (3), the first and second editions of which were printed in America; by 1805 eight editions had appeared. A study of this work shows remarkable similarities with the current United States Army theory and practice. Alexander Bruce's 1717 work on the *Institution of Military Law* (54), was an early landmark in the separation of military and civil law. Sullivan's *Thoughts on Military Law* (250) appeared in London in 1784, three years before the third edition of Adye was issued there. Robert G. Scott's *Military Law of England* (233), which cited the authorities for then-current practices, appeared in 1810. No official manual was printed until the 1884 *Manual of Military Law* was issued by the Stationery Office.

Court-martial records will be found in both the files of the Judge Advocate General and those of the Board of General Officers—one reason being that the Judge Advocate General was also the secretary to the Board until after the Seven Years' War. Those who are interested in procedures of an eighteenth-century army court martial will find the complete text of the trial of Major Robert Rogers, held at Quebec in 1767, in volume II (de luxe edition) of Kenneth Robert's *Northwest Passage*. (See also, Chapter XXV)

MILITARY MEDICINE. There were individuals who by observation or inspiration forged ahead of their own day. Hunter's *Observations* (148) dealing with tropical disease in the West Indies, was published in 1788; Donald Monro (189) wrote in 1764 on preventive medicine and the operation of hospitals, and Sir John Pringle's *Observations on the Diseases of the Army* (215) was printed in 1775. Sinnott's criticism of the Army Medical Department (242) is dated 1796, and the War Office in 1795 attempted to certify the existing situation by issuing *Regulations to be Observed by Troops Embarked in Transports* (270) and further regulations for troops after arrival in the West Indies (267).

Surgeons were authorized by Establishment Warrant, nomination being one of the colonel's prerogatives and qualifications usually being attested to by either the Physician General, the Surgeon General, or sometimes by the London College of Physicians and Surgeons. For actual experience of a medical officer with the troops, see *Surgeon James' Journal* (150).

Staff surgeons and allocation of personnel to hospitals was determined by Establishment, these being found in *War Office Papers,* Series 24 and 26 (292); *Treasury Papers* (290), Classes 1, 52, and 64; and in the *Audit Office Papers* (291), Classes 1, 3, and 16. Normally there were no enlisted men assigned to medical duties by Establishment; a list of medical officers exists for the period from 1727 through the remainder of the century (153).

CHAPLAINS. Chaplains were authorized by Establishment as were the medical officers; like them, the appointment was at the disposal of the colonel of the regiment. Chaplains were also usually authorized for expeditionary staffs and for hospitals. The office of Chaplain General appears in the Establishment for 1718, and at other times on the staff of the Captain General. Although the Bishop of London appears to have had no official position of Military Vicar, overseas chaplains complained to him about ill-treatment, notably in the case of Chaplain Jackson of the Newfoundland garrison in Queen Anne's day.

OFFICIAL PUBLICATIONS. This particular group of books (265–270) has been included as a sample of the change in administrative viewpoint of the War Office under the Duke of York. Previously, books had been written or compiled by individuals and printed at private expense; or the War Office had ordered the printing accomplished, as during the American Revolution. Bland's *Military Discipline* (46), for example, had been made an official document by Royal Warrant; the Duke of Marlborough's *New*

Exercise (16) was made official by an order from him as Captain General. Books of the period of the American Revolution and some earlier ones were made official by virtue of having been authorized by the Adjutant General. This particular group was selected because of its probable interest to researchers, and a much more varied lot can be found in the *British Museum Catalog of Printed Books,* under "ENGLAND. Army," where the evolution of official publications is shown chronologically.

PRIMARY SOURCES. As has been previously mentioned, a great deal of information about the eighteenth-century British army will be found outside the War Office Papers as such, particularly for the first half of the century. (See Bibliography, Nos. 284 through 291 and 293). These should be consulted if only to correlate or corroborate information found elsewhere.

Outside the Public Record Office itself, the British Museum manuscripts are rich in material for the early part of the century, and the rare books and pamphlets collection there is unexcelled. *Parliamentary Papers* (213 and 295) need looking into, as do the India House records if one's investigation includes the Far East. For the American Army, particularly for the last half of the century (after 1767), the Canadian Archives have the records [Record Group] not the Public Record Office. And the collections in the great libraries must not be overlooked (299 and 300).

COMMANDS AND CONTROL. The King nominally commanded the army, but after the Battle of Dettingen (1743) no English king again actually exercised field command. Even before this, control of the use of the army—as distinguished from command—had fallen into the province of the Principal Secretaries of State. The general who was to command an expedition was selected after civilian planning had been done, and then and only then did strictly military planning begin. To this factor we can assign most of the horrible disasters of the amphibious expeditions of the reign of William III and the first half of the eighteenth century.

Command was to remain the weakest part of the British army until the middle of the nineteenth century, for Parliament remained distrustful of a standing army throughout our period. It is only in this context that the seeming abnormality whereby the artillery was removed from the army command structure except in time of war or domestic emergency can be rationalized.

Further, the army was without an effective head through most of the eighteenth century. From the time of the fall of John Churchill in 1711 to the period when Cumberland became Captain-General in the 1740's, the army was supervised by the civilian Secretary-at-War who was primarily responsible to Parliament. Again, this was true in the last quarter of the century until Frederick, Duke of York, became Commander-in-Chief in 1795.

Worse than the state of the troops at home was the situation of the overseas garrisons before 1750, as Fortescue shows. The Secretary-at-War considered that his jurisdiction did not extend beyond England, Scotland,

Wales and the Channel Islands; the Secretary of State for the Southern Department virtually ignored them. They thus suffered in a sort of Limbo that was only relieved when operation overseas forced attention on them—often too late. Essentially again this was the fault of Parliament for not fixing responsibility.

SUGGESTIONS FOR FURTHER INVESTIGATION. Numerous topics in the military history of eighteenth-century England need further attention. Deserving of attention are: the disbanded units of the British army, the British garrisons of the West Indies, British troops in India—although there were not many regular regiments of Royal troops there during the eighteenth century—biographies of such individuals as Sir Jeffrey Amherst, Lord Rawdon, later the Marquis of Hastings, the Earl of Cornwallis, and certainly an investigation of James II and Cumberland as administrators.

We badly need a study of the development of British military thought. Contemporary publications show that there was much consideration of military problems. Further consideration is needed of the development of the technical services of the army, including transport, subsistence, pay, medical services, and the other phases. Some basic work has been done in the histories of the various technical services, and White's *Bibliography* has listed the printed secondary material. But still ahead is the giant task of synthesis and analysis to make the material meaningful in the sense of readily available information arranged by subject.

Some of the *War Office Papers* remain virtually untouched; particularly the *Audit Office Papers* need critical winnowing for information on the overseas garrisons before 1750, the area where the *War Office Papers* show an almost total blank.

The medical department of the army could bear inquiry. The operation of hospital ships with expeditions and the field hospitals in America, Germany, and elsewhere should be looked into particularly.

In addition, there is no list of commissions held in the army overseas for the period 1697–1737, although lists for the Irish Army, Scots Army, and English Home Army were kept. There was almost certainly a parallel Plantations Commission Register, now lost or strayed, which possibly may slumber peacefully unrecognized in some collection. This ledger, if found, will shed significant light on the participation of army officers in local colonial affairs. Lacking the names of all the officers, we cannot accurately gauge this for the American colonies as a whole although we can do this for New York, South Carolina, and Nova Scotia. Even so, the situation in the West Indies remains vague, especially in the Leeward Islands, although from such information as is available we know that officers became landlords, soldiers acted as overseers, and the garrisons generated political storms.

BIBLIOGRAPHY

PRINTED SOURCES

1. Adjutant General's Office. *A New Exercise to be observed by His Majesty's Troops on the establishment of Great Britain and Ireland.* London, 1757. New York: J. Parker, 1757.
2. Adjutant General's Office. *The Manual Exercise as ordered by His Majesty, in 1764. Together with plans and explanations of the method generally practiced at reviews and field days.* [London: March 26, 1759] Lancaster, Penn.: Francis Bailey, 1775. New York: H. Gaine, 1775.
3. Adye, R. W. *The Bombardier and Pocket Gunner.* London: William Greenough, 1802.
4. Adye, Stephen Payne. *A Treatise on Courts Martial, with an Essay on Military Punishment and Rewards.* New York: H. Gaine, 1769. 2nd ed., Philadelphia: 1779, subsequent editions in London.
5. Aldington, Major John. *A Short Essay on the Construction and Advantages of Light Artillery,* London, 1808.
6. Aldington, Richard. *The Duke: being an account of the life and achievements of Arthur Wellesly, 1st Duke of Wellington.* New York: Viking Press, 1943.
7. Alison, Archibald. *The Military Life of John, Duke of Marlborough.* New York: Harper & Brothers, 1848.
8. Anderson, Aeneas. *A Journal of the Forces which sailed from the Downs in April 1800, . . . till their arrival in Minorca and continued . . . in the Mediterranean and Egypt.* London: J. Debrett, 1802.
9. Anderson, J. H. *Precis of Great Campaigns, 1796–1817.* London: Hugh Rees, 1907.
10. Anon. *An Abridgement of the English Military Discipline, Printed by Special Command for the Use of His Majesty's Forces.* London: Charles Biel, 1686.
11. ———. *The Army in India and its Evolution.* Calcutta: 1924.
12. ———. *British Military Library or Journal, Comprehending a Complete Body of Military Knowledge.* London: 1799–1801.
13. ———. *Compleat Gentleman Soldier; or a Treatise of Military Discipline, Fortifications and Gunnery.* London: T. Ballard, 1702.
14. ———. *Commands for the Exercise of Foot, Armed With Firelock Muskets and Pikes; with the Evolutions . . .* London: 1690.
15. ———. *Considerations on the Establishment of the British Engineers.* London: T. Cadell, 1768.
16. ———. *The Duke of Marlborough's New Exercise of Firelocks and Bayonets; appointed by His Grace to be used by all the British forces and the Military with instructions . . . By an officer in Her Majesty's Footguards.* London: J. Read, 1712.

17. ———. *Elements of Military Arrangement, and of the Discipline of War, adapted to the Practice of the British Infantry.* London: T. Egerton, 1780.

18. ———. *English Military Discipline, or the way and method of exercising Horse & Foot, according to the practice of this present time. With a treatise of all sorts of Arms and Engines of War . . .* London: R. Harford, 1680.

19. ———. *Essay on Field Fortification, (by an officer of experience in the Prussian Service).* J. C. Pleydell, tr. London: for J. Nourse, 1768.

20. ———. *Exercise for the Horse, Dragoons and Foot Forces.* London: John Baskett, 1740.

21. ———. *The Exercise of the Foot: with the evolutions . . . To which is added, the Exercise of the horse, grenadiers of horse, and dragoons.* Dublin: R. Thorston; M. Gunne, 1701.

22. ———. *The Field of Mars, being an Alphabetical Digest of the Principal Naval and Military Engagements in Europe, Asia, Africa, and America . . . particularly of Great Britain and her Allies from the Ninth Century to the Present Period.* London, 1801.

23. ———. *Impartial Enquiery Into the Duke of Ormonde's Conduct in the Campaigne of 1712.* London: J. Roberts, 1715.

24. ———. *Journal of the Campaign on the Coast of France, 1758.* London, 1758.

25. ———. *Military Dictionary Explaining All Difficult Terms in Martial Discipline, Fortifications, and Gunnery.* London: for F. Nutt, 1702.

26. ———. *Operations of the Allied Army under Ferdinand, Duke of Brunswick, . . . 1759–62. By an officer who served in the British forces.* London, 1764.

27. ———. *Operations of the British and Allied Arms during the campaigns of 1743 and 1744. By an eye witness.* London; 1744.

28. ———. *The Principles of War, exhibited in the practice of the camp; and as developed in . . . general orders . . . in the . . . Peninsula with parallel orders of George the Second, the Duke of Cumberland, the Duke of Marlborough, etc. . . . .* London: William Clowes, 1815.

29. ———. *The Rudiments of War, comprising the principles of military duty in a series of orders issued by Commanders in the English Army, etc.* London, 1799.

30. ———. *A Short Narrative of the late campaign (in Zealand) of the British army, under the orders of the Right Honorable, the Earl of Chatham.* London: p. for James Ridgway, 1810.

31. ———. *System of Camp Discipline . . . for the land forces . . . in which are included Kane's discipline for a battalion in action . . . General Kane's campaigns of King William and the Duke of Marlborough.* 2nd ed. London: Milon, 1757.

32. *Army Lists.* The first printed list appeared in 1740, the second in 1754, and annually from 1756 through the eighteenth century.

33. Aspin, J. *The Naval and Military Exploits which have distinguished the Reign of George the Third.* London, 1820.
34. Atkinson, Christopher T. *Marlborough and the Rise of the British Army.* London: G. P. Putnam's Sons, 1921.
35. Bajwa, Fauja Singh. *The Military System of the Sikhs.* Delhi: Motilal Banarsidass, 1964.
36. Ballard, Brigadier-General C. *The Great Earl of Peterborough.* London: Skeffington & Son, 1929.
37. Banks, John. *The History of the Duke of Marlborough, including . . . a Methodical Narrative of the Late War upon the Danube.* London, 1755.
38. Batty, Captain. *A Sketch of the Late Campaign in the Netherlands.* London, 1815.
39. Beatson, Robert. *Naval and Military Memoirs of Great Britain 1727–1783.* London, 1790.
40. Belcher, Henry. *The First American Civil War; first period 1775–1778.* London, 1911.
41. Bell, Douglas Herbert. *Wellington's Officers.* London: Collins, 1938.
42. Beresford, Lieutenant-General Lord. *Peninsula Cavalry Journal, (1811–1813) of Lieutenant-General R. B. Long, Lord Beresford.* T. H. McGuffie, ed. London: George G. Harrap & Co., 1951.
43. Biddulph, Colonel John. *Stringer Lawrence, the father of the Indian Army.* London: J. Murray, 1901.
44. Biggs, William. *The Military History of Europe, etc., from the commencement of the War with Spain in 1739 to 1748.* London: Baldwin, R., 1755.
45. Blackmore, Howard L. *British Military Firearms, 1650–1850.* London: Herbert Jenkins, 1961.
46. Bland, Major-General Humphrey. *A Treatise of Military Discipline, in which is Laid down and Explained the Duty of the Officer and Soldier Thro' the several Branches of the Service.* London: S. Buckley, 1727. Dublin: Andrew Croate, 1727.
47. Bonneauville, M. de. *An Essay on Fortifications . . . with supplement containing Marshal Saxe's new system of fortifications and construction of new wooden forts.* C. Vallencey, tr. Dublin, 1757.
48. Bouquet, Henri. *The Papers of Col. Henry Bouquet.* Harrisburg, Pa: Historical Records Survey, 1941–42. 11 vols.
49. Bredrick, T. *A Complete history of the late war in the Netherlands together with an abstract of the Treaty of Utrecht.* London, 1713.
50. Brindley, J. *The Theatre of the Present War in the Netherlands and upon the Rhine . . . Also a Military Dictionary . . . explaining all the Technical Terms in the Science of War.* London, 1745.
51. Broome, Captain A. *History of the Rise and Progress of the Bengal Army.* London, 1850.
52. Browne, J. A. *England's Artilleryman, A Historical Narrative of the Services of the Royal Artillery, from the formation of the Regiment to . . . 1862.* London, 1865.

53. Browning, B. *The Life and Letters of Sir John Moore*. Oxford: Oxford Univ. Press, 1923.

54. Bruce, Alexander. *The Institution of Military Law, Ancient and Modern; Wherein the most Material Questions and Cases relating to Martial Discipline are fully examined and cleared from the Principles of Civil Law*. Edinburgh: Lias and successors of Andrew Anderson, 1717.

55. Bryant, Arthur. *The Years of Endurance, 1793–1802*. New York and London: Harper & Brothers, 1942.

56. Bryant, Arthur. *Years of Victory, 1802–1812*. New York and London: Harper & Brothers, 1944.

57. Burnbury, Lieutenant-General Sir H. *A Narrative of Military Transaction in the Mediterranean 1805–1815*. London: 1851.

58. Burne, Alfred. *The Noble Duke of York; the military life of Frederick, Duke of York and Albany*. London and New York: Staples Press, 1949.

59. Campbell, Brevet Major, and Captain Shaw. *Standing Orders as given out and enforced by the late Major Genl. Robt. Crawford for the use of the Light Division . . . serving under his command in the army of the Duke of Wellington*. Corfu: Government Printing Office, 1814; reprinted, Dublin, 1844 and London, 1852.

60. Cannon, Richard, *Historical Records of the British Army, comprising the history of every Regiment in His Majesty's Service*. London: 1835–53. 70 vols.

61. Carmichael-Smyth, Major-General Sir James. Sir James Carmichael, ed. *A Precis of the Wars in Canada, from 1755 to the Treaty of Ghent in 1814*. London: Tinsley Brothers, 1862.

62. Charteris, Evan. *William Augustus, Duke of Cumberland, and the Seven Years' War*. London: Hutchinson and Co., Ltd., 1925.

63. Charteris, Evan. *William Augustus, Duke of Cumberland: His Early Life and Times, 1721–1748*. London: Edward Arnold, 1913.

64. Chichester, H. M. and G. Burges-Short. *Records and Badges of Every Regiment and Corps in the British Army*. 2nd ed. London: Gale & Polden, 1902.

65. C. H. S., a Staff Officer. *Essay on the Military System of Bonaparte*. London, 1811.

66. Churchill, John. *Letters and Dispatches of John Churchill, first Duke of Marlborough, from 1702–1712*. Gen. Sir George Murray, ed. London: J. Murray, 1845. 5 vols.

67. Churchill, Winston. *Marlborough, His Life and Times*. New York: Charles Scribners Sons, 1933–1938. 4 vols.

68. Clairac, M. de. *The Field Engineer*. John Muller, tr. London, 1757.

69. Clode, Charles M. *Military Forces of the Crown*. London: John Murray, 1869. 2 vols.

70. Coehorn, Baron de (or Koehoorn). *New Methods of Fortification for Low and Wet Terrain*. Thomas Savery, tr. London, 1705 and the Hague, 1706.

71. Colby, Eldridge. *Masters of Mobile Warfare.* Princeton University Press, 1943.

72. Conolie, M. de la. *Chronicles of an old Campaigner.* London, 1737. Reprinted, London: John Murray, 1904.

73. Cooper, Leonard. *British Regular Cavalry, 1644–1914.* London: Chapman & Hall, 1965.

74. Cornwallis, Charles. *Correspondence of Charles, 1st Marquis Cornwallis.* Charles Ross, ed. London: J. Murray, 1859. 3 vols.

75. *Court and City Register . . . containing Lists of the Army and Navy, 1742 through 1809.* London, 1742–1808.

76. Coxe, William. *Memoirs of John, Duke of Marlborough, with his original correspondence.* 2nd ed. London: Longman, Hurst, Rees, Orme, and Brown, 1820. 6 vols.

77. Creswell, Capt. John (R. N.). *Generals and Admirals: the story of amphibious command.* London: Longmans, Green, 1952.

78. Crisse, Count Turpin de. *An Essay on the Art of War.* London, 1761. (trans.) 2 vols.

79. Curling, John. *Observations on the Campaign in the Netherlands Terminated by the Battle of Waterloo, etc.* London: Hitchin, 1858.

80. Curtis, Edward Ely. *The Organization of the British Army in the American Revolution.* New Haven: Yale University Press, 1926.

81. Dalrymple, Campbell. *A Military Essay, containing; reflections on the raising, arming, clothing and discipline of the British infantry and cavalry.* London: for D. Wilson, 1761.

82. Dalton, Charles. *English Army Lists and Commission Registers, 1661–1714.* London: Eyre and Spottiswoode; reprinted London: Francis Edwards, 1960. 6 vols.

83. Dalton, Charles. *George the First's Army.* London: Eyre and Spottiswoode, 1910–12. 2 vols.

84. D'Antonio, Alexandro Victorio. *A Treatise on Gunpowder; A Treatise in Firearms; A Treatise on the Service of Artillery in time of War.* Captain Thomas, R. A., tr. London, 1789.

85. Davies, Godfrey. *Wellington and His Army.* Oxford: Basil Blackwell, 1954.

86. Dawney, Major Nicolos P. *The Distinction of Rank of Regimental Officers, 1684–1855.* London: Society for Army Historical Research, 1960.

87. Deuteil (or Duteil), Jean Chevalier. *The formations and maneuvers of infantry, calculated for the effectual resistance of cavlary, and for attacking them successfully, on a new principle of tactics.* John MacDonald, tr. London: T. Edgerton, 1810. (Metz; Collignon, 1782).

88. Devize, M. *The History of the Siege of Toulon.* A. Boyce, tr. London: Arthur Collins, 1708.

89. Diron, Major. *A Narrative of the Campaign in India which terminated the War with Tippos Sultan, in 1792.* London, 1794.

90. Dodwell and Miles, eds. *Alphabetical List of the Officers of the Indian Army; with the Dates of their Respective Promotions, Re-*

tirements, Resignation, or Death, . . . 1760–1834. London, 1838.

91. Donkin, Robert. *Military Collections and Remarks.* New York; H. Gaine, 1777.

92. Douglas, William. *A Summary, Historical and Political, of the First Planting, Progressive Improvements, and Present State of the British Settlements in North America.* London, 1755. 2 vols.

93. Downing, Clement. *A History of the Indian Wars.* William Foster, ed. London: Humphrey Milford, 1924.

94. Drinkwater, John. *A History of the late Siege of Gibraltar with a Description and Account of the Garrison from the Earliest Period.* 3rd ed. London: T. Spilsbury, 1786.

95. Dundas, Colonel Sir David. *Principles of Military Movements, chiefly applied to infantry. Illustrated by maneuvers of the Prussian troops, and by an outline of the British campaigns in Germany during the war of 1757.* London: T. Cadell, 1788.

96. East India Company. *Amalgamation of the Indian Army with Her Majesty's Service, and the schemes of the Amalgamation Commission for the retirement of the Indian Officers.* London, 1861.

97. ———. *Collection of Treaties and Engagements with the Native Princes and States of Asia concluded on the behalf of the East India Company, by the British Government in India, etc. from 1739–1809.* London, 1812.

98. ———. *Copies and Extracts of Advices to and from India, relative to the cause, progress, and successful termination of the war with the late Tippos Sultaun.* London: printed for the Proprietors, 1800.

99. ———. *List of the Company's Civil and Military Servants . . .* London, 1788.

100. ———. *New Arrangement, with respect to the rank and formations of the Army, etc. in the East Indies; relating to European artillery and infantry, native cavalry and infantry, with the peace establishment for each presidency.* London: John Stockdale, 1796.

101. ———. *Notes relative to the Peace concluded between the British Government (i.e., the East India Company) and the Manhattan Chieftain, etc.* London: J. Stockdale, 1805.

102. ———. *Proceedings relative to the sending out of four of His Majesty's regiments to India.* London, 1788.

103. Edwardes, Michael. *The Battle of Plassey and the Conquest of Bengal.* London: Batsford, 1963.

104. Emmerich, Andrew. *The Partisan in War; or the use of a corps of light troops to an army.* London: Reynell, 1789.

105. Entick, John. *The General History of the Late (Seven Years') War.* London: Edward Dilly, 1763–64.

106. Esposito, Brigadier-General V. J. and Colonel John R. Elting. *A Military History and Atlas of the Napoleonic Wars.* London: Faber and Faber, 1964.

107. Ettinger, Amos A. *James Edward Oglethorpe, Imperial Idealist.* Oxford: Clarendon Press, 1936.

108. Fawcett, William, tr. *Regulations for the Exercise of Riflemen and Light Infantry and Instructions for the Conduct in the Field*. London, 1803.

109. ————. *Regulations for the Prussian Cavalry*. London: J. Haberkorn, 1757. (transl.)

110. ————. *Regulations for the Prussian Infantry*. London, 1754. (transl.)

111. Ffoulkes, Charles. *The Gun-Founders of England, with a list of English and Continental Gun-Founders from the XIV to the XIX Centuries*. Cambridge: Cambridge Univ. Press, 1937.

112. Esher, Oliver Sylvain, 3rd Viscount Brett. *Wellington*. Garden City, New York: Doubleday, Doran & Co., 1928.

113. Forbes, Arthur. *A History of the Army Ordnance Services*. London, 1929. 3 vols.

114. Forrest, Sir George. *Life of Lord Clive*. London: Cassell and Company, 1918. 2 vols.

115. Fortescue, Sir John. *The British Army, 1783–1802*. London, 1905.

116. ————. *County Lieutenants and the Army 1803–1814*. London: Macmillan and Company, 1909.

117. ————. *History of the British Army*. London: MacMillan and Company, 1910–1935. 13 vols, plus maps.

118. ————. *Six British Generals* (Cromwell, Marlborough, Abercromby, Stuart, Moore, Wellington). London: Williams & Norgate, 1928.

119. Francis, Alan David. *The Methuens and Portugal*. Cambridge: Cambridge Univ. Press, 1966.

120. Frederick the Great. *Military Instructions from the late King of Prussia to his Generals*. Major Foster, tr. Sherborne, 1797.

121. Freind, J. *Account of the Earl of Peterborough's Conduct in Spain chiefly since the raising of the Siege of Barcelona, 1706*. London, 1707.

122. Frischauer, Paul. *England's years of danger, a new history of the World War, 1792–1815*. New York: Oxford Press, 1938.

123. Fuller, Colonel J. F. C. *Sir John Moore's System of Training*. London, 1924.

124. George, John Nigel. *English Pistols and Revolvers; a historical outline of the development and design of English hand firearms from the seventeenth century to the present day*. Anslow County, N. C.; Small Arms Technical Pub. Co., 1938 & New York: Arco Publishing Co., 1962.

125. Gipson, Lawrence H. *The British Empire Before the American Revolution*. New York: Alfred Knopf, 1943–1967. 13 vols.

126. Gleig, Rev. George R. *Life of Major General Sir Thomas Munro, (India-Burma)*. London: H. Colburn and R. Bentley, 1830. 3 vols.

127. ————. *The Life of Arthur, Duke of Wellington*. New York & London: J. M. Dent & Co. 1900, 1911.

128. Glover, Richard. *Peninsula Preparation; the Reform of the British Army, 1795–1809*. Cambridge Univ. Press, 1963.

129. Gopal, Ram. *How the British Occupied Bengal; a corrected account of the 1756–1765 events.* London: Asia Publishing House, 1963.

130. Gordon, Anthony. *A Treatise on the Science of Defence for the Sword, Bayonet, and Pike in Close Action.* London: T. Egerton, 1805.

131. Gordon, Lawrence L. *British Battles and Medals; a description of every campaign medal and bar awarded from the Armada, to . . . 1946, together with the names of all the regiments . . . entitled to them.* Aldershot: Gale and Polden, 1947.

132. Grose, Francis (supposed author). *Advice to the officers of the British Army with the addition of some hints to the drummer and private soldier, embellished after drawings in color and line by Frank Wilson.* London, 1782 & London: J. Copes, 1946. (Satire)

133. ————. *Military antiquities respecting a history of the English Army from the Conquest to the present time.* London: S. Harper, 1786–88. 2 vols.

134. Grant, George. *The New Highland Discipline, or a Short Manual Exercise.* Bickham, 1757.

135. Guibert, Jacques Antoine Hypolite de. *General Essay on Tactics with an introductory Discourse upon the Military Science in Europe.* London, 1781 (*trans.*) 2 vols.

136. Gurwood, Lieutenant-Colonel John. *The General Orders of Field Marshal the Duke of Wellington . . . in Portugal, etc. from 1809 to . . . 1815 compiled alphabetically from the second printed volumes.* London: W. Clowes, 1832.

137. Hanway, Jonas. *The Soldier's Faithful Friend, being Political Moral and Religious Monitions to Officers and Private Men in the Army and Militia.* London: F. Dodsley, 1766.

138. ————. *An Account of the Society for the encouragement of the British troops in Germany and North America, with the motives to the making a present to these troops, also to the widows and orphans . . .* London, 1760.

139. Harness, W. H. *Clive, the Conqueror of India.* London: Massie Publishing Co., 1939.

140. Heriot, John. *A Historical Sketch of Gibraltar, with an Account of the Siege which that Fortress stood against the Combined Forces of France and Spain.* London, 1792.

141. Hervey, William. *Journals of the Hon. William Hervey in North America and Europe, 1755–1814, with Orderly Books at Montreal 1760–63.* London: Bury St. Edmunds, Paul and Mathew, 1906.

142. Hibbert, Christopher. *Wolfe at Quebec.* London: Longmans, Green, 1959.

143. Hinde, Captain (Royal Regt. of Foresters). *The Discipline of the Light Horse.* London: W. Owen, 1778.

144. Hitsman, J. Mackay. *The Incredible War of 1812: a Military History.* Toronto, Ont.: Toronto Univ. Press, 1966.

145. Hogg, Major-General Oliver F. G. *English Artillery, 1326–1716.* London: Royal Artillery Institution, 1963.

146.   Hogg, Major-General Oliver F. G. *The Royal Arsenal; its Back-ground, Origin and Subsequent History.* London: Oxford Univ. Press, 1963. 2 vols.

147.   Hook, T. E. *Life of General, the Right Honorable Sir David Baird, Bart.* London: Bentley, 1832. 2 vols.

148.   Hunter, John. *Observations on the Diseases of the Army in Jamaica and on the Best Means of Preserving the Health of Europeans in that Climate.* London: G. Nicol, 1788.

149.   James, Charles. *A New and Enlarged Account of the Military Oc-currences of the late War between Great Britain and the United States of America.* London, 1818. 2 vols.

150.   James, Dr. Huddy. *Surgeon James' Journal, 1815.* James Yansittart, ed. London, 1964.

151.   Jennings, William. *A General System of Attack and Defence with One General Rule for Erecting Fortifications* . . . London, 1804.

152.   Jenny (or Jeney), M. de. *The Partisan; or the Art of Making War in Detachments with plans proper to facilitate* . . . *the Several Dis-positions and Movements Necessary* . . . *to Accomplish their Marches, Ambuscades, Attacks, and Retreats with Success.* London: for R. Griffiths, 1760.

153.   Johnson, William. *Roll of commissioned officers in the medical Service of the British Army, who served on full pay within the period between the Ascension of George II and the formation of the Royal Army Medical Corps.* Lieut. Col. A. L. Howell, ed. Aberdeen, 1919.

154.   Jones, Colonel J. T. *Journals of the Sieges Carried on by the Army under the Duke of Wellington in Spain, 1811–14.* London: J. Weale, 1827. 2 vols.

155.   Jones, Captain. *Artificial Fireworks* . . . *also Mr. Muller's Fire-works, for Sea and Land Service, his Tables for Sea and Land Serv-ices* . . . London: for J. Millan, 1776.

156.   Jones, Captain L. T. *A Historical Journal of the British Campaign on the Continent in the year 1794, with the Retreat through Hol-land, 1795.* London, 1797.

157.   Jones, William D., comp. *Records of the Royal Military Academy, 1741–1840.* Woolwich: Royal Military Academy, 1851.

158.   Kane, Major-General Richard. *Campaigns of King William and Queen Anne: from 1689 to 1712, also, a new system of military discipline, for a battalion of foot on action; with the most essential exercise of the cavalry* . . . London: Millan, 1745.

159.   Kaye, J. W. *Lives of Indian Officers, Illustrative of the History of the Civil and Military Service of India.* London, 1867. 2 vols.

160.   Kearsley, Alexander H. *Marlborough and his Campaigns, 1702–1709, with the battles described in conjunction with Field Service Regulations.* Aldershot: Gale & Polden, 1929 and 1931. 2 vols.

161.   Knox, Captain John. *Historical Journal of the Campaigns in North America.* Arthur G. Doughtry, ed. Toronto, Ont.: the Champlain Society, 1914. 3 vols.

162. Laffin, John. *British Campaign Medals.* London: Aberlard-Schuman, Ltd., 1964.
163. Larpent, F. Seymour. *The Private Journal of F. Seymour Larpent.* (Larpent was Deputy Judge Advocate to Wellington's headquarters in the Peninsula.) Sir G. Larpent, ed. London: R. Bentley, 1853. 2 vols.
164. Latrille, General. *Reflections on Modern War.* Major H. Le Mesurier, tr. London, 1809.
165. Laws, Lieutenant-Colonel M.E.S., comp. *Battery Records of the Royal Artillery, 1716–1859.* Woolwich: Royal Artillery Institution, 1952. (A second volume is in press, 1968.)
166. Lawson, Cecil C. P. *A History of the Uniforms of the British Army.* London: P. Davies, 1940–1968. 5 vols. to date.
167. le Blond, Guillaume. *Treatise of Artillery, or of the Arms and Machines used in War since the invention of Gunpowder; being the first part of le Blond's ELEMENTS OF WAR.* London; 1746: Ottawa, Ontario: Museum Restoration Service, 1969. (trans.)
168. le Cointe, M. *The Science of Military Posts, for the use of Regimental Officers, who frequently Command Detached Parties.* London: for T. Payne, 1761. (trans.)
169. Lediard, T. *Life of John, Duke of Marlborough . . . with a great number of original letters and papers. London,* 1736. 3 vols.
170. Lenk, Torsten. *The Flintlock; its Origin and Development.* J. E. Hayward, ed.; G. A. Urquhart, tr. London, 1965.
171. Lloyd, Christopher. *The Capture of Quebec.* London: Batsford, 1959 and New York: Macmillan, 1959.
172. Lloyd, Major-General Henry: *History of the Late War in Germany.* London: 1776–1790. 3 vols.
173. Lochée, Lewis. *An essay on Military Education (by the master of the Little Chelsea Military Academy).* London, 1773.
174. Lovett, Major Alfred C. *The Armies of India.* London: Adam and Charbo Black, 1911.
175. McGuffin, T. H. *The Siege of Gibraltar, 1779–1783.* London: Batsford, 1965.
176. Mackesy, Piers. *The War in the Mediterranean, 1803–1810.* London: Longmans, Green & Co., 1957.
177. ———. *The War for America, 1775–1783.* Cambridge: Harvard Univ. Press, 1964.
178. Malleson, Col. G. B. *The Decisive Battles of India, 1746–1849.* London: W. H. Allen & Co., 1914.
179. Mante, Thomas. *The History of the Late War in North America and the Islands of the West Indies, including the Campaigns of 1763 and 1764 against His Majesty's Indian Enemies.* London: for W. Stranhan & T. Cadell, 1772.
180. Marshall, Henry. *Military Miscellany; comprehending a history of the Recruiting of the Army, Military Punishments, etc.* London: J. Murray, 1846.

181. Martemont, Malosti de. *The Spirit of the Modern System of War, by a Prussian General Officer.* William Fawcett, tr. London, 1757.

182. Martin, Colonel. *A Plan for Establishing and Disciplining a National Militia in Great Britain, Ireland and in all the British Dominions of America.* London: for A. Millan, 1745.

183. Maxwell, Sir Herbert E. *The Life of Wellington.* Waterloo Centenary edition. London: S. Low, Marston and Company, 1914. 2 vols.

184. Maycock, Captain F. W. O. *The Invasion of France, 1814.* London: Macmillan, 1914.

185. Millner, J. *A Compendious Journal of all the marches . . .* (*of the allied armies, 1701–12*). London, 1733.

186. Milne, Samuel. *The Standards and Colours of the Army from the Restoration 1661 to the Introduction of the Territorial System 1881.* Leeds: Goodall & Suddick, 1893.

187. Minney, R. J. *Clive of India.* London: Jarrolds, 1931 and 1957.

188. Molyneux, Thomas More. *Conjunct expeditions; or Expeditions that have been carried on jointly by the fleet and the army, with a commentary on a littoral war.* London, 1759.

189. Monro, Donald. *Observation on the Means of preserving the Health of Soldiers and of Conducting Military Hospitals.* London; J. Murray, 1780. (original work, 1764.)

190. Moodie, John. *Remarks on the Most Important Military Operations of the English Forces, on the West Side of the Peninsula of Hindoostan in 1783, and in 1784.* London, 1788.

191. Moore, James Carrick. *A Narrative of the Campaigns of the British Army in Spain, commanded by His Excellency Sir John Moore.* 4th ed. London: J. Johnson, 1809.

192. Moore, Sir John. *The Diary of Sir John Moore.* Major General Sir J. F. Maurice, ed. London, 1904. 2 vols.

193. Morris, William O'Connor. *Wellington, soldier and statesman, and the revival of the military power of England.* New York: G. Putnam's Sons, 1904.

194. Moyse-Bartlett, Lieutenant-Colonel H. *The Pirates of Trucial Oman.* London: Macdonald & Co., 1966.

195. Muller, John. *The Attack and Defence of Fortified Places.* London: J. Egerton, 1747.

196. ———. *Elements of Mathematics . . . Projectiles, Gunnery, etc.* London, 1765.

197. ———. *Treatise of Artillery.* 3rd ed. London: For John Millan, 1757. Reprinted Philadelphia, 1777. Reprinted, Ottawa, Ontario: the Museum Restoration Service, 1965. Includes Charles W. Rudyerd's plates.

198. ———. *Treatise of Fortifications, Regular and Irregular, with Remarks on the Construction of Vauban and Coehorn . . .* London, 1756. Reprinted, Ottawa, Ontario: Museum Restoration Service, 1968.

199. ———. *Treatise of Mines.* London, 1757.

200. Napier, Major-General Sir William. *A History of the War in the Peninsula and in the South of France, 1807–1814.* 2nd ed. Sir Charles Oman and Sir John Fortescue, eds. London: T. and W. Boone, 1832–1833. 5 vols.

201. Nicholson, Colonel Francis. *Journal at the Capture of Annapolis, 1710. Collections of the Nova Scotia Historical Society,* vol. I. Halifax, 1879.

202. Norman, C. B. *Battle Honors of the British Army, from Tangiers, 1662, to the Commencement of the Reign of King Edward VII.* London: J. Murray, 1911.

203. Oman, Carola. *Sir John Moore.* London: Hodder & Stoughton, 1953.

204. Oman, Sir Charles. *A History of the Peninsular War.* Oxford: Clarendon Press, 1902–30. 5 vols.

205. ———. *Wellington's Army, 1809–1814.* New York: Longmans, Green & Company, 1912. Reprinted, London: Francis Edwards, 1969. Appendix III, "Bibliography of British Diaries, Journals, and Memoirs."

206. Omond, Lieutenant-Colonel John Stuart. *Parliament and the Army.* Cambridge: Cambridge Univ. Press, 1933.

207. O'Rourke, John (Count). *Treatise on the Art of War; or Rules for Conducting an Army.* London, 1778.

208. Pares, Richard. *War and Trade in the West Indies.* London: Frank Cass Co., 1963.

209. Parker, R. *Memoirs of Military Transactions, 1683–1718, in Ireland and Flanders.* London, 1747.

210. Pargellis, Stanley M. *Lord Loudoun in North America.* New Haven: Yale Univ. Press, 1933, and London: Humphrey Milford, Oxford Univ. Press, 1933.

211. ———. *Military Affairs in North America, 1748–65.* New York: D. Appleton-Century Co., 1936.

212. Parkinson, C. Northcote. *War in the Eastern Seas, 1793–1815.* London: George Allen & Unwin, 1954.

213. Parliament. *Report from the Committee Appointed to Consider the State of H. M. Land Forces and Marines, etc. Extract from Reports of the Committees of the House of Commons . . . not inserted in the Journals . . . ordered reprinted by the House.* London, 1803–1806. 16 vols.

214. Petrie, Sir Charles. *Wellington; a reassessment.* London: Barrie, 1956.

215. Pringle, Sir John. *Observations on the Diseases of the Army.* London: W. Strahan, later ed., 1775.

216. Railton, J. *The Army's Regulator, or the British Monitor. Discovering . . . infringements upon his Majesty's Articles of War.* London: for W. Smith, 1738.

217. Ramsey, David. *Military Memoirs of Great Britain or a History of the War, 1775–1763.* Edinburgh, 1779.

218. Rankin, M. F. *The American Revolution.* New York: Putnam, 1964.

219. Reide, Thomas. *A Treatise on the Duty of Infantry Officers and the Present System of British Military Discipline.* London, 1795.

220. Rennell, James. *Marches of the British Armies in the Peninsula of India, during the Campaign of 1790 and 1791.* London: Palmer, 1892.

221. Robins, Benjamin. *New Principles of Gunnery.* London, 1742.

222. Roger, A. B. *The War of the Second Coalition, 1798 to 1801; a Strategic Commentary.* Oxford: Clarendon Press, 1964.

223. Rolt, Richard. *An Impartial Representation of the Conduct of the Several Powers of Europe, engaged in the late general war; . . . from 1739 to 1748.* London: S. Birt, 1749–50. 2nd ed., 1754. 4 vols.

224. Ropes, John C. *The Campaigns of Waterloo; a Military History.* New York: Charles Scribner's Son, 1893.

225. Royal Artillery. *List of Officers of the Royal Artillery as they stood in . . . 1703, with a continuation to the present, etc.* John Kane, comp. London, 1815 and 1819.

226. Royal Artillery. *List of Officers of the Royal Regiment of Artillery as they stood in . . . 1763, with a continuation to the present time (incl. military medical department of the Ordnance).* John Cave, comp. Greenwich, 1815. Revised 4th edition, London, 1900.

227. *Royal Military Academy, Records of the.* Woolwich: Royal Military Academy, 1892.

228. Russell, Captain John. *Movements and Changes of Position of a Battalion of Infantry, in strict conformity to his Majesty's Rules and Regulations.* London, 1802.

229. Russell, Lieutenant John. *Remarks on the Inutility of the Third Rank of Firelocks, and the Proprietory of Increasing the Effective Force of the Country by drawing up the Musquetry Two Deep, and forming the Third Rank of Pikemen.* London, 1805.

230. Sackville, Charles. *A Treatise Concerning the Militia in Four Sections.* London: for J. Millan, 1758.

231. Savory, Lieutenant-General Sir Reginald. *His Britannic Majesty's Army in Germany During the Seven Years' War.* Oxford: the Clarendon Press, 1966.

232. Saxe, Marshal Count Maurice de. *Reveries; or, Memoirs upon the Art of War.* William Fawcett, trans. London, 1757.

233. Scott, Robert Bisset. *The Military Law of England (with all the principal authorities), adapted to the general use of the Army . . . and the Practice of Courts Martial.* London: T. Goddard, 1810.

234. Scott, Sir Sibbald D. *The British Army, Its Origins, Progress, and Equipment.* London: Cassell, Petler, and Galpin, 1868–80. 3 vols.

235. Scouller, Major R. E. *The Armies of Queen Anne.* Oxford: Clarendon Press, 1966.

236. Sheppard, E. W. *Coote Bahadur.* London: W. Laurie, 1956.

237. Shy, John. *Toward Lexington—The Role of the British Army in the Coming of the American Revolution.* Princeton: Princeton Univ. Press, 1965.
238. Simcoe, John. *Journal of the Operations of the Queen's Rangers from the end of . . . 1777 to the conclusion of the late American War.* Exeter, England, 1787.
239. Simes, Thomas. *The Military Course for the Government and Conduct of a Battalion, designed for their Regulations in Quarter Camp or Garrison with useful Observations and Instructions for their Manner of Attack and Defence.* London, 1777.
240. Simes, Thomas. *The Military Guide for Young Officers.* London: J. Humphreys, R. Bell, and R. Aitken, 1772. Reprinted Philadelphia, 1776. 2 vols.
241. Simes, Thomas. *The Regulator; or Instructions to form the Officer, and complete the Soldier . . . to which is added, Proceedings of General Courts Martial, with the nature of the Office and duties of the Judge-Advocate.* London, 1780
242. Sinnott, N. *Observations, Tending to Show the Mismanagement of the Medical Department in the Army.* London: J. Murray and S. Gighly, 1796.
243. Skrine, Francis H. *Fontenoy and Great Britain's Share of the War of the Spanish Succession, 1741–1748.* Edinburgh and London: W. Blackwood and Sons, 1906.
244. Smelser, Marshall *The Campaign for the Sugar Islands, 1749; a study in Amphibious Warfare.* Chapel Hill: Univ. of North Carolina Press, 1955. Reprinted, Ottawa, Ontario: Museum Restoration Service, 1969.
245. Smith, Captain George. *An Universal Military Dictionary, a copious explanation of the Technical Terms. . . .* London: 1779.
246. Smith, William. *A Historical Account of the Expedition against the Ohio Indians in the Year MDCCLXIV under the Command of Henry Bouquet, Esq. . . . to which are annexed military papers containing reflection on the War with Savages.* London, 1766. Reprinted Cincinatti; Ohio Valley Historical Society, Series No. 1, 1868.
247. Smyth, Brigadier-General Sir John. *The History of the Royal Military Academy, Woolwich, the Royal Military College; Sandhurst, and the Royal Military Academy, Sandhurst, 1741–1961.* London, 1961.
248. Stewart, Charles. *The Service of British Regiments in Canada and North America; a résumé with a chronological list of uniforms portrayed in sources consulted.* Ottawa: Canadian Defence Library, 1962.
249. Stuart, Major-General J. *Correspondence during the indisposition of the Commander in Chief in India.* London, 1783.
250. Sullivan, R. G. *Thoughts in Martial Law, with a Mode Recommended for Conducting the Proceedings of General Courts Martial.* London: for T. Becket, 1784.

251. Taylor, Frank. *The Wars of Marlborough, 1702–1709.* Oxford, 1921. 2 vols.

252. Thomason, K. and Francis Buist. *Battles of the '45.* London, 1962.

253. Thorn, Major W. *Memoir of the Conquest of Java with the Subsequent Operations of the British Forces in the Orient.* London, 1815.

254. Thorn, William. *Memoir of the Wars in India, (1803–1806), conducted by . . . Lord Lake . . . and Sir Arthur Wellesley from . . . 1803 to its termination in 1800 . . .* London: Egerton, 1818.

255. Townshend, Lieutenant-Colonel Charles V. F. *The Military Life of Field Marshal George First Marquis Townshend, 1724–1807 . . . Dettingen, Fontenoy, Culloden, Laffeldt, Quebec.* London: J. Murray, 1901.

256. Trenchard, John. *A Short History of Standing Armies in England.* London: Dick Thomas, 1698.

257. Tylden, Major G. *Horses and Saddlery; an Account of the Animals used by the British and Commonwealth Armies from the Seventeenth Century to the present day with a description of their equipment.* London: J. A. Allen, 1965.

258. Vauban, Marshal Sebastian le Prestre de. *A Manual of Siegecraft and Fortification.* George A. Rothrock, tr., from the *Mémoire pour servir d'instruction dans la conduite des sièges et dans la defense des place* (Leiden in 1740). Ann Arbor, Michigan: University of Michigan Press, 1969.

259. Walker, T. J. *The Depot for Prisoners of War at Norman Cross, Huntingdonshire, 1796–1816.* London: Constable and Company, 1913.

260. Walpole, Horatio (1st Baron). *The Case of the Hessian Forces in the Pay of Great Britain, impartially and fully examined; with some recollections on the present conjuncture of affairs.* London: R. Franklin, 1731.

261. Walsh, Thomas. *Journal of the Late Campaign in Egypt.* London: T. Cadell and W. Davies, 1803.

262. Walton, Colonel Clifford. *History of the British Standing Army, AD 1660–1700.* London: Harrison & Sons, 1894.

263. Warburton, E. *Memoir of Charles Mordaunt, Earl of Peterborough and Monmouth, with selections from his Correspondence.* London, 1853. 2 vols.

264. Ward, S. G. P. *Wellington's Headquarters; a study of the administrative problems in the peninsula.* Oxford University Press, 1957. 6 vols.

265. War Office. *Instructions and Regulations for the Formations and Movements of the Cavalry (17 June, 1796).* London: War Office, 1799.

266. ———. *Manual and Platoon Exercise for the Light Cavalry.* London: War Office, 1812.

267. ———. *Regulations for the use of His Majesty's Troops upon their*

arrival in the West Indies (10 October, 1795). London: War Office, 1795.

268. ———. *Rules and Regulations for the Formations, Field Exercise, and Movements of His Majesty's Forces.* London: War Office, 1803.

269. ———. *Rules and Regulations for the Manual and Platoon Exercises, Formations, Field Exercises, and Movements of His Majesty's Forces, For the use of the Non-Commissioned Officers of the British Army.* London: War Office, 1807.

270. ———. *Regulations to be observed by Troops embarked in Transports for service abroad, particularly by those designed for the West Indies.* London: War Office, 1795.

271. Waugh, W. T. *James Wolfe, Man and Soldier.* London, 1928.

272. Webster, John C., ed. *Journal of Sir Jeffery Amherst . . . 1758–1763.* Toronto, Ontario: Ryerson Press, 1931. Chicago: Univ. of Chicago Press, 1931.

273. Wellesley, Arthur. *The Dispatches of Wellington.* Lt. Col. Gurwood, comp. London: Clarendon and Bedford, 1837–72. 36 vols.

274. Welsh, Colonel James. *Military Reminiscences; extracted from a journal of nearly forty years active service in the East Indies.* London: Smith, Elder, & Co., 1830. 2 vols.

275. Western, J. R. *The English Militia in the Eighteenth Century: the Study of a Political Issue, 1660–1802.* London: Routledge and Kegan Paul, 1965.

276. White, A. S. *Bibliography of Regimental Histories of the British Army.* London: Society for Army Historical Research, 1965.

277. Whitworth, Col. Rex. *Field Marshal Lord Ligonier; a Study of the British Army, 1702–1770.* Oxford: Clarendon, 1958.

278. Wilkinson, Spencer, ed. *From Cromwell to Wellington; Twelve Soldiers.* London: Lawrence and Bullen, 1899.

279. Williamson, John. *A Treatise on Military Finance; containing the Pay, Subsistence, Deductions, and Arrears of the Forces on the British and Irish Establishments . . . with an inquiry into the Method of Cloathing and Recruiting the Army.* London, 1782.

280. Willson, Beckles. *The Life and Letters of James Wolfe.* New York and London: W. Heinemann, 1909.

281. Wilson, Lieutenant-Colonel W. J. *History of the Madras Army, 1746–1826.* Madras, 1882–1888. 5 vols.

282. Windham, William. *A Plan of Discipline for the use of The Norfolk Militia.* London, 1759. Reprinted (extract) Boston, 1768. Reprinted Ottawa, Ontario: Museum Restoration Service, 1969.

283. Wolfe, General James. *Instructions to Young Officers; also his orders for a Battalion and an Army. Together with the Orders and Signals used in Embarking and Debarking an Army by Flatbottom'd Boats, etc. . . . .* London: J. Millan, 1768, 1780. Reprinted Ottawa, Ontario: Museum Restoration Service, 1967, from the second (1780) edition.

MANUSCRIPT SOURCES

OFFICIAL PAPERS: (Public Record Office)

284. *Admiralty Papers,* Class 36; *Ship Muster Books, 1688–1808.*
Class 37; *Ship Muster Books, 1804–1842.*
Class 50; *Admiral's Journals, 1702–1911.*
Class 51; *Captain's Logs, 1669–1852.*
Class 52; *Master's Logs, 1672–1840.*
Class 53; *Ship's Logs, 1799–1920.*

285. *Colonial Office Papers,* Class 1; *General Series, 1574–1757.*
Class 5; *American and West Indies, 1606–1807.*
(Individual colonies listed in *P.R.O. List XXXVI.*)

286. *State Paper Office,* Class 41; *State Papers, Domestic, Military
1640–1782.*
Class 44; *Entry Books, 1661–1828.*
Class 34; *State Papers, Domestic, Anne, 1702–1714.*
Class 35; *State Papers, Domestic, George I, 1714–1727.*
Class 36; *State Papers, Domestic, George II, 1727–1760.*
Class 37; *State Papers, Domestic, George III, 1760–1782.*
Class 87; *State Papers: Foreign, Military Expeditions, 1695–
1763.*

287. *Home Office Papers, Domestic and General,*
Class 42; *George III (continuing S.P. 37), 1782–1798.*
Class 43; *Entry Books, 1782–1898.*
Class 50; *Correspondence, Military, 1782–1840.*
Class 51; *Entry Books, 1758–1855* (Militia, yeomenry, vol-
unteers, Ordnance correspondence).

288. *Paymaster General's Office,* Class 2; *Ledgers, 1757–1840.*
Class 4; *Half Pay, 1737–1921.*
Class 14, *Miscellaneous Books, 1720–1861.*

289. *Public Record Office,* Class 30/11; *Cornwallis Papers* (1st Mar-
quis).
Class 30/37; *Ordnance Board Papers* (Arms order).
Class 30/55; *Dorchester (Carleton) Papers.* (Calendared by
Historical Manuscripts Commission, 1904–1909).

290. *Treasury Papers,* Class 1; *Treasury Board Papers, 1557–1920.*
Class 2; *Registers of Papers, 1777–1920.*
Class 3; *Skeleton Registers, 1783–1920* (transfers).
Class 27; *Letters-Out, General, 1688–1920.*
Class 30; *Accounts, General Yearly, 1688–1854.*
Class 38; *Departmental Accounts, 1588–1881.*
Declared Accounts, 1686–1767.
Supply Books, 1700–1835 (appropriated funds).
Class 48; *Lowndes Papers, 1661–1886* (Treasury chief
clerk).
Class 64; *Accounts, Various, Army, 1685–1845.*
Commissariat, 1689–1822.

Class 52; *King's Warrants, 1667–1857* (Entry Book)'.
Class 56; *Warrants, Various, War Office, 1795–1861.*

291. *Exchequer and Audit Office,* Class 1; *Declared Accounts, 1536–1828.*
Class 3; *Accounts Various, 1539–1866.*
Class 16; *Miscellaneous, 1568–1910.*

292. *War Office Papers,* Class 1; *Letters-In, 1732–1868.*
Class 2; *Indexes of Correspondence, 1759–1858.*
Class 4; *Secretary's Letter Books, 1715–1782.*
Class 7; *Departmental Letter Books, 1715–1782.*
Class 24; *Establishment Warrants, 1661–1846.*
Class 25; *Registers, Various, 1660–1938.*
Class 26; *Miscellaneous Books, 1670–1818.*
Class 34; *Amherst Papers, 1712–1784.*
Class 44 through 55; *Ordnance Board Papers, 1568–1923.*

293. *Public Record Office Lists and Indexes* (Annotated and corrected *Manuscript* and *Printed Army Lists* transferred from WO 64 and WO 65).
Indexes 5436–5438; Manuscript Army Lists, 1737–42, 1742–52, 1752–59. *Index 5440* is alphabetical, 1751–1823.
Indexes 5441 et. sec.; Printed *Army Lists,* from 1740.

294. *Official Papers* (British Museum).
Class 50; *Military Manuscripts.*
Arundel Manuscripts.
Burney Manuscripts.
Cottonian Manuscripts.
Egerton Manuscripts.
Harleian Manuscripts.
Lansdowne Manuscripts.
Sloan Manuscripts.
Stowe Manuscripts.
Additional Manuscripts (this group includes the *Montague, Haldimand, Bouquet,* and other useful groups of papers).

295. *Official Papers* (Houses of Parliament).
House of Lords Manuscripts: reports, lists of officers and troops, etc.

296. *Official Papers* (Government of India, Sixteenth, Seventeenth, and Eighteenth Centuries) India House, London (by appointment only).
Papers, records, and reports respecting the administration of India by the Honorable East India Company.

297. *Official Records* (Canadian Archives, Ottawa, Ontario).
Amherst Papers; transcripts of material in WO 34, plus other documents deposited by the Amherst family (not in P. R. O.).
Record Group 8; *British Military, Ordnance, and Admiralty Records, 1757–1903* (Class 18 contains the American Loyalist Regimental muster rolls).

Record Group 9; *Canadian Defence Records, 1776–1867* (pre-Confederation).

PRIVATE MANUSCRIPT HOLDINGS

298. *Blenheim Manuscripts*—papers of John Churchill, 1st Duke of Marlborough at Blenheim Palace.
299. *Henry E. Huntington Manuscripts,* Henry E. Huntington Library, San Marino, California.
   Abercrombie Papers (as Commander-in-Chief, America).
   Loudoun Papers (as Commander-in-Chief, America).
   Amherst Papers (Papers left with Major General Thomas Gage when Amherst was recalled; not duplicated in WO 34).
300. *William L. Clements Manuscripts,* William L. Clements Library, Ann Arbor, Michigan.
   George Clinton Papers, 1697–1759.
   Sir Henry Clinton Papers, 1750–1812.
   Thomas Gage Papers, 1754–1783.
   George III, King of Great Britain—Typescript of Correspondence (1784–1810). This group of papers continues the printed six-volume set by Sir John Fortescue, *Correspondence of George III, 1760–1783.*
Note: These Private Manuscript holdings are available only under restricted conditions and by special permission of the institutions or libraries involved.

SUPPLEMENT TO BIBLIOGRAPHY

301. Longford, Elizabeth. *Wellington: the years of the sword.* London: Weidenfeld and Nicolson, 1969.
302. Ward, S. G. P. *Wellington.* London: Batsford, 1963.
303. Ward, S. G. P. *Faithful: The story of the Durham Light Infantry.* London: Thomas Nelson, n.d. [1963].
304. Muller, John. *Treatise of Mines.* London, 1757.
305. Pringle, Sir John. A lecture Pringle gave at the Royal Society on 30 November 1778 on the theory of artillery; published as a pamphlet.
306. Paret, Peter. *Yorck and the Era of Prussian Reform.* Princeton, 1966.
307. Braubach, Max. *Prinz Eugen von Savoyen.* Munich, 1963–1967. 5 vols.
308. Delbrück, Hans. *Geschichte der Kriegskunst im Rahmen der politischen Geschichte.* Berlin, new edition, 1962.
309. Jähns, Max. *Geschichte der Kriegswissenschaften vornehmlich in Deutschland.* Muncih-Leipzig, 1891.
310. Colin, Jean. *L'Éducation militaire de Napoléon.* Paris: 1900.
311. Colin, Jean. *La Tacticque et la discipline dans les armées de la Révolution.* Paris, 1902.

312. Colin, Jean. *L'Infanterie au XVIIIe siècle: la tacticque.* Paris, 1907.

313. Anon. *Songs and Music of the Redcoats.* London: Leo Cooper, 1970.

314. Haswell, Jock. *The First Respectable Spy* [Colonel Grant of British Military Intelligence, 1789–1829]. London: Hamish Hamilton, 1969.

315. Gleig, G. R. *The Subaltern: a chronicle of the Peninsular War.* London: Leo Cooper, 1969.

VI

THE NAVY IN THE
EIGHTEENTH CENTURY

Christopher Lloyd

PRIMARY SOURCES. The wealth of material available for the study of eighteenth-century naval history makes it advisable to ensure that the records are not already in print before embarking on research in the public repositories. The aim of the Navy Records Society of London for the past eighty years has been to make such records, whether private or public, available in print, and from the number of titles listed below it will be seen how much has already appeared, though there is still a gap in mid-century. The American War of Independence is particularly well covered, especially as some years ago the Naval Historical Society of New York printed the correspondence of Admirals Sir Thomas Graves (17) and Lord Rodney (3). The appearance of the *Naval Documents of the American Revolution* under the editorship of William Bell Clark (20), now in course of publication, promises to provide every kind of relevant document.

The best available bibliography for the century is the naval section of Pargellis and Medley's *Bibliography of British History: the eighteenth century* (85). Since its publication in 1951 much valuable work has appeared, but it remains essential for its references to contemporary pamphlets and specialised articles in learned journals. Albion's bibliography, previously mentioned, is useful on account of the wider scope of its references to works dealing with the activities of Britain's enemies in this century of warfare.

In the manuscript field the main sources of material are the Admiralty records deposited in the Public Record Office. For most purposes, the Secretary's In and Out Letters (Adm. 1 and 2) provide the richest material, but as there are over 8000 volumes it is advisable to know exactly what one is looking for. The Minutes of the Board (Adm. 3) are useful for the study of naval policy, though formal minutes were not kept after 1802. The Returns of Officers Services (Adm. 9) are important for biographical purposes, especially the 1817 volume. Other biographical details may be gleaned from the Passing Certificates (Adm. 107) or from the registers of surgeons and chaplains. A useful handbook for the student of genealogy is Fothergill's *Records of Naval Men* (34), of which there is a copy in the Office which lists the types of records worth consulting.

For the history of privateering and the defence of trade, the registers of convoys (Adm. 7) and the issue of Letters of Marque are essential (see Digest Index 4857–87), as are the Prize Cases indexed in the High Court of Admiralty records. Since the defence of trade cannot be studied without a thorough knowledge of the nature of such trade, its importance to the nation, and the main lines of overseas communications, it is necessary to study the chief sources for maritime commercial activity at that time. A good introduction to the subject will be found in the collection of essays on a variety of such topics collected by C. Northcote Parkinson in *The Trade Winds* (86). Schumpeter's analysis of commercial statistics throughout the century (113) and Macpherson's four enormous volumes containing a great deal of original material, entitled *Annals of Commerce* and published in 1805 (63), will be found essential. Primary sources also include the Custom House Ledgers in the Board of Trade archives, though most of these were unfortunately burned in the Customs House fire of 1834. Statistics on the state of trade between 1780 and 1802 will also be found in the Board of Trade records (Public Record Office, 6/185).

Lloyd's of London became the leading maritime insurance body in the world towards the end of the century. The advice of the corporation to the Admiralty on the subject of enemy privateers and its collaboration with the naval authorities on the business of organising convoys of merchant shipping was of the utmost importance, as was the issue of the annual Register of Shipping. For such naval activities, see Lloyd's correspondence with the Admiralty in the Public Record Office (Adm. 1/3992), as well as the Proceedings of the Committee of Lloyd's which are preserved in the corporation's own library. The standard history of the corporation is by Wright and Fayle (125).

Logs are arid documents except for minutiae. Those of Admirals will be found in Adm. 50, those of Captains in Adm. 51 and Ship's Logs are arranged alphabetically in Adm. 53; other logs by lieutenants or masters are of lesser importance.

Administrative and financial history, where much work remains to be done, must begin with the papers of the Treasurer of the Navy, listed under the Accountant-General's Department (Adm. 14, 15). The papers of the Surveyor, who was responsible for ships and dockyards, are in Adm. 95. The records of the Navy Board are more scattered and less well listed than those of the Admiralty. Some will be found in Adm. 106, others at the National Maritime Museum, Greenwich. The same division of material obtains with the papers of subsidiary boards, such as the Sick and Wounded and the Victualling Boards, so that both repositories must be used. The General Orders of the Admiralty to the other Boards are mostly at the Maritime Museum.

Here also will be found an almost complete collection of the original drafts (plans) of ships, many dockyard records, as well as the personal papers of such officers as Lord Nelson, Lord St. Vincent, Lord Keith, Edward Vernon and Lord Exmouth (most of which have been printed at one time or another), as well as those of Sir Edward Codrington, Lord Duncan, Samuel and Alexander Hood, Sir John Duckworth and Augustus Keppel (many of which have not been printed).

The British Museum is also rich in naval material, notably in collections of private letters of men like Nelson, St. Vincent or Sir John Norris. The large collection of miscellaneous manuscripts left by Lord Liverpool will be found to contain much material of naval interest towards the end of the century. Volume 49 of the Museum's Class Catalogue, entitled "Naval and Maritime," lists such material chronologically under such headings as Tactics, Prizes, Expeditions, Dockyards, Signals, etc. These references are particularly valuable when they refer to items in larger collections which are hard to trace.

Other libraries whose catalogues should be consulted are the National Library of Scotland and the Wellcome Medical Historical Library, where, for example, there are the orders and accounts of Nelson's fleet in the Mediterranean which illustrate the logistical problems of that date.

The most important collections of papers published by the Navy Records Society are the following: those of Admiral Edward Vernon (94), the elder Byng, Lord Torrington, and his son John (118); the Barham (Charles Middleton) (49) and Sandwich (John Montague) (4) papers form an essential source for the study of the American War and a corrective to some of the views expressed in Albion's earlier book on the timber problem (1); the papers of George, Earl Spencer (24), Cuthbert Collingwood (43), St. Vincent (John Jervis) (12) and Lord Keith (George Elphinstone) (56) are all important for the war against Napoleon during the French Revolution.

CHRONICLES AND HISTORIES. Of contemporary chronicles which contain a mass of miscellaneous information, mention must be made of Beatson's *Naval and Military Memoirs, 1727–83* (11), which will be found extremely useful for amphibious expeditions, and Derrick's *Memoirs of the Rise and Progress of the Royal Navy* (28), which contains lists of ships and men from Tudor times onwards. The 40 volumes of the *Naval Chronicle* should be consulted for the period 1789 to 1818, though the indexing is unsatisfactory; it may be mentioned in passing that it was the perusal of these untidy volumes which inspired the late C. S. Forester to write the Hornblower series of novels. A detailed chronicle rather than a history of that war is William James's *Naval History of Great Britain, 1793–1827* (47). The six volumes of the later editions have been indexed for the Navy Records Society by C. G. Toogood; the first or 1822 edition of James should be avoided.

POLICY AND STRATEGY. Naval policy and strategy, being empirical in its nature, is better delineated in later histories than in contemporary documents. Primary sources for such study would of course be the papers of the Prime Minister of the time, or the First Lord of the Admiralty. Thus to supplement the Spencer Papers for the war against the French Revolution (24), it is necessary to consult his unpublished correspondence with Dundas in the National Library of Scotland, or the papers of the younger Pitt in the Public Records Office (Gifts and Deposits 30/8).

Mahan's well-known book on sea power (64) was the first to attempt such an evaluation of naval policy, but since it was a pioneer effort, and since it was chiefly based on French secondary sources, many of his findings may be questioned today. By his emphasis on fleet actions, his influence in modern times has often been deleterious on the writing of naval history, which until recently was far too preoccupied with battles and tactics rather than with strategy and the defence of trade. Hence the value of modern guides to the exercise of maritime power such as Graham's *Empire of the North Atlantic* (39) and above all Sir Herbert Richmond's magisterial *Statesmen and Sea Power* (97). Unfortunately the more extensive work on which Richmond's lectures were based, *The Navy as an Instrument of Policy, 1558–1727* (98), was left unfinished at the time of the author's death. Marcus' *Naval History of England* (69), though it ends in 1783, is the most recent general narrative history and contains useful lists for further reading.

TACTICS. The tactics employed in the age of sail are described in the official "Fighting Instructions," which have been edited by Corbett (22), and, from the French point of view, by Castex in his *Idées militaires* (16). Numerous personal signal books used by various commanding officers still remain unprinted. What has been called the "formalism" of British tactics was attacked by Clerk of Eldin in 1782 (21), the year in which Rodney broke the enemy line of battle at the battle of the Saints and Howe issued a new signal book in collaboration with Kempenfelt, which altered the traditional pattern because it was based on French methods of signalling. Clerk's essay has a complicated bibliographical history because it was first issued for private circulation; the enlarged edition of 1804 is to be preferred. The tactics of Nelson's generation are best studied in the battle logs which have been printed by the Navy Records Society (45). The most recent narratives are in Warner's *Nelson's Battles* (121), where reference is made to more specialised studies.

GENERAL HISTORIES OF THE WARS. General histories of the principal wars must be considered before we list the biographies of the leading protagonists, because their activities covered more than one war, nor can any theatre of operations be considered in isolation. A definitive history of the war of 1739–48 is by Richmond (99). Corbett's *England in the Seven Years' War* (23) is more open to criticism, though more readable. Particular incidents in that war may be studied in the documents relating to the loss of Minorca (100), or in Dudley Pope's lively book on the famous shooting of Admiral Byng (91), or in monographs on the battle of Quiberon Bay (23), or the capture of Quebec (23). A classic study of the inter-relation of naval and commercial policy at that period is Professor Pares' *War and Trade in the West Indies, 1739–63* (83). Piers Mackesy's *War for America, 1775–83* (61) is the best balanced account of that war and is fully documented. Morison's biography of Paul Jones should also be consulted (72). The French angle has been well studied by Lacour-Gayet (48), and by Richmond in his *Navy in India, 1763–83* (101).

No modern narrative account of the whole of the twenty-years' war with France and Napoleon during the French Revolution exists, probably because of the daunting mass of material available. Mahan attempted the task in two volumes (65), which are not nearly as satisfactory as his two volumes on the war of 1812–14 (65). Particular aspects have, however, been studied in detail—e.g., Rodger's *War of the Second Coalition, 1798–1801* (107); Parkinson's *War in the Eastern Seas* (88); Mackesy's *War in the Mediterranean, 1803–10* (62); or the documents on the blockade of Brest (53). The economic blockade, which proved decisive, is still best discussed in Hecksher's *Continental System* (42), though much new material is provided in the more recent volumes by Crouzet in France (26).

The Anglo-American war of 1812–14 has always roused much partisan writing on both sides, notably in American textbooks, in which it figures more largely than in English ones. By far the best account remains that by Mahan (65). The first scholarly account of one of the principal causes of the war, that of impressment of American seamen by the British, was made by Zimmerman in 1925 (126). A popular account of the war was written by the late C. S. Forester (33). More detailed books worth consulting are those by Peter Padfield entitled *Broke and the Shannon* (82), which is particularly good on the gunnery question, and Morison's life of Matthew Calbraith Perry (73), which includes something about his brother, Oliver Hazard Perry. Most of the contemporary literature on the subject provides more heat than light.

BIOGRAPHICAL COLLECTIONS. The chief biographical collections are those by John Charnock, *Biographia Navalis* (18), of which volumes five and six deal with the period from 1740 to 1793. John Marshall's more extensive *Royal Naval Biography* (71) covers the next twenty years, but it is not easy to use because of the lack of a printed index. If an officer survived till 1849 he will be found in William O'Byrne's *Naval Biographical Dictionary* (80) printed that year; most of the subjects wrote their own biographies in this compilation. A brief list of the promotions of all officers, compiled from the official Navy Lists (or Sea Officers Lists, as they were then called) will be found in *The Commissioned Sea Officers of the Royal Navy, 1660–1815*, of which copies will be found in the larger libraries, though the work was never actually printed or published. These volumes were compiled after the appearance of the bibliographical paper on biographical collections by G. F. James in 1937 (46).

NELSON. A useful guide to the vast literature on Nelson is Oliver Warner's *Lord Nelson: a guide to reading* (120). The basis of all books about Nelson is the edition of his letters and despatches in seven volumes made by Sir Harris Nicolas in 1846 (78). These are supplemented by Alfred Morrison's privately printed collection of letters from the Nelson-Hamilton

correspondence, which first illuminated that famous affair (74). Most of
the series of Lady Hamilton's letters in the National Maritime Museum
have been transcribed by Hugh Tours in his *Life and Letters of Emma
Hamilton* (117). Nelson's letters to his wife have been published by the
Navy Records Society (77). Biographies of Nelson range from Southey's
classic (115) of 1813, which superseded the books which appeared soon
after the admiral's death, to Carola Oman's monumental *Nelson* (81),
which appeared in 1947. This draws on much new material, but it is not
a study of Nelson as a naval officer. For the more professional aspects of
his career, Mahan's life of Nelson as "the embodiment of sea power"
(66), which was published in 1897, is still useful, though the Trafalgar
campaign must be studied in the works of Desbrière (29) and Sir Julian
Corbett (25). Shorter modern biographies which may be recommended
are those by Russell Grenfell (40) and Oliver Warner (122).

OTHER ADMIRALS. Many important admirals remain to be studied
in detail, e.g., Sir John Norris, Richard Kempenfelt, Sir John Duckworth
and Sir William Cornwallis, but most of the naval heroes have earned
some sort of a biography. The old-style life and letters, written from family papers, is not to be despised, though the editing of the documents often
leaves much to be desired. Thus, for Lord Anson we still depend on Barrow's life of 1839 (5), though his voyage is fully treated in Williams' edition of the relevant documents published by the Navy Records Society
(5). Barrow first suggested that the best-selling narrative of Anson's voyage round the world was not, as is still generally supposed, written by his
chaplain, Rev. Richard Walter, but by Benjamin Robins; Williams prints
documents to prove this beyond question. Anson's work at the Admiralty
and his part in the direction of the Seven Years' War still remains to be
studied; unfortunately he left very few personal letters.

Barrow's life of Richard, Earl Howe (6) is also old-fashioned but useful, since the family papers have never been printed. Ruddock Mackay's
life of Lord Hawke (60) is a model of a modern biography. Mundy's life
of Rodney (75), though printed in 1830, contains much of the admiral's
private correspondence, however badly it is edited; there is a reliable modern life by Captain Macintyre (58). The biography of Admiral William
Bligh by George Mackaness (59) covers the extensive literature on the
mutiny of the *Bounty*. This famous episode has captured the imagination
of succeeding generations. It was first fully described by Barrow in 1831,
though his book appeared anonymously (7). In modern times, owing to
the success of many films on the subject, much work has been done on
Bligh and the *Bounty,* for example by Owen Rutter and Geoffrey Rawson
(95). Dudley Pope recalls another famous mutiny, that of the *Hermione,*
in his *The Black Ship* (92).

Parkinson's life of Exmouth (Edward Pellew) (87) and Sherrard's of
St. Vincent (John Jervis) (114) are both scholarly. The Earl of Camperdown's biography of his ancestor, Lord Duncan, (15) and the memoirs of
Lord de Saumarez edited by Sir John Ross (111), which were published
in 1838, contain much original material. The latter has recently been sup-

plemented by documents illustrating the command of Saumarez in the Baltic during the Napoleonic war which A. N. Ryan has edited for the Navy Records Society (108); he has also contributed valuable articles on the war in the Baltic to the *English Historical Review* (109) (110). Mention may also be made of the present writer's life of Lord Cochrane (55), which refers to the admiral's *Autobiography of a Seaman,* which he wrote after he became Earl of Dundonald. Oliver Warner has recently published a life of Nelson's Collingwood which draws extensively on the admiral's vivid letters which have been printed at various times (123).

PERSONNEL. For the study of manning and life at sea it is best to begin with the Regulations and Instructions, the first edition of which appeared in 1731; after thirteen editions, in which little alteration was made, a much enlarged one appeared in 1808. Two works by Professor Michael Lewis illuminate the officer structure—*England's Sea Officers* (50) and *A Social History of the Navy, 1793–1815* (51). An older and less scholarly book is Robinson's *British Tar in Fact and Fiction* (105). Hutchinson's *Press Gang* (44) is superseded by Lloyd's *The British Seaman, 1200–1860* (54). This book is not only a study of impressment and recruiting in general, but provides information about life at sea, pay, food, etc. A useful contemporary pamphlet on the subject of impressment is by Charles Butler (13). Grievances about pay and living conditions at sea reached a climax in the great mutinies of 1797, of which the best account is by Manwaring and Dobrée (68). An older book on the subject is by Conrad Gill (37), but this attributes too much importance to the influence of revolutionary ideas in the fleet. Dugan's more recent *Great Mutiny* (30) is more popular than scholarly. A number of journals and memoirs by officers and a few by seamen have survived from the latter part of the century: there are singularly few for the earlier half. The best are those by Admiral Augustus Hervey, 1746–1759 (32); Commander James Anthony Gardner, 1775–1814, a most amusing book (36); and Admiral Sir William Dillon (52), which Professor Lewis edited for the Navy Records Society. Five journals of the Nelsonian period were edited for the same Society by H. G. Thursfield (116). These are very illuminating, those by Edward Mangin and Robert Wilson being the best available accounts of life afloat. Other memoirs from the lower deck are extremely vivid but must be treated with caution as historical evidence because they were written many years after the event and often for reasons of personal justification. The best of these are by William Richardson (96), Robert Hay (41), C. R. Pemberton, who wrote under the pseudonym of Pel Verjuice (89) and Jack Nasty-Face, whose real name was William Robinson (106). Such accounts, and others of the same kind, are evaluated in *The British Seaman* mentioned above.

ADMINISTRATION AND FINANCE. An area of study which is beginning to attract more attention than in the past is naval administration and finance. The best general study of the organisation of the Admiralty is contained in the articles contributed by Sir Oswyn Murray to the *Mariner's Mirror* in 1937–39 (76). A definitive study for the first part of the century is Daniel Baugh's *British Naval Administration in the Age of Walpole* (9), which contains a detailed bibliography. Light on the business methods of those days is provided by Professor Albion's well-known *Forests and Sea Power* (1) and the more recent study of naval contracts by Bernard Pool (90). The latter part of the century has not been properly studied, nor have St. Vincent's attempts to reorganise the ramshackle structure of the Navy Board, in spite of the formidable amount of evidence of corruption in the subordinate boards and in the dockyards which will be found in the numerous reports of the Commission of Naval Enquiry which he set up and which reported after his fall from power. These were printed as Parliamentary Papers, as were the equally voluminous reports of the Commission for Revising and Digesting the Civil Affairs of the Navy which was set up by his successor, Lord Barham, who as Sir Charles Middleton had proved himself the ablest administrator of his time. A comparatively unexplored source for administration at the end of the period is Dupin's *Voyages dans la Grande-Bretagne* (31), the third and fourth volumes of which deal fully with the subject because Dupin was sent to England to study, among other things, the whole question of naval administration as soon as the war was over. The autobiography of Sir John Barrow (8), who was Secretary of the Admiralty longer than any other person, is interesting for his comments on how the Admiralty was run during the Nelsonian era.

PRIVATEERING AND THE DEFENCE OF TRADE. The defence of trade, not only from the depredations of enemy fleets, but by the convoy system against enemy privateers is another comparatively neglected subject, much of the best work having been done from the American or French angles. For English privateering (of which the naval authorities never really approved), the second volume of Marsden's *Law and Custom of the Sea* (70) is useful, and there are good studies of Bristol privateers by Damer Powell (93) and of Liverpool privateers by Gomer Williams (124). The wealth of material in the records of the High Court of Admiralty remains as yet unexploited.

MISCELLANEOUS. The third volume of Charnock's *History of Marine Architecture* (19) is still useful for shipping in general. The services and sizes of almost every warship are listed in Manning and Walker's *British Warship Names* (67). Except for the introduction of the carronade, there was little development in gunnery during the century, so Robertson's *Evolution of Naval Armament* (103) remains a good general account.

Alexander Dalrymple (who still lacks a biographer) was appointed as the first official hydrographer in 1795 to give Britain a lead in cartography after Cook had led the way and a more precise method of finding the longitude had been discovered. The 54 volumes of the Board of Longitude now at Herstmonceux (the present site of the Royal Observatory) have not been much used, but there is a definitive history of the chronometer by R. T. Gould (38) and a valuable study of the behaviour of early time-keepers at sea (79).

The main geographical achievement of the century was the exploration of the Pacific, a matter of national even more than geographical importance after the loss of the American colonies and therefore involving the use of naval ships and officers. The narratives of Cook's predecessors, John Byron (35) and Philip Carteret (119) have recently appeared in scholarly editions under the auspices of the Hakluyt Society, which has also published Professor Beaglehole's monumental edition of the journals of James Cook and his associates (10). The four massive volumes of this edition constitute one of the most impressive editorial achievements of modern times. Every scrap of material connected with Cook's voyages is printed, as well as an accurate text: for the first time we now know what Cook actually wrote and thought. For the work of his successors, Admiral Bern Anderson's biography of Vancouver (2) and James Mack's life of Matthew Flinders (57) should be consulted.

Important studies in cartography are those by A. H. W. Robinson, *Marine Cartography in Britain* (104), and Admiral Ritchie's very readable account of naval surveyors in his *Admiralty Chart* (102). An official history of the hydrographical department has recently been compiled by Admiral Sir Archibald Day (27).

A work which the student will find useful at every turn in maritime research is the 1815 expansion by William Burney of Falconer's marine dictionary, printed in 1769, which is entitled *A New and Universal Dictionary of the Marine* (14). This contains long articles on a variety of topics, as well as succinct definitions of nautical terms and many illuminating diagrams.

FURTHER RESEARCH. Although naval history in the eighteenth century is a well-worked field, some of the aspects which merit further exploration have already been mentioned above. More attention needs to be paid to the administrative and financial sides of the story, notably during the latter part of the century. Privateering and the effects of war on trade are subjects which have seldom been satisfactorily studied, though the organisation of the convoy system in the latter part of the century has been the subject of some unpublished doctoral theses. Certain figures—Sir John Norris, Lord Anson, Sir Richard Kempenfelt, Sir John Duckworth—merit modern critical biographies, as does Cook's rival, Alexander Dalrymple. No doubt the tactics employed in particular battles have been studied frequently, but there is still room for a strategic conspectus of how Britain employed her fleets and conducted her amphibious expeditions during the long and critical struggle for mastery at sea and the winning (and losing) of a maritime empire. Logistics, recruitment, health and victualling are all legitimate and important areas of study. Mahan's thesis has been too easily accepted: it needs to be evaluated in the wider light of modern research, and the influence of his writings about the age of sail upon the age of warfare under steam should be more critically assessed.

BIBLIOGRAPHY

1. Albion, R. G. *Forests and Sea Power: the timber problem of the Royal Navy.* Cambridge, Mass.: Harvard University Press, 1926.
2. Anderson, Bern. *Surveyor of the Sea: the life of Captain George Vancouver.* Toronto University Press, 1960.
3. Barck, D. E., ed. *Letter books of Lord Rodney, 1780–82.* New York: Naval Historical Society of New York, 1932.
4. Barnes, R. G. and J. H. Owen, ed. *The Sandwich Papers.* London: Navy Records Society, 1932–38. 4 vols.
5. Barrow, Sir John. *Life of George, Lord Anson.* London: Murray, 1839. Much new material has been collected by G. Williams in *Documents Relating to Anson's Voyage Round the World.* Navy Records Society, 1967.
6. Barrow, Sir John. *Life of Richard, Earl Howe.* London: Murray, 1838.
7. Barrow, Sir John. *The Mutiny and Piratical Seizure of HMS Bounty.* London: Murray, 1831.
8. Barrow, Sir John. *Autobiographical Memoir.* London: Murray, 1848. *See* Lloyd, Christopher. *Mr. Barrow of the Admiralty.* London: Collins, 1969.
9. Baugh, D. A. *British Naval Administration in the age of Walpole.* Princeton University Press, 1965.
10. Beaglehole, J. G., ed. *The Journals of Captain James Cook.* London: Hakluyt Society, 1955–67. 3 vols.
11. Beatson, R. *Naval and Military Memoirs of Great Britain, 1727–83.* London: Longmans, 1790. 3 vols.
12. Bonner, Smith D., ed. *The Letters of Lord St. Vincent.* Navy Records Society, 1922–27. 2 vols.
13. Butler, C. *On the Impressment of Seamen.* London, 1778.
14. Burney, W. and W. A. Falconer. *New and Universal Dictionary of the Marine.* London: Cadell, 1815. Falconer's Dictionary first appeared in 1769; the later edition of Burney's revision is 1830.
15. Camperdown, Earl of. *Admiral Duncan.* London: Longmans, 1898.
16. Castex, R. *Les Idées Militaires de la Marine du XVIIIe siècle.* Paris, 1911.
17. Chadwick, F. E., ed. *The Graves Papers, 1781.* New York: Naval Historical Society of New York, 1916.
18. Charnock, J. *Biographia Navalis.* London: Faulder, 1794. 6 vols. Only vols. 5 and 6 concern the period 1740–93.
19. Charnock, J. *History of Marine Architecture.* London: Faulder, 1800. 3 vols. Vol. 3 covers the eighteenth century.
20. Clark, William Bell, ed. *Naval Documents of the American Revolution.* Washington: U.S. Navy Dept. 1964–   .
21. Clerk, J. of Eldin. *An Essay on Naval Tactics.* Edinburgh: Con-

stable. The second edition of 1804 is the fullest; the first was not actually published until 1790.

22. Corbett, Sir Julian, ed. *Fighting Instructions* and *Signals and Instructions*. Navy Records Society, 1905, 1908.
23. Corbett, Sir Julian. *England in the Seven Years' War*. London: Longmans, 1907. 2 vols. Special studies of episodes during that war are by G. Marcus, *Quiberon Bay*, London, 1960, and C. Lloyd, *The Capture of Quebec*, London: Batsford, 1959.
24. Corbett, Sir Julian and H. W. Richmond, ed. *The Private Papers of George, Earl Spencer*. Navy Records Society, 1913–14. 4 vols.
25. Corbett, Sir Julian. *The Campaign of Trafalgar*. London: Longmans, 1910.
26. Crouzet, F. L. *'Economie britannique and le Blocus Continentale*. Paris, 1958. 2 vols.
27. Day, Sir Archibald. *The Admiralty Hydrographic Service*. London: Her Majesty's Stationery Office, 1967.
28. Derrick, C. *Memoirs of the Rise and Progress of the Royal Navy*. London: Cadell, 1806.
29. Desbrière, E. *La Campagne maritime de 1805*. Trans. C. L. Eastwick under the title of *The Trafalgar Campaign*. London: Oxford University Press, 1933. 2 vols.
30. Dugan, James. *The Great Mutiny*. New York: Putnam, 1965.
31. Dupin, F. C. F. *Voyages dans la Grande-Bretagne*. Paris: 1820. 4 vols. English translation, London, 1822.
32. Erskine, D., ed. *Augustus Hervey's Journal*. London: Kimber, 1953.
33. Forester, C. S. *The Naval War of 1812*. London: Joseph, 1957.
34. Fothergill, G. *The Records of Naval Men*. Walton, 1910.
35. Gallagher, R. E., ed. *Byron's Journal of his Circumnavigation*. London: Hakluyt Society, 1964.
36. Gardner, James Anthony. *Recollections, 1775–1814*. Ed. J. K. Laughton for the Navy Records Society, 1906, and reprinted under the original title of *Above and Under Hatches* by C. Lloyd. London: Batchworth Press, 1955.
37. Gill, C. *The Naval Mutinies of 1797*. Manchester University Press, 1913.
38. Gould, R. T. *The Marine Chronometer*. London: Potter, 1923.
39. Graham, G. S. *Empire of the North Atlantic*. Toronto University Press, 1950.
40. Grenfell, Russell. *Nelson the Sailor*. London: Faber, 1949.
41. Hay, M. D., ed. *Landsman Hay*. London: Hart Davis, 1953.
42. Hecksher, E. F. *The Continental System, an economic interpretation*. London: Oxford University Press, 1922.
43. Hughes, E., ed. *The Private Correspondence of Lord Collingwood*. Navy Records Society, 1957.
44. Hutchinson, J. R. *The Press Gang Afloat and Ashore*. London: Nash, 1913.
45. Jackson, T. Sturges, ed. *Logs of the Great Sea Fights, 1794–1805*. Navy Records Society, 1899, 1900. 2 vols.

46. James, G. F. *Bibliographical Aids to Research: Collected Naval Biography*. Inst. Hist. Res. Bull. vol. 16, 1937.

47. James, W. *The Naval History of Great Britain, 1793–1827*. London: Macmillan, 1822. 6 vols. The later editions of 1837, 1886 and 1902 are to be preferred and have been indexed for the Navy Records Society by C. G. Toogood in 1895.

48. Lacour-Gayet, G. *La Marine militaire de la France sous la règne de Louis XV*. Paris, 1902.

49. Laughton, J. K., ed. *The Letters of Lord Barham*. Navy Records Society, 1907–11. 3 vols.

50. Lewis, M. A. *England's Sea Officers: the story of the naval profession*. London: Allen and Unwin, 1939.

51. Lewis, M. A. *Social History of the Royal Navy, 1793–1815*. London: Allen and Unwin, 1960.

52. Lewis, M. A., ed. *A Narrative of my Professional Adventures* by Sir William Dillon. Navy Records Society, 1953. 2 vols.

53. Leyland, J., ed. *The Blockade of Brest*. Navy Records Society, 1899, 1902. 2 vols.

54. Lloyd, C. *The British Seaman, 1200–1860*. London: Collins, 1968.

55. Lloyd, C. *Lord Cochrane*. London: Longmans, 1947.

56. Lloyd, C. ed. *The Keith Papers*. Navy Records Society, 1927, 1950, 1955. 3 vols.

57. Mack, J. D. *Matthew Flinders*. London: Nelson, 1966.

58. Macintyre, D. *Admiral Rodney*. London: Davis, 1962.

59. Mackaness, G. *Life of Vice-Admiral William Bligh*. Sydney: Angus and Robertson, 1931. 2 vols.

60. Mackay, Ruddock F. *Admiral Hawke*. London: Oxford University Press, 1965.

61. Mackesy, Piers. *The War for America, 1775–1783*. London: Longmans, 1964.

62. Mackesy, Piers. *The War in the Mediterranean, 1803–1810*. London: Longmans, 1957.

63. Macpherson, D. *Annals of Commerce*. London, 1805. 4 vols.

64. Mahan, A. T. *The Influence of Sea Power on History, 1660–1783*. London: Sampson Low, 1890.

65. Mahan, A. T. *The Influence of Sea Power upon the French Revolution and Empire, 1793–1815*. London: Sampson Low, 1892. 2 vols. See also his *Sea Power in its Relation to the War of 1812*. London: Sampson Low, 1905.

66. Mahan, A. T. *The Life of Nelson*. London: Sampson Low, 1897.

67. Manning, T. D. and C. F. Walker. *British Warship Names*. London: Putnam, 1959.

68. Manwaring, G. E. and B. Dobrée. *The Floating Republic*. London: Bles, 1935.

69. Marcus, G. *A Naval History of England: The formative centuries*. London: Longmans, 1961.

70. Marsden, R. G., ed. *The Law and Custom of the Sea*. Navy Records

Society, 1916. 2 vols. The second volume deals with the eighteenth century.

71. Marshall, J. *Royal Naval Biography*. London: Longmans, 1823. 4 vols. in two parts and 3 supplementary volumes.

72. Morison, S. E. *John Paul Jones*. London: Faber, 1959.

73. Morison, S. E. *Old Bruin: the life of Matthew Calbraith Perry*. London: Oxford University Press, 1968.

74. Morrison, A. *Collection of Autograph Letters: The Hamilton and Nelson Papers*. Privately printed, 1893. 2 vols.

75. Mundy, G. B. *Life and Correspondence of Lord Rodney*. London: Murray, 1830.

76. Murray, Sir Oswyn. Articles in *The Mariner's Mirror* on "The Admiralty," 1937–39.

77. Naish, G. B., ed. *Nelson's Letters to his Wife*. Navy Records Society, 1958.

78. Nicolas, Sir Harris. *Letters and Despatches of Lord Nelson*. London: Colbourn, 1844–46. 7 vols.

79. Nockholds, G. W. "Early Timekeepers at Sea," in *Proc. Antiq. Horological Soc.*, 1963–64.

80. O'Byrne, W. R. *A Naval Biographical Dictionary*. London: Murray, 1849.

81. Oman, Carola. *Nelson*. London: Hodder and Stoughton, 1947.

82. Padfield, Peter. *Broke and the Shannon*. London: Hodder and Stoughton, 1968.

83. Pares, Sir Richard. *War and Trade in the West Indies, 1739–63*. London: Macmillan, 1936.

84. Pares, Sir Richard. "The Manning of the Navy in the West Indies," in *Trans. R. Hist. Soc.*, 1937.

85. Pargellis, S. and D. J. Medley. *Bibliography of British History: the eighteenth century*. London: Oxford University Press, 1951.

86. Parkinson, C. Northcote. *The Trade Winds*. London: Allen and Unwin, 1948.

87. Parkinson, C. Northcote. *Edward Pellew, Lord Exmouth*. London: Methuen, 1934.

88. Parkinson, C. Northcote. *War in the Eastern Seas, 1793–1815*. London: Allen and Unwin, 1954.

89. Partridge, Eric, ed. *The Autobiography of Pel Verjuice* (C. R. Pemberton). London: Scolartis Press, 1929. See also Pitcairn Jones in *Mariner's Mirror*, 1953.

90. Pool, Bernard. *Navy Board Contracts, 1660–1832*. London: Longmans, 1966.

91. Pope, Dudley. *At 12 Mr. Byng was Shot*. London: Weidenfeld, 1962.

92. Pope, Dudley. *The Black Ship*. London: Weidenfeld, 1963.

93. Powell, J. Damer. *The Bristol Privateers*. Bristol: J. W. Arrowsmith, 1930.

94. Ranft, B. M., ed. *The Vernon Papers*. Navy Records Society, 1958.

95. Rawson, G. *Pandora's Last Voyage*. London: Longmans, 1963. See

also Rutter, Owen, *Court Martial of Bounty Mutineers*. London: Hodge, 1931.

96. Richardson, W. A. *Mariner of England*. S. Childers, ed. London: Murray, 1908.

97. Richmond, Sir Herbert. *Statesmen and Sea Power*. London: Oxford University Press, 1946.

98. Richmond, Sir Herbert. *The Navy as an Instrument of Policy, 1558–1727*. E. A. Hughes, ed. Cambridge: Cambridge University Press, 1953.

99. Richmond, Sir Herbert. *The Navy in the War of 1739–48*. Cambridge: Cambridge University Press, 1920.

100. Richmond, Sir Herbert, ed. *The Loss of Minorca*. Navy Records Society, 1913.

101. Richmond, Sir Herbert. *The Navy in India, 1763–83*. London: Benn, 1931.

102. Ritchie, G. S. *The Admiralty Chart*. London: Hollis and Carter, 1967.

103. Robertson, F. L. *The Evolution of Naval Armament*. London: Constable, 1921.

104. Robinson, A. H. W. *Marine Cartography in Britain*. Leicester University Press, 1962.

105. Robinson, C. N. *The British Tar in Fact and Fiction*. London: Harper, 1909.

106. (Robinson, W.) *Nautical Economy by Jack Nasty-Face*. Ann Arbor: University Microfilms. See also Pitcairn Jons in *Mariner's Mirror*, 1953.

107. Rodger, A. B. *The War of the Second Coalition, 1798–1801*. London: Oxford University Press, 1964.

108. Ryan, A. N., ed. *The Saumarez Papers*. Navy Records Society, 1968.

109. Ryan, A. N. "The Attack upon Copenhagen, 1807," in *English Historical Review*, 1953.

110. Ryan, A. N. "The Defence of British Trade in the Baltic, 1807–13," in *English Historical Review*, 1959.

111. Saumarez, Sir Ross. *Memoirs and Correspondence of Lord De Saumarez*. London: Bentley, 1838. 2 vols.

112. Schomberg, Isaac. *The Naval Chronology, or an Historical Summary of Naval and Maritime Events*. London: Egerton, 1802. 5 vols.

113. Schumpeter, E. B. *English Overseas Trade Statistics, 1697–1808*. London: Oxford University Press, 1960.

114. Sherrard, O. A. *Life of Lord St. Vincent*. London: Allen and Unwin, 1933.

115. Southey, Robert. *The Life of Horatio, Lord Nelson*. London: Murray, 1813. 2 vols. Frequently reprinted.

116. Thursfield, J. R., ed. *Five Naval Journals*. Navy Records Society, 1951.

117. Tours, Hugh. *The Life and Letters of Emma, Lady Hamilton*. London: Gollancz, 1963.

118. Tunstall, B., ed. *The Byng Papers*. Navy Records Society, 1930–2. 3 vols.
119. Wallis, Helen, ed. *Carteret's Voyage Round the World*. London: Hakluyt Society, 1965. 2 vols.
120. Warner, Oliver. *Lord Nelson: a guide to reading*. London: Caravel Press, 1955.
121. Warner, Oliver. *Nelson's Battles*. London: Batsford, 1965.
122. Warner, Oliver. *Portrait of Lord Nelson*. London: Chatto and Windus, 1958.
123. Warner, Oliver. *Life and Letters of Vice-Admiral Lord Collingwood*. London: Oxford University Press, 1968.
124. Williams, Gomer. *History of the Liverpool Privateers*. London: Heinemann, 1897.
125. Wright, C. and E. Fayle. *A History of Lloyd's*. London: Macmillan 1928.
126. Zimmerman, J. F. *Impressment of America Seamen*. New York: Columbia University Studies in History, CXVIII, 1925. See also A. Steel in *Cambridge Historical Journal,* 1949.

SUPPLEMENT TO BIBLIOGRAPHY

127. Baynham, Lieutenant-Commander H. *From the Lower Deck: the old navy, 1780–1840*. London: Hutchinson, 1969.
128. Howarth, David. *Trafalgar: the Nelson touch*. London: Collins, 1969.
129. Pugh, Surgeon-Commander P. D. G. *Nelson and his Surgeons*. Edinburgh: Livingstone, 1968.
130. *Catalogue of the Library of the National Maritime Museum*. M. Sanderson, ed. Volume I: Voyages and Travels; Volume II: Biography. London: HMSO, 1969.
131. Spinney, David. *Rodney*. London: Allen and Unwin, 1969.

VII

THE SCIENTIFIC, TECHNOLOGICAL AND ECONOMIC BACKGROUND TO 1815

W. H. G. Armytage

FIRST REFERENCE STAGE: SOME GUIDEPATHS TO SOURCE MATERIAL. On first entry, the wealth of material awaiting the investigation of the interrelationships of the Armed Forces of the Crown with the technological, scientific, economic, political, and social life of Great Britain up to the time of the Battle of Waterloo seems bewildering. But it need not be so. Adequate guides exist to alleviate the tedium of time-wasting enquiries locating source material as are noted in the Introduction.

Since bibliographies on the foreign wars are given in other chapters, here it suffices to indicate studies of the wars against Wales, Scotland and Ireland, and of the Cinque Ports (45). A Welsh bibliography is provided by Jenkins and Rees (215); further studies are by E. I. Bromberg (38), Harries (175), Lynn Nelson (302), accounts by A. H. and D. Williams (427) and (428), E. A. Lewis (242), W. J. Lewis (248), Morris (284, 285) Edwards (116), Dodd (109–111) and a summary by Lloyd (254). Scottish wars can be followed through a bibliography by H. W. Meikle (277), E. M. Barron (24), J. M. W. Bean (26), catalogues by Terry and Matheson (see Introduction) of local publications and works, supplemented by Joseph Bain (21), William Burns (44), Pryde (332), Hume Brown (41), Edward Miller (280), J. E. Morris (284), R. H. Campbell (47), W. C. Dickinson (102), Scottish wars effect on the growth of York [Bean (26)], Broome (40), financial loans to the Crown (Hay (182)), the growth of shipping (W. S. Reid (341)) and the union lords (Simont (369)). Here the *Scottish Historical Review* has invaluable specialist articles. A masterly case study of the effect of Scotland on the third civil war is afforded by H. R. Trevor-Roper (408). A bibliography of Irish economic affairs is given by Prendeville (325). A study of Elizabethan wars is given by Falls (121), of the Williamite confiscations by J. R. Simms (368), a guide to Irish bibliographical material by Eager (115), and an overview by J. C. Beckett (27).

On the history of science the annual bibliographies in *Isis* (210) are indispensable, and those of E. S. Ferguson (125) in the history of technology are useful; *Ambix* (4) is good for early chemistry. So, after the Renaissance, is the *Annals of Science* (8). *Osiris* (310) embraces learning and culture. For general help Bloch (31) Bonsor *et alii* (32) and Bernal (29) are suggested. So is Kirby (230) and Kranzberg and Pursell (231). For a general economic background Lipson (250) is still a mine of information.

THEMATIC HISTORIES. Finally, apart from general histories of science pure and applied by Bernal (29), de Solla Price (330), Hull (164), Kirby *et alii* (230), Merton (278), Pledge (321) and Wolf (433, 434), there are a number of thematic histories that should be consulted in any attempt to discover the scientific technological and economic background to war. Alphabetically these range from books on aeronautics (198) (256) (373); agriculture (221) (281); arsenals (199) (436); assurance (218) (435); astronomy (220); castles (405); chains (223); chronology (201); colonies (50); contraception (193); diaries (273) (334); economic growth (322) (352); electricity and magnetism (287); firearms (49); food and drink (53) (423); heraldry (415); lighting (306); medieval military architecture (400); merchant marine (207) (213); metals (2) (362); naval armament (347); marine engineering (380); navigation (396); obituaries before 1800 (209) (288); press gangs (208); sailors (349); sea-officers (245); scientific periodicals (232); steam engines (100) (294) (350) (393); tinplate (281); and water turbines (432).

THE CHAIN REACTIONS IN NORMAN TIMES. From the neolithic days described by V. G. Childe (57) and the Roman mines identified by O. Davies (89) up till the eighteenth century, the increasing use of iron and steel, especially in warfare, has been documented in masterly fashion by A. Steensberg (386), H. H. Coghlan (71), R. E. Oakeshott (303), L. Aitchison (2) and H. R. Schubert (362) who show how Roman forts in Britain stimulated its mining. Metallurgy has also been authoritatively treated by R. F. Tylecote (409).

With the beginning of the Norman conquest, and especially with the documentation in Doomsday Book (83), clearer pictures are available of the political (312), social (387) and technological background.

After Doomsday Book, the Great Roll of the Exchequer, consisting of various "pipes" or annual enrolled accounts of sheriffs and others, afford the earliest qualified accounts of the needs of the army and navy. From this too, authors of various volumes of the Victoria County Histories (412) have quarried information about the two great early medieval armament centres, Gloucester plus the Forest of Dean (180) and the County Palatine of Durham. For a bibliography of early towns, see Gross (157).

The defeat of Harold's troops at Hastings (where they dismounted to do battle on foot) reveals that, as Lynn White, Jr., writes, "the Anglo-Saxons used the stirrup, but did not comprehend it; and for this they paid a fearful price" (421). Side by side with the deployment of the horse in wartime went his employment in peace. Here the horse collar—which enabled powerful horses to be bred both for carrying armed men and for pulling ploughs—

is relevant as Chevalier Lefebure de Nöettes (239) and F. G. Payne (316) have shown. Certainly in Doomsday Book nearly all refer to ox-ploughs (126) and not till the twelfth century, as Lennard (241) shows, did horses begin to take over. These "oat-burning engines" were led by the three-field system. This provided, in addition to oats for the horses and barley for beer, legumes for vitality, and, in Lynn White's view, "goes far towards explaining . . . the startling expansion of population, the growth and multiplication of cities, the rise in industrial production, the out-reach of commerce, and the new exuberance of spirits" since "the Middle Ages from the tenth century onwards were full of beans" (421). For the road system, see Stenton (388). We can also trace the increasing importance of the "smith" since he made weapons for agricultural, domestic and personal use as well as weapons for military use.

"The whole history of the development of Anglo-Norman administration is intelligible only in terms of the scale and pressing needs of war finance" wrote J. O. Prestwich (328). Here the use of mercenaries—*stipendiarii,* hired for service in particular campaigns—was, in the opinion of Hollister (200), "the most significant military expense." A good picture of English warfare in 1066 is given by R. Glover (151).

As traditional skirmishes with small bodies of knights gave way to ever larger forces, protracted wars, and more distant theatres of operations, more money was necessary to pay more mercenaries (339). This, as Bryce D. Lyon shows, stretched "the fabric of feudal relations" (257). For feudal levies see N. B. Lewis (246, 247), for feudal military service I. J. Saunders (360), for "bastard feudalism" K. B. MacFarlane (259, 260) and for army "wages" A. E. Prince (331).

To pacify the country some 327 castles were built in the period 1154–1216 in the Angevin Kingdom of England, as R. A. Brown notes (42) and Painter (312) discusses. Each castle had its smith—who forged quarrels (iron bolts for crossbows) horseshoes, hinges and nails. For a catalogue of masons' marks see Davis (93), for the effect of the crusades on military architecture and other matters see Oman (306), Hamilton Thompson (400), Toy (405), Braun (37), Smail (372), La Monte (233), Runciman (356) and Setton (366). Chinese knowledge of gunpowder (90) (249 and 152) was, as Wang Ling points out, brought to Europe. Its effects are examined by Singer, Holmyard, Hall and Williams (370).

The effect of the Hundred Years' War on the merchant marine has most recently been considered by Dr. K. B. McFarlane (261). Further clues can be obtained from H. J. Hewitt (190). Postan on the other hand considers it to have been not so much "the mainspring as a makeweight of economic development" (324).

Further examples of the feedback from weaponry to civil technology are, as Lynn White shows (421), the spring (from the bow) to operate lathes, pestles and sawmills, and, according to Roth (353) clocks and mousetraps. For chainmail see C. Stanley Smith (379). For "booty" and "spoils of war" see D. Hay (182, 183), for medieval cities H. Pirenne (319, 320), and for ships see Arenhold (9).

Medieval science in England can be explored through Rashdall (338). Gunther (158) is especially valuable for his picture of the "Merton" school, whose interest in, and importance for, navigation can be deduced. For more detail Thorndike (401) and Sarton (361) are valuable, whilst J. C. Russell, in addition to estimating medieval population (357), has given a valuable dictionary of thirteenth-century English writers (358).

Medieval technology can be surveyed in volume ii of Singer, Holmyard, Hall and Williams (370) and Usher (411).

Prediction and forecasting the future were also fostered by war as Thorndike (401) and Taylor (396) note.

THE DEVOURING CANNON: SALTPETRE, METALLURGY AND CHARCOAL. Crecy and subsequent battles in the Hundred Years' War (20) established the usefulness of guns so, as T. F. Tout (403) showed, responsibility for producing them rested with the Keeper of the Wardrobe from 1345 onwards. In the Wars of the Roses (262) Germans were hired to use hand guns and spread the knowledge and use of firearms in England as Oman (307), Doucet (114) and V. G. Kiernan (229) argue. However, Schubert considers it "very probable that the art of casting iron bullets and guns was introduced from France" (362). Further study of French trade (e.g. in 342) is needed.

For a good history of gunpowder see Hime (192). Until the sixteenth century saltpetre came from Spain. Working from Escales (119) and Oscar Guttman (159) one can see its importance. In 1515 Hans Wolf was appointed to go from shore to shore with his band to find saltpetre, and in 1531 Thomas à Lee was given a similar appointment. By 1561 Queen Elizabeth was bargaining with Gerard Honricke, "an almayne Captain," to come over and teach her subjects the art of making saltpetre as good as that made "beyond the seas." When he arrived she resigned her bargain to Philip Cockeram and John Barnes to make saltpetre for ten years (*Engineering,* 15 June, 1894). As Helen Evelyn (120) shows, saltpetre was the basis of the Evelyn fortune (97). George and John Evelyn (together with Richard Hills) obtained an eleven-year grant in 1589, and, two years later, an even more comprehensive grant empowering them to enter any land where saltpetre might be found. They inaugurated the first large-scale manufacture of gunpowder. Bovill (33) is helpful here. And on Armada guns see Michael Lewis (244).

The quest for saltpetre led the East India Company from 1625 onwards to import it from India. In the following year it was licensed to erect powder mills in Surrey, Kent and Sussex (their first attempt in Windsor Forest was stopped because it interfered with the King's deer). By 1695 it was obliged to supply 500 tons a year to the Ordnance. Not unnaturally, a later chief inspector to the Indian Ordnance Department, Arthur Marshall, gave us a classic history of explosives (269).

Guns or soap? By the time of Charles I saltpetre men found themselves competing with the soap-boilers for wood ashes—then required for potash and for the conversion of sodium nitrate into the potassium compound. Gunpowder had civil uses too: in stopping the great fire of London, and in the Cornish Mines (243). For a picture of the supply in 1776 see Stephenson (389).

WARS AND CAPITAL FORMATION. The whole system of medieval war involved the crown in raising money both at home and abroad. For loans raised before and during the Hundred Years' War, see J. F. Willard (426) and E. P. Fryde (138, 139). Such loans, aids, and subsidies to foreign powers were quite complex, as Ehrenberg (117) shows.

The cost of hiring German pikemen, Spanish arquebusiers, Albanian horsemen and Italians led Henry VIII to ransack the monasteries to find money to pay them. Elizabeth had to make do with the militia; when she hired troops, she got, as L. Stone has shown (392), into deep financial trouble in doing so. True, Scotland and Ireland were sources of recruits and Drake's voyages brought in some dividends, but this was not enough. Elizabeth got herself into low water by hiring continental troops to help the Dutch in 1578, as L. Stone (392) describes. "These hundred years and more never any king of this land was able to continue wars beyond sea above one year." Dr. Bartholomew Clerk's opinion in 1586/7 reflected the fact that the 6,000 troops in the Netherlands cost the Queen half her revenue (apart from parliamentary grants). To this should be added troops and subsidies in France (which between 1589 and 1595 cost a whole year's parliamentary grant) and the even greater expense of crushing Tyrone's rebellion (some £1,924,000 in 1593 alone). The implications of all this on war aims and strategy have been explored by R. B. Wernham (419). For further exhaustive analysis of Tudor and Stuart finance the studies of F. C. Dietz (104–107) are essential.

The need for revenue even led the Crown to trench on future oak supply. Despite the Acts of 1543 and 1570 and Burleigh's policy of "plantations" (V. C. H. Berkshire, ii), Elizabeth sold licenses to cut in the woods, and James I disafforested a considerable proportion of Crown lands as well as granting a patent to Sir Giles Mompesson in 1617 for this purpose. Charles I went further and even sold two forests to provide for the fleet when it returned from the expedition to the Isle of Rhé. For the story of the growth of the National Debt see W. A. Shaw (367).

From the Armada onwards we can discern the rise of government backers and contractors in various buccaneering enterprises (7) and (39) in the war against Spain which brought at least one of them what A. H. Dodd calls "fabulous gains" (110), which were invested in copper works at Neath and the publication of Welsh religious works. For further information on the Crown's operations on the money market see Robert Ashton (10). For marine risks and their impact on insurance V. Barbour (22) is illuminating. For war and society as a whole in the seventeenth century see G. N. Clark (62, 63).

WAR AND ECONOMIC GROWTH (I) 1540–1689. Patents reflect the increasing needs of the services. Here Hyde Price (330) and E. W. Hulme (204, 205) and M. B. Donald (113) are essential. The use of "earth coal, sea coal, turf or peat" to make iron, steel and lead, flasks for touch-

boxes, powder boxes, and bullet boxes for small arms have all been catalogued by Hume (204), as are patents for "instruments of war," sackbuts,
trumpets, train oil, salt, shorthand, nails, writing paper, mathematical instruments and even playing cards.

Agents abroad were busy. Cardinal Wolsey had Spinelly in Flanders to
contract with the great master founder of Malines, Hans Poppenruyter.
Sometimes foreigners were tempted to England to further the Crown's policy
of inaugurating and promoting industries bearing on national defence by
the granting of licenses. Such licenses, as N. B. Donald (112) shows, were
given to Burchard Cranich for mining and melting metals in 1554, to John
Medley for draining mines in 1562, to George Gylpin and Peter Stough-
berken to make ovens and furnaces in 1563, to Cornelius de Vos to make
alum and copperas in 1564, to Daniel Hochstetter and Thomas Thurland
to mine in eight English counties. Armour for man and horse—a light bullet
proof fabric without any metal "mingled or wrought in the same"—was to
be provided, under patent, for seven years from 1587 by John Purchise.

Attempts to obtain English steel from ores containing silica or manganese
began, as Schubert shows, in Robertsbridge (Sussex) and Boxhurst (Kent)
in 1566 (362). Sheffield too was making its own steel by the end of the
century and attempts were made to start it in Ireland. By the following century its manufacture by the cementation process spread to the Forest of
Dean, the Midlands and to Newcastle-on-Tyne, probably through the
agency of Ambrose Crowley on whom Flinn is very informative (131, 134).
Other improvements like "shearing" for cutting tools and crucible or cast
steel followed.

Apart from the Spanish raid on Newlyn scarcely a shot was fired in anger
on English ground from 1569 to 1639, whereas on the continent there were
no less than eight wars. So, argued Professor Nef (298), if war was such a
decisive economic determinant "we should expect the French and the Germans to have been the leaders more than either the Italians or the English."
He considered that England's "remarkable progress" was "made possible in
no small measure by the peaceful conditions the country enjoyed. Continental wars seem to have hindered the growth of scientific knowledge more
than they stimulated it." So too Lawrence Stone (391) argues that "the
direct results of war in sixteenth-century England were small." See also John
Hale (160). Because "problems of warfare seemed to occupy a smaller
place in English than in continental scientific and technical publications at
the turn of the sixteenth and the beginning of the seventeenth century," Nef
argued that salt and alum making, coal mining, printing, glass and paper-
making, soap boiling, brewing and sugar refinery did not depend so much
on war orders as on the influx of Huguenots and the growth of the population. The former led to the expansion of the new draperies of East Anglia
and to the rise of sugar refining (owing to the sack of Antwerp in 1576 and
1583); the latter led to a demand for ironware in homes.

But even Nef argues that England supplied foreign armies with cannon,
being "not backward in furnishing the weapons with which foreign armies
blew each other to bits" (299). He therefore agrees that the growth of
metallurgical industries was due to cast iron and brass cannon. So too

Ernest Straker (394) shows that the large cannon foundries in Sussex and Kent "shipped many, if not most of their guns to the Continent," and he cites diversion of merchant capital from commerce to privateering.

Margaret Hodgen (197) ascribes the acceleration of technological innovation at this time to the migration of craftsmen to Surrey, Sussex and Kent. Elsewhere (299) Nef asks, "If war had been the principal taskmaster for the British technician, would he not have accomplished more between 1625 and 1775 to meet the most urgent need of the armed forces—a great addition to the supplies of metal?"

Here early regional studies like those of J. W. Gough on seventeenth-century entrepreneur engineers like Sir Hugh Myddleton (154), Thomas Bushell (155) and the Mines of Mendip (153) are especially rewarding, as is C. E. Hart's on the free miners of the Royal Forest of Dean (180). For a survey of overseas trade at this time see G. C. D. Ramsey (337).

The answer seems to be in the growth of a governmental war machine. From the dry dock at Portsmouth in 1496, and Deptford in 1517, clusters of storehouses and growing naval establishments grew along the Medway, needing a Navy Board to administer them. Its story has been authoritatively chronicled by C. S. L. Davies (86). The rise of Trinity House has been told by A. A. Ruddock (355). Davies has also given what looks like the only authoritative account of a similar movement in the army which led to the establishment of the Ordnance Office (87). Both Board and Office actually ordered supplies for the armed forces, which must have stimulated the so-called Industrial Revolution of the 1560's which Nef himself (296) has so patiently chronicled. Yet a third central government office was the Mastership of the Woods, established in 1542 from the surveyorship of woods of suppressed monasteries (created in 1538). This became the office of Surveyor General of His Majesty's Woods and Forests. This as Albion shows (3) was a treasury jurisdiction. As the American colonies developed as a naval storehouse, an office was created there in 1685.

Food policy was affected by the needs of the armed forces as Brian Pearce shows (317). So too the Navigation Acts can be seen through the eyes of Lawrence A. Harper (174) as a seventeenth-century experiment in social engineering. Certainly the British naval needs, as L. A. Harding (172) and E. G. R. Taylor (396, 397, 398) show, contributed much to mathematics.

When continental manufacturers were disorganised by the religious wars on the continent in the last half of the sixteenth century, English undressed and undyed products were rushed in to take their place. P. J. Bowden (34) shows how Alderman Cockayne tried to ensure that such exports were both dressed and dyed in England.

Since, as Albion (3) shows and the Clowes (67) confirm, timber was so increasingly required for ships (5 and 6), that English forests were protected and timber was imported. The need for Naval Stores also stimulated the Eastland Trade, described by R. W. K. Hinton (195) and Ralph Davis (91 and 92). For heating coal came into more general use: annual shipments of this relatively new commodity increasing, as Nef shows (297), between 1564 and 1634 by a factor of 14. Need drove the miners to dig deeper, at levels which made necessary new pumping devices and new transport on rails to save making subterranean roadways. New knowledge was also dearly bought about the dangers (e.g. gases) to be encountered underground.

Further efforts to substitute coal for wood in smelting iron coupled with those of Germans in England, like Sturtevant and Blauenstein, culminated in the success of Abraham Darby I who revived an old ironworks at Coalbrookdale in 1709 for this purpose in order to supply the workshops of Sheffield and Birmingham. This led to a rapid expansion of the coal trade (297), as Nef shows, as well as of the coasting trade (425) and other ancillary industries (431).

FROM CANNON TO STEAM ENGINE. Wartime demands on mining "gave," as Professor John indicates, "a powerful impetus to the development of the steam engine" (216). One should read R. E. Scouller's study of the armies of Queen Anne (365) before turning to L. T. C. Rolt's account of Savery's and Newcomen's attempt to cope with West Country mining problems (350). By the end of the War of the Spanish Succession (in 1713) steam engines were draining many copper and coal mines. Arthur Stowers explores its development after Newcomen's death in 1729 (393). The War of the Austrian Succession (1739–1748) still further accelerated their construction and dispersal throughout other parts of the country like Tyneside (335), Durham (203), Merseyside (178), Derbyshire (301) and Lancashire (289). Its overall development has been surveyed by H. W. Dickinson (100). The consequent stimulus to improving rivers and canals (371), and to surveying needs little emphasis, for the first survey of the Clyde was made by James Sterling (66) (known as "the Venetian" because of his penetration of the glass-making secrets of that city), manager of the Scots Mining Company of Leadhills (known as "God's Treasure House in Scotland"). His friend, J. T. Desaguliers, lectured on the steam engine. A third F.R.S., Henry Beighton, erected steam engines and made a full scale survey of Warwickshire by triangulation.

Not only did the construction of these steam engines in the eighteenth century coincide with the rise of the travelling lecturer in science (169), but its employment in drainage led to the development of early scientific societies in Lincolnshire and of new developments in education, which can be explored with copious bibliographic assistance in Hans (169) and Taylor (396, 397, 398). This in turn improved and profited from the making of guns, when another ironmaking patentee, John Roebuck, began making large calibre guns (with a special chamber for the powder) called "carronades" after his foundry, the Carron Iron Works. This employed the bellows from 1761 onwards with air cylinders (made by John Smeaton, the civil engineer) (16). From air cylinders and boring cannon was but a short step to improving the cylinders for the steam engine (43, 48). So the stage was set for the introduction by Roebuck of James Watt to Matthew Boulton, and for the building of such an engine in 1771 by the great ironmaker John Wilkinson.

Chains and shot, like cannon, need iron. Coke pig iron was, at first, only suitable for foundries. Here the innovative skills of the Darbys (286 and 333) and William Wood (132) and the stimulus of the Wars of the Austrian Succession (1739–1748) and the Seven Years' War (1756–1763) provided an enormous impetus for blast furnaces. For a guide to commercial statistics see Clark and Franks (63).

THE ORGANISATION OF SCIENCE. On the equally complex question of the contribution of sixteenth- and seventeenth-century war to science, Professor A. R. Hall considers that "the practice of artillery contributed nothing to seventeenth-century science but the convenient illustration of dynamical principles" and that "its influence on science or of science upon it, was negligible." He considers that "there is simply no relationship at all between the theory of ballistics, which was an integral part of the revolution in dynamics, and the implausible proposals for destruction or defence which were the natural products of a warlike but unmechanical age." Advancing knowledge severed rather than strengthened the leads between biology and medicine, astronomy and navigation, mathematics and mensuration; scientific renaissance had deeper roots. Chemists rather than ballisticians favoured "military conservatism and the fact that war concerned only a small proportion of the population spared Europe the development of its ordnance from the sixteenth to the nineteenth century" (161). Yet even Professor Nef admitted that "war needs provided some of the subject matter and stimulated the development of some of the methods used in the natural sciences," and agreed that "no doubt the new relation, which was felt to exist between science and military or naval success, increased the prestige of the scientists (299). Drebbel is a case in point (402).

The activities and organisation of those scientists has been described by Sprat (385), Merton (278), D. McKie (264), Stimson (390), Macaulay (258), Sir Harold Hartley (181), H. T. Pledge (321), G. N. Clark (61) and A. R. Hall (163, 164). It can be monitored in periodicals like *Ambix* (4), *The Annals of Science* (8), *Isis* (210), *Osiris* (310) and especially in *Notes and Records of the Royal Society of London* (302).

The Royal Society caught up the enthusiasm of men like Henry Oldenburg, who had written to Hartlib in 1658 about the "engine of war" devised by Küffler "thought to have aurum fulminans in it" (163). The experimental spirit which led Caspar Kalthoff and Edward Somerset to devise pumps at Raglan Castle (mentioned in Nos. 68 and 98–100 of the latter's *Century of Inventions* (1663)) was abroad.

Ideas from other countries, were, as Francis Bacon had suggested, eagerly tried out by some returning exiles. Thus Sir Richard Weston (a Royalist exile in the Low Countries whose *Discours of Husbandrie used in Brabant and Flanders* was actually published by the Commonwealth man Samuel Hartlib in 1650 and 1652) returned to improve the navigation of the Wey for which he was granted timber from the King's estates at Oatlands and Richmond. He also included nonesuch grass, grew hay by irrigating the meadows, and introduced a rotation of crops (clover, flax and turnips).

The Royal Society commanded Lord Brounckner "to make some experiments of the Recoiling of Guns." Read before the Society on 10 June 1661 his paper was included by Sprat (385) in his history, together with Henshaw's "History of the Making of Saltpetre" read before the Society on 18 September 1662. Indeed the latter excited the hostility and criticism of an early critic of the Society, Henry Stubbs, who accused him in *Legends no Histories* of plagiarising from Johann Glauber's *Prosperity of Germany* and cited his own personal investigations into the production of saltpetre at Warwick and Coventry. The controversy between them is outlined by H. W. Jones (222).

Robert Hooke, its first experimenter, tried to devise a movable keel for warships, and translated the treatise of Francesco de Lana-Terzi on a lighter-than-air craft for the *Philosophical Transactions of the Royal Society* (1679). But it was envisaged as causing a "disturbance to the Civil Government of men" since "no city can be secure against attack . . . and the same would happen to private houses and ships on the sea" (94).

Sir George N. Clark (61) considered that after 1664 the Dutch war absorbed the energies of the most active fellows of the Society, like John Evelyn (who became a commissioner for the sick and wounded prisoners), with the result that it was "at a low ebb" by 1680. He also felt tempted to throw the blame on the wars of Louis XIV for its "enfeeblement altogether" in the early years of the eighteenth century. Unlike Professor Hessen (189), Sir George Clark regarded economic man and man the fighting animal as "two distinct abstractions" whose motives may interpenetrate (61).

Pepys' friend, Sir Anthony Deane (F.R.S.), a Harwich master shipwright, became commissioner of the navy in 1675, devised the "punchinello" cannon, and was elected to the Royal Society in 1681. For other naval advances see Coleman (72 and 73). For the Navy under William III see J. P. Ehrman (118), and under Queen Anne, J. H. Owen (311).

The argument that the application of scientific methods to society (like improving rivers (371), encouraging industry and establishing a land bank) were preferable to war was argued in *England's Improvement by Sea and land to outdo the Dutch without fighting* (1677, 1681) by Andrew Yarranton, a former captain in the Parliamentary Army who had opened an ironworks in 1652 and was busy improving water navigation. For the impact of the Dutch wars on England see Charles Wilson (430 and 431). Some members of the Royal Society acted as if that were their view too, but others continued to contribute knowledge of explosives. Thus when Francis Hawksbee was Curator of Experiments at the Royal Society he published the results of work on the combustion of gunpowder (*Phil. Trans.* XXIV, 1705, pp. 1806–7; XXV, 1707, pp. 2409).

The President of the Royal Society was also made the chief examiner at the Military Academy at Woolwich (158), many of whose teachers, like Benjamin Robins (whose *New Principles of Gunnery* (1742) led J. U. Nef (299) to regard him as "one of the first English natural philosophers to combine, with a good conscience, speculative scientific work and practical engineering for destructive purposes") were elected F.R.S. Scientific ideas were diffused through publications (115), teachers (169 and 265), itinerant lecturers in science (144), international contacts (137, 149, 150, 167).

Here A. E. Musson and Eric Robinson (289 and 290) are especially rewarding and their articles can be chased through various journals.

WAR AND ECONOMIC GROWTH, (II) 1689–1776. For an overview of economic growth from 1688 onwards Deane and Cole (95) are indispensable. For the so-called War of Jenkins' Ear to the Seven Years' War economic chauvinism was fanned by an outburst of pamphlets. "Our commerce, in general," argued one, "will flourish more under a vigorous and well-managed naval war, than under any peace, which should allow an open intercourse between nations," whilst three years later in 1748, the Archbishop of York told Newcastle that the clothiers of Wakefield did not rejoice at the peace as their trade prospered by war (314). The part played by the Royal Society of Arts in encouraging such trade (and technology) after 1754 is well described by Hudson and Luckhurst (202), and the growth of the shipping industry which carried it by Ralph Davis (91).

Contemporary pamphlets are listed by Hanson (170) on the expense of the War of the Spanish Succession (No. 5719) and on the possible consequences of the War of the Austrian Succession (Nos. 5687–8, 5861, 5969–70). Discussions concerning gunsmiths (761, 1093, 1125, 1310, 1569), gunpowder (778–9, 1309, 2495–9, 3450, 4190, 5207, 6251), and various other industrial activities connected with war can be followed up in his 263-page index. He has also given us a good study of the relations of government with the press (171). Patriotism in poetry has been explored by Dobrée (108). There was also much tough patriotic piety abroad among clergymen of the Church of England, like Richard Watson, Bishop of Llandaff, consultant to the government in 1787 about improvements in gunpowder (his advice is said to have saved the government some £100,000 a year) and an enthusiastic and energetic advocate of improving the efficiency of farming methods during the Napoleonic war. (Wordsworth in his *Description of the Lakes* (1820) sneered at his "vegetable manufactory"). Watson's *Address to the People of Great Britain* urging the vigorous prosecution of the war went to fourteen editions as well as being widely pirated. It outraged men like Gilbert Wakefield (the colonist) and Benjamin Flower (who later emigrated to America). Two such other bellicose clergy were the Rev. Alexander Forsyth of Aberdeen (who improved the flintlock and in 1807 patented a percussion carbine) and James Puckle (who devised for his quick-firing guns round bullets for Christians and square bullets for Turks). Indeed an exhortation was engraved on Puckle's guns:

"Defending King George your country and lawes
Is defending yourself and the Protestant cause."

So it is not surprising that after examining economic growth in England from the War of the Grand Alliance (1689 to 1697) to the Seven Years' War (1756 to 1763) A. H. John should have concluded "there does not seem to be any theoretical reason why, given a favourable conjuncture of circumstances, war should not prove an impetus to growth of the victorious power" (219). "Most striking" in his opinion was its impact on the copper trade (see also 177). After reading Richmond (344) one can see why the need for sheathing ships and making brass revived the dormant Cornish industry, till by 1758 it was more important than tin (354). It also encouraged the South Wales coal industry, since 30–35 tons of coal were needed to produce a ton of copper. It also stimulated further growth in Birmingham —a centre of brass manufacture. On the brass and copper industries in general to 1880 see Hamilton (165).

Similar interaction is visible in other regions. One must study overviews by Witt Bowden (35), Phyllis Deane (96) and M. W. Flinn (132) before embarking on detailed studies like that on the woollen trade of Yorkshire by Herbert Heaton (187), the Leeds woollen industry in particular by W. G. Crump (79), M. W. Beresford and G. R. J. Jones (28), the Irish linen industry by C. Gill (148), the Lancashire cotton trade by G. W. Daniels (82), or A. P. Wadsworth and Julia de L. Mann (414). The important arms centre round Birmingham has been explored by W. H. B. Court (77), Sheffield cutlery by G. I. H. Lloyd (253) and lead mining in Wales by W. J. Lewis (248). The Strutts of Derbyshire have been exhumed by Fitton and Wadsworth (127), the hosiery and other trades of Nottingham by J. D. Chambers (55, 56), the Derwent valley of Northumberland and Durham by M. W. Flinn (130), the larder counties of Norfolk by Naomi Riches (343), and Lincolnshire by M. W. Barley (23). More modern studies are those of G. R. Lewis (243) and A. H. Dodd on North Wales (109), J. Rowe on Cornwall (354), A. Fell (124) and J. D. Marshall (270) on Furness, and C. W. Chalklin (52) on Kent. See also Cordeaux and Merry's bibliography of Oxfordshire (76) and Conisbee's bibliography of Bedfordshire (74). On Scotland see Hamilton (166) and the Clows (65). More technical are the studies of W. K. V. Gale on iron and steel (143). J. D. Marshall (270) especially calls attention to the rapid local expansion of Furness in 1746 when gun-making and shot manufacture were begun there in 1745 and Furness bar iron was being exported to Liverpool for the manufacture of anchors, chains and other shipbuilding requirements. For ships' chronometers see Gould (156) and for nomenclatures Charles Gill (147). Another naval necessity—cooping—led to some 634,-000 wooden hoops being exported in 1807. Contemporary estimates of sheep and wool production are "given" by Fussell and Goodman (142) whilst Smiles (376) can still be read with pleasure and profit.

Another consequence, not so much of the War of Austrian Succession as of the Pretender's success in penetrating so far down into England in 1745, was the impetus it gave to road making (211 and 212). This should be compared with the work on canals described by A. W. Skempton (371). Mantoux (268) shows how turnpike trusts increased from 160 to 530 between 1748 and 1760 "proper for the passage of troops, horses and carriages, at all times of the year." As the Webbs showed, some 452 Acts were passed to keep up roads between 1760 and 1774 (418). The surveys for some of these roads were commissioned by the Board of Ordnance to prevent another rebellion. In carrying it out, their surveyor, William Roy, thought of mapping the whole of the British Isles by triangulation and astronomical "fixes." Promoted to become Inspector-General of Coasts in

1765 he pressed the idea upon the Board, citing the example of France. The advent of the Duke of Richmond as Master-General of Ordnance in 1782, the ending of the War of American Independence, and the suggestion of the French Academy to the Royal Society that triangulations of the two countries should be linked were, as E. G. R. Taylor shows (398) decisive, for the successful completion of the Anglo-French triangulation led to the establishment of the Ordnance Survey Office for the Triangulation in 1791. Roy having died the year before, Colonel Williams, then Captain Mudge, were put in charge. Here Close (64) is very suggestive. The development of surveys also owed much to "plantations" in America, Africa (88) and Australia (128). Health problems of the navy and their relevance to modern medicine can be seen from Lloyd (251) and Lloyd and Coulter (252).

WAR AND ECONOMIC GROWTH (III) 1776–1789. The expense of the Seven Years' War, said Adam Smith in 1776, was not defrayed by the exportation of gold and silver but by "British commodities of some kind or other." The expense of 1761, "more than nineteen millions," would have drawn on nearly four times the annual import of gold and silver into both Spain and Portugal—were that available. Hence the enormus stimulus to the manufacture of commodities to pay the cost of provisions for the army, subsidies (where necessary) and loans. Thus "a very expensive foreign war" could "be carried on for many years without either exporting any considerable quantity of gold and silver, or even having any such quantity to export" (377).

Published as England was embarking on another war, this time with the rebellious American colonists (80), Adam Smith's *Wealth of Nations* of 1776 was deservedly influential. It stressed the underlying principle of the commercial system that manufacturers, during the war, would sustain "a double demand . . . , first, by working up goods to be sent abroad, to pay the bills drawn upon foreign countries for the pay and provisions of the army; and, secondly, by working up others necessary for purchasing items usually being consumed at home." He concluded that "in the midst of the most destructive foreign war, therefore, the greater part of manufacturers may frequently flourish greatly and on the contrary they may decline on the return of the peace" (377). Yet Professor John finds in the wars against the rebellious American colonists (1775–1783) and the French (1793–1802, 1802–1805) "considerable counterbalancing factors to the war-time expansion of industry" which "on the whole, probably negative the advance of war." Though he cites the contraction of investment and fall in employment in the export industries in the first and the fall of the consumer goods industries in the second, a good case be made out for the stimuli of these as well (217).

Some industries are worth mentioning here. The manufacture of "Yorkshire cloths" which Herbert Heaton (187) saw as "especially suited for military garments" and which "enjoyed the favour of many European governments until the rise of the native industries dispensed with the need for the imported article" increased tenfold from 28,990 pieces in 1727 to 285,-851 in 1800 in several West Riding fulling mills. Though from 1750 to

1765 production actually dropped from 60,477½ pieces to 54,660 pieces, it increased during the American War, making a vast jump (172,588 to 285,851 pieces) during the French Revolutionary Wars. Here Heaton's study of Benjamin Gott (186) is especially revealing.

Amongst the firms which prospered making guns for the American War was Samuel Walker, who began making nails in the intervals between "teaching the school at Grenoside" near Rotherham. With his brothers the firm extended to making frying pans and guns: a role in which they attracted the attention of Thomas Paine, the man who virtually coined the title of the United States of America.

The early cotton industry, as Daniels (82) shows, is important too, affecting the growth of ports, as Darby (83) indicates. Eventually building materials (84), agriculture (228) follow suit.

Sheathing of ships with copper to prevent the worm and fouling was, according to A. H. John (219), common on ships in the African and West India trades by the 1720's, but according to J. R. Harris was still not common practice in 1761 (176). Certainly during the war of American Independence Sir Charles Middleton (279), the controller of the navy, was still pressing the matter on the First Lord, Lord Sandwich.

Instead of casting the cannon and drawing it to the rotating boring head, Wilkinson, the great ironmaster, cast his cannon solid and rotated as the cutter was fed against it. H. W. Dickinson (99) finds it "difficult to overestimate the importance of this invention" since it was "really the introduction of the guide principle into machine tools."

The war against the American colonies led to the cancellation of Wilkinson's patent (No. 1063) for solid casting and boring of cannon. Sir Lewis Namier shows (291) how Anthony Bacon, a lessor of all the mines within an area of 40 miles around Merthyr Tydvil, who had previously had an agreement with Wilkinson, prepared to cast them from his own works. Addis (1) gives an account of Bacon's partnership with Richard Crawshay, pointing out that Bacon requested the transfer of the contract to Francis Homfray at the end of the war and did not use it because he was suspected of supplying cannon to the American government as well as the British. Bacon also became one of the chief contractors for provisioning British troops in America. After he retired, a very wealthy man, he sold Dowlais, Cyfartha, Plymouth and Pen-y-Darran to Samuel Homfray and Richard Crawshay, who developed them still further.

Crawshay began to use the "puddling" process for purifying iron devised by Henry Cort, former Admiralty agent who had bought a foundry at Fareham in 1775 to do so (103). But Crawshay flourished, whereas Cort was ruined by his very connections with the Admiralty. His partner Adam Jellicoe, after abusing his trust as Deputy-Paymaster of seamen's wages, committed suicide, so Cort, in selling up to pay for Jellicoe's defalcations, had to allow his patent to lapse. This enabled Cort's now unpatented process to spread even more rapidly than ever before (12).

Another result of the American war was the reorganisation of the Ordnance Department. This was undertaken by Thomas Blomefield, a former Woolwich cadet who had served in the Navy at Quiberon Bay and in the

Army in the American war of independence returning, on being wounded, to become Superintendent of the Royal Brass Foundry. He inspected the fleet in 1799 and condemned no less than 496 guns (123). A good essay on the American war and its impact on the emergent United States is that by Brooke Hindle (194). The conflict provided an even greater fillip to the English copper industry (165 and 346), which became intensively occupied with providing the sheathing and bolts for ships. The chief supplier, Williams of Anglesea, also supplied dockyards in Holland, Spain and France. With France as an enemy, it was natural that such trade was forbidden by the Government in 1780. The French promptly set up their own rolling mills.

In addition to ship sheathing, copper was also needed for the boilers and tubes in the steam engines of Boulton and Watt (100), and demand for copper led to Watt's engine being used to work Cornish veins, which was hitherto uneconomic (354).

But above all as war intensified, and France, Spain and Holland came in against Britain, supplies of iron were cut off. So, as T. S. Ashton (15, 16) and Mantoux (268) show, great developments took place in ironmaking in Yorkshire and Derbyshire. When the war ended all these foundries began to experiment with water pipes, domestic stores, cast iron barges (like that launched by the Carron Ironworks on the Clyde Canal in 1789), or iron bridges (like that across Coalbrookdale). Above all iron cylinders for steam engines were bored by the 1774 patent that Wilkinson had devised for boring cannon. For their demands on the coal industry see Ashton and Sykes (11).

Prosper as they might through war orders, many of these manufacturers were by no means warlike—indeed the reverse. As Raistrick (333, 336) shows, a large number of them were Quakers, whilst Sir Gavin de Beer (98) insists the sciences were never at war.

Among the loyalists taken away by the British after Bunker Hill in 1776 was Benjamin Thompson, who later conducted an important series of experiments "to determine the most advantageous situation for the vent in firearms and to measure the velocities of bullets, and the recoil, under various circumstances." Practical experiments in the firing of guns during a cruise in the *Victory* and election to the Royal Society widened his experimental interests; he went on to design a frigate of some 1,000 tons, as well as a new signalling system for ships at sea.

As Under-Secretary of State in the American Department in 1780 he improved the design of "horse furniture and accoutrements" as well as the clothing of dragoons, obtaining the Copley Medal for experiments in this field. He then went to Munich where he established an iron foundry and continued to experiment making guns. Here he was struck by "the very considerable degree of heat which a brass cannon acquires in a short time in being bored, and with the still more intense heat of the metallic chips separated from it by the borer." This observation led him to discard the caloric theory of heat (i.e., that heat was a kind of fluid as held by Black, Lavoisier, and Dalton) and to redefine it as a form of motion. His main paper on this subject was published in the *Philosophical Transactions* in

1798, and sustained in papers later read before the *Institut National*. A good account of these, with a full bibliography setting the discovery in perspective, has been given by W. J. Sparrow (384); Rumford's work in establishing the Royal Institution of Great Britain in 1800 has been explored by T. Martin (271). A superb synthesis of recent work (much of it their own) is given by Musson and Robinson (290).

THE GREAT INCUBATOR OF CHANGE: THE WAR AGAINST FRANCE 1792–1815. The Napoleonic wars led Crawshay's works at Cyfartha and Merthyr Tydvil to become "by far the largest in this Kingdom; probably, indeed, the largest in Europe; and in that case, as far as we know the largest in the world." Addis (1) stresses that in addition to new inventions, war demand and the generalised use of steam power, improved communications—the Glamorgan canal was begun in 1791 and completed in 1798—helped as well. Trouble in Russian imports stimulated other English ironmakers even more so that by 1803 English iron was substituting for the first time for Russian and Swedish iron in the navy and other government services (13). A recent overview is by Hobsbawm (196). As the festschrift edited by L. S. Pressnell (326) indicates, Ashton (16) is still the authority, in addition to providing a good bibliography (14) and an estimate of the standard of living (17).

The impact of the war on Welsh agriculture is examined in a novel way by David Thomas (399). Its impact on the iron industry is examined by A. H. Birch (30). For the rise of Leeds see Heaton (186).

The influence of French on English science at this time is well described by Scott (364).

Two basic features of the English factory system appeared during the Napoleonic war—the principle of interchangeable parts and the assembly line. The first seems to have begun with the manufacture of ship's blocks by the Taylors of Southampton (313). Walter Taylor was also regarded as the inventor of the circular saw (101). But Tait, Marc, Isambard, Brunel and Maudsley generally get the credit for the machines in the Portsmouth dockyard which, on 24 March 1805, enabled the Admiralty to discontinue their contracts with Taylor and Dunsterville (146). Maudsley's went on to become the nursery of the great Victorian engineers. Another illustration of the importance of the principle of interchangeable parts is seen in the "Brown Bess" which up to 1799 was often made in Germany, though some were made by gunsmiths in the Minories or in Dublin. So confusing was it to match the outside of the barrel with the bayonet ring that in 1812 the government took over the small arms factory at Enfield to make barrels; by 1859 it was a monopolist in the trade (122).

The second, the assembly line, was according to Siegfried Giedion (145) used in the victualling office at Deptford. He illustrates and quotes from *The Book of Trades, or Library of the Useful Arts* (London, 1804) to show how moulders, markers, splitters, chuckers and depositors working at specialised tasks deposited 70 biscuits a minute *"with the regularity of a clock,* the clacking of the peel, operating like the motion of the pendulum." By 1833 this was mechanised, becoming what Giedion calls "probably the first assembly line in the food industries."

Other imaginative deployments of new techniques were Vincent Lunardi's balloon ascents (256) from the artillery ground at Moorfields (where guns had been cast for over a century). His scientific adviser was the chemist, George Fordyce, who provided the hydrogen apparatus. Three weeks later another chemist, John Sadler, became the first known Englishman to make a balloon ascent (198). Sadler abandoned ballooning to join the Admiralty where he became Inspector of Chemistry in 1807. After him the post was suppressed.

Just as the French formed a balloonist corps which helped the revolutionary armies to win its victories, so Rear-Admiral Sir Charles Knowles suggested that balloons should be used from ships to observe enemy preparations in Brest and other ports "without the expense of intelligence by spies" (94). Another imaginative use of balloons was made by Lieut. (later Admiral) Lord Cochran who towed them behind his brig *Pallas* to release pamphlets along the French coast.

More directly concerned with the artillery was another technological device: the rocket. Devised by a member of the Royal Laboratory, Woolwich, Sir William Congreve, in 1808, the rocket was so successful that its inventor was directed to form two rocket companies, serving with one of them at Leipzig in 1813 and Southern France in 1814 (103). Congreve's rockets were also deployed against the Americans at Bladensburg and Baltimore in 1814, as Francis Scott Key records in *The Star-Spangled Banner.* Congreve's father, who was the director of the laboratory, was an inventor too. In 1793 he removed the two opposing sails of a windmill and used the remaining two as a semaphore.

Congreve and his father, with Admirals Keith and Exmouth, were also members in 1811 of the Prince Regent's committee which examined Cochrane's plan for asphyxiating the garrison of Cherbourg by sulphur fumes. The project reappeared in 1845 and again at the outbreak of the Crimean War, but was rejected by the Ordnance Department (122). Indeed Cochrane's inventiveness was inexhaustible. He had previously (11 April 1809) attacked the French Fleet in the Basque Roads with eight fire ships and three floating explosive hulks. He was later, as an admiral in the Greek Navy (1827), to employ steam warships, and when reinstated in the British Navy, to urge the adoption of screw-propellers (68).

Yet another invention was the "Artillery" wheel with iron tyres, devised by Samuel Miller (98). This, together with the contemporary patenting of the laminated elliptical or semi-laminated springs of Obadiah Elliot for carriages, helped the concomitant development of the steam road vehicles pioneered by Murdoch and Trevithick.

Mechanical semaphores by posts with three movable arms were also devised by the brothers Chappe in 1792. Four years later shutters containing letters on both sides were devised by Lord George Murray for the transmission of code signals. Murray became the first director of telegraphs at the Admiralty and set up a chain of 24 stations at three-mile intervals from London to Portsmouth.

To protect British merchant shipping from French privateers and enable the fleet to deploy more quickly, the government accepted Thomas Telford's suggestion (made originally by Watt and Rennie) of a Caledonian Canal from Fort William to Inverness (348).

The "social retrogression and evils which marked the industrial revolution" were attributed by Daniels (82) primarily to "the war in which the country was engaged," but Ashton (16) describes the war orders for cannon, gun-carriages, shot, firearms, swords and bayonets as "Food for the Gods" adding "the industry grew in proportion as the need for munitions increased." So Lecky was amply justified in saying "England might well place the statues of Watt and Arkwright by the side of Wellington and Nelson." Spending up to £100 million a year and creating by 1816 a national debt of £885 million, England was only able to carry the war through to a triumphant conclusion "largely if not mainly" (as Lecky said) "due to the cotton mill and the steam engine" (238).

As Mahan said the contestants "meet in a deadly strife in which no weapon was drawn." The Imperial soldiers were turned into coast guardsmen to shut out Britain from her markets: the British ships became revenue cutters to prohibit the trade of France (267). It is especially interesting, in view of the theme of centralisation stressed at the beginning of this note, that Dr. Hobsbawn should argue that the Industrial Revolution would not have occurred without a monopoly of the world export markets, and that that was assured by a series of aggressive wars between 1702 and 1815 which gave Britain a colonial empire unrivalled by that of any other European power.

Perhaps the most effective instrument for shaping social structure emerged in 1799: the Income Tax. Like all previous forms of direct taxation—Danegeld, scutage, taxes on movables, poll taxes, ship money, taxes on female students, culminating in others on horses, on houses and windows, on hair powder, on dogs, on clocks and watches—it was generated by wartime needs. Imposed by Pitt in 1799 it was, as B. E. V. Sabine remarks in his authoritative study, "the tax that beat Napoleon." It survived to become the most powerful weapon for redistribution of the national income (359).

Overseas trade has been dealt with by a group edited by C. N. Parkinson (315). Other facets of the war, like the press, have been explored by A. Aspinall (18) and Laws (237), the development of civil engineering by Rolt (351), the use of foreign regiments by C. Atkinson (19), farmers' tools by G. E. Fussell and C. Goodman (142), iron by Birch (30), firearms by Carman (49), colonies by Carrington (50), zinc smelting by Cocks and Walters (70) and labour supply by J. D. Chambers (54).

AGENDA FOR FURTHER WORK. (1) Having been opened up by the historians of science and technology, the common ground existing between economic and military historians (each, in their way, concerned with polemics) needs exploring and surveying. From the breeding of horses (neglected since Ridgeway (345) in 1905) to the rise of chemical industries (saltpetre, pitch, turpentine, bay salt and naphtha) many linkages with the army and navy are traceable in the Pipe Rolls. Therefore some graduate students of medieval military history might undertake vertical (i.e. evolutionary) studies of particular industries, in the light of a series of wars, whilst others might undertake horizontal (i.e. interaction) studies of the impact of individual wars along the whole line of military supplies and technology. There is scope for "prevised" as well as "provided" technologies. Yet other students could supplement these studies by examining the interaction of tactics and technology following the helpful suggestions of Lynn White, Jr. (421). A fifth field for study contains the reactions of individual wars on insurance, trade, and other social developments. Contemporary military historians need to plot interactions rather than describe actions. They must be technologically as well as tactically minded, progressing beyond the robust empiricism of Major-General J. F. C. Fuller (140) or Montross (283) and rounding out the suggestive contours of Preston, Wise and Werner (327).

(2) Tudor, Stuart and Hanoverian specialists can, with the greater material at their disposal, follow the fruitful example of, amongst others, A. H. John (216, 217, 218), and examine the wider social impact of wars on such problems as banking, credit, and the rise of standardisation. E.g., did the need for standardised parts become apparent only in the sixteenth century as Carman (49) suggests in his account of the caliver? How far was the "experimental method" facilitated by the work of Colonel Wemyss (103) in the seventeenth century or of the Duke of Richmond at the end of the eighteenth? Can a "technical fall out" from the work of technocrats like this be discerned? Can we trace operational research before the establishment of centres like Lambeth, Woolwich and Shoeburyness?

(3) In addition to intensive work on Army Lists and Commission Registers as listed by Dalton (81), studies of the hospitals (e.g. Haslar) and other institutions (e.g. Woolwich) under the navy or army are badly needed to examine the area and method of recruitment, and types of occupation undertaken on leaving. Can such personnel be shown to have helped in the dissemination of scientific knowledge in the eighteenth century? From this data hypotheses and concepts revealed by the role of the army in developing countries today can also be tested. When and to what extent did the army and navy provide avenues of mobility, serve as instruments of social sedation, sustainers of researchers, or centres of rehearsal for solving social problems?

(4) So too detailed biographical theses on the personnel attached to these institutions, and to the army and navy in general are needed. For example, John Arderne, a fourteenth-century army physician, proposed incendiary-carrying dogs and birds, whilst James Lind, the famous eighteenth-century naval physician, devised a rifled gun with telescopic sights. These studies could be collated as E. G. R. Taylor has done (397, 398).

(5) From 1369 when Chaucer served in France, to 1793 when S. T. Coleridge enlisted in the 15th dragoons as Silas Tomkyn Comberback, many of the great names in English literature have had experience of the

armed forces. How did such service affect them? We also need more studies of the type of Commander Charles Robinson (349), which indicates the esteem in which various writers held the forces? We also need the assistance of bibliographers to continue the type of work begun by Cockle (69).

(6) Generalised, and at times intense, apprehensions of the intentions (as opposed to the actions) of foreign powers has influenced home policy. It has also prompted close scrutiny and comparison of home institutions and the assimilation and adaptation of foreign practices. This field is of particular interest to the present author.

(7) Lastly, and perhaps most difficult of all, how has the general tone of life (sanitation, cleanliness, social discipline) been affected by the needs of the army and navy in particular periods?

BIBLIOGRAPHY

1. Addis, John P. *The Crawshay Dynasty: a study in industrial organisation and development 1765–1867.* Cardiff: The University of Wales Press, 1957, pp. 7–8.
2. Aitchison, Leslie. *A History of Metals.* London: Macdonald & Evans, 1960, II, pp. 420–471.
3. Albion, R. G. *Forests and Sea Power: the timber problem of the Royal Navy 1652–1826.* Cambridge, Mass.: Harvard Economic Studies, 1926.
4. *Ambix, The Journal of the Society for the Study of Alchemy and Early Chemistry.* Cambridge: Heffer, 1937.
5. Anderson, R. C. "French Masts and Spars in 1780." *The Mariners' Mirror,* XLV (1959), pp. 224–6.
6. Anderson, R. C. *A List of English Men of War 1509–1649.* Society for Nautical Research, Occasional Publications, Vol. VII, 1959.
7. Andrews, Kenneth R. *Elizabethan Privateering.* Cambridge University Press, 1964.
8. *Annals of Science. A quarterly review of the history of science and technology since the Renaissance.* London: Taylor & Francis, 1936.
9. Arenhold, L. "Ships Earlier Than 1300." *The Mariners' Mirror,* I (1911).
10. Ashton, Robert. *The Crown and the Money Market 1603–1640.* Oxford: University Press, 1960.
11. Ashton, T. S. and J. Sykes. *The Coal Industry of the Eighteenth Century.* Manchester: Publications of the University of Manchester, Economic History Series No. 5, 1929.
12. Ashton, T. S. *An Economic History of England: the 18th century.* London: Methuen & Co., 1955.
13. Ashton, T. S. *An Eighteenth-Century Industrialist: Peter Stubs of Warrington, 1756–1806.* Manchester University Press, 1939.
14. Ashton, T. S. *The Industrial Revolution: a study in bibliography.*

London: Economic History Society, Bibliographies and Pamphlets No. 3, 1937.

15. Ashton, T. S. *The Industrial Revolution*. London: Geoffrey Cumberlege, Oxford University Press, 1948.

16. Ashton, T. S. *Iron and Steel in the Industrial Revolution*. 2nd ed. Manchester University Press, 1920, 1951.

17. Ashton, T. S. "The Standard of Life of the Workers in England 1790–1830." *Journal of Economic History*, Supplement 9 (1949), pp. 19–38a.

18. Aspinall, A. *Politics and the Press, c. 1780–1850*. London: Home and Val Thal, 1949.

19. Atkinson, C. "Foreign Regiments in the British Army, 1793–1802." *Society for Army Historical Research, Journal* XXI (1942), XXII (1943–4), pp. 2–14, 45–52, 107–115, 132–142, 187–197, 234–50, 265–76, 313–324.

20. Bagley, J. J. *Life in Medieval England*. London: Batsford, 1960.

21. Bain, Joseph. *The Edwards in Scotland 1296–1377*. Edinburgh: David Douglas, 1901.

21a. Balleine, G. R. *A Biographical Dictionary of Jersey*. London: Staples Press, 1948.

22. Barbour, V. "Marine Risks and Insurance in the Seventeenth Century." *Journal of Economic and Business History*, I (1929–1930), pp. 580–588.

23. Barley, M. W. *Lincolnshire and the Fens*. London: Batsford, 1952.

24. Baron, E. M. *The Scottish Wars of Independence*. Inverness: R. Carruthers, 1934.

25. Bauer, P. T. *The Rubber Industry*. London: Longmans, Green & Co., 1948.

26. Bean, J. M. W. "The Percies and Their Estates in Scotland." *Archaeologia Aeliana*, 4th Series, XXXV (1957), pp. 91–9.

27. Beckett, J. C. *The Making of Modern Ireland 1603–1923*. London: Faber & Faber, 1966.

28. Beresford, M. W. and G. R. J. Jones. *Leeds and Its Region*. Leeds: Leeds Local Executive Committee for the British Association for the Advancement of Science, 1967.

29. Bernal, J. D. *Science in History*. 3rd ed. London: C. A. Watts & Co., 1965.

30. Birch, Alan. "The British Iron Industry in the Napoleonic Wars" in his *Economic History of the Iron and Steel Industry*. London: Frank Cass, 1967, pp. 44–46.

31. Bloch, Marc. *Feudal Society*. Trans. by L. A. Manyon with a preface by M. M. Foster. London: Routledge & Kegan Paul, 1962.

32. Bonsor, W., ed. *An Anglo-Saxon and Celtic Bibliography (A.D.450–1087)*. Oxford: Blackwell, 1957.

33. Bovill, E. W. "Queen Elizabeth's Gunpowder." *Mariners' Mirror*, XXXIII (1947), pp. 179–186.

34. Bowden, Peter J. *The Wool Trade in Tudor and Stuart England*. London: Macmillan & Co., 1962.

35. Bowden, Witt. *Industrial Society in England Towards the End of the Eighteenth Century.* New York: Macmillan, 1925.
36. Boyle, Vernon C. "West Country Shipping and Practice in the Days of Wooden Ships." *Mariners' Mirror,* XLV (1959), pp. 227–233.
37. Braun, H. S. *The English Castle.* London: B. T. Batsford, 1936.
38. Bromberg, E. I. "Wales and the Medieval Slave Trade." *Speculum.* XVII (1942), pp. 263–9.
39. Bromley, J. S. "The French Privateering War" in H. E. Bell and R. L. Ollard, *Historical Essays 1600–1750.* London: A. C. Black, 1964.
40. Broome, Dorothy. "Exchequer Migrations to York in the Thirteenth and Fourteenth Centuries" in A. G. Little and F. M. Powicke, eds., *Essays in Medieval History Presented to T. F. Tout,* pp. 291–300.
41. Brown, P. Hume. *History of Scotland.* Cambridge University Press, 1899–1909. 3 vols.
42. Brown, R. A. "A List of Castles, 1154–1216." *English Historical Review,* LXXIV (1959), p. 249.
43. Bruce, A. K. "On the Origin of the Internal Combustion Engine." *Engineer,* Cl, XXIV (1942).
44. Burns, William. *The Scottish War of Independence.* Glasgow: James Maclehose, 1874.
45. Burrows, Montague. *History of the Cinque Ports.* London: Longman & Co., 1888.
46. *The Cambridge Economic History.* Cambridge University Press, 1941, Vol. II, 1942, Vol. III.
47. Campbell, R. H. "The Anglo-Scottish Union of 1707 II. The Economic Consequences." *The Economic History Review, XVI* (1963–4), pp. 468–477. See also his *Canon.* Edinburgh, 1960.
48. Cardwell, D. S. L. "Power Technologies and the Advance of Science 1700–1825." *Technology and Culture,* VI (1965), pp. 188–207.
49. Carman, W. Y. *The History of Firearms.* London: Routledge & Kegan Paul, 1955.
50. Carrington, C. E. *The British Overseas: Exploits of a Nation of Shopkeepers.* Cambridge University Press, 1956.
51. Cartwright, A. P. *The Dynamite Company.* London: Macdonald, 1964.
52. Chalklin, C. W. *Seventeenth-Century Kent.* London: Longmans, Green & Co., 1965.
53. Chaloner, W. H. "Food and Drink in British History: a bibliographical guide." *Amateur Historian,* Summer 1960, pp. 315–9.
54. Chambers, J. D. "Enclosure and Labour Supply in the Industrial Revolution." *Economic History Review,* 2nd Series, 5 (1953), pp. 319–43.
55. Chambers, J. D. *Nottinghamshire in the Eighteenth Century: a study in life and labour under the squirearchy.* London: P. S. King, 1932.
56. Chambers, J. D. "The Vale of Trent 1670–1800." *Economic History Review,* Supplement 3 (1957).

57. Childe, V. G. *Prehistoric Communities of the British Isles.* 2nd ed. London: W. & R. Chambers, 1947.

58. *Chymia: Annual Studies in the History of Chemistry.* Oxford: 1948—.

59. Clapham, J. H. *An Economic History of Modern Britain.* Cambridge University Press, 1926.

60. Clark, G. N. *The Dutch Alliance and the War Against France Trade 1688–1697.* Manchester University Press, 1923.

61. Clark, G. N. *Science and Social Welfare in the Age of Newton.* 2nd ed. Oxford: Clarendon Press, 1949.

62. Clark, G. N. *War and Society in the Seventeenth Century.* Cambridge University Press, 1958.

63. Clark, G. N. and Barbara M. Franks. *Guide to English Commercial Statistics 1696–1782.* London: Royal Historical Society, 1938.

64. Close, Colonel Sir Charles. *The Early Years of the Ordnance Survey.* Reprinted from the *Royal Engineers Journal.* Published by the Institution of Royal Engineers, 1926.

65. Clow, Archibald and Nan L. *The Chemical Revolution.* London: Batchworth, 1946.

66. Clow, Archibald and Nan L. "The Timber Famine and the Development of Technology." *Annals of Science,* XII (1957), pp. 85–102.

67. Clowes, G. S. Laird. *Sailing Ships, Their History and Development.* London: HMSO, 1936. A Science Museum monograph.

68. Cochrane, Thomas, Tenth Earl of Dundonald. *The Autobiography of a Seaman.* London: Richard Bentley, 1861.

69. Cockle, M. J. D. *A Bibliography of Military Books up to 1642.* London: Simpkin, Marshall, 1900, reprinted 1957.

70. Cocks, E. J. and B. Walters. *A History of the Zinc Smelting Industry in Britain.* London: Harrap, 1968.

71. Coghlan, H. H. *Notes on Prehistoric and Early Iron in the Old World.* Oxford: Pitt Rivers Museum, Occasional Papers on Technology, No. 8, 1956.

72. Coleman, D. C. "Labour in the English Economy of the Seventeenth Century." *The Economic History Review,* 2nd Series, VIII (1956).

73. Coleman, D. C. "Naval Dockyards Under the Later Stuarts." *Economic History Review,* 2nd Series, VI, No. 2 (1953).

74. Conisbee, L. R. *A Bedfordshire Bibliography.* Bedford: Historical Society, 1962.

75. Corbett, Sir Julian. *England in the Seven Years' War.* London: Longmans, Green & Co., 1907.

76. Cordeaux, E. H. and D. H. Merry. *A Bibliography of Printed Works Relating to Oxfordshire (excluding the University and City of Oxford).* Oxford: Historical Society, 1955.

77. Court, W. H. B. *The Rise of the Midland Industries, 1600–1838.* London: Oxford University Press, 1938.

78. Crombie, A. C., ed. *Scientific Change, Historical Studies in the Intel-*

lectual Social and Technical Conditions for Scientific Discovery and Technical Invention, from Antiquity to the Present. London: Heinemann, 1963.

78a. Crone, John Smyth. *A Concise Dictionary of Irish Biography*. Dublin: Talbot Press, 1928.

79. Crump, W. B., ed. "The Leeds Woollen Industry." *Publications of the Thoresby Society*. Leeds, Vol. 32, 1931.

80. Curtis, E. E. *The Organisation of the British Army in the American Revolution*. London: Humphrey Milford, 1926.

81. Dalton, Charles. *English Army Lists and Commission Registers 1661–1714*. London: Eyre & Spottiswoode, 1892–1904. 6 vols.

82. Daniels, G. W. *The Early English Cotton Industry*. Publications of the University of Manchester, Historical Series, No. 36, 1920.

83. Darby, H. C. *An Historical Geography of England Before A.D. 1800*. Cambridge University Press, 1948.

84. Davey, Noonan. *A History of Building Materials*. London: Phoenix House, 1961.

85. Davie, Donald. *The Language of Science and the Language of Literature*. London: Sheed and Ward, 1963.

86. Davies, C. S. L. "The Administration of the Royal Navy Under Henry VIII: the origin of the Navy Board." *English Historical Review*, LXXX (1965), pp. 268–288.

87. Davies, C. S. L. "Provisions for Armies 1509–50: a study in the effectiveness of early Tudor government." *Economic History Review*, XVII (1964–5), pp. 234–248.

88. Davies, K. G. *The Royal African Company*. London: Longmans, 1957.

89. Davies, O. *Roman Mines in Europe*. Oxford: Clarendon Press, 1935.

90. Davies, T. L. and J. R. Ware. "Early Chinese Military Pyrotechnics." *Journal of Chemical Education*, XXIV (1947), pp. 522–37.

91. Davis, Ralph. *The Rise of the English Shipping Industry in the Seventeenth and Eighteenth Centuries*. London: Macmillan, 1962.

92. Davis, Ralph. *The Trade and Shipping of Hull 1500–1700*. East Yorkshire Local History Series, No. 17, Micklegate, 1964.

93. Davis, Ralph Henry Carless. "A Catalogue of Mason's Marks as an Aid to Architectural History." *Journal of the British Archaeological Association*, Series 3, Vol. 17 (1954), pp. 43–76.

94. Davy, J. B. *Interpretive History of Flight*. London: HMSO, 1948.

95. Deane, Phyllis and W. A. Cole. *British Economic Growth 1688–1959*. Cambridge University Press, 1962.

96. Deane, Phyllis. *The First Industrial Revolution*. Cambridge University Press, 1965.

97. de Beer, E. S., ed. *The Diary of John Evelyn*. Oxford: Clarendon Press, 6 vols., 1955.

98. de Beer, Sir Gavin. *The Sciences Were Never at War*. London: Thomas Nelson, 1960.

99. Dickinson, H. W. *John Wilkinson, Ironmaster*. Ulverstone: Hume Mitchen, 1914.

100. Dickinson, H. W. *A Short History of the Steam Engine*. Cambridge: Printed for Babcock & Wilcox Ltd. at the University Press, 1935.

101. Dickinson, H. W. "The Taylors of Southampton: their ships' blocks, circular saws and ships' pumps." *Newcomen Society Transactions*, XXIX (1953–5), pp. 169–178.

102. Dickinson, W. C. *Scotland from the Earliest Times to 1603*. London: Thomas Nelson & Sons, 1961.

103. *The Dictionary of National Biography* (Oxford University Press, 1903–61) *together with Dictionary of National Biography corrections and additions culmulated from the Bulletin of the Institute of Historical Research 1923–1963*.

104. Dietz, Frederick C. *English Government Finance 1485–1558*. Urbana: *University of Illinois Studies in the Social Sciences*, Vol. IX, No. 3, 1920.

105. Dietz, Frederick C. *The Exchequer in Elizabeth's Reign. ibid.*, Vol. VIII, No. 2, 1923.

106. Dietz, Frederick C. *Finances of Edward VI and Mary*. Northampton, Mass.: *Smith College Studies in History*, Vol. III, No. 2, 1918.

107. Dietz, Frederick C. *The Receipts and Issues of the Exchequer During the Reigns of James I and Charles I. ibid.*, Vol. XIII, No. 4, 1928.

108. Dobrée, Bonamy. *The Theme of Patriotism in the Poetry of the Early Eighteenth-Century London. Warton Lectures on English Poetry*. British Academy, 1949.

109. Dodd, A. H. *The Industrial Revolution in North Wales*. Cardiff: University of Wales Press Board, 1933.

110. Dodd, A. H. "Mr. Myddleton, the Merchant of Tower Street," in S. T. Bindoff, J. Hurstfield and C. H. Williams, ed., *Elizabethan Government and Society*. London: The Athlone Press, 1961.

111. Dodd, A. H. *Studies in Stuart Wales*. Cardiff: University of Wales Press, 1952.

112. Donald, Maxwell Bruce. *Elizabethan Copper, the History of the Company of Mines Royal 1568–1605*. London: Pergamon Press, 1955.

113. Donald, Maxwell Bruce. *Elizabethan Monopolies. The History of the Company of Mineral and Battery Works from 1565 to 1604*. Edinburgh and London: Oliver and Boyd, 1961. Maps and plates.

114. Doucet, R. *Les Institutions de la France au XVIe siècle*. Paris, 1948.

115. Eager, A. R. *A Guide to Irish Bibliographical Material*. London: Library Association, 1964.

116. Edwards, J. G. "The Normans and the Welsh March." *Proceedings of the British Academy*, XLII (1956), pp. 155–177.

117. Ehrenberg, Richard. *Capital and Finance in the Age of the Renaissance*. London: Jonathan Cape, 1928.

118. Ehrman, John. *The Navy in the War of William III 1689–1697: its state and direction*. Cambridge University Press, 1957.

119. Escales, Richard R. *Die Explosivstoffe.* Leipzig, 1904, 1908–15.
120. Evelyn, Helen. *History of the Evelyn Family.* London: E. Nash, 1915.
121. Falls, Cyril. *Elizabeth's Irish Wars.* London: Methuen & Co., 1950.
122. Ffoulkes, C. J. *Arms and Armament: a historical survey of the weapons of the British Army.* London: G. Harrap & Co., 1945, p. 24.
123. Ffoulkes, C. J. *The Gunfounders of England.* Cambridge: University Press, 1937.
124. Fell, A. *The Early Iron Industry of Furness and District.* Ulverston: Hume Kitchin, 1908.
125. Ferguson, Eugene S. "Contributions to Bibliography in the History of Technology." Parts I, II and III. *Technology and Culture,* 3 (1962), pp. 73–84, 167–174.
126. Finberg, H. P. R. "The Doomsday Ploughman." *English Historical Review,* LVI (1941), pp. 67–71.
127. Fitton, R. S. and A. P. Wadsworth. *The Strutts and the Arkwrights 1758–1830.* Manchester University Press, 1958.
128. Fitzpatrick, Brian. *British Imperialism and Australia 1783–1833: an economic history of Australasia.* London: George Allen & Unwin, 1939.
129. Flinn, M. W. *An Economic and Social History of Britain 1066– 1939.* London: Macmillan, 1961.
130. Flinn, M. W. "Industry and Technology in the Derwent Valley of Durham and Northumberland in the Eighteenth Century." *Newcomen Society Transactions,* XXIX (1935–5), p. 262.
131. Flinn, M. W. *Men of Iron: the Crowleys in the early iron industry.* Edinburgh: Edinburgh University Press, 1962.
132. Flinn, M. W. *The Origins of the Industrial Revolution.* London: Longmans, Green, 1966.
133. Flinn, M. W. "Williams Wood and the Coke Smelting Process." *Transactions of the Newcomen Society,* XXXIV (1961–2), pp. 55– 71.
134. Flinn, M. W. and A. Birch. "The English Steel Industry Before 1856" *The Yorkshire Bulletin of Economic and Social Research,* VI (1954), pp. 166–167.
135. Forbes, Eric G. "The Foundation and Early Development of *The Nautical Almanac." Journal of the Institute of Navigation,* XVIII (1965), pp. 391–401.
136. Forward, E. A. "Simon Goodrich and His Work as an Engineer, Pt. I, 1796–1805." *Transactions of the Newcomen Society,* III (1922– 3), pp. 1–15.
137. Franklin, B. *The Papers of Benjamin Franklin.* L. W. Larabee, ed. Vol. 8. New Haven: Yale University Press, 1965.
138. Fryde, E. B. "Loans to the English Crown 1328–1331." *English Historical Review,* IXX (1955), pp. 198–21.
139. Fryde, E. B. "Materials for the Study of Edward III's Credit Operations 1327–1348." *Bulletin of the Institute of Historical Research,* XXII (1949), pp. 105–38, XXIII (1950), pp. 1–30.

140. Fuller, Major General J. F. C. *Armaments and History*. London: Eyre & Spottiswoode, 1946.

141. Fussell, G. E. *The Farmers Tools: from A.D. 1500–1900*. London: Andrew Melrose, 1952.

142. Fussell, G. E. and C. Goodman. "Eighteenth Century Estimates of British Sheep and Wool Production." *Agricultural History,* IV (1930), pp. 131–151.

143. Gale, W. K. V. *The British Iron and Steel Industry: a technical history*. Newton Abbott: David and Charles, 1967. See also his *Black Country Iron Industry*. London: Iron and Steel Institute, 1966.

144. Gibbs, F. W. "Itinerant Lectures in Natural Philosophy." *Ambix,* vi (1960), pp. 111–117.

145. Giedion, Siegfried. *Mechanisation Takes Command: a contribution to Anonymous History*. New York: Oxford University Press, 1948.

146. Gilbert, K. R. *The Portsmouth Block-Making Machinery, A Pioneering Enterprise in Mass Production*. London: H.M.S.O., 1965. A Science Museum monograph.

147. Gill, Charles S. *The Old Wooden Walls; Their Construction, Equipment etc. Being an Abridged Edition of Falconer's Celebrated Marine Dictionary*. London: W. & G. Foyle, 1930.

148. Gill, Conrad. *The Rise of the Irish Linen Industry*. Oxford: Clarendon Press, 1925.

149. Gille, Paul. "Les Mathematiques et la construction navale." *Archives Internationales d'Histoire des Sciences,* viii (1956), pp. 57–63.

150. Gillispie, Charles Colston, ed. *A Diderot Pictorial Encyclopaedia of Trades and Industry. Manufacturing and the technical arts in plates selected from L'Encyclopédie, ou Dictionnaire Raisonné des Sciences, des Arts et des Métiers of Denis Diderot*. New York: Dover, 1959. 485 plates.

151. Glover, R. "English Warfare in 1066." *English Historical Review,* lxvii (1952), pp. 1–18.

152. Goodrich, Carrington L. and Feng Chia-sheng. "The Early Development of Firearms in China." *Isis,* xxxvi (1946), 114–123, and addenda and corrigenda, 250.

153. Gough, John Wiedhofft. *The Mines of Mendip*. 2nd rev. ed. Newton Abbott: David and Charles, 1967.

154. Gough, John Wiedhofft. *Sir Hugh Middleton, Entrepreneur and Engineer*. Oxford: Clarendon Press, 1964.

155. Gough, John Wiedhofft. *The Superlative Prodigall: a life of Thomas Bushell*. Bristol: University of Bristol, 1932.

156. Gould, Rupert T. *The Marine Chronometer: its history and development* with a foreword by Sir Frank W. Dyson. London: The Holland Press, 1960.

157. Gross, Charles. *A Bibliography of British Municipal History Including Gilds and Parliamentary Representation*. 2nd ed. with a preface by G. H. Martin. Leicester University Press, 1966.

158. Gunther, R. T. *Early Science in Oxford*. Oxford: University Press for the Oxford Historical Society, 1923–1945. 12 vols.

159. Guttman, Oscar. *The Manufacture of Explosives: a theoretical and practical treatise on the history, the physical and chemical properties and the manufacture of explosives.* London: The Specialist Series, Symons & Co., later Whittaker & Co., and Sir I. Pitman & Sons, 1895.

160. Hale, John. "War and Public Opinion in the Fifteenth and Sixteenth Centuries." *Past and Present,* No. 22 (July 1962), pp. 18–35.

161. Hall, Alfred Rupert. *Ballistics in the Seventeenth Century. A Study in the relation of science and war with reference principally to England.* Cambridge University Press, 1952.

162. Hall, Alfred Rupert. "Military Technology," in C. Singer *et alii* (q.v.).

163. Hall, Alfred Rupert and Marie Boas Hall. *The Correspondence of Henry Oldenburg.* Madison: University of Wisconsin Press, Vol. I, 1941–1962, 1965.

164. Hall, Alfred Rupert. *The Scientific Revolution 1500–1800. The Formation of the Modern Scientific Attitude.* 2nd ed. London: Longmans, Green & Co., 1962.

165. Hamilton, H. *The English Brass and Copper Industries to 1800.* London: Longmans & Co., 1926.

166. Hamilton, H. *The Industrial Revolution in Scotland.* London: Clarendon Press, 1932.

167. Hamilton, Stanley B. "Continental Influences on British Civil Engineering up to 1800." *Archives Internationales d'Histoire des Sciences.*

168. Hanham, H. J. "Some Neglected Sources of Bibliographical Information: county biographical dictionaries, 1890–1914." *Bulletin of the Institute of Historical Research,* XXXIV (1961), pp. 55–66.

169. Hans, Nicholas. *New Trends in Education in the Eighteenth Century.* London: Routledge & Kegan Paul, 1951.

170. Hanson, Laurence William. *Contemporary Sources for British and Irish Economic History 1701–1750.* Cambridge University Press, 1963.

171. Hanson, Laurence William. *Government and the Press 1695–1763.* Oxford University Press, 1936.

172. Harding, Louis Allen. *A Brief History of the Art of Navigation.* New York: The William Frederick Press, 1952.

173. Hargreaves, E. L. *The National Debt.* London: Frank Cass & Co., Ltd., 1966.

174. Harper, Lawrence A. *The English Navigation Laws. A Seventeenth-Century Experiment in Social Engineering.* New York: Columbia University, 1939.

175. Harries, F. J. *The Welsh Elizabethans.* Pontypridd: Glamorgan County Times, 1924.

176. Harris, J. R. *The Copper King. a biography of Thomas Williams of Llanedan.* Liverpool University Press, 1964.

177. Harris, J. R. "Copper and Shipping in the Eighteenth Century." *Economic History Review,* 2nd Series, XIX (1966), pp. 550–568.

178. Harris, J. R. "The Newcomen Engine on Merseyside." *Historical Society of Lancashire and Cheshire,* cvi (1955), p. 109.
179. Harriss, G. L. "The Struggle for Calais: an aspect of the rivalry between Lancaster and York." *English Historical Review,* IXXV (1960), pp. 30–53.
180. Hart, C. E. *The Free Miners of the Royal Forest of Dean and Hundred of St. Briavels.* Gloucester: British Publishing Co., 1953.
181. Hartley, Sir Harold. *The Royal Society: its origins and founders.* London: Royal Society, 1960.
182. Hay, Denys. "Booty in Border Warfare." *Transactions of the Dumfriesshire and Galloway Natural History and Antiquarian Society,* 3rd Series, XXXI (1952–3), pp. 145–66.
183. Hay, Denys. "Division of the Spoils of War in Fourteenth-Century England." *Transactions of the Royal Historical Society,* 5th Series, IV, 1954, pp. 91–109.
184. Hay, Denys. *Europe. The Emergence of an Idea.* Edinburgh University Press. Studies in History, Philosophy and Economics, No. 7, 1957.
185. Hay, Denys, ed. *The Renaissance Debate.* New York: Holt, Rinehart and Winston, 1965.
186. Heaton, Herbert. "Benjamin Gott and the Industrial Revolution in Yorkshire." *Economic History Review,* iii (1931).
187. Heaton, Herbert. *The Yorkshire Woolen and Worsted Industries From the Earliest Times up to the Industrial Revolution.* 2nd ed. Oxford: Clarendon Press, 1965, p. 147.
188. Hepworth, Philip. *How to Find Out in History.* Oxford: Pergamon Press, 1966.
189. Hessen, B. "The Social and Economic Roots in Newton's *Principia,*" in *Science at the Cross Roads.* London: Kniga, 1931.
190. Hewitt, H. J. *The Organisation of War under Edward III.* Manchester University Press, 1968.
191. Hill, J. E. C. *The Century of Revolution, 1603–1714.* London: Nelson, 1966.
192. Hime, Henry William Lovett. *Gunpowder and Ammunition: their origin and progress.* London: Longmans & Co., 1904.
193. Himes, Norman Edwin. *Medical History of Contraception.* Washington, D.C.: U.S.A. National Committee on Maternal Health, 1936.
194. Hindle, Brooke. *The Pursuit of Science in Revolutionary America.* Chapel Hill, North Carolina: Institute of Early American History and Culture, Williamsburg, Virginia, 1956, pp. 219–247.
195. Hinton, R. W. K. *The Eastland Trade and the Common Weal in the Seventeenth Century.* Cambridge University Press, 1959, p. 95.
196. Hobsbawn, E. J. *Industry and Empire.* London: Weidenfeld & Nicholson, 1968.
197. Hodgen, Margaret T. *Change and History: a study of the dated distributions of technological innovations in England.* New York: Viking Fund Publications in Anthropology, (Wenner Gren Foundation for Anthropological Research), 1954, pp. 171–202.

198. Hodgson, J. E. *The History of Aeronautics in Great Britain from the Earliest Times to the Latter Half of the Nineteenth Century.* London: Humphrey Milford, 1924.

199. Hogg, O. F. G. *The Royal Arsenal: its background, origin and subsequent history.* London: Oxford University Press, 1963. 2 vols.

200. Hollister, C. Warren. *The Military Organisation of Norman England.* Oxford: Clarendon Press, 1965.

201. Hood, Peter. *How Time is Measured.* London: Geoffrey Cumberlege, Oxford University Press, 1955.

202. Hudson, D. and K. W. Luckhurst. *Royal Society of Arts 1754–1954.* London: John Murray, 1954.

203. Hughes, E. "The Newcomen Engine in the Durham Coalfield." *Archaeologia Aeliana,* 1949, p. 29.

204. Hulme, Edward Wyndham. "A Sketch of the Early History of the Patent System." *Law Quarterly Review,* xii (1896), pp. 141–154, xiii (1897) pp. 312–8, xvi (1900) pp. 44–56, xviii (1900) pp. 280–8, revised and condensed as *The Early History of the English Patent System with a list of Monopoly Grants for New Industries and Inventions A.D. 1554–1603.* Boston: Little, Brown & Co., 1909.

205. Hulme, Edward Wyndham. *Statistical Bibliography in relation to the Growth of Modern Civilization.* London: Grafton & Co. for the author, 1923.

206. Hulme, Harold. *Sir John Eliot and the Vice-Admiralty of Devon.* London: Camden Miscellany, Vol. XVIII, 1940.

207. Hunter, H. C. *How England got its Merchant Marine 1066–1776.* New York: National Council of American Shipbuilders, 1935.

208. Hutchinson, J. R. *The Press-Gang Afloat and Ashore.* London: Eveleigh Nash, 1913.

209. *An Index to the Biographical and Obituary Notices in the Gentleman's Magazine 1731–1780.* London: British Record Society, 1891.

210. *Isis. An International Review devoted to the History of Science and Its Cultural Implications.* Baltimore: The Johns Hopkins Press, 1912– .

211. Jarvis, Rupert C. "Army Transport and the English Constitution: with special reference to Jacobite risings." *Journal of Transport History,* II (1955–6), pp. 101–120.

212. Jarvis, Rupert C., ed. *The Jacobite Risings of 1715 and 1745.* Cumberland County Council Record Series, Vol. I, 1954.

213. Jarvis, Rupert C. "Sources for the History of Ships and Shipping." *Journal of Transport History,* III (1957–8), pp. 212–234.

214. Jenkins, Rhys. *Links in the History of Engineering and Technology from Tudor Times. The Collected Papers of Rhys Jenkins.* Cambridge University Press, 1936.

215. Jenkins, Rhys T. and W. Rees. *A Bibliography of the History of Wales.* Cardiff: University of Wales Press Board, 1931.

216. John, A. H. "Aspects of English Economic Growth in the First Half of the Eighteenth Century," in E. M. Carus-Wilson, *Essays in Economic History,* II (1962).

217. John, A. H. *The Industrial Development of South Wales 1750–1880.* Cardiff: University of Wales Press, 1950.

218. John, A. H. "The London Assurance Company and the Marine Insurance Market of the Eighteenth Century." *Economica,* n.s. XXV, 1958.

219. John, A. H. "War and the English Economy, 1700–1763." *Economic History Review,* 2nd Series, VII, No. 3 (April, 1955), pp. 329–344.

220. Johnston, F. R. *Astronomical Thought in Renaissance England.* Baltimore: Johns Hopkins Press, 1937.

221. Jones, E. L., ed. *Agriculture and Economic Growth in England.* London: Methuen, 1967.

222. Jones, H. W. "Mid-Seventeenth Century Science: some polemics." *Osiris,* IX (1950), pp. 254–274.

223. Jump, P. "Chains throughout the Ages." *Proceeds of the Staffordshire Iron and Steel Institute,* XLIV, Stourbridge: 1928–9.

224. Kaye, F. B., ed. *Bernard Mandeville, The Fable of the Bees.* Oxford University Press, 1924.

225. Keen, M. H. *The Laws of War in the Late Middle Ages.* London: Routledge & Kegan Paul, 1965.

226. Kellaway, William. *Bibliography of Historical Works issued in the United Kingdom 1957–1960.* University of London: Institute of Historical Research, 1962, pp. 55–142.

227. Kellaway, William. *Bibliography of Historical Works issued in the United Kingdom 1961–1965.* University of London: Institute of Historical Research, 1967, pp. 76–184.

228. Kerridge, Eric. *The Agricultural Revolution.* London: George Allen & Unwin, 1967.

229. Kiernan, V. G. "Foreign Mercenaries and Absolute Monarchy," in Trevor Aston, ed., *Crisis in Europe, 1560–1660.* London: Routledge & Kegan Paul, 1956, pp. 117–140.

230. Kirby, Richard Shelton, Sidney Withington, Arthur B. Darling and Frederick Grindley Kingour. *Engineering in History.* London: McGraw-Hill Book Co., 1956.

231. Kranzberg, Melvin and Carroll W. Pursell. *Technology and Western Civilisation.* London: Oxford University Press, 1967, 2 vols., pp. 745–774.

232. Kronick, D. A. *A History of Scientific and Technical Periodicals: the origins and development of the scientific and technical press 1665–1790.* London: Scarecrow Press, 1962.

233. La Monte, J. L. "Some Problems in Crusading Historiography." *Speculum,* XV (1940).

234. Lancaster, Joan C. *Bibliography of Historical Works issued in the United Kingdom 1946–1956.* University of London: Institute of Historical Research, 1957, pp. 89–248.

235. Latham, Bryan. *Timber, its development and distribution, a historical survey.* London: G. Harrap & Co., 1957.

236. Laughton, Sir J. K., ed. *Letters and Papers of Charles Lew Barham*

(*Sir Charles Middleton*), *Admiral of the Red Squadron, 1758–1813*. London: Naval History Society, 1907–11. 3 vols.

237. Laws, M. E. S. "Foreign Artillery Corps in the British Service." 1. "The French Emigrant Artillery." *Journal of the Royal Artillery,* LXV (1938), pp. 356–367. 2. "The Dutch Immigrant Artillery." LXXIII (1946), pp. 250–60. 3. "The Royal Foreign Artillery." LXXV (1948).

238. Lecky, W. E. H. *History of England in the Eighteenth Century.* London: Longmans, 1878–1890, Vol. VI, p. 217.

239. Lefebure de Noëttes, Richard Joseph Edward Charles. *L'Attelage.* Paris: 1931.

240. Lefebure de Noëttes, Richard Joseph Edward Charles. *La Force matrice animale à travers les âges.* Paris, Strasbourg: Berger-Levrault, 1931.

241. Lennard, R. "The Composition of demesne plough-teams in twelfth-century England." *English Historical Review,* XXV (1960), pp. 193–207.

242. Lewis, E. A. "The Development of Industry and Commerce in Wales during the Middle Ages." *Transactions of the Royal Historical Society,* New Series, XVII (1903), pp. 121–173.

243. Lewis, G. R. *The Stannaries: a study of the English tin mines.* Boston: Houghton, Mifflin & Co., 1908.

244. Lewis, Michael. *Armada Guns: a comparative study of English and Spanish armaments.* London: George Allen & Unwin, 1961.

245. Lewis, Michael. *England's Sea Officers. The Story of the Naval Profession.* London: George Allen and Unwin, 1939.

246. Lewis, Norman Bache. "The Organisation of Indentured Retainers in Fourteenth-Century England." *Transactions of the Royal Historical Society,* 4th Series, XXVII (1945), pp. 29–39.

247. Lewis, Norman Bache. "The Last Medieval Summons of the English Feudal Levy, 13th June 1385." *English Historical Review,* LXXIII (1958), pp. 1–26.

248. Lewis, W. J. *Lead Mining in Wales.* Cardiff: University of Wales Press Board, 1967.

249. Ling, Wang. "On the Invention and Use of Gunpowder and Firearms in China." *Isis,* XXXVII (1947), pp. 160–178.

250. Lipson, E. *The Economic History of England.* London: A. & C. Black, 1947. 3 vols.

251. Lloyd, Christopher. "The Introduction of Lemon Juice as a Cure for Scurvy." *Bulletin of the History of Medicine,* XXXV (1961), pp. 123–132.

252. Lloyd Christopher and J. L. S. Coulter. *Medicine and the Navy.* E. & S. Livingstone, Vol. III, 1961.

253. Lloyd, G. I. H. *The Cutlery Trades.* London: Longmans & Co., 1913.

254. Lloyd, J. E. *A History of Wales.* 3rd ed. London: Longmans, 1949.

255. Loomie, Albert J. *The Spanish Elizabethans.* New York: Fordham University Press, 1963.

256. Lunardi, Vincent. *An Account of the First Aerial Voyage in England.* London: J. Bell, 1784.

257. Lyon, Bryce D. *From Fief to Indenture.* Cambridge, Mass.: Harvard University Press, 1957.

258. Macaulay, Lord. *The History of England from the accession of James the Second.* London: Longmans, Green & Roberts, 1849. 8 vols.

259. MacFarlane, K. B. "Bastard Feudalism." *Bulletin of the Institute of Historical Research,* XX (1943–5), pp. 161–80.

260. MacFarlane, K. B. "The Investment of Sir John Falstaff's profits of War." *Transactions of the Royal Historical Society,* 5th Series, VII, 1957.

261. MacFarlane, K. B. "War, the Economy and Social Change." *Past and Present,* No. 22 (July, 1962), pp. 3–17.

262. MacFarlane, K. B. "The Wars of the Roses." *The Raleigh Lecture on History.* British Academy, London: Oxford University Press, 1964.

263. MacInnes, Charles Malcolm. *An Introduction to the Economic History of the British Empire.* London: Rivingtons, 1935.

264. McKie, D. "The Arrest and Imprisonment of Henry Oldenburg." *Notes and Records of the Royal Society,* VI (1949).

265. MacLachlan, H. *English Education under the Test Acts.* Manchester University Press, 1931.

266. Mahan, Captain A. T. *The Influence of Sea Power upon History 1660–1783.* London: Sampson Low, Marston & Co., 1890.

267. Mahan, Captain A. T. *The Influence of Sea Power on the French Revolution and Empire.* London: Sampson Low, Marston & Co., 2 vols., 1892.

268. Mantoux, Paul. *The Industrial Revolution in the Eighteenth Century, An Outline of the Beginnings of the Modern Factory System in England.* Rev. ed. Marjorie Vernon, tr. London: Jonathan Cape, 1947.

269. Marshall, Arthur. *Explosives: their manufacture, properties, tests and history.* 2nd ed. London: J. & A. Churchill, 1915.

270. Marshall, J. D. *Furness and the Industrial Revolution: an economic history of Furness (1711–1900) and the town of Barrow (1757–1897),* with an epilogue. Barrow-in-Furness: Library and Museum Committee, 1958.

271. Martin, T. *The Royal Institution.* 3rd ed. London: The Institution, 1961.

272. Matthews, Leslie G. *The Royal Apothecaries.* London: The Wellcome Historical Medical Library, 1968.

273. Matthews, William. *British Diaries.* Berkeley: University of California, 1950.

274. Matthews, William. *British Autobiographies.* Berkeley: University of California Press, 1955.

275. Matthias, Peter. *The Brewing Industry in England, 1700–1830.* Cambridge University Press, 1959.

276. May, W. E. "The Last Voyage of Sir Clowdisley Shovell." *Journal of the Institute of Navigation,* XIII (1960), pp. 324–32.

277. Meikle, H. W. and others. *Scotland: a select bibliography.* Cambridge University Press, 1956.

278. Merton, R. K. "Science, Technology and Society in the Seventeenth-Century England." *Osiris,* IV (1938), pp. 360–632.

279. Middleton, Sir Charles (Comptroller of the Navy from 1778–1790). "Memorandum of Advice, Forethought and Preparation." *Navy Records Society Publications,* Vol. XXIX (1910), p. 29.

280. Miller, Edward. *War in the North.* Hull University Press, 1960.

281. Minchinton, W. E. *The British Tinplate Industry.* Oxford: Clarendon Press, 1957.

282. Minchinton, W. E., ed. *Essays in Agrarian History.* 2 vols. Reprinted for the British Agricultural History Society. Newton Abbot: David & Charles, 1968, pp. 163–165.

283. Montross, L. *War through the Ages.* New York: Harper Brothers, 1944.

284. Morris, J. E. *Bannockburn.* Cambridge University Press, 1914.

285. Morris, J. E. "Mounted Infantry in Medieval Warfare." *Transactions of the Royal Historical Society,* 3rd Series, VIII (1914), pp. 77–102.

286. Mott, R. A. "Abraham Darby (I and II) and the Coal Iron Industry" and "The Coalbrookdale Group Horsebay Works." *Newcomen Society Transactions,* XXXI (1957–8, 1958–9), pp. 49–93 and 271–287.

287. Mottelay, P. F. *Bibliographical History of Electricity and Magnetism.* London: Griffin, 1922.

288. Musgrave, Sir William. *Obituary prior to 1800.* London: Harleian Society, 1899–1901.

289. Musson, Albert Edward and Eric Robinson. "The Origins of Engineering in Lancashire." *Journal of Economic History,* XX (1960), 209–233.

290. Musson, Albert Edward and Eric Robinson. *Science and Technology in the Industrial Revolution.* Manchester: The Manchester University Press, 1969.

291. Namier, L. B. *England in the Age of the American Revolution.* 2nd ed. London: Macmillan, 1961, pp. 229, 230.

292. Napier, Mark. *Memoirs of John Napier of Merchiston.* Edinburgh: William Blackwood, 1834.

293. Natan, A., ed. *The Silver Renaissance: essays in eighteenth-century history.* London: Macmillan, 1961, especially C. A. Ronan, "Science in Eighteenth-Century Britain."

294. Needham, Noël Joseph Terence Montgomery. "The pre-natal history of the Steam Engine." *Transactions of the Newcomen Society* XXXV (1962–3) pp. 3–58.

295. Needham, Noël Joseph Terence Montgomery, with the collaboration of Wang Ling. *Science and Civilisation in China.* Cambridge University Press, 1954– .

296. Nef, John U. *Cultural Foundations of Industrial Civilisation.* The Wiles Lectures . . . at Queen's University, Belfast. Cambridge University Press, 1958.

297. Nef, John U. *The Rise of the British Coal Industry.* London: George Routledge, 1932.

298. Nef, John U. "War and Economic Progress, 1540–1640." *Economic History Review,* XII (1942), pp. 13–38.

299. Nef, John U. *War and Human Progress: an essay on the rise of industrial civilisation.* London: Routledge & Kegan Paul, 1950; Cambridge, Mass.: Harvard University Press, 1950.

300. Nelson, Lynn H. *The Normans in South Wales, 1070–1171.* Austin and London: The University of Texas Press, 1960.

301. Nixon, Frank. "The Early Steam Engine in Derbyshire." *Newcomen Society Transactions,* XXXI (1957–8, 1958–9), pp. 1–28.

302. *Notes and Records of the Royal Society of London,* 1938– .

303. Oakeshott, R. Ewart. *The Archaeology of Weapons: arms and armour from prehistoric times to the age of chivalry.* London: Butterworth Press, 1960.

304. Oakeshott, Walter. *Founded Upon the Seas.* Cambridge University Press, 1942.

305. O'Dea, W. T. *The Social History of Lighting.* London: Routledge & Kegan Paul, 1958.

306. Oman, Sir Charles. *A History of the Art of War in the Middle Ages.* Revised and edited by John H. Beeler, Ithaca, N. Y.: Cornell University Press, 1953.

307. Oman, Sir Charles. *A History of the Art of War in the Sixteenth Century.* London: Methuen & Co., 1937.

308. O'Neil, Brian Hugh. St. John. *Castles and Cannon. A Study of Early Artillery Fortification in England.* Oxford: Clarendon Press, 1960.

309. Oppenheim, M. *A History of the Administration of the Royal Navy and of Merchant Shipping in relation to the Navy: from MDIX to MDCLX.* London: J. Lane, 1896; reprint 1961.

310. *Osiris, Studies on the history and philosophy of science and on the history of learning and culture.* Bruges: St. Catherine's Press, 1936– .

311. Owen, J. H. *War at Sea under Queen Anne 1702–1708.* Cambridge University Press, 1938.

312. Painter, S. "English Castles in the Middle Ages. Their numbers, location, and legal position," in *Feudalism and Liberty.* F. A. Cazel, ed. Baltimore: Johns Hopkins Press, 1961.

313. Pannell, J. P. M. "The Taylors of Southampton: pioneers in mechanical engineering." *Proceedings of the Institution of Mechanical Engineers.* London: 1955, CLXIX, No. 46, pp. 924–931.

314. Pares, Richard. *War and Trade in the West Indies.* Oxford: Clarendon Press, 1936, p. 62.

315. Parkinson, Cyril Northcote, ed. *The Trade Winds: a study of British overseas trade during the French Wars, 1793–1815.* London: George Allen & Unwin, 1948.

316. Payne, F. G. "The British Plough: some stages in its development." *Agricultural History Review,* V (1957), pp. 74–84.

317. Pearce, Brian. "Elizabethan Food Policy and the Armed Forces." *Economic History Review,* XII (1942), pp. 39–45.

318. Pepys, Samuel. *Diary.* H. B. Wheatley, ed. London: G. Bell and Sons, 3 vols., 1923.

319. Pirenne, H. *Economic and Social History of Medieval Europe.* London: Kegan, Paul & Co., 1936.

320. Pirenne, H. *Medieval Cities.* Princeton: University Press, 1925.

321. Pledge, H. T. *Science Since 1500.* London: H.M.S.O., 1966.

322. Pollard, S. "Laissez Faire and Shipbuilding." *Economic History Review,* V (1952), pp. 98–115.

323. Postan, M. M. "The Fifteenth Century." *Economic History Review,* IX, (1938–9), pp. 160–7.

324. Postan, M. M. "Some Social Consequences of the Hundred Years' War." *Economic History Review,* XII (1942).

325. Prendeville, P. L. "A Select Bibliography of Irish Economic History." *Economic History Review,* 1931–2.

326. Pressnell, L. S., ed. *Studies in the Industrial Revolution Presented to T. S. Ashton.* London University Press, 1960.

327. Preston, Richard Arthur, Sidney F. Wise, and Herman O. Werner. *Men in Arms: a history of warfare and its interrelationships with western society.* London: Atlantic Press, 1956.

328. Prestwich, J. O. "War and Finance in the Anglo-Norman State." *Transactions of the Royal Historical Society,* 5th Series, IV (1954), pp. 19–43.

329. Price, Derek de Solla. "Automata and the Origins of Mechanism and Mechanistic Philosophy." *Technology and Culture,* V (1964), pp. 9–23.

330. Price, W. Hyde. *English Patents of Monopoly.* Cambridge: Harvard Economic Studies, 1913.

331. Prince, A. E. "The Payment of Army Wages in Edward III's Reign." *Speculum,* XIX (1944), pp. 137–60.

332. Pryde, G. G. *Scotland from 1603 to the Present Day.* London: Thomas Nelson & Co., 1962.

333. Raistrick, A. *Dynasty of Ironfounders: the Darbys and Coalbrookdale.* London: Longmans & Green, 1953, pp. 338, 274.

334. Raistrick, A., ed. *The Hatchet Diary: a tour through the country of England . . . in 1796.* Truro: Bradford, 1967.

335. Raistrick, A. "Newcomen Steam Engines on Tyneside." *Newcomen Society Transactions,* xvii (1936–7), p. 131.

336. Raistrick, A. *Quakers in Science and Industry, being an account of the Quaker Contribution to Science and Industry during the 17th and 18th Centuries.* London: Bannisdale Press, 1950.

337. Ramsey, G. C. D. *English Overseas Trade During the Centuries of Emergence.* London: Macmillan, 1957.

338. Rashdall, Hastings. *The University in the Middle Ages.* New edition

ed. by F. M. Powicke and A. B. Emden. Oxford: Clarendon Press, 1936.

339. Redstone, V. B. "Some mercenaries of Henry of Lancaster 1327–1330." *Transactions of the Royal Historical Society,* 3rd Series, VII (1913), pp. 151–166.

340. Reid, Major General Sir Alexander Forsyth. *The Rev. A. J. Forsyth.* Aberdeen University Press, 1909.

341. Reid, W. Stanford. "Seapower in the Anglo-Scottish War, 1296–1328." *The Mariners' Mirror,* XIVI (1960), pp. 7–23.

342. Rich, E. E. *The Ordnance Book of the Merchants of the Staple.* Cambridge University Press, 1937.

343. Riches, Naomi. *The Agricultural Revolution in Norfolk.* Chapel Hill: University of North Carolina Press, 1937.

344. Richmond, Sir Herbert. *The Navy in the War of 1739–48.* Cambridge University Press, 1920.

345. Ridgeway, William. *Origin and Influence of the Thoroughbred Horse.* Cambridge: The University Press, 1905.

346. Roberts, R. O. "Copper and Economic Growth in England 1729–84." *National Library of Wales Journal,* X, No. 1 (1949).

347. Robertson, F. L. *The Evolution of Naval Armament.* London: 1921.

348. Robertson, M. L. "Scottish Commerce and the American War of Independence." *Economic History Review,* 2nd Series, IX (1956–7), pp. 123–131.

349. Robinson, Commander Charles N. *The British Tar in Fact and Fiction.* London and New York: Harper and Brothers, 1909.

350. Rolt, L. T. C. *Thomas Newcomen: the prehistory of the steam engine.* London: Macdonald, 1963.

351. Rolt, L. T. C. *Thomas Telford.* London: Longmans Green & Co., 1958, pp. 80–92.

352. Rostow, W. W. *The Process of Economic Growth.* Oxford: University Press, 1952, pp. 144–164.

353. Roth, C. "Medieval illustrations of mouse-traps." *Bodleian Library Record,* X (1956), pp. 244–51.

354. Rowe, J. *Cornwall in the Age of the Industrial Revolution.* Liverpool University Press, 1953.

355. Ruddock, A. A. "The Trinity House at Deptford in the Sixteenth Century." *English Historical Review,* xv (1950), pp. 467–8.

356. Runciman, Sir Stephen. *A History of the Crusades.* Cambridge: University Press, 1951–1952. 3 vols.

357. Russell, Josiah Cox. *British Medieval Population.* Albuquerque: University of New Mexico, 1948.

358. Russell, Josiah Cox. *Dictionary of Writers of Thirteenth-Century England.* Institute of Historical Research Bulletin: special supplement 3. London: Longmans Green & Co., 1936.

359. Sabine, B. E. V. *A History of Income Tax.* London: George Allen & Unwin, 1966.

360. Sanders, I. J. *Feudal Military Service in England.* Oxford University Press, 1956.

361. Sarton, George. *Introduction to the History of Science.* Washington: Carnegie Institution, publication No. 376, 1927–1948. 3 vols.

362. Schubert, H. R. *History of the British Iron and Steel Industry from c.450 B.C. to 1775 A.D.* London: Routledge & Kegan Paul, 1957.

363. Schubert, H. R. "The King's Ironworks in the Forest of Dean 1612–1674." London: Reprinted from the *Journal of the Iron and Steel Institute,* 1953.

364. Scott, Wilson L. "The Impact of the French Revolution in English Science." *Mélanges Alexandre Koyré,* ii. Paris: Harmann, 1964, pp. 475–495.

365. Scouller, Major R. E. *The Armies of Queen Anne.* Oxford: Clarendon Press, 1966.

366. Setton, Kenneth M., ed. *A History of the Crusades.* Philadelphia: University of Pennsylvania Press, I. *The First Hundred Years,* M. W. Baldwin, ed., 1955. II. *The Later Crusades 1189–1311,* Robert Lee Wolff, ed., 1962. III. *The Fourteenth and Fifteenth Centuries,* H. W. Hazard, ed. IV. *Civilizations and Institutions,* Jeremiah O'Sullivan, ed. V. *Influences and Consequences with Genealogies and Bibliography,* Gray C. Boyce, ed.

367. Shaw, W. A. "The Beginnings of the National Debt." in T. F. Tout and James Tait, ed. *Historical Essays by Members of Owens College, Manchester.* Manchester: Longmans Green & Co., 1902, pp. 391-432.

368. Simms, J. G. *The Williamite Confiscations in Ireland 1690–1703.* London: Faber & Faber, 1956.

369. Simont, T. C. "The Anglo-Scottish Union of 1707. I. The Economic Background." *Economic History Review,* pp. 455–477.

370. Singer, Charles, E. J. Holmyard, A. R. Hall, Trevor I. Williams, ed. *A History of Technology.*
Vol. ii (assisted by E. Jaffe, Nan Clow and R. H. G. Thomson). *The Mediterranean Civilisations and the Middle Ages.* Oxford: Clarendon Press, 1956.
Vol. iii. *From the Renaissance to the Industrial Revolution c.1500–c.1750.* London: Oxford University Press, 1957.
Vol. iv (assisted by Y. Peel, J. R. Petty, M. Rieve). *The Industrial Revolution c.1750–c.1859.* Oxford: Clarendon Press, 1958.

371. Skempton, A. W. "The Engineers of the English river navigations 1620–1760." *Newcomen Society Transactions,* XXIX, (1953–55), 25–54.

372. Smail, R. C. *Crusading Warfare (1097–1193).* Cambridge University Press, 1956.

373. Smeaton, W. A. "The First and last balloon ascents of Pilatre de Rozier." *Archives Internationales d'Histoire des Sciences,* XI, 1958, pp. 263–269.

374. Smeaton, W. A. *Fourcroy: chemist and revolutionary, 1755–1809* Cambridge: W. Heffer, 1962.

375. Smeaton, W. A. "Jean Pilatre de Rozier (1757–1785), the first aeronaut." *Annals of Science,* XI (1955), pp. 349–355.

376. Smiles, Samuel. *Lives of the Engineers.* London: Murray, 1905. 5 vols.

377. Smith, Adam. *The Wealth of Nations.* London: J. M. Dent, 1933, ii, pp. 388–390.

378. Smith, A. H. "Place-names and the Anglo-Saxon Settlement." *Proc. Brit. Acad.* XLII (1956), pp. 67–88.

379. Smith, Cyril Stanley. "Methods of making chain mail (14th to 18th Centuries) a metallographic note." *Technology and Culture,* 1959, 1, pp. 60–67.

380. Smith, Engineer Captain Edgar C. *A Short History of Naval and Marine Engineering.* Cambridge University Press, 1935.

381. Smythe, Brigadier Sir John. *Sandhurst.* London: Weidenfeld & Nicolson, 1961.

382. Sombart, Werner. *Krieg und Kapitalismus.* Munich: Duncker and Humblot, 1913.

383. Sombart, Werner. *Der Moderne Kapitalismus.* Munich: Duncker and Humblot, 1921.

384. Sparrow, W. J. *Knight of the White Eagle: a biography of William Thompson Count Rumford 1753–1814.* London: Hutchinson, 1964, pp. 214–239.

385. Sprat, Thomas. *History of the Royal Society edited with critical apparatus by Jackson I. Cope and Harold Whitmore Jones.* St. Louis, Missouri: Washington University Studies, 1958.

386. Steensberg, A. *Ancient Harvesting Implements.* Copenhagen: 1943.

387. Stenton, F. M. "The Development of the Castle in England and Wales," in G. Barraclough, ed., *Social Life in Early England.* London: Routledge & Kegan Paul, 1960.

388. Stenton, F. M. "The Road System of Medieval England." *The Economic History Review,* VII (1936–7), pp. 1–21.

389. Stephenson, Orlando W. "The Supply of Gunpowder in 1776." *American Historical Review,* XXX (1924–5), p. 277.

390. Stimson, Dorothy. *Scientists and amateurs: a history of the Royal Society.* London: Schuman, 1948.

391. Stone, L. Contribution to "War and Society 1300–1600," in *Past and Present,* No. 22 (1962), p. 15.

392. Stone, L. *An Elizabethan: Sir Horatio Palavicino.* Oxford: University Press, 1956.

393. Stowers, Arthur. "The Development of the atmospheric steam engine after Newcomen's death in 1779." *Transactions of the Newcomen Society,* XXXV (1962–3), pp. 87–96.

394. Straker, Ernest. *Wealden Iron.* London: G. Bell & Sons, 1931.

395. Surtees. *Publications of the Surtees Society.* Durham and London: 1834–   . A history of the society was published as vol. 150 by A. Hamilton Thompson in 1939.

396. Taylor, E. G. R. *The Haven-finding Art: a history of navigation from Odysseus to Captain Cook*. London: Hollis and Carter, 1956.
397. Taylor, E. G. R. *The Mathematical Practitioners of Tudor and Stuart England*. Cambridge University Press for the Institute of Navigation, 1954.
398. Taylor, E. G. R. *The Mathematical Practitioners of Hanoverian England 1714–1840*. Cambridge University Press for the Institute of Navigation, 1966.
399. Thomas, David. *Agriculture in Wales During the Napoleonic Wars: a study in the geographical interpretation of historical sources*. Cardiff: University of Wales Press, 1963.
400. Thompson, A. Hamilton. *Military Architecture in England during the Middle Ages*. London: Henry Frowde, 1912, p. 65.
401. Thorndike, Lynn. *A History of Magic and Experimental Science*. New York: Columbia University Press, Vol. i 1923, ii 1923, iii & iv 1934. The remaining four volumes (v 1941, vi 1941, vii 1958, viii 1958) carry the story up to the seventeenth century.
402. Tierie, Gerrit. *Cornelis Drebbel 1572–1633*. Amsterdam: H. J. Paris, 1932.
403. Tout, T. F. *Chapters in English Administrative History*. Manchester University Press, 1928–1937. 5 vols.
404. Tout, T. F. *Collected Papers*. Manchester University Press, 1934, 238ff.
405. Toy, S. *Castles: a short history of fortifications from 1600 B.C. to A.D. 1600*. London: William Heinemann 1939, p. 90.
406. Trevelyan, G. M. *England under Queen Anne*. Vol. i *Blenheim*. Vol. ii *Ramillies*. Vol. iii *The Peace*. London: Longmans Green & Co., 1930, 1932, 1934, pp. 97. See Vol. 1 pp. 223ff., 350ff.
407. Trevelyan, G. M. *English Social History*. London: Longmans, Green & Co., 1946.
408. Trevor-Roper, H. R. "Scotland and the Puritan Revolution." *Historical Essays 1600–1750 Presented to David Ogg*. H. E. Bell and R. L. Ollard, ed. London: A. & C. Black, 1964, pp. 78–130.
409. Tylecote, R. F. *Metallurgy in Archaeology: a prehistory of metallurgy in the British Isles*. London: Edward Arnold, 1962.
410. Upton, E. S. *Guide to Sources of English History from 1603 to 1660 in Early Reports of the Royal Commission on Historical Manuscripts*. New York: Scarecrow Press, 1964.
411. Usher, A. P. *History of Mechanical Inventions*. 2nd ed. Cambridge, Massachusetts: Harvard University Press, 1954.
412. *The Victoria County Histories of England*.
413. Vinogradoff, Paul. *English Society in the Eleventh Century*. Oxford: Clarendon Press, 1908, pp. 140–1.
414. Wadsworth, A. P. and Julia de L. Mann. *The Cotton Trade and Industrial Lancashire, 1600–1780*. Manchester: Publications of University of Manchester, 1931.
415. Wagner, A. R. *Heralds and Heraldry in the Middle Ages*. Oxford University Press, 1956, pp. 13–17.

416. The War Office (W.O.) papers in the Public Record Office.
417. Webb, Henry J. *Elizabethan Military Science. The Books and the Practice*. Madison: University of Wisconsin Press, 1965.
418. Webb, Sidney and Beatrice. *The Story of the King's Highway*. London: Longmans, 1913, pp. 118–164. (From this has been compiled by Ballen, Dorothy. *A Bibliography of Road-Making and Roads in the United Kingdom*. London: Studies in Economic and Political Science Bibliographies, No. 3.)
419. Wernham, R. B. "Elizabethan War Aims and Strategy," in S. T. Bindoff, J. Hurstfield and C. H. Williams, ed. *Elizabethan Government and Society*. London: The Athlone Press, 1961.
420. Western, J. R. *The English Militia in the Eighteenth Century*. London: Routledge & Kegan Paul, 1965.
421. White, Lynn. Jr. *Medieval Technology and Social Change*. Oxford: Clarendon Press, 1962.
422. Whitehorne, P. *Certain Waies for the Ordering of Souldiers in battelray*. A translation of Machiavelli's *libro dell'Arte della Guerra*. London: John Kingston for Nicolas Englande, 1560.
423. Wilbraham, Anne and J. C. Drummond. *The Englishman's Food*. London: Jonathan Cape, 1935.
424. Wilbur, C. M. "The History of the Cross-Bar." *Annual Report of the Smithsonian Institution*, Washington, 1936.
425. Willan, T. S. *The English Coasting Trade 1600–1750*. Manchester University Press, 1938.
426. Willard, J. F. "The Crown and its creditors, 1327–1333." *English Historical Review*, xiii (1927), pp. 12–19.
427. Williams, A. H. *An Introduction to the History of Wales*. Cardiff: University of Wales Press Board, 1941. Vol. i, *Prehistoric Times to 1603*, 1941, Vol. iii *1663–1784*, 1948.
428. William, David. *Modern Wales*. London: John Murray, 1950.
429. Williams, T. T. *Biographical Dictionary of Scientists*. London: A. & C. Black, 1969.
430. Wilson, C. *Profit and Power, A Study of England and the Dutch Wars. Cambridge* University Press, 1957.
431. Wilson, Charles. *England's Apprenticeship 1603–1763*. London: Longmans, 1965.
432. Wilson, Paul N. "Early Water Turbines in the United Kingdom." *Newcomen Society Transactions*, XXXI (1957–58), pp. 219–241.
433. Wolf, A. *History of Science, Technology and Philosophy in the 16th and 17th Centuries*. 2nd ed. London: Allen and Unwin, 1950.
434. Wolf, A. *History of Science, Technology and Philosophy in the Eighteenth Century*. 2nd ed., revised by Douglas McKie. London: G. Allen & Unwin, 1952.
435. Wright, Charles and C. E. Fayle. *A History of Lloyd's, from the Foundry of Lloyd's Coffee House to the Present Day*. London: Macmillan, 1926.
436. Young, Henry Ayerst, *The East India Company's Arsenals and Manufactories*. Oxford: Clarendon Press, 1937.

VIII

THE ARMY IN THE
NINETEENTH CENTURY

Albert Tucker

Study of the army has never been integrated into the broader scope of English history in the nineteenth century. The Victorians themselves were largely responsible, since to them military affairs were a peripheral matter. The soldier became a more vital figure later in the century with the expansion of empire, but on the whole, as Michael Howard pointed out in 1956, Victorians tended to see war "as simply a vested interest of the Establishment, . . . and the predominance of this bourgeois tradition . . . has resulted in an underestimation of the subject." (67) Neglect of the army has continued into recent historical writing on the period. Though there are brief and selective bibliographies in the two volumes of the *Oxford History of England* by Woodward (128) and Ensor (40), and a few pages on the army were included in volume XI of *English Historical Documents,* military organization was specifically excluded from Volume XII (1) of this series, covering the years from 1833 to 1874 (35). Even the two latest essays on the historiography of the nineteenth century by Roger Prouty and John Clive (47) find no place for the mention of military subjects, though Clive has rightly pointed to the deeper understanding of Victorian England which has developed through the integration of specialized studies into the life of the whole society.

Another reason for this neglect has been the tendency of military historians to maintain the approach of specialists, producing technical studies of armed forces and campaigns which have often been of more immediate use to officers in training than to students of history. The classic example of this deficiency is Sir John Fortescue's *History of the British Army* (43), the last three volumes of which cover the years from 1815 to 1870. There are sixty chapters in these three volumes and fifty are preoccupied with campaigns, including the Crimean War and the Indian Mutiny. The other ten discuss domestic and foreign affairs. Only four chapters make any attempts to analyse conditions within the army or the relation between military and imperial policy. Of these, it should be said that the first and the last chapters contain some fine descriptions of the lot of the soldier, if allowance is made for Fortescue's Tory views and his dependence on debates in Hansard after the Crimean War.

Fortescue's approach to the army in society hardly compares with the brief, twenty-five page section on the Armed Forces in Élie Halévy's *England in 1815* (58), which concentrates on the central question of why and how "military and political institutions [in England] were in perfect harmony." Though his analysis, like the much earlier work of Dupin (38), treats of the thirty years prior to 1815, it provides also a point of departure for the period from the end of the Napoleonic to the Crimean Wars, since nothing substantially changed during those forty years. The only discussion which approaches the integration of Halévy is that of Alfred Vagts in his *History of Militarism* (118), but there the references to the English experience are scattered and brief; they do not easily fit the patterns of France and Germany in the nineteenth century.

Indeed, any account of European militarism in the nineteenth century must consider English military organization to have been anomalous, a view which was explained as early as 1883 by Captains Hozier (68) and Norman (92) in the English monthly, the *Nineteenth Century*. Through most of the period, in spite of the Industrial Revolution, the army belonged to an aristocratic and rural England. It was one of the last of English institutions to adjust to the world of steam and rail. The two finest of English military writers in the twentieth century, J. F. C. Fuller (46) and Liddell Hart (78), have commented on this comparatively backward state of English military institutions at the very height of the Pax Britannica. The student of history, however, should set their interpretations against the older but more objective surveys on "Army" and "War" which were written between 1878 and 1888 by G. P. Colley (27) and J. F. Maurice (87) respectively for the ninth edition of the *Encyclopaedia Britannica*.

JOURNALS. Of the journals on military affairs none are more relevant than the *Journal of the Royal United Service Institution*, which was founded in 1858 (73). The War Office Librarian wrote in 1920 that "it is difficult to estimate the debt which English military literature owes to the RUSI and the lectures and discussion held there." (69) The talks ranged over a wide variety of military subjects, with prominent military figures often participating; the publication of these discussions in the journal, along with prize essays on problems of defense and tactics, makes it one of the richest sources in print for the nineteenth century. The older *United Service Magazine* was published intermittently through the nineteenth century and was succeeded in 1920 by the *Army Quarterly* (see Introduction). Significant articles occasionally appeared in the *Civil and Military Gazette* and the *Army Review*. The *Journal of the Society for Army Historical Research,* begun in 1921 (see Introduction), contains essays of varied quality; most are not relevant for the nineteenth century but there are some which bear directly on Victorian military campaigns and on regiments which took part in them. The *Royal Engineers Journal* was first issued in 1870 and is a source for accounts by officers of the technical and certainly best educated branch of the army. For details on commissions, appointments, and promotions there are the annual volumes of the *Army List* (62) and the *Army and Navy Gazette.*

The French publication, *Revue Militaire des Armées Étrangères,* issued under the Ministry of War in Paris, sometimes gave interesting details not easily found in English publications on British military organization. Its nearest English parallel was *The Armed Strength of Foreign Nations,* which was published annually, first by the Topographical Section in the 1860's and later by the Intelligence Section. When it ceased publication in the later eighties, J. F. Maurice sought to revive the *United Service Magazine* as its replacement, but the attempt lasted only a few years. In 1907 the General Staff sanctioned a review called *Recent Publications of Military Interest,* but it too went out of existence in 1911. The British were never as consistent as the French in considering it vital that their army be seen against the military organization of other powers.

Periodicals with no particular focus on military affairs nevertheless published essays on the army. The number of these increased with the expansion of empire and the growth of the reading public in the last third of the century. Discussion of the army is to be found frequently in the *Contemporary Review,* the *Fortnightly Review, Blackwood's Edinburgh Magazine,* the *Nineteenth Century* (begun in 1878), and the *National Review* (founded in 1883).

OFFICIAL PAPERS. There are three sources for official papers—the War-Office Library, the Public Record Office, and the large series of Sessional or Parliamentary Papers which can most easily be consulted in the State Paper Room of the British Museum. The collection of official papers at the War-Office Library is selective, but all are printed and are ably catalogued. One of the most valuable bibliographical aids at this library is the List of War-Office Committees which reported on various aspects of the nineteenth-century army. There is also a small printed collection of War-Office records in the British Museum under index numbers 2666, 2677, and 2683–93. The second volume of C. M. Clode, *The Military Forces of the Crown* (26), contains some three hundred pages of appendixes taken from War-Office papers and statutes, on subjects that range from savings banks and education to the need for maintaining a clear separation between the financial control of Parliament and the military command and patronage which derived from the royal prerogative.

Less selective and certainly more abundant are the War-Office papers at the P.R.O. They are entirely open but they are not of even quality for the nineteenth century. Many are routine office memoranda of a miscellaneous nature, and unfortunately some have recently been destroyed. The student needs to be clear about his questions before consulting the catalogues of the Round Room at the P.R.O. He should also be aware first of the rich sources of information which lie comparatively neglected in the Parliamentary Papers. Those that bear on the army have never been catalogued. They were omitted from the *Select List* and the *Breviate* of P. and G. Ford (131). The only guide in print is the *Index to the Parliamentary Papers* that was published every six years after 1832 and every decade after 1870. These indexes up to 1899 are listed in the Catalogue of 1904 (130). The reports and the minutes of evidence to be found in the *Parliamentary Papers* can easly be supplemented by the debates in *Hansard,* where discussion of the annual army estimates often leads into issues of policy and organization. The debates are seldom adequate as sources, however, even for graduate theses, since they were badly reported during a good part of the century, and neither politicians nor soldiers could reveal as much in Parliament as they did in diaries and in their private papers.

PRIVATE PAPERS. Among private papers the most significant have now been deposited in the British Museum or the P.R.O. Those of the Duke of Wellington are still at Apsley House. There are no substantial collections on the pre-Crimean Army, but a large number of private papers exists for the half-century after the Crimean War. All relate to the higher administration of the army, to the making of policy and to issues of reform. At the P.R.O. there are the papers of Lords Cardwell and Kitchener, as well as those of Sir Redvers Buller and Sir John Ardagh, a Royal Engineer who rose to high rank and corresponded with most of the military leaders from the seventies to the Boer War.

The Manuscript Room of the British Museum now has the papers of most politicians who influenced military policy in this period—e.g. of Lord Ripon, of Gladstone, Campbell-Bannerman, Balfour, St. John Broderick (Lord Middleton) and Arnold-Forster. Less centralized are the papers of four Secretaries of State for War. Those of Gathorne Hardy (1874–78) have been deposited in the County Record Office at Ipswich (157); those of Edward Stanhope (1887–92) are still at Chevening (161); the papers of Lord Lansdowne (1895–1900) are at Bowood (159); and the National Library of Scotland has for some time been the custodian of the papers of both Lord Haldane and General Sir Douglas Haig (158).

Letters from the Duke of Cambridge, Commander-in-Chief from 1856 to 1895, can be found in most of these collections, though the main body of his correspondence is in the Royal Archives at Windsor (156). It is an appropriate depository for the papers of the man who maintained for so long the facade of royal command over the army. The letters of his successor, Lord Wolseley (1895–1900), are divided between the library of King's College, University of London, and the Public Library at Hove (162), where they were deposited by his daughter. The last Commander-in-Chief before the formation of the General Staff was Lord Roberts; a few of his papers are in PRO/WO/105, but most are in the custody of the Ogilvie Trust and are accessible through the National Register of Archives (160), which is also the source for the papers of Spenser Wilkinson, the military writer with views about army organization and imperial defense that coincided with those of Lord Roberts. Closer still to politicians and to the making of policy at the end of the century was Sir George Clarke (Lord Sydenham), who served as the first Secretary of the Colonial Defense Committee after 1885, and then of the Committee of Imperial

Defense after 1904. His papers are all in the Manuscript Room of the British Museum. The first Viscount Esher has left both published (163) and unpublished materials (164) of great importance.

Taken together, these collections of official and private papers form the most basic source for the organization and administration of the nineteenth-century army. They should be consulted only after full use has been made of the abundant secondary sources which will be discussed here according to the following chronological divisions: the pre-Crimean Army, the Crimean War and After, the Cardwell Reforms, the Boer War, and Reform and Change before the First World War, with a subsequent short discussion on Technical Developments, Education, and suggestions for further research.

THE PRE-CRIMEAN ARMY. The figure of the Duke of Wellington still tends to dominate writing on the pre-Crimean army. His indifference to military change is briefly discussed in Fortescue's biography (44), but it is a biased book lacking in documentation. More useful are the volumes of the duke's despatches and speeches edited by Gurwood (56). The influence of Wellington throughout the army was profound during this whole period from 1815 to 1852, but it is misleading to attribute the static quality of military organization to Wellington alone. His post-Napoleonic career should be interpreted in the perspective of that Tory, aristocratic leadership over the army which was unaffected by any of the legislation of these years, and which relegated the technical branches to a secondary role. The result was an exaggeration of seniority and patronage. This appears in the biographies of the Duke of York (16) and of the Marquess of Anglesey (5); it is evident also in the description of the early career of Lord Raglan by Christopher Hibbert (64), and in the *Life and Correspondence of Sir John Burgoyne* (129). The only biographical treatment of Lord Hill, Commander-in-Chief 1827–42; of Lord Hardinge, Commander-in-Chief 1852–56; and of Sir Willoughby Gordon, who held the office of Quartermaster-General for forty years, from 1811–51, is in the *Dictionary of National Biography*.

The careers of such men are not worth extended treatment, since each accepted uncritically the premises on which the army was based. More to the point is a study of the functions of the army, its reflection of the social structure, and the implications of the conviction that command must remain firmly in the hands of the crown. For this approach one can begin with the biography of Lord Palmerston (10), who was Secretary-at-War 1809–28, and with the older constitutional studies of Anson (6) and Dicey (33); but the most rewarding sources are the *Parliamentary Papers*. There were in particular three royal commissions and one parliamentary committee during these years (132, 134, 135, 136), whose reports and minutes of evidence are basic for an understanding of the pre-Crimean army. They make clear that there was no conflict between the civil and the military power so long as the nation was not called upon to fight a major war that would require substantial increases in the size of the army. According to a

Parliamentary Return of 1835 (133), the army numbered hardly more than 100,000 men and its chief function was to police the colonies.

This colonial role, with the focus on the small military campaign, emerges vividly from the biographies of Sir Harry Smith (103) and Sir Hugh, later Viscount Gough (94). The Victorian military campaign has been the subject of more recent study in an excellent book edited by Brian Bond (13). It reveals again and again that the army was seldom prepared or organized even for this limited role. Talented commanders nursed a continuous grievance against the patronage, nepotism, and confusion of the War Office. The problems are evident in the lives of Smith, Gough, and Burgoyne; they are central to the brief biography of Sir Charles Napier by William Butler (17); and they are confirmed in studies of the War Office itself by Owen Wheeler (122) and Hampden Gordon (51), both of which can be supplemented by the much older account of J. H. Stocqueler (110), the pseudonym of J. H. Siddons, who had been a civil servant in the War Office. The criticism that runs throughout these studies was fully justified by the persistence of confusion and the failure of leadership in the Crimean War.

THE CRIMEAN WAR. The most basic source for the performance of the British Army in the Crimea lies again in the *Parliamentary Papers,* particularly in the five reports from the Select Committee of 1855 (138), the so-called Roebuck Committee. It was followed by the Report of the McNeill and Tulloch Commission of 1856 (139), which investigated the whole problem of supplies. Then came the Royal Sanitary Commission of 1857–58 (141), chaired by Sidney Herbert, whose role may have been exaggerated in his official biography (109), since the directing hand of Florence Nightingale was clearly at work behind the scenes.

Any study of the war leads inevitably to her career, because she so dramatized for the English public the terrible losses from disease and wounds. According to her latest biographer, Mrs. Woodham-Smith (127), the blame lay entirely with the incompetence of old men in charge of hospital services; but students of the period would be better advised to comprehend the broad moral and bureaucratic framework by returning to the older biography by Sir Edward Cook (30), to the biography of Sir John Hall by S. M. Mitra (90), and beyond both of these to the still more dated work of A. A. Gore, *The Story of Our Services Under the Crown* (52). The most recent and expert study is Sir Zachary Cope, *Florence Nightingale and the Doctors* (32), while W. H. Greenleaf in *Victorian Studies* (54) has done a succinct and unusual comparison of the two biographies by Cook and Woodham-Smith.

Treatment of the sick and wounded in war became for the first time an issue of public controversy. So too did the leadership of Lord Raglan. Both controversies were largely due to the despatches of W. H. Russell, the original English war correspondent. Apart from the pages of the *Times* through 1854–55, his impressions and conclusions can be found in three books which he published between 1855 and 1895 (100). Raglan's leadership was placed in more sympathetic perspective by Kinglake (74), and he has recently been made the central figure in a small and lively study of the Crimean War by Christopher Hibbert, *The Destruction of Lord Raglan* (64). Hibbert acknowledges the artistic and sustained quality of Kinglake's prose but, apart from suggesting that the latter was "often prejudiced and sometimes wrong," he makes no attempt to point up where and how his own book differs. This is a minor gap, however, in what is otherwise a fine piece of military history, based on the papers of Lord Raglan and on numerous letters from officers and soldiers who fought in the Crimea. Hibbert's use of these sources gives to his book a quality that is superior to *The Reason Why* by Cecil Woodham-Smith (127). The latter goes directly and simply after a thesis, again on the culpable conduct of certain individuals. A biographical emphasis on the careers of Lucan and Cardigan brings it close to the form of a novel, a criticism which is further explained in the scholarly bibliographical essay by Brison Gooch, "The Crimean War in Selected Documents and Secondary Works since 1940" (49). Gooch is one of the few writers in English to study the war in European terms, enabling him to write of English leadership in the context of an allied command.

Certainly Raglan was handicapped by the fact that he had to co-operate with a temperamental French commander, yet the heavy British losses must still be attributed to fundamental weaknesses in the organization of transport and supplies, to the poor training of officers, and to confusion between civil and military power in the War Office. These conclusions emerge forcefully from *The Panmure Papers* (36), as well as from three books that continue to be essential reading for any analysis of the war: Sir H. E. Wood, *The Crimea in 1854 and 1894* (125); the Countess of Airlie, *With the Guards We Shall Go* (1); and Sir George MacMunn, *The Crimea in Perspective* (82). Two recent articles by M. Robbins (96) and J. M. Merrill (89) examine problems of transportation and amphibious operations. Reflection on reading like this, moreover, leads beyond the Crimean War to the whole background of the Cardwell Reforms.

THE CARDWELL REFORMS. The three chief reforms of Cardwell followed directly from reaction against British performance in the Crimean War. They were the abolition of purchase, the introduction of short service, and the physical transfer of the Horse Guards to the War Office. All are covered in what is still the standard work on the subject, R. Biddulph, *Lord Cardwell at the War Office* (11). A. B. Erickson has written a more recent study of Cardwell's public life, which contains a brief, thirty-page section on his army reforms (41). It is based on the papers of Cardwell and Gladstone, and on a selection of War-Office papers. The reforms become more vital, however, by studying each in turn through other sources.

The first, which did away with purchase and therefore with the whole system of over-regulation prices and army agency, can be studied through five reports of royal commissions which sat between 1840 and 1870 (136, 137, 140, 144, 145). That of 1857 contains the most controversial debate on the subject, with the arguments of Sir Charles Trevelyan predominating.

Trevelyan's campaign for the abolition of purchase was a continuation of his interest in civil service reform. In three short books on the army (114), he deplored the fact that middle-class principles of selection by merit and education were to be found only in the Artillery and Engineers. Trevelyan's arguments are borne out by the Memoranda Papers of the Commander-in-Chief in PRO/WO/31, which are the files containing applications for commissions and promotions until 1870.

The second reform of Cardwell—the introduction of short service—was the answer to lack of a trained reserve, which had so weakened the British military position in the Crimea. This is evident in a short article by Brian Bond, "Prelude to the Cardwell Reforms, 1856–68" (13). In 1859 an attempt was made to build a reserve through a force of Volunteers that would be separate from the regular army. They were organized under the terms of a War-Office circular which is printed in a superficial book on the Volunteers by C. Sebag-Montefiore (102). The force is also discussed in B. Rose, "The Volunteers of 1859" (99), but the most basic source is in nine bundles of papers in PRO/WO/32, covering the years 1859–1908. Wolseley's opinion of them in 1880 is part of the second bundle (paper No. V/Gen.No./6857a). The movement may have stirred patriotic sentiment, but it constituted only the semblance of an organization for defense. A royal commission on the Volunteers in 1862 [C. *3053*] criticized the excessive social activities which seemed the real purpose for many who joined.

After Sadowa in 1866 it became more than ever apparent that Britain must find some means of obtaining a more effective reserve that would have to be combined with the regular rotation of troops in India and the colonies. This need lay behind the Royal Commission on Recruiting of 1867 (142). A First and a Second Reserve were created but by 1870 neither had achieved the anticipated figure of 80,000. This was the immediate background to Cardwell's Enlistment and Localization Acts, the problems of which are explained in Sir Archibald Alison, *On Army Organization* (2), and in Cardwell's two long speeches before the House of Commons in 1871 and 1872 (22). Additional factors bound up with the requirements of the army in India are explained by the evidence of Ralph Knox before the Committee on the Militia and Brigade-Depot System of 1877 (147). Knox was one of Cardwell's closest advisers in the War Office; he had sat on the Localization Committee of 1872 (146), and his evidence of 1877 suggests why the reforms never succeeded as Cardwell had hoped. Brian Bond has taken the defects of the short-service system as the subject of another article in the *J.R.U.S.I.* (13).

The third reform of Cardwell—removal of the Horse Guards to the War Office—did not achieve its goal until the turn of the century. Cardwell had hoped to develop a chief of staff, but the long reign of the Duke of Cambridge prevented such an appointment. The duke was the subject of an excellent two-volume biography in 1909 (119). The author, Willoughby Verner, tempered his sympathy by a judicious selection of the duke's letters, which make the book still superior to a recent rather trivial biography by Giles St. Aubyn (101). The issue of the Horse Guards versus the War Office is discussed in books already cited by Biddulph (11), Gordon (51), and Wheeler (122). The most serious consequence was failure to develop a staff system by the time of the Boer War, but that the fault lay not with the duke alone is clear from the Report of the Harting-ton Commission in 1890 (151), which should be read in conjunction with the Stanhope Memorandum of 1891 (152). These two documents, together with the biography of Campbell-Bannerman (108), emphasize political resistance to any "thinking" department that would plan for a European war.

In sum, the Cardwell Reforms had a limited effect. Through the eighties and nineties a continuous debate developed in periodicals between sup-porters and critics, the latter insisting that the Cardwell short-service system could not provide for the complex military needs of an expanding sea-borne empire. Most participants in this debate were experienced officers attending evening sessions of the Royal United Service Institution. The best of their papers were printed in the *J.R.U.S.I.* (73), but longer and more general essays were also printed in the *Nineteenth Century*. Interest in this printed debate, together with access to the Cardwell papers and to various other papers in the P.R.O. and the British Museum, led to the re-cent article by Albert Tucker, "Army and Society in England 1870–1900" (115), in which the reforms as a whole are integrated with social and political problems of the period.

All accounts of the Cardwell scheme come back to the fact that the army attained greater prominence during the last third of the century, not through any large-scale war or threats from Europe, but through its suc-cess in the small imperial campaign. Every officer of ability and ambition had to find his career through these expeditions, and Sir Garnet, later Viscount Wolseley, was only the most outstanding of those whose careers followed this pattern. The latest biography of him is that of Joseph Leh-man (77), but Lehman's judgments do not add anything to those of F. B. Maurice and G. Arthur, who wrote the official biography in 1924 (85). Wolseley's own autobiography, *The Story of a Soldier's Life* (124), only goes to 1873, when the most significant part of his career was just be-ginning. More to the point on the imperial expedition are the memoirs of Sir William Butler (17) and Sir Evelyn Wood (126). The tactical lessons from these minor expeditions were analysed in a lucid little book by C. R. Callwell on *Small Wars* (20) which formed the point of departure for the recent study edited by Brian Bond (13). In the latter, the writers con-tradict the tendency to dismiss the later Victorian campaign; they pay tribute to the special talents required of British commanders on un-mapped terrain, where transport and supply presented a diversity of chal-lenges that were vitally different from those of European warfare.

The tactical genius of Wolseley for these limited wars emerges also from the official narrative, the *Military History of the Campaign of 1882 in Egypt,* prepared with painstaking care by J. F. Maurice (86), then a colonel in the Intelligence Section of the War Office. The diary of Wolseley's expedition to relieve Gordon in 1884 has recently been edited by Adrian Preston (93). Despite the success of these campaigns, however, and the prominence of the Wolseley "ring," British officers did not gain the experience of handling large numbers of troops, and this lack was compounded by failure of the Duke of Cambridge to press for more professional training. Substance for these conclusions may be found in the autobiographies of Sir Neville Lyttelton (80), Sir Horace Smith-Dorrien (104), Lord Grenfell (55), Sir George Greaves (53), and Sir William Robertson (98). Their accounts can be set in the objective context of *The Army Book for the British Empire* (50) and the *Chronology of Events Connected with Army Administration* (24). A royal commission of 1887 into civil establishments of government (150) reported with a long section on the War Office, so that leadership of the army at the turn of the century can easily be placed in context with its higher administration.

THE BOER WAR. The main primary sources for the Boer War are in the Cabinet papers among PRO/CAB. 37. Volumes 43–61 cover the years 1896–1902. Individual papers are described in the *List of Cabinet Papers 1880–1914* (19). These papers are better understood by studying first the Report of the Royal Commission on the War in South Africa, with its two volumes of evidence (153). Campaigns and battles are narrated in the official History of the *War in South Africa 1899–1902* (107), which was planned by G. F. Henderson and taken over after his death in 1903 by J. F. Maurice. Restrictions placed on this work by the Army Council are described in *Sir Frederick Maurice, a Record and Essays* (84). Much more articulate and filled with critical judgment and personal bias is the *Times History of the South African War,* written in six volumes by Leo Amery (3), who later admitted that his task "was in essence propagandist—to secure the reform of our Army in preparation for coming dangers. . . ." Basil Collier in *Brasshat* (28) argues that Amery was strongly influenced by Sir Henry Wilson. He wrote indeed while some of the most far-reaching reforms were already taking place, each of them attributable to military deficiencies revealed by the campaign in South Africa. Amery's polemics can be placed in perspective through biographies of the men who commanded—of *Lord Roberts* by David James (71), of *Kitchener* by Philip Magnus (83), which is more penetrating than the older biography by Sir G. Arthur (8), and of Buller through Julian Symons, *Buller's Campaign* (111). None of these compares, however, with the spirited and condensed story by Rayne Kruger, *Good-bye Dolly Gray* (75).

The impact of the Boer War on military and strategic thinking can most fully be realized by comparing the outcome of the Hartington Report of 1890 (151) with that of the Esher Committee in 1904 (154). The first had been largely ignored; the second led to more formal organization of the Committee of Imperial Defense, and to formation of the General Staff and the Army Council. The official sources on these developments are described in two booklets: *List of Papers of the Committee of Imperial Defence to 1914* (29), and *The Records of the Cabinet Office to 1922* (18). These records can be supplemented by the Balfour and Sydenham papers in the British Museum. Much of this material formed the basis for the article by J. P. Mackintosh, "The Role of the C.I.D. Before 1914." (81) More comprehensive and administrative in emphasis is the work of an American political scientist, F. A. Johnson, *Defense by Committee* (72), which suffers from the fact that the papers of the Cabinet Office and those of Clarke and Balfour were not open when he wrote the book. The subject takes on added life from the published memoirs of Clarke (25) and Esher (14), but all the related issues of imperial strategy, of military preparation, and of a general staff were raised to a high level of debate by Spenser Wilkinson in two books, *The Brain of an Army* and *Britain at Bay* (123). Together with Leo Amery (4) and Lord Roberts (97), Wilkinson urged a closer association between the nation and the army, with a view to some form of compulsory service. The opposite view was pressed in Ian Hamilton's *Compulsory Service* (60), which was written as a semi-official defense of the Haldane reforms. The most objective summaries relating military organization to the broader issue of imperial defense are still the two chapters by W. C. B. Tunstall in volume three of the *Cambridge History of the British Empire* (116).

REFORM AND CHANGE BEFORE THE FIRST WORLD WAR. The Boer War had revealed once again that a system of voluntary enlistment, given the demands on the British army, could not produce enough men to sustain a trained reserve. This weakness prompted the report of the Norfolk Commission in 1904 (155), which concentrated on the Militia and the Volunteers. Its findings pointed to the reasons for failing to attract recruits, reasons which were closely involved with the conditions of the private soldier. The life of the soldier in a volunteer army has ever since been the subject of interesting, if not always scholarly study, beginning with an article in the *J.R.U.S.I.* of 1889 (34), proceeding with the autobiography and a novel by Robert Blatchford (12), and coming finally to three recent books by H. de Watteville, *The British Soldier* (121), John Laffin, *Tommy Atkins* (76), and Tom McGuffie, *Rank and File* (88), all of which describe improvements in the lot of the soldier during the thirty years before 1914. To understand why it was so difficult to obtain and to sustain larger numbers, one has to examine issues of policy and organization in the War Office.

The most successful Secretary for War after Cardwell was clearly Lord Haldane. His success emerges more clearly when it is compared with the failure of his two predecessors in the War Office—St. John Brodrick and H. O. Arnold-Forster. Their attempts at reform are covered in John K. Dunlop, *The Development of the British Army 1899–1914* (37), which is now showing signs of age because it was based on the *Parliamentary Papers* and on secondary sources, before the official and private archives on the period were opened. Two articles by Albert Tucker (115) get inside those politics of the Unionist Government which so hampered military reorganization immediately after the Boer War. On the formation of Haldane's expeditionary and territorial forces in 1907, the impression of achievement is best realized by comparing Arnold-Forster, *The Army in 1906* (7) with R. B. Haldane, *Army Reform* and *Before the War* (57).

The implications of this reorganization of the infantry are fully discussed in Charles Repington, *The Foundations of Reform* (95). The book is a collection of articles which Repington wrote as military correspondent of the *Times* between 1906 and 1908. His admiration of the new Territorial Force should be compared with the description of the old Militia as a source of recruits in Sir Gerald Ellison, *Home Defence* (39). Neither book has been superseded by Haldane's latest biographer, Donald Sommer (106), who considers his five years at the War Office as merely one facet in a complex career. Had Haldane still been Secretary of State for War in 1913, instead of Sir John Seely, it is not likely that the Curragh Incident would have created the crisis that it did in civil-military relations. The Incident is lucidly analysed by Sir James Fergusson in a book (170) which contains a complete bibliography on the subject.

Like Cardwell before him, Haldane may have accomplished far-reaching reforms chiefly because of his willingness to consult with young reformers in uniform—with men such as Sir William Nicholson, Sir Gerald Ellison, Sir Henry Wilson, and Sir Douglas Haig. The first three brought to bear their experience in India under the command of Lord Roberts, and one can see something of this influence in two articles by Ellison, one in 1912 and the other in 1932 (39). It plays no part in John Terraine's account of the career of Haig before the First World War (112). Wilson's role during these years is interpreted by Basil Collier in *Brasshat* (28), and more fully in the older biography by Sir C. E. Callwell (21). The view of Hankey that British military plans may have become too closely tied to those of France is discussed by Liddell Hart in *The British Way in Warfare* (78), which should be compared with J. E. Tyler, *The British Army and the Continent* (117).

TECHNICAL DEVELOPMENTS AND EDUCATION. Adequate studies of the Artillery and Engineers have not been written. The sources are at the P.R.O. and at Woolwich. But ordnance production and the whole organization at Woolwich have been studied historically by O. F. Hogg in *The Royal Arsenal* (66). Volume two covers the period since the Crimean War. Altogether the work is based on more than 3,000 volumes of War-Office papers in the P.R.O. It is a thorough, comprehensive history of the Ordnance that is not likely ever to be superseded. Greater immediacy is attained, however, by adding to Hogg's narrative the Report of the Strathnairn Committee of 1867 on transport and supply (143), that of the Morley Committee in 1887 on the military manufacturing departments (149), and the Report of the Royal Commission on Warlike Stores of the same year (148). These are all more basic sources than Fortescue's history of the Army Service Corps (45).

The functions of the Inspector-General of Fortifications become clear from biographies of Sir John Burgoyne (129) and Sir Andrew Clarke (120). Supply and finance at mid-century were explained by E. B. de Fonblanque (42). The Commissariat was the focus for the career of Arthur, Lord Haliburton, who wrote *Army Administration in Three Centuries* (59), and was himself the subject of a biography by J. B. Atlay (9). Weapons and tactics are related to each other in the essay "War" by J. F. Maurice (87). The impact of the machine-gun was profound, particularly in the Russo-Japanese War, which led to the study by Lt. V. A. Jackson, *Machine Guns and Their Tactical Uses* (70). Whether the cavalry would continue to be a useful force was the central question of *War and the Arme Blanche* by E. Childers (23), and Leonard Cooper in a recent history of British cavalry (31) has devoted chapters 12–15 to the hundred years before the First World War.

On military education the most direct sources are the Report of the Royal Commission of 1869 (144) and the various reports of the Director-General of Education after the establishment of that office in 1870; they are listed among the indexes to the *Parliamentary Papers*. The influence of the public schools on the officer class is part of "Army and Society . . ." by Albert Tucker (115), while David Newsome has done a definitive *History of Wellington College* (91). Two slighter books on Sandhurst appeared in 1961, by Sir John Smyth (105) and Hugh Thomas (113). There is no comparable work on the Royal Military Academy at Woolwich. The Staff College at Camberley did little to advance professional study until the end of the nineteenth century, in spite of the efforts of Wolseley. The standard text is still *The Staff and the Staff College* by A. R. Godwin-Austen (48), but Jay Luvaas in *The Education of an Army* (79) has excellent chapters on Edward Hamley, J. F. Maurice, and G. F. Henderson, each of whom was successively an influential teacher at the Staff College.

The difference between Hamley's *The Operations of War* (61) and Henderson's far more brilliant *Science of War* (63) reflects the tactical changes induced by new artillery and infantry weapons, by larger formations of men, and by increased mobility. Few men at the time could foresee the consequences of these factors for a continental war, and those who did had little impact on military thinking either at the Staff College or in the War Office.

SUGGESTIONS FOR FURTHER RESEARCH. One of the most remarkable features of the nineteenth-century army was its autonomy from the navy. The result was a failure to develop amphibious operations. Liddell Hart asked in a recent article (78): "why is it that in Britain, the country most dependent on sea power, the marines have never been developed as they have been in America?" He suggests one or two answers but the question could be pursued more comprehensively. One answer is bound up with the background and training of the officers in the Infantry and Cavalry, whose education was always inferior to that of officers in the Engineers and Artillery. This whole subject of education would make an interesting study, but more specifically research and reflection are needed on the role and status of Engineer and Artillery officers. Their social origins and their professional outlook were free of those overtones of class and snobbery which came from the system of purchase.

The history of purchase would itself make a significant monograph, from its origins in the seventeenth century to its abolition in 1870. Generalizations abound on its effects, but the actual working of the system through

Army Agency and the office of Military Secretary has not yet been adequately explained. The idea that the officer was a gentleman and an amateur lasted well beyond the abolition of purchase, partly because he commanded units that did not seem essential to defense of the country. Regiments were raised entirely by voluntary enlistment and large numbers of soldiers came from Ireland. Again, as a base for recruiting and as a focus for occupation, Ireland deserves more serious examination than it has so far received.

Poverty and unemployment drove many young Irishmen to enlist, but the British army remained essentially one of voluntary recruits. Their origins as English society became industrialized and urbanized were closely related to the increasing number of rejections by the end of the century; it is a subject which could throw a good deal of light on the difference between town and country. Many young men were drawn into regular regiments through the Militia, but neither the Militia nor the Volunteers established in 1859 have been studied with much concentration. Research here would have implications for social as well as military history.

Much the same could be said for two final suggestions: an examination of the system of army contracts, which would have distinct political and social overtones; and study of the War Office in the context not simply of campaigns and personalities, but of those far-reaching changes which took place in administrative and civil-service reform. Such studies would go far to integrating the history of military organization more successfully into the life of the whole society.

BIBLIOGRAPHY

1. Airlie, Countess of. *With the Guards We Shall Go.* London: Hodder and Stoughton, 1933.
2. Alison, (Sir) Archibald. *On Army Organization.* London and Edinburgh: originally published in Blackwood's Magazine, 1869.
3. Amery, Leo. *The Times History of the War in South Africa.* London: Sampson Low, 1900–1909. 7 vols.
4. Amery, Leo. *The Problem of the Army.* London, 1903.
5. Anglesey, Marquess of. *One-Leg, the Life and Letters of Henry William Paget, First Marquess of Anglesey, 1768–1854.* New York: Morrow, 1961.
6. Anson, (Sir) Wm. *Law and Custom of the Constitution.* Volume II, *The Crown.* A. B. Keith, ed. Oxford: Clarendon Press, 1935.
7. Arnold-Forster, H. O. *The Army in 1906.* London: Murray, 1906. See also *The War Office, the Army, and the Empire.* London and New York: Cassell, 1900.
8. Arthur, (Sir) George. *Life of Lord Kitchener.* London and New York: Macmillan, 1920. 3 vols.
9. Atlay, J. B. *Lord Haliburton.* London: Smith, Elder, 1909.

10. Bell, H. C. F. *Lord Palmerston*. London: Longmans, Green, 1936. 2 vols.

11. Biddulph, (Sir) Robert. *Lord Cardwell at the War Office*. London: Murray, 1904.

12. Blatchford, Robert. *My Life in the Army*. London: no date. *Tommy Atkins of the Ramchunders*. London, 1895.

13. Bond, Brian, ed. *Victorian Military Campaigns*. London: Hutchinson, 1967. New York: Praeger, 1967. "Recruiting the Victorian Army." *Victorian Studies,* V (1962). "Prelude to the Cardwell Reforms 1856–68," *J.R.U.S.I.,* CVI (1961), 229–36. "The Effect of the Cardwell Reforms on Army Organization 1878–1904," *J.R.U.S.I.,* CV (1960), 515–24.

14. Brett, Reginald Baliol (2nd Viscount Esher). *Journals and Letters of Reginald, Viscount Esher.* M. V. Brett, ed. London: Nicholson and Watson, 1934–38. 4 vols.

15. Brodrick, St. John (Midleton, Earl of). *Records and Reactions 1856–1939.* London: Murray, 1939.

16. Burne, (Colonel) A. H. *The Noble Duke of York*. London: Staples Press, 1950.

17. Butler, (Sir) William Francis. *Sir Charles Napier*. London: Macmillan, 1890. *The Life of Sir George Pomeroy-Colley*. London: Murray, 1899. *An Autobiography*. London: Constable, 1911.

18. *Cabinet Office to 1922, Records of.* P.R.O. Handbook No. 11. London: H.M.S.O., 1966.

19. *Cabinet Papers 1880–1914, List of.* P.R.O. Handbook No. 4. London: H.M.S.O., 1964.

20. Callwell, C. R. *Small Wars*. London: H.M.S.O., 1896; 3rd ed., 1906.

21. Callwell, (Sir) C. E. *Sir Henry Wilson: life and diaries*. New York: Scribner's, 1927. 2 vols.

22. Cardwell, Edward T. Speeches in *Hansard's Parliamentary Debates*. Third Series. CCIV (16 Feb. 1871); and CCIX (22 Feb. 1872).

23. Childers, E. *War and the Arme Blanche*. London: Arnold, 1910.

24. *Chronology of Events Connected with Army Administration 1858–1907*. London, 1908.

25. Clarke, (Sir) George (Lord Sydenham of Combe). *My Working Life*. London: Murray, 1927.

26. Clode, Charles M. *The Military Forces of the Crown*. London: Murray, 1869. 2 vols.

27. Colley, George P. "Army." *Encyclopedia Britannica*. 9th ed. New York: Samuel Hall, 1878–1889.

28. Collier, Basil. *Brasshat*. London: Secker and Warburg, 1961.

29. *Committee of Imperial Defence to 1914, List of Papers of.* P.R.O. Handbook No. 6. London: H.M.S.O., 1964.

30. Cook, (Sir) Edward. *Florence Nightingale*. London: Macmillan, 1913. 2 vols.

31. Cooper, Leonard. *British Regular Cavalry 1644–1914*. London: Chapman, 1965.

32. Cope, (Sir) Zachary. *Florence Nightingale and the Doctors.* London: Museum Press; New York: Lippincott, 1958.
33. Dicey, A. V. *Introduction to the Study of the Law of the Constitution.* 9th ed. Introduction by E. C. S. Wade. London: Macmillan, 1945.
34. Don, Deputy-Surgeon W. G. "Recruits and Recruiting." *J.R.U.S.I.,* XXXIII (1889), 827–53.
35. Douglas, D. C., gen. ed. *English Historical Documents.* [Aspinall, A., and Smith, E. A., eds., XI, *1783–1832.* London: Eyre and Spottiswoode, 1959.] [Young, G. M., and Handcock W. D. eds., XII(1), *1833–1874.* London: Eyre and Spottiswoode, 1956.]
36. Douglas, (Sir) George, ed. *The Panmure Papers.* London: Hodder, 1908. 2 vols.
37. Dunlop, John K. *The Development of the British Army, 1899–1914.* London: Methuen, 1938.
38. Dupin, F. P. C. *View of the History and Actual State of the Military Forces of Great Britain.* London, 1822. 2 vols.
39. Ellison, (Sir) Gerald. *Home Defence.* London: Stanford, 1898. "Our Army System in Theory and Practice." *Army Review,* III (1912), 382–97. "Lord Roberts and the General Staff." *Nineteenth Century and After, CXII* (December, 1932), 722–32.
40. Ensor, R. C. K. *England 1870–1914.* Oxford: Clarendon Press, 1936.
41. Erickson, Arvel B. *Edward T. Cardwell: Peelite.* Philadelphia: American Philosophical Society, 1959.
42. Fonblanque, E. B. de. *Treatise on the Administration and Organization of the British Army.* London: Longmans, 1858. "Reform in Army Administration." *J.R.U.S.I.,* XIII (1869), 88–109.
43. Fortescue, (Sir) John W. *History of the British Army.* London and New York: Macmillan, 1899–1930. 13 vols. [XI (1923), XII (1927), XIII (1930)].
44. Fortescue, (Sir) John W. *Wellington.* London: Williams and Norgate, 1925.
45. Fortescue, (Sir) John W. *The Royal Army Service Corps; a history of supply and transport in the British army.* Cambridge University Press, 1930–31. 2 vols.
46. Fuller, J. F. C. *War and Western Civilization 1832–1932.* London: Duckworth, 1932.
47. Furber, E. H., ed. *Changing Views in British History.* Cambridge: Harvard, 1966. The essays by Prouty and Clive cover the period 1820–1914.
48. Godwin-Austen, A. R. *The Staff and the Staff College.* London: Constable, 1927.
49. Gooch, Brison. "The Crimean War in Selected Documents and Secondary Works since 1940." *Victorian Studies,* I (March, 1958), 271–79.
50. Goodenough, W. H., and J. C. Dalton. *The Army Book for the British Empire: a record of the development and present composition of*

the military forces and their duties in peace and war. London: H.M.S.O., 1893.

51. Gordon, Hampden. *The War Office.* London: Putnam, 1935 (Whitehall Series).

52. Gore, Albert A. *The Story of Our Services under the Crown.* A historical sketch of the Army Medical Staff. London, 1879 (reprinted from *"Colburn's" United Service Magazine*).

53. Greaves, (Sir) George. *Memoirs.* London: Murray, 1924.

54. Greenleaf, W. H. "Biography and the 'Amateur' Historian: Mrs. Woodham-Smith's 'Florence Nightingale.'" *Victorian Studies,* III (1959–60), 190–202.

55. Grenfell, Lord. *Memoirs of Field-Marshal Lord Grenfell.* London: Hodder and Stoughton, 1925.

56. Gurwood, (Lieutenant-Colonel) John, ed. *The Dispatches of Field Marshal the Duke of Wellington.* London, 1844–47. 8 vols. [Vol. VIII contains selections for the period 1815–33]. See also Gurwood, ed. *Speeches of the Duke of Wellington in Parliament.* London, 1854. 2 vols.

57. Haldane, R. B. *Army Reform.* London: Unwin, 1907. *Before the War.* London: Cassell, 1920.

58. Halévy, Élie. *England in 1815.* 2nd rev. ed. London: Benn, 1949. New York: Barnes and Noble, 1949.

59. Haliburton, Arthur (1st baron). *Army Organization.* London: Stanford, 1898. *Army Administration in Three Centuries.* London, 1901.

60. Hamilton, (Sir) Ian. *Compulsory Service.* London: Murray, 1910.

61. Hamley, (Sir) Edward. *The Operations of War.* London and Edinburgh: Blackwood, 1866 (new edition, brought up to the latest requirements by L. E. Kiggell, 1914).

62. *Hart's Annual Army List.* London: Murray, 1840–1915. 67 vols.

63. Henderson, G. F. R. *The Science of War.* Capt. Neill Malcolm, ed. London: Longmans, 1905.

64. Hibbert, Christopher. *The Destruction of Lord Raglan.* London: Longmans, 1961; and Penguin, 1963.

65. Higham, Robin, ed. *The Consolidated Author and Subject Index to the JRUSI, 1857–1963.* Ann Arbor, Mich., University Microfilms, 1964.

66. Hogg, O. F. *The Royal Arsenal.* London and New York: Oxford, 1963. 2 vols.

67. Howard, Michael. "Military History as a University Study." *History,* XLI (1956), 184–91.

68. Hozier, H. M. "The German and the British Armies." *Nineteenth Century,* XIV (August, 1883).

69. Huddleston, F. J. "The War Office Library." *Army Quarterly,* I (1920), 366–75.

70. Jackson, Lieutenant V. A. *Machine Guns and Their Tactical Uses.* London: Foster, Groom, 1910.

71. James, David. *Lord Roberts.* London: Hollis and Carter, 1954.

72. Johnson, F. A. *Defence by Committee: the British Committee of Imperial Defence 1885–1959.* London and New York: Oxford, 1960.

73. *Journal of the Royal United Service Institution.* London, 1857– . See also Higham, Robin, ed., *The Consolidated Author and Subject Index to the [J.R.U.S.I.], 1857–1963.* Ann Arbor, Mich., University Microfilms, 1964.

74. Kinglake, A. W. *The Invasion of the Crimea: its origin and an account of its progress down to the death of Lord Raglan.* London: Blackwood, 1863–87. 8 vols.

75. Kruger, Rayne. *Good-Bye Dolly Gray.* London: Cassell, 1959; New York: Lippincott, 1960.

76. Laffin, John. *Tommy Atkins.* London: Cassell, 1966.

77. Lehman, Joseph. *All Sir Garnet.* London: Cape, 1964.

78. Liddell Hart, Basil Henry. *The British Way in Warfare.* London: Faber, 1932. *Deterrent or Defence.* London: Stevens, 1960. "The Value of Amphibious Flexibility and Forces." *J.R.U.S.I.,* CV (1960), 483–92.

79. Luvaas, Jay. *The Education of an Army: British military thought 1815–1940.* Chicago: University of Chicago, 1964.

80. Lyttelton, (Sir) Neville. *Eighty Years.* London: Hodder, 1927.

81. Mackintosh, J. P. "The Role of the C.I.D. Before 1914." *English Historical Review,* LXXVII (1962), 490–503.

82. MacMunn, (Sir) George. *The Crimea in Perspective.* London: Bell, 1935.

83. Magnus, Philip. *Kitchener: portrait of an imperialist.* London: Murray, 1958.

84. Maurice, (Sir) Frederick, ed. *Sir Frederick Maurice, a Record and Essays.* London: Arnold, 1913.

85. Maurice, (Sir) F., and (Sir) George Arthur. *The Life of Lord Wolseley.* London: Heinemann, 1924.

86. Maurice, J. F. *Military History of the Campaign of 1882 in Egypt.* London: H.M.S.O., 1887.

87. Maurice, J. F. "War." *Encyclopaedia Britannica.* 9th ed. New York: Samuel Hall, 1878–1889. This essay was published in expanded form as *War.* London: Macmillan, 1891.

88. McGuffie, Tom. *Rank and File: the common soldier in peace and war 1642–1914.* London: Hutchinson, 1964.

89. Merrill, James M. "British-French Amphibious Operations in the Sea of Azov, 1855." *Military Affairs,* XX (1956), 16–27.

90. Mitra, S. M. *Life and Letters of Sir John Hall.* London: Longmans, 1911.

91. Newsome, David. *History of Wellington College.* London: Murray, 1959.

92. Norman, C. "The French Army of Today." *Nineteenth Century,* XIV (November, 1883).

93. Preston, Adrian, ed. *In Relief of Gordon: Lord Wolseley's Campaign Journal of the Khartoum Relief Expedition 1884–85.* London: Hutchinson, 1967.

94. Rait, R. S. *The Life and Campaigns of Field-Marshal Viscount Gough.* London: Constable, 1903. 2 vols.
95. Repington, Charles. *The Foundations of Reform.* London: Simpkin, Marshall, 1908.
96. Robbins, M. "The Balaclava Railway." *Journal of Transport History,* I (1953), 28–43.
97. Roberts, F. M. Earl. *A Nation in Arms.* London: Murray, 1907.
98. Robertson, (Sir) William. *From Private to Field-Marshal.* London: Constable, 1921.
99. Rose, B. "The Volunteers of 1859." *J.S.A.H.R.* (September, 1959).
100. Russell, William H. *The War in the Crimea.* London, 1855. [Revised as *The British Expedition to the Crimea.* London: Routledge, 1858.] *My Diary During the Last Great War.* London, 1874 (reprinted from the *Army and Navy Gazette* 1872–74). *The Great War with Russia, a personal Retrospect.* London: Routledge, 1895.
101. St. Aubyn, Giles. *Royal George.* London: Constable, 1963.
102. Sebag-Montefiore, C. *A History of the Volunteer Forces from the Earliest Times to the Year 1860.* London: Constable, 1908.
103. Smith, G. C. M., ed. *The Autobiography of Lieut. General Sir Harry Smith.* London: Murray, 1903.
104. Smith-Dorrien, (Sir) Horace. *Memories of Forty-Eight Years' Service.* London: Murray, 1925.
105. Smyth, (Sir) John. *Sandhurst.* London: Weidenfeld and Nicholson, 1961.
106. Sommer, Donald. *Haldane of Cloan.* London: Allen, 1960.
107. *South Africa, History of the War in, 1899–1902.* London: H.M.S.O., 1906–1910. 4 vols.
108. Spender, J. A. *Life of Sir Henry Campbell-Bannerman.* London: Hodder, 1923. 2 vols.
109. Stanmore, Lord. *Sidney Herbert: a memoir.* London: Murray, 1906. 2 vols.
110. Stocqueler, J. H. *A Personal History of the Horse Guards 1750–1872.* London, 1873.
111. Symons, Julian. *Buller's Campaign.* London: Cresset, 1963.
112. Terraine, John. *Douglas Haig the Educated Soldier.* London: Hutchinson, 1963.
113. Thomas, Hugh. *The Story of Sandhurst.* London: Hutchinson, 1961.
114. Trevelyan, (Sir) Charles. *The Purchase System.* London, 1867. *The British Army in 1868.* London, 1868. *A Standing or a Popular Army.* London, 1869.
115. Tucker, Albert. "Army and Society in England 1870–1900: a reassessment of the Cardwell Reforms." *Journal of British Studies,* II (May, 1963), 110–41. "Politics and the Army in the Unionist Government in England 1900–05." *Canadian Historical Association, Annual Report* (1964). "Army Reform in the Unionist Government 1903–05." *Historical Journal,* IX (1966), 90–100.
116. Tunstall, W. C. B. "Imperial Defence 1870–1897," and "Imperial

Defence 1897–1914." *Cambridge History of the British Empire*, II, chs. 7, 15.

117. Tyler, J. E. *The British Army and the Continent 1900–1914*. London: Arnold, 1938.

118. Vagts, Alfred. *History of Militarism*. New York: Meridan, 1959.

119. Verner, Willoughby. *The Military Life of H.R.H. the Duke of Cambridge*. London: Murray, 1909. 2 vols.

120. Vetch, R. H. *Life of Lieut. General Sir Andrew Clarke*. London: Murray, 1905.

121. Watteville, H. G. de. *The British Soldier*. London: Dent, 1954.

122. Wheeler, Owen. *The War Office Past and Present*. London: Methuen, 1914.

123. Wilkinson, Spenser. *The Brain of an Army*. London: Constable, 1895. *Britain at Bay*. London: Constable, 1909.

124. Wolseley, (Sir) Garnet. *The Story of a Soldier's Life*. London: Constable, 1903. 2 vols.

125. Wood, (Sir) H. Evelyn. *The Crimea in 1854 and 1894*. London: Chapman and Hall, 1895.

126. Wood, (Sir) H. Evelyn. *From Midshipman to Field-Marshal*. London: Methuen, 1906. 2 vols.

127. Woodham-Smith, Cecil. *Florence Nightingale*. London: Constable, 1950. *The Reason Why*. London: Constable, 1953; and Penguin, 1958.

128. Woodward, E. L. *The Age of Reform 1815–1870*. 2nd ed. Oxford: Clarendon Press, 1962.

129. Wrottesley, George, ed. *Military Opinions of Sir John Burgoyne*. London: Bentley, 1859. *Life and Correspondence of Sir John Burgoyne*. London: Bentley, 1873. 2 vols.

PARLIAMENTARY PAPERS

130. *Catalogue of Parliamentary Papers 1801–1900*. London: King and Son, 1904.

131. Ford, P. and G. *Select List of British Parliamentary Papers 1833–1899*. Oxford, 1953. *Breviate of Parliamentary Papers 1900–1916*. Oxford, 1956.

132. 1833 (650) VII. 1. Report of the Select Committee on Army and Navy Appointments.

133. 1835 (473) VI. 96. Return of the number and distribution of the effective forces of the British Army in the various colonies of Great Britain, since 1815.

134. 1836 [59] XXII. 1. Report of Commissioners for Inquiring into the System of Military Punishments in the Army.

135. 1837 [78] XXXIV. 1. Report of the Commission on Consolidating the Different Departments Connected with the Civil Administration of the Army.

136. 1840 [234] XXII. 1. Report of Commissioners into Naval and Military Promotions.
137. 1854 [1802] XIX. 833. Report of Commissioners on Promotion in the Army.
138. 1855 (80) (156) (218) (247) (318). IX, Parts 1–3. First to Fifth Reports from the Select Committee on the Army before Sebastopol (Roebuck Committee).
139. 1856 [2007] XX. 1. Report of the Commission into the supplies of the British Army in the Crimea (McNeill and Tulloch Commission).
140. 1857 [2267] XVIII. 1. Report of Commissioners into the System of Purchase and Sale of Commissions in the Army.
141. 1857–58 [2318] XLIII. 1. Report of the Commission into the Regulations affecting the Sanitary Condition of the Army (The Royal Sanitary Commission).
142. 1867 [Cd.3752] XV. 1. Report of the Royal Commission on Recruiting.
143. 1867 (3848) XV. 343. Report of a Committee on the Administration of the Transport and Supply Departments of the Army (Strathnairn Committee).
144. 1869 [4221] XXII. 1. First Report of a Royal Commission into the present state of Military Education and the Training of Candidates for Commissions in the Army.
145. 1870 [C.201] XII. 199. Report of Commissioners into Over-Regulation Payments on Promotion in the Army.
146. 1872 [C.493] XXXVII. 386. Report of the Committee on the Organization of the Various Military Land Forces of the Country.
147. 1877 [C.1654] XVIII. 29. Report of the Committee on the Militia and Brigade-Depot System.
148. 1887 [Cd.5062] XV. 1. Report of the Royal Commission on Warlike Stores (Fitzjames Stephen Committee).
149. 1887 [C.5116] XIV. 1. Report of a Committee on the Organization and Administration of the Manufacturing Departments of the Army (Morley Committee).
150. 1887 [C.5226] XIX. 1. First Report of the Royal Commission into the civil establishments of the different offices of state at home and abroad.
151. 1890 [Cd.5979] XIX. 1. Report of Commissioners on the Civil and Professional Administration of the Naval and Military Departments (Hartington Report).
152. 1901 [Cd.607] XXXIX. 255. Paper by the Secretary of State laying down the requirements from our Army, dated 1st June, 1891 (Stanhope Memorandum).
153. 1904 [Cd.1789–92] XL. XLI. XLII. Report of the Royal Commission on the War in South Africa (Elgin Commission).
154. 1904 [Cd.1932, 1968, 2002] VIII. 101. Report of a Committee to Inquire into the Reconstitution of the War Office (Esher Committee).

155. 1904 [Cd.2061–64] XXX. XXXI. Report of the Royal Commission on the Militia and the Volunteers (Norfolk Commission).

PRIVATE PAPERS

156. Cambridge, Duke of, Papers. Royal Archives. Write: Mr. Mackworth Young, Royal Archivist, Windsor Castle, Berks.
157. Gathorne Hardy (Lord Cranbrook) Papers, County Record Office, Ipswich, Suffolk.
158. Haig and Haldane Papers, Department of Manuscripts, National Library of Scotland, Edinburgh 1.
159. Lansdowne Papers, Bowood Park, Calne, Wilts. Write: The Secretary, The Marquis of Lansdowne, Bowood Park, Calne, Wilts.
160. National Register of Archives, Quality Court, Chancery Lane, London, W.C. 2.
161. Stanhope Papers, Chevening, Sevenoaks, Kent. Write: Dr. Aubrey Newman, Department of History, University of Leicester, Leicester.
162. Wolseley Papers. Public Library, Hove, Sussex. Write. Borough Librarian and Curator, Public Library, Hove, Sussex. Wolseley's official papers are in the War Office Library.

SUPPLEMENT TO BIBLIOGRAPHY

163. National Army Museum. *The Army in India, 1850–1914: a photographic record.* London: Hutchinson, 1968.
164. The Esher Papers are at Watlington Park, Watlington, Oxford.
165. Blanco, Richard L. "The Attempted Control of Venereal Disease in the Army of Mid-Victorian England." *Journal of the Society for Army Historical Research,* 1967.
166. Papers in the Manuscript Room of the British Museum:
    H. O. Arnold-Forster
    A. J. Balfour
    Sir Henry Campbell-Bannerman
    W. E. Gladstone
    St. John Broderick, Viscount Middleton
    G. F. S. Robinson, first Marquis Ripon
167. Young, Lieutenant-Colonel F. W. *The Story of the Staff College, 1858–1958.* Camberley, 1958.
168. Sutherland, John. *Men of Waterloo.* London: Muller, 1967.
169. Waterfield, Private R. *The Memoirs of Private Waterfield: a soldier in Her Majesty's 32nd Regiment of Foot (Duke of Cornwall's Light Infantry), 1842–1857.* London: Cassells, 1968.
170. Fergusson, (Sir) James. *The Curragh Incident.* London: Faber and Faber, 1964.

IX

THE NAVY IN THE
NINETEENTH CENTURY

PART I, 1815–53

C. J. Bartlett

The late eighteen-seventies and early eighteen-eighties have been described as the "dark ages" in the history of the British navy. But for contemporary writing on naval matters this is true of a much longer period starting about 1840. In the early and middle years of Queen Victoria's reign few works produced on the navy were larger than pamphlets. William James (19) and Edward Brenton (9) both completed their naval chronicles in the eighteen-thirties, carrying the story of main events down to about 1836. Subsequent operations, such as those off the coast of Syria in 1840, were described at some length by observers or participants in a journalistic fashion. But in general a new era of naval writing had to await the emergence of such figures as Philip and Sir John Colomb, Sir John Laughton, and Sir William Laird Clowes and others later in the century. The information available when interest in naval history revived was thus too sketchy to offset the predisposition to treat the post-Napoleonic and Victorian Navy as a conservative and unenlightened force—a dull interlude between the glories of Nelson and the revivalism of "Jacky" Fisher. Nevertheless, the British nation and empire were in general well served by the navy during this period, and at a comparatively low cost. Once misleading phrases such as the *Pax Britannica* have been discarded, it is possible to see the navy in proper perspective as a vital instrument of policy, exerting influence in a multitude of ways. This was also a period of exciting technological change, the course of which has yet to be properly charted.

GENERAL WORKS. Not surprisingly the treatment of the years 1815–53 by most general histories tends to be uneven. A sequel to Geoffrey Marcus' (28) history of the navy, which stops in 1783, is expected. The best short introduction is provided by Michael Lewis (22). Of the older histories that by Clowes (12) is uneven, though it contains much of value.

Just how thin the field is can readily be seen from the general bibliography provided by Robert Greenhalgh Albion.

NAVAL ADMINISTRATION. If one turns to the more specialised works, the position is also disappointing. On naval administration there is, for instance, no equivalent of Daniel Baugh's study of the Walpole era (see chapter VI). Fortunately, Bernard Pool (34) has placed everyone in his debt with his study of Navy Board Contracts, not least because he has rescued the Board itself from much ill-informed criticism. For naval administration in general there is only the fragment of an uncompleted work by Sir Oswyn Murray (30), a general study by Sir Richard Hamilton (17), and the memoirs of Sir John Briggs (10). The quality of the latter varies sharply and is sometimes no more than anecdotal. It does, however, capture the flavour of the period admirably. Published work on specific Boards of Admiralty is limited to biographies of Sir James Graham by Arvel B. Erickson (14) and John Ward (38), and of the 1st Earl of Ellenborough by Albert Imlah (18). The work of those two very energetic First Lords cannot be seen in proper perspective without reference to their predecessors and successors. The long tenure of office by the 2nd Viscount Melville in particular has been neglected, though it is a subject of much abusive comment, and here the official records can be supplemented by the private papers of John Wilson Croker (47), Sir Thomas Byam Martin (41), and Melville himself (43, 46, 47). Unfortunately, the papers of the latter are now scattered through several libraries in Britain and the United States. A partial guide is to be found in *The American Archivist* (1963, xxvi. 449–62), but it omits the large collection in the Scottish Record Office, Edinburgh. The papers of the 2nd Earl of Minto (44) and of Lord Ellenborough (45) are readily available, as are those of two admirals, Sir George Cockburn (42) and Sir Alexander Milne (44), who saw much service at the Admiralty. Much light is also thrown on naval administration by the papers of Sir Robert Peel (41) and Lord John Russell (45), especially their correspondence with their respective First Lords of the Admiralty. Lesser figures such as Sir Charles Wood, later the 1st Viscount Halifax (41), should also be noted.

NAVAL POLICY. Although Britain's naval strength was at its peak in 1815, a constant watchfulness was needed to maintain the necessary margin of safety. The consequent discussions and decisions as to size, type and distribution of the navy have been examined by Christopher Bartlett (3). This work draws upon a variety of sources, including official and private papers, in an attempt to explain the thinking of successive governments and Boards of Admiralty on such matters as the introduction of steam warships, the scale of naval spending in the light of Britain's relations with other states, and the use of the navy as an instrument of policy. A variety of published works too numerous to mention here, which impinge on these matters are noted in the bibliography. Much basic information on naval expenditure and distribution of ships has been published in *Parliamentary Papers* (32). Even so the British Navy cannot be seen in proper perspec-

tive without reference to the archives of the other leading naval powers—
not least those of the United States. More work on the lines of the unpublished thesis by J. W. McCleary (27) on Anglo-French naval rivalry between 1815 and 1848 is needed. There is also much of interest to the naval
historian in Kenneth Bourne's (8) new study of Anglo-American relations
in the nineteenth century. This book makes it possible to compare British
and American appraisals of their respective naval needs and prospects in
the event of a further war between the two countries. It also refers to many
important sources. A valuable set of documents on the role of the navy in
the Latin American struggle for independence has been assembled by Professors Gerald Graham and Robert Humphreys (16). Charles G. Pitcairn
Jones (20) has edited documents on the suppression of piracy in the Levant, while a model picture of the battle of Navarino has been produced
by Christopher Woodhouse (40). This is how naval battles should really
be analysed, with generous reference to non-British sources, and with full
treatment of the political and strategic aspects as well as of the immediate
conduct of the battle itself. Christopher Lloyd (24) has written a useful
account of the navy and the slave trade, but the difficulty of establishing
the precise contribution of the fleet as opposed to other forces is well illustrated in an unpublished thesis by L. A. Bethell (6). This very judi-
ciously examines political conditions in Brazil, the complex diplomatic negotiations between Britain and that country, as well as examining the role
of the anti-slave trade squadrons as instruments of policy.

THE DEVELOPMENT OF WARSHIPS AND GUNS. The second
quarter of the nineteenth century witnessed the beginnings of a revolution
in naval *matériel*. The last years of the sailing navy await their historian.
The career of the controversial designer, Sir William Symonds, has been
narrated by James A. Sharp (36), while the closing chapters of Albion's
(1) vital monograph explain the problems associated with timber supplies.
But an historian with the necessary technical expertise will not easily be
found to analyse the problems of sailing-ship design. The history of steam-
ships, together with the introduction of iron hulls, has fared rather better.
There is James P. Baxter's (4) model study of the birth and early evolution of the ironclad warship, which delves deeply into British and other
sources. It reveals that prejudice alone was not responsible for the slow introduction of iron warships, and in general treats the whole problem with
admirable detachment. Further useful works on the development of steam
and iron warships are listed in Albion (2) and Bartlett (3). Among important private papers to reinforce the official records (among which Admiralty 2/1387–91 serve as an introduction) are those of Admiral Sir
Baldwin Wake Walker, Surveyor of the Navy (44). The broader implications of the introduction of steam power are analysed by Bernard Brodie
(11), while there is an interesting examination of some contemporary publications in *The Edinburgh Review* of July 1852 (pp. 194–231). Some of
the contemporary discussion of the invasion scares precipitated by the
steamship revolution is also to be found in the biographies and memoirs of
leading statesmen of the time, as well as much that remains untapped in

their private papers [see Bartlett's bibliography (3)]. It is worthy of note, however, that Sir George Biddlecombe (7) had occasion to preface a general study of naval tactics in 1850 with the remark, "It may be a matter of surprise that a work of this kind, up to the present period, should not have been undertaken by a more competent authority." It is possible that a detailed examination of official sources might reveal something of the nature of strategic and tactical thinking during this period, including the problems of amphibious warfare which was to play no small part in the impending Crimean War. The evolution of naval gunnery has been examined by Baxter (4) and F. L. Robertson (35); additional key works may be found in their bibliographies and in other works already mentioned (2, 3).

THE DOCKYARDS. The obvious starting point for any history of the dockyards is the report of the committee for their revision, presented on 14 December 1848, and to be found in Admiralty Records 1/5591. A Select Committee on political influence in the yards published a revealing report in 1852 (32). The papers of Sir Alexander Milne (44) are another mine of information, Milne being the naval lord in mid-century with the main responsibility for running the yards. So important was his professional skill that he was the first nineteenth-century lord of the Admiralty to survive the fall of a ministry, thereby striking a major blow against the political considerations which had become so formidable a force in naval administration since the previous century. Some of the official sources for the study of Portsmouth and Chatham have been deposited at Greenwich. There is an interesting thesis on an overseas naval base, Trincomalee, by H. A. Colgate (13).

SOCIAL HISTORY. The social historian of the navy of this period is undoubtedly Michael Lewis (21), though much original material remains to be tapped. There is a useful article by Lloyd (26) on the education of officers at Portsmouth and Greenwich. The health of seamen has been examined in one of the most exhaustive of all naval monographs by Lloyd and Jack Coulter (23). On the important question of manning the navy there are two useful articles by R. Taylor (37), though not all authorities had abandoned thoughts of impressment so completely as he claims.

BIOGRAPHIES. This is a thin period for biographies and memoirs, that of Sir William Parker by Sir Augustus Phillimore (33) being the most informative. Sir John Briggs (10) provides some thumb-nail sketches, and there is a great deal of basic information in the contemporary works of John Marshall (29) and William O'Byrne (31).

SUGGESTIONS FOR FURTHER STUDY. It should already be evident that there exist ample opportunities for original research into this period. Few historians have worked seriously in the Admiralty records deposited in the Public Record Office in London, and there must surely remain much of interest in the private papers of such distinguished naval officers as Sir Edward Codrington, Lord Exmouth, Sir Alexander Milne, Sir

William Parker and Sir Robert Stopford, all of which are readily accessible at Greenwich (44). Those of Sir Charles Napier (41, 45) Sir Thomas Byam Martin (41), and Sir George Cockburn (42) should also be noted. It is surprising, too, that there should exist no adequate biography of Sir Thomas Masterman Hardy (Nelson's Hardy). Lack of private material may be a deterrent, yet he could surely be studied through official sources and the correspondence of his colleagues and contemporaries. Although the most dramatic portion of his career was over by 1815, his command of the squadron in Latin American waters between 1819 and 1823, when the struggle for the independence of that continent was at its height, and similarly his service as First Sea Lord in the early eighteen-thirties, a time of administrative and technical change, should provide much of interest. Equally, Sir William Parker, despite the valuable work of Phillimore (33), may repay further study as one of the hardest worked admirals of the long "peace." The temperamental Sir Charles Napier similarly awaits an able student.

The navy as an instrument of policy has not been analyzed with sufficient depth or sensitivity. Too often British naval writers have uncritically portrayed the navy as an international policeman of unquestioned repute without reference to foreign opinion, or indeed to the complaints of some British interests and political groups. Gunboat diplomacy during its formative years in the second quarter of the nineteenth century has been particularly neglected (But see Part II). It could only succeed in certain conditions; it was not a panacea. Its irrelevance in some incidents in Argentina has been well brought out by Henry Ferns (15) in the course of a study with much broader interests. But until naval historians are prepared to study the internal histories of countries subjected to naval pressure of this type, the real history of gunboat diplomacy will never be written.

There is no recent study of the British naval operations against Mehemet Ali off the coast of Syria in 1840. Reference to the papers of Minto and Sir Robert Stopford (44) alone add much to the story as it is usually presented. A work on the lines of Woodhouse's *Navarino* (40) would be much appreciated. Minto's papers, with those of Admirals Sir William Parker (44) and Sir Charles Napier (41, 45), require examination to illustrate the role of the navy in the Spanish and Portuguese civil wars of the eighteen-thirties. No student of the navy as an instrument of policy should neglect the private papers of leading British politicians of the period. Sir Robert Peel (41), for instance, has not usually been viewed as a statesman with great interest in naval matters, yet his papers are a veritable mine of information for the early eighteen-forties. One cannot discuss all the possibilities here, but occasional references to the navy are likely to be found in the correspondence of most leading ministers of the period. In particular, there should still be a great deal to learn from the papers of that most militant of British politicians, the 3rd Viscount Palmerston (48), despite the several important works devoted to his career (5, 39). In passing one might also mention the papers of Lord John Russell (45), the 4th Earl of Aberdeen, and William Ewart Gladstone (41). In general far too little use has been made of original material by naval historians for these years, especially of non-British sources, and the approach to naval history has too often been marred by neglect of political and other broader considerations.

BIBLIOGRAPHY

1. Albion, Robert Greenhalgh. *Forests and Sea Power: 1652–1862*. Cambridge, Mass.: Harvard University Press, 1926. Now reprinted: Hamden, Conn.: Archon Books, 1965.
2. ———. *Naval and Maritime History: an annotated bibliography*. Mystic, Conn.: Marine Historical Association, 1963, and 1966 supplement.
3. Bartlett, Christopher John. *Great Britain and Sea Power: 1815–53*. Oxford: Clarendon Press, 1963.
4. Baxter, James Phinney, III. *The Introduction of the Ironclad Warship*. Cambridge, Mass.: Harvard University Press, 1933.
5. Bell, Herbert Clifford Francis. *Lord Palmerston*. London: Frank Cass, reprint 1966.
6. Bethell, L. M. *Great Britain and the Abolition of the Brazilian Slave Trade: 1830–52*. Ph.D. thesis, London University, 1963.
7. Biddlecombe, Sir George. *Naval Tactics and Trials of Sailing*. London: Charles Wilson, 1850.
8. Bourne, Kenneth. *Great Britain and the Balance of Power in North America: 1815–1908*. London: Longmans, 1967.
9. Brenton, Edward Pelham. *The Naval History of Great Britain: 1783–1836*. London: Henry Colburn, 1837.
10. Briggs, Sir John Henry. *Naval Administration: 1827–92*. London: Sampson Low & Co., 1897.
11. Brodie, Bernard. *Sea Power in the Machine Age*. Princeton: Princeton University Press, 1941.
12. Clowes, Sir William Laird. *The Royal Navy. A History from the earliest times to the present*. London: Sampson Low & Co., 1897–1903. 7 vols.
13. Colgate, H. A. *Trincomalee and the East Indies Squadron: 1746–1844*. M. A. thesis, London University.
14. Erickson, Arvel Benjamin. *The Public Career of Sir James Graham*. Oxford: Basil Blackwell, 1952.
15. Ferns, Henry Stanley. *Britain and Argentina in the nineteenth century*. Oxford: Clarendon Press, 1960.
16. Graham, Gerald, and Robert Arthur Humphreys. *The Navy and South America: 1807–23*. Navy Records Society, vol. CIV., 1962.
17. Hamilton, Sir Richard Vesey. *Naval Administration*. London: George Bell & Sons, 1896.
18. Imlah, Albert Henry. *Lord Ellenborough*. Cambridge: Harvard University Press, and London: Oxford University Press, 1939.
19. James, William. *The Naval History of Great Britain: 1793–1827*. London: R. Bentley & Son, 1886.

20. Jones, Charles Gray Pitcairn. *Piracy in the Levant: 1827–28*. Navy Records Society, vol. LXXIII, 1934.
21. Lewis, Michael. *The Navy in Transition: a social history: 1814–64*. London: Hodder and Stoughton, 1965.
22. ———. *The Navy of Britain: a historical portrait*. London: George Allen & Unwin, 1948.
23. Lloyd, Christopher, and Jack Lionel Sagar Coulter. *Medicine and the Navy: 1815–1900*. London: Livingstone (E & S) Ltd., 1963.
24. Lloyd, Christopher. *The Navy and the Slave Trade*. London: Longmans, 1949.
25. ———. "The origins of H. M. S. *Excellent.*" *Mariner's Mirror,* vol. XLI, pp. 193–97.
26. ———. "The Royal Naval Colleges at Portsmouth and Greenwich" *Mariner's Mirror,* vol. LII, pp. 145–56.
27. McCleary, J. W. *Anglo-French Naval Rivalry: 1815–48*. Ph.D. thesis, Johns Hopkins University, 1947.
28. Marcus, Geoffrey. *A Naval History of England: the formative centuries*. London: Longmans, 1961.
29. Marshall, John. *Royal Naval Biography*. London, 1823–25.
30. Murray, Sir Oswyn. "The Admiralty." *Mariner's Mirror,* vols. XXIII-XXV, especially XXIV, pp. 458–78.
31. O'Byrne, William Richard. *A Naval Biographical Dictionary*. London: John Murray, 1849.
32. *Parliamentary Papers. General Index to the Accounts and Papers, Reports of Commissions, Estimates etc.* Printed by order of the House of Commons or presented by command, the index for 1801–52 being published in 1853; that for 1852/3–68/9 in 1870.
33. Phillimore, Sir Augustus. *The Life of Admiral of the Fleet Sir William Parker*. London, 1876–80.
34. Pool, Bernard. *Navy Board Contracts: 1660–1832*. London: Longmans, 1966.
35. Robertson, F. L. *The Evolution of Naval Armament*. London: Constable & Co., 1921.
36. Sharp, James A. *Memoirs of the Life and Services of Rear Admiral Sir William Symonds*. London, 1858.
37. Taylor, R. "Manning the Royal Navy: the reform of the recruiting system, 1852–62." *Mariner's Mirror,* vol. XLIV, pp. 302–13, and vol. XLV, pp. 46–58. Note also his thesis, *Manning the Royal Navy: the reform of the recruiting system: 1847–61* (M. A., London, 1954).
38. Ward, John Towers. *Sir James Graham*. London: Macmillan, 1967.
39. Webster, Sir Charles Kingsley. *The Foreign Policy of Lord Palmerston: 1830–41*. London: G. Bell & Sons, 1951.
40. Woodhouse, the Hon. Christopher Montague. *The Battle of Navarino*. London: Hodder and Stoughton, 1965.

PERSONAL COLLECTIONS OF PRIVATE PAPERS

41. British Museum, London: Papers of Sir Robert Peel, the 4th Earl of Aberdeen, William Ewart Gladstone, Sir Charles Wood, Sir Charles

Napier, and Sir Thomas Byam Martin. A selection of the Martin papers has been published by the Navy Records Society, edited by Sir Richard Vesey Hamilton, see especially vol. XIX, 1900.

42. Library of Congress, Capitol Hill, Washington, D. C.: Papers of Sir George Cockburn.

43. National Library of Scotland, Edinburgh: Papers of 2nd Viscount Melville.

44. National Maritime Museum, Greenwich, England: Papers of Sir Edward Codrington, Lord Exmouth, 2nd Earl of Minto, Sir David and Sir Alexander Milne, Sir William Parker, Sir Robert Stopford and Sir Baldwin Wake Walker.

45. Public Record Office, London: Papers of 1st Earl of Ellenborough, Sir Charles Napier and Lord John Russell.

46. Scottish Record Office, Edinburgh: Papers of 2nd Viscount Melville.

47. William Clements Library, Ann Arbor, Michigan: Papers of John Wilson Croker and 2nd Viscount Melville.

48. The papers of 3rd Viscount Palmerston are now deposited both in the British Museum and, temporarily, at the National Register of Archives in London.

SUPPLEMENT TO BIBLIOGRAPHY

49. Lewis, Captain A. F. P. *Captain of the Fleet; the career of Admiral Sir William Domett, GCB, 1751–1828*. London: Keepsake Press, 1967.

50. Graham, Gerald S. *Great Britain in the Indian Ocean: a study of maritime enterprises, 1810–1850*. Oxford: Clarendon Press, 1968.

51. Colomb, Vice-Admiral P. H. *Slave-Catching in the Indian Ocean: a record of naval experiences*. London: (1873) reprinted by Pall Mall Press, 1968.

52. Sullivan, Captain G. L. *Dhow Chasing in Zanzibar Waters and on the Eastern Coast of Africa* . . . London: (1873) reprinted by Cass, 1968.

53. Ward, W. E. F. *The Royal Navy and the Slavers*. London: Allen & Unwin, 1969.

54. Baynham, Harry. *The Royal Navy, 1780–1840*. Barre, Mass.: Barre Publishers, 1970.

Part II, 1854–1914

Ruddock F. Mackay

The comparative lack of operational interest in the period 1815 to 1914 accounts for the allocation of only a single chapter to the century concerned; yet a good case can be made out for regarding 1854 as a cardinal landmark in British naval history. The whole story may be divided simply into the Age of Sail ending in 1854, and the Age of Technology extending to the present. Not only does the character of the events change radically after 1854; the nature and, above all, the quantity of the source-material inevitably reflects the mechanization of the new Age. Under these circumstances it will not be surprising to find that the style and method adopted here do not always conform very closely with those to be found in Part I of this chapter.

The year 1854 marked the beginning of a spell of naval activity, stimulated by the Crimean War and by subsequent invasion scares, which lasted till 1861. From 1862 to 1883 British governments were able to keep down naval expenditure because of the lack of serious foreign competition. In 1884 the policies of Russia, France and to some extent Germany appeared to threaten British predominance, and questions about how warships were to be used, strategically and tactically, suddenly came to the fore. From this date there is a dramatic increase in the relevant materials available to the historian, whether in the form of published books and articles, or in the form of confidential Admiralty and Cabinet papers. Tactics, foreign intelligence, organization for war, and to a lesser extent strategy, received more attention. Meanwhile, despite restricted expenditure on construction, technical development had gone ahead during the sixties and seventies. After 1884, the researcher finds a spectacular increase in the quantity of published and unpublished materials, both technical and non-technical.

ARCHIVES. (1) THE PUBLIC RECORD OFFICE. The first step, certainly, is to make a careful study of the *Guide to the Contents,* Vol. II. (See Introduction.) Under ADMIRALTY AND SECRETARIAT will be found the various classes of papers in the Secretary's Department. As for earlier periods in naval history, the main class (Adm. 1) bulks large. Most researchers will need to spend a good deal of time on it. But it is essential to realize that many important papers (from 1852 onwards) were placed in another class, namely *Cases* (Adm. 116). In the *Guide,* one should look under INDEXES AND COMPILATIONS to find the valuable index volumes called "the Admiralty Digest and Indexes" (*Series III:* Adm. 12). These assist investigation of Adm. 1 and Adm. 116 (though a list of contents for the latter is more readily available on the open shelves). Expert advice from a supervisor is needed when requisitioning the relevant Index or Digest; also when, having found the old Admiralty reference in the Digest or Index, one wishes to convert it into the (modern P.R.O.) reference in Adm. 1 or Adm. 116. At the time of writing (June 1970) researchers are advised to work in the Rolls Room: only here will one find a complete set of the lists needed for finding references appertaining to this period.

Otherwise, as far as the Admiralty archives are concerned, attention is drawn to the STATION RECORDS. The volumes relating to Africa (Adm. 123) deal with the slave trade, Boer War, etc. The correspondence of the China Station (Adm. 125) likewise runs right through the period. Several classes of STATION RECORDS, including those just mentioned, have indexes.

For the years after 1884, much information on naval subjects may be found in the Cabinet Papers. The relevant handbook (70) should be obtained and studied before research gets seriously under way. The same advice applies to the handbook listing the papers of the Committee of Imperial Defence (71). These papers will be a major source for those interested in the broader aspects of naval policy from 1901 to 1914.

(2) THE NATIONAL MARITIME MUSEUM. The Manuscripts Department is the main repository in Britain of the personal collections of naval officers and others connected with the Navy. It has much to offer for the years 1854 to 1914, some indication of which is given in the sections which follow.

(3) THE NAVAL LIBRARY, MINISTRY OF DEFENCE. Besides its unequalled collection of books on naval subjects (see Introduction), the Library holds much primary material relating to the period. There is a complete set of *Parliamentary Papers,* with indexes. Reports of inquiries into naval matters are separately available. Of great interest is the collection of Admiralty prints (catalogued as "Pamphlets"). These embody material on tactics, manoeuvres, ordnance, etc. (See the Subject Catalogue.) Fisher had a great deal of printing done; he also had some sets of prints bound up. There are volumes relating to Lords Selborne, Cawdor, and Tweedmouth in the post of First Lord. Finally, the collection of *N. I. D. Reports* is noteworthy: the series begins in 1883 with reports of the Foreign Intelligence Committee and, after the formation of the Naval Intelligence Department in 1887, continues (not quite completely) up to 1908. The reports of British naval attachés are here.

(4) THE BRITISH MUSEUM. Outstanding amongst the relevant personal collections are the Balfour Papers (85). These are of great importance for defence policy from 1902 to 1914 and after.

DOCUMENTS PUBLISHED BY THE NAVY RECORDS SOCIETY. In a class by themselves are the Navy Records Society volumes of documents relating to the period. In *The Russian War, 1854* (58) will be found the Admiralty's correspondence with Sir Charles Napier about operations in the Baltic and with Sir James Deans about operations in the Black Sea. *Russian War, 1855, Baltic* (59) and *Russian War, 1855, Black Sea* (60) contain the Admiralty's correspondence with the Hon. Richard Dundas and Sir Edmund Lyons. The documents in *The Second China War* (61) come mainly from the Foreign Office archives at the Public Record Office. They concern the capture of the *Lorcha Arrow* and the British countermeasures (1856), the appointment of Lord Elgin and the capture of Canton (1857–8), the expedition to the Peiho and the Treaty of Tientsin (1858), the end of Lord Elgin's first mission to China and the two final engagements at the Peiho (1859–60). (A recent book by M. Banno (7) may be noticed here. It shows how, under the reigning political circumstances, such limited operations could achieve success.) *The Papers of Admiral Sir John Fisher* (62) include much of the material printed by Fisher in *Naval Necessities* (1904–6) and also a number of tentative War Plans (printed in 1907). But a typescript attributable to Fisher, which covers the file of War Plans now at the P.R.O. (Adm. 116/1043B), is not included. Only 37 pages of *The Jellicoe Papers,* vol. I (63) bear directly on the pre-War period.

PERIODICALS. The *Transactions* of the Institution, of Naval Architects (see Introduction; also (8) in the Bibliography below) are a major source for technical development. The *Journal of the Royal United Service Institution* first appeared in 1857 and it provides an invaluable guide to the thinking of the more articulate officers of both services during this period. The *Mariner's Mirror* did not start coming out until 1911, but since then a number of contributions have thrown valuable light on the nineteenth century, for example Admiral George Ballard's articles on early ironclads. Edward J. Reed's quarterly journal *Naval Science* was a remarkable, if short-lived feature of the 1870's. The articles were often highly technical, but comprised naval education and even strategy—an unfashionable subject at the time, as Schurman has shown (75).

GENERAL WORKS. There is, as yet, no comprehensive general history for the period 1854 to 1914, although Clowes' last two volumes (see Part I) do contain a great deal of useful information. Apart from the lack of obvious operational interest, the main reason for this gap is the difficulty presented by the technical material. It seems that it may be some time before the second volume of G. J. Marcus' history of the Navy appears (see chapter IV). Indeed, until more specialized studies have been undertaken in the technical field, it will hardly be possible to write a firmly-based general account of the period. Studies relating technical developments within the naval sphere to those outside it would also be appropriate and welcome.

Another factor likely to delay the writing of a general history is the improved availability of certain personal collections of papers. Several collections of this type are now awaiting inspection at the National Maritime Museum and Churchill College. (See Bibliography below under *Collections of Personal Papers.*)

At present the best substitute for a general history of the period is probably Parkes's monumental work on *British Battleships* (66). Unfortunately reasons of economy precluded full bibliographic treatment, but the book remains without a rival in its overall technical expertise. While principally concerned with the construction of battleships, it also includes valuable summaries of all major developments in policy and administration. However, these latter items should not be regarded as definitive. On a lesser scale, Hovgaard's book (41) is still useful as is Richard Hough's *Dreadnought: a history of the modern battleship* (40): they both summarize the main aspects of technical development carried out by all the navies significant in the period.

For the early years (1854–85), attention should be drawn to H. N. Sulivan's life of Admiral Sir Bartholomew Sulivan (81) and to Philip Colomb's biography of Admiral Sir Astley Cooper Key (25). As a Captain, Sulivan influenced the formation of the R.N.R. and rose to prominence through his surveys in the Baltic, 1854–5. Colomb's book ranks as a classic. Though he did not apparently have access to the Admiralty's files when writing, his work is very strong on technical development and comments on policy, such as it was. (More biographies of general reference will be found under *Biographical materials* below.)

After 1880 the student is working in what has come to be regarded as "the Marder period," for the latter has produced no less than four thoroughly researched works relating to these years (52, 53, 54, 55). A great variety of references can be gleaned from his footnotes, especially in *The Anatomy of British Sea Power* and in *From the Dreadnought to Scapa Flow.* Although concerned primarily with policy and strategy, Marder has much of value to say about most facets of British naval history from 1880 to 1914. But because of its very nature, the field of naval policy offers readier scope for reinterpretation than does the technical sphere treated by Parkes (66), March (51) and others. The linking piece at present between Bartlett's own earlier work [see Part I of this chapter (3)] and Marder's books is Bartlett's essay, "The Mid-Victorian Reappraisal of Naval Policy" in Bourne and Watt (10), while Moon (57) tackles the invasion problem.

Specialist works with a bearing on the general history of the period include Preston and Major's *Send a Gunboat* (69). This is good on the characteristics of the vessels and on their operational activities. Very useful is Schurman's *Education of a Navy* (75), which in addition to being bibliographically helpful, is a fine analysis of the writings of Sir John Colomb and his brother Philip, Alfred Thayer Mahan, Sir John Laughton, Sir Herbert Richmond, and Sir Julian Corbett. Schurman's forthcoming biography of Corbett should also be of interest. Other facets of naval development are covered in Lloyd's *The Navy and the Slave Trade* [see Part I (24)], Michael Lewis' social history [see Part I of this chapter (21)], and Penn's account of the vicissitudes of the naval engineers (68).

Much older, and less useful because of its lack of references is Brassey's *The British Navy* (16).

The Navy also played an important role in diplomatic operations, either directly as in the case of the gunboats (69) or as the velvet fist behind the Union Jack. Here, several of the Navy Records Society volumes (58–61) are useful sources. In addition, students should see such works as Banno's *China and the West, 1858–1861* (7), and the books by Bartlett (10) and Brassey (16). Monger (56), Woodward (83) and Steinberg (78) treat aspects of the Anglo-German naval rivalry with which, of course, Marder also deals in some detail.

BIOGRAPHICAL MATERIALS. The later nineteenth century is rich in memoirs, biographies, and in the raw materials for such portraits. Of the Prime Ministers of the period apart from Balfour (85), only Asquith's personal papers (103) contain much worth using. These have correspondence with the First Lords for the years 1908 to 1914, as well as a number of papers of the Committee of Imperial Defence. Then, of course, there are the materials on the First Lords themselves.

Of these, only three have, so far, had biographies. First is Chilston's *W. H. Smith* (21) which contains a good chapter on the Admiralty years. though there is no evidence that the author made use of the Admiralty materials at the Public Record Office. There is only a weak study of McKenna written by his nephew Stephen (50). Then there are the Churchilliana ranging from Gretton's new book (37), which while not presenting many new materials, does have new interpretations, to the mammoth work (22) of the late Randolph Churchill with its textual and documentary volumes. These are in themselves important primary sources as are Churchill's own volumes comprising *The World Crisis* (23). In addition, there are papers in various libraries for McKenna (99), Cawdor (104), Selborne (106), and Tweedmouth (105), not to mention that ubiquitous diarist, Viscount Esher (102), whose published journals and letters are also important (110).

Obviously the most important First Sea Lord of the period was "Jacky" Fisher. For this reason he is the central figure in Marder's researches (52–5) and a remarkable amount of detail about the Admiral is incorporated in Marder's edition of Fisher's correspondence, not to mention Bacon's life (3) and the recent biography by Richard Hough (40a). Fisher himself published memoirs (32–3) and left in the Naval Library four volumes of important prints, *Naval Necessities* (108), relating to his proposed reforms and projects. Many of these papers have been published in Kemp's Navy Records Society volumes (62). A huge collection of Fisher's papers is kept at Lennoxlove (101) and there are also some manuscripts at Kilverstone (100). A number of those associated with Fisher have also left materials. Thus we have some of the papers of his Naval Assistant, Captain T. E. Crease (109). While the papers of Fisher's protégé Bacon have been lost, those of Jellicoe [see Chapter XIV (276)] have survived. Many of the admirals mentioned below came into contact with Fisher one way or another during their careers, not always with happy results. Fisher was a great propagandist as his own letters show and as can be seen in Gollin's study of *The Observer*'s editor J. L. Garvin (36).

Some of the key figures of the pre-1914 period like Wilson (15) and Battenberg (46) await satisfactory biographies. Better served is the gunnery expert Sir Percy Scott in Padfield's *Aim Straight* (65); also Sir Geoffrey Phipps Hornby in Mrs. Egerton's hands (31). While Stuart's life of Sir Henry Keppel (79) is an excessively detailed treatment, it does possess the merit of being based upon the Victorian admiral's journals and diaries. Captain Bennett's recent life of Lord Charles Beresford (11) makes able use of the latter's published memoirs (12) as well as a good range of other sources. Officers who were younger and whose fame largely rests upon their careers during and even after the First World War nevertheless have had a good deal to say about the pre-war Navy. Among these are Sir Reginald Bacon (5, 6), K. G. B. Dewar (30), whose papers have also been preserved (89), Mark Kerr (45), who is quite informative, Sir Roger Keyes (47, 48), who always managed to arrive in the right spot at the right time, his sometime chief, de Robeck [papers only (97)], Chatfield (20), Fremantle (34), and James (43). Important biographies of a similar genre are the short authorized one of Sir Henry F. Oliver by Sir William James (42), Lady Wester Wemyss' life and letters of her husband (82), Rear-Admiral Chalmers' authorized life and letters of Earl Beatty (19), and Bacon's *Jellicoe* (4).

Further down the ladder are a number of autobiographies which deal with life as seen by the regular officer, such as Oswald Frewen's *Sailor's Soliloquy* (35), based on his diaries for the years 1887–1910, and Lionel Dawson's *Flotillas: a hard-lying story* (28) and *Gone for a Sailor* (29). From the lower deck there is Lionel Yexley's *The Inner Life of the Navy* (84); Yexley was an unofficial spokesman for the matelots. And lastly, there is Geoffrey Penn's descriptively entitled history of the midshipmen, *Snotty* (67) and Geoffrey Lowis' amusing *The Fabulous Admirals* (49).

The personal papers of many of the above have been preserved in various repositories, the largest of which is at the National Maritime Museum at Greenwich. Here, particularly interesting and impressive is the collection of Admiral Sir Geoffrey Phipps Hornby (88): it contains much material on tactics, Admiralty organization, naval education and technical matters, especially from 1873 to 1894. The papers of Sir Gerard H. U. Noel (87) give insight into the activities of an officer who was often progressive in the technical field but reactionary in the sphere of policy and strategy. The collection of Sir Alexander Milne (86), who was twice Senior Naval Lord during the sixties and seventies, seems to be of general importance. It certainly has special relevance for policy on the North American station during the American Civil War. Other notable collections are those of Kenneth G. B. Dewar (89), Sir William H. May (90), Sir Albert H. Markham (91), Augustus Phillimore (93), Sir Herbert W. Richmond (94), Sir Edmond J. W. Slade (95), and Sir James R. Thursfield (a distinguished journalist who wrote about the Navy for *The Times*) (96).

The Naval Library has amongst its collections the papers of Cmdr. Charles N. Robinson (107), who was on the staff of *The Times* from

1895 to 1936. The papers of Sir Roger, later Admiral of the Fleet, Lord
Keyes (98) are at Churchill College, Cambridge, together with those of
Admiral Sir John de Robeck (97), Reginald McKenna (99), and Lord
Hankey (112). See also chapter XIV (277). At Watlington are the
materials accumulated by Viscount Esher (102), that ubiquitous counsellor
of the early twentieth century.

THE CONDITION OF THE FLEETS. The post-1854 period saw
great changes in naval material. As yet these have not been closely explored. Parkes' (66) and Hough's (40) work on battleships and March's
on destroyers (51) together with Preston and Major on gunboats (69)
are about all that has so far appeared devoted to the development of
specific classes. Barnaby's history of the Institution of Naval Architects
(8) not only provides a brief summary of the *Transactions* from 1860 onwards, but also makes illuminating comments. Manning's life of Sir William White (111) contains much information about naval construction
from 1870 to 1902. Additional material of this sort may be gleaned from
Sir Westcott Abell's short treatise on the shipwright's trade (1) and from
two company histories—*Vickers* by J. D. Scott (76) and *Two Hundred
and Fifty Years* by Scotts of Greenock (77); also from Appleyard's *Charles
Parsons* (2), Barnes' *Alfred Yarrow* (9), Hovgaard's *History of Warships* (41), and Sandler's unpublished dissertation on the emergence of
the British capital ship (74). (For Baxter's work on ironclads, see Part I
(4) above.) Bernard Brodie's *Sea Power in the Machine Age* (18) may
also be mentioned here. Useful accounts of early submarines are provided
by Admiral Jameson (44), and by Sueter (80), who was involved under
Bacon in their introduction. To these must be added Cowie's small book on
mines and mine-laying (27). But much work remains to be done on
technical developments such as engines, hulls, tank-testing, armourplate
and rifled guns, though Hogg has some information in *The Royal Arsenal*
(38) on the latter.

TACTICS AND STRATEGY. Not much has yet been written on this
important field. Richard Hough's *Admirals in Collision* (39) shows that
even shiphandling sometimes left something to be desired. The emphasis in
the period tended to be on tactics rather than strategy, though on this see
Schurman (75). Few naval officers wrote on these subjects; a fairly typical
example of what was produced is Admiral Sir Cyprian Bridge's *The Art
of Naval Warfare* (17). By far the best thinking came from the American
Mahan, whose studies were either historical or provincial, or from the pen
of Sir Julian Corbett, a civilian, whose *Some Principles of Maritime
Strategy* (26) was the major theoretical work of the leading British naval
historian. Lumby's Navy Records Society volume (64) and Moon's recent
dissertation (57) as well as I. F. Clarke's *Prophesying War* (24) should be
mentioned here. Moon's recent dissertation (57) uses War Office, Admiralty, and other papers to investigate the details of the invasion question.
I. F. Clarke (24) provides a study of the literature of public pressure,
while Lumby (64) may be expected to make a useful contribution re the

Mediterranean. Marder's life and papers of Sir Herbert Richmond (55) as well as his other works and Schurman's *Education of a Navy* (75) are basic.

SUGGESTIONS FOR FURTHER STUDY. Gaps and opportunities have been indicated under *Biographical Materials* above; also under *The Condition of the Fleets*. Stress has been laid on the need for more studies of technical development, but the difficulty presented by such work must not be under-rated. Engineering or scientific knowledge is a desirable qualification. However, a recent thesis on battleship-construction indicates the kind of effort which is required (74). Guns and ammunition, electricity, the torpedo, and communications all invite attention. Incidentally, a work on cruisers has been commissioned by Seeley Service.

On the operational side, the logistics of the Crimean War might repay closer study. The Navy's part in the Egyptian affair of 1882, together with the attempts to wrest technical and tactical lessons from the experience, might be worth a monograph. Nor do the possibilities of African gunboat activity appear to have been exhausted. Steinberg (78) has indicated the need for full investigation of the German documents now available for the Tirpitz period.

Histories of the Naval Intelligence Department (see Naval Library above) and the Royal Corps of Naval Constructors are attractive possibilities. So is the sphere of biography, for which the many collections of papers mentioned above are relevant. Admiral Sir Reginald Bacon might provide a good subject for a biography; his two volumes of memoirs (5, 6) would assist the researcher. See also Chapter XIV (6).

The relationship between the Navy and the press could make a worthwhile subject. For the Fisher period, Gollin's book about J. L. Garvin (36) will be useful, as will the Garvin papers (113).

Finally, a history of administration during this period would be welcome; the works by Briggs (see Part I) and Brassey (16) provide a start, together with the last volume of Clowes' history (see Part I). Naval education and training offer possibilities; and Arctic exploration, especially, might prove a rewarding field, for which the material at the Maritime Museum should prove valuable.

BIBLIOGRAPHY

1. Abell, Sir Westcott. *The Shipwright's Trade*. Jamaica, New York: Caravan Book Service, 1962 (reprint).
2. Appleyard, Rollo. *Charles Parsons*. London: Constable, 1933.
3. Bacon, Admiral Sir Reginald. *The Life of Lord Fisher of Kilverstone*. London: Hodder & Stoughton, 1929. 2 vols.
4. ———. *The Life of John Rushworth, Earl Jellicoe*. London: Cassell, 1936.

5. ———. *A Naval Scrapbook, 1877–1900*. London: Hutchinson, 1925.
6. ———. *From 1900 Onward*. London: Hutchinson, 1940.
7. Banno, Masataka. *China and the West, 1858–1861*. Cambridge, Mass.: Harvard University Press, 1964.
8. Barnaby, K. C. *The Institution of Naval Architects, 1860–1960*. London: Royal Institution of Naval Architects, 1960.
9. Barnes, Eleanor C. *Alfred Yarrow: his life and work*. London: Edward Arnold, 1924.
10. Bartlett, C. J. "The Mid-Victorian Reappraisal of Naval Policy." See Bourne (14) below.
11. Bennett, Captain Geoffrey. *Charlie B*. London: Peter Dawnay, 1968.
12. Beresford, Admiral Lord Charles. *The Memoirs of Lord Charles Beresford*. 4th ed. London: Methuen, 1916.
13. Bourne, Kenneth. *Britain and the Balance of Power in North America, 1815–1908*. London: Longmans, 1967.
14. Bourne, Kenneth, and Watt, D. C., ed. *Studies in International History: essays presented to Professor W. N. Medlicott*. London: Longmans, 1967.
15. Bradford, Vice-Admiral Sir Edward E. *Life of Admiral of the Fleet Sir Arthur Knyvet Wilson*. London: Murray, 1923.
16. Brassey, Sir Thomas (later Lord). *The British Navy: its strength, resources, and administration*. London: Longmans, Green, 1882–3. 5 vols.
17. Bridge, Admiral Sir Cyprian. *The Art of Naval Warfare*. London: Smith, Elder, 1907.
18. Brodie, Bernard. *Sea Power in the Machine Age*. Princeton: Princeton University Press, 1941.
19. Chalmers, Rear-Admiral W. S. *The Life and Letters of David, Earl Beatty*. London: Hodder & Stoughton, 1951.
20. Chatfield, Admiral of the Fleet Lord. *The Navy and Defence*. London: Heinemann, 1942.
21. Chilston, Viscount. *W. H. Smith*. London: Routledge, 1965.
22. Churchill, Randolph S. *Winston Churchill*. I and II. London: Heinemann, 1966–67.
23. Churchill, Winston. *The World Crisis*. London: Butterworth, 1923–31. 5 Vols in 6.
24. Clarke, I. F. *Prophesying War, 1763–1984*. New York: Oxford, 1966.
25. Colomb, Vice-Admiral Philip H. *Memoirs of Sir Astley Cooper Key*. London: Methuen, 1898.
26. Corbett, Julian S. *Some Principles of Maritime Strategy*. London: Longmans, 1911.
27. Cowie, J. S. *Mines, Minelayers and Minelaying*. London: Oxford University Press, 1949.
28. Dawson, Captain Lionel. *Flotillas: a hard-lying story*. London: Rich & Cowan, 1933.
29. ———. *Gone for a Sailor*. London: Rich & Cowan, 1936.

30. Dewar, Vice-Admiral K. G. B. *The Navy from Within.* London: Gollancz, 1939.

31. Egerton, Mrs. E. *Admiral of the Fleet Sir Geoffrey Phipps Hornby.* Edinburgh and London, 1896.

32. Fisher, Admiral of the Fleet Lord. *Memories.* London: Hodder & Stoughton, 1919.

33. ————. *Records.* London: Hodder & Stoughton, 1919.

34. Fremantle, Admiral Sir Sydney R. *My Naval Career, 1880–1928.* London: Hutchinson, 1949.

35. Frewen, Oswald. *Sailor's Soliloquy.* G. P. Griggs, ed. London: Hutchinson, 1961.

36. Gollin, Alfred M. *The "Observer" and J. L. Garvin, 1908–1914: a study in a great editorship.* London: Oxford University Press, 1960. (The Garvin Papers are now at the University of Texas, Austin, Texas.)

37. Gretton, Vice-Admiral Sir Peter. *Former Naval Person: Winston Churchill and the Royal Navy.* London: Cassell, 1968.

38. Hogg, Brigadier O. F. G. *The Royal Arsenal.* London: Oxford University Press, 1963. 2 Vols.

39. Hough, Richard. *Admirals in Collision.* New York: Viking; London: H. Hamilton, 1959.

40. Hough, Richard. *Dreadnought: a history of the modern battleship.* London: Michael Joseph, 1965.

40a. ————. *First Sea Lord: an authorized biography of Admiral Lord Fisher.* London: Allen & Unwin, 1969.

41. Hovgaard, William. *Modern History of Warships.* London: E. & F. N. Spon; New York: Spon & Chamberlain, 1920.

42. James, Admiral Sir William. *A Great Seaman: the life of Admiral of the Fleet Sir Henry F. Oliver.* London: Witherby, 1956.

43. ————. *The Sky was Always Blue.* London: Methuen, 1951.

44. Jameson, Rear Admiral Sir William. *The Most Formidable Thing: the story of the submarine from its earliest days to the end of World War I.* London: Hart-Davis, 1965.

45. Kerr, Admiral Mark. *Land, Sea, and Air: reminiscences of Mark Kerr.* London: Longmans, 1927.

46. ————. *Prince Louis of Battenberg, Admiral of the Fleet.* London: Longmans, 1934.

47. Keyes, Admiral Sir Roger. *Adventures Ashore and Afloat.* London: Harrap, 1939.

48. ————. *The Naval Memoirs of Admiral of the Fleet Sir Roger Keyes.* London: Butterworth, 1934–35, 2 vols. Vol. I deals with 1910–1915.

49. Lowis, Geoffrey. *The Fabulous Admirals.* London: Putnam, 1957.

50. McKenna, Stephen. *Reginald McKenna, 1863–1943.* London: Eyre and Spottiswoode, 1948.

51. March, Edgar. *British Destroyers.* London: Seeley Service, 1967.

52. Marder, Arthur J. *The Anatomy of British Sea Power: a history of British naval policy in the pre-dreadnought era, 1880–1905.* Ham-

den, Conn.: Archon Books, 1964. (Same as original ed. of 1940, published in Britain as *British Naval Policy, 1880–1905.*)

53. ———. *From the Dreadnought to Scapa Flow: the Royal Navy in the Fisher era, 1904–19.* London: Oxford University Press, 1961–1970. 5 vols. Vol. I covers 1904–1914. See Vol. V for a full bibliography.

54. ———. *Fear God and Dread Nought: the correspondence of Admiral of the Fleet Lord Fisher of Kilverstone.* London: Cape, 1952–59. 3 vols.

55. ———. *Portrait of an Admiral: the life and papers of Sir Herbert Richmond.* London: Cape, 1952.

56. Monger, G. W. *The End of Isolation: British foreign policy, 1900–1907.* London: Nelson, 1963.

57. Moon, Howard. *The Invasion of the United Kingdom: public controversy and official planning, 1888–1918.* Unpublished Ph.D. thesis, London University, 1968.

58. Navy Records Society. *Russian War, 1854, Baltic and Black Sea, Official Correspondence.* D. Bonner-Smith and A. C. Dewar, eds. 1943.

59. ———. *Russian War, 1855, Baltic: official correspondence.* D. Bonner-Smith, ed. 1944.

60. ———. *Russian War, Black Sea: official correspondence.* A. C. Dewar, ed. 1945.

61. ———. *The Second China War, 1856–60.* D. Bonner-Smith and E. W. R. Lumby, eds. 1954.

62. ———. *The Papers of Admiral Sir John Fisher.* P. K. Kemp, ed. 1960 and 1964. 2 vols.

63. ———. *The Jellicoe Papers.* Vol. I (1893–1916). A. Temple Patterson, ed. 1966.

64. ———. *Papers Relating to Naval Policy and Operations in the Mediterranean, 1911–1915.* E. W. R. Lumby, ed. [1971 or 1972]

65. Padfield, Peter. *Aim Straight: a biography of Admiral Sir Percy Scott.* London: Hodder & Stoughton, 1966.

66. Parkes, Oscar. *British Battleships: Warrior 1860 to Vanguard 1950: a history of design, construction and armament.* Rev. ed. London: Seeley Service, 1966.

67. Penn, Commander Geoffrey. *Snotty: the story of the midshipman.* London: Hollis & Carter, 1957.

68. ———. *Up Funnel, Down Screw: the story of the naval engineer.* London: Hollis & Carter, 1955.

69. Preston, Anthony and John Major. *Send a Gunboat.* London: Longmans, 1967.

70. Public Record Office: *List of Cabinet Papers, 1880–1914.* London: H.M.S.O., 1964.

71. ———. *List of Papers of the Committee of Imperial Defence to 1914.* London: H.M.S.O., 1964.

72. Reed, E. J., ed. *Naval Science.* A quarterly journal. London: Lockwood & Co., 1872–5.

73. Ritchie, G. S. *The Admiralty Chart: British hydrography in the nineteenth century*. London: Hollis & Carter, 1967.
74. Sandler, S. "The Emergence of the British Capital Ship, 1863–70." Unpublished Ph.D. thesis, London University, 1965. (See Bulletin of the Institute of Historical Research, May 1967, for a summary, including sources.)
75. Schurman, D. M. *The Education of a Navy: the development of British naval strategic thought, 1867–1914*. London: Cassell, 1965.
76. Scott, J. D. *Vickers: a history*. London: Weidenfeld and Nicholson, 1962.
77. Scotts at Greenock. *Two Hundred and Fifty Years of Shipbuilding by the Scotts at Greenock*. 4th ed. with new title. Glasgow: Scott Shipbuilding, 1961.
78. Steinberg, Jonathan. *Yesterday's Deterrent: Tirpitz and the birth of the German battlefleet*. London: Macdonald, 1965.
79. Stuart, Vivian. *The Beloved Little Admiral: Admiral of the Fleet the Hon. Sir Henry Keppel*. London: Robert Hale, 1967.
80. Sueter, Cmdr. Murray F. *The Evolution of the Submarine Boat, Mine, and Torpedo from the Sixteenth Century to the Present*. Portsmouth: J. Griffin, 1907.
81. Sulivan, H. N. *The Life and Letters of Admiral Sir Bartholomew James Sulivan, 1810–1890*. London: J. Murray, 1896.
82. Wester Wemyss, Lady. *The Life and Letters of Lord Wester Wemyss*. London: Eyre & Spottiswoode, 1935.
83. Woodward, E. L. (Sir Llewllyn). *Great Britain and the German Navy*. Oxford: Clarendon Press, 1935.
84. Yexley, Lionel. *The Inner Life of the Navy*. London: Pitman, 1908.

COLLECTIONS OF PERSONAL PAPERS

The British Museum, London
85. The A. J. Balfour Papers
The National Maritime Museum, Greenwich
86. The Papers of Admiral Sir Alexander Milne
87. The Papers of Admiral of the Fleet Sir Gerard Noel
88. The Papers of Admiral of the Fleet Sir Geoffrey Phipps Hornby
89. The Papers of Vice-Admiral K. G. B. Dewar
90. The Papers of Admiral of the Fleet Sir William H. May
91. The Papers of Admiral Sir Albert H. Markham
92. The Papers of Admiral of the Fleet Sir Henry Oliver
93. The Papers of Admiral Sir Richard Phillimore
94. The Papers of Admiral Sir Herbert Richmond
95. The Papers of Vice Admiral Sir Adolphus Slade
96. The Papers of Sir James R. Thursfield

There are, of course, many other collections. Researchers with specific queries are advised to seek an interview with the Custodian of Manuscripts. Although extremely busy, he will make his expert knowledge available to researchers as far as practicable.

Churchill College, Cambridge
97. The Papers of Admiral of the Fleet Sir John de Robeck
98. The Papers of Admiral of the Fleet Lord Keyes (On loan and possibly sold by 1969.)
99. The Papers of Reginald McKenna
    Here again, other collections are held and more acquisitions are likely. The collections have in many cases been deposited with conditions attached, so intending researchers should make application to the Archivist well ahead of their proposed visits.

Kilverstone, Thetford, Norfolk
100. Papers of Admiral of the Fleet Lord Fisher. These are quite extensive personal and family materials. Apply to Lord Fisher.

Lennoxlove, Haddington, East Lothian, Scotland
101. The main collection of Papers of Admiral of the Fleet Lord Fisher, some 6,000 items. These belong to the Duke of Hamilton and application to use them should be made to him. They have now been indexed.

Watlington, Watlington Park, Watlington, Oxford
102. The Papers of Viscount Esher.
    Application to use these must be made to the present Viscount.

The Bodleian Library, Oxford
103. The Papers of H. H. Asquith. For a full description, see Chapter XIV.

The Naval Library, Ministry of Defense, London
104. The Papers of Lord Cawdor
105. The Papers of Lord Tweedmouth
106. The Papers of Lord Selborne
107. The Papers of C. N. Robinson
108. The only edition of Fisher's *Naval Necessities* containing a fourth volume (mostly printed items)
109. The Papers of Captain T. E. Crease

SUPPLEMENT TO THE BIBLIOGRAPHY

110. Brett, Maurice V., and Oliver, Viscount Esher. *Journals and Letters of Reginald, Viscount Esher*. London: Nicholson & Watson, 1934–1938. 4 vols.
111. Manning, Frederic. *The Life of Sir William White*. London: J. Murray, 1923.

X

ECONOMIC, SCIENTIFIC, AND TECHNOLOGICAL BACKGROUND FOR MILITARY STUDIES, 1815–1914

W. H. G. Armytage

No student of military studies can ignore in the nineteenth century the reciprocality and interrelationship of economic, scientific and technological factors. As in earlier centuries, these factors were affected by war. Pressures for raw materials and markets motivated the building of bigger navies, "showing the flag," the prosecution of colonial campaigns and the establishment of colonial garrisons. Linking much of this was the "corridor" to India, with the side effects that the policy entailed. The "spatial dynamics" of making the Indian Ocean a British lake, when analysed, show a complex interrelationship of necessitarian ethics and noble intentions that stretched the sinews of the "mother country" to the limit.

Clues to the interrelationship of war technology and social change can be found under (2), (10), (15), (21), (31), (32), (47), (49), (83), (85), (90), (133), (136), (177), (246), (266), (267), (336), (341), (355), (459), (478), (488), (492), (496), (498), (499), (501), (506), (508), (510), (516), (520), (524), (527), (529), (532), (545), (565), (568), (582), (585), (586), (607), (620), (624), (629), (637), (640), (645), (648), (650), (654), (656), (658), (659), (669), (670), (673), (680), (698–700), (704), (715), (717). This can be evaluated in the light afforded by the general surveys of economic development provided by Ashley (51), Ashworth (53), Beard (76), Briggs (102), Cairncross (119), The Cambridge Economic History (122), J. D. Chambers (145), S. G. Checkland (148), Sir John Clapham (153, 154), Cole and Postgate (163), Court (173), Crombie (182), Foy (249), the Hammonds (315, 317, 318), Heaton (333),

251

Hoffman (348, 349), A. E. Kahn (390), Levi (408), Lipson (416), Meier and Baldwin (452), J. R. Meyer (454), Mulhall (472), Redford (540), B. C. Roberts (557), Thorold Rogers (560), W. W. Rostow (567), Thomson (642), Toynbee (652), Woodward (703) and Woolf (707). For "hindsight" evaluation, Mowat (469), Pigou (515), Plummer (518), Putnam (533) and Ball (67) are useful background reading.

Further analysis can best begin with those fact-finding groups, the Parliamentary committees and commissions (169), (170), (386), (387), which offer vast quarries of information from which much remains to be dug. Other valuable sources are contemporary journals (106), (568), (569), (570), (623), (682–4), the international exhibitions held from 1851 onwards of which Merle Curti (189) has been so helpful an analyst and the welter of guides for theses, records and statistics given under (16), (19), (29), (30), (45), (88), (95), (96), (179), (251), (331), (353), (359), (455), (463), (474), (497) and (539).

Two basic industries of the period are shipbuilding and railways. Shipping (8), sea power and its problems (71), (108), (296), ironclads (74), naval administration (103) bring up questions of comparative costs (521) and mass production (398). Here the steel industry is important (190), (293), (354), (411), (419), (438–440), (616). For specific naval personnel, recourse may be made to O'Byrne (489).

Similarly the relationship of railways to economic growth has been explored by Mitchell (462) and to war by E. A. Pratt (527). Interesting cross links between railway innovation and the volunteers can be found in (572).

Many studies exist of firms like John Brown (293), Mushets (494) and Vickers (669), or of firms like Unilever (688), D. Napier (689) or Siemens (585), (593). They should be consulted to see what interrelationships have already been established. Regional studies like those on Tyneside (125), Widnes (321), St. Helens (69), Crewe (144), the Midlands (174), Coventry (338), Wales (5), (383), the Black Country (11) and Liverpool (62) exist in abundance but must be tracked down.

Nor should the impact on agriculture be forgotten. From Orwin and Whetham (493a) a picture can be obtained of the impact of the Crimean, Franco-Prussian, and Boer Wars on farm prices, whilst Fussell (269), in one of his many informative books on agricultural history, gives the story of farmers' tools before the tractor came. For the general history of food, written by a natural scientist, see Drummond (223).

Substantial help can be obtained from *The Times,* the *Economist,* and the *Journal of the Royal Statistical Society.* The annual bibliographies in the *Economic History Review* and in *Isis* are invaluable. So is the *Journal of Economic History.* Detailed historical studies will be found in the Liverpool publication *Business History* (117) which, biennially since 1958, has also included a select list of business histories, and in the even newer *Industrial Archaeology,* founded in 1964 as the *Journal of Industrial Archaeology,* which carries articles on the history of particular industries and on technology. Published by a firm specialising in books on such topics—David and Charles of Newton Abbot—it is edited from the new Technological University at Bath.

Initially an unofficial periodical of the armaments industry published from 1892 to 1920 was *Arms and Explosives*. Complete runs only exist in England at the Patent Office Library, the British Museum and the Bodleian.

A list of local record offices is given by Emmison and Gray (238) and of municipal corporation archives by Andrews (19).

In the last thirty years, attempts have been made to indicate hitherto inaccessible resource material afforded by theses housed in British University libraries; Luxmoore Newcombe (485), P. D. Record (538) and A.S.L.I.B. (45) have done much to remedy this, and, in certain fields like transport history, J. H. Dyos (231) has compiled a good bibliography.

Since Victorian scientists often wrote, sometimes pseudonymously, in the general periodicals, recourse might be made to Poole's *Index to Periodical Literature* (523a). For these general periodicals, subsequent indices can be gleaned from Walter E. Houghton (353) whose own *Wellesley Index to Victorian Periodicals 1824-1900* is currently under way. For books and pamphlets Halkett and Laing (308) is also useful.

OVERVIEWS. (a) Science. For stimulating "overviews" of science see Charles Singer (600) and C. C. Gillispie (283 and 284) and the by no means outmoded necklace of biographical studies by R. H. Murray (476) and collaborative volumes like those edited by Herbert Dingle (217), E. A. Underwood (660), Howard Mumford Jones (385) and I. Bernard Cohen (161), A. C. Crombie (180 and 182) and Taton (626).

(b) Overviews of engineering in general have been provided by Kirby, Withington, Darling and Kilgour (397), Westcott and Spratt (679) and Armytage (33); of civil engineering by Straub (620), Norrie (488) and Pannell (496); of mechanical engineering by Cressy (178) and Burstall (115) and the Institution itself (372); of electrical engineering by Dunsheath (230) and Sharlin (590).

(c) Technology. Among the spate of general histories of technology over the last thirty years the most stimulating are Mumford (475), Giedion (279) and Usher (664); the most informative are Forbes (262), the fourth and fifth volumes of Singer, Holmyard, Hall and Williams (601), Klemm (400), Derry and Williams (209), Eco and Zorzoli (232), Forbes and Dyksterhuis (261) and Lilley (412). The most recent bibliography, Ferguson's (251), contains a good evaluation (pp. 17–33) of preceding bibliographies, as well as excellent subject lists of books with critical comments.

Thanks to the Science Museum, Her Majesty's Stationery Office now issue invaluable reference works: H. P. Pledge (517) and G. F. Westcott (679) give a general history of the sciences and a synopsis of historical events in engineering and ordnance. Other developments include aeroplanes by C. H. Gibbs-Smith (278), cycles, motor cycles, light cars and motor cars by C. F. Caunter (137–141), aeronautics by M. J. B. Davy

(201–203), sailing ships by G. S. L. Clowes (158), merchant steamers and motor ships by H. P. Spratt (614), time measuring devices by F. A. B. Ward (675), steam road vehicles by C. St. C. B. Davison (200) and submarine cables by G. R. M. Garratt (272).

BIOGRAPHICAL MATERIAL. Smiles (603) is still as stimulating and relevant on early Victorian engineers as most subsequent biographers, with the additional merit of giving the flavour of the period. Even more helpful than the *D.N.B.* (and its supplements), since it is concerned entirely with the nineteenth century, is Boase (93), hitherto virtually unobtainable, now happily reprinted.

As an antidote to determinism one should look at the history of science through the careers of the scientists. Here a model is L. Pearce Williams' book (685), the most comprehensive of many lives of Faraday (176, 247, 248). Also essential are J. G. Crowther's many books (186–7) W. Irvine (375), Gavin de Beer (206) and Gertrude Himmelfarb (343) on Darwin; Sir George Thomson on his father (643); Sir Edward Bailey on Lyell (60); Wilma George on Alfred Russell Wallace (276); and Rollo Appleyard on Parsons (24). Further biographical material is available in the *Philosophical Transactions* or in *Obituary Notices of the Royal Society* or in *Notes and Records of the Royal Society*. Here the biographical dictionary of T. I. Williams is enormously helpful (686).

METALS. As Sir John Clapham wrote "the war departments of states were the metal-working inventors' ideal clients, clients whose demand for absolute strength of material and absolute perfection of workmanship was, or at least should have been, completely inelastic at all times, and in war time might become unlimited" (153). As makers of half the pig iron in the world from 1848 to 1866, British metallurgists were also more capable of applying the exact methods of science to them. Bessemer (88), Siemens (593) and Gilchrist Thomas (639) were all indirectly affected by war demands, as were those who exploited and improved their discoveries: Whitworth (680), Armstrong (28), Firth (440), Cammell (124), Laird (404), Mushet (494), and Vickers (669).

MACHINE TOOLS AND METALS. Engineers need machine tools, and L. T. C. Rolt (564) has shown the variety they created. The increasing perfection of specialist gear-cutting machines (693), grinding machines (694), lathes (695) and milling machines (696) has been illuminated by R. S. Woodbury. The superb machine tool collection at the Science Museum has been catalogued by K. R. Gilbert (282), who has also added a bibliography.

Tools and engines need new and improved metals, and their history has been consecutively studied by Aitchison (9), Wertime (676) and Duckworth (225). The utilization of nickel, platinum, copper, zinc and brass have been reviewed by Howard-White (357), McDonald (430) and W. O. Alexander (14) respectively.

The steel industry can be further monitored through the *Iron and Coal*

Trades Review, the *Journal of the Iron and Steel Institute* and the Reports of the British Iron Trade Association. Factors in its development in the early nineteenth century are discussed by Walter Isard (376) and in the late nineteenth century by W. A. Sinclair (598), Charlotte Erickson (242), T. J. Orsagh (493) and Peter Temin (629). But the authentic overviews are still D. L. Burn (112), T. H. Burnham and G. O. Hoskins (113), and J. C. Carr and W. Taplin (130). Much valuable information is also contained in the *Royal Commission on the Depression of Trades and Industry.* (1886)

Power and new metallurgy create new arms. Artillery, machine guns, pistols, revolvers and rockets are surveyed by H. B. C. Pollard (520), W. Y. Carman (128), R. Held (335), and D. Pope (524).

POWER. Improved metallurgical techniques are essential for the development of power. Here the best short history of the steam engine is that of H. W. Dickinson (213), which should be supplemented by D. B. Barton's specialist study of the Cornish Beam engine (72). Its application to boats is explored by H. P. Spratt (616) and E. C. Smith (607). A copious and authoritative bibliography of its application to railways in Britain has been compiled by G. Ottley (495). Locomotives are comprehensively and competently reviewed by E. L. Ahrons (6) and continued by O. S. Nock (488). Railway systems and companies are overviewed by C. H. Ellis (236) and J. Simmons (595), whilst numerous histories of individual railways exist for the enthusiast. These also find much stimulus in the *Railway Review* and the Journal of the *Stephenson Locomotive Society.*

THE PRIME MOVER: COAL. For the coal industry see *The Colliery Guardian, The Iron and Coal Trades Review,* the *Transactions of the Institute of Mining Engineers,* the *Transactions of the National Association of Colliery Managers,* and the *Colliery Year Book and Coal Trades Directory.* The technological innovation within the industry is examined by S. F. Walker (674) and A. J. Taylor (625), its labour structure by the *Departmental Committee on Miners Eight-Hour Day,* H.M.S.O., 1907, *Cd. 3426–8* and *3505–6,* its labour unions by R. Page Arnot (48) and J. E. Williams (682), its economic position by W. S. Jevons (381) and D. A. Thomas (634). The extent of Britain's reserves was calculated by the *Royal Commission on Coal Supplies,* H.M.S.O., 1903, *Cd. 1725–6,* H.M.S.O., 1904, *Cd. 1990–2,* H.M.S.O., 1905, *Cd. 2353–65.*

More work was got out of coal after 1891 when Parsons (499, 501) patented his condensing turbine and, three years later, his exhaust steam turbine. Its most dramatic use was at the Diamond Jubilee Review of the fleet in 1897; by 1904 it was mandatory for the navy. More revolutionary was its employment in large generating plants (117). Cheap electrical power made possible the working of aluminum (148 and 153).

CHEMISTRY, PHYSICAL CHEMISTRY AND CHEMICAL ENGINEERING. Coal utilisation incubated organic chemistry, and here the fourth volume of J. R. Partington's massive (1007-page) history with its copious bibliography (503) offers a starting point, followed chronologically by the third edition of A. Findlay's survey of chemistry since Liebig (252). The industrial background is sketched with special reference to its relevance to modern developments by Sherwood Taylor (629), L. F. Haber (302), D. W. F. Hardie and J. D. Platt (321); Chalmers (143) and Cajori (120) are helpful too.

Increasing sophistication of new power sources like electricity, new industrial processes, elicited refined conceptual keys. Here the development of mathematics and physics is of cardinal importance. The specifically British contribution can be obtained from D. E. Smith (606), Sir Edmund Whittaker (681) and W. Wilson (690). As Tennant (632), Miall (456) and Haber (302) have shown, from it sprang the gas industry, fertilisers, coal tar, hydrochloric acid (and chloride of lime for the cotton and paper industries) and dyes. With the salt of Cheshire it fired the Leblanc process. Though improved after 1863 by the Solvay process, the industry producing washing soda (sodium carbonate), cooking soda (bicarbonate of soda) and caustic soda (sodium hydroxide), which was located in Widnes (321), St. Helens (69) and Tyneside (125), so polluted the air that the first of the Alkali Acts was passed in that year to check it. The alkali inspectors, Robert Angus Smith, F. R. S., and his assistants, Alfred Fletcher, Brereton Todd, Charles Blatherwick and John T. Hobson mark, as Roy MacLeod has ably shown (431), the emergence of the Civil Scientist, whose work expanded with his own creation of a scientific method of control, and provides a classical example of the growth of statute and administrative law out of relevant scientific knowledge.

RUBBER. The rubber industry's growth has been described by P. Schidrowitz and T. R. Dawson (583), W. Woodruff (702) and A. G. Donnithorne (222). Rubber artifacts with social effects were contraceptives (559), the macintosh, shoes and fountain pens. Others like the hollow ball, the balloon, the provision of insulating material, to say nothing of the bicycle and later the motor car tyre, were to so stimulate demand that a search for artificial rubber began (73).

THE EMERGENCE OF PROFESSIONAL SCIENTISTS AND ENGINEERS. Even richer harvests of information can be reaped from the transactions, journals, proceedings or minutes of the numerous professional associations, institutions or societies that took shape after 1818. Following the general medical practitioners who secured, in the year of Waterloo, an act allowing them to examine postulants for admission (35), the first professional association of engineers was founded in 1818 by those who, like Telford (563) had obtained unparalleled experience in the twenty-three years of war.

By 1831 a virtual "parliament" of scientists, organised in professional sections, took shape in the British Association, a body which threw up proposals for a Ministry of Science (39). Its *Annual Report* is itself a valuable source book of the progress of science during the period, so is its main splinter group, the British Science Guild (formed to act as a pressure group for science in 1905), of which I have given an account elsewhere (36).

The growth of other service corps of an increasing technological society can be further monitored through the *Proceedings* or *Transactions* of the four major engineering societies—Civil (founded in 1818), Mechanical (founded in 1848), Electrical (founded as telegraph engineers in 1871) and Chemical (founded in 1922). Histories of these have been provided by Pendred (507), Parsons (500) and Appleyard (27). Others like the Institution of Naval Architects [founded in 1860, see Barnaby (70)], of Gas Engineers (founded in 1863), of the Royal Aeronautical Society (founded in 1866) and the Institution of Marine Engineers (founded in 1889) also have a direct relevance. Insights may also be gleaned from publications of the Royal Institute of British Architects (founded in 1834), the Royal Agricultural Society (founded in 1838), and the Institutions of Mining Engineers (founded in 1889) and of Mining and Metallurgy (founded in 1892). Nor should the work of the Royal Engineers (525) be forgotten.

Illumination can be found in the publications of the Chemical Society (founded in 1841) and the Institute of Chemistry (founded in 1877), the Society of Chemical Industry (founded in 1851), the Iron and Steel Institute (founded in 1809), the Institutions of Municipal Engineers (founded in 1873), the Society of Analytical Chemistry and the Physical Society (both founded in 1874), the Royal Society of Health (founded in 1876), the Institute of Brewing (founded in 1886).

Professionalism leads to tests of competence. Just as the Apothecaries Act of 1815 (35) elicited provincial medical schools, so after the foundation of Sandhurst in 1812 the only way of obtaining a commission without purchasing it was to go through Sandhurst and pass an examination in Euclid, military surveying and higher mathematics, together with three subjects from the following six: general history, Latin, French and German, conic sections, attack and defence of fortresses. As Hugh Thomas has written "a comparatively formidable mathematical knowledge was regarded as essential for a commission" (637). The mathematics professor from 1814 to 1858, John Narrien, a self-educated F.R.S., author of several textbooks, and noted in Boase (93), taught by what would now be regarded as practical "modern" methods.

As R. J. Montgomery shows (465), the Civil Service Commissioners were established in 1856. From their annual reports can be traced their increasing influence over the entrance examinations for India (which they took over in 1859), over Sandhurst and Woolwich (which they took over in 1870) and over the whole Civil Service. By 1900 they were examining the Naval and Colonial entrants too.

In the army a Council for Military Education was organised in 1857 to regulate the qualifying test established in 1849. Tests were instituted for admission to the "staff college" for senior officers at Camberley and the ordinary college for officer entrants at Sandhurst (637), as well as to the centre for the training of artillery and engineers at Woolwich. These tests, in the opinion of the commissioners, would raise the standards in schools generally. They were right as the first school leaving examinations began at this time in the form of Oxford and Cambridge locals.

Contemporaneously, the abolition of purchase for commissions also saw the rise of the civic universities (35), both stemming from the steady demand for technically trained personnel in society, and both paced by foreign examples (40, 41, 44). Professional standards interacted with this.

With the intensification of the industrial pacemaking by Germany, the foundation of the British Standards Institution (founded in 1901) inaugurated a new intensification of technological specialisms. The Institutes of British Foundrymen (founded in 1904), of Metals (1908) and of Petroleum (founded in 1913) speak for themselves. So do the Institutions of Automobile Engineers (founded in 1906), of Structural Engineers (founded in 1908) and of Locomotive Engineers (founded in 1911). The war with Germany intensified the movement, for during it the Society of Aircraft Constructors was founded in 1915 whilst as a result of it was formed the Institutes of Physics (in 1918), of Production Engineers (in 1921), of Chemical Engineers (in 1922) and of Radio Engineers (in 1925). The journals of these and other bodies await a thorough combing, for both presidential addresses, papers, and, where available, obituary notices.

THE IMPORTANCE OF INDIA. Crouzet (185) sees the Napoleonic Wars as transferring the location of continental industries from the seaboard inland, to the "golden triangle" of Paris, Hamburg and Milan. England developed its own triangle of trade by exporting manufactures to India, which then exported foodstuffs to Europe.

The increasing focus on India and China is reflected in the numerous small wars in that subcontinent, seven before the Mutiny. As Saul (576) and Fletcher (256) show, the exploitation of the Suez Canal led to India's becoming a lynch-pin in the balance of payments, for just before the First World War it financed 2/5 of Britain's total deficits.

Early arsenals and "manufactories" in India have been explored in (715), the men who ruled it in (701), investment in (405), (469), (645), its historians in (514) and the areas around it in (311), its impact on technology in (123), (226), (256), its mutiny in (587). Overviews, apart from the *Cambridge History,* are (109), (199) and (492). A general assessment of the British impact has been made by Griffith (297).

Interest in India also led Kew to be transformed from a mere extended Royal Garden to a redistribution centre for the vegetable products of the empire. As a result of a Treasury committee's recommendation in 1840, its administration was transferred from the Board of Green Cloth to the Commissioners of Woods and Forests. Kew became, under Sir William Jackson Hooker (13), a world clearing centre for plants.

Apart from the aesthetic properties of his favourite, the rhododendron, Hooker was very much alive to the economic aspects of botany. A teaching museum was opened in 1847, the gardens were extended, and from 1865 to 1885 plans for 12 colonial floras were drawn up under the direction of his son. Clothing, paper-making, gums, resins and drugs all came

from plants. It supplied plane trees for the London parks, cork oaks for
South Australia, tobacco to Natal, tea to Assam, coffee, ginger, cinnamon,
mango, tamarind and cotton to Brisbane. But perhaps the most dramatic
of all was H. A. Wickham's capture of the seeds of *Hevea brasiliensis* for
Kew. From them all the rubber trees in the Asian plantations have sprung
(13).

The stimulus of building railways in India up to 1849 can be gleaned
from D. Thorner (645) and from 1845 to 1895 from W. J. MacPherson
(432), while earlier descriptions of Indian railways are by Davidson (198)
and Bell (77). Irrigation works are studied by Harris (322) and Hart
(326). Further information can be obtained from the India Office records,
of which H. C. Hughes gives a good account (360).

Ironically, service in India kindled in engineer officers like Colonel
Alexander Strange a desire to extend facilities for scientific research in
England, and, as D. S. L. Cardwell has shown (127), he returned in 1861
"with revolutionary ideas as to the role of science in society and the duties
of society towards science." These, as Cardwell shows, involved the establishment of a Ministry of Science. A similar scientific pioneer, Colonel
R. E. B. Crompton (183), returned to England ten years later to play a
great part in the development of electrical engineering and road transport.

India, in short, was a social laboratory where ideas were tested, not only
on the spot, but in London. Hence the remark of a late nineteenth-century
M.P., "We are all of us, members for India" (102). For an analysis of
modern historical writing on India, C. H. Philips (514) is perhaps the most
recent.

THE SCIENCE OF SOCIETY. From 1815 to 1851, calculated G. R.
Porter (525), national defence cost the country £579 millions as opposed to the £630 millions from 1800 to 1815. He presents yet another
science that goes back to Petty and Graunt: the application of quantitative
techniques to the study of human society. Thirty-nine years earlier, another such assessor had remarked, "War, accounted in former days a sea-
son of embarrassment and poverty, assumed in the present age the appearance of a period of prosperity." So P. Colquhoun, the well-known statis-
tician, wrote in 1812 (165). Between these two statistical assessors come
J. R. McCulloch (428, 429), a founder of the political economy club,
Thomas Tooke (649), and W. F. Spackman (613).

After 1851 such assessments multiplied in the hands of Braithwaite Pool,
William Newmarsh, W. S. Jevons, Leone Levi, J. E. Thorold Rogers and
M. G. Mulhall. These set a style of social assessment and evaluation well
described from 1870 onwards by T. W. Hutchison (366).

Here the growth of statistics must be studied, especially in connection
with the Board of Trade whose statistical activities expanded under Sir
Robert Giffen (280) and Sir H. Llewellyn Smith (608). The Annual *Abstract of Labour Statistics* began in 1889. At a more impressionistic level
there is good contemporary assessment edited by T. H. Ward in 1887
(708).

In 1838 the first military statistical reports began to be published in

Europe—those of T. G. Balfour (66), who, after being elected F.R.S., became in 1859 head of the first statistical branch of the army.

INTERNATIONAL COMPARISONS. This self assessment had its implications notably in A. Shadwell's *Industrial Efficiency* (1908), which compared British industries to those in America and Germany. Such comparisons stretch back and were affected especially in the case of the French by war scares. A Veterinary College (for servicing the cavalry) was like an English imitation of the Ecole Polytechnique [see Pugh (532)] and, as indicated by Pritchard (531), the result of French example. Other such French stimulants are suggested (37), (47), (118), (152), (223), (259), (329), (411).

Past mid-century, Germany became the industrial pacemaker, intensifying with every decade (224) up to 1914. Copious as the literature on this theme is, here it suffices to offer (37), (42), (46), (150), (152), (223), (285), (286), (290), (298), (305), (307), (336), (349), (356), (364), (399), (414), (442), (453), (468), (512), (565), (566), (582), 584), (599), (619) and (704).

Also looming up with ever increasing technical mastery of its own environment was the United States of America, whose Civil War had repercussions in Britain (20), (98), (240), (425), (529) and (640), and whose generalised stimulus can be explored from (41), (111), (166a), (217), (228), (300, (319), (467), (491), (534), (558), (590), (597), (624), (640), (666) and (667). More generalised comparisons of British economic development, especially with the continent, are provided by Fox-Bourne (263), Henderson (337), Hoseltz (352), Lewis (409), and Temin (630). Indeed the whole question of the "depression" and "retardation" of British economic growth between 1870 and 1913 should be explored through (478), (505), (553), (575), (579), (581), (635) and (687). The "state of mind" of that time is examined in (516), (586) and (691) and economic doctrines in (366). Imlah (370) examines the export of capital and balance of payments over the whole period 1816–1913.

SCIENTIFIC MANPOWER. Such comparisons kindled the spirit of emulation, and schools were affected by the need to train those who would enable the economic war to be won. Here efforts were numerous from H.M.S. *Excellent* (717), to Sandhurst (637), Woolwich (349) and Addiscombe (668). The curricula of the schools preparing boys for the academies is a relatively untilled field. Excellent surveys of the published material have been given by Trevor Hearl (332) and a good account of the pioneering work of Army schools by A. C. T. White (680). But more examination is needed of schools preparing for the military academies, such as the program at Wimbledon founded by J. M. Brackenbury (99); studies are also needed of lecturers in these schools like C. L. Bloxham (92), and of the books written for them (97), (244), (555). Here (254) and (255) are useful jumping off grounds.

From here the field extends to the naval gunnery schools (714) and technical education generally (1), (44), (50), (55), (81), (91), (164), (172), (260), (407), (434), (458), (609), (636), agricultural schools (168), schools of design (78), schools for mechanics (324), (393), (657), scholarships given by armaments manufacturers like Whitworth (422) and the general encouragement of science teaching (394), (638), (655). Even "elementary" schools are affected (673).

Reverberations of foreign competition can be detected in the universities (35), (80), (82), (114), (146), (421), (592), (647), and the school of mines (541), in the rise of examinations (241), (255), (449), public libraries (295) and consequently in the general organisation of education (66), (234), (258), (591), (608), (614). Working-men's clubs (310) and colleges (323) should not be forgotten, nor should the efforts of the Royal Society of Arts (358).

The organisation of science [Lyon Playfair (543) was one of the first government scientists] is an important area, not least because of the role of army (544) and naval officers (59), (63), (64), (184). Further studies of their surveys and cartographic efforts are needed to supplement Kirwan (399). There are some stimulating estimates of the social function of science (83) and its social relations (187) and a bibliography of its sociology (68). Standard works (18), (57), (58), (127), (385), (426) need supplementing [especially since "civil science" is being exhaustively studied by, amongst others, McLeod (431)] by a study of the service fellows in the Royal Society (569).

SCIENCE AND SOCIAL WELFARE. Inspectorates for Factories (1833), Prisons (1835), Anatomy (1839), Mines (1840), to say nothing of Noxious Trades (1854) and the Merchant Marine (1850), together with others for Railways and Schools, fashioned the Welfare State (557), as David Roberts has shown.

The passage of the Contagious Diseases Acts in 1864, 1866 and 1869 made it necessary to register, license and medically examine prostitutes in some eighteen garrisons or dockyard towns. An agitation was initiated by the Ladies National Association for the Repeal of the Contagious Diseases Acts. Its secretary was Josephine Butler and its political champion was James Stansfeld, the liberal M.P. for Halifax (316). After seventeen years' agitation, the repealing act became law in 1886.

One of the most decisive areas in which science impinged on society was in the lengthening of the life span and the improvements in public health. W. M. Frazer's account of the development of environmental hygiene and the public health acts, especially that of 1875 (264), is a good starting off point. This should be followed up by Royston Lambert's more recent study of Sir John Simon and English social administration, which has an excellent bibliography that includes location of unpublished material, up to 1963. Of special interest here is the research on cholera by Surgeon Major Timothy Richards Lewis included in an earlier work by M. E. M. Walker (673) and that of Sir Ronald Ross on malaria by Sir William Hall-White (313). The best overview of scientific medicine, with superb bibliographies, is that of Douglas Guthrie (299). His essay on medicine in the navy should be supplemented by Lloyd and Coulter (420), which also has an excellent bibliography.

The growth of these and other regulatory activities of the state, based on fact finding, social diagnosis and remedies, facilitated the mobilization when necessary of the resources of the nation in a total war. The Warfare State, as Professor Titmus has suggested, had to be a Welfare State as well (648).

AGENDA FOR FURTHER RESEARCH

(1) Contemporary interest on science in government demands clearer apprehension of the work of men like Colonel Strange (127), the advocate of a Ministry of Science, Generals Sabine and Strachey and Captain Galton. So too the growth of statistical branches of the services and of their topographical departments need study.

(2) The political work of service officers might also be investigated. Sir Andrew Clark (and the Suez Canal), Goldie in Nigeria, Kenyon-Slaney in Parliament, H. H. Grenfell and the Navy League are all examples worth following up.

(3) Historians of science might find some interesting contributions to ballistics from William Burnside, electricity from Philip Cardew, hydraulics from H. H. Grenfell, servo-mechanisms from P. Brotherhood, submarine defence from Sir William Crossman, shipbuilding from Francis Elgar, and wireless from Sir Henry B. Jackson.

(4) High on the agenda of all military histories should be the Indian Army and its role collectively and individually in British economic and scientific development. The work of medical officers like J. Forbes Royle (1799–1851) on cinchona, or of W. H. Sleeman (1788–1856) on the development of the sugar cane, or of Surgeon-Major William Jameson (1815–1882) on the development of tea planting (he died in a tea garden) are well worth exploring as George Bruce has recently shown (109). Then there are engineers like David Reid (1841–1892) who, after many years of building railways in India and Ceylon, introduced Ceylon tea into England.

(5) Other wars also need examination as theatres of rehearsal (e.g. Steam vessels in the Burmese War of 1824 and the Maxim Gun in the Matabele War 1893–4). Thus the Crimean War is slowly being reassessed as an example of economic warfare (17), and in terms of improvements in technology (88), (556), sanitation (312) and other aspects (166), (314), (670), (698), (699). The American Civil War has interest from the point of view of Confederate purchasing (640), its impact on Europe (425) and the blockade (98), (240), to say nothing of its lessons (20), (529). The Boer War's impact on health has been well explored by Bentley W. Gilbert (281). Indeed war and Social Darwinism (192–6), (585) might well be reassessed in the light of the volunteer movement (506) and the Territorial Army (421).

(6) The armaments industry itself is virtually unexplored as such. In-

novative manufacturers like William Westley Richards (1790–1865) (who brought out the Enfield Rifle in 1853) need study. Others can be revealed by diligent examination of contemporary observers like G. L. M. Strauss (620a), who gives accounts of sword, bayonet and rifle works in Birmingham.

(7) Strauss, himself a former surgeon in the French army, indicates that a major survey of foreign military exiles in England like C. A. Redl (inventor of the core telegraph) would show how they endowed the country of their adoption with new ideas.

(8) The "inner dynamics" of war "scares" in the nineteenth century have a technological background (155, 708). For example, talk of a channel tunnel generated fears of invasion. C. J. Bartlett (71) has found that Admiralty records and papers, like those of the Foreign and Colonial Offices, "can be explored almost indefinitely" (p. 346) with a view to identifying innovators. Did, for example, T. C. Croker (180) introduce lithography into the Admiralty, or did he spend his time writing about Ireland?

(9) Lists of engineer officers in the navy (which begin in 1837) need study to see how far skills were fed back into civilian life. Further studies are also needed on the industries of the naval dockyards at Malta, Keyham and Portsmouth. Thus the school of naval architecture (established in 1806, discontinued in 1832, and whose history can be found in *Parliamentary Papers* XXIV (1833), pp. 315–330) needs further investigation to round out the statement of J. D. Chambers (145) that the navy passed out "a thin stream" of engineers "trained with the aid of foreign textbooks since none existed in Britain." Chambers considered that they helped to revive the British shipbuilding industry between 1837 and 1851. The influence of the Army schools and those of the East India Company—like Addiscombe and Haileybury—is currently (1969) being assessed by Trevor Hearl (332).

(10) Here the views of nineteenth-century men of letters are important [e.g. (208)] and need investigation. Are there also military counterparts to the virtual dynasty of naval novelists like Captain Marryat, G. A. Henty, W. H. G. Kingston, Joseph Conrad, John Masefield and E. S. Forster? Though from the time of Mrs. Sherwood the army at home and overseas threw up writers, they have not been noticed or examined by belle-lettrists or literary historians. Here an excellent example has been set by I. F. Clarke (155). Indeed, the select list of war studies (pp. 217–226) and check list of imaginary wars (pp. 227–249) which he gives will stimulate all research workers in the field. Similar check lists of specifically military writers and correspondents are needed: Howard Russell (268) and C. B. Brackenbury (99) of *The Times,* or R. E. Childers (150) of the *Daily News,* or the *Illustrated London News*'s J. A. Crowe (93) would of course figure in them.

(11) Closely allied to this field are the "curiosities" of war, as explored by Thomas Carter (133–4), the antiquarian-minded clerk in the Adjutant-General's office. Biographical studies are needed of the administrators in the army and of the administrative ideas of generals like Napier (480).

(12) On the horizon of every student of nineteenth-century science and

technology is the navy. Apart from its anti-slavery activities (675), the hydrological (147) and meteorological research of its scientifically and technically minded naval officers made possible such contemporary conveniences as weather forecasts. Here men like Captain Fitzroy (Darwin's friend) need reassessment. Studies are also needed of the five (later seven) departments (those under the surveyor, accountant-general, comptroller of victualling, medical director-general, comptroller of steam machinery, and director of engineering and public works ashore) that replaced the old Navy Board in 1832. For example, under the new arrangement Sir William Symonds, the first surveyor, spent some time looking for wood for ships in the Apennines, even after Sir Edward Perry, comptroller of steam machinery, was appointed in 1837. Here one gets a good case history of the transition from a plantocratic to a technocratic Britain which is such a feature of the age.

(13) The rise of technological factors in national rivalries also deserves study. We lack, for instance, a good modern evaluation of the fight over petroleum fields. Here C. T. Marvin (93) might prove an interesting subject for investigation, especially in view of his fear that Russian petroleum would virtually drown the British Empire. In spite of the efforts of Major W. E. Gowan of the Bengal Infantry to index his writings, they have still to be chased through the columns of the *Army and Navy Magazine* and the *United Service Gazette.*

BIBLIOGRAPHY

1. Abbott, A. *Education for Industry and Commerce in England.* London: Oxford University Press, 1933.
2. Acton Lord. *Essays on Freedom and Power.* Gertrude Himmelfarb, ed. Glencoe: Free Press, 1949.
3. *Accounts and Papers. Vol. LXX. Indexes to Bills and Reports 1801–1852.* London: 1854.
4. Adamson, J. W. *English Education 1789–1902.* Cambridge: Cambridge University Press, 1930.
5. Addis, John P. *The Crawshay Dynasty, 1765–1867.* Cardiff: University of Wales Press, 1957.
6. Ahrons, E. L. *The British Steam Railway Locomotive 1825–1924.* London: Locomotive Publishing Co., 1927.
7. *Aims and Objects, Sixty Years of Progress: the Institution of Public Health Engineers.* London: The Institution, 1955.
8. Aldcroft, D. H. "The depression in British Shipping." *Journal of Transport History,* May, 1965.
9. Aitchison, L. *A History of Metals.* London: Macdonald & Evans, 1960, 2 vols.
10. Allen, Frances, *et al. Technology and Social Change.* New York: Appleton-Century-Crofts, 1957.

11. Allen, G. C. *The Industrial Development of Birmingham and the Black Country, 1860–1927*. London: Allen & Unwin, 1929.

12. Allen, G. C. & A. G. Donnithorne. *Western Enterprise in Far Eastern Economic Development: China and Japan*. London: Allen & Unwin, 1954.

13. Allen, Mea. *The Hookers of Kew 1785–1911*. London: Michael Joseph, 1967.

14. Alexander, W. O. "A Brief Review of the Development of the Copper, Zinc and Brass Industries in Great Britain from A.D. 1500 to 1900." *Murex Review*, Vol. 1, No. 15, 1955, p. 389–423.

15. Ames, E. and N. Rosenberg. "Changing Technological Leadership and Industrial Growth." *Economic Journal*, lxxiii, 1963.

16. "Analytical bibliography of the history of engineering and applied science," in *Newcomen Society for the Study of the History of Engineering and Technology, Transactions,* v. II, 1921–2, v. XXII, 1941–2, and v. XXV, 1945–47.

17. Anderson, Olive. "Economic Warfare in the Crimean War." *Economic History Review,* 2nd Series xiv, 1961–2, pp. 34–47.

18. Andrade, E. N. Da C. *Brief History of the Royal Society*. London: Royal Society, 1960.

19. Andrews, A. *Archives*. No. 5, 1951, pp. 11–21.

20. Andrews, J. Cutler. *The North Reports the Civil War*. Pittsburgh: University of Pittsburgh Press, 1955.

21. Anlage, I. and Eberhard Scherbening. *Wirtschaftsorganisation im Kriege*. Jena: 1938.

22. Anshen, Ruth Nanda. *Science and Man*. New York, 1942.

23. Appert, C. *L'Art de conserver pendant plusieurs années toutes les substances animales et végétales*. Paris: Patris, 1810.

24. Appleyard, Rollo. *Charles Parsons, his Life and Work*. London: Constable & Co., 1933.

25. Appleyard, Rollo. *Pioneers of Electrical Communication*. London: Macmillan, 1930.

26. Appleyard, Rollo. "With but after." Reprinted from the *Fortnightly Review*. London: Chapman & Hall, 1900.

27. Appleyard, Rollo. *The History of the Institution of Electrical Engineers (1871–1931)*. London: The Institution of Electrical Engineers, 1931.

28. Armstrong, W. G. *et al. The Industrial Resources of the District of the Three Northern Rivers*. London: Longmans, 1864.

29. *The Architect*. A journal of art, civil engineering, etc. London: 1869.

30. *The Architect and Building Operative*. London, 1889. Merged with *The Civil Engineer Architects Journal*, started in 1837, in 1867.

31. Armada. *The Second Armada. A Chapter of Future History*. [By A. Haywood]. Reprinted, with more details, from *The Times*. London: Harrison and Sons, 1871.

32. *Armaments Yearbook*.

33. Armytage, W. H. G. *A Social History of Engineering*. Boston: M.I.T. Press, 1966, pp. 122–4.
34. Armytage, W. H. G. *A. J. Mundella, 1825–1897*. London: Ernest Benn, 1951.
35. Armytage, W. H. G. *Civil Universities: aspects of a British tradition*. London: Ernest Benn, 1955, pp. 169–70.
36. Armytage, W. H. G. *Sir Richard Gregory*. London: Macmillan, 1957.
37. Armytage, W. H. G. *Four Hundred Years of English Education*. Cambridge: Cambridge University Press, 1964.
38. Armytage, W. H. G. *A Social History of Engineering*. London: Faber & Faber, 1961.
39. Armytage, W. H. G. *The Rise of the Technocrats*. London: Routledge & Kegan Paul, 1965.
40. Armytage, W. H. G. *The French Influence on English Education*. London: Routledge & Kegan Paul, 1967, pp. 39–40.
41. Armytage, W. H. G. *The American Influence on English Education*. London: Routledge & Kegan Paul, 1967.
42. Armytage, W. H. G. *The German Influence on English Education*. London: Routledge & Kegan Paul, 1969.
43. Armytage, W. H. G. *The Russian Influence on English Education*. London: Routledge & Kegan Paul, 1969.
44. Armytage, W. H. G. "Some sources for the history of technical education in England." *British Journal of Educational Studies*, I, II, VI, 1956–57.
45. *ASLIB Manuals*. Theodore Besterman, ed. London: A.S.L.I.B., 1945.
46. Armstrong, E. V. & H. S. Lukens. "Jean Antione Chaptal, Comte de Chanteloupe." *Journal of Chemical Education*, xiii, 1936, pp. 257–62.
47. Arnold, Matthew. *Collected Works*. R. H. Super, ed. Ann Arbor, Michigan: 1963 onwards.
48. Arnot, R. Page. *The Miners*. London: Vol. i, 1949; Vol. ii, 1949.
49. Aron, Raymond. *War and Industrial Society*. Mary Bottomore, tr. London: 1958.
50. Ashby, Sir Eric. *Technology and the Academies*. Macmillan, 1958.
51. Ashley, W. J. *The Economic Organization of England*. London: Longmans, 1914.
52. Ashton, T. S. *The Industrial Revolution, 1760–1830*. Oxford: Home University Library, 1948.
53. Ashworth, W. *An Economic History of England, 1870–1939*. London: Methuen, 1960.
54. Aston, G. G. *Letters on Amphibious Wars*. London: John Murray, 1911.
55. A.T.T.I. *The First Half-Century, 1904–1954*. London: A.T.T.I., 1954.
56. *Australian Dictionary of Biography, 1788–1850*. Melbourne University Press, 1966. 2 vols.

57. Babbage, C. *Passages from the Life of a Philosopher*. London: Longmans, 1864.

58. Babbage, C. *Reflections on the Decline of Science in England*. London: B. Fellowes, 1830.

59. Bagrow, L. *History of Cartography*. Revised by R. A. Skelton. London: Watts, 1964.

60. Bailey, Sir Edward B. *Charles Lyell*. London: Nelson, 1962.

61. Baines, Sir E. *History of the Cotton Manufacture in Great Britain*. London: Fisher & Co., 1835.

62. Baines, Thomas. *History of Liverpool*. London: Longmans, 1852.

63. Baker, J. N. L. *A History of Geographical Discovery and Exploration*. 2nd ed. London: Harrap, 1937.

64. Baker, John R. *The Controversy on Freedom in Science in the Nineteenth Century*. Oxford: Society for the Freedom in Science, Occasional Pamphlets No. 22, 1962.

65. Baldwin, F. G. C. *The History of the Telephone in the United Kingdom*. London: Chapman and Hall, 1925.

66. Balfour, Graham. *The Educational Systems of Great Britain and Ireland*. Oxford: Clarendon Press, 1903, 2nd ed.

67. Ball, M. Margaret. *N.A.T.O. and the European Union Movement*. London: Stevens and Son, 1959.

68. Barber, Bernard. *Sociology of Science: a trend report and a bibliography*. U.N.E.S.C.O., Paris: 1956.

69. Barker, T. C. and J. R. Harris. *A Merseyside Town in the Industrial Revolution: St. Helens 1750–1900*. Liverpool: University Press, 1954. Reprinted with corrections by Frank Cass, London, 1959.

70. Barnaby, K. C. *The Institution of Naval Architects 1860–1960*. London: The Institution and George Allen and Unwin, 1960.

71. Bartlett, C. J. *Great Britain and Sea Power 1815–1883*. Oxford: Clarendon Press, 1963.

72. Barton, D. B. *The Cornish Beam Engine*. Truro: D. B. Barton, 1965.

73. Bauer, Peter Tamas. *The Rubber Industry: a study in competition and monopoly*. London: Longmans, 1948.

74. Baxter, James P. *The Introduction of the Ironclad Warship*. Cambridge, Mass.: Harvard University Press, 1933.

75. Beales, A. C. F. *The History of Peace: a short account of the movements for organised peace*. New York: C. MacVeagh, the Dial Press, 1931.

76. Beard, C. *The Industrial Revolution*. London: Swan Sonnenschein & Co., 1901.

77. Bell, Horace. *Railway Policy in India*. London: Rivington, Percival & Co., 1894.

78. Bell, Quentin. *The Schools of Design*. London: Routledge, 1963.

79. Bellamy, E. *Looking Backward 2000–1887*. With a foreword by E. Fromm, New York: New American Library, 1960.

80. Bellot, H. H. *University College London, 1826–1926*. U.L.P., 1929.

81. Benge, R. C. *Technical and Vocational Education in the United Kingdom: a bibliographical survey.* U.N.E.S.C.O., n.d.
82. Berdahl, Robert O. *British Universities and the State.* University of California Press, 1959.
83. Bernal, J. D. *Science and Industry in the Nineteenth Century.* London: Routledge & Kegan Paul, 1953.
84. Bernal, J. D. *The Social Function of Science.* London: Routledge, 1939.
85. Bernard, L. L. *War and Its Causes.* New York: Holt & Co., 1944.
86. Bernhardi, Friedrich von. *Germany and the Next War.* Allen H. Powles, tr. New York: Longmans, Green and Co., 1914. [By this time it had reached 14 impressions since first publication in 1912 in England.]
87. Bernhardi, Friedrich von. *War of Today.* II, 28–29; 72–74. London: Hugh Rees, 1912.
88. Bessemer, Sir Henry. *Autobiography.* London: *Engineering,* 1905, p. 156.
89. Bibby, Cyril. *T. H. Huxley: scientist, humanist and educator.* London: Watts, 1959.
90. Blair, J. "Technology and Size." *American Economic Review,* XXXCIII, 1948, p. 121.
91. Blanchet, Jeremy. *Science, Craft and the State: a study of English technical education and its advocates, 1867–1906.* Unpublished thesis, D. Phil., Oxford, 1953.
92. Bloxham, Charles London. *Laboratory Teaching: or progressive exercises in practical chemistry.* London: J. Churchill and Sons. This went to 6 editions by 1893. [His *Chemistry, Organic and Inorganic* published by the same publishers at the same time went to 11 by 1923.]
93. Boase, F. *Modern English Biography.* London: Frank Cass, 1965. 6 vols.
94. Boetem, Eric H. and Adolphus Lalit. *Historical Periodicals.* Santa Barbara, California: Clio Press, 1961, pp. 216–244 and pp. 265–268.
95. Bolton, Henry Carrington. *A Catalogue of Scientific and Technical Periodicals, 1665–1895.* Together with Chronological Tables and a Library Check-List. Washington: Smithsonian Miscellaneous Collections, Vol. XL, 1989.
96. Bond, M. F. "Materials for Transport History amongst the Records of Parliament." *Journal of Transport History,* IV, No. 1, 1959, pp. 48–50.
97. Boucher, John Sidney. *Mensuration, plain and solid: for the use of schools and colleges, civil, military and naval and specially adapted for self instruction.* London: Longmans, Green & Co., 1857.
98. Bradlee, Francis B. C. *Blockade Running During the Civil War.* Salem, Mass.: 1925.
99. Brackenbury, Charles Booth. *Men of the Time.* London: Kegan Paul (1887), p. 140.

100. Brackenbury, John Matthew. *Guardian*, 4 Sept. 1895, p. 1299; 25 Sept. 1895, p. 1414.
101. Brief, R. P. "The Origin and Evolution of 19th-Century Asset Accounting." *Business History Review*, XL, 1966.
102. Briggs, Asa. *The Age of Improvement 1783–1867*. London: Longmans, 1960, pp. 7, 129–183.
103. Briggs, John Henry. *Naval Administrations, 1827 to 1892*. London: Sampson, Low and Co., 1897.
104. Bright, Sir Charles Tilson. *Telegraphy, Aeronautics and War*. London: Constable and Co., 1918. (Sir Charles wrote prolifically on the history of telegraphs. One history, published by C. Lockwood of London in 1898 is worth citing.)
105. Brinley, Thomas. *Migration and Economic Growth: a study of the Atlantic economy*. Cambridge: Cambridge University Press, 1954.
106. British Association for the Advancement of Science. *Transactions*, Vol. 1, 1832.
107. *British National Bibliography*. London, 1950. Weekly issues.
108. Brodie, Bernard. *Sea Power in the Machine Age*. Princeton University Press, 1944.
109. Bruce, George. *The Stranglers*. New York: Harcourt Brace and World, 1969.
110. Bruce, R. V. *Lincoln and the Tools of War*. Indianapolis: Bobbs Merrill, 1956.
111. Buckell, George Teasdale. *Experts on Guns and Shooting*. London: Sampson, Low and Co., 1900.
112. Burn, D. L. *The Economy History of Steelmaking, 1867–1939*. Cambridge: Cambridge University Press, 1940.
113. Burnham, T. H. & Hoskins, G. O. *Iron and Steel in Britain, 1870–1930*. London: Allen & Unwin, 1943.
114. Burns, C. D. *A Short History of Birkbeck College*. London University Press, 1924.
115. Burstall, A. F. *History of Mechanical Engineering*. London: Faber & Faber, 1963.
116. Bush, Vannevar. *Modern Arms and Free Men: a discussion of the rôle of science in preserving democracy*. New York: Simon & Schuster, 1949; London: William Heinemann, 1950.
117. *Business History*. Liverpool: University Press, 1958– .
118. Cady, John F. *The Roots of French Imperialism in Eastern Asia*. Ithaca, N. Y.: Cornell University Press, 1954.
119. Cairncross, A. K. *Factors in Economic Development*. London: George Allen & Unwin, 1962.
120. Cajori, F. *A History of Physics in its Elementary Branches (through 1925) including the Evolution of Physical Laboratories*. New York: Dover, 1929, 2nd ed., 1960.
121. Callwell, C. E. *Military Operations and Maritime Preponderance*. London & Edinburgh: W. Blackwood & Sons, 1905.
122. *Cambridge Economic History of Europe*, vol. VI, Pt. 1. Cambridge: Cambridge University Press, 1965.

123. Cameron, John G. P. *A Short History of the Royal Indian Engineering College, Coopers Hill.* London: Coopers Hill Society, 1960.

124. Cameron, John, ed. *Ordnance Survey. Metereological Observations taken during the years 1829–1852.* London: H.M.S.O., 1856.

125. Campbell, W. A., *et al. The Old Tyneside Chemical Trade.* Newcastle, 1961.

126. Carbutt, Edward Hamer. "Fifty Years of Progress in Gun-Making." *Transactions of the Institute of Mechanical Engineers,* 1887.

127. Cardwell, D. S. L. *The Organisation of Science in England.* London: Heinemann, 1957, pp. 92–98.

128. Carman, W. Y. *A History of Firearms From the Earliest Times to 1914.* London: Routledge & Kegan Paul, 1955.

129. Carpenter, R. C. and H. Diederichs. *The Development of the Internal Combustion Engine to 1860.* London: C. Lockwood & Son, 1908.

130. Carr, J. C. and W. Taplin. *History of the British Steel Industry.* Oxford: Basil Blackwell, 1962.

131. Carswell, J. *The Prospector.* London: Cresset Press, 1950.

132. Carter, C. F. & B. R. Williams. *Industry and Technical Progress.* Oxford: Oxford University Press, 1957.

133. Carter, Thomas. *Curiosities of War and Military Studies: anecdotal, descriptive and statistical.* London: Groombridge, 1860. 2nd edition illustrated, 1871.

134. Carter, Thomas. *War Medals of the British Army.* Revised, enlarged and continued to the present time by W. H. Long. London: Norie and Wilson, 1893.

135. Castro, José de. *Geography of Hunger.* London: Gollancz, 1952.

136. *A Catalogue of Modern Works on Science and Technology . . .* London: Chapman and Hale. 42 editions. [The British Museum lacks the first to the fourth, the sixth, the fifteenth, the twenty-first, twenty-second and twenty-sixth editions.] 1876–1914.

137. Caunter, C. F. *The History & Development of Cycles as illustrated by the collection of cycles in the Science Museum. Pt. 1. Historical Survey,* 1955.

138. Caunter, C. F. *Handbook of the collection illustrating cycles. Pt. 2. Catalogue of Exhibits with Descriptive Notes.* London: H.M.S.O., 1958.

139. Caunter, C. F. *Handbook of the Collection Illustrating Motor Cars, Pt. 2.* London: H.M.S.O., 1959.

140. Caunter, C. F. *The History and Development of Motor Cycles as Illustrated by the Collection of Motor Cycles in the Science Museum.* London: H.M.S.O., 1955–58.

141. Caunter, C. F. *The History and Development of Light Cars.* London: H.M.S.O., 1957.

142. Chadwick, G. F. "The Army Works Corps in the Crimea." *Journal of Transport History,* vi. 1963–4, pp. 129–141.

143. Chalmers, T. W. *Historic Researches: chapters in the history of*

physical and chemical discovery. London: Morgan Bros. Ltd., 1949.

144. Chaloner, W. H. *The Social and Economic Development of Crewe, 1780–1923.* Manchester University Press, 1950.

145. Chambers, J. D. *The Working of the World.* Oxford: Opus 32. Oxford Paperbacks University Series, 2nd ed., 1968, p. 42.

146. Chapman, Arthur W. *The Story of a Modern University.* Oxford: University Press, 1955.

147. *Charting the Seas in Peace and War. The Story of the Hydrographic Department of the Admiralty over a hundred and fifty years, 12th August, 1795 to 12th August 1945.* London, H.M.S.O., 1947.

148. Checkland, S. G. *The Rise of Industrial Society in England 1815–1885.* London: Longmans, 1964.

149. Chevalier, J. *Le Creusot, berceau de la grande industrie française.* Paris: Dunod, 1946.

150. Childers, Robert Erskine. *German Influence on British Cavalry.* London: E. Arnold, 1911. [A bibliography of his writings has been published by Patrick S. O'Hegarty in 1948.]

151. *Chymia. Annual Studies in the History of Chemistry.* I, O.U.P., University of Pennsylvania Press, 1948.

152. Clapham, J. H. *The Economic Development of France and Germany 1815–1914.* 4th ed. Cambridge University Press, 1936.

153. Clapham, J. H. *An Economic History of Modern Britain; the early railway age 1820–1914; free trade and steel 1850–1886; machines and national rivalries (1887–1914) with an epilogue (1914–1929).* Cambridge: Cambridge University Press, 1939–1952.

154. Clapham, J. H. "The Industrial Revolution and the Colonies." *Cambridge History of the British Empire.* Vol. II, Cambridge: Cambridge University Press, 1940.

155. Clarke, I. F. *Voices Prophesying War 1763–1984.* London: Oxford University Press, 1966.

156. Clay, R. S. and T. H. Court. *The History of the Microscope.* London: Griffin, 1932.

157. Clow, A and Nan L. Clow. *The Chemical Revolution: a contribution to social technology.* London: Batchworth Press, 1952.

158. Clowes, G. S. L. *Sailing Ships, their History and Development, as Illustrated by the Collection of Ship-Models in the Science Museum.* London: H.M.S.O., 1930–52.

159. Cobden, Richard. *Three Panics.* London: Ward & Co., 1862.

160. Cobt, H. S. "Sources for Economic History amongst the Parliamentary Records in the House of Lords Record Office." *Economic History Review,* XIX, 1966, 154–174.

161. Cohen, I. B. and Howard Mumford Jones. *A Treasury of Scientific Prose: a nineteenth-century anthology.* Boston: Little, Brown, 1963.

162. Cohen, J. M. *The Life of Ludwig Mond.* London: Methuen and Co., 1956.

163. Cole, G. D. H. and Raymond Postgate. *The Common People, 1746–1938.* 2nd ed. London: Methuen, 1945.

164. Cole, Sir Henry. *Fifty Years of Public Work*. London: Bell, 1884. 2 vols.
165. Colquhoun, P. *Treatise on the Population, Wealth, Power, and Resources of the British Empire*. London: J. Mawman, 1814 (but see Griffin's criticisms in *Growth of Capital* [1890], p. 121).
166. Colvile, R. F. "The Baltic as a Theatre of War." *J.R.U.S.I.*, LXXXVI (1941), pp. 72–80.
166a. Colvile, R. F. "The Navy and the Crimean War." *J.R.U.S.I.*, LXXXV, 1940, pp. 73–8.
167. Colvin, F. H. and D. J. Duffin. *Sixty Years with Men and Machines*. New York: Whittlesey House, McGraw-Hill Book Co. Inc., 1947.
168. Comber, N. M. *Agricultural Education in Great Britain*. London: Longmans for British Council, 1948.
169. *Committee of Inquiry into the Organisation and Administration of the Manufacturing Departments of the Army*. London: H.M.S.O., 1888, C.5116.
170. *Committee on War Office Contracts*. London: H.M.S.O., 1898, *Cd. 313*.
171. Copeland, M. T. "Technical Development in Cotton Manufacturing since 1860." *The Quarterly Journal of Economics*, November, 1909.
172. Cotgrove, Stephen F. *Technical Education and Social Change*. London: Allen & Unwin, 1958.
173. Court, W. H. B. *Concise Economic History of Britain*. Cambridge: Cambridge University Press, 1954.
174. Court, W. H. B. *The Rise of Midland Industries*. London: Oxford University Press, 1938.
175. "Courtauld, Samuel." *Illustrated London News*, 13 Oct. 1855, pp. 445–6.
176. Cramp, W. *Michael Faraday and Some of His Contemporaries*. London: Pitman & Sons, 1931.
177. Craven, W. Frank. *Why Military History?* Colorado: United States Air Force Academy, 1959.
178. Cressy, Edward. *A Hundred Years of Mechanical Engineering*. London: Duckworth, 1937.
179. "Critical bibliography of the history of science and its cultural influences." *ISIS*, V. I, 1913.
180. Croker, T. F. D. *Fairy Legends of the South of Ireland by T. C. Croker*, with a memorial of the author by his son. London: John Murray, 1834.
181. Cromb, James. *The Highland Brigade. Its battles and heroes*, edited and brought down to the end of the Boer War by D. E. Cromb. Stirling: Eneas Mackay, 1902.
182. Crombie, A. C., ed. *Scientific Change: historical studies in the intellectual, social and technical conditions for scientific discovery and technical invention, from antiquity to the present*. London: Heinemann, 1963.
183. Crompton, R. E. B. *Reminiscences*. London: Constable, 1928.
184. Crone, G. R. *Maps and their makers: an introduction to the history of cartography*. 3rd ed. London: Hutchinson, 1966.

185. Crouzet, Francois. "Wars, Blockade, and Economic Change in Europe." *Journal of Economic History,* 2, XXIV (1964), pp. 567–588.
186. Crowther, J. G. *Discoveries and Inventions of the 20th Century.* 4th ed. London: Routledge, 1955.
187. Crowther, J. G. *The Social Relations of Science.* London: Macmillan, 1941.
188. "Current Bibliography in the History of Technology," *Technology and Culture.* 1st annual (1962), v. 5 No. 1 Winter 1964, pp. 138–48.
189. Curti, Merle. "America at the World Fairs 1851–1893." *American Historical Review,* LV (1950), pp. 833–856.
190. Daly, Robert W. *How the "Merrimac" Won: the strategic story of the C.S.S. Virginia.* New York: Crowell, 1957.
191. Danilevskii, V. V. *Russkaya Tekhnika.* Moscow: 1948.
192. Darwin, C. R. *A Naturalist's Voyage.* London: John Murray, 1860.
193. Darwin, C. R. *The Effects of Cross and Self Fertilization in the Vegetable Kingdom.* London: John Murray, 1876.
194. Darwin, C. R. *The Expression of the Emotions in Man and Animals.* London: John Murray, 1872.
195. Darwin, C. R. *The Formation of Vegetable Mould Through the Action of Worms.* London: John Murray, 1881.
196. Darwin, C. R. *The Origin of Species.* London: John Murray, 1895.
197. Daumas, M. *Les instruments scientifiques aux xviiᵉ et xviiiᵉ siècles (Bibliothèque de philosophie contemporaine: philosophie des sciences.)* Paris: Presses Universitaires de France, 1953.
198. Davidson, Edward. *The Railways of India.* London: E. and F. N. Spon, 1868.
199. Davis, H. W. C. *The Great Game in Asia 1800–1844.* London: Oxford University Press, 1927. [British Academy: Raleigh Lecture in History, 1926].
200. Davison, C. St. C. B. *History of Steam Road Vehicles.* London: H.M.S.O., 1953.
201. Davy, M. J. B. *Handbook of the Collections Illustrating Aeronautics —I. Heavier-than-Air Craft.* London: H.M.S.O., 1935.
202. Davy, M. J. B. *Handbook of the Collection Illustrating Aeronautics —II. Lighter-than-Air Craft.* London: H.M.S.O., 1934.
203. Davy, M. J. B. *Interpretive History of Flight.* London: H.M.S.O., 1948.
204. Davy, Richard. *New Inventions in Surgical Mechanisms.* London: Smith Elder and Co., 1875.
205. Deane, Phyllis and W. A. Cole. *British Economic Growth, 1688–1959, Trends and Structure.* Cambridge University Press, University of Cambridge Department of Applied Economic Monographs, 8, 1962.
206. de Beer, G. *Charles Darwin: a scientific biography.* New York: Doubleday, 1965.
207. Department of Explosives Supply. *Second Report on Costs and*

Efficiencies for H.M. Factories controlled by Factories Branch.
London: H.M.S.O., 1919.

208. De Quincey, Thomas. "On War" in *De Quincey's Writings.* ed.
J. T. Fields, ed. V. 8, Boston: Ticknor, Reed and Fields, 1854, pp.
191–232. [A copy of this essay, interleaved and prepared with numerous alterations by the author, is in the British Museum under
C.61 a.2(1)].

209. Derry, T. K. and Trevor I. Williams. *A Short History of Technology.
From the earliest times to 1900.* Oxford: Clarendon Press, 1960.

210. Dicey, Albert Venn. *Lectures on the relation between law and
public opinion in England during the nineteenth century.* London:
Macmillan, 1905.

211. Dicey, Sir Edward. *The Egypt of the Future.* London: William
Heinemann, 1907.

212. Dickinson, H. W. "Richard Roberts, his Life and Inventions."
T.N.S., XXV (1950), pp. 123–37.

213. Dickinson, H. W. *James Watt.* Cambridge: Cambridge University
Press, 1936.

214. Dickinson, H. W. "Joseph Bramah and his Inventions." *T.N.S.,*
XXVI, (1946), pp. 169–86.

215. Dickinson, H. W. *A Short History of the Steam Engine.* Introd. by
A. E. Musson, 2nd ed. London: Frank Cass, 1963.

216. Dickinson, H. W. and A. Titley. *Richard Trevithick.* Cambridge:
Cambridge University Press, 1934.

217. Dingle, Herbert, ed. *A Century of Science 1851–1951.* London:
Hutchinson's Technical and Scientific Publications, 1951.

218. Dircks, H. *Perpetuum mobile or Search for Self Motive Powers.*
London: 1861–1870.

219. Dircks, H. *Inventors and Inventions.* London: n.p., 1867.

220. Dodds, J. W. *The Age of Paradox.* London: Gollancz, 1953.

221. Domt, Cyril. *Clerk Maxwell and Modern Science.* Six Commemora-
tive Lectures. London: Athlone Press, 1963.

222. Donnithorne, Audrey G. *British Rubber Manufacturing. An Economic Study of Innovations.* London: Gerald Duckworth and Co.,
1953.

223. Drummond, Sir Jack Cecil and Anne Wilbraham. *The Englishman's
Food: A history of five centuries of English Diet.* Rev. and ed. by
Dorothy Hollingsworth, London: Jonathan Cape, 1959.

224. Dubos, R. J. W. *Louis Pasteur.* London: Gollancz, 1951.

225. Duckworth, W. E. *A Guide to Operational Research.* London:
Methuen, 1962.

226. Dugan, James. *The Great Iron Ship.* London: Hamish Hamilton,
1953.

227. Dunkin, Edwin. *Obituary notices of Astronomers, Fellows and Associates of the Royal Astronomical Society.* London: The Society,
1879.

228. Dunning, J. H. *American Investment in British Manufacturing Industry.* London: Allen and Unwin, 1958.

229. Dunsheath, Percy, ed. *A Century of Technology.* London: Hutchinson, 1951.

230. Dunsheath, Percy. *A History of Electrical Engineering.* London: Faber and Faber, 1962.

231. Dyos, H. J. "Transport History in University Theses." *Journal of Transport History,* IV (1959–60), pp. 161–173.

232. Eco, U. and G. B. Zorzoli. *A Pictorial History of Inventions from Plough to Polaris.* Trans. from the Italian by A. Lawrence. London: Weidenfeld and Nicolson, 1962.

233. von Edelsheim, Franz Freiherr. *Operations upon the Sea.* Alexander Gray, tr. New York: The Outdoor Press, 1914.

234. Edwards, H. J. *The Evening Institute.* London: National Institute of Adult Education, 1961.

235. Ehrman, John. *Cabinet Government and War, 1890–1940.* London and New York: Cambridge University Press, 1958.

236. Ellis, C. H. *British Railway History: an outline from the accession of William IV to the nationalisation of railways, 1830–1947.* London: Allen and Unwin, 1954–9. 2 vols.

237. Ellis, Ellen Deborah. *An Introduction to the History of Sugar as a Commodity.* Bryn Mawr, Monograph Series No. 4, 1905.

238. Emmison, F. G. and I. Gray. *County Records.* London: Historical Association, 1948.

239. Engels, F. *The Condition of the Working Class in England in 1844.* London: Allen and Unwin, 1892.

240. Engerman, Stanley L. "The Economic Impact of the Civil War." *Explorations in Entrepreneurial History.* 2nd series, III (1965–6), pp. 176–199.

240a. *The Engineer.* Especially Centenary Number 4, January, 1956.

241. Erickson, Arvel B. "Abolition of Purchase in the British Army." *Military Affairs,* XXIII, Summer 1959, pp. 65–76.

242. Erickson, C. "The Recruitment of British Management." *Explorations in Entrepreneurial History.* October, 1953.

243. Erickson, C. *British Industrialists: steel and hosiery, 1850–1950.* Cambridge: Cambridge University Press, 1959.

244. Ewing, Sir J. A. Preface to *Examples on Mathematics, Mechanics, Navigation, and Nautical Astronomy . . . for the use of junior officers afloat.* England: Miscellaneous Official Publications, 1911.

245. Eyre, J. Vargas. *H. E. Armstrong: pioneer of technical education.* London: Butterworth, 1958.

246. Falls, Cyril. *A Hundred Years of War.* London: C. Duckworth and Co., 1953.

247. Faraday, M. *Experimental Researches in Electricity.* London: 1839–1855. 3 vols.

248. Faraday, M. *Faraday's Diary.* T. Martin, ed. London: Royal Institution, 1932–36.

249. Fay, C. R. *Great Britain from Adam Smith to the Present Day.* London: Longmans, Green and Co., 1928.

250. Fay, C. R. *Palace of Industry, 1851.* Cambridge: Cambridge University Press, 1951.

251. Ferguson, Eugene S. *Bibliography of the History of Technology.* Published jointly by the Society for the History of Technology and the M.I.T. Press, Cambridge, Mass., 1968.

252. Findlay, A. *A Hundred Years of Chemistry.* Rev. by T. I. Williams. 3rd ed. London: Duckworth, 1965.

253. Finer, S. E. *The Life and Times of Sir Edwin Chadwick.* London: Methuen, 1952.

254. *First Report of the Council on Military Education, C.2603. Parliamentary Paper* XXIX, 1860, *et seq.*

255. *First Reports of Her Majesty's Civil Service Commissioners, C.2038.* London: H.M.S.O., *et seq.*

256. Fletcher, Max E. "The Suez Canal and World Shipping 1869–1914." *Journal of Economic History,* XVIII (1958), pp. 556–573.

257. Fletcher, W. *The History and Development of Steam Locomotion on Common Roads.* London: E. and F. N. Spon, 1891.

258. Fleure, H. J. "The Manchester Literary and Philosophical Society." *Endeavour,* VI (1947), pp. 147–151.

259. Foch, Ferdinand. *Principles of War.* H. Belloc, tr. London: Chapman and Hall, 1918.

260. Foden, F. E. *A History of Technical Examinations in England to 1918: with special reference to the examination work of the City and Guilds of London Institute.* Unpublished thesis, Ph.D., Reading, 1961.

261. Forbes, R. J. and E. J. Dijksterhuis. *A History of Science and Technology.* London: Penguin Books, 1963. 2 vols. Vol. 1, Ancient times to the seventeenth century. Vol. 2, The eighteenth and nineteenth centuries.

262. Forbes, R. J. *Man the maker: history of technology and engineering.* London: Constable, 1958.

263. Fox-Bourne, H. R. "Foreign Rivalries in Industrial Products." *The Great Industries of Great Britain.* London: Cassell & Co., 1877–80. 3 vols.

264. Frazer, W. M. *A History of English Public Health 1834–1939.* London: Bailière, Tindall and Cox, 1950.

265. Fuller, Claud E. and Richard D. Stuert. *The Rifled Musket.* Harrisburg: Stackpole Co., 1958.

266. Fuller, J. F. C. *War and Western Civilisation 1832–1932.* London: Duckworth, 1932.

267. Fuller, J. F. C. *The Last of the Gentlemen's Wars.* London: Faber and Faber, 1937.

268. Furneaux, Rupert. *William Howard Russell of the Times.* London: Cassell, 1944.

269. Fussell, George Edwin. *The Farmers' Tools, 1500–1900: a history of British farm impliments, tools, and machinery before the tractor came.* London: Andrew Melrose, 1952.

270. Gale, W. K. V. *The British Iron and Steel Industry.* Newton Abbot: David and Charles, 1967.
271. Galton, Sir F. *Hereditary Genius.* London: Watts and Co., 1950.
272. Garratt, G. R. M. *A History of Submarine Cables.* London: H.M.S.O., 1950.
273. Garrett, Alexander A. *History of the Society of Incorporated Accountants 1885–1957.* Oxford University Press, 1961.
274. Gartmann, Heinz. *Science as History.* A. G. Readett, tr. London: Hodder and Stoughton, 1960.
275. Geddes, P. *Cities in Evolution.* London: Williams and Norgate, 1915.
276. George, Wilma. *Biologist, Philosopher. A Study of the Life and Writings of Alfred Russell Wallace.* London: Abelard-Schuman, 1964.
277. Gibbs-Smith, C. H. *The Aeroplane: an historical survey of its origins and development.* London: H.M.S.O., 1960.
278. Gibbs-Smith, C. H. *A History of Flying.* London: Batsford, 1953.
279. Giedion, S. *Mechanization takes command: a contribution to anonymous history.* New York: Oxford University Press, 1948.
280. Giffen, Sir Robert. *The Growth of Capital.* London: G. Bell and Sons, 1889.
281. Gilbert, Bentley W. "Health and Politics: the Physical Deterioration Report of 1904." *Bulletin of the History of Medicine,* Vol. 39, 1965, pp. 143–153.
282. Gilbert, K. R. *Catalogue of exhibits with historical introduction: the machine tool collection.* London: H.M.S.O., 1966.
283. Gillispie, Charles Coulston. *Genesis and Geology.* Cambridge, Mass.: Harvard University Press, 1951.
284. Gillispie, Charles Coulston. *The Edge of Objectivity. An Essay in the History of Scientific Ideas.* Princeton: Princeton University Press, 1960.
285. Von der Goltz, W. L. C. *Conduct of War.* Major G. F. Levenson, tr. Wolseley Series, No. 4. London: Kegan Paul, 1910.
286. Von der Goltz, W. L. C. *The Nation in Arms.* New ed. London: Hugh Rees, 1906.
287. Gooding, P. and P. E. Halstead. "The Early History of Cement in England." *Proceedings of the Third International Symposium on the Chemistry of Cement.* London, 1954, pp. 1–26.
288. Gordon, Alexander. *Elemental Locomotion by means of Steam Carriages on Common Roads.* London: T. Tegg and Sons, 1836. [Evidence given before a Select Committee of the House of Commons.]
289. Gordon, Lord Dudley. *Engineering.* CLXXVI (1953), p. 381.
290. Gordon, H. J. *The Reichswehr and the German Republic, 1919–1926.* Princeton: Princeton University Press, 1957.
291. Gough, Hubert. *Soldiering On.* London: Arthur Barker, 1954.
292. Graham, G. S. "The Transition from Paddle Wheel to Screw Propeller." *Mariners' Mirror,* XLIV (1958), pp. 35–48.

293. Grant, Sir Allan. *Steel and Ships: the history of John Brown's*. London: M. Joseph, 1950.
294. Gray, Alexander. *The Socialist Tradition, Moses to Lenin*. London: Longmans, 1946.
295. Greenwood, Thomas. *Free Public Libraries*. London: Simpkin, Marshall, 1886.
296. Grenfell, Russell. *Sea Power*. Garden City: Doubleday, 1941.
297. Griffiths, Sir Percival. *The British Impact on India*. London: Macdonald, 1952.
298. Groos, O. *Der Krieg in der Nordsee*. Berlin: E. S. Mittler and sohn, 1920.
299. Guthrie, Douglas. *A History of Medicine*. Rev. ed. London: Thomas Nelson, 1958, pp. 266–420.
300. Habbakkuk, H. J. *British and American Technology in the 19th Century*. Cambridge: Cambridge University Press, 1962.
301. Habbakkuk, H. J. and P. Deane. "The Take-off in Britain." *The Economics of Take-off into Sustained Growth*. W. W. Rostow, ed. London: Macmillan and Co., 1963.
302. Haber, L. F. *The Chemical Industry During the Nineteenth Century*. Oxford: Clarendon Press, 1958.
303. Hadfield, Sir R. A. *Faraday and His Metallurgical Researches*. London: Chapman and Hall, 1931.
304. Hadfield, Sir R. A. *Metallurgy and its Influence on Modern Progress*. London: Chapman and Hall, 1925.
305. Hagen, Hans. *Wilhelm II als Kaiser und König: eine historische Studie*. Berlin, 1954.
306. Hague, D. C. *The Economics of Man-made Fibres*. London: Duckworth, 1957.
307. Haines, George IV. *German Influence upon English Education and Science, 1800–1866*. Connecticut College, New London, 1957.
308. Halkett, Samuel and John Laing. *Dictionary of Anonymous and Pseudonymous Literature*. Edinburgh: Oliver and Boyd, 1926–1962. 9 vols.
309. Hall, A. R. and Marie Boas. *A Brief History of Science*. New York: New American Library, 1961.
310. Hall, B. T. *Our Sixty Years: the story of the Working Men's Club and Institute Union*. London: W.M.C. and I.U., 1922.
311. Hall, D. G. E., ed. *Historians of South East Asia*. London: Oxford University Press, 1962.
312. Hall, Sir John. *Observations on the report of the Sanitary Commissioners in the Crimea 1855–1856*. London: 1857. See also his life and letters by S. M. Mitra. London: Longmans, 1911.
313. Hall-White, Sir William. *Great Doctors of the Nineteenth Century*. London: Edward Arnold, 1935.
314. Hamley, Edward. *The War in the Crimea*. London: Seeley and Co., 1891.
315. Hammond, J. L. and B. *The Bleak Age*. London: Penguin, 1947.
316. Hammond, J. L. and B. *James Stansfeld*. London: Longmans, 1932.

317. Hammond, J. L. and B. *The Rise of Modern Industry*. London: Methuen and Co., 1925.
318. Hammond, J. L. and B. *The Town Labourer*. London: Gollancz, 1937.
319. Hammond, P. Y. *Organizing for Defense: the American military establishment in the twentieth century*. Princeton: Princeton University Press, 1961.
320. Hancock, W. *Narrative of Twelve Years of Experiments, 1824–36 (with Steam Carriages)*. London: J. Weale, 1839.
321. Hardie, D. W. F. *A History of the Chemical Industry in Widnes*. London: I.C.I., 1950.
322. Harris, D. G. *Irrigation in India*. London, Bombay: Oxford University Press, 1923.
323. Harrison, J. F. C. *A History of the Working Men's College, 1854–1954*. London: Routledge, 1954.
324. Harrison, J. F. C. *Learning and Living, 1790–1960*. London: Routledge, 1961.
325. Hart, B. H. Liddell. "Responsibility and Judgment in Historical Writing." *Military Affairs*, XXIII, Spring, 1959, pp. 35–36.
326. Hart, Henry C. *New India's Rivers*. Bombay: Orient Longmans, 1956.
327. Hartley, Sir Harold. *Polymorphism: an historical account*. Oxford: Holywell Press, 1902.
328. Hauser, E. A. *Latex*. New York: Chemical Catalog Company Inc., 1930.
329. Hayes, Carlton J. H. *France, a Nation of Patriots*. New York: Columbia University Press, 1930.
330. Head, Sir John. *Rise and Progress of Steam Locomotion on Roads*. London: Institution of Civil Engineers, 1873.
331. Headicar, B. M., C. Fuller, and later, others. *London Bibliography of the Social Sciences*. 1931–37, 13 vols.
332. Hearl, Trevor. "Military Academies and English Education: a review of some published material." *History of Education Society Bulletin*, No. 2, pp. 11–20.
333. Heaton, H. "Benjamin Gott and the Industrial Revolution in Yorkshire." *Economic History Review*, III (1931), p. 61.
334. Heaton, Herbert. *A History of Trade and Commerce with Especial Reference to Canada*. Toronto: T. Nelson and Sons, 1939.
335. Held, R. *The Age of Firearms: a pictorial history*. London: Cassell, 1959.
336. Henderson, W. O. *The Zollverein*. Cambridge University Press, 1939.
337. Henderson, W. O. *Britain and Industrial Europe 1750–1870*. Liverpool University Press, 1954.
338. Herbert, Sir Alfred. *The Development of Machinery in Coventry*. Coventry: A. Herbert, 1930.
339. Hesner, Ervin. *The International Steel Cartel*. University of North Carolina Press: 1943.

340. Heywood, H. "Solar Energy, Past, Present and Future Application." *Engineering, Section D, British Association,* CLXXVI (1953), pp. 377, 409.

341. Higgins, Benjamen Howard. *Economic Development, Problems, Principles and Policies.* New York: W. W. Norton and Co., 1959.

342. Hilton, Richard. *The Indian Mutiny: a centenary history.* London: Hollis and Carter, 1957.

343. Himmelfarb, Gertrude. *Darwin and the Darwinian Revolution.* New York: Doubleday, 1963.

344. "Historic Tinned Foods." *Journal of the Society of Chemical Industry,* vol. LVII, 1938.

345. H. M. Treasury: *Official Publications.* London: H.M.S.O., 1958.

346. Hodgson, J. E., ed. *Notebook of Sir George Cayley.* Cambridge: Newcomen Society, 1933.

347. Hoffmann, W. *British Industry 1700–1955.* W. O. Henderson and W. H. Chaloner, trs. Oxford: Blackwell, 1955.

348. Hoffmann, W. "The Growth of Industrial Production in Britain: A Quantitative Survey." *Economic History Review,* II (1949), 165ff.

349. Hogg, O. F. G. *The Royal Arsenal. Its Background, Origin and Subsequent History.* London: Oxford University Press, 1963.

350. Holt, Edgar. *The Boer War.* London: Putnam, 1958.

351. Horowitz, Irving Louis. *The Idea of War and Peace in Contemporary Philosophy.* New York: Paine-Whitman, 1957.

352. Hoselitz, Bert F. *Sociological Aspects of Economic Growth.* "Entrepreneurship and Capital Formation in France and Britain since 1700." *Capital Formation and Economic Growth.* Glencoe: Free Press, 1960.

353. Houghton, Walter E. "Reflections on indexing Victorian periodicals." *Victorian Studies,* VII (1963–64), pp. 192–196.

353a. Houseman, Lorna. *The House that Thomas Built: the story of De La Rue.* London: Chatto and Windus, 1968.

354. Hovgaard, William. *Modern History of Warships.* London: E. and F. N. Spon, 1920.

355. Howard, Michael, ed. *Soldiers and Governments.* London: Rupert Hart-Davis, 1957.

356. Howard, Michael. *The Franco-Prussian War: the German invasion of France, 1870–1871.* London: R. Hart-Davis, 1961.

357. Howard-White, F. B. *Nickel: an historical review.* London: Methuen, 1963.

358. Hudson, Derek and Kenneth W. Luckhurst. *The Royal Society of Arts, 1754–1954.* London: Murray, 1954.

359. Hudson, K. *Industrial archaeology: an introduction.* 2nd ed. London: John Baker Ltd., 1966.

360. Hughes, H. C. "India Office Railway Records." *Journal of Transport History,* VI (1963–4), pp. 241–248.

361. Hughes, H. C. "The Scinde Railway." *Journal of Transport History,* V (1961–3), pp. 219–225.

362. Humfrey, J. H. *Concise Review of the Campaigns of the British Legion in Spain.* London: 1838.

363. Hunt, B. C. *Development of the Business Corporation in England, 1800–1867.* Cambridge, Mass.: Harvard University Press, 1936.

364. Hurd, Archibald and Henry Castle. *German Sea Power: its rise, progress, and economic basis.* London: John Murray, 1913.

365. Hutchinson, G. S. *Machine Guns: their history and tactical employment.* London: Macmillan and Co., 1938.

366. Hutchison, T. W. *A Review of Economic Doctrines, 1870–1929.* Oxford: Clarendon Press, 1953.

367. Hyde, F. E. *Blue Funnel: a history of Alfred Holt and Company of Liverpool from 1865–1914.* Liverpool: Liverpool University Press, 1957.

368. Ihde, Aaron J. *The Development of Modern Chemistry.* London: Harper and Row, 1965.

369. Ihde, A. J. "Chemical Industry, 1780–1900." *Journal of World History,* IV (Paris, 1958), pp. 957–84.

370. Imlah, A. H. "British Balance of Payments and Export of Capital, 1816–1913." *Economic History Review,* 2nd series, V (1952).

371. Imlah, Albert H. *Economic Elements in the Pax Britannica: studies in British foreign trade in the nineteenth century.* Cambridge, Mass.: Harvard University Press, 1958.

372. Institution of Naval Architects. *Proceedings.* Vol. 1. 1866.

373. Institution of Royal Engineers. *Detailed History of the Railways in the South African War 1899–1902.* Chatham: the Institution, 1904.

374. *Inventor and Entrepreneur. Recollections of Werner von Siemens.* London: Lund Humphries, 1966.

375. Irvine, W. *Apes, Angels and Victorians.* London: Weidenfeld and Nicholson, 1955.

376. Isard, Walter. "Some Locational Factors in the Iron and Steel Industry Since the Early Nineteenth Century." *Journal of Political Economy,* LVI (1948).

377. James, Sir Henry, ed. *Accounts of the methods and processes adopted for the production of maps of the Ordnance Survey of the United Kingdom . . .* London: Longmans and Co., 1875.

378. Jeffreys, Rees. *The King's Highway.* London: Batchworth Press, 1949.

379. Jevons, W. S. *The Principles of Science: a treatise on logic and scientific method.* London: Oxford (printed), 1874. 2 vols.

380. Jevons, W. S. *The Principles of Economics: a fragment of a treatise on the industrial mechanism of society.* London: Macmillan, 1905.

381. Jevons, W. S. *The Coal Question.* A. W. Flux, ed. London: Macmillan & Co., 1906.

382. Jewkes, John *et al. The Sources of Invention.* London: Macmillan, 1958.

383. John, A. H. *The Industrial Development of South Wales, 1750–1850.* Cardiff: University of Wales Press, 1950.

384. Johnson, John and W. L. Randell. *Colonel Crompton.* London: Longmans, Green and Co., 1946.
385. Jones, Howard Mumford and I. Bernard Cohen, eds. *Science before Darwin: A Nineteenth-Century anthology.* London: Andre Deutsch, 1963.
386. Jones, H. V., ed. *Parliamentary Papers from 1801 to 1900.* London: P. S. King, no date.
387. Jones, H. V., ed. *Catalogue of Parliamentary Papers 1901–1910. Being a Second Supplement to the Catalogue of Parliamentary Papers 1801–1900.* London: P. S. King, no date.
388. Jones, H. V., ed. *Second Supplement 1911–1920.* London: P. S. King, no date.
389. *Journal of the Institute of Water Engineers,* X (1956), pp. 509–14.
390. Kahn, A. E. *Great Britain in the World Economy.* New York: Columbia University Press, 1946.
391. Keen, P. A. "The Channel Tunnel Project." *Journal of Transport History,* III (1957–8), pp. 132–144.
392. Kelly, Thomas. *George Birkbeck: pioneer of adult education.* Liverpool University Press, 1957.
393. Kelly, Thomas. *A History of Adult Education in Great Britain.* Liverpool University Press, 1962.
394. Kerr, J. F. "Some Sources for the History of the Teaching of Science in England." *British Journal of Educational Studies,* VII, 2, 1959.
395. Keyes, D. B. "History and Philosophy of Chemical Engineering Education." *Chemical Engineering Progress,* XLIX (1935), p. 635.
396. Kidner, R. W. *The First Hundred Road Motors.* South Goldstone: Oakwood Press, 1958.
397. Kirby, Richard Shelton, *et al. Engineering in history.* New York: McGraw-Hill, 1956.
398. Kirchner, Walter. "Samuel Bentham and Siberia." *Slavonic and East European Review,* XXXVI (1958), pp. 471–80.
399. Kirwan, L. P. *A History of Polar Exploration.* Harmondsworth, Middlesex: Penguin Books, 1959.
400. Klemm, F. *A History of Western Technology.* Trans. from the German by Dorothea W. Singer. London: Allen and Unwin, 1959.
401. Kuznets, Simon Smith. "Quantitative Aspects of the Economic Growth of Nations: VI, Long-Term Trends in Capital Formation Proportions." *Economic Development and Cultural Change,* July, 1961, p. 56.
402. Kuznets, Simon Smith. *Modern Economic Growth: rate, structure and spread.* Yale University Studies in Comparative Economics, No. 7. New Haven and London: Yale University Press, 1966.
403. Messrs. Laird Brothers and "the Alabama," [being a letter to the Editor of *The Times* by Messrs. Laird dated May 25th 1869 relating to the building of the Alabama]. Liverpool and Birkenhead, 1869.
404. Larsen, E. *A History of Invention.* London: Phoenix House Ltd., 1961.

405. Larwood, H. J. C. "Science in India before 1850." *British Journal of Educational Studies,* VII (1958–9), pp. 36–49.
406. *Lectures on the Results of the Great Exhibition of 1851.* London: David Bogue, 1852.
407. Leese, John. *Personalities and Power in English Education.* Leeds: E. J. Arnold, 1950.
408. Levi, Leone. *History of British Commerce.* London: John Murray, 1880.
409. Lewis, W. A. "International Competition in Manufactures." *American Economic Review,* 1957.
410. Lewis, Winifred. *The Light Metals Industry.* Toronto: S. J. R. Saunders, 1949.
411. "L'Expansion coloniale et la stratégie navale." *Académie de Marine Mémoires et Communications,* IX, 1930.
412. Lilley, S. *Men, Machines and History: the story of tools and machines in relation to social progress.* Rev. ed. London: Lawrence and Wishart, 1966.
413. Lilley, S., ed. *Essays on the Social History of Science.* Copenhagen: *Centaurus* vol. III, No's. 1/2, 1953.
414. Linstead, Sir Patrick. *The Prince Consort and the Founding of the Imperial College.* London: Imperial College, 1961.
415. Lipset, Seymour Martin and Reinhard Bendix. *Social Mobility in Industrial Society.* London: Heinemann, 1959.
416. Lipson, E. *The Growth of English Society.* London: A. and C. Black, 1949.
417. Lloyd, Christopher. *The Nation and the Navy.* London: Cresset Press, 1954.
418. Lloyd, Christopher. *The Navy and the Slave Trade.* London: Longmans, Green and Co., 1949.
419. Lloyd, Christopher. *Short History of the Royal Navy, 1805–1918.* 3rd ed. London: Methuen and Co., 1942.
420. Lloyd, Christopher and Jack L. S. Coulter. *Medicine and the Navy 1200–1900.* Vol. IV, 1815–1900. Edinburgh and London: E. and S. Livingstone, 1963.
421. Logan, Sir Douglas. *Haldane and the University of London.* Birkbeck College: University of London, 1960.
422. Low, D. A., ed. *The Whitworth Book.* London: Longmans, 1926.
423. Lowndes, G. A. N. *The Silent Social Revolution.* Oxford University Press, 1937.
424. Luckhurst, K. W. *The Story of Exhibitions.* London: Studio Publications, 1951.
425. Luvaas, Jay. *The Military Legacy of the Civil War: the European inheritance.* Chicago: University of Chicago Press, 1959.
426. Lyons, Sir H. *The Royal Society, 1660–1940: a history of its administration.* Cambridge: Cambridge University Press, 1944.
427. MacClellan, G. B. *Report of Captain G. B. MacClellan . . . in Europe in 1855 and 1856.* Washington: Senate Documents 34th Congress, Special Session, 1857.

284 · A GUIDE TO THE SOURCES OF BRITISH MILITARY HISTORY

428. McCulloch, J. R. *Dictionary of Commerce.* London: Longmans and Co., 1882. [The first edition was published in 1832.]

429. McCulloch, J. R. *Statistical Account of the British Empire.* London: Longmans and Co., 1837.

430. McDonald, D. *A History of Platinum from the Earliest Times to the 1880's.* London: Johnson Mathey, 1960.

431. MacLeod, Roy M. "The Alkali Acts Administration 1863–84: the emergence of the civil scientist." *Victorian Studies,* Vol. IX (1965–6), pp. 85–112.

432. Macpherson, W. J. *British Investment in Indian Guaranteed Railways 1845–1875.* Cambridge Ph.D. thesis.

433. Maddison, F. "Early Astronomical and Mathematical Instruments: a brief survey of sources and modern studies." In *History of Science, an annual review of literature, research and teaching,* Vol. II, 1963, pp. 17–50.

434. Magnus, Sir Philip. *Educational Aims and Efforts, 1880–1910.* London: Longmans, 1910.

435. Magnus, Sir Philip. *Kitchener.* London: John Murray, 1958.

436. Maguire, T. M. *Military Education in England.* London: J. J. Keleher & Co., 1903. (A prolific writer on all aspects of war.)

437. Mantoux, P. *The Industrial Revolution in the Eighteenth Century.* (English trans. of the French original of 1906.) London: Jonathan Cape, 1928.

438. Marder, Arthur J. *The Anatomy of British Sea Power: a history of British naval policy in the pre-dreadnought era, 1880–1905.* London: Frank Cass & Co., 1964.

439. Marder, Arthur J. *Fear God and Dread Nought: the correspondence of Admiral of the Fleet Lord Fisher of Kilverstone.* London: Cape, 1952–59. 3 vols.

440. Marder, Arthur J. *From the Dreadnought to Scapa Flow: I: The Road to War, 1904–1914.* London: Oxford University Press, 1961.

441. Marder, Arthur J. *Portrait of an Admiral: the life and papers of Sir Herbert Richmond.* London: Jonathan Cape, 1952.

442. Marienfeld, Wolfgang. *Wissenschaft und Schlachtflottenbau in Deutschland, 1897–1907.* Berlin, 1957.

443. Marshall, A. C. and Herbert Newbould. *The History of Firths (1842–1918).* Sheffield: Thomas Firth and Sons, Norfolk Works, 1924.

444. Martin T. *The Royal Institution.* 3rd ed. London: The Royal Institution, 1961.

445. Marx, Karl. *Capitol.* G. D. H. Cole, ed. Everyman Edition. London: J. M. Dent, 1934, II, pp. 864–5.

446. Masse, Charles Henri. *The Predecessors of the Royal Army Service Corps.* Aldershot: Gale & Polden, 1948.

447. Mathews, Joseph James. *Reporting the Wars.* Minneapolis: University of Minnesota Press, 1957.

448. Maxcy, George and Audrey Gilbertson. *The Motor Industry.* London: Allen and Unwin, 1959.

449. Maxwell, J. C., ed. *The Scientific Papers of the Hon. H. Cavendish.* Cambridge: Cambridge University Press, 1921. 2 vols.

450. Mead, Margaret. *Cultural Patterns and Technical Change.* New York: Mentor Books, 1957.

451. Meeks, C. L. B. *The Railroad Station: an architectural history.* New Haven: Yale University Press, 1956. Yale Historical Publications History of Art, vol. II.

452. Meier, G. M. and R. E. Baldwin. *Economic Development, Theory, History, Policy.* New York: John Wiley and Sons, 1957.

453. Meisner, Heinrich. *Militärattaches und Militärbevollmächtige in Preussen und im Deutchen Reich.* Berlin, 1957.

454. Meyer, J. R. "An Input-Output Approach to Evaluating the Influence of Exports on British Industrial Production in the late 19th Century." *Explorations in Entrepreneurial History,* October, 1955.

455. Meyrfiat, Jean and Jean Viet. *World List of Social Science Periodicals.* 3rd ed. Paris: U.N.E.S.C.O., 1966.

456. Miall, Stephen. *History of the British Chemical Industry.* London: Ernest Benn, 1931.

457. Middleton, W. E. K. *A History of the Theories of Rain and other Forms of Precipitation.* London: Oldbourne, 1965.

458. Millis, C. T. *Education for Trades and Industries.* London: E. Arnold, 1932.

459. Millis, Walter, *et al. Arms and the State: civil-military elements in national policy.* New York: Twentieth Century Fund, 1958.

460. *Minutes of the Institution of Civil Engineers,* XXVIII, 1868, 573 ff.

461. Mirskaya, Jeannette and Allan Nevins. *The World of Eli Whitney.* New York: Collier Books, 1962.

462. Mitchell, B. R. "The Coming of the Railway and United Kingdom's Economic Growth." *Journal of Economic History,* XXIV, 1964, pp. 315-336.

463. Mitchell, B. R. and Phyllis Deane. *Abstract of British Historical Statistics.* Cambridge: Cambridge University Press, 1962.

464. Mond, Alfred Moritz. *Questions of Today and Tomorrow.* London: Methuen and Co., 1912.

465. Montgomery, R. J. *Examinations: an account of their evolution as administrative devices in England.* London: Longmans, 1965, p. 27.

466. Moorehead, Alan. *Gallipoli.* New York: Harper, 1956.

467. Morton, Louis. "The Origins of American Military Policy." *Military Affairs,* XXII, 1958.

468. Mosse, W. E. *The European Powers and the German Question, 1848-71.* Cambridge University Press, 1958.

469. Mowat, Charles Loch. *Britain Between the Wars, 1918-1940.* London: Methuen, 1955.

470. Moyse-Bartlett, Hubert. *The King's African Rifles: a study in the military history of East and Central Africa, 1890-1945.* Aldershot: Gale and Polden, 1956.

471. Moyse-Bartlett, Hubert. *From Sail to Steam. The Final Development*

and Passing of the Sailing Ship. London: Stapler Press, 1946. (Historical Assocation leaflet G.4).

472. Mulhall, M. G. *Dictionary of Statistics*. 20th ed. London: G. Routledge and Sons, 1886.

473. Mulhall, Michael. *Industries and Wealth of Nations*. London: Longmans and Co., 1896, p. 105.

474. Mullins, E. C. L. *Texts and Calendars: an analytical guide to serial publications*. London: Royal Historical Society, 1958.

475. Mumford, L. *Technics and Civilization*. London: Routledge, 1934.

476. Murray, Robert H. *Science and Scientists in the Nineteenth Century*. London: The Sheldon Press, 1925.

477. Muspratt, Edward K. *My Life and Work*. London: John Lane, 1917.

478. Musson, Albert Edwin. "The Great Depression in Britain, 1873–1896: a reappraisal." *Journal of Economic History*, XIX (1959).

479. Musson, A. E. "James Nasmyth and the Early Growth of Mechanical Engineering." *Economic History Review*, X (1957), pp. 121–7.

480. Napier, Sir William Francis Patrick. Six Letters, in vindication of the British Army, *Exposing the calumnies of the Liverpool Financial Reform Association*, London, 1849.

481. Nasmyth, J. *Autobiography*. London: John Murray, 1883.

482. Naunton, W. J. S. *Synthetic Rubber*. London: Macmillan and Co., 1937.

483. *Nautical Magazine, The*. London, 1832.

484. *Naval Science, a quarterly magazine for promoting the improvement of naval architecture*. London, 1872–5.

485. *Newcomen Society for the Study of the History of Engineering and Technology. Transactions*. London, 1920.

486. Newitt, D. M. "The Origins of Chemical Engineering," in H. W. Cremer, ed., *Chemical Engineering Practice*, I (1956), pp. 1–52.

487. Nock, O. S. *The British Steam Railway Locomotive 1925–1965*. London: Ian Allen, 1966.

488. Norrie, C. M. *Bridging the Years: a short history of British civil engineering*. London: Arnold, 1956.

489. O'Byrne, Robert H. *Naval Annual*. London, 1855.

490. O'Callaghan, Sean. *The Easter Lily; the Story of the I.R.A*. New York: Roy, 1956.

491. Oliver, John W. *History of American Technology*. New York: Ronald Press, 1956.

492. O'Malley, L. S. S., ed. *The Indian Civil Service 1601–1930*. 2nd ed. London: Frank Cass & Co., 1965.

493. Orsagh, T. J. "Progress in Iron and Steel; 1870–1913." *Comparative Studies in Society and History*, 1961.

493a. Orwin, Christabel and Edith H. Wetham. *History of British Agriculture, 1846–1914*. London: Longmans, 1964.

494. Osborn, Fred M. *The Story of the Muchets*. London: Thomas Nelson, 1951.

495. Ottley, G. *A Bibliography of British Railway History*. London: George Allen and Unwin, 1965.

496. Pannell, John Percival Masterman. *An Illustrated History of Civil Engineering.* London: Thames and Hudson, 1964.

497. Parke, Nathan Grier, III. *Guide to the Literature of Mathematics and Physics, including related works on engineering science.* 2nd rev. ed. New York: Dover Publications, 1958, pp. 240–243.

498. Parkes, Oscar. *British Battleships: Warrior 1860 to Vanguard 1950: a history of design, construction and armament.* London: Seeley, 1958.

499. Parsons, R. H. *The Development of the Parsons Steam Turbine.* London: Constable, 1936.

500. Parsons, R. H. *The Institution of Mechanical Engineers, 1847–1947.* London: Constable, 1936.

501. Parsons, R. H. *The Steam Turbine and Other Inventions of Sir Charles Parsons, O.M.* London: Longmans, Green and Co., 1948.

502. Partington, C. F., ed. *The British Cyclopaedia of Arts and Sciences.* London, 1835–8. 10 vols.

503. Partington, J. R. *The Alkali Industry.* London: Baillière and Co., 1925

504. Partington, J. R. *A History of Chemistry.* Vol. IV. London: Macmillan, 1964.

505. Patel, S. J. "Rates of Industrial Growth in the Last Century, 1860–1958." *Economic Development and Cultural Change,* April, 1961.

506. Payne, J. B. *Proofs of A. B. Richard's claim to be Chief Promoter of the Volunteer Movement.* London: Swift & Co., 1867.

507. Pendred, S. St. L. *British Engineering Societies.* London: Longmans for British Council, 1947.

508. Penn, Geoffrey. *"Up Funnel, Down Screw!" The Story of the Naval Engineer.* London: Hollis and Carter, 1955.

509. P.E.B. Engineering Reports. *Motor Vehicles,* 1950.

510. *The Perkin Centenary Volume: 100 years of synthetic dye-stuffs.* London: Pergamon Press, 1958.

511. Perrin, W. G. *Nelson's Signals: the evolution of the signal flags.* London: H.M.S.O., 1908.

512. Perry, John. *England's Neglect of Science.* London: T. Fisher Unwin, 1900.

513. Petrie, J. F. "Maudslay Sons and Field as General Engineers." *Transactions of the Newcomen Society,* XV (1934), pp. 39–61.

514. Philips, C. H., ed. *Historians of India, Pakistan and Ceylon.* London: Oxford University Press (for the School of Oriental and African Studies), 1961.

515. Pigou, A. C. *Aspects of British Economic History, 1918–1925.* London: Macmillan, 1947.

516. Playne, Carolyn. *The Pre-War Mind in Britain.* London: G. Allen and Unwin, 1928.

517. Pledge, H. T. *Science since 1500: a short history of mathematics, physics, chemistry, biology.* 2nd ed. London: H.M.S.O., 1966.

518. Plummer, A. *New British Industries in the Twentieth Century.* London: Pitman and Sons, 1937.

519. Pole, William. *Some Short Reminiscences of Events in My Life and Work.* Abbreviated from MS notes. London: printed for private circulation, 1898.

520. Pollard, H. B. C. *A History of Firearms.* London: Bles, 1926. (He edited *The Territorial* from 1912 onwards).

521. Pollard, S. "British and World Shipbuilding, 1890–1914: a study in comparative costs." *Economic History Review,* 1957.

522. Pollard, S. "Laissez Faire and Shipbuilding." *Economic History Review,* V (1952), pp. 98–115.

523a. Poole, William Frederick. *Index to Periodical Literature. 1802–1881* with the assistance of W. I. Fletcher, rev. ed. London: Routledge, Kegan Paul, 1891.

524. Pope, D. *Guns.* London: Weidenfeld and Nicolson, 1965.

525. Porter, G. R. *Progress of the Nation.* London: C. Knight and Co., 1851, p. 506.

526. Porter, Whitworth *et al. History of the Corps of Royal Engineers.* 5 vols. 1–3, 8, 9. London: Longmans & Co., Chatham Royal Engineer Institution, 1889–1958.

527. Pratt, E. A. *The Rise of Rail-Power in War and Conquest, 1833–1914.* London: P. S. Knight and Son, 1915.

528. Presland, John (Gladys Skelton). *Vae Victis: the life of Ludwig von Benedek.* London: Hodder & Stoughton, 1934.

529. Preston, R. A. "Military Lessons of the American Civil War." *Army Quarterly,* LXV (1953), pp. 229–237.

530. Price, Don K. *Government and Science.* New York: Oxford University Press, 1962.

531. Pritchard, John Laurence. *Sir George Cayley: the inventor of the aeroplane.* London: Parrish, 1961.

532. Pugh, L. P. *From Farriery to Veterinary Medicine, 1785–1795.* Cambridge: Heffer, 1962.

533. Putnam, P. C. *Energy in the Future.* New York: D. Van Nostrand Co., 1954.

534. Rae, J. B. *American Automobile Manufacturers.* Philadelphia: Chilton, 1959.

535. Randell, W. L. *S. Z. de Ferranti and his Influence upon Electrical Development.* London: Longmans, Green and Co., for British Council, 1946.

536. Rawlinson, H. G. *The British Achievement in India.* London: W. Hodge and Co., 1948.

537. Read, J. *Prelude to Chemistry: an outline of alchemy, its literature and relationships.* 2nd ed. London: Bell, 1939 (reprint, Oldbourne, 1961).

538. Record, P. D. *Index to Theses accepted for Higher Degrees in the Universities of Great Britain and Ireland.* A.S.L.I.B., 1950–1, 1953.

539. Record, P. D. *Survey of Thesis Literature in British Libraries.* London: Library Association, 1950.

540. Redford, A. *The Economic History of England, 1760–1860.* London: Longmans and Co., 1931.

541. Reeks, Margaret. *The Royal School of Mines*. London: Royal School of Mines, 1920.

542. Reeves, John. "An account of some of the articles of the Materia Medica employed by the Chinese." *Transactions of the Medico-Botanical Society*, 1828.

543. Reid, Sir Thomas Wemyss. *Memoirs and Correspondence of Lyon Playfair*. London: Cassell, 1900.

544. Reid, Sir William. *An Attempt to develop the law of storms*. London, 1838.

545. Rennie, David Field. *The British Arms in North China and Japan*, London: 1864.

546. Rennie, George, 1791–1866. *Proc. Roy. Soc.* XVI (1868), pp. 33–5.

547. Resenthal, Eric. *General De Wet*. Cape Town.

548. Reynolds, O. *Memoir of James Prescott Joule*. Manchester: Literary and Philosophical Series, 1888.

549. Reynolds, O. *Proc. Roy. Soc.*, LXXXVIII, A. 1912–13.

550. Ricardo, John Lewis. *The War Policy of Commerce*. London, 1855.

551. Richards, B. D. "Tidal Power: its development and utilisation." *Journal of the Institution of Civil Engineers*, XXX (1948), pp. 104–149.

551a. Richardson, Benjamin Ward. *Hygeia, a city of health*. London, 1855.

552. Richardson, H. W. "The Development of the British Dyestuffs Industry before 1939." *Scottish Journal of Political Economy*, IX (1962), pp. 110–129.

553. Richardson, H. W. "Retardation in Britain's Industrial Growth, 1870–1913." *Scottish Journal of Political Economy*, XII (1965).

554. Rimmer, W. G. *Marshalls of Leeds, Flax-Spinners, 1788–1886*. Cambridge: Cambridge University Press, 1960.

555. Rippin, C. R. and M. W. Crofton. *Solutions of the Mathematical Questions at the examination to the Royal Military Academy, Woolwich*. Woolwich, 1865.

556. Robbins, M. "The Balaclava Railroad." *Journal of Transport History*, I (1953), pp. 28–43, and II (1955), pp. 51–2.

557. Roberts, David. *Victorian Origins of the British Welfare State*. New Haven: Yale University Press, 1960.

558. Roe, J. W. *English and American Toolbuilders*. New Haven: Yale University Press, 1916.

559. Roff, W. J. *Fibres, Plastics and Rubber*. London: Butterworth's Scientific Publications, 1956.

560. Rogers, J. E. Thorold. *Six Centuries of Work and Wages*. London: Sonnenschein and Co., 1884.

561. Rolt, L. T. C. *Horseless Carriage: the motor car in England*. London: Constable, 1950.

562. Rolt, L. T. C. *Isambard Kingdom Brunel*. London: Longmans, 1957.

563. Rolt, L. T. C. *Thomas Telford*. London, Longmans, 1958.

564. Rolt, L. T. C. *Tools for the Job*. London: Batsford, 1965.
565. Rosenberg, H. R. A. Brady and M. E. Townshend. "The Economic Impact of Imperial Germany" in *The Tasks of Economic History*. Papers presented at the Third Annual Meeting of the Economic History Association. Princeton Supplemental Issue of the *Journal of Economic History*, December 1943, pp. 101–134.
566. Rosinski, Herbert. *The German Army*. London: Hogarth Press, 1939.
567. Rostow, W. W. *The Process of Economic Growth*. Oxford: Clarendon Press, 1960, enlarged edition of 1953 original.
568. Royal Artillery Institution. *Proceedings*.
569. Royal Society. *Biographical Memoirs of the Royal Society*. Vol. I, 1955; *Notes and Records of the Royal Society of London*. Vol. I, 1938, *Proceedings of the Royal Society of London*, Vol. I.
570. Sabine, Sir Edward, ed. *The North Georgia Gazette*, 1821–
571. Sadler, M. E., ed. *Continuation Schools in England and Elsewhere*. Manchester University Press, 1907.
572. Samuda, Joseph D'Agiular. *A Treatise on the adaptation of atmospheric pressure to the purpose of locomotion on railways*. London, 1841.
573. Sandes, Edward Warren Caulfield. *The Military Engineer in India*, Chatham: Institution of Royal Engineers, 1933, 1937. 2 vols.
574. Sandes, Edward Warren Caulfield. *The Royal Engineers in Egypt and the Sudan*. Chatham: Institution of Royal Engineers, 1937.
575. Saul, S. B. "Britain and World Trade 1870–1914." *Economic History Review*, 2nd series, VII (1954–5), p. 61.
576. Saul, S. B. "The Market and the Development of the Mechanical Engineering Industries in Britain 1860–1914." *Economic History Review*, 2nd series, XX (1967).
577. Saul, S. B. "The Motor Industry in Britain to 1914." *Business History*, v (1962).
578. Savage, Christopher Ivor. *The Economic History of Transport*. London: Hutchinson and Co., 1959.
579. Saville, J. "Some Leading Factors in the British Economy before 1914." *Yorkshire Bulletin of Economic and Social Research*, XXI, 1961.
580. Saville, J., ed. "Studies in the British Economy 1870–1914." *Yorkshire Bulletin of Social and Economic Research*, XVII (1957).
581. Sayers, R. S. *A History of Economic Change in England 1880–1939*. Oxford: Oxford University Press, 1967.
582. von Scheliha, Viktor E. K. R. *A Treatise on Coast Defence*. London, 1868.
583. Schidrowitz, P. and T. R. Dawson. *History of the Rubber Industry*. London: Institution of the Rubber Industry, 1953.
584. Schüssler, Wilhelm. *Weltmachtstreben und Flottenbau*. Witten/Ruhr, 1956.
585. Scott, John Dick. *Siemens Brothers, 1858–1958*. London: Weidenfeld and Nicolson, 1958.

586. Semmel, Bernard. *Imperialism and Social Reform: English social-imperial thought 1895–1914*. London: George Allen and Unwin, 1960.
587. Sen, Surendra Nath. *Eighteen Fifty-Seven*. Delhi: Government of India, 1957.
588. Shakespear, Charles. *In the Company's Service: a reminiscence written anonymously*. 1883.
589. Shackleton, Sir Ernest Henry. *The Heart of the Antarctic: being the story of the British Antarctic Expedition 1907–1909,* London: William Heinemann, 1909.
590. Sharlin, H. I. *The Making of the Electrical Age*. New York: Abelard-Schuman, 1963.
591. Sheehan, Donald. "The Manchester Literary and Philosophical Society." *Isis,* XXXIII (1941–2), pp. 519–523.
592. Shimmin, A. N. *The University of Leeds*. Cambridge University Press, 1954.
593. Siemens, G. *History of the House of Siemens*. A. F. Rodger, tr. Munich, 1957.
594. Sigsworth, E. M. "Science and the Brewery Industry." *Economic History Review,* 2nd Series, XVII (1964–5), pp. 536–550.
595. Simmons, Jack. *The Railways of Britain: an historical introduction*. London: Routledge and Kegan Paul, 1961.
596. Simon, J. *English Sanitary Institutions*. London: Cassell and Co., 1890.
597. Simon, Matthew and David E. Novak. "Some Dimensions of the American Commercial Invasion of Europe, 1871–1914." *Journal of Economic History,* XXIV (1964), pp. 591–607.
598. Sinclair, W. A. "The Growth of the British Steel Industry in the Late Nineteenth Century." *Scottish Journal of Political Economy,* VI (1959).
599. Siney, M. C. *The Allied Blockade of Germany, 1914–1916*. Ann Arbor, Michigan: University of Michigan Press, 1957.
600. Singer, Charles. *A Short History of Scientific Ideas to 1900*. Oxford: Clarendon Press, 1959.
601. Singer, Charles, E. J. Holmyard, A. R. Hall, and Trevor I. Williams, eds. *A History of Technology*. Vol. IV. The Industrial Revolution, c.1750–c.1850. Vol. V. The Late Nineteenth Century, c.1850–c.1900, Oxford: Clarendon Press, 1958.
602. Smellie, K. B. *A Hundred Years of English Government*. London: Duckworth, 1950.
603. Smiles, S. *Lives of the Engineers*. London: John Murray, 1861–2. 5 vols.
604. Smiles, S. *Self Help*. With an introduction by Asa Briggs. London: John Murray, 1950.
605. Smiles, Samuel. *Industrial Biography*. New ed. London: John Murray, 1889.
606. Smith, D. E. *History of Mathematics*. London: Constable, 1958. 2 vols.

607. Smith, E. C. *A Short History of Naval and Marine Engineering.* Cambridge: Cambridge University Press, 1938.

608. Smith, Sir Hubert Llewellyn and Sir A. N. D. Acland. *Studies in Secondary Education.* London: Percival and Co., 1892.

609. Smith, Sir Swire. *Educational Comparisons, or, remarks on industrial schools in England, Germany and Switzerland.* London: Bradford, 1873.

610. "William Smith, Civil Engineer, Geologist, 1769–1839." *T.N.S.,* (1948), pp. 93–8.

611. "The Society of Civil Engineers." *Transactions of the Newcomer Society,* XVII (1938), pp. 51–71.

612. Spackman, W. F. *An Analysis of the Occupations of the People, showing the relative importance of the agricultural, manufacturing, shipping, colonial, commercial, and mining interests . . . of Great Britain.* London, 1847.

613. Spackman, W. F. *Statistical Tables of the United Kingdom and its Dependencies.* London, 1843.

614. Spalding, Thomas Alfred. *The Work of the London School Board.* 2nd ed. London: P. S. King, 1900.

615. Spiro, R. H. "John Loudon McAdam and the Metropolitan Turnpike Trust." *Journal of Transport History,* II (1955), pp. 207–13.

616. Spratt, H. P. *Handbook of the Collection Illustrating Merchant Steamers and Motor-Ships.* London: H.M.S.O., 1949.

617. Stevenson, Louis Tillotson. *An Index of the Basic Demand for Paper.* New York: American Paper, Pulp Assoc., 1949.

618. Story, Noah. *The Oxford Companion to Canadian History and Literature.* Toronto: Oxford University Press, 1967.

619. Strachey, Alix. *The Unconscious Motives of War, a Psychoanalytical Contribution.* London: Allen and Unwin, 1957.

620. Straub, Hans. *A History of Civil Engineering.* English translation by E. Rockwell. London: Hill, 1952.

620a. Strauss, G. L. M. *et al. England's Workshops.* London: Groombridge and Sons, 1867.

621. Swan, Sir K. R. *Sir Joseph Swan.* London: Longmans Green and Co., for British Council, 1946.

622. Swindin, N. *Transactions of the Institution of Chemical Engineers,* XXXI (1953), p. 187.

623. Swinton, Ernest. *The Defence of Duffer's Drift.* New ed. Oxford: George Ronald, 1949.

624. Taft, Robert. *Photography and the American Scene: a social history 1839–1889.* New York: Dover Publications, 1964.

625. Taton, Rene. "The French Revolution and the Progress of Science." *Centaurus,* III, pp. 73–9.

626. Taton, Rene. *Science in the Nineteenth Century.* A. J. Pomerans, tr. London: Thames and Hudson, 1965.

627. Taylor, A. J. "Labour, Productivity and Technological Innovation in the British Coal Industry 1850–1914." *Economic History Review,* 2nd Series, XIV (1961).

628. Taylor, A. J. P. *The Struggle for Mastery in Europe, 1848–1914.* Oxford: Clarendon Press, 1965.
629. Taylor, F. S. *A History of Industrial Chemistry.* London: Heinemann, 1957.
630. Temin, Peter. "The Relative Decline of the British Steel Industry 1880–1913," in Henry Rosovsky, ed., *Industrialisation in Two Systems: essays in honour of Alexander Gerschenkron.* New York: Wiley and Sons, 1966.
631. Temi, Peter. "Steam and Waterpower in the Early Nineteenth Century." *Journal of Economic History,* XXVI (1966).
632. Tennant, E. W. D. "The Early History of the St. Rollox Chemical Works." *Chemistry and Industry,* LXVI (1947), p. 667.
633. Thackeray, Sir Edward Talbot. *Biographical Notices of the Royal (Bengal) Engineers,* London: Smith Elder & Co., 1900.
634. Thomas, Brinley. *Migration and Economic Growth. A Study of the Atlantic Economy.* Cambridge: Cambridge University Press, 1954.
635. Thomas, D. A. "The Growth and Direction of our Foreign Trade during the last Half Century." *Journal of the Royal Statistical Society,* LXVI (1903).
636. Thomas, D. H. *The Development of Technical Education in England, 1851–1889.* Unpublished thesis, Ph.D., London, 1940.
637. Thomas, Hugh. *The Story of Sandhurst.* London: Hutchinson, 1961, p. 86.
638. Thompson, D. "Queenwood College, Hampshire." *Annals of Science,* XI (1956), pp. 246–540.
639. Thompson, Lilian Gilchrist. *Sidney Gilchrist Thomas.* London: Faber & Faber, 1940.
640. Thompson, S. B. *Confederate Purchasing Operations Abroad.* Chapel Hill: University of North Carolina Press, 1935.
641. Thompson, Silvanus P. *The Life of William Thomson.* London: Macmillan and Co., 1910. 2 vols.
642. Thomson, David. *England in the Nineteenth Century.* Harmondsworth: Penguin, 1950.
643. Thomson, Sir George P. *J. J. Thompson and the Cavendish Laboratory in His Day.* London: Nelson, 1964.
644. "Thormanby" [W. Willmott Dixon]. *Kings of the Rod, Rifle and Gun.* London: Hutchinson and Co., 1899.
645. Thorner, D. *Investment in Empire: British Railway and Steam Shipping Enterprise in India, 1825–1849.* Philadelphia: University of Pennsylvania Press, 1950.
646. Thornton, A. P. *The Imperial Idea and Its Enemies: a study in British power.* London: Macmillan & Co., 1959.
647. Tillyard, A. I. *A History of University Reform.* Cambridge: W. Heffer, 1913.
648. Titmus, R. M. "War and Social Policy" in *Essays on "The Welfare State."* London: George Allen and Unwin, 1958, pp. 75–87.
649. Tooke, Thomas. *History of Prices.* Vol. I and II 1838, III 1840, IV 1848, V and VI 1857.

650. Tooley, R. V. *Maps and Map-Making.* 2nd ed. London: Batsford, 1952 (new imp. 1961).
651. Toulmin, S. and J. Goodfield. *The Fabric of the Heavens. The Ancestry of Science.* London: Hutchinson, 1961.
652. Toynbee, A. *Lectures on the Industrial Revolution in England.* London: Rivingtons, 1844.
653. *Transactions of the Institution of Chemical Engineers,* I (1923), vii–x.
654. Trebilcock, R. C. "A 'Special Relationship'—Government, Rearmament and the Cordite Firms." *Economic History Review,* XIX (1966), pp. 364–79.
655. Turner, D. M. *History of Science Teaching in England.* London: Chapman and Hall, 1927.
656. Tylden, Major G. *The Armed Forces of South Africa.* Johannesburg: Juta and Co., 1954.
657. Tylecote, Mabel. *The Mechanics' Institutes of Lancashire and Yorkshire before 1851.* Manchester University Press, 1957.
658. Tyler, J. E. *The British Army and the Continent, 1904–1914.* London: E. Arnold and Co., 1938.
659. Ubbelohde, A. R. "Towards Tektopia." *The Twentieth Century,* September 1955, pp. 226–235.
660. Underwood, E. A., ed. *Science, Medicine and History.* Essays on the evolution of scientific thought and medical practice written in honour of Charles Singer. Oxford: University Press, 1953. 2 vols.
661. Unwin, G. *Samuel Oldknow and the Arkwrights. The Industrial Revolution at Stockport and Marples.* Manchester University Press, 1924.
662. Ure, Andrew. *Dictionary of Arts, Manufactures and Mines.* Seventh edition by Robert Hunt assisted by F. W. Rudler. London: Longmans and Co., 1875–78. 4 vols.
663. Ure, Andrew. *The Philosophy of Manufactures.* London: Charles Knight, 1835.
664. Usher, A. P. *A History of Mechanical Inventions.* Rev. ed. Cambridge, Mass.: Harvard University Press, 1954.
665. Vagts, Alfred. *Landing Operations.* Harrisburg: Military Service Publishing Co., 1946.
666. Vandiver, Frank E. *Confederate running through Bermuda 1861–1865. Letters and Cargo Manifests.* Austin: University of Texas Press, 1947.
667. Vandiver, Frank E. *Ploughshares into Swords: Josiah Gorgas and Confederate ordnance.* Austin: University of Texas Press, 1952.
668. Vibart, Henry Meredith. *Addiscombe. Its heroes and men of note.* With an introduction by Lord Roberts of Kandahar. Westminster: A. Constable and Co., 1894.
669. Vickers Sons and Maxims Ltd. "Their Works and Manufactures." Reprinted from *Engineering* LXIV (1898), pp. 403, 430, 457, 521, 555, 583, 607, 639, 674, 703, 729, 760, 791.
670. Vulliamy, C. E. *Crimea.* London: Jonathan Cape, 1939.

670a. Walford, Alfred John. *Guide to Reference Material*: I. *Science and Technology*, 2nd ed., 1966. II. *Social and Historical Sciences, Philosophy and Religion*. London: Library Association.

671. Walford, E. W. *Early Days in the British Motor Cycle Industry*. Coventry: British Cycle and Motor Cycle Manufacturers' and Traders' Union, 1931.

672. Walker, Edmond. *The Organisation of a National Army based on the general and free education of the People*. London, 1869. British Museum copy has MS notes.

673. Walker, M. E. M. *Pioneers of Public Health*. London: Oliver and Boyd, 1930.

674. Walker, Sydney Ferris. *Coal Cutting by Machinery in the United Kingdom*. London: Colliers Guardian, 1902.

675. Ward, W. E. F. *The Royal Navy and the Slavers*. London: George Allen and Unwin, 1969.

676. Webb, Sidney and Beatrice. *The History of Liquor Licensing in England, principally from 1700 to 1830*. London: Longmans and Co., 1903.

677. Webb, Sidney and Beatrice. *The Story of the King's Highway*. London: Longmans, Green and Co., 1926.

678. Wertime, T. A. *The Coming of the Age of Steel*. Leiden: E. J. Brill, 1961.

679. Wescott, George Foss. *Mechanical and Electrical Engineering: synopsis of historical events*. Revised by H. P. Spratt. London: H.M.S.O., 1960.

680. White, A. C. T. *The Story of Army Education 1643-1963*. London: George Harrap and Co., 1963.

681. Whittaker, Sir E. *A History of the Theories of Aether and Electricity*. London: Nelson, 1951-3.

682. Williams, J. E. *The Derbyshire Miners*. London: G. Allen and Unwin, 1962.

683. Williams, John. *A General Index to the first thirty-eight volumes of the Memoirs of the Royal Astronomical Society*. London, 1871.

684. Williams, John. *A General Index to the first twenty-nine volumes of the monthly notices of the Royal Astronomical Society*. London, 1870.

685. Williams, L. Pearce. *Michael Faraday: a biography*. London: Chapman and Hall, 1965.

686. Williams, T. I. *A Biographical Dictionary of Scientists and Engineers*. London: A. and C. Black, 1969.

687. Wilson, Charles. "Economy and Society in Late Victorian Britain." *Economic History Review*, XVIII (1965).

688. Wilson, Charles. *History of Unilever*. London: Cassell, 1954. 2 vols.

689. Wilson, Charles and W. Reader. *Men and Machines: a history of D. Napier and Son, Engineers, Ltd., 1808-1958*. London: Weidenfeld and Nicolson, 1958.

690. Wilson, W. *A Hundred Years of Physics*. London: Duckworth, 1950.

691. Winslow, E. M. *The Pattern of Imperialism.* New York: Columbia University Press, 1948.
692. Wood, Ethel M. *The Polytechnic and Quintin Hogg.* Rev. ed. London: Nisbet, 1932.
693. Woodbury, R. S. *History of the Gear-Cutting Machines: a historical study in geometry and machines.* Technology Monographs Historical Series No. 1. Massachusetts Institute of Technology: The Technology Press, 1958.
694. Woodbury, R. S. *History of the Grinding Machine: a historical study in tools and precision production.* Technology Monographs Historical Series No. 2. Massachusetts Institute of Technology: The Technology Press, 1959.
695. Woodbury, R. S. *History of the Lathe to 1850: a study in the growth of a technical element of an industrial economy.* Monograph Series No. 1. Cleveland, Ohio: Society for the History of Technology, 1961.
696. Woodbury, R. S. *History of the Milling Machine: a study in technical development.* Technology Monographs Historical Series No. 3. Massachusetts Institute of Technology: The Technology Press, 1960.
697. Woodcroft, Bennett. *Brief Biographies of the Inventors of Machines for Textile Fabrics.*
698. Woodham-Smith, C. B. *Florence Nightingale.* London: Constable and Co., 1950.
699. Woodham-Smith, C. B. *The Reason Why.* London: Constable and Co., 1953.
700. Woodrooffe, Thomas. *The Enterprise of England: an account of her emergence as an oceanic power.* London: Faber and Faber, 1958.
701. Woodruff, Philip. *The Men Who Ruled India.* London: Jonathan Cape, 1954–5. 2 vols.
702. Woodruff, William. *The Rise of the British Rubber Industry during the Nineteenth Century.* Liverpool University Press, 1958.
703. Woodward, Ernest Llewellyn. *The Age of Reform: 1815–1870.* Oxford: Clarendon Press, 1938.
704. Woodward, Ernest Llewellyn. *Great Britain and the German Navy.* Oxford: Clarendon Press, 1935.
705. Woodward, Horace Bolingbroke. *History of the Geological Society of London.* London: Geological Society, 1908.
706. Wooley, Joseph, ed. *Naval Science.* Vols. 3 and 4. London, 1872.
707. Woolf, L. S. *After the Deluge.* London: L. and V. Woolf, 1931–53. 3 vols.
708. Woolley, Charles. *Phases of Panics: a brief historical review.* London: H. Good and Son, 1896.
709. Worby, W. Beaumont. *Motor Vehicles and Motors.* 1900.
710. Woytinsky, E. S. and W. S. *World Population and Production.* New York: Twentieth Century Fund, 1953.
711. Wright, J. F. "British Economic Growth, 1688–1959." *Economic History Review,* XVIII (1965), pp. 397–412.

712. Wyse, Sir Thomas. *Education Reform,* London: Longman, Rees, Orme, Brown, Green & Longman, 1836.
713. Yolland, William. *An elementary course of mathematics prepared for the use of the Royal Military Academy.* London, 1850–3.
714. Yolland, William. *Ordnance Survey Observations made . . . from 1842 to 1852, for the determination of the latitudes of various trigonometrical stations.* London, 1857.
715. Young, Brigadier-General Henry Ayerst. *The East India Company's Arsenals and Manufactories.* Oxford: Clarendon Press, 1937.
716. Young, Sir Frederick. *Exit Party: an essay on the rise and fall of "party" as the ruling factor in the formation of the Governments of Great Britain.* London: Chapman and Hall, 1900. [Young also wrote much in favour of imperial federation].
717. Young, R. T. *The House that Jack Built. The Story of H.M.S. Excellent.* Aldershot: Gale and Polden, 1955.

XI

COLONIAL WARFARE, 1815–1970

Donald C. Gordon

Most of the British colonial wars of the nineteenth and twentieth centuries bear the somewhat pejorative label of "small wars." Charles Edward Callwell, a closer student of such conflicts than most of his fellows, defined the term as

> Practically . . . all campaigns other than those where both the opposing sides consist of regular troops. It comprises the expeditions against savages and semi-civilized races by disciplined soldiers, it comprises campaigns undertaken to suppress rebellions and guerrilla warfare in all parts of the world where organized armies are struggling against opponents who will not meet them in the open field, and it thus obviously covers operations very varying in their scope and in their conditions.

The major military intellectuals of Britain have paid scant attention to these wars. Military doctrines and ideas developed and elaborated by such men as MacDougall, Hamley, Maurice, Henderson, Liddell Hart and Fuller have generally ignored the British experience in colonial warfare; this in spite of the fact that many of these intellectuals served in colonial wars. The clash of mighty armies in Europe had a far greater appeal than the small wars in Africa or Asia; it was in the conflicts of European powers and in the great war between the American states that the new and intriguing aspects of war were revealed.

There was, then, during most of the nineteenth century an obvious schism between the problems that interested the military student and the actual operations of the British army. That army was organized largely for colonial wars, against savage or semi-civilized peoples, and the reputations of most of its commanders were made or lost in such affairs. Wolseley, "our only general," won his accolades in Canada, West Africa and Egypt; Buller, a prominent member of the Ashanti ring, made and lost his reputation in Africa. Roberts, "our only other general," was the victor in Kandahar and Paardeberg. Most of the officers who were also military thinkers served and fought in colonial wars. Yet certainly the thrust of their thought and writings seems to have been governed much more by battles on the European and

American continents than by the wars in which they actually participated.

Nor was the instruction in the Staff College pointed towards small wars. One officer remarked that strategic studies there had never involved the movement of less than 100,000 men. The study of Indian hill warfare was not part of the instruction until the turn of the century.

Despite this professional indifference to the small wars of empire, however, there was a vast public interest in them. The quarterlies opened their columns generously not only to articles on the problems of defense, to debate on such matters as long and short term service, the abolition of purchase, and general training of military leaders, but also to accounts of victories and defeats on faraway fields. And the spread of literacy created a new public eager to read, and hence a new popular press eager to print, exciting reports of heroic deeds of the fighting men on the battlefields of empire. Thus, to the annoyance of many military leaders, began the age of the war correspondents. Reporting the wars became a glamorous and increasingly professional calling. William Howard Russell, the British pioneer in the trade, never took much satisfaction from the fact of his priority; he referred to himself as "the miserable parent of a luckless tribe." But his reportorial gifts and the varying abilities of those who followed him not only filled the columns of the press but weighed the shelves of libraries with works dealing with the miseries, burdens and grandeurs of empire. The general subject of "deeds that won the empire" inspired many writers; more than three hundred works about General Gordon, for example, have rolled off the presses since the tragedy at Khartoum.

BIBLIOGRAPHIES. An effective introduction into this vast mass of literature, most of it pure ephemera, demands the extensive use of bibliographical aids. The printed catalogues of those Imperial Government departments most involved in the empire and its problems provide the most obvious record of this outpouring of words. The *Catalogue of the War Office Library* (56, 57, 58), the annual index of bibliographies published by the Ministry of Defence Library (54), and the printed catalogue of the Naval Library of the Ministry of Defence (55) are all basic sources.

The *Catalogue of Printed Books in the Library of the Colonial Office* (52), published in 1896, with supplementary volumes following, has been supplanted in usefulness by the *Catalogue of the Colonial Office Library* (53). The first two volumes, covering pre-1950 accessions, are an author catalogue; the post-1950 accessions are arranged by author and title. Volumes 14 and 15 are a classified catalogue of the post-1950 accessions, constituting essentially a shelf list of the Library's holdings, a most useful approach. The whole runs to some 176,000 titles.

The highly regarded *Subject Catalogue of the Library of the Royal Empire Society* (115) is no longer the guide to the holdings of the Society's Library that it once was, due in part to the ravages of bombing, but it is still a most useful guide to many aspects of imperial history, including the military. A more recent Society publication is Donald H. Simpson, *Biography Catalogue of the Library of the Royal Commonwealth Society* (123). The listing of books and periodical material about Britons and others prominent and not so prominent in the history of empire offers considerable help to the student.

The recently published *Wellesley Index to Victorian Periodicals, 1824–1900* (138) is a most significant addition to the list of bibliographical aids. There is a wealth of material in major nineteenth-century British periodicals on the problems of defense of the empire and on the campaigns in India. The *Wellesley Index* lists the articles and authors from material published in eight major British quarterlies. A large portion of the writings of men such as Hamley, Kaye, Spenser Wilkinson, John Frederick Maurice, and J. K. Laughton among others are in it.

Journals not included, however, are those devoted to military and naval affairs. The most venerable of these, and one whose pages are rich in material pertaining to British colonial wars and imperial defense in general, is the *Journal of the Royal United Service Institution* (116). Though somewhat antiquarian in tone, the *Journal of the Society for Army Historical Research* (125) also has much of value. The naval counterpart is the *Mariner's Mirror* (93), a publication of the Society for Nautical Research. Somewhat more professional in emphasis than the above is the *Army Quarterly* (5), while the American *Military Affairs* (99) occasionally prints British historical material. Several branches of the British military services also have their own publications.

OFFICIAL HISTORIES. There is, of course, a substantial *corpus* of British official military and naval history. The highlights of this are those massive and imposing collections that deal with operations in the two World Wars. But the writing and publication of official British histories goes back to the mid-nineteenth century and the Crimean War. Between that war and the War of 1914–18, they chronicled only Indian or colonial wars. Lord Napier's campaign against the Emperor Theodore was reported in the excellent and detailed work by T. J. Holland and H. M. Hozier, *Record of the Expedition to Abyssinia* (67). After 1873, the newly created Intelligence Branch of the Army was responsible for the preparation and publication of official histories. Sir Frederick Maurice added a new dimension to the pattern of official histories in his *Military History of the Campaign of 1882 in Egypt* (97) influenced, perhaps, by his earlier experience as both staff officer and newspaper correspondent during the Ashanti campaign. His version of official history was short and, while far from light and gossipy, was far more journalistic in tone than those that had appeared so far. It suffered, however, from the decided limitation of an almost adulatory tone towards Wolseley; such displeasing topics as the latter's treatment of Hamley, for example, were simply not mentioned.

This effort to strike out on a new path was not followed, however, either by others or by Maurice himself. As the latter confessed "there are some things that an Official Historian must conceal." Either military or political reputations had to be protected if the work was to see publication. Major-General H. E. Colvile saw his *History of the Sudan Campaign* (27) published in a mutilated form because of statements distasteful to some of the political leaders. Colonel G. F. R. Henderson encountered the same problems in the preparation of the first volume of the official work on the Boer War. His death in 1903 left the completion of the work in the hands of Frederick Maurice, so the multi-volume *History of the War in South Africa* (96) was not published until 1906–1910. Maurice found himself handicapped by the feeling that bureaucrats, both military and civilian, were reading over his shoulder, and the work suffered in general from the inhibiting effect of such scrutiny. His was, of course, the last of the major official histories until World War I challenged another generation of military historians.

Many of the problems of the authors of these official histories arose from their varying conceptions of their readership. Most intended their studies to inform and educate the military mind, and anything in the way of a larger readership was little thought of. But Maurice took a different view. He was concerned with education of the British public rather than of the British officer, and for this reason eschewed detail in the interest of clarity, generalization and readability. But he had no notable successors, and as we have noted even he was overborne by the weight of convention in the shaping of those volumes of the history of the Boer War with which he was involved.

Another sort of official history and record is to be found in the medical volumes and in the reports and journals of medical officers, which are discussed in Chapter XXIII.

OTHER HISTORIES. Sir John Fortescue's mammoth *History of the British Army* (40) stands apart, in dimension if in no other way, in the writing of British military history. It is the campaign history of the Old British Army, the long-service institution that essentially ended with the adoption of the Cardwell reforms in 1870. Only the final three volumes of this major work deal with the colonial campaigns: India down through the Mutiny, the early Kaffir wars in South Africa, Napier's invasion of Abyssinia, the Chinese wars, and those against the Maoris in New Zealand. Fortescue had his prejudices, naturally enough, and in so massive a work there were bound to be some errors in detail, but his *History* is a solid and permanent contribution to British and imperial history, and certainly likely to be one of the lasting achievements of his generation of historians. It is a work of fundamental significance to any student of the colonial or Indian wars. Fortescue's other contributions, such as his study of the *Royal Army Service Corps* (42) and a shorter, very general work entitled simply *Military History* (41), are of peripheral interest here.

Otherwise, the professional historian has shown little interest in British colonial wars as military operations, though highly readable and dramatic works on some battles and campaigns have recently been written by journalists and others. To the professional historian, military history has never occupied a place of great esteem; Marx has seemed more important than Mars in the explanation of events that have helped shape the pattern of history. Surely part of the reason for this is the essentially urban and urbane liberal-humanistic tradition in which most historians have been reared. This has tended to denigrate interest in military history as somewhat uncouth and unsophisticated. To write military history is to pay tribute to the power of brute force in controlling the destinies of men, and thus to perpetuate the authority of that force in men's minds; and this opens the military historian to the charge of being militaristic.

In addition, in many of the colonial wars there was a sense of inevitability in the final triumph of Western arms and advanced technology over the swords, gingals, bows and assegai of non-European folk. This tended to rob battles of much of their drama. Such events as the charge at Omdurman were the exception; more typical were the campaigns in the north-western frontiers of India, controlled more by logistics than by serious military clashes. It is revealing that greater historical interest has centered in defeats than in victories. Gordon, besieged and murdered at Khartoum, the fearful and costly retreat from Kabul, the triumph of Cetawayo's (Ketshwayo) *impis* at Isandhlwana, seem to have exercised a greater fascination than the obvious successes of a superior technology.

And of course the same factor that limited the concern of the military intellectuals with colonial wars, the fact that they were, with few exceptions, "small wars," has also cost them the scrutiny of historians. The remoteness of many of the theatres of combat and the lack of bibliographical aids and other supports for scholarship have also restricted historical interest and production.

The most serious study of the colonial wars in which the British were so frequently involved was by a scholarly officer, Colonel C. E. Callwell. His *Small Wars* (18) went through several editions, with revisions by the author to keep it abreast of developments. Callwell wanted to help the British officer to understand the problems of directing regular armies against irregular forces, problems which might be confronted in wars of conquest or annexation, in the suppression of insurrection or lawlessness, or in what were essentially punitive expeditions undertaken to wipe out an insult or avenge a wrong. He devoted the work largely to exposition of the strategical and tactical problems in such wars, and most of his material was drawn from British experience, though not entirely so. Callwell's work was the only one to attempt a consideration of the military tasks in all of the theaters of operation in which British forces were likely to operate, and its frequent republication attests to the reputation that the work achieved.

Callwell was concerned with just the sort of question asked by Charles B. Wallis, a British officer whose most substantial experience had been in West Africa. Wallis asked:

> Is our training in the art of war sufficient for our needs in every part of the Empire? Is it sufficiently practical and elastic to be able to cope with the Boer on the Veldt, the Afridi on the North-West Frontier, the Dervish in the Soudan, the savage in the West African forest and our numerous other possible foes in different parts of the civilized and uncivilized world?

To dispel some of the ignorance which was all too apparent to him, Wallis himself published a short work on *West African Warfare* (137), a handbook of advice to officers going to serve in that area of empire. It is perhaps less useful than W. C. G. Heneker's *Bush Warfare* (65), which also dealt chiefly with the problems of campaigns in West Africa.

An old hand in Indian campaigns, Colonel George J. Younghusband, also tried to define the principles on which operations in Indian Frontier areas should be based. His *Indian Frontier Warfare* (146) dealt with the tactical problems presented by frontier wars during the last two or three decades of the century and was largely based on operations during the second Afghan war and the Chitral campaign. He placed a good deal of emphasis on the desirability of political pacification accompanying the use of military power, but in this he cited not British experience but rather Hoche's campaign against the royalists of the Vendee.

A variety of other works advised the British officer on the problems and difficulties of savage and guerrilla warfare, though none attained the position of Callwell's work. Macguire's *Guerrilla or Partisan Warfare* (89), Bartlett's *Battalion and Brigade Drill for Savage Warfare* (7), General Sir Wilkinson Dent Bird's *Some Principles of Frontier Mountain Warfare* (8) and Gordon Casserley's *Manual of Training for Jungle and River Warfare* (22) all reflected the problems of policing the imperial frontiers.

A later work dealing not with the maintenance of frontiers, but with the frequent responsibility of assisting civilian police forces in the securing of domestic order, was Sir Charles Gwynn's *Imperial Policing* (60). Gwynn drew examples largely from the British experiences in India, Egypt, Shanghai and Palestine in discussing the handling of riots and other domestic turmoil likely to boil up in city streets and marketplaces. Among the case studies was a very critical analysis of General Dyer's handling of the Amritsar mobs.

THE ASHANTI WAR. Few of the small wars have attracted such a wealth of talented military writers as the Ashanti War of 1873–74. Two of the leading members of the Wolseley ring were among the prominent historians and commentators on the campaign against Kofi Karikari in his capital of Kumasi. Indeed, Wolseley seems to have controlled the writing of its history with the same care with which he planned the campaign itself. Henry Brackenbury, the author of the major work on the campaign, *The Ashanti War* (12), was Wolseley's military secretary, and his private secretary, J. F. Maurice (later Major-General Sir Frederick Maurice), was a special correspondent for the *London Daily News* and the author of *The Ashantee War* (95). Histories of a campaign written by those so close to the commander are not likely greatly to diminish his reputation in the public mind.

In addition, some of the more famous of the early war correspondents accompanied Wolseley in the West African campaign. The young Henry M. Stanley, already with one experience of war reporting under his belt in the march with Napier into Abyssinia, was now on the other side of Africa to report Wolseley's triumphs. Also with him was G. A. Henty, another veteran of the Magdala campaign and in the early years of attaining his formidable reputation for the novels that introduced so many boyish readers to the robust joys of British imperialism. Both Stanley, in *Coomassie and Magdala: the story of two British campaigns in Africa* (127), and Henty in *The March to Coomassie* (66) reveal the journalist's eye for detail. Other works of the same character dealing with the Ashanti war were Frederick Boyle's

Through Fanteeland to Coomassie (11) and Winwood Reade's *The Story of the Ashanti Campaign* (112). Both Stanley and Reade were critical of Wolseley; the former of the general's conduct in Kumasi, the latter of some of the commander's diplomacy during the campaign. W. D. McIntyre's "British Policy in West Africa: The Ashanti Expedition of 1873–4" in *The Historical Journal* (90) is an excellent short account of the background of the expedition and of some important questions arising from it.

OTHER AFRICAN CAMPAIGNS. There are innumerable so-called Kaffir wars in the history of European expansion into the interior of southern Africa. But the purely military aspect of these wars is so inseparable from the history of frontier policy and action, and the military forces, generally Boer commandos, are so small, that no exclusively military history of these various minor operations has yet been written.

The first major conflicts are those of the Zulu war of 1879 and the first Anglo-Boer war. Donald R. Morris has commented that the literature of the Zulu war is in a sorry condition, a comment certainly applicable to many of the other small wars of the nineteenth-century empire. Morris' own *The Washing of the Spears* (100) has done much to remedy the condition of which he complained. The later chapters in this splendid work deal largely with the military campaigns, and the author's set-battle pieces are admirable. It is an excellent account of the cultural clash between the advancing frontier of European settlement and the vigorous native people of Southern Africa. One notable flaw is the lack of footnotes. Other works dealing with this Zulu war suffer either from brevity or a lack of objectivity. Sir Reginald Coupland's *Zulu Battle Piece: Isandlhwana* (28) was largely confined to an account of the British defeat and the subsequent action of Rorke's Drift based largely on official reports.

Brian Bond has contributed an excellent essay on the first Boer war in his edited volume, *Victorian Military Campaigns* (9), and Oliver Ransford covers much the same ground in *The Battle of Majuba Hill: The first Boer war* (111). Half or more of this work is devoted to a discussion of the background and aftermath of the war; the account of the military actions is limited, something not surprising considering their small scale.

THE BOER WAR. Befitting the impact and the dimensions of the war itself, the literature of the South African war is considerably more imposing than that stimulated by any of the other colonial wars, with the possible exception of the Indian revolt of 1857. By far the most important of all of the works that deal primarily with the military aspects of the conflict is *The Times History of the War in South Africa* (3). Leopold Amery was the general editor of this seven-volume work, and the sole author of the first three volumes; he was assisted in the later ones by Basil Williams and Erskine Childers.

Neither so sweeping nor so powerful a book as Amery's was the commentary and history of thte South African war prepared and written by the Historical Section of the German Great General Staff. But *The War in South Africa* (48) is a surprisingly readable work in spite of its official authorship, managing nicely to combine the narrative of events with the professional analysis of a staff study. It found much to praise in the British military effort, even though some of its comments on Roberts' Paardeberg campaign seem to reveal a misunderstanding of his objective in that campaign.

The difficulties involved in the writing of the British official *History of the War in South Africa* (96) have been discussed above. The work as it was finally published was largely a compilation of the facts and minutiae of the campaigns, generally lacking in reader interest.

While there were many gifted journalists in South Africa to report the progress of the struggle, perhaps the most acute comments in the first year of the war appeared in the London *Morning Post* from the pen of one of England's leading military intellectuals, Spenser Wilkinson. He was kept informed of the movements in the theaters of operations by a number of correspondents, some of whom were obviously pushing the limits of security pretty far. His pieces were published as *Lessons of the War* (139).

Another of Britain's leading military thinkers, J. F. C. Fuller, then a subaltern, was among the first of the reinforcements dispatched to South Africa after the outbreak of the conflict. He was crippled by illness for most of the early operations but served for some eighteen months during the guerrilla phase of the war. *The Last of the Gentleman's Wars* (45) contains much on life in the army during the war and reflects the author's regret for the disappearance of the time when sportsmanship was the essence of soldiering.

There has been a revival of interest in some of the military aspects of the Boer war during the last few years. Two works of roughly comparable quality, Edgar Holt's *The Boer War* (69) and Rayne Kruger's *Good-bye Dolly Gray* (81), are both effective and polished presentations of some of the larger aspects of the conflict. Another work of stature is John Selby, *The Boer War* (121a). Julian Symons' *Buller's Campaign* (132) focuses not only on the disastrous operations about Ladysmith and along the Tugela River, but also on the problem of Buller himself. Oliver Ransford, *The Battle of Spion Kop* (111b) is also concerned with a central engagement of this same campaign. The first volume of Sir Keith Hancock's biography *Smuts: the sanguine years* (63), gives some insight into modern guerrilla warfare in one of its embryonic stages. Hancock's and Jean van der Poel's editing of the Smuts papers, *Selections from the Smuts Papers,* Vol. I (62), sheds much light on Smuts's ideas of Boer strategy and the nature of their military operations.

EGYPT AND THE SUDAN. The literature of the campaigns in Egypt and the Sudan is enormous, much of it concerned chiefly with the enigmatic personality and career of General Charles Gordon. Maurice's official history (97) of the operations culminating in Wolseley's victory at Tel-el-Kebir has already been mentioned; the comparable official history of the Gordon relief expedition is that of Major-General H. E. Colvile, *History of the Sudan Campaign* (27), two relatively slight volumes compared with the usual dimensions of official histories. A German officer and observer, Hermann Vogt, wrote a crisp and effective account of Wolseley's operations leading to Tel-el-Kebir, *The Egyptian War of 1882* (135). More flamboyant is Winston Churchill's, *The River War* (24). Randolph Churchill's *Winston S. Churchill: Companion Volume I, Parts 1 and 2* (23) gives not only an insight into the wars in which the young Churchill participated, but an even better insight into the mind of the author. A more fervid work on the Sudan campaign is that of George Warrington Steevens, *With Kitchener to Khartoum* (128). On a much larger scale is that of Thomas Archer, *The War in Egypt and the Soudan* (4). This massive work is devoted to the Egyptian rising under Arabi, the bombardment of Alexandria, Wolseley's subsequent campaign and the failure of the Gordon relief expedition. It is rich in detail, with considerable grasp of the military operations of the 1882 campaign and of Gordon's activities in the Sudan. Another work of substance dealing with the same campaigns is Charles Royle's *The Egyptian Campaigns* (117). Two highly placed military officers contributed to the literature of the Nile Valley operations: General Sir Henry Brackenbury in *The River Column* (13) and General Sir William Butler in *The Campaign of the Cataracts* (16). Adrian Preston is responsible for a newly edited edition of Wolseley's campaign journal, *In Relief of Gordon* (109).

The Gordon relief operations have some place in British imperial history because of the use of imperial manpower. The need for transportation up the Nile reminded Wolseley of his Canadian experiences in the first Louis Riel uprising, and led to the recruitment of Canadian river men and loggers to assist in handling the boats over the Nile cataracts. The Canadian Colonel C. P. Stacey has edited the *Records of the Nile Voyageurs, 1884–1885* (126). The other colonial contingent came from New South Wales and served in the minor operations from the port of Suakin, for which see Frank Hutchinson's and Francis Myers' *The Australian Contingent* (73) and Stanley Brogden's *The Sudan Contingent* (14).

The difficulties in transporting the relief forces up the Nile led to the creation of a Camel Corps, and the problems and confusions involved in the use of these animals are related in Major-General Lord Edward Gleichen's *With the Camel Corps up the Nile* (49). The problems of transportation are also described in Colonel George A. Furse's *Report on the Formation and Working of the Land Transport of the Nile Expeditionary Force* (47). Furse was the Director of Transport and later author of *Military Expeditions beyond the Seas* (46), which was largely an instructional manual in logistical problems.

Until recently, comparatively little effort was devoted to an attempt to understand the "other side of the hill" in the operations against the Madhi and his followers. This deficiency has been substantially remedied by works such as those of A. B. Theobald, *The Mahdiya* (133), and the more scholarly P. M. Holt, *Mahdist State in the Sudan, 1881–1898* (72). Any history of the Mahdist period is likely to have a substantial element of military history, and the Theobald study is perhaps more inclined in this direction and somewhat more traditional in tone than the later Holt.

Edward W. C. Sandes' *The Royal Engineers in Egypt and the Sudan* (121) is a rich and well researched account of the work of the sappers in both war and peace in the Nile Valley. Among more swash-buckling descriptions of the campaigns in the Nile, the brilliant story of Kitchener's campaign, culminating in the classic account of the charge at Omdurman, is found in Winston Churchill's *The River War* (23) and in the even more high-pitched work of one of the best known of the newspaper correspondents of the period, George Warrington Steevens' *With Kitchener to Khartum* (128).

INDIA AND BURMA. Military history also has a small place in the general body of historical writing about India. With few exceptions, historians have been more interested in the social, political and economic aspects of the British impact on India. The wars of conquest have not been ignored, but they have seldom actively engaged the minds of historians.

The major official history of the campaigns of the Indian army is *Frontier and Overseas Expeditions from India* (74). The studies which comprise this work were compiled by the Intelligence Branch of the Chief of Staff, Army Headquarters. They cover operations along the borders of India from the period of the first Burmese war to the campaign against the Abors in 1911–12. The sixth volume is particularly far-ranging, dealing with the campaigns in Africa and Asia in which Indian troops engaged. These cover a span of time extending from the Napoleonic operations in Egypt through the South African war and the Boxer rebellion. Supplementing these is *The Second Afghan War, 1878–1880* (75), prepared by the Intelligence Branch of Army Headquarters, and followed, appropriately, by *The Third Afghan War, 1919* (76).

Again the work of Sir John Fortescue stands out as a major contribution to non-official military history. Volumes XI, XII and XIII of his great work (40) have a strong Indian theme. The Pindari war, the two Afghan wars, the two Burmese wars, and, naturally, the events of the Mutiny appear in considerable detail. Fortescue's assumptions were frankly imperialist, he was frequently unjust in his appraisals of those who ruled India, especially political officers, and as he confesses, he wrote at times from somewhat limited material. But no student of British military activity can safely ignore his fundamental contribution.

Fortescue's sole rival for distinction would be Sir John Kaye. As with Fortescue, Kaye's work was influenced by his conception of the essential justness and need for Britain's civilizing role in India, but Kaye was too much of an historian to be blind to the claims of truth and justice when dealing with Britain's foes. Considering the fact that Kaye wrote his part of his *History of the Indian Mutiny of 1857–58* (79) while the passion of the Mutiny was still smoldering and while many of the participants were still alive, it is a remarkable work. This is the more apparent when the tone of his contribution is compared with that of G. B. Malleson, who finished the work after Kaye's death. Some of the harshest words of criticism that Fortescue ever penned were directed at Malleson.

Others who wrote of the Mutiny in the tradition established by Kaye were T. Rice Holmes and Sir George Forrest. Holmes's *History of the Indian Mutiny* (68) sought to be objective but was not free from British preconceptions of the Mutiny nor from a certain amount of special pleading. Forrest's *History of the Indian Mutiny* (39) also strove for objectivity. Of all of the British historians of the Mutiny, Edward J. Thompson in *The Other Side of the Medal* (134) is the most critical of his countrymen and reveals more of the brutality in its suppression.

Of the Indian accounts, that of Professor S. N. Sen, *Eighteen Fifty-Seven* (122) is by all odds the most valuable. Though the military aspects of the uprising and its suppression are effectively handled, much attention is given to causes and meanings in Indian history. This work supplants nearly all other general histories of the Mutiny, either British or Indian.

The best accounts of that military disaster to British arms, the first of the Afghan wars, are the earliest and the latest to be written. Sir John Kaye, preeminent in this as he was later in the history of the Mutiny, wrote his *History of the War in Afghanistan* (78), some eight years after the event. Patrick A. Macrory, in *Signal Catastrophe* (91) relied substantially on Kaye's work in his retelling of the political blundering that led to the effort to place Shah Suja on the Afghan throne and hold him there by British bayonets. The author also draws heavily upon the eyewitness accounts in Vincent Eyre's *The Military Operations at Cabul* (36) and Lady Sale's *A Journal of the Disasters in Afghanistan, 1841–42* (119). A recent work by the historian J. A. Norris, *The First Afghan War, 1838–42* (105), offers a strong defense of Lord Auckland and Alexander Burnes against what the author regards as the prejudiced judgments of Kaye and all others who have taken their line from him.

H. B. Hanna's *The Second Afghan War, 1878–1880* (64) is an outstanding three-volume study of a conflict that ended in happier circumstances for British arms than did the first. Hanna's criticism was not confined to the political leadership of the war; he had harsh things to say also about Lord Roberts' command. The other point of view is given in Roberts' own work, *Forty-One Years In India* (114), and by David James in *Lord Roberts* (77).

On the general topic of Indian frontier wars, H. L. Nevill's *Campaigns on the North-West Frontier* (104) attempted a student's history of all campaigns. Nevill covered the period from 1850 to 1908; he did not discuss the second Afghan war, though he did consider some side-effects of that conflict. George J. Younghusband's *Indian Frontier Warfare* (146) and Arthur Swinson's recent *North-West Frontier* (130) also deal with the same area and its problems. C. E. Callwell, of *Small Wars,* also wrote a highly useful professional study of the problem of fighting irregular forces in the rugged frontier regions in *Tirah* (20), which describes the difficulties in dealing with an enemy "who fights when he chooses and runs away when he chooses without being the worse for doing so." Winston Churchill's *The Malakand Field Force* (24a) gives a vivid picture of Indian frontier warfare. Major General J. G. Elliott's *The Frontier, 1839–1947* (35a) is a recent addition to this literature.

Colonel E. W. C. Sandes, whose admirable account of the work of the Royal Engineers in Egypt and the Sudan, was mentioned earlier, also wrote *The Military Engineers in India* (120). In addition to recording the military services of the sappers, he presents full accounts of their civil work in road construction, irrigation, water supply, railroad building, telegraphic communication and other fields.

Volume V of *Frontier and Overseas Expeditions from India* (74) is devoted to the three Burmese wars. A professor of Sanskrit, Horace H. Wilson, was the compiler and author of two basic works on the first of these wars, *Documents Illustrative of the Burmese War* (140) and *Narrative of the Burmese War, 1824–26* (141). A source on whom Fortescue relied substantially for his account of this war was Frederick B. Doveton's *Reminiscences of the Burmese War in 1824–5–6* (35). Major John J. Snodgrass, military secretary to the commander of the British forces, was the author of *Narrative of the Burmese War* (124). The most detailed account is G. W. de Rhe Philipe's *A Narrative of the First Burmese War* (108). A short account of some of the naval operations is Lieutenant John Marshall's *Narrative of the Naval Operations in Ava during the Burmese War in the years 1824, 1825 and 1826* (94).

Less has been written about the later Burmese wars. Colonel William F. B. Laurie's *The Second Burmese War* (83) is a first-hand account of the conflict. Material on the third Burmese war is even more scarce; perhaps the most relevant work is Sir Charles Crosthwaite's *The Pacification of Burma* (32).

CHINA. The pioneering works of Hosea B. Morse are still a starting point for any study of Chinese relations with the West, especially during the nineteenth century when western states were forcing their trade upon China. While Morse's works are certainly not military histories, they do contain much of interest for the student of naval and military affairs in the opening of China. The first volume of his *International Relations of the Chinese Empire* (101) covers the period of the wars with the western states, most notably Britain. One of Morse's leading successors is John K. Fairbank, whose two-volume *Trade and Diplomacy on the China Coast* (37) has little about the military aspects of the first Chinese war, but deals extensively with the political problems of this period of Anglo-Chinese relations. A work that substantially continues Fairbank's study is Masataka Banno's *China and the West, 1858–61* (6).

Edgar Holt's *The Opium Wars in China* (70) places stronger emphasis upon the military features of the Sino-western confrontation. This is a superior journalistic introduction to the period and its conflicts, although Holt is largely dependent on British sources and does not have a command of materials comparable to that of recognized scholars such as Fairbank and Banno. John Selby's essay in Bond's *Victorian Military Campaigns* (9) is an admirable account of the later phases of these wars.

Grace Fox's *British Admirals and Chinese Pirates, 1832–1869* (43) deals with naval action of a wider scope than the participation in the Chinese wars. It is essentially a study of the formation and implementation of British naval policy on the China coast. British naval forces were gravely concerned with the suppression of piracy in Chinese waters, but this study makes it clear that the larger matters of policy were in the hands of the

Foreign and Colonial Offices and not in those of local naval commanders. The record of naval participation in the Chinese wars of 1856 to 1860 as reported in the dispatches of commanders is contained in D. Bonner-Smith and E. W. R. Lumby, eds., *The Second Chinese War, 1856–1860* (10).

Somewhat lighter in tone, but still worth attention, is Maurice Collis' *Foreign Mud* (26). This is more an account of the background and beginnings of the first Chinese war than a description of the military aspects of that conflict, but it is an easy and readable work. Pin Chia Kuo's *A Critical Study of the First Anglo-Chinese War* (82) also has little to say about the purely military aspects of the struggle, though much of the discussion is pertinent to the problem of the fighting efficiency and the morale of the Chinese soldier. Arthur Waley's *The Opium War through Chinese Eyes* (136) is a notable effort to see the war from the other point of view.

The observations of participants in the Chinese wars are naturally a mixed bag. Among the more significant are the comments of the then Lieutenant-Colonel Garnet Wolseley, who wrote of the third Chinese war in *Narrative of the War with China* (143) and also in his later *Story of a Soldier's Life* (144). Other participants who contributed works of interest were R. James MacGhee, in *How We Got to Pekin* (88) David F. Rennie, in *The British Arms in North China and Japan* (113), and Robert Swinhoe, in *Narrative of the North China Campaign of 1860* (129).

NEW ZEALAND. Some of the smallest of the small wars of the nineteenth century were the Maori wars in New Zealand. They have also been examined recently in two works. Edgar Holt, who has become the agent for the introduction of many modern readers to some of the military contests of the last century, has also given us an excellent account of the Maori war in *The Strangest War* (71). A new study is *War and Politics in New Zealand, 1855–1870* (34), by B. J. Dalton, whose excellent article in *Historical Studies: Australia and New Zealand* (33), argues that British commanders and troops were far more competent than generally pictured.

Perhaps because of his four years' residence in New Zealand, Fortescue's discussion of the Maori wars in Vol. VIII has a distinction that sets it apart from his treatment of other topics. Older works not to be overlooked are J. E. Alexander's *Bushfighting* (2), William Fox's *The War in New Zealand* (44), and J. A. Cowan's *The New Zealand Wars* (29), though these works are stronger on detail than on conception of what the wars were about, and too critical of British officialdom, both civil and military.

THE NAVY. Except, as we have seen, in China, the "small wars" made fewer demands on British naval power than on the military. Of course, the freedom of movement available for the transport of men and material rested on British command of the sea. The fundamental purpose of the British navy was not so much to defend the waters adjacent to the British Isles as to make the oceans and seas of the world free and safe for all who might "pass through them on their lawful occasions." Its usual tasks were the suppression of piracy and the slave trade, and the latter's Pacific Ocean counterpart, the "blackbirding" traffic. Major actions were limited in number: Navarino and the Crimean war alone provided those officers who had served Nelson any real opportunity to emulate the deeds of those heroic days. For the most part any other chances for distinction came from such limited operations as those of the Burmese and Chinese wars.

The major account of the Royal Navy during these long decades of the *Pax Britannica* is William Laird Clowes's *The Royal Navy* (25). Volumes VI and VII are devoted to the history of the Navy in the nineteenth century in both its civil and military aspects. While Clowes wrote the bulk of these volumes himself, as editor he also secured contributions from such men as Theodore Roosevelt and Sir Clement Markham. The work has an encyclopedic quality about it; a host of small and occasionally bloody encounters are described.

Edward Cardwell, the great War Secretary, said that he did not know of a nobler page in British history than that which recorded the activities of the Royal Navy in halting the slave trade, a story well told in Christopher Lloyd's *The Navy and the Slave Trade* (85).

From the time of the Crimean war until the Fisher reorganization of 1904, the most extensively used vessel of the Royal Navy was the gunboat. They were everywhere from the Baltic, where they had their birth, to the South Seas, from Chinese waters to the Great Lakes. Antony Preston and John Major recount much of the history of this vessel in *Send a Gunboat* (110). The work is shaky in its historical generalizations but rich in details about the gunboats themselves. The gunboat stands as a symbol of that era when, as Prof. Gerald Graham points out in *The Politics of Naval Supremacy* (51), the other major powers of the world acquiesced in British control of the world's greatest naval force.

MALAYA. The struggle against Communist insurgency in Malaya is the most fully recounted of the British experiences in modern guerilla warfare. Operations against the insurgents by a British tactical unit are described in Major Anthony Crockett's *Green Beret, Red Star* (31); Arthur Campbell writes of the three-year part that the Suffolk Regiment played in the operations in Malaya in *Jungle Green* (21); Oliver Crawford (30) discusses the training methods of the Jungle Warfare School and some of the psychological and physical effects of jungle maneuvres. The experiences in Malaya also form a part of Franklin Mark Osanka's *Modern Guerrilla Warfare* (107), a collection of essays by thirty-seven authorities on the military and social aspects of such operations, and are the focus of O'Ballance's volume (147).

CYPRUS, PALESTINE AND KENYA. Other areas of guerrilla warfare in recent years have been Cyprus and Palestine. The Eoka side of the Cyprus struggle is reported in such works as George Grivas' *General Grivas on Guerrilla Warfare* (59), Charles Foley's editing of *The Memoirs of General Grivas* (38) and Doros Alastos' *Cyprus Guerrilla* (1). In the Palestinian conflicts, Harry Sacher's *Israel* (118) is an intensive record of the years of struggle against the British down to the first Arab-Israeli conflict. Major R. D. Wilson's *Cordon and Search* (142) is an account of the arduous duties of a British airborne division in Palestine from 1945 to 1948. Major Frank Kitson's *Gangs and Counter-Gangs* (80) is perhaps most important for its account of the military struggle against the Mau-Mau in Kenya.

The whole subject of colonial warfare in British possessions in the twentieth century is badly in need of an adequate bibliography, let alone of more scholarly accounts.

BIOGRAPHY AND AUTOBIOGRAPHY. British military biography has largely dealt with those generals, admirals, and air marshals who reached the heights of power during one or other of the two World Wars. Works by and about these men nearly all contain appreciable material on colonial affairs because nobody reached high rank who did not serve abroad. The two conflicts not only made publishers more willing to accept such works, but also saw a steady trickle of memoirs of colonial wars authored by heroes of far-off engagements or by the independently wealthy. Of the biographies dealing with the great of the purely colonial wars, Joseph Lehmann's excellent and highly readable *All Sir Garnet* (84) supplants in many respects the more pedestrian and eulogistic *Life of Lord Wolseley* (98) by Sir Frederick Maurice and Sir George Arthur. David James's *Lord Roberts* (77) is a readable though somewhat conventional biography of the hero of Khandahar and of the South African war. The standard work on the commander of the Abyssinian campaign is *Lord Napier of Magdala* (103), by his son, Lieutenant-Colonial H. D. Napier. The work contains substantial material from Napier's private correspondence. Edward McCourt has written an interesting account of one of the more independent-minded of the Wolseley ring, General Sir William Butler, in *Remember Butler* (87). Sir Philip Magnus's *Kitchener: portrait of an imperialist* (92) is a superior assessment of the life and character of the conqueror of the Sudan. Christopher Sykes's *Orde Wingate* (131), is a recent work on one of the more unconventional of British military leaders.

Of the autobiographies, Wolseley's *The Story of a Soldier's Life* (144) is most important, even though it covers only a part of Wolseley's long career. Field Marshal Earl Roberts' *Forty-one Years in India* (114) is another incomplete work; the author's command in the Boer War and later activities for conscription are missing. Others of this genre are Sir William Butler's *Autobiography* (15) and General Sir Neville Lyttelton's *Eighty Years Soldiering* (86). General Sir William Munro's *Records of Service and Campaigning in Many Lands* (102) covers a lengthy career in the medical corps; General Sir Desmond O'Callaghan recounts his experience as artillery officer in *Guns, Gunners and Others* (106). Other notable works are Sir Ian Hamilton's *Listening for the Drums* (61), General Sir Charles E. Callwell's *Service Yarns* (17) and *Stray Recollections* (19), and Sir Evelyn Woods's *From Midshipman to Field Marshal* (145). Sir John Glubb, *A Soldier with the Arabs* (50) tells of the career of another of Britain's military romantics.

POSSIBLE RESEARCH. There is much yet to be done in the field of the history of Britain's colonial wars. Perhaps the most obvious possibility for interesting research lies in a further reconsideration of military leaders. Lehmann has shown what can be done in his excellent work on Wolseley; so has Magnus in his dissection of Kitchener. Julian Symons touched on some aspects of the problem presented by Redvers Buller in his *Buller's Campaign* (132), but this enigmatic man needs further assessment. Others also deserve attention: Sir Evelyn Wood and Percy Girouard, the railroad builder, among them.

The role of military and naval men in civil office awaits study. Their use as colonial governors was commonplace; Sir William Jervois and Sir George Clarke are notable instances. How well did such men carry out their political duties and accept the fact that the orderly military values were not suitable to political tasks? The problems of civilian-military relationships during colonial wars remains largely unexplored, as does the civilian work of military forces not engaged in active combat. The political, economic and social impact of imperial garrisons on the lives of emerging colonies is a topic of interest yet to be examined.

It is easy to think of the army as an imperial police force, but just when and where it assumed police duties and how effectively it carried them out needs to be assessed. The role of the military in support of civil authority cannot all have been of Amritsar character.

The pattern of promotion within the army could be of interest. The fact that Buller was among the more prominent of the Wolseley ring and that both he and Sir George Colley, another member of the group, revealed their incapacity for high command on battlefields in South Africa suggests the need for further investigation into the nature of and the relationships existing between members of the "ring." Did Wolseley so over-awe and dominate his subordinates that they lost capacity for decision when they held command themselves? Growing up in Wolseley's shadow may have been a vitiating experience. And this suggests that the career patterns of general officers might be a revealing study.

There is no satisfactory study of the effects of railroad development on warfare, and the evolution of military transport generally could well be usefully examined. Another area of interest might be the stimulus of colonial wars, fought in out-of-the-way corners of the world, on medical research. And above all, there are numerous conflicts that can be freed from the old assumptions of imperialism and placed in new and more scholarly contexts, thereby revealing more clearly the nature of the cultural clash between the forces of European expansion and the non-European peoples who felt its impact.

BIBLIOGRAPHY

1. Alastos, Doros (pseud.) [Eurodos Ioannides]. *Cyprus Guerrilla.* London: Heinemann, 1960.
2. Alexander, J. E. *Bushfighting: illustrated by remarkable actions and incidents of the Maori wars in New Zealand.* London: Sampson Low, 1873.

3. Amery, L. S., ed. *The Times History of the War in South Africa, 1899–1902*. London: Sampson Low, 1900–1909. 7 vols.
4. Archer, Thomas. *The War in Egypt and the Soudan*. London: Blackie, 1886–87. 4 vols.
5. *Army Quarterly*. London: 1920–   .
6. Banno, Masataka. *China and the West, 1858–61*. Cambridge, Mass.: Harvard University Press, 1964.
7. Bartlett, Eric. *Battalion and Brigade Drill for Savage Warfare*. London: W. Clowes, 1904.
8. Bird, Wilkinson Dent. *Some Principles of Frontier Mountain Warfare*. London: Hugh Rees, 1909.
9. Bond, Brian, ed. *Victorian Military Campaigns*. New York: Praeger, 1967.
10. Bonner-Smith, D. and E. W. R. Lumby, eds. *The Second Chinese War, 1856–1860*. London: Navy Records Society, 1954. (Publications of the Navy Records Society, Vol. XCV.)
11. Boyle, Frederick. *Through Fanteeland to Coomassie*. London: Chapman & Hall, 1874.
12. Brackenbury, Henry. *The Ashanti War*. Edinburgh: Blackwood, 1874. 2 vols.
13. ————. *The River Column: a narrative of the advance of the River Column of the Nile Expeditionary Force*. Edinburgh: Blackwood, 1885.
14. Brogden, Stanley. *The Sudan Contingent*. Melbourne: Hawthorne Press, 1943.
15. Butler, William. *Autobiography*. London: Constable & Co., 1911.
16. ————. *The Campaign of the Cataracts*. London: Sampson Low, 1887.
17. Callwell, Charles Edward. *Service Yarns and Memories*. London: Blackwood, 1912.
18. ————. *Small Wars*. London: Stationery Office, 1896; new and rev. ed. 1899; 3rd ed. 1906.
19. ————. *Stray Recollections*. London: E. Arnold, 1923.
20. ————. *Tirah*. London: Constable, 1911.
21. Campbell, Arthur. *Jungle Green*. Boston: Little, Brown, 1953.
22. Casserley, Gordon. *Manual of Training for Jungle and River Warfare*. London: T. Werner Laurie, 1915.
23. Churchill, Randolph S., ed. *Winston S. Churchill: Companion Volume I,* parts 1 and 2. Boston: Houghton Mifflin, 1967.
24. Churchill, Winston. *The River War*. London: Longmans, 1899. 2 vols.
24a. Churchill, Winston. *The Story of the Malakand Field Force*. London: Longmans, 1898.
25. Clowes, W. Laird. *The Royal Navy, a History from the Earliest Times to the Present*. London: Sampson Low, 1897–1903. (Reprinted New York, 1966). 7 vols.
26. Collis, Maurice. *Foreign Mud*. London: Faber & Faber, 1946.

27. Colvile, Henry Edward. *History of the Sudan Campaign*. London, 1889.
28. Coupland, Reginald. *Zulu Battle Piece: Isandlhwana*. London: Collins, 1948.
29. Cowan, J. A. *The New Zealand Wars: a history of the Maori campaign and the pioneering period*. Wellington: W. A. G. Skinner, 1922. 2 vols.
30. Crawford, Oliver. *The Door Marked Malaya*. London: Hart-Davis, 1958.
31. Crockett, Anthony. *Green Beret, Red Star*. London: Eyre & Spottiswood, 1954.
32. Crosthwaite, Charles. *The Pacification of Burma*. London: Edward Arnold, 1912.
33. Dalton, B. J. "A New Look at the Maori War of the Sixties." *Historical Studies: Australia and New Zealand*, XII, no. 46, April, 1966.
34. ———. *War and Politics in New Zealand, 1855–1870*. Sydney: Sydney University Press, 1967.
35. Doveton, Frederick B. *Reminiscences of the Burmese War in 1824–5–6*. London: W. H. Allen, 1852.
35a. Elliott, Major-General J. G. *The Frontier, 1839–1947*. London: Cassell, 1970.
36. Eyre, Vincent. *The Military Operations at Cabul*. London: John Murray, 1843.
37. Fairbank, John K. *Trade and Diplomacy on the China Coast: the opening of the Treaty Ports, 1842–54*. Cambridge, Mass.: Harvard University Press, 1953. 2 vols.
38. Foley, Charles, ed. *The Memoirs of General Grivas*. New York: Praeger, 1965.
39. Forrest, George. *History of the Indian Mutiny*. Edinburgh: Blackwood, 1904–12. 3 vols.
40. Fortescue, John. *History of the British Army*. London: Macmillan, 1899–1930. 13 vols.
41. ———. *Military History*. Cambidge: Cambridge University Press, 1914.
42. ———. *The Royal Army Service Corps*. Cambridge: Cambridge University Press, 1930–31. 2 vols.
43. Fox, Grace. *British Admirals and Chinese Pirates, 1832–1869*. London: Kegan Paul, 1940.
44. Fox, William. *The War in New Zealand*. London, 1866.
45. Fuller, J. F. C. *The Last of the Gentleman's Wars*. London: Faber & Faber, 1937.
46. Furse, George A. *Military Expeditions Beyond the Seas*. London: Clowes, 1897.
47. ———. *Report on the Formation and Working of the Land Transport of the Nile Expeditionary Force*. London, 1885.
48. Germany. General Staff. *The War in South Africa from October 1899 to September 1900*. (Authorized English translation by W.

H. Waters and H. DuCane.) London: John Murray, 1904–06. 2 vols.
49. Gleichen, Edward. *With the Camel Corps up the Nile.* London: Chapman & Hall, 1888.
50. Glubb, John Bagot. *A Soldier with the Arabs.* London: Hodder & Stoughton, 1957.
51. Graham, Gerald. *The Politics of Naval Supremacy.* Cambridge: Cambridge: Cambridge University Press, 1965.
52. Great Britain. Colonial Office. Library. *Catalogue of the Printed Books in the Library of the Colonial Office.* London, 1896; Supplement, 1907.
53. ————. Colonial Office. Library. *Catalogue of the Colonial Office Library, London.* Boston: G. F. Hall, 1964. 15 vols.
54. ————. Ministry of Defence. Library (Central and Army). *Index of Book Lists.* Issued annually and available on request. [Ministry of Defence Library (Central and Army), Old War Office Bldg., London S. W. 1].
55. ————. Ministry of Defence. Naval Library. *Author and Subject Catalogues of the Naval Library.* Boston: G. K. Hall, 1967. 5 vols.
56. ————. War Office. Library. *Catalogue of the War Office Library.* London: Stationery Office, 1906–12. 3 vols.
57. ————. *Supplement to War Office Library Catalogue.* Pts. I & II. Comp. by F. J. Hudleston London: Stationery Office, 1916.
58. ————. ————. Pt. III (Subject Index). Annual Supplement. 1st— . Jan. 1912– .
59. Grivas, George. *General Grivas on Guerrilla Warfare.* New York: Praeger, 1965. (English edition as *Guerrilla Warfare and Eoka's Struggle.* London: Longmans, 1964.)
60. Gwynn, Charles. *Imperial Policing.* London: Macmillan, 1934.
61. Hamilton, Ian. *Listening for the Drums.* London: Faber & Faber, 1944.
62. Hancock, Keith and Jean van der Poel. *Selections from the Smuts Papers.* Vol. I. Cambridge: Cambridge University Press, 1966.
63. ————. *Smuts: the sanguine years.* Cambridge: Cambridge University Press, 1962.
64. Hanna, H. B. *The Second Afghan War, 1878–1880.* London: Constable, 1899. 3 vols.
65. Heneker, W. C. G. *Bush Warfare.* London: Hugh Rees, 1907.
66. Henty, G. A. *The March to Coomassie.* 2nd ed. London, 1874.
67. Holland, T. J. and H. M. Hozier. *Record of the Expedition to Abyssinia.* London, 1870. 2 vols.
68. Holmes, T. Rice. *History of the Indian Mutiny.* London: W. H. Allen, 1883.
69. Holt, Edgar. *The Boer War.* London: Putnam, 1958.
70. ————. *The Opium Wars in China.* London: Putnam, 1964.
71. ————. *The Strangest War.* London: Putnam, 1962.
72. Holt, P. M. *The Mahdist State in the Sudan, 1881–1898.* London: Oxford University Press, 1958.

73. Hutchinson, Frank and Francis Myers. *The Australian Contingent.* Sydney: T. Richards, 1885.
74. India. Army. Intelligence Branch. *Frontier and Overseas Expeditions from India.* Simla and Calcutta, 1907–13. 6 vols. with supplements.
75. ———. *The Second Afghan War, 1878–80.* Simla, 1905.
76. ———. *The Third Afghan War, 1919.* Simla, 1926.
77. James, David. *Lord Roberts.* London: Hollis & Carter, 1954.
78. Kaye, John. *History of the War in Afghanistan.* London: 1857–58. 3 vols.
79. ———. *Kaye's and Malleson's History of the Indian Mutiny of 1857–8.* Col. Malleson, ed. London: Longmans, Green, 1897–98. 6 vols.
80. Kitson, Frank. *Gangs and Counter-Gangs.* London: Barrie and Rockliff, 1960.
81. Kruger, Rayne. *Good-bye Dolly Gray: The story of the Boer war.* London: Cassell, 1959.
82. Kuo, Pin Chia. *A Critical Study of the First Anglo-Chinese War.* Shanghai: Commercial Press, 1935.
83. Laurie, William F. B. *The Second Burmese War.* London: Smith, Elder & Co., 1853.
84. Lehmann, Joseph. *All Sir Garnet.* London: Jonathan Cape, 1964.
85. Lloyd, Christopher. *The Navy and the Slave Trade.* London: Longmans, Green, 1949.
86. Lyttelton, Neville. *Eighty Years Soldiering.* London: Hodder & Stoughton, 1927.
87. McCourt, Edward. *Remember Butler.* London: Routledge & Kegan Paul, 1968.
88. MacGhee, Robert James. *How We Got to Pekin: a narrative of the campaign in 1860.* London: R. Bentley, 1862.
89. MacGuire, Thomas M. *Guerrilla or Partisan Warfare.* London, 1904.
90. McIntyre, W. D. "British Policy in West Africa: the Ashanti Expedition of 1873–4." *Historical Journal,* vol. 1, 1962.
91. Macrory, Patrick A. *Signal Catastrophe.* London: Hodder & Stoughton, 1966.
92. Magnus, Philip. *Kitchener: portrait of an imperialist.* London: J. Murray, 1958.
93. *Mariner's Mirror.* London: Society for Nautical Research, 1911– .
94. Marshall, John. *Narrative of the Naval Operations in Ava during the Burmese War in the Years 1824, 1825 and 1826.* 1830.
95. Maurice, John Frederick. *The Ashantee War.* London: H. S. King, 1874.
96. ———. *History of the War in South Africa, compiled by direction of H. M. Gov't.* London, 1906–08. 3 vols.
97. ———. *Military History of the Campaign of 1882 in Egypt.* London: Stationery Office, 1877; Rev. ed. 1908.
98. ——— and George C. Arthur. *Life of Lord Wolseley.* London, 1924.

99. *Military Affairs.* Washington, D. C.: 1937–1968; Manhattan, Kansas, 1968– .

100. Morris, Donald R. *The Washing of the Spears.* New York: Simon & Schuster, 1965.

101. Morse, Hosea B. *The International Relations of the Chinese Empire.* London: Longmans, 1910–1918. 3 vols.

102. Munro, William. *Records of Service and Campaigning in Many Lands.* London: Hurst & Blackett, 1887.

103. Napier, H. D. *Lord Napier of Magdala: a memoir.* London: E. Arnold, 1927.

104. Nevill, H. L. *Campaigns on the North-West Frontier.* London: John Murray, 1912.

105. Norris, J. A. *The First Afghan War, 1838–42.* Cambridge: Cambridge University Press, 1967.

106. O'Callaghan, Desmond. *Guns, Gunners and others.* London: Chapman & Hall, 1925.

107. Osanka, Franklin Mark. *Modern Guerilla Warfare.* New York: Free Press of Glencoe, 1962.

108. Philipe, G. W. de Rhe. *A Narrative of the First Burmese War.* Calcutta: Gov't. Printer, 1905.

109. Preston, Adrian, ed. *In Relief of Gordon.* London: Hutchinson, 1967.

110. Preston, Antony and John Major. *Send a Gunboat.* London: Longmans, 1967.

111a. Ransford, Oliver. *The Battle of Majuba Hill: The first Boer war.* London: J. Murray, 1967.

111b. Ransford, Oliver. *The Battle of Spion Kop.* London: John Murray, 1969.

112. Reade, William Winwood. *The Story of the Ashanti Campaign.* London: Smith, Elder, 1874.

113. Rennie, David F. *The British Arms in North China and Japan.* London: J. Murray, 1864 .

114. Roberts, Frederick. *Forty-One Years in India.* London: Bentley, 1897. 2 vols.

115. Royal Commonwealth Society, London. Library. *Subject Catalogue of the Library of the Royal Empire Society, formerly Royal Colonial Institute,* by Evans Lewin. London: Society, 1930–37. 4 vols.

116. Royal United Service Institution, London. *Journal. 1857–* . See also Higham, R., ed., *Consolidated Author and Subject Index to the J.R.U.S.I.* Ann Arbor: University Microfilms, 1965.

117. Royle, Charles. *The Egyptian Campaigns.* London: Hurst & Blackett, 1886. 2 vols.

118. Sacher, Harry. *Israel.* London: Weidenfeld, 1952.

119. Sale, Florentia. *A Journal of the Disasters in Afghanistan; 1841–42.* London: J. Murray, 1843.

120. Sandes, E. W. C. *The Military Engineers in India.* Chatham: Institution of Royal Engineers, 1933. 2 vols.

121. ———. *The Royal Engineers in Egypt and the Sudan.* Chatham: Institution of Royal Engineers, 1937.
121a. Selby, John. *The Boer War.* Edinburgh: James Thin, 1970.
122. Sen, S. N. *Eighteen Fifty-Seven.* New Delhi: Publications Division, Ministry of Information & Broadcasting, Gov't. of India, 1957.
123. Simpson, Donald H. *Biography Catalogue of the Library of the Royal Commonwealth Society.* London: Royal Commonwealth Society, 1961.
124. Snodgrass, John J. *Narrative of the Burmese War.* London: J. Murray, 1827.
125. Society for Army Historical Research, London. *Journal.* Sheffield, 1921– .
126. Stacey, C. P. *Records of the Nile Voyageurs, 1884–1885.* Toronto: the Champlain Society, 1959.
127. Stanley, Henry M. *Coomassie and Magdala: the story of two British campaigns in Africa.* New York: Harper, 1874.
128. Steevens, George Warrington. *With Kitchener to Khartum.* Edinburgh: Blackwood, 1898.
129. Swinhoe, Robert. *Narrative of the North China Campaign of 1860.* London: Smith, Elder, 1861.
130. Swinson, Arthur. *North-west Frontier: people and events, 1839–1947.* London: Hutchinson, 1967.
131. Sykes, Christopher. *Orde Wingate.* London: Collins, 1959.
132. Symons, Julian. *Buller's Campaign.* London: Cresset Press, 1963.
133. Theobald, A. B. *The Mahdiya: a history of the Anglo-Egyptian Sudan, 1881–1899.* London: Longmans, Green, 1951.
134. Thompson, Edward J. *The Other Side of the Medal.* London: L. & V. Woolf, 1925.
135. Vogt, Hermann. *The Egyptian War of 1882.* London: Kegan Paul, 1883.
136. Waley, Arthur. *The Opium War Through Chinese Eyes.* London: Allen & Unwin, 1958.
137. Wallis, Charles B. *West African Warfare.* London. Harrison, 1905.
138. *Wellesley Index to Victorian Periodicals, 1824–1900.* Walter E. Houghton, ed. Toronto: University of Toronto Press, 1966– .
139. Wilkinson, Spenser. *Lessons of the War; Being Comments from Week to Week to the Relief of Ladysmith.* London: Constable, 1900.
140. Wilson, Horace H. *Documents Illustrative of the Burmese War.* Calcutta, 1827.
141. ———. *Narrative of the Burmese war, 1824–26.* London: W. H. Allen, 1852.
142. Wilson, R. D. *Cordon and Seach.* Aldershot: Gale, 1949.
143. Wolseley, Garnet. *Narrative of the War with China.* London: Longmans, 1862.
144. ———. *The Story of a Soldier's Life.* London: Constable, 1903. 2 vols.
145. Woods, Evelyn. *From Midshipman to Field Marshal.* London: Methuen, 1906.

146. Younghusband, George J. *Indian Frontier Warfare*. London: Kegan Paul, 1898.

SUPPLEMENT TO BIBLIOGRAPHY

147. O'Ballance, Edgar. *Malaya: the communist insurgent War, 1948–1960*. Hamden, Conn.: Anchor Books, 1966.

148a. Bruce, George. *Six Battles for India*. London: Arthur Barker, 1969.

148b. Henderson, Ian with Philip Goodhart. *The Hunt for Kimathi* (U.S. title: *Manhunt in Kenya*). London: Hamish Hamilton, 1958.

148c. Martin, C. The Boxer Rebellion. London: Abelard-Schuman, 1968.

149. The Kitchener Papers are located at the Public Record Office.

150. Imperial War Museum lists of manuscript holdings.

151. Reports of the Army Medical Department:
    1880. Appendix 3, *Medical History of the Wars in Afghanistan*.
    1867. Appendix 6. *Medical History of the Abyssinian Expedition*.
    1880. Appendix 4, *Natal and the Transvaal in the Boer War*.

152. Norrie, Colonel W. M. *Official Account of the Military Operations in China, 1900–1901,* London: H.M.S.O., 1903.

153. Elton, Lord. *General Gordon*. London: Collins, 1954.

154. Featherstone, D. *At them with the bayonet! The First Sikh War*. London: Jarrolds, 1968.

155. Gardner, Brian. *Mafeking: a Victorian legend*. London: Cassell, 1966.

156. Hurd, D. *The Arrow War: an Anglo-Chinese confusion, 1856–1860*. London: Collins, 1967.

157. James, Harold, and Denis Sheil-Small. *The Ghurkas*. Harrisburg, Pa.: Stackpole, 1966.

158. Martin, Colonel D. R. *The Postal History of the First Afghan War, 1838–1842*. London: Postal History Society, 1964.

159. Selby, John. *The Paper Dragon: an account of Britain's wars against and relations with China in the nineteenth century*. London: Arthur Barker, 1968.

160. Singh, Brigadier Rajendra. *History of the Indian Army*. New Delhi: Army Educational Stores, 1963.

XII

RESOURCES IN THE DOMINIONS

PART I: BRITISH MILITARY HISTORY
IN SOUTH AFRICA

Neil D. Orpen

The study of British military history in South Africa involves a preliminary semantic problem which has an important bearing on the scope of any research to be undertaken within the present-day Republic of South Africa. The problem is to decide just what the term "British" implies with respect to events in South Africa, where the local population of European descent— at least in the former Cape Colony and Natal—were largely British after 1820 and remained so even until the Statute of Westminster in 1931 clearly established the autonomy of the Union of South Africa, with a distinct South African nationality.

Taking it that in the military sphere the student is concerned primarily with the history of the British Army as such, it will be found that in South Africa two further complications arise as regards source material. The first of these complications stems from the fact that it is almost impossible to make a clear separation between the history of the purely "Imperial" and the Colonial forces. Reasons for this difficulty can be found in the second complication, which is the fact that in virtually no other part of the future Commonwealth was warfare conducted so continuously or on so large a scale as in South Africa. Operations ranged from minor actions to wrest the Cape from the Dutch in 1795 and again in 1806, through numerous Frontier clashes and so-called Kaffir Wars against natives pressing in from the East, or brushes with the Boers, to the disastrous defeat at Isandhlwana in the Zulu War of 1879, followed by rout at the hands of the Boers at Majuba in 1881 and the full-scale three-year South African War of 1899–1902, involving Britain in warfare on a scale she had not known since the days of Napoleon.

Thus it can be seen that in South Africa British troops—in the sense of British Army units—acted as garrisons not merely to defend the country against possible foreign aggression, but even more continuously to guard against armed opposition to Her Majesty's policies within the country itself or along its immediate borders. Such being the case, the Newcastle-Cardwell System, aimed at concentrating British regiments at home from 1868 onwards, could never be fully applied to the Cape Colony, a subject dealt with in detail in the contemporary documents and correspondence in "The Military Defence of South Africa–1867" in the Africana section of the South African Library in Cape Town. British garrison troops were in fact maintained right up until the beginning of World War I, when they were only released as a result of South Africa's offer to replace them with units drawn from the newly constituted Union Defence Force.

Even this step did not spell a final severing of the closest possible links between South Africa and British military history, however, for there were South African units involved as integral parts of a British Division—in France from 1916 until the end of the Great War. There were South African troops fighting in Egypt and Palestine under Allenby and, at one stage, there were British battalions forming part of the South African Infantry brigade on the Western Front.

Thus, though Union and the outbreak of World War I saw the departure of British troops from South Africa, and post-war developments resulted in South Africa also taking over the landward defence of the naval base at Simonstown, very close links between the British and South African forces remained. By 1939 they were tenuous indeed, but World War II, with the North African theatre for so long the only one in which Commonwealth troops were in direct contact with the enemy, once again created conditions in which the history of these different forces became inextricably entangled with one another.

South Africa, in contrast to Australia and New Zealand, made no stipulation against the splitting of her formations under overall British command, with the result that in the East African Campaign on 1940–41, there were South Africans not only among specialist Force troops but also fighting with all the British African Divisions involved; whilst in North Africa, British troops fought under South African command and numerous South African units fought beside or actually as part of British divisions. The process reached a peak in the Italian Campaign during 1944–45, when the British 24th Guards Brigade actually became part of the 6th South African Armoured Division, whilst thousands of South Africans in Engineering and other technical units were completely integrated in the British 8th Army, and even in the American 5th Army.

Bearing the above in mind, a comprehensive study of the British military history in South Africa must therefore take into account that in the old Cape Colony and Natal, Volunteer corps or regiments were founded as long ago as 1855, to relieve Imperial battalions urgently needed for the Crimean War and—shortly afterwards—for the Indian Mutiny. A number of these regiments—like the Natal Carbineers, the Cape Town Rifles, the Cape Field Artillery, Prince Alfred's Guard, the Durban Light Infantry, Natal Mounted Rifles, and the Umvoti Mounted Rifles, exist to this day and their colours are heavy with battle honours earned beside Imperial troops not only in South Africa itself but also in two World Wars. Other units of later foundation have similar records. One or two, such as the Light Horse

Regiment (previously Imperial Light Horse) earned fame on the British side in the South African War and have added to their laurels since then, whilst the Pretoria Regiment, fighting in tanks, became so closely associated with the British 24th Guards Brigade in World War II that—for historical purposes—their records are virtually inseparable over 1944–45.

It nevertheless remains obvious that the main primary sources on British Military History will have to be sought in the United Kingdom, in the records of the War Office or of the individual units concerned. Much local colour and, especially in the case of the Boer War of 1881 and the South African War of 1899–1902, a considerable amount of information will, on the other hand, be found only in South Africa or—more readily in some cases—in authoritative books written or published in that country.

Official documents bearing upon British Military History pure and simple are very rare in South African archives or collections, by reason of their having been returned to England. However, certain despatches to and from the Secretary of State for the Colonies, the Military Secretary's papers, letters from naval and military officers and some other records in the Cape Archives could be profitably studied, whilst research in the Natal Archives at Pietermaritzburg could also be fruitful as far as military operations during the last century are concerned.

The richest source of material is likely to be unearthed in the Transvaal and Orange Free State Archives, in Pretoria and Bloemfontein respectively, for here will be found the "other side of the story" as far as the fighting against the Boers is concerned, without which no history of either the first or second Boer Wars can be complete. An invaluable guide in regard to the war of 1899–1902 can be found in the comprehensive Lists of Sources published in the two completed volumes of Prof. J. H. Breytenbach's *Die Tweede Vryheidsoorlog,* both of which are the result of exhaustive research of both published and unpublished sources in English and Dutch or Afrikaans (10).

Other fruitful sources of information are the first-hand accounts contained in reminiscences of prominent Boers themselves, of which General Christiaan de Wet's *Three Years War* (15), published very shortly after the event, and Colonel Deneys Reitz's famous *On Commando* (36), are both in English. A considerable amount of eye-witness information, not only on this drawn-out conflict but also on earlier campaigns, is also available in the files of South African newspapers, whose contemporary accounts of actions may in a number of cases be closer to the truth than embroidered official accounts written specifically "for the record." *The Cape Argus,* established 1857, and the *Cape Times* (1876) have both been in circulation regularly since their foundation in Cape Town, and *The Diamond Fields Advertiser* has likewise appeared regularly since 1875 in Kimberley, whilst in Natal the *Natal Witness* of Pietermaritzburg dates right back to 1846 and the *Natal Mercury* of Durban is also more than a century old. In the Orange Free State, *The Friend* of Bloemfontein dates back to 1850, and Johannesburg's well-known *Star* first appeared in 1889. These are but a handful of the scores of newspapers, living and extinct, which may be consulted in public libraries and sometimes in excellent privately-owned reference libraries of the papers themselves. They contain a wealth of information on British military operations, often conveniently including complete official despatches, in addition to their own correspondents' reports.

South African units which fought on the British side in the unfortunate conflict of 1899–1902 have in some cases produced authoritative unit histories, making mention of operations involving British units or British formations in which they themselves fought. Fortunately, in almost all cases, these same units saw action in both world wars, with particularly close association with British units in World War II. Their unit histories thus repay study, whilst no British Military History could be complete without reference to the official story of the South African Infantry Brigade in World War I, written by John Buchan under the title of *The History of the South African Forces in France* and relating the events on the Somme, at Ypres, Delville Wood, Marrieres Wood and elsewhere in which the South Africans were involved as an integral part of the 9th (Scottish) Division, which was for much of the time actually commanded by the South African, Major-General Sir Henry T. Lukin.

With respect to World War II, unit histories again contain much useful information on British operations, but an even wider canvas is covered in the two excellent official histories on land operations published by the Union War Histories before its offices closed some years ago. These two volumes, *The Sidi Rezeg Battles* (2) and *Crisis in the Desert* (3) are among the most authoritative yet produced anywhere on the North African Campaign between November 1941 and July 1942, with considerable reference to British units and operations, based on official sources not yet available to the public.

On the East African Campaign, which covers the conquest of Italian Somaliland and the liberation of Abyssinia in 1940–41, another volume has recently been completed under the title of *East African and Abyssinian Campaigns* (30). Written by Commandant Neil Orpen on behalf of the S.A. Ex-Services National Council, with access to all official records and with active assistance from senior British and South African officers, this history is primarily South African, but nevertheless forms an essential part of any study of operations conducted by the British under Middle East Command in the early days of the war against Italy.

During the Second World War South Africa provided a fairly considerable quantity of arms and other supplies to Britain and the Allies including motor vehicles, guns and vast quantities of ammunition. This was done through the Eastern Group Organization, much of the material going to the Middle East and India. Details can be found in the *Union Yearbook* (56). Details of the Empire Air Training Scheme are probably as available in London as in South Africa.

Going back to earlier times, it will be discovered that records of the Cape Mounted Riflemen, through an unusual set of circumstances, provide some information on the doings of British forces in South Africa even as far back as 1797. This arises from the fact that on the British first occupying the Cape in 1795, they employed and then actually embodied the Hottentot soldiers who had been in the service of the Dutch. Generally known as the Cape Corps or Pandours, these men returned to British service at the second occupation in 1806. They then became known as the Cape Regiment. Their early history was recorded in Richard Cannon's rare *History of the Cape Mounted Riflemen* (1841) and continued up to and beyond the regiment's disbandment as an Imperial unit after 1870, in P. J. Young's *Boot and Saddle* (50). The latter covers the regiment's continued existence as a Colonial unit until its final absorption into the South African Mounted Riflemen, which was the basis of the still existing South African Permanent Force.

It was not the last of the name "Cape Corps," however, and in World War I yet another Cape Corps was raised from among the Cape Coloured people, fighting with distinction against the Turks, under British command. In World War II, the corps rendered yeoman service once more, but this time as part of the South African Forces.

On the Kaffir Wars along the Eastern Frontier, much scattered material may be found in the regimental histories of the relative British Army units themselves. Few official records are available in South Africa, except in cases where the troops participating were almost entirely Colonial, but an invaluable record of conditions and events during the War of the Axe (or Seventh Kaffir War) of 1846–47 has fortunately become available in a Van Riebeeck Society edition of *Buck Adams' Narrative,* written by a private of the 7th. (Princess Royal's) Dragoon Guards, and evidently compiled from notes taken at the time (17).

Thomas Baines' Journal in the same privately printed series devotes three of its eight chapters to the Eighth Kaffir War, covering the period December 1850 to the end of 1851. The book is valuable in that it includes as an Appendix a five-page list of sketches and paintings by this well-known artist with the forces, with their reference numbers in three different collections.

Andrew Geddes Bain, later a renowned road-builder, was in command at Fort Thomson. His day-to-day account of patrol activities in 1836 is preserved in his Military Journal, comprising Chapter IV of the Van Riebeeck Society edition of his *Journals,* which gives a contemporary picture of life and problems facing the British in Kaffraria in those days (22).

Of the Zulu War of 1879, Sir Reginald Coupland's *Zulu Battle Piece* (13) provides an admirable account, complete with bibliography, but it is significant that the Natal Carbineers—as good cavalry as he had ever commanded, according to Lord Chelmsford—do not even figure in the index, though their presence at the Isandhlwana disaster is recorded, as is that of the Natal Native Contingent and the Natal Police, all of whose records could help to throw light on this tragic episode and other aspects of the war. Similarly, of course, the background to the Cameron Highlanders' moves during the Zulu Rebellion in 1906 cannot be properly appreciated without reference to the operations of the Natal militia, whose records are to be found in their own regimental histories and local archives. Many such cases could be cited, but with the subject as a whole still awaiting the true researcher, it is quite impossible to state with any degree of definiteness what volume of information may repose in any particular source or type of source in South Africa.

The truth is, of course, that research within South Africa itself has been primarily concerned with the compilation of histories of distinctly South African units and formations. The history of the British Army has been left to authors and researchers in England or to a very small handful of military enthusiasts in South Africa whose work is not to be found in archives or public records of any nature, and may well be lost to posterity unless the necessary funds and effort can be expended to preserve the results of their individual researches. In this respect, the field for research into British Military History in South Africa is wide open and, with naval and air force history included, it could well involve considerable work over many years.

It is impossible to gauge the volume of material available or worthy of study, but a small inkling of the vastness of the subject may be gained from the fact that the Johannesburg Library's "Catalogue of British Regimental Histories with notes on their Service in Africa," compiled in 1953, runs to 64 pages, and many times that number of volumes, many of which include details of service in South Africa dating right back to the First British Occupation of 1795. The subject thus presents a considerable challenge to anyone with the courage to undertake it.

BIBLIOGRAPHY

1. Adler, F. B., A. E. Lorch, and H. H. Curson. *The South African Field Artillery, German East Africa and Palestine, 1915–1919*. Pretoria: Van Schaik, 1958.
2. Agar-Hamilton, J. A. I. and L. C. F. Turner. *The Sidi Rezeg Battles*. Cape Town: Oxford Univ. Press, 1957.
3. Agar-Hamilton, J. A. I. and L. C. F. Turner. *Crisis in the Desert*. Cape Town: Oxford Univ. Press, 1952.
4. Amery, L. S. *The Times History of the War in South Africa*. London, 1900–1909. 6 vols.
5. Anderson, Ken. *Nine Flames*. Cape Town: Purnell, 1964.
6. Bengough, Major-General H. M. *Notes and Reflections on the Boer War*. London: William Clowes, 1900.
7. Birkby, Carel. *Springbok Victory*. Johannesburg: Libertas, 1941.
8. Birkby, Carel, ed. *The Saga of the Transvaal Scottish Regiment*. Cape Town: Timmins, 1950.
9. Blaney, Major A. E. *A Company Commander Remembers*. Pietermaritzburg: Publ. privately, 1963.
10. Breytenbach, Prof. J. H. *Die Tweede Vryheidsoorlog*. Vols. 1 and 2. Cape Town: Nasionale Pers, 1948–49.
11. Burleigh, B. *The Natal Campaign*. London: Chapman & Hall, 1900.

12. Caddell, Captain W. W. *Secret Service in South Africa*. London: Cassell, 1911.
13. Coupland, Sir Reginald. *Zulu Battle Piece*. London: Collins, 1948.
14. Curson, Dr. H. H. *The History of the Kimberley Regiment*. Kimberley, 1963.
15. De Wet, General Christiaan. *Three Years' War*. London: Constable, 1902.
16. Fielding, W. L. *With the 6th. Div*. Pietermaritzburg: Shuter & Shooter, 1946.
17. Gordon-Brown, A., ed. *Buck Adams' Narrative*. Cape Town: Van Riebeeck Society, 1941.
18. Hattersley, Prof. A. E. *Carbineer—History of the Royal Natal Carbineers*. Aldershot: Gale & Polden, 1950.
19. Hart, Lieutenant-General Sir Reginald. *Standing Orders for the South Africa Command*. London: H.M.S.O., 1912.
20. Kennedy, R. F., ed. *Journal of Residence in Africa, 1842–1853,* by Thomas Baines. Vol. II. Cape Town: Van Riebeeck Society, 1964.
21. Klein, Harry. *Springboks in Armour*. Cape Town: Purnell, 1965.
22. Lister, Margaret, ed. *Journals of Andrew Geddes Bain*. Cape Town: Van Riebeeck Society, 1949.
23. Lee, A. *The History of the Tenth Foot*. Vol. II. Aldershot: Gale & Polden, 1911.
24. Lorch, Major A. E. *A Story of the CMR and 1st. Regiment, S.A. Mounted Riflemen*. Cape Town, 1926.
25. McKenzie, A. G. *The Dukes, 1855–1956*. Cape Town: Regimental Council, Duke of Edinburgh's Own Rifles, 1956.
26. Orpen, Neil. *Gunners of the Cape*. Cape Town: Cape Field Artillery Regimental History Committee, 1965.
27. Orpen, Neil. *Prince Alfred's Guard*. Cape Town: Books of Africa, 1967.
28. Orpen, Neil. Articles in *The Encyclopedia of South Africa*.
29. Orpen, Neil. *The Cape Town Highlanders*. Cape Town: Cape Town Highlanders Trustees, 1970.
30. Orpen, Neil. *East African and Abyssinian Campaigns*. Cape Town: Purnells, 1968.
31. Parry, D. H. *The Death or Glory Boys*. London: Cassell, 1899.
32. Paton, Colonel G., Colonel F. Glennie, and Colonel W. Penn-Symons. *Historical Records of the 24th. Regiment*. London: Simpkin, Marshall, 1892.
33. Pieterse, H. I. C. *Oorlogsavonture van Generaal Wynand Malan*. Cape Town: Nasionale Pers, 1941.
34. Pilcher, Col. T. D. *Some Lessons from the Boer War, 1899–1902*. London: Isbister, 1903.
35. Preller, Dr. G. S. *Scheepers se Dagboek*. Nasionale Pers, 1940.
36. Reitz, Colonel Deneys. *Commando*. Bloemfontein: White, 1929.
37. Robley, Lieutenant-Colonel H. G. and P. J. Aubin. *History of the 1st Battalion, Princess Louise's Argyll & Sutherland Highlanders*. Cape Town: Publ. privately, 1883.

38. Rosenthal, Eric. *General de Wet*. Johannesburg: Central News.
39. Schmidt, H. W. *With Rommel in the Desert*. Durban: Albatross, 1950.
40. Simpkins, Major B. G. *Rand Light Infantry*. Cape Town: Timmins, 1965.
41. Stalker, J. *The Natal Carbineers*. Pietermaritzburg: Davis, 1912.
42. Strydom, Dr. C. J. S. *Kaapland en die Tweede Vryheidsoorlog*. Cape Town, Nasionale Pers, 1943.
43. Tomasson, W. H. *With the Irregulars in the Transvaal and Zululand*. London: Remington, 1881.
44. Tungay, Captain R. W. *The Fighting Third*. Cape Town: Unie-Volkspers, 1947.
45. Turner, L. C. F., H. R. Gordon-Cumming, and J. E. Betzler. *War in the Southern Oceans*. Cape Town: Oxford Univ. Press, 1961.
46. Viljoen, General Ben. *My Reminiscences of the Anglo-Boer War*. London: Hood, Douglas and Howard, 1902.
47. Williams, B. *Record of the Cape Mounted Riflemen*. London: Causton, 1909.
48. Wood, Walter. *The Rifle Brigade*. London: Richards, 1901.
49. Wood, Walter. *The Northumberland Fusiliers*. London: Richards, 1901.
50. Young, P. J. *Boot and Saddle*. Cape Town: Maskew Miller, 1955.
51. *A Militia Unit in the Field: 6th Lancashire Fusiliers*. Publ. for private circulation.
52. *Centurions of a Century*: 12th. or Suffolk Regiment. In Africana Section of S. A. Library, Cape Town.
53. *Catalogue of British Regimental Histories with Notes on Their Service in South Africa*. Johannesburg Public Library, 1953. (Note: This catalogue of 64 pages contains details of ALL regimental histories of British units insofar as the publications are available in the Johannesburg Public Library. More have undoubtedly been added since 1953.)
54. *Official Record of the Guards' Brigade in South Africa*. London: Keliher, 1904.
55. *The Military Defence of South Africa*. Documents and correspondence relating to the proposed withdrawal of troops. Cape Town, 1867.
56. *The Union Yearbook*, No. 23, 1946, Chapter XXIX.
57. South Africa. General Staff. *The Union of South Africa and the Great War, 1914–1918*. Pretoria, 1924.
58. Martin, A. C. *The Durban Light Infantry, 1854–1960*. Durban, 1969. 2 vols.

NEWSPAPERS AND PERIODICALS:

Cape Times, Cape Argus.	Cape Town.
The Star.	Johannesburg.
Natal Witness.	Pietermaritzburg.
Natal Mercury.	Durban.

Diamond Fields Advertiser.   Kimberley.
Friend.   Bloemfontein.
Commando. (Official journal of the S.A. Defence Force) Pretoria.

ARCHIVES:
The Provinces of the Republic each have their own archives, with a central archives also, in Pretoria. It is therefore advisable to apply direct to the Chief Archivist at Cape Town (Cape Province), Pietermaritzburg (Natal), Bloemfontein (Orange Free State) or Pretoria (Transvaal) for details of archives available. The following is merely an indication of what may be found, but considerable research may be required.

CAPE ARCHIVES:
Co. 1/16. 5111–5128. Letters from Naval and Military Officers.
DEF. 1/34. Miscellaneous published Defence Papers and Cape Mounted Riflemen files.
    Four volumes of Imperial Forces HQ, D.A.G. and D.Q.M.G. papers.

TRANSVAAL ARCHIVES:
Commandant-General Archives (K–G) and correspondence files (G.R.)
Dr. W. J. Leyds Archives (re S.A. War, 1899–1902)
Prof. S. P. Engelbrecht collection (ditto)
Gen. S. W. Burger   "   "
Dr. G. S. Preller   "   "
Gen. J. H. de la Rey   "   "

PART II: CANADIAN AND BRITISH
MILITARY HISTORIOGRAPHY

J. Mackay Hitsman

Canadian military history, from the British conquests of Acadia and New France during the eighteenth century until the conclusion of the Second World War of the twentieth century, is primarily an imperial story. Prime responsibility for defence against a foreign aggressor devolved upon British military and naval forces that took their direction from Whitehall. A different trend only began to develop after the creation of a Canada-United States Permanent Joint Board on Defence in 1940. Since the creation of the North Atlantic Treaty Organization in 1948, responsibility for planning the defence of North America has been assumed by a Canada-United States Regional Planning Group.

The strategy employed during the years leading to the withdrawal of British troops from Quebec in 1871 is set forth in the present writer's *Safeguarding Canada, 1763–1871* (10). Colonel C. P. Stacey's *Canada and the British Army, 1846–1871* (15) is likely to remain the definitive account of British efforts, finally crowned with success, to withdraw the costly garrisons of regular troops from Ontario, Quebec, New Brunswick, and Prince Edward Island. The story of the later attempts to get Canada to contribute to the defence of the rest of the British Empire is best told by Richard A. Preston in *Canada and "Imperial Defense" 1867–1919* (14). Donald C. Gordon's similar study is less comprehensive in scope (4). Although British troops were withdrawn from Halifax and Esquimalt in 1906 and the Royal Navy's dockyards were transferred to Canadian control in 1910 and 1911, it was agreed that British warships might continue to use these facilities and that naval ordnance and stores might be stockpiled there for use in the event of war (22). With certain exceptions during the course of the Great War, 1914–1919 (2), the munitions requirements for Canada's own tiny armed forces continued to be most economically met by direct purchases from British stocks. Following the outbreak of the Second World War, large British orders were placed in North America. Manufacture was assisted by a joint Inspection Board of the United Kingdom and Canada (7). Official histories of Canada's military and naval forces describe Anglo-Canadian cooperation in imperial defence (12, 13, 16, 17, 22 and 23). Gerald S. Graham's *Empire of the North Atlantic* covers the whole period from a

330

more purely naval point of view, but he has not nearly enough to say about the freshwater fleets that once plied the "inland lakes of Canada" (6). All of the above volumes contain bibliographies and/or footnote references to all the detailed articles or short studies that may be considered authoritative and worthy of notice.

Special reference must be made to George F. G. Stanley's extremely interesting and well written survey volume *Canada's Soldiers: the military history of an unmilitary people* (20). Yet readers should realize that Stanley took a calculated risk when he accepted the findings of certain earlier Canadian military historians. These "Saturday Night Soldiers" were enthusiastic and prolific, but they had not been trained to evaluate their source material. Some of their opinions have been proved incorrect by the present small group of capable military historians, and other statements must be suspect until shown to be otherwise. Such remarks do not apply, of course, to the confidential study that Major-General Sir James Carmichael-Smyth, R.E., submitted to the Duke of Wellington in 1826 (1).

Nowadays students are better served in Canada. The Library of the Depatment of National Defence in Ottawa holds virtually complete sets of British *Army* and *Navy Lists,* copies of most British military and naval works of reference and most of the many autobiographical books written by British officers who were in North America during the late eighteenth and early nineteenth centuries. In addition to its own holdings, the National Library of Canada in Ottawa maintains a master card index of all books held in Canadian libraries, and these may generally be borrowed on inter-library loan. The most likely libraries to interest the student of military history are those of the Royal Canadian Military Institute in Toronto, the Royal Military College of Canada and Queen's University at Kingston, McGill University in Montreal, the University of Toronto and the Toronto Public Library. These institutions and certain provincial archives (particularly that of Nova Scotia at Halifax) hold manuscripts relating to the service of the British Army and Royal Navy in the part of North America that is now Canada. Such holdings are listed at the Public Archives of Canada in Ottawa, where, naturally enough, the bulk of manuscript holdings are to be found.

The accumulated records of the British forces stationed in Canada during the eighteenth and nineteenth centuries were turned over to the Public Archives when the garrisons left. Included are volumes relating to the Provincial Marine, which was operated on the Great Lakes and Lake Champlain by the Q. M. G. Department of the British Army in North America, and to the Royal Navy which absorbed it during the War of 1812. These records are generally known as the "C" Series and form part of Record Group 8. Also in this group are the Admiralty Lake Service Records, 1814–1833, the Admiralty Pacific Station Records, 1858–1903, and copies of various reports on Canadian defence. Record Group 7 consists of the records of the Governor General's Office. Record Group 9 contains the records of the Canadian Department of Militia and Defence, certain of which relate to Anglo-Canadian military matters generally and to imperial defence in particular. Similar records of the succeeding Department of

National Defence are being gathered into a Record Group 24. Manuscript Groups 23 and 24 consist of odd-lots of private papers, many of which concern British military or naval personalities. Manuscript Group 24 also contains "Lake Service Letters Received, 1815–1817 (F. 25)," covering the post-war demobilization period leading to the Rush-Bagot Convention.

Over the years the Public Archives of Canada have acquired microfilm or transcripts of British documents relating to Canada which are in the Public Record Office in London, England. Most of the official correspondence is in the Colonial Office papers, because it was between governors (who were also soldiers) and a political Secretary of State for War and the Colonies. The correspondence is arranged by colony and is held as Manuscript Group 11. C. O. 43. Entitled "Entry Books, Canada," it includes copies of what would now be considered TOP SECRET instructions to the governors of Canada; these are not to be found in the Governor General's Papers. The most useful copies of War Office Papers are in-letters from North America (W.O.1) and monthly strength returns of regular troops (W.O.17). Microfilm of Despatches from naval Commanders-in-Chief of the North America and West Indies Stations, and Captain's Letters from the "inland lakes of Canada" are in Admiralty 1 Series. The growing mass of Admiralty and War Office Papers is held as Manuscript Group 12. Students would be well advised to obtain printed Preliminary Inventories of the material in the Public Archives relevant to their needs.

Students might check through the quarterly *Canadian Historical Review,* the annual reports of the Canadian Historical Association, and issues of the *Canadian Defence Quarterly* (1923–1939) and of the *Canadian Army Journal* (1946–1964) for possible leads, bearing in mind the fact that some of the articles therein are unsound.

In conclusion it may be safely stated that detailed studies are needed for the entire period. Probably the greatest lack is a good military study of the British defence of Canada during the American Revolution, similar in approach to Colonel Stacey's account of the capture of Quebec in 1759 (18) and the present writer's volume on the War of 1812 (9).

BIBLIOGRAPHY

1. Carmichael, Sir James, ed. *Precis of the Wars in Canada, from 1755 to the Treaty of Ghent in 1814. With Political and Military Reflections.* By the late Maj.-Gen. Sir James Carmichael-Smyth, London: Ginsley Brothers, 1862.
2. Carnegie, David. *The History of Munitions Supply in Canada, 1914–1918.* London: Longmans, Green & Co., 1925.
3. Glover, Richard A. *Peninsular Preparation: The Reform of the British Army, 1795–1809.* Cambridge, England: Cambridge University Press, 1963.

4. Goodspeed, Lieutenant-Colonel D. J. *The Armed Forces of Canada, 1867–1967*. Ottawa: Queen's Printer, 1967.
5. Gordon, Donald C. *The Dominion Partnership in Imperial Defence, 1870–1914*. Baltimore, Maryland: Johns Hopkins University Press, 1965.
6. Graham, Gerald S. *Empire of the North Atlantic: The Maritime Struggle for North America*. Toronto: University of Toronto Press, 1950.
7. Hitsman, J. Mackay. *Military Inspection Services in Canada, 1855–1950*. Ottawa: Queen's Printer, 1962.
8. ———. "How Successful was the 100th Royal Canadians?" *Military Affairs*, XXXI, No. 3, Fall 1967, pp. 139–145.
9. ———. *The Incredible War of 1812: A Military History*. Toronto: University of Toronto Press, 1965.
10. ———. *Safeguarding Canada, 1763–1871*. Toronto: University of Toronto Press, 1967.
11. Kealy, J. D. F., and E. C. Russell. *A History of Canadian Naval Aviation*. Ottawa: Queen's Printer, 1967.
12. Nicholson, Colonel G. W. L. *Official History of the Canadian Army in the First World War, Canadian Expeditionary Force, 1914–1919*. Ottawa: Queen's Printer, 1962.
13. ———. *Official History of the Canadian Army in the Second World War*. Vol. II. *The Canadians in Italy, 1943–45*. Ottawa: Queen's Printer, 1956.
14. Preston, Richard A. *Canada and "Imperial Defense": a study of the origins of the British Commonwealth's defense organization, 1867–1919*. Durham, N. C.: Duke University Press, 1967.
15. Stacey, Colonel C. P. *Canada and the British Army 1846–1871: a study in the practice of responsible government*. London: Longmans, Green, & Co., 1936. Revised Edition, Toronto: University of Toronto Press, 1963.
16. ———. *Official History of the Canadian Army in the Second World War*. Vol. I. *Six Years of War: the Army in Canada, Britain and the Pacific*. Ottawa: Queen's Printer, 1955.
17. ———. *Official History of the Canadian Army in the Second World War*. Vol. III. *The Victory Campaign: the operations in North-West Europe, 1944–1945*. Ottawa: Queen's Printer, 1960.
18. ———. *Quebec, 1759: the siege and the battle*. Toronto: The Macmillan Company of Canada, 1959.
19. ———. *Records of the Nile Voyageurs 1884–1885: the Canadian Voyageur Contingent in the Gordon Relief Expedition*. Toronto: The Champlain Society, 1959.
20. Stanley, George F. G. *Canada's Soldiers: the military history of an unmilitary people*. Toronto: The Macmillan Company of Canada, 1954. Revised edition, 1960.
21. Thorgrimsson, Thor and E. C. Russell. *Canadian Naval Operations in Korean Waters*. Ottawa: Queen's Printer, 1965.

22. Tucker, Gilbert N. *The Naval Service of Canada: its official history.* Ottawa: Queen's Printer, 1952. 2 vols.

23. Wood, Lieutenant-Colonel H. F. *Strange Battleground: official history of the Canadian Army in Korea.* Ottawa: Queen's Printer, 1966.

PART III: AUSTRALIAN AND BRITISH

MILITARY HISTORY—A NOTE

Robin Higham*

Those studying British military history will find that the isolated continent of Australia provided little of interest in terms of military history outside the usual colonial model until the First World War. It is true that there were garrisons down under and that there were the usual problems of colonial government. Then came Australian participation in the Sudan in 1885, in the Boer War and in the two World Wars, Korea and Vietnam.

The obvious place to start is with the indefatigable C. E. Dornbusch's *Australian Military Bibliography* of 1963 (38).

PERIODICALS. The best are the Australian *Army Journal* which is an official publication started in 1948, the *Australian Military Journal* founded in 1911, but closing in 1916, and *Stand-To* originating in 1956. The latter is the journal of the Australian Capital Territory Branch of the Returned Servicemen's League. It frequently features historical articles and reminiscences by Australians who served at all levels. It occasionally has essays by outside scholars. Its book reviews are generally useful, and from time to time it carries obituaries of leading Australian military figures. Other journals are to be found in Dornbusch (pp. 21, 31, and 63).

OFFICIAL HISTORIES. An Australian team led by C. E. W. Bean set the style for many other official histories with a series of readable volumes on World War I (1–15) which in themselves set standards for the Second World War historians. What made the Australian contribution distinctive was the approach. On the one hand there was a breadth of view, which had only previously existed in the little known Japanese volumes on the Russo-Japanese War and which provided for works dealing not only with the fighting fronts but also with the home. On the other hand there was the technique of comparing the reports of commanders with what witnesses in the front lines had observed and noted. Moreover, in the First World War Australians served very closely alongside British units in Gallipoli and

---

* A two-years' search by correspondence failed in spite of the help of numerous persons both within and without Australian academia to produce an author for this section. Therefore, the Editor, with great reluctance, undertook the task.

Palestine as well as on the Western Front. The volumes in the series, including both the medical and the special photographic tomes, have more feel for the war than the equivalent British works. In both Bean's *Official History of Australia in the War of 1914–1918* (1–15) and Long's *Australia in the War 1939–45* (16–37), the same technique was evolved of integrating the volumes on each service into the general pattern, a model which the British histories of World War II followed.

Disappointingly, there has been little written otherwise about Australian military history. T. B. Millar of the Australian National University has provided some very condensed background in his *Australia's Defence* (40), but it is more concerned with current Australian policy than with history and the same is true of his work on the impact of Britain's withdrawal from Asia (41). Sir Frederick Shedden, a retired permanent under-secretary at the Ministry of Defence is writing a history of Australian defence policy, G. L. Macandie (44) and F. M. McGuire (45) have books on the Royal Australian Navy and George Odgers, one of the official historians, an illustrated history of the RAAF (46).

Owing to the fact that Australia denuded her forces in peacetime and had a very sparse military establishment, she had few officers who reached high rank in wartime, either in 1914–18 or 1939–45. In the First World War the most important of these was Sir John Monash, whose success seems in part to have been due to the fact that he was not a regular but a civilian engineer. Thus there are few memoirs of note, though these would be most useful as giving a non-English slant on many British operations and personalities.

Possible sources of help are the Military Historical Society of Australia in Melbourne and the Royal Australian Historical Society (8 Young Street, Sydney). It is believed, however, by those down under that much of the material relating to Australian military and naval history is lodged in the Public Record Office or in the War Office and Admiralty archives in London.

One aspect of military history worth noting—the Returned Serviceman's League—is in G. L. Kristianson's *The Politics of Patriotism* (39).

RESEARCH NEEDED. There is the possibility that Anglo-Australian defence arrangements would prove a fruitful study with plenty of untapped material to be found in the Australian Parliamentary debates and reports. In a land where a spade was often called a spade in public, discussion was frequently franker and less beclouded than in Britain. Australian reaction to Jellicoe's 1919 proposals for a British Pacific Fleet largely composed of aircraft carriers might be a fruitful starting point. The whole question of the standardization of weapons and the opening of manufacturing facilities down under had a direct relationship to British defence problems, especially after war broke out in Europe in 1939 and the Japanese began at the same time to threaten Singapore and thus Australia itself. Sociological studies of the officer corps of all three Services and the exchange patterns with British officers and schooling in Britain would also probably yield material of interest, as would a contrast of Australian attitudes towards authority and discipline with those of English other ranks.

BIBLIOGRAPHY

OFFICIAL HISTORY OF AUSTRALIA IN THE WAR OF
1914–1918 (General Editor: C. E. W. Bean). All items published by
the Australian War Memorial, Canberra.

1. Vol. I. C. E. W. Bean. *The Story of Anzac. From the outbreak of war to the end of the first phase of the Gallipoli campaign, May 4, 1915* (1921).
2. Vol. II. C. E. W. Bean. *The Story of Anzac. From May 4, 1915 to the Evacuation of the Gallipoli Peninsula* (1924).
3. Vol. III. C. E. W. Bean. *The Australian Imperial Force in France 1916* (1929).
4. Vol. IV. C. E. W. Bean. *The Australian Imperial Force in France 1917* (1933).
5. Vol. V. C. E. W. Bean. *The Australian Imperial Force in France During the Main German Offensive, 1918* (1937).
6. Vol. VI. C. E. W. Bean. *The Australian Imperial Force in France During the Allied Offensive, 1918* (1942).
7. Vol. VII. H. S. Gullett. *The Australian Imperial Force in Sinai and Palestine 1914–1918* (1923).
8. Vol. VIII. F. M. Cutlack. *The Australian Flying Corps in the Western and Eastern Theatres of War 1914–1918* (1923).
9. Vol. IX. Arthur W. Jose. *The Royal Australian Navy 1914–1918* (1928).
10. Vol. X. S. S. Mackenzie. *The Australians at Rabaul. The Capture and Administration of the German Possessions in the Southern Pacific* (1927).
11. Vol. IX. Ernest Scott. *Australia During the War* (1936).
12. Vol. XII. *Photographic Record of the War. Reproductions of Pictures taken by the Australian Official Photographers . . . and others.* Annotated by C. E. W. Bean and H. S. Gullett (1923).

THE AUSTRALIAN ARMY MEDICAL SERVICES IN THE WAR
OF 1914–1918.

13. Vol. I. Part I: A. G. Butler. *The Gallipoli Campaign.* Part II: R. M. Downes. *The Campaign in Sinai Palestine.* Part III: F. A. Maguire and R. W. Cilento. *The Occupation of German New Guinea* (1930).
14. Vol. II: A. G. Butler. *The Western Front* (1940).
15. Vol. III. A. G. Butler. *Special Problems and Services* (1943).

AUSTRALIA IN THE WAR OF 1939–45. All items published by the
Australian War Memorial, Canberra:

SERIES 1 (ARMY)
16. I. Gavin Long. *To Benghazi* (1952).

17. II. Gavin Long. *Greece, Crete and Syria* (1953).
18. III. Barton Maughan. *Tobruk and El Alamein* (1967).
19. IV. Lionel Wigmore. *The Japanese Thrust* (1957).
20. V. Dudley McCarthy. *South-West Pacific Area—First Year* (1959).
21. VI. David Dexter. *The New Guinea Offensives* (1961).
22. VII. Gavin Long. *The Final Campaigns* (1963).

SERIES 2 (NAVY)
23. I. G. Hermon Gill. *Royal Australian Navy, 1939–42* (1957).
24. II. G. Hermon Gill. *Royal Australian Navy, 1942–45* (1969).

SERIES 3 (AIR)
25. I. Douglas Gillison. *Royal Australian Air Force, 1939–42* (1962).
26. II. George Odgers. *Air War Against Japan, 1943–45* (1957).
27. III. John Herington. *Air War Against Germany and Italy, 1 1939–43* (1954).
28. IV. John Herington. *Air Power Over Europe, 1944–45* (1963).

SERIES 4 (CIVIL)
29. I. Paul Hasluck. *The Government and the People, 1939–41* (1952).
30. II. Paul Hasluck. *The Government and the People, 1942–45* (1970).
31. III. S. J. Butlin. *War Economy, 1939–42* (1955).
32. IV. S. J. Butlin. *War Economy, 1942–45* (in preparation).
33. V. D. P. Mellor. *The Role of Science and Industry* (1958).

SERIES 5 (MEDICAL)
34. I. Allan S. Walker. *Clinical Problems of War* (1952).
35. II. Allan S. Walker. *Middle East and Far East* (1953).
36. III. Allan S. Walker. *The Island Campaigns* (1957).
37. IV. Allan S. Walker and others. *Medical Services of R.A.N. and R.A.A.F.* (1961).

ADDITIONAL BIBLIOGRAPHY

38. Dornbusch, C. E. *Australian Military Bibliography.* Cornwallville, N.Y.: Hope Farm Press, 1963.
39. Kristianson, G. L. *The Politics of Patriotism.* Canberra: Australian National University Press, 1966.
40. Millar, T. B. *Australia's Defence.* Melbourne: Melbourne University Press, 1968.
41. Millar, T. B. *Britain's Withdrawal from Asia: its implications for Australia.* Canberra: Australian National University Press, 1968.
42. *The Australian National Biographical Dictionary* (in process).
43. Moorehead, Alan. *Gallipoli.* London: Hamilton, 1967. (re-issue)
44. Macandie, G. L. *The Genesis of the Royal Australian Navy.* Sydney, 1949.

45. McGuire, F. M. *The Royal Australian Navy: its origin, development, and organization.* Melbourne: Oxford University Press, 1949.
46. Odgers, George. *The Royal Australian Air Force: an illustrated history.* Sydney: Ure Smith, 1965.
47. Vazenry, G. R. *Australian Military Forces: reorganization (and historical notes).* Melbourne: Military History Society of Australia, 1967.
48. Rhodes James, Robert. *Gallipoli.* London: Batsford, 1965.
49. Roskill, Captain S. W. *Naval Policy between the Wars, I. The Period of Anglo-American Antagonism, 1919–1929.* London: Collins, 1968.
50. Hall, H. Duncan. *Commonwealth: a history of the British Commonwealth of Nations.* Princeton, New Jersey: van Nostrand, 1969.

PART IV: A NOTE ON NEW ZEALAND

MILITARY HISTORY

*Robin Higham**

Having been founded in a rather different manner from Australia, New Zealand enjoyed very little military history from the colonial period until the end of the nineteenth century. Like Australia she was in an isolated part of the world and largely protected from external problems by the combination of the Foreign Office and the Admiralty in London. But several decades of peace ended with New Zealand participation in the Boer War, the official account of which was not, however, produced until 1949 (1). There followed widespread action in the First and Second World Wars.

Despite the closeness to Australia, Bean's work there apparently had little influence in New Zealand. The history of the First World War was the standard sort on the British model (2–6). And even when the history of the Second World War came to be written, as Walker notes (78), there was little influence from across the Tasman Sea—the project came into being and grew by itself (7–76).

While information on other than official military history in New Zealand remains scattered, for the historian of British military affairs the New Zealand official series provides an additional perspective and its use is much to be recommended.

BIBLIOGRAPHY

SOUTH AFRICAN WAR (1899–1902)

1. Hall, D. O. W. *The New Zealanders in South Africa, 1899–1902.* 1949.

FIRST WORLD WAR. There were 5 official or semi-official histories of New Zealand's part in the 1914–1918 war.
2. Vol. I. Waite, Major F. *The New Zealanders at Gallipoli.* 1919.

* Like the Australian section, this was to have been written by a native; unfortunately, press of other work made it necessary for the Editor to add this strictly limited contribution.

3. Vol. II. Stewart, Colonel H. *The New Zealanders in France, 1916–1919.* 1921.
4. Vol. III. Powles, Lieutenant-Colonel C. G. *The New Zealanders in Sinai and Palestine.* 1922.
5. Vol. IV. Drew, Lieutenant H. T. B., ed. *The War Effort of New Zealand.* 1923.
6. Studholme, Lieutenant-Colonel J., comp. *Some Records of the New Zealand Expeditionary Force.* (Unofficial, but based on official records.) 1928.

SECOND WORLD WAR. The following publications were prepared by the War History Banch, Department of Internal Affairs, Wellington, New Zealand.

7. *New Zealand Official War Histories.* (*1939–1945*).
8. Anson, T. V. *New Zealand Dental Services.* (1960).
9. Baker, J. V. T. *War Economy.* 1965.
10. Bates, P. W. *Supply Company.* 1960.
11. Borman, C. A. *Divisional Signals.* 1954.
12. Burdon, R. M. *24 Battalion.* 1953.
13. Cody, J. F. *21 Battalion.* 1953.
14. Cody, J. F. *New Zealand Engineers in the Middle East.* 1961.
15. Cody, J. F. *28 (Maori) Battalion.* 1956.
16. Davin, D. M. *Crete.* 1953.
17. Dawson, W. D. *18 Battalion and Armoured Regiment.* 1961.
18. Gillespie, Oliver A. *The Pacific.* 1952.
19. Henderson, J. H., *RMT; Official History of the 4th and 6th Reserve, Mechanical Transport Companies.* 1954.
20. Henderson, J. H. *22 Battalion.* 1958.
21. Kay, R. L. *27 (Machine Gun) Battalion.* 1958.
22. Kay, R. L. *Italy, Vol. II. From Cassino to Trieste.* 1967.
23. Kidson, A. L. *Petrol Company.* 1961.
24. Llewellyn, S. P. *Journey Towards Christmas (Official History of the 1st Ammunition Company, 2nd N.Z.E.F.)* 1949.
25. Loughnan, R. J. M. *Divisional Cavalry.* 1963.
26. McClymont, W. G. *To Greece.* 1959.
27. McKinney, J. B. *Medical Units of 2 N.Z.E.F. in the Middle East and Italy.* 1952.
28. Mason, W. W. *Prisoners of War.* 1954.
29. Murphy, W. E. *The Relief of Tobruk.* 1961.
30. Murphy, W. E. *2nd New Zealand Divisional Artillery.* 1966.
31. Norton, F. D. *26 Battalion.* 1952.
32. Phillips, N. C. *Italy, Vol. I. Sangro to Cassino.* 1957.
33. Pringle, D. J. C., and W. A. Glue. *20 Battalion and Armoured Regiment.* 1957.
34. Puttick, Sir Edward. *25 Battalion.* 1960.
35. Ross, Angus. *23 Battalion.* 1959.
36. Ross, J. M. S. *Royal New Zealand Air Force.* 1955.
37. Scoullar, J. L. *Battle for Egypt; the Summer of 1942.* 1955.

38. Sinclair, D. W. *19 Battalion and Armoured Regiment*. 1954.
39. Stevens, W. G. *Problems of 2 N.Z.E.F.* 1958.
40. Stevens, W. G. *Bardia to Enfidaville*. 1962.
41. Stout, T. D. M. *New Zealand Medical Services in New Zealand and the Pacific*. 1958.
42. Stout, T. D. M. *New Zealand Medical Services in the Middle East and Italy*. 1956.
43. Stout, T. D. M. *War Surgery and Medicine*. 1954.
44. Thompson, H. L. *New Zealanders with the Royal Air Force*: Vol. I (1953); Vol. II (1956); Vol. III (1959).
45. Underhill, M. L., and others. *New Zealand Chaplains in the Second World War*. 1950.
46. Walker, Ronald. *Alam Halfa and Alamein*. 1967.
47. Waters, S. D. *The Royal New Zealand Navy*. 1956.
48. Wood, F. L. W. *The New Zealand People at War, Political and External Affairs*. 1958.

DOCUMENTS. WAR HISTORY BRANCH.

49. Vol. I. *European Theatres from Outbreak of War to June 1941*. 1949.
50. Vol. II. *European Theatres from July 1941 to End of War*. 1951.
51. Vol. III. *Documents Relating to New Zealand's Participation in the Second World War, 1939–1945*. 1963.
52. *Episodes and Studies, Vols. I and II* (Bound volumes incorporating the following):
53. Clare, B. G. *Early Operations with Bomber Command*. 1950.
54. Dean, H. R. *The Royal New Zealand Air Force in South-East Asia, 1941–42*. 1952.
55. Faircloth, N. W. *New Zealanders in the Battle of Britain*. 1950.
56. Hall, D. O. W. *Women at War*. 1948.
57. Hall, D. O. W. *Prisoners of Germany*. 1949.
58. Hall, D. O. W. *Prisoners of Italy*. 1949.
59. Hall, D. O. W. *Prisoners of Japan*. 1949.
60. Hall, D. O. W. *Coastwatchers*. 1951.
61. Hall, D. O. W. *Escapes*. 1954.
62. Kay, R. L. *Long Range Desert Group in Libya, 1940–1941*. 1949.
63. Kay, R. L. *Long Range Desert Group in the Mediterranean*. 1950.
64. Llewellyn, S. P. *Troopships*. 1949.
65. McGlynn, M. B. *Special Service in Greece*. 1953.
66. McKinney, J. B. *Wounded in Battle*. 1950.
67. Murphy, W. E. *Point 175, The Battle of Sunday of the Dead*. 1954.
68. Ross, J. M. S. *The Assault on Rabaul*. 1949.
69. Smith, E. H. *Guns Against Tanks*. 1948.
70. Thompson, H. L. *Aircraft Against U-Boats*. 1950.
71. Wards, I. McL. *Takrouna*. 1951.
72. Wards, I. McL., and others. *The Other Side of the Hill*. 1952.
73. Waters, S. D. *Achilles at the River Plate*. 1948.

74. Waters, S. D. *German Raiders in the Pacific.* 1949.
75. Waters, S. D. *Leander.* 1950.
76. Whelan, J. A. *Malta Airmen.* 1951.
77. Ross, Rear-Admiral John O'Connell. *The White Ensign in Early New Zealand.* London: Bailey Brothers, 1967.
78. Walker, Ronald. "The New Zealand Second World War History Project." *Military Affairs,* XXXII, No. 4, February 1969, pp. 173–181.

SUPPLEMENT TO BIBLIOGRAPHY

79. Rhodes James, Robert. *Gallipoli.* London: Batsford, 1965.
80. Roskill, Captain S. W. *Naval Policy between the Wars, I. The Period of Anglo-American Antagonism, 1919–1929.* London: Collins, 1968.
81. Hall, H. Duncan. *Commonwealth: a history of the British Commonwealth of Nations.* Princeton, New Jersey: van Nostrand, 1969.

ADDITIONAL BIBLIOGRAPHY

101. On South African logistics in World War II, see *The Union* [of South Africa] *Yearbook,* No. 23., 1946, XXIX.
102. Barclay, Brigadier C. N. *The First Commonwealth Division: the story of the British Commonwealth Land Forces in Korea, 1950–1953.* Aldershot: Gale & Polden, 1954.
103. Beckerling, J. L. *The Medical History of the Anglo-Boer War: a bibliography.* Cape Town: Cape Town University School of Librarianship, 1967.
104. Bourne, Kenneth. *Britain and the Balance of Power in North America, 1815–1908.* London: Longmans, 1967.
105. Carew, Tim. *Korea: the Commonwealth at war.* London: Cassells, 1967. First-hand accounts.
106. Eayrs, James. *In Defence of Canada.* Toronto: University of Toronto Press, 1965. 2 vols.
107. McLin, J. B. *Canada's Changing Defence Policy, 1957–1963: the problems of a middle power in alliance.* Baltimore: The Johns Hopkins Press, 1967.

XIII

THE FIRST WORLD WAR ON LAND

M. J. Williams

In the First World War, the British Army experienced the greatest ordeals and achieved the largest triumphs in its history. Despite enormous casualties from the middle of 1916 to the end of the war (113), the British Army bore the main burden of operations on the Western Front against the bulk of the German Army and in 1918, played the leading role in the Advance to Victory. Moreover, the Army was principally responsible for Turkey's defeat; in Italy it played an important part in accelerating the collapse of Austria-Hungary.

GENERAL BIBLIOGRAPHY. The records of these achievements, unparalleled in British military history, are enormous in volume. Unfortunately there is only one general history of real scholarly value which can introduce the student to the subject—Liddell Hart's *A History of the World War* (71). Even more regrettable is the absence of any adequate bibliographical survey even of secondary sources, although a fine attempt has been made by A. S. White in his *A Bibliography of Regimental Histories of the British Army* (123) to compile one for unit histories.

It is advisable to consult the catalogues and subject indexes of the British Museum to obtain full information on published secondary sources. Further assistance can be obtained from the bibliographies and book lists of the Imperial War Museum (56) and the Ministry of Defence Library (Central and Army), whose monthly and yearly accessions lists are published by H.M.S.O. Useful aids to research are the Parliamentary Debates (98); the Army Lists (124); Army Orders, and the now very rare *Field Service Regulations 1914*. Thus, despite the absence of adequate bibliographical guides, there should be no difficulty in consulting secondary sources.

PRIMARY SOURCES. With regard to primary sources, the position is far from satisfactory. The formerly confidential Army Council Instructions can be used in the Ministry of Defence Library. Although great quantities of Cabinet papers and military records can now be studied in the Public Record Office, many important collections of private papers are not accessible, while large-scale destruction of military records has occurred. Not only have nearly all the personnel records of officers and men been destroyed, but also unit muster-rolls, parade-states and Part I and Part II orders, the general orders of unit commanders and the unit orders recording the granting of leave, postings, casualties and movements of individual soldiers. Furthermore, the records of the War Office, G.H.Q.'s, formations and units now in the Public Record Office are very incomplete. Here Class W.O.900, specimens of destroyed documents, might be noted. Moreover, certain P.R.O./W.O. classes—including court martial records of the Judge Advocate-General, many Irish records and W.O./154 (documents removed from War Diaries)—are closed for a hundred years.

In order to use Cabinet records in the P.R.O., the student must begin by studying the guides published by H.M.S.O. (78) and then the Class Lists in the Public Record Office itself. Since no guides to the W.O classes, the military records in the P.R.O., have yet been published, it is advisable to consult the general *Guide to the Contents of the Public Record Office* (52) and then the W.O. Class Lists in the Public Record Office itself.

An invaluable guide to the location of private papers is the National Register of Archives, whose Bulletins are published by H.M.S.O. Determined efforts are being made by the Imperial War Museum, the Military Archives Centre, King's College, London, Churchill College, Cambridge, and Manchester University to acquire collections, and already an appreciable degree of success has been achieved. But in view of the extensive destruction since 1939 of First World War military records, the Official Military Histories edited by Brigadier-General Sir J. E. Edmonds (29), (based in many cases upon records which have since disappeared), remains and seems likely to remain, indispensable for the study of the period. Why these records did not go to the P.R.O. remains a mystery. CAB 45, which is open to 1938, contains drafts of the Official Histories with the accompanying correspondence about and comments upon them from both senior and junior officers.

JOURNALS. While many service journals such as those of the Royal Artillery, the Royal Engineers and Royal Tank Corps (later Royal Armoured Corps) contain occasional articles of importance, only two are of great value for the whole period. Firstly, the *Army Quarterly* from 1920–1940 contains articles and anonymous reviews by Edmonds (29) and a number of very important articles by one of his assistants, Captain G. C. Wynne (161), on the evolution of the German Defensive Battle. Secondly, the *Journal of the Royal United Service Institution* (see introduction) contains a host of articles by those with experience in the war.

THE HIGH COMMAND. The way in which the Cabinet, the War Cabinet and their Committees, and the General Staff made and carried out war policy can be studied in the main Cabinet records in the Public Record Office, the classes CAB 1, 21, 22, 23 (the War Cabinet), 24, 25 (the

Supreme War Council), 27, 28, 41 and 42, and in the classes of military records W.O. 163 (the records of the Army Council), W.O. 162 (the Adjutant-General) and W.O. 106 (the Directorates of Military Operations and Intelligence).

These must be supplemented by Hankey, *The Supreme Command* (57), an important though reticent study by the Secretary of the War Cabinet and of the Committee of Imperial Defence (C.I.D.), and a number of memoirs and biographies. Roy Jenkin's *Asquith* (67) does not deal adequately with his wartime role and needs to be supplemented by study of Asquith's private papers (131). Lloyd George's *War Memoirs* (79), although unreliable, are also very important and his private papers are now accessible (148). Randolph Churchill's *Derby* (25) and Gollin's study of Milner (46), are both important for their material on the relations between generals and politicians. Unhappily, Sir Winston Churchill's own account, *The World Crisis* (26) must be treated with great caution, especially in its account of the Dardanelles, but Volume III of his son's extensive life will help provide balance here. (See Chapter XIV) *The World Crisis: a criticism* (88) by Maurice, Bacon, Oman, etc., seems hardly worth mentioning now, since nearly all the essays are of little value. No satisfactory study of the work of Kitchener has yet been produced. Both Sir George Arthur's official *The Life of Lord Kitchener* (3a) and Philip Magnus' recent *Kitchener* (84) are quite inadequate, and thus a great gap remains to be filled. It should be noted that the papers of Bonar Law (134), Balfour (132), Austen Chamberlain (137), Carson (136), Crewe (139), and Kitchener (145) are on public repository, while, on conditions, the papers of Milner (151) and Philip Kerr (149) are also accessible.

STRATEGY. The need to support France and the struggle between "Westerners" and "Easterners" dominated the strategy of the war. (See Chapter XV.) Here, in addition to the classes of Cabinet and W.O. records in the Public Record Office already cited, the classes W.O./73, W.O./114, W.O./157 (Intelligence material) and W.O./158 (the correspondence of G.H.Q.'s, H.Q.'s and missions) are relevant. Modern scholarship has so far added little to the accounts of the Chief of the Imperial General Staff 1915–18, Sir William Robertson in *Soldiers and Statesmen* (103) and *From Private to Field Marshal* (102). C. E. Callwell, the Director of Military Operations in the War Office 1914–15, edited the extraordinarily candid *Field Marshal Sir Henry Wilson* (19), and the famous military critic and writer, C. à C. Repington wrote *The First World War* (101), which are classic statements of the case of the "Westerners." However, Liddell Hart, in his *History of the World War* (71), *The British Way in Warfare* (72) and *Through the Fog of War* (73) puts forward ingenious arguments for the "Easterners." The meretricious survey by Paul Guinn, *British Strategy and Politics, 1914–18* (53), adds little that is really new, whereas John Terraine's *The Western Front* (118) is a cogent, if too dogmatic, restatement of the "Westerners" case. The reader may also wish to consult the Robertson Papers (155).

THE WESTERN FRONT. This theatre, where the main mass of the British Army was committed and Germany finally defeated, has attracted most historical attention and British operations have aroused heated controversies, especially over the Somme 1916, Third Ypres 1917 and the reasons for the March Retreat in 1918, that are yet to be resolved.

Here, in addition to the P.R.O. classes already cited, W.O./95, the collection of War Diaries, is indispensable. It might be noted that this Class, like W.O./158, is relevant for operations in all other theatres as well. The Official History, edited by the chief of the military-historical branch of the Committee of Imperial Defense later the Cabinet Office, Brigadier-General Edmonds, formerly Deputy Chief Engineer at G.H.Q., *Military Operations, France and Belgium* (29), now, like all the World War I official histories (63), out of print, is a remarkably detailed work, with full accounts of operations and of casualties down to battalion level and often lower. But, quite apart from inevitable reticences, it is marred by persistent attempts to distort German casualty figures (125), and, in the early 1918 volumes, its criticisms of Lloyd George's alleged failure to provide a sufficient flow of reinforcements and replacements are questionable (31). Further, the operational narrative, in too many cases in the later volumes, is identical with that of the unreliable divisional histories. The most controversial volume is that dealing with Third Ypres, 1917 Volume II (30). Here the compiler, Captain G. C. Wynne, as an objection to the way in which the volume was edited, refused to have his name used upon the title page. Nevertheless, in fairness, the *British* casualty figures quoted are almost certainly genuine. *The Order of Battle* volumes (13) are also important for this and other theatres. Edmonds' Official History is supplemented and to some extent corrected by C. E. W. Bean's Australian Official History, *The Australians in France* (11), which is incredibly detailed.

Turning to the leaders themselves, the work of Sir John French remains to be adequately covered (French's own *1914* (40) is so inaccurate that it can only be mentioned as an "awful warning"), although his son, the Hon. E. G. French, published a number of accounts. But neither *The Life of Field Marshal Sir John French* (41) nor *French Replies to Haig* (42), the main works, are convincing. They are essentially apologiae. A definitive study of Haig has yet to be written though the three main biographies, General Charteris' (Haig's Chief of Intelligence 1915–18) *Field Marshal Earl Haig* (23); Duff Cooper's *Haig* (27); and Terraine's *Douglas Haig* (116) all supplement one another. Charteris himself gives valuable information both on his work as Chief of Intelligence at G.H.Q., 1915–18, and on Haig himself in *At G.H.Q.* (24), though studies of G.H.Q. and Haig's chief advisors, Charteris himself, Kiggell, Lawrence and Dill, remain to be written. Extracts from Haig's papers are in Robert Blake's *The Private Papers of Douglas Haig* (15) but the Haig Papers and Diaries should, if possible, be consulted (143).

It is now possible to consult a number of important collections of private papers—those of Haig's Chief of Staff 1915–18, Sir Launcelot Kiggell

(144); Sir Herbert Lawrence, Haig's Chief of Staff 1918 (146); the Commander of the Fourth Army, Rawlinson (154); the unlucky commander of the Second Army 1915, Smith-Dorrien (156); the great tank expert, Fuller (141); the Fifth Army's Chief artillery advisor, Uniacke (159); and Wynne (161), the main assistant of General Edmonds. Further, the important Grant (142) and Liddell Hart (147) papers may be accessible.

Certain important secondary works cannot be neglected: Plumer's Chief of Staff, "Tim" Harington's *Plumer* (58) and his own *Tim Harington Looks Back* (59); the celebrated Director of Military Operations 1915–18 Maurice's *Life of General Lord Rawlinson* (87); the commander of the Fifth Army until March 1918 Gough's *The Fifth Army* (50); and Gough's eventual successor, Birdwood's *Khaki and Gown* (14) are important biographies of and accounts by Army Commanders. To these must be added the Australian Monash's *War Letters* (93) and J. F. C. Fuller's *Memoirs of an Unconventional Soldier* (43). Classic accounts of Anglo-French military relations are in Sir Edward Spears' *Liaison 1914* (111) and *Prelude to Victory* (112). These can be supplemented by Liddell Hart's *Foch* (74) and Lieutenant-General Sir J. P. du Cane's *Marshal Foch* (28). The most authoritative critique of British tactical methods is G. C. Wynne's *If Germany Attacks* (127).

The distinguished writer C. E. Montague's *Disenchantment* (94) stands out from a great mass of personal accounts as a survey of and commentary upon the conditions of war on the Western Front and the outlook of the fighting troops. Here a useful guide to the personal accounts of junior officers is Cyril Falls's *War Books* (36). Apart from Terraine's work, modern scholarship has added nothing of note. An important critique of some recent works is in Terraine's "Instant History" (117).

In addition to the memoirs of the men at the top and to volumes such as A. J. P. Taylor's *Illustrated History* (115), there are a host of personal memoirs which should be consulted for the light they shed on life as it was seen by ordinary officers and men. Most of the recent scholarly works list these items in their bibliographies for each campaign, and no scholar can neglect works such as Graves's *Goodbye to All That* (51) or Sassoon's *Memoirs* (107, 108), both of which were part of the later anti-war literature, or C. E. Carrington's *A Subaltern's War* (22) or *Soldier from the Wars Returning* (21), the latter of which looks back from the vantage point of experience in another war, or Lord Moran's classic *Courage* (96) and Major Baynes's *Morale* (9). Moreover, there are some classics which are worth reading as literature and are nevertheless useful. In this category must go Wolff's *In Flanders Fields* (126) which started the revival of interest in the 1914 war, Alan Moorehead's *Gallipoli* (95) which is the work of a crack World War II war correspondent bringing the insights of that amphibious conflict to bear, and Brigadier Anthony Farrar-Hockley's *Death of an Army* (37).

There is a serious shortage of General Staff studies of operations and only three appear to be available, based upon Staff Tours—one on Le

Cateau (47), one on the Marne (49), 8th–10th September, 1914, and the other on the crossing of the Aisne in September, 1914 (48); all published by H.M.S.O., 1934–7.

It is regrettable that the report of Lieutenant-General Sir Walter Kirke's Committee, appointed in 1932 to investigate the lessons of the war and largely concerned with the Western Front, has never been published. It was made a confidential document by the former Chief of Staff of the Fourth Army, Sir A. A. Montgomery-Massingberd when C.I.G.S. (75). However it can now be studied in W.O. 33.

GALLIPOLI AND THE DARDANELLES. Second only in importance to the Western Front, as a campaign, is Gallipoli—the great "lost opportunity" of the war, with its tantalizing prospects of a Balkan League and a life-line to Russia. Previously published accounts of the campaign are superseded by Robert Rhodes James's *Gallipoli* (66). But it should be noted that the most authoritative study is Lieutenant-Colonel F. A. Raynfield's unpublished *The Dardanelles Campaign,* now in the Imperial War Museum (100). Modern scholarship is reverting to the anti-Churchillean standpoint of C. E. W. Bean's *The Story of Anzac* (12). For the naval aspect, Arthur J. Marder's *Dreadnought to Scapa Flow* (85) is indispensable (and see Chapter XIV). A number of important collections—the Birdwood (133); Dawnay (140) and Orlo Williams (160) papers—can now be consulted. It should also be noted that the P.R.O. Class CAB/19 contains the complete reports of the Dardanelles Commission set up in 1916 by the government in response to the Parliamentary and public outcry at the Dardanelles failure, with copies of statements, documents and minutes.

In addition to the standard accounts already mentioned, to which, of course, must be added Brigadier Aspinall-Oglander's official volume *Gallipoli* (3), researchers should look at Ashmead-Bartlett's *The Uncensored Dardanelles* (8), General Sir Ian Hamilton's *Gallipoli Diary* (162), Joseph Murray's *Gallipoli as I Saw It* (163) and Aitken's *Gallipoli to the Somme: the recollections of a New Zealand infantryman* (1).

MACEDONIA OR SALONIKA. Although many historians have regretted the "lost opportunity" of Gallipoli, little attention has been paid to Macedonia, condemned by the "Westerners" as a useless "sideshow," and which arose partly because of the declining prospects of the Gallipoli campaign as well as the desire to support Serbia. The need to assist Serbia was realized by Asquith as early as September 1915, and thanks to much co-operation and agreement with the Greek Premier, Venizelos, troop movements to Salonika began at the end of September. Once launched, the pressure of the French government prevented abandonment of the campaign. The British role was, however, subsidiary to that of the French and the Serbs, and London always treated it as a sideshow. While there is a good recent study by Alan Palmer, *The Gardeners of Salonica* (97), still the main reliance must be the discreet official history by Cyril Falls (34). The story of the Germans' "largest internment camp," so-called by the Germans because of the large force that remained idle for nearly three years, 1915–1918, needs more attention from students.

While the "Westerners" condemned the diversion of resources to Salonika, their condemnation of the "sideshows" in the Middle East as distractions from the task of defeating Germany was, and is, much more emphatic, as for instance in Robertson's *Soldiers and Statesmen* (103) and Terraine's *Haig* (116).

PALESTINE. Palestine was the main theatre of war against Turkey because the original aim of ensuring the security of Egypt, ever present in Kitchener's mind and which seemed the more necessary after the Gallipoli failure, became transformed by Murray, the Commander-in-Chief, Egypt, 1916–17, the War Cabinet and Allenby, Commander-in-Chief, 1917–18, into an offensive campaign that, in 1918, destroyed the main Turkish forces.

The campaign as a whole is solidly covered in the official volumes by Sir George MacMunn and Cyril Falls, *Egypt and Palestine* (82), which should be supplemented by Gullett's Australian history (54) and by Falls's brilliant study of Allenby's final offensive, *Armageddon, 1918* (35). It is unfortunate that no study of Sir Archibald Murray, a former C.I.G.S. and G.O.C.-in-C. Egypt, 1916–17, exists. Allenby's career is better covered, with a good biography by one of his former staff officers, Lord Wavell (121), whose *The Palestine Campaign* (122) is the best short account. Colonel Richard Meinertzhagen, the famous intelligence officer, includes an interesting account of his work in his *Army Diary* (90).

LAWRENCE OF ARABIA. There is a vast T. E. Lawrence literature. Apart from his own works (69, 70), there are two main biographies, Liddell Hart's eulogistic *T. E. Lawrence* (76) and the savagely hostile one by Richard Aldington, *Lawrence of Arabia* (2). Private collections that can be consulted for the campaign are those of Dawnay (140) and Chetwode (138); the Robertson-Murray correspondence (152); and the various collections of Lawrence correspondence (68).

MESOPOTAMIA. Mesopotamia was another "sideshow" condemned by "Westerners" and one that contributed little to the defeat of Turkey despite a considerable commitment of troops, although these were largely from the Indian Army. Here again, a campaign, inspired largely by the Admiralty and the India Office's desire to protect the oilfields near the Persian Gulf, and defensive in origin, was transformed by Nixon, Commander-in-Chief in 1916, and Maude, Commander-in-Chief 1916–17, into an offensive campaign that not only gained Baghdad but also, after the Turkish collapse began in September 1918, cleared the whole of Iraq and North-West Persia and even penetrated briefly into Armenia and the Caucasus.

The most recent study is Barker, *The Neglected War* (5), a good introduction. F. J. Moberly's official history, *Mesopotamia* (91) is very thorough, but should be supplemented by A. H. Burne's *Mesopotamia* (18). Despite its lack of importance compared to the Palestine campaign, Mesopotamia is richer in important memoirs and biographies. The Commander of the ill-fated first thrust at Baghdad was captured at Kut. Townshend's *My Campaign in Mesopotamia* (119) is an unreliable apologia and both his biography by his cousin Erroll Sherson, *Townshend of Chitral and Kut* (110) and Barker's recent *Townshend of Kut* (6) are unsatisfactory. But Callwell's *Life of Sir Stanley Maude* (20) is still an indispensable work, as are Maude's successor Sir William Marshall's *Memoirs of Four Fronts* (86); Sir George MacMunn's (responsible for supply, and transport from 1916) *Behind the Scenes in Many Wars* (83); and Sir Aylmer Haldane's *A Soldier's Saga* (55). The Hon. Aubrey Herbert, who took a prominent part in the attempt to bribe the Turks to raise the siege of Kut gives an interesting account of this episode in *Mons, Anzac and Kut* (61).

The full report and papers of the Mesopotamia Commission, set up in August 1916, in response to Parliamentary pressure to investigate the Kut disaster are contained in CAB/19.

THE ITALIAN CAMPAIGN. While Italy was also, in a sense, a "sideshow," the dispatch of British divisions to Italy in November 1917, under the command first of General Sir Herbert Plumer, then of General Lord Cavan, was a necessity as it was imperative to help prop up the crumbling Italian front after Caporetto. Subsequently the British divisions in the mixed Anglo-Italian Tenth Army under Lord Cavan played a large part in the Vittorio Veneto campaign and in the essential crossing of the Piave, which was the final blow to the already disintegrating Austro-Hungarian Army.

However, the campaign has been very thinly covered so far and only the Edmonds' official history *Italy 1915–1919* (32) contains a full accourt. This, however, can be supplemented by General Gathorne-Hardy's (Cavan's Chief of Staff) *A Summary of the Campaign in Italy* (45) and by the P.R.O. classes, W.O. 158, W.O. 106 and W.O. 95.

INTERVENTION IN RUSSIA. Even less well covered than the Italian is the Russian intervention campaign of 1918, whose motives were partly political—a vague hope of assisting the Whites—and partly military—to prevent a possible German occupation of the ports of Murmansk and Archangel with their Allied supply stores. There are few published accounts of value. The works of the G.O.C. at Archangel, Ironside, in his *Archangel 1918–19* (65), Sir Charles Maynard's *Murmansk Venture* (89), the account of the commander of the Murmansk force, and Higham's *Armed Forces in Peacetime* (62) must be noted. Here there is a genuinely neglected campaign needing scholarly attention.

COLONIAL CAMPAIGNS. To a very considerable extent these were the responsibility of Dominion Forces. Thus Australian and New Zealand troops were responsible for the conquest of the German colonies in Australasia and the Pacific (12), while Japanese troops took Tsing Tao (7). The conquest of the German African colonies was mainly due to the efforts of the Union of South Africa, whose Premier, General Botha, organized the conquest of German South-West Africa and the Cameroons, while first Smuts and then Van Deventer cleared German East Africa. Here the South African official history, *The Union of South Africa in the Great War* (120) can be consulted. Nevertheless, British forces were enaged and two official histories have been compiled: Moberly's *Togoland and the Cameroons* (92) and Hordern's incomplete and now lost *East Africa 1914–16* (64). This needs to be supplemented by Meinertzhagen's *Army Diary* (90) and a good recent study, Gardner's *The German East* (44). The accomplished writer Brett Young's *Marching on Tanga* (129) is an interesting memoir of the campaign. Although the African theatre is of comparatively little importance, nevertheless it merits more scholarly attention.

TECHNICAL DEVELOPMENTS. The 1914 War was the first really modern war in British history in which scientists began to have a direct influence upon the battlefield. Yet in spite of this, the topic has not been much explored and has been generally neglected by scholars. Liddell Hart's *The Tanks* (77) is the most authoritative account of the development of the tank and the operations of the Tank Corps. This can be supplemented by Stern's *Tanks 1914–18* (114), an account of tank development and Whitehall battles; and by the Anderson (130), Fuller (141), Stern (157) and Swinton Papers (158). W.O. 158 contains many files on tank development and policy. It might also be noted that CAB 17/167 contains a file on the tank. The actual importance of the tank in military operations is a controversial subject, and Edmonds' final France and Belgium volumes, *1918* Volumes IV and V (29) are very critical of their use. On the other hand, great claims are made for the tank by Liddell Hart's work and by previous Tank Corps histories.

It is very regrettable that no comprehensive history of the Royal Artillery exists, since artillery technique was revolutionised in 1914–18. Lieutenant-Colonel S. W. H. Rawlins, Chief of Staff to Sir Noel Birch, the Chief Artillery Adviser, G.H.Q. France, prepared a typescript history of the development of the R.A. in France. Though this has not been published, a copy is in the Rawlins Papers (153). *The Royal Artillery War Commemoration Book* (105) contains some articles of interest. The story of the development of artillery observation work by the R.F.C. and R.A.F. and their liaison system with the artillery, has also been greatly neglected. Only brief references can be found in the British Official Military History. The main authority on artillery observation work and liaison by the R.F.C. and R.A.F. is Raleigh and Jones', *The War in the Air* (99). Lord Brabazon, who as an R.F.C. officer was a pioneer in the development of aerial photography, has some interesting information on this in his *Brabazon Story* (17).

While the study of the work of the Royal Artillery has been neglected, the Royal Engineers and Signals (at this time a branch of the Royal Engineers) have been much better served. The official *Work of the Royal Engineers in the European War* (106) is most comprehensive.

The development and operational use of the machine-gun can be followed in Seton-Hutchinson's *Machine-Guns* (109) and Baker-Carr's *From Chauffeur to Brigadier* (4). For small arms in general the records of the Hythe School of Musketry are in W.O./140 and a useful guide is H. C. B. Rogers' *Weapons of the British Soldier* (104).

Essential if unspectacular services like the Army Service Corps and Ordnance Services lack major histories. However, Beadon's short *The R.A.S.C.* (10) is useful, as is Forbes's *History of the Ordnance Services* (38); while W.O./111 contains some records of the Ordnance Service.

One revolutionary new weapon, gas, has been well described both as to development and employment by a Director of Gas Services in France, C. H. Foulkes, in *Gas* (39). Here again it should be noted that W.O./142 contains the records of the Directorate of Chemical Warfare. On medical developments see Chapter XXIII.

TRAINING. Although technical developments made possible a tactical revolution between 1914 and 1918, these developments could only be effective if the general state of training was reasonably satisfactory. Training, a topic that awaits a scholarly survey, was, however, a great problem. The training in established methods and the introduction of new ones was made exceedingly difficult by the enormous expansion of the Army. Although by 1916 Army Schools were in existence to teach new methods and the principles and methods of co-operation between arms, and specialist training schools for the different arms had been established, training programmes remained largely in the hands of the divisional commands, as General Sir Ivor Maxse, G.O.C. XVIII Corps, remarked during the Cambrai Inquiry of December 1917 (which is available in W.O. 158). The partial reverse at Cambrai during the German counter-attack was attributed by Maxse, Byng (the Third Army Commander) and G.H.Q. primarily to faulty training of junior officers and other ranks.

Not until 1917 was there a training section of the General Staff at G.H.Q. France, the most important theatre, to prepare manuals and notes for general issue. Further, although the decline in skill with the rifle was inevitable, G.H.Q.'s patronage of Colonel "Ronnie" Campbell's famous bayonet fighting "Circus" did more harm than good. It was necessary to establish, after the Somme, an infantry school at Pont Remi to remind the infantry that the rifle was not an inferior pike.

The War Office itself did not issue a really practical infantry guide, *S.S. 143, Instructions for the Training of Platoons for Offensive Action*, until late 1917. In the meanwhile, to train its infantry for the Somme offensive, the Fourth Army Staff prepared its own pamphlet of 17th May 1916, "The Little Red Book," with unhappy results; while for Messines the Second Army used its own *S.S. 155* (71) a training manual compiled by its engineers.

Infantry training, in particular, suffered a bad set-back with the introduction of the wave-type attack in 1916–17. Reform began in August

1917, but not until the second half of 1918 was infantry training in particular and training in general in a satisfactory state in France, largely thanks to the efforts of the Inspector-General of Training, Sir Ivor Maxse (150), appointed in July 1918. One other point worthy of note was the failure of G.H.Q. France to prepare a suitable manual for defensive warfare until May 1918 (*S.S. 210*). Training at home has been completely neglected. On conscription see Chapter XV.

Here, apart from scattered references in the Official History, Liddell Hart (75); Fuller (43); and Wynne's *If Germany Attacks* (127) and *The Schlieffen Plan* (128) contain information of value. Private collections that should be consulted are those of Maxse himself (150) and Sir Charles Bonham Carter (135), Director of Military Training at G.H.Q. France, 1917–18.

MILITARY THEORY AND LITERATURE. During the war itself, the General Staff strongly supported by G.H.Q. France upheld the long-established Clausewitzian theory of maximum concentration of forces at the decisive point. This view was opposed by the Lloyd George and Churchill or "Easterner" school of 1915–17, which aimed at striking at the "props" mainly in an attempt to minimise the cost in life to Britain.

Further, during the war the Tank Corps in France, whose main spokesman was Fuller, held strongly by 1917 that the *technique* of war was wrong—dependence on the artillery to clear the way for the infantry meant, they held, crippling the scope of the tank, which should have been developed much more fully. But the Tank Corps officers were not "anti-Western" as such.

Only after the war did the theoretical conflict begin in earnest, with the growing attacks of Liddell Hart on Clausewitzian concepts which led him to formulate both his theory of the Indirect Approach and also what was basically an "Easterner" view. Further, Fuller became increasingly critical of the neglect of the tank. A good survey of both Fuller's and Liddell Hart's theories is in Jay Luvaas' *The Education of an Army* (80). The "Westerner" approach is now once again in the ascendant with Terraine its principal spokesman. However, little fresh material has been brought forward by either side since 1945.

RESEARCH. A vast amount of important work remains to be done. The conflicts between the strategic conceptions of the "Easterners" and "Westerners" of what war policy should have been and how operations should have been conducted remains to be decided. Further probing studies are needed in many other spheres. The work and role of the War Office and the General Staff require thorough investigation. The Western Front continues to present many difficult problems—the planning and conduct of the great attrition campaigns of 1916–17, whether or not the Somme and Third Ypres were successes or defeats; the wisdom or unwisdom of the preparations to meet the German offensives of March–April 1918. The role of the tank and the questions of casualties and strengths all have yet to be definitively studied. The work and importance of Haig and his chief assistants at G.H.Q. France require reappraisal on the basis of the new evidence available.

Other fronts and campaigns also need more attention from the scholar. With regard to the Palestine campaign, studies of the work of Allenby and the contributions of his chief staff officers, Sir Louis Bols, Guy Dawnay and Bartholomew are wanted, as is one of Sir Archibald Murray, while no thorough, scholarly study of the Arab revolt and its contribution to Turkish defeat is yet available. Campaigns like Italy and the intervention in Russia in 1918 have been almost completely neglected.

With regard to the technical developments of the war, much remains to be done. The importance of the tank and tank policy and development need further study. Likewise it is regrettable that no real history of the development and work of the Royal Artillery is in fruit. The Machine Gun Corps is not yet satisfactorily covered, and a study of the work of G. M. Lindsay, that pioneer in machine-gun tactics, is much wanted. Moreover, the story of the development of artillery observations work and the liaison system with the artillery of the Royal Flying Corps and R.A.F. has been greatly neglected. Only brief references to aerial photography, the photographic services and the system of disseminating the results of aerial photography to formations and units can be found in Edmonds' histories. The important topic of training has been also neglected. All these important topics demand scholarly attention.

It will be necessary for scholars to investigate thoroughly the military records now becoming available in the P.R.O. and to continue the search for missing records, while beginning serious study of the important private collections now beginning to become accessible in order to resolve the very large number of unresolved problems and to study topics previously neglected, in order that much needed progress be made in the military historiography of the First World War.

BIBLIOGRAPHY

1. Aitken, Alexander. *Gallipoli to the Somme.* London: Oxford University Press, 1963.
2. Aldington, Richard. *Lawrence of Arabia.* London: Collins, 1955.
3. Aspinall-Oglander, Cecil. *Military Operations: Gallipoli.* London: History of the Great War from Official Documents, 1929–32.
3a. Arthur, Sir George. *The Life of Earl Kitchener.* Vol. III. London: Macmillan, 1920.
4. Baker-Carr, Brigadier C. D'A. B. *From Chauffeur to Brigadier.* London: Edward Benn, 1930.
5. Barker, A. J. *The Neglected War: Mesopotamia 1914–18.* London: Faber & Faber, 1967.
6. Barker, A. J. *Townshend of Kut.* London: Cassell, 1967.
7. Barnardiston, Major-General N. W. Diaries, covering the Tsing-

Tao Operation 1914. Write Mr. Antony Grant, Head of the Military Archive Centre, King's College, London.

8. Bartlett, Ellis Ashmead. *The Uncensored Dardanelles.* London: Hutchinson, 1928.

9. Baynes, John. *Morale: a study of men and courage.* . . . *1915.* New York: Praeger, 1967.

10. Beadon, R. H. *The R.A.S.C.* Cambridge: The University Press, 1931.

11. Bean, C. E. W. *The Australians in France (The Official History of Australia in the War of 1914–1918,* Vols. III–VI, 1929–42), Sydney: Angus & Robertson.

12. Bean, C. E. W. *The Story of Anzac* (Vols. I and II of the Australian Official History). 12th ed. Sydney: Angus & Robertson, 1941. Vol. I also covers the conquest of the German colonies in Australasia.

13. Becke, Major A. F. *The Order of Battle of Divisions.* H.M.S.O., 1935–45. 4 parts. Part 4 covers the Army Council, G.H.Q.'s, Armies and Corps.

14. Birdwood, Field Marshal Lord. *Khaki and Gown.* London: Ward Lock, 1941.

15. Blake, Robert, ed. *The Private Papers of Douglas Haig, 1914–19.* London: Eyre & Spottiswoode, 1952.

16. Bonham-Carter, Victor. *Soldiers True.* London: Muller, 1963.

17. Brabazon, Lord. *The Brabazon Story.* London: Heinemann, 1956.

18. Burne, Col. A. H. *Mesopotamia: the last phase.* Gale & Polden, Aldershot, 1931.

19. Callwell, Major-General Sir C. E. *Field Marshal Sir Henry Wilson.* London: Cassell, 1927. 2 vols.

20. Callwell, Major-General Sir C. E. *The Life of Sir Stanley Maude.* Constable, 1920.

21. Carrington, C. E. *Soldier from the Wars Returning.* London: Hutchinson, 1964.

22. "Charles Edmonds." *A Subaltern's War.* London: P. Davies, 1929. Reissued, 1964.

23. Charteris, Brigadier-General John. *Field Marshal Earl Haig.* London: Cassell, 1929.

24. Charteris, John. *At G.H.Q.* London: Cassell, 1931.

25. Churchill, Randolph. *Lord Derby.* London: Heinemann, 1960.

26. Churchill, Sir Winston. *The World Crisis.* Vols. I–IV. London: Thornton Butterworth, 1923–27.

27. Cooper, A. Duff. *Haig.* London: Faber, 1935–6. 2 vols.

28. du Cane, Lieutenant-General Sir J. P. (Head of British Liaison Mission with Foch.) *Marshal Foch.* Privately printed 1920, in Imperial War Museum.

29. Edmonds, Brigadier-General Sir J. E., ed. *Military Operations, France and Belgium.* London: Macmillan to 1940, then H.M.S.O., 1922–49. 14 vols.

   Vol. I—*1914 August–October.* 1st ed. 1922, 3rd, completely revised, ed. 1933.

Vol. II—*1914 October–November*. 1925.

Vol. III—*December 1914–May 1915*. Compiled by G. C. Wynne. 1927.

Vol. IV—*1915*. (Aubers Ridge, Festubert, Loos). 1928.

Vol. V—*1916 to 1st July*. 1932.

Vol. VI—*2nd July 1916—end Somme*. By Captain Wilfrid Miles, 1938.

1917 Vol. I covers Arras. Compiled by Captain Cyril Falls, 1940.

1917 Vol. II *Messines and Third Ypres,* 1948.

1917 Vol. III *Cambrai*. Compiled by Captain Wilfrid Miles, 1948.

1918 Vol. I *March Offensive*. 1935.

Vol. II *March–April*. 1937.

Vol. III *May–July*. 1939.

Vol. IV *8th August–26th September*. 1947.

Vol. V *26th September–11th November*. 1947.

In compiling the 1918 volumes, General Edmonds was assisted by General H. R. Davies and Lieutenant-Colonel R. G. B. Maxwell-Hyslop.

30. *Military Operations France and Belgium,* 1917, Vol. II. (See above 29).

31. *Military Operations France and Belgium,* 1918 Vols. I and II. (See 29).

32. Edmonds, Brigadier-General Sir J. E. *Military Operations Italy 1915–1919*. H.M.S.O., 1949 (the concluding volume of the Military Histories).

33. *Military Operations France and Belgium,* Vol. IV and V. (See 29).

34. Falls, Captain Cyril. *Military Operations, Macedonia*. H.M.S.O., 1933–5. 2 vols.

35. Falls, Captain Cyril. *Armageddon, 1918*. London: Weidenfeld & Nicolson, 1964.

36. Falls, Captain Cyril. *War Books*. London: Peter Davies, 1930.

37. Farrar-Hockley, Brigadier Anthony. *Death of an Army*. London: Barker, 1967.

38. Forbes, Major-General A. *A History of the Ordnance Services*. Vol. III. London: Medici Society, 1929.

39. Foulkes, Major-General C. H. *Gas*. London: Blackwood, 1934.

40. French, Field Marshal Lord. *1914*. London: Constable, 1919.

41. French, The Hon. E. G. *The Life of Field Marshal Sir John French, Earl French of Ypres*. London: Cassell, 1931.

42. French, The Hon. E. G. *French Replies to Haig*. London: Hutchinson, 1936. (Note also The Hon. E. G. French's *Some War Diaries, Addresses and Correspondence of Sir John French,* Herbert Jenkins, 1937, and *The Kitchener-French Dispute: a last word,* Glasgow: Wm. MacLellan, 1960.)

43. Fuller, Major-General J. F. C. *Memoirs of an Unconventional Soldier*. London: Nicolson and Watson, 1936.

44. Gardner, Brian. *The German East*. London: Cassell, 1963.

45. Gathorne-Hardy, Lieutenant-General. The Hon. Sir Francis (Cavan's Chief of Staff). "A Summary of the Campaign in Italy." *The Army Quarterly,* October 1921.
46. Gollin, A. *Proconsul in Politics.* (A study of Milner.) London: Blond, 1964.
47. General Staff Studies. *The Battle of Le Cateau.* London: H.M.S.O., 1934.
48. General Staff Studies. *The Battle of the Aisne.* London: H.M.S.O., 1934.
49. General Staff Studies. *The Battle of the Marne.* London: H.M.S.O., 1935.
50. Gough, General Sir Hubert. *The Fifth Army.* London: Hodder & Stoughton, 1931.
51. Graves, Robert. *Goodbye to All That.* London: Jonathan Cape, 1929.
52. *Guide to the Contents of the Public Record Office,* Part II, London: H.M.S.O., 1963.
53. Guinn, Paul. *British Strategy and Politics, 1914–18.* Oxford: Clarendon Press, 1965.
54. Gullett, Sir H. *The Australian Expeditionary Force in Sinai and Palestine.* 4th ed. Sydney: Angus and Robertson, 1937. (Vol. VII of Australian Official History.)
55. Haldane, General Sir Aylmer. *A Soldier's Saga.* London: Blackwood, 1948.
56. *Handbook: The Imperial War Museum.* London: H.M.S.O., 1967.
57. Hankey, Lord. *The Supreme Command.* London: Allen & Unwin, 1961. 2 vols. The Hankey Papers are now in Churchill College, Cambridge, but not yet accessible.
58. Harington, General Sir Charles. *Plumer of Messines.* London: Murray, 1935.
59. Harington, General Sir Charles. *Tim Harington Looks Back.* London: Murray, 1940.
60. Henniker, Colonel A. M. *Transportation on the Western Front 1914–1918.* London: H.M.S.O., 1937.
61. Herbert, Aubrey. *Mons, Anzac and Kut.* London: Arnold, 1919.
62. Higham, Robin. *Armed Forces in Peacetime.* London: Foulis, 1962.
63. Histories of the First and Second World Wars, Sectional List No. 60, H.M.S.O., 1962.
(It should be noted that the Official History of Gallipoli, Brigadier-General C. F. Aspinall-Oglander's *Gallipoli,* Heinemann, 1929–1932, 2 vols., is not included in this list.)
64. Horden, Lieutenant-Colonel Charles. *Military Operations East Africa.* Vol. I, Aug. 1914–September 1916 (incomplete). H.M.S.O., 1941.
65. Ironside, Field Marshal Lord. *Archangel, 1918–19.* London: Constable, 1953.

66. James, Robert Rhodes. *Gallipoli*. London: Batsford, 1965.
67. Jenkins, Roy. *Asquith*. London: Collins, 1965.
68. The T. E. Lawrence Letters. Letters of T. E. Lawrence to G. B. and Charlotte Shaw are in the British Museum. Many other letters are in the possession of Harvard and the University of Texas.
69. Lawrence, T. E. *The Seven Pillars of Wisdom*. London: Cape, 1926. 2 vols.
70. Lawrence, T. E. *Revolt in the Desert*. London: Cape, 1927.
71. Liddell Hart, Sir Basil Henry. *A History of the World War, 1914–1918*. London: Faber, 1934. [U.S. reprint *The Real War* (1966)].
72. Liddell Hart, Sir Basil Henry. *The British Way in Warfare*. London: Faber, 1932.
73. Liddell Hart, Sir Basil Henry. *Through the Fog of War*. London: Faber, 1938.
74. Liddell Hart, Sir Basil Henry. *Foch: man of Orleans*. London: Eyre & Spottiswoode, 1931.
75. Liddell Hart, Sir Basil Henry. *Memoirs*. Vol. I. London: Cassell, 1965.
76. Liddell Hart, Sir Basil Henry. *T. E. Lawrence: in Arabia and after*. Cape, 1934.
77. Liddell, Sir Basil Henry. *The Tanks: the history of the Royal Tank Regiment*. Vol. I. London: Cassell, 1959.
78. The Records of the Cabinet Office, H.M.S.O., 1966.
"List of Cabinet Papers 1880–1914," published by the P.R.O., H.M.S.O., 1964.
"List of Cabinet Papers 1915 and 1916," P.R.O., H.M.S.O., 1966.
"The Records of the Cabinet Office to 1922," P.R.O., H.M.S.O., 1966.
79. Lloyd George, David. Earl Lloyd George of Dwyfor. *War Memoirs*. London: Nicolson & Watson, 1933–36. 6 vols.
80. Luvaas, Jay. *The Education of an Army*. London: Cassell, 1965.
81. Luvaas, Jay. *The Military Legacy of the American Civil War*. University of Chicago Press, 1959.
82. MacMunn, Lieutenant-General Sir George (with Cyril Falls). *Military Operations Egypt and Palestine*. London: H.M.S.O., 1928–30. 2 vols.
83. MacMunn, Lieutenant-General Sir George. *Behind the Scenes in Many Wars*. London: Murray, 1930.
84. Magnus, Philip (Sir Philip Magnus-Allcroft). *Kitchener*. London: Murray, 1958.
85. Marder, Arthur J. *From Dreadnought to Scapa Flow*. Vol. II. London: Oxford University Press, 1965.
86. Marshall, Lieutenant-General Sir William (Maude's successor). *Memoirs of Four Fronts*. London: Ernest Benn, 1929.
87. Maurice, General Sir Frederick. *The Life of General Lord Rawlinson of Trent*. London: Cassell, 1928.
88. Maurice, General Sir Frederick. *The World Crisis: a criticism*.

London: Hutchinson, 1927 (in BM catalogue under Churchill).

89. Maynard, Sir Charles. *The Murmansk Venture*. London: Hodder & Stoughton, 1928.

90. Meinertzhagen, Richard. *Army Diary, 1899–1926*. Oliver and Boyd, 1960. (See also Meinertzhagen: *Middle East Diary, 1917–56*. Cresset Press, 1959.)

91. Moberly, F. J. *Military Operations: Mesopotamia*. London: H.M.S.O., 1923–27. 4 vols.

92. Moberly, F. J. *Togoland and the Cameroons, 1914–16*. London: H.M.S.O., 1931.

93. Monash. *The War Letters of General Monash*. F. M. Cutlack, ed. Sydney: Angus & Robertson, 1934.

94. Montague, C. E. *Disenchantment*. London: Chatto & Windus, 1922.

95. Moorehead, Alan. *Gallipoli*. New York: Harper, 1956.

96. Moran, Lord. *The Anatomy of Courage*. Boston: Houghton, Mifflin, 1967.

97. Palmer, Alan. *The Gardeners of Salonica*. London: Andre Deutsch, 1965.

98. Parliamentary Debates, 5th Series.
Vols. LXV–CX (Commons)
Vols. XVII–XXXII (Lords)
Unfortunately there are no records of secret sessions.

99. Raleigh, Sir Walter, and H. A. Jones. *The War in the Air*. Oxford: Clarendon Press, 1922–37. 6 vols.

100. Raynfield, F. A. *The Dardanelles Campaign*. Unpublished. Imperial War Museum.

101. Repington, C. à C. *The First World War, 1914–18*. London: Constable, 1920. 2 vols.

102. Robertson. Field Marshal Sir William. *From Private to Field Marshal*. London: Constable, 1921.

103. Robertson, Field Marshal Sir William. *Soldiers and Statesmen*. London: Cassell, 1926. 2 vols.

104. Rogers, H. C. B. *Weapons of the British Soldier*. Imperial Service Library/Seeley Service, 1961.

105. *The Royal Artillery War Commemoration Book*. Compiled by R. A. War Commemoration Fund. London: George Bell, 1920.

106. The Royal Engineers Institution. *The Work of the Royal Engineers in the European War, 1914–1919*. Chatham, Kent: The R. E. Institution, 1921–27. 9 vols.

107. Sassoon, Siegfried. *Memoirs of an Infantry Officer*. London: Faber, 1931.

108. Sassoon, Siegfried. *Memoirs of a Fox-Hunting Man*. London: Faber, 1928.

109. Seton-Hutchinson, Graham. *Machine-Guns*. London: Macmillan, 1938.

110. Sherson, Erroll. *Townshend of Chitral and Kut*. London: Heinemann, 1928.

111. Spears, Sir E. L. *Liaison 1914*. London: Heinemann, 1930.

112. Spears, Sir E. L. *Prelude to Victory*. Cape, 1939.
113. *Statistics of the Military Effort of the British Empire*. The War Office, 1922.
        (See also, "Casualties and Medical Statistics," T. J. Mitchell and G. M. Smith, H.M.S.O., 1931, and Command Paper 1193, H.M.S.O., 1921, "The General Annual Report on the British Army for the period 1st October 1913-30th September 1919," Part IV, and the Annual Reports of the Imperial War Graves Commission, in the major repositories.)
114. Stern, Sir Albert. *Tanks 1914–18. The Log Book of a Pioneer*. London: Hodder & Stoughton, 1919.
115. Taylor, A. J. P. *Illustrated History of the First World War*. London: Hamish Hamilton, 1963.
116. Terraine, John. *Douglas Haig: The Educated Soldier*. London: Hutchinson, 1963.
117. Terraine, John. "Instant History." *J.R.U.S.I.*, May 1962, The Royal United Service Institution, Vol. 107.
118. Terraine, John. *The Western Front*. London: Hutchinson, 1964.
119. Townshend, C. V. F. *My Campaign in Mesopotamia*. London: Thornton Butterworth, 1920.
120. The Union of South Africa General Staff. *The Union of South Africa in the Great War 1914–1918*. Pretoria: The Government Printing and Stationery Office, 1924.
121. Wavell, Field Marshal Lord Archibald. *Allenby: a study in greatness*. London: Harrap, 1940.
122. Wavell, Field Marshal Lord Archibald. *The Palestine Campaign*. London: Constable, 1928.
123. White, A. S. *A Bibliography of Regimental Histories of the British Army*. London: Francis Edwards Ltd., 1965.
124. White, A. S. "The Army List." *Journal of the Society for Army Historical Research*, Vol. XXV (1947) and Vol. XLV/181 (1967).
125. Williams, M. J. "The Treatment of the German Losses on the Somme in the British Official History." *J.R.U.S.I.*, February, 1966, Vol. CXI.
126. Wolff, Leon. *In Flanders Fields*. New York: Viking, 1958.
127. Wynne, G. C. *If Germany Attacks*. London: Faber, 1940.
128. Wynne, G. C. "The Schlieffen Plan." *J.R.U.S.I.*, November, 1958, Vol. CIII.
129. Young, F. Brett. *Marching on Tanga*. London: Collins, 1938.

PAPERS

130. The Anderson Papers. The papers of Percy Anderson (who worked with Sir Albert Stern). The Imperial War Museum. Write to Miss R. Coombs, the Librarian.
131. The Asquith Papers. Papers of H. H. Asquith, Earl of Oxford and Asquith. The Bodleian Library, Oxford. Write to Keeper of Manuscripts, Department of Western MSS.

132. The Balfour Papers. The papers of A. J. Balfour (Earl Balfour). The British Museum.
133. The Birdwood Papers. The Australian War Memorial, Canberra, New South Wales.
134. The Bonar Law Papers. The papers of the Rt. Hon. Andrew Bonar Law. Write the Librarian, the Beaverbrook Library, 33 St. Bride Street, London, E.C.4.
135. The Bonham-Carter Papers. Papers of General the Hon. Sir Charles Bonham-Carter, Director of Training at G. H. G. France 1917–18. Write Mr. Edwin Welch, Archivist, Churchill College, Cambridge.
136. The Carson Papers. The papers of Lord Carson. The Public Record Office of Northern Ireland, May Street, Belfast 1.
137. The Chamberlain Papers. The papers of the Rt. Hon. Austen Chamberlain. Write the Librarian, Birmingham University Library, Birmingham, England.
138. The Chetwode Papers. Papers of General Sir Philip Chetwode. The Imperial War Museum.
139. The Crewe Papers. The papers of Lord Crewe. Write the Librarian Cambridge University Library.
140. The Dawnay Papers. Papers of Lieutenant-General Guy Dawnay. The Imperial War Museum.
141. The Fuller Papers. The Military Archive Centre, King's College, London.
142. The Grant Papers. The papers of Sir Charles Grant, second in command to du Cane in 1918, are in the possession of C. R. A. Grant, Esq., Pitchford Hall, Shrewsbury, Shropshire, England.
143. The Haig Papers. The papers of F. M. Earl Haig of Bemersyde are in the National Library of Scotland, George IV Bridge, Edinburgh 1. (Keeper of MSS Mr. Wm. Park, M. A.) Written permission of the present Earl Haig is necessary for access. Duplicate copies of Earl Haig's War Diaries are in the Scots Record Office, H. M. General Register House, Edinburgh 2. (Keeper of the Records of Scotland, Sir James Ferguson of Kilkerran, Bt., Ll.D.) Here again written permission of Earl Haig is necessary.
144. The Kiggell Papers. Papers of Lieutenant-General Sir Launcelot Kiggell, Haig's Chief of Staff 1915–18, Military Archive Centre, King's College, London.
145. The Kitchener Papers. The papers of F. M. Earl Kitchener of Khartoum, P.R.O., Class 30/57.
146. The Lawrence Papers. The papers of General the Hon. Sir Herbert Lawrence, Chief of Staff 1918, are in the National Library of Scotland, Edinburgh. Write Keeper of MSS, National Library of Scotland, George IV Bridge, Edinburgh 1.
147. The private papers of Sir Basil Liddell Hart are in his home, States House, Medmenham, Marlow, Bucks. King's College, London, will eventually acquire this collection.
148. The Lloyd George Papers are in the Beaverbrook Library.
149. The Lothian Papers. Papers of the Marquess of Lothian (Philip

Kerr, Secretary to Lloyd George). The Scottish Record Office (G.D. 40 Sec. 17). Consent of present Marquess needed.

150. The Maxse Papers. The bulk of General Sir Ivor Maxse's papers are in the Imperial War Museum. Some are in the West Sussex Record Office, Chichester. Write the County Archivist, County Hall, Chichester.

151. The Milner Papers. The papers of Lord Milner are in the Bodleian. Written permission of the Librarian of New College, Oxford, is needed for access.

152. The Murray Papers. Correspondence of Sir Archibald Murray with Sir William Robertson, 1916–17. British Museum.

153. The Rawlins Papers. The papers of Lieutenant-Colonel S. W. H. Rawlins, Chief of Staff to Sir Noel Birch, Artillery Adviser to G. H. Q. 1916–18. Write Major R. Bartelot, Assistant Secretary (Historical), the Library of the Royal Artillery Institution, Woolwich, London, S.E.18.

154. The Rawlinson Papers. The papers of F. M. Lord Rawlinson of Trent are in the National Army Museum, Camberley, Surrey. Write Mr. Boris Mollo, Head of Dept. of Books. The Rawlinson Diaries: Churchill College, Cambridge.

155. The Robertson Papers: King's College, London.

156. The Papers of General Sir H. L. Smith-Dorrien. The British Museum.

157. The Stern Papers: King's College, London.

158. The Swinton Papers. Papers of Sir Ernest Swinton are in King's College, London.

159. The Uniacke Papers. The papers of Major-General H. C. Uniacke (Artillery Adviser Fifth Army), The Royal Artillery Institution Library, Woolwich, London, S.E.18.

160. The Orlo Williams Papers: The Imperial War Museum.

161. The G. C. Wynne Papers: King's College, London.

SUPPLEMENT TO BIBLIOGRAPHY

162. Hamilton, General Sir Ian. *Gallipoli Diary.* London: E. Arnold, 1920. 2 vols.

163. Murray, Joseph. *Gallipoli as I Saw It.* London: Kimber, 1965 (reprint).

164. Barclay, Brigadier C. N. *Armistice, 1918.* London: Dent, 1968.

165. Chandos, Lord [Oliver Lyttleton]. *From Peace to War: a study in contrast, 1857–1918.* New York: New American Library, 1968.

165a. Davies, W. J. K. *Light Railways of the First World War: a history of tactical rail communications on the British fronts, 1914–18.* Newton Abbot; David and Charles, 1967.

166. Green, Lieutenant-Colonel H., *The British Army in the First World War: the Regulars, the Territorials, and Kitchener's Army with some campaigns into which they fitted.* London: Clowes, 1968.

167. Professor John Campbell of McMaster University, Hamilton, On-

tario, has underway a study of historiography of the First World War including the debunking-revisionist cycle.

168. Duncan, G. S. *Douglas Haig as I Knew Him.* London: George Allen & Unwin, 1968.

169. Money Barnes, Major R. M. *The British Army 1914 and Its History.* London: Seeley Service, 1968.

170. Bidwell, Brigadier Shelford. *Gunners at War: a tactical study of the Royal Artillery in the twentieth century.* London: Arms and Armour Press, 1969.

171. Braddon, Russell. *The Siege (Kut, 1915/16).* London: Johnathan Cape, 1969.

172. Coppard, George. *With a Machine-Gun to Cambrai.* London: Imperial War Museum, 1969.

173. Inchbald, Major G. *Camels and Others: the Imperial Camel Corps in World War I.* London: Johnson, 1968.

174. Millar, Ronald. *Death of an Army: the siege of Kut, 1915–1916.* Boston: Houghton Mifflin, 1969. (See item 171 above; not to be confused with 37 above on the BEF.)

175. Sixsmith, Major-General E. K. G. *British Generalship in the Twentieth Century.* London: Arms and Armour Press, 1969.

176. *Soldier and Sailor Words and Phrases including the slang of the trenches and the air force; British and American war-words and service terms and expressions in everyday use; nicknames, soubriquets, and titles of regiments, with their origins: the battle-honours of the Great War awarded to the British Army.* Detroit: Gale Research, 1968 (reprint of the 1925 edition).

XIV

THE FIRST WORLD WAR AT SEA

Arthur Marder

There is already a vast literature on the naval aspects of 1914–1918. This is easily accounted for by the number of participants who wrote up their experiences, the continuing fascination of the war for the post-war generations, and the extra stimuli to authorship provided more recently by the fiftieth anniversary of the war and the availability of a mass of primary source material. Scholarly works, however, are none too abundant.

OFFICIAL PAPERS AND HISTORIES. The Admiralty Record Office material (296) is, naturally, the most important single source. Though successive First Lords of the Admiralty and First Sea Lords carted off much of their own records, more than enough remains to keep a researcher happy. All wartime records are open for the inspection of scholars, except for unnamed categories of documents which are withheld for reasons of "public policy." These include court-martial proceedings, which are subject to a special 100-year rule. The P.R.O. material is staggering in quantity and is not made manageable by the haphazard way in which the Admiralty arranged the documents. There are, however, helpful indexes at the Public Record Office, and the bibliography in the concluding volume of Marder's study of the "Fisher Era" (160) contains a rough guide to the Admiralty records. The Cabinet Office Papers (296) are of prime importance for the study of many naval topics, and most of these papers are indexed. There is a convenient listing of Parliamentary papers for the war years (85).

The Naval Staff Histories of the war (268) are an invaluable, if deliberately uncritical, source for operations. The Corbett and Newbolt *Naval Operations* (57), for all its restrained judgments and at times excessive detail, is absolutely essential. The other key official published histories are Fayle's *Seaborne Trade* (78) for trade warfare and defense, Hurd's *The Merchant Navy* (114), and Raleigh and Jones's *The War in the Air* (192).

Necessary complements to the British archival material and monographs are the records of the United States Navy Department (297), the German Ministry of Marine archives (293), and the volumes in the official German history of the war at sea (86). Extremely important for the German side of the naval war, and above all the testimony of Vice-Admiral Adolf von Trotha (Scheer's Chief of Staff), are the naval proceedings (1919–25) of the Reichstag Committee of Inquiry which debated the causes of Germany's defeat in the war and subsequent collapse (238). The highly critical testimony of Alboldt, a pre-war warrant officer and wartime subordinate dockyard official, who was appointed by the Reichstag Committee in 1926 as its special authority for the naval proceedings, must be used with extreme caution. Alboldt's evidence and other material were published separately by him (3).

PERIODICALS. Two Service journals are indispensable: the *Royal United Service Institution Journal* and the *Naval Review,* the latter restricted. The *Naval Review,* in particular, is filled with more or less authoritative articles on all facets of the war at sea.

GENERAL HISTORIES. Covering most naval aspects of the war are Vols. II–V of Marder's *From the Dreadnought to Scapa Flow* (160), which have made use of all the above-mentioned categories of material. The best one-volume narrative is that by Captain Bennett (25). Launched in 1969 is a popular weekly periodical (128 numbers are projected) devoted to all aspects of the war (108), and whose naval charts, illustrations, and essays are generally of high quality. Sir Llewellyn Woodward's book on the war (241), though making no pretence to considerable original scholarship, is an excellent general treatment of the British war effort on land and sea, as well as of the home front.

THE HIGH COMMAND: WHITEHALL, or the "war behind the war." Asquith's impact on the war at sea was peripheral—confined pretty much to the genesis of the Dardanelles operation. The naval material in his papers (270) consists mainly of some correspondence with First Lords and a large number of Cabinet papers (the latter now available in the Cabinet Office Records). Most of the useful material in his *Memories and Reflections* (180) is indexed under "Fisher" and "Churchill." The biography by Spender and Asquith (217) is worth no more than a glance. Jenkins' outstanding life (131) contains many references to naval matters, but does not fully bring out Asquith's weaknesses as a war leader. Lloyd George's influence on the naval war was mainly in connection with the introduction of the convoy system, on which one must consult his *War Memoirs,* Vol. III (151). None of the biographies of him is worth anything to the naval historian. The skillfully indexed Lloyd George Papers (284) have a scattering of material pertaining to naval affairs, mostly in 1917 correspondence.

Turning to the wartime First Lords of the Admiralty, we have Churchill's skillful *apologia* in his *The World Crisis* (55). Not always reliable, it yet remains an absolutely indispensable source on the Navy in the first ten months of the war. The period is being treated in the biography of his father which Randolph Churchill started (89). The Churchill Papers (277) are not yet available. Neither Violet Bonham Carter's appreciation (28)

nor Admiral Gretton's fine account of Churchill's love affair with the Royal
Navy (95) goes far beyond the published record, but the former does add
some interesting Churchill-and-Fisher sidelights, and the latter has a number of fresh insights. The official and still standard biography of Balfour,
by his niece Blanche Dugdale (73), is sketchy on his time as First Lord.
The more recent biography by Young (245) is no less disappointing in
this respect. The Balfour Papers (291), a rich hoard, include his papers
as First Lord. Colvin's authorized life of Sir Edward Carson (56) has several chapters on his time as First Lord. Montgomery Hyde's life of Carson
(116) ably summarizes his service as First Lord with some new material.
There are Carson Papers, mostly in Belfast (275). There is nothing of consequence in print on the last, and in respects the ablest, of the wartime
First Lords, Sir Eric Geddes, though Baron Geddes' family chronicle (84)
has a few pages on his brother's Admiralty experience and some insights
on the manner of man he was. Geddes's First Lord papers are to be found
among the Admiralty records at the Public Record Office (281).

The First Sea Lords have fared better. Admiral Kerr's life of Prince
Louis of Battenberg (141) is barely adequate, largely through no fault of
his own: Prince Louis apparently left few papers. Only recently have several boxes of his papers (hitherto believed to have been destroyed) turned
up (272). Very few of the papers are concerned with the war period, however. John Terraine is preparing a new authorized life. Admiral Bacon's authorized biography of Fisher (10), sympathetic to his subject but not slav-
ishly so, is still useful. A new biography, by Richard Hough (111), is especially strong on the personal side of Fisher's life in his latter years. Another
Fisher biography, by Mackay, is in preparation (156). Much of Fisher's
correspondence has been selected and annotated by Marder (159), with
biographical essays prefacing each section; it is perhaps basic to a study of
Fisher in the war. One should also consult the Crease Papers (295), especially for the inside story of Fisher's resignation in May 1915. The Admiral's explosive memoirs (79) (80) contain disorganized material on his
wartime policies and ideas. His papers are divided between Kilverstone
Hall and the much larger and more valuable indexed collection at Lennoxlove (280). Admiral Sir Henry Jackson, who succeeded Fisher, wrote
nothing for publication and has had no biographer. His First Sea Lord
papers (295) are important for the letters from Jellicoe, Beatty, and other
commanding officers. Jellicoe is the subject of a good short biography by
Altham (4) and a well-done (if not without bias for his subject) large one
by Bacon (9). Bacon did not have access to all the Jellicoe Papers, one
reason why the standard biography is now the recent authorized one by A.
Temple Patterson (184). Jellicoe's own writings are mentioned below. The
second volume of A. Temple Patterson's ably edited selection of the Admiral's correspondence (183), mainly from the Admiralty records in the
P.R.O. and the Beatty and Jellicoe papers, deals with Jellicoe's time as
First Sea Lord and beyond. The *Jellicoe Papers* (291) are a most important collection. A valuable source on Wemyss is his wife's volume (240):
extracts from his letters and diaries, with connecting passages and commentary. The Admiral's papers (290), best on his initial year as First Sea

Lord, feature a voluminous correspondence with the C.-in-C., Grand Fleet, Beatty. (Much of this file is duplicated in the Beatty MSS.) The papers of the Chief of the Admiralty War Staff, 1914–17, Admiral Sir Henry Oliver (294), are worth consulting for his unpublished reminiscences.

Lord Hankey's *The Supreme Command* (101) (he was in possession of every defense secret) is based on his diaries and recollections. It is far more useful for grand strategy and military matters, yet contains many important references to naval affairs. The same can be said about the excellent authorized biography by Captain Roskill (202), based on the Hankey Papers (292)—a formidable mass featuring his full wartime diaries, family correspondence, copies of his letters to prominent people, and the more important letters he received. Franklyn Johnson made the first detailed study of the C.I.D. (133) at a time when most of the pertinent records were not available. Guinn's examination of the politico-military factors which influenced strategy, and the ideas and role played by the leading politicians, soldiers, and seamen (97), is much fuller on the military side. Captain Puleston's *High Command in the World War* (190) is not very revealing about naval affairs. Lord Beaverbrook's *Politicians and the War* (19), like its sequel, the more valuable *Men and Power* (18), was "designed to emphasise the immense importance of what may be called the civilian aspect of war direction—a thing which war-books tend to neglect."

We get glimpses of the wartime workings of the Admiralty in Admiral Fremantle's autobiography (81), Chapters 3 and 7 of Marder's study of the brilliant, acerbic Richmond (161), leader of the "Young Turks," Lieutenant-Commander Kenworthy's strongly biased (against the Admiralty) autobiography (138), Admiral Dewar's autobiography (68), which is full of information and insights on the central direction of the war, though excessively critical of the Establishment, and Admiral James's short authorized biography of Admiral Oliver (123). Also important for Admiralty policies and activities are the Fremantle, Oliver, Duff, Dewar, Richmond, Graham Greene, and Sir Frederick Hamilton Papers (279) (294).

The story of the famed secret intelligence branch of the Navy, "Room 40," will be found in Alfred Ewing's autobiography (76) (it was he and his small band who began to work at the deciphered signals early in the war); Admiral James's readable and authorized life of "Blinker" Hall (122), the remarkable Director of Naval Intelligence, under whose overall direction Room 40 operated in the latter part of the war; James's own memoirs (122) (he headed up Room 40 in 1917–18); Francis Toye's brief sketches of Room 40 and its personnel in his autobiography (228); and Hoy's anecdotal *40 O.B.* (113). Hoy was private secretary to Admiral Hall, though not himself a worker in Room 40. Kahn's history of cryptology (134) has a chapter on Room 40 which has made a skillful use of the published sources. Bywater and Ferraby's *Strange Intelligence* (33) is an entertaining volume by two naval journalists without benefit of access to Admiralty records. Hall's Papers (283) are of value only for some five typescript chapters (of which Admiral James made good use) for an autobiography which was to run to fifteen or twenty chapters. It is a pity he discontinued the work after the Admiralty told him that he would not be allowed to publish. Hall's assistants—Cozens-Hardy, Leeson, Lord Herschell, H. B. Irving—are dead, and there is no one now about, except for Admiral James, who could throw much light on Hall's work in the field of intelligence, although the Naval Library, Ministry of Defence, possesses a miscellany of N.I.D. material of formidable proportion. (But see below, p. 21n.)

GRAND FLEET, NORTH SEA, AND HOME WATERS. Basic are the Jellicoe Papers (291), Vol. I of the Temple Patterson edition of the Admiral's papers and the first part of Vol. II (183), his biography of Jellicoe (184) and Bacon's (9), Jellicoe's *The Grand Fleet* (129), its complement, by his opposite number, Scheer (208), and the Bellairs (295), Sturdee (287), and Beatty (273) Papers. The last-named, one of the most important collections, are being prepared for publication (13). Beatty has been well served in the authorized biography by Admiral Chalmers (39), who was on his staff for most of the war. His is a sympathetic treatment, as one would expect (the Admiral emerges as a good deal more than an impetuous fighter), yet judicious at the same time. A new authorized biography, by John Barnes, is in preparation. Shane Leslie's memoirs (150) contain a perceptive sketch of Beatty and his reactions to Jutland. Admiral Sir A. L. Duff left a Grand Fleet diary (1914–16) (294) of considerable interest and value. The papers of Admiral Sir Reginald Plunkett-Ernle-Erle-Drax (292) have a plethora of source material on Grand Fleet tactics, and those of Admiral Sir Walter Cowan (294) some interesting correspondence.

The gossipy recollections of the Russian Attaché to the Grand Fleet, von Schoultz (211), are a good source but must be used with some caution. Lionel Dawson's biography of one of the most offensively-minded of Grand Fleet officers, Walter Cowan (66), is thin on the war years. The autobiography of de Chair (67), who made his mark as commander of the Northern Patrol, is not very revealing or interesting, except for the story of Jellicoe's dismissal as First Sea Lord. Better on the Northern Patrol are the *Reminiscences* of his successor, Admiral Tupper (230), those of Admiral Humphrey Smith (216), and Chatterton's *The Big Blockade* (44). Among the more informative of Grand Fleet reminiscences and autobiographies are those by Admiral Dreyer (72) (best on Jutland), though wordy and badly organized, Fremantle (81), James (124), Usborne (233), and Goodenough (91). Richmond's diaries and letters (161) (294) contain much information. One of Goodenough's young officers, Stephen King-Hall, who was present in all the main North Sea actions, wrote two accounts of them (144) (145). His diary and letters constitute the last segment of Louise King-Hall's *Sea Saga* (143). Admiral Tweedie's recollections of service in Grand Fleet destroyers (231) (as well as in the eastern Mediterranean and in monitors on the Belgian coast) are of some value. Captain Munro wrote an unsatisfactory account of Scapa Flow (174), Cousins, a readable popular one (58). A Naval Staff publication on East Coast operations (263) has some worth. Part II of the proceedings of a U. S. Air Force military history symposium (232) contains a paper by Marder comparing Jellicoe and Beatty as Cs.-in-C. Grand Fleet, and a number of commentaries on the paper, by Professor Donald Schurman and senior officers of the Royal Navy.

On the battle cruisers we have Filson Young's popular account (244) (he served in the *Lion,* 1914–15); the autobiography of Pelly (185) (Captain of the *Tiger*); Lady Seymour's memoir of her son, Ralph Seymour (212), Beatty's ill-fated Signal Officer; and the first volume of Beatty's Flag-Captain, Chatfield's, autobiography (41), which studiously avoids controversial matters. Patterson is doing the authorized life of Chatfield, based on the Chatfield Papers (276). The papers of Admiral Drax (292) contain material relating to his service in the *Lion,* 1913–16.

The famed Harwich Force is the focus of interest in books by Woolard (242), Carr (36), and Domvile (69), as well as in the voluminous diaries of Domvile (278), Tennant (294), and Louis Hamilton (294), and the papers of the very able Commander of the Force, Reginald Tyrwhitt (289), and of Keyes (292). The last named include a file of Tyrwhitt correspondence. Patterson is writing the authorized biography of Tyrwhitt. The two most revealing books on the Dover Straits are Bacon's *The Dover Patrol* (6) and the second volume of Roger Keyes's memoirs (142), each a useful corrective to the other. Keyes's Papers (292) are, as just noted, extant, but Bacon's have, alas, disappeared. The breezy autobiography of "Evans of the *Broke*" (172) is best on the Dover Patrol and the *Broke* destroyer action of 1917. Reginald Pound has done a first-class biography of the rather flamboyant Evans (189). On the Zeebrugge-Ostend operations of 1918, apart from Keyes's indispensable Vol. II, we have the detailed account by Carpenter (35), Captain of the *Vindictive,* and Barrie Pitt's lively popular work (187), which claims more from the results of the raid than the facts warrant. Aspinall-Oglander's authorized biography of Keyes (5) falls into the same trap. Sanford Terry has brought together certain primary sources on the operations (225)—Keyes's dispatches, etc.

Then there is Jutland, where we have in recent years come a long way since the polemical and biased accounts of Pollen (188), Bellairs (21), Bacon (8) (11), Churchill (55), and Harper (88) (102). The detailed study by Commander Frost, U.S.N. (82) was a vast improvement, though hypercritical of British strategy and tactics, and with a tendency to be wise after the event. In rapid succession have come four much better balanced Jutland studies: Captain Macintyre's popular work (154), based on standard sources, Captain Bennett's straightforward account (23), which makes use of fresh material, Commander Irving's (118), an especially vivid narrative, by one who was there, and Marder's (160), which stresses analysis and incorporates a considerable body of new material. The Jellicoe chapter in Correlli Barnett's *The Sword-Bearers* (14) goes too far in attributing the unsatisfactory aspects of Jutland to the "decadent and uncreative" pre-war social system. Pastfield's fine little booklet (182) is concerned mainly with the technical aspects of the battle. Fawcett and Hooper's collection of vivid personal narratives of the action (77) is a gem. And of course there are the *Official Despatches* (1); Corbett's Vol. III (57); as well as the Admiralty *Narrative of the Battle of Jutland* (2) (essentially the *Naval Staff*

Appreciation of Jutland (268) without the judgments and criticisms; Jellicoe's recently discovered full notes on the *Narrative* are in the Naval Library); and the *Harper Record* (103), which is substantially the unpublished and disputed *Harper Record* of 1919 but without the diagrams. In addition to the Jellicoe (291) and Beatty (273) Papers, the student of Jutland will want to examine the Evan-Thomas (291), Frewen (282) (291), Roskill (285), Godfrey (295), Jerram (294), and Tennant (294) Papers. (The last-named include a three-volume 1914–18 diary—Harwich Force, Mediterranean, Grand Fleet—as well as his Naval Staff College lectures on Jutland.) The BBC has post-war recordings of Jutland impressions by Admirals Chatfield, Dreyer, and Goodenough (247), the last particularly good! The Harper Papers (291) are of value mainly for the post-war controversy. They include a Harper memorandum of extraordinary interest: "Facts Dealing with the Official Record of the Battle of Jutland and the Reason It Was Not Published." It has been reproduced as an appendix to the *Jellicoe Papers,* Vol. II (183). The complementary document, the minutes of the Beatty Board, will appear in the *Beatty Papers* (13). Important for Jutland material matters are the naval proceedings of the post-war Reichstag Committee of Inquiry (238).

MEDITERRANEAN, DARDANELLES. On the *Goeben* episode, which got the war off on the wrong foot for the Royal Navy, we have Admiral Sir A. Berkeley Milne's unconvincing *apologia* in book form (167) and in his papers (294), and Admiral Sir Ernest Troubridge's version in his sister-in-law's account (229) and in his papers (288).

The proceedings of the Dardanelles Commission (P.R.O.: Cab. 19/33) are the obvious prime source for a study of the genesis and development of the Dardanelles/Gallipoli operations. They replace the published reports of the Dardanelles Commission (63), which cited only a few tantalizing fragments. Other basic sources include the scarcely known Mitchell Committee Report (260), the Keyes Papers (292), the first volume of his strongly opinionated memoirs (142), the de Robeck Papers (292), and Wemyss' vivid and highly critical account (239). The Navy Records Society will be publishing editions of the Keyes Papers (98), the de Robeck Papers (218), and, somewhat further off, papers on Mediterranean operations to the end of 1914 (153). Keble Chatterton's *Dardanelles Dilemma* (46) leans heavily (as do all his books) on eyewitness accounts. General Sir Ian Hamilton's diary (99) has a good deal on the Navy's role in the operation. Robert Rhodes James's *Gallipoli* (119) is the outstanding work of scholarship on the whole operation. Alan Moorehead's book (170), despite the many (on the whole, minor) inaccuracies, remains a standard work, if only for the extraordinary skill with which the story is told. Both James and Moorehead are much stronger on the military side than the naval. There are three eminently readable books on the fabulous exploits of the British submarines which penetrated the Marmora—by Jameson (127), Brodie (30), and Shankland and Hunter (213). Admiral of the Fleet Cunningham's autobiography (61) contains some interesting pages on the work of the destroyers.

On the Mediterranean theatre in general, noteworthy are Captain Weldon's volume (237), which is essentially his diary; Admiral Usborne's *Smoke on the Horizon* (234), a detailed examination of selected operations in the theatre, and his *Blast and Counterblast* (233), on Grand Fleet activity, etc., but most valuable for the Eastern Mediterranean naval scene in the latter part of the war; Chatterton's *Seas of Adventures* (51); Admiral Mark Kerr's two volumes of chatty reminiscences (139) (140); and a doctoral dissertation by Chrisman (52). The papers of Admiral Sir Howard Kelly (294) are good on the Mediterranean in 1914 and the Adriatic in 1917–18, and Marder's *Portrait of an Admiral* (161) has material on the Adriatic theatre in 1915. Fremantle's memoirs (81) include material on the Aegean. Volume II of Admiral Godfrey's *Naval Memoirs* (90), several cuts above the usual naval memoirs, are particularly good on the Dardanelles in 1915 and the Mediterranean in 1917–18. See also his collection of Mediterranean papers (295).

CLEARING THE SEAS OF COMMERCE RAIDERS. This dramatic phase of the naval operations, which bulked so large in the first six months of the war, is well told by Middlemas (166) (though with a number of errors in technical matters), by Chatterton (50), and by Langmaid (147) in a condensed account of German surface raiders in both wars. On the central actions, Coronel and the Falklands, there are the three older and still useful accounts, by Hirst (107), who took part in both actions, by Verner (235) on the Falklands (he served in the battlecruiser *Inflexible*), and Irving (117). Barrie Pitt's book (186) has made thorough use of the standard printed sources, Captain Bennett has written the now standard work on the two battles (24), which have never been described more graphically, and Admiral Hickling, in his autobiography (105), has contributed a valuable first-hand account. Richard Hough has written an excellent account (112), with new German material and focusing on the German side. A Naval Staff publication on German cruiser warfare (264) has some useful material.

THE U-BOAT PROBLEM AND THE CONVOY SYSTEM. The unrestricted submarine campaign and the British counter-measures constitute, of course, the central thread in the war at sea during 1917 and 1918. Still of value is Laurens' older account (148). Better is another vintage publication, by Gibson and Prendergast (87). Based on all the available published sources, including the works of the German authorities Gayer (83) (a U-Boat flotilla commander and afterward a department head in the U-boat office of the Ministry of Marine) and Michelsen (165) (Senior Officer, U-boats, June 1917 till the end of the war), it remains standard. It must, however, be supplemented by Admiral Spindler's official German account (86); the writings of Bauer (15) (16) (Senior Officer, U-boats, until June 1917); and the raw material on the anti-submarine campaign in the Naval Library, which includes the reports of the Anti-Submarine and Air Divisions, Admiralty (256), (257), (258), and past-war Naval Staff commentaries on the subject (261), (265). Professor Bryant Ranft is editing a volume of source material on trade defense (193). Admiral James's thin biography of Admiral Sir William Fisher (120) (who left few papers (294), Director of the Anti-Submarine Division, Admiralty, 1917–18, has a few bits. On the whole subject of trade warfare and defense the official volumes by Fayle, *Seaborne Trade* (78), are indispensable, as are the Barley-Waters Naval Staff papers on trade defense in 1917–18 (271) and an Admiralty "Statistical Review" (251). Hurd's official *The Merchant Navy* (114) is an inspiring story told in an unemotional style. David Bone (27) wrote a sympathetic and charming account of British merchant shipping in the war. There is a Parliamentary Paper on losses of British merchant and fishing vessels by enemy action: names, dates, etc. (164), and a Command Paper on merchant tonnage losses by enemy action and marine risk, merchant shipbuilding output, and enemy vessels captured and brought into service (163).

Grant has done an excellent succinct volume on the circumstances under which each U-boat was lost (92), and a sequel (93) in which the N.I.D. factor is emphasized. See also the final approved Admiralty list (249). Gordon Campbell's fascinating story of the Q-ships (34), Carr's anecdotes on the anti-submarine campaign (38), and several of Keble Chatterton's books (42), (43), (45), (47), (49) cover various facets of that campaign in entertaining style. Admiral Bayly's straightforward biography (17) is best on his command of the Western Approaches, where the U-boat for long gave the most trouble.

For the controversial story of the introduction of the convoy system one should above all consult the Duff Papers (279), (294), the Newbolt Papers (295), two excellent studies by Lieutenant-Commander Waters (236) (269), Lloyd George's *War Memoirs,* Vol. III (151), and Jellicoe's two books on all aspects of the anti-submarine campaign (128), (130), the second of which was written in part as a reply to Lloyd George's charges that the Admiralty had dragged their feet and had to be pushed into convoy —by the Prime Minister. The Bethell Papers (274)—he was C.-in-C., Plymouth, 1916–18—have some interesting bits and pieces. See also the autobiography of the American Secretary of the Navy, Josephus Daniels (62), Admiral Sims's *The Victory at Sea* (214), and Elting Morison's authorized biography of Sims (171). All three, as well as the light wartime memoirs of Admiral Rodman (200), who commanded the U.S. battle squadron attached to the Grand Fleet, also throw light on the Anglo-American naval relationship generally in 1917–18. Lord Salter's *Memoirs* (206) include chapters on his experiences as Director of Ship Requisitioning (1917–18), which touched on the introduction of convoy and related matters. Valuable on all aspects of the convoy system are several of the Technical History monographs (255) and two post-war Ministry of Shipping surveys (253), (254). Rutter's *Red Ensign* (205) is a convenient history of convoy. Captain Munro's war reminiscences (173) are largely concerned with his experiences as a Commodore of Convoy.

Chapter 4 of Mancur Olson's book (179) deals effectively with the successful British attempts to circumvent the U-boat blockade, Siney wrote a scholarly treatment of the Allied blockade of Germany, 1914–16 (215), and Bell, the official history of the blockade, 1914–18 (20).

TECHNICAL DEVELOPMENT, SHIP DESIGN, SHIP HISTORIES. There is a plethora of unpublished British official works in the first two categories (nearly all are available in the Naval Library), among them the *Records of Warship Construction* (250), the fifty monographs collectively known as *The Technical History* (255), *Grand Fleet Gunnery and Torpedo Memoranda* (259), and *The History of British Minefields* (265). *The Technical History,* together with the printed records of Lord Fisher's Board of Invention and Research (B.I.R.) (248), are the basic sources for a study of the applications of science to naval warfare. (A student at the University of California, Irvine, Mr. Jack K. Gusewelle, is completing a doctoral dissertation on scientists and the Navy, 1914–18.) Sir J. J. Thomson's memoirs (227) and the biography of that distinguished scientist by Rayleigh (194) have some material on his work as a member of the B.I.R.

The autobiography of Tennyson d'Eyncourt (224), Director of Naval Construction, 1912–14, is disappointing. Le Fleming's *Warships of World War I* (149) is a convenient little reference volume. The standard work on British battleships is Oscar Parkes's monumental classic (181), with a vast array of plans, diagrams, photographs, and an excellent text. Hough's *Dreadnought* (110) is a useful supplement. Hough has also done an interesting biography of the dreadnought *Agincourt* (109), and Roskill, a model job on the seven *Warspites* (201), featuring the last of them and her service at Jutland. British destroyers have found their historians in Kemp (136) and Manning (157), the latter's a reference work, the former a pithy, well-written story. The classic work on the subject, a veritable encyclopedia, is by March (158). "Taffrail's" *Endless Story* (222) is a vividly written work on the light craft, and Lionel Dawson's interesting, and often amusing, recollections (65) focus on his service with the torpedo craft. The British submarine in World War I figures prominently in the histories of that craft by Hezlet (104), Kemp (137), and Jameson (126). Kenneth Edward's *We Dive at Dawn* (74) and Carr's charming little *By Guess and By God* (37) narrate many of the principal British submarine exploits during the war. Everitt's *The K Boats* (75) is a very graphic, harshly critical account of this class of submarine that contains much information but lacks balance. Chalmers' biography of Max Horton (40), the great submariner of World War II, has a section on his Baltic exploits of the First War, which had already made him a legendary figure.

The best books in English on mines and mining, including their role in 1914–18, are by Langmaid (146) and Cowie (59); one should also consult the official *Mining Manual* (252). There is an official history of British minesweeping (267). "Taffrail's" *Swept Channels* (223) is not so much a history of minesweeping as an attempt, very successful, to capture the atmosphere of the work of this force.

NAVAL AVIATION. British naval aviation made great strides in the last year or two of the war, holding out tremendous possibilities to its supporters. Captain Stephen Roskill's volume of source materials on the Naval Air Service through the First War (203) is basic. Included in his materials are excerpts from the papers of a pioneer of maritime air power, Group Captain H. A. Williamson (292). The official account of all facets of the war in the air, by Raleigh and Jones (192), is not always reliable in its treatment of the Royal Naval Air Service. One should also consult the recollections of six pioneers: Grey (96) (the co-founder and Editor of *Aeroplane,* 1911–39), Longmore (152), Moore (169), Davies (64), Sueter (219), and Samson (207), and the biography of a seventh, Rutland (243). Thetford's *British Naval Aircraft Since 1912* (226) is the standard reference work on the subject, and Macintyre (155), Kemp (135), and Popham (188a) have done general histories of naval aviation which include concise, clearly told accounts of the Fleet's air arm from its beginning in 1911. Major-General Sykes's autobiography (220) (he was a founder of the R.F.C.) contains a number of references to the R.N.A.S. in the war, especially to its role in the Dardanelles operation. Wedgwood Benn's volume (22) has material on the wartime exercise of naval air power in the Adriatic and Near East. Boyle's *Trenchard* (29), though not always fair to the Navy, has good material on naval air power in the war and the amalgamation of the R.N.A.S. and R.F.C. in 1918 to form the R.A.F. Lloyd George's *War Memoirs,* Vol. IV (151), has a good chapter on the latter. Robin Higham's study of the British rigid airship (106) is easily the best volume on the subject, as is Robinson's on the Zeppelin (199), which gives the other side of airship operations over the North Sea.

A MISCELLANY. The beautifully indexed Royal Archives (286) contain some nuggets in the correspondence of King George V with high political and naval personages. Lord Riddell's *War Diary* (198) (he was a press lord close to Lloyd George), the wartime experiences and reflections of *The Times* Military Correspondent, Repington (195), and Harold Nicolson's authorized *George the Fifth* (178) have many references to naval affairs and personalities. Good sketches of the civilian and professional leaders of the Navy will be found in such works as Bacon's *From 1900 Onward* (7) (Fisher, Jellicoe, Churchill), Jameson's *The Fleet that Jack Built* (125) (Fisher, Jellicoe, Beatty, Tyrwhitt, Keyes), Taprell Dorling's *Men O'War* (71) (Fisher), Hurd's *Who Goes There?* (115) (Churchill, Fisher, Jellicoe), and Churchill's *Great Contemporaries* (53) (Fisher, Balfour).

The splendid work done by the Royal Naval Division is chronicled by Jerrold (132). On what conditions were like in the lower deck, one should consult the wartime issues of the lower-deck organ, *The Fleet,* as well as the post-war recommendations of the Jerram Committee on naval pay (176), and for officers' pay, the recommendations of other committees (175).

Sir Frederick Maurice has contributed a valuable study of the co-ordination, or lack of co-ordination, in the Allied war effort in all spheres (162). Much source material on the same topic will be found in the printed *Reports* (records of the six extended meetings) of the Allied Naval Council in 1918 (246). Anglo-American naval relations are the theme of a major work by Professor Warner R. Schilling (209). It is founded on an exhaustive analysis of the American naval records and private collections of papers.

There are interesting footnotes to the war at sea in Admiral Brownrigg's *Indiscretions of the Naval Censor* (31) and in Hampshire's *The Phantom Fleet* (100), which is an absorbing tale of maritime deception: the mocked up merchant vessels that represented modern capital ships.

Works dealing in part with naval tactics and strategy generally in the war include a sound and thoughtful statement by Creswell (60), Bacon and McMurtrie's persuasively argued treatise (12), Roskill's classic summing up of the strategic aspects of the war (204), and books by Richmond (196) (197) and Grenfell (94) (221). Professor Donald Schurman's forthcoming life of Corbett (210) should fit into this category. Moon's doctoral dissertation on the invasion problem, 1888–1918 (168), two-thirds of which deals with the war years, is a thorough study of all aspects of this hardy perennial. Domville-Fife's *Evolution of Sea Power* (70) has chapters on such large topics as anti-submarine warfare, the capital ship, etc., with many references to World War I. World War I tactical material will be found in a post-war Naval Staff study (266).

Also worth noting are Churchill's *Thoughts and Adventures* (54), with chapters on the U-boat war and the Dover Barrage; Barry Bingham's personal account of the Falklands, Jutland, and the Heligoland Bight (1914) actions (26); Keble Chatterton's *Gallant Gentlemen* (48), a miscellany of naval actions, including the *Goeben* episode, Coronel, and the Falklands; Admiral James's attractive sketches of the Bight action of 1914, the *Goeben* episode, and Jutland (121); Bywater's detailed record of the actions in which the light cruisers, British and German, played a prominent role (32); and Pollen's *The Navy in Battle* (188), which is of interest as recording how much, or how little, was known about the principal actions in 1918. Good on German naval personalities and the German side of the main actions in the North Sea (including Jutland) and unrestricted submarine warfare is Admiral Raeder's autobiography (191). Useful for reference is the Parliamentary Paper on Navy losses (177): names of ships, dates, etc.

RESEARCH OPPORTUNITIES. Wanted are analyses in depth of naval leadership in the war and of the relations between the admirals and the politicians. The exciting story of the Dover Patrol needs to be told without the special pleading of a Bacon or a Keyes. Studies of Balfour, Carson, and Geddes as First Lords, and of Jackson and Wemyss as First Sea Lords, are worth doing. The work of the Naval Intelligence Department (N.I.D.), and of Room 40 in particular, would make fascinating topics, though they would require some digging. Mr. Donald McLachlan (author of *Room 39,* London 1968, the story of Naval Intelligence in World War II) writes "I expect soon to do a rather fuller study than has yet been possible of Blinker Hall. By using knowledge of the second war intelligence to re-examine Hall's work there is quite a lot of new material to be looked for and appreciated. Hall's son is assisting me." (Letter to the author, 28 May 1970.) A study of the Admiralty War Staff ("Naval Staff" from May 1917) is needed. Mr. George Walker, Lecturer in History at the Britannia Royal Naval College, Dartmouth, has such a project in mind: to enquire into the Naval Staff of 1914–1918 and to discover why it was so bad. (Letter to the author, 11 June 1970.) Other lacunae are studies in depth of naval materiel and the whole of naval procurement, an overall treatment of submarine design, of ammunition and mine development, the development of amphibious warfare materiel and doctrine, and the outlook and problems of the lower deck. There is no good detailed history of the R.N.A.S., especially one with an accent upon material, nor has the evolution of ship-borne aircraft and the aircraft-carrier been studied in detail. A student of Anglo-American affairs might find Allied naval relations, on both Fleet and Admiralty levels, a suggestive topic. This would, of course, involve, *inter alia,* an examination of the U. S. naval records in the National Archives, Navy Section. Highly recommended is the Jutland Controversy, beginning in *1916,* which could be made a provocative study in naval intellectual—and psychological—history. There are promising opportunities in the area of trade defense. The Cabinet Office Papers, supplemented by the Admiralty and Foreign Office Papers, all at the P.R.O., open up the possibility of a profitable examination of such topics as the naval terms of an armistice and a peace settlement and strategic and political factors in Britain's relations with the Northern Neutrals. Finally, there is the muddied relationship between the so-called blockade and German submarine policy: between the continual stiffening of the contraband regulations and the various German declarations of what used to be called the "sink at sight" zones. Each country has accused the other of being the initiator of all these steps; that is, the British say they undertook them because the Germans embarked on further steps of U-boat frightfulness, while the Germans say they kept extending the zone, etc., because the British kept stiffening up the contraband list, and so on. No one has really had a look to see who did what, or who started the race. The whole question, too, is bound up with the defensive arming of merchant ships, the Germans claiming that it was offensive and thus forcing them to sink without warning, the British counter-claiming that it was entirely defensive, that guns were mounted only on the sterns of ships, and so forth and so on. It would make an interesting study to chase down, step by step, exactly what happened, and why, in the escalation of British and German policy.

BIBLIOGRAPHY

PUBLISHED WORKS

1. Admiralty. *Battle of Jutland, 30th May to 1st June, 1916. Official Despatches, with Appendices,* Cmd1068. London: H.M.S.O., 1920.
2. ———. *Narrative of the Battle of Jutland.* London: H.M.S.O., 1924.
3. Alboldt, E. *Die Tragödie der alten deutschen Marine.* Berlin: Deutsche Verlagsgesellschaft für Politik und Geschichte, 1928.
4. Altham, Captain Edward. *Jellicoe.* London: Blackie, 1938.
5. Aspinall-Oglander, Brigadier-General Cecil F. *Roger Keyes.* London: Hogarth Press, 1951.
6. Bacon, Admiral Sir Reginald. *The Dover Patrol, 1915–1917.* London: Hutchinson, 1919. 2 vols. *The Concise Story of the Dover Patrol,* London: Hutchinson, 1932, is a condensation.
7. ———. *From 1900 Onward.* London: Hutchinson, 1940.
8. ———. *The Jutland Scandal.* 2nd ed. London: Hutchinson, 1925.
9. ———. *The Life of John Rushworth, Earl Jellicoe.* London: Cassell, 1936.
10. ———. *The Life of Lord Fisher of Kilverstone.* London: Hodder & Stoughton, 1929. 2 vols.
11. ———. and others. *The World Crisis by Winston Churchill: a criticism.* London: Hutchinson, 1927.
12. ———, and Francis E. McMurtrie. *Modern Naval Strategy.* London: Muller, 1940.
13. Barnes, John, ed. *The Beatty Papers,* Vol. I (1908–16). London: Navy Records Society, 1970.
14. Barnett, Correlli. *The Swordbearers: studies in Supreme Command in the First World War.* London: Eyre & Spottiswoode, 1963.
15. Bauer, Admiral Hermann. *Als Führer der U-Boote im Weltkriege, 1914–1918.* 2nd ed. Leipzig: Koehler & Amelang, 1943.
16. ———. *Reichsleitung und U-Bootseinsatz, 1914–1918.* Lippoldsberg: Klosterhaus, 1956.
17. Bayly, Admiral Sir Lewis. *Pull Together: the memoirs of Admiral Sir Lewis Bayly.* London: Harrap, 1939.
18. Beaverbrook, Lord. *Men and Power, 1917–1918.* London: Hutchinson, 1956.
19. ———. *Politicians and the War, 1914–1916.* London: Butterworth, 1928.
20. Bell, A. C. *A History of the Blockade of Germany and of the Countries Associated with Her in the Great War, Austria-Hungary, Bulgaria, and Turkey, 1914–1918* (1937). London: H.M.S.O., 1961.
21. Bellairs, Commander Carlyon. *The Battle of Jutland.* 2nd ed. London: Hodder & Stoughton, 1920.

22. Benn, Captain Wedgwood. *In the Side Shows*. London: Hodder & Stoughton, 1919.
23. Bennett, Captain Geoffrey. *The Battle of Jutland*. London: Batsford, 1964.
24. ———. *Coronel and the Falklands*. London: Batsford, 1962.
25. ———. *Naval Battles of the First World War*. London: Batsford, 1968.
26. Bingham, Commander the Hon. Barry. *Falklands, Jutland, and the Bight*. London: Murray, 1919.
27. Bone, David W. *Merchantmen-at-Arms: the British Merchant Service in the War*. London: Chatto & Windus, 1919.
28. Bonham-Carter, Lady Violet. *Winston Churchill as I Knew Him*. London: Collins, Eyre & Spottiswoode, 1965.
29. Boyle, Andrew. *Trenchard*. London: Collins, 1962.
30. Brodie, C. G. *Forlorn Hope 1915: the Submarine Passage of the Dardanelles*. London: W. J. Bryce, 1956.
31. Brownrigg, Rear-Admiral Sir Douglas. *Indiscretions of the Naval Censor*. London: Cassell, 1920.
32. Bywater, Hector C. *Cruisers in Battle: Naval "Light Cavalry" under fire, 1914–1918*. London: Constable, 1939.
33. ———, and H. C. Ferraby. *Strange Intelligence: memoirs of Naval Secret Service*. London: Constable, 1931.
34. Campbell, Rear-Admiral Gordon. *My Mystery Ships*. London: Hodder & Stoughton, 1928.
35. Carpenter, Captain A. F. B. *The Blocking of Zeebrugge*. London: Herbert Jenkins, 1922.
36. Carr, Lieutenant William G. *Brass Hats and Bell-Bottomed Trousers: unforgettable and splendid feats of the Harwich Patrol*. London: Hutchinson, 1939.
37. ———. *By Guess and By God: the story of the British submarines in the War*. London: Hutchinson [1930].
38. ———. *Good Hunting*. London: Hutchinson, 1940.
39. Chalmers, Rear-Admiral William S. *The Life and Letters of David, Earl Beatty*. London: Hodder & Stoughton, 1951.
40. ———. *Max Horton and the Western Approaches*. London: Hodder & Stoughton, 1954.
41. Chatfield, Admiral of the Fleet Lord. *The Navy and Defence*. London: Heinemann, 1942.
42. Chatterton, E. Keble. *The Auxiliary Patrol*. London: Sidgwick & Jackson, 1923.
43. ———. *Beating the U-Boats*. London: Hurst & Blackett, 1943.
44. ———. *The Big Blockade*. London: Hurst & Blackett, 1932.
45. ———. *Danger Zone: the story of the Queenstown Command*. London: Rich & Cowan, 1934.
46. ———. *Dardanelles Dilemma: the story of the naval operations*. London: Rich & Cowan, 1935.
47. ———. *Fighting the U-Boats*. London: Hurst & Blackett, 1942.
48. ———. *Gallant Gentlemen*. London: Hurst & Blackett, 1931.

49. ————. *Q-Ships and Their Story.* London: Sidgwick & Jackson, 1922.

50. ————. *The Sea-Raiders.* London: Hurst & Blackett, 1931.

51. ————. *Seas of Adventures: the story of the naval operations in the Mediterranean, Adriatic, and Aegean.* London: Hurst & Blackett, 1936.

52. Chrisman, Herman Henry. *Naval Operations in the Mediterranean during the Great War, 1914–1918.* Stanford University Ph.D. dissertation, 1931, unpublished.

53. Churchill, Winston S. *Great Contemporaries.* London: Butterworth, 1937.

54. ————. *Thoughts and Adventures.* London: Butterworth, 1932.

55. ————. *The World Crisis.* London: Butterworth, 1923–31. 5 vols. in 6, Vols. I–III. Vol. I includes the war through 1914; II, 1915; III (in two Parts), Part I, includes Jutland.

56. Colvin, Ian. *The Life of Lord Carson.* London: Gollancz, 1932–36. 3 vols. (Vol. I by Edward Marjoribanks), Vol. III.

57. Corbett, Sir Julian S., and Sir Henry Newbolt. *History of the Great War. Naval Operations.* London: Longmans, 1920–31. 5 vols. Rev. ed. of I (the events of 1914), 1938, of III (includes the Jutland material), 1940. Corbett was the author of I–III, Newbolt, of IV–V. There are also map volumes for each volume except II, which has its own maps in a pocket. Map volumes I and III are in revised editions.

58. Cousins, Geoffrey. *The Story of Scapa Flow.* London: Muller, 1965.

59. Cowie, Captain J. S. *Mines, Minelayers and Minelaying.* London: O.U.P., 1949.

60. Creswell, Commander John. *Naval Warfare: an introductory study.* 2nd ed. London: Sampson, Low, 1941.

61. Cunningham of Hyndhope, Admiral of the Fleet Viscount. *A Sailor's Odyssey.* London: Hutchinson, 1951.

62. Daniels, Josephus. *The Wilson Era: years of war and after.* Chapel Hill, North Carolina: University of North Carolina Press, 1946.

63. Dardanelles Commission. *First Report,* Cd.8490, and *Final Report,* Cmd.371. London: H.M.S.O., 1917, 1919.

64. Davies, Vice-Admiral Richard Bell. *Sailor in the Air.* London: Peter Davies, 1967.

65. Dawson, Captain Lionel. *Flotillas: a hard-lying story.* London: Rich & Cowan, 1933.

66. ————. *Sound of the Guns: being an account of the wars and service of Admiral Sir Walter Cowan.* Oxford: Pen-in-Hand, 1949.

67. de Chair, Admiral Sir Dudley. *The Sea is Strong.* Somerset de Chair, ed. London: Harrap, 1961.

68. Dewar, Vice-Admiral K. G. B. *The Navy from Within.* London: Gollancz, 1939.

69. Domvile, Admiral Sir Barry. *By and Large.* London: Hutchinson, 1936.

70. Domville-Fife, Charles W., ed. *Evolution of Sea Power*. London: Rich & Cowan, 1939.
71. Dorling, Captain Taprell. *Men O'War*. London: P. Allan, 1929.
72. Dreyer, Admiral Sir Frederic. *The Sea Heritage: a study of maritime warfare*. London: Museum Press, 1955.
73. Dugdale, Blanche E. C. *Arthur James Balfour, First Earl Balfour*. London: Hutchinson, 1936. 2 vols.
74. Edwards, Lieutenant-Commander Kenneth. *We Dive at Dawn*. London: Rich & Cowan, 1939.
75. Everitt, Don. *The K Boats*. London: Harrap, 1963.
76. Ewing, Alfred W. *The Man of Room 40: the life of Sir Alfred Ewing*. London: Hutchinson, 1939.
77. Fawcett, Lieutenant-Commander H. W., and Lieutenant G. W. W. Hooper, eds. *The Fighting at Jutland*. London: Macmillan, 1921. There is also an abridged edition (1921).
78. Fayle, C. Ernest. *History of the Great War. Seaborne Trade*. London: Murray, 1920–24. 3 vols.
79. Fisher, Admiral of the Fleet Lord. *Memories*. London: Hodder & Stoughton, 1919.
80. ———. *Records*. London: Hodder & Stoughton, 1919.
81. Fremantle, Admiral Sir Sydney R. *My Naval Career, 1880–1928*. London: Hutchinson, 1949.
82. Frost, Commander Holloway H. *The Battle of Jutland*. London: B. F. Stevens & Brown, 1936.
83. Gayer, Lieutenant-Commander Albert. *Die deutschen U-Boote in ihrer Kriegführung, 1914–1918*. Berlin: Mittler, 1930.
84. Geddes, Baron. *The Forging of a Family*. London: Faber, 1952.
85. *General Index to Parliamentary Papers, 1900–1949*. London: H.M.S.O., 1960. Pages 776–8 list the naval report and papers for 1914–18.
86. Germany, Ministry of Marine. *Der Krieg zur See, 1914–1918*. A series of seven sets. Berlin: Mittler—
    Der Krieg in der Nordsee (1920–65, 7 vols.). I–V, by Captain Otto Groos, VI–VII, by Admiral Walther Gladisch. There is a supplementary volume of Jutland maps for V.
    Der Handelskrieg mit U-Booten (1932–66, 5 vols.), by Rear-Admiral Arno Spindler.
    Der Krieg in den türkischen Gewässern (1928–38, 2 vols.), by Rear-Admiral Hermann Lorey.
    Der Kreuzerkrieg in den ausländischen Gewässern (1922–37, 3 vols.). I–II, by Captain Erich Raeder (rev. ed. of I, 1927), III, by Vice-Admiral Eberhard von Mantey.
    Der Krieg in der Ostsee (1922–64, 3 vols.). I, by Captain Rudolph Firle, II, by Lieutenant Heinrich Rollmann, III, by Admiral Ernst von Gagern.
    Die Kämpfe der kaiserlichen Marine in den deutschen Kolonien (1935), Vice-Admiral Kurt Assmann, ed.

Die Überwasserstreitkräfte und ihre Technik (1930), by Captain Paul Köppen.

87. Gibson, R. H., and Maurice Prendergast. *The German Submarine War, 1914–1918.* 2nd ed. London: Constable, 1931.

88. Gibson, Langhorne, and Vice-Admiral J. E. T. Harper. *The Riddle of Jutland.* London: Cassell, 1934.

89. Gilbert, Martin. *Winston Churchill,* Vol. III (1914–16). London: Heinemann, 1971. Vol. IV (1917–23) will be published in 1973, two "companion" volumes of sources for III, in 1972, and three for IV, in 1974.

90. Godfrey, Admiral John H. *The Naval Memoirs of Admiral J. H. Godfrey.* Privately printed, 1964–66. 7 vols. in 10. Copy in the Naval Library.

91. Goodenough, Admiral Sir William. *A Rough Record.* London: Hutchinson, 1943.

92. Grant, Robert M. *U-Boats Destroyed.* London: Putnam, 1964.

93. ————. *U-Boat Intelligence, 1914–1918.* London: Putnam, 1969.

94. Grenfell, Commander Russell. *The Art of the Admiral.* London: Faber, 1937.

95. Gretton, Vice-Admiral Sir Peter. *Former Naval Person: Winston Churchill and the Royal Navy.* London: Cassell, 1968.

96. Grey, C. G. *Sea-Flyers.* London: Faber, 1942.

97. Guinn, Paul. *British Strategy and Politics, 1914–18.* London: O.U.P., 1965.

98. Halpern, Paul, ed. *The Keyes Papers,* Vol. I (to 1928). London: Navy Records Society, 1972?

99. Hamilton, General Sir Ian. *Gallipoli Diary.* London: Arnold, 1920. 2 vols.

100. Hampshire, A. Cecil. *The Phantom Fleet.* London: Kimber, 1960.

101. Hankey, Lord. *The Supreme Command.* London: Allen & Unwin, 1961. 2 vols.

102. Harper, Rear-Admiral J. E. T. *The Truth about Jutland.* London: Murray, 1927.

103. ————, and others. *Reproduction of the Record of the Battle of Jutland,* Cmd.2870. London: H.M.S.O., 1927.

104. Hezlet, Vice-Admiral Sir Arthur. *The Submarine and Sea Power.* London: Peter Davies, 1967.

105. Hickling, Vice-Admiral Harold. *Sailor at Sea.* London: Kimber, 1965.

106. Higham, Robin. *The British Rigid Airstrip, 1908–1931.* London: Foulis, 1961.

107. Hirst, Paymaster Commander Lloyd. *Coronel and After.* London: Davies, 1934.

108. *History of the First World War.* Barrie Pitt, ed. London: Purnell, 1969–.

109. Hough, Richard. *The Big Battleship: the curious career of H.M.S. Agincourt.* London: Michael Joseph, 1966. U. S. edition: *The*

Great Dreadnought: the strange story of H.M.S. Agincourt. New York: Harper & Row, 1967.

110. ———. *Dreadnought: a history of the modern battleship.* London: Michael Joseph, 1965.

111. ———, *First Sea Lord: an authorized biography of Admiral Lord Fisher.* London: Allen & Unwin, 1969. U. S. edition: *Admiral of the Fleet: the life of John Fisher.* New York: Macmillan, 1970.

112. ———. *The Pursuit of Admiral von Spee: a study in loneliness and bravery.* London: Allen & Unwin, 1969.

113. Hoy, H. C. *40 O.B.* London: Hutchinson, 1932.

114. Hurd, Sir Archibald. *History of the Great War. The Merchant Navy.* London: Murray, 1921–29. 3 vols.

115. ———. *Who Goes There?* London: Hutchinson, 1942.

116. Hyde, H. Montgomery. *Carson.* London: Heinemann, 1953.

117. Irving, Lieutenant-Commander John. *Coronel and the Falklands.* London: Philpot, 1927.

118. ———. *Jutland.* London: Kimber, 1966.

119. James, Robert Rhodes. *Gallipoli.* London: Batsford, 1965.

120. James, Admiral Sir William. *Admiral William Fisher.* London: Macmillan, 1943.

121. ———. *Blue Water and Green Fields.* London: Methuen, 1940.

122. ———. *The Eyes of the Navy: a biographical study of Admiral Sir Reginald Hall.* London: Methuen, 1955. U. S. edition: *The Code Breakers of Room 40: the story of Admiral Sir Reginald Hall.* New York: St. Martin's Press, 1956.

123. ———. *A Great Seaman: the life of Admiral of the Fleet Sir Henry F. Oliver.* London: Witherby, 1956.

124. ———. *The Sky Was Always Blue.* London: Methuen, 1951.

125. Jameson, Rear-Admiral Sir William. *The Fleet that Jack Built: nine men who made a modern navy.* London: Hart-Davis, 1962.

126. ———. *The Most Formidable Thing.* London: Hart-Davis, 1965.

127. ———. *Submariners V.C.* London: Peter Davies, 1962.

128. ———. *The Crisis of the Naval War.* London: Cassell, 1920.

129. Jellicoe, Admiral of the Fleet Earl. *The Grand Fleet, 1914–16: its creation, development and work.* London: Cassell, 1919.

130. ———. *The Submarine Peril.* London: Cassell, 1934.

131. Jenkins, Roy. *Asquith.* London: Collins, 1964.

132. Jerrold, Douglas. *The Royal Naval Division.* London: Hutchinson, 1923.

133. Johnson, Franklyn A. *Defence by Committee: the British Committee of Imperial Defence, 1885–1959.* London: O.U.P., 1960.

134. Kahn, David. *The Codebreakers.* New York: Macmillan, 1967.

135. Kemp, Lieutenant-Commander P. K. *Fleet Air Arm.* London: Jenkins, 1954.

136. ———. *H.M. Destroyers.* London: Jenkins, 1956.

137. ———. *H.M. Submarines.* London: Jenkins, 1952.

138. Kenworthy, Lieutenant-Commander J. M. (Lord Strabolgi). *Sailors, Statesmen—and Others: an autobiography.* London: Rich & Cowan, 1933.

139. Kerr, Admiral Mark. *Land, Sea, and Air: reminiscences of Mark Kerr*. London: Longmans, 1927.

140. ———. *The Navy in My Time*. London: Rich & Cowan, 1933.

141. ———. *Prince Louis of Battenberg, Admiral of the Fleet*. London: Longmans, 1934.

142. Keyes, Admiral Sir Roger. *The Naval Memoirs of Admiral of the Fleet Sir Roger Keyes*. London: Butterworth, 1934–35. 2 vols.

143. King-Hall, Louise, ed. *Sea Saga: being the naval diaries of four generations of the King-Hall family*. London: Gollancz, 1935.

144. King-Hall, Commander Stephen. *My Naval Life, 1906–1929*. London: Faber, 1952.

145. ———. *A North Sea Diary, 1914–1918*. London: Newnes, 1936.

146. Langmaid, Captain Kenneth. *The Approaches Are Mined!* London: Jarrolds, 1965.

147. ———. *The Sea Raiders*. London: Jarrolds, 1963.

148. Laurens, Commander Adolphe. *Histoire de la guerre sous-marine allemande (1914–1918)*. Paris: Société d'Éditions Géographiques, Maritimes et Coloniales, 1930.

149. Le Fleming, H. M. *Warships of World War I*. London: Ian Allan, [1962?].

150. Leslie, Sir Shane. *Memoirs of Sir Shane Leslie*. London: Murray, 1966.

151. Lloyd George, David. *War Memoirs of David Lloyd George*. London: Nicholson & Watson, 1933–36. 6 vols.

152. Longmore, Air Chief Marshal Sir Arthur. *From Sea to Sky, 1910–1945*. London: Geoffrey Bles, 1946.

153. Lumby, E. W. R., ed. *Papers Relating to Naval Policy and Operations in the Mediterranean, 1912–1914*. London: Navy Records Society, 1971?

154. Macintyre, Captain Donald. *Jutland*. London: Evans, 1957.

155. ———. *Wings of Neptune: the story of Naval Aviation*. London: Peter Davies, 1963.

156. MacKay, Ruddock F. *Fisher of Kilverstone*. Oxford: Clarendon Press, 1971?

157. Manning, Captain T. D. *The British Destroyer*. London: Putnam, 1961.

158. March, Edgar J. *British Destroyers: a history of development, 1892–1953*. London: Seeley Service, 1966.

159. Marder, Arthur J. *Fear God and Dread Nought: the correspondence of Admiral of the Fleet Lord Fisher of Kilverstone*. Vol. III. London: Cape, 1952–59. 3 vols.

160. ———. *From the Dreadnought to Scapa Flow: the Royal Navy in the Fisher Era, 1904–1919*. London: O.U.P., 1961–70. 5 vols. Vols. II–V: II, the war to the eve of Jutland; III, Jutland and aftermath, to December 1916; IV, December 1916–December 1917; V, 1918–summer, 1919.

161. ———. *Portrait of an Admiral: the life and papers of Sir Herbert Richmond*. London: Cape, 1952.

162. Maurice, Major-General Sir Frederick. *Lessons of Allied Co-Operations: naval, military, and air, 1914–1918.* London: O.U.P., 1942.
163. "Mercantile Losses." Cd.9221 (November 1918). Abbreviated title.
164. "Merchant Shipping. War Losses." Parliamentary Paper 199 (1919).
165. Michelsen, Vice-Admiral Andreas. *Der U-Bootskrieg, 1914–1918.* Leipzig: Koehler, 1925.
166. Middlemas, Keith. *Command the Far Seas: a naval campaign of the First World War.* London: Hutchinson, 1961.
167. Milne, Admiral Sir A. Berkeley. *The Flight of the "Goeben" and the "Breslau."* London: Eveleigh Nash, 1921.
168. Moon, Howard. *The Invasion of the United Kingdom: public controversy and official planning, 1888–1918.* University of London Ph.D. dissertation, 1968, unpublished.
169. Moore, Major W. Geoffrey. *Early Bird.* London: Putnam, 1963.
170. Moorehead, Alan. *Gallipoli.* London: Hamish Hamilton, 1956.
171. Morison, Elting E. *Admiral Sims and the Modern American Navy.* Boston: Houghton Mifflin, 1942.
172. Mountevans, Admiral Lord. *Adventurous Life.* London: Hutchinson, 1946.
173. Munro, Captain D. J. *Convoys, Blockades and Mystery Towers.* London: Sampson Low [1932].
174. ———. *Scapa Flow: a naval retrospect.* London: Sampson Low, 1932.
175. "Navy Pay, Half Pay, Retired Pay, and Allowance of Officers" (recommendations of committees). Cmd.270 (1919). Abbreviated title.
176. "Navy Pay, Allowances, and Pensions of the Royal Navy and Royal Marines" (recommendations of Admiral Jerram's Committee). Cmd.149 (1919). Abbreviated title.
177. "Navy War Losses." Parliamentary Paper 200 (1919).
178. Nicolson, Harold. *King George the Fifth: his life and reign.* London: Constable, 1952.
179. Olson, Mancur, Jr. *The Economics of Wartime Shortage: a history of British food supplies in the Napoleonic War and in World Wars I and II.* Durham: Duke University Press, 1963.
180. Oxford and Asquith, Earl of. *Memories and Reflections, 1852–1927.* Vol. II. London: Cassell, 1928. 2 vols.
181. Parkes, Oscar. *British Battleships.* Rev. ed. London: Seeley Service, 1966.
182. Pastfield, Rev. John L. *New Light on Jutland.* London: Heinemann, 1953.
183. Patterson, A. Temple, ed. *The Jellicoe Papers.* London: Navy Records Society, 1966–68. 2 vols. Vol. I closes with Jellicoe's Jutland dispatch.
184. ———. *Jellicoe.* London: Macmillan, 1969.
185. Pelly, Admiral Sir Henry. *300,000 Sea Miles: an autobiography.* London: Chatto & Windus, 1938.
186. Pitt, Barrie. *Coronel and Falkland.* London: Cassell, 1960. U. S. edition: *Revenge at Sea.* New York: Stein & Day, 1964.

187. ———. *Zeebrugge*. London: Cassell, 1958.

188. Pollen, Arthur Hungerford. *The Navy in Battle*. London: Chatto & Windus, 1918. U. S. edition: *The British Navy in Battle*. New York: Doubleday, Page, 1918.

188a. Popham, Hugh. *Into Wind: a history of British naval flying*. London: Hamish Hamilton, 1970.

189. Pound, Reginald. *Evans of the Broke*. London: O.U.P., 1963.

190. Puleston, Captain William D. (U.S.N.). *High Command in the World War*. London: Scribner's, 1934.

191. Raeder, Grand-Admiral Erich. *My Life*. Annapolis, Maryland: U. S. Naval Institute, 1960. A condensation of his *Mein Leben*. Tübingen: Schlichtenmayer, 1956–57. 2 vols.

192. Raleigh, Sir Walter, and H. A. Jones. *History of the Great War. The War in the Air*. Oxford: Clarendon Press, 1922–37. 6 vols. Raleigh wrote Vol. I, Jones, the other five. There are, in addition, map volumes for I and III and a volume of Appendices.

193. Ranft, Bryan, ed. *Defence of Trade, 1914–18*. London: Navy Records Society, no date fixed.

194. Rayleigh, Lord. *The Life of Sir J. J. Thomson*. Cambridge University Press, 1942.

195. Repington, Lieutenant-Colonel Charles à Court. *The First World War, 1914–1918*. London: Constable, 1920. 2 vols.

196. Richmond, Admiral Sir Herbert W. *National Policy and Naval Strength and Other Essays*. London: Longmans, 1928.

197. ———. *Statesmen and Sea Power*. London: O.U.P., 1946.

198. Riddell, Lord. *Lord Riddell's War Diary, 1914–1918*. London: Nicholson & Watson, 1933.

199. Robinson, Douglas H. *The Zeppelin in Combat: a history of the German Naval Airship Division, 1912–1918*. Rev. ed. London: Foulis, 1966.

200. Rodman, Admiral Hugh. *Yarns of a Kentucky Admiral*. Indianapolis, Indiana: Bobbs-Merrill, 1928.

201. Roskill, Captain S. W. *H.M.S. Warspite*. London: Collins, 1957.

202. ———. *Hankey: man of secrets*. Vol. I (through World War I). London: Collins, 1970.

203. ———, ed. *Papers Relating to the Royal Naval Air Service, 1908–1918*. London: Navy Records Society, 1969.

204. ———. *The Strategy of Sea Power*. London: Collins, 1962.

205. Rutter, Owen. *Red Ensign: a history of convoy*. London: Robert Hale, 1942.

206. Salter, Lord. *Memoirs of a Public Servant*. London: Faber, 1961.

207. Samson, Air-Commodore Charles R. *Fights and Flights*. London: Benn, 1930.

208. Scheer, Admiral Reinhard. *Germany's High Sea Fleet in the World War*. London: Cassell, 1920.

209. Schilling, Warner R. *Admirals and Foreign Policy, 1913–1919*. New York: Columbia University Press, 1971?

210. Schurman, Donald M. *Sir Julian Corbett and the Royal Navy*. London: 1971?
211. Schoultz, Commodore G. von. *With the British Battle Fleet: war recollections of a Russian naval officer*. London: Hutchinson, 1925.
212. Seymour, Lady. *Commander Ralph Seymour, R.N.* Glasgow: The University Press, 1926.
213. Shankland, Peter, and Anthony Hunter. *Dardanelles Patrol*. London: Collins, 1964.
214. Sims, Rear-Admiral William S. *The Victory at Sea*. London: Murray, 1920.
215. Siney, Marion C. *The Allied Blockade of Germany, 1914–1916*. Ann Arbor: The University of Michigan Press, 1957.
216. Smith, Vice-Admiral Humphrey H. *A Yellow Admiral Remembers*. London: Arnold, 1932.
217. Spender, J. A., and Cyril Asquith. *Life of Herbert Henry Asquith, Lord Oxford and Asquith*. London: Hutchinson, 1932. 2 vols.
218. Steinberg, Jonathan, ed. *The de Robeck Papers*. London: Navy Records Society, no date fixed.
219. Sueter, Rear-Admiral Murray F. *Airmen or Noahs*. London: Pitman, 1928.
220. Sykes, Major-General Sir Frederick. *From Many Angles: an autobiography*. London: Harrap, 1942.
221. T 124 (Captain Russell Grenfell). *Sea Power*. Rev. ed. London: Cape, 1941.
222. Taffrail (Captain Taprell Dorling). *Endless Story: being an account of the work of the destroyers, flotilla-leaders, topedo-boats and patrol boats in the Great War*. London: Hodder & Stoughton, 1931.
223. ———. *Swept Channels: being an account of the work of the minesweepers in the Great War*. London: Hodder & Stoughton, 1935.
224. Tennyson d'Eyncourt, Sir Eustace H. W. *A Shipbuilder's Yarn*. London: Hutchinson, 1948.
225. Terry, C. Sanford, ed. *Ostend and Zeebrugge, April 23: May 10, 1918: the dispatches of Vice-Admiral Sir Roger Keyes and other narratives of the Operations*. London: O.U.P., 1919.
226. Thetford, Owen. *British Naval Aircraft Since 1912*. 2nd ed. London: Putnam, 1962.
227. Thomson, Sir J. J. *Recollections and Reflections*. London: Bell, 1936.
228. Toye, Francis. *For What We Have Received: an autobiography*. New York: Knopf, 1948.
229. Troubridge, Laura. *Memories and Reflections*. London: Heinemann, 1925.
230. Tupper, Admiral Sir Reginald. *Reminiscences*. London: Jarrolds, 1929.
231. Tweedie, Admiral Sir Hugh. *The Story of a Naval Life*. London: Rich & Cowan, 1939.
232. United States Air Force Academy. *Command and Commanders in*

Modern Warfare. Lieut.-Col. William Geffen, ed. Colorado: U. S. Air Force Academy, 1969.

233. Usborne, Vice-Admiral C. V. *Blast and Counterblast: a naval impression of the War.* London: Murray, 1935.

234. ———. *Smoke on the Horizon: Mediterranean fighting, 1914–1918.* London: Hodder & Stoughton, 1933.

235. Verner, Commander Rudolf. *The Battle Cruisers at the Action of the Falkland Islands.* Colonel Willoughby Verner, ed. London: John Bale Sons, Danielsson, 1920.

236. Waters, Lieutenant-Commander D. W. "The Philosophy and Conduct of Maritime War," Part I, 1815–1918, *Journal of the Royal Naval Scientific Service,* May 1958. *A restricted publication.*

237. Weldon, Captain L. B. *'Hard Lying': Eastern Mediterranean, 1914–1919.* London: Jenkins, 1925.

238. *Das Werk Untersuchungsausschusses der Verfassungsgebenden deutschen Nationalversammlung und des deutschen Reichstages 1919–1930.* Vol. X/1 of 4th series, *Die Ursachen des deutschen Zusammenbruches in Jahre 1918.* Berlin: Deutsche Verlagsgesellschaft für Politik und Geschichte, 1928.

239. Wester Wemyss, Admiral of the Fleet Lord. *The Navy in the Dardanelles Campaign.* London: Hodder & Stoughton, 1924.

240. Wester Wemyss, Lady. *The Life and Letters of Lord Wester Wemyss.* London: Eyre & Spottiswoode, 1935.

241. Woodward, Sir Llewellyn. *Great Britain and the War of 1914–1918.* London: Methuen, 1967.

242. Woolard, Commander Claude L. A. *With the Harwich Naval Forces, 1914–1918.* (Privately printed, Antwerp, 1931.)

243. Young, Desmond. *Rutland of Jutland.* London: Cassell, 1963.

244. Young, Filson. *With the Battle Cruisers.* London: Cassell, 1921.

245. Young, Kenneth. *Arthur James Balfour.* London: Bell, 1963.

* * *

246. Allied Naval Council: its minutes will be found in the Naval Library, Ministry of Defence, the "I.C." series of the Cabinet Office Records (Cab.28), and the War Department, Archives of the National Archives in Washington, D.C.

247. Sound Archives, British Broadcasting Corporation, Broadcasting House, London, W.1. Chatfield: 3789/92; Dreyer, SLP 22872; Goodenough, 719/22.

BRITISH OFFICIAL WORKS—UNPUBLISHED

Except as noted, all are available in the Naval Library, Ministry of Defence.

248. Board of Invention and Research. *Reports and Minutes of Meetings, 1915–17.* 6 vols. Abbreviated title.

249. "Chronological List of German U-Boats Sunk in First World War, 1914–1918" (n.d.).

250. Director of Naval Construction Depatment, Admiralty. *Records of Warship Construction during the War, 1914–1918* (1919).

251. Director of Statistics, Admiralty. "Statistical Review of the War Against Shipping" (23 December 1918).

252. Director of Torpedoes and Mining Department, Admiralty. *Mining Manual* (1922–24, 3 vols.).

253. Ministry of Shipping. *A Report of Shipping Control during the War. The Work of the Transport Department and Ministry of Shipping up to the Armistice, 11th November, 1918* (post-war). There is a copy in Lord Salter's papers. (The Lord Salter, P.C., G.B.E., K.C.B., West House, Glebe Place, London, S.W.3.)

254. ————. *The System of Convoys for Merchant Shipping in 1917 and 1918* (post-war). There is a copy in Lord Salter's papers.

255. Technical History Section, Admiralty: fifty monographs (1919-20), collectively known as *The Technical History,* and whose most useful volumes for most purposes are:

TH 1 *Submarine v. Submarine*
TH 4 *Aircraft v. Submarine. Submarine Campaign, 1918*
TH 7 *The Anti-Submarine Division of the Naval Staff. December 1916–November 1918*
TH 8 *Scandinavian and East Coast Convoy Systems, 1917–1918*
TH 13 *Defensive Arming of Merchant Ships*
TH 14 *The Atlantic Convoy System, 1917–1918*
TH 15 *Convoy Statistics and Diagrams*
TH 21 *Submarine Administration, Training, and Construction*
TH 23 *Fire Control in H.M. Ships*
TH 24 *Storage and Handling of Explosives in Warships*
TH 28 *Guns and Gun Mountings*
TH 29 *Ammunition for Naval Guns*
TH 30 *Control of Mercantile Movements. Part I. Text*
TH 31 *Control of Mercantile Movements. Part II. Appendices*
TH 32 *Control of Mercantile Movements. Part III. Plans*
TH 37 *Inception and Development of the Northern Base* (Scapa Flow)
TH 39 *Miscellaneous Convoys*
TH 40 *Anti-Submarine Development and Experiments Prior to December 1916*
TH 51 *Development of the Paravane*

The others are on more or less esoteric subjects, such as *Naval Medical Transport during the War* (TH 3), *Naval Anti-Gas Devices* (TH 26), *The Development of the Gyro-Compass Prior to and during the War* (TH 20), *Admiralty Airship Sheds* (TH 43), etc. TH 38 was not issued.

NAVAL STAFF STUDIES

256. Anti-Submarine Division. *Monthly Reports, 1917–18* (May 1917–November 1918).

257. ————. *R.N.A.S. Anti-Submarine Reports* (Monthly, June 1917–March 1918). Continued in (258).

258. Air Division. *Naval Air Operations* (Monthly Reports, April–October 1918).
259. Gunnery Division. *Grand Fleet Gunnery and Torpedo Memoranda on Naval Actions, 1914–1918* (1922).
260. ———. *Report of the Committee Appointed to Investigate the Attacks Delivered on and the Enemy Defences of the Dardanelles Straits. 1919* (1921). The "Mitchell Committee Report."
261. Historical Section. *History of the Second World War. Defeat of the Enemy Attack on Shipping, 1939–1945* (1957, 2 vols.). The first chapter of Vol. 1A is on "Some Lessons from the First World War," and there are excellent plans and tables in Vol. 1B. *A restricted publication.*
262. Leith, Captain Lockhart. *The History of British Minefields* (n.d., 2 vols.).
263. *Operations off the East Coast of Great Britain, 1914–1918* (1940).
264. *Review of German Cruiser Warfare, 1914–1918* (1940).
265. Torpedo Division. *Remarks of the Naval Staff on Anti-Submarine Operations* (1927).
266. Training and Staff Duties Division. *Addendum No. 1 to Naval Tactical Notes, Vol. i, 1929* (1931).
267. ———. *History of British Minesweeping in the War* (1920). Actually written by Captain Lionel L. Preston, Director of Minesweeping at the Admiralty, 1917–19.
268. ———. "Monographs (Historical)" on the war: thirty-nine (including one that was later withdrawn), the most important of which for most purposes are:

Monograph No.	Title	Year of Publication
8	*Naval Operations Connected with the Raid on the North-East Coast, December 16th, 1914*	1921
11	*The Battle of Heligoland Bight, August 28th, 1914*	1921
12	*The Action off Dogger Bank, January 24th, 1915*	1921
13	*Summary of the Operations of the Grand Fleet, August 1914 to November 1916*	1921
18	*The Dover Command,* vol. I, (No vol. II was produced, as the subject was considered to be adequately covered in the Official History, *Naval Operations.*)	1922
19	*Tenth Cruiser Squadron,* vol. I. (Covers 1914–Feb. 1916; no Vol. II was issued.)	1922
21	*The Mediterranean, 1914–1915* (Superseded No. 4, *Goeben and Breslau,* of 1920.)	1923
23	*Home Waters—Part I. From the Outbreak of the War to 27 August 1914*	1924
24	*Home Waters—Part II. September and October 1914*	1924
27	*Battles of Coronel and Falkland Islands* (Superseded No. 1, *Coronel,* of 1920, and No. 3, *Falklands,* of 1920.)	1922

Monograph No.	Title	Year of Publication
28	*Home Waters—Part III. From November 1914 to the End of January 1915* (Includes a revised No. 8.)	1925
29	*Home Waters—Part IV. From February to July 1915*	1925
30	*Home Waters—Part V. From July to October 1915*	1926
31	*Home Waters—Part VI. From October 1915 to May 1916*	1926
32	*Lowestoft Raid. 24th–25th April 1916*	1927
33	*Home Waters—Part VII. From June 1916 to November 1916*	1927
34	*Home Waters—Part VIII. From December 1916 to April 1917*	1933
35	*Home Waters—Part IX. 1st May, 1917, to 31st July, 1917.* (No monographs were issued for Home Waters between August 1917 and November 1918.)	1939
—	*Mediterranean Staff Papers relating to Naval Operations from August 1917 to December 1918.* (No monographs were issued for the Mediterranean between 1916 and July 1917.)	1920
—	*The Naval Staff of the Admiralty. Its Work and Development*	1929
—	*Naval Staff Appreciation of Jutland.* (Withdrawn in about 1928 and most copies destroyed. See *From the Dreadnought to Scapa Flow,* Vol. III, viii–ix.) The Naval Library does not have a copy. There is one with the Harper Papers (291) and another in the Library of the University of California, Irvine.	1922

The other monographs are concerned with the German Cruiser Squadron in the Pacific, 1914 (No. 2), Cameroons, 1914 (No. 5), passage of the British Expeditionary Force, August 1914 (No. 6), the Patrol Flotillas at the start of the war (No. 7), the White Sea Station (No. 9), East Africa, 1914–15 (No. 10), the first Australian convoy, 1914 (No. 14), operations in Mesopotamia and the Persian Gulf, 1914–16 (No. 15), the China Squadron, 1914 (No. 16), the East Indies Squadron, 1914 (No. 17), the Cape of Good Hope Station, 1914 (No. 20), the Atlantic Ocean, 1914 (No. 22), the Baltic, 1914 (No. 25), the Atlantic, from the Falklands to May 1915 (No. 26), the Archangel River Flotilla, 1919 (un-numbered).

269. Waters, Lieutenant-Commander D. W. *Notes on the Convoy System of Naval Warfare, Thirteenth to Twentieth Centuries,* Part II, *First World War, 1914–18* (1960). (Part I, covering the earlier period, was issued in 1957.)

MANUSCRIPTS

270. *Asquith Papers:* Department of Western MSS., Bodleian Library, Oxford.

271. *Barley-Waters Papers:* Naval Historical Branch, Ministry of Defence, Old War Office Building, Whitehall, London, S.W.1. A mass of valuable papers and raw material on trade defence, by Lieutenant-Commander D. W. Waters and Commander F. Barley. There is a duplicate set (not quite complete) in the Naval Library, Ministry of Defence.

272. *Battenberg Papers:* Lord Brabourne (senior Trustee of the Broadlands Archives Trust), Newhouse Mershan, Ashford, Kent. At the present time, however, the papers are not available to scholars.

273. *Beatty Papers:* the 2nd Earl Beatty, D.S.C., Chicheley Hall, Newport Pagnell, Buckinghamshire.

274. *Bethell Papers:* Mrs. Agatha Marsden-Smedley, 31 Draycott Place, London, S.W.3. Important for the Duff and Jellicoe letters, 1917–18, to Admiral the Hon. Sir Alexander Bethell.

275. *Carson Papers:* the Hon. Edward Carson, Cleve Court, Minster-in-Thanet, Ramsgate, Kent. The great bulk of Carson's Admiralty papers, some 200 items, are in the Public Record Office of Northern Ireland (Law Courts Building, May Street, Belfast), catalogued under D.1507/4. Material on Jellicoe's dismissal (December 1917) is in D.1506/1/2. The Belfast material includes a number of interesting items, but the cream of Carson's naval papers appear to have been destroyed in the Blitz.

276. *Chatfield MSS.:* 2nd Baron Chatfield, 46 Academy Road, Westmount, Quebec, Canada. Family correspondence; some post-war Jutland material.

277. *Churchill Papers:* the Chartwell Trust. They are expected to be made available (in the Churchill College Library, Cambridge) after the completion of the authorized biography. One should then write to Mr. Winston Churchill, Broadwater House, Chailey, Sussex.

278. *Domvile Papers:* Admiral Sir Barry Domvile, K.B.E., C.B., C.M.G., Robin's Tree, Roehampton Vale, London, S.W.15. Destined eventually for the National Maritime Museum.

279. *Duff Papers:* Lieutenant-Commander Peter Dolphin, R.N. (ret.), Saxonbury, Betsham, Gravesend, Kent. Some correspondence and minutes pertaining to his work are at the Admiralty. The main collection is at the National Maritime Museum.

280. *Fisher Papers:* the 3rd Baron Fisher, Kilverstone Hall, Thetford, Norfolk; the Duke of Hamilton, P.C., KT., LL.D., etc., Lennoxlove, Haddington, East Lothian, Scotland.

281. *Geddes Papers:* Admiralty Papers, Public Record Office: Adm.116/1804–1810. The first volume has an excellent index to all the papers.

282. *Frewen Papers:* Mrs. Lena Frewen, Sheephouse, Brede, Sussex. The well-written 55 volumes of Captain Frewen's diaries (1903–57), of which the first 44 are indexed.

283. *Hall Papers:* Commander Richard A. Hall, R.N. (ret.), 18 River-

mead Court, London, S.W.6. The papers, as stated, are few. The Captain's memory might be helpful to a scholar.

284. *Lloyd George Papers:* The Beaverbrook Library, 33 St. Bride Street, London, E.C.4. Apply to the Librarian, Mr. A. J. P. Taylor, at least one week in advance, indicating preference in dates. Do *not* call at the Library without an appointment.

285. *Roskill Papers:* Captain S. W. Roskill, D.S.C., R.N. (ret.), Blounce, South Warnborough, Basingstoke, Hampshire. Important unpublished papers and correspondence on Jutland.

286. *Royal Archives:* Windsor Castle, Berkshire; Mr. R. C. Mackworth-Young, M.V.O., Librarian.

287. *Sturdee Papers:* Captain W. D. M. Staveley, R.N., Ivy Hatch, Kent.

288. *Troubridge Papers:* Lieutenant-Commander Sir Peter Troubridge, Bt., R.N. (ret.), The Manor House, Elsted, Midhurst, Sussex. A few score letters from well-known people of the period, but almost entirely social, and a notebook in which the Admiral had drafted some reminiscences, including a *pièce justicative* on the *Goeben* affair.

289. *Tyrwhitt Papers:* Lady Agnew, Pinehurst, South Ascot, Berkshire.

290. *Wester Wemyss Papers:* The Hon. Mrs. F. Cunnack, Saint-Suliac, Ile et Vilaine, France.

291. *British Museum,* Department of Manuscripts, Bloomsbury, London, W.C.1: *Balfour Papers* (Add. MSS. 49683–49962; particularly valuable, the personal and official correspondence when First Lord, 1915–16, with the First Sea Lord, Admiral Sir Henry Jackson, and the C.-in-C., Grand Fleet, Jellicoe, in 49714); *Admiral Sir Hugh Evan-Thomas Papers* (Add. MSS. 52504–52506, correspondence of the Rear-Admiral Commanding 5th Battle Squadron at Jutland); *Captain Oswald M. Frewen Papers* (Add. MSS. 53738, post-war letters from Jellicoe dealing with Jutland); *Harper Papers* (Add. MSS. 54477–54480); *Jellicoe Papers* (Add. MSS. 48989–49057, correspondence with the Admiralty as C.-in-C., Grand Fleet, in 48990–48992, letters from Fisher, Madden, Beatty, Jackson in 49006–49009, the Jutland material in 49014, 49027–49028, 49040–49042, and autobiographical notes in 49038).

292. *Churchill College Library.* Cambridge. Dr. J. T. Killen, Librarian: de Robeck, Drax, Hankey, Keyes, and Williamson Papers. The Keyes Papers are on loan by Lord Keyes. The Hankey Papers may be made available when his authorized biographer, Captain S. W. Roskill, is through with them. The de Robeck and Keyes Papers will not be available until no longer needed by their Editors, Drs. Steinberg and Halpern, respectively. Application to see papers should be made in advance to the Librarian.

293. *Germany, Ministry of Marine Archives:* Bundesarchiv-Militärarchiv, *7800 Freiburg im Breisgau,* Wiesentalstrasse 10. Among the more valuable records are the "Akten des kaiserlichen Marine-Kabinetts," 1890–1918 (the office headed by Admiral Georg von Müller), the voluminous papers of Rear-Admiral Magnus von Lovetzow (Chief of the Operations Section of Scheer's staff, and, from August 1918,

Chief of Staff of the Operations Department of the *Admiralstab*), and the folders on the major naval actions which were prepared by the German Office of Naval History in the interwar period and consist of the War Diary of the Kommando der Hochseestreitkrafte, letters, and action reports. The National Archives, Washington, have microfilm copies of all the Ministry of Marine records; the Naval Library, Ministry of Defence, has microfilm copies of selected "Atken," all the Levetzow material and the K.d.H. War Diary.

294. *National Maritime Museum Library.* Greenwich, London, S.E.10, Mr. A. W. H. Pearsall, Custodian of Manuscripts: the papers of *Sir W. Graham Greene,* Secretary of the Admiralty, 1911–17, and Admirals *Sir Walter Cowan, K. G. B. Dewar, Sir Alexander Duff, Sir William Wordsworth Fisher, Sir Sydney Fremantle, Sir Frederick Hamilton, Sir Louis Hamilton, Sir Martyn Jerram, Sir Howard Kelly, Sir Berkeley Milne, Sir Henry Oliver, Sir Herbert Richmond,* and *Sir William Tennant.*

295. *Naval Library, Ministry of Defence,* Empress State Building, Earls Court, London, S.W.7, Rear-Admiral P. N. Buckley, C.B., D.S.O., Librarian: *Rear-Admiral Roger M. Bellairs Papers* (1917–18 Grand Fleet papers of Bellairs, who was then on Beatty's Staff, but these papers are now unaccountably missing; possibly lost or mislaid when the Library moved from Whitehall in 1963); *Captain T. E. Crease Papers* (he served as Lord Fisher's Secretary during much of his appointments as First Sea Lord and in the first year of his chairmanship of the B.I.R.); *Admiral John H. Godfrey Papers* (his Naval Staff College Jutland lectures and supplementary papers, and *Naval Memoirs*); *Admiral of the Fleet Sir Henry Jackson Papers; Sir Henry Newbolt Papers* (correspondence and minutes pertaining to the Admiralty vetting of *Naval Operations,* Vols. IV and V).

296. *Public Record Office,* Keeper of the Public Record Office, Chancery Lane, London, W.C.2: *Admiralty Record Office Papers,* particularly classes Adm. 1, 116, and, above all, 137: Adm. 1 (*Papers*) contains the registered files of the Admiralty which were selected for permanent preservation; Adm. 116 (*Cases*) contains registered files which were detached by the Admiralty registry from the main series of registered files and put into cases, simply on account of their larger size: and Adm. 137 (*1914–1918 War Histories*) contains registered and unregistered papers and various operational papers which passed through the hands of the Naval Historical Section; *Cabinet Office Records,* especially the minutes of the Committee of Imperial Defence (C.I.D.), 1902–1939 (Cab. 2), the War Council (Nov. 1914–May 1915), Dardanelles Committee (June–Oct. 1915), and War Committee (Nov. 1915–Nov. 1916) (Cab. 22), and the War Cabinet and Imperial War Cabinet (Dec. 1916–Oct. 1919) (Cab. 23); the Cabinet letters in the Royal Archives, 1868–1916 (Cab. 41); the papers of the C.I.D. (Cab. 3 to 6, especially Cab. 3, "Home Defence" series), the War Council, Dardanelles Committee, and War Committee (Cab. 24); and the papers of the Dardanelles Commis-

sion (Cab. 19). Indispensable aids to the efficient use of the Cabinet Office materials are: *List of Cabinet Papers, 1880–1914* (P.R.O. Handbook No. 4), *List of Papers of the Committee of Imperial Defence to 1914* (P.R.O. Handbook No. 6), *List of Cabinet Papers, 1915 and 1916* (P.R.O. Handbook No. 9), and *The Records of the Cabinet Office to 1922* (P.R.O. Handbook No. 11), all skillfully prepared by Mr. A. W. Mabbs and colleagues.

297. *United States Navy Department Records,* National Archives, Washington, D.C. Chiefly valuable for Admiral Sim's reports from London, 1917–18, in Record Group 45, Admiral Benson's personal papers and correspondence as Chief of Naval Operations, also in Record Group 45, and assorted materials for 1917–18 in the Records of the Chief of Naval Operations in Record Group 38. An inventory of the last-named is available through the General Services Administration, National Archives and Records Service, the National Archives, Washington, D.C. 20408.

XV

THE WAR ON THE
HOME FRONT, 1914–1918

Paul Guinn

The focus of this chapter is the British nation at home with concentration upon the political and administrative superstructure, the economic and social base, and the mental and emotional responses to the war and all that it brought with it. The subject is not so much the war as the society which waged it.

PRIMARY SOURCES. The student of the 1914–18 war now has at his disposal a multiplicity of previously unavailable primary sources. The Public Record Office, depository for government archives, has published a series of *Handbooks* (3) to aid the researcher in locating material of interest to him. The Cabinet Office records are obviously basic; and American students may well be grateful to the Public Record Office for having further made available some of these records on microfilm. The reader is referred to Professor Marder's chapter (XIV above) for more detailed information and references to the Public Record Office material and publications.

Documents and studies issued during the war itself by the government for public or parliamentary use are often important sources for the historian. The most useful guides to these are the official *General Alphabetical Index* to, and the scholarly *Breviates* of, parliamentary papers (4). Among the more significant of the wartime command papers which reveal the workings of the Higher Direction, are the reports of the Dardanelles and Mesopotamia Commissions (105) (108); the extracts from the two wartime proceedings of the Imperial War Conference (107); the two annual reports of the War Cabinet (114); the reports of the Commission of Enquiry into Industrial Unrest (104) and of the "Whitley" Reconstruction committee (111); the report and evidence of the Royal Commission on the Irish revolt (113); the Censorship, 1914–1916 (112); the Derby report on military service (106); and the Instructions of the Ministry of National Service (110).

Some of the relevant private paper collections are listed in the appendix. Special mention must be made of the newly-established Beaverbrook Library

(1), described in its fly sheet as "a private collection . . . the property of the Trustees of the Beaverbrook Foundations . . . of books and papers, relating to twentieth-century politics." The collection, located in London, contains the long-awaited Lloyd George and Bonar Law papers, as well as those of Lord Beaverbrook himself ("not open to readers" while A. J. P. Taylor prepares the biography) and others. "Descriptive Lists" are available.

By far the most impressive collection of non-literary sources—photographs, films, sound recordings, and official art—is to be found in the Imperial War Museum. The Museum's *Handbook* (2) gives much information on the nature, variety, and accessibility of these, and is itself a model of design and good taste. The *Handbook* warns that neither the official photographic nor the official art programs became organized before 1916.

NEWSPAPERS AND PERIODICALS. The newspaper press, as is well known, played a unique role in the history of the war. The stifling of Parliament by the political establishment of both major parties doubtless had much to do with this. There exists a full-length critical *The History of The Times* (133), conservative imperialist in 1914–18, written by its staff. These volumes are a valuable and somewhat neglected source of contemporary British political history. The extreme High Tory *Morning Post* is the subject of a less ambitious book by Hindle (132). Col. Repington, the picaresque wartime "military correspondent" of both these journals (he shifted employers in January 1918), published his lengthy wartime diary and reminiscences (193). "Press Lords"—i.e., proprietors—Beaverbrook and Northcliffe, but not his brother Rothermere, have been the subject of biographies (87) (218) (188); while Lord Riddell, who was close to Liberal leaders, published a *War Diary* (194). There are biographies of at least four newspaper editors—Dawson of *The Times* (221), Donald of the Liberal *Daily Chronicle* (207), Scott of the non-conformist *Manchester Guardian* (124), and Spender of the Asquithian Liberal *Westminster Gazette* (127). Spender also wrote his memoirs (202).

There is not much available by way of analysis of the weekly political and other journals, some of which were quite influential. Brief histories have been written of the Socialist *New Statesman* (135), and the conservative humorous magazine, *Punch* (190). *Mr. Punch's History of the Great War* (191), a selection from the wartime issues, remains of interest as a record of right-thinking reactions to unprecedented events.

Garvin (97) and St. Loe Strachey (204), editors respectively of the conservative Sunday newspaper, *The Observer,* and of the influential responsible conservative weekly, *The Spectator,* are both the subjects of memorials written by their widows. Strachey also left his rather slight memoirs (203). Professor Gollin's study of Garvin's editorship of *The Observer* (99) is limited to the prewar period. Professor A. F. Havighurst is working on a study of H. W. Massingham, editor of the radical *The Nation* (128).

The Economist is an important source for economic and social policy.

There is an early description of *The Press and the General Staff* (156), written from the point of view of the latter, a few interesting pages on the political role of the press in Churchill's *World Crisis* (73), and a little book on the *Press in War-Time* by an official of the Press Bureau (78). There is room, however, for a general analysis of this subject.

SECONDARY ACCOUNTS. The only book-length general account which attempts to describe all aspects of British involvement in the war is the veteran historian Sir Llewellyn Woodward's *Great Britain and the War of 1914–1918* (219). It consists of (p. xi) a number of "the essential facts and a running commentary."

The general surveys of twentieth-century British history by Havighurst (117), Medlicott (170), and Taylor (205) all include excellent chapters on the war period. Taylor's account is characterized by bite, Medlicott's by balance, and Havighurst's by sensitivity.

Cameron's *1916* (68) consists largely of unreferenced quotations, but some of these, drawn from the Beaverbrook collections, appear to be otherwise unpublished. The contemporaneous 21-volume *The Times History of the War* (211) contains a good deal of miscellaneous information.

CONDUCT OF THE WAR: LLOYD GEORGE AND CHURCHILL AS WAR MINISTERS. The "grand strategy" of the war was hammered out, not without stress, in London. Guinn's *British Strategy and Politics* (116) is an interpretation of British grand strategy against the background of national politics. It contains a select bibliography. Cruttwell's earlier short essay, *The Role of British Strategy* (79), attempts to evaluate the specifically British contribution to the Entente's over-all war policy. The multi-volume *World Crisis* (73) by Winston Churchill—First Lord of the Admiralty, member of the Dardanelles Committee, field-grade officer on the Western Front, member of parliament, and Minister of Munitions—is not only a personal testimony of distinction, but also a valuable and penetrating general account. The overly discreet *Supreme Command* by Sir Maurice Hankey (126)—secretary of the successive Cabinet war committees—is the only memoir specifically concerned with the central direction, or lack of it, of the war. It can now be read in conjunction with Roskill's biography (271). Among other numerous records of personal experience may be singled out the biographies of Secretary of War Kitchener by Arthur (50) and Magnus (162); the biographies of the Director of Military Operations and Chief of Imperial General Staff, Henry Wilson, by Callwell (67), Collier (76) and Ash (262); the *War Diaries* (223) and *1914* (222) by the first commander of the British forces in France and Belgium, Sir John French; the *Private Papers* (120) of his successor, Sir Douglas Haig; two works by Chief of Imperial General Staff Sir William Robertson (195) (196); the tittle-tattle of Military Correspondent of *The Times* Col. Repington, preserved in his *The First World War* (193); two biographies (125) (172) of General Smuts, member of the War Cabinet; and, above all, the *War Memoirs* (152) of the second wartime Prime Minister, Lloyd George.

The official histories of the war, though written under the direction of the Committee of Imperial Defence, contain no volume on the central strategic direction.

There was no unified command of the services nor any Minister of Defence at any time during the war. On the other hand, Cabinet control of the armed services remained continually, if theoretically, in effect.

One aspect of military policy—the "Westerners-versus-Easterners" controversy—continues to dominate the historiography of British grand strategy. The non-Western Front operations continue to be condemned as poor "strategy," with little appreciation of their political and territorial benefits. On the other hand, discussion of "Western Front" policy, despite the destructive criticism of Liddell Hart (149) (150) (151) and others, is still sometimes conducted with more partisanship than scholarship. Thus Terraine's recent biography of Haig, the Western Front commander, extols his subject's military virtues despite the overwhelming evidence of Haig's lack of understanding of the realities of the 1914–1918 military environment (208). By way of contrast, Bonham-Carter's somewhat slight biography of Chief of the Imperial General Staff Sir William Robertson admits his subject's partisanship (60). Tendencies toward idealization, "loyalty," and optimism remain; the spectacle of vain battle seems still to be too unendurable to gaze at without blinking or distortion.

In retrospect, the figures of "Lloyd George and Churchill as War Ministers," the title of a searching comparative essay on the subject by John Ehrman (90), tower above their contemporaries. Asquith did not attempt to assume this role; and Kitchener, who as Secretary of State for War was assigned it by the Prime Minister, proved ineffective in an unfamiliar environment.

Randolph Churchill's full-scale and much-acclaimed biography of his father (72)—complemented by separate extensive documentation—is a major source, though he died before completing Volume III, *The War Years,* which is now being written by Martin Gilbert. The "intimate portrait" by Asquith's daughter, Violet Bonham-Carter (61), has a few revealing touches.

Lloyd George's biographies, several of which are listed below (142) (153) (154) (179), are all more or less unsatisfactory or insufficiently informative. Neither journalist nor son nor brother nor secretary provides more than a partial view. The Wizard of Wales continues to elude "definitive" treatment.

As applied to Churchill and Lloyd George in 1914–18, the concept of war minister encompasses three major areas: policy, administration, and politics. Both statesmen had the vision to see beyond and behind the German armies in the West; both were outstanding mobilizers of enthusiasm and ideas. Lloyd George was a more successful operator in the then existing political arena; without his advent to the prime ministership, the Entente could hardly have prevailed. Great Britain was certainly very fortunate to have men of this quality among her political leadership. The contrast with Wilhelmine Germany is striking.

POLITICS AND ADMINISTRATION. Much good—and some highly creative—work has been and continues to be done in this area, though some of the principal issues and questions have not yet been posed, let alone analyzed.

Pride of place must be given to Beaverbrook's volumes on party politics during the war, *Politicans and the War, 1914–1916* (54) and *Men and Power, 1917–1918* (55). These are classic studies, written with vigour, perceptiveness, and distinction, and will always be required reading for students of the subject. They are also, however, idiosyncratic and occasionally in error, and they somewhat neglect the underlying issues in favour of the spectacle of the clash of highly charged personalities. Even so, they comprise, together with Churchill's *World Crisis,* a magnificent work.

Attempts at providing a synthetic account of party politics and political history during the war include, in addition to the general histories of twentieth-century Britain mentioned earlier, Taylor's lecture on *Politics in the First World War* (206), Guinn's study on *Strategy and Politics* (116), Chambers' earlier *War Behind the War* (69), and Robert Blake's introduction to his edition of the Haig papers (120). Trevor Wilson's *Downfall of the Liberal Party* (217) is the best study now available on British politics from the outbreak of the war to Lloyd George's seizure of power in December 1916. The field, however, remains an open one, and there is room for a major study.

Students whose principal concern is with public administration are advised to consult P.R.O. handbook No. 11 on Cabinet Office records (3), Hankey's *Supreme Command* (126), an early volume by Fairlie in the Carnegie series (14), and the general works on British government by Daalder (80), Jennings (139), Mackintosh (161), and Smellie (199). Ehrman's elegant and sophisticated *Cabinet Government and War* (89) is primarily concerned with the administrative aspects of civilian policy direction of the military services. F. S. Oliver's *Ordeal by Battle* (178) is a contemporary conservative imperialist critique. R. McGregor Dawson wrote several articles on the same theme with particular reference to 1914–18 (83) (84). Professor Naylor is preparing a work on the establishment of the War Cabinet Secretariat (174). A study of Lloyd George's personal secretariat, the notorious "Garden Suburb," has been written by Joseph Davies, one of its members (81).

The crucial political event of the period is, of course, the fall of Asquith and the consequent decline and eventual break-up and defeat of the Liberal Party. The most recent treatments of this theme are Trevor Wilson's book (217) and a *Journal of Modern History* article by McGill (159). Both authors have made considerable use of private papers of Liberal politicians, while Wilson has in addition exploited the minutes of local Liberal Federations. These valuable and painstaking studies are somewhat limited in their conclusions as a result of their refusal to look beyond the record of party politics, as is also true of Koss's article on May 1915 (148a).

The issues involved in the Maurice Debate of May 1918 are the principal subject of General Maurice's pamphlet, *Intrigues of the War* (169).

Some sidelights on the formation of the Second Coalition, December 1916, are furnished by the account in *The History of The Times* (133), by a recent article on Milner's entry into the War Cabinet (155), and by contemporary recollections of Samuel (198), and Buckmaster (130). Other Liberal leaders who have published memoirs include Addison (47), (48); Asquith [inadequate] (52), Fisher (93), Grey (115), Haldane (121) and Lloyd George [profuse, revealing, and highly biased] (152). Asquith has been the subject of several biographies. The authorized one (201) is substantial but not very revealing. Jenkins recent urbane book (138) is agreeable reading and competent writing, but does not add much to the historical record save for Asquith's letters to one confidante and the diary of another. Biographies also exist of a number of other Liberal politicians: among them Grey (212), Haldane (168), (200), McKenna (160), Masterman (166), Montagu (213), Reading (137), and Samuel (62).

Unfortunately there is nothing comparable to Mr. Wilson's book for the waxing fortunes of the Conservative Party, which finally returned to a position of preponderant power in all but name in December 1916. Robert Blake's superb biography of the Conservative Leader, Bonar Law (59), does not quite fill this gap. Other biographies, memoirs, or other memorials of Tory figures and their confidants—among them Amery (49), Balfour (88) (273), Carson (77) (136), Austen Chamberlain (182), Derby (71), Esher (92), Fitzroy (94), Hewins (131), Lansdowne (175), Walter Long (183), F. S. Oliver (177), Milner (220), Salvidge (197), and F. E. Smith (58) are numerous—but they, with the exception of Gollin's *Milner* (100), furnish raw material rather than historical analysis. By way of contrast there does exist a solid if obsolescing study by Brand (64) on the British Labour Party during the war, to be supplemented by a study of the Fabians (157), Dowse's recent book on the Independent Labour Party (86), Middlemas' *Clydesiders* (171) and Graubard's study of Labour Party reactions to the Russian Revolution (102), though this last work is mainly devoted to postwar development. Brand and G. D. H. Cole have each written good general histories of the Party (63) (74). Unfortunately neither the biography of Henderson (123) nor the memoir by Barnes (53)—the two succeeding Labour Cabinet members in the British coalition government—is revealing. Lord Elton wrote a *Life* of MacDonald (91), Postgate one of Lansbury (187); Clynes's Memoirs (75) and Bullock's biography of Bevin (66) are both important for Labour Party affairs. There are two studies of John Redmond, the Irish Nationalist leader (118) (119). King George V is the subject of a good professional biography (176) by Harold Nicolson.

ECONOMY AND SOCIETY. Any student of British society during the war will have to consult some of the 25 volumes of the *Economic and Social History of the World War, British Series,* sponsored by the Carnegie Endowment for International Peace. Before delving into these, however, he would be well advised, for the economic aspect, to begin with the 1914–18 chapters in two recent studies of British economic history by Ashworth (51) and Pollard (186), and, for the social aspect, to read Arthur Marwick's *The Deluge: British Society and the First World War* (164). This last is a perceptive, level-headed, and well-written study. Marwick speculates further on the subject in a new article in the *Journal of Contemporary History* (165), and in his book *Britain in the Century of Total War* (163). Hurwitz's analysis of the expansion of governmental control and public reactions thereto is still required reading not least because of its analysis of the general socio-political environment (134). The government's response to labor "unrest" during 1917 and after is the subject of two contemporary essays, "The Policy of Social Peace in England: The Whitley Councils" and "The Problem of Worker Control," by a great French historian, Elie Halévy (122).

The Carnegie Endowment series (21) was an audacious enterprise. Written well before primary sources were generally available, these volumes were entrusted in large part to civil servants and others who played some active role in the events or organizations described. The general editor of the series and president of the Endowment, James T. Shotwell, reached (in 1934, the depth of the Depression) the comforting conclusion (36) that (p. xi, Editor's Preface):

> The principles tested by previous experience and imprinted with the authority of great economists and social, moral and political philosophers have survived the mighty cataclysm which seemed at first to have shattered all preconceived notions.

For the most part, the authors of the series shared the Liberal ethos, with its devotion to free trade and its distrust of state action. G. D. H. Cole expressed, to be sure, the viewpoint of the skilled unionists. Less predictably, civil servant Arthur Salter forcibly pointed out (43) that (p. 19), despite the withdrawal of "between one-half and two-thirds of the productive capacity of the country . . . into combatant or other war service," the country was, on the whole, *better* fed than before the war. The maintenance and even improvement of the "home front's" health and well-being was the direct result, as Salter insisted, of the process of state control of civilian production and of state allocation of goods and services. This important message, however, which Salter transmitted with legitimate pride on behalf of the civil service and in implicit lessons for the future, tended to be muffled by the free-enterprise bias, real or prudential, of most of the authors of the series.

Shotwell divided the Carnegie Endowment British series into three categories: works of reference, descriptions of wartime management, and studies in economic and social history. The volumes, of course, vary greatly in quality and in nature of presentation. Among the monographs which retain value as independent historical analyses, one would include Beveridge on food control (22), Cole's three volumes on the labour movement (25–27), Fayle (31), and Salter (43) on shipping, Lloyd on the War Office and Ministry of Food (40), Redmayne on the coal industry (42), Stamp on taxation (45), and Wolfe (46) on labour supply and regulation. There is a *Bibliographical Survey of Contemporary Sources* (24). Among the earlier Carnegie series of *Preliminary Economic Studies of the War,* note M. B. Hammond's study of labour conditions (16).

Apart from the Carnegie series and the works cited in the first paragraph of this section, special mention should be made of the very wide-ranging official *History of the Ministry of Munitions* (109) (the production of

which is described in an article in the *Economic History Review* (129)),
two books by Grady (101) and Morgan (173) on financial policy, and
Pratt on the railways (189). Paul Johnson's recent *Land Fit for Heroes*
(141) is a pioneering study of the reconstruction effort in its wartime
ideological context.

In addition to Marwick's work (164), accounts of British social life have
been left by four ladies: Sylvia Pankhurst (180), C. S. Peel (181), Caroline
Playne (184) (185), and Irene Willis (216). *Everyman at War* (192) is an
anthology of personal narratives.

MENTAL AND EMOTIONAL REACTIONS. The nature and quality
of "public opinion," still more of emotional states, is difficult for the historian to analyze with accuracy and impossible with precision. A section of
Marwick's *Deluge* (164) is devoted to the subject; it is about all the exists.

Hatred of Germany, Germans, and all things German virtually subsumed
all other attitudes for the bulk of the British "stay-at-home" population. The
enemy, in Prime Minister Asquith's words, was "Prussian militarism"—
the supreme political evil. There is no general scholarly survey of what might
be called civilian mental and emotional reactions to the phenomenon of total
war. [Professor Graubard is working on the thought of selected intellectual
groups on the problems of war and peace (103).] In default, one can turn
to memoirs and literature. Many of the former are listed in Marwick and
used both by him and by Caroline Playne in her two rather overwrought—
but informative—volumes on *Society at War* (184) and *Britain Holds On*
(185). Vera Brittain's *Testament of Youth* (65) is still very moving.

The literature of the war is the subject of Bergonzi's *Heroes' Twilight*
(57)—an intelligent analysis, which is, however, primarily concerned with
the writings of those who fought. It includes a chronology of publications.
Much of the contemporary "home front" literature—and virtually all of the
plays produced during the period—was either escapist or simply irrelevant
to the war. Some of the finest writings of Conrad, Joyce, Lawrence, and
Maugham were published during the war—but none reflected it, unless in a
need to escape from its presence.

Two "romans-fleuves," by Ford Madox Ford (95) and Henry Williamson
respectively (215), are concerned with aspects of wartime Britain. The
former is difficult to read through; the second is a faithful chronicle. Arnold
Bennett's novel, *Lord Raingo* (56), includes fascinating evocations of the
political atmosphere of the Lloyd George coalition.

There are, furthermore, at least two writers of stature—Rudyard Kipling
and H. G. Wells—whose wartime writing is still readable and of value as
having crystallized widely held feelings. These two writers can be seen as
representative of the two main strands of contemporary English thought on
social and political issues: conservative-imperial (Kipling) and liberal-hu-
manitarian (Wells). Kipling's wartime short stories and accompanying
poems (144–146) are hymns of hate for the enemy and scorn for neutrals.
His finest wartime accomplishment was the series of terse and epigrammatic
Epitaphs (147), bright flashes in an overwhelming darkness. H. G. Wells's
Mr. Britling Sees It Through (214) published in September, 1916, was the

one best-selling novel to be published during the war itself. It is a story of disillusionment.

RESEARCH OPPORTUNITIES. The opening of the archives has created an embarrassment of riches. On the conduct of the war, the "Easterners-versus-Westerners" controversy needs to be seen not in purely military terms but as a distinction between a military concept of victory over Germany through battle and a political view of operations designed to improve the British Imperial position. In default of such an intellectual framework, the non-Western-Front operations continue to be condemned as poor "strategy," with little appreciation of their territorial and political benefits. Air operations, including air defence, need to be examined in terms of the overall military environment.

One of the obvious—and doubtless deliberate—gaps in the official histories were the related subjects of propaganda, intelligence, and covert operations. These last may have had a significant bearing on political and military events. Are any official records or accounts available?

On the administrative side, the "war behind the war" in the critical months of 1917 and 1918, when Smuts arrived on the English scene, the Air Ministry was formed, and the Royal Air Force created, has to be set into the whole context of both politics and grand strategy. The politics of administration is still a lucrative field for research and analysis.

Apart from the levels of general studies, party politics, and political biography, little of substance has been written on some of the central questions of war politics. There is no published monograph on British foreign policy, war aims, and related questions, though there is an American Ph.D. thesis (82). Aside from a University of London M.A. thesis by Malcolm Thomis (209) and a French article (85) of 40 years ago, both oriented toward the military aspect of the problem, there is no analysis of the question of "National Service"—that is to say industrial as well as military conscription. [Professor Theodore Ropp of Duke is working on conscription in the Empire (196a.)] Yet National Service is perhaps the central political issue of the war period.

There is a valuable—indeed pioneering—study by Hurwitz (134) on the general topic of "war socialism," the process of state control of the economy and labour; but there is nothing extant on the conscious and deliberate movement away from free trade and toward a policy of permanent economic autarchy, a policy which received its expression in the Allied Economic Conference in Paris of June 1916. No up-to-date monograph exists on the Lloyd Georgian "Revolution" in government administration. Lloyd George created both a Supreme War Cabinet with a secretariat and a host of new ministries —Shipping, Labour, Food, National Service—which took control of the economy.

Johnson's insightful and suggestive study of the rise and fall of the Ministry of Reconstruction is supplemented by an analysis of the entire "Reconstruction" movement of 1917 and after—an aspect of wartime idealism—of which the two lasting results appear to have been the franchise reform of 1918 and Fisher's education act of the same year. Almost by way of postscript, one might comment that there does not appear to be a study of the effect of the Irish question on British wartime politics. Perhaps this would be good for at least an article. One hopes that some of these themes will find their historian.

All the four themes of war politics just identified—National Service, economic autarchy, governmental expansion, and the maintenance of British rule over Ireland—are variations on one basic thrust. What was taking place was an expansion of state control and direction in all fields and in the interests of state power and efficiency, to the detriment of autonomy and liberty. At the same time the war speeded reform, social change, and concern for community interests in the opposite direction. To what extent were these processes due to the pressures of war, to what extent to internal forces? That is the basic question for historical analysis.

BIBLIOGRAPHY

DEPOSITORIES

1. Beaverbrook Library, 33 St. Bride Street, London, E.C.4. Private collection on twentieth-century politics; applications to use to be made "at least one week in advance."
2. Imperial War Museum, Lambeth Road, London, S.E.1. See *Handbook of the Imperial War Museum: 1914 to the present day*. London: H.M.S.O., 1963.

GOVERNMENT DOCUMENTS AND PUBLICATIONS

Unpublished:
3. Public Record Office [P.R.O.], Chancery Lane, London, W.C.2. Depository for government archives. See Public Record Office Handbooks No. 4, *List of Cabinet Papers, 1880–1914,* London: H.M.S.O., 1966; No. 6, *List of Papers of the Committee of Imperial Defence to 1914,* 1964; No. 9, *List of Cabinet Papers, 1915 and 1916,* 1966; No. 10, *Classes of Departmental Papers for 1906–1939,* 1966; and No. 11, *The Records of the Cabinet Office to 1922,* 1966.
   The following classes, or parts of classes, are available on microfilm: Photographic copies of Cabinet letters in the Royal archives, 1868–1916 (Cab. 41).
   Photographic copies of Cabinet papers, 1880–1916 (Cab. 37).
   Photographic copies of Minutes and Memoranda of the Committee of Imperial Defence, 1884–1914 (Cab. 38).
   Minutes and Conclusions (with indexes) of the War Cabinet and Cabinet, 1916–1922 (Cab. 23).
   Indexes to papers in the G, GT and CP series (Cabinet memoranda), 1916–1922 (Cab. 24).

Enquiries about positive copies should be addressed to the Secretary, P.R.O.

Published:
4.   The various categories of published official materials are discussed in P. and G. Ford, *A Guide to Parliamentary Papers,* Oxford: Basil Blackwell, 1956, 2nd edition. Non-parliamentary official publications are listed in a *Quarterly List of Official Publications,* London: H.M.S.O., 1914–1918. The parliamentary procedures themselves can be followed in Great Britain. Parliament. *Parliamentary Debates: House of Commons* and *House of Lords, 1914–1918,* London: H.M.S.O.
The parliamentary papers are listed in the *Quarterly List of Parliamentary Publications,* London: H.M.S.O., 1914–1918; indexed in Great Britain. Parliament. House of Commons. *General alphabetical index to the bills, reports, estimates, accounts and papers, printed by order of the House of Commons and to the papers presented by command 1910–1919.* Parliament, 1927. H. of C. Repts. and papers no. 189. London: H.M.S.O., 1927; and to a considerable extent analyzed in P. and G. Ford, *A Breviate of Parliamentary Papers, 1900–1916: the foundation of the welfare state,* Oxford: Basil Blackwell, 1957 and *A Breviate of Parliamentary Papers, 1917–1939,* Oxford, Basil Blackwell, 1951.
Some specific works are listed in Individual References under Great Britain.

NEWSPAPERS AND PERIODICALS

A listing and brief description of national newspapers is to be found in David Butler and Jennie Freeman, *British Political Facts, 1900–1960,* New York: St. Martin's Press, 1963 [Br. edn., London: Macmillan] pp. 205–214, together with a description of sources, including press directories. This listing may be supplemented by the chart in *The History of the Times* Vol. IV, *1912–1948,* London, *The Times,* 1952, Pt. II, pp. 1130–36. The most useful of the various directories is probably *Willing's Press Guide,* London: James Willing, published annually. This includes periodicals and reviews as well as newspapers.

CARNEGIE ENDOWMENT FOR INTERNATIONAL
PEACE SERIES

5.   Carnegie Endowment for International Peace. Division of Economics and History. *Preliminary Economic Studies of the World War.* New York: Oxford University Press, 1918–1923. This was a planned series of 25 volumes, of which 23 were actually published. The following list excludes those volumes not devoted to Great Britain.
6.   Andrews, Irene Osgood, assisted by Margaret A. Hobbs. *Economic*

Effects of the War upon Women and Children in Great Britain. 2nd rev. ed. 1921. No. 4.

7. Baker, Charles Whiting. *Government Control and Operation of Industry in Great Britain and the United States during the World War.* 1921. No. 18.

8. Bogart, Ernest L. *Direct and Indirect Costs of the Great World War.* 2nd rev. edn. 1920. No. 24.

9. Carver, Thomas Nixon. *Government Control of the Liquor Business in Great Britain and the United States.* 1919. No. 13.

10. Carver, Thomas Nixon. *War Thrift.* 1919. No. 10.

11. Crowell, J. Franklin. *Government War Contracts.* 1920. No. 25.

12. Devine, Edward T., assisted by Lillian Brandt. *Disabled Soldiers and Sailors: pensions and training.* 1919. No. 12.

13. Dixon, Frank Haigh and Julius H. Parmelee. *War Administration of the Railways in the United States and Great Britain.* 2nd rev. edn. 1919. No. 3.

14. Fairlie, John A. *British War Administration.* 1919. No. 8.

15. Gephart, William F. *Effects of the War Upon Insurance, with Special Reference of the Substitution of Insurance for Pensions.* 1918. No. 6.

16. Hammond, M. B. *British Labor Conditions and Legislation during the War.* 1919. No. 14.

17. Hibbard, Benjamin H. *Effects of the Great War upon Agriculture in the United States and Great Britain.* 1919. No. 11.

18. Litman, Simon. *Prices and Price Control in Great Britain and the United States during the World War.* 1920. No. 19.

19. McKey, Frank L. *The Financial History of Great Britain, 1914–1918.* 1918. No. 7.

20. Smith, J. Russell. *Influence of the Great War upon Shipping.* 1919. No. 9.

21. Carnegie Endowment for International Peace, Division of Economies and History. *Economic and Social History of the World War. British Series.* New Haven: Yale University Press, 1921–1940. 25 vols. [Br. edn. Oxford: Clarendon Press and London: H. Milford, Oxford University Press.]

22. Beveridge, Sir William H. *British Food Control.* 1928.

23. Bowley, Arthur L. *Prices and Wages in the United Kingdom, 1914–1920.* 1921.

24. Bulkley, M. E. *Bibliographical Survey of Contemporary Sources for the Economic and Social History of the War.* 1922.

25. Cole, G. D. H. *Labour in the Coal-Mining Industry (1914–1921).*

26. Cole, G. D. H. *Trade Unionism and Munitions,* 1923.

27. Cole, G. D. H. *Workshop Oganization.* 1923.

28. Dearle, N. B. *Dictionary of Official War Time Organizations.* 1928.

29. Dearle, N. B. *An Economic Chronicle of the Great War for Great Britain and Ireland.* 1929.

30. Dearle, N. B. *The Labour Cost of the Great War to Great Britain.* 1940.

31. Fayle, C. Ernest. *The War and the Shipping Industry.* 1927.

32. Hall, Hubert. *British Archives and the Sources for the History of the World War.* 1925

33. Henderson, Hubert D. *The Cotton Control Board.* 1922.

34. Hill, Norman and others. *War and Insurance.* 1927.

35. Hirst, F. W. and J. E. Allen. *British War Budgets.* 1926.

36. Hirst, Francis W. *The Consequences of the War to Great Britain.* 1934.

37. Jenkinson, Hilary. *A Manual of Archive Administration, including the Problems of War Archives and Archive Making.* 1922.

38. Jones, D. T. and others. *Rural Scotland during the War.* 1926.

39. Keith, Arthur Berriedale. *War Government of the British Dominions.* 1921.

40. Lloyd, E. M. H. *Experiments in State Control: at the War Office and the Ministry of Food.* 1934.

41. Middleton, Sir Thomas Hudson. *Food Production in War.* 1923.

42. Redmayne, Sir R. A. S. *The British Coal-Mining Industry During the War.* 1923.

43. Salter, J. A. *Allied Shipping Control: an experiment in international administration.* 1921.

44. Scott, W. R. and J. Cunnison. *The Industries of the Clyde Valley during the War.* 1924.

45. Stamp, Sir Josiah. *Taxation During the War.* 1932.

46. Wolfe, Humbert. *Labour Supply and Regulation.* 1923.

INDIVIDUAL REFERENCES

47. Addison, Christopher, *Four and a Half Years: from June 1914 to January 1919.* London: Hutchinson, 1934. 2 vols.

48. Addison, Christopher. *Politics from Within, 1911–1918, including some records of a great national effort.* London: H. Jenkins, 1924. 2 vols.

49. Amery, Leopold. *My Political Life.* Vol. II: *War and Peace, 1914–1929.* London: Hutchinson, 1953.

50. Arthur, Sir George, *Life of Lord Kitchener.* London and New York: Macmillan, 1920. 3 vols.

51. Ashworth, William. *An Economic History of England, 1870–1939.* London: Methuen, 1961. [U. S. edn., N. Y.: Barnes and Noble, 1961.]

52. Asquith, Earl of Oxford and. *Memories and Reflections, 1852–1927.* London: Cassell, 1928. [U. S. edn. Boston: Little, Brown, 1928.] 2 vols.

53. Barnes, George. *From Workshop to War Cabinet.* London: H. Jenkins, 1923.

54. Beaverbrook, Lord. *Politicians and the War, 1914–1916.* London: T. Butterworth, 1928–32. 2 vols. [U. S. edition of volume one, Garden City, N. Y.: Doubleday Doran, 1928.] One-volume edition, London: Oldbourne, 1960.

55. Beaverbrook, Lord. *Men and Power, 1917–1918.* London: Hutchinson, 1956. [U. S. edn., N. Y.: Duell, Sloan and Pierce, 1957.]
56. Bennett, Arnold. *Lord Raingo.* London: Cassell, 1926. [U. S. edn., N. Y.: George H. Doran, 1926.]
57. Bergonzi, Bernard. *Heroes' Twilight: a study of literature of the Great War.* N. Y.: Coward-McCann, Inc., 1966. [British edn., London: Constable, 1965.]
58. Birkenhead, Lord. *F. E.: the life of F. E. Smith, First Earl of Birkenhead.* London: Eyre and Spottiswoode, 1960.
59. Blake, Robert. *The Unknown Prime Minister: the life and times of Andrew Bonar Law, 1858–1923.* London: Eyre & Spottiswoode, 1955. [U. S. edn., entitled: *Unrepentant Tory: the life and times of Andrew Banar Law, 1858–1923, Prime Minister of the United Kingdom.* New York: St. Martin's Press, 1956.]
60. Bonham-Carter, Victor. *Soldier True: the life and times of Field-Marshal Sir William Robertson, Bart, G. C. B., G. C. M. B., K. C. V. O., D. S. O., 1860–1933.* London: F. Muller, 1963. [U. S. edn., entitled: *The Strategy of Victory, 1914–1918: the life and times of the master strategist of World War I: Field-Marshal Sir William Robertson.* N. Y.: Holt, Rinehart and Winston, 1964.]
61. Bonham-Carter, Violet. *Winston Churchill as I Knew Him.* London: Eyre & Spottiswoode and Collins, 1965. [U. S. edn., entitled: *Winton Churchill: an intimate portrait.* N. Y.: Harcourt, Brace, 1965.]
62. Bowle, John. *Viscount Samuel: a biography.* London: Gollancz, 1957.
63. Brand, Carl F. *The British Labour Party: a short history.* Stanford: Stanford University Press, 1964.
64. Brand, Carl F. *British Labour's Rise to Power: eight studies.* Stanford: Stanford University Press, 1941. [Br. edn., London: H. Milford, Oxford University Press, 1941.]
65. Brittain, Vera. *Testament of Youth: an autobiographical study of the years 1900–1925.* London: V. Gollancz, 1933. [U. S. edn., N. Y.: Macmillan, 1933.]
66. Bullock, Alan. *The Life and Times of Ernest Bevin:* Vol. I, *Trade Union Leader, 1881–1940.* London: Heinemann, 1960.
67. Callwell, Major-General Sir C. E. *Field-Marshal Sir Henry Wilson: his life and diaries.* London: 1927. [U. S. edn., N. Y.: C. Scribner's, 1927.] 2 vols.
68. Cameron, James. *1916–Year of Decision.* London: Oldbourne, 1962.
69. Chambers, Frank P. *The War Behind the War, 1914–1918: a history of the political and civilian fronts.* London: Faber & Faber, 1939. [U. S. edn., N. Y.: Harcourt, Brace, 1939.]
70. Chester, D. N., ed and F. M. G. Willson, writer. *The Organization of British Central Government, 1914–1956: a survey by a study group of the Royal Institute of Public Administration.* London: George Allen and Unwin, 1957.

71. Churchill, Randolph. *Lord Derby, King of Lancashire: the official life of Edward, Seventeenth Earl of Derby, 1865–1948.* London: Heinemann, 1959. [U. S. edn., N. Y.: Putnam, 1960.]

72. Churchill, Randolph. *Winston S. Churchill.* Boston: Houghton Mifflin, 1966–   . [Br. edn., London: Heinemann, 1966–   ]. This multi-volumed biography is being continued by Martin Gilbert.

73. Churchill, Winston S. *The World Crisis, 1911–1918.* London: T. Butterworth, 1923–1929, 4 vols. [U. S. edn., N. Y.: C. Scribner's 1923–1929.]

74. Cole, G. D. H. *A History of the Labour Party from 1914.* London: Routledge and Kegan Paul, 1948.

75. Clynes, J. R. *Memoirs.* London: Hutchinson, 1937. 2 vols.

76. Collier, Basil. *Brasshat: a biography of Field-Marshal Sir Henry Wilson.* London: Secker & Warburg, 1961.

77. Colvin, Ian. *The Life of Lord Carson.* Vol. III. London: V. Gollancz, 1936.

78. Cooke, Sir Edward. *The Press in War-time, with some account of the official Press Bureau: an essay.* London: Macmillan, 1920.

79. Cruttwell, C. R. M. F. *The Role of British Strategy in the Great War.* Cambridge: Cambridge University Press, 1936.

80. Daalder, Hans. *Cabinet Reform in Britain, 1914–19.* Stanford: Stanford University Press, 1963.

81. Davies, Joseph. *The Prime Minister's Secretariat, 1916–1920.* Newport, Mon: R. H. Johns, 1951.

82. Davis, Rodney Oliver. *British policy and opinion on war aims and peace proposals, 1914–1918.* Ph. D. Thesis, Duke University, n.d.

83. Dawson, R. McGregor. "The Cabinet Minister and Administration: Asquith, Lloyd George, Curzon." *Political Science Quarterly* (N. Y.: Columbia University Press), Vol. 55 (1940), pp. 348–77.

84. Dawson, R. McGregor. "The Cabinet Minister and Administration: The British War Office, 1903–16." *Canadian Journal of Economics and Political Science* (Toronto: University of Toronto Press), November 1939, pp. 451–78.

85. Debyser, Felix. "Le Gouvernement britannique et la question du service militaire obligatoire." *Revue d'Histoire de la Guerre Mondiale* (Paris: A. Costes), 1929, pp. 289–317.

86. Dowse, Robert E. *Left in the Centre: The Independent Labour Party, 1893–1940.* London: Longmans, 1966. [U. S. edn., Evanston: Northwestern University Press, 1966.]

87. Driberg, Tom. *Beaverbrook: a study in power and frustration.* London: Weidenfeld and Nicholson, 1956.

88. Dugdale, Blanche E. C. *Arthur James Balfour, first earl of Balfou.* London: Hutchinson, 1936. [U. S. edn., N. Y.: G. P. Putnam's 1937.]

89. Ehrman, John. *Cabinet Government and War, 1890–1940.* Cambridge: Cambridge University Press, 1958.

90. Ehrman, John. "Lloyd George and Churchill as War Ministers." *Transactions of the Royal Historical Society* (London: Offices of the

Royal Historical Society), 1961, Fifth Series, vol. II, pp. 101–115.

91. Elton, Lord. *The Life of James Ramsay MacDonald (1866–1937)*. London: Collins, 1939. [U. S. edn., N. Y.: C. Scribner's, 1939.]

92. *Esher, Reginald Viscount, Journals and Letters of Maurice V. Brett* (ed.). London: Nicholson and Watson, 1934–38. 4 vols. [U. S. edn., entitled: *The Captains and the Kings Depart: journals and letters of Reginald, Viscount Esher*. N. Y.: C. Scribner's, 1938.] 2 vols.

93. Fisher, H. A. L. *An Unfinished Autobiography*. London and N. Y.: Oxford University Press, 1940.

94. Fitzroy, Sir Almeric. *Memoirs*. London: Hutchinson, 1925. 2 vols.

95. Ford, Ford Madox. *Parade's End*. Rev. edn. N. Y.: Knopf, 1961. [Br. edn.: *The Bodley Head Ford Madox Ford*. Graham Greene, ed. London: Bodley Head, 1962–63. 4 vols.] Includes *Some Do Not*. London: Duckworth, 1924 and N. Y.: T. Seltzer, 1924; *No More Parades*. West Drayton: Penguin, 1938 and N. Y.: A. C. Boni, 1925; and *A Man Could Stand Up*. London: Duckworth, 1926 and N. Y.: A. C. Boni, 1926.

96. Gallacher, William. *Revolt on the Clyde: an autobiography*. London: Lawrence and Wishart, 1936.

97. Garvin, Katharine. *J. L. Garvin: a memoir*. London: William Heinemann, 1948.

98. George, William. *My Brother and I*. London: Eyre and Spottiswoode, 1958.

99. Gollin, Alfred M. *The Observer and J. L. Garvin, 1908–1914: a study in a great editorship*. London and N. Y.: Oxford University Press, 1960.

100. Gollin, A. M. *Proconsul in Politics: a study of Lord Milner in opposition and in power*. London: A. Blond, 1964. [U. S. edn., N. Y.: Macmillan, 1964.]

101. Grady, Henry F. *British War Finance, 1914–1919*. N. Y.: Columbia University Press, 1927.

102. Graubard, Stephen R. *British Labour and the Russian Revolution*. Cambridge, Mass.: Harvard University Press, 1956.

103. Graubard, Stephen, ed. *Daedalus*. Analysis of "how various [intellectual] groups thought about the problems of war and peace" (Ltr. to author). Unpublished, in process.

104. Great Britain. Commission of Enquiry into Industrial Unrest. *Reports,* (Cd. 8662–9), and *Summary* by G. N. Barnes, (Cd. 8696), in Parliament, *Sessional Papers,* 1917–1918, vol. XV, pp. 1–133, 149.

105. Great Britain. Dardanelles Commission. *First Report, Supplement and Final Report,* (Cd. 8490, Cd. 8502, and Cmd. 371), in Parliament, *Sessional Papers,* 1917–18, vol. X, p. 419 and 481, and 1919, vol. XIII, p. 715.

106. Great Britain. *The Earl of Derby's Report on Recruiting,* Cd. 8149, in Parliament. *Sessional Papers,* 1914–16, vol. XXXIX, p. 517.

107. Great Britain. Imperial War Conference. *Proceedings: Extracts from*

Minutes of Proceedings and Papers laid before the Conference, 1917–18, (Cd. 8566, Cd. 9177), in Parliament, *Sessional Papers,* 1917–1918, vols. XXIII, p. 319 and XVI, p. 691.

108. Great Britain. Mesopotamia Commission. *Report of the Commission Appointed by Act of Parliament to Enquire into the Operations of War in Mesopotamia,* (Cd. 8610) in Parliament, *Sessional Papers,* 1917–1918, vol. XVI, p. 773.

109. Great Britain. Ministry of Munitions. *History of the Ministry of Munitions.* London: H.M.S.O., 1920–1924. 12 vols. (see 129).

110. Great Britain. Ministry of National Service. *Instructions* (Cd. 8833–8840), in Parliament, *Sessional Papers,* 1917–18, vol. XXXVIII, pp. 283–345.

111. Great Britain. Ministry of Reconstruction, Committee of. *Interim Report of the Sub-committee on Relations between Employers and Employed* (Cd. 8606), in Parliament. *Sessional Papers* [SP], 1917–1918, vol. XVIII, p. 415; Committee on Employers and Employed, *Second Report on Joint Standing Industrial Councils* (Cd. 9002), *SP,* 1918, vol. X, p. 659; *Supplementary Report on Works Committees,* (Cd. 9001), *SP,* 1918, vol. XIV, p. 951; *Report on Conciliation and Arbitration,* (Cd. 9099), *SP,* 1918, vol. VII, p. 763; *Final Report* (Cd. 9153), *SP,* 1918, vol. VIII, p. 629.

112. Great Britain. Parliament. *The Censorship,* (Cd. 7679), in *Sessional Papers,* 1914–16, vol. XXXIX, p. 529.

113. Great Britain. Royal Commission on the Rebellion in Ireland. *Report,* (Cd. 8279), *Evidence and Appendix,* (Cd. 8311), in Parliament, *Sessional Papers,* 1916, vol. XI, pp. 171, 185.

114. Great Britain. The War Cabinet. Reports for the years 1917 and 1918. (Cd. 9005), (Cmd. 325), in Parliament, *Sessional Papers,* 1917–1918, vol. XIV, p. 379, and 1919, vol. XXX, p. 453.

115. Grey of Fallodon, Viscount. *Twenty-Five Years, 1892–1916.* London: Hodder and Stoughton, 1925. [U. S. edn., N. Y.: Frederick A. Stokes, 1925.] 2 vols.

116. Guinn, Paul. *British Strategy and Politics, 1914–1918.* Oxford: Clarendon Press, 1965.

117. Havighurst, Alfred F. *Twentieth-Century Britain.* 2nd edn. N. Y.: Harper and Row, 1966.

118. Gwynn, Denis. *The Life of John Redmond.* London: G. G. Harrap, 1932.

119. Gwynn, Stephen. *John Redmond's Last Years.* London: Edward Arnold, 1919. [U. S. edn., N. Y.: Longmans, Green, 1919.]

120. *The Private Papers of Douglas Haig, 1914–1919: being selections from the private diary and correspondence of Field-Marshal the Earl Haig of Bemersyde.* Robert Blake, ed. London: Eyre and Spottiswoode, 1952.

121. *Richard Burdon Haldane; an autobiography.* London: Hodder and Stoughton, 1929. [U. S. ed., Garden City, N. Y.: Doubleday, 1929.]

122. Halévy, Élie. "The Policy of Social Peace in England: The Whitley Councils" [originally published in French in the *Revue d'économie politique* (Paris), 383–431 (July–August 1919)], and "The Problem of Worker Control" [Lecture to the Comité' National d'Etudes Politiques et Sociales (March 1921)] in *The Era of Tyrannies: essays on socialism and war.* R. K. Webb, tr. Garden City, N. Y.: Doubleday, Anchor Books, 1965, pp. 105–181. [Fr. ed., *L'èra des tyrannies.* Paris: Callimard, 1938.]

123. Hamilton, Mary Agnes. *Arthur Henderson.* London: W. Heinemann, 1938.

124. Hammond, J. L. *C. P. Scott of the Manchester Guardian.* London: G. Bell, 1934.

125. Hancock, W. K. *Smuts: the sanguine years, 1870–1919.* Cambridge: Cambridge University Press, 1962.

126. Hankey, Lord. *The Supreme Command, 1914–1918.* London: Allen and Unwin, 1961. 2 vols.

127. Harris, Wilson. *J. A. Spender.* London: Cassell, 1946.

128. Havighurst, Alfred F., Department of History, Amherst College. Study of Massingham, editor of the *Nation.* Unpublished, in process.

129. Hay, Denys. "The Official History of the Ministry of Munitions, 1915–1919." *Economic History Review* (London: A & C Black), vol. XIV (1944–45), pp. 185–90.

130. Heuston, R. F. V. *Lives of the Lord Chancellors, 1885–1940.* Oxford: Clarendon Press, 1964. Lives of Lords Buckmaster and Haldane are included.

131. Hewins, W. A. S. *The Apologia of an Imperialist: forty years of empire policy.* London: Constable, 1929. 2 vols.

132. Hindle, Wilfred. *The Morning Post, 1772–1937: portrait of a newspaper.* London: G. Routledge, 1937.

133. *The History of The Times.* Vol. iv. *1912–1948.* London: The Times, 1952. 2 parts.

134. Hurwitz, Samuel J. *State Intervention in Great Britain: a study of economic control and social response, 1914–1919.* N. Y.: Columbia University Press, 1949. Reprinted, Cass, 1968.

135. Hyams, Edward. *The New Statesman: the history of the first fifty years, 1913–1963.* London: Longmans, 1963.

136. Hyde, H. Montgomery. *Carson: the life of Sir Edward Carson, Lord Carson of Duncairn.* London: Heinemann, 1953.

137. Hyde H. Montgomery. *Lord Reading: the life of Rufus Isaacs, First Marquess of Reading.* London: Heinemann, 1967. [U. S. edn., N. Y.: Farrar, Straus and Giroux.]

138. Jenkins, Roy. *Asquith.* London: 1964. [U. S. edn., N. Y.: Chilmark Press, 1964.]

139. Jennings, Sir Ivor. *Cabinet Government.* 3rd edn. N. Y. and Cambridge: Cambridge University Press, 1959.

140. Johnson, Franklyn Arthur. *Defence by Committee.* New York: Oxford University Press, 1960.

141. Johnson, Paul Barton. *Land Fit for Heroes: the planning of British reconstruction, 1916–1919.* Chicago and London: University of Chicago Press, 1968.

142. Jones, Thomas. *Lloyd George.* Cambridge, Mass.: Harvard University Press, 1951. [Br. edn., London: Oxford University Press, 1951.]

143. Jones, Sir Thomas G. *The Unbroken Front: Ministry of Food, 1916–1944. Personalities and Problems.* London: Everybody's Books, 1944.

144. Kipling, Rudyard. "Mary Postgate" (1915) and "The Beginnings" [Poem], *A Diversity of Creatures.* N. Y.: Charles Scribner's, 1917, pp. 489–515. [Br. edn., London: Macmillan, 1917. 2 vols.]

145. Kipling, Rudyard. "The Children" [poem], *A Diversity of Creatures.* N. Y.: Charles Scribner's, 1917, pp. 150–5. [Br. edn., London: Macmillan, 1917. 2 vols.]

146. Kipling, Rudyard. "Sea Constables: A Tale of '15," *Debits and Credits.* N. Y.: Charles Scribner's Sons, 1926, pp. 29–56. [Br. edn., London: Macmillan, 1927. 2 vols.]

147. Kipling, Rudyard. "Epitaphs," *The Years Between and Poems from History.* N. Y.: Charles Scribner's 1919, pp. 113–23. [Br. edn., London: Macmillan, 1919.]

148. Koss, Stephen E. "The Destruction of Britain's Last Liberal Government." *Journal of Modern History* (Chicago, Ill.: University of Chicago Press) vol. XL, no. 2 (June, 1968), pp. 257–277.

148a. Koss, Stephen E. *Lord Haldane: scapegoat for Liberalism.* New York: Columbia University Press, 1969.

149. Liddell Hart, B. H. *Through the Fog of War.* London: Faber and Faber, 1938. [U. S. edn., N. Y.: Random House, 1938.]

150. Liddell Hart, B. H. *Reputations.* London: John Murray, 1928. [U. S. edn., Boston: Little, Brown, 1928.]

151. Liddell Hart, B. H. *A History of the World War, 1914–1918.* London: Faber and Faber, 1934. [U. S. edn., Boston: Little, Brown, 1935, reprinted 1966 as *The Real War.*]

152. Lloyd George, David. *War Memoirs.* London: I. Nicholson and Watson, 1933–36. [U. S. edn., Boston: Little, Brown, 1933–37.] 6 vols.

153. Lloyd George, Earl. *Lloyd George.* London: F. Muller, 1960. [U. S. edn., entitled: *My Father, Lloyd George.* N. Y.: Crown, 1961.]

154. Lloyd George, Frances. *The Years that are Past.* London: Hutchinson, 1967.

155. Lockwood, P. A. "Milner's Entry into the War Cabinet, December 1916." *The Historical Journal* (Cambridge: Cambridge University Press) vol. VII, no. 1 (1964), pp. 120–134.

156. Lytton, Neville. *The Press and the General Staff.* London: W. Collins, 1921.

157. McBriar, A. M. *Fabian Socialism and English Politics, 1884–1918.* Cambridge and N. Y.: Cambridge University Press, 1962.

158. MacDonagh, Michael. *In London During the Great War: the diary of a journalist.* London: Eyre and Spottiswoode, 1935.

159. McGill, Barry. "Asquith's Predicament, 1914–1918." *Journal of Modern History* (Chicago: University of Chicago Press) vol. XXXIX, no. 3 (September, 1967), pp. 283–303.

160. McKenna, Stephen. *Reginald McKenna, 1863–1943: a memoir.* London: Eyre and Spottiswoode, 1948.

161. Mackintosh, John P. *The British Cabinet.* Toronto: University of Toronto Press, 1962. [Br. edn., London: Stevens and Sons, Ltd., 1962.]

162. Magnus, Philip. *Kitchener: portrait of an imperialist.* London: J. Murray 1958. [U. S. edn., N. Y.: Dutton, 1959.]

163. Marwick, Arthur. *Britain in the Century of Total War: war, peace, and social change.* London: Bodley Head, 1968.

164. Marwick, Arthur. *The Deluge: British society and the First World War.* London: Bodley Head, 1965. [U. S. edn., Boston: Little, Brown, 1965.]

165. Marwick, Arthur. "The Impact of the First World War on British Society." *The Journal of Contemporary History* (London: Weidenfield and Nicholson) vol. III, no. 1 (January, 1968), pp. 51–63.

166. Masterman, Lucy. *C. F. G. Masterman: a biography.* London: Nicolson and Watson, 1939.

167. Masterman, Lucy. "Recollections of David Lloyd George." *History Today* (London) Vol. IX, Nos. 3 and 4 (1959), pp. 160–169, 274–81.

168. Maurice, Major-General Sir Frederick. *Haldane: the life of Viscount Haldane of Cloan.* London: Faber and Faber, 1937–39. 2 vols.

169. Maurice, Major-General Sir Frederick. *Intrigues of the War: startling revelations hidden until 1922, important secrets now disclosed.* London: Loxley, 1922.

170. Medlicott, W. N. *Contemporary England, 1914–1964.* London: Longmans, Green, 1967.

171. Middlemas, R. K. *The Clydesiders: a left wing struggle for parliamentary power.* London: Hutchinson, 1965.

172. Millin, Sarah Gertrude. *General Smuts.* London: Faber and Faber, 1936. [U. S. edn., Boston: Little, Brown, 1936.] 2 vols.

173. Morgan, E. Victor. *Studies in British Financial Policy, 1914–25.* London: Macmillan, 1952.

174. Naylor, John F., Department of History, State University of New York at Buffalo. "The Establishment of the Cabinet Secretariat." [In progress; to be published in *Historical Journal,* Cambridge, England.]

175. Newton, P. C. *Lord Lansdowne: a biography.* London: Macmillan, 1929.

176. Nicolson, Harold. *King George the Fifth: his life and reign.* London: Constable, 1952. [U. S. edn., N. Y.: Doubleday, 1953.]

177. *The Anvil of War: letters between F. S. Oliver and his brother, 1914–1918.* Stephen Gwynn, ed. London: Macmillan, 1936.

178. Oliver, Frederick S. *Ordeal by Battle.* London: Macmillan, 1915. [U. S. edn., N. Y.: Macmillan, 1916.]

179. Owen, Frank. *Tempestuous Journey: Lloyd George, his life and times.* London: Hutchinson, 1954. [U. S. edn., N. Y.: McGraw, Hill, 1955.]

180. Pankhurst, Estelle. *The Home Front: a mirror to life in England during the World War.* London: Hutchinson, 1932.

181. Peel, Mrs. C. S. *How We Lived Then, 1914–1918: a sketch of social and domestic life in England during the war.* London: John Lane, 1929.

182. Petrie, Sir Charles. *Life and Letters of the Right Hon. Sir Austen Chamberlain.* London: Cassell, 1939–40. 2 vols.

183. Petrie, Sir Charles. *Walter Long and His Times.* London: Hutchinson, 1936.

184. Playne, Caroline E. *Britain Holds On, 1917, 1918.* London: G. Allen and Unwin, 1933. Reprinted, New York: Howard Fertig, 1969.

185. Playne, Caroline E. *Society at War, 1914–1916.* London: Allen and Unwin, 1931. [U. S. edn., N. Y.: Houghton Mifflin, 1931.] Reprinted 1969 by Howard Fertig, New York.

186. Pollard, Sidney. *The Development of the British Economy, 1914–1950.* London: Edward Arnold, 1962.

187. Postgate, Raymond. *The Life of George Lansbury.* London and N. Y.: Longmans, Green, 1951.

188. Pound, Reginald and Geoffrey Harmsworth. *Northcliffe.* London: Cassell, 1959. [U. S. edn., N. Y.: Praeger, 1960.]

189. Pratt, Edwin A. *British Railways and the Great War: organization, efforts, difficulties and achievements.* London: Selwyn and Blount, 1921. 2 vols.

190. Price, R. G. G. *A History of Punch.* London: Collins, 1957.

191. *Mr. Punch's History of the Great War.* London: Cassell, 1919.

192. Purdom, C. B., ed. *Everyman at War: sixty personal narratives of the war.* London and Toronto: J. M. Dent, 1930. [U. S. edn., N. Y.: E. P. Dutton, 1930.]

193. Repington, Lieutenant-Colonel C. à Court. *The First World War, 1914–18: personal experiences.* London: Constable, 1920. [U. S. edn., Boston: Houghton Mifflin, 1920.]

194. *Lord Riddell's War Diary, 1914–1918.* London: I. Nicholson and Watson, 1933.

195. Robertson, Field-Marshal Sir William. *From Private to Field-Marshal.* London: Constable, 1921. [U. S. edn., Boston and N. Y.: Houghton Mifflin, 1921.]

196. Robertson, Field-Marshal Sir William. *Soldiers and Statesmen, 1914–1918.* London: Cassell, 1926. 2 vols.

196a. Ropp, Theodore (Duke University). A study of conscription in the Empire. In progress.

197. Salvidge, Stanley. *Salvidge of Liverpool: behind the political scene.* London: Hodder and Stoughton, 1934.

198. Samuel, Viscount. *Memoirs.* London: Cresset, 1945. [U. S. edn., entitled: *Grooves of Change: a book of memoirs.* 1946.]

199. Smellie, K. B. *A Hundred Years of English Government.* 2nd edn., rev. London: Gerald Duckworth and Co., 1950.
200. Sommer, Dudley. *Haldane of Cloan: his life and times, 1856–1928.* London: Allen and Unwin, 1960.
201. Spender, J. A. and Cyril Asquith. *Life of Herbert Henry Asquith, Lord Oxford and Asquith.* London: Hutchinson, 1932. 2 vols.
202. Spender, J. A. *Life, Journalism, and Politics.* London: Cassell, 1927. 2 vols.
203. St. Loe Strachey, John. *The Adventure of Living: a subjective autobiography (1860–1922).* N. Y. and London: G. P. Putnam's, 1922.
204. Strachey, Amy. *St. Loe Strachey: his life and his paper.* London: Gollancz, 1930.
205. Taylor, A. J. P. *English History, 1914–1945.* New York and Oxford: Oxford University Press, 1965. The paperback edition (1970) has an additional bibliographical note.
206. Taylor, A. J. P. *Politics in the First World War.* The Raleigh Lecture on History, 1959. London: British Academy, Oxford University Press, London, 1959. Also in *Proceedings of the British Academy, 1959.* London: Oxford University Press, 1960, pp. 67–95.
206a. Taylor, A. J. P. Biography of Lord Beaverbrook. In progress.
207. Taylor, Henry A. *Robert Donald: being the authorized biography of Sir Robert Donald, G.B.E., LL.D. journalist, editor and friend of statesmen.* London: Stanley Paul, 1934.
208. Terraine, John. *Douglas Haig: the educated soldier.* London: Hutchinson, 1963. [U. S. edn., *Ordeal of Victory.* Philadelphia: Lippincott, 1963.]
209. Thomis, M. I. *The labour movement in Great Britain and compulsory military service, 1914–1916.* M. A. thesis, University of London: King's College (Mr. M. E. Howard), 1959.
210. Thomson, Malcolm. *David Lloyd George: the official biography.* London and New York: Hutchinson, 1948.
211. *The Times History of the War.* London: The Times, 1914–21. 22 vols. (pts. 1–273.)
212. Trevelyan, G. M. *Grey of Fallodon: the life and letters of Sir Edward Grey, afterwards Viscount Grey of Fallodon.* London: Longmans, 1937. [U. S. edn., Boston: Houghton Mifflin, 1937.]
213. Waley, Sigmund D. *Edwin Montagu: a memoir and an account of his visits to India.* New York: Asia Pub. House, 1964.
214. Wells, H. G. *Mr. Britling Sees It Through.* London: Cassell, 1916. [U. S. edn., N. Y.: Macmillan, 1916.] Later published under title of *Mr. Britling.* London: T. Fisher Unwin, 1924.
215. *Williamson, Henry. A Chronicle of Ancient Sunlight.* London: MacDonald, 1953—. The volumes relating to the war are *How Dear Is Life,* 1954; *A Fox under my Cloak,* 1955; *The Golden Virgin,* 1957; *Love and the Loveless,* 1958; and *A Test to Destruction.* 1960. All were revised for the paperback edition of 1963–64, London: Panther.
216. Willis, Irene Cooper. *England's Holy War: a study of English Liberal

idealism during the great war. N. Y.: A. A. Knopf, 1928. [One volume edn. of three volumes published in England: *How We Went into the War.* Manchester and London: National Labour Press, 1919; *How We Got on with the War.* Manchester and London: National Labour Press, 1920; and *How We Came Out of the War.* London: International Bookshop, 1921.]

217. Wilson, Trevor. *The Downfall of the Liberal Party, 1914–1935.* London: Collins, 1966. [U. S. edn., Ithaca, N. Y.: Cornell University Press, 1966.]

218. Wood, Alan. *The True History of Lord Beaverbrook.* London: Heinemann, 1965.

219. Woodward, Sir Llewellyn. *Great Britain and the War of 1914–18.* London: Methuen, 1967. [U. S. edition, N. Y.: Praeger, 1967.]

220. Wrench, John Evelyn. *Alfred Lord Milner: The Man with no Illusions.* London: Eyre and Spottiswoode, 1958.

221. Wrench, Sir Evelyn. *Geoffrey Dawson and our Times.* London: Hutchinson, 1955.

222. French of Ypres, Field-Marshal Viscount. *1914.* London: Constable, 1919. [U. S. edn., Boston: Houghton Mifflin, 1919.]

223. French, Gerald, ed. *Some War Diaries, Addresses, and Correspondence of Field-Marshal the Right Honourable the Earl of Ypres.* London: H. Jenkins, 1937.

PRIVATE PAPERS

The only general listing of these is in the indexes maintained by the National Register of Archives [NRA] at Quality House, Quality Court, Chancery Lane, London, W.C.2. The register's "aim is to record the location, content and availability of all collections of documents, both large and small, in England and Wales (other than those of the central government) without limit of date" (Flysheet, Historical Manuscripts Commission. National Register of Archives, Facilities Offered to Students, n.d.). The following private paper collections have been identified primarily among the Register's indexes.

224. Asquith, Herbert H. Prime Minister. Papers, Bodleian Library, Oxford University, Oxford.

225. Baldwin, Stanley. Conservative politician: Joint Financial Secretary to Treasury, 1917–21. Papers, Cambridge University Library. These were listed in the Library's *Summary Guide,* 1966, as not being open to inspection before 1970.

226. Balfour, Arthur J. Conservative politician: First Lord of Admiralty 1915–16, Foreign Secretary, 1916–19. Papers, British Museum, London.

227. Beaverbrook, Lord (Max Aitken). Newspaper proprietor and friend of Bonar Law. Beaverbrook Library, London. Papers "not open to readers."

227a. Bennett, Arnold. Novelist. *Journal,* City Museum, Stoke-on-Trent.

THE WAR ON THE HOME FRONT · 419

228. Birrell, Augustine. Liberal politician: personal letters, British Museum; papers, Liverpool University Library.
229. Bonar Law, Andrew. Leader of unionist party, Colonial Secretary 1915–16, member of war cabinet and Chancellor of Exchequer, 1916–18. Papers, Beaverbrook Library, London.
230. Carson, Edward. Conservative politician: First Lord of Admiralty, 1916–Jul. 1917; member, war cabinet, Jul. 1917–Jan. 1918. Papers, Public Record Office, Northern Ireland, Belfast.
231. Cecil, Robert. Conservative politician: Minister for Blockade, 1916–18. Correspondence, British Museum, London; papers, 1915–1919, Public Record Office, (F. O. 800/195–198), London.
232. Chamberlain, Austen. Conservative politician: Secretary for India, 1915–17; member, war cabinet from Apr. 1918. Papers, Birmingham University Library, Birmingham.
233. Chamberlain, Neville. Conservative politician and businessman. Director-General of National Service, 1916–17. Papers, to be bequeathed to Birmingham University Library, Birmingham (on death of widow).
234. Churchill, Winston S. Liberal politician: First Lord of Admiralty to May 1915; Minister of Munitions from July 1917. Papers, Chartwell Trust. Applications to be made to A. F. Moir, Esq., c/o Messr. Flodgates, 8 Waterloo Place, London, S.W.1. Availability uncertain.
235. Crewe Milnes, Robert. Liberal politician. Papers, Cambridge University Library, Cambridge. Closed till 1973 at wish of family.
236. Curtis, Lionel. Publicist. Papers. These are "temporarily" at the office of the *Round Table* and *Annual Register,* 166 Piccadilly, London, W.1, but are expected "finally" to go to the Bodleian Library, Oxford University. Applications for the papers, "not normally available," are to be made to Sir Ivison MacAdam, editor of the *Annual Register* and Curtis executor.
237. Curzon, George. Conservative politician, President of Air Board, 1916, member of war cabinet. Papers, private possession. Consult NRA.
238. Davies, Joseph. Secretary, prime minister's personal secretariat, Dec. 1916 on. Papers, National Library of Wales, Aberystwyth.
239. Dawson, Geoffrey. Editor of *The Times.* Papers, *The Times,* London. These, according to a 1965 letter to the National Register of Archives, "are inaccessible, as material in *The Times* is not made available to anyone outside their staff."
240. Fisher, H. A. L. Educator and Coalition liberal, President of Board of Education, 1916 on. Papers, Bodleian Library, Oxford University, Oxford.
241. Garvin, J. L. Editor of *The Observer.* Papers. University of Texas Library.
241a. George V, King. Papers. Royal Archives, Windsor.
242. Haig, Douglas. British commander, western front, 1915–1918. Papers, National Library of Scotland, Edinburgh. Access requires written permission of the present Earl Haig.

243. Haldane, Richard. Liberal politician. Papers, National Library of Scotland, Edinburgh.
244. Harcourt, Lewis. Liberal politician: Secretary for Colonies to 1915. Papers, in possession of Lord Harcourt, Stanton Harcourt, Oxon.
245. Hardinge, Charles. Administrator: Viceory of India 1910–16; Under-Secretary for Foreign Affairs, 1916–20. Papers, Cambridge University Library, Cambridge.
246. Kitchener, Herbert H. Secretary for War, 1914–1916. Papers, Public Record Office, London.
247. Lansbury, George. Labor leader. Papers, British Library of Political and Economic Science, London School of Economics, London.
248. Lloyd George, David. Prime Minister, 1916–1922. Papers, Beaverbrook Library, London.
249. Kerr, David (Lord Lothian). Editor, *Round Table,* 1910–16; private secretary to Lloyd George, 1916–21. Papers, Scottish Record Office, Edinburgh.
249a. McKenna, Reginald. Liberal politician. Papers, The Library, Churchill College, Cambridge University.
250. Milner, Alfred. Conservative politician: member of war cabinet 1916–18; Secretary of War, 1918. Papers, Bodleian Library, Oxford University, Oxford. Written consent of the librarian of New College, Oxford University, is required.
251. Montagu, Edwin. Liberal politician, Secretary for India from 1917. Papers as Secretary, India Office Library, Commonwealth Relations Office, King Charles Street, London, S.W.1.
252. Morel, E. D. Publicist, Secretary of Union of Democratic Control. Papers, British Library of Political and Economic Science, London School of Economics, London.
253. Runciman, Walter. Liberal politician; President of Board of Trade, 1914–1916. Papers, private possession, enquire at National Register of Archives.
254. Samuel, Herbert. Liberal politician. Papers, House of Lords Record Office, London.
255. Scott, C. P. Proprietor and editor of *Manchester Guardian.* Papers, British Museum, London.
256. Spender, J. A. Editor, *Westminster Gazette,* and friend of Asquith. Papers, British Museum, London.
257. Wargrave, Lord (Edward Goulding). Conservative M. P. Papers, Beaverbrook Library, London.
258. Webb, Beatrice and Sidney. "Fabians." Letters, London School of Economics, London, British Library of Political and Economic Science.

PARTY ARCHIVES
259. The Labour Party, Transport House, London.
260. The Conservative Party, London.

261. Minutes of various local Liberal associations may be found referred to in Trevor Wilson (217 above).

ADDITIONS TO BIBLIOGRAPHY

262. Ash, Bernard. *The Lost Dictator: Field-Marshal Sir Henry Wilson.* London: Cassells, 1968.

263. Asquith, Lady Cynthia. *Diaries, 1915–1918.* London: Hutchinson, 1968. [N. Y.: Knopf, 1969.]

264. Beloff, Max. *Imperial Sunset.* Vol. I. *Britain's Liberal Empire, 1897–1921.* London: Methuen, 1969. [N. Y.: Knopf, 1970.]

265. *Memoirs of a Conservative: J. C. C. Davidson's Memoirs and Papers, 1910–1937.* James, R. R., ed. London: Weidenfeld and Nicolson, 1969.

266. Gregory, Ross. *Walter Hines Page: ambassador to the court of St. James's.* Lexington: University Press of Kentucky, 1969.

267. Hinds, L. M. *Franco-British Economic Cooperation during the First World War.* Thesis under J. B. Duroselle, Faculty of Arts and Letters, University of Paris. N.d., but was scheduled to be completed, 1968.

268. Jones, Thomas. *Whitehall Diary.* Vol. I, *1916–1925.* Keith Middlemas, ed. London: Oxford University Press, 1969.

269. Middlemas, Keith and John Barnes. *Baldwin: a biography.* London: Weidenfeld and Nicolson, 1969. [N. Y.: Macmillan, 1969.]

270. Northedge, F. S. *The Troubled Giant: Britain among the Great Powers, 1916–1939.* London: G. Bell, 1966. [N. Y. and Washington: Frederick A. Praeger, 1966.]

271. Roskill, Stephen. *Hankey, man of secrets.* London: Collins. Volume I, *1877–1918,* 1970.

272. Sullivan, A. E. "Colonel Repington." *Army Quarterly* (London). October 1968, pp. 86–92.

273. Young, Kenneth. *Arthur James Balfour: The happy life of the politician, prime minister, statesman, and philosopher.* London: G. Bell, 1963.

XVI

THE DEVELOPMENT OF THE
ROYAL AIR FORCE, 1909–1945

Robin Higham

The scholarly history of the British flying services is, except for the war periods, largely non-existent. Researchers have been handicapped by the Fifty- (now Thirty-) Year Rule (see Introduction), by the premature destruction of records, especially at the Air Ministry Archives at Hayes, by the necessity to have some familiarity with terminology, technology and Service attitudes. Apart from studies of aircraft, more scholarly works simply have not appeared. There is not even a general one-volume history of the RAF of later date than Saunders' *Per Ardua* (260) of 1944, though there is one bibliography (361) and another one is in process (120).

JOURNALS. Outside of the official histories, the principal sources are the standard military periodicals (see Introduction) and the specialized aeronautical publications. The principal Service organ is the *R.A.F. Quarterly* (250), which is supplemented by *The Hawk* (114), published by the Staff College at Andover. Neither of these has a cumulative index. On the civilian side there is the long-established *Journal of the Royal Aeronautical Society,* for which there are cumulative indices and most recently a new one which includes the papers published (150). More specialized are *The Aeroplane* (1) and *Flight* (88), founded in 1911 and 1909 respectively, and merged in 1968. *The Engineer* and *Engineering* are also worth consulting. Both are covered in *Engineering Index* (see Introduction). Occasionally useful articles and item-type materials are to be found in *Air Britain, Air Pictorial,* and the like. The letters columns, especially of *The Aeroplane,* periodically provide corrections of articles or of claims made as well as bits of historical minutiae (2).

OFFICIAL HISTORIES AND PAPERS. For the history of the RAF these are almost in a class by themselves, since sometimes they are in effect summaries of official papers. The two major sets are *The War in the Air* (226) on the First World War, which covers the Royal Flying Corps, the Royal Naval Air Service, and their descendant, the RAF itself to 1919, and the various volumes of the *United Kingdom History of the Second World War,* discussed below. The six volumes of *The War in the Air* were originally to have been written by Sir Walter Raleigh, a professor of English literature at Oxford. But he died after completing the first, and the remainder were written by Captain H. A. Jones, RFC, who served in the Cabinet Historical Office and later in the Air Ministry. As a series it suffers from a number of difficulties, including lack of perspective, and supervision by Trenchard, one of the principal wartime participants. The naval parts, in some cases verbatim drafts handed in by junior officers, were not covered in the Corbett and Newbolt volumes on naval operations (see Chapter XIV). High policy does not receive nearly so searching a treatment as in the volumes on the Second World War. Two basic subjects are treated more fully in separate series: aircraft production in the twelve-volume *History of the Ministry of Munitions* (196), and aviation medicine in Macpherson *et al., Diseases of War, II, . . . the medical aspects of aviation* (189).

In between the wars the RAF published a short history (14), and during the Second World War a number of popular paperbacks appeared (195), of which *The Battle of Britain* sold 4,250,000 copies. Bridging the gap between these pieces of instant history and the official accounts of the 1939–45 struggle are the three volumes of Saunders and Richards, *The Royal Air Force, 1939–1945* (262). Designed as part of a popular history to assuage public thirst until the official volumes could appear, they are the only place in which an albatross' eye view of RAF activities during the war may be obtained. Otherwise, except for the four volumes of *The Strategic Air Offensive against Germany* (305), the RAF story is buried in the campaign and other tomes of *The History of the Second World War* (see Introduction). There is no air equivalent to Roskill's *The War at Sea* [see Chapter XVIII (13)]. However, a great deal of information can be gleaned from a careful perusal of Rexford-Welch's *R.A.F. Medical Services* (233). Webster and Frankland's work (305) on Bomber Command's campaign against Germany is controversial; unlike the other campaign sub-series all four volumes were published as a unit in 1961. The last volume contains a number of useful documents pertaining to the pre-1939 period. Equally important for the history of a technological service are the volumes in the civil series dealing with all aspects of war production, especially those by Scott and Hughes (265) Postan, Hay, and Scott (223), and Hall (108, 109).

The official histories are based almost exclusively upon official papers, now being deposited in the Public Record Office. In addition several special collections exist. At the Air Historical Branch (319) are kept operational records of the Second World War together with some papers from the First. Papers which do not contain materials on the Higher Direction may be used with prior permission, as may those at the Air Ministry Archives at Hayes. All manuscripts based on these materials must be cleared with the Air Publications Branch. Fortunately, the head of all three organizations in 1967 was the same person (319). Unfortunately, the disposals system being employed in 1959 was such that only documents which bore the signature of the Secretary of State for Air or of the Chief of the Air Staff were sure to survive and eventually to be transferred to the Public Record Office. Personnel Records are kept at the RAF Records Center at Gloucester but admission to them is very restricted, as under the British system, unlike under the American, personnel are not allowed to see their own fitness reports. This is an obstacle to biographers.

Parliamentary debates are not a very useful source except for occasional remarks by back-benchers and official statements. Questions, however, can be quite revealing, for members with professional aviation knowledge often tried to catch out inexperienced ministers. Parliamentary indices involve some semantic problems and should be checked for words such as "aircraft," "air force," "aviation," "air," "air service," "Air Ministry," "Supply," not to mention "War Office," "Admiralty," "Fleet Air Arm," "Ministry of Aircraft Production," and "Ministry of Defence." The Sessional Papers are a largely untapped mine with their Estimates, Appropriations Accounts, Reports of the Comptroller and Auditor-General, Command Papers, and Reports of the Estimates and Public Accounts Committees. *The General Index to House of Commons Papers, 1900–1949* (117) provides many suggestions starting with AIR (see Introduction). The state of the art may be found in civil accident reports, though these were not published until almost the end of the interwar period. For Air Staff thinking, consult the specifications for types of aircraft and other equipment, which even if not available from official sources can often be obtained from either aircraft manufacturers themselves or from the many works now dealing either with specific types (176, 210, 240, 241, 268, 269), or with the products of one company (30, 191A, 321). See also the work by Schlaiffer and Heron on aircraft engines and fuels (264).

PRIVATE PAPERS. It is possible that collections of these exist, but so far this field has not been explored. Conditions in the RAF with journeys by air were not conducive to the accumulation of private files. The sponsored biographies that have so far appeared (40, 41, 74, 75, 123, 161) have not given much indication that they were based upon important private archives. Nor was the RAF in general historically minded so that people did not accumulate papers as they did in other services.

GENERAL HISTORIES of the RAF are lacking. The few which do exist are either badly dated, not scholarly, or concentrate upon only a short period. In general they have been written either by retired officers like Chamier (57), Gossage (98), Charlton (59), Macmillan (187), and Joubert de la Ferte (149), or by journalists, or they have been written for boys. The only recent work of any depth is David Divine's polemic *The Broken Wing* (79). Robin Higham has covered various aspects of the development of British air power to 1939 (119, 121, 122). Geoffrey Norris' *The Royal Flying Corps* (211) merely skims the surface, and apart from Raleigh's first volume (226), little is available. Spaight's *The Beginnings of Organized Air Power: an historical study* (279) is by one of Trenchard's subordinates at the Air Ministry, while C. G. Grey ("C.G.G.")'s *A History of the Air Ministry* (101) is prejudiced and unreliable. Eugene Emme, Historian of NASA in the United States, provides some documentation in *The Impact of Air Power* (85). But that is about the limit. Nor is there much to go on in the way of topical histories. Air Vice Marshal "Johnnie" Johnson has tackled air fighting (142), Air Vice Marshal Peter Wykham Fighter Command (318), Air Marshal Sir Robert Saundby air bombardment (259) and George Quester deterrence (225), though these latter two should be used with care, Air Chief Marshal Sir Philip Joubert de la Ferte the ground crews (146) and Coastal Command (144), and John W. R. Taylor the Central Flying School (288). Potted Squadron histories are the field of Peter Lewis (172) and Moyes (204). The Air Ministry was not included in the New Whitehall series, nor has such an important place as Farnborough had more than some brief official histories (62, 197, 254) and public relations brochures (291). The one thing that can be said is that there is plenty of room for scholarly work.

On the other hand, the R.A.F. being a technical Service there is almost a surfeit of useful books on the quasi-technical and antique historical background. Most of these deal with such things as one type of aircraft or the invention of the aeroplane. They really provide the raw material for scholarly work, especially in the way in which they reveal what were Air Ministry specifications, thus reflecting Air Staff tactical and strategic thinking. Moreover, they contain the statistical materials for a more accurate assessment of the role of the R.A.F. and the magnitude of air warfare, especially in the First World War. The uninitiated will want to start with Nayler and Ower's *Aviation: its technical development* (206), Gibbs-Smith's *The Aeroplane* (96), Sir Graham Sutton's *Mastery of the Air; an account of mechanical flight* (282), and the books on early British aviation by Brett (44), Hodgson (128), Spaight (279), Snowden Gamble (276), Penrose (220), Wheeler (306), Lewis (169), and Stewart (281), not to mention Geoffrey Dorman's *Fifty Years Fly Past* (81). Meteorology and Navigation may also be necessary, in which case Air Vice Marshal D. C. T. "Pathfinder" Bennett (32) or W/Cdr. E. W. Anderson (17) can be consulted, while for a history of the art there are the shorter works of E. G. R. Taylor (286) and Arthur Hughes (134). RAF maps were catalogued in the War Office Directorate of Military Surveys (100).

In the field of aircraft themselves, there is first of all the annual *Jane's All the World's Aircraft* (140). More easily afforded are the series published by Putnam and Macdonald (321) respectively. Owen Thetford has a volume each on naval since 1912 (293) and RAF aircraft since 1918 (292). In addition there are volumes dealing with most of the principal manufacturing companies and some especially detailed books on single types such as the Hurricane (192), Spitfire (241), Lancaster (240) and Mosquito (269) of World War II. The most detailed work on the 1914–18 British aeroplanes is that by J. M. Bruce (50), while Bruce

Robertson covers serial numbers (239) and camouflage (238), and Peter Lewis has studied fighters (171) and bombers (170). In addition, the Profile series (224) is worth checking on individual types, while real examples may be seen by consulting the *Journal of the Royal Aeronautical Society* list (322).

The ceremonial side of the Service is in Air Publication *A. P. 818* (12), *Colours and Standards of the RAF* (7), Hering's *Customs and Traditions of the Royal Air Force* (118), and in Wing/Cmdr. Norman Macmillan's article, "Uniform Habits" (188). Eric Partridge's *A Dictionary of Forces' Slang, 1939–1945* (218) is a guide to the humour of types like Pilot/Officer Prune of World War II notoriety, while *The Aeroplane* has provided one for nicknames (5). Songs, mess games, and sports, some inherited and some invented, also have their literature (2, 4, 147, 253, 331). Turner has catalogued the Air V.C.'s (298).

AUTOBIOGRAPHIES AND BIOGRAPHIES. The newness of the Flying Service and the youth of its personnel in the First World War resulted in a lot of ephemeral books by and about passing heroes. Very few officers were senior enough to retire at the end of the conflict. There is thus a paucity of other than action memoirs until the Second World War. In addition to this, few biographies have been published and most lack depth. John Laffin on Salmond (161) is very thin; Collier hardly does Dowding (75) justice (though "Stuffy" may well not have been the easiest person with whom to work), but is better with Brancker (74), as is Macmillan (185); above all Boyle's *Trenchard* (41) suffers from the author's lack of familiarity with the world about the Chief of the Air Staff. That side of life is well shown in his secretary's *Flying-Corps Headquarters, 1914–1918* (24), and in Slessor's autobiographical *The Central Blue* (274a). It is also to be seen in Mark Kerr's *Land, Sea and Air* (155), in Sir Frederick Sykes's *From Many Angles* (285), in Tedder's recent *With Prejudice* (290), in Sir Philip Joubert de la Ferte's *The Fated Sky* (145), in Lord Douglas' *The Years of Combat* (82), and in Sir Arthur Harris' *Bomber Offensive* (111). Sir Arthur Longmore, who retired in 1942, wrote his own book (179), but Sir Roderic Hill, who did much pioneer work, has only a life written by his daughter (123). Those who retired during or after World War II were mostly at more junior ranks, but their books cover a wide field from armament research to medicine (135, 95, 70, 175).

In the formative years the Ministers were all anxious to tell their side of the story, so we have Churchill (64), Seely (202), Hoare (124, 125, 126), Londonderry (178), and Swinton (284), but the practice has been less contagious after the Second World War, perhaps because of the declining prestige of the office of Secretary of State for Air.

One prolific writer of the period is Capt. Norman Macmillan (183ff), a sometime test pilot for Handley Page, whose works provide usable insights into people and flying. His four-volume history of the RAF (187) suffered from being written without access to sources and from its very contemporaneous nature.

THE FIRST WORLD WAR. Much of what has already been said applies to the 1914–1918 period, when the British air force was the world's *second* largest; the French were first. The Thirty-Year Rule has now rolled back past the basic materials housed in the Imperial War Museum, the Air Historical Branch and the Air Ministry Archives (319). Contemporary journals, such as *Flight* and *The Aeroplane,* suffer, of course, from wartime censorship, and there were stories, such as that of the rigid airship program (121), which were never discussed. The journals usually have annual indices, but the trouble with using them is that a strong familiarity with names and terms is necessary, and the same is at least partially true for Parliament. Private papers for the period are largely still an unknown quantity, while most of the contemporary books are limited to the fighter-pilot type memoirs such as those of Ball (156), Mannock (180) and McCudden (181), Norman Macmillan (184), Duncan Grinnell-Milne (103), and C. Day Lewis (167, 168), to mention some of the best and to Snowden Gamble's *The Story of a North Sea Air Station* (277) and Pattinson's *History of 99 Squadron* (219) and Burge's *The Annals of 100 Squadron* (52). These can be supplemented by reference to Robertson's *Air Aces of the 1914–18 War* (237) and Cole's *McCudden, V. C.* (72).

The War in the Air (226) is the basic source. But there are other materials in print, notably *The History of the Ministry of Munitions* (196), and the three official investigations into the administration, command and supply of the R.F.C. (*Cd.8191, 8192* and *8194*) which helped precipitate the formation of the Air Ministry and the RAF in 1918. Brigadier-General Guy Livingston's *Hot Air in Cold Blood* (174), the lives of Brancker (74, 185) and Higham's *The Military Intellectuals* (122) as well as Boyle's *Trenchard* (41) amplify the story, but it is notable that there are considerable omissions on this subject even in Lloyd George's memoirs (see Chapter XV). Additional background is available from three sources: Admiral Mark Kerr (155) prints an important memorandum of 1917 and Sykes (285) one of 1918, while two American missions, the Crowell (301) and the Gorell (11), published their findings.

Aircraft of the First World War are now covered in some detail. In addition to the works already mentioned, there is a small series by J. M. Bruce on British aircraft (50), Thetford and Grey on German (294), Lamberton and Cheesman on fighters (162), and Lamberton on bombers of all air forces (163).

Special aspects of the war have as yet not received much treatment. The classic analysis of the use of air power on the Western Front is Sir John Slessor's *Air Power and Armies* (273). Two recent books are McKee's *The Friendless Sky* (182) and Alan Morris' *Bloody April* (199). The one area which has received detailed treatment is the matter of air defence, since the 1914 war was the first in centuries in which the Channel ceased to be an effective moat. Major-General E. B. Ashmore (20) commanded the defences and Lt/Col. A. Rawlinson (227) was a subordinate; Capt. Joseph Morris (200) and Frank Morison (246) wrote on it in the interwar years; but the best accounts are recent studies by Fredette, *The Sky on Fire: the First Battle of Britain* (91) and by Robinson, *The Zeppelin in Combat* (243), which make use of both British and German sources. Robinson, a psychiatrist, has also just produced a one-volume history of aviation medicine (242). On the role of women see Douglas-Pennant (83).

While naval aviation in the First World War is covered in Chapter XIV, researchers should consult the documentary collection being edited for the Navy Records Society by the official naval historian of the 1939–45 War, Captain Roskill (244), the relevant chapters in *The War in the Air* (226), and P. K. Kemp, *The Fleet Air Arm* (153). Thetford has a volume devoted to naval aircraft since 1912 (293), while Higham covers airships (121). C. R. Samson (257) was one of the early birds who stayed with the RAF, as was Longmore (179).

THE INTERWAR YEARS. Much the same remarks which hold true for the First World War and the history of the RAF in general also apply to the years 1918–1939. However, the United Kingdom histories of the Second World War are useful for certain aspects of the period. Basil Collier (73) goes into much of the background of air, while Terence O'Brien (212) provides more on civil, defence. Webster and Frankland (305) sum up the reasons for the early weakness of the bombing offensive to 1942 and provide some of the key interwar papers. The ramifications of the counter-strike policy may also be found in the volumes on *Food* (110) and *Emergency Medical Services* (84). More background is contained in Rexford-Welch's volumes (233) of the RAF medical series, often tucked away in chapters dealing with specific problems. Higham (119) provides a wide bibliographical introduction as well as a brief survey of the RAF and of the aircraft industry.

As already noted, the Secretaries of State of the period, Churchill, Hoare, Londonderry, and Swinton, have written their memoirs. In addition those of Liddell Hart (173) should be consulted not only for a general view, but because Trenchard fed him information up till they parted in 1935. Lord Rothermere has told his side of rearmament (247). Also of interest are T. E. Lawrence's account of his time as an airman, *The Mint* (164), and Charles Sims's *Camera in the Sky* (272). The homes of the Air Ministry are briefly touched upon in Geoffrey Dorman's "Adastral Houses" (80).

These were the years of discussions of air power and here the guide is Higham's *Military Intellectuals* (122). However, he made no attempt to explore the influence of writers and editors of the technical and popular press, leaving such people as C. G. Grey and Oliver Stewart for others to study.

Airmen had to prove themselves, and a series of record-breaking flights from the Schneider Cup races to long-distance hops were undertaken. The start was made immediately the war ended with a rash of attempts in 1919. Alcock and Brown crossed the Atlantic (308), as did *R-34* (190), but Hawker and Grieve (115) did not. The Smith brothers reached

Australia (275), C. R. Samson went from Cairo to the Cape and back (258), and Fellowes was first over Everest (87). Equally importantly, they claimed that aircraft could be used economically for frontier and tribal pacification. The great testing ground was Iraq in which Harris (111), Charlton (58), "H.W." and Sidney Hay (137) served. But for a different side of the story see Glubb Pasha (99), Sir Arnold Wilson (312), and Ismay (138). Slessor (274) and Kingston-McCloughry (159) served on the North-West Frontier. Yet despite the fact that these operations were supposed to be showcases for air power and despite the fact that air power has been used in defence of Aden for decades now, this is a subject which has never had a history, though articles exist in the JRUSI and elsewhere and many survivors are still alive. [Lt/Col. Julian Paget has one in process (330).]

THE SECOND WORLD WAR. The 1939–1945 war was really an air war, whereas the 1914–1918 one was not. Not only was the RAF four times its earlier size in terms of manpower, but through much improved training, many more people survived, while a better educated public provided a ready market for many more books. The result is somewhat the same as earlier in terms of many personal accounts, but at the same time there was a greater official output both during and after the conflict. In addition, historians were appointed to each ministry almost from the very beginning, where they were deluged with about two million *files* for the six-year period. On the other hand, although communiques were fed to the press, the official dispatches did not begin to appear in the *London Gazette* until Dowding's on the Battle of Britain was published in 1946. Students of RAF history will have to look to foreign sources, as Telford Taylor's new study (289) of the Battle of Britain shows. Where so many of the early campaigns are concerned, either the British have successfully thrown a smoke-screen over the real picture, or, as was so often the case in the first thirty months of the war, they were retreating and most of their records were lost. Moreover, care must be taken to avoid, as the official histories do not always, giving the picture from London.

The general history is the official *The Royal Air Force, 1939–1945* (262), which must, however, be used in conjunction with later volumes of the larger official campaigns series, especially Webster and Frankland (305). In addition, a number of one-volume works now cover Coastal Command (144, 278), RAF torpedo-bombers (28), Fighter Command (318), photographic reconnaissance (PRU) (22, 194), testing aircraft (70, 307), operational scientists (boffins) (67, 263), and the development of rockets (148, 323). Then, too, there are the official histories of associated air forces which did not exist for the First World War—notably the Indian (105), Australian (21), New Zealand (209), Canadian (55), and American (the latter being split between three groups) (97, 129, 299, 300). Then there are the memoirs of many commanders, the more important of which were mentioned earlier, but which must also include Sir Basil Embry's *Mission Completed* (86), Kingston-McCloughry's *The*

Direction of War (158), Lee's *Special Duties* (166), and of a technical nature Sir Frank Whittle's *Jet* (309), the behind-the-scenes story of the British development of the jet engine, to which must be coupled Shacklady's *The Gloster Meteor* (268). Hector Bolitho served in the Air Ministry and recorded his experiences in *Penguin in the Eyrie: a RAF diary 1939–1945* (37). Marshal of the RAF Lord Portal's memoirs had not by October 1967 yet appeared in print.

Fighter operations remained as glorious, if not more so, than in the First World War, especially after "the Few" won the Battle of Britain. Glamorization of fighter pilots started with Noel Monks's *Squadrons Up* (198) and Charles Gardner's *A.A.S.F.* (93). (The Advanced Air Striking Force in France), and continued throughout the conflict. A start may be made with Shores and Williams' *Aces High; the Fighter Aces of the British and Commonwealth Air Forces in World War II* (271) and continued with "Johnnie" Johnson's *Wing Leader* (141) and Pierre Clostermann's *The Big Show* (69), both of which are first-hand accounts. Thereafter it becomes a matter of selection from a large number of memoirs and biographies. Special mention needs to be made of the more technical night interception business (43, 63, 228). Sometimes, of course, the odds were much against the RAF as at Malta (33, 177).

The Battle of Britain itself has attracted a lot of attention, including the philatelic commemoration of the 25th anniversary. The Air Ministry's *The First Great Air Battle in History: the Battle of Britain* (195) was a major propagandic coup; it sold 4,250,000 copies! The modern reconstructions by Middleton (193), Collier (76), Wood and Dempster (316), Clark (66), and Telford Taylor (289), supplement the official account in Collier (73) and the German Galland's *The First and the Last* (92). On the American volunteer group, see Boebert's article "The Eagle Squadrons" (35). The Royal Observer Corps (333) played a major role in the battle as did radar (chapter XXI). Many pilots were saved by parachutes and thus were entitled to join the Caterpillar Club (362), while others became the "guinea pigs" of the skilled plastic surgeon, Sir Archibald McIndoe (201). Two of the famous fighter stations have had their roles preserved in Sutton's *Raiders Approach!* (283) on Hornchurch and Graham Wallace's *R.A.F. Biggin Hill* (304). Once offensive sweeps (127) were undertaken across the Channel, escaping became a major pastime as related by Crawley (78), Brickhill (46, 47, 48), Reid (229, 231), Nabarro (205) and Embry (86); see also Hutton's *Official Secret* (136).

Even during the Battle of Britain the attack on Germany began. Whether or not it was wise remains a moral and strategic issue which has been raised both by Herr Rumpf in *The Bombing of Germany* (255) and by David Irving in *The Destruction of Dresden* (139), but ignored by Martin Caidin in *The Night Hamburg Died* (54), when more damage was done than at Hiroshima. Noble Frankland's *The Bombing Offensive against Germany; outlines and perspectives* (90) is a more useful starting point, while Ralph Barker *The Thousand Plan* (29) deals with the first really big raid. The views of the Commander-in-Chief are forcefully stated in

Marshal of the RAF Sir Arthur Harris' *Bomber Offensive* (111) which supplemented the official account for a number of years. D. C. T. Bennett's acid remarks in *Pathfinder* (31) are supported by Constance Babington-Smith in *Air Spy* (22) and less strongly by Anderson's *Pathfinders* (16) and Saward's *The Bomber's Eye* (263), which deals with radar. The combination of Guy Gibson's own account, *Enemy Coast Ahead* (97), with Brickhill's story of his 617 Squadron, *The Dam Busters* (45), may be supplemented by Braddon's *Cheshire V. C.* (42), Boyle's *No Passing Glory* (40), Lawrence's *No. 5 Bomber Group, RAF* (165), Saunders' *Return at Dawn* (261), and Walker's *Strike to Defend* (303). The tail-gunner's view can be found in works by Henry (116), Clark (65), and Rivas (235). Bullmore's *Dark Haven* (51) discusses the history of wartime flying control. Not everyone returned from these raids: Barker's *Down in the Drink* (26), Nicholl's *Supermarine Walrus* (210), and Whittle and Borissow's *Angels without Wings* (310) tell what happened to some of them. The most successful Bomber Command aircraft was the Mosquito, now suitably enshrined in Sharp and Bowyer's *Mosquito* (269), while Robertson has done the same for the Lancaster (240).

Analysis of the offensive against Germany began as soon as the war was over and is contained in the *U. S. Strategic Bombing Survey* (302) and in the British Intelligence Objectives Sub-Committee reports (49) and those of the British Bombing Survey Unit. The last named had a very peculiar history which is related in detail in Webster and Frankland, IV, 40–58 (305). The Stanford Research Institute (280), the Home Office (131), and the National Fire Protection Association in the United States (39) all have analysed the results. The science of firefighting itself has been attempted by James Kenyon (154) and more recently by the Home Office (130).

OPERATIONS OVERSEAS. Here the official campaign histories provide much data that has not yet been pulled into single volumes. Neither the six volumes on the Mediterranean (221) nor the five on the war against Japan (160) have yet been completed. However, both Anzac series are out (21, 209). In addition, Tedder's *With Prejudice* (290) has a great deal to say on the war from 1942 onwards. But, particularly in the early days of campaigns overseas, which means Norway, France, Greece, Burma, and Malaya, most records were lost.

The small RAF unit aiding the Russians was chronicled by Hubert Griffith (102). Operations from Malta are covered by the commander, Air Vice Marshal Sir Hugh Lloyd in *Briefed to Attack* (177), Coffin in *Malta Story* (71), and by the Canadian ace "Buzz" Beurling in *Malta Spitfire* (33), as well as by an official New Zealand account, *Malta Airmen* (209). Operations in Greece and Libya are the province of various volumes by Wisdom (314, 315), Ogilvie (213), Netherwood (207), Gavshon (94), Houart (132), and Houghton (133), while a more analytical approach is taken by Philip Guedalla in *Middle East, 1940–1942, a study in air power* (104), by Roderic Owen in *Tedder* (216), and by Frank Owen in *The Desert Air Force* (217). Overseas areas were ones in which both the British Overseas Airways Corporation and the RAF Ferry and Transport Commands operated. Their stories have been told in *Merchant Airmen* (195) and in *Atlantic Bridge* (195), but both now leave much to be desired. In particular, neither deals with the political struggle over operations and routes nor with the RAF's lack of interest in transport aircraft. Farther to the East in Burma, air transport played a major role not only in the Chindit operations, but also in the advance of the Fourteenth Army in general. But the war in Burma was a forgotten war and few correspondents witnessed it. The tone is set by Russell's *Forgotten Skies* (256) and Moxon's *After the Monsoon* (203). The official histories start with *Wings of the Phoenix* (195), and continue with the various volumes on the Indian, Anzac, and British efforts, notably *The War against Japan* (160). Lastly there is the USAF Historical study of *Air Supply in the Burma Campaigns* (287). Ferrying aircraft to various units is covered in Cheesman's story of the Air Transport Auxiliary (61).

THE WAR AT SEA. Naval operations are covered in Chapter XVIII. In addition to Joubert on Coastal Command (144), the standard work is Roskill's official series *The War at Sea* (245). The memoirs of Embry (86), Joubert (145) and Slessor (274) give the AOC'-in-C's picture. Australian crews did much flying over the North Atlantic and this is recorded in their official history (21) and in Southall's *They Shall Not Pass Unseen* (278). But so far the emphasis has been upon operations and aircraft, and little has been done on the materiel side.

AIRBORNE OPERATIONS. Though largely part of the Army story (chapter XIX), the RAF did have a hand in its work as told by Newnham, *Prelude to Glory: the story of the creation of Britain's Parachute Army* (208), Chatterton, *Winged Pegasus: the story of the Glider Pilot Regiment* (60), Seth, *Lion with Blue Wings* (226), and Wright, *The Wooden Sword* (317). The RAF Regiment's history is recounted in Sherbrooke-Walker's *Khaki and Blue* (270). Odd items remain. Tickell's *Moon Squadron* (297) chronicles the special airlift to France for agents, and Harrison deals with the Special Air Service in *These Men are Dangerous* (112). See also *S.O.E.* (324). So far the WAAF has only Dame Gwynne-Vaughan's manuscript narrative in the Imperial War Museum (106), and Settle's *All the Brave Promises* (267). Pigeons, which were used for rescue work have been treated by Osman (214), bomb-disposal by Haarer (107), Thomas (296), and Hartley (113), and camouflage in general by Barkas (25).

Various views of the RAF are to be found in the memoirs of foreigners who served in it. A list of these is included in the special bibliography mentioned at the beginning of this chapter (120).

RESEARCH NEEDED. The history of the RAF remains at present one of omissions. As has been noted, even the official volumes do not provide a comprehensive overview nor do any of the works so far produced deal with some of the less glamorous, but no less important subjects which make up the whole entity of air power. Almost the whole of the training system has been neglected; there is nothing, apparently, on Halton and the apprentice scheme, on Cranwell, nor on the Staff College at Andover, now to be merged with those of the other Services.

The story of medicine in the British air services deserves a one-volume treatment.

While the beginnings of the Royal Air Force are fairly clear, the period of the First World War leaves much to be desired. Scholars without sentimental or emotional prejudices need to tackle the problems of command, the training and effectiveness of the fighting force, production, maintenance, repair and salvage, perhaps as part of larger studies. The use of air power in the Middle East, where a few aircraft made a considerable difference, has yet to be seen as a whole. Anyone who tackles these subjects might well follow the Webster and Frankland approach of plans, operations, and analysis.

A great deal of the RAF's operational effort and much of its material in the interwar years and after the Second World War were employed in keeping the peace in the Near and Far East, yet no studies exist of the activities in Aden, Iraq, on the Northwest Frontier and in Malaya. It would be worth knowing how effective air control really was, what it cost, how many hours were flown, and what effect operations in a frontier atmosphere against personnel unequipped with anti-aircraft weapons had upon the development of the RAF as a whole. And this analysis should be extended to climatic and diurnal conditions as well, not to mention personnel linkages.

Studies are also needed of record-breaking as a whole, of displays, such as the annual affair at Hendon, of the development of specifications and of procurement techniques, and of testing in all phases. Here at least Clouston (70), Keith (152) and Huskisson (135) provide a start. Perhaps more important are the development of strategical and tactical doctrines, including Cabinet reaction to them, and of the wherewithal to implement them. Above all else, the whole subject of relations with the Army and Navy, especially in the interwar years, is a fertile but untilled land, though Roskill will cover some of it in his history of the Royal Navy between the wars.

The impact of disarmament upon aeronautical technology has been much neglected. In fact the whole problem has not much more than Carlton's article (56) on its side as yet.

The Empire Air Training Scheme of World War II for air crew has not been touched, nor has the development of maintenance in the RAF, nor has the Royal Auxiliary Air Force. What studies may have been done are regarded as secret. The bomber offensive against Germany has been put into focus, but not bomber operations in other theaters. The story of the development of the tactical air forces might well be picked up where Slessor left off in 1936. Not much is known of the development and testing of bombs and bombsights. Repair and salvage is another important logistical area which is mentioned in official histories, but for which treatment in depth is lacking. All of these subjects can probably be tackled without too much delay, since the Thirty-Year Rule will soon open most archives. More importantly, some sociological studies of the officer corps might be revealing, and most important of all would be a good look at how the Air Council functioned from 1918 to 1945 and after.

BIBLIOGRAPHY

1. *Aeroplane.* London, 1911–1968.
2. *Aeroplane.* "The Dying Aviator." 10 & 17 June, 1960, pp. 721, 753. [See also Neville Duke & Edward Lanchberry. *The Crowded Sky* (1959) 144. Bryden, H. G. "Songs They Sang in the RFC, 1914–1918," in *Wings* (1942).]
3. *Aeroplane.* 40th RAF Anniversary issue 28 March 1958 (includes table of all RAF aircraft issued to squadrons).
4. *Aeroplane.* "RAF Mess Games." 3 February, 1961, pp. 129, 217, 218.
5. *Aeroplane.* "RAF Nicknames." 14 February, 1947, 186.
6. *Air-Britain Digest.* London, 1949– .
7. Air Ministry. *Colours and Standards of the RAF.* London: H.M.S.O. 1957.
8. Air Ministry. *Dress Regulations for Officers.* London: H.M.S.O., 1961 and older editions.
9. [Air Ministry]. *Meteorology for Aviators.* London: H.M.S.O. (reprinted and amended), 1953.
10. Air Ministry. *Operational Research in the Royal Air Force, (A.P. 3368).* London: H.M.S.O., 1963.
11. Air Ministry *Cmd. 384* (1919), *Report of the American Aviation Mission.* 19 July 1919. The Gorell Report.
12. Air Ministry. *Royal Air Force Manual—Drill and Ceremonial (A.P. 818).* 5th Edition. 1961.
13. Air Ministry. *The Rise and Fall of the German Air Force (1933–1945).* 1948.
14. Air Ministry. *A Short History of the Royal Air Force, (A.P. 125).* 1929.
15. *Air Pictorial: Journal of the Air League.* London, 1939– .
16. Anderson, W/Cdr. William. *Pathfinders.* London: Jarrolds, 1946.
17. Anderson, W/Cdr. E. W. *The Principles of Navigation.* New York: American Elsevier Pub. Co., 1966.
18. Anderson, H. Graeme. *The Medical and Surgical Aspects of Aviation.* London: Hodder & Stoughton, 1919.
19. Anon. "Historical Group." *Journal of the Royal Aeronautical Society,* LXIII, August 1959, 479–482.
20. Ashmore, Major-General Edward Bailey. *Air Defence.* London: Longmans, Green & Co., 1929.

21. Australia: official history of the Royal Australian Air Force:
Gillison, Douglas. *Royal Australian Air Force, 1939–1942.* Canberra: Australian War Memorial, 1962.
Herington, John. *Air War against Germany and Italy, 1939–43.* Canberra: Australian War Memorial, 1954.
Herington, John. *Air Power over Europe, 1944–45.* Canberra: Australian War Memorial, 1963.
Odgers, George. *Air War against Japan, 1943–45.* Canberra: Australian War Memorial, 1957.
Walker, Allan S. *et al. Medical Services of the R.A.N. and the R.A.A.F.* Canberra: Australian War Memorial, 1961.
22. Babington-Smith, Constance. *Evidence in Camera.* London: Chatto and Windus, 1958; New York: Harper (Ballantine), 1957, with the title *Air Spy.*
23. Babington-Smith, Constance. *Testing Time.* London: Cassells, 1961.
24. Baring, Maurice. *R.F.C.H.Q., 1914–1918.* London: G. Bell & Sons, 1920. Retitled in 1930 *Flying Corps Headquarters, 1914–1918* by Heinemann. Reissue 1968.
25. Barkas, Geoffrey. *The Camouflage Story, from Aintree to Alamein.* London: Cassell, 1952.
26. Barker, Ralph. *Down in the Drink.* London: Pan Books, 1958.
27. Barker, Ralph. *Strike Hard, Strike Sure, epics of the Bombers.* London: Chatto and Windus, 1963.
28. Barker, Ralph. *The Ship-Busters: the story of the R.A.F. torpedo-bombers.* London: Chatto and Windus, 1957.
29. Barker, Ralph. *The Thousand Plan.* London: Chatto & Windus, 1965.
30. Barnes, C. H. *Shorts Aircraft Since 1900.* London: Putnam, 1967.
31. Bennett, D. C. T. *Pathfinder.* London: Muller, 1958.
32. Bennett, D. C. T. *The Complete Air Navigator.* London: Pitman, 1936, revised 1967.
33. Beurling, George F. *Malta Spitfire.* Toronto: Oxford University Press, 1943.
34. Bishop, Edward. *The Guinea Pig Club.* London: Macmillan, 1963.
35. Boebert, Earl. "The Eagle Squadrons." *Journal of the American Aviation Historical Society,* IX, No. 1, 1964, 3–20.
36. Bolitho, Hector. *Command Performance: the authentic story of the last battle of Coastal Command, RAF.* New York: Howell, Soskin, 1946.
37. Bolitho, Hector. *Penguin in the eyrie: a RAF diary 1939–1945.* London: Hutchinson, 1955.
38. Bolitho, Hector. *Task for Coastal Command: the story of the battle for the Southwestern approaches.* London: Hutchinson, 1946.
39. Bond, Horatio, ed. *Fire and the Air War.* Boston, Mass.: National Fire Protection Association, 1946.
40. Boyle, Andrew. *No Passing Glory.* London: Collins, 1955.
41. Boyle, Andrew. *Trenchard: man of vision.* London: Collins, 1962.
42. Braddon, Russell. *Cheshire V.C.* London: Evans Bros., 1954.

43. Braham, W/Cdr. John Randall Daniel. *Scramble.* London: Frederick Muller, 1961. *Night Fighter.* New York: Norton, 1962.
44. Brett, R. Dallas. *History of British Aviation, 1908–14.* London: John Hamilton, 1933.
45. Brickhill, Paul. *The Dam Busters.* London: Evans Bros., 1951; new edition, 1966.
46. Brickhill, Paul. *Escape or Die: authentic stories of the RAF Escaping Society.* London: Evans Bros., 1952.
47. Brickhill, Paul. *Escape to Danger.* London: Faber, 1946.
48. Brickhill, Paul. *The Great Escape.* London: Faber, 1951.
49. British Intelligence Objectives Sub-Committee. *B.I.O.S. Final Report.* London: H.M.S.O., 1945. (There were at least 1595 reports made.)
50. Bruce, J. M. *British Aeroplanes 1914–18.* London: Putnam, 1957.
51. Bullmore, W/Cdr. F. T. K. *The Dark Haven.* London: Jonathan Cape, 1956.
52. Burge, S/Ldr. C. Gordon. *The Annals of 100 Squadron: being a record of the war activities of the pioneer night bombing squadron in France during the period March 1917 to November 11th, 1918, including its operations against German towns whilst serving in the independent force of the RAF.* London, 1919.
53. Burke, Edmund. *Guy Gibson, V.C.* London: Arco Publications, 1961.
54. Caidin, Martin. *The Night Hamburg Died.* New York: Ballantine, 1960.
55. Canada. Royal Canadian Air Force. *The R.C.A.F. Overseas.* Toronto, 1944–49. 3 vol.
56. Carlton, David. "The Problems of Civil Aviation in British Air Disarmament Policy, 1919–1934." *Journal of the Royal United Service Institution,* No. 644, Nov., 1966, 307–316.
57. Chamier, J. A. *The Birth of the RAF.* London: Sir Isaac Pitman, 1943.
58. [Charlton, L. E. O.] *Charlton.* London: Faber & Faber, 1931.
59. Charlton, L. E. O. *The RAF and the USAAF.* New York: Hutchinson, [1941–1947]. 5 vols.
60. Chatterton, Brigadier George. *Winged Pegasus.* London: Macdonald, 1962.
61. Cheesman, E. C. *Brief Glory: the story of A.T.A.* Leicester: Harborough Publishing Co., 1946.
62. Child, S. and C. F. Counter. "Royal Aircraft Establishment, Farnborough. 1878–1918." Farnborough, [Mimeograph], [n.d.] [copy in Air Historical Branch Library].
63. Chisholm, Air Commodore Roderick. *Cover of Darkness.* London: Chatto and Windus, 1953.
64. Churchill, Winston. *The World Crisis and the Aftermath, 1918–1928.* New York: Charles Scribner's Sons, 1923–1929.
65. Clark, Denis. *Tail-end Charlie.* London: Lutterworth Press, 1947.

66. Clark, Ronald W. *Battle for Britain: sixteen weeks that changed the course of history*. London: Harrap, 1965.
67. Clark, Ronald W. *The Rise of the Boffins*. London: Phoenix House, 1962.
68. Clarke, S/Ldr. D. M. *What were They like to Fly?* London: Ian Allen, 1964.
69. Clostermann, Pierre. *The Big Show*. New York: Random House, 1951.
70. Clouston, A. E. *The Dangerous Skies*. London: Cassell & Co., 1954.
71. Coffin, Howard Macy. *Malta Story: based on the diary and experiences of Flying Officer Howard M. Coffin, RAF*. W. L. River, ed. New York: E. P. Dutton, 1943.
72a. Cole, Christopher. *McCudden, V.C.* London: Kimber, 1967.
72b. Cole, Christopher, ed. *Royal Flying Corps, 1915–16*. London: Kimber, 1969.
73. Collier, Basil. *The Defence of the United Kingdom*. London: H.M.S.O., 1957.
74. Collier, Basil. *Heavenly Adventurer: Sefton Brancker and the dawn of British aviation*. London: Secker and Warburg, 1959.
75. Collier, Basil. *Leader of the Few: the authorized biography of Air Chief Marshal The Lord Dowding of Bentley Priory, G.C.B., G.C.V.O., C.M.G.* London: Jarrolds, 1957.
76. Collier, Richard. *Eagle Day: the Battle of Britain, August 6–September 15, 1940*. London: Hodder, 1966.
77. Craven, Wesley Frank and James Lea Cate, eds. *The Army Air Forces in World War II*. Chicago: University of Chicago Press, 1948–1958.
78. Crawley, Aiden. *Escape from Germany: a history of RAF escapes during the war*. London: Collins, 1956.
79. Divine, David. *The Broken Wing: a study in the British exercise of air power*. London: Hutchinson, 1966.
80. Dorman, Geoffrey. "Adastral Houses." *Aeroplane,* 18 February 1955, 201–202.
81. Dorman, Geoffrey. *Fifty Years Fly Past: from the Wright brothers to the Comet*. London: Forbes Robertson, 1951.
82. Douglas, Marshal of the RAF, Lord Douglas of Kirtleside. *Years of Combat*. London: Collins, 1963. *Years of Command*. London: Collins, 1966. (Published in United States as *The Years of Combat and Command*. New York: Simon and Schuster, 1966.)
83. Douglas-Pennant, Violet. *Under the Searchlight*. London: Allen and Unwin, 1922.
84. Dunn, Cuthbert Lindsay. *The Emergency Medical Services*. London: H.M.S.O., 1952–1953. 2 vols.
85. Emme, Eugene M. *The Impact of Air Power: national security and world politics*. New York: D. Van Nostrand, 1959.
86. Embry, Air Chief Marshal Sir Basil. *Mission Completed*. London: Methuen, 1957.

87. Fellowes, P. F. M., L. V. Stewart Blocker, P. T. Etherton, Marquis of Douglas & Clydesdale. *First over Everest.* London: John Lane, & Bodley Head, Ltd., 1933.
88. *Flight.* London, 1909– . (Originally a supplement of *Auto*).
89. Frankland, Noble. *Some Reflections on the Strategic Air Offensive, 1939–1945: a lecture.* JRUSI 1962, Reprint 17p.
90. Frankland, Noble. *The Bombing Offensive against Germany: outlines and perspectives.* London: Faber, 1965. (The Lees Knowles Lectures.)
91. Fredette, Raymond H. *The Sky on Fire: the first Battle of Britain.* New York: Holt, Rinehart and Winston, 1966.
92. Galland, Adolf. *The First and the Last.* New York: Holt, 1954.
93. Gardner, Charles. *A.A.S.F.* London: Hutchinson, 1940.
94. Gavshon, Arthur L. *Flight for Freedom: the story of the S.A.A.F. and its aces.* Johannesburg: Electric Printing Works, 1941.
95. Gibbs, Air Marshal Sir Gerald. *Survivor's Story.* London: Hutchinson & Co., 1956.
96. Gibbs-Smith, Charles. *The Aeroplane: an historical survey.* London: H.M.S.O., 1960. See also his *The Invention of the Aeroplane.* London: Faber, 1966.
97. Gibson, W/Cdr. Guy. *Enemy Coast Ahead.* London: Michael Joseph, 1946.
98. Gossage, Air Vice-Marshal E. L. *The Royal Air Force.* London: William Hodge & Co., Ltd., 1937.
99. Glubb, Sir John Bagot. *War in the Desert.* New York: Norton, 1961.
100. Great Britain. War Office. Directorate of Military Surveys. *R.A.F. Maps.*
101. Grey, C. G. *A History of the Air Ministry.* London: George Allen and Unwin, Ltd., 1940.
102. Griffith, Hubert Freeling. *RAF in Russia.* London: Hammond, 1942.
103. Grinnell-Milne, Duncan. *Wind in the Wires.* London: Mayflower-Dell Paperback, 1966. Revision of 1933 edition.
104. Guedalla, Philip. *Middle East, 1940–1942, a Study in Air Power.* London: Hodder, 1944.
105. Gupta, S. C. *History of the Indian Air Force, 1933–1945.* New Delhi: Government Printer, 1961.
106. Gwynne-Vaughan, Dame Helen. *The Women's Auxiliary Air Force.* Narrative MS in th Imperial War Museum.
107. Haarer, S/Ldr. A. F. *A Cold-Blooded Business.* [Staples, 1958]. London: Panther, 1960. 189p.
108. Hall, H. Duncan. *North American Supply.* London: H.M.S.O., 1955.
109. Hall, H. Duncan, and Christopher Compton Wrigley. *Studies of Overseas Supply.* London: H.M.S.O., 1956.
110. Hammond, Richard James. *Food.* London: H.M.S.O., 1951–1962. 3 vols.

111. Harris, Marshal of the RAF Sir Arthur. *Bomber Offensive.* London: Collins, 1947.
112. Harrison, Derrick Inskip. *These Men are Dangerous: the Special Air Service at war.* 2nd ed. London: Cassell, 1957.
113. Hartley, Arthur Bamford. *Unexploded Bomb: a history of bomb disposal.* London: Cassell, 1958.
114. *The Hawk.* RAF Staff College, Andover, 1928– .
115. Hawker, H. G., and K. Mackenzie Grieve. *Our Atlantic Attempt.* London: Methuen & Co., Ltd., 1919.
116. Henry, Mike. *Air Gunner.* London: Foulis, 1966.
117. H.M.S.O. *General Index to the Bills, Reports and Papers . . . of the House of Commons . . . 1900 to 1948/1949.* London: H.M.S.O. 1960. pp. 26–33 "Air."
118. Hering, S/Ldr. P. G. *Customs and Traditions of the Royal Air Force.* Aldershot, Gale and Polden, 1961.
119. Higham, Robin. *Armed Forces in Peacetime: Britain 1918–1940.* London: Foulis, 1963.
120. Higham, Robin. *A Bibliography of the RAF.* Manhattan, Kans., Farrell Library, 19—
121. Higham, Robin. *The British Rigid Airship, 1908–1931: a study in weapons policy.* London: Foulis, 1961.
122. Higham, Robin. *The Military Intellectuals in Britain, 1918–1940.* New Brunswick, N.J.: Rutgers University Press, 1966.
123. Hill, Prudence. *To Know the Sky: the life of Air Chief Marshal Sir Roderic Hill.* London: Kimber, 1962.
124. [Hoare, Sir Samuel] Lord Templewood. *Empire of the Air, the advent of the air age, 1922–1929.* London: Collins, 1957.
125. Hoare, Sir Samuel. *A Flying Visit to the Middle East.* Cambridge: Cambridge University Press, 1925.
126. Hoare, Sir Samuel. *India by Air.* London: Longmans, Greene & Co., Ltd., 1927.
127. Hodgkinson, Colin. *Best Foot Forward.* London: Odhams, 1957.
128. Hodgson, J. E. *The History of Aeronautics in Great Britain.* Oxford: The University Press, 1924.
129. Holley, I. B., Jr. *Buying Aircraft: material procurement for the Army Air Forces.* Washington: Department of the Army; Office of the Chief of Military History, 1964.
130. Home Office. Fire Service Department. *Manual of Firemanship: a survey of the science of firefighting.* 1964.
131. Home Office. Civil Defence Dept. *The effects of Saturation raids upon the German civil defence system.* 1946.
132. Houart, Victor. *Desert Squadron.* London: Souvenir Press, Ltd., 1959.
133. Houghton, George William. *They Flew through Sand.* 2nd ed. London: Jarrolds, 1942.
134. Hughes, Arthur J. *History of Air Navigation.* London: George Allen and Unwin, 1946.

135. Huskinson, Patrick. *Vision Ahead.* London: Laurie 1949.
136. Hutton, Clayton. *Official Secret.* London: Max Parrish, 1960.
137. "H. W." [E. L. Howard-Williams] and Sidney Hay. *By Order of the Shah.* London: Cassell & Co., 1937.
138. Ismay, General Lord. *The Memoirs of General Lord Ismay.* New York: Viking, 1960.
139. Irving, David. *The Destruction of Dresden.* London: Kimber, 1963.
140. Jane's *All the World's Aircraft.* London: Sampson, Low., 1909—.
141. Johnson, James Edgar. *Wing Leader.* London: Chatto and Windus, 1956.
142. Johnson, Air Vice-Marshal J. E. "Johnnie." *Full Circle: the story of air fighting.* London: Chatto and Windus, 1964.
143. Jones, W/Cdr. Ira. *Tiger Squadron.* London: W. H. Allen, 1954.
144. Joubert de la Ferte, Air Chief Marshal Sir Philip. *Birds and Fishes: the story of Coastal Command.* London: Hutchinson, 1960.
145. Joubert de la Ferte, Air Chief Marshal Sir Philip. *The Fated Sky.* London: Hutchinson, 1952.
146. Joubert de la Ferte, Air Chief Marshal Sir Philip. *The Forgotten Ones: the story of the ground crews.* London: Hutchinson, 1961.
147. Joubert de la Ferte, Air Chief Marshal Sir Philip. *Fun and Games.* London: Hutchinson, 1964.
148. Joubert de la Ferte, Air Chief Marshal Sir Philip. *Rocket.* London: Hutchinson, 1957.
149. Joubert de la Ferte, Air Chief Marshal Sir Philip. *The Third Service.* London: Thames and Hudson, 1955.
150. *The Journal of the Royal Aeronautical Society.* London, 1866–   .
   The Journal of the Royal Aeronautical Society. Consolidated Subject Index. Volumes I–XXX, 1897–1926; *Classified List of Papers published in . . . . 1927–1950;* Consolidated index, 1968.
151. *Journal of the Royal Air Force College.* Cranwell, 1920–   .
   (2–3 numbers yearly to 1939, then suspended until 1948.)
152. Keith, Claude Hilton. *I Hold My Aim.* London: Allen and Unwin, 1946.
153. Kemp, Lt/Cdr. P. K. *The Fleet Air Arm.* London: Jenkins, 1954.
154. Kenyon, James W. *The Fourth Arm.* London: George G. Harrap & Co., 1948.
155. Kerr, Admiral Mark. *Land, Sea and Air.* London: Longmans, Green & Co., Ltd., 1927.
156. Kiernan, R. H. *Capt. Albert Ball V. C.* London: John Hamilton, 1933.
157. King, Alison. *Golden Wings.* London: C. Arthur Pearson, Ltd., 1957.
158. Kingston McCloughry, Air Vice-Marshal E. J. *The Direction of War: A Critique of the Political Direction and High Command in War.* London: Jonathan Cape, 1955.
159. Kingston-McCloughry, Air Vice-Marshal E. J. *Winged Warfare: air problems of peace and war.* London: 1936.

160. Kirby, S. Woodburn. *The War Against Japan.* London: H.M.S.O., 1957–   . 5 vols.

161. Laffin, John. *Swifter than Eagles: the biography of Marshal of the RAF Sir John Maitland Salmond.* London: Blackwood, 1964.

162. Lamberton, W. M., E. F. Cheesman, ed. *Fighter Aircraft of the 1914–1918 War.* Letchworth: Harleyford Publications, 1960.

163. Lamberton, William M. *Reconnaissance and Bomber Aircraft of the 1914–1918 War.* Letchworth: Harleyford Publications, 1962.

164. Lawrence, T. E. *The Mint.* London: Jonathan Cape, 1955.

165. Lawrence, W. J. *No. 5 Bomber Group, RAF.* London: Faber, 1951.

166. Lee, Air Vice-Marshal Arthur Stanley Gould. *Special Duties: reminiscences of a Royal Air Force Staff officer in the Balkans, Turkey and the Middle East.* London: Sampson Low, 1946.

167. Lewis, Cecil Day. *Farewell to Wings.* London: Temple Press, 1964.

168. Lewis, Cecil Day. *Sagitarius Rising.* London: P. Davies, 1936.

169. Lewis, Peter. *British Aircraft, 1809–1914.* London: Putnam, 1962.

170. Lewis, Peter. *The British Bomber Since 1914: fifty years of design and development.* London: Putnam, 1967.

171. Lewis, Peter. *The British Fighter Since 1912.* London: Putnam, 1963.

172. Lewis, Peter. *Squadron Histories: RFC, RNAS and RAF, 1912–1959.* London: Putnam, 1959.

173. Liddell Hart, B. H. *Memoirs.* London: Cassell, 1965. 2 vols.

174. Livingston, General Guy. *Hot Air in Cold Blood.* Selwyn and Blount, 1933. (See also *Aeroplane,* 19 May 1950, 71.)

175. Livingston, Air Marshal Sir Philip. *Fringe of the Clouds.* London: Johnson, 1962.

176. Lloyd, F. H. M. *Hurricane.* Leicester: Harborough, 1946.

177. Lloyd, Air Marshal Sir Hugh. *Briefed to Attack: Malta's part in African victory.* London: Hodder, 1949.

178. Londonderry, Charles Stewart Henry Vane-Tempest-Stewart, Marquis of . . . . *Wings of Destiny.* London: Macmillan, 1943.

179. Longmore, Sir Arthur. *From Sea to Sky, 1910–1945.* London: Geoffrey Bles., 1946.

180. Mannock, Maj. Edward. *The Personal Diary of Major Edward "Mick" Mannock, V.C., DSO (2 bars), M.C. (1 bar), Royal Flying Corps and Royal Air Force.* London: Spearman, 1966.

181. McCudden, Maj. J. T. B., RFC. *Five Years in the Royal Flying Corps,* The Aeroplane Co., 1919.

182. McKee, Alexander. *The Friendless Sky.* New York: Morrow, 1964.

183. Macmillan, Norman. *Great Airmen.* London: G. Bell, 1955.

184. Macmillan, Norman. *Into the Blue.* London: Duckworth, 1929.

185. Macmillan, Norman. *Sir Sefton Brancker.* London: William Heinemann, Ltd., 1935.

186. Macmillan, Norman. *Tales of Two Air Wars.* London: G. Bell, 1967.

187. Macmillan, Norman. *The Royal Air Force in the World War.* I,

1919–1940, II *May 1940–May 1941,* III & IV, *1940–1945.* London: Harrap, 1942–50.

188. Macmillan, Norman. "Uniform Habits." *Aeronautics* [London], August 1961, 26–32.

189. Macpherson, Major-General Sir W. G., *et al. Diseases of the War, II, Including the Medical Aspects of Aviation and Gas Warfare, and Gas Poisoning in Tanks and Mines.* London: 1922, taken over in 1947 by H.M.S.O.

190. Maitland, Air Commodore E. M. *The Log of HMA R-34.* London: Hodder and Stoughton, 1920.

191. Mason, Francis K. *Battle Over Britain.* London: McWhirter Twins, 1969.

191a. Mason, Francis K. *Hawker Aircraft Since 1920.* London: Putnam, 1961.

192. Mason, Francis K. *The Hurricane.* London: Macdonald, 1962.

193. Middleton, Drew. *The Sky Suspended.* London: Longmans, Green, 1960.

194. Millington, Air Commodore E. G. L. *The Unseen Eye.* London: Gibbs & Phillips, 1961.

195. Ministry of Information, prepared for the Air Ministry (*Popular World War II Histories*):

The Air Battle of Malta: the offical account of the R.A.F. in Malta, June 1940 to November 1942 (1944).

Atlantic Bridge: the official account of R.A.F. Transport Command's Ocean Ferry. By John Pudney (1945).

The Battle of the Atlantic; the official account of the fight against the U-boats, 1939–1945 (1946).

Bomber Command; the Air Ministry account of Bomber Command's offensive against the Axis, September 1939–July 1941 (1941).

Bomber Command Continues: the Air Ministry account of the rising offensive against Germany, July 1941–June 1942 (1942).

The Campaign in Burma (prepared for South-East Asia Command by the Central Office of Information by Lt/Col. Frank Owen) (1946).

Coastal Command; the Air Ministry account of the part played by Coastal Command in the battle of the seas, 1939–1942 (1942).

The First Great Air Battle in History: The Battle of Britain: an Air Ministry record of the Great Days from August 8th to October 31st 1940 (First American Edition, Garden City Publishing Co., Inc., 1941).

Merchant Airmen: the Air Ministry account of British civil aviation, 1939–1944. By John Pudney (1946).

R.A.F. Middle East: the official story of air operations in the Middle East from February 1942 to January 1943 (1945).

Roof Over Britain: the official story of Britain's anti-aircraft defences, 1939–1942 (1943).

There's Freedom in the Air: the official story of the Allied Air Forces from the occupied countries (1944).

Wings of the Phoenix: the official story of the air war in Burma (1949).

Report by the Supreme Commander to the Combined Chiefs of Staff on Operations in Europe of the Allied Expeditionary Force, 6 June 1944 to 8 May 1945 (1946).

Report by the Supreme Allied Commander Mediterranean to the Combined Chiefs of Staff on Greece, 12th December 1944 to 9th May 1945 (1949).

Report by the Supreme Allied Commander Mediterranean to the Combined Chiefs of Staff on the Italian Campaign: [Part One] *8 January 1944 to 10 May 1944* (1946) Part II—*10th May 1944 to 12th August 1944* [and] Part III —*13th August 1944 to 12th December 1944* (1948).

[*ibid.*] *on the Operations in Southern France, August 1944* (1946).

Despatch by the Supreme Commander of the ABDA Area to the Combined Chiefs of Staff on Operations in South-West Pacific, 15th January 1942 to 25th February 1942 (1948).

196. Ministry of Munitions. *History of the Ministry of Munitions,* Vol. XII—*The Supply of Munitions, Part I—Aircraft,* [H.M.S.O], 1921.

197. Ministry of Supply. *Laboratory of the Air: an account of the Royal Aircraft Establishment of the Ministry of Supply, Farnborough.* London: H.M.S.O., 1948.

198. Monks, Noel. *Squadrons up! a first hand history of the R.A.F.* New York: McGraw, 1941.

199. Morris, Alan. *Bloody April.* London: Jarrolds, 1967.

200. Morris, Capt. Joseph. *The German Air Raids on Great Britain.* London: Sampson Low, Marston & Co., Ltd. [c. 1922–23].

201. Mosley, Leonard. *Faces from the Fire: the biography of Sir Archibald McIndoe.* London: Weidenfeld & Nicolson, 1962.

202. Mottistone, J. E. B. Seely, Lord. *Fear, and be Slain: adventures by land, sea and air.* London: Hodder and Stoughton, 1931.

203. Moxon, Oliver. *After the Monsoon.* London: Robert Hale, Ltd., 1958.

204. Moyes, Philip John Richard. *Bomber Squadrons of the R.A.F.* London: Macdonald, 1964.

205. Nabarro, Derrick. *Wait for the Dawn.* London: Cassell & Co., 1952.

206. Nayler, J. L. and E. Ower. *Aviation: its technical development.* London and New York: Peter Owen and Vision Press, 1965.

207. Netherwood, George. *Desert Squadron: the Royal Air Force, Egypt and Libya, August 1940 to April 1942.* Cairo: R. Schindler, c. 1944.

208. Newnham, Group Captain Maurice. *Prelude to Glory: the story of*

the creation of Britain's Parachute Army. London: Sampson Low, Marston & Co., 1947.

209. New Zealand, Department of Internal Affairs, The Royal New Zealand Air Force:

>> Ross, John Macaulay Sutherland. *Royal New Zealand Air Force*. Wellington, 1955.

>> Thompson, H. L. *New Zealanders with the RAF*. Wellington, 1956–1959. 3 vols.

>> Whelan, John Allison. *Malta Airmen*. Wellington, 1951.

210. Nicholl, Lt/Cdr. G. W. R. *The Supermarine Walrus; the story of a unique aircraft*. London: Foulis, 1966.

211. Norris, Geoffrey. *The Royal Flying Corps: a history*. London: Frederick Muller, 1965.

212. O'Brien, Terence. *Civil Defence*. London: H.M.S.O., 1955.

213. Ogilvie, Eain G. *Libyan Log: empire air forces in the Western Desert, July 1941–July 1942*. London: Oliver & Boyd, 1943.

214. Osman, W. H. *Pigeons in World War II*. London: Racing Pigeon Club Pub. Co., 1950.

215. Oughton, Frederick, and Cmdr. Vernon Smyth. *Ace with One Eye: the life and combats of Major Edward Mannock*. London: 1963.

216. Owen, Roderic. *Tedder*. London: Collins, 1952.

217. Owen, R. Fenwick. *The Desert Air Force*. London: Hutchinson, 1948.

218. Partridge, Eric. *A Dictionary of Forces Slang, 1939–1945*. London: Secker & Warburg, 1948.

219. Pattinson, Sir Lawrence Arthur. *History of 99 Squadron Independent Force, Royal Air Force, March 1918–November 1918*. Cambridge: W. Heffer and Sons, 1920.

220. Penrose, Harald J. *British Aviation: the pioneer years*. London: Putnam, 1967.

221. Playfair, Major-General I. S. O. *et al. The Mediterranean and the Middle East*. London: H.M.S.O., 1954–   . 6 vols.

222. Pollock, P. Hamilton. *Wings on the Cross: a padre with the R.A.F.* Dublin: Clonmore, 1958.

223. Postan, M. M., Denys, Hay, and J. D. Scott. *The Design and Development of Weapons*. London: H.M.S.O., 1964.

224. Profile Publications. "Aircraft Series." Leatherhead, Surrey, 1965–   .

225. Quester, George H. *Deterence before Hiroshima*. New York: Wiley, 1966.

226. Raleigh, Sir Walter Alexander, and H. A. Jones. *The War in the Air*. Oxford: Clarendon Press, 1922–1937. 6 vols.

227. Rawlinson, A. *The Defence of London, 1915–1918*. London: Andrew Melrose, Ltd., 1923.

228. Rawnsley, C. F., and Robert Wright. *Night Fighter*. London: Collins, 1957.

229. Reid, Patrick R. *The Colditz Story*. London: Hodder and Stoughton, 1952.

230. Reid, Patrick R. *The Latter Days*. London: Hodder and Stoughton, 1953.
231. Reid, Patrick R. *Men of Colditz*. Philadelphia: Lippincott, 1954.
232. Reid, Patrick R. *Winged Diplomat . . . Air Commodore "Freddie" West*. London: Chatto & Windus, 1962.
233. Rexford-Welch, S/Ldr. S. C. *Royal Air Force Medical Services*. London: H.M.S.O., 1954–1958. 3 vols.
234. Rivaz, F/Lt. Richard Charles. *Tail Gunner*. London: Jarrold's, 1943.
235. Rivaz, Richard Charles. *Tail Gunner Takes Over*. London: Jarrold's, 1945.
236. Roberts, Leslie. *There Shall be Wings—an informal history of the RCAF*. London: George Harrap, 1960.
237. Robertson, Bruce. *Air Aces of the 1914–1918 War*. Letchworth: Harleyford Publications, 1959.
238. Robertson, Bruce. *Aircraft Camouflage and Markings, 1907–1954*. Rev. ed. Letchworth: Harleyford Publications, 1961.
239. Robertson, Bruce. *British Military Aircraft Serials, 1912–1963*. London: Ian Allen, 1964 (revised 1966).
240. Robertson, Bruce. *Lancaster*. Letchworth: Harleyford Publications, 1964.
241. Robertson, Bruce. *Spitfire*. Re-issue. Letchworth: Harleyford Publications, 1962.
242. Robinson, Douglas H. *The Dangerous Sky*. Seattle: University of Washington Press, 1972.
243. Robinson, Douglas H. *The Zeppelin in Combat*. Rev. ed. London: Foulis, 1966.
244. Roskill, Captain S. W. *The Naval Air Service* (I. *The First World War* and II. *To 1939*). London: Navy Records Society, 1970–   .
245. Roskill, Capt. S. W. *The War at Sea*. London: H.M.S.O., 1954–1961. 3 vols. in four.
246. [Ross, Albert Henry]. *War on Great Cities, a Study of the Facts,* by Frank Morison [pseud.]. London: Faber & Faber, 1937.
247. Rothermere, Harold Sydney Harmsworth, 1st Viscount. *My Fight to Rearm Britain*. London: Eyre & Spottiswoode, 1939.
248. *Royal Air Force Flying Review, 1946–   .*
249. *Royal Air Force College Journal, 1920–   .*
250. *Royal Air Force Quarterly, 1930–   .*
251. *Royal Air Force Review. 1946–   .* (Founded by the Air Ministry in 1946 under S/Ldr Peter Hering. In Jan. 1952 the Air Ministry gave it to a commercial publisher.)
252. *R.A.F. Coastal Command's War Record, 1939–1945*. London: Rowan Press, 1957.
253. Royal Air Force Sports Board. *The Royal Air Force Athletic and Games Handbook, 1965–1966*. London: H.M.S.O., 1965.
254. Royal Aircraft Establishment. *Aero. 2150—A Historical Summary of the Royal Aircraft Factory and its Antecedents, 1878–1918*. Farnborough: RAE, 1947.

255. Rumpf, Hans. *The Bombing of Germany.* New York: Holt, Rinehart and Winston, 1963.
256. Russell, W/Cdr. Wilfred W. *Forgotten Skies; the Story of the Air Forces in India and Burma.* London: Hutchinson, 1946.
257. Samson, Charles R. *Fights and Flights.* London: Ernest Benn, 1930.
258. Samson, Charles Rumney. *A Flight from Cairo to Cape Town.* London: Ernest Benn, 1931.
259. Saundby, Air Marshal Sir Robert. *Air Bombardment; the story of its development.* New York: Harper, 1961.
260. Saunders, Hilary St. G. *Per Ardua: the rise of British air power, 1911–1939.* London: Oxford University Press, 1944.
261. Saunders, Hilary St. G. *Return at Dawn: the official Story of the New Zealand Bomber Squadron of the RAF from June 1939 to July 1942.* Wellington: New Zealand Director of Publicity, [1942?].
262. Saunders, Hilary St. G., and Dennis Richards. *Royal Air Force, 1939–45.* London: H.M.S.O., 1953–54. 3 Vols.
263. Saward, Group Captain Dudley. *The Bomber's Eye.* London: Cassell, 1959.
264. Schlaiffer, Robert, and S. D. Heron. *The Development of Aircraft Engines and Fuels.* Boston: Harvard Business School, 1950.
265. Scott, J. D., and Richard Hughes. *The Administration of War Production.* London: H.M.S.O., 1955.
266. Seth, Ronald. *Lion with Blue Wings: the story of the Glider Pilot Regiment.* London: Gollancz, 1955.
267. Settle, Mary Lee. *All the Brave Promises; the memories of Aircraftwoman 2nd Class 2146391.* London: Heinemann, 1966.
268. Shacklady, Edward. *The Gloster Meteor.* London: Macdonald, 1962.
269. Sharp, C. Martin, and Michael J. F. Bowyer. *Mosquito.* London: Faber, 1967.
270. Sherbrooke-Walker, Colonel Ronald. *Khaki and Blue.* London: St. Catherine Press, 1952.
271. Shores, Christopher, and Clive Williams. *Aces High: the fighter aces of the British and Commonwealth Air Forces in World War II.* London: Spearman, 1966.
272. Sims, Charles. *Camera in the Sky.* London: Temple Press, 1958.
273. Slessor, J. C. (now Marshal of the R.A.F. Sir John). *Air Power and Armies.* London: Oxford University Press, 1936.
274a. Slessor, Marshal of the RAF Sir John. *The Central Blue.* London: Cassell, 1956.
274b. Slessor, Marshal of the RAF Sir John. *These Remain: a personal anthology—memories of flying, fighting, and field sports.* London: Michael Joseph, 1969.
275. Smith, Sir Ross. *14,000 Miles Through the Air.* New York: Macmillan, 1922.
276. Snowden Gamble, Charles Frederick. *The Air Weapon; British military aeronautics from 1784–1929.* London: Oxford University Press, 1931. 3 Vols. of which only one published.

277. Snowden Gamble, Charles Frederick. *The Story of a North Sea Air Station: being some account of the early days of the Royal Flying Corps (Naval Wing) and of the part played thereafter by the air station at Great Yarmouth and its opponents during the War 1914–1918.* London: Oxford University Press, 1928.

278. Southall, Ian. *They Shall Not Pass Unseen.* Sydney, Australia: Angus and Robertson, 1956.

279. Spaight, J. M. *The Beginnings of Organized Air Power: a historical study.* London: Longmans, Green, & Co., 1927.

280. Stanford Research Institute, Stanford University. *Impact of air attack in World War II: selected data for civil defence planning.* Washington: USGPO, 1953.

281. Stewart, Maj. Oliver. *Aviation: the creative ideas.* New York: Praeger, 1966.

282. Sutton, Sir Graham. *Mastery of the Air: an account of the science of mechanical flight.* London: Hodder & Stoughton, 1966.

283. Sutton, S/Ldr. H. T. *Raiders Approach!* Aldershot: Gale and Polden, 1956.

284. Swinton, (Phillip Cunliffe-Lister, 1st Viscount). *I Remember.* London: Hutchinson and Co., 1948.

285. Sykes, Major General Sir Frederick Hugh. *From Many Angles: an autobiography.* London: George G. Harrap, 1942.

286. Taylor, Prof. E. G. R. *The Haven-Finding Art.* London: Hollis and Carter, 1957.

287. Taylor, Joe G. *Air Supply in the Burma Campaigns.* Maxwell AFB: USAF Historical Division, Air University, 1957.

288. Taylor, John W. R. *C.F.S.—Birthplace of Air Power.* London: Putnam, 1958.

289. Taylor, Telford. *The Breaking Wave.* London: Weidenfeld and Nicolson, 1967.

290. Tedder, Marshal of the RAF Lord. *With Prejudice.* London: Cassell, 1966.

291. The Times. *Survey of British Aviation.* Annually to coincide with Farnborough Show in September. See also the Society of British Aircraft (now Aerospace) Constructors' materials.

292. Thetford, Owen. *Aircraft of the Royal Air Force, 1918–1957.* London: Putnam, 1958 and later editions, especially the 1968 Golden Jubilee issue.

293. Thetford, Owen. *British Naval Aircraft, 1912–1958.* London: Putnam, 1959.

294. Thetford, Owen, and Peter Gray. *German Aircraft of the First World War.* London: Putnam, 1962.

295. Thetford, O. G. and E. J. Riding. *Aircraft of the 1914–1918 War.* Letchworth: Harleyford Publications, 1954.

296. Thomas, Cpl. W. *Life in My Hands.* London: Heinemann, 1960.

297. Tickell, Jerrard. *Moon Squadron.* London: Wingate, 1956.

298. Turner, J. F. *V. C.'s of the Air.* London: Harrap, 1960.

299. United States Air Force, Air University, Air Historical Division,

Historical Studies: Some studies, like Joe Taylor's (287), have been published. For further information inquire of the Director of the Historical Studies Program, Maxwell AFB, Alabama, 36112.

300. U. S. Army Air Force. *Target: Germany.* New York: Simon & Schuster, 1943.

301. U. S. Congress, House, Subcommittee on Military Affairs, *Hearings, United Air Service,* 66th Cong., 2nd Sess., 1919, Part I, pp. 16–31. "The Crowell Report."

302. United States Strategic Bombing Survey. *Overall Report.* Washington: USGPO, 1945.

303. Walker, S/Ldr. N. *Strike to Defend; a book about some of the men who served in R.A.F. Bomber Command during World War II.* London: Spearman, 1963.

304. Wallace, Graham. *R.A.F. Biggin Hill.* London: Putnam & Co., 1957. *Aeroplane,* 1 Nov. 1957, 654.

305. Webster, Sir Charles, and Noble Frankland. *The Strategic Air Offensive against Germany.* London: H.M.S.O., 1961. 4 Vols.

306. Wheeler, Air Commodore A. H. *Building Aeroplanes for "Those Magnificent Men."* London: Foulis, 1965.

307. Wheeler, A. H. *. . . that nothing failed them: testing aeroplanes in war.* London: Foulis, 1963.

308. Whitten-Brown, Sir Arthur. *Flying the Atlantic in Sixteen Hours.* New York: Frederick A. Stokes, 1920.

309. Whittle, Sir Frank. *Jet.* London: Muller, 1953.

310. Whittle, P., and M. Borissow. *Angels without wings: the dramatic inside stories of the RAF's Search and Rescue Squadrons.* Maidstone: Angley Book Co., 1966.

311. Wilson, A. J. *Skysweepers . . . the story of Fighter Command's offensive operations against the enemy in 1941 and the spring of 1942 and the battle with the German night bombers over Britain.* London: Jarrolds, 1942.

312. Wilson, Sir Arnold Talbot. *Mesopotamia, 1917–1920; a Clash of Loyalties; a Personal and Historical Record.* London: Oxford University Press, 1931.

313. Wilson, S/Ldr. Michael C. D. and F/Lt A. S. L. Robinson. *Coastal Command Leads the Invasion.* London: Jarrolds, 1945.

314. Wisdom, Thomas Henry. *Triumph over Tunisia, being the story of the part of the Royal Air Force in the African victory.* London: G. Allen and Unwin, 1944.

315. Wisdom, Thomas Henry. *"Wings over Olympus"; the story of the Royal Air Force in Libya and Greece.* London: G. Allen and Unwin, 1942.

316. Wood, Derek, and Derek Dempster. *The Narrow Margin.* London: Hutchinson & Co., 1961.

317. Wright, Lawrence. *The Wooden Sword.* London: Elek, 1967.

318. Wykeham, Peter. *Fighter Command.* London: Putnam, 1960.

319. Access to official records: For materials prior to 1922, write the

Secretary, the Public Record Office, Chancery Lane, London, W.C.2. For post-1922 materials application should be made to the Head of the Air Historical Branch, Ministry of Defence, Queen Anne's Chambers, 41 Tothill Street, London, S.W.1,; he also controls the Archives.

320. Clearance of manuscripts which have used official RAF materials must be obtained from the Publications Clearance Branch (Air), Ministry of Defence. At the time of writing (July 1967), S/Ldr. L. A. Jackets was head of both AHB and PCB(A). Access to the collections of the Royal Aeronautical Society is obtainable by writing The Secretary, 4 Hamilton Place, London, W. 1. The papers of Group Captain Hugh A. Williamson are at Churchill College and there are a few papers in the Imperial War Museum (see their list), but the Trenchard and Tizard papers are in private hands. The Ministry of Defence Library (Central and Army) List No. 1642 contains by squadron a list of all known published histories.

ADDITIONS TO BIBLIOGRAPHY

321. Jackson, A. J. *Avro Aircraft since 1908*. London: Putnam, 1965.
Barnes, C. H. *Bristol Aircraft since 1910*. London: Putnam, 1964.
Jackson, A. J. *De Havilland Aircraft*. London: Putnam, 1962.
Sharp, C. Martin. *DH—an outline of de Havilland History*. London: Faber, 1960.
de Havilland, Sir Geoffrey. *Sky Fever*. London: Hamish Hamilton, 1961.

322. *Journal of the Royal Aeronautical Society*. August, 1959, 479–482.

323. Irving, David. *The Mare's Nest*. Boston: Little Brown, 1965.

324. Foote, M. R. D. *S. O. E.* London: H.M.S.O., 1966. (Reissued in revised form, 1968.)

325. Cole, Christopher, ed. *Royal Air Force, 1918*. London, Kimber, 1968. The weekly communiques from RAF headquarters in France.

326. Taylor, J. W. R. and P. J. R. Moyes. *Pictorial History of the RAF*. London: Ian Allen, 1968–   . Vol. I covers to 1939.

327. Barker, Ralph. *Aviator Extraordinary: the Sidney Cotton Story*. London: Chatto & Windus, 1968.

328. Brown, S/Ldr. A. J. *Ground Staff*. London: Eyre and Spottiswoode, 1943.

329. Green, William. *Warplanes of the Third Reich*. London: Macdonald, 1968.

330. Paget, Lt/Col. Julian. *The Last Post: Aden, 1964–67*. London: Faber, 1969.

331. Ward-Jackson, C. H. and Leighton Lucas. *The Airman's Song Book*. London: Blackwood, 1968.

332. Zahn, G. C. *Chaplains in the R.A.F.: a study in role tension*. London: , 1968.

333. Winslow, T. E. *Forewarned is Forearmed: a history of the Royal Observer Corps.* London: Hodge, 1948.

334. Bekker, Cajus. *The Luftwaffe War Diaries.* London: Macdonald, 1967.

335. Green, William. *Warplanes of the Second World War.* Various series. London: Macdonald, 1957–   .

336. Lee, Air Vice-Marshal A. S. G. *No Parachute: a fighter pilot in World War I; letters written in 1917 by Lt. A. S. G. Lee, Sherwood Foresters, attached Royal Flying Corps.* London: Jarrolds, 1968.

337. Morris, Alan. *First of Many: the Independent Air Force, 1918.* London: Jarrolds, 1968.

338. Forrester, L. *Fly for Your Life.* London: Collins, 1961.

339. Oulton, Tom. *The Flying Sword.* London: Macdonald, 1964.

340. Bishop, Lt/Col. William A. *Winged Warfare.* New York: Ace Books reprint 1967.

341. Bishop, William Arthur. *The Courage of the Early Morning.* Toronto: McClelland and Stewart, 1965. The son's biography of his father (340).

342. Bowyer, M. J. F. *Fighting Colours: RAF fighter heraldry, 1939–1969.* London: Stephens, 1969.

343. Coughlin, Tom. *The Dangerous Sky* (The RCAF in World War II). London: Kimber, 1969.

344. Emmott, N. W. "RAF—The Impossible Dream." *United States Naval Institute Proceedings,* December 1969, 26–39.

345. Erdmann, James M. *Leaflet Operations in the Second World War.* Denver: The author, Department of History, University of Denver, 1969.

346. *German Aviation Medicine in World War II.* Washington: USGPO, 1950.

347. Halley, J. J. *Royal Air Force Unit Histories, I, Nos. 1–200 Sqdns., 1 April 1918 to 1 April 1968.* Brentwood, Essex: Air-Britain Publications, 1969.

348. Killen, John. *A History of Marine Aviation, 1911–1968.* London: Muller, 1968.

348a. Killen, John. *The Luftwaffe: a history.* London: Muller, 1967.

349. Leighton, Sir R. T. *Pilots' Notes for the handling of World War I Warplanes and their Rotary Engines.* Biggleswade, Beds.: Shuttleworth Collection, 1969.

350. Moseley, Leonard. *"Battle of Britain"—the making of a film.* New York: Ballantine, 1969.

351. Reilly, Robin. *Sixth Floor* (The Mosquito raid on Shell House, Copenhagen in 1945). London: Frewin, 1969.

352. Shores, Christopher, and Hans Ring. *Fighters over the Desert* (the first of three volumes). London: Spearman, 1969.

353. Shorrick, N. *Lion in the Sky; the history of Seletar.* Singapore: Federal Publications SDN, 1969.

354. Smith, S/Ldr. S. *Wings Day: the man who led the RAF's epic battle in German captivity.* London: Collins, 1968.

355. Thompson, H. L. *Aircraft against U-Boats*. Wellington, New Zealand: War History Branch, 1950.

356. Beamont, W/Cdr. Roland. *Phoenix into Ashes*. London: Kimber, 1968.

357. Winterbotham, F. W. *Secret and Personal*. London: Kimber, 1970. Chief of the Secret Air Intelligence Section, 1930–1945.

358. Otway, Lt/Col. T. B. H. *The Second World War 1939–45: Army Airborne Forces*. London: War Office, 1951.

359. Norton, G. C. *By Air to Battle: the story of the Airborne Forces*. London: Leo Cooper, 1970.

360. Ministry of Technology. *Productivity of the National Aircraft Effort*. London: HMSO, 1969.

361. National Book League; *Story of the Royal Air Force*: a selected list; compiled in association with the Ministry of Defence, Air Historical Branch (RAF). London: The League, 1968.

362. Mackersey, Ian. *Into the Silk*. London: Muller, 1957.

XVII

THE INTER-WAR YEARS*

John Keegan

Military affairs in Britain in the inter-war years were initially too unpopular, subsequently too uneventful, finally too heavily overshadowed by the crucial issue of peace itself to have generated much contemporary writing. There are of course exceptions to this statement, but as a general rule it holds good. During the last ten years scholarly interest in the period has quickened, but has been frustrated until recently by the operation of the fifty-year rule.

It seems likely that this situation is now about to change. The introduction of the thirty-year rule has opened the records down to 1938 and the relevant Cabinet, Foreign Office and Service Ministry papers are now lodged at the Public Record Office; what gaps exist have not yet been clearly established. Much work needs to be done on them. Many personal papers, the majority still in private possession, have also recently become available; a complete list, which includes information on their location and attached conditions of access, will be found in the first chapter of Watt's *Contemporary History* (116b). Bibliographies of printed material are scarce. Professor Higham's *Armed Forces in Peacetime* (54a) is the obvious starting point. It contains, besides references to government publications, very full lists of books and articles, including such modern scholarship as there is. In the nature of things there is no older scholarship to speak of. Captain Roskill's *Naval Policy* (98c) has an excellent bibliography and many references to the naval documents. An additional bibliographical source of great value is the Ministry of Defence Library book lists, which are indexed (82).

NATIONAL POLICY. The first object of British defence policy in the aftermath of the Great War was to disarm Germany and keep her disarmed. Its enactment is formally recorded in Temperley's *History of the Peace Conference* (109): the official documents have long been available in the American *Papers Relating to Foreign Relations* (111). Brigadier Morgan (85) describes the successes and failures of the Allied Control commission

* This survey excludes the affairs of the R.A.F. for which see Chapter XVI.

in enforcing the disarmament provisions of Versailles. Meanwhile the government had to demobilize its own armed forces. No complete study has been made of the process, but Professor Higham's *Armed Forces in Peacetime* (54a) contains valuable references to articles and documents.

The most important principle to guide British defence policy thereafter was that propounded by Lloyd George in 1919 and maintained by Winston Churchill on a day to day basis from 1928 to 1932, which laid down that the United Kingdom would be involved in no major war for the next ten years. Much derided after the Second World War, when its existence became generally known, the Ten-Year Rule has now found defenders, notably A. J. P. Taylor who argues in his survey of the period (106)—by far the most stimulating published—that even though "it came in for much criticism later when it seemed that British disarmament had been carried too far and had gone on too long . . . it was a sound political judgment when it started and even its prolongation could be justified . . . [moreover] it was agreed doctrine between the party leaders!"

A non-policy, for that is what the Ten-Year Rule amounted to, provides little fodder for the historian. And there is indeed no comprehensive study of British defence policy between the wars, though Captain Roskill's *Naval Policy* (98c) will, when complete, shed much incidental light. Professor Higham's book is useful in the management of the armed services, and Professor Johnson's treatise on the Committee of Imperial Defence (62) has an important section on policy making at the highest level. More is promised, most enticingly the papers of Lord Hankey, Secretary of the Cabinet, C.I.D., Chief of Staff Sub-committee and of the Privy Council for most of the period. They are at present lodged at Churchill College, Cambridge, where Captain Roskill is doing a two-volume biography. It is unlikely that anything more revealing of material defence policy exists; Hankey's published works (49a, 49b) however are guarded in tone.

Failing specialist studies, the student must fall back on histories of British foreign policy in general and, for the first fifteen years of the period, disarmament in particular. The most important primary source is the unfinished series on British Foreign Policy (26), the most important secondary source the *Survey of International Affairs* (96). There is no good modern account though Medlicott (81) and Reynolds (93) may be consulted. The most comprehensive study of disarmament is by Chaput (17) which may be supplemented from Wheeler-Bennett's contemporary summaries of progress made (119a,b,c).

From 1932 to 1935 Britain hovered between disarmament and re-armament, the debate crystallising in so far as it did around the issue of "collective security," which meant support for the dying League of Nations. Again there is no complete treatment of Britain's involvement with that body though Walters' *History* (113) reveals a good deal incidentally. After the collapse of the League in 1935 the government embarked reluctantly upon a policy of re-armament and bi-lateral security treaties, tempered by appeasement (which falls outside the scope of this bibliography). The progress of re-armament is nowhere adequately dealt with, though the references in Higham (54a) provide an excellent index to what scattered material there is and the essays, references and splendid bibliography in D. C. Watt (116a) should not be overlooked by anyone interested in this half of the period. The opening chapters of several of the official histories are also essential, particularly Collier's (20) which emphasises the government's obsession with German air attack, to which it subordinated all other defence considerations. Much will become known of general defence planning when the first volume of *Grand Strategy* (43) is published.

Few biographies or memoirs of political leaders, numerous though they are, are of use, if only because so few interested themselves in defence questions (many, of course, are now actively antipathetic). Exceptions are those by Churchill (19), Duff Cooper (22) and Amery (2). This paucity of personal material will make the student's search among the official papers of the period, where the dry bones of defence policy are interred, all the more difficult.

THE HIGH COMMAND. So strong is the tradition of civilian control in the British Services, and so little had they to do between the wars, that a study of the High Command during that period lacks both interest and excitement. That of the R.A.F., a service in the making, is of course an exception to that rule. Its commanders and their policies did make fireworks, which sometimes shed sparks over their rival services' territory; as Roskill (98c) shows *re* the naval-aviation controversy.

High Command continued to be exercised on a single-service basis, though there was some progress towards unification. The most important steps were the establishment of a Chiefs of Staffs Sub-Committee of the C.I.D. in 1924, as a result of their misunderstandings over Chanak, and the establishment of the Imperial Defence College in 1926, intended to provide a common training for future commanders. Neither led on to the creation of a unified Defence Ministry, though such a body was frequently advocated. In 1936 a Minister for the Co-ordination of Defence was appointed, but the personality of the first, Sir Thomas Inskip, precluded any chance of this substitute arrangement leading to worthwhile results. He took a view of his duties Gladstonian in its narrowness, wrote few papers and no books. His successor, Lord Chatfield, has left two highly readable volumes of autobiography (18a,b) but much of it concerns his earlier naval career. Prof. A. Temple Patterson has a biography of Chatfield in progress. For concrete information and documentary references, the student must turn again to Johnson (62) and Higham (54a).

There are few relevant biographies or memoirs of service chiefs, since those who held high command between the wars were either distinguished veterans like Beatty (15) and Wemyss (118) or nonentities like Deverell. Memoirs of the former concentrate naturally on their war services; there are none of the latter sort. Wilson's involvement in the Irish troubles has attracted some attention; the most recent biography (4) advances the absurd notion that he was a potential dictator. More realistic accounts of civil-military relations are provided by Ismay (59) and Macready (75);

Wavell's life (21) has some interesting chapters in the pre-war career of an officer already marked for high command.

Personal papers of service chiefs may yet however have matters of interest to reveal. The Centre for Military Archives at King's College, London (where Liddell Hart's papers are to go) is making a business of collecting them.

THE NAVY IN PEACETIME. The Royal Navy had survived the ordeal of the Great War successfully, yet not triumphantly. The only major engagement with its principal opponent had ended inconclusively—a profoundly unsettling outcome for a service which since Trafalgar had trained for nothing less than total victory.

For that reason alone, the inter-war years were to be unhappy ones for the navy. Its uneasiness was compounded by a dramatic decline in strength, by the difficulties of adjustment to war in two new dimensions, the aerial and submarine, and by the need to co-operate in and yet resist the politicians' plans for exemplary disarmament. Most important, it was to lack for most of the twenties and early thirties any clear perception of its future or even of its present role: Germany's fleet lay at the bottom of Scapa Flow; the gunboat years had passed (for their Baltic twilight, see Bennett (9)); France was not a credible opponent; Japan was too recently an ally and anyhow too distant to think of as a future enemy (though see Bywater (13)); America too obviously a friend to make a convincing foe.

It was nevertheless American strength against which the Admiralty chose to measure its own during the twenties. The strategic ambiguities to which this led are brilliantly exposed by Captain Roskill in the first volume of his study of *Naval Policy between the Wars* (98c) which when complete, will leave very little to be discovered or said about any British—or American —naval question of the period. In the meantime, Higham (54a) offers a wealth of useful references, and there are scattered passages of interest on naval policy in the biographies of Admirals Wemyss (118), Keyes (66), Dreyer (28) and Dewar (25)—the last two well known controversialists —as well as Beatty (on whom see chapter XIV). *Brassey's Naval Annual* (12), the *Naval Review* (88), and the *Mariner's Mirror* (78), the latter in particular containing some important articles on the Admiralty by its Permanent Secretary, Sir Oswyn Murray, provide essential teaching on currents of naval thought and policy. Much of it concerns the professionally doleful subject of disarmament. The approach of war which quickened the navy's pulse is badly documented, pressure of space perhaps having forced Captain Roskill to curtail discussion of the subject in the first chapters of the Official History (98a). No doubt he will expand in the second volume of his *Naval Policy*.

The literature of naval life between the wars is scanty, reflecting its pinched quality. The navy had little to do save watch its ships go to the breakers, its pay scales diminish both relatively and absolutely, and its officers compete for shorter and shorter spells of sea-going command. Command and pay generated, in fact, the only two moments of drama in the peacetime navy: the *Royal Oak* courts-martial, recently recounted by Leslie Gardner (41) and the Invergordon mutiny of which there is only a dated account by Kenneth Edwards (31a). The same author has written a narration of the navy's sole spell of active service between the wars, the policing of the Spanish coast during the Civil War (31b). Vice-Admiral Sir Peter Gretton is doing a wider study of the same period.

The navy might have been expected to spend its years of indecision and inactivity in debate. Traditionally, however, it is not a theorising service; there was little writing by naval authors between the wars, nor was the quality of that writing distinguished. Most were content to mention the growing importance of the submarine and the aeroplane, the depressive effect of disarmament on morale, and latterly the menace of Japanese naval expansion. Students may confirm these impressions by a glance at the works of Ackworth (1a, 1b), T 124 (105), Drage (27) and Hearnshaw (51). Higham deals with some of their work in his *Military Intellectuals* (54b).

In an entirely different class are the writings of Admiral Richmond, first Director of the Imperial Defence College and later Professor of Naval History at Cambridge. His most important book, *Statesmen and Seapower*, was not published until 1945, but he laid the ground for this masterly analysis of the relationship between national policy and naval strategy in a number of smaller studies published between the wars (94a, b, c). The irony is that the navy should have at last produced a man with a capacity to explain the navy to the nation and vice versa, as Schurman (99) characterises his achievement, at a moment when their joint power had begun its final decline. Richmond's diary, 1909–20, has been edited by Professor Marder (76), and his papers are lodged at the National Maritime Museum, Greenwich.

If strategic debate is traditionally not a preoccupation of the navy, tactical experiment is. And there was indeed much covert effort expended in the refinement of anti-submarine and aerial equipment between the wars. A little has been published about submarine warfare of which the best is summarised by Admiral Hezlet (53). Curiously nothing has been written about the development of carrier design or doctrine. There is equally little about the administration or organisation of the navy; information on that, as on so much else, must be disinterred from the annual Estimates, Hansard, Comptroller General's Reports, and Admiralty papers now open at the P.R.O.

NAVAL PROCUREMENT AND DISARMAMENT. The Royal Navy, at the end of the Great War was stronger than it had ever been before or would be again. It counted 58 capital ships, 104 cruisers, 34 coast defence vessels, 13 aircraft carriers (an elastic term), 521 destroyers and 135 submarines. Within nine years its strength had fallen to 18 capital ships, 42 cruisers, 8 carriers (though these better merited the name), 100 destroyers and 55 submarines—a level at which it was to stand until the outbreak of war.

This decline was due in unequal measure to demobilisation, to financial stringency and to the adoption of a policy of exemplary disarmament. That policy, made possible by Scapa Flow, was forced upon Britain by America, whose navy wished, if not for superiority to Britain's, since Congress was unlikely to foot the bill, then for parity. It sought to achieve it by threatening a building programme it judged the British Treasury would refuse the means to match. Its judgment was accurate, and at the Washington Conference of 1922 the British and American governments united to impose fixed levels of armament on the naval powers, favoring themselves at the expense of Japan and even more of France and Italy. This treaty set the pattern for those to follow it in 1930 and 1935. By far the best survey of their proceedings is in Chaput (17) who also provides a very full bibliography; Roskill (98c) has some new material on the first two treaties. The League of Nations *Armaments Year Book* (69) is an essential guide to the fluctuations of naval strength between the wars, and *Jane's* (61) is of course indispensable.

Disarmament and retrenchment combined to keep procurement to a low level; consequently there is little relevant literature. The only British capital ships built were the awkward *Nelson* and *Rodney,* of which details appear in Parkes (90); the modernised *Warspite* is the subject of a book by Captain Roskill (98b). A number of properly-built carriers were launched, of which *Ark Royal* has a history (60); Commander Kemp's *Fleet Air Arm* (63a) is useful on this underworked topic. Cruisers, which escaped limitation until 1930, are the subject of no detailed study. Commander Lipscombe has written on the *British Submarine* (72) and Commander Kemp on *British Destroyers* (63b), Captain Cowie's work on mine warfare is excellent (24); Commander King-Hall recalls in his biography (67) that he pointed out to the Admiralty in the twenties that no coherent policy seemed to guide British naval construction between or within classes. It is possible that research could re-inforce that judgment.

There is no study of naval re-armament, though the early chapters of Scott (100a) on *War Production* are useful on Admiralty organisation and plans.

THE ARMY IN PEACETIME. The army's first task at the end of the war was to demobilise, a task for which plans, unsatisfactory as it turned out, were to hand and which was complete by 1920. The most succinct account may be found in Higham (54a) together with copious documentary references.

The end of the war also meant a return to "real soldiering," a well-worn armistice joke which proved more true than the jokers reckoned. For "real soldiering" had always meant the well-ordered round of regimental life, as lived in any of the thirty cavalry or seventy infantry regiments, each an historic institution with strong social and regional identity and considerable domestic autonomy. Wartime expansion had temporarily cramped them, but they re-emerged intact at its end and resumed their traditional way of life. Its intense family flavour is caught perhaps best in John Master's memoir of a Gurkha battalion in the thirties (80).

Because the regimental relationship was so strong and non-regimental institutions consonantly weak, the affairs of the British army between the wars are rarely described at a much higher level. The student's best guide to any life of the period is in the memoirs of soldiers like Smyth (101a), Belhaven (7), Morris (86) or Vandeleur (112); particularly valuable is Robert Henriques' novel *No Arms No Armour* (52) which perfectly evokes the manners of a horsey, paternalistic officer class. Two excellent regimental histories describing battalion life between the wars are those of the Manchester Regiment (8) and the Royal West Kents (16).

Given the social primacy of the regiments, it is not surprising that the need to reduce their numbers in the aftermath of the war should have created a furor. The southern Irish regiments, whose recruiting grounds were lost in 1922, and the surplus cavalry regiments fought bitterly against it, but the first had all to be disbanded and the latter suffer amalgamation. Colonel ffrench-Blake's history of the 17th/21st Lancers (36) provides an illuminating account of the efforts made by two proud cavalry regiments to avoid consummating an arranged match.

Some issues, however, could unite the army, notably pay, promotion and conditions of service. All were poor between the wars and poorer after the retrenchments of 1931. It was particularly galling to the middle-class career officer that promotion was noticeably slower in his sort of regiment than in the less serious-minded Guards or Cavalry. Grenfell's (45) and Kennedy's books (65) are contemporary protests by disgruntled ex-regulars.

The officers of the army continued however to be drawn from the traditional classes, though in diminishing numbers, and to be educated at Sandhurst (infantry, cavalry and Indian Army) or Woolwich (artillery and engineers). John Masters (80) provides an entertaining account of life at Sandhurst, Sir John Smyth (101b) a sober history of the college; Godwin-Austen does the same for the Staff College (44), which more officers had begun to make their goal. Personal memoirs of the course there may be found in Martel (79b) and Fuller (39d).

Like other army affairs, recruiting and most training remained in regimental hands. Recruits were hard to come by, but unemployment acted as a spur. The statistics may be turned up in the *General Annual Report* (114) and in the *Estimates*. The training manuals, for all tactical levels between platoon and division, were re-written after the war, though not radically enough to suit most reformers' thinking (see the comments of Hobart (74), Liddell Hart (70c), Fuller (39c) and Martel (79b)). A list of the manuals current at any time can be found in Lindsell (71), which is useful itself on military administration, but they make dreary reading and can be positively misleading unless checked against accounts of what took place in practice, to which memoirs provide a guide.

Internal development in the different branches of the army may be studied in a number of corps and regimental histories. Of these, Liddell Hart's *Tanks* (70b) is far and away the best, but several cavalry histories are good on mechanisation: notably ffrench-Blake (36). Others are the *Engineers* (95), Beadon's *Service Corps* (6), Fernyhough's *Ordnance*

(35), Nalder's *Signals* (87), and White's *Education* (120). There is nothing on the Medical Corps; a grave deficiency is the Artillery, except for the early chapters about anti-aircraft in Pike (91). A very great deal may be gleaned from the journals of the Royal Artillery, Signals, Cavalry, Service Corps, Tank Corps and Ordnance, files of which are kept at the main Ministry of Defence Library. *The Army Quarterly* (3) founded in 1920 provides an untrammelled organ of opinion and the *R.U.S.I. Journal* (97), splendidly indexed by Professor Higham, offers material for a more general survey of army affairs.

The last years of peace are better served by printed material. Most important, as they are for the whole 1918–1939 period, are Liddell Hart's *Memoirs* (70c), which reveal how entrenched traditional attitudes were at the summit of the military hierarchy. The biography of the minister he served, Hore-Belisha (83), is much less revealing than it might be. That, however, is a general verdict on the available literature. Once again the student must be referred to Higham's admirable documentation (54a) and to the official papers which await scouting at the P.R.O.

COLONIAL OPERATIONS. After 1918 the army quickly reverted to its traditional role of a colonial police force. Throughout the inter-war years, when its combatant strength stood at about 135 battalions of infantry, half were always overseas; the proportions were roughly: U.K., 67; India, 45; Egypt and the Sudan, 8; the Far East, 5; the Mediterranean, 4; and in the twenties, there were 8 on the Rhine. Cavalry and artillery were distributed in like measure but most of the Tank Corps stayed at home. The Army List provides year-to-year details.

The army's colonial duties were two-fold. It had to maintain peace within the imperial colonial and mandated territories and to protect their frontiers from foreign attack. It was frequently called upon to discharge both. The most serious internal disturbances with which it had to deal were those in India in 1919, Iraq, 1920, and Palestine, 1936–38. There are useful accounts of the Punjab troubles of 1919 by Furneaux (40) and Swinson (103) and of those in Iraq by Haldane (47). The Palestine Rebellion is treated partially and incompletely by a number of authors, Courtney (23), Sykes (104), Marlowe (77) and Farago (34). Besides these, there were a rush of minor disorders: in Egypt and the Sudan, 1920–24; in Moplah Country in India, 1921; in Palestine, 1929; in India, 1930–31; in Burma, 1930–32; and in Cyprus, 1931. Accounts of operations are best turned up in the histories of the regiments involved, to which White's bibliography (121) is an invaluable guide, or in their journals of which the main Ministry of Defence Library keeps files. There is also a general treatment of the theme of Imperial Policing, with succinct accounts of its raw material, in Gwynn (46).

The Army's most important frontier operations were those of the Third Afghan War, 1919, and in Waziristan, 1919 and 1936–38. Fighting on that frontier of India was of course endemic if only because the tribesman pursued it as a way of life. The British were glad to entertain them because these operations provided relatively cheap and highly realistic training. There are official accounts of all three campaigns (42a, b, c, d), exhaustive but dull, which Molesworth (84) and de Watteville (117) paraphrase.

Falling rather outside the colonial context are the operations in Ireland, 1918–21, and on the periphery of Russia, 1918–20. The lack of any extensive narrative or analysis of the British Army's experience in Ireland, by a private if not an official hand, is very strange. Until something more complete is published the student must make do with the limited studies of the Black and Tans (10), of Michael Collins (107) and of the Irish guerrillas, notably a racy memoir by Commandant Tom Barry (5). The best short history of the troubles is Edgar Holt's (57), whose focus is political rather than military. Callwell's life of Wilson (14) provides useful information on the principal British commander in Ireland.

There is very much more and better printed material on the intervention in Russia: for the operations in the north, Ironside's diary (58); Strakhovsky's (102) and Halliday's histories (48) and the official account (33) for the Siberian front; Peter Fleming's gripping story of Kolchak's fate (37); a memoir of the British Mission by a member (55); a regimental history by its commander (115) and the official account (30); and for Transcaspia and the Caucasus, General Dunsterville's history of his Force (29), and C. H. Ellis' admirable little *Transcaspian Episode* (32). Footman's *Civil War in Russia* (38) furnishes an overview of the period, as does Kennan (64) from an American viewpoint, while Ullman's first volume (110) promises a definitive history of British involvement as a whole. Bradley (11) has an excellent bibliographical preface.

The services' part in the international crisis at Shanghai, 1927, is barely described anywhere. Watt (116a), Roskill (98c) and Kinross (68) deal with the Chanak crisis, 1922, at a governmental level, and Walder (123) has recently published a comprehensive and racy history of the episode.

ARMY MUNITIONS. The official historian of British War Production in the Second World War (92) resorts to the description "The Disarmed Army" in his account of its munitioning and equipment between the wars. This literature is consequently sparse.

This is least true of the development of the tank and of the progress of mechanisation in general. Richard Ogorkiewicz provides the best historical commentary in *Armour* (89), which measures British progress against French, German, American, and Russian. Liddell Hart (70b) best describes the battle over mechanisation between traditionalists and progressives, and Martel's memoir (79a) is a valuable account by a pioneer of armour. An important biography of the most enlightened, if most insubordinate, serving soldier of the period is Macksey's life of Hobart (74). *The Tank* (108), the journal of the Corps, has much of detailed interest.

There is very little on the design, development or supply of other weapons or equipment. The most comprehensive treatment is in Postan (92) which has excellent chapters on artillery, small arms, and transport. Hogg (56) and Scott (100b) have chapters on the manufacture of weapons, the first by a state, the second a private undertaking; Hay describes the re-establishment of the Royal Ordnance Factories (50). Nalder (87) on the development of Signals, and the Royal Engineers history (95) on searchlights and mechanical equipment are both useful; Fernyhough's history of the Ordnance Corps (35) describes its internal organisation in a book which could hardly fail to be dull.

Higham (54a) has on this as on all other topics a valuable bibliography to offer. But he does not refer to a restricted series of War Office publications, prepared since the war, which may not be cited here but would probably be made available to the serious student. It is unlikely, however, that he would uncover much of interest, for the army went to war in 1939 with equipment—apart from tanks, wireless sets and some artillery pieces —almost unchanged since 1918.

MILITARY THEORISTS AND THEIR OPPONENTS. Before the First World War, Britain had produced no military theorist of note, as a critical reading of Jay Luvaas' *Education of an Army* (73) will make clear. In the twenty years following, European military thought was dominated by Englishmen. It is unrewarding to speculate why this should have been. Perhaps it was that no other country saw the rise of the quality of Liddell Hart or J. F. C. Fuller; perhaps none offered its writers an audience.

Not that Britain lent to either of its literary strategists a very ready ear; indeed both were read more widely abroad than at home and often in pirated editions. Not until Liddell Hart caught Hore-Belisha's attention in the late thirties did the ideas of either begin to influence national policy. What were their ideas?

Briefly, they were those of young officers who had suffered and rebelled against the mass tactics of the war and had seen in the tank the means of sparing their successors a similar experience. They were to differ over the details of employing tanks but in tactical fundamentals they agreed. The best summary of the development of their ideas, those of their disciples and of their critics, intellectually ineffective though they were, is Higham's *Military Intellectuals* (54b). Luvaas (73) also has a perceptive essay on each.

Fuller, a regular infantryman who had risen to high rank in the Tank Corps during the war, germinated the plan for Cambrai and outlined a scheme to end the war in 1919 with a mechanised army. In his post-war career he achieved less than his rise promised since official favour fell away, and he increasingly sought fulfillment in writing. Much of his literary work was historical, but it was slight in scope and marred by didacticism. Not until the publication after 1945 of his volumes on decisive battles did he strike his best form as a historian. His early military writing suffers from the same fault. His discussion of the nature of war, for example, in *The Science of War* (39b) and *The Reformation of War* (39a) is philosophical in the worst sense, cloudy, abstract and naive. It is only when he confines himself to narrower tactical topics, as in *Armoured Warfare* (39c), that he impresses the modern reader. It was these tactical tracts, moreover, which made his name among his contemporaries. A parallel effect, however, was the blighting of his career, which ended in 1930. Naturally embittered, he took up in compensation the problems of geo-politics and civil-military relations, for which he advocated increasingly authoritarian solutions. It was perhaps a natural progression that in the mid-thirties he should have joined the British Fascists, a step which lost him his public.

Liddell Hart, unlike Fuller only a wartime soldier, began his military writings with no thought of criticizing the high command. Wounded in the Somme, he whiled away his convalescence by putting into order some ideas he had formed in training. The resulting booklet so impressed the War Office that after the armistice he was found a place in the New Education Corps. By then he had taken up military studies in earnest and found his ideas diverging increasingly from the official line. Unable to develop them truly as an officer, he took a medical discharge and began a career as a military correspondent, first on *The Daily Telegraph,* later on *The Times,* appointments he owed in the first instance to official patronage. He also began to publish military historical and strategic studies. Very much less philosophical than Fuller's early works, these books are as readable today as when first written, and by the mid-thirties he was undisputed leader of military thought in the country. He had, however, already begun to alarm orthodox military opinion. When in 1936 he became unofficial advisor to the War Minister, he encountered openly hostile resistance to his ideas. In the last minutes of peace, however, his thinking reversed course. Having hitherto always advocated mechanised attack as the best form of defence, in *The Defence of Britain* (70a) he argued the case for a more traditional "maritime" strategy.

The scope and bulk of both men's writings is too large to treat here. Higham (54a) and Luvaas (73), the former in particular, should be consulted as a bibliographical guide. If there is anything left to explore in the work of either, it is perhaps that most intractable of questions attaching to the history of ideas: what exactly has been the nature of their influence on men and events?

RESEARCH NEEDED. Given the almost unworked character of the field, it is difficult to isolate accurately which subjects most need investigation. A number are indicated in the sections above. But it would not perhaps be exaggerated to say that the whole field stands open, except for naval affairs, a patch in which Captain Roskill has broken ground on an impressive scale. The twin subjects of disarmament and re-armament, in all their aspects, would perhaps most repay scholarly attention but many others come to mind: inter-service relations, with special reference to the role of the R.A.F.; civil-military relations; naval technology, especially aircraft-carriers; almost all army affairs; imperial defence; war plans; operations, particularly those in Ireland, China, and Palestine; service education; and the sociology of the services. It will indeed for some time be difficult to know where to begin.

BIBLIOGRAPHY

1. Ackworth, Captain Bernard. *The Navies of Today and Tomorrow*. London: Eyre and Spottiswoode, 1930.
1b. Ackworth, Captain Bernard. *The Navy and the Next War*. London: Eyre and Spottiswoode, 1934.
2. Amery, L. S. *My Political Life*. Vols. II and III. London: Hutchinson, 1953 and 1955.
3. *Army Quarterly, The*. London: William Clowes, 1920– .
4. Ash, Bernard. *The Lost Dictator*. London: Cassell, 1968.
5. Barry, Commandant Tom. *Guerrilla Days in Ireland*. Cork: Mercier Press, 1964.
6. Beadon, Colonel R. H. *The Royal Army Service Corps*. Cambridge: Cambridge University Press, 1931.
7. Belhaven, Lord. *The Uneven Road*. London: John Murray, 1950.
8. Bell, A. C. *History of the Manchester Regiment 1922–48*. Altrincham: John Sherrat, 1954.
9. Bennett, Geoffrey. *Cowan's War*. London: Collins, 1964.
10. Bennett, R. *The Black and Tans*. London: Hulton, 1959.
11. Bradley, John. *Allied Intervention in Russia*. London: Weidenfeld and Nicolson, 1958.
12. *Brassey's Naval Annual*. London: William Clowes, 1886– .
13. Bywater, H. C. *Sea Power in the Pacific*. London: Constable, 1934.
14. Callwell, Major-General Sir C. E. *Field Marshal Sir Henry Wilson*. London: Cassell, 1927.
15. Chalmers, W. S. *The Life and Letters of David, Earl Beatty*. London: Hodder and Stoughton, 1951.
16. Chapin, H. D. *The Queens Own Royal West Kent Regiment 1920–1950*. London: Michael Joseph, 1954.
17. Chaput, R. A. *Disarmament in British Foreign Policy*. London: Allen and Unwin, 1935.
18a. Chatfield, Lord. *The Navy and Defence*. London: Heinemann, 1942.
18b. Chatfield, Lord. *It Might Happen Again*. London: Heinemann, 1947.
19. Churchill, Winston S. *The Second World War*. Vol. I. London: Cassell, 1948.
20. Collier, Basil. *The Defence of the United Kingdom*. London: H.M.S.O., 1957.
21. Connell, John. *Wavell*. London: Collins, 1904.
22. Cooper, Duff (Lord Norwich). *Old Men Forget*. London: Hart-Davis, 1953.
23. Courtney, R. *Palestine Policeman*. London: Herbert Jenkins, 1939.
24. Cowie, Captain J. S. *Mines, Minelayers and Mining*. London: Oxford University Press, 1949.
25. Dewar, Vice-Admiral K. G. B. *The Navy from Within*. London: Allen and Unwin, 1939.

26. *Documents on British Foreign Policy, 1919–39.* (Various editors) London: H.M.S.O., 1947–   . (See H.M.S.O. Sectional List No. 58.)
27. Drage, Geoffrey. *Sea Power.* London: John Murray, 1931.
28. Dreyer, Vice-Admiral Sir Frederick. *The Sea Heritage.* London: Museum Press, 1955.
29. Dunsterville, Major-General L. C. *The Adventures of Dunsterforce.* London: Arnold, 1920.
30. *Eastern Siberia.* London: H.M.S.O., 1920.
31a. Edwards, Kenneth. *The Mutiny at Invergordon.* London: Rich and Cowan, 1937.
31b. Edwards, Kenneth. *The Grey Diplomatists.* London: Rich and Cowan, 1938.
32. Ellis, C. H. *The Transcaspian Episode.* London: Hutchinson, 1963.
33. *Evacuation of North Russia, The.* London: H.M.S.O., 1920.
34. Farago, L. *Palestine on the Eve.* London: Putnam, 1936.
35. Fernyhough, Brigadier A. H. *History of the Royal Army Ordnance Corps.* London: The Royal Army Ordnance Corps, n.d. (about 1967).
36. ffrench-Blake, R. L. V. *A History of the 17th/21st Lancers, 1922–59.* London: Macmillan, 1962.
37. Fleming, Peter. *The Fate of Admiral Kolchak.* London: Hart-Davis, 1963.
38. Footman, David. *Civil War in Russia.* London: Faber, 1956.
39a. Fuller, Major-General J. F. C. *The Reformation of War.* London: Hutchinson, 1923.
39b. Fuller, Major-General J. F. C. *Foundations of the Science of War.* London: Hutchinson, 1926.
39c, Fuller, Major-General J. F. C. *Lectures on F. S. R. III.* London: Eyre and Spottiswoode, 1932. (Re-issued in 1943 as *Armoured Warfare.*)
39d. Fuller, Major-General J. F. C. *Memoirs of an Unconventional Soldier.* London: Ivor Nicholson, 1936.
40. Furneaux, Rupert. *Massacre at Amritsar.* London: Allen and Unwin, 1963.
41. Gardner, Leslie. *The Royal Oak Courts Martial.* Edinburgh: Blackwood, 1956.
42a. General Staff, India. *The Waziristan Campaign, 1919–20.* Calcutta: Government of India Press, 1921.
42b. General Staff, India. *Official Account of the Third Afghan War.* Calcutta: Government of India Press, 1926.
42c. General Staff, India. *Official History of Operations on the North Most Frontier of India, 1936–7.* New Delhi: Government of India Press, 1943.
42c. General Staff, India. *Official History of Operations on the Northern Most Frontier of India, 1920–35.* New Delhi: Government of India Press, 1945.

43. Gibbs, Norman. *Grand Strategy.* Vol. I. London: H.M.S.O. (in preparation) [1972.]
44. Godwin-Austen, A. R. *The Staff and the Staff College.* London: Constable, 1927.
45. Grenfell, Commander Russell. *The Men Who Defend Us.* London: Eyre and Spottiswoode, 1938.
46. Gwynn, C. W. *Imperial Policing.* London: Macmillan, 1934.
47. Haldane, Lieutenant-General Sir Aylmer. *The Insurrection in Mesopotamia, 1920.* Edinburgh: Blackwood, 1922.
48. Halliday, E. M. *The Ignorant Armies.* London: Weidenfeld and Nicolson, 1958.
49a. Hankey, Lord. *Government Control in Wartime.* Cambridge: Cambridge University Press, 1945.
49b. Hankey, Lord. *The Supreme Command, 1914–1918.* London: Allen and Unwin, 1963.
50. Hay, Ian. *R.O.F.: the Story of the Royal Ordnance Factories 1939–48.* London: H.M.S.O., 1949.
51. Hearnshaw, J. F. C. *Sea Power and Empire.* London: Harrap, 1940.
52. Henriques, Robert. *No Arms No Armour.* London: Secker and Wartung, 1938.
53. Hezlet, Admiral Arthur. *The Submarine and Seapower.* London: Peter Davies, 1967.
54a. Higham, Robin. *Armed Forces in Peacetime.* London: G. T. Foulis, 1962. (The bibliography in this book is by far the fullest available on the period.)
54b. Higham, Robin. *The Military Intellectuals in Britain 1918–39.* New Brunswick, New Jersey: Rutgers University Press, 1966. (Contains an excellent checklist of periodicals.)
55. Hodges, Major Phelps. *Britmis.* London: Cape, 1931.
56. Hogg, Brigadier O. F. G. *The Royal Arsenal.* Vol. II. London: Oxford University Press, 1963.
57. Holt, Edgar. *Protest in Arms.* London: Putnam, 1960.
58. Ironside, Field Marshal Lord. *Archangel Diary 1918–19.* London: Constable, 1953.
59. Ismay, Lord. *The Memoirs of Lord Ismay.* London: Heinemann, 1960.
60. Jameson, Rear-Admiral Sir W. *Ark Royal.* London: Hart-Davis, 1957.
61. *Jane's Fighting Ships.* Various editors. London: Sampson Low, annually since 1896.
62. Johnson, F. A. *Defence by Committee. The British Committee of Imperial Defence 1885–1959.* London: Oxford University Press, 1960.
63a. Kemp, Lieutenant-Commander P. K. *Fleet Air Arm.* London: Herbert Jenkins, 1954.
63b. Kemp, Lieutenant-Commander P. K. *H. M. Destroyers.* London: Herbert Jenkins, 1956.

64. Kennan, George F. *The Decision to Intervene.* London: Faber, 1958.
65. Kennedy, Captain J. R. *This Our Army.* London: Hutchinson, 1935.
66. Keyes, Sir Roger. *Naval Memoirs, II.* London: Thornton Butterworth, 1935.
67. King-Hall, Sir Stephen. *My Naval Life.* London: Faber, 1952.
68. Kinross, Lord. *Ataturk: the rebirth of a nation.* London: Weidenfeld and Nicolson, 1964.
69. *League of Nations Armaments Year Book.* Geneva: League of Nations, annually 1925–39.
70a. Liddell Hart, Sir Basil. *The Defence of Britain.* London: Faber, 1939.
70b. Liddell Hart, Sir Basil. *The Tanks.* Vol. I, 1914–39. London: Cassell, 1959.
70c. Liddell Hart, Sir Basil. *Memoirs.* London: Cassell, 1965. 2 vols.
71. Lindsell, Lieutenant-General W. G. *Military Organisation and Administration.* Aldershot: Gale and Polden, 1939.
72. Lipscombe, Commander F. W. *The British Submarine.* London: Charles Black, 1954.
73. Luvaas, Jay. *The Education of an Army. British Military Thought, 1815–1940.* London: Cassell, 1965.
74. Macksey, Kenneth. *Armoured Crusader.* A Biography of Major-General Sir Percy Hobart. London: Cassell, 1967.
75. Macready, Lieutenant-General Sir Gordon. *In the Wake of the Great.* London: William Clowes, 1965.
76. Marder, Arthur J. *Portrait of an Admiral. The Life and Papers of Sir Herbert Richmond.* London: Cape, 1952.
77. Marlowe, John. *The Seat of Pilate.* London: Cresset Press, 1946.
78. *Mariner's Mirror, The.* Journal of the Society for Nautical Research. London: Cambridge University Press. Quarterly since 1911. (Murray's articles in issues for 1937–39 particularly.)
79a. Martel, Lieutenant-General Sir Giffard Le Q. *In the Wake of the Tank.* London: Sifton Praed, 1935.
79b. Martel, Lieutenant-General Sir Giffard Le Q. *An Outspoken Soldier.* London: Sifton Praed, 1949.
80. Masters, John. *Bugles and a Tiger.* London: Michael Joseph, 1956.
81. Medlicott, W. N. *British Foreign Policy since Versailles.* London: Methuen, 1940.
82. Ministry of Defence. *Index of Book Lists.* London: Ministry of Defence Library (Central and Army).
83. Minney, R. J. *The Private Papers of Hore-Belisha.* London: Collins, 1960.
84. Molesworth, Lieutenant-General G. N. *Afghanistan 1919.* London: Asia Publishing House, 1962.
85. Morgan, Brigadier-General J. H. *Assize of Arms.* London: Methuen, 1945.
86. Morris, John. *Hired to Kill.* London: Hart-Davis, 1960.
87. Nalder, Major-General R. F. H. *The History of British Army Sig-*

nals in the Second World War. London: Royal Signals Institute, 1953.

88. *Naval Review, The*. London, 1911– . (Confidential for twelve years from publication. Available to approved students in the R.U.S.I. Library, Whitehall, S.W. 1.)
89. Ogorkiewicz, Richard. *Armour*. London: Atlantic Books, 1960.
90. Parkes, Oscar. *British Battleships*. Revised. London: Seely Service, 1966.
91. Pike, General Sir Frederick. *Ack Ack*. London: Harrap, 1949.
92. Postan, M. M., ed. *Design and Development of Weapons*. London: H.M.S.O., 1964.
93. Reynolds, P. A. *British Foreign Policy in the Inter-War Years*. London: Longmans, 1954.
94a. Richmond, Admiral Sir Herbert. *Economy and National Security*. London: Ernest Bell, 1931.
94b. Richmond, Admiral Sir Herbert. *Imperial Defence*. London: Hutchinson, 1932.
94c. Richmond, Admiral Sir Herbert. *Sea Power in the Modern World*. London: Bell, 1934.
95. Royal Engineers, Institution of. *History of the Corps of Royal Engineers*. Vol. VII, 1919–38. Chatham: Institution of Royal Engineers, 1952.
96. Royal Institute of International Affairs. *Survey of International Affairs*. London: Oxford University Press, annually since 1920.
97. *Royal United Service Institution Journal*. London: The Royal United Service Institution, quarterly since 1857.
98a. Roskill, Captain S. W. *The War at Sea*. Vol. I. London: H.M.S.O., 1954.
98b. Roskill, Captain S. W. *H.M.S. Warspite*. London: Collins, 1957.
98c. Roskill, Captain S. W. *Naval Policy Between the Wars*. Vol. I, *The Period of Anglo-American Antagonism, 1921–1929*. London: Collins, 1968.
99. Schurman, Donald. *The Education of a Navy*. London: Cassell, 1965.
100a. Scott, J. D. *The Administration of War Production*. London: H.M.S.O., 1955.
100b. Scott, J. D. *Vickers: a history*. London: Weidenfeld and Nicolson, 1962.
101a. Smyth, Brigadier Sir John. *The Only Enemy*. London: Hutchinson, 1959.
101b. Smyth, Brigadier Sir John. *Sandhurst*. London: Weidenfeld and Nicolson, 1961.
102. Strakhovsky, Leonid. *Intervention at Archangel*. Princeton: University Press, 1944.
103. Swinson, Arthur. *Six Minutes to Sunset*. London: Peter Davies, 1964.
104. Sykes, Christopher. *Orde Wingate*. London: Collins, 1959.
105. T 124, *Sea Power*. London: Cape, 1940.

106. Taylor, A. J. P. *English History 1914–45*. Oxford: Clarendon Press, 1965.
107. Taylor, Rex. *Michael Collins*. London: Hutchinson, 1958.
108. *Tank, The*. Journal of the Royal Tank Regiment. London: Royal Tank Regiment Publications, 1 Elverton Street, S.W.1., monthly since.
109. Temperley, H. W. V., ed. *A History of the Peace Conference of Paris*. London: Hodder and Stoughton, 1920–4. 6 vols.
110. Ullman, R. H. *Anglo-Soviet Relations 1917–1921*, I, *Intervention and the War*, II, *Britain and the Russian Civil War*. Princeton University Press, (1968).
111. U. S. State Department. *Papers Relating to the Foreign Relations of the United States, 1919*. Washington: U. S. Government Printing Office, 1942–3.
112. Vandeleur, Brigadier J. O. E. *A Soldier's Story*. Aldershot: Gale and Polden, 1967.
113. Walters, F. P. *A History of the League of Nations*. London: Oxford University Press, 1958. 2 vols.
114. War Office. *The General Annual Report of the British Army*. London: H.M.S.O., annually, 1920–39.
115. Ward, Colonel John, M. P. *With the "Diehards" in Siberia*. New York: Doran, 1920.
116a. Watt, D. C. *Personalities and Policies*. London: Longmans, 1965 (contains an extremely valuable bibliography).
116b. Watt, D. C., ed. *Contemporary History in Europe*. London: Allen and Unwin, 1969 (the first chapter refers to all the collections of papers of the period now open to students).
117. de Watteville, H. *Waziristan, 1919–20*. London: Constable, 1925.
118. Wemyss, Lady Wester. *The Life and Letters of Lord Wester Wemyss*. Admiral of the Fleet. London: Eyre and Spottiswoode, 1935.
119a. Wheeler-Bennett, Sir John. *The Reduction of Armaments*. London: Allen and Unwin, 1925.
119b. Wheeler-Bennett, Sir John. *Disarmament and Security Since Locarno*. London: Allen and Unwin, 1932.
119c. Wheeler-Bennett, Sir John. *The Disarmament Deadlock*. London: Routledge, 1934.
120. White, Colonel A. C. T. *The Story of Army Education 1643–1963*. London: Harrap, 1963.
121. White, A. S. *A Bibliography of Regimental Histories of the British Army*. London: Society for Army Historical Research, 1965.

SUPPLEMENT TO BIBLIOGRAPHY

122. Hacker, Barton C. *The Military and the Machine: an analysis of the controversy over mechanization—the British Army 1919–1939*. Ph.D. dissertation, University of Chicago, 1967.
123. Walder, David. *The Chanak Affair*. London: Hutchinson, 1969.

124. Medlicott, W. N. *Britain and Germany: the search for agreement, 1930–1937*. London: University of London Athlone Press, 1969. (a lecture).
125. Buckley, Thomas H. *The United States and the Washington Conference, 1921–1922*. University of Tennessee Press, 1970.

XVIII

ROYAL NAVY, 1939–45

Lieutenant-Commander P. K. Kemp

The naval records of World War II, meaning the official contemporary records in the form of Admiralty papers and dockets, Reports of Proceedings, official correspondence, ships' logs, and so on, are probably more extensive and more all-embracing than those of any other conflict in which Britain has been engaged. The welcome relaxation of the closed period from 50 years to 30 is going to mean that almost all of this material will be open in 1972. This relaxation is, however, likely to be tempered with some exceptions. For example, it is most unlikely that the SIC (Secret Intelligence Centre) papers will be released at the same time as the purely operational papers, and it is reasonably certain that there will be other categories, mainly within the Intelligence sphere but also possibly including some of the wartime Cabinet papers, which may be withheld from public inspection for varying periods beyond the initial 30 years. Another such class of paper which has already been accorded similar treatment are the minutes of Service Courts-Martial which now linger under an official ban of 100 years.

Perhaps at this stage a note of caution should be sounded in the ear of the future naval researcher. So much of the planning and operational activities of the war were on a two-or-three-Service basis that the naval historian can only neglect the records of the other two Services—Army and Royal Air Force—at his peril. Thus, the sheer volume of paper which will become available for research when the war records as a whole emerge from the closed period into the public domain may well form a daunting sea through which any historian might well find difficulty in plotting a steerable course.

There are, however, some possible short cuts. Still within the official category of records are the war histories which have been written by teams of military and civilian historians attached to the Cabinet Office Historical Section. There is a broad division into two series, Military and Civil, the first under the general editorship of Sir James Butler, Emeritus Professor of Modern History in Cambridge University, the second under that of Sir Keith Hancock, sometime Chichele Professor of Economic History in Oxford University, now of the Australian National University. These particular histories will be considered in more detail later in this chapter, but the point which could well be made now is that when these histories were initiated the 50-year rule was still in force.

> "In the published series, footnotes have been confined to material that is already accessible. The completed documentation has been given in confidential print. There it will be immediately available to critical readers within the Government service. No doubt it will become available in due time to the historians of a future generation. The official historians of this generation have consciously submitted their work to the professional verdict of the future."

Readers of this chapter should note these four sentences from the Introduction to Captain Roskill's *The War at Sea,* I (13). Copies of all these official histories which contain the full documentation exist in the Naval Historical Branch, Ministry of Defence. When the relevant papers are released into the Public Record Office, the fully documented histories should also be found on the open shelves in the Naval Library. The five volumes in the Military series which are still to be published (*Grand Strategy,* Vols. I and IV, *Mediterranean and Middle East,* Vols. V and VI, and *War Against Japan,* Vol. V) are now likely to appear with all their references added in the public edition.

Two further aspects of these official histories are worth a mention. One is that each department whose papers were seen by the official historians took pains to identify each paper actually used and to stamp it to the effect that it had been used for this purpose. Such stamped papers should be quickly recognizable to any toiler at the Public Record Office. The second aspect is that, in addition to unlimited access to all official papers from Cabinet level downwards, all the historians engaged were also able to call upon the advice and help of senior commanders and participants in the war. Most of them therefore amassed a fairly considerable correspondence in the course of their labours. At the time of writing it is the intention also to deposit this correspondence in the Public Record Office, though whether it thus automatically acquires the status of official records is perhaps problematical. But whatever its status, it could well form a valuable background of explanatory information and amplification.

Still on the official side, but purely on the operational level, are the publications of the Naval Historical Branch known as the Naval Staff Histories. These were written during and after the war (those written during the war were later amended or rewritten in the light of subsequent information and analysis, and of the capture and exploitation of the German naval archives) with the purpose of providing for the fleet a detailed narrative of particular actions, stressing in many cases the tactical lessons to be learned and drawing attention to any errors which may have been made. Some of these Naval Staff Histories deal broadly with major campaigns, e.g., *Defeat of the Enemy Attack on Shipping,* which is a detailed analysis of the Battle of the Atlantic, but the majority are devoted to particular naval actions. Each volume has a short bibliography of the official numbered papers used in the course of compilation. There are some 65 volumes in this series, but they have never been published in the generally accepted sense of the word, i.e., they were never put on public sale, since they were issued as, and in fact still are, classified documents. Complete sets of these publications are held in the Naval Library and will of course be available for consultation as the papers on which they are based emerge from beneath the blanket of the 30-year rule. Other countries engaged in the naval war have produced official histories, and these should not be overlooked.

THE TAMBACH ARCHIVES. One other considerable archive on the official side which requires a mention was made available through the capture at Schloss Tambach after the war of the main body of all German records, diplomatic and political as well as military. With the exception of certain limited categories, notably the B. d U. [Befehlshaber der U-Boote] War Diaries and U-boat logs of the Second World War, all this material has been returned to the Militärgeschichtliches Forschungsamt, Freiburg-im-Breslau, but microfilm copies of all the more important Second World War material exist in the Naval Historical Branch. In addition, the Naval Historical Branch has a miscellaneous collection of associated material, partly in the form of official Intelligence Division publications on various aspects of German naval development and war direction, and partly studies in depth on particular subjects made by historians and other students based on these German records.

A prerequisite to successful historical research in the German naval archives will always be an understanding of the organisation of the German navy as well as the functions of the various constituent departments. Source material for this is available. A detailed list of the German records is given in Appendix I to this chapter.

The above, broadly, covers what might be called the official archival background to the naval history of World War II. They are the main source of research and are endemic to serious study of the subject in all its aspects. There are also on the official side some peripheral aids in understanding the political background to the conflict in the various Parliamentary White Papers and the two Foreign Office series of *Documents on British Foreign Policy* and *Documents on German Foreign Policy*.

Also in this category of peripheral official aid can be placed the wartime Intelligence summary issued under the title of *Weekly Intelligence Report,* becoming monthly after the war, and quarterly later still. These wartime reports were classified as Secret when they were issued, but are generally considered to be no more than Restricted at present, and no doubt will emerge into the public sector with the other official wartime papers under the 30-year rule. They contain occasional articles of operational interest, but on the whole deal more with pure Intelligence matters (movements, identifications, etc.) of little permanent interest. A complete set is held in the Naval Library.

Two valuable sources of naval information are the *Journal of the Royal United Service Institution* and the *Naval Review,* both mentioned in the Introduction. The naval lectures in the former publication are often of particular value since they have been prepared by experts with extensive knowledge and experience of their subjects.

No chapter such as this would be complete without a reference to the Imperial War Museum in Lambeth Road. Quite apart from the exhibits there, which show many naval weapons and items of equipment in their entirety, the Museum contains the pictures painted by the official war artists in all theatres of war and copies of all photographs taken by official and accredited photographers, supplemented by many others from private sources presented by individuals. Mention too must be made of the Museum's Library. It has a very fine collection of naval books on the war in all languages, but in addition has been the depository of a number of personal accounts of war experiences which will not be found elsewhere. No serious historian on any naval aspect of World War II should omit the Museum from his itinerary.

THE HIGH COMMAND. In the official sphere, the War Cabinet Papers and the Committee of Imperial Defence and Chiefs of Staff Papers are the main source of prime information. Somewhere below them will come the First Sea Lord papers, which consist mainly of correspondence between the First Sea Lord and local Commanders-in-Chief. Admiral of the Fleet Sir Dudley Pound, who was First Sea Lord from the outbreak of war until October 1943, was, unfortunately for the historian, not a man who kept much correspondence, and his official papers are sparse and contain less of interest than one would have hoped. He left virtually no private papers. Admiral of the Fleet Sir Andrew Cunningham, who succeeded him, was kinder to the historians, and his official papers are more voluminous. His private papers, though still of course within the closed period, are deposited in the British Museum and will certainly have much of interest in them.

A series of official publications which are quite invaluable for this subject are the six volumes in the Grand Strategy series of the official histories of the Second World War (1–6). So far four volumes have been published; the two remaining ones are well advanced and publication is expected shortly (1968). The annotations give the lead to the official papers. All the official histories, both in the Military series and the Civil series, have been listed under the number 1.

The official histories, mentioned earlier, virtually cover the war period in all its aspects, operational, strategical, and industrial. They are to a large extent interacting, in that many of the civilian and thus partly industrial series affect such purely naval topics as logistics, convoy, production, etc. The purely naval history, written by Captain S. W. Roskill under the title *The War at Sea* (3 vols.) is a model of lucidity and accuracy and has the advantage over its World War I predecessor in that death did not intervene to force a change of author half way through the venture. There was, too, no unhappy clash of temperament after this war to exercise its censorship upon the author as had happened after World War I, and Roskill's work is commendably objective throughout. After its publication he produced a shorter version for a more general readership under the title *The Navy at War* (109) (U. S. title, *White Ensign*) published in 1960. While accurate and valuable, it has not the command or detail of his official history. Much the same can be said of Kemp's *Victory at Sea* (81), which was an attempt by the Admiralty to produce a short, popular, single-volume history which might attract those readers who might be daunted by the sheer bulk of the official history.

Among the official histories, mention should be made of the Medical series. The Navy contributes two volumes to this series, both by Surgeon-Captain J. L. S. Coulter, the first volume on administration and the second on operations (19).

Just as valuable in its way, though perhaps a little glib in parts, is Sir Winston Churchill's six-volume history, *The Second World War* (54), as useful for its Appendices as for its text. As the supreme architect of victory, and combining as he did the office of Minister of Defence with that of Prime Minister, he was at the very heart of the direction of the war. There are a number of books about Churchill, most of them of little worth, and we shall have to await Randolph Churchill's biography of his father, with the companion volumes of his relevant papers, before we can begin to see the man as a whole and can measure his full impact on the direction of the war. Lord Alanbrooke's diaries (47), edited by Sir Arthur Bryant, have a few points of naval interest; Sir John Kennedy's *The Business of War* (83) and Leasor's *War at the Top* (85) are both interesting in their insights into the Chiefs of Staff Committee and Churchill's conduct of the war generally. Lord Hankey's three little books, *Government Control in War,* (67) *Diplomacy in Public Affairs* (68), and *Politics, Trials and Errors* (69), are useful background reading, and one assumes that he left some private papers, presumably in the possession of the present Lord Hankey, which could possibly be of extreme value. A full, authorised biography of Lord Hankey in two volumes is in the course of preparation by Captain S. W. Roskill, of which the first has been published. It is thought that the ultimate destination of the Hankey papers is likely to be Churchill College, Cambridge. S. E. Morison's *Strategy and Compromise* (98) gives some light on the decision, on the highest levels, to open the 1942 Campaign in North Africa rather than in North-West Europe, and Trumbull Higgins' *Winston Churchill and the Second Front* (132) is also useful in this respect. Lord Avon (Sir Anthony Eden's) memoirs, *The Reckoning* (44), gives an interesting picture of the general war direction, but has very little of purely naval interest. Lord Cunningham's autobiography, *A Sailor's Odyssey* (59), on the other hand, has a great deal to say about the higher direction of the war, written largely from a position of high command away from the centre. A biography of Admiral Pound is expected.

Admiral Sir William James, who was Commander-in-Chief at Portsmouth from 1940–1943, has some useful contributions in his *The Sky was Always Blue* (77), while there are other books of the same genre in Sir Philip Joubert's *Birds and Fishes* (79) and *The Fated Sky* (80) and Sir John Slessor's *The Central Blue* (116), which should be consulted for the Royal Air Force side, particularly Coastal Command's activities during the Battle of the Atlantic. Lord Tedder's controversial and aptly named *With Prejudice*

(118) has much to say on the Royal Air Force side of the major Mediterranean operations.

STRATEGY AND PLANNING. The basic official material consists of the Defence Committee Papers, the Chiefs of Staff Papers, and those of the Joint Planners. The collection of the "Hush" signals, now in the Naval Historical Branch, are also useful, although they deal almost entirely with the operational aspect of planning. The First Sea Lord Papers do not contain as much as might be expected, but nevertheless they should not be overlooked.

It is not easy to say how much the various collections of private papers will reveal when they are released; only in a very few cases has the present author been able to look into them, and then only sporadically and in no great depth. The invaluable Cunningham Papers are deposited in the British Museum, as also are those of Sir Geoffrey Leyton and Sir Arthur Power. Churchill College has an extensive collection of naval papers, including the wartime diaries of Sir Ralph Edwards, who as a Director of the Operations Division in the early war years was privy to much of the operational planning; Sir John Edelsten, a wartime ACNS [Assistant Chief of the Naval Staff] in charge of the anti-submarine war; Sir James Somerville, who served both in the Mediterranean and the Indian Ocean; and Sir Reginald Drax, who for a long period was Commander-in-Chief at the Nore. Other collections which are expected to come to Churchill College in due course are those of Sir Bertram Ramsay, Sir Algernon Willis, and Captain Stephen Roskill. Sir Louis Hamilton's papers are at the National Maritime Museum, which also has some lesser collections.

Captain Roskill's official history, *The War at Sea* (13), and his *Strategy of Sea Power* (109) are both invaluable. Kemp's *Victory at Sea* (81), which was a shorter history written with Admiralty backing to fill a "popular" role, is useful. It also gives references to numbered Admiralty papers which were used in its compilation. Churchill's six volumes (54) must not be overlooked, while the six volumes of the Grand Strategy series (1–6) of the official war history are quite invaluable. Many of the campaign volumes of the official history—Norway, France, Flanders, Mediterranean and Middle East, Japan (7–14)—give details of major strategy and planing decisions. Captain Cresswell's *Sea Warfare* (58) is also useful in giving a broad view of the course of the naval war. Two biographies of Admiral Sir Bertram Ramsay are worth consulting for the various major operations of which he was in overall naval command; they are David Woodward's *Ramsay at War* (125) and Rear-Admiral Chalmers' *Full Cycle* (52). Captain Macintyre has written a biography of Admiral of the Fleet Sir James Somerville (89) which covers his wartime activities in command of Force H and as Commander-in-Chief in the East Indies, while an autobiography which should not be overlooked, although not so outspoken or forceful as one might expect, is that of Admiral of the Fleet Sir Philip Vian (120). F. H. Hinsley's *Hitler's Strategy* (72) is useful as a well-informed look on "the other side of the hill."

THE BATTLE OF THE ATLANTIC AND THE RUSSIAN ROUTE. Throughout the course of the war, the Anti-Submarine Division of the Naval Staff issued *Monthly Anti-Submarine Reports*; they contain a great deal of day-to-day detail of the Atlantic and North Russian battles, and are the main official source of information. There is a set of these in the Naval Library. The individual *Convoy Packs* will amplify these where necessary. The *Reports of Proceedings* of convoy escort commanders also tell the individual convoy stories. The Naval Historical Branch has produced a volume, *Defeat of the Enemy Attack on Shipping*, which is a mine of detailed information; a companion volume of charts and diagrams provides the vital statistics, while a third volume, *Arctic Convoys*, as its name suggests, covers the main convoy battles along that icy highway. The Air Historical Branch has compiled a detailed history of Coastal Command, written by Captain Peyton-Ward, which is an essential source for any study of the Atlantic Battle. In Sir John Edelston's private collection of papers now deposited in Churchill College, Cambridge, there may be some which deal with this subject. A history of the Naval Intelligence Division in World War II, Donald McLachlan's *Room 39* (95), has an interesting chapter on the organisation and activity of the Submarine Tracking Room in the war.

A fair amount of general literature exists. Captain Donald Macintyre's *The Battle of the Atlantic* (90) is an excellent short overall account of the campaign, while his *U-Boat Killer* (91) describes his personal experience as commander of an escort group. Admiral Gretton's *Escort Group Commander* (65) is another in this category, concise, unemotional, and objective; both of them are valuable in that they are written from personal experience and do not overplay the drama. Three books cover the activities of Captain F. J. Walker's support group in the Atlantic battle, perhaps the most successful U-boat killing group throughout the war. They are Commander Wemyss' *Relentless Pursuit* (122) and *Walker's Groups in the Western Approaches* (123), and Terence Robertson's *Walker, R. N.* (107). Ronald Seth's *The Fiercest Battle* (113) is a good account of the passage of Convoy ONS 5, which proved to be the turning point of the Atlantic war, while Rear-Admiral Creighton's *Convoy Commodore* (57) gives a view of the battle from the Merchant Convoy itself. Commander D. A. Rayner's *Escort* (106) and Nicholas Monserrat's *Three Corvettes* (97) on which his famous novel *The Cruel Sea* (133) was partly based, are valuable in giving the experience in operation of individual captains of escort ships, and Rear-Admiral Pugsley's *Destroyer Man* (105) is another useful book in this category. H. Busch's *U-boats at War* (48) is useful as giving the enemy's point of view. But all these books must take second place to Rear-Admiral Chalmers' *Max Horton and the Western Approaches* (53), which is invaluable for the post-1942 scene.

On the northern convoy route to Russia, the best account is *The Kola Run* (51) by Vice-Admiral Sir Ian Campbell and Captain Macintyre. Vice-Admiral Schofield's *The Russian Convoys* (112) is a steady, accurate piece of work with some useful statistics. A recent book by David Irving (76) deals in detail with the ill-fated Convoy PQ 17, while Godfrey Winn's *PQ 17*

(124), as one might imagine, is a highly sentimentalised account of the same convoy.

THE MEDITERRANEAN. The Mediterranean War Diary, among the official records, gives the overall operational picture of the naval war in the Mediterranean and is a useful starting point. There is the personal correspondence between the Commander-in-Chief and the First Sea Lord bound up in the First Sea Lord Papers, and of course the various despatches and Reports of Proceedings which cover all operations in those waters. The Cunningham, and, when they are deposited, the Willis Papers should obviously be consulted. The reports covering the operations of Force H, which was an independent command attached to the North Atlantic Command operating at Gibraltar, should not be overlooked as, until about mid-1942, it played an important part in Mediterranean operations. There are in addition various Naval Staff Histories which cover particular operations in that area.

There are six volumes (two still to be published) of the official history of the Second World War which are valuable for the detail and balance with which they have been written. General Playfair and his inter-Service staff are publishing *The Mediterranean and Middle East* (12). Roskill's official history (13) is invaluable, as also is Cunningham's *A Sailor's Odyssey* (59). Captain H. T. Dorling's *Western Mediterranean 1942–1945* (60), is an excellent account of operations in that area. W. E. Benyon-Tinker's *Dust upon the Sea* (46) is useful as it covers the operations of the little known Levant Schooner Flotilla, and Rear-Admiral de Belot's *The Struggle for the Mediterranean* (45) has its value as a concise account of the main operations, while Dudley Pope's *Flag 4* (104) is equally valuable for the coastal force operations. Ian Cameron has covered the Malta Convoys in *Red Duster, White Ensign* (49); so too do Peter Shankland and Anthony Hunter in *Malta Convoy* (115). The Battle of Cape Matapan has its historians in Ronald Seth (114) and Captain Pack (101). Two books on the German capture of Crete are Clark's *The Fall of Crete* (55) and Stewart's *The Struggle for Crete* (117). The unfortunate encounter at Mers-el-Kebir between the French Mediterranean squadron and Force H is described in Heckstall-Smith's *The Fleet That Faced Both Ways* (70), but his account needs verification and checking against the official records when they are released. Finally, Captain Macintyre's concise overall picture, *The Battle for the Mediterranean* (92), should not be overlooked.

Fiction does not often play much part in serious historical research, but C. S. Forester's *The Ship* (63) is based largely on the experiences of H.M.S. *Arethusa* in the Battle of Sirte, fought against the Italian fleet by Rear-Admiral Vian's squadron during the passage of a convoy from Alexandria to Malta in 1942.

THE INDIAN AND PACIFIC OCEANS. In addition to the normal official records which will be found in the naval papers in the Public Record Office, Lord Mountbatten produced a massive and detailed despatch (100) which is invaluable, though naturally it only covers the period of his own command in the area. Admiral Sir Geoffrey Layton deposited his papers in the British Museum; they are of interest, particularly over the fall of Singapore. Sir Arthur Power's papers, in Churchill College, are likely also to contain something of interest.

In the official history series, General Kirby has written five volumes of *The War Against Japan* (11), (the fifth, at the moment of writing [1967], is in the press) where although the main emphasis is on the military operations in Burma, the naval operations are reasonably well covered. Among the Naval Historical Branch's publications are six volumes dealing with the naval side of the war against Japan, with individual battle summaries covering other main actions in which British or Commonwealth ships were engaged.

The great burden of the Pacific War was, of course, carried by the U. S. Navy, and no bibliography of naval books which deal with this area would be complete without including Rear-Admiral Morison's massive history of *U. S. Naval Operations in World War II* (99). His many volumes contain much information on the operational aspects of the Royal Navy in the Pacific and should on no account be missed. Valuable, also, are Whitehill's *Fleet Admiral King* (84) and Fleet Admiral Halsey's *Admiral Halsey's Story* (66), for although they deal mainly with U. S. naval operations, there are pages in them both which cover the British naval operations.

The ubiquitous Captain Macintyre has written an excellent small history of the naval war in the Pacific (93), which, although much condensed, gives an accurate overall picture. Captain Hopkins, who was a British naval liaison officer attached to the U. S. Pacific Fleet wrote an account of his experiences (73) which is useful. So also is Admiral Sir John Collins' *As Luck Would Have It* (56), a record of his experiences in that campaign. But on the whole, apart from the published official despatches which are too condensed to provide more than an overall glance, very little has been written on this theatre of war from the British angle, since the major preoccupation with the Pacific, of course, always lay with the United States.

Not very much more has been written about the Indian Ocean operations, though naturally enough the fall of Singapore and the loss of the *Prince of Wales* and *Repulse* have attracted the attention of naval writers. Singapore will continue to be a barren subject until the official papers become fully available; until then Kirby's official history (11) and Roskill's *War at Sea* (13) remain the most objective and reliable reports. Captain Grenfell's *Main Fleet to Singapore* (64) is a fairly savage indictment of British Far East policy; the story of the *Prince of Wales* and *Repulse* is recorded, not very objectively by Bernard Ash in *Someone had Blundered* (43) and more objectively by Richard Hough in *The Hunting of Force Z* (74).

AMPHIBIOUS OPERATIONS. Reports by the various force commanders will be the main source of information among the official records, with the papers of Combined Operations Headquarters as essential reading on the general background, such as planning and logistics, etc., of all major and minor combined operations. The official histories cover them all in fairly considerable detail on a three-service basis, while the Naval Historical Branch Staff Histories give the purely naval side. A history, produced in 1956 by Amphibious Warfare Headquarters, the post-war successor to Combined Operations Headquarters, under the title *History of the Combined Operations Headquarters, 1940–1945,* is quite invaluable as a source of information not only on the operations themselves and their initial planning but also on the development of techniques and equipment. This was published with a confidential security classification, but should become available with other official papers as they emerge into the public sector. It is additionally useful as it prints references to numbered papers within the general corpus of official records. Bernard Fergusson's *The Watery Maze,* (62), though not included in the Official History series, is to some extent officially inspired and was written with access to the official combined operations papers.

Individual operations are well covered by a variety of books, a few good, more indifferent, and some frankly "scissors and paste." Admiral Maund's *Assault from the Sea* (96) is one of the better ones; Admiral Hickling's *Sailor at Sea* (71) is useful in some respects. The attack on St. Nazaire is well told by Commander Ryder in his book of that name (111), and Lucas Phillips' *The Greatest Raid of All* (87) deals thoroughly with the same operation. His *Cockleshell Heroes* (88) is the story of the famous operation in the Gironde River, well told and authentic. The assault on North-West France has, naturally, attracted many authors. Kenneth Edwards' *Operation Neptune* (61) and Ryan's *The Longest Day* (110) are useful, though neither can be compared with Ellis's majestic account (10) in the official history series.

TECHNICAL DEVELOPMENTS, MATERIEL, AND THE F. A. A.

The technical departmental papers will be released with other war records, and those of the Director of Naval Construction, Engineer-in-Chief, and Director of Naval Ordnance will comprise the more important sources of information. After the First World War, the Admiralty D. N. C. department produced two useful publications entitled *Records of Naval Construction*; a similar publication was planned after the Second World War, but finance was not forthcoming to enable copies to be printed. A draft of the proposed publication is held in the Ship Department at Bath, and it is hoped eventually to acquire a copy for the Naval Library. On the scientific side, the papers of the Director of Scientific Research will be useful.

Fleet Air Arm papers are extensive, ranging from those of the Fifth Sea Lord on the top level to squadron line books on the bottom. Between them come such official papers as Reports of Proceedings, carrier logs, F. A. A. station reports, and so on. Roskill's official history (13) deals accurately with the major wartime carrier operations, and the Naval Historical Branch has produced three volumes on naval aviation (Vol. III awaiting publication) which go into policy and operations in considerable detail.

Technical development and materiel have not attracted much attention among naval authors; although the various official publications in the Technical History Series are still restricted, they must not be overlooked. Gerald

Pawle's *The Secret War* (102) on miscellaneous weapons and Edward Terrell's *Admiralty Brief* (119) are useful in their descriptions of various technical developments in the design of new weapons, etc. Sir Robert Watson Watt's *Three Steps to Victory* (121) is invaluable for his description of the birth and development of radar.

The Fleet Air Arm has a reasonably large bibliography. *Flight Deck,* started in 1944, is a monthly publication devoted to problems, etc., of naval air, and although a restricted publication, will presumably move into the public sector in due course under the 30-year rule. Hurren's *Perchance* (75) is a useful overall history, as also are Kemp's *Fleet Air Arm* (82), Cameron's *Wings of the Morning* (50), and Macintyre's *Wings of Neptune* (94). Peter Lewis has compiled a book of squadron histories (86) which gives some useful operational details. Histories of individual carriers include Admiral Jameson's admirably detailed *Ark Royal* (78) and Kenneth Poolman's *Illustrious* (103).

LOGISTICAL PROBLEMS. Beyond the papers of the various Admiralty supply divisions, there is little literature on this subject. Some of the volumes of the official history, civil series, edited by Sir Keith Hancock, are useful in this connection, particularly the war production series, but they deal with the problems more on a national than a naval scale. Occasional articles and lectures in the *Journal of the R. U. S. I.* and *Brassey's Annual* deal with aspects of the problem, while three useful cyclostyled [mimeographed] reports, of which copies are held in the Naval Library, are *History of Naval Store Department in North America, History of the British Admiralty Technical Mission,* and *History of the British Admiralty Delegation, Washington.* All these three were issued with a confidential security classification; but should become fully available in due course under the new 30-year ruling.

REAPPRAISALS AND SUBJECTS NEEDING INVESTIGATION. Virtually the whole of naval warfare 1939–1945 will be open for reappraisal when the actual records become available for examination under the 30-year rule. Few of the books mentioned above, with the exception of course of the official histories, have been written with full access to the naval papers. The great majority of those which have will not have had the benefit of access to the Cabinet Papers, which are in most cases the prime source of information and authority. This lack of access has, not unnaturally, led to errors, both in fact and in emphasis, being repeated from book to book, so that a considerable field of essential reappraisal remains open.

Very little work indeed has been done in Britain on what one might call the "nuts-and-bolts" aspect of the naval war: the technical design and development of ships and weapons, the evolution of the various types of beaching or landing craft used in amphibious warfare, aircraft development and supply, or the assembly and operation of the fleet train in the Pacific, and a host of other similar subjects suggest themselves. Even in the operational field there are gaps waiting to be filled—the British side of the invasion of North Africa in November 1942, for example, still awaits its historian. The field is wide, and with the release in 1972 of the whole corpus of official war records, the opportunities of rewarding research are prodigious. On the sociological side there is room for research on officers and men, the impact of civilian expansion with Hostilities Only personnel, methods and intensity of training, the place of women in the Navy, and a number of related problems.

BIBLIOGRAPHY

OFFICIAL HISTORIES OF THE SECOND WORLD WAR

U. K. MILITARY SERIES, SIR JAMES BUTLER, ED.

Grand Strategy:
1. Butler, J. R. M. Vol. II, *September 1939 to June 1941.* 1957.
2. Ehrman, John. Vol. V, *August 1943 to September 1944.* 1956.
3. Ehrman, John. Vol. VI, *October 1944 to August 1945.* 1956.
4. Gibbs, Norman. Vol. I, *1933 to September, 1939.* (Uncertain)
5. Gwyer, J. M. A., and J. R. M. Butler. Vol. III, *June 1941 to October 1942.* 1964.
6. Howard, Michael. Vol. IV, *October 1942 to August 1943.* In progress.

Campaigns:
7. Collier, Basil. *The Defence of the United Kingdom.* 1957.
8. Derry, Thomas Kingston. *The Campaign in Norway.* 1952.
9. Ellis, Lionel Frederic. *The War in France and Flanders.* 1953.
10. Ellis, Lionel Frederic. *Victory in the West.* 1962–1969. 2 vols.
11. Kirby, Stanley Woodburn. *The War Against Japan.* 1957, 1958, 1962, —. 5 vols.
12. Playfair, Ian Stanley Ord. *The Mediterranean and the Middle East.* 1954. 6 vols.
13. Roskill, Captain Stephen Wentworth. *The War at Sea.* 1954–1961. 3 vols.
14. Webster, Sir Charles, and Arthur Noble Frankland. *The Strategic Air Offensive against Germany, 1939–1945. 1961.* 4 Vols.

Civil Affairs and Military Government:
15. Donnison, Frank Stegfried Vernon. *British Military Administration in the Far East.* 1956.
16. Donnison, Frank Stegfried Vernon. *Civil Affairs and Military Government: North-West Europe, 1944–1946.* 1961.
17. Donnison, Frank Stegfried Vernon. *Civil Affairs and Military Government: general principles.* In progress.
18. Harris, Charles Reginald Schiller. *Allied Military Administration of Italy, 1943–1945.* 1957.

Medical Histories of the Second World War:
19. Coulter, Surgeon-Captain Jack Leonard Sagar. *Royal Naval Medical Services*: Vol. I, *Administration,* 1954; Vol. II, *Operations,* 1956.

U. K. CIVIL SERIES, SIR KEITH HANCOCK, ED.

Introductory:

20. Central Statistical Office. *Statistical Digest of the War*. 1951.
21. Hancock, William Keith. *British War Economy*. 1952.
22. Postan, Michael Moissey. *British War Production*. 1952.
23. Titmuss, Richard Morris. *Problems of Social Policy*. 1950.

General Series:

24. Behrens, Catherine Betty Abigail. *Merchant Shipping and the Demands of War*. 1955.
25. Court, William Henry Bassano. *Coal*. 1951.
26. Ferguson, Sheila, and Hilde Fitzgerald. *Studies in the Social Services*. 1954.
27. Hammond, Richard James. *Food*. 1951, 1956, 1962. 3 Vols.
28. Hargreaves, Eric Lyde, and Margaret Mary Gowing. *Civil Industry and Trade*. 1952.
29. Medlicott, William Norton. *The Economic Blockade*. 1952, 1959. 2 vols.
30. Murray, Keith Anderson Hope. *Agriculture*. 1955.
31. Parker, Henry Michael Denne. *Manpower: a study of wartime policy and administration*. 1957.
32. Payton-Smith, D. J. *Oil*.
33. Savage, Christopher Ivor. *Inland Transport*. 1957.
34. Sayers, Richard Sidney. *Financial Policy, 1939–1945*. 1956.
35. Weitzman, S. *Education*.

War Production Series:

36. Ashworth, William. *Contracts and Finance*. 1953.
37. Hall, H. Duncan. *North American Supply*. 1955.
38. Hall, H. Duncan, and Christopher Crompton Wrigley. *Studies of Overseas Supply*. 1956.
39. Hornby, William. *Factories and Plant*. 1958.
40. Hurstfield, Joel. *The Control of Raw Materials*. 1953.
41. Inman, Peggy. *Labour in the Munitions Industries*. 1957.
42. Scott, John Dick, and Richard Hughes. *The Administration of War Production*. 1955.

GENERAL BIBLIOGRAPHY

43. Ash, Bernard. *Someone Had Blundered*. London: Michael Joseph, 1960.
44. Avon, Earl of. *The Eden Memoirs, The Reckoning*. London: Cassell, 1965.
45. de Belot, Rear Admiral R. *The Struggle for the Mediterranean, 1939–1945*. New Jersey: Princeton University Press, 1951.
46. Benyon-Tinker, W. E. *Dust Upon the Sea*. London: Hodder and Stoughton, 1947.
47. Bryant, Sir A., ed. *Turn of the Tide* (Vol. I), *Triumph in the West* (Vol. II). Based on the diaries of Field-Marshal Lord Alanbrooke. London: Collins, 1957 and 1959.

48. Busch, H. *U-Boats at War*. London: Clowes, 1955.
49. Cameron, Ian. *Red Duster, White Ensign*. London: Muller, 1959.
50. Cameron, Ian. *Wings of the Morning*. London: Hodder and Stoughton, 1962.
51. Campbell, Vice-Admiral Sir Ian and Captain D. Macintyre. *The Kola Run*. London: Muller, 1958.
52. Chalmers, Rear-Admiral W. S. *Full Cycle*. London: Hodder and Stoughton, 1959.
53. Chalmers, Rear-Admiral W. S. *Max Horton and the Western Approaches*. London: Hodder and Stoughton, 1954.
54. Churchill, Winston S. *The Second World War*. London: Cassell and Co., 1947–54. 6 vols.
55. Clark, Alan. *The Fall of Crete*. London: Blond, 1967.
56. Collins, Vice-Admiral Sir John. *As Luck Would Have It*. Melbourne: Angus and Robertson, 1965.
57. Creighton, Rear-Admiral Sir K. *Convoy Commodore*. London: Kimber, 1956.
58. Cresswell, Captain John. *Sea Warfare*. London: Oxford University Press, 1967.
59. Cunningham, Admiral of the Fleet Lord of Hyndhope. *A Sailor's Odyssey*. London: Hutchinson, 1951.
60. Dorling, Captain H. Tapprell. *Western Mediterranean 1942–1945*. London: Hodder and Stoughton, 1947.
61. Edwards, Commander K. *Operation Neptune*. London: Collins, 1946.
62. Fergusson, Bernard. *The Watery Maze*. London: Collins, 1961.
63. Forester, C. S. *The Ship*. London: Michael Joseph, 1943.
64. Grenfell, Captain R. *Main Fleet to Singapore*. London: Faber and Faber, 1951.
65. Gretton, Vice-Admiral Sir Peter. *Escort Group Commander*. London: Cassell, 1964.
66. Halsey, Fleet Admiral W. F., and Lieutenant Commander J. Bryan. *Admiral Halsey's Story*. New York: McGraw Hill, 1947.
67. Hankey, Lord. *Government Control in War*. Cambridge University Press, 1945.
68. Hankey, Lord. *Diplomacy in Public Affairs*. London: Benn, 1946.
69. Hankey, Lord. *Politics, Trials, and Errors*. Oxford University Press, 1950.
70. Heckstall-Smith, A. *The Fleet that Faced Both Ways*. London: Blond, 1962.
71. Hickling, Vice-Admiral H. *Sailor at Sea*. London: Kimber, 1965.
72. Hinsley, F. H. *Hitler's Strategy*. Cambridge University Press, 1951.
73. Hopkins, Captain H. *Nice to Have You Aboard*. London: Allen and Unwin, 1964.
74. Hough, R. *The Hunting of Force Z*. London: Collins, 1963.
75. Hurren, B. J. *Perchance*. London: Nicholson & Watson, 1949.
76. Irving, D. *The Destruction of Convoy PQ 17*. London: Cassell, 1968.

77. James, Admiral Sir William. *The Sky was Always Blue*. London: Methuen, 1957.

78. Jameson, Rear-Admiral Sir William. *Ark Royal*. London: Hart-Davis, 1957.

79. Joubert, Air Chief Marshal Sir Philip. *Birds and Fishes*. London: Hutchinson, 1960.

80. Joubert, Air Chief Marshal Sir Philip. *The Fated Sky*. London: Hutchinson, 1952.

81. Kemp, Lieutenant-Commander P. K. *Victory at Sea*. London: Muller, 1957.

82. Kemp, Lieutenant-Commander P. K. *Fleet Air Arm*. London: Jenkins, 1954.

83. Kennedy, Major General Sir John. *The Business of War*. London: Hutchinson, 1957.

84. King, Admiral Ernest J., and W. W. Whitehill. *Fleet Admiral King*. New York: Norton & Co., 1952.

85. Leasor, James (in conjunction with General Sir Leslie Hollis). *War at the Top*. London: Michael Joseph, 1959.

86. Lewis, P. *Squadron Histories*. London: Putnam, 1959.

87. Lucas Phillips, C. E. *The Greatest Raid of All*. London: Heinemann, 1958.

88. Lucas Phillips, C. E. *Cockleshell Heroes*. London: Heinemann, 1956.

89. Macintyre, Captain D. *Fighting Admiral*. London: Evans, 1961.

90. Macintyre, Captain D. *The Battle of the Atlantic*. London: Batsford, 1961.

91. Macintyre, Captain D. *U-Boat Killer*. London: Weidenfeld & Nicolson, 1956.

92. Macintyre Captain D. *The Battle for the Mediterranean*. London: Batsford, 1964.

93. Macintyre, Captain D. *The Battle for the Pacific*. London: Batsford, 1966.

94. Macintyre, Captain D. *Wings of Neptune*. London: Peter Davies, 1963.

95. McLachlan, D. *Room 39*. London: Weidenfeld & Nicolson, 1968.

96. Maund, Rear-Admiral L. E. H. *Assault from the Sea*. London: Methuen, 1949.

97. Monserrat, N. *Three Corvettes*. London: Cassell, 1945.

98. Morison, Rear-Admiral S. E. *Strategy and Compromise*. Boston: Little Brown, 1958.

99. Morison, Rear-Admiral S. E. *History of U. S. Naval Operations in World War II*. Boston: Little Brown, 1947–62. 15 vols.

100. Mountbatten, Vice-Admiral Lord of Burma. *South-East Asia, 1943–45, A Report to the Combined Chiefs of Staff by the Supreme Allied Commander*. London: H.M.S.O., 1951.

101. Pack, Captain S. W. C. *The Battle of Matapan*. London: Batsford, 1961.

102. Pawle, G. *The Secret War*. London: Harrap, 1963.

103. Poolman, Kenneth. *Illustrious*. London: Kimber, 1955.
104. Pope, Dudley. *Flag 4*. London: Kimber, 1954.
105. Pugsley, Rear-Admiral A. F. *Destroyer Man*. London: Weidenfeld and Nicolson, 1957.
106. Rayner, Commander D. A. *Escort*. London: Kimber, 1955.
107. Robertson, Terence. *Walker, R. N.* London: Evans, 1956.
108. Roskill, Captain S. W. *The Navy at War*. London: Collins, 1960.
109. Roskill, Captain S. W. *The Strategy of Sea Power*. London: Collins, 1962.
110. Ryan, C. *The Longest Day*. London: Gollancz, 1960.
111. Ryder, Commander R. E. D. *The Attack on St. Nazaire*. London: Murray, 1947.
112. Schofield, Vice-Admiral B. B. *The Russian Convoys*. London: Batsford, 1964.
113. Seth, R. *The Fiercest Battle*. London: Hutchinson, 1961.
114. Seth, R. *Two Fleets Surprised*. London: Bles, 1960.
115. Shankland, P., and A. Hunter. *Malta Convoy*. London: Collins, 1962.
116. Slessor, Air Chief Marshal Sir John. *The Central Blue*. London: Cassell, 1956.
117. Stewart, I. McD. G. *The Struggle for Crete*. London: O. U. P., 1966.
118. Tedder, Marshal of the R. A. F. Lord. *With Prejudice*. London: Cassell, 1966.
119. Terrell, E. *Admiralty Brief*. London: Harrap, 1958.
120. Vian, Admiral of the Fleet Sir Philip. *Action this Day*. London: Muller, 1960.
121. Watt, Sir R. Watson. *Three Steps to Victory*. London: Odhams, 1957.
122. Wemyss, Commander D. E. G. *Relentless Pursuit*. London: Kimber, 1955.
123. Wemyss, Commander D. E. G. *Walker's Groups in the Western Atlantic*. Liverpool: Daily Post, 1948.
124. Winn, G. *P. Q. 17*. London: Hutchinson, 1917.
125. Woodward, David. *Ramsay at War*. London: Kimber, 1957.

SUPPLEMENT TO BIBLIOGRAPHY

126. Warner, Oliver. *Admiral of the Fleet Cunningham of Hyndhope: the Battle for the Mediterranean*. Athens, O.: Ohio University Press, 1967.
127. Drake, Sir Eugen Millington. *The Drama of the Graf Spee and the Battle of the Plate: a documentary anthology, 1914–1964*. London: P. Davies, 1964.
128. Goodhart, Philip. *Fifty Ships that Saved the World: the foundations of the Anglo-American Alliance*. London: Heinemann, 1965.
129. Schofield, Vice-Admiral B. B., and Lieutenant-Commander L. F. Martin. *The Rescue Ships*. Edinburgh: Blackwood, 1968.

130. Terraine, John. *The Life and Times of Lord Mountbatten.* London: Hutchinson, 1968.

131. Wright, Bruce S. *The Frogmen of Burma: the story of the Reconnaissance Unit.* Toronto: Clarke, Irwin, 1968.

132. Higgins, Trumbull. *Winston Churchill and the Second Front.* New York: Macmillan, 1963.

133. Monserrat, Nicholas. *The Cruel Sea.* London: Cassell, 1951.

134. Lenton, H. T. *Navies of the Second World War* series. London: Macdonald, 1966– .

135. Lloyd's Register of Shipping. *Index of War-built Vessels, 1940 to 1945.* 2nd ed. London, 1967.

136. Waters, Lieutenant-Commander D. W. "The Philosophy and Conduct of Maritime War," II, "1918–1945." *Journal of the Royal Naval Scientific Service,* July 1958.

137. von der Porter, Edward P. *The German Navy in World War II.* New York: Crowell, 1969.

138. Gretton, Vice-Admiral Sir Peter. *Former Naval Person: Winston Churchill and the Royal Navy.* London: Cassell, 1968.

139a. Smith, Peter *Task Force 57* (the British Pacific Fleet). London: Kimber, 1969.

139b. Smith, Peter. *Destroyer Leader* (HMS *Faulknor*). London: Kimber, 1968.

140. Winton, John. *The Forgotten Fleet: the British Navy in the Pacific, 1944–1945.* New York: Coward-McCann, 1970.

APPENDIX I

For practical purposes the Tambach collection should be looked upon as the records of the *Seekriegsleitung* or Naval Staff with the *Oberbefehlshaber der Marine* (Ob.d.M.) or Chief of Staff (Raeder and later Dönitz), the *Chef des Stabes der Seekriegsleitung* or C.o.S. of Naval Staff and subordinate to him the *Chef. 1./Skl* or Chief of Naval Staff Operations Division. It is with this latter that we are mainly concerned here.

1. SEEKRIEGSLEITUNG (Naval Staff Operations Division). The records were laid down in the archive according to a strict pattern and mainly on the principle of subject matter and/or areas. The following is a broad outline:

1./Seekriegsleitung (1.Skl.) *TEIL A* (Part A) is the War Diary containing brief accounts of daily events on all aspects of the war and in all theatres. Frequently a specific item would refer for further details to another section or file in the archive.

1./Seekriegsleitung—TEIL B gives weekly surveys and considerations of a general military nature. This too has its sub-divisions:

    TEIL B.I = Survey—cruiser warfare in foreign waters

    TEIL B.IIa = Survey—North Sea/Norway

    TEIL B.IIb = Survey—Western theatre, Channel, Atlantic coast

    TEIL B.III = Survey—Baltic

    TEIL B.IV = Survey—U-boat war

    TEIL B. V. Miscellaneous appendices to TEIL A

    TEIL B.VI = Remarks of Radio Communications, Radio Intelligence

    TEIL B.VII = Merchant shipping

    TEIL B.VIII = Political, International Law, Propaganda

    TEIL B.IX = Survey—Mediterranean theatre

    TEIL B.X = Survey—East Asia

1./Seekriegsleitung—TEIL C deals with specific considerations of individual questions and problems of naval war. Operational directives and operational evaluation. This section is sub-divided as follows:

    TEIL C. I = Cruiser warfare in foreign waters

    TEIL C. IIa = North Sea/Norway

    TEIL C. IIb = Western theatre, Atlantic coast, fleet operations

    TEIL C. III = Baltic

    TEIL C. IV = U-boat war

    TEIL C. V = War in the air

    TEIL C. VI = Mine warfare

TEIL C. VII = Chief of Naval Staff, notes on Führer Conferences

TEIL C. VIII = International Law and War, Propaganda, Political

TEIL C. IX = Questions of supply

TEIL C. X = Coastal- and Flak-defence

TEIL C. XI = Merchant shipping

TEIL C. XII = Economic warfare

TEIL C. XIII = Italy's war effort

TEIL C. XIV = Germany—War in the Mediterranean, Aegean

TEIL C. XIVa = Germany—War in the Black Sea

TEIL C. XV = Co-operation with Japan

TEIL C. XVI = France and Germany—relations,

TEIL C. XVII = Special questions concerning U. S. A., war against U. S. A.

TEIL Ca = Fundamental questions concerning conduct of the war

TEIL Cb = Bases, Colonies

TEIL Cc = Post-war fleet building

TEIL Cd = Distribution of forces

TEIL Ce = Personal

1./Seekriegsleitung—TEIL D is a chronological collection of daily reports from all areas. This section is of little value from the point of view of serious research. Much more valuable is the *1./Skl. Fernschreib- und Funkspruch-Sammlung.*

In addition to the above *TEILE A, B, C* and *D,* the archive contains a vast number of specific files usually bearing an archival number (e.g. Akte X, 3). These files were usually of a highly classified nature and, although having some relevance to the main archival TEILE, warranted special and separate filing. Among these *AKTEN* or *CHEF—AKTEN* there are, e.g., the *Hitler Directives* (Chef—Akte IV, 1, Vols. 1–4), special operations such as *Fall Weiss* (attack on Poland), *Seelöwe* (invasion of England), *Weserübung* (invasion of Norway), *Barbarossa* (invasion of Russia), *Co-operation with Japan, Invasion 1944* (Normandy and South of France), *Bismarck*—operation, *Scharnhorst*-operation, *Channel Breakthrough, Dieppe landing,* attacks on the *Arctic convoys,* important events in the *Mediterranean, Aegean, Adriatic, Black Sea, Achse* (Italian capitulation etc., etc.). These are but examples of the special files.

To supplement the main sections of the naval archive, there are the records of a number of the *departments of the Seekriegsleitung.* The information contained in these affiliated sections is in many respects closely related to that found in *TEILE A, B* and *C,* but frequently in much more detail (inter-departmental). A few examples here are:

1/Skl. Ic = the section or officer dealing with foreign-political questions of the war, liaison with the Auswärtiges Amt (Foreign Office), collaboration in questions of International Law.

1./Skl. Ii = International Law and its application to the war at sea, Prize-Law, etc.

These two offices together submitted to the archive a considerable collection of files on Germany's conduct of the war in relation to enemy countries and neutral countries. In the archive they are laid down according to individual countries. Subjects dealt with are, e.g., Armistice negotiations with France, Control Commission questions, Italian Control Commission questions, French navy and merchant navy, Co-operation with Russian, Co-operation with Italy (pre- and post-capitulation), relations with Sweden, relations with Finland, relations with Spain, Portugal, Contraband questions, etc., etc.

1./Skl. I E = The department or officer dealing with all questions of offensive and defensive mining.

1./Skl. I k = Operational planning and the conduct of cruiser warfare.

1./Skl. I L = Co-operation with the Luftwaffe in air matters affecting the navy.

1./Skl. I m = Operational questions concerning the Mediterranean area.

1./Skl. I op = Operational planning for all theatres, excluding cruiser warfare.

1./Skl. I u = All questions of U-boat warfare.

1./Skl. I Nord dealt with the daily situation as well as operations in the area of Naval Group Command North, which included Norway.

1./Skl. I West ditto in the area of the Naval Group Command West (France).

Whereas it will be seen that the designation *1./Skl. I a,* etc., indicated naval operations, another department, i.e., *1./Skl. II* dealt with merchant shipping in all its aspects—movements, arming and equipment, production of instructional handbooks, shipping losses, etc.

The archive contains a limited collection from this department.

Apart from the purely operational aspect of the *Seekriegsleitung,* a considerable section of the archive is devoted to the records of the *Chef Marinenachrichtendienst (Chef MND)* or radio communications. This department was directly subordinated to the *Chef Skl.* or Chief of Naval Staff, and with its various sub-divisions handled all aspects of naval communications, including radio intelligence, development of equipment, decoding and de-cryption, military evaluation of de-coded enemy signals, deception, information on foreign navies and merchant shipping, foreign press, etc.

This completes a broad outline of the records of the *Seekriegsleitung.* In order of importance we now come to the records of the:

SHORE-BASED COMMANDS AND THEIR SUBORDINATE FORMATIONS.

MARINEOBERKOMMANDO OSTSEE (MOK Ostsee) = Naval Group East, with subordinate commands such as:

Befehlshaber der sicherung der Ostsee = F.O. Sea Defences, Baltic.

Küstenbefehlshaber westl., östl., mittl, Ostsee = F.O. Coastal Defences, east, west, central Baltic.

Kommandant im Abschnitt Wesermünde, Pillau, = S.O. . . . . . . *Gotenhafen,* etc., etc.

ADMIRAL DÄNEMARK/SKAGERRAN = Admiral Commanding Denmark with the various local sub-commands.

MARINE-GRUPPEN-KOMMANDO NORD = Naval Group Command North with subordinate commands such as:

Admiral Norwegen = Admiral Commanding, Norway, with sub-commands such as:

Admiral norw. Westküste = Admiral Norwegian west coast

Admiral norw. Nordküste = Admiral Norwegian north coast

Admiral norw. Polarküste = Admiral Norwegian Arctic coast, each with its subordinate commands or S.O.'s/N.o.i.C's, etc., etc.

MARINEOBERKOMMANDO NORDSEE = F.O. North Sea area with subordinate commands such as Heligoland Bight, West coast Denmark, Frisian Is Netherlands, etc.

MARINE-GRUPPEN-KOMMANDO WEST = Naval Group Command, West, with subordinate commands such as:

Admiral Kanalküste = Admiral Channel Coast, with local commands

Admiral Atlantikküste = Admiral Atlantic coast, with local commands

Admiral franz. Südküste = Admiral South coast of France, with local (after 1942) commands

Befehlshaber der Sicherung, West = F.O. Sea Defences West, with local commands

MARINE-GRUPPEN-KOMMANDO SÜD = Naval Group Command, South, with subordinate commands such as:

Admiral Schwarzes Meer = Admiral Black Sea, with local commands

Admiral Aegaenis = Admiral Aegean, with local commands

Admiral Adria = Admiral Adriatic, with local commands

DEUTSCHES MARINEKOMMANDO, ITALIEN = German Flag Officer, Italy, with (after Sept. 1943) subordinate local commands

DEUTSCHES MARINEKOMMANDO, TUNESIEN = German Naval Command, Tunisia, with local commands

CHEF DER SEETRANSPORTSTELLEN, NORDAFRIKA = S.O. Sea Transport, North Africa, with N.o.i.C.'s at such places as Bengasi, Biserta, Mersa Matruh, Tobruk, etc., etc.

For all the above commands, the archive contains war diaries and, in the case of the senior commands, such as Gruppe West, Gruppe Nord, B.S.W., etc., there are in addition many files dealing with specific operations or aspects of the war, relative to their respective areas.

BEFEHLSHABER DER U-BOOTE. For the greater part of the war, the U-Boats came under a separate command, directly responsible to the *Oberbefehlshaber der Marine* (Ob.d.M.)—C. in C. Navy. Control of the U-Boat arm remained throughout the war the prerogative of the *B.d.U.*, i.e., Dönitz. Quite apart from the collection of U-Boat records in the *Seekriegsleitung* section of the archive, there is a considerable, self-contained, group comprising the *War Diary of the Befehlshaber der U-Boote* together with some related files, the *War Diary* of the S.O. U-Boats in *Norway* and in the *Mediterranean*, and the *War Diaries* of the U-Boats themselves.

COMMANDS AFLOAT. In logical sequence to the records of the Shore Commands come those of the Commands afloat, i.e., the *Seebefehlshaber* functioning under the *Flottenkommando* or C. in C. Fleet. The more important of these commands were:

Seebefehlshaber West (later *Flottenkommando*) = C. in C. Fleet
Befehlshaber der Aufklärungsstreitkräfte later) = F.O. Scouting
Befehlshaber der Kreuzer later) Forces/ Cruisers
Befehlshaber der Kampfgruppe later) Battle-Group
Führer der Zerstörer (F.d.Z) formerly = S.O. Destroyers/Torpedoboats
Führer der Torpedoboote (F.d.T)
Führer der Schnellboote = S.O. Motor-torpedo-boats (E-boats)
Führer der Minenschiffe = S.O. Minelayers

In addition to the war diaries or operational files of these commands, there are in the archive the war diaries of all the major warships from battleship to minelayer. This same system applies in very many instances also to the:

Minensuchflottillen = minesweeping flotillas (Fleet sweepers and auxs.)
Räumbootsflottillen = motor-minesweeping flotillas
Kanonenboote = gun-boats
Geleitboote = escort vessels
Vorpostenflottillen = patrol flotillas (aux. war vessels)
U-Jagdflottillen = anti-submarine flottilas (mainly aux. war vessels)
Sperrbrecherflottillen = ex-merchant ships equipped for mine clearance etc., etc.

For tactical purposes the flotillas mentioned above were subordinated to the local commands such as the *Sicherungsdivision* or *Sicherungsflottille* (*Sea Defence Division/Sea Defence Flottille*) in the respective Command areas. E.g. The *Befehlshaber der Sicherung, West,* had subordinated to his command at first 4 and later 3 such *Sicherungsdivisionen* for minesweeping, escort and general defence purposes on a coastline stretching from the Dutch/Belgian border round the west coast of France as far as the Spanish border (Biscay).

A further separate section of the archive is that concerning the various *Hilfskreuzer* (A.M.C's), *Blockadebrecher* (Blockade-runners) and *Versorgungsschiffe* (Supply-ships). There are war diaries for each Hilfskreuzer as well as for some of the blockade-runners, but the high rate of loss incurred by the Germans in this part of their war effort meant the inevitable loss of war diaries, so that there are many gaps. One important factor here is that these ships came under the direct control (operational) of the naval war staff.

A very important, if by no means complete, collection of records is that of the various *German Naval Attachés*. Allied to these files are those of the *Etappendienst* or organisation for the supply of German ships in foreign ports and also for the provision of Intelligence. (This service did not function to any great extent after 1942).

In the course of its normal duties, the *Kriegswissenschaftliche Abteilung* or German Naval Historical Section collected its own departmental records. There are numerous studies written by the historians as well as by members of the naval staff on specific aspects of the war, some of Admiral Raeder's personal papers, collected papers of Admiral Gladisch, Admiral Assmann, etc.

This bibliography does not pretend to give more than a broad outline of the captured German naval archive and its content for the Hitler period. There should nevertheless be sufficient information to indicate the potential for serious research.

In 1960, the Ministry of Defence, Navy Department, approved a project for the microfilming of the records of the Hitler era. To have filmed the entire collection would have been prohibitive financially as well as in time; therefore the programme had to be restricted to selective filming, with the object of retaining in this country copies of the more important records. This project was completed at the end of 1964, by which time approximately 1300 reels of film had been completed, and a valuable collection of historical records made available to official and other historians and scholars. A catalogue for the project—about 1000 pages—provides a satisfactory guide to the broad categories, but this is at present classified and has a limited distribution list.

In 1955, the task of returning the German Naval Archive to the Federal German Republic was started and, by 1965, restitution had been virtually completed, with the exception of a few restricted categories.

APPENDIX II

THE GERMAN NAVAL RECORD COLLECTION OF THE U.S. NAVAL HISTORY DIVISION

Rear-Admiral E. M. Eller, USN

In April 1945, the German Naval Archives were captured by Allied forces at Tambach Castle near Coburg. These records represented the complete holdings of the War Historical Division of the German Naval Staff and dated as early as 1850. The archives included the records of the Prussian Navy, the Imperial German Navy, and the naval establishments of the Weimar Republic and the Third Reich.

While it was agreed that the records would be under the joint control of the British Admiralty and the U. S. Navy, the Admiralty took actual possession of the material. The Admiralty also arranged the archives and registered each document. During this registration project, the current identification numbers (PG numbers) were assigned to the records and superimposed on the original registry symbols (KR numbers) used by the Germans. The British registration books provide the best overall guide to the German Naval Archives.

At the same time that the British registration project was underway, a team from the U. S. Office of Naval Intelligence began to microfilm selected portions of the records. Upon the completion of this program in 1949, about 3900 reels of 35-millimeter microfilm were obtained and forwarded to Washington. Each reel included several PG-numbers and the reels themselves were designated with either a "T" number (for records dating after about 1922) or with a "TA" number (for records prior to 1922). As each shipment of microfilm was sent into Washington, an accession list was also forwarded. The accession lists, now bound together, represent an important finding aid for the microfilm collection. Another useful finding aid prepared by the U. S. Navy filming team and forwarded to Washington was a subject card index to the microfilms.

The U. S. Navy's filming program was selective. As a rough estimate, approximately 60% of the captured German records were duplicated. The greatest stress was placed on filming the operational records of World Wars I and II. It is estimated that about 55% of the microfilms bear on World War II, 30% on World War I, and the remaining 15% on the periods between the two World Wars and prior to 1914.

Since 1962, the British Admiralty has returned most of the original records to the Militärgeschichtliches Forschungsamt, Freiburg. The chief exception is the operational logs of German Submarine Commands for World War II. The microfilms of these U-boat records represent the only portion of the U. S. collection that is closed for unofficial research.

In 1967, the U. S. Navy began to transfer the pre-1922 (TA) reels to the U. S. National Archives. To date (July 1968), 500 of the approximately 1700 reels in this group have been forwarded. The National Archives is preparing research copies of the master reels and intends to publish a checklist of the total collection when the transfer is complete.

The USN holdings are in the Classified Archives, Building 210, Washington Navy Yard, 8th and M Streets, SE.

XIX

THE SECOND WORLD WAR ON LAND

M. J. Williams

In World War II, the role of the Army was much less significant than in 1914–18. Between 1939 and 1945 the Army did not engage the main forces either of Germany or Japan. It played a major role only in the defeat of the Italian army in the North and East African campaigns. From 1942, Britain was a junior partner in the Grand Alliance, and even in Burma, operations were heavily dependent upon United States transport aircraft. Hence, despite many very able commanders and many heroic deeds, the performance of the Army could not compare with its achievements in 1914–18.

BIBLIOGRAPHIES. In studying the Army in World War II, the scholar is handicapped by the lack of comprehensive bibliographic guides to secondary sources. As for the First World War, it is necessary to consult the catalogues of the British Museum and the booklists obtainable from the Imperial War Musem (31) and the Ministry of Defence (Central and Army) Library. A. S. White's "The Army List" (93) is a useful guide, and the *London Gazette* (H.M.S.O.) should be consulted for dispatches, awards and appointments. King's Regulations and Army Orders can be studied in the copyright libraries, the Ministry of Defence Library, the Imperial War Museum and the Royal United Service Institution.

PRIVATE PAPERS. Apart from the absence of any comprehensive bibliographies of secondary sources, a further handicap is that, for practical purposes, important collections of private papers are not accessible. The scholar would do well to study the Bulletins of the National Register of Archives and to contact the four main repositories which hold collections of private papers: the Imperial War Museum; the Military Archive Centre, King's College, London; Churchill College, Cambridge; and Manchester University. Nevertheless, even these centres can be of little assistance at present, since, as yet, few major collections have been deposited there and some of these are not yet open to the student.

OFFICIAL PAPERS. An even more formidable handicap to the

scholar is the fact that official documentary sources are not yet accessible (except to the especially privileged). They are still in the custody of the Army Records Centre, the Cabinet Office and the Ministry of Defence. Under the Thirty-Year Rule (See Introduction), which may, of course, be shortened or lengthened at the discretion of the Lord Chancellor, official documentary records will not start becoming available in the Public Record Office until January 1970. Thus, as yet, the records of the War Cabinet and its Defence Committees; of the Joint Chiefs of Staff Committee and its numerous sub-committees—the Deputy-Chiefs of Staff Committee, the Joint Planning and Joint Intelligence Committees and the Combined Operations Committee—are not open. Nor are the papers of the British Representatives upon the Combined Chiefs of Staff Committee, of military missions and of the War Office, G.H.Q.'s, formations and units available to the student. The personal papers of troops are not likely to become available and many classes of records have been, or will be, destroyed. It must be noted that apart from the *ad hoc* "weeding" of records that always occurs during the course of operations themselves, extensive "weeding" is carried out by the War Office and Army Records Centre for various reasons. Thus it is customary to destroy a great deal of basic unit documentation such as Part I (General C.O.'s orders) and Part II (orders which record individual movements, casualties and postings) after a given period. It will be interesting to see what proportion of the total of some twenty million documents at the disposal of the Cabinet Office Historical Section, which compiles the Official Military Histories, reaches the Public Record Office. Moreover even when, from 1 January 1970, records start to become accessible in the P.R.O., certain classes—court-martial records, intelligence material, and confidential reports—are unlikely to be open in the foreseeable future.

OFFICIAL HISTORIES. The scholar is thus still forced to rely upon secondary sources ranging from the Official Histories, compiled under the general direction of Sir James Butler by the Cabinet Office Historical Section (33), to popular works which may contain information of value. While, unlike the First World War Official Histories, the present "Grand Strategy" series deals with war policy and strategy, it may be noted that the Official Military Histories are not compiled upon the same plan as were General Edmonds' volumes. The Second World War Military Histories are to some extent inter-service histories, for an attempt is made to show the part played by each of the Services; there is certainly more reference in them to the operations of the other Services than in the First World War Military Histories. No attempt is made to provide a detailed narrative of operations. Whereas the First World War volumes gave an exceedingly detailed account of operations down to and beyond the battalion level, this has not been the aim of the present series. It was planned to leave detailed operational narratives to the divisional and regimental histories, although in practice this plan has been modified to some extent. A fine survey of the World War II British Official Histories can be found in Higham's "A Government at War" (102).

Further, the detailed statements of casualties, such a marked feature of Edmonds' work, have been avoided on the grounds that the records are too uncertain to provide reliable information. Here at present, for total losses the *Statistical Digest of the War* (82) must be relied upon. Also, on similar grounds, despite having large quantities of German records at its disposal, the Cabinet Office Historical Section is reluctant to attempt many comparative assessments of fighting strengths. In fact little information about this important question can be obtained from the Official Histories. Certainly the volumes are well written, and their literary merit may be superior to that of General Edmonds' volumes. But in general the reader only obtains a conspectus of operations, and on the whole they compare unfavourably with the Official Military Histories of the First World War.

Formation and unit histories must therefore, in many cases, be extensively consulted to obtain detailed accounts of operations, though these have, of course, to be used with caution. Excellent collections of these are available in the Ministry of Defence Library, the Imperial War Museum and the Royal United Service Institution in England and in the New York Public Library and the Library of Congress. A. S. White's *Bibliography of the Regimental Histories of the British Army* (94) is the only bibliography of unit histories and even this is incomplete. As for other secondary works, despite their enormous quantity, those with scholarly value are few.

THE HIGH COMMAND. While no authoritative studies exist of the work of the General Staff and its relations with the Government and the other services, the relationship between the Premiers, Chamberlain and Churchill, and the General Staff and the influence of the General Staff upon war policy can be studied in a number of important works. Feiling's (25) is the official biography of Chamberlain, but some additional material can be obtained from Ian Macleod's *Neville Chamberlain* (48). It is premature, however, to attempt an assessment of Chamberlain's strength and weakness as a wartime Prime Minister as cabinet records and many private collections of importance are not yet open. Churchill's *The Second World War* (15) contains material of great value and gives a very valuable insight into the mind of the great leader, but is scarcely impartial or balanced.

Two valuable sources of information for the Chamberlain period are Minney's *Private Papers of Hore-Belisha* (54), which is critical both of Chamberlain and Churchill, and Macleod and Kelly's *The Lord Ironside Diaries* (49), which is in turn critical of Hore-Belisha but does not enhance the reputation of General Sir Edmund Ironside as C.I.G.S. Liddell Hart's *Memoirs* (40) only cover the Hore-Belisha incident; volume III may never appear.

For the period of Churchill's dominance, the most important and most controversial works are Bryant's two volumes of extracts from the diaries and papers of Sir Alan Brooke, later Lord Alanbrooke (8, 9), which are not only very critical of Churchill but make excessive claims for Alanbrooke's grand strategical conceptions. At present they are indispensable for the work of the General Staff, its relations with other services, and Alanbrooke's views on the war, his subordinates and his colleagues. It is unfortunate that no study of Sir John Dill, C.I.G.S. from May 1940 to November 1941 and then Chief British representative on the Combined Chiefs of Staff Committee until his death in November 1944, has yet appeared.

Sir John Kennedy's *The Business of War* (26) tells the story from the point of view of the Director of Military Operations to 1943 and later ACGIS (operations) and is worthy of note. Lord Avon (Anthony Eden's) *The Reckoning* (4) has much valuable information on the High Command, especially in the 1940–41 period when Eden was Secretary of War. R. J. Casey's *Personal Experiences* (14) are also valuable but unfortunately the reminiscences of Earl Attlee (3) are disappointingly reticent.

Ismay's *Memoirs* (35) and Leasor's *War at the Top* (38) must also be noted for their information on the relationship of the General Staff with the other services' staffs.

GRAND STRATEGY AND STRATEGY. Despite the desire of the General Staff to build up a great mass army of 55 imperial divisions by 1942, this target was never achieved, partly owing to the needs of the other services. No more than 24 purely British divisions could ever be made operational. This in itself restricted the role of the Army, but even more important than this was the basic decision of Britain's war leadership, taken by Chamberlain before the war, consistently adhered to by Churchill and supported by the General Staff with equal consistency, to avoid a repetition of the costly attrition battles of 1914–18. This decision was greatly strengthened by the Fall of France. Not until "Overlord" in 1944, about which the C.I.G.S. Sir Alan Brooke, was far from enthusiastic, was the Army committed to a major land campaign against large German forces, by which time the German army had been bled white on the Russian front. In the meantime, the Army's most striking successes, until the autumn of 1942, had been over the Italian army in Africa, so that until 1943 the Middle Eastern theatre absorbed nearly half of the operational formations. In the Far East, the task of defeating the Japanese was mainly the responsibility of the Indian Army, using British units and supplies.

The *Grand Strategy* series of Official Histories (33), is indispensable for a study of wartime military policy and strategy and the Army's relations with the other services although it is, unfortunately, as yet incomplete. Volume I by Professor N. H. Gibbs (the pre-war period) and Volume IV by Professor Michael Howard (August 1942–August 1943) have yet (Summer, 1968) to appear. However, Butler's Volume II (10) (to June 1941) and Butler and Gwyer's Volume III (11) (to August 1942) are somewhat complacent and uncritical. The most valuable and informative volumes are Ehrman's Volumes V and VI (21, 22), which cover from August 1943 to the end of the war. Furthermore, Churchill's *The Second World War* (15) contains many important minutes and documents and cannot be neglected, while Howard's *The Mediterranean Strategy in the Second World War* (34) is a brilliant short analysis covering the whole period up to the autumn of 1944. It is valuable both for its emphasis on the opportunism of British strategy in general and its criticism of the claims made by Bryant in his two volumes, *The Turn of the Tide* (8) and *Triumph in the West* (9), for Alanbrooke's strategical conceptions, and as a lucid account of the role alloted to the Army by the Chiefs of Staff and Churchill.

For the early war period Minney's *Private Papers of Hore-Belisha* (54) and Macleod and Kelly's *Ironside Diaries* (49) are important. Connell's *Wavell* (16) and *Auchinleck* (17) are likewise valuable for their material on the views of these two commanders in the Middle East and their relations with Churchill in 1940–42. Lord Montgomery's *Memoirs* (55) has to be approached with caution, as has Wilmot's *Struggle for Europe* (97), as both put forward the thesis that the war in the West could have been won in 1944 after Normandy with a single concentrated thrust. This thesis is very dubious and is contested by Tedder, Eisenhower's Deputy, in his own memoirs, *With Prejudice* (86), which are severely critical of Montgomery in particular and the Army in general. The scholar should also refer to Liddell Hart's "Western War Strategy" (39). Joslen's *Orders of Battle* (36) must be consulted for dispositions of formations and units.

THE "PHONEY WAR." The first theatre of operations was France. Here the British Expeditionary Force, under Lord Gort, was handicapped by its own smallness, by imperfect liaison with the French, and by strained relations between Gort and Hore-Belisha.

The best account of the fall of Hore-Belisha is Liddell Hart's *Memoirs* (40). The official *France and Flanders 1939–40* (23), has many shortcomings—it gives no adequate account of Gort's plans or his relations with his allies. Spears's *Assignment to Catastrophe,* volume I (80), can be referred to in this connection. Gort's period of command has yet to be evaluated authoritatively.

NORWAY. The official *The Campaign in Norway* is too brief and is unfair to General Mackesy, the scapegoat of the Narvik fiasco. Connell (17) makes some interesting criticisms of Derry, as does Moulton (100), a former commandant of the Royal Marines.

THE FALL OF FRANCE. The German Offensive that overran the West in May and June 1940 narrowly missed destroying the main operational forces of the British Army. However, this campaign is very inadequately dealt with by Ellis (23), and only the Dunkirk campaign itself is properly covered, where much valuable information from the German side is given. However, Montgomery (55) gives an interesting account of G.H.Q. in the last stages of the Dunkirk evacuation.

THE MEDITERRANEAN AND THE MIDDLE EAST. While the French collapse and the loss of much equipment was a grave blow to the Army, a new theatre of operations developed in the Middle East with Italy's entry into the war. Wavell's early victories over the Italians in

North and East Africa have been well described. The British Official History, Playfair's *Mediterranean and the Middle East,* Volume I (69), is weak in detail and the Indian Official History, Bharucha's *The North African Campaign* (7), although very detailed, relies too much upon despatches. There is, however, a fine account of the Eighth Army's successes against Marshal Graziani in Liddell Hart's *The Tanks* (41), which may be supplemented by the Australian Official History, Gavin Long's *To Benghazi* (45). For East Africa, the Indian Official History, Prasad's *The East African Campaign* (71), is very detailed.

Successes against the Italians were still not fully complete when the controversial Greek expedition was decided upon. The best published accounts of this reverse are Long's (46) and McClymont's (53), the Australian and New Zealand Official Histories respectively.

The loss of Crete following the withdrawal from Greece in May 1941 is well covered in Davin's New Zealand Official History (18), while Stewart's *The Struggle for Crete* (84) adds some interesting new information on the British commanders and units.

In the meantime Rommel had attacked in the Western Desert. The spring and summer of 1941 are well handled by Liddell Hart (41), while the Australian official history (52) gives a detailed account of the siege of Tobruk in 1941.

Although Wavell's failures against Rommel led to his supersession in June 1941, he had already planned the campaign against French Syria carried out by Sir Henry Maitland Wilson and completed after Auchinleck's arrival. Here Wilson's *Eight Years Overseas* (98) and the Long's *Greece, Crete and Syria* (46) should be consulted. The Indian Official History, *Campaigns in Western Asia* (64), covers in detail not only this campaign but the important Iraq operation launched mainly from India in April, and the move into Persia in August 1941.

Auchinleck's assumption of command in the Middle East was followed by the completion of the subsidiary moves against Syria and Persia, as already noted, and by the great Crusader offensive of November 1941. Here Playfair's *The Mediterranean and the Middle East,* Volume III (69), is important for its elaboration of statements already made in Volume II that face-hardened armour was used on German tanks in 1941 and that this was even more prevalent in 1942, and its conclusion that for this and other reasons, German tanks were technically superior until Shermans arrived in the desert. This is questioned by both the South African (1) and New Zealand (58) official histories and in Liddell Hart. Here R. M. P. Carver's "Auchinleck's Desert Battles" (12), should be noted, as well as his *Tobruk* (13). The best published account of the Crusader Offensive is in Agar-Hamilton and Turner's *Sidi Rezegh Battles* (1), which should be supplemented by W. E. Murphy's *The Relief of Tobruk* (58). Two questions that remain to be resolved are the extent of the danger to the Eighth Army during Rommel's dash to the wire of November 24–26th, and whether he should have been allowed to get away to El Agheila.

Rommel's counterstroke of early 1942—the "Gazala Gallop"—is well described in *The Tanks* (41). The main operations of 1942 began with

Rommel's offensive on the Gazala front in May and are best described in the South African Official History, L. C. F. Turner's *Crisis in the Desert* (88). The New Zealand Official History (78) is the best account and analysis of Rommel's checking and Auchinleck's counter-offensives in July 1942. Both studies clearly establish the failures in British training, especially in regard to co-operation between armour and other arms. The attempts made by Connell (17) and Correlli Barnett's *The Desert Generals* (5) to rehabilitate Auchinleck are more ingenious than convincing.

The supersession of Auchinleck in August 1942 has given rise to much controversy over the question of whether he contemplated the evacuation of Egypt and also over the question of the credit for the planning of Alam Halfa. Both questions have yet to be definitively answered. It should be noted that de Guingand (30), Brigadier General Staff of Eighth Army when Auchinleck fell, definitely supports the Auchinleck "school." Rommel's last effort, at Alam Halfa, is described in detail by the New Zealand Official History (91), though whether Montgomery was too cautious is another problem as yet unresolved.

North's edition of the Alexander memoirs (61) cannot be recommended, while Montgomery's (55) are principally valuable for the insight into his mind (for which see also his Chief of Staff, de Guingand's *Operation Victory* (29)). El Alamein is well described by Playfair and Molony's *The Mediterranean and the Middle East,* Vol. IV (69), a considerable improvement on the earlier volumes in this series. Very detailed accounts of El Alamein itself can be found in Walker's *Alam Halfa and El Alamein* (91) and Maughan's *Tobruk and El Alamein* (52). The reader may also wish to consult the Lindsell Papers (43) for the battle and the pursuit. Stevens' *From Bardia to Enfidaville* (83) is a full, though somewhat reserved, account of Eighth Army operations from El Alamein to the close of the campaign, but a full study of First Army operations is needed. General Tuker's *Approach to Battle* (87) is a severe critique of British tactical methods especially interesting for the period from El Alamein to the end in Africa.

SICILY. Here the only adequate accounts of operations which were the prelude to the invasion of Italy are the official G. W. L. Nicholson's *The Canadians in Italy* (60) and Linklater's popular official history, *The Italian Campaign* (44). The reader should also consult the United States Army Official History by Albert N. Garland and Howard McGaw Smith (103).

With regard to minor operations in the Mediterranean in 1943–1945, it may be noted that no good accounts exist of the unsuccessful operations in the Dodecanese in 1943 or of the eventual occupation of Greece.

ITALY. Despite the scale of forces employed and the hopes Alanbrooke and Churchill placed upon it, Italy is a theatre sadly neglected by historians, although it witnessed the hardest fighting of the war for the British Army, sustained for over eighteen months against German formations on an average of much higher quality than those encountered in North West Europe after Normandy.

Nicholson, while adequate for Sicily (60), is not reliable, nor can Pal's official Indian *Campaign in Italy* (65) be recommended. The best history of Eighth Army operations up to the spring of 1944, which includes a fine account of the Cassino battles of February/March, is N. C. Phillips's Official New Zealand *Italy*, Vol. I (68). The only detailed account of the campaign as a whole is Linklater's *The Italian Campaign* (44).

SPECIAL SERVICES AND COMBINED OPERATIONS. Fergusson's *The Watery Maze* (27) is semi-official but too brief. A detailed account of the Commandos is Hilary St. George Saunders' *The Green Beret* (75), while he also covers airborne forces in *The Red Beret* (76), as does the War Office's *Airborne Forces* (2). Robertson's *Dieppe* (74) is the best published account of that unhappy operation. Full studies of the work of the Chiefs of the Combined Operations Staff, Sir Roger Keyes, Lord Mountbatten and Major-General Sir Robert Laycock are much needed.

NORTH-WEST EUROPE, 1944–5. The best general strategic survey of the campaign at high command level is the American Official History by Pogue (104). Morgan's *Overture to Overlord* (57), the account by "Cossac" of the preparations for the invasion of Europe can be supplemented by Wilmot (97) and Liddell Hart (41). The Normandy campaign, where British forces encountered a number of first-class Panzer divisions, especially those of the Waffen SS, has been described at length. The Canadian Official History, C. P. Stacey's *The Victory Campaign* (81), is an excellent account which is also of great value for all operations of 1st Canadian Army, 1944–45. It is far superior to the British Official History, Ellis' *Victory in the West*, Vol. I (24), which is inaccurate and superficial. The puzzle of Montgomery's intentions—whether he did in fact have a Master-Plan to which he consistently adhered (55)—a claim accepted by Wilmot and Ellis, but contested by Tedder in *With Prejudice* (86) is unresolved. Here Blumenson (105) should also be consulted. Wigglesworth's "The Invasion of Normandy" (95) is an interesting commentary on Ellis; a noteworthy assessment of the British performance is Liddell Hart's "Lessons of Normandy" (42). The intelligence summaries of General Dempsey, the G.O.C.-in-C. 2nd Army, are accessible and may be of interest (19).

The great dispute between Montgomery and Eisenhower over Montgomery's proposals for a concentrated thrust after Normandy north of the Ruhr is best studied in Pogue (104), Ruppenthal (106) and Tedder (86), while operations in late August and early September 1944, the pursuit phase, have been described by Wilmot (97). The "Market Garden" operation, Montgomery's last hope of carrying out his concentrated thrust, can be studied in Wilmot and in Hibbert's *Arnhem* (32), both of which are critical of the failure to relieve the First Airborne Division, and in Urquhart's *Arnhem* (89), the memoirs of the G. O. C. of the First

Airborne Division. The operations which freed the mouth of the Scheldt are well described by Stacey (81) and Saunders (76).

Unfortunately, except for Stacey's volume, which covers First Canadian Army's operations thoroughly, the final offensives from October 1944 to the end of the campaign are very inadequately covered. At present only formation and unit histories are really useful, as no authoritative studies of the Second Army offensives south of the Maas in autumn 1944; of the role of 30 Corps in the Ardennes; 12 Corps operations in "Blackcock" in January 1945; of the Rhine crossing by Second Army and its final advances, exist. However, Montgomery's *Normandy to the Baltic* (56) provides a brief general account, and North's popular military history, *North-West Europe 1944–45* (62), a somewhat fuller one to which the reader may like to refer.

THE FAR EAST. The early reverses against Japan were so painful that their full story, especially that of the Malayan debacle, is unlikely ever to be told. Woodburn Kirby's *The War Against Japan,* Vol. I (99), covers discreetly the loss of Hong Kong and Malaya. The Australian Official History, Wigmore's *The Japanese Thrust* (96), is highly critical of all non-Australian formations in Malaya, while the Indian Official History, Bhargava and Sastri's *Campaigns in South Eastern Asia* (6) must be treated with caution. General Perceval, the G. O. C.-in-C. Malaya, has provided a reticent personal account (67) as has the Malayan Secretary for Defence, Vlieland in *Disaster in the Far East* (90). Also worthy of note is Grenfell's *Main Fleet to Singapore* (28) for its comments on the military position after the loss of command of the sea.

The Malayan disaster was followed by the loss of Burma. Here Woodburn Kirby's *The War Against Japan,* Vol. II (99), covers the retreat from Burma, the abortive first Arakan offensive and the first Chindit expedition, again with discretion. The Indian Official accounts, Prasad's *The Retreat from Burma 1941–42* (72) and Madan's *The Arakan Operations* (50) (which covers this area to the end of the war), are very detailed but not always reliable. Smyth's *Before the Dawn* (107) has some interesting comments although this account, written by the unlucky commander of the 17th Division, must be treated with caution.

There is an extensive "Chindit" literature. Sykes's *Orde Wingate* (85) is the authorized but very biased biography of the Chindit leader. Slim's *Defeat into Victory* (79) is valuable, not only for its criticisms of Wingate, but as perhaps the best memoirs of a British military commander. One important question about the Chindits remains to be answered— whether, despite the general unprofitability of their ventures, the 1943 expedition did not encourage the Japanese command to launch its Assam offensive in 1944.

The campaigns of 1944–45 were the period of victory and the ending of the dangerous moral ascendancy of the Japanese. Woodburn Kirby's *The War Against Japan,* Vol. III (99), covers the great Kohima-Imphal struggle and his Volume IV (99) takes the story to May 1945 and the re-occupation of Rangoon, by which time victory was assured. But these volumes are deficient in information on the tactical methods evolved in 1944–5 to overcome the Japanese and need to be supplemented by the detailed Indian Official Histories: S. N. Prasad (73) and P. N. Khera's *The Reconquest of Burma* Vol. II (37). Connell's *Auchinleck* (17) is valuable for its account of the relations between the C.-in-C. India and the forces in the field. Unhappily Connell did not complete his biography of Wavell, Commander in Chief 1942–3, because he died and no studies of the work of Wavell's Deputy, General Sir Alan Hartley, Lord Mountbatten (the "Supremo" from October 1943) or the two C.-in-C's Allied Land Forces, South East Asia, General Sir George Giffard and General Sir Oliver Leese, are yet available.

TECHNICAL DEVELOPMENTS. The topic of Army-Air co-operation has been scantily covered in the official military histories. Tedder (86) is interesting but, at present, Parham and Belfield's study of A. O. P.'s, *Unarmed into Battle* (66), and Saunders' *The Royal Air Force, 1939–45* (77) must be relied upon. (See also Chapter XVI.)

Another neglected topic, though of lesser importance, is the development of gas, stocks of which, although not used, were kept in readiness in certain theatres.

Pakenham-Walsh's *History of the Corps of Royal Engineers* (63) covers this essential arm well, while Nalder's *Royal Corps of Signals* (59) is a major work. Unfortunately there is no real history of the Royal Artillery although the confidential War Office Manual on its development will become available for study, along with other such works, when the Thirty-Year Rule permits.

In the meanwhile, although not altogether satisfactory, Postan, Hay and Scott's *Design and Development of Weapons* (70) and Weeks' *Organization and Equipment for War* (92) can be consulted for artillery and weapons development in general. Nor is there any adequate account of the work of the Royal Army Service Corps, the Royal Army Ordnance Corps and the Royal Pioneer Corps, but a history of R. E. M. E. is in preparation.

Tank development and policy is authoritatively studied in Liddell Hart (41), which should be supplemented by Martel's *An Outspoken Soldier* (51) and Mackesy's life of Hobart: *Armoured Crusader* (47), not only for the specialised armour of the 79th Armoured Division, but also for the disputes over the policy to be adopted in developing armoured forces. But the differences between the General Staff and Martel (while Commander Royal Armoured Corps) on the one hand and Hobart on the other, need further examination. Additional material is in the Reports of the Public Accounts Committee of the House of Commons (108).

One great want is a study of the development of infantry tactics and of the great improvement in communications that enabled it to get air and artillery support much more easily than in 1914–18. Also, the reasons for the continued inferiority of British machine-guns and mortars against the German M. G. 42 and Nebelwerfer, from 1942, need fuller explanation than they receive in Postan, Hay and Scott's work. Here the reader should also refer to Ronald Clark's chapter "Science and Technology 1919–1945" for a fuller study of the sources for the history of weapons development.

TRAINING. In general, until 1942 this was very inadequate and a major cause of early set-backs. Commanders like Montgomery, Paget (C.-in-C. Home Forces and 21 Army Group, 1943) and Slim worked very hard to improve standards. The Battle School was pioneered by Brigadier J. E. Utterson Kelso. The General Staff in 1942 established a Directorate of Research (later Tactical Investigation) to apply operational research methods. But even so, training remained largely in the hands of the divisional commands and, especially in view of the presence of so many Dominion and Imperial troops, who always tended to go their own way, was very difficult to standardize. It is regrettable that only scattered references to this vital subject are made in published works. The New Zealander, Kippenberger (101), has interesting comments on World War II infantry tactics in North Africa and Italy. Here again there is scope and need for a major study.

REAPPRAISALS. It is striking how the immediate post-war enthusiasm for Montgomery and, to a lesser extent, for Alexander, has died down. Their campaigns have been subjected to heavy criticism as too cautious and pedestrian, not only by the enthusiasts for Auchinleck such as Connell and Correlli Barnett but detached critics like Liddell Hart. Further, criticism of the performance of the troops themselves has mounted. While the old stubborn determination in defence is not denied, even an Official Historian, Michael Howard, criticizes their excessive caution and casualty-consciousness (34). These criticisms may possibly be invalid, but there is general recognition that the Army could not, and did not, have the importance in World War II that it had in World War I, that it was subsidiary to the other services as Britain herself was a junior partner in the Grand Alliance.

RESEARCH OPPORTUNITIES. Scholarly research is needed in almost every sphere of the history of the Army. The role of the leadership of the Army; on the General Staff itself; on British war policy and strategy; on the contributions of the C. I. G. S., from Ironside to Alanbrooke to success and the organization of the War Office await thorough and scholarly study. No adequate studies of numerous campaigns yet exist. Thus thorough scholarly research into the performance of the Army in the early campaigns from the "Phoney War" period to the Fall of France has scarcely begun. With regard to the North African campaigns, battles such as "Crusader" and Alam Halfa need further study, and much yet remains to be discovered about the role of Auchinleck. Later campaigns like Sicily, Italy, and North-West Europe after Normandy—where Montgomery's strategy and achievement also require further study—are quite inadequately covered. In the Far East, the causes of the early reverses need penetrating study as do the role of the senior commanders Alexander, Slim and their leading assistants. More work is needed on combined operations.

Much neglected topics are the matters of the tactical and logistical organization of the Army and the course of changing developments in their fields. Technical developments—Army-Air co-operation, the development of the Royal Artillery, communications and essential supply services have been sadly neglected. Training and tactics have so far received too little attention and the same is true of weapons development.

However, by 1970, great quantities of documents will start to become available to scholars and great opportunities to remedy the deficiencies in scholarly study and to make great contributions to the historiography of the Army in World War II will be presented.

BIBLIOGRAPHY

1. Agar-Hamilton, J. A. I. and L. C. F. Turner. *Sidi Rezegh Battles* (South African Official History). Oxford University Press, 1957.
2. *Airborne Forces (The Second World War 1939–1945)*. War Office, Otway, 1951.
3. Attlee, C. R. *As It Happened*. London: Heinemann, 1954.
4. Avon, Lord (Anthony Eden). *The Reckoning*. Vol. III of the Memoirs of Lord Avon. London: Cassell, 1965.
5. Barnett, Correlli. *The Desert Generals*. London: Kimber, 1960.
6. Bhargava, K. D. and K. N. V. Sastri. *Campaigns in South Eastern Asia, 1941–43*. Calcutta: Orient Longmans, 1960.
7. Bharucha, P. C. *The North African Campaign, 1940–43*. Calcutta: Orient Longmans, 1956.
8. Bryant, Sir Arthur. *The Turn of the Tide*. London: Collins, 1957.
9. Bryant, Sir Arthur. *Triumph in the West*. London: Collins, 1959.
10. Butler, Sir J. R. M. *Grand Strategy,* II (Sept. 1939–June 1941). H.M.S.O., 1957.
11. Butler, Sir J. R. M. *Grand Strategy,* III (with J. M. A. Gwyer). In two parts. Part I by Gwyer covers June 1941 to the Washington Conference; Part II by Butler goes up to August 1942. H.M.S.O., 1964.
12. Carver, R. M. P. "Auchinleck's Desert Battles." *J.R.U.S.I.,* July, 1960.
13. Carver, R. M. P. *Tobruk*. London: Batsford, 1964.
14. Casey, Lord R. J. *Personal Experiences, 1936–46*. London: Constable, 1962.
15. Churchill, Sir Winston. *The Second World War*. 6 vols. Vol. I, "The Gathering Storm," 1948; Vol. II, "Their Finest Hour," 1949; Vol. III, "The Grand Alliance," 1950; Vol. IV, "The Hinge of Fate," 1951; Vol. V, "Closing the Ring," 1952; Vol. VI, "Triumph and Tragedy," 1954. London: Cassell, 1948–54.

16. Connell, John. *Wavell, Soldier and Scholar. To June 1941.* London: Collins, 1964.
17. Connell, John. *Auchinleck.* London: Cassell, 1959. (N. B. Auchinleck's papers in Manchester University are not yet accessible.)
18. Davin, D. M. *Crete.* Oxford University Press and Whitcombe & Tombs, Auckland and Wellington, 1953. (New Zealand Official History, compiled by the War History Branch, Department of Internal Affairs, Wellington.)
19. Dempsey, General Sir Miles. Intelligence Summaries, lodged in the Military Archive Centre, King's College, London.
20. Derry, T. K. *The Campaign in Norway.* H.M.S.O., 1952.
21. Ehrman, John. *Grand Strategy.* Vol. V (August 1943–September 1944). H.M.S.O., 1956.
22. Ehrman, John. *Grand Strategy.* Vol. VI (October 1944–August 1945). H.M.S.O., 1956.
23. Ellis, L. F. *France and Flanders 1939–1940.* H.M.S.O., 1953.
24. Ellis, L. F. *Victory in the West.* Vol. I (Normandy). H.M.S.O., 1962. (Vol. II, when published, will cover the rest of the N.W. Europe campaign.)
25. Feiling, Keith. *Neville Chamberlain.* London: Macmillan, 1946.
26. Fergusson, Bernard, ed. *The Business of War: the war narrative of Major-General Sir John Kennedy.* London: Hutchinson, 1957.
27. Fergusson, Bernard. *The Watery Maze.* London: Collins, 1963.
28. Grenfell, Russell. *Main Fleet to Singapore.* London: Faber, 1951.
29. Guingand, Sir Francis de. *Operation Victory.* London: Hodder and Stoughton, 1947.
30. Guingand, Sir Francis de. *Generals at War.* London: Hodder and Stoughton, 1964.
31. *Handbook.* The Imperial War Museum, H.M.S.O., 1967.
32. Hibbert, C. *Arnhem.* London: Batsford, 1962.
33. "Histories of the First and Second World Wars." H.M.S.O., 1967. (Sectional List No. 60.)
34. Howard, Michael. *Mediterranean Strategy in the Second World War.* London: Weidenfeld and Nicolson, 1968.
35. Ismay, General Lord. *The Memoirs of Lord Ismay.* London: Heinemann, 1960. (Ismay was Deputy Secretary of the War Cabinet, Chief of its Military Secretariat and Churchill's representative on the Joint Chiefs of Staff Committee.) N.B. The Ismay papers in King's College are not yet accessible, though they may become available.
36. Joslen, H. F. *Orders of Battle, 1939–45.* H.M.S.O., 1960. 2 vols.
37. Khera, P. N. and S. N. Prasad. *The Reconquest of Burma.* Vol. II. Calcutta: Orient Longmans, 1959.
38. Leasor, James (with Major-General Sir Leslie Hollis). *War at the Top.* 1959. (Hollis was Ismay's assistant.)
39. Liddell Hart, Sir Basil. "Western War Strategy." *J.R.U.S.I.,* February 1960 (Vol. 105).
40. Liddell Hart, Sir Basil. *Memoirs.* Vol. II. London: Cassell, 1965.

41. Liddell Hart, Sir Basil. *The Tanks: The History of the Royal Tank Regiment.* Vol. II. London: Cassell, 1959.
42. Liddell Hart, Sir Basil. "Lessons of Normandy." *Journal of the Royal Armoured Corps,* 1956.
43. The Lindsell Papers. The papers of Lieutenant-General Sir Wilfred Lindsell (Q.M.G. to 8th Army) on "Q" matters are in King's College.
44. Linklater, Eric. *The Italian Campaign.* H.M.S.O., 1951.
45. Long, Gavin. *To Benghazi.* Canberra, 1952. (The Australian Official History, published by the Australian War Memorial, Canberra, New South Wales.)
46. Long, Gavin. *Greece, Crete and Syria.* Canberra, 1953.
47. Mackesy, K. *Armoured Crusader: Major-General Sir Percy Hobart.* London: Hutchinson, 1967.
48. Macleod, Ian. *Neville Chamberlain.* London: Muller, 1961.
49. Macleod, Roderick and Denis Kelley. *The Lord Ironside Diaries.* London: Constable, 1962. (U. S. title, *Time Unguarded.*) (N.B. Col. Macleod has deposited a narrative of his own and Ironside's career in King's College, London.)
50. Madan, N. N. *The Arakan Operations, 1942–5.* Calcutta: Orient Longmans, 1954.
51. Martel, Lieutenant-General Sir Giffard le Q. *An Outspoken Soldier.* London: Sifton Praed, 1949.
52. Maughan, Barton. *Tobruk and El Alamein.* Canberra, 1966.
53. McClymont, W. G. *To Greece.* Auckland, Whitcombe and Tombs, 1959.
54. Minney, R. J. *The Private Papers of Hore-Belisha.* London: Collins, 1960.
55. Montgomery, Field Marshal the Viscount. *The Memoirs of Field Marshal the Viscount Montgomery of Alamein.* London: Collins, 1958.
56. Montgomery, Field Marshal Lord. *Normandy to the Baltic.* London: Hutchinson, 1947.
57. Morgan, General Sir Frederick ("Cossac"). *Overture to Overlord.* London: Hodder and Stoughton, 1950.
58. Murphy, W. E. *The Relief of Tobruk.* Auckland: Whitcombe and Tombs, 1961.
59. Nalder, Major-General R. F. H. *The Royal Corps of Signals.* The Royal Signals Institution, 1958.
60. Nicholson, Lieutenant-Colonel G. W. L. *The Canadians in Italy.* (Vol. II of the Canadian Official History, compiled by the Department of National Defence.) Ottowa: Queen's Printer, 1957.
61. North, John, ed. *The Memoirs of Field Marshal Lord Alexander of Tunis.* London: Cassell, 1962.
62. North, John. *North-West Europe 1944–45.* H.M.S.O., 1953.
63. Pakenham-Walsh, Major-General R. P. *The History of the Corps of Royal Engineers.* Vols. VIII–IX. Institution of Royal Engineers, Chatham, Kent, 1958.

64. Pal, Dharm. *Campaigns in Western Asia.* New Delhi: Orient Longmans 1957.
65. Pal, Dharm. *The Campaign in Italy.* New Delhi: Orient Longmans 1960.
66. Parham, Major-General H. J. and E. M. G. Belfield. *Unarmed into Battle.* London: Warren and Son, 1956.
67. Perceval, Lieutenant-General A. E. *The War in Malaya.* London: Eyre and Spottiswoode, 1949.
68. Phillips, N. C. *Italy.* Vol. I. Auckland: Whitcombe and Tombs, 1957
69. Playfair, Major-General I. S. O., ed. *The Mediterranean and the Middle East.* H.M.S.O., Vol. I, 1954; Vol. II, 1956; Vol. III, 1960; Vol. IV, 1966. (Completed by Brigadier C. J. C. Molony.) N.B. Two volumes remain to come, to cover Sicily and Italy.
70. Postan, M. M., D. Hay and J. D. Scott. *Design and Development of Weapons.* H.M.S.O., 1964.
71. Prasad, Bisheshwar, ed. *The East African Campaign, 1940–41.* Calcutta: Orient Longmans, 1963.
72. Prasad, Bisheshwar. *The Retreat from Burma, 1941–42.* Calcutta: Orient Longmans, n.d. (Dr. Prasad is the chief editor of the Indian Official Histories compiled by the Combined Inter-Services Historical Section of India and Pakistan.)
73. Prasad, S. N., K. D. Bhargava and P. N. Khera. *The Reconquest of Burma.* Vol. I. Calcutta: Orient Longmans, 1958.
74. Robertson, Terence. *Dieppe: The Shame and the Glory.* London: Hutchinson, 1963.
75. Saunders, H. St. G. *The Green Beret.* London: Michael Joseph, 1949.
76. Saunders, H. St. G. *The Red Beret.* London: Michael Joseph, 1950.
77. Saunders, H. St. G. (with Denis Richards). *The Royal Air Force.* Vol. III. H.M.S.O., 1954.
78. Scoullar, Lieutenant-Colonel J. C. *The Battle for Egypt.* Oxford University Press and Whitcombe and Tombs, 1955.
79. Slim, Field Marshal Lord. *Defeat into Victory.* London: Cassell, 1956.
80. Spears, Sir E. L. *Assignment to Catastrophe.* Vol. I. *Prelude to Dunkirk.* London: Heinemann, 1954.
81. Stacey, Colonel C. P. *The Victory Campaign.* Ottowa: Queen's Printer, 1960.
82. *The Statistical Digest of the War.* H.M.S.O., 1951. (N.B. The Reports of the Imperial and Commonwealth War Graves Commission —H.M.S.O.—are available in the major repositories.)
83. Stevens, Major-General W. G. *From Bardia to Enfidaville.* Auckland: Whitcombe and Tombs, 1962.
84. Stewart, I. McD. G. *The Struggle for Crete.* Oxford University Press, 1966.
85. Sykes, Christopher. *Orde Wingate.* London: Collins, 1959.

86. Tedder, Marshal of the R.A.F. *With Prejudice*. London: Cassell, 1966.
87. Tuker, Lieutenant-General Sir Francis. *Approach to Battle*. London: Cassell, 1963.
88. Turner, L. C. F. *Crisis in the Desert*. Oxford University Press, 1952.
89. Urquhart, Major-General R. E. (with Wilfrid Greatorex). *Arnhem*. London: Collins, 1958.
90. Vlieland, C. A. "Disaster in the Far East, 1941–42." In King's College, London. (Memoirs of service as Secretary for Defence Malaya.)
91. Walker, Ronald. *Alam Halfa and El Alamein*. Wellington: R. E. Owen, 1967.
92. Weeks, Lieutenant-General Sir Ronald (Deputy C.I.G.S. Supply). *Organization and Equipment for War*. Cambridge University Press, 1950.
93. White, A. S. "The Army List." *Journal of the Society for Historical Research,* XXV (1947), XLV/181 (1967).
94. White, A. S. *A Bibliography of the Regimental Histories of the British Army*. Francis Edwards Ltd., 1965.
95. Wigglesworth, Air Marshal Sir Philip. "The Invasion of Normandy." *J.R.U.S.I.,* May 1963, Vol. 108 (a review of Major Ellis's "Victory in the west," Vol. I).
96. Wigmore, Lionel. *The Japanese Thrust,* Canberra: Australian War Memorial, 1957.
97. Wilmot, Chester. *The Struggle for Europe*. London: Collins, 1952.
98. Wilson, Field Marshal Lord. *Eight Years Overseas, 1939–1947*. London: Hutchinson, 1948. (Lord Wilson, having been G.O.C.-in-C. in Egypt and Syria, 1939–42, then became G.O.C.-in-C. Iran and Iraq, 1942–3, Supreme Allied Commander in the Mediterranean 1943–4 and in 1945 Head of the British Mission in Washington and Chief Representative on the Combined Chiefs of Staff Committee.)

SUPPLEMENT TO BIBLIOGRAPHY

99. Kirby, Major-General Woodburn, ed. *The War Against Japan*. H.M.S.O., Vol. I, 1957; Vol. II, 1958; Vol. III, 1961; Vol. IV, 1965.
100. Moulton, J. L. *The Norwegian Campaign of 1940*. London: Eyre and Spottiswoode, 1966. (U. S. *A Study of Warfare in 3 Dimensions.*)
101. Kippenberger, S. Howard. *Infantry Brigadier*. Oxford University Press, 1949.
102. Higham, Robin. "A Government at War," in *Stand To*. The Journal of the Australian Capital Territory Branch. Returned Sailors, Soldiers and Airmen's Imperial League of Australia, Canberra, Vol. VIII, No. 2, March–April 1963 and Vol. VIII, No. 4, July–August 1963.

103. Garland, Albert N. and Howard McGaw Smith. "The United States Army in World War II: The Mediterranean Theater of Operations: *Sicily and the Surrender of Italy*." Office of the Chief of Military History, Department of the Army, Washington, D.C., 1965.
104. Pogue, Forrest C. "The United States Army in World War II: The European Theater Operations: *The Supreme Command*." Office of the Chief of Military History, Department of the Army, Washington, D.C., 1954.
105. Blumenson, Martin. "The United States Army in World War II: The European Theater Operations: *Breakout and Pursuit*." Office of the Chief of Military History, Department of the Army, Washington, D.C., 1961.
106. Ruppenthal, Roland G. "The United States Army in World War II: The European Theater: *The Logistical Support of the Armies*." Vol. I, 1953; Vol. II, 1959. Office of the Chief of Military History, Department of the Army, Washington, D.C.
107. Smyth, Brigadier Sir John V. C. *Before the Dawn*. London: Cassell, 1954.
108. *Cmd. 6865. Wartime Tank Production*. (1946).
109. Bowlby, Alex. *Recollections of Rifleman Bowlby: Italy, 1944*. London: Leo Cooper, 1969.
110. Carew, Tim. *The Fall of Hong Kong*. London: Pan, 1968.
111. Chamberlain, Peter and Chris Ellis. *British and American Tanks of World War II; the complete illustrated history of British, American and Commonwealth tanks, gun motor carriages and special purpose vehicles, 1939–1945*. London: Arms and Armour Press, 1969.
112. Clabby, Brigadier J. *The History of the Royal Army Vetinary Corps, 1919–1961*. London: J. A. Allen, 1969.
113. Conniford, M. P. *A Summary of the Transport used by the British Army, 1939–1945*. Bracknell, Berks.: Bellona Publications, 1969. Multiple parts.
114. Essame, General H. *The Battle for Germany*. London: Batsford, 1969.
115. Jackson, Major-General W. E. F. *The Battle for Rome*. London: Batsford, 1969.
115a. Jackson, Major-General W. G. F. *The Battle for Italy*. London: Clowes, 1967.
116. Lewin, Ronald, ed. *The War on Land, 1939–45*. London: Hutchinson, 1969.
117a. Mays, Spike. *Reuben's Corner*. London: Eyre and Spottiswoode, 1967.
117b. Mays, Spike. *Fall out the Officers*. London: Eyre and Spottiswoode, 1969.
118. Simson, Ivan. *Singapore—too little, too late*. London: Leo Cooper, 1970.

JOURNALS OF SPECIAL VALUE.
The Royal United Service Institution Journal (Vol. 90–   ).
The Journal of the Royal Armoured Corps.
The Royal Engineers Journal.
The Journal of the Royal Artillery.

Apart from the photographic and film collections in the Imperial War Museum, once again the Radio Times Hulton Picture Library, 35 Marylebone High Street, London, W.1., must be consulted.

XX

BRITAIN IN THE SECOND WORLD WAR*

Margaret Gowing and A. H. K. Slater

This chapter is a residual one which deals with all those parts of the war not covered by others. It is divided into two broad parts, the one dealing with government policy and machinery and the other with the impact of war upon British individuals, institutions and culture. Much of the subject matter is the province of the historians of political, economic and social trends and institutions and because of the multiplicity of interests involved, this list is not confined to works of scholarship. When this chapter was first drafted many of these historians appeared to regard the war as no more than an incident, rather than the watershed it seemed to be twenty-five years ago. However, since 1967 a new generation of young historians has begun to concern itself with these aspects of the war: Arthur Marwick (322) and Angus Calder (330) (who includes his own very good bibliography) have written histories of the war from the point of view of society in general.

GENERAL INFORMATION: INDEXES. It is impossible to list here the many thousands of specialist or personal books on the Second World War. The essential guide to these is the quinquennial British Museum (B.M.) *Subject Index of Modern Books* (30), where the main entry is "European War, 1939–1945." Researchers should peruse all the many sub-entries, for even "war memorials, rolls of honour" may be of use to the social historian. The sub-entry "General History" includes some relevant bibliographies. Political and military memoirs must be sought elsewhere in the *Index,* usually under the entry "England, History" or under the appropriate professional entry, e.g., civil engineering. *The British National Bibliography* has appeared in annual volumes since 1950. Its entry "World War 2" together with specialist entries should be consulted, particularly for

* This chapter was written in the summer of 1967 in order to meet the date laid down in the contract with the volume editor. The delay in publication, which has been due to various causes, means that it is inevitably out of date. Some minor additions have been made to include books published more recently, but the authors wish to emphasize, first, that they would have written the chapter differently if they had been writing it in 1970; second, that while the information about private archives was accurate in 1967, they cannot vouch for its accuracy as of 1970.

the years not yet covered by the B. M. *Subject Index.* The Imperial War Museum (I.W.M.) has an unprinted subject index, but in 1967 the library there was undergoing a major re-organisation so this work will have to be used with care. This index is especially useful for government papers and circulars and for unpublished works; it includes for example a monthly chronicle and photographic record of the impact of the war in all its phases on the small town of Grantham.

GOVERNMENT PUBLICATIONS. Statutory documents and Parliamentary papers are available in the usual bound volumes, while publications in printed book form can be traced through the B. M. Library and Indexes. Other government papers—pamphlets, circulars, handbooks, leaflets and publicity material—are much more elusive. Sometimes complete sets are held by departmental libraries—e.g. by the Ministry of Agriculture, Fisheries and Food—while the I.W.M. is the depository for the war-time information material of the Ministry of Information, War Office, Admiralty and Air Ministry. It also has much of the Ministry of Home Security material.

FILMS. All the documentaries of the war period are listed in *The British Film and Television Year Book for 1949,* while features can be located in *The Monthly Film Bulletin* published by the British Film Institute. War-time films considered worth saving are in the *National Film Archive* (see Introduction), which also has a card index of news films. The I.W.M. also has large holdings of films.

STILL PHOTOGRAPHS. The I.W.M. has huge collections. The magazines, *Picture Post* and *The Illustrated London News,* also provided much material. For information on obtaining copies, see the Introduction. There are various illustrated books about the war (13, 14, 125, 189, 195, 227).

RECORDINGS AND BROADCAST MATERIAL. The chief source is the British Broadcasting Corporation (See Introduction).

MUSIC. Wartime sheet music is included in the nine volumes of the published *B.B.C. Music Library Catalogue.* Copies of this are available at all large public and university libraries in the U.K. In case of doubt over anything in this section, apply to The Librarian of the B.B.C.

GRAMOPHONE OR PHONOGRAPH RECORDS. The British Institute of Recorded Sound Ltd. (29 Exhibition Road, London, S.W.7.) keeps lists of all gramophone records issued.

MISCELLANEOUS. The I.W.M. has large collections of (a) Press-cuttings of the war years from British daily newspapers, arranged in chronological order by days; also some U. S. press material for the same period. (b) Posters, official and unofficial from both sides in the war. (c) Original records of surveys made in wartime by Mass Observation and the Government Social Survey.

As for cartoons, there is a complete set of the famous ones by David Low in the Library of the London School of Economics (277). Apparently there are also many cartoons in the Beaverbrook papers (285). Otherwise see newspaper files.

We return now to our two broad subjects—(I) government policy and machinery, and (II) the impact of war on Britain.

GOVERNMENT POLICY AND MACHINERY. Here the main themes are the mobilisation of the economy and the organisation of munitions production; the organisation of civil defence; social policy; foreign, Commonwealth and colonial policy; postwar reconstruction policy; the machinery of government. Another theme is closely linked with these— political life during the war. These themes were so entangled in policy and administration that no sharp demarcation of material into topics can be made. Instead the types of material available have been surveyed indicating the main themes covered.

The main types of printed material on government policy and machinery are (i) the biographies and memoirs of the men who were in positions of power, (ii) the civil series of the official war histories, (iii) other academic works. In addition there is (iv) primary material.

(1) MEMOIRS AND BIOGRAPHIES. There are many memoirs by, or biographies about, people who held government or quasi-government positions during the war. These books mostly cover a much wider span than the war, and they vary enormously in their candor and quality. They are often useful for general war background as well as government policy. We have not attempted to evaluate these books because even the least meritorious literary effort may yield some information to someone on some specialist topic, but we have indicated the particular fields of interest of the people concerned. Churchill's memoirs (51), despite a summary index, are of course in a class apart; although they are highly personal, they do include a great deal of primary material. Churchill's speeches (52, 53) are also primary material. We have included no biographical material about Churchill, apart from Lord Moran's book (166) and a volume by Lord Swinton about six Prime Ministers (226), because that field is so large that it is now a specialist subject. Other "Government" people covered by memoirs, diaries and biographies are as follows: King George VI (241); Archbishops of Canterbury (130, 148); John Anderson [Viscount Waverley] (civil defence, war economy, manpower, finance) (242); Clement Attlee (Deputy Prime Minister, home affairs, Commonwealth affairs) (11, 132, 226); Lord Beaverbrook (munitions production) (83, 253); William Beveridge (manpower, postwar reconstruction) (17, 18); Ernest Bevin (manpower, postwar reconstruction) (35); Robert Boothby (food) (24); Robert Bruce-Lockhart (political warfare) (34); R. A. Butler (foreign policy, education) (215); Neville Chamberlain (89, 152); R. G. Casey (Middle East affairs) (43); Lord Cherwell (war economy, scientific affairs, general aide to Churchill) (20); Lord Citrine (316); Duff Cooper [Viscount Norwich] (War Office, information, security) (174); Stafford Cripps

(foreign policy, munitions production, India) (62); Henry Page Croft [Lord Croft] (War Office) (71); Hugh Dalton (economic warfare, Board of Trade) (76); Lady Denman (Women's Land Army) (126); Anthony Eden [Earl of Avon] (War Office, foreign and Commonwealth policy) (12); Walter Elliot (health) (65); Lionel Fraser (Treasury) (98); Hugh Gaitskell (economic warfare, Board of Trade) (193); P. J. Grigg (War Office) (105); Lord Halifax (foreign policy) (19, 106); Oliver Harvey (foreign policy) (340); Samuel Hoare [Viscount Templewood] (foreign policy) (121, 229); Leslie Hore-Belisha (War Office) (164); Thomas Johnston (Scottish affairs) (135); J. M. Keynes (Treasury) (114); Ivone Kirkpatrick (political warfare) (139); Lord Lloyd (colonial policy) (3); Lord Lothian (foreign policy) (38); Oliver Lyttelton [Lord Chandos] (Board of Trade, munitions production) (47); Harold Macmillan (munitions production, colonial and foreign policy), (153); G. Mallaby (Cabinet Secretariat) (156); D. Maxwell-Fyfe [Earl of Kilmuir] (legal affairs) (138); Robert Menzies (Commonwealth and Foreign policy) (315); Herbert Morrison (munitions production, civil defense, Home Office) (169); Harold Nicolson (information) (173); Montagu Norman (Bank of England) (27, 55); John Boyd Orr (food) (176); F. W. Pethick-Lawrence (India) (31); John Reith (B.B.C., information, building programmes) (188); Arthur Salter (shipping, Anglo-U.S. affairs) (197, 197a); Harold Scott (civil defense) (201); Lord Simon (legal affairs) (209); Edward Spears (Anglo-French affairs) (216); E. Thurtle (information) (231); George Tomlinson (manpower) (22); Cecil Weir (munitions production) (239); Lord Woolton (food, postwar reconstruction) (250).

In addition to the Ministers and officials listed above there are a great number of memoirs by other members of the diplomatic and colonial services. These are listed in an appendix to a volume by D. C. Watt (234).

Many of the above books clearly contain general political material. There are also memoirs or biographies of people who were in the penumbra of wartime power—mostly M.P.s or peers. Those covered are Lord Addison (165), L. S. Amery (5) (this does not cover ministerial office), George Bell, Bishop of Chichester (131), Aneurin Bevan (95), Fenner Brockway (32), Thelma Cazalet-Keir, (45), Henry Channon (48), Diana Cooper (63), A. P. Herbert (117), Thomas Jones (136), Harold Laski (78, 158), Jennie Lee (144), D. N. Pritt (186), Eleanor Rathbone (222), Lord Samuel (198), Emanuel Shinwell (206), Edith Summerskill (224), Josiah Wedgwood (237, 238), Lord Winterton (248).

Because of the close link between foreign affairs and strategy, the memoirs of many of the generals, British and American, are also relevant here (see chapter XIX). Some other American memoirs are also useful for foreign affairs and Allied cooperation—Harry Hopkins' papers (205), Cordell Hull's, Stimson's and Winant's memoirs (123, 221, 247) and Stettinius' book on lend-lease (220) (not exactly a memoir). Of other Allied memoirs those of General de Gaulle (99), Maisky (155), and Raczynski (187) are important, and Stalin's *Correspondence* (218) is essential primary material.

(II) THE CIVIL SERIES OF OFFICIAL WAR HISTORIES, consisting of 27 volumes, was a completely new enterprise for the government; there had been official military histories before but no government-sponsored series to describe the organisation of economic and social life in wartime. The Carnegie volumes were not official (see Chapter XV). Since the whole idea of official history is distasteful to many historians, it is worth adding something about the credentials of this particular series. In 1943 at one of the worst points in the war, the War Cabinet decided that a team of historians should be employed to write narratives which would "fund experience for Government use" (no one thought seriously of atomic warfare then). A distinguished historian, Professor Keith Hancock, was appointed Supervisor, and his team was given access even in wartime to top secret papers. After the war it was decided that the narratives should be prepared for publication instead of just for government use. (The official military histories began after the war.) The historians were bound to stick to such conventions of the British constitution as the unanimity of Cabinet decision and the anonymity of permanent civil servants. Moreover, the histories went to departments for official comment before publication, and in one or two cases there were conflicts between official wishes and the historian's judgment. Nevertheless, one of us, Margaret Gowing, worked on the war histories and can say that in each case the historian stood up to examination; faults in the books are due to the historians' fallibility rather than official censorship. Confidential print copies, containing very full references to official documents, have been prepared and will be available to scholars when the documents themselves are made public. A wide range of miscellaneous narratives written in the course of the historians' work also exists and will become available in accordance with the arrangements made under the Public Records Act.

The civil official histories consist of four synoptic volumes—a *Statistical Digest of the War* (146), *British War Economy* (112), *British War Production* (181), and *Problems of Social Policy* (232). Specialist volumes deal with agriculture (170), civil defence (175), civil industry and trade (113), coal (70), economic warfare (161), financial policy (200), food (110, 111), manpower (178), shipping (15), studies in the social services (91), transport (199), works and buildings (141). In a war production series there are volumes on administration of war production (202), contracts and finance (10), design and development of weapons (182), factories and plants (122), labour in the munitions industries (129), overseas supply (107, 108), raw materials (124). The oil volume is (in July 1970) in process of publication. One volume, education, did not appear as the author died before finishing it, but her work is being used by Dr. Peter Godsden of Leeds University for a history outside the official series.

In a series as large as the civil histories the quality of the volumes inevitably varies, but several are distinguished. It is worth pointing in particular to R. M. Titmuss's *Problems of Social Policy*. The author came from an insurance office to the war histories without a university education. R. H. Tawney said that any university should be proud to give the author of *Problems of Social Policy* a chair; Titmuss subsequently became a professor at the London School of Economics and a world authority on social policy and administration.

The civil series did not include foreign policy, but E. L. Woodward wrote an official history on this subject under Cabinet Office auspices (249, 249a). Foreign policy in war was so closely interwoven with military strategy that the official military histories (see Chapter XVIII) should also be consulted. Several of the civil histories have sections on inter-Allied economic affairs which also affected foreign policy—notably those on economic blockade, financial policy, overseas supply, food, shipping plus *British War Economy* and *British War Production*. There are also foreign-policy implications in the official wartime atomic energy story (100).

An important officially sponsored but independently edited volume of wartime documents about Indian affairs (157b) has been published outside the civil series.

An official history of Northern Ireland at war was commissioned by the Government of Northern Ireland (23).

Material relevant to the chapter will be found in the Civilian Medical Series edited by Sir Arthur S. McNalty (320).

(III) OTHER ACADEMIC STUDIES AND CONTEMPORARY COMMENT. It is surprising how relatively few scholarly studies there have been of the non-military aspects of the war, and indeed how discussion of many of these aspects almost ceased after the immediate postwar years. A. J. P. Taylor's *English History 1914–1945* (228) fits together much material on many themes in little space. The biggest crop of specialist studies during and immediately after the war was on the war economy, economic planning, and manpower problems. During the war itself Keynes's booklet *How to Pay for the War* (137), written before he entered the Treasury, was outstandingly important in its effects: it opened a new era of government economic policy. Two other wartime books, one on saving and spending (154) and one on taxation (207), influenced financial policy. After the war several economists by profession or by conversion wrote books or delivered lectures which were a mixture of memoirs and theoretical exposition. *Lessons of the British War Economy* (49) was a collection of such studies. There also were studies of economic planning by Ely Devons (80), Oliver Franks (96), Hubert Henderson (116), John Jewkes (134), James Meade (160) and Lionel Robbins (191). A. J. Brown wrote generally on inflation (33). Two books, one by J. C. R. Dow (82) and one by a group of Oxford dons (251), are especially good on the economic no man's land between war and postwar. Recently Alan Milward has published a guide, *The Economic Effects of the World Wars on Britain* (342).

Books on more specialist aspects of government economic policy or on economic affairs in wartime will be found in the B.M. subject indexes. Several which include the war in a longer perspective are those on the levelling of incomes (204), on strikes (140), on the State and the trade unions (4), on national wages policy (192), on industrial relations (92), on gov-

ernment expenditure (317), and on government economic policy generally
(331). There is an important account of the forced wartime sale of Courtaulds' U. S. subsidiary (337).

There are some wartime and early postwar articles on wartime economic
problems in *Economica, The Economic Journal, Oxford Economic Papers,
The Manchester School, Transactions of the Manchester Statistical Society*
and the *Bulletin of the Oxford University Institute of Statistics*. Some of the
articles from the *Bulletin* were collected into a book *Studies in War Economics* (177). For information on the war, it is necessary to comb journals
up to about 1950. The wartime publications of Political and Economic
Planning (PEP) are also important. *The Economist* is the fullest (though
not always the wisest) source for contemporary economic comment; it is
also worth looking at *The Banker* and at the individual bank reviews. A
few basic articles from miscellaneous journals on special topics—on agriculture (256), transport (257), mutual aid (254), and shipbuilding (255),
have been listed at the end of the "Printed Works" section of the bibliography for this chapter.

The Second World War changed Britain's whole attitude to economic
policy: Keynes had entered the Treasury. Similarly the war was a most
powerful agent of social reform. Some of the impulse to reform grew from
the altruism and idealism which common danger bred, while much of it
grew out of civil defense measures—the need to cope with the problems
caused by air raids and evacuation. There was a vast outpouring of writing
at the time, especially on the traumatic experiences of evacuation from the
big cities. This alone prompted well over 200 studies of various kinds. We
have not included lists, because in 1945 the literature was surveyed in *The
Psychoanalytic Study of the Child* (258). Titmuss' official history is extremely well documented from a very wide range of specialist journals and
publications, although the references are in innumerable footnotes and are
not gathered together. Accounts by, or about, organisations closely linked
with the government should also be consulted—to take just two examples,
the publications and contemporary papers of the National Council of Social
Service (some in I.W.M.) and of the Women's Voluntary Services (again
I.W.M. and see 102). Since the war and the official histories, further study
of wartime social policy and of the social effects of the war was almost non-
existent until Marwick's (322) and Calder's (330) general books. Dent's
book on education (79) was written during the war, and there is little else
except general education history (74, 341). Abel-Smith's histories of hospitals and the nursing profession (1 and 2) and Marion Bowley's book on
housing policy (26) have something on the war. Mackintosh wrote about
the war and mental health (151). Asa Briggs's life of Seebohm Rowntree
(29) is worth looking at for the war pages.

On civil defense proper, air raid precautions and military defense are
well documented in official histories (175, 59, 332), and the I.W.M. holds
many books about the contribution of the various services—Home Guard,
police, fire service, etc., etc. Less has been written about the area where civil
defense or home security merge into justice and civil liberty. There is a
book on the internment of aliens (142) and another on the contribution of

aliens to the war effort (16), but nothing much on the detention of pro-Germans, except in the appropriate memoirs (e.g. 81). There is a book about conscientious objectors (115). Government attitudes to "dangerous" press comment are found in the books about troubles with *The Daily Mirror* (73, 84) and *The Daily Worker* and *The Week* (56). There is no comprehensive study of the government's information policy and its relations with the mass media. The wartime volume of Asa Briggs's history of the B.B.C. will probably have appeared before this book is published. A number of books deal with newspaper affairs in wartime, in addition to those already mentioned (7, 50, 66, 127, 158a, 167, 252).

The fields of government wartime foreign, Commonwealth, Indian, and colonial policy have been left remarkably untilled by scholars until recently. On foreign policy there are the wartime volumes of the Survey of International Affairs (196), Langer and Gleason's book about the early part of the war from the U. S. side (143), a history by Herbert Feis (90), and a study of the Combined Boards (194). On Commonwealth and Colonial policy, where the wartime change in direction was so marked, there are few books (87, 157, 244), the one with the clearest perspective being Margery Perham's (180); but Mansergh's book of documents is also important (157a). The government's postwar reconstruction policy has never been studied as a whole. There are short sections in some of the official histories (e.g. 112, 200, 232) and in the life of Keynes (114), while the various textbooks on the welfare state discuss the social aspects (e.g. 323, 324). But anyone interested needs to study the primary material, especially the contemporary publications such as Beveridge's book on full employment (18a) and the government documents noted under sub-section iv below.

On the machinery of government there is nothing devoted solely to Second World War developments and their influence, but *Lessons of the British War Economy* (49) and the official histories are useful. Many of the modern textbooks on British government barely mention the war but some pay a little more attention to it (40, 42, 75, 133, 168, 210); F. M. G. Willson's book has perhaps the most (245). The "New Whitehall Series," which consists of books on individual government departments, also covers the war in varying degrees (318). The lectures by Sir John Anderson (6 and 6a) and John Ehrman (86) should be read. There seems to be no study at all of the functioning and the composition of the Civil Service although it performed better in the Second World War than ever before or since. A lecture by Oliver Franks (97) is illuminating, and Max Nicholson's recent criticism of the Civil Service (172) includes the war.

Studies of political life in wartime are also lacking, and there seems to be very little apart from the material in some of the biographies and memoirs listed above and a recent book by George Malcolm Thomson (325). *British Political Facts 1900–1960* (see Introductory chapter) gives factual information and there are books on the Labour Party (28, 57, 58), the Communist Party (179), and the Fascists (72); there is nothing on the Conservative or Liberal Parties, nor about the splinter movements of the Left, and the wartime bye-elections. The 1945 General Election was the subject of special study (149, 37). See also the many useful articles in the periodicals, *Public Administration* and *The Political Quarterly*.

(IV) PRIMARY SOURCES: The great bulk of the Cabinet and Departmental records for the whole war period are becoming available by 1972. For private manuscript collections see (259–   ). The most important single collection is that of Lord Cherwell (264), who had a vital role as Churchill's economic as well as scientific adviser. He was a law unto himself; he had all his official papers removed to Oxford at the change of government in 1945, and managed to keep nearly all of them. The bulk of his papers have been available to *bona fide* students for some years, yet very few people have used them: scholars can be slow to "nose out" a good find. Almost all the other manuscript sources listed are of "government policy" people, but they are mostly private papers; Ministers and officials other than Lord Cherwell apparently obeyed the rules.

Primary material on government policy, apart from files and manuscripts, consists of Parliamentary Debates and government publications (see introductory chapter and earlier notes in this chapter on the vast "sub-species" of government circulars, pamphlets, etc.). We would emphasize the usefulness of P. & G. Ford, *Breviate of Parliamentary Papers, 1940–1954* (see introductory chapter). The official histories also have copious references to government papers, some of which are reproduced in Le May's collection of documents (147). The Reports of the Select Committees of Parliament, especially those on national expenditure, are important while two regular government newspapers, *The Board of Trade Journal* and *The Ministry of Labour Gazette,* contain a great deal of detailed information.

In the penumbra of political life there are large sources of primary material in the form of pamphlets. Some of the outpouring was overtly partisan, for example the series of Gollancz books of which *Guilty Men* (44) (about quarter of a million copies sold) was most famous. Much of the flood concerned postwar aspirations, and researchers should study the pamphlets of the political parties. Apart from records at Party H.Q.'s, the I.W.M. and the Library of Nuffield College, Oxford, have big pamphlet collections.

We have so far been concerned with the central government. Local government is also important. Local authorities' rules on access to files are as, or more, stringent than those of the central government. But minutes of council meetings and of the main committees, including reports from officers, are usually available in local record offices. There are printed guides to most of the county record offices, but one of the snags is that smaller authorities do not have record offices. There is a great deal of untapped material in this whole area. The Historical Manuscripts Commission issues a list of record repositories (120) which includes the local record offices and many more besides.

What gaps remain in research into the field of government policy during the Second World War? Enough has been said to show that there are some very large holes. There is a great deal to be done on foreign policy, on Commonwealth and Colonial policy. There are plenty of smaller topics

within these big ones—for example, the extraordinarily successful Middle
East Supply Centre, or relief policy. In domestic policy there is the postwar
reconstruction planning, which began in one of the darkest periods of the
war, many aspects of education, the whole machinery of central government, the civil service and the development of local government in war.
There is information policy and security policy. Besides the many big subjects still left for research, myriads of smaller ones must suggest themselves
to any reader of the official histories.

THE IMPACT OF WAR ON BRITAIN. The second main subject division—the impact of the war on the life of the citizens and on institutions
—is so enormous, both in the subject sub-divisions and in the contemporary
literature, that this can be only a very broad guide to topics and to sources.
It is here that recourse to the indexes of the B.M. and the I.W.M. is essential. The Mass Observation and Social Surveys are invaluable, while
hundreds of people wrote about what the war meant to them—servicemen,
their wives, air raid wardens, firemen, nurses, newspaper reporters, merchant seamen, university dons, farmers' boys conscripted into the coal-
mines, teachers, munitions workers, village housewives, a London cook,
women indeed of every type and dwelling place. Many reached print, the
personal experiences of many others are lodged unprinted in the I.W.M.,
while still more must remain in private drawers. Child evacuees have recently recollected their experiences (329). Innumerable boroughs and
firms wrote with pride of their wartime achievements: again, some are
printed publicly, some privately, and the I.W.M. holds many of the latter
as well as of the former but again some are still held privately. In addition
to these accounts, there are the contemporary records and annual reports
of every conceivable kind of organisation—from the Chambers of Commerce to the National Council of Civil Liberties or the Central Board for
Conscientious Objectors. Again the I.W.M. holds many such reports, and
some local bodies have deposited war papers in their local record offices or
libraries. The annual returns of accessions to the National Register of
Archives published by the Historical Manuscripts Commission since 1955
are helpful here. But the bulk of this paper must still be in private hands.
Similarly every conceivable professional and technical journal for the war
years is full of information about wartime problems and achievements.
From such a multitude of experiences of individuals, organisations and
professions it is impossible to list specific items, for different research workers will be interested in different activities or different localities.

Of the events of the war in Britain, the best documented are the air raids
and their effects. We have already partly dealt with this in discussing government civil defense policy. For the effects of attack there are also the
volumes of the Stanford Research Institute on the impact of air attack in
World War II (219). There are other less technical books (e.g. 21, 60).
There are several records of the bombed buildings of Britain (e.g. 36, 190).
At the civil defense working level there are many records—instructions, reports, log books, handbooks, reminiscences. The I.W.M. has a great deal
of material, and some local libraries have log books of air raid wardens'

posts and fire guards [the Home Guard was under the Army, but see Graves's book (101)]. From the huge collection of books of contemporary experiences of the blitz and air raid precautions we have listed the reports of the U. S. correspondent, Ed Murrow (171), John Strachey's *Post D* (223), Ritchie Calder's *Carry on London* (39), and the war chapter of the autobiography of the poet, Stephen Spender (217). Many of the memoirs and biographies listed above also describe the blitz. Three novels, one by Elizabeth Bowen (25) and two by Graham Greene (103, 104) evoke the blitz particularly well. The precautions against German invasion are also well documented in contemporary material in the I.W.M. and in two books on the subject (93, 240). No other period of the war has called forth so much writing as 1940 and the blitz. E. S. Turner recently wrote a book about the first nine months of the war, the phoney war (233), but there is very little on the long hard slog from 1941 to the end.

Indeed great scope exists for a really probing study of economic and social life in this period and the longer term effects of the upheavals of war. There are many obvious themes. On the economic front there has been no re-consideration in the perspective of twenty years of the economic costs of the war. A. R. Conan's work (319) suggests the great need for revision of the picture accepted just after the war. Work also needs to be done on the impact of war on industry—on investment, innovation and management. Some clues are to be found in M. M. Postan's recent *Economic History of Western Europe 1945–1964* (183). There are the many wartime histories of individual firms already mentioned and some longer histories, for example of Vickers (203) and Courtaulds (337). There are also one or two memoirs or biographies of industrialists such as Lord Nuffield (8) and Sir Miles Thomas (230). There is very little on the trade unions apart from a book on the miners (9) and Lord Citrine's memoirs (316). At the end of the war a variety of industrial studies were made and these too will be helpful—the studies of the Social Reconstruction Survey (94, 208) and the reports of the Board of Trade Working Parties on various industries which were written in 1946–48. Unfortunately these reports only cover textiles and consumer goods industries. There is nothing on engineering, but there were additional especially important reports in 1944 and 1945 on the coal mining, cotton and gas industries (see the Fords' *Breviate of Parliamentary Papers* on the last three). D. L. Burns covers the steel industry in wartime (321). On the social side, themes lie hidden beneath the reports of the various ministries for the war years (see the Fords' *Breviate*), the figures of the Registrar General's *Statistical Review of England and Wales for the Years 1940–1945,* or in the figures for the mobilization of women or the numbers of foreign troops in Britain. There is, for example, no study of the effects of the war, long-term and short-term, on women. (If anyone pursues this they will find a specialist library, the Fawcett Library, at 27 Wilfred Street, London, S.W.1. and a rich but neglected source material in the wartime volumes of the women's magazines.) There is virtually no history at all on the impact of Commonwealth and foreign, especially American, troops in Britain. One or two books about international mingling in Britain are listed (41, 159, 162. See also 307).

Another theme of social history that has been neglected is the effect of the war on "culture," broadly interpreted. Several works by men of learning and literature are relevant: the autobiographies of Bertrand Russell (334), Leonald Woolf (335), Compton Mackenzie (336) and John Lehmann (145) and the collected essays, letters and journals of George Orwell (326). There was a remarkable upsurge in attention to matters of the intellect during the war. The Army had a lively Bureau of Current Affairs (ABCA pamphlets are in the I.W.M.). State patronage of the arts crept in through the Council for the Encouragement of Music and the Arts (CEMA). This story is told in the annual reports of the Pilgrim Trust for 1940–42, in two CEMA reports, one for 1942–43 and one for 1944, and in a book, *The Arts in England* (88). See, too, the biography of Keynes (114) and Thomas Jones's *Diary* (136). Artists were commissioned to paint the war, as in the First World War, and a splendid collection resulted. It is catalogued by the I.W.M. (128). There was some superb theatre in London in the later war years, but the dramatic fare of the troops was not on the same level (77). Writing flourished. Poets were perhaps less eloquent than in the First World War—there is an anthology of World War II poetry (109) and those interested can work outwards from there. A. P. Herbert produced topical jingles (118, 119). Literary periodicals were good—see especially *Horizon* and *Our Time. New Writing,* edited by John Lehmann, appeared in book form regularly (146). A very small sample of the novels with a war background might include Evelyn Waugh's *Put Out More Flags* and *Sword of Honour* (235, 236), two of Anthony Powell's big series (184, 185), Norman Collins' *London Belongs to Me* (61), two by Henry Williamson (243, 243a), one by Muriel Spark (214), the wartime volumes of C. P. Snow's series (211, 212, 213), a novel by William Cooper (64), and an Angus Wilson novel (246) and a short story (246a). Readers who are sceptical about the lowering of class barriers in wartime might find confirmation in the novels of a popular writer of the time, Angela Thirkell.

At the receiving end, there was an immense wartime thirst for print. For example G. M. Trevelyan's *English Social History* appeared in 1944 and immediately sold like a best-selling novel. Publishers launched (and sold) series on all kinds of topical affairs. This was not just because there was nothing else to do in the blackout. An important part of the war was the serious-minded aspiration of people at large for a better world in specific terms. The 1940 broadcasts of J. B. Priestley, mostly published in *The Listener,* the Beveridge Report and the reconstruction speeches of Herbert Morrison had very great influence and should be studied.

How significant is all this after a quarter of a century? Here is the theme above all which needs to be pursued by historians. How did the economic costs and benefits of the war turn out? What was the long term effect of the war on society, on the small children of wartime who are now adults, on the class structure? What was the cost of victory in terms of international power? *Was* the war an incident or a watershed in British History?

BIBLIOGRAPHY

PRINTED WORKS

Places of publication are not always given for university press books unless different from university name. "Official Civil Series" denotes a volume in the series *History of the Second World War, United Kingdom Civil Series,* edited by Sir Keith Hancock. H.M.S.O. designates Her (or His) Majesty's Stationary Office. Square brackets are used for authors' names when supplied from other than the publication cited.

1. Abel-Smith, Brian. *A History of the Nursing Profession.* London: Heinemann, 1960.
2. Abel-Smith, Brian. *The Hospitals, 1800–1948.* London: Heinemann, 1964.
3. Adam, Colin F. *Life of Lord Lloyd.* London: Macmillan, 1948.
4. Allen, V. L. *Trade Unions and the Government.* London: Longmans, 1960.
5. Amery, L. S. *My Political Life.* Vol. 3., *The Unforgiving Years, 1929–1940.* London: Hutchinson, 1955.
6. Anderson, Sir John [Viscount Waverley]. *The Machinery of Government.* London: Oxford University Press, 1946.
6a. Anderson, Sir John [Viscount Waverley]. *The Organisation of Economic Studies in Relation to the Problems of Government.* (Stamp Memorial Lecture, 1947.) London: Oxford University Press, 1947.
7. Andrews, Linton. *Linton Andrews.* London: Benn, 1964.
8. Andrews, P. W. S. and E. Brunner. *The Life of Lord Nuffield.* Oxford: Blackwell, 1955.
9. Arnot, R. Page. *The Miners in Crisis and War.* London: Allen and Unwin, 1961.
10. Ashworth, W. *Contracts and Finance* (Official Civil Series). H.M.S.O., 1953.
11. Attlee, C. R. *As It Happened.* London: Heinemann, 1954.
12. Avon, the Earl of [Anthony Eden]. *The Eden Memoirs.* Vol. 2, *The Reckoning.* London: Cassell, 1965.
13. Beaton, Cecil. *Time Exposure.* London: Batsford, 1941.
14. Beaton, Cecil. *The Years Between: diaries 1939–44.* London: Weidenfeld and Nicolson, 1965.
15. Behrens, C. B. A. *Merchant Shipping and the Demands of War* (Official Civil Series). H.M.S.O., 1955.
16. Bentwich, Norman. *I Understand the Risks.* London: Gollancz, 1950.
17. Beveridge, Janet. *Beveridge and His Plan.* London: Hodder and Stoughton, 1954.
18. Beveridge, Lord [Sir William]. *Power and Influence.* London: Hodder and Stoughton, 1953.

18a. Beveridge, Lord [Sir William]. *Full Employment in a Free Society*. London: Allen and Unwin, 1944.

19. Birkenhead, the Earl of. *Halifax, the Life of Lord Halifax*. London: Hamish Hamilton, 1965.

20. Birkenhead, the Earl of. *The Prof in Two Worlds; The Official Life of Professor F. A. Lindemann, Viscount Cherwell*. London: Collins, 1961.

21. Bishop, E. *The Battle of Britain*. London: Allen and Unwin, 1960.

22. Blackburn, Fred. *George Tomlinson*. London: Heinemann, 1954.

23. Blake, J. W. *Northern Ireland in World War II*. H.M.S.O., Belfast, 1956.

24. Boothby, Robert. *I Fight to Live*. London: Gollancz, 1947.

25. Bowen, Elizabeth. *The Heat of the Day*. London: Cape, 1949.

26. Bowley, Marion. *Housing and the State, 1919–1944*. London: Allen and Unwin, 1945.

27. Boyle, Andrew. *Montagu Norman*. London: Cassell, 1967.

28. Brand, Carl F. *The British Labour Party, a short history*. Stanford University Press; Oxford University Press, 1965.

29. Briggs, Asa. *Seebohm Rowntree, 1871–1954*. London: Longmans, 1961.

30. British Museum. *Subject Index of Modern Books*. 1936–1940 out of print; 1941–1945 pub. 1953 at 8vo. £8.8s; 1946–1950 in 4 vols. pub. 1961 at £24; 1956–1960 in 6 vols. pub. 1966 at £60; 1951–1955 in preparation.

31. Brittain, Vera. *Pethick-Lawrence, A Portrait*. London: Allen and Unwin, 1963.

32. Brockway, Fenner. *Outside the Right*. London: Allen and Unwin, 1963.

33. Brown, A. J. *The Great Inflation, 1939–51*. London: Oxford University Press, 1955.

34. Bruce-Lockhart, Robert. *Comes The Reckoning*. London: Putnam, 1947.

35. Bullock, Alan. *The Life and Times of Ernest Bevin*. Vol. 2, *Minister of Labour, 1940–1945*. London: Heinemann, 1967.

36. Butler, A. S. G. *Recording Ruin*. London: Constable, 1942.

37. Butler, D. E. *The Electoral System in Great Britain since 1918*. 2nd ed. London: Oxford University Press, 1963.

38. Butler, J. R. M. *Lord Lothian (Philip Kerr) 1882–1940*. London: Macmillan, 1960.

39. Calder, Ritchie. *Carry on London*. London: English Universities Press, 1941.

40. Campion, Sir Gilbert and others. *British Government since 1918*. London: Allen and Unwin, 1950.

41. Canadian Department of National Defense. *The Canadians in Britain, 1939–1944*. Ottawa: King's Printer, 1945.

42. Carter, Byrum E. *The Office of Prime Minister*. London: Faber, 1956.

43. Casey, Lord. *Personal Experience, 1939–46.* London: Constable, 1962.
44. "Cato" [M. Foot, F. Owen and P. Howard]. *Guilty Men.* London: Gollancz, 1940.
45. Cazalet-Keir, Thelma. *From The Wings.* London: Bodley Head, 1967.
46. Central Statistical Office. *Statistical Digest of the War* (Official Civil Series). H.M.S.O., 1951.
47. Chandos, Lord [Oliver Lyttelton]. *The Memoirs of Lord Chandos.* London: Bodley Head, 1962.
48. Channon, Sir Henry. *Chips: the diaries of Sir Henry Channon.* London: Weidenfeld and Nicolson, 1967.
49. Chester, D. N., ed. *Lessons of the British War Economy.* Cambridge: Cambridge University Press, 1951.
50. Christiansen, Arthur. *Headlines All My Life.* London: Heinemann, 1961.
51. Churchill, Winston S. *The Second World War.* Vols. II–VI. London: Cassell, 1949–1954.
52. Churchill, Winston S., compiled by Charles Eade. *War Speeches.* London: Cassell, 1951. 3 vols.
53. Churchill, Winston S., compiled by Charles Eade. *Secret Session Speeches.* London: Cassell, 1946.
54. Citrine, Lord. *Men and Work.* London: Hutchinson, 1964.
55. Clay, Henry. *Lord Norman.* London: Macmillan, 1957.
56. Cockburn, Claud. *I Claud.* London: Penguin Books, 1967.
57. Cole, G. D. H. *A History of the Labour Party from 1914.* Routledge, Kegan Paul, 1948.
58. Cole, G. D. H. *A Short History of the British Working-Class Movement, 1789–1947.* 3rd ed. London: Allen and Unwin, 1948.
59. Collier, Basil. *The Defence of the United Kingdom* (Official Military Series). H.M.S.O., 1957.
60. Collier, Richard. *The City that Wouldn't Die.* London: Collins, 1959.
61. Collins, Norman. *London Belongs to Me.* London: Collins, 1945.
62. Cooke, Colin. *The Life of Richard Stafford Cripps.* London: Hodder and Stoughton, 1957.
63. Cooper, Diana. *Trumpets from the Steep.* London: Hart-Davis, 1960.
64. Cooper, William. *The Struggles of Albert Woods.* London: Cape, 1952.
65. Coote, Colin C. *A Companion of Honour: the story of Walter Elliot.* London: Collins, 1965.
66. Coote, Colin C. *Editorial: memoirs.* London: Eyre and Spottiswoode, 1965.
67. Coupland, R. *Indian Politics, 1936–1942.* Oxford: Oxford University Press, 1943.
68. Coupland, R. *The Cripps Mission.* Oxford: Oxford University Press, 1942.

69. Coupland, R. *India: a restatement.* Oxford: Oxford University Press, 1945.
70. Court, W. H. B. *Coal* (Official Civil Series). H.M.S.O., 1951.
71. Croft, Lord [Sir Henry Page-Croft]. *My Life of Strife.* London: Hutchinson, [1948].
72. Cross, Colin. *The Fascists in Britain.* London: Barrie and Rockcliff, 1961.
73. Cudlipp, Hugh. *Publish and Be Damned: the astonishing story of the Daily Mirror.* London: Andrew Dakers, 1953.
74. Curtis, S. J. *History of Education in Great Britain.* 6th ed. London: University Tutorial Press, 1965.
75. Daalder, Hans. *Cabinet Reform in Britain, 1914–1963.* Stanford: Stanford University Press, 1964.
76. Dalton, Hugh. *The Fateful Years, Memoirs 1931–1945.* London: Muller, 1957.
77. Dean, Basil. *The Theatre at War.* London: Harrap, 1956.
78. Deane, Herbert A. *The Political Ideas of Harold J. Laski.* New York: Columbia University Press, 1955.
79. Dent, H. C. *Education in Transition, 1939–43.* London: Kegan Paul, 1944.
80. Devons, E. *Planning in Practice: essays in aircraft planning in wartime.* London: Cambridge University Press, 1950.
81. Domvile, Barry. *From Admiral to Cabin Boy.* London: Boswell Publishing Co., 1947.
82. Dow, J. C. R. *The Management of the British Economy, 1945–1960.* Cambridge: Cambridge University Press, 1964.
83. Driberg, Tom. *Beaverbrook, A Study in Power and Frustration.* London: Weidenfeld and Nicolson, 1956.
84. Edelman, Maurice. *The Mirror, A Political History.* London: Hamish Hamilton, 1966.
85. Edwardes, M. *The Last Years of British India.* London: Cassell, 1963.
86. Ehrman, John. *Cabinet Government and War, 1890–1940.* Cambridge: Cambridge University Press, 1958.
87. Elliott, W. Y. and H. Duncan Hall. *The British Commonwealth at War.* New York: Knopf, 1943.
88. Evans, B. Ifor and Mary Glasgow. *The Arts in England.* London: Falcon Press, 1949.
89. Feiling, Keith. *The Life of Neville Chamberlain.* London: Macmillan, 1946.
90. Feis, Herbert. *Churchill, Roosevelt and Stalin: the war they waged and the peace they sought.* Princeton: Princeton University Press, 1957.
91. Ferguson, S. M. and H. Fitzgerald. *Studies in the Social Services* (Official Civil Series). H.M.S.O., 1954.
92. Flanders, Allan and H. A. Clegg, ed. *The System of Industrial Relations in Great Britain.* Oxford: Blackwell, 1961.
93. Fleming, Peter. *Invasion 1940.* London: Hart-Davis, 1957.

94. Fogarty, M. P., ed. *Further Studies in Industrial Organisation*. London: Methuen, 1948.
95. Foot, Michael. *Aneurin Bevan*. Vol. 1. London: MacGibbon and Kee, 1962. See also "Cato."
96. Franks, Oliver. *Central Planning and Control in War and Peace*. London: Longmans, 1947.
97. Franks, Oliver. *The Experience of a University Teacher in the Civil Service*. Oxford: Oxford University Press, 1947.
98. Fraser, Lionel. *All to the Good*. London: Heinemann, 1963.
99. de Gaulle, Charles. *War Memoirs*. Vol. 1, Collins, 1955; Vol. II, Weidenfeld and Nicolson, 1959. Each with separate volume of documents.
100. Gowing, Margaret. *Britain and Atomic Energy, 1939–45*. London: Macmillan, 1964.
101. Graves, Charles. *The Home Guard of Britain*. London: Hutchinson, 1943.
102. Graves, Charles. *Women in Green: the story of the W.V.S.* London: Heinemann, 1948.
103. Greene, Graham. *The End of the Affair*. London: Heinemann, 1951.
104. Greene, Graham. *The Ministry of Fear*. London: Heinemann, 1943.
105. Grigg, P. J. *Prejudice and Judgment*. London: Cape, 1948.
106. Halifax, Earl of. *Fulness of Days*. London: Collins, 1957.
107. Hall, H. Duncan. *North American Supply* (Official Civil Series). H.M.S.O., 1955.
108. Hall, H. Duncan and C. C. Wrigley. *Studies of Overseas Supply* (Official Civil Series). H.M.S.O., 1956.
109. Hamilton, Ian, ed. *The Poetry of War, 1939–45*. London: Alan Ross, 1965.
110. Hammond, R. J. *Food* (Official Civil Series). H.M.S.O., 1951, 1956 and 1962. 3 vols.
111. Hammond, R. J. *Food and Agriculture in Britain, 1939–45; Aspects of Wartime Control*. Stanford: Stanford University Press, 1954.
112. Hancock, W. K. and M. M. Gowing. *British War Economy* (Official Civil Series). 2nd impression with amendments. H.M.S.O., 1953.
113. Hargreaves, E. L. and M. M. Gowing. *Civil Industry and Trade* (Official Civil Series). H.M.S.O., 1952.
114. Harrod, R. F. *The Life of John Maynard Keynes*. London: Macmillan, 1951.
115. Hayes, Denis. *Challenge of Conscience, The Story of the Conscientious Objectors of 1939–1949*. London: Allen and Unwin, 1949.
116. Henderson, Hubert D. (Henry Clay, ed.). *The Inter-War Years and Other Papers*. Oxford: Oxford University Press, 1955.
117. Herbert, A. P. *Independent Member*. London: Methuen, 1950.
118. Herbert, A. P. *Let Us be Glum*. London: Methuen, 1941.
119. Herbert, A. P. *Light the Lights*. London: Methuen, 1945.

120. Historical Manuscripts Commission. *Record Repositories in Great Britain.* 2nd ed. H.M.S.O., 1966.

121. Hoare, Sir Samuel [Viscount Templewood]. *Ambassador on Special Mission.* London: Collins, 1946. See also Templewood, Viscount (229).

122. Hornby, W. C. *Factories and Plant* (Official Civil Series). H.M.S.O., 1958.

123. Hull, Cordell. *Memoirs of Cordell Hull.* New York: Macmillan, 1948; London: Hodder and Stoughton, 1948.

124. Hurstfield, J. *The Control of Raw Materials* (Official Civil Series). H.M.S.O., 1953.

125. Hutchinson, Walter, ed. *Hutchinson's Pictorial History of the War.* London: Hutchinson, [1939–45]. 15 vols.

126. Huxley, Gervas. *Lady Denman, G.B.E.* London: Chatto & Windus, 1961.

127. Hyams, Edward. *The New Statesman: the history of the first fifty years, 1913–1963.* London: Longmans, 1963.

128. Imperial War Museum. *Catalogue of Paintings, Drawings and Sculpture of the Second World War.* 2nd ed. H.M.S.O., 1964.

129. Inman, P. *Labour in Munition Industries* (Official Civil Series). H.M.S.O., 1957.

130. Iremonger, F. A. *William Temple, Archbishop of Canterbury.* Oxford: Oxford University Press, 1948.

131. Jasper, Ronald C. D. *George Bell, Bishop of Chichester.* Oxford: Oxford University Press, 1967.

132. Jenkins, Roy. *Mr. Attlee, An Interim Biography.* London: Heinemann, 1948.

133. Jennings, Ivor. *Cabinet Government.* 3rd ed. Cambridge: Cambridge University Press, 1961.

134. Jewkes, John. *Ordeal by Planning.* London: Macmillan, 1948.

135. Johnston, Thomas. *Memories.* London: Collins, 1952.

136. Jones, Thomas. *Diary with Letters.* Oxford: Oxford University Press, 1954.

137. Keynes, J. M. *How to Pay for the War.* London: Macmillan, 1940.

138. Kilmuir, the Earl of. *Political Adventure, Memoirs.* London: Weidenfeld and Nicolson, 1964.

139. Kirkpatrick, Ivone. *The Inner Circle: memoirs.* London: Macmillan, 1959.

140. Knowles, K. G. J. C. *Strikes: a study in industrial conflict.* Oxford: Blackwell, 1952.

141. Kohan, C. M. *Works and Buildings* (Official Civil Series). H.M.S.O., 1952.

142. Lafitte, F. *The Internment of Aliens.* London: Penguin Books, 1940.

143. Langer, W. L. and S. E. Gleason. *The Undeclared War 1940–41.* Oxford: Oxford University Press, 1953.

144. Lee, Jennie. *This Great Journey: a volume of autobiography, 1904–1945.* London: MacGibbon and Kee, 1963.

144a. Lehigh University—see Stanford Research Institute.

145. Lehmann, John. *I Am My Brother: autobiography II*. London: Longmans, 1960.
146. Lehmann, John, ed. *New Writing* (1936–39, continued as *Folios of New Writing*, 1940–41, and *New Writing and Daylight*, 1942–1946). All the wartime volumes published by Hogarth Press.
147. Le May, G. H. L. *British Government, 1914–1953: select documents*. London: Methuen, 1955.
148. Lockhart, J. G. *Cosmo Gordon Lang*. London: Hodder and Stoughton, 1949.
149. McCallum, R. B., and A. Readman. *The British General Election of 1945*. Oxford: Oxford University Press, 1947.
150. Macdonald, D. F. *The State and the Trade Unions*. London: Macmillan, 1960.
151. Mackintosh, James M. *The War and Mental Health in England*. New York: The Commonwealth Fund, 1944.
152. Macleod, Iain. *Neville Chamberlain*. London: Muller, 1961.
153. Macmillan, Harold. *The Blast of War, 1939–1945*. London: Macmillan, 1967.
154. Madge, Charles. *The War-time Pattern of Saving and Spending*. Cambridge: Cambridge University Press, 1943.
155. Maisky, Ivan. *Memoirs of a Soviet Ambassador*. London: Hutchinson, 1967.
156. Mallaby, George. *From My Level: unwritten minutes*. London: Hutchinson, 1965.
157. Mansergh, Nicholas. *Problems of Wartime Co-operation and Postwar Change, 1939–1952* (Survey of British Commonwealth Affairs, Royal Institute of International Affairs). Oxford: Oxford University Press, 1958.
157a. Mansergh, Nicholas, ed. *Documents and Speeches on British Commonwealth Affairs, 1931–1952*. (Royal Institute of International Affairs.) Oxford: Oxford University Press, 1952.
157b. Mansergh, Nicholas and E. W. R. Lumby, eds. *Documents on the Transfer of Power in India, 1942–1947*. Vol. I, H.M.S.O., 1970.
158. Martin, Kingsley. *Harold Laski*. London: Gollancz, 1953.
158a. Martin, Kingsley. *Editor*. London: Hutchinson, 1968.
159. Mead, Margaret. *The American Troops and the British Community*. London: Hutchinson [1944].
160. Meade, J. E. *Planning and the Price Mechanism*. London: Allen and Unwin, 1948.
161. Medlicott, W. N. *Economic Blockade* (Official Civil Series). H.M.S.O., 1952, 1959. 2 vols.
162. Mengin, Robert. *De Gaulle à Londres*. Paris: Editions de la Table Ronde, 1965. English trans., *No Laurels for de Gaulle*. Michael Joseph, 1967.
163. Menon, V. P. *The Transfer of Power in India*. London: Longmans, 1957.
164. Minney, R. J. *The Private Papers of Hore-Belisha*. London: Collins, 1960.

165. Minney, R. J. *Viscount Addison.* London: Odhams, 1958.
166. Moran, Lord. *Winston Churchill: the struggle for survival, 1940–1965.* London: Constable, 1966.
167. [Morison, Stanley.] *The History of The Times, 1912–1948.* Vol. IV, Part II. The Times, 1952.
168. Morrison of Lambeth, Lord. *Government and Parliament: a survey from the inside.* Paperback ed. Oxford University Press, 1964.
169. Morrison of Lambeth, Lord. *Herbert Morrison: an autobiography.* London: Odhams, 1960.
170. Murray, K. A. H. *Agriculture (Official Civil Series).* H.M.S.O., 1955.
171. Murrow, Ed. *This is London.* London: Cassell, 1941.
172. Nicholson, Max. *The System: the misgovernment of modern Britain.* London: Hodder & Stoughton, 1967.
173. Nicolson, Harold (ed. Nigel Nicolson). *Diaries and Letters, 1939–1945.* London: Collins, 1967.
174. Norwich, Viscount. *Old Men Forget: the autobiography of Duff Cooper,* London: Hart-Davis, 1954.
175. O'Brien, T. H. *Civil Defence (Official Civil Series).* H.M.S.O., 1955.
176. Orr, John Boyd. *As I Recall.* London: MacGibbon and Kee, 1966.
177. Oxford University Institute of Statistics. *Studies in War Economics.* Oxford: Blackwell, 1947.
178. Parker, H. M. D. *Manpower (Official Civil Series).* H.M.S.O., 1957.
179. Pelling, H. M. *The Communist Party.* London: A. & C. Black, 1958.
180. Perham, Margery. *Colonial Sequence, 1930–1949.* London: Methuen, 1967.
181. Postan, M. M. *British War Production (Official Civil Series).* H.M.S.O., 1952.
182. Postan, M. M., D. Hay and J. D. Scott. *Design and Development of Weapons (Official Civil Series).* H.M.S.O., 1964.
183. Postan, M. M. *An Economic History of Western Europe, 1945–1964.* London: Methuen, 1967.
184. Powell, Anthony. *The Kindly Ones.* London: Heinemann, 1962.
185. Powell, Anthony. *The Valley of Bones.* London: Heinemann, 1964.
186. Pritt, D. N. *Autobiography of D. N. Pritt.* Parts 1 and 2. London: Lawrence and Wishart, 1965 and 1966.
187. Raczynski, Edward. *In Allied London.* London: Weidenfeld and Nicolson, 1962.
188. Reith, Lord. *Into the Wind.* London: Hodder and Stoughton, 1949.
189. Reynolds, Quentin. *Britain Can Take It.* London: John Murray, 1941.
190. Richards, J. M. *The Bombed Building of Britain.* 2nd ed. London: The Architectural Press, 1947.
191. Robbins, Lionel. *The Economic Problem in Peace and War.* London: Macmillan, 1947.
192. Roberts, B. C. *National Wages Policy in War and Peace.* London: Allen and Unwin, 1958.

193. Rodgers, W. T., *Hugh Gaitskell, 1906–1963*. London: Thames and Hudson, 1964.

194. Rosen, S. McKee. *The Combined Boards of the Second World War*, New York: Columbia University Press, 1951.

195. Ross, Alan. *The Forties: a period piece*. London: Weidenfeld and Nicolson, 1950.

196. Royal Institute of International Affairs. *Survey of International Affairs*. Wartime Series was ed. variously by A. J. Toynbee, F. T. Ashton-Gwatkin and V. M. Boulter. 11 vols. published 1952–1958, Oxford University Press. Also *Documents on International Affairs, 1939–46*, Oxford University Press, 1956. See also Mansergh, Nicholas.

197. Salter, Lord [Sir Arthur]. *Memoirs of a Public Servant*. London: Faber, 1961.

197a. Salter, Lord [Sir Arthur]. *Slave of the Lamp*. London: Weidenfeld and Nicolson, 1967.

198. Samuel, Viscount. *Memoirs*. London: Cresset Press, 1945.

199. Savage, C. I. *Inland Transport* (Official Civil Series). H.M.S.O., 1957.

200. Sayers, R. S. *Financial Policy* (Official Civil Series). H.M.S.O., 1956.

201. Scott, Harold. *Your Obedient Servant*. London: Andre Deutsch, 1959.

202. Scott, J. D. and Richard Hughes. *Administration of War Production* (Official Civil Series). H.M.S.O., 1955.

203. Scott, J. D. *Vickers, a history*. London: Weidenfeld and Nicolson, 1962.

204. Seers, D. *The Levelling of Incomes since 1938*. Oxford: Blackwell, 1951.

205. Sherwood, Robert. *The White House Papers of Harry Hopkins: an intimate history*. London: Eyre and Spottiswoode, 1948. 2 vols.

206. Shinwell, Emanuel. *Conflict without Malice*. London: Odhams, 1955.

207. Shirras, G. F., and L. Rostas. *The Burden of British Taxation*. Cambridge University Press, 1942.

208. Silverman, H. A., ed. *Studies in Industrial Organization*. London: Methuen, 1946.

209. Simon, Viscount. *Retrospect*. London: Hutchinson. 1952.

210. Smellie, K. B. *A History of Local Government*. 3rd ed. London: Allen and Unwin, 1958.

211. Snow, C. P. *The New Men*. London: Macmillan, 1954.

212. Snow, C. P. *Homecomings*. London: Macmillan, 1956.

213. Snow, C. P. *The Light and the Dark*. London: Faber, 1947.

214. Spark, Muriel. *The Girls of Slender Means*. London: Macmillan, 1963.

215. Sparrow, Gerald. *"R.A.B." The Career of Baron Butler of Saffron Walden*. London: Odhams, 1965.

216. Spears, Edward. *Assignment to Catastrophe*. London: Heinemann, 1954. 2 vols.
217. Spender, Stephen. *World within World*. London: Hamish Hamilton, 1951.
218. Stalin, J. V. *Stalin's Correspondence with Churchill, Attlee, Roosevelt and Truman, 1941–45*. London: Lawrence & Wishart, 1958. English ed. in 1 vol.
219. Stanford Research Institute. *Impact of Air Attack in World War II: selected data for civil defense planning*.
Division I. Physical Damage to Structures, Facilities and Persons.
Division II. Effects on the General Economy.
Division III. Social organisation, Behavior and Morale under Stress of Bombing.
Division I, Lehigh University, Bethlehem, Pa., 1953.
Divisions II & III, Stanford Research Institute, 1953.
220. Stettinius, Edward R., Jr. *Lend-Lease, Weapon for Victory*. New York and London: Macmillan, 1944.
221. Stimson, Henry L. and McGeorge Bundy. *On Active Service in Peace and War*. New York: Harper, 1948; London: Hutchinson, 1949.
222. Stocks, Mary. *Eleanor Rathbone*. London: Gollancz, 1949.
223. Strachey, John. *Post D*. London: Gollancz, 1941.
224. Summerskill, Lady. *A Woman's World*. London: Heinemann, 1967.
225. Swinton, Viscount. *I Remember*. London: Hutchinson, 1948.
226. Swinton, the Earl of [Viscount]. *Sixty Years of Power*. London: Hutchinson, 1966.
227. Tabori, Pal. *20 Tremendous Years, World War II and After*. London: Oldbourne [1961].
228. Taylor, A. J. P. *English History, 1914–1945*. Oxford University Press, 1965.
229. Templewood, Viscount [Sir Samuel Hoare]. *Nine Troubled Years*. London: Collins, 1954.
230. Thomas, Miles. *Out on a Wing*. London: Michael Joseph, 1964.
231. Thurtle, Ernest. *Time's Winged Chariot*. London: Chaterson, 1945.
232. Titmuss, R. M. *Problems of Social Policy* (Official Civil Series). H.M.S.O., 1950.
233. Turner, E. S. *The Phoney War on the Home Front*. London: Michael Joseph, 1961.
234. Watt, D. C. *Personalities and Policies*. London: Longmans, 1965.
235. Waugh, Evelyn. *Put Out More Flags*. London: Chapman and Hall, 1942.
236. Waugh, Evelyn. *Sword of Honour* (The wartime trilogy, comprising *Men at Arms, Officers & Gentlemen*, and *Unconditional Surrender*). London: Chapman and Hall, 1965. In one volume.
237. Wedgwood, C. V. *The Last of the Radicals*. London: Cape, 1951.
238. Wedgwood, Josiah. *Memoirs of a Fighting Life*. London: Hutchinson [1941].

239. Weir, Cecil M. *Civilian Assignment.* London: Methuen, 1953.
240. Wheatley, R. R. A. *Operation Sealion: German plans for the invasion of England, 1939–1942.* Oxford University Press, 1958.
241. Wheeler-Bennett, John W. *King George VI: his life and reign.* London: Macmillan, 1958.
242. Wheeler-Bennett, John W. *John Anderson, Viscount Waverley.* London: Macmillan, 1962.
243. Williamson, Henry. *A Solitary War.* London: Macdonald, 1967.
243a. Williamson, Henry. *Lucifer Before Sunrise.* London: Macdonald, 1967.
244. Williamson, James, A. *A Short History of British Expansion.* London: Macmillan, 1964.
245. Willson, F. M. G. (ed. D. N. Chester). *The Organisation of British Central Government, 1914–1956.* London: Allen and Unwin, 1957.
246. Wilson, Angus. "Christmas Day in the Workhouse" from *Such Darling Dodos.* London: Secker and Warburg, 1954.
246a. Wilson, Angus. *No Laughing Matter.* London: Secker and Warburg, 1967.
247. Winant, John C. *A Letter from Grosvenor Square.* London: Hodder and Stroughton, 1947.
248. Winterton, Earl. *Orders of the Day.* London: Cassell, 1953.
249. Woodward, Llewellyn. *British Foreign Policy in the Second World War,* (Official War History). H.M.S.O., 1962.
249a. Woodward, Llewellyn. *British Foreign Policy in the Second World War.* Vol. I. *September 1939–June 1941.* (Official War History.) H.M.S.O., 1970.
250. Woolton, the Earl of. *Memoirs.* London: Cassell, 1959.
251. Worswick, G. D. N. and P. Ady, ed. *The British Economy, 1945–1950.* Oxford University Press, 1952.
252. Wrench, John Evelyn. *Geoffrey Dawson and Our Times.* London: Hutchinson, 1955.
253. Young, Kenneth. *Churchill and Beaverbrook.* London: Eyre and Spottiswoode, 1966.

ARTICLES REFERRED TO

254. Allen, R. G. D. "Mutual Aid between the U.S. and the British Empire." *Journal of the Royal Statistical Society,* Part III, 1946. This is reprinted in R. S. Sayers, *Financial Policy* but without the discussion.
255. Ayre, Sir Amos. "Merchant Shipbuilding during the War." *Proceedings of the Institution of Naval Architects,* 1945.
256. Kirk, J. H. "Output of British Agriculture during the War." *Proceedings of the Agricultural Economics Society.* June, 1946.
257. Hurcomb, Sir Cyril. "The Coordination of Transport in Great Britain during the years 1935–1944." *Journal of the Institute of Transport,* Vol. 22, No. 3.

258. Wolf, K. M. "Evacuation of Children in Wartime: a survey of the literature." *The Psychoanalytic Study of the Child,* Vol. 1, 1945.

LIST OF MANUSCRIPT SOURCES. On the assumption that many of the people in positions of power and influence in Government in the Second World War and many people who were engaged in political life had some residue of papers, there must be large numbers of such collections. It is clearly impossible to identify all these, and this list is confined primarily to papers which have already been consigned to a place of deposit. For other papers there is plenty of room for researchers' individual approaches to the persons concerned or their families. Listed are all deposits which may conceivably be of interest, but in most cases the contents of the collection are not known; often the collections are still unsorted.

The contemporary papers of those not in Government or politics must be enormous; this group, after all, covers millions of individuals, firms and associations of different kinds. A note about places of deposit for such papers is included in the text. In the following list a few collections of non-political papers are noted, but these are mainly those of figures in the literary world.

Permission for access to the papers listed below should be addressed to the Librarian of the Institution of deposit unless otherwise stated. None of these papers are on open shelves, and terms of access vary from fairly free access for *bona fide* scholars to very restricted or partial access or access only at some date in the future. In some cases details are given, but in other cases researchers will have to apply to the Librarian for up-to-date information. Notes about spheres of interest are only given for less well-known people.

Three depositories specialise in the government political papers with which this chapter is concerned—Churchill College, Cambridge, Nuffield College, Oxford, and the British Library of Political and Economic Science at the London School of Economics, Houghton Street, London, W.C.2. Two other manuscript deposits should be mentioned. The Oxford Colonial Records Project, under the aegis of the Institute of Commonwealth Studies of Oxford University, collects papers of officers of the former Colonial Service and could have some relevance for the development of colonial policy in wartime, as seen in the field. The India Office Library, Orbit House, Blackfriars Road, London, S.E.1., has manuscript material relating to British policy (civil and military) in India.

CHURCHILL COLLEGE (apply Librarian) is setting out to acquire in particular papers of Winston Churchill's contemporaries in political, military and scientific life. On the political side it already has:

259. Lord Hankey's diaries, letters and papers, 1899–1963 (closed until the official biography finished).
260. Lord Vansittart's papers, 1933–1941.
261. Lord Lloyd's papers, letters and photographs, 1889–1940.
262. Earl Alexander of Hillsborough's papers (A. V. Alexander, wartime First Lord of Admiralty).

263. Ernest Bevin's papers.
Anyone contemplating research in this period should write to the Librarian at Churchill College for an up-to-date list of their collection, as the Archives are only just getting under way.

NUFFIELD COLLEGE (apply Librarian) holds Viscount Cherwell's papers. These are voluminous and, as noted in the text, extremely valuable. They are listed and divided into four categories:
264. (a) papers which can only be consulted with permission of the Cabinet Office.
  (b) and (c) papers which can only be consulted by persons willing to submit anything written on the basis of these papers to the Cabinet Office.
  (d) mainly personal rather than official papers, to be made available only to persons having a serious research interest.
Presumably the restrictions on (a), (b), (c) will be relaxed to accord with the opening of papers in the Public Record Office.
265. Henry Clay's papers. He was concerned with the Bank of England, wartime financial policy and wartime Board of Trade reconstruction policy.
266. G. D. H. Cole's papers—some political papers and papers useful for a study of wartime reconstruction policy.
267. Stafford Cripps's papers. Part received, others still to come. Lady Cripps's permission is needed in order to consult them.
268. Lord Gainford's papers [J. E. Pease] (general political interest).
269. Hubert Henderson's papers (wartime Treasury adviser).
270. Lord Morrison of Lambeth's personal papers.
271. Viscount Nuffield. A very few personal papers.
272. Lord Rennell's papers (general political).
273. Fabian Society records. Not yet sorted or catalogued but where possible available to research workers.

BRITISH LIBRARY OF POLITICAL AND ECONOMIC SCIENCE (apply to Librarian) holds:
274. Lord Beveridge's papers. A very large collection covering all his activities.
275. Hugh Dalton's papers. No list. Diaries are complete and full. Some files.
276. George Lansbury's papers. Some letters cover the period from the outbreak of war to his death on 7th May 1940.
277. David Low's cartoons. A complete set.
278. Violet Markham's papers. (Wartime manpower.)
279. Passfield papers [Beatrice and Sidney Webb]. A large correspondence of political interest, and Beatrice Webb's diary which she kept until the day before her death on 30th April 1943. At present and possibly for some time all the correspondence is at Sheffield University where a scholar is working on them. Any inquires to the British Library of Political and Economic Science.

COLLECTIONS IN OTHER DEPOSITS

280. Winston Churchill's papers are owned by the Chartwell Trust except the papers which are public records. All his papers have been listed by the Public Record Office but are closed at present. Any applications to see them should be sent to J. A. McCracken, Esq., Fladgate & Co., 8 Waterloo Place, London, S.W.1.

281. Earl Attlee's papers (non-official). Some are in the Library of University College, Oxford, and some later ones in Churchill College, Cambridge.

282. Earl Baldwin's papers [Stanley Baldwin] are in the Library of Cambridge University, to be open in 1970.

283. Neville Chamberlain's papers (non-official). These are expected within the very near future (position at August 1967) in the University of Birmingham Library. When they have arrived there and been sorted and listed, they will be available to scholars.

284. F. O. Barnford's diary is in the British Museum. He was Secretary to the Director of Naval Construction.

285. Lord Beaverbrook's papers are in the Beaverbrook Library, London, which is under the supervision of A. J. P. Taylor, the historian. The papers are not at present (1967) open to researchers. The address of the Library is 33 St. Bride Street, London, E.C.4.

286. Viscount Cecil of Chelwood's papers [Lord Robert Cecil] are in the British Museum (general political interest). Application to see them should be made to the Marquess of Salisbury, Hatfield House, Hatfield, Hertfordshire.

287. Clement Davies' papers, an extensive collection of political and personal papers, are in process (August 1967) of being handed over to the National Library of Wales, Aberystwyth, Cardiganshire. Terms of deposit and conditions of access are not yet decided. Clement Davies was an M.P. and postwar Leader of the Liberal Party.

288. Geoffrey Dawson's papers are in the possession of *The Times* (his editorship extended into the war) but are inaccessible.

289. Chuter Ede's diaries are in the British Museum but are not open till 1976. He was a junior minister at the Board of Education in the war and his diaries are very important for the 1944 Education Act.

290. Viscount Elibank's papers are in the National Library for Scotland (general political interest).

291. H. A. L. Fisher's papers are in the Bodleian Library, Oxford (education, politics).

292. The first Earl of Halifax's personal papers are in the Archives of the Wood family at Garrowby, York. Microfilm of some of his official papers will in due course go to Churchill College, Cambridge. There is a detailed catalogue of the Archives, copies of which are at the British Museum, the National Register of Archives (at Historical Manuscripts Commission), York City Library and the East Riding

County Record Office, Beverley. Enquiries concerning the papers should be addressed to Major T. L. Ingram, 3 Darnley Terrace, London, W.11.

293. Sir Patrick Hannon's papers are in the Beaverbrook Library, London, on the same terms of access as those of Lloyd George (*q.v.*). He was an M.P. and a prominent industrialist.

294. Arthur Creech Jones's papers are to go to Rhodes House, Oxford. He was an M.P. especially concerned with colonial affairs (Secretary of State for Colonies after the war).

295. Lord Keynes's papers—an extensive collection—are in King's College, Cambridge, but contain none of his wartime official papers.

296. Harold Laski's correspondence with Benjamin Huebsch, U. S. publisher (twenty letters from Laski during 1939–45) are in the National Archives in Washington. Xerox copies in British Library of Political and Economic Science.

297. Earl Lloyd George's papers are in the Beaverbrook Library (see under Beaverbrook) and are open to readers without restriction. There are lists and indexes. They include some material on the Second World War, particularly about a compromise peace. Intending researchers (over 21 years of age) should write to the Librarian giving their particular subject of study. Except for those holding academic appointments listed in the normal reference books, applicants should enclose a letter of reference.

298. Lord Lothian's papers are in the Scottish Record Office, Registry House, Edinburgh 2.

299. Gilbert Murray's papers are in the Bodleian Library, Oxford (general political interest).

300. H. W. Nevinson's journals are in the Bodleian Library, Oxford.

301. Lord Pethick-Lawrence's papers are in the India Office Library. He was Secretary of State for India, 1942–47.

302. Lord Quickswood's papers [Lord Hugh Cecil] are at Hatfield House, Hatfield, Hertfordshire and applications to see them should be made to the Marquess of Salisbury at Hatfield House (general, political, education, Church affairs).

303. Eleanor Rathbone's papers are in the University Library, Liverpool, and are freely available. She was an M.P. and an important social reformer. There are also papers on aliens in wartime.

304. Viscount Samuel's papers are in the House of Lords Record Office and nearly all of them up to 1946 are available to students. They cover a wide political field and a file on colonial policy is useful. Files on Jewish affairs and Israel are in the Israel State Archives (microfilms in House of Lords). Applications to Clerk of the Records, Record Office, House of Lords, London, S.W.1.

305. Lord Simon of Wythenshawe's papers [Ernest Simon] are in the Manchester Central Library and include wartime papers on the Universities and education generally, and on planning. Lord Simon was a noted public figure with interests in education, industry, economic and social thought and local government. Applications to

see the papers by *bona fide* scholars and sponsored students to The City Librarian, Central Library, St. Peter's Square, Manchester 2.

306. Lord Templewood's papers [Samuel Hoare] other than India Office papers are in the Cambridge University Library but are not in 1967 open to inspection.

307. Mme. Guillot's collection of documents and souvenirs of the Free French Forces in London is in the Imperial War Museum.

NON-POLITICAL RECORDS: These mainly concern "cultural" records of the period. Collections registered but contents unknown are:

308. Sir Sidney Cockerell (general literary interests) 80 volumes of personal diaries till his death in 1962 and 70 volumes of letters are in the British Museum, but diaries from 1932 are closed until 1994 and letters of living persons are closed during their lifetime.

309. C. S. Forester, author. Papers are in the University of California at Berkeley.

310. J. L. and Barbara Hammond, historians. Papers are in the Bodleian Library, Oxford.

311. Edward Marsh, official and patron of the arts. Correspondence files are in the Berg Collection, New York Public Library.

312. Dr. Herbert Thompson, music and art critic. His diary, in 71 volumes, continued to his death in 1945. Applications to the Brotherton Library, University of Leeds, Leeds 2.

313. Michael Sadleir, author and publisher. Collection at Houghton Library, Harvard University.

314. George Orwell's papers including wartime diaries are in the Library of University College, London. See entry 326 in this list.

ADDITIONS TO BIBLIOGRAPHY

315. Menzies, Robert. *Afternoon Light*. London: Cassell, 1967.
316. Citrine, Lord [Sir Walter]. *Two Careers*. London: Hutchinson, 1968.
317. Peacock, Alan T. and Jack Wiseman. *The Growth of Public Expenditure in the United Kingdom*. 2nd ed. London: Allen and Unwin, 1967.
318. The complete New Whitehall series is as follows:
    1. *The Home Office:* Sir Frank Newsam, 2nd ed., 1955.
    2. *The Foreign Office:* Lord Strang, 1957.
    3. *The Colonial Office:* Sir Charles Jeffries, 1955.
    4. *The Ministry of Works:* Sir Harold Emmerson, 1956.
    5. *The Scottish Office:* Sir David Milne, 1958.
    6. *The Ministry of Pensions and National Insurance:* Sir Geoffrey King, 1958.
    7. *The Ministry of Transport and Civil Aviation:* Sir Gilmour Jenkins, 1959.
    8. *The Ministry of Labour and National Service:* Sir Godfrey Ince, 1960 (out of print).

9. *The Department of Scientific and Industrial Research:* Sir Harry Melville, 1962 (out of print).
10. *Her Majesty's Customs and Excise:* Sir James Crombie, 1962.
11. *The Ministry of Agriculture, Fisheries and Food:* Sir John Winnifrith, 1962.
12. *The Treasury:* Lord Bridges, 2nd ed., 1967.
13. *The Inland Revenue:* Sir Alexander Johnston, 1965.

319. Conan, A. R. *The Problem of Sterling.* London: Macmillan, 1966.
320. Dunn, Cuthbert Lindsay, ed. *The Emergency Medical Services.* London: H.M.S.O., 1952–1953. 3 vols.
McNalty, Sir Arthur Salusbury. *Civilian Health and Medical Services.* London: H.M.S.O., 1953 and 1955. 2 vols.
321. Burn, D. L. *The Steel Industry, 1939–1959.* Cambridge: Cambridge University Press, 1961.
322. Marwick, Arthur. *Britain in the Century of Total War.* London: Bodley Head, 1968.
323. Bruce, Maurice. *The Coming of the Welfare State.* 3rd ed. London: Batsford, 1966.
324. Gregg, Pauline. *The Welfare State.* London: Harrap, 1967.
325. Thomson, George Malcolm. *Vote of Censure.* London: Secker and Warburg, 1968.
326. Orwell, George. *Collected Essays, Letters and Journals.* Sonia Orwell and Ian Angus ed. London: Secker and Warburg, 1968.
327. Mosley, Oswald. *My Life.* London: Nelson, 1968.
328. Anthony Powell. *The Military Philosophers* [a novel]. London: Heinemann, 1968.
329. S. B. Johnson, ed. *The Evacuees.* London: Gollancz, 1968. Recollections of those evacuated in 1939.
330. Calder, Angus. *The People's War: Britain, 1939–45.* London: Jonathan Cape, 1969.
331. Winch, Donald. *Economics and Policy.* London: Hodder and Stoughton, 1970.
332. Hodson, H. V. *The Great Divide: Britain-India-Pakistan.* London: Hutchinson, 1969.
333. Home Office. *W.V.S. Civil Defence, 1938–1963,* H.M.S.O., 1963.
334. Russell, Bertrand. *The Autobiography,* Vol. II, 1914–1944 and Vol. III, 1944–1967. London: Allen and Unwin, Vol. II, 1968, Vol. III, 1969.
335. Woolf, Leonard. *The Journey not the Arrival Matters.* London: Hogarth Press, 1969.
336. Mackenzie, Compton. *My Life and Times, Octave 8, 1939–1948.* London: Chatto and Windus, 1969.
337. Coleman, D. C. *Courtaulds: An Economic and Social History,* Vol. II. Oxford University Press, 1969.
338. Philips, C. H. with H. L. Singh and B. N. Pandey, ed. *The Evolution of India and Pakistan, 1858 to 1947: Select Documents Vol. 4.* Oxford University Press, 1962.
339. Philips, C. H. and Wainwright, Mary, ed. *The Partition of India:*

Policies and Perspectives, 1935–1947. London: Allen and Unwin, 1970.

340. Harvey, Oliver (ed. John Harvey,) *The Diplomatic Diaries of Oliver Harvey,* London: Macmillan, 1970.
341. Armytage, W. H. G. *Four Hundred Years of English Education.* 2nd ed. Cambridge University Press, 1970.
342. Milward, Alan S. *The Economic Effects of the World Wars on Britain.* London: Macmillan, 1970.

XXI

SCIENCE AND TECHNOLOGY, 1919–1945*

Ronald W. Clark

The British decision not to describe in a full-scale Cabinet history the part which science and technology played in the Second World War was no doubt historically regrettable. It was also understandable, particularly in the context of the late 1940's in which it was made, for the question of security, perpetual if diminishing, was still augmented by others which would have encouraged bowdlerisation. Among them was the continuing influence of the nuclear bomb on Anglo-U. S. relations, the fact that many wartime scientific developments impinged on post-war civilian pride and prosperity, the controversial impact of Churchill and Cherwell on scientifico-military decisions, and the immediate post-war Allied treatment of German scientists and industrialists, a treatment sometimes more reminiscent of gang-members arguing over the loot than of a band of brothers. The mixture of protest, legal steps, argument and recrimination which followed *S.O.E.* (92) in a different field, might well have been a pale shadow compared with the reactions which would have followed a full-scale and honest government account of wartime scientific development. One need think only of the proximity fuse. To be fair, there may also have been in some official circles a lingering hope that the new importance of science to the Services would be purely ephemeral, and that the cavalry would soon return as queen of the battlefield.

One result of these factors has been that the accounts of wartime science and technology are as patchy in quantity and as variable in quality as those of its overall and casual impingement on the Services during the inter-war years. The scope for research remains great, and vast gaps show in what is admittedly a vast subject. So do the difficulties, one of which stems from the fact that the writer on the subject needs to be part scientist, part researcher-journalist, and, in view of the human issues involved as deeply here as elsewhere, wholly sceptic. A second major problem arises from the huge spread of sources.

* The author wishes to point out that the following essay was completed in 1967, that considerable additions have since been made to the literature, and that details of MS sources may well have changed since then.

OFFICIAL HISTORIES. In this respect the whole period from 1919 to 1945 can be considered as one, and it is significant that two of the volumes in the Cabinet's series of military histories which are of greatest value—Collier's *Defence of the United Kingdom* (60) and Webster and Frankland's history of the strategic bombing offensive (247)—carry the record in one uninterrupted story from the end of the First World War to the end of the Second. Other volumes in the series; notably Roskill's on the war at sea (197) and Ellis' Normandy landings (78), contain material of interest but it is naturally enough those in the war production and civil series, where science is less intermingled with operations, which are most important. Much of their material lies on the munitions side of the border which divides that subject from science and technology, but *Design and Development of Weapons* (181) has an adequate if brief account of radar, while some advances in civil engineering are touched on in *Civil Defence* (169). The raw or only partly-cooked material for a number of other volumes, notably a massive account of radar and what appears to have been considered at one time as a potential history of the Ministry of Aircraft Production, are still believed to lie in the Cabinet Offices. Excluding such full-blown histories, the most comprehensive single government publication is Crowther & Whiddington's account of *Science at War* (65), even though this was written and produced far too soon after 1945 to be more than tentatively unwrapped from the swaddling clothes of censorship.

On a different level, the amount of official material is vast, ranging from such obvious H.M.S.O. publications as *The Aircraft Builders: an account of aircraft production, 1935–1946* (5) to those dealing with the work of the Aeronautical Research Council (3), from the account of high speed aerodynamics at the Royal Aircraft Establishment (202) to Astbury's story of the Research and Experiments Department of the wartime Ministry of Home Security (15) and the design requirements of aircraft (69). Of great importance, especially for the inter-war years, are the annual reports of the Department of Scientific and Industrial Research (216), of the groups such as the Radio and Chemical Research Boards which operated under its aegis (192) and (44), and in addition the Department's immediate post-war publications such as the account of the Road Research Laboratory's wartime work (196).

The usual guides to government publications (95) may give clues to such items as the four useful Reports of the Royal Commission on Awards to Inventors (122). But there is also the Summary of Claims prepared by the Commission for the Imperial War Museum (123), while one of the most important transcripts of evidence, that of the radar claim, is now lodged in the Science Museum, South Kensington. These, as well as much other official material such as the reports and summaries issued by the Ministry of Information and the Ministry of Petroleum Warfare (among other agencies) particularly during the closing months of the last war, are beyond the scope of official guides; some, such as the 16-page and 191-page accounts of radar and radio (191) and (189), contain much information not easily available elsewhere. But there are no short cuts for the researcher if he wants to do his job properly and search beyond the rule-of-thumb guides compiled by other people; he will have to use his brains and his boot-leather.

The line between official and non-official publications is frequently indistinct; in the area around it there jostle both the invaluable volumes of Jane (126) and Brassey (31), and the personal stories which have been privately written though obviously published with official blessing—a class perhaps epitomised by Bernard Fergusson's story of Combined Operations (86) which contains scientific sidelights on an organisation which could at the same time claim both Professor Bernal and Professor Zuckerman on its staff.

BIOGRAPHIES. The number of biographies and autobiographies which have been written with varying degrees of official help, lucidity, and hagiography is considerable for the inter-war period and immense after that. Boyle's life of Trenchard (29), Ludovici's life of Sir Alliot Verdon-Roe (151), and the two lives of Sefton Brancker by Norman Macmillan (154) and Basil Collier (62) are good specimens from one field, just as *The Brabazon Story* (30) and Weir's account of work on such disparate subjects as penicillin and the jerrican (248) are typical from another. Some privately-produced volumes such as Wernher's (249) are particularly useful.

UNIT AND COMPANY HISTORIES. Few of the seemingly endless regimental histories, squadron histories or campaign accounts can be read without the discovery of something worth-while—Brickhill's *The Dam-Busters* (32), almost in this *genre,* contains some popular but useful material on the "bouncing bombs"—but most of the information thus gained is marginal. Of obviously much greater use, but much rarer, are such books as Gerald Pawle's account of the "Wheezers and Dodgers," the Admiralty Department of Miscellaneous Weapons Development (172), Terrell's story of naval inventions used in the Battle of the Atlantic (238), and Rowe's autobiographical account of the Telecommunications Research Establishment (198), which concentrate their light on one particular scientific or technological aspect of the war. The subject-indexes of the Imperial War Museum, the British Museum, and the *Journal of the Royal United Service Institution,* as well as the Accessions List of the Ministry of Defence Library and the American *Engineering Index* (80) are among the best guides through these particular jungles.

They are also useful, although obviously less so, in dealing with company histories—the many thousands of books, booklets, pamphlets and brochures, varying immensely in quality and relevance but possibly containing more raw material on this subject than any other group of sources. The stories of Marconi (93), of Siebe Gorman (244), de Havilland (220), Vickers (246), Dunlop (228), Shell (142), and Baird and Tatlock (146) are only random samples from the hundreds whose interest is scientific as well as purely industrial. Many are privately-printed or roneo'd [mimeographed]; of some, such as the Ferranti War Record (20) only a few copies have been produced. Others, such as Threlfall's story of phosphorus

(241), largely an account of Albright & Wilson, illuminate a wide field of science and war. Many "trade and industry" accounts almost inextricably tangle science and industry, as does *Timber at War* (117). However, books and booklets by no means exhaust the sources of relevant company information, as is illustrated by *The Dyeing of Government Services Material* (*Wool*) (75), a brief but interesting I.C.I. pamphlet, and "Plastics at War," in *British Plastics* for July, 1950 (176).

JOURNALS. This brings us to the stickiest as well as the largest of the morasses through which the student of science and war is forced to wade his way—the vast collection of journals which fall into three roughly overlapping divisions: Service, scientific, and technical-cum-industrial. Of prime importance of course are the main naval (167, 168) and Air Force (201) journals, as well as those of the Royal Corps of Signals (206), the Royal Engineers (207), the Royal Electrical and Mechanical Engineers (194), and the Royal Army Service Corps (204). In addition, the *Army Quarterly* (12)—where one can find such items as Brownlow's article on invention (34)—*The Royal Armoured Corps Journal* (11), the *Journal of the Royal United Service Institution* (210), and the *Journal of the Royal Naval Scientific Service* (208)—the last still technically "Restricted"—should be consulted, particularly for the months following the end of the last war. So, of course, should the *Radar Bulletin* (186). These are only the more obvious examples; the Imperial War Museum catalogue lists 15 journals dealing with Army Signals alone.

The Service journals naturally tend to deal with the end-product of science and technology, operations. Genesis and birth must be sought not only in such publications as the *Proceedings* of the Royal Society (209)— "Critical Conditions in Neutron Multiplication," an important paper leading to the bomb, was published in the *Proceedings* of the Cambridge Philosophical Society (37)—but in the publications of the leading professional organisations, which include, among a long list, those of the Institution of Civil (51), Structural (230), Mechanical (159), and Electrical Engineers (77), as well as of the Royal Aeronautical Society (200).

Considerable use must also be made of such basic publications as *Nature* (166), not only for news of progress, but for such biographical notices as that on Cherwell (133); *Discovery* (71); and *Engineering* (81), whose issues during the second half of 1945 surveyed a great deal of the war's technological advances. In addition, there is the immense range of week-by-week technical and specialist magazines and journals: *The Aeroplane* (4) and *Flight* (91), *Aircraft Production* (6), *The Electrical Review* (76), *Motor Transport* (165), and *Shipping World & Shipbuilder* (221), are random examples. Few can be studied without gain, and the same is equally true of the literally hundreds of house-journals which form part of the field for basic, preliminary research. Students appalled at the quantity of material available will gain little solace from the fact that two important articles, A. P. Rowe's "From Scientific Idea to Practical Use" (198), and R. V. Jones's "Scientists and Statesmen: the example of Sir Henry Tizard," were contained in *Minerva* (135); that *Research* contained R. V. Jones's important "Scientific Intelligence" (134); and that *Chemistry and Industry* (43) has published in recent years a long series of review-articles dealing with various aspects of science and war. And it is unwise to ignore such varied publications as the *Oxford Magazine* (171) or *The Illustrated London News* (120), both of which can provide useful tit-bits.

MANUSCRIPT MATERIALS. Among manuscript sources the most important—at least for the war years—are the Cherwell Papers (259), and those of Churchill held by the Chartwell Trust (261). Sir Henry Tizard's (54) are particularly relevant to the wartime work of the Ministry of Aircraft Production (Tizard was, after all, unofficial scientific adviser to four successive Ministers), while the Hankey Papers (260) are of direct concern to the inter-war years and to the first years of the Second World War. Also of interest—and held at Churchill College as are the Hankey Papers—are those of Professor A. V. Hill (261), Sir George Thomson, chairman of the Maud Committee which led to the nuclear bomb (265), and of Dr. Barnes Wallis (266), the College also holds a number of papers relating to the Maud Committee itself (264), while among other items which are likely to throw new if perhaps marginal light on science and war are the papers of Admiral Lord Keyes (262) and Admiral Sir James Somerville (263). The Trenchard Papers used in Boyle's life (29) are of course of immense interest to the inter-war story of the Royal Air Force.

So far as illustrations are concerned, the Imperial War Museum with its millions of photographs is the largest source. Articles as varied as turbine blades and leather boots, wind tunnels and rubber washers are all involved, and the sources range from private institutions and organisations such as the Fire Protection Association (88) to private companies, and from government departments to the commercial photographic libraries of which the Radio Times Hulton Picture Library (193) is the biggest. It is quite impossible even to hint at all the possibilities; the researcher will have to use his own common sense and initiative.

The usefulness of the various components of this huge agglomeration of material differs for each of the three over-lapping eras into which the years 1919–1945 tend to divide themselves. During the first of these, running from 1919 to the rearmament programmes of the mid-1930's, both arms and the application of science to armaments savoured decidedly of the indecent, and little action is recorded in relatively little material. So far as the higher organization of science for the Services is concerned, one of the most important sources is likely to be the Hankey Papers (260). It was, in fact, almost certainly due to Hankey's prodding that there were set up in the early 1920's three Co-ordinating Boards of the Department of Scientific and Industrial Research to deal with Physics, Chemistry and Engineering. These, together with the existing Radio Research Board, then brought under D.S.I.R. control, would "co-ordinate the technical work of the various naval, military, and aeronautical establishments" in the words of the D.S.I.R. annual report (216). The experience of the Co-ordinating Boards was unhappy, as is clear from Melville's history of D.S.I.R. (160) and from Clark's biography of Sir Henry Tizard (54), the

Departmental Secretary who tried to nourish them into permanence. Nevertheless, the Department's impact on the Services continued. Bernal later concluded in *The Social Function of Science* (23) that by 1937 more than a third of the D.S.I.R.'s expenditure could "be credited to war and is fairly closely connected with possible war uses."

In the Royal Navy in the 1920's, where the benefits were felt of the appointment of Frank Smith as Director of Scientific Research and of the setting up of a Department of Scientific Research and Experiment with a laboratory next door to the National Physical Laboratory at Teddington— its story briefly told by Cheshire (46)—most work was concentrated on underwater detection and on mining and mine-sweeping. Underwater detection owed much to Rutherford, whose earlier work on Asdic is noted in more than one biography (83) and (82). Mining and mine-sweeping are admirably covered in Langmaid's *The Approaches are Mined* (147). But the Admiralty's scientific record of the inter-war years is not unduly encouraging; its position can be judged by the fact that Admiral of the Fleet Lord Chatfield in his autobiographical record of the years from 1921 to 1939 (41) devotes only two of his 291 pages to the subject of research. However, during the Second World War the Admiralty became notable for developing Operational Research under Professor Blackett— among others—while to its scientific credit there must also go the defeat of the magnetic mine (35) and the main body of anti-submarine work of various kinds.

In the Army, the last of the three Services to accept the appointment of a Scientific Adviser, the most important story is that of the successful rear-guard action fought against the tank. Liddell Hart (107) (108) and (109) and Martel (156 and 157) are the most important sources—as well, of course, as the Service journals. Liddell Hart also noted (110) in 1937 that "the way that decisions are reached on questions of strategy, tactics, organisation, etc. is lamentably unscientific. It is due in part to the lack of any staff organ devoted to research. . . ." What went wrong is popularly described in Divine's *The Blunted Sword* (72), while Hore-Belisha's Papers (163) help to explain why so little could be put right. The miserable results cannot be concealed in the official accounts of the British campaigns in the Low Countries (78) and Norway (68) following the outbreak of war, nor in *The Ironside Diaries* (153).

By comparison with the two senior services, the Royal Air Force, whose early years have been described by Chamier (39), had much to report. The successive reorganisations which made this possible can be followed not only in the Service Journals (201) and (210) and in *Flight* (91), but in the pages of Grey's *History of the Air Ministry* (98), while further details are filled in by Taylor's *C.F.S.: the birthplace of air power* (234). The most important single collection of MS material is the Trenchard Papers. Both Sir John Salmond, who commanded the Air Defence of Great Britain from 1925 to 1929, and Lord Dowding, Air Member for Research and Development on the Air Council from 1930 to 1936, have been the subjects of good biographies (144) and (61). Joubert's books (138), (139), (140), are occasionally illuminating but tend to be unreliable. For light relief there is the story of Grindell Matthews (18), one of those persistent near-inventors forever trying to stake a claim to the £1,000 which the Air Ministry had seriously offered to anyone successfully demonstrating a death-ray. He was no doubt a forerunner of those optimists described in "Doctor Strabismus at War" (229).

The second section of our period, starting with the realisation of the Nazi threat in the mid-1930's and ending with the fall of the Chamberlain Government in May 1940, saw the ground work laid for the wartime co-operation between science and the Services, largely in the R.A.F. and largely despite the opposition or disinterest of the authorities. The start of the air rearmament programme, the genesis and flowering of radar, and the early speculative work which was to help produce the first nuclear weapons all fall within the period.

During these years, as Europe slid slowly down the slope to war, the energies of those responsible for the Services' scientific needs were largely turned, so far as they were turned at all, to defence against the bomber. The problem had been discussed in Ashmore's book (13) and it was later to be described in greater detail in the earlier chapters of Pile's *Ack-Ack* (175), Collier's *Defence of the U.K.* (60), and Peter Wykeham's *Fighter Command* (257), three books which consider the same question over three decades from three different points of view. The reasons for so little being done so late are suggested in David Divine's *The Broken Wing* (73).

In practice, defence was to be concentrated, as far as science and technology were concerned, on the expanding aircraft programme and on radar. For both subjects, the amount of material available in company histories, in company house journals, and, to a lesser extent, in technical and trade journals, is massive. No major account of the aircraft industry between 1933 and 1935 has yet been published, although *The Aircraft Builders* (5) gives the overall picture, and many specialised subjects are covered piece-meal. A good deal of information is contained in a number of Cabinet histories, particularly those dealing with British War Production (180) and with *Design and Development of Weapons* (181), while Devons' *Planning & Practice* (70) is useful and Huskinson's personal story (118) throws a good deal of light on the M.A.P. There is a mass of material in the Technical Reports of the Aeronautical Research Committee (2), while an extremely useful account of A.R.C. work is given in Professor Collar's Third Tizard Memorial Lecture (57), which deals with Sir Henry Tizard's membership in the A.R.C. from 1920 until 1933 and with his chairmanship for the following decade. Pudney has produced an admirable history of the Royal Aircraft Establishment (183), while flight-testing is covered in at least two good and popular volumes (224) and (251). The more famous planes of the day have been described in detail, among them the Spitfire (235), the Hurricane (149) and the Mosquito (25), while Grey (96) and (97) and Thetford (240) are among the other reliable guides. Many wartime reminiscences throw light on the pre-war re-armament programme, although naturally well watered-down with operations. Most of the ever-voluble air marshals' own accounts of the war and its prelude—by Bennett (21), Harris (104), Saundby (211),

Tedder (237), Douglas (74) and Slessor (222) among others—contain occasional, and frequently partial, references to the growing technology of war in the air. Prudence Hill's biography of her father (116), an Air Marshal with a long record of technical appointments, is pleasantly un- bumptious. One particular aspect of air rearmament has been chronicled in some detail. This is the story of the jet, described by Whittle himself (252). Lancelot Law Whyte's *Focus and Diversions* (253) and Clark's *Tizard* (54) deal with various aspects of the subject, as do the memoirs of some Fellows of the Royal Society, including those of David Pye (184), Sir Henry Tizard (242), and Lord Cherwell (45).

RADAR. The most important technological key to the defence of the United Kingdom was, of course, provided by radar, which in the last three decades has produced enough books to fill a score of libraries. Most of the raw material for the history of the subject—the minutes of the Tizard Com- mittee, the records of Bawdsey and the subsequent Telecommunications Research Establishment, and of the Ministry of Aircraft Production—are only now becoming available for inspection. Exceptions are documents in private collections. Both Cherwell's papers (259) and Tizard's are valuable. Both also throw much light on that patch of triangular ground where science, industry, and the Services meet—and on the Tizard-Cherwell controversy, which was to play such an important part in the scientific ordering of the war. This has been well-ventilated not only in the biog- raphies of the two men (242) and (24), but also by Lord Snow (225), and (226), and by R. V. Jones in a series of articles in *The Times* (136) and in *The Oxford Magazine* (130). Directly linked with the argument was the development of infra-red defence methods, which have also been described in detail by Jones (131).

Much of the official raw material on radar was put through the sausage- machine to produce one large but unpublished history. What has officially appeared is largely limited to the relevant chapters of Crowther and Whiddington (65); of *Design and Development of Weapons* (180) and of Webster and Frankland's book on the strategic bombing offensive (247); to Brigadier Sayers' *Army Radar* (213), published in 1950, but still tech- nically a restricted document; and, if they are to be considered official, to the accounts by Sir Edward Appleton, Secretary of the D.S.I.R., in the *Journal of the Institution of Electrical Engineers* (9) and (10). By far the most valuable single item is the account of the proceedings of the radioloca- tion convention held in London in March 1946 and printed by the same *Journal* (190). Next comes the massive transcript of evidence on the radar claim put to the Royal Commission on Awards to Inventors (121).

The unofficial accounts of radar are numerous and frequently con- tentious. One of the first was Rowe's small but admirable book about T.R.E. (199). Later came Watson-Watt's *Three Steps to Victory* (246). There is of course an extensive technical literature typified by Appleton's "Scientific Principles of Radiolocation" (9), and F. E. Jones's account of "Oboe" (129). The large number of specialist books include Saward's *The Bomber's Eye* (212), and Chisholm's *Cover of Darkness* (47) which deal with airborne radar, and Price's *Instruments of Darkness* (182), while *Engineering's* 1945 account (187) and Addison's "The Radio War" (1) were the first published accounts of electronic counter-measures. Much of the story can be disinterred from the Service journals—typically in such items as "Royal Signals and the Early Days of Radar" in *The Wire* (188) and "Sealion's" "Naval Radar" in *The Navy* (218); but the immense possibilities are suggested by R. W. Feachem's "A Naval Shore Radar Station in North-West Iceland," which can be found in *The Polar Record* (85), and by the MS material available in varied forms, typified by A. C. Lock's *Diary and Notes Relating to Radar Equipment, 1940–43* in the Imperial War Museum (150).

OPERATIONAL RESEARCH. From radar there grew Operational Research. While its post-war proliferations have been amply described, major works dealing with its wartime evolution are relatively scanty. The most important single document is the invaluable Air Ministry account of its growth in the Royal Air Force (170). Pile's *Ack-Ack* (175) describes the work of Operational Research as it was developed by "Blackett's Circus," and Blackett himself has written on the subject both in the proceedings of the British Association for the Advancement of Science (26) and in his book of collected essays (27)—much of the work being done under the benevolent eyes of the Admiralty which quickly showed the enthusiasm of most converts. Once again the researcher will have to work his own way through the Service journals.

THE ATOMIC BOMB. By comparison with radar, whose antennae were already turned towards the Continent as Big Ben chimed the nation into war on September 3rd, 1939, work on the possibilities of a nuclear weapon had barely begun, despite the intermittent speculation about such a weapon since the early days of H. G. Wells. A play dealing with the subject was running in London when Cockcroft and Walton split the atom artificially in 1932, while Leo Szilard had postulated such a weapon during his brief stay in England during the 1930's. Most of this has gone unrecorded. None of those intimately involved in the British work on nuclear energy have written their full stories, and the standard works, except for the skimpy official White Paper of 1945 (16), are Margaret Gowing's admirable history (94), written with access to all the documents and virtually a Cabinet history, and Clark's *The Birth of the Bomb* (52), produced largely from interviews with those concerned. David Irving's *The Virus House* (125) throws additional light on the Allied scientific intelligence work involved, although primarily concerned with the German nuclear effort.

The British work on nuclear weapons, begun in earnest only a few weeks before the end of "the phoney war" and the fall of the Chamberlain Government in the Spring of 1940, was typical of the more determined scientific and technological effort that was now being mobilised—although it is clear from Butler's *Grand Strategy* (36) in the Cabinet histories that the new Scientific Advisory Committee of the Cabinet was set up only in the face of opposition from the new Prime Minister. The need for this fresh effort was underlined by the emergency Penguin published anonymously in the August of 1940 (215). A key paragraph concerned the reduction to numerical values of certain factors in military operations. "This has, indeed, been done to a certain extent with the tactical problems of naval and air fighting, but it could be extended to many more," this went. "The scientific staffs of the Services need to play a much larger part than they seem to do in the formulation and solution of strategical and tactical problems."

HIGHER SCIENTIFIC CONTROL, 1940–1945. The higher direction of the scientific war during the final third of our period, of which this hope was to be part-fulfilment, has not yet been described coherently or in detail, although it is touched upon in many of the books which have already been mentioned: (93), (225) and (53). This gap is not surprising in view of the inaccessibility of the vital documents and the labyrinthine and counter-crossing chains of command by which the direction was exercised. No account exists, it may be noted in passing, either of the Ministry of Supply's massive, unwieldy and potentially important Advisory Committee on Scientific Research and Technical Development or, at the other end of the scale, of the Cherwell-supported M.D.I., run by Major-General Willis Jefferis. The work of the S.A.C., which ran from such mundane subjects as manpower to investigation of reports that the enemy was building a Channel Tunnel, has also gone unchronicled. Judging from the passing references to it which have been made, Tizard's private comment was justified: that the Committee was "really very ineffective." More effective, for better or for worse, was the personal judgment of Churchill, much of whose scientific attitude is revealed in *The War and Colonel Warden* (173); whose minutes, printed as appendices in his own volumes of *The Second World War* (48), are illuminating and whose overall attitude to science is discussed in the Royal Society memoir (49). On this subject Birkenhead's biography of Cherwell (24) is useful, and the Cherwell papers themselves (259) essential, quite apart from Churchill's own papers.

RETREAT AND RETURN. The reorganisation of the war's scientific effort was only beginning when all had to be concentrated on the threat of invasion. Some of the ingenious technological devices suggested for meeting it are mentioned in Peter Fleming's *Invasion* (90); another is described in detail in Banks's *Flame Over Britain* (17)—one aspect of petroleum warfare whose varied uses and horrors are described in other publications (87) and (254). Simultaneously, there came the first great test of radar in the Battle of Britain. Few books give it due credit. Exceptions include *The Narrow Margin* (255) and *The Breaking Wave* (236), the chapters of Basil Collier's two books which cover the subject (58) and (60), and those of Peter Wykeham (257). *Unexploded Bomb* (113) does for the army experts at the receiving end of the attack what Bullard's account of how the magnetic mine was defeated (35) did for the earlier assault.

From the end of 1940, much of Britain's scientific and technological effort became concentrated on the war in the air, particularly the radio and radar war, and on the Battle of the Atlantic. However, two groups which between them began to cream off the rest of the scientific potential consisted of the Combined Operations Executive and those others preparing for a return to the Continent. For the first, the official history produced by the Amphibious Warfare Headquarters is a basic document (63). Bernard Fergusson (86) is both enlightening and readable, as is Maund's *Assault from the Sea* (158) and the life of Roger Keyes (14). Less flattering accounts of the impact of science on the organisation are provided by the biography of Pyke (145) and by the accounts of "Habbakuk," the ill-fated plan to create an iceberg aircraft-carrier. These latter include "The Mystery of the Iceberg Ship" (119) and an illuminating account in *The Illustrated London News* (120).

Such variety of documentation is typical of the whole gamut of scientific and technological devices which in a different field made the Normandy landings possible. Many of the sources throw additional light on the rest of the nation's scientific effort; their extent is so vast that it is possible here only to illustrate, by example, the range available. Thus the bibliography on the Mulberry Harbours includes such items as Sir Harold Wernher's history (250), articles in the technical press such as "The Pre-Fabricated Port of Arromanches" (233) and Hamilton's "Floating Wharves and Jetties" (103). Admiral Hickling has described the harbours in the R.U.S.I. *Journal* (114), while the entire subject has more recently been admirably covered by Michael Harrison's *The Return in Triumph* (106). "Pluto," the pipeline under the ocean which supplied the armies in North-West Europe with petrol, has a similarly complicated bibliography which includes papers read to the Worshipful Company of Shipwrights (111) and the Institution of Naval Architects (184); articles in *The Detonator* (128), *The Quartermaster Review* (179), *The Engineer,* (174), the *Journal of the R.A.S.C.* (178), and *The Civil Engineer at War* (112); a pamphlet issued by W. T. Henley's Telegraph Works (177); and numerous references in such books as Norman Kemp's *The Devices of War* (141), which covers Pluto, the piat and Sommerfeld track among other subjects. A comparable spread of references is involved in the made-to-measure armoured vehicles used for the invasion, and fought by the 79th (specialised) Armoured Division, "the Funnies," raised and led by Hobart whose story is covered in a recent biography (152).

Much of the pre-invasion work was of a civil engineering nature and is described in the three special volumes issued by the Institution of Civil Engineers (50). *Overture to Overlord* (164) deals with some of the problems. Once the troops were ashore, "Open the Ports" was the order—the title of a book (100) describing the work of the human minesweepers. Somewhat comparable achievements are the subject of *Above Us the Waves* (245), the story of the midget submarines, and *The Frogmen* (243). The story of long-distance communications for the invasion is told in *Signal Venture* (105), and almost every facet of the operation is of course described in regimental or Corps publications.

The months that followed the invasion of Europe witnessed two developments of great scientific interest. One was the unleashing of Hitler's "secret weapons," the V 1 or "doodlebug," and the V 2 rocket. The British ingenuity which was deployed to meet this threat is described in the official despatch (7), in *Ack-Ack* (175), Collier's *The Battle of the V-Weapons* (59), the same author's *Defence of the United Kingdom* (60), and Prudence Hill's life of her father (116). *The Mare's Nest* (124) concentrates on the Intelligence side. Much of the British success stemmed from the development of photographic interpretation and intelligence, a subject finely covered by Babington Smith's *Evidence in Camera* (223), an European complement to Millington's *The Unseen Eye* (161), which describes the photo-reconnaissance problems of the Desert War.

The second post-invasion development was the progressive uncovering by British and U. S. forces of the enemy's scientific effort. Much of this was carried out by T-Force ("T" for Technical), whose operations have so far been described only in the *History of T-Force Activities in Rhine Army* (239), although the subject is touched on in Bar-Zohar's interesting little book (19). Note should be taken here of the many publications issued in Northern Germany by Rhine Army. *Some Notes on the Tactical Handling of Flame Throwers (Wasps and Crocodiles)* (89), the Royal Engineers' story of bridging (33), and the histories of the 11th (231), and the 7th (219) Armoured Divisions and of the 3rd Assault Division (214) are merely some that are of more than purely Service interest.

OTHER SCIENTIFIC WORK. In much post-war summary it is as difficult to draw a line between technology and operations as it is to define the extent of science and technology itself. There are accounts of the gliders (42), (66) and (256), of the Fleet Air Arm (38) and the anti-submariners (143) which, among many others, illustrate this point. As to the line between science and industry, the researcher must decide for himself whether his brief includes "The Story of the Jerrican" (40), certainly a device that helped to make victory possible; "Drinking Water from Sea Water by a Chemical Method" (8), which was very relevant to the Battle of the Atlantic; the story of "DDT" as given by the *Society of Dyers and Colourists Journal* (67); or the work on fabric research which was just as essential in its own way (84). All describe the impact of science on war, while at least one volume of Sir G. I. Taylor's scientific papers (232) and at least one post-war paper in the Proceedings of the Royal Society (99) concern the very mechanics of death and destruction.

Almost any of the works so far listed could be multiplied many times over to illustrate the vastness of the field covered by that much-used but woollily ill-defined portmanteau phrase "the application of science and technology to the Services." Of the gaps, British efforts to unearth German scientific and technological secrets is but one. No account exists of the wartime work of Porton, the British chemical and biological warfare establishment, and the work of such organisations as the London Inter-Service Sub-Committee on Biological Warfare must be inferred from references in U. S. sources. So must the rest of Britain's preparations for biological warfare. Prising this particular door open is unlikely to be easy—one notes that even following the recent 30-year rule, items in the Public Record Office in London specially starred "This piece is closed for 75 years" include not only "1934–38 Chemical Warfare" but also "1939–42: Destruction of German harvest by incendiary aircraft actions." Whereas Service leaders have given their stories *in extenso,* Cockcroft, Blackett and Zuckerman are only three of the scientific leaders who have remained comparatively silent—although the last two have incorporated a certain amount of personal experience in their books of collected essays and papers (27) and (258), and Cockcroft has provided some interesting reminiscences in the *Deep River Review* (55). Other scientists have made relatively minor contributions in papers and lectures. As already mentioned, no public account exists of the work of the Ministry of Supply's Advisory Committee on Scientific Research and Technical Development, let alone of the Cabinet's S.A.C. No one has yet chronicled the exploits of the Earl of Suffolk, a man of curious wartime scientific assignments who was eventually killed while de-fusing a new mine. Most of the attempts to describe the wartime work of specific Service research establishments have been made from outside by professional writers rather than from inside by professional scientists, which may make for intelligibility but is apt to produce patchy coverage of a subject.

The larger issues have, moreover, so far been largely ignored, although Snow's *Science and Government* (225) did open the subject, to the relish of some and the annoyance of others. Bernal (22), Hill (115), Cockcroft (56), Crowther (64) have all touched on them, while into even popular books on the war effort such as *War at the Top* (148) there has crept an acknowledgment that at some point in mid-twentieth century Clausewitz' dictum about war being nothing more than a continuation of politics by other means stumbled over a precipice into the ridiculous. Contrariwise, one of the most important results of the demands which the British Services have made on science and technology during the last half-century has been the translation of the scientist and technologist into a Fifth Estate which holds the vital clues to national survival, a translation against which a definite, partly healthy, but inevitably Luddite reaction is now developing. Little of this, or of the developing moral responsibilities of science *vis-à-vis* the Services in the nuclear age, has been more than touched upon outside the purely nuclear argument. In addition, one other aspect of the subject has so far gone relatively unchronicled. This is the international character of the foundation upon which both industry and science have come to rest in the twentieth century. This international foundation has been temporarily fractured by the exigencies of two world wars, but in the long run may be seen to have been reinforced. However, it seems slightly more likely that a new law of Nature should be discovered than that this story should be told in the detail that history may think it deserves.

BIBLIOGRAPHY

1. Addison, E. B. "The Radio War." *The Journal of the Royal United Service Institution,* Vol. XCII No. 565, 1947.

2. Aeronautical Research Committee: see H.M.S.O. Sectional List No. 8 (especially back issues), 1909– .

3. Aeronautical Research Council. *Review for the Years 1939–1948.* H.M.S.O., 1950.

4. *The Aeroplane.* 1911–1968.

5. *The Aircraft Builders: an account of aircraft production 1935–1945.* Ministry of Aircraft Production and Central Office of Information, 1947.

6. *Aircraft Production.* 1938–1963.

7. "Air Operations by Air Defence of Great Britain and Fighter Command in connection with the German Flying Bomb and Rocket Offensive 1944–45." Supplement to *The London Gazette,* October 19, 1948.

8. Akeroyd, E. I., E. L. Homes, and A. Klein. "Drinking Water from Sea Water by a Chemical Method." *Water and Water Engineering,* October, 1945.

9. Appleton, Sir Edward, K.C.B., M.A., D. Sc., Lld.F.R.S. "The Scientific Principles of Radiolocation." *The Journal of the Institution,* Vol. 92, Part I, No. 57, September 1945, The Institution of Electrical Engineers.

10. Appleton, Sir E. V. "The Scientist in Wartime." 32nd Thomas Hawksley Lecture, *The Proceedings of the Institution of Mechanical Engineers,* 1946, Vol. 154, No. 3.

11. *The Royal Armoured Corps Journal* (including *The Royal Tank Corps Journal*—itself first *The Tank Corps Journal* and then *The Tank*). Aldershot, 1946– .

12. *The Army Quarterly and Defence Journal.*

13. Ashmore, General E. B. *Air Defence.* London: Longmans, Green, 1929.

14. Aspinall-Oglander. *Roger Keyes.* London: Hogarth Press, 1951.

15. Astbury, A. R., comp. *Research and Experiments Department, Ministry of Home Security, 1939–1945 (History of the).* Ministry of Works, 1948.

16. *Atomic Bomb, Statements Relating to the.* H.M.S.O., 1945.

17. Banks, Sir Donald. *Flame Over Britain: a personal narrative of petroleum warfare.* London: Sampson, Low, Marston & Co., Ltd., 1946.

18. Barwell, Ernest H. G. *The Death Ray Man: the biography of Grindell Matthews, inventor and pioneer.* Hutchinson, 1943.

19. Bar-Zohar, Michael. *The German Hunt for German Scientists.* London: Arthur Barker, 1965.

20. Beardsall, Charles P. *Ferranti Limited War Record, 1939–1945.* Manchester, (1967).

21. Bennett, Air Vice-Marshal D. C. T. *Pathfinder.* London: Muller, 1958.

22. Bernal, J. D. *Science in History.* London: Watts, 1965.

23. Bernal, J. D. *The Social Function of Science.* London: Routledge, 1939.

24. Birkenhead, The Earl of. *The Prof in Two Worlds.* London: Collins, 1961.
25. Bishop, Edward. *The Wooden Wonder: the story of the de Havilland Mosquito.* London: Parrish, 1959.
26. Blackett, P. M. S. "Operational Research." *The Advancement of Science,* London, Vol. V, No. 17, 1948.
27. Blackett, P. M. S. *Studies of War.* Edinburgh: Oliver and Boyd, 1962.
28. Blackett, P. M. S. "Tizard and the Science of War." *Nature,* March 5, 1960.
29. Boyle, Andrew. *Trenchard, Man of Vision.* London: Collins, 1962.
30. Brabazon of Tara, Lord. *The Brabazon Story.* Heinemann, 1950.
31. *Brassey's Naval Annual.* London: Wm. Clowes & Son, 1899–   .
32. Brickhill, Paul. *The Dam Busters.* London: Evans, 1951.
33. *Bridging, Normandy to Berlin.* Royal Engineers, BAOR, 1945.
34. Brownlow, C. A. L. "Invention: Machinery and War." *The Army Quarterly,* Vol. LXVII, No. 1, 1953.
35. Bullard, E. C. "The Protection of Ships From Magnetic Mines," delivered to Royal Institution of Great Britain, February 15, 1946, London, n.d.
36. Butler, J. R. M. *Grand Strategy.* II, *September 1939–June 1941.* H.M.S.O., 1957.
37. *Proceedings of the Cambridge Philosophical Society.* 1843–   .
38. Cameron, Ian. *Wings of the Morning, The Story of the Fleet Air Arm in World War Two.* London: Hodder and Stoughton, 1962.
39. Chamier, Air Commodore J. A. *The Birth of the R.A.F.* London: Pitman, 1943.
40. Chase, J. C. "The Story of the Jerrican." *The Royal Army Service Corps Review,* Vol. 1. No. 2, 1949.
41. Chatfield, Admiral of the Fleet Lord. *The Navy and Defence, It Might Happen Again.* Vol. II. Heineman, 1947.
42. Chatterton, Brigadier George. *The Wings of Pegasus.* London: Macdonald, 1962.
43. *Chemistry and Industry.* 1881–   .
44. Chemistry Research Board, *Report, for the Period, 1936–1946.* London: H.M.S.O., 1948.
45. "Frederick Alexander Lindemann, Viscount Cherwell." By Sir George Thomson, with a note by Sir William Farren. *Biographical Memoirs of Fellows of the Royal Society.* Vol. 12, November, 1966.
46. Cheshire, R. W. "The Admiralty Research Laboratory." *Journal of the Royal Naval Scientific Service,* Vol. 2, No. 2, 1947.
47. Chisholm, R. *Cover of Darkness.* London: Chatto & Windus, 1953.
48. Churchill, Winston S. *The Second World War.* Vols. I–VI. London: Cassell, 1948–1954.
49. "Winston Leonard Spencer Churchill." By Professor R. V. Jones. *Biographical Memoirs of Fellows of the Royal Society.* Vol. 12, November, 1966.

50. "The Civil Engineer in War." *Institution of Civil Engineers*. London, 1948. 3 vols.
51. *Proceedings of the Institution of Civil Engineers, 1952–* .
52. Clark, Ronald W. *The Birth of the Bomb*. London: Phoenix House, 1961.
53. Clark, Ronald W. *The Rise of the Boffins*. London: Phoenix House, 1962.
54. Clark, Ronald W. *Tizard*. London: Methuen, 1965.
55. Cockcroft, Sir John. "R.D.F." *Deep River Review*, October 1946.
56. Cockcroft, Sir John, ed. *The Organisation of Research Establishments*. Cambridge: Cambridge University Press, 1965.
57. Collar, A. R. "Tizard and the Aeronautical Research Committee." *Journal of the Royal Aeronautical Society*, Vol. 71, No. 680, August, 1967.
58. Collier, Basil. *The Battle of Britain*. London: Batsford, 1962.
59. Collier, Basil. *The Battle of the V-Weapons, 1944–45*. London: Hodder & Stoughton, 1964.
60. Collier, Basil. *The Defence of the United Kingdom*. H.M.S.O., 1957.
61. Collier, Basil. *Leader of the Few: the authorised biography of Air Chief Marshal the Lord Dowding of Bentley Priory*. London: Jarrolds, 1957.
62. Collier, Basil. *Heavenly Adventurer: Sefton Brancker and the dawn of British aviation*. London: Secker and Warburg, 1959.
63. *History of Combined Operations Organization, 1940–1941*. Amphibious Warfare Headquarters, London, 1956.
64. Crowther, J. G. *The Social Relations of Science*. London: Macmillan, 1941.
65. Crowther, J. G. and R. Whiddington. *Science at War*. H.M.S.O., 1947.
66. Cumming, Michael. *The Powerless Ones: gliding in peace and war*. London: Muller, 1966.
67. "D.D.T." *Journal of the Society of Dyers and Colourists*. Bradford, 1884– .
68. Derry, T. K. *The Campaign in Norway*. H.M.S.O., 1952.
69. *Design Requirements for Aeroplanes for the Royal Air Force and Royal Navy*. H.M.S.O., 1948.
70. Devon, Ely S. *Planning and Practice*. Cambridge: Cambridge University Press, 1950.
71. *Discovery*. 1920–
72. Divine, David. *The Blunted Sword*. London: Hutchinson, 1964.
73. Divine, David. *The Broken Wing, A Study in the British Exercise of Air Power*. London: Hutchinson, 1966.
74. Douglas of Kirtleside, Marshal of the Royal Air Force Lord (with Robert Wright). *Years of Command*. London: Collins, 1966.
75. *Dyeing of Government Services Material (Wool) I.C.I.* Birmingham: Kynoch Press, n.d.
76. *The Electrical Review*. 1872– .
77. *Proceedings of the Institution of Electrical Engineers, 1949–* .

78. Ellis, Major L. F. *The Campaign in France and Flanders, 1939–1940.* H.M.S.O., 1956.
79. Ellis, Major, L. F. *Victory in the West.* Vol. I, *The Battle of Normandy.* H.M.S.O., 1962.
80. *The Engineering Index.* Chicago annually, 1898– .
81. *Engineering.* 1866–
82. Evans, Ivor Burford Needham. *Man of Power. The life story of Baron Rutherford of Nelson.* London: Stanley Paul, 1939.
83. Eve, A. S. *Rutherford.* Cambridge: Cambridge University Press, 1939.
84. "Secret Fabric That Saved Thousands of Lives." *The Navy, Army, Air and Munitions Journal,* Vol. 15, No. 3, 1947.
85. Feachem, R. W. "A Naval Shore Radar Station in North-West Iceland." *The Polar Record,* Vol. 5, No. 39, Scott Polar Research Institute, Cambridge, 1950.
86. Fergusson, Sir Bernard. *The Watery Maze: the story of Combined Operations.* London: Collins, 1961.
87. "Fido." *Aeronautics.* Vol. 13, No. 1, 1945.
88. Fire Protection Association, Aldermary House, Queen Street, London, E.C.4.
89. *Flame Throwers (Wasps and Crocodiles). Some Notes on the Tactical Handling of.* 21 Army Group Training Pamphlet, 1945.
90. Fleming, Peter. *Invasion, 1940. An account of the German preparations and the British counter-measures.* London: Rupert Hart-Davis, 1957.
91. *Flight,* 1909–
92. Foot, M. R. D. *S.O.E., an Account of the work of the Special Operations Executive in France, 1940–1944.* H.M.S.O., 1966.
93. Godwin, George. *Marconi 1939–1945.* London: Chatto & Windus, 1946.
94. Gowing, Margaret. *Britain and Atomic Energy.* London: Macmillan, 1964.
95. *Government Publications: official indexes, lists, guides, catalogues.* London: H.M.S.O., 1957.
96. Grey, C. G. *Bombers.* London: Faber, 1941.
97. Grey, C. G. *British Fighter Planes.* London: Faber, 1941.
98. Grey, C. G. *A History of the Air Ministry.* London, 1940.
99. Grime, G. and H. Sheard. "The Experimental Study of the Blast from Bombs and Bare Charges." *Proceedings,* Royal Society Series A., Vol. 187, No. 10, 1946.
100. Grosvenor, Joan and Leonard Maurice Bates. *Open the Ports.* London: Kimber, 1956.
101. "Habbakuk." *The Illustrated London News,* March 2, 1946, London.
102. Haigh, J. S. "Royal Signals and the Early Days of Radar." *The Wire,* Vol. I, No. 6.
103. Hamilton, R. M. "Floating Wharves and Jetties." *Dock and Harbour Authority Journal,* April 1946.

104. Harris, Marshal of the Royal Air Force Sir Arthur. *Bomber Offensive.* London: Collins, 1947.
105. Harris, Brigadier L. H. *Signal Venture.* Aldershot: Gale & Polden, 1951.
106. Harrison, Michael. *Mulberry: the return in triumph.* London: W. H. Allen, 1965.
107. Hart, B. H. Liddell. *The Memoirs of Captain Liddell Hart.* London: Cassell, 1965. 2 vols.
108. Hart, B. H. Liddell. *Dynamic Defence.* London: Faber & Faber, 1940.
109. Hart, B. H. Liddell. *The Tanks. The History of the Royal Tank Regiment and its predecessors, Heavy Branch Machine-Gun Corps, Tank Corps and Royal Tank Corps, 1914–1945.* London: Cassells, 1959.
110. Hart, B. H. Liddell. *Thoughts on War.* London: Faber, 1944.
111. Hartley, A. C. "Oil Pipelines Across the Channel." *Paper No. 17 of Shipbuilding and Ships.* London: Worshipful Company of Shipwrights, 1947.
112. Hartley, A. C. "Operational Pluto." *The Civil Engineer at War,* Vol. 3, Institution of Civil Engineers, London, 1948.
113. Hartley, Major A. P. *Unexploded Bomb: a history of bomb disposal.* London: Cassell, 1958.
114. Hickling, Rear-Admiral H. "The Prefabricated Harbours." *The Journal of the Royal United Service Institution,* Vol. XL, No. 559, 1945.
115. Hill, A. V. *The Ethical Dilemma of Science.* London: O.U.P., 1960.
116. Hill, Prudence. *To Know the Sky: the life of Air Chief Marshal Sir Roderic Hill.* London: Kimber, 1962.
117. House, Frank. *Timber at War: an account of the activities of the Timber Control, 1939–1945.* London: Ernest Benn Ltd., 1965.
118. Huskinson, Air Commodore P. *Vision Ahead.* London: Werner Laurie, 1949.
119. "The Mystery of the Iceberg-Ship." *United Service Review,* March 18, 1946.
120. *Illustrated London News,* 1842– .
121. Royal Commission on Awards to Inventors. *Transcript of Evidence in the Radar Case.* Science Museum, South Kensington, London.
122. Royal Commission on Awards to Inventors. *Reports 1–4, Cmd. 7586* (1948).
123. Royal Commission on Awards to Inventors. "Summary of Claims." Imperial War Museum, London. Typewritten.
124. Irving, David. *The Mare's Nest.* London: Kimber, 1964.
125. Irving, David. *The Virus House.* London: Kimber, 1964.
126. Jane, F. T. *All the World's Aircraft.* London: Sampson, Low, 1909 and annually except for 1915.
127. Jane, F. T. *Fighting Ships.* London: Sampson, Low, 1897 annually.
128. JDS. "Coxe and Pluto: the part played by Combined Operations

Experimental Establishment Westward Ho! in the development of Pluto." *The Detonator,* Vol. II, No. 3, 1952.

129. Jones, F. E. "Oboe: a precision ground-controlled blind-bombing system." *The Journal of the Institution of Electrical Engineers,* Vol. 93, Part IIIA, No. 2, 1946.

130. Jones, R. V. "Cherwell's Judgement in World War II." *The Oxford Magazine,* May 9, 1963.

131. Jones, R. V. "Infra-Red Detection in British Air Defence, 1936–37." *Infra-Red Physics,* 1961.

132. Jones, R. V. "Research Establishments." *Chemistry and Industry,* 1966.

133. Jones, R. V. "The Right Hon. Viscount Cherwell, P.C., C.H., F.R.S." *Nature,* Vol. 180. Sept. 21, 1957.

134. Jones, R. V. "Scientific Intelligence." *Research,* Vol. 9, September, 1956.

135. Jones, R. V. "Scientists and Statesmen: the example of Henry Tizard." *Minerva,* Vol. IV, No. 2, Winter, 1966.

136. Jones, R. V. "Scientists at War." *The Times,* London, April 6–8, 1961.

137. Jones, R. V. "Sir Henry Tizard 1885–1959." *Journal of the Royal Aeronautical Society,* London, Vol. 68, No. 648, December, 1964.

138. Joubert de la Ferté, Air Chief Marshal Sir Philip. *The Fated Sky.* London: Hutchinson, 1952.

139. Joubert de la Ferté, Air Chief Marshal Sir Philip. *Rocket.* London: Hutchinson, 1957.

140. Joubert de la Ferté, Air Chief Marshal Sir Philip. *The Third Service: the story behind the Royal Air Force.* London: Thames & Hudson, 1955.

141. Kemp, Norman. *The Devices of War.* London: Werner Laurie, 1956.

142. Kerr, Wing-Commander George P. *Time's Forelock; a record of Shell's contribution to aviation in the Second World War.* London: S.P.C., 1948.

143. Kirkby, J. M. "Some Mechanical Features in Anti-Submarine Weapons." *Institution of Mechanical Engineers,* 1941.

144. Laffin, John. *Swifter than Eagles: the biography of Marshal of the Royal Air Force, Sir John Maitland Salmond, G.C.B., C.M.G., C.V.O., D.S.O., D.C.L., L.D.* London: Blackwood, 1964.

145. Lampe, David. *Pyke, the Unknown Genius.* London: Evans, 1959.

146. Langdon-Davies, J. *Measuring the Future. Scientific Progress illustrated by the wartime experience of Messrs. Baird & Tatlock (London) Ltd.* Glasgow: Maclehose, 1947.

147. Langmaid, Captain Kenneth. *The Approaches are Mined.* London: Jarrolds, 1965.

148. Leasor, James and Sir Leslie Hollis. *War at the Top: based on the experiences of General Sir Leslie Hollis.* London: Michael Joseph, 1959.

149. Lloyd, F. H. M. *Hurricane, The Story of a Great Fighter.* Leicester: Harborough Publishing Co., 1945.
150. Lock, Archibald C. *Diary and Notes relating to Radar Equipment, 1940–1943.* MS in Imperial War Museum, London.
151. Ludovici, Laurence James. *The Challenging Sky: the life of Sir Alliott Verdon-Roe.* London: Jenkins, 1956.
152. Macksey, Major Kenneth John. *Armoured Crusader: a biography of Major-General Sir Percy Hobart.* London: Hutchinson, 1967.
153. MacLeod, Roderick, and Kelly, Denis, eds. *The Ironside Diaries.* London: Constable, 1962.
154. Macmillan, Norman. *Sir Sefton Brancker.* London: Heinemann, 1935.
155. Martel, Sir Giffard. "The Development of Mechanisation 1933–1939." *The Journal of the Royal United Service Institution,* Vol. XCI, No. 564, 1946.
156. Martel, G. le Q. *In the Wake of the Tank: the First Eighteen Years of Mechanisation in the British Army.* London: Sifton Praed, 1936.
157. Martel, Sir Giffard le Quesne. *An Outspoken Soldier.* London: Sifton Praed, 1949.
158. Maund, Rear-Admiral L. E. H. *Assault from the Sea.* London: Methuen, 1949.
159. *Proceedings of the Institution of Mechanical Engineers.* 1847– .
160. Melville, Sir Harry. *The Department of Scientific and Industrial Research.* London: Allen and Unwin, 1962.
161. Millington, Air Commodore G. *The Unseen Eye.* London: Anthony Gibbs & Phillips, 1961.
162. *Minerva, A Review of Science, Learning and Policy.* London: Quarterly, 1962– .
163. Minney, R. J. *The Private Papers of Leslie Hore-Belisha.* London: Collins, 1960.
164. Morgan, Lieutenant-General Sir Frederick. *Overture to Overlord.* London: Hodder & Stoughton, 1950.
165. *Motor Transport.* 1905– .
166. *Nature.* 1869– .
167. *The Navy.* 1895– .
168. *The Naval Review* (for private circulation). 1913– .
169. O'Brien, Terence H. *Civil Defence.* H.M.S.O., 1955.
170. *The Origins and Development of Operational Research in the Royal Air Force.* H.M.S.O., 1963.
171. *Oxford Magazine.* 1882– .
172. Pawle, Gerald. *The Secret War.* London: Harrap, 1956.
173. Pawle, Gerald. *The War and Colonel Warden.* Based on the recollections of Commander C. R. Thomson. London: Harrap, 1963.
174. "Petrol Pipeline Under the English Channel." *The Engineer,* May 25, June 8, and June 15, 1945, London.
175. Pile, Sir Frederick. *Ack-Ack: Britain's defence against air attack during the Second World War.* London: Harrap, 1949.

176. "Plastics at War." *British Plastics,* July, 1950.
177. "Cable for Operation Pluto." W. T. Henley's Telegraph Works, (I.W.M.)
178. "Pluto." *The Journal of the Royal Army Service Corps,* Vol. LXIX, No. 6, 1945.
179. "Operation Pluto." *The Quartermaster Review,* Vol. XXV, July–August, 1948.
180. Postan, M. M. *British War Production.* H.M.S.O., 1952.
181. Postan, M. M., D. Hay, and J. D. Scott. *The Design and Development of Weapons: studies in government and industrial organisation.* H.M.S.O., 1965.
182. Price, *Instruments of Darkness: the struggle for supremacy.* London: Kimber, 1967.
183. Pudney, John. *Laboratory of the Air: an account of the Royal Aircraft Establishment of the Ministry of Supply, Farnborough.* Ministry of Supply, 1948.
184. Purvis, M. K. "Craft & Cable Ships for Operation Pluto." *I.N.A. Paper No. 8,* Institution of Naval Architects.
185. "David Randall Pye." By O. A. Saunders. *Biographical Memoirs of Fellows of the Royal Society,* Vol. 7, 1961.
186. *Radar Bulletin* (later *Radar and Electronics*). 1946– .
187. "Radar Counter-Measures." *The Engineer,* Dec. 7, 1945.
188. "The Royal Signals and The Early Days of Radar." *The Wire.* (I.W.M.)
189. "Radio Industry Grows Five-fold in Secret." No source, London, 1945. (Copy located at I.W.M.)
190. Proceedings of the Radiolocation Convention. *Journal of the Institute of Electrical Engineers,* Part 93, III A 1/10, 1946 VI (1) 5–1620.
191. *The Story of Radiolocation.* Ministry of Information, 1945.
192. Radio Research Board. *Annual Reports.* London, 1920– .
193. Radio Times Hulton Picture Library. (See Introduction.)
194. *R.E.M.E. Magazine, The Journal of the Corps of Royal Electrical and Mechanical Engineers.* 1951– .
195. *Research.* 1947–1962.
196. *The Road Research Board, The Wartime Activities of.* H.M.S.O., London, 1949.
197. Roskill, Stephen W. *The War at Sea.* Vol. 2, *The Balance of Power*; Vol. 3, Part I, *The Offensive.* H.M.S.O., 1956 and 1960.
198. Rowe, A. P. "From Scientific Idea to Practical Use." *Minerva,* London, spring, 1964.
199. Rowe, A. P. *One Story of Radar.* London: Cambridge University Press, 1948.
200. *The Journal of the Royal Aeronautical Society.* 1866– .
201. *Royal Air Forces Quarterly,* 1961.
202. *Research on High Speed Aerodynamics at the Royal Aircraft Establishment from 1942–1945.* W. A. Mair, ed. H.M.S.O., 1956.
203. *The Royal Armoured Corps Journal* (including *The Royal Tank*

Corps Journal which was first the *Tank Corps Journal* and then *The Tank*). 1946–   .

204. *Royal Corps of Transport Review* (1966 as *Royal Army Corps Quarterly*). 1905–   .

205. *Journal of the Royal Corps of Electrical and Mechanical Engineers.* 1951–   .

206. *Royal Signals Quarterly Journal.* 1933–   . (After 1954 as *Journal of the Royal Signals Institution.*)

207. *The Royal Engineers Journal.* Institution of Royal Engineers, Chatham: 1905–   .

208. *Journal of the Royal Naval Scientific Service.* 1946–   .

209. *Proceedings of the Royal Society.* 1832–   .

210. *Journal of the Royal United Service Institution.* 1858–   . (See Introduction.)

211. Saundby, Air Marshal Sir Robert. *Air Bombardment.* New York: Harper, 1961.

212. Saward, Dudley. *The Bomber's Eye.* London: Cassell, 1959.

213. Sayer, Brigadier A. P. *Army Radar.* London: War Office, 1950.

214. Scarfe, Norman. *Assault Division: a history of the 3rd. Division.* London: Collins, 1947.

215. *Science in War.* Harmondsworth Mddx: Penguin Books, 1940.

216. Department of Scientific and Industrial Research. *Annual Reports.* London, 1916–

217. Scott, J. D. *Vickers.* London: Weidenfeld & Nicholson, 1962.

218. "Sealion." "Naval Radar." *The Navy,* Vol. LIII, No. 7, 1948.

219. *History of the 7th Armoured Division, June 1943–July 1945.* British Army of the Rhine, 1945.

220. Sharp, C. Martin. *D.H.: an outline of de Havilland history.* London: Faber, 1961.

221. *Shipping World & Shipbuilder.* 1883–   .

222. Slessor, Marshal of the R.A.F. Sir John. *The Central Blue.* London: Cassell, 1956.

223. Smith, Constance Babington. *Evidence in Camera.* London: Chatto & Windus, 1958. (U. S. title: *Air Spy.*)

224. Smith, Constance Babington. *The Testing Time: the story of British test flying.* London: Cassells, 1961.

225. Snow, Sir Charles. *Science and Government.* London: Oxford University Press, 1961.

226. Snow, Sir Charles. *A Postscript to Science and Government.* London: Oxford University Press, 1962. (Included in #225 in U. S. Edition.)

227. Southall, Ivan. *Softly Tread the Brave.* London: Angus & Robertson, 1960.

228. Storrs, Sir Ronald. *Dunlop in War and Peace.* London: Hutchinson, 1946.

229. "Dr. Strabismus at War." *R.A.F. Weekly Bulletin,* March 6, 1941.

230. *The Structural Engineer.* 1923–   .

231. *Taurus Pursuant: a history of the 11th. Armoured Division*. British Army of the Rhine, 1945.

232. *The Scientific Papers of Sir Geoffrey Ingram Taylor*. Vol. III, *Aerodynamics & the Mechanics of Projectiles and Explosives*. G. K. Batchelor, ed. Cambridge: Cambridge University Press, 1963.

233. Taylor, John P. "The Pre-Fabricated Port of Arromanches, (Mulberry B)." *Shipbuilding and Shipping Record*, London, 1945.

234. Taylor, John W. R. *C.F.S.: birthplace of air power*. London: Putnam, 1958.

235. Taylor, John W. R., and Maurice F. Allward. *Spitfire*. Leicester: Harborough Publishing Company, 1945.

236. Taylor, Telford. *The Breaking Wave: the German defeat in the summer of 1940*. London: Weidenfeld & Nicholson, 1967.

237. Tedder, Marshal of the Royal Air Force Lord. *With Prejudice*. London: Cassell, 1966.

238. Terrell, Edward. *Admiralty Brief: the story of inventions that contributed to victory in the Battle of the Atlantic*. London: Harrap, 1958.

239. *History of T-Force Activities in Rhine Army*. BAOR, 1946.

240. Thetford, O. G. *Aircraft of the Royal Air Force, 1918–57*. London: Putnam, 1957 and later editions.

241. Threlfall, R. E. *The Story of 100 Years of Phosphorus Making, 1851–1951*. Oldbury: Albright & Wilson, 1951.

242. "Sir Henry Thomas Tizard." By Sir William S. Farren with a note by Professor R. V. Jones. *Biographical Memoirs of Fellows of the Royal Society*, Vol. 7, 1961.

243. Waldron, T. J. and James Gleeson. *The Frogmen*. London: Evans, 1950.

244. *A Record of War and Peace, 1819–1946*. London: Siebe Gorman & Co, 1946.

245. Warren, C. E. T. and James Benson. *Above Us the Waves*. London: Harrap, 1953.

246. Watson-Watt, Sir Robert. *Three Steps to Victory*. London: Odhams, 1958.

247. Webster, Sir Charles and Noble Frankland. *The Strategic Air Offensive Against Germany, 1939–1945*. H.M.S.O., 1961. 4 vols.

248. Weir, Sir Cecil M. *Civilian Assignment*. London: Methuen, 1953.

249. Wernher, Major-General Sir Harold. *World War II: personal experiences*. Privately printed, 1950.

250. Wernher, Major-General Sir Harold. *History of the Mulberry Project, August 1943–April 1944 embracing Phoenix, Whale, Bombardon and Gooseberry. 1944*. (Unpublished manuscript in the official archives, London.)

251. Wheeler, A. H. ". . . *and that nothing failed them*." London: G. T. Foulis, 1963.

252. Whittle, Air Commodore Sir Frank. *Jet*. London: Muller, 1953.

253. Whyte, Lancelot Law. *Focus & Diversions*. London: Cressett Press, 1963.

254. Wilson, Captain Andrew. *Flame Thrower*. London: Kimber, 1956.
255. Wood, Derek, and Derek Dempster. *The Narrow Margin*. London: Hutchinson, 1961.
256. Wright, Lawrence. *The Wooden Sword*. London: Elek, 1967.
257. Wykeham, Peter. *Fighter Command*. London: Putnam, 1960.
258. Zuckerman, Sir Solly. *Scientists at War*. London: Hamish Hamilton, 1966.
259. *Manuscript sources:* It is quite impossible to give detailed information on the availability of much MS material. Thus the Hankey papers will not be available for study until the biography of Lord Hankey now being written is complete, while the Cherwell papers, in the hands of Nuffield College, Oxford, are divided into various categories to which different rules apply regarding access and publication. Others, such as the Tizard and Trenchard papers are in private hands.
260. The Hankey Papers (Churchill College).
261. The Papers of Professor A. V. Hill (Churchill College).
262. The Papers of Admiral Keyes (Churchill College).
263. The Papers of Admiral Somerville (Churchill College).
264. Papers of the Maud Committee (Churchill College).
265. Papers of Professor Sir George Thomson (Churchill College).
266. Papers of Dr. Barnes Wallis (Churchill College).

INITIALS GIVEN IN TEXT

S.O.E. Special Operations Executive
H.M.S.O. His Majesty's Stationery Office
D.S.I.R. Department of Scientific and Industrial Research
C.F.S. Central Flying School
A.R.C. Aeronautical Research Committee
T.R.E. Telecommunications Research Establishment
M.D.I. Military Defence I
S.A.C. Scientific Advisory Committee (of the Cabinet)

XXII

BRITISH DEFENCE POLICY SINCE 1945

Martin Edmonds and A. J. R. Groom

The relatively high rate of innovation in both strategic thinking and weaponry is the most salient characteristic of British defence policy since 1945. This has led to the involvement of a large sector of the population in, and the allocation of a considerable proportion of the country's resources to, defence. In a situation of "non-war" this degree of concern for defence is a new feature of modern British history.

The doctrines of massive retaliation, broken-backed warfare and the many guises of graduated deterrence were debated, and in some cases adopted, with an alacrity that was not reflected in the hardware in service. Nevertheless, within two decades the development, firepower and weapons systems of the armed forces changed beyond recognition. Moreover, the proportion of the country's resources devoted to defence constituted a great burden, as it was large in both absolute and relative terms. Annual expenditure was never less than six per cent of the G.N.P. and sometimes rose to more than 10 per cent; in terms of total government expenditure the proportions spent on defence fluctuated between a quarter and a third.

National Service, which ended in 1962, brought the Armed Services into much closer contact with the public than either had been accustomed to in peacetime: and the new relationship was generally considered by both parties to be an unpleasant necessity. The mass media brought the "colonial policing" activities of the Services vividly into the purview of the public at large in a manner not possible before 1945. Thus the traditional activities of the Services were no longer an isolated part of the life of the country. Furthermore, the advent of the nuclear age created general interest in "Grand Strategy"—that potent mixture of strategic and foreign affairs.

The experience of the Second World War and the destructive capability of nuclear weapons allied to startling advances in air power brought a fundamental change in Britain's geostrategic position. The impregnable island fortress defended by a powerful navy was a fact of life that had been instilled into the subconsciousness of generations of Britons. In 1945, this sense of assurance was no more. Indeed it became increasingly evident that the foundations of *Pax Britannica* had been eroded. The Royal

Navy no longer "ruled the waves" nor was it relevant: and the sun was about to set on the British Empire. While Britain continued to play a world role and claimed Great Power status partly by virtue of its prospective nuclear weapons, the United States and the Soviet Union alone could aspire to the role of a Super Power. Britain was both over-committed and vulnerable, yet only partly willing to acknowledge that its role in International Society had changed. No longer was it the dominant partner in an alliance, more sought after than seeking; the security of the British Isles rested henceforth on the United States alliance within the NATO framework.

A decade after the Second World War, the brutalisation of society engendered by total war had dissipated, but there remained the drabness of austerity, the disillusion with the welfare state, the frustration of decolonisation entailing the search for a new role and the fear of, and vulnerability to, a nuclear holocaust. The very fabric of British society was being questioned at home and abroad. The values epitomised by the resistance to Hitler were now no longer relevant; the problem was one of readjustment to a world of rapid social, economic and political change. In defence this challenge was felt alike, but in a different manner, by the Aldermaston marchers and the Cranwell cadet. This, indeed, was the context of British defence policy since 1945: welfare demands and perceived defence exigencies often clashed because Britain's leaders did not always realise the nature of the challenge nor, when they saw it, did they always meet it.

SOURCES. 1. A SURVEY. Despite the importance of defence throughout the years since 1945, there are few sources immediately available to the historian because of the Thirty-Year rule. The archives of the Ministry of Defence, the Service Ministries, the Ministries of Supply, Aviation and Technology, the Foreign Office and the Cabinet Office are all closed. Government publications are few in number and limited in content. The usual practice has been to publish an annual Defence White Paper (121) in February, followed by Estimates for the Services (122) later in the year. These statements have provided a bare outline of policy and a minimum of data relating to deployment, weaponry and planning. While it is in the nature of current defence planning that there is an element of secrecy, the rate of change—political, technological and conceptual—has been such that access to archives for the immediate post-war years would be unlikely to prove prejudicial to the public interest. However, these sources seem destined to remain unavailable for some years so that, for the time being, study of the government's policy must be based on its own publications and press releases supplemented by Ministerial presentation of policy to Parliament. In most years the annual White Paper is presented to the House of Commons in early March, and the Service Estimates have followed at an appropriate interval. The standard of debate (140) is low, and its influence on policy is limited. Members of Parliament have substantially no greater access to information than the public and thus, given their ignorance and the relatively little electoral kudos that defence engenders, they show a minimal interest. Indeed, apart from debates on special issues such as the cancellation of the Blue Streak, defence debates are carried on by a coterie of some fifty members drawn from both sides of the House.

While contemporary defence analysis suffers from lack of access to documents, access is possible to some of the actors. However, the Official Secrets Act seals most lips and takes the life blood out of memoirs. Moreover, memoirs are notoriously fickle and men are vain. The testimony of actors is thus of no great moment.

A large number of books have been published on British defence problems since 1945. The general quality is low although there are some notable exceptions. These are usually of a prescriptive rather than an analytical nature and are not confined to defence policy alone. Periodicals and the press are of a higher standard when allowance is made for their journalistic nature. A selection of periodicals and the daily and weekly press that gives a worthwhile coverage to defence problems is included in the bibliography. Finally, books on British defence problems are comprehensively reviewed in *International Affairs* (157), the *Royal United Services Institution Journal* (176), *Survival* (179), *Yearbook of World Affairs* (181), some Service journals and the trade and national press.

Libraries which contain a useful collection of material relevant to British defence policy since 1945 are few in number. In London, both the Royal Institute of International Affairs and the Institute for Strategic Studies have good general and press libraries; other important collections are to be found in the Royal United Services Institution and the various libraries of the University of London. The British Museum is the deposit library for all publications in Britain. Elsewhere in Britain, Cranwell, Dartmouth, Greenwich and Shrivenham, the principal Service Colleges, in addition to University libraries, house the main collections and may be used on application.

The study of contemporary British defence problems has increased in the last decade along with the general rise of interest in strategic studies. Apart from the political parties and the professional commentators, both the Institute for Strategic Studies and the Royal Institute of International Affairs have shown some interest in British problems, many of which have been published in the *Adelphi Papers* (190) and *J.R.U.S.I. Pamphlets* (225) respectively, and there are courses on Strategic Studies at several Universities, notably London (Kings College, London School of Economics and Political Science, and University College), Lancaster, Aberystwyth, Manchester and Southampton. Nevertheless, British defence policy since 1945 is largely a virgin field in which there are no standard works.

2. TECHNIQUES OF ANALYSIS. Forced to accept immediate material difficulties in pursuit of his research into British defence policy in the last two decades, the historian has to seek information wherever he can find it. This is not an easy task; it can only be achieved successfully after several years of the patient and systematic collection of items of information from a wide variety of disparate sources. The ordeal is arduous and not immediately rewarding. It is only after a long period of time and after developing techniques of using material as collateral evidence, as a test

both of that material and of official pronouncements and immediately available commentary, that a more detailed and accurate picture emerges.

The different provenance of the data—ranging from Defence Ministry advertisements in scientific journals mentioning specific qualifications for particular research projects to the deliberations of Learned Societies, or from recruiting posters to Banking Reviews—requires that the defence analyst be careful, versatile and possess an intuitive sense for significant pieces of information which might otherwise have gone unnoticed or ignored. The principles of aerodynamics, nuclear physics, economics, organisational theory, engineering and psychology are but some of the areas with which the scholar must have a working acquaintance; otherwise he must have access to others who can interpret the significance of technical information.

With experience, it becomes easier to identify and evaluate pertinent items, and likely sources themselves become more readily apparent. One interesting phenomenon in this respect is that very often trade, service and professional journals published outside the United Kingdom are the best informed on the details of British defence policy and planning, particularly in relation to the technicalities of British weaponry. Worthy of mention in this respect is the United States journal *Aviation Week* (148), the Swiss aviation magazine *Interavia* (156), and the French *Revue Générale Militaire* (173). Among regular British sources on defence is *Flight International* (153) which pays particular attention to defence contracts and weaponry. It is, however, to give a false impression to say that there are *regular* sources of information. The analyst does not know when and in what form the information will come to him; his task is to be cognisant of it when it is before him.

Although this process is lengthy and sometimes tedious, it is important to know what can be done with the plethora of small items that has been collected. It has already been mentioned that it can be used to build up an overall picture, or as collateral evidence in relation to official sources. It is this sort of technique that is employed by *Aviation Studies International* (a private research organisation run by Richard Worcester) (192), based on their detailed analysis of the technicalities of advanced weapons systems, their number, performance parameters and costs. However, the material can be used for other purposes, equally pertinent to the analysis of defence policy: for example, to gain an insight into problems of training, education and socialisation in the armed forces, to find out details of force levels and structures, and to provide a quantitative basis for assessment of British defence capabilities in relation to commitments in various parts of the world and in different operational environments. Alternatively, it can lead to rewarding fields of enquiry within the broad context of the economics of defence and the consequent issues of opportunity cost. Contractual procedures for weapons systems and sub-systems, the structure and size of the armaments industry, resource constraints in terms of capital investment, technical know-how and materials, and the weapons acquisition process can sometimes give detailed insights into defence feasibilities, weaponry and, ultimately, policy. By systematically working backwards in time, and tabulating chronologically production and prototype contracts and research innovations—for which the *New Scientist* (166), *Nature* (163), and *Discovery* (150) are rewarding sources—and by relating these with defence policy announcements, the patterns and continuity of defence decision-making and the probable criteria upon which these decisions were made, can be revealed.

For the most part, this approach to defence analysis provides evidence which, at best, is circumstantial. The machinations of the responsible Departments for defence planning and procurement remain behind locked doors, and access to primary evidence is denied. However, the greater the understanding of the decision-making processes within these Ministries, the technical and research information upon which decisions are made, the economic, financial and industrial constraints upon defence expenditure, and the issues raised by problems of research lead times and time horizons, coupled with an acquaintance with specific Service problems, the more the evidence becomes acceptable within a tolerable margin of credibility.

Until primary sources are released, analysis of British defence policy must depend upon techniques of this laborious nature. It is to be hoped that Ministers responsible will concede the significance of independent research in this important field of enquiry, as has been so forcefully demonstrated by independent institutions in the United States. Until some gesture is made from official quarters, either in terms of active assistance or the removal of obstruction, so much of which is petty, the defence analyst, unless he is content with journalistic and impressionistic comment, is obliged to conduct his research employing a time-wasting *modus operandi* that may best be described as a way of life.

NUCLEAR AND ALLIANCE PROBLEMS—GRAND STRATEGY.

1. GENERAL WORKS. Despite the intellectual debate over massive retaliation and graduated deterrence, and the political furor over the independent deterrent, there are only two published general historical accounts of British defence policy since 1945 that are worthy of note. Like several other studies of British problems, these are by Americans: William P. Snyder, *The Politics of British Defence Policy 1945–62* (106) and Richard Rosecrance, *Defence of the Realm* (93). These are supplemented by A. J. R. Groom's volume (48) tracing British thinking about nuclear weapons from 1940 until 1962 as seen by the political parties and the military intellectuals, as well as by the Unions and the Churches. It pays particular attention to the nuclear disarmament movement. It is mainly concerned with "Grand Strategy"; alliance problems and disarmament are therefore not ignored, nor are the developments in delivery systems. Good summaries of the main issues can be found in articles by Goldberg (40 and 41) and Gott (45). Finally, a dissertation on British bases by a United States officer, De Witt Armstrong (3), contains an outline of the decision-making process in defence.

2. WARTIME PROJECT. It is difficult to understand Britain's post-

war policy in the nuclear domain without a background knowledge of Britain's heavy involvement in the wartime project to build the atomic bomb. Here the first volume of the official history by Margaret Gowing (46) provides a good full account.

3. THEORETICAL PROBLEMS. Two schools of thought have dominated Western strategic thought since 1945. Both found an early formulation (and perhaps their origin) in Britain. One may be broadly termed that favouring some form of massive retaliation, and the other could be loosely classified under the label "graduated deterrence." British policy was, on the whole, dominated by the former until the advent of the 1964 Labour government, while most military intellectuals favoured the latter. In British and NATO circles during the late forties and early fifties, Sir John Slessor was closely associated with the policy of strategic nuclear bombing, and his ideas were embraced both by the Conservative government in Britain and the Republican administration in the United States. After his retirement from active service, Slessor wrote *Strategy for the West* (101), but later modified his ideas in two books (102 and 103) and a host of articles.

The arrival, or anticipation, of mutual deterrence between East and West evident in the middle and late fifties gave rise to concern over the credibility of the Western deterrent; this provided a new "justification" for the British independent deterrent. Graduated deterrence was soon to become "conventional wisdom" outside government circles, and its principal advocates included a retired high-ranking naval officer, Anthony Buzzard, and a leading Labour Party defence expert, Denis Healey. Both wrote numerous articles (17–19, 44). However, the Tory government's answer to mutual deterrence and its doubts about the credibility of the United States deterrent against a limited attack in Europe was to adopt a "massive retaliation" policy as an action as well as declaratory policy. It was also felt that this policy could yield economies, preserve British independence, prestige and Great Power status, and augment British influence in Washington. Duncan Sandys was the Defence Minister charged with reshaping the armed forces. He reduced their numbers by nearly half; apart from a colonial policing capability, they were almost entirely nuclearised. The Sandys Five-Year Plan was outlined in the Defence White Papers of 1957 and 1958 (121). An intriguing article by Laurence Martin (71) surveys the market for strategic ideas at that time. During the same period Montgomery was commenting on alliance problems in his role as Deputy Supreme Allied Commander Europe (76–79).

After an initially favourable reception, Sandys' policy met with general opposition. For a brief period, servicemen gave public expression to their dissent, as an article by Cowley (24) demonstrates, although some, such as Moulton (81), waited until their retirement. This outburst was contrary to the British tradition in civil-military relations as can be gauged by Howard's article (57). During this period major treatises of a general theoretical nature were published by Liddell Hart (67), Strachey (107 and 108), and Blackett (9): they all differed substantially from the government's line. Moreover, the government's defence policy was no longer consistent with that of the United States under the McNamara doctrine. Although these differences were played down by both parties, Zuckerman (119), then the government's Chief Scientist, wrote a veiled criticism of the McNamara line.

After the appointment of Denis Healey as the Labour government's Secretary of State for Defence, Sandys' framework was dropped. Labour's policy vacillated as the White Papers of 1965, 1966 and 1967 (123) indicate. However, by 1967 a thorough review was completed, and an attempt to abandon Britain's world role was made in order to make commitments commensurate with capabilities. This policy was hastened by devaluation and the subsequent cuts in defence expenditure.

4. DISARMAMENT AND ARMS CONTROL. There is no single work which covers British policy since the war. British policy has been active in this area, and the best guide to it can be found in the occasional White Paper and the accounts of such politicians and diplomats as Noel-Baker (83), Nutting (84), and Wright (117). British diplomacy (and political opinion) was the most responsive in the West to the proposals for disengagement in Europe that were current in the late fifties. The volumes by Howard (54) and Hinterhof (53) are a reliable guide to these proposals. More recently, nuclear proliferation has been a major concern of British policy, and Leonard Beaton (5) has made the subject very much his preserve. One major theoretical work on disarmament and arms control has been produced in Britain—Hedley Bull's *The Control of the Arms Race* (15)—and a second, by April Carter, is to be published in the near future (20).

5. THE PROTEST MOVEMENT. The Campaign for Nuclear Disarmament, the Committee of 100 and the Direct Action Committee organised a massive and colourful campaign during the years 1958–1963. The best single account of this is by Christopher Driver, *The Disarmers* (29). The intellectual content of the movement was not commensurate with its size, but it was greater than its influence. The movement's most prominent leader, Bertrand Russell, wrote two books (94 and 95) which are more accessible than the protestor's many pamphlets. A similar but separate point of view can be found in King-Hall (64 and 65). An excellent sociological analysis of the protest movement is Frank Parkin's *Middle Class Radicalism* (214).

6. ECONOMICS AND DELIVERY SYSTEMS. A more thorough treatment will be given below. However, the Economist Intelligence Unit volume, *The Economic Effects of Disarmament* (30), is a useful introduction to many aspects of the economics of British defence policy. Examples of the difficulty in finding an adequate delivery system for the deterrent can be found in Burns (16), Field (35), and Fletcher (37). An article by Groom puts a similar problem in an alliance framework (50).

7. ALLIANCES. There is no volume analysing British nuclear policy

in NATO, SEATO, or CENTO: this reversal of a traditional policy of "splendid isolation" has evoked no major study. There are, however, many articles by Buchan and Healey analysing alliance problems. In addition, there are three important studies of alliance problems by P. M. S. Blackett (8), Alistair Buchan (13), and Fred Mulley (82)—a future Labour Minister.

DEFENCE—SUBSTANTIVE ISSUES IN RESPECT OF POLICY, SYSTEM AND ENVIRONMENT. 1. GENERAL COMMENTS. In an examination of defence policy, it is misleading to divorce any single aspect from its context, whether temporal, spatial or technical. The substantive issues below must be seen within the context of the Grand Strategy involving nuclear weapons, alliances, and the theoretical and conceptual problems that these two specifically raise. Further, in any survey of bibliographical material on substantive issues in defence policy, the inter-relationship and interdependence of the many facets relevant to defence must be borne in mind. It would be misleading to suggest that they can be studied separately while at the same time giving an accurate overall picture. For example, as the Defence White Paper of 1965 rightly stressed, political change throughout the world required constant revision of Britain's defence posture, and assumptions behind defence policy had to be worked out in relation to the forces required, the weapons that they should bear, and the organisation and control of the total defence effort. Policy, organisation and equipment, it might be argued, are the three most salient variables in any examination of defence. They are interdependent at various levels of capability and commitment, ranging from the more mundane problems of civil defence to nuclear deterrence within the strategic context of the East-West debate.

It is therefore only for purposes of simplicity that this examination of British defence policy is separated into three sections, corresponding to these three variables, conceding that in doing so, there will be an element of distortion. In addition, any defence problem must be seen in context; for this reason, the defence environment has been included in a separate section. The external environment in which political and military change is going on throughout the world has an immediate bearing upon British defence capability. The internal environment, in which interact the forces of economic, political and social priorities, sets parameters within which defence has to be contained. There is an interrelationship between these two types of environment, as, for example, in 1951, where the external situation regarding first Berlin, and secondly Korea, led the Government to embark upon a programme of controlled reallocation of scarce industrial, economic and material resources to defence.

2. DEFENCE POLICY—CONSISTENT OBJECTIVES AND MARGINAL ADJUSTMENT. Within the context of Grand Strategy, there are a number of defence policy objectives which represent a continuum since 1945. The impression they give, as illustrated in Martin's *The Long Recession,* (216) is not one of long-term political goals so much as legacies of past

policies that await discredit or obsolescence as a result of the dynamics of change in the external international environment. Such policies have marginally been changed in response to influences, but the ultimate objectives have remained unaltered. Among these are Britain's commitments to the Commonwealth. Malaya is a case in point. The anti-guerrilla operations in that country have been assessed in part by a participant in Thompson's *Defeating Communist Insurgency* (109), as well as in Paret and Shy's *Guerillas in the 60's* (87), and O'Ballance's *Malaya: the Communist insurgent war* (85). These, however, concern themselves more with the techniques of guerilla operations. The recent Malaysian confrontation with Indonesia has not been fully assessed, though sporadic coverage may be found in military and professional journals and newspapers. Other Commonwealth commitments have to be found in non-British sources, and some reference by way of illustration can be made to Britain's commitment to Australia in Millar's *Australia's Defence* (73).

There is a distinction to be made between Britain's Commonwealth commitments and her obligations to countries through bi-lateral treaty in which Britain guarantees military support and assistance. Although such commitments diminished throughout the period under examination, culminating in the decision early in 1968 to bring forward the military withdrawal from the Indian Ocean and the Far East, no work of substance on any of them has yet emerged. Military journals, such as *Brassey's Annual* (149), *Army Quarterly* (146), and the *Royal United Services Institution Journal* (176), will serve the historian best.

Britain's commitments in Europe, the Middle and Far East, and to the United Nations have presented a constant element in her defence policy. There is no substantial work on Britain's policy towards the Brussels Treaty, EDC, WEU or NATO. Several books make reference to NATO but do so only within a general alliance context. Sources already mentioned fall into this category. Works of less immediate significance but which, nevertheless, help to build up a general picture include, for example, a chapter by Beloff in *The Atlantic Community* edited by Wilcox and Haviland (113). Of special note is the *Rand Corporation* series of memoranda and papers on NATO, of which perhaps deWeerd's *British Defence Policy and NATO* (112) might be singled out because of its immediate relevance. Among journals containing useful articles that add to the overall picture should be mentioned the *Atlantic Community Quarterly* (147), *NATO's 15 Nations* (162), and the official *NATO Letter* (161). For an earlier insight, Ismay, *NATO: the first five years* (59), serves as a point of departure. With regard to other alliances, Modelski's *SEATO* (75) alone contains anything relevant—and only then in the first section. There is nothing on CENTO, nor on Britain's military policy towards the United Nations. It is only with reference to Britain's contribution to the United Nations forces in Korea that anything concrete can be found, as, for example, in Rees's *Korea: the limited war* (86), and Goodwin's *Britain and the United Nations* (41).

A policy which Britain has maintained since 1945, which, in recent years has become known as the "East of Suez" policy, became, in the middle sixties, a centre of controversy among servicemen, politicians and journalists. Significantly, the differences of opinion were less about the policy itself and more about the equipment necessary to fulfill that policy: for example, there are articles in *International Affairs* by Buchan (14) and Howard (55). These references may be used to discover the major issues in respect of that policy, and the controversy surrounding the choice between carriers and strategic bombers.

An important and unquestioned feature of British defence policy is the close relationship between Britain and the United States. This policy is within the framework of the Atlantic Alliance and is manifest in bilateral discussion, planning and technical cooperation. Within this general field, technological information and favourable arms agreements are afforded Britain by the United States. The familiar pattern again emerges that there is no work which traces the form and extent to which Britain's defence policy, effort or capability is geared to, or dependent upon, its relationship with the United States. Only the more technical and professional articles in respect of arms deals, notably Skybolt, Polaris, and the F.111, give any detailed information. After the Nassau Conference oblique references were made to this aspect of British defence policy; though most journals on international affairs in Britain and the United States contained articles on that conference, the important questions were in the main left unanswered.

There are other constant aspects of British defence policy but their importance has varied according to the changed international environment. One such feature is the defence of Britain and its airspace. After 1945 vulnerability to air attack indicated a fundamental need for a viable air defence capability and the prosecution of Britain's existing lead in aerodynamics and jet propulsion. The arguments for air defence during the post-war period, and especially soon after the 1957 White Paper, can be found in several sources, among which are Divine's *Broken Wing* (27) and Fedden's *Britain's Air Survival* (34). These two could be fruitfully supplemented by the many books on the development and history of British aircraft built during the period which include Higham's *Production and Politics* (52) and Rae's *The British Automobile and Aircraft Industries* (90). Of particular note also is the coverage provided by the aviation journals, *Flying Review* (154), *Aeroplane* (144), and *Flight International* (153). These can be supplemented by the *RAF Quarterly* (175), the *Royal Aeronautical Society Journal* (175), *Aeronautics* (143), and *Aeronautical Quarterly* (142). Later, discussion concerning air defence became submerged within the broader spectrum of passive defence, deterrence and early warning systems.

Alongside Britain's air defence policies must come her world naval role, and the consistent policy that she has pursued in respect of maritime patrol and surveillance. Naval policy since 1945 has involved the demise of capital ships and the initiation and completion of a construction programme of aircraft carriers and a substantial number of destroyers and frigates with anti-submarine capabilities. Recently, several books have been published making reference to naval policy. Gretton's *Maritime Strategy* (47) is

576 · A GUIDE TO THE SOURCES OF BRITISH MILITARY HISTORY

the best, and to this can be added both the traditional Schofield's *British Sea Power: naval policy in the twentieth century* (97) and Martin's *Sea in Modern Strategy* (72), which is of a more theoretical nature. *Navy* (165), the publication of the Navy League, and *Naval Review* (164), an independent publication, are useful general sources. As with air power, Britain's naval policy has become somewhat overshadowed by the big strategic debates: the development of missile ships, Polaris, and the cancellation of the carrier programme in 1968 reflect this changing emphasis.

The Cinderella of the armed services is the Army. For the most part, the service has had to maintain the brunt of operations in the many trouble spots throughout the world in which Britain has been involved. It is difficult to identify any government policy towards the Army, other than the continual development of techniques of armour, mobility, and, for a brief period, medium-range missile capability. The fortunes of the Army can be traced in Verrier's *An Army for the Sixties* (110), Divine's *The Blunted Sword* (26), and in Barnett's *Britain and Her Army* (222).

Although constant aspects of British defence policy can be found, it is the fluctuations and alterations which are most significant. It is the changes in defence policy that give the analyst some information with which to get to grips, and with which he can use his methodically gathered material as collateral evidence for the change. Most alterations concern new and different weapons systems, thereby indicating that this approach to defence is immediately the most rewarding; furthermore, it is often the most politically significant. Sometimes, the alterations are on a grand scale, as in 1951, 1957 and 1967.

The first, following five years of post-war defence rundown and demobilisation with commitments being met with existing *matériel* and resources, was the decision to rearm. A programme over three years amounting to £4,700 million was instigated in response to a perceived Soviet threat and the outbreak of the Korean war. It involved a scramble to acquire new weapons systems whose progress had fallen behind as a result of specific government decisions not to devote too much time and technical expertise to weapons research and development. The details of the rearmament programme and the problems that it involved are best discovered among official sources, namely, the Report and minutes of evidence before the *Select Committee on Estimates on Rearmament, 1950–1952* (132), and the *Select Committee on Estimates on the Supply of Military Aircraft, 1955–6* (133) and the *Public Accounts Committee Reports* (131) for the period. The 1957 White Paper precipitated considerable reaction and comment, as have the recent decisions in respect of weapons cancellations and Far East commitments.

3. DEFENCE ORGANISATION. Taking a broad definition of defence organisation, this section is designed to include not only the organisation and structure of the Defence Ministry, but also the political control of defence through the Defence Committee of the Cabinet and Parliament, the structure and organisation of the individual armed services, and the many other government departments that have some responsibility for aspects of de-

fence. The task becomes markedly simpler if it is stated immediately that there are no substantial references to the structure and organisation of the armed services individually or collectively. There are no management studies of the military establishment as can be found in the United States. Interservice joint planning, particularly under simulated or combat conditions, is treated in a few articles which can be found in a number of professional journals. There are, however, a number of references to military training: for example, Smyth's *Sandhurst* (105). Perhaps the examination of *Recruitment* by the 1958 Advisory Committee (125) is a better point of departure.

The main issues arising out of Defence Organisation centre around the unification of the services and the increase in the control and influence of the Ministry of Defence over military decisions. In 1946 the importance of the experience of the Second World War in coordinating the efforts of the three Services became institutionalised in the formation of the Ministry of Defence. A small Ministry, its function was primarily one of responsibility for the formulation and general application of a unified policy. Broad responsibility for administration rested with the Service Departments. The background to this new element in the Establishment can be found in Johnson's *Defence by Committee* (62) and Kingston-McCloughry's *The Direction of War* (66). An outline of the new Ministry can be found in *Public Administration Review* in an article by Robinson (92). Throughout the 1950's the Ministry of Defence steadily increased in size and influence. This trend was continued by the reorganisation of defence in 1958 which reflected not only the increased power and sphere of competence of the Ministry, but also the changed military environment brought about by the 1957 White Paper. The new organisation and its background is described in an article by Willson in *Public Administration* (114), but there was little response to either the reorganisation of 1963 (127) or the recent changes involving the replacement of Service Ministers for what are described as "functional" Ministers for Administration and Equipment. The most recent and comprehensive study of central organisation for defence since 1945 is that of Howard, *Central Organisation for Defence* (215) though the study confines itself specifically to the Whitehall Departments rather than to the broader defence organisational structure.

The tendency is to see the organisation for defence only in terms of the Ministry that bears its name; this is, however, only a part of the picture. The Ministries of Supply, Aviation and (more recently) Technology are important, and their relationship with the Ministry of Defence and the Services is vital for an understanding of all the aspects of the defence decision-making processes. The contribution and influence of the Government Research Establishments, which are predominantly within the sphere of responsibility of the "supply" Ministries, is a case in point. The work at Farnborough, the Royal Aircraft Establishment, is briefly outlined in Cockroft's *The Organisation of Research Establishments* (23), and the general contribution of the scientific community to defence decision-making can be found in Zuckerman's *Scientists and War* (120), and Clark's biography of Tizard (21).

Other Departments that may loosely be considered to come within the general orbit of Defence Organisation are the Treasury, the Cabinet Office and the Foreign Office. The influence of the Treasury on defence is a rewarding way of gaining an insight into defence decision-making, partly as defence decisions involving expenditure have to be justified in reasonably detailed terms. The Select Committee on Estimates enquiry into the *Treasury Control of Expenditure, 1958–9* (134) and the following Command paper on the *Control of public expenditure, 1961* (126), under the Chairmanship of Lord Plowden, are good places to start. This can be supplemented by Bridges' general account, *The Treasury* (11), Beer's *Treasury Control* (6) and Brittain's *Treasury under the Tories* (10), all of which make reference to defence. The Foreign Office and Cabinet Office relationship to defence decision-making is more difficult to discern. The student has to resort to slight references in memoirs, as for example, Shinwell's *Conflict without Malice* (100), and Eden's *Full Circle* (31). Defence Ministers, however, are not prone to writing their memoirs.

Theoretically, the political control of defence is the province of the Defence Committee of the Cabinet. The relationship between the Cabinet and the Services is an interesting one, and is outlined, though not in detail, in Snyder's *Politics of British Defence Policy* (106). Parliamentary influence over defence is a matter of speculation, and its debates are but a limited source of information. Important questions to the Minister, particularly those of interest to the historian, are invariably deflected. An assessment of Parliamentary interest is made in Finer, Berrington and Bartholomew's *Backbench Opinion in the House of Commons* (36). If this is a point of interest for research, direct reference to Hansard, *Parliamentary Debates* (140 and 141), is the best place to start.

Organisation for defence relates to the decision-making processes in defence. This is the link between defence policy and the many influences that can and do come into play where defence problems are concerned. The formal organisation is only a guide; the patterns of communication, information, and opinion between servicemen, politicians and civil servants, and the defence issues themselves are the most important things to discover. If the scholar cannot have the arguments and the explanations documented before him, at least the individuals, groups, vested interests, scientific data, and constraints within the context of the formal organisation are a good starting point for research. The patterns of defence decision-making in the Defence Departments and the Services were based, until the early sixties, on the notion of the "operational requirement," rather than the new and complex techniques based on the weapons systems philosophy, indicating that studies of weapons procurement are fruitful fields of enquiry.

4. EQUIPMENT. The process of weapons procurement is outlined in a number of articles, of which the clearest introduction is "From Westminster to West Raynham" in *Flying Review* (39). From official sources there is the Zuckerman/Gibbs Report on the *Management and Control of Research and Development* (139), which can be supplemented with *Public Accounts Committee Reports* as, for example, that of 1961–2 on the de-

velopment of the air-to-surface missile Blue Steel (131). Select Committee on Estimates Reports are valuable in studying weapons procurement, and in identifying relationships within the various Ministries. The *Supply of Military Aircraft* (133) already mentioned and the Lang Reports on *Contractual Procedure in the Ministry of Aviation* (129 and 130) are good examples as is the more recent *Supply of Electrical and Electronic Equipment for the Services 1964–1965* (135). A detailed analysis of British Defence contracting is by Edmonds in Smith (ed.), *Issues in Public Accountability* (218). Books on the subject are harder to find and sometimes overgeneralised; however, Hastings' *Murder of the TSR-2* (51) has some illuminating comments, and Worcester's *Roots of British Air Policy* (115) and Williams' *Crisis in Procurement* (217) contain useful points. An interesting development recently is the formation of the *Select Committee on Science and Technology* (136); the first investigation of matters outside the civilian context was in *Defence Research*; considerable valuable information was revealed, and it must be hoped that this precedent will be continued. Very general information can be found in the numerous government department publications which are published spasmodically; one that exemplifies this type and the generality of its content, is the Ministry of Aviation's pamphlet *Aviation in Britain* (138). Political party sources are to be found in the parties' headquarters but should be used with care, although they can be illuminating.

On the industrial side, there is much information to be found. Most valuable of all is the *Plowden Committee Enquiry into the Aircraft Industry, 1965* (128). *The Times'* Surveys of Industry, and editions devoted to particular industries, such as ship-building, aircraft, and electronics, are most helpful. Other worthwhile sources are professional and trade journals, (194) among which might be mentioned *The Engineer* (152), which has also done surveys of particular industries, and *The Aeroplane* (144). Some books have been written on industries connected with the defence field, of which Scott's *Vickers* (99), is a good example. Indeed, a rewarding field would be comprehensive studies of firms like Hawker, Fairey, Swann-Hunter and Rolls-Royce. The house magazines of industrial firms are a source that should not be ignored. Back numbers of these are to be found in the Libraries of the firms concerned.

For an early insight into the problems of defence procurement, Postan, Hay and Scott's *Design and Development of Weapons* (89) is most valuable; although it is concerned with the wartime period, many of the conceptual problems involved in procurement are outlined. For current trends in procurement, especially in relation to European collaboration and cooperation, Edmonds' "The implications of international collaboration in weapons procurement" in *International Affairs* (32) and the Institute for Strategic Studies' *Reports* (190) on European technical cooperation are points of departure.

THE DEFENCE ENVIRONMENT. The general tenor of the defence environment has been covered in the introduction to this paper. Without making reference to too many peripheral and diffuse sources and issues, only the most significant internal and external forces impinging upon defence policy will be mentioned. Internally, the economy, and financial constraints upon defence policy, are most significant. The geometrical increase in the cost of weapons systems and the armed forces in general has made demands on the economy that are not commensurate with the returns in terms of security, capability and spin-off. It is this problem which engages Blackaby and Paige in an article on defence expenditure in *Survival* (7) and by Paige alone in the *National Institute Economic Review* (81). The unhappy record of wastage and misappropriation in the armed forces, involving cancellations and expensive overcommitment, has exacerbated this situation. As an endeavour to counter the upward trend in defence costs, various steps have been taken. This has entailed the imposition of an absolute ceiling in defence expenditure on the one hand, and the adoption of techniques of economic analysis within the defence Departments on the other. Such techniques include cost effectiveness, a critique of which can be found in Day's article in the *Scottish Journal of Political Economy* (25), weapons systems management, long-range costing, and operations research—the origins of which are described in *Operations Research in the RAF* (2), published by the Air Ministry. The cost of defence throughout the period has been a source of interest for journalists and defence commentators alike. This aspect of the defence scene is consistently covered in the weekly press, such as the *Economist* (152), *New Statesman* (167) and *Spectator* (178). The background to the economic constraints on defence is not well covered, and a thorough examination of the British economy since 1945 is urgently required. For the moment, such books as Peacock and Wiseman's *Growth of Public Expenditure in the United Kingdom* (88), Dow's *The Management of the British Economy 1945–60* (28), Shonfield's *British Economic Policy since the War* (98), and Worswick and Ady's *The British Economy in the 50's* (116) must serve as sources of explanation why economic constraints on defence expenditure are as important as they have become.

The external environment is essentially that dominated by the nuclear debate and the situation regarding alliances, the nature and extent of the Soviet threat, and more recently, the impact of the European Economic Community. The defence implications of these aspects of the external environment are, again, covered above. However, with a shift in British defence policy towards Europe, both in respect of the Plowden Committee recommendations regarding weapons procurement and Britain's application to enter the European Economic Community, a call for some examination of Britain's defence relationship with Europe and its possible implications within a wider, nuclear context, must soon be made.

CONCLUSION. Research into British defence policy since 1945 is a fascinating but arduous enterprise. Restrictions regarding material sources can be overcome given patience and luck. The best starting point is either in the article reference service provided by the library of the Royal United Services Institution or the monthly reference list supplied by the Military Science College at Shrivenham, and the War Office Library List. A glance at any of these sources at once illustrates the wide variety and number of possible sources for defence analysis, but at the same time it points to the enormous size and complexity of the field and the incompleteness of the overall picture.

The student of British defence policy since 1945 is likely to be struck by the paucity of theoretical analysis and, above all, by the absence of major studies of British civil-military relations and of the decision-making process in defence although a study of the latter has been announced (196). There are few, if any, theoretical insights available in the British literature that cannot be found in that of the United States, although the converse does not hold. Civil-military relations are a major concern of all states large and small, developed and developing. The contemporary British record seems to be good, and there is a great need to understand why this should be so. To date there are only two serious enquiries into this phenomenon (1, 219). Finally, no section on decision-making in defence or sociological aspects of the Armed Services has been included in this paper because of the relative lack of suitable material. Yet both are major growth areas of fundamental importance in international relations; the latter has only recently become the focus of attention in the University of Edinburgh studies (220, 221). It remains, however, imperative that this void in the study of British defence policy be filled.

BIBLIOGRAPHY

ARTICLES AND BOOKS
1. Abrams, P. "Democracy, technology and the retired British Officer" in S. Huntington. *Military Politics*. New York: Free Press, 1962.
2. Air Ministry. *Operations Research in the R. A. F.* London: H.M.S.O., 1965.
3. Armstrong, De Witt. *The Changing Strategy of British Bases*. MS. Institute for Strategic Studies Library, 1959.
4. Banks, F. R. "The importance of time in aircraft manufacture," *Royal Aeronautical Society Journal,* January, 1957.
5. Beaton, L. *Must the Bomb Spread?* Harmondsworth: Penguin, 1963.
6. Beer, S. *Treasury Control*. London: Oxford University Press, 1957.
7. Blackaby, F. T. and D. C. Paige. "Defence expenditure: burden or stimulus." *Survival*, vol. 2, No. 6, 1960.
8. Blackett, P. M. S. *Atomic Weapons and East-West Relations*. London: Cambridge University Press, 1956.
9. Blackett, P. M. S. *Studies of War*. London: Oliver and Boyd, 1962.
10. Brittain, S. *Treasury under the Tories, 1951–1964*. Harmondsworth: Penguin, 1964.
11. Bridges, E. B. *The Treasury*. London: Allen and Unwin, 1964.
12. "Britain and the nuclear deterrent." *Political Quarterly,* January, 1960.

13. Buchan, A. *NATO in the Sixties.* London: Weidenfeld and Nicholson, 1960.
14. Buchan, A. "Britain in the Indian Ocean." *International Affairs,* April, 1966.
15. Bull, H. *The Control of the Arms Race.* London: Weidenfeld and Nicholson, 1961.
16. Burns, A. L. "Military technology and International politics." *Yearbook of World Affairs,* 1961.
17. Buzzard, A. "Massive retaliation and graduated deterrence." *World Politics,* January, 1956.
18. Buzzard, A. "Crux of defence policy." *International Relations,* April, 1956.
19. Buzzard, A., J. Slessor, and R. Lowenthal. "The H-Bomb, massive retaliation, and graduated deterrence." *International Affairs,* April, 1956.
20. Carter, April. *Disarmament: a question of unilateralism.* Anticipated, 1970.
21. Clark, R. W. *Tizard.* London: Methuen, 1965.
22. Cockburn, R. "Technology and Air Power." *Royal Aeronautical Society Journal,* March, 1964.
23. Cockroft, J. *The Organisation of Research Establishments.* London: Cambridge University Press, 1965.
24. Cowley, J. "Future Trends in warfare." *Yearbook of World Affairs,* 1960.
25. Day, A. C. L. "Cost benefit analysis and defence expenditure." *Scottish Journal of Political Economy,* February, 1963.
26. Divine, D. *The Blunted Sword.* London: Hutchinson, 1964.
27. Divine, D. *The Broken Wing.* London: Hutchinson, 1966.
28. Dow, J. C. R. *The Management of the British Economy, 1945–60.* London: Cambridge University Press, 1964.
29. Driver, C. *The Disarmers.* London: Hodder and Stoughton, 1964.
30. The Economist Intelligence Unit. *The Economic Effects of Disarmament.* London: E.I.U., 1963.
31. Eden, A. *Full Circle.* London: Cassell, 1959.
32. Edmonds, M. H. A. "International Collaboration in weapons procurement: the Anglo-French case." *International Affairs,* April, 1967.
33. Edmonds, M. H. A. "The Academic Teaching of Management— Appendix: The British Aircraft Industry Project," *ATM Occasional Papers,* D. Pugh, ed. Oxford: Blackwell, 1966.
34. Fedden, R. *Britain's Air Survival.* London: Cassell, 1957.
35. Field, T. F. "Britain's deterrent and the discussion to abandon the Blue Streak missile." *NATO's 15 Nations,* February, 1962.
36. Finer, S. E., H. Berrington, and D. Bartholomew. *Backbench opinion in the House of Commons.* Oxford: Pergammon, 1961.
37. Fletcher, R. *£60 a Second on Defence.* London: MacGibbon and Kee, 1963.

38. Flight International. "The Ten-Year Gap." *Flight International,* December 19, 1963.
39. Flying Review. "From Westminister to West Raynham." *Flying Review,* March–April, 1964.
40. Goldberg, A. "The atomic origins of the British nuclear deterrent." *International Affairs,* July, 1964.
41. Goldberg, A. "The military origins of the British nuclear deterrent." *International Affairs,* October, 1965.
42. Goldstein, W. *The Dilemma of British Defence.* Columbus: Ohio State University Press, 1966.
43. Goodwin, G. V. *Britain and the United Nations.* London: Oxford University Press, 1957.
44. Goold-Adams, R., A. Buzzard, and D. Healey. *On Limiting Atomic War.* London: Royal Institute of International Affairs, 1956.
45. Gott, R. "Evolution of the British Independent deterrent." *International Affairs,* April, 1963.
46. Gowing, M. *Britain's Atomic Energy; 1939–45.* London: Macmillan, 1966.
47. Gretton, P. *Maritime Strategy.* London: Cassell, 1965.
48. Groom, A. J. R. *British Thinking about Nuclear Weapons.* Anticipated, 1971.
49. Groom, A. J. R. "US-Allied relations and the atomic bomb in the second world war." *World Politics,* October, 1962.
50. Groom, A. J. R. "The United States and the British Independent Deterrent." *Yearbook of World Affairs,* 1964.
51. Hastings, S. *Murder of the TSR-2.* London: Cassell, 1966.
52. Higham, Robin. *Politics and Production.* Anticipated, 1975.
53. Hinterhoff, E. *Disengagement.* London: Stevens, 1959.
54. Howard, M. *Disengagement in Europe.* Harmondsworth: Penguin, 1958.
55. Howard, M. "Britain's strategic problem East of Suez." *International Affairs,* April, 1966.
56. Howard, M. "British defence commitments and capabilities." *Foreign Affairs,* Vol. 39, 1960–1.
57. Howard, M. "Civil-military relations in Great Britain and the United States, 1945–58." *Political Science Quarterly,* March, 1960.
58. Institute for Strategic Studies. *Defence, Technology and the Western Alliance Sections, I–VI.* London: Institute for Strategic Studies, 1967.
59. Ismay, Lord. *NATO: the first five years.* Paris: NATO, 1955.
60. Jacob, I. "Principles of British Military Thought." *Foreign Affairs,* Volume 29, 1950–51.
61. Jacobson, H. K. and E. Stein. *Diplomats, Scientists and Politicians.* Ann Arbor: University of Michigan Press, 1966.
62. Johnson, F. A. *Defence by Committee.* London: Oxford University Press, 1960.
63. de Kadt, E. J. *British Defence Policy and Nuclear War.* London: Cass, 1964.

64. King-Hall, S. *Power Politics in the Nuclear Age.* London: Gollancz, 1962.
65. King-Hall, S. *Defence in the Nuclear Age.* London: Gollancz, 1958.
66. Kingston-McCloughry, E. J. *Direction of War.* London: Cape, 1955.
67. Liddell Hart, B. H. *Deterrence and Defence.* London: Stevens, 1960.
68. Liddell Hart, B. H. "Is gas better defence than atomic weapons?" *Survival,* September–October, 1959.
69. Liddell Hart, B. H. "Will small atomic weapons create a new revolution?" *Marine Corps Gazette,* December, 1959.
70. Mayhew, C. *Britain's Role Tomorrow.* London: Hutchinson, 1967.
71. Martin, L. W. "The market for strategic ideas in Britain: the Sandys Era." *American Political Science Review,* March, 1962.
72. Martin, L. W. *The Sea in Modern Strategy.* London: Chatto and Windus, 1967.
73. Millar, T. B. *Australia's Defence.* Melbourne: Melborne University Press, 1965.
74. Millar, T. B. *Britain's Withdrawal from Asia: its implications for Australia.* Canberra: Australian National University Press, 1968.
75. Modelski, G. *SEATO.* Vancouver: University of British Columbia, 1962.
76. Montgomery, Lord. "A look through the window at World War III." *Royal United Services Institution Journal,* November, 1964.
77. Montgomery, Lord. "Organising for War in modern times." *Royal United Services Institution Journal,* November, 1955.
78. Montgomery, Lord. "The panorama of warfare in a nuclear age." *Royal United Services Institution Journal,* November, 1956.
79. Montgomery, Lord. "The present state of the game in the contest between East and West." *Royal United Services Institution Journal,* November, 1958.
80. Morgan, M. B. "Some aspects of science in support of the RAF." *Royal Aeronautical Society Journal,* January, 1962.
81. Moulton, J. L. *Defence in a changing world.* London: Eyre and Spottiswoode, 1964.
82. Mulley, F. *Politics of Western Defence.* London: Thames and Hudson, 1962.
83. Noel-Baker, P. *The Arms Race.* London: Calder, 1958.
84. Nutting, A. *Disarmament. Outline of negotiations.* London: Oxford University Press.
85. O'Ballance, E. *Malaya: the communist insurgent war.* London: Faber, 1966.
86. Paige, D. C. "Defence Expenditure." *National Institute Economic Review,* Nov. 10, 1960, pp. 28–39.
87. Paret, P. and J. W. Shy. *Guerillas in the 60's.* New York: Praeger, 1962.
88. Peacock, A. T. and J. Wiseman. *Growth of Public expenditure in the United Kingdom.* Princeton: Princeton University Press, 1959.

89. Postan, M., D. Hay, and J. D. Scott. *Design and Development of Weapons.* London: H.M.S.O., 1964.
90. Rae, John. *British Automobile and Aircraft Industries.* Cambridge, Mass.: M.I.T., 197?.
91. Rees, D. *Korea: the limited war.* London: Macmillan, 1964.
92. Robinson, C. F. "British Organisation for Defence." *Public Administration Review,* Vol. 8., 1948.
93. Rosecrance, R. *Defence of the Realm.* New York: Columbia University Press, 1968.
94. Russell, B. *Commonsense and Nuclear Warfare.* London: Allen and Unwin, 1959.
95. Russell, Bertrand. *Has Man a Future?* London: Allen and Unwin, 1961.
96. Sabine, J. *British Defence Policy.* London: Allen and Unwin, 1969.
97. Schofield, B. B. *British Sea Power: naval policy in the twentieth century.* Batsford, 1967.
98. Schonfield, A. *British Economic Policy since the War.* Harmondsworth: Penguin, 1958.
99. Scott, J. D. *Vickers.* London: Weidenfeld and Nicholson, 1965.
100. Shinwell, E. *Conflict without Malice.* London: Odhams, 1955.
101. Slessor, J. *Strategy for the West.* London: Cassell, 1954.
102. Slessor, J. *The Great Deterrent.* New York: Praeger, 1957.
103. Slessor, J. *What Price Co-existence?* New York: Praeger, 1961.
104. Smith, A. "Behind the Aeroplane: massive research effort." *Aeronautics,* September, 1959.
105. Smyth, J. *Sandhurst.* London: Weidenfeld and Nicholson, 1961.
106. Snyder, W. P. *The Politics of British Defence Policy, 1945-62.* London: Benn, 1964.
107. Strachey, J. *On the Prevention of War.* London: Macmillan, 1962.
108. Strachey, J. *Scrap all the H-Bombs.* Labour Party. April, 1958.
109. Thompson, R. *Defeating Communist Insurgency.* London: Chatto and Windus, 1966.
110. Verrier, A. *An Army for the 60's.* London: Secker and Warburg, 1966.
111. Wallace, W. "World Status without tears," in *Politics in the 50's: the age of affluence.* R. Skidelsky and V. Bogdanor, eds. London: Macmillan, 1968.
112. deWeerd, H. *British Defence Policy and NATO.* Santa Monica: Rand, 1964.
113. Wilcox, F. O., and H. F. Haviland, eds. *Atlantic Community.* New York: Praeger, 1963.
114. Willson, F. M. G. "Defence organisation: 1958 style." *Public Administration.* Winter, 1958.
115. Worcester, R. *Roots of British Air Policy.* London: Hodder and Stoughton, 1966.
116. Worswick, G. D. N., and P. Ady. *The British Economy in the 60's.* London: Oxford University Press, 1962.
117. Wright, M. *Disarm and Verify.* London: Chatto and Windus, 1964.

118. Young, W. *Strategy for Survival.* Harmondsworth: Penguin, 1959.
119. Zuckerman, S. "Judgement and control in modern warfare." *Foreign Affairs,* January, 1962.
120. Zuckerman, S. *Scientists and War.* London: Hamilton, 1966.

OFFICIAL SOURCES

COMMAND PAPERS
121. Defence White Papers. 1945–1964. Published annually by the Ministry of Defence.
122. Service Estimates. 1945–1964. Published annually by the three Services.
123. *Statement on Defence Estimates.* 1965–   . Published annually and replaces both the Defence White Paper and the Service Estimates.
124. *The Supply of Military Aircraft. Cmd. 9388.* 1954/5.
125. *Report of the advisory committee on recruiting. Cmnd. 545,* 1958/9.
126. *Control of public expenditure. Cmnd. 1432.* 1961/2.
127. *Central Organisation for defence. Cmnd. 2097.* 1963/4.
128. *Committee of enquiry into the aircraft industry.* The Plowden Report. *Cmnd. 2853.* 1964/5.
129. *The Lang Report: the Ferranti case. Cmnd 2428.* 1965.
130. *The Lang Report: proposals for improvement in contracting. Cmnd 2581.* 1965.

House of Commons Papers
        Public Accounts Committee Reports: 1945–   .
131. Report 1961/2. *Development of the air-surface missile Blue Steel HC 94-1.*
        Select Committee on Estimates Reports. 1945–   .
132. *Report on Rearmament. HC 260 & HC 288.* 1950–1952.
133. *Report on the Supply of military aircraft. HC 34.* 1956/7.
134. *Report on Treasury control of Expenditure. HC 254/1.* 1958/9.
135. *Report on Electrical and Electronic Equipment for the Services, HC 358.* 1964/5.
136. *Select Committee on Science and Technology: Defence Research* HC 213. 1968/9.

Government Department Publications
137. Sectional Lists: Ministry of Defence, No. 67. March, 1964.
138. Ministry of Aviation. *Aviation in Britain.* London: H.M.S.O., 1964.
139. Ministry of Science. *Management and Control of Research and Development.* London: H.M.S.O., 1961.

Parliamentary Debates
140. Hansard: House of Commons Debates. 1945–   .
141.   House of Lords Debates. 1945–   .

PERIODICALS. In alphabetical order; referred to either in the text, or the bibliography.

142. *Aeronautical Quarterly.* 1949– . London. Indexed: Br Tech Ind; Eng Ind.
143. *Aeronautics.* 1939–1963. London. Not indexed.
144. *Aeroplane.* 1911–1968. London. Indexed: Br Tech Ind; Eng Ind.
145. *American Political Science Review.* 1906– . Washington. Indexed: P. A. I. S.; Soc Sci & Hum Ind; Int Bib Soc Sci (Pol Sci).
146. *Army Quarterly and Defence Journal.* 1829– . Indexed: P. A. I. S.; Air Univ Lib Ind.
147. *Atlantic Community Quarterly.* 1963– . Washington. Indexed: Soc Sci & Hum Ind.
148. *Aviation Week and Space Technology.* 1916– . New York. Indexed: B. P. I.; R. G.
149. *Brassey's Annual.* 1890– . London. Not Indexed.
150. *Discovery.* 1920– . London. Indexed: Br Tech Ind.
151. *Economist.* 1843– . London. Indexed: Br Hum Ind; Soc Sci & Hum Ind.
152. *Engineer.* 1856–– . London. A. E. & T Ind; Br Tech Ind; Eng Ind.
153. *Flight International.* 1909– . London. Indexed: Air Univ Lib Ind; Br Tech Ind; Eng Ind.
154. *Flying Review International* (formerly *R. A. F. Flying Review*). 1946– . London. Not Indexed.
155. *Foreign Affairs.* 1922– . New York. Indexed: P. A. I. S.; Soc Sci & Hum Ind; Int Bib Soc Sci (Pol Sci).
156. *Interavia.* 1946– . Geneva. Not Indexed.
157. *International Affairs.* 1922– . R. I. I. A. London. Indexed: Br Hum Ind; P. A. I. S.; Soc Sci & Hum Ind; Int Bib Soc Sci (Pol Sci).
158. *International Relations.* 1954– . London. Indexed: Int Bib Soc Sci (Pol Sci).
159. *Marine Corps Gazette.* 1916– . Virginia. Indexed: Air Univ Lib Ind.
160. *National Institute Economic Review.* 1959– . London. Indexed: P. A. I. S.
161. *NATO Letter.* 1953– . Paris. Not Indexed.
162. *NATO's 15 Nations.* 1956– . Amsterdam. Indexed: Air Univ Lib Ind.
163. *Nature.* 1869– . London. Indexed: Br Tech Ind; Eng Ind; Sci Abstr.
164. *Naval Review.* 1911– . London. Not Indexed and restricted (See Introduction).
165. *Navy.* (Navy League) 1895– . London. Not Indexed.
166. *New Scientist.* 1956– . London. Indexed: Br Tech Ind.
167. *New Statesman.* 1913– . London. Indexed: Br Hum Ind; Soc Sci & Hum Ind.
168. *Parliamentary Affairs.* 1947– . London. Indexed: Br Hum Ind; P. A. I. S.

169. *Political Quarterly*. 1930–   . Edinburgh. Indexed: Br Hum Ind; P. A. I. S.; Soc Sci & Hum Ind; Int Bib Soc Sci (Pol Sci).
170. *Political Science Quarterly*. 1886–   . New York. Indexed: P. A. I. S.; Soc Sci & Hum Ind; Int Bib Soc Sci (Pol Sci).
171. *Public Administration*. 1923–   . London. Indexed: Br Hum Ind; P. A. I. S.; Int Bib Soc Sci (Pol Sci).
172. *Public Administration Review*. 1940–   . Washington. Indexed: P. A. I. S.; Soc Sci & Hum Ind; Int Bib Soc Sci (Pol Sci).
173. *Revue Militaire Generale*. 1956–   . Paris. Not Indexed.
174. *Royal Aeronautical Society Journal*. 1897   . London. Indexed: Br Tech Ind; Eng Ind.
175. *Royal Air Force Quarterly*. 1930–   . London. Indexed: Air Univ Lib Ind.
176. *Royal United Services Institution Journal*. 1857–   . London. Indexed: P. A. I. S.; Br Hum Ind; Air Univ Lib Ind.
177. *Scottish Journal of Political Economy*. 1954–   . Edinburgh. Indexed: Br Hum Ind; P. A. I. S.; Int Bib Soc Sci (Pol Sci).
178. *Spectator*. 1828–   . London. Indexed: Br Hum Ind.
179. *Survival*. 1959–   . ISS London. Not Indexed.
180. *World Politics*. 1948–   . Princeton. Indexed: P. A. I. S.
181. *Yearbook of World Affairs*. 1947–   . London. Indexed: Int Bib Soc Sci (Pol Sci).

DAILY AND WEEKLY PRESS

182. *The Times*. (Inc The Times surveys of industry.)
183. *The Guardian*. (Previously *The Manchester Guardian*.)
184. *The Daily Telegraph*.
185. *The Observer*.
186. *The Sunday Times*.
187. *The Financial Times* (including their Surveys of Industry).
188. *Peace News*.
189. *The Times Literary Supplement*.

MISCELLANEOUS SOURCES

190. *Adelphi Papers*. Published occasionally by the Institute for Strategic Studies. London.
191. *ATM Occasional Papers*. Birmingham.
192. *Aviation Studies International*. Edited by R. Worcester. Wimbledon, London.
193. Bank Reviews. (See those of various banks.)
194. Journals of particular industries and firms; access by enquiry to the firms concerned.
195. Royal Military College of Science, Shrivenham. *Monthly article reference list*.
196. *Jane's All the World's Aircraft*.

197. *Jane's Fighting Ships.*
198. War Office Library List. London. (See Introduction.)

ABBREVIATIONS USED FOR PERIODICALS INDEXES.

199. A. S. and T. Ind. *Applied Science and Technology Index.*
200. Air Univ Lib Ind: *Air University Library Index to Military Periodicals.*
201. B. P. I.: *Business Periodicals Index.*
202. Br Hum Ind: *British Humanities Index.*
203. Br Tech Ind: *British Technology Index.*
204. Eng Ind: *Engineering Index.*
205. Int Bib Soc Sci (Pol Sci) *International Bibliography of Social Science* (Political Science).
206. P. A. I. S. *Public Affairs Information Service.*
207. R. G. *Readers Guide to Periodical Literature.*
208. Sci Abstr. *Science Abstracts.*
209. Soc Sci & Hum Ind: *Social Science and Humanities Index.*

SUPPLEMENTARY BIBLIOGRAPHY

210. Beaufré, General André. *The Suez Expedition, 1956.* London: Faber, 1969.
211. Gimbel, John. *The American Occupation of Germany.* Stanford: Stanford University Press, 1968.
212. Paget, Lieutenant-Colonel Julian. *The Last Post: Aden, 1964–67.* London: Faber, 1969.
213. Wilson, Andrew. *The Bomb and the Computer.* London: Barrie and Jenkins, 1969.
214. Parkin, Frank. *Middle Class Radicalism.* Manchester: Manchester University Press, 1968.
215. Howard, Michael. *Central Organization for Defence.* London: Royal United Service Institution, 1970.
216. Martin, L. W. *British Defence Policy; the long recessional.* London: Institute for Strategic Studies. November, 1969.
217. Williams, G., and J. Simpson. *Crisis in Procurement.* London: Royal United Service Institution, 1969.
218. Edmonds, Martin. "Some observations on defence contracting: the cases of Bristol Siddeley and Ferranti" *in* Smith, J., ed. *Issues in Public Accountability.* London: Macmillan, 1970.
219. Ottley, S. "Social origins of the British Army elite" *in* van Doorn, J., ed. *Armed Forces and Society.* Amsterdam: Moulton, 1968.
220. University-Services Study Group, *The Services and Society in the 1970's.* Edinburgh University, 1968.
221. University-Services Study Group, *Continuity and Change in Military Institutions.* Edinburgh University, 1969.
222. Barnett, Correlli. *Britain and Her Army.* London: Allen Lane Press, 1970.

223. P. I. B. Report No. 116. *Armed Forces Pay*. London: H.M.S.O., June, 1969.
224. Layton, C. *European Advanced Technology*. London: Allen and Unwin, 1969.
225. Further Miscellaneous Sources: The JRUSI Pamphlets, 1969–   .

XXIII

THE EVOLUTION
OF MILITARY MEDICINE

F. N. L. Poynter

The history of military medicine is a field of study which has long been awaiting development. Despite the fact that inadequate and badly organised medical services, with consequent heavy losses of troops from disease and the infection of minor wounds, have decided the issue in many battles, campaigns, and even wars until the present century, historians have failed to give this factor the close attention that it deserves. This may have been due to lack of expert guidance from medical historians, for they too have neglected it. There is only one brief essay by Fielding H. Garrison (38) the British section of which is worth consulting. There is no single work on British military medicine parallel to Keevil, Lloyd and Coulter's *Medicine and the Navy,* but many aspects of it, both general and special, have been treated in books and journal articles by army doctors. Those which have been published since January, 1954, will be found in the Wellcome Library's quarterly index *Current Work* (127), and most of the earlier publications may be traced under appropriate headings in the *Index-Catalogue* (123). It should be remembered that the medical literature contemporary with particular wars or campaigns also offers much evidence of a primary character on the medical services of the time and the profession's view of their organization, especially from the Crimean War onwards. Official papers also contain a variety of information. The State Papers, Domestic and Foreign, as well as the Home Office and Foreign Office Papers should be consulted at the Public Record Office, while at the War Office, established in 1794, will be found substantial records for the nineteenth century and later.

One of the best general historical reviews of the organization of the services of the British Army, with a very clear exposition of the significance and duties attached to particular offices at different periods, is the Introduction to Johnston's *Roll* (67). This important work is too little known and rarely found in libraries, for only 250 copies were printed during the First World War (1917). It is a register, with biographical data wherever it could be found, of all the officers in the army medical service from the

591

accession of George II until the formation of the Royal Army Medical Corps (23rd June, 1898). Eight years later, in 1925, one of Colonel Johnston's collaborators, Colonel Peterkin, supplemented the *Roll* with a similar list of medical officers serving between 1660 and 1727 (93). This has been even more difficult to find, but when the present Director General, Sir Robert Drew, decided to publish a continuation of Johnston's *Roll* that had been compiled under his command, it was suggested that a reprint of Peterkin and Johnston should be issued with it, so that we now have a complete and readily available Roll of all the medical officers from the formation of the standing army to 1960 (29). It is hoped that the provision of this basic reference work will stimulate many new related studies. The Introduction of the new volume, by the late Colonel Young, is a valuable account, based on official papers, of the formation of the Royal Army Medical Corps and its subsequent history. Peter Lovegrove's short but well illustrated history of the Corps (74) should also be consulted. Other general articles on medicine and the army are those by Drew (30, 31), Drummond (32), Hargreaves (50), and Barnsley (2–6), while Gore's little book (43) contains inaccuracies and should be used with caution.

ARMY MEDICAL SERVICES TO 1815. Turning now to work on the army medical services, in the various historical periods, we find very little indeed on the earlier centuries. G. E. Gask (39) has written on the surgeons who supported Henry V's army at Agincourt; C. G. Cruickshank (23) has an excellent and well documented chapter in his book *Elizabeth's Army*; Firth's book on Cromwell's Army (36) contains a useful chapter on the treatment of the sick and wounded. Other contributions to the history in the seventeenth and eighteenth centuries have been made by Barnsley (5), Drew (31), Gask (40, 41), Gordon-Taylor (42), MacNaughton (81), and Stevenson (114). But anybody embarking on a serious study would need to read (not merely consult) contemporary writings such as Pringle's *Observations,* 1752 (97), Brocklesby's *Oeconomical and Medical Observations,* 1764 (12), and Millar's *Observations,* 1798 (88), for conditions in the American War of Independence. Sir John Pringle (1707–1782) is regarded as one of the founders of modern military medicine; his book, like Brocklesby's, is a classic of military hygiene and contains the first proposal for mutual respect by the combatants of the neutrality of military hospitals in the battle area.

The Napoleonic Wars eventually brought home to the politicians the lessons which Pringle and others had tried to give. A casual and utterly incompetent medical service could bring defeat as surely as bad generals or lack of men and arms. The disaster at Walcheren in 1809 was the turning point; the subsequent inquiry led to the appointment of a man, James Mac-Grigor (77), who was to transform their organization and lay the foundations of the modern Corps. St. Clair (108) has left us a first-hand account of the expedition and there are good modern studies by McGuffie (76), Brett-James (10), and Van Loo (72), while Feibel (35) has recently discussed the primary medical sources for its history.

A good deal of important source material for the whole period of the wars, including documents and illustrations, is listed, with notes, in the guide to the Wellcome Museum's Exhibition, *Medicine in 1815* (128). An archive concerning the medical history of the Peninsular War has been calendared by Dorothy Smith (111), and contemporary *Memoirs* by Thomas (118) provide useful information. The articles by Howell (52) and Matheson (86) on the medical aspects of Waterloo should also be noted, together with Surgeon James's journal (66) and Arnold Chaplin's (17) discussion of the mortality rate, while Greenwood (49) has made statistical studies of the rates for the whole period. A special study of the diseases of the army in Jamaica at this time was published by Lemprière (69) in 1799, and the official *Instructions* (65) issued by the Army Medical Board of Ireland in 1806 offers useful data for another area.

THE CRIMEAN WAR. The cathartic effect of the Crimean War is amply documented in an extensive literature. As is well known, this war led to the development of the modern nursing profession by Florence Nightingale, who was also responsible to a large degree for the establishment of the Royal Army Medical College. The best published guide to the voluminous official reports and to Miss Nightingale's decisive evidence given to the Commission is the section on the Army (Chapter II) of Bishop and Goldie's *Bio-Bibliography* (7). The views of Sir Alexander Tulloch (122) on the work of the Commission should not be overlooked, while the official history—the first official medical history of any war—is of great importance. Florence Nightingale's opponent and spokesman of the orthodox army view was Sir John Hall, who has left an archive of unpublished papers, listed by Miss Ward (126), of which General Barnsley has given us a glimpse (6). The same writer has also drawn attention to the unpublished memoirs of William Cattell (3), which also cover this period, while among the published memoirs are interesting accounts by McCormick (75), Reid (99), and Robinson (103), with a nursing sister's reminiscences by Sister Mary Aloysius (1a). Mrs. Woodham-Smith's biography of Florence Nightingale (130) gives a vivid, if somewhat biased view of the medical situation at Scutari, and a contemporary work by Charles Bryce (13) gives a comparative view of the medical services of the allied armies at Sebastopol. The experience of the Crimean War gave the stimulus for Surgeon-General Longmore's official—and now classic—monograph (45) on the transport of the sick and wounded. It also provided valuable lessons for other armies, and the Union medical histories of the American Civil War followed their British precedent.

MINOR WARS. The minor wars in which the British were engaged in the nineteenth century also led to accounts, official or unofficial, of their medical aspects. Typical of these is Inspector-General Currie's medical history of the Abyssinian Campaign (24, 44), which appeared in the Report on the Health of the Army in 1867, J. H. Thornton's *Memories of Seven Campaigns* (119) covering India, China, Egypt and the Sudan, and Sir Anthony' Hume's *Service Memoirs* (54) containing recollections of the Crimean War, the Indian Mutiny, and the New Zealand War of 1860.

THE BOER WAR of 1899–1901 turned out to be yet another war in which the British lost far more of their troops from disease than from enemy action. Almroth Wright had already developed his anti-typhoid inoculation, but had failed to convince a sceptical Army Medical Department of its value in protecting troops against infection. (In September, 1914, he wrote to the *Times* again urging that it should be used for protecting the British Expeditionary Force in the First World War.) This episode and Wright's unhappy relations with the Army Medical Service are recounted in Leonard Colebrook's biography (18). Reports and enquiries on the Crimean model followed the end of the war, and a great deal of first hand evidence was given to two Royal Commissions (46, 47). Reports of the work of the Imperial Yeomanry hospitals in South Africa (53), as well as of the Edinburgh (125) and Portland (94, 95) hospitals there were published at the time. Bowlby (8) and Treves (121) also wrote accounts of the war hospitals and the reminiscences of Daly (25), Fremantle (37), and Makins (85) are worth noting.

THE FIRST WORLD WAR. When the medical history of the Great War came to be written the materials were so voluminous that although the official history needed twelve volumes (84), there is still much awaiting professional historical study, especially if certain aspects and special topics are to be written up in depth and in detail. The medical journals of the whole period, especially the *British Medical Journal* and the *Lancet,* contain a wealth of information which can be further expanded by following up the references given in them. To commemorate the jubilee of the Armistice in 1918 the Wellcome Institute of the History of Medicine opened an extensive exhibition on Medicine and Surgery in the Great War (November, 1968). The published catalogue (129) lists some 350 items, of which many are important references for the medical history of this war, especially on the British side. A great deal of relevant data is also to be found in the official publications of other Commonwealth governments, such as the Mesopotamia inquiries and other reports of the Government of India's Medical Advisory Committee (57–64), as well as the *Official History of the Canadian Forces in the Great War, 1914–1919; the Medical Services* (82), *The Australian Medical Services in the War of 1914–1918* (15), and *The New Zealand Medical Service in the Great War, 1914–1918* (16). Unofficial and more personal accounts are such books as Brereton's *The Great War and the R. A. M. C.* (9), Souttar's *A Surgeon in Belgium* (113), and Isabel Hutton's *With a Woman's Unit in Serbia, Salonika and Sebastopol* (55). Also worth consulting are McLaren's *History of the Scottish Women's Hospitals* (78) and Lord's *Story of the Horton War Hospital* (73). The development of modern plastic surgery sprang from the pioneer work of Sir Harold Gillies on war shattered faces at the Sidcup Hospital, and a good account of this is contained in Pound's biography of Gillies (96).

The first serious use of psychology also developed during this war. From 1917 on, the Binet system of measuring intelligence, devised and first applied in 1905, was employed in Britain for testing recruits. Despite some reluctance on the part of the British medical profession to accept the claims of psychiatrists, war neurosis and shell-shock proved a problem which could not be tackled successfully by other means. An account of psychiatric treatment in the British Army was written by T. W. Salmon as early as 1917 (109).

THE INTERWAR YEARS AND THE SECOND WORLD WAR. The period between the wars is well served by the medical series of the official History of the Second World War (80), for there was a long-standing controversy between the British Medical Association and the War Office which is covered in some detail in Professor Crew's volumes on administration (22). The substantial and well documented accounts of medicine and pathology, medical research, the civilian and emergency services are all invaluable. On the technical side a special journal appeared throughout the war with the title *Bulletin of War Medicine* (14). This war made much greater demands on the services of psychiatrists, and Ahrenfeldt (1) has given us a systematic account of psychiatry in the British Army in this period. A brief and more personal view has been put on record by two of its leading British protagonists, William Sargent and Eliot Slater (110). Again there are official medical histories for the other Commonwealth countries, Feasby on Canada (34), Walker on Australia (124), Stout on New Zealand (115), and Raina on India (99). In addition there is the special Indian investigation of medical services in the Third Afghan War of 1919 (56) and the subsequent move to reorganize the Indian medical service. Cotterell's *R. A. M. C.* (20) is a rather journalistic account of the work of the Corps in this war.

INDIA. The history of the Indian Medical Service over more than three centuries was written by D. G. Crawford in 1914 (21) and is the standard work on this service. Many of its officers have also published volumes of autobiography or reminiscences which offer a good insight into conditions in the service at particular periods. Outstanding among these are those of Fayrer (33), and Leonard Rogers (104), whose life-span covered the introduction and establishment of scientific tropical medicine and hygiene in India. Historians seeking to work in this field would need to study the whole history of tropical medicine, for the majority of the pioneers (e.g., Ross, Leishmann, Bruce) were serving officers at the time of their discoveries.

ROYAL ARMY MEDICAL COLLEGE AND CHELSEA HOSPITAL. Among the important institutions directly connected with British military medicine are the Royal Army Medical College and the Royal Chelsea Hospital. In 1955 the College celebrated the centenary of its first department—pathology—an event which produced a number of useful articles in the *Times* (120), the *British Medical Journal,* the *Lancet* (68), *Medical Officer* (87), and the *Journal of the Royal Army Medical Corps.* Others on the history of the College are those of Neal (91), Barnsley (2), and Morrison (89). The history of the hospital which Charles II founded at Chelsea for army veterans has been well written by Captain Dean (26), and more recently the origins of the hospital have been directly connected with the Invalides in Paris by Carson Ritchie in his edition of Thomas Povey's contemporary account of the French hospital (101). Ian Hay's *Hundred Years of Army Nursing* (51) records the development of an important branch of the medical service, and an article by Jessie Dobson (28) offers a glimpse of army nursing in pre-Nightingale times. A valuable guide to another aspect of the service which should not be forgotten is Brittain's bibliography of military medical jurisprudence (11).

Finally, nobody thinking of researching in this field should go too long without consulting the librarian of the Royal Army Medical College at Millbank in London. The library's Muniments Room contains unpublished archives and volumes of cuttings which are of the greatest interest. A small catalogue was published from the College in 1965, with a Supplement in 1967 (105).

MEDICAL HISTORY AND THE AIR FORCE. Aviation being a twentieth-century discovery has had a voluminous literature, but few histories. Yet in Robinson's *The Dangerous Sky* (102) it does at least have a general one which gives researchers a starting point. The growth of aviation was so rapid that during the First World War many of the problems went largely unexplored. After the war the Royal Air Force saved money by stopping most aviation research, in part because it was decreed that fighting would not be at heights where medical considerations would become a problem. Thus aviation medical problems were covered for the First World War only as a subsidiary part of the second volume in Macpherson's series *Diseases of the War* (83). Perhaps this limited coverage was also due to the fact that since airmen did not wear parachutes, there were fewer survivors than there might have been. This lack of medical history is made up for in the Second World War with S/Ldr. S .C. Rexford-Welch's three volumes on Royal Air Force Medical Services (100). For additional background, the Army volumes (80) should be consulted.

Few books have been written by R.A.F. medical officers. Air Marshal Livingstone has written a general autobiography (71) and Victor Tempest (pseudonym) *Near the Sun: the impressions of a medical officer in Bomber Command* (116), but that is about all. The plastic surgeon, Sir Archibald McIndoe, and his work are covered in three books (27, 90, and 79). Then there is Paterson's *Morale in War and Work: an experiment in the management of men* (92) which used the R. A. F. as a guinea pig. Two American studies suggest what might be done: *Medical Support of the Army Air Forces in World War II* (70) and on a lower level, *Medical Support in a Combat Air Force: a study of medical leadership in World War II* (112).

Studies of the work done by the Royal Aircraft Establishment at Farnborough on physiological problems in connection with aircraft design and testing may be possible, especially if the Fifty-Year Rule is relaxed. The R. A. F.'s Institute of Aviation Medicine and its work could make a fascinating study. The development of standards and means of testing and evaluating these for the selection of aircrew and the relationship of these to medical practice outside the services is another topic worth looking into. So too is the development of survival equipment from both medical and technological aspects.

As in the case of the Army, much that has been noted here must be rather tentative owing to the paucity of printed histories and to the dearth of specialists in the field.

BIBLIOGRAPHY

1.   Ahrenfeldt, R. H. *Psychiatry in the British Army in the Second World War*. London: Routledge and Kegan Paul, 1958.
1a. Sister Mary Aloysius. *Memories of the Crimea*. London: Burns & Oates, 1897.
2.   Barnsley, R. E. *Mars and Aesculapius: an address given in the Royal Army Medical College*. London: Sapphire Press, 1963.
3.   ———. "The Memoirs of William Cattell, 1828–1919." *J. roy. Army med. Corps*, 1962, *108*, 10–16.
4.   ———. "Miss Nightingale and the College." *Ibid.*, 1965, III, 66–73.
5.   ———. "King Charles II's medical Services." *Army med. Serv. Mag.*, 1960, *12*, 94–6.
6.   ———. "Teeth and tails in the Crimea" [Notebooks of Sir John Hall, Principal Medical Officer to Lord Raglan]. *Med. Hist.*, 1963, 7, 75–9.
7.   Bishop, W. J. and S. Goldie. *A Bio-Bibliography of Florence Nightingale*. London: Dawsons, 1962.
8.   Bowlby, Sir A. A. *The Hunterian Oration on British Military Surgery in the Time of Hunter and in the Great War*. London: Adland & West Newman, 1919.
9.   Brereton, Lieutenant-Colonel F. S. *The Great War and the R. A. M. C.* London: Constable, 1919.
10. Brett-James, A. "The Walcheren Failure." *Hist. Today*, 1963, *13*, 811–20; 1964, *14*, 60–8.
11. Brittain, R. P. "A Bibliography: military medical jurisprudence." *J. roy. Army med. Corps*, 1963, *109*, 220–2.
12. Brocklesby, R. [1722–97]. *Oeconomical and Medical Observations . . . tending to the Improvement of Military Hospitals, and to the Cure of Camp Diseases, incident to Soldiers*. London: T. Becket & P. A. de Hondt, 1764. This is the best 18th c. book on military sanitation.
13. Bryce, C. *England and France before Sebastopol, looked at from a Medical Point of View*. London: Churchill, 1857.
14. *Bulletin of War Medicine*. Vols. 1–6. London: Med. Res. Council, 1940–46.
15. Butler, A. G., ed. *The Official History of the Australian Army Medical Services in the War of 1914–1918*. 2 ed. Melbourne, 1930–1943. 3 vols.

16. Carbery, A. D. *The New Zealand Medical Service in the Great War.* Auckland: Whitcombe & Tombs, 1924.

17. Chaplin, A. "The Rate of Mortality in the British Army 100 Years Ago." *Proc. roy. Soc. Med. (Sect. Hist. Med.),* 1914, *9,* 89–99.

18. Colebrook, L. *Almroth Wright, Provocative Doctor and Thinker.* London: Heinemann, 1954.

19. Cope, Sir V. Z. *Medicine and Pathology. (History of the Second World War. U. K. Medical Series.)* London: H.M.S.O., 1952.

20. Cotterell, A. *R. A. M C.* London: Hutchinson, n.d.

21. Crawford, D. G. *A History of the Indian Medical Service 1600–1913.* London: W. Thacker, 1914. 2 vols.

22. Crew, F. A. E. *The Army Medical Services. Administration; Campaigns [History of the Second World War. United Kingdom Medical Series. ed. Sir A. S. MacNalty.]* London: H.M.S.O., 1953–62. 6 vols.

23. Cruickshank, C. G. *Elizabeth's Army.* 2nd ed. Oxford: Clarendon Press, 1966.

24. Insp. Gen. Currie. "Medical History of the Abyssinian Expedition" in Great Britain. Army Medical Dept., *Report on the Health of the Army.* 1867, vol. 9, Appendix pp. 267–299. London: Harrison, 1869.

25. Daly, F. A. B. *Boer War Memories: personal experiences.* London, 1935.

26. Dean, C. G. T. *The Royal Hospital Chelsea.* London: Hutchinson, 1950.

27. Dennison, E. J. *A Cottage Hospital grows up: the story of the Queen Victoria Hospital, East Grinstead.* London: A. Blond, 1963.

28. Dobson, J. "The Army Nursing Service in the Eighteenth Century." *Ann. roy. Coll. Surg. Eng.,* 1954, *14,* 417–9.

29. Drew, Sir R. *Commissioned Officers in the Medical Services of the British Army, 1660–1960.* London: Wellcome Institute of the History of Medicine, 1968. 2 vols.

30. ———. "Medicine's Debt to the Army: a review of the army's Contributions to medical science." *Jl. roy. Army med. Corps,* 1964, *110,* 5–12.

31. ———. "John Hunter and the Army" (Hunterian Oration, 1966). *Ibid.,* 1967, *113,* 5–17.

32. Drummond, Sir A. "Medicine and the Army." *St. Bart's Hosp. Jl.,* 1958, *62,* 20–5.

33. Fayrer, Sir J. *Recollections of my Life.* Edinburgh & London: W. Blackwood, 1900.

34. Feasby, W. R. *Official History of the Canadian Medical Services, 1939–1945.* Ottawa: E. Cloutier, Queen's Printer, 1953–6. 2 vols.

35. Feibel, R. M. "What happened at Walcheren: the primary medical sources." *Bull. Hist. Med.,* 1968, *42,* 62–77.

36. Firth, Sir C. *Cromwell's Army.* London: Methuen, 1902. 3rd ed. published in 1921.

37. Fremantle, F. E. *Impressions of a Doctor in Khaki.* London: Murray, 1901.

38. Garrison, F. H. *Notes on the History of Military Medicine.* Washington: Assoc. Military Surg., 1922.

39. Gask, G. E. "The Medical Services of Henry the Fifth's Campaign of the Somme in 1415." *Proc. roy. Soc. Med. (Sect. Hist. Med.),* 1922, *16,* 1–10. Also in his *Essays in the History of Medicine,* pp. 94–102. London: Butterworth, 1950.

40. Gask, G. E. "A Contribution to the History of the Care of the Sick and Wounded during Marlborough's March to the Danube in 1804, and at the Battle of Blenheim." *Jl. roy. Army med. Corps.,* 1922, *38,* 274–288. Also in his *Essays in the History of Medicine,* pp. 103–115. London: Butterworth, 1950.

41. ———. "John Hunter in the Campaign in Portugal; 1762–3." *Brit. Jl. Surg.,* 1936/7, *24,* 640–668. Also in his *Essays in the History of Medicine,* pp. 116–144. London: Butterworth, 1950.

42. Gordon-Taylor, G. "The Medical and Surgical Aspects of 'the Forty-Five.' " *Brit. Jl. Surg.,* 1945, *33,* 1–16.

43. Gore, A. A. *The Story of our Services under the Crown: a historical sketch of the Army Medical Staff.* London: Baillière, 1879.

44. Great Britain. Army Medical Dept. *Report for the Year 1859– .* London: Harrison, 1861– .

45. ———. *A Treatise on the Transport of Sick and Wounded Troops.* By T. Longmore. London: Stationery Office, 1869.

46. ———. Royal Commission on S. African Hospitals. *Report of the Royal Commission appointed to consider and report upon the Care and Treatment of the Sick and Wounded during the S. African Campaigns. With Evidence and Appendix.* (Cd. 453–455.) London: Wyman & Sons, 1901. 3 vols.

47. ———. Royal Commission on the War in S. Africa. *Report of H. M. Commissioners appointed to inquire into the Military Preparations and other Matters connected with the War in S. Africa.* (Cd. 1789–1792.) London: Wyman & Sons, 1903. 4 vols.

48. ———. War Office. Medical Services. *Medical and Surgical History of the British Army which served in Turkey and the Crimea during the War against Russia, in the Years 1854–6.* London: Harrison & Sons, 1858. 2 vols. First official medical and surgical history of a war.

49. Greenwood, M. "British Loss of Life in the Wars of 1794–1815, and in 1914–1918." *Jl. roy. statist. Soc.,* 1942, *105,* 1–16.

50. Hargreaves, R. "The Medico and the Armed Services." *Practitioner,* 1963, *191,* 670–7.

51. Hay, I. *One Hundred Years of Army Nursing: the story of the British Army Nursing Services from the time of Florence Nightingale . . .* London: Cassell, [1953].

52. Howell, H. A. L. "The British Medical Arrangements during the Waterloo Campaign." *Proc. roy. Soc. Med. (Sect. Hist. Med.),* 1924, *17,* 39–50.

53. Howe, Countess, ed. *The Imperial Yeomanry Hospitals in South Africa, 1900–1902*. London: A. L. Humphreys, 1902. 3 vols.
54. Hume, Sir A. *Service Memoirs*. London: Edward Arnold, 1912.
55. Hutton, Lady I. E. *With a Woman's Unit in Serbia, Salonika, and Sebastopol*. London: Williams & Norgate, 1928.
56. India. General Staff British Army Headquarters. *The Third Afghan War, 1919*. Calcutta: Government of India Central Publication Branch, 1926.
57. India. Government. Medical Advisory Committee. *Report on Amoebic Dysentery and other Protozoal Infections of the Intestine*. Delhi: Super. Gov. Printg., 1917.
58. ———. ———. ———. *Suggestions regarding General Policy of Preventive Action against Malaria in Force "D" (1917) (Provisional)*. Delhi: Super. Gov. P., 1917.
59. ———. ———. ———. *Mesopotamia Inquiries. Report on Basrah Base*. Simla: Gov. Monotype Press, 1916.
60. ———. ———. ———. *Mesopotamia Inquiries. Report on Lines of Communications. (Skeikh Saad to Basra.)* Delhi: Super. Gov. Printg., 1917.
61. ———. ———. ———. *Mesopotamia Inquiries. Report on 3rd Indian Army Corps*. Delhi: Super. Gov. Printg., 1917.
62. ———. ———. ———. *Mesopotamia Inquiries. Report as to Sheikh Saad*. Delhi: Super. Gov. Printg., 1916.
63. ———. ———. ———. *Mesopotamia Inquiries. Report on remaining Inspections (Euphrates and Karun.) December 20th, 1916– January 12th, 1917.)* Delhi: Super. Gov. Printg., 1917.
64. ———. ———. ———. *Mesopotamia Inquiries (September 1916 to January 1917). Final Report*. Delhi: Super. Gov. Printg., 1917.
65. Ireland. Army Medical Board. *Instructions from the Army Medical Board of Ireland to Regimental Surgeons serving on that Establishment for regulating the Concerns of the Sick and of the Hospital. With an Appendix and Index*. Dublin: G. Grierson, 1806.
66. James, J. H. *Surgeon James's Journal, 1815*. Ed. J. Vansittart. London: Cassell, 1964.
67. Johnston, Colonel W. *Roll of Commissioned Officers in the Medical Service of the British Army . . . 1727 to . . . 1898*. Aberdeen: University Press, 1917. (See also 29.)
68. The Lancet. "A Century of Army Pathology." *Lancet*, 1955, I, 955–6.
69. Lemprière, W., [d. 1834]. *Practical Observations on the Diseases of the Army in Jamaica, as they occurred between the Years 1792 and 1797: on the Situation, Climate, and Diseases of that Island; and on the most Probable Means of Lessening Mortality . . .* London: Longman and Rees, 1799. 2 vols.
70. Link, M. M., and H. A. Coleman. *Medical Support of the Army Air Forces in World War II*. Washington, D. C.: U.S.G.P.O. 1955.
71. Livingston, Sir P. C. *Fringe of the Clouds*. London: Johnson, 1962.

72. Loo, Dr. Van. *Les Fièvres zélandaises et leur influence sur l'expédition anglaise en 1808.* Gouda: G. B. van Goor Zonen, 1910.

73. Lord, J. R. *The Story of the Horton (Co. of London) War Hospital, Epsom; its Inception and Work and Some Reflections.* London: Heinemann, 1920.

74. Lovegrove, P. *Not least in the Crusade: a short history of the Royal Army Medical Corps.* Aldershot: Gale & Polden, 1951.

75. McCormick, R. C. *A Visit to the Camp before Sebastopol.* New York: Appleton, 1855.

76. McGuffie, T. H. "The Walcheren Expedition and the Walcheren Fever." *Eng. Hist. Rev.* 1947, *62*, 191–202.

77. MacGrigor, Sir J. *The Autobiography and Services. With an Appendix of Notes and Original Correspondence.* London: Longmans, Green, Longman & Roberts, 1861.

78. McLaren, E. S., Ed. *History of the Scottish Women's Hospitals.* London: Hodder and Stoughton, 1919.

79. McLeave, H. *McIndoe: plastic surgeon.* London: Muller, 1961.

80. MacNalty, Sir A. S., ed. *History of the Second World War. U. K. Medical Series.* London: H.M.S.O., 1952–[in progress].

81. MacNaughton, W. A. "Medical Heroes of the 'Forty-Five.' " *Caledon. Med. Jl.,* 1932–6, *15,* 59–68; 110–124; 142–150.

82. MacPhail, Sir A. *Official History of the Canadian Forces in the Great War. 1914–1919: The Medical Services.* Ottawa: F. A. Acland, 1925.

83. Macpherson, Major-General Sir W. G. *Medical Services Diseases of the War* . . . Edited by . . . Sir W. G. Macpherson . . . Sir W. P. Herringham . . . T. R. Elliott . . . and A. Balfour. (*History of the Great War*) London: H.M.S.O., 1922. 2 vols.

84. Macpherson, Major-General Sir W. G., et al., eds. *History of the Great War based on Official Documents.* Medical Services. London: H.M.S.O., 1921–31. 12 vols.

85. Makins, Sir G. H. *Surgical Experiences in South Africa, 1899–1900. Being mainly a Clinical Study of the Nature and Effects of Injuries produced by Bullets of Small Calibre.* London: Smith, Elder & Co., 1901.

86. Matheson, J. M. "Comments on the Medical Aspects of the Battle of Waterloo, 1815." *Med. Hist.,* 1966, *10,* 204–7.

87. Medical Officer. "100 Years of Army Pathology." *Med. Offr.,* 1955, *93,* 272–3.

88. Millar, J., [1733–1805]. *Observations on the prevailing Diseases in Great Britain together with a Review of the History of those of former Periods, and in other Countries. To which are now prefixed Observations on the Conduct of the War, in an Appeal to the People of Great Britain on the State of Medicine in England; and of the Military Medical Arrangements in the Army and Navy.* London: the Author, 1798.

89. Morrison, R. J. G., et al. "Centenary of the Royal Army Medical College." *Jl. roy. Army med. Corps,* 1961, *107,* 11–32.

90. Mosley, L. *Faces from the Fire*. The Biography of Sir Archibald MacIndoe. London: Weidenfeld and Nicolson, 1962.

91. Neal, J. B. "The History of the Royal Army Medical College." *Jl. roy. Army med. Corps*, 1957, *103*, 163–72.

92. Paterson, T. T. *Morale in War and Work: an experiment in the management of men*. London: M. Parrish, 1955.

93. Peterkin, Colonel A. *A List of Commissioned Medical Officers of the Army, 1660–1727*. Aberdeen University Press, 1925. (See also 29.)

94. Portland Hospital. *A Civilian War Hospital. Being an Account of the Work of the Portland Hospital, and of Experience of Wounds and Sickness in South Africa, 1900 . . . By [Sir] A. A. Bowlby, et al.* London: Murray, 1901.

95. ———. *Report of the Committee*. London: Murray, 1901.

96. Pound, R. *Gillies: surgeon extraordinary*. London: M. Joseph, 1964.

97. Pringle, Sir J., [1707–82]. *Observations on the Diseases of the Army*. London: Millar and Wilson, 1752. Pringle, founder of modern military medicine, was Physician-General of the British Army from 1744 to 1752. His book lays down the principles of military sanitation and the ventilation of barracks, gaols, hospital ships, etc. He did much to improve the lot of soldiers, and it was due to remarks in his book that foot-soldiers were given blankets when on service. The preface of the book includes an account of the origin of the Red Cross idea (the neutrality of military hospitals on the battlefield); for a further note on this, see *Lancet*, 1943, *2*, 234.

98. Raina, B. L. *Medical services: medicine, surgery and pathology*. (*Official History of the Indian Armed Forces in the Second World War, 1939–45. Medical series, vol. 2*.) [Kanpur]: Combined Interservices Historical Section, India and Pakistan, 1955.

99. Reid, D. A. *Memories of the Crimean War, January 1855 to June 1856*. London: St. Catherine Press, 1911. (See also No. 138.)

100. Rexford-Welch, S. C. *The Royal Air Force Medical Services* (*History of the Second World War. U. K. Medical series. Ed. Sir A. MacNalty*.) London: H.M.S.O., 1954–58. 4 vols.

101. Ritchie, C. "The Hostel of the Invalides" by Thomas Povey [1682]. (Lambeth Palace Library MS. 745); edited, with an introduction and notes. *Med. Hist.*, 1966, *10*, 1–22; 177–197.

102. Robinson, Douglas H. *The Dangerous Sky*. Seattle: University of Washington Press, 1971.

103. Robinson, F. *Diary of the Crimean War*. London: R. Bentley, 1856.

104. Rogers, Sir L. *Happy toil; fifty-five years of tropical medicine*. With a foreword by Sir J. W. D. Megan. London: F. Muller, 1950.

105. Royal Army Medical Corps Historical Museum. *Catalogue of the contents of the Muniment Room at the Royal Army Medical College, Millbank, London, S.W.1.*, p. 11: para 2. London: R. A. M. C., September 1965, Supplement 1. January 1967.

106. Sachs, A. "The Centenary of British Military Pathology." *Jl. roy. Army med. Corps*, 1955, *101*, 100–121.

107. ————. "One hundred years of Army Pathology." *Brit. med. Jl.*, 1955, *i*, 1087.

108. St. Clair, T. S. *A Resident in the West Indies and America, with a Narrative of the Expedition to the Island of Walcheren.* London: R. Bentley, 1834. This gives a first hand account of the expedition. It was also published with the title *A Soldier's Recollections of the West Indies and America.* London: R. Bentley, 1834. 2 vols.

109. Salmon, T. W. *The Care and Treatment of Mental Diseases and War Neuroses (Shell shock) in the British Army.* New York: Nat. Committee for Mental Hygiene, 1917. (Duplicated typescript, pp. 102.)

110. Sargent, W., and Eliot Slater. "De l'Influence de la Guerre 1939–1945 sur la psychiatrie britannique." *J. brasil. Psiquiatria*, 1952, *1*, 298–414.

111. Smith, D. "The Fergusson Papers: a calendar of 92 manuscript letters and documents concerning the medical history of the Peninsular War (1808–14)." *Jl. Hist. Med.*, 1964, *19*, 267–71.

112. South, O. P. *Medical Support in a Combat Air Force: a study of medical leadership in World War II.* Maxwell Air Base, Ala., Documentary Research Division, Research Studies Institute, Air University, 1956.

113. Souttar, H. S. *A Surgeon in Belgium.* London: Arnold, 1915.

114. Stevenson, L. G. "John Hunter, Surgeon-General 1790–1793." *Jl. Hist. Med.*, 1964, *19*, 239–66.

115. Stout, T. D. M. *War Surgery and Medicine.* (Official History of New Zealand in the Second World War, 1939–1945.) Wellington, N. Z.: War History Branch, Dept. of Internal Affairs, 1954.

116. Tempest, V. [pseud.]. *Near the sun: the impressions of a medical officer in Bomber Command.* Brighton: Crabtree Press, 1946.

117. Terman, L. M., et al. *The Stanford Revision and Extension of the Binet-Simon Scale for Measuring Intelligence.* Baltimore: Warwick and York, 1917.

118. Thomas, W. *Memoirs of Portugal, Historical and Medical.* London: the Author, 1819.

119. Thornton, Sir J. H. *Memories of Seven Campaigns. A Record of Thirty-Five Years' Service in the Indian Medical Department in India, China, Egypt, and the Sudan (1856–91).* Westminster: Constable, 1895.

120. The Times. "The Army's other Victories. A Hundred Years of Battle against Disease." *Times*, 1955, March 14, p. 9.

121. Treves, Sir F. *The Tale of a Field Hospital.* London: Cassell, 1900.

122. Tulloch, Sir A. M. *The Crimean Commission and the Chelsea Board: being a Review of the Proceedings and Report of the Board.* London: Harrison, 1857.

123. U. S. Army. Surgeon-General Office. Library. *Index-Catalogue.* 1st–3rd series, 4th series (-M), 5th series. Washington: Gov. Printing Office, 1880–1961.
    The main section to consult is "Medicine, military," especially

in Vol. XI, 4th series, (pp. 289–1226). Abundant cross-references are provided, e.g., to "Armies"; "Hygiene, Military"; "Surgery, Military"; "Hospitals"; "Red Cross"; etc.

124. Walker, A. S. *Series 5 (Medical)* of *Australia in the War of 1939–1945.*
        Vol. 1. Clinical problems of war.
        Vol. 2. Middle East and Far East.
        Vol. 3. The Island Campaigns.
    Vol. 4. Medical Services of R. A. N. and R. A. A. F. Canberra: Australian War Memorial, 1952–61.

125. Wallace, D., and F. C. Boyd, eds. *Report of the Work of the Edinburgh and East of Scotland South African Hospitals.* Edinburgh: Oliver & Boyd, 1901.

126. Ward, P. M. "Sir John Hall MSS." *Bull. nat. Reg. Arch.,* 1964, No. 13, pp. 7–13.

127. Wellcome Historical Medical Library. *Current Work in the History of Medicine.* 1. — . London: W. H. M. L., 1954– [in progress].

128. Wellcome Historical Medical Museum. *Medicine in 1815, (Exhibition Cataolgue No. 2.).* London: W. H. M. M., 1965.

129. Wellcome Institute of the History of Medicine. *Medicine and Surgery in the Great War, 1914–1918, (Exhibition Catalogue No. 4).* London: W. I. H. M., 1968.

130. Woodham-Smith, C. *Florence Nightingale, 1820–1910.* London: Constable, 1950.

131. Manson-Bahr, Sir Patrick. *Patrick Manson; the founder of tropical medicine.* London: Nelson, 1962.

ADDITIONS TO BIBLIOGRAPHY

132. Begg, R. Campbell. *Surgery on trestles. A saga of suffering and triumph.* Norwich: Jarrold, 1967. A first hand account of surgery in the Mesopotamian campaign of World War I.

133. Dearden, Harold. *Medicine & Duty: a war diary.* London: Heinemann, 1928.

134. Donald, Charles. *With the Eighth Army in the field.* London: British Medical Association, 1944. (Brigadier Donald was consulting surgeon to the Eighth Army in North Africa and Italy.)

135. James, John Haddy. *Surgeon James's journal, 1815.* Edited by J. Vansittart. London: Cassell, 1964.

136. Laffin, John. *Surgeons in the field.* London: Dent, 1970. A general history, but with substantial accounts of British services.

137. Lawson, George. *Surgeon in the Crimea.* The experiences of George Lawson recorded in letters to his family, 1854–1855. Edited, enlarged and explained by V. Bonham-Carter, assisted by M. Lawson. London: Constable, 1968.

138. Reid, Douglas A. *Soldier-surgeon. The Crimean War Letters of Dr. Douglas A. Reid, 1855–1856.* Edited by Joseph O. Baylen and Alan Conway. Knoxville, University of Tennessee Press, 1968. (See also No. 99.)

139. Thapar, D. R. *The morale builders. Forty years with the military medical services of India.* London: Asia Publishing House, 1965.

XXIV

THE EVOLUTION OF NAVAL MEDICINE

Christopher Lloyd

Since naval medicine is only an aspect of the wider annals of medicine, general histories of medicine and of the medical profession cannot, of course, be neglected. Thus the background of naval surgeons and their training will be found in the histories of the Barber-Surgeons (49, 54). The history of epidemiology is still well served by Creighton's two volumes (14) though, since these are based on an erroneous theory of causation, they must naturally be supplemented by modern works such as those by Winslow (51), or Scott on tropical medicine (39), a work which contains much material of relevance to the student of naval medicine.

A comprehensive history of naval medicine in Britain up to 1900, with full bibliographies, will be found in the four volumes of *Medicine and the Navy,* of which the first two volumes are by J. J. Keevil, the last two by C. Lloyd and J. L. S. Coulter (26). Volume I takes the story up to 1649, volume II to 1714, volume III to 1815, and volume IV to 1900. For the twentieth century there is no continuous narrative, though the shorter histories of naval medicine in general by Allison (2) and Roddis (37) should be consulted, the latter being somewhat wider in scope since it includes other navies, such as the American.

After the war of 1914–18 the Admiralty printed a series of essays on particular topics (1), but nothing was done on a scale to rival the multi-volume history of Army medicine in that war. The naval aspect therefore deserves further research. The war of 1939–45, on the other hand, is comprehensively treated in two volumes of the official history of the war by Coulter (13). A valuable comparative study of the health of the navy in two world wars has also recently been made (22).

For the earlier centuries of naval history, much information about the incidence of disease, victualling etc. will be found in the histories of naval administration previously cited in other sections.

Manuscript sources are scanty before the eighteenth century, and early medical statistics must be regarded with suspicion, partly because they are so incomplete, being based on odd lists from hospitals or particular ships, and partly because the changes in the nomenclature and diagnosis of disease have been so bewildering: for a long time almost any ailment could be classed under "fever."

Nor is the material relating to the administration of the Sick and Hurt (or as it was later called, the Sick and Wounded) Board more satisfactory. An attempt has been made to describe the Board as it existed in 1664–67 (40), and some of its activities later in the century are illustrated by the documents printed by R. D. Merriman (33, 34). A history of the Medical Department in general was attempted by Surgeon-Captain Turnbull in 1903, but the manuscript (which is in the library of Haslar Hospital, Portsmouth) was never completed, nor was it based on earlier records. Hence the general history of the Board is best studied in the volumes of *Medicine and the Navy* previously cited.

The official records of the Board are defective in that the earliest is dated 1727, and there are large lacunae, e.g., for the period 1765–94. Part of the Board's correspondence is at the Public Record Office (Ad. 1/3528–9), part at the National Maritime Museum (series E.F.). There are letters from the Medical Department from 1742 (Ad. 97, 98), but they are not continuous. The earliest surviving surgeon's journal is dated 1793; from that date all those which have been preserved will be found in Ad. 101. They often contain curious essays on medical topics, as well as on the topography of out-of-the-way places around the world, so that there is much geographical and anthropological information to be gleaned about areas still untouched by civilisation.

The Board was also responsible for the welfare of Prisoners of War, and the records in Ad. 103 relating to these are of interest. Hospital musters will be found in Ad. 102. The extensive records of Greenwich Hospital and the Chatham Chest deal with administration, so they contain little of medical interest.

The modern history of naval medicine must be based on the Statistical Reports on the Health of the Navy. The first of these was printed in 1840, covering the years 1830–36, and again in 1849. These were the first attempts to collate nosological returns from surgeon's journals as well as hospitals, nearly all previous records having been drawn from the latter alone. Since 1856 these Reports have been published annually, except during the years 1916–20 and 1937–52. For an evaluation of their value and their subsequent history, a paper by Surgeon-Captain Ellis should be consulted (19). For a complete run of the Reports it is advisable to enquire of the librarian at the R.N. Medical School, Gosport, Hants. The earlier volumes contain interesting excerpts from surgeon's journals, but the later ones are confined to statistical abstracts.

Other official publications to be noted are the Regulations for Medical Officers in the Admiralty Regulations and Instructions, 1805 and 1825 editions. Among Parliamentary Papers relevant to the history of surgeons and naval hospitals, the most important are the Milne Committee report on medical officers, 1866; that on naval hospitals in 1868, which relates to the Florence Nightingale reforms; that on the training of medical officers in 1899; and the Skey report on venereal disease in the Army and Navy in 1867. Naval surgeons were for a time employed on convict ships, and regulations for their conduct were printed in Parliamentary Papers in 1840, 1846, and 1869. This aspect of naval medicine has been explored in Bateson's book on the convict ships (6).

Since ten times the number of sailors and soldiers have died of disease compared with the number killed in action, a valuable evaluation of statistical material relating to casualties was made by Major Greenwood (23), which is discussed by Professor Lewis in so far as it relates to the Napoleonic period (27), and in the paper by Ellis previously referred to.

Textbooks of medical practice at sea in the past are not numerous, nor have many copies survived, because nothing goes out of date as quickly as a medical handbook. The earliest and rarest is by William Clowes in 1588 (11). More widely used both in the Navy and the East India Company was John Woodall's *Surgeon's Mate,* which ran through several editions (52). The dissertations on sea diseases by Cockburn at the end of the seventeenth century were frequently reprinted and, because of the fallacies they contain, very mischievous (12). The only surviving diary of a naval surgeon is that by James Yonge, covering the years 1647 to 1721, which has been recently printed, but most of it is about topics which have nothing to do with medicine (53). Another diary supposed to have been written by John Knyveton in 1756–1809 should be regarded as suspect, since it has all the appearance of a modern pastiche. More genuine and practical are handbooks for the use of those employed in the slave trade or on the African coast such as that by Atkins in 1742 (4).

The father of nautical medicine was Dr. James Lind. His biography has been briefly written by Admiral Roddis (38), but more details about him will be found in volume III of *Medicine and the Navy.* His classic treatise on scurvy was re-edited and brought up to date by Stewart and Guthrie on the occasion of its bicentenary (30). His *Essay on Preserving the Health of Seamen* (29) is invaluable on such subjects as hygiene and victualling. It has been reprinted, with excerpts from the works of Blane and Trotter, in a Navy Records Society volume entitled *The Health of Seamen* (31). Lind's other work (28), which was the first and only handbook on tropical medicine for a long time, was written for the benefit of colonists, so it is not of specific naval interest.

Sir Gilbert Blane's most important work was based on his experience in the American War; the second and expanded edition is to be recommended (7). Though not, like Lind, an original thinker, he set the fashion for collecting medical statistics, and his prominence as a Commissioner for Sick and Wounded enabled him to achieve essential reforms in the service. After the Napoleonic war was over he wrote an important paper on the comparative health of the navy at the beginning and end of that war, which was reprinted in 1822 (8) and will also be found in *The Health of Seamen,* volume cited above.

Two of his contemporaries throw much light on medical affairs in the American and French wars. Dr. Trotter's miscellany entitled *Medicina Nautica* appeared in 1797 and Dr. Robertson wrote a number of dissertations which were collected in 4 volumes in 1804 (47). These include many statistics relating to the American War, his experience with old age pensioners at Greenwich, and his enthusiastic reports on the use of Peruvian Bark to combat fever.

More specifically of a textbook nature, rather than being dissertations or reminiscences, are, for the eighteenth century, those by Northcote (36) and Turnbull (48); for the nineteenth, those by Wilson on naval surgery (50) and Armstrong on naval hygiene (3).

On particular topics, accounts of tropical diseases encountered on the West African station are of great interest in the history of colonisation, especially Bryson's report of 1847 (9) and the narrative of the exploration of the Niger by naval vessels by Baikie in 1854 (5). It was Baikie who really established the use of quinine as a prophylactic, thus opening up the interior of Africa, and his papers in the British Museum (MSS 32,449) are worth consulting. Sir William Burnett's report on the incidence of cholera in the Black Sea fleet during the Crimean War is important (10). Two modern essays by Sir Sheldon Dudley on Yellow Fever and Pulmonary Tuberculosis as seen by naval surgeons gather together much scattered information (17, 18). For the whole history of scurvy, the chief scourge of the sea, an invaluable paper by Miss Henderson Smith lies buried in the journal of the Royal Army Medical Corps (45).

On conditions afloat, hygiene, victualling and habitability, apart from the general histories cited above and the present writer's book on British seamen (31), there are contemporary studies by Gavin Milroy (35), J. D. MacDonald (32) and for the modern period T. B. Shaw (42). A book such as Drummond and Wilbraham's *The Englishman's Food* (16) contains much interesting information.

The history of naval hospitals up to 1900 is covered in *Medicine and the Navy,* but monographs and articles by Tait (46) on Haslar, Hughes on the nursing service (24) or James on medical officers at Greenwich Hospital (25) are worth consulting. The history of the hospital ship has only been partially studied 41), and further research on the activities of such ships would be rewarding.

For developments in naval medicine in the twentieth century it is best to consult the files of *The Journal of the Royal Navy Medical Service* which, since it began to appear in 1915, devotes most of its space to contemporary problems and advances in medicine. It is a privately printed journal, and a run of its volumes may be found at the R. N. Medical School, Gosport, or at Haslar Hospital. The results of much contemporary research will be found in the Reports of the Medical Research Council's Royal Naval Personnel Research Committee, available at the same libraries. The problems associated with the habitability of submarines and of warships in hot climates has received attention at the hands of Surgeon-Captain Ellis and others (15, 20, 21, 43), as well as those of naval architects (44). The extent of American experience in these matters in recent years must supersede British research.

For further research into the evolution of naval medicine it is advisable to consult the librarian of the Wellcome Medical Historical Library, Euston Road, London.

BIBLIOGRAPHY

1. Admiralty. *Naval Medical History of the War (1914–18)*. London, n.d.
2. Allison, R. S. *Sea Diseases*. London: Hale, 1943.
3. Armstrong, A. *Observations on Naval Hygiene and Scurvy*. London: Churchill, 1858.
4. Atkins, J. *The Navy Surgeon*. London: Hodges, 1743.
5. Baikie, W. B. *Narrative of a Voyage up the Niger in 1854*. London: Murray, 1856.
6. Bateson, C. *The Convict Ships, 1787–1868*. Glasgow: Brown and Ferguson, 1959.
7. Blane, Sir G. *Observations on the Diseases Incident to Seamen*. 2nd ed. London: Cooper, 1789.
8. Blane, Sir G. *The Comparative Health of the Navy,* reprinted in his *Select Dissertations*. London: Underwood, 1822.
9. Bryson, A. *Report on the Climate and Principal Diseases of the African Station,* London: Clowes, 1847.
10. Burnett, Sir W. *Report on the Cholera in the Black Sea*. London: Admiralty, 1854.
11. Clowes, W. *A Proved Practice for all Young Chirurgians*. London: 1588.
12. Cockburn, W. *Sea Diseases*. 3rd ed. London, 1736. The first edition is dated 1696.
13. Coulter, J. L. S. *The Royal Naval Medical Service*. London: H.M. Stationery Office, 1954. 2 vols.
14. Creighton, C. *A History of Epidemics in Britain*. Cambridge University Press, 1891. 2 vols.
15. Critchley, M., "Problems of Naval Warfare under Climatic Extremes." *Brit. med. j.,* 1945.
16. Drumond, Sir J. and A. Wilbraham. *The Englishman's Food*. London: Cape, 1957.
17. Dudley, Sir S. "Yellow Fever as seen by Medical Officers of the Royal Navy." *Proc. R. Soc. Med.,* 26, 1933.
18. Dudley, Sir S. "Pulmonary Tuberculosis in the Royal Navy." *Ibid.* 34, 1941.
19. Ellis, F. P. "Naval Medical Statistics." *J. Roy. Nav. med. Serv.,* 1959.
20. Ellis, F. P. "Tolerable Levels of Warmth in the Royal Navy." *Annals of Roy. Coll. Surgeons,* 1953.
21. Ellis, F. P. "Underwater respiration and Submarine Atmosphere." *J. royal Nav. med. Serv.,* 1951.
22. Ellis, F. P., and Sir A. Rowlands. "Health of the Navy in Two World Wars." *J. Roy. nav. med. Serv.,* 1966.
23. Greenwood, Major. "British loss of life in the Wars of 1794–1815, and 1914–18." *J. Roy. Statist. Soc.,* 1942.

24. Hughes, M. L. "The Naval Nursing Service." *J. Roy. nav. med. Serv.*, 1922.
25. James, R. R. "The Medical Officers of Greenwich Hospital, 1695–1800." *J. roy. Nav. med. Serv.*, 1834.
26. Keevil, J. J., C. Lloyd, and J. L. S. Coulter. *Medicine and the Navy 1200–1900*. Edinburgh: Livingstone, 1957–63.
27. Lewis, M. A. *Social History of the Royal Navy, 1793–1815*. London: Allen and Unwin, 1960.
28. Lind, J. *An Essay on Diseases incidental to Europeans in Hot Climates*. London: Becket, 1768.
29. Lind, J. *An Essay on the most effectual means of Preserving the Health of Seamen*. London: Wilson, 1757 (and see Lloyd, C. below).
30. Lind, J. *A Treatise of the Scurvy*. Edinburgh: Sands, 1753. A modern edition by Stewart, C. P. and D. Guthrie was published in Edinburgh in 1953 by Livingstone.
31. Lloyd, C. *The British Seaman, 1200–1860*. London: Collins, 1968. Also an edition of the writings of Lind, Blane and Trotter entitled *The Health of Seamen*, Navy Records Society, 1965; and see Keevil above.
32. MacDonald, J. D. *Outlines of Naval Hygiene*. London: Smith, Elder, 1881.
33. Merriman, R. D., ed. *The Sergison Papers*. Navy Records Society, 1950.
34. Merriman, R. D., ed. *Queen Anne's Navy*. Navy Records Society, 1961.
35. Milroy, G. *The Health of the Royal Navy Considered*. London: Hardwicke, 1862.
36. Northcote, W., *The Marine Practice of Physic and Surgery*. London: Richardson, 1770. 2 vols.
37. Roddis, L. H. *A Short History of Nautical Medicine*. New York: Schuman, 1941.
38. Roddis, L. H. *James Lind*. New York: Schuman, 1950.
39. Scott, H. H. *A History of Tropical Medicine*. London: Arnold, 1939. 2 vols.
40. Shaw, J. J. S. "The Commission of Sick and Wounded, 1664–67." *Mariner's Mirror*, 1939.
41. Shaw, J. J. S. "The Hospital Ship, 1608–1740." *Mariner's Mirror*, 1936.
42. Shaw, T. B. *Manual of Naval Hygiene*. Oxford Univ. Press, 1929.
43. Shaw, T. B. "Ventilation in H.M. Ships." *J. Roy. nav. med. Serv.*, 1926.
44. Sims, Sir A. J. "Habitability of Naval Ships under wartime conditions." *Trans. Inst. of Naval Architects*, 1945.
45. Smith, A. Henderson. "Historical Enquiry into the Efficacy of Lime Juice for the Prevention of Scurvy." *J.R. Army med. Corps.*, 1919.
46. Tait, W. *The History of Haslar Hospital*. London: Simpkin, 1906.

47. Trotter, T., *Medicina Nautica*. London: Cadell, 1797–1803. 3 vols. R. Robertson. *Works*. London, 1804. 4 vols.
48. Turnbull, W. *The Naval Surgeon*. London: Phillips, 1806.
49. Wall, C. *History of the Surgeon's Company, 1745–1800*. London: Hutchinson, 1937.
50. Wilson, J. *Outline of Naval Surgery*. Edinburgh: Maclachlan, 1846.
51. Winslow, C. E. A. *The Conquest of Epidemic Diseases*. Princeton University Press, 1943.
52. Woodall, J. *The Surgeon's Mate*. London, 1639.
53. *Yonge, J., Journal of*. F. N. L. Poynter, ed. London: Longmans, 1963.
54. Young, S. *The Annals of the Barber-Surgeons of London*. London: Blades, 1890.

XXV

THE HISTORY OF MILITARY
AND MARTIAL LAW

F. H. Dean

This chapter traces the history of military law from its mediaeval origins in the Articles of War administered in the Court of the Constable and Marshal, through its developments in the sixteenth, seventeenth and eighteenth centuries into a system of law administered in courts-martial (with particular reference to the constitutional change in the Army's position which occurred in 1689) up to the re-organization in the 1880's which introduced the modern system. There are references to the original sources, to the printed works on the subject from the sixteenth century onwards, to reports of Royal Commissions and other inquiries and to relevant Acts of Parliament and cases. The history of naval law and of martial law are treated more briefly. The chapter concludes with suggestions of topics for further study, and a detailed bibliography is attached.

In this chapter the expressions "military law," "air force law" and "naval law" will be used to denote jurisdiction over the members of the armed forces of the Crown and certain classes of civilians associated with the forces, and the expression "martial law" will be used to denote jurisdiction over all citizens in times of rebellion and riot. This distinction is now well settled, although the use of the term "martial law" to mean what is strictly "military law" can be found as late as the middle of the nineteenth century; see Cockburn, C. J. (32)

The sources for the study of this subject are as follows:

    (1) Acts of Parliament. The more important of these are reproduced in many text books, and all up to 1865 are to be found among the Statutes at Large, and since that date among the Statutes as published by Her Majesty's Stationery Office and also as printed as part of the Law Reports. All these series are available in all English legal libraries.

    (2) Commissions to Commanders-in-Chief, the Judge Advocate General and judge advocates.

    (3) Articles of War.

(4) Court-Martial proceedings.
(5) Other original records.
(6) Reports of Royal Commissions and Committees of Inquiry.
(7) Periodicals and books.

The places where the items under headings (2) to (7) can be found in London are stated in the text of this chapter or in the list of authorities at the end of it. As the history of military and martial law involves no security considerations, there is unrestricted access to virtually all sources of material except records of courts-martial less than one hundred years old. Facilities for bona fide students to peruse these can sometimes be obtained on application to the Judge Advocate General.

The military law of England, like that of other western European countries, originated as part of the mediaeval law of arms. That law embraced much wider topics than military discipline itself; it included, for instance, the law as to who were entitled to the status of combatants, and the complicated rules as to spoil and ransom: Keen (50). These matters are outside the scope of this chapter.

Although during the reign of Charles II (1660–1685) the King maintained his own Guards and other regiments as a standing military force, there was no precise legal authority for their maintenance, and prior to 1688 there was in England no statutory or other legal basis for a standing professional army.

Every male adult had military obligations, at first feudal and later statutory in origin, and had to perform them from time to time as necessity arose. When citizens were thus embodied for military service, from the earliest times some form of legal discipline was required to control them, and there had to be tribunals in which this discipline was enforced. These were the origins of military law, and for the reasons stated it originally operated only in times of actual war.

When a campaign occurred, either the Crown, with the advice of the Constable and Marshal, enacted regulations called Articles of War for the discipline of the troops, or such Articles were issued by the Commander-in-Chief by virtue of a commission issued to him by the Crown: see specimen of such commissions in Rymer's *Foedera* (71). Many collections of these early codes of Articles exist; Grose (45) prints translations of several of them, from Richard I's Articles for his troops who went on the Third Crusade in 1189 up to 1643. Walton (86) gives others up to 1700. Several books on military topics published during the reign of Elizabeth I contain accounts of the administration of discipline under the Articles of War then current: see especially Digges (38), Rich (68), Styward (79), Garrard and Hitchcock (44), and Sutcliffe (80). A modern work containing useful references is Cruikshank (34). The developments during the Civil War period are discussed in Firth (41). Towards the end of the seventeenth century a contemporary writer, Turner (84), gives an account of the Articles current in his time, while a modern writer who discusses them is Walton (86).

In early times we find high military officers being tried before Parliament for their conduct in war; see for the trial before Parliament of Henry de Essex in 1157 the translation from the Parliament Rolls in Speed (77) and for the similar trials of William de Weston and Sir John de Gomenes (1377) and of the Bishop of Norwich in his capacity as Commander of an expedition (1383) the translations in Grose (45). These, however, were in the nature of state trials rather than the ordinary administration of military discipline under the Articles of War.

The Articles of War were administered at first as it has been generally believed in the Court of the High Constable and Marshal of England, which was part of the Curia Regis, the King's Council and Supreme Court, composed of his great officers of state, out of which the common law courts developed. There are several accounts of the offices of Constable and Marshal and of their Court, notably in Tytler (85); see also the curious seventeenth-century manuscript account by Phillips (67). The Court also had a non-military jurisdiction, in which capacity it was known as the Court of Chivalry, an account of which is given in Squibb (77A) who, incidentally, believes that this Court was distinct from the Courts of the Constable and Marshal which exercised jurisdiction in matters of military discipline. On its military side it followed the Army in time of war. Its jurisdiction in military matters was regulated from time to time by statutes, of which early examples are 13 Richard II, c.2 (1390), 18 Henry VI, c.19 (1440), 2 and 3 Edward VI, c.2 (1549) and 4 and 5 Philip and Mary, c.3 (1557).

The Office of High Constable fell into abeyance in 1521 and was not revived, but that of Marshal continues to the present day. It was ultimately decided that in the absence of the Constable the Marshal had no judicial authority in military matters: see Tytler (85). Thereafter (except when otherwise ordered by the Crown in special cases up to the reign of Charles I; e.g., see his order of 1631 in Rushworth (70) Part II, Volume I, page 112) military cases were tried in accordance with the current Articles of War by Commanders-in-Chief and/or their deputies or appointees under authority contained in the Commander-in-Chief's commission of appointment: see, for example, the Parliamentary Commission appointing the Earl of Essex to be Captain-General of the Parliamentary Army, and giving him power to issue rules and orders for the punishment of crime "according to the custom of the wars and the law of the land," reproduced in Firth and Rait (42). At first these tribunals of officers were termed Councils of War, but in the seventeenth century the term "Court-Martial" appears, derived from the Court of the Marshal which it superseded: see Tytler (85). Before long, varieties of courts-martial emerged for dealing with cases of varying degrees of seriousness; general and regimental courts were the first of these to appear: see the Regulations for the Musters (1663) and the Articles of War (1673) both reproduced in Walton (86). These developments are discussed by Cruikshank (34) for the Elizabethan period, by Firth (41) for the Civil War period and by Walton (86) for the period 1660–1700.

Even before the court of the Constable and Marshal was replaced by courts-martial consisting of officers appointed by the Commander-in-Chief, it seems that a need was found for the Court to have the guidance of a professional lawyer. This official became known as the Judge Marshal and developed into the modern Judge Advocate. A useful short account of the office of judge advocate, with references to sources, is given in Stuart-Smith (78). An account of the judge marshal at the end of the sixteenth century appears in Sutcliffe (80), and Markham (59) describes the office as it was in the early seventeenth century. A specimen of the patent of appointment of a judge advocate to serve in Ireland in 1597 appears in the *Liber Munerum Publicorum Hiberniae* and is reproduced in translation in Walton (86). Parliamentary Ordinances as to judge advocates during the Civil War are reproduced in Firth and Rait (42).

After the Restoration (1661) there came into existence an official known as the King's Judge Marshal and Advocate-General, appointed as a permanent official by patent from the Crown; he carried out numerous administrative functions in regard to the assembly of courts, summoning of witnesses, and presenting the proceedings after the trial to the Sovereign or other confirming authority, as well as sitting or providing a deputy to sit at the trial itself. By this time the Judge Advocate General or his deputy had come to perform at the trial both prosecuting and judicial functions. He also had at this time some civil responsibilities within the Army, e.g., verification of wills and contracts, the fixing of prices and the regulation of weights and measures; see Tytler (85), the Articles of War of the time (*supra*) and the Judge Advocates' patents and warrants of appointment and other sources referred to in Walton (86).

Accounts of the procedure of courts trying military offenders in early times are scarce, although reference has been made to the records of four mediaeval cases tried before Parliament. Markham (59) gives a short description of the Court of the Marshal about his own time; see also Phillips (67). From about 1640 onwards, there is ample material. For the Civil War period there is extant a considerable number of re-prints of the proceedings of notable trials by court-martial in pamphlet form. These are among the Thomasson Tracts (81), and some are in the Ministry of Defence Library in the Old War Office Building (1). About 1680, Turner (84) gives an account of the varieties of courts-martial with which he was acquainted and of their procedure. It is clear that courts-martial up to the eighteenth century exercised a jurisdiction to try civil disputes between members of the army in addition to their usual criminal jurisdiction, and also that general courts-martial sat to hear appeals from lesser courts-martial.

For a long period there was controversy as to the proper scope of military law and of the jurisdiction of its tribunals. It was maintained that it could not be applied in England, at least in time of peace; thus during the reign of Edward II (c. 1326) the conviction of the Earl of Lancaster under military law in time of peace was reversed; see the citation from the Parliamentary Rolls in Walton (86), page 532. Earlier statutes regulating the jurisdiction of the Court of the Constable and Marshal have already been mentioned. These controversies were very active during the seventeenth century and are reflected in a clause in the Petition of Right

(1629). A negative answer to the question whether any form of military justice could lawfully be administered within the realm of England, carried to extremes, would have made the maintenance of discipline in the Army impossible, as was pointed out by one of Charles I's generals in a letter of 1640 protesting against the suggestion that Councils of War were illegal; see Rushworth (70) Volume 3, page 1199ff, also reproduced in Clode II (31). There are numerous seventeenth-century instances of soldiers being tried in the civil courts under sixteenth-century statutes for desertion and other military offences, and late in that century it was acknowledged that the Articles of War ought not to have any application in England in peacetime, at least in regard to the power to inflict any punishment affecting life or limb. Nevertheless, the maintenance of some troops in England was tolerated though not legalised in the time of Charles II, and discipline was administered from day to day according to the laws and customs of war; a law which was itself unlawful.

The year 1689 is the dividing line between the system so far described and that of modern times. After the Revolution of 1688 Parliament recognised the necessity to maintain military forces in England and to provide for their discipline, but determined to keep such matters under their control. These were the objects of the first Mutiny Act (1 William and Mary, c.5) reproduced in Walton (86), Clode II (31) and in many other works. This Act operated only for seven months and subsequent Mutiny Acts only for one year at a time, a system which in essence continued until 1955. A detailed account of the first Mutiny Act and the developments to be found in later acts is in Clode II (31). The first Mutiny Act had no application outside England, and within the realm provided for trial by court-martial only for mutiny, sedition and desertion. Thus the everyday discipline of the Army continued to be governed by Articles of War in spite of their illegality in England in peacetime, and the Act did not purport to take away the Crown's prerogative to make such Articles in time of war or for overseas; this was expressly acknowledged in the Act of 1702. The year 1712 marked another development, necessitated by an outbreak of peace; the Crown was given power to make Articles of War for operation overseas "in such manner as might have been done (by royal prerogative) beyond the seas in time of war." In 1718 the Crown was empowered to make Articles of War providing for the trial of a considerable range of offences both in the United Kingdom and in the King's dominions overseas, and this power was not limited to wartime. Thus the Crown had gained *from Parliament* and for a year at a time the power to maintain standing forces in the United Kingdom and in its overseas dominions in peacetime, and of providing for their discipline by Articles of War, and still retained its prerogative power to maintain forces in foreign territories and to discipline them also under Articles of War. Finally, in 1803 the Mutiny Act and the statutory power of making Articles of War were extended to provide for the Army whether it was in the United Kingdom, the King's overseas dominions or in foreign territories; this was done because the Peace of Amiens had brought the previous state of war to an end and yet it was necessary to keep troops overseas, so that the power to provide for their discipline by prerogative Articles became open to question. Meanwhile the Acts had become more detailed, and dealt expressly with numerous offences, so that to some extent they overlapped the Articles of War; in case of inconsistency the Act prevailed. Jurisdiction to try certain civil offences by court-martial was first conferred in 1717, was more closely defined in 1750 and 1784 and simplified in 1814. The jurisdiction was limited, however, to places outside the United Kingdom where no British civil courts were available; this limitation remained until the Mutiny Acts were replaced by the Army Act in 1881 and has still not been completely removed: see the Army Act 1955 and the Air Force Act 1955, section 70.

The legal and constitutional position of the Army remained substantially unchanged until 1879. During the nineteenth century the practice developed of issuing King's or Queen's Regulations covering in detail the whole area of military organisation and administration. These Regulations, which are still issued, have no statutory authority, and if a Regulation were found to be inconsistent with the general or statute law it would be invalid.

During the two centuries between 1689 and 1879 there were naturally developments in court-martial procedure. Numerous text books of the period give accounts of the whole process from the charging of the accused to the execution of the sentence; the most notable are perhaps Adye (26) of which the 4th Edition (1796) is the most famous, Tytler (85) first published in 1799, Simmons (76) dated about 1830, D'Aguiler (35) published in 1850 and Hough (49) in 1855. Clode II (31) describes the system as it was immediately before the changes introduced in 1879. By that time the judge advocate had shed his function as prosecutor and his responsibility had come to be limited, as today, to ensuring the proper conduct of the trial, recording the proceedings, and acting as a judicial adviser to the Court; see Clode I (30) Vol. 2, pages 363–364 and Appendix CXLV and Clode II (31) page 110. The Judge Advocate General himself and his Deputy were, as they always had been, barristers, but the judge advocates who normally officiated in court, though usually appointed by the Judge Advocate General, at least in the United Kingdom (hence the term "Deputy Judge Advocate") were serving officers who had had some legal training but were not barristers; one became a Canon of York Minster!

The best method of coming to understand the gradual changes in procedure, the functions of the judge advocate, representation of the accused and so forth, is to study the records of actual cases. The proceedings of many notable trials were issued in book form, e.g., that of Lord George Sackville (1760) arising out of the Battle of Minden (72). An interesting feature of this case was that after the trial had gone on for some time the current Mutiny Act lapsed, and as the new Act had not yet received the Royal Assent the jurisdiction of the Court also lapsed and the trial had to be re-commenced later. Apart from these books relating to notable trials, hundreds of the original manuscript proceedings of trials from 1668 onwards are in the War Office Records. These include records in the Courts-Martial Books (into which original proceedings were copied) and in the Order Books of formations on whose orders trials were held.

There is also much information available as to the general administration of military discipline and the position and functions of the Judge Advocate General, in the War Office Records, ranging from high constitutional issues to arguments about his establishment and the pay of his clerks. In addition to his duties already described, in 1695 (under William III's Warrant of 18th February 1694–5 quoted in Clode II (31) page 77 from the War Office Records) he became secretary and legal adviser to the Board of Officers by which, under the Crown, the Army was administered from 1715 until the appointment of a Commander-in-Chief in 1793; the minutes of this Board are in the War Office Records. This duty ultimately led to the Judge Advocate General becoming a Minister with a seat in Parliament, where he had to defend the actions of the military authorities taken on his advice; necessarily, he went out of office with each change in the Government. This history of the office from 1715 onwards is described in Clode I (30) Volume II, where the original documents are cited and an example is given of the Judge Advocate General's patent of appointment in Victoria's reign, together with a memorandum prepared in the 1860's setting out the duties of the office. The Judge Advocate General continued to sit in the House of Commons until 1893.

In 1868 a Royal Commission on courts-martial and the system of punishment for military offences was appointed. Its first report (July 1868; 17b) dealt entirely with punishment; flogging had recently been abolished and other ameliorations were proposed. The main concern appears to have been the control of drunkenness, for which there were 9,736 trials by court-martial in 1860. More important was the final report of 1869 (17b) which after a further Committee on the Mutiny Acts had reported in 1878 (17c) led to the reforms of 1879. The object of these was to bring to an end the system whereby military law was contained in two frequently overlapping codes, the Mutiny Act and the Articles of War, of which the second was subordinate to the first, and to simplify and modernise the whole system. This was achieved by the Army Discipline and Regulation Act 1879, soon repealed and re-enacted as the Army Act 1881. This Act contained a modern code embodying the whole law relating to military offences and their trial and punishment both summarily by commanding officers and by courts-martial. The Act had in itself no force, but had to be brought into operation each year and for only a year at a time by the Army (Annual) Act; this system both preserved the constitutional principle maintained since 1689 and provided opportunities for amending the Army Act. The Act also gave power to the Secretary of State for War to make Rules of Procedure for the conduct of disciplinary proceedings. The issue of non-statutory Queen's Regulations was not affected by the new legislation.

This re-organisation of military law was closely followed by the issue for the first time of an official publication entitled the *Manual of Military Law* (57), which virtually brought to an end the publication of privately produced works on the subject. Consequently, in order to trace the development of military law since 1881, reference must be made to the *Manual,* of which the present edition of the main part is the 11th (57).

In March 1918, under the Air Force (Constitution) Act 1917, the Royal Air Force was created. The legal arrangements for this force have from the beginning closely corresponded to those for the Army. From 1918 onwards there was an Air Force Act, almost verbally identical (*mutatis mutandis*) with the Army Act and kept in operation year by year by the statute thereafter known as the Army and Air Force (Annual) Act. There was also a set of Air Force Rules of Procedure, corresponding to those made under the Army Act, and Air Force King's or Queen's Regulations. There was and is a *Manual of Air Force Law* (56).

Until the legislation of 1879–1881 was passed, the accused at a court-martial could not be represented by an advocate, whether a lawyer or a serving officer, though he could be attended by either who as "prisoner's friend" could advise and assist him without putting questions or addressing the Court. Under the new law the accused was given the right to be represented either by a professionally qualified advocate or by a serving officer. No provision was made, however, for the prosecution to be represented, and from 1860 (when the judge advocate ceased to act as prosecutor) prosecutions were usually conducted by regimental adjutants, sometimes advised by counsel. The Darling Committee on Courts-Martial (17d), which reported in 1919, led to the formation in 1923 of military and air force departments of the Judge Advocate General's Office, staffed by barristers and solicitors commissioned as officers, whose function it was to advise on the drafting of charges and the preparation and conduct of prosecutions, and themselves to prosecute at courts-martial in important cases; they were also made responsible for legal education in the Army and the Royal Air Force.

This system continued in its main essentials until after the Second World War. There was a Committee of Inquiry (the Oliver Committee) into courts-martial in 1938 (17e), whose principal recommendation was that the independence of the Judge Advocate General should be made clear by placing him under a Minister other than the Secretaries of State for War and Air and freeing him from responsibility for his military and air force departments, thus leaving him with exclusively judicial functions; the military and air force departments were to be re-organised as a Directorate or Directorates within the War Office and Air Ministry. There were also proposals as to legal aid, appeals, and legal education within the forces. Before effect could be given to this report war ensued and nothing could be done. In 1946 yet another Committee, the Lewis Committee, was appointed and reported in 1948 (17g) making recommendations as to the re-organisation of the Judge Advocate General's office, appeals, legal aid, and other matters. The recommendations of these two Committees were partially implemented between 1948 and 1951. Directorates of Army and Air Force Legal Services, staffed by serving officers with legal qualifications, were formed to replace the military and air force departments of the Judge Advocate General's office, and the functions of the Judge Advocate General and his staff of barristers became exclusively judicial, consisting in the main of sitting as judge advocates and giving post-trial advice; they ceased to be responsible to the Service Ministries and instead came to be appointed by and responsible to the Lord Chancellor as head of the judiciary and paid out of Supreme Court funds. A Courts-Martial Appeal Court was also instituted to hear appeals from the findings of courts-martial, and was composed of the judges of the (civil) Court of Criminal Appeal; from this Court a limited right of appeal to the House of Lords was provided. This system is in operation today and is described in detail in the current edition of the Manuals of Military and Air Force Law (57 and 56).

In the early 1950's it was thought that the Army and Air Force Acts, which since 1881 had been amended piecemeal year by year, required thorough re-drafting. This was done, and the outcome was the Army Act 1955, the Air Force Act 1955, and their accompanying Rules of Procedure, which came into operation on 1st January 1957. The Acts are based on the reports of a Select Committee of the House of Commons, which were published together with the evidence received and memoranda submitted by a drafting committee (17i). The provisions for the two services are virtually identical. A constitutional innovation was made, however, in that it was provided that each Act should expire after twelve months but, subject to Parliamentary approval, could be renewed annually without amendments for a further year by an Order in Council approved by Parliament until the expiration of five years from its commencement. The limitation of renewals to a total period of five years was intended to provide the opportunity for the regular revision of the Acts after each such period of time, and this was in fact carried out in 1961 and 1966. A noteworthy feature of the new Acts is the considerable extension of the application of military and air force law to dependants of members of the forces and several other categories of civilians working for or in association with the armed forces: see section 209 of each Act, and the treatment of this topic in Wiener (87).

There is space only for a short note as to Naval law, which has developed quite independently. What follows is condensed from a memorandum kindly prepared for me by Mr. Basil S. Hall, M.C., T.D., of the Treasury Solicitor's Office. In early times the Sovereign called on merchant ships and their crews to supplement his own in time of war, and not until the seventeenth century did the British Navy consist entirely of the King's ships. There does not, however, seem to have been the same reluctance to tolerate a permanent Navy as there was to accepting a standing Army, and consequently there is no such clear dividing line in the development of Naval law as occurred in the growth of military law in 1689.

Conduct at sea, including the discipline of mariners, was regulated by the laws and customs of the sea; many of these originated from the Island of Rhodes and an early collection is the twelfth-century Laws of Oleron. These were supplemented in time of war by directions of the Admiral. A version of the Laws of Oleron, with guidance to Admirals as to directions to be given in war time, appears in the English fifteenth-century *Black Book of the Admiralty* (27, 62 and 83).

Such were the origins of the Naval Articles of War (many of which applied also in time of peace) contained in successive Naval Discipline Acts, of which the first was 13 Car.II St.1 c.13 (1661); it dealt with offences, punishments, court-martial procedure and the appointment of judge advocates. Various subsequent Acts were passed between 1749 and 1866. Provisions as to court-martial procedure became more detailed and punishments less severe. An amendment of 1813 enabled the King to substitute other punishments for the death penalty, but only in 1949 was corporal punishment finally abolished in the Navy. Jurisdiction over offences committed on shore dates from 1749, and from 1866 any offence against the law of England could be tried by court-martial, although if such offences were committed on shore in the United Kingdom and outside Naval establishments they were left to be tried in the civil courts; this restriction largely disappeared some fifty years later. From the eighteenth century the Naval Discipline Acts were supplemented by Admiralty Instructions.

After the Second World War, at about the same time as the Lewis Committee (*supra*) investigated Army and Air Force courts-martial, the Pilcher Committee (17j) dealt with the administration of justice in the Navy. Their report led to the Naval Discipline Act 1957, which contains the code now in operation. There is a Naval publication analogous to the Manuals of Military and Air Force Law (25). General works which may be consulted include those by Brook (29), Clowes (33), Gardiner (43), Hannay (46), Lewis (53), McArthur (54), Nicholas (62), Oppenheim (64), Robinson (69), and Thring (82).

The next statutory renewal of the Army Act and Air Force Act 1955 will come into operation on the 1st January 1972, and in preparation for this work on the further revision of these Acts is going on at the time of writing (1970). Students should therefore look out for the report of the Select Committee of the House of Commons, or possibly of both Houses of Parliament, which will probably be set up some time in 1971 to consider the amending legislation in detail. This opportunity is being taken to bring the Army and Air Force Acts and the Naval Discipline Act 1957 into much closer accord with one another, and it may be that in due course, although probably not for some years, it will be possible to draft and enact a code of discipline common to the three services. This process must, however, be rendered more difficult by the differing traditions and to some extent the differing needs of the Navy on the one hand and the Army and Royal Air Force on the other.

Only brief reference can be made to the subject of martial law as defined in the opening paragraph of this chapter. The extent to which military force can be used to restore order when the civil authority has broken down, due to rebellion or some such situation, can only be judged by the necessity of the case. A proclamation of the introduction of martial law is usual but not essential. It is settled that civilians must not under a pretext of martial law be brought before military tribunals, tried and punished, unless the civil courts are suspended and not available to deal with them. These and other legal and constitutional issues are fully discussed in Dicey (37) Chapter 8 and Note 12 in the Appendix; although this work was first published more than 80 years ago its statement of general principles remains sound. A historical account of the subject from the seventeenth century, with references to authorities, reported cases, inquiries and Parliamentary debates will be found in Clode I (30) Volume II, Chapter 18 and Note II and Illustrations 106–113; see also Clode II (31), Chapter 8. Both these works were written in the middle of the nineteenth century, when the use of military power to suppress the rebellions in Jamaica in 1831 and 1865 was fresh in men's minds. Two other nineteenth-century works which reflect the contemporary interest in the subject are those by Finlason, I and II (39 and 40). Reference should also be made to the cases arising out of the Jamaica rebellion of 1865, in which attempts were made to prosecute for murder the Governor, who had proclaimed martial law, and the General Officer Commanding and the President of a military court, who in pursuance of the proclamation had arrested a civilian, tried him before a military court, and executed him; see R. v. Nelson and Brand, Special Report 1867 (32) and R. v. Eyre, Special Report 1868 (28). The current law is succinctly stated in the current edition of the Manual of Military Law, Part I (57) Chapter 1, paragraphs 10–12.

A subject related to martial law but distinct from it is the use of the military to aid the civil power in any emergency, for example a riot, a strike, a flood or an earthquake. A historical account of this subject is in Clode I (30) Volume II, Chapter 17 and Notes GG and HH and Illustrations 98–105, and the current law, which is largely governed by statute, is stated in Section 6 of Part II of the Manual of Military Law (58) where references to the relevant authorities and statutes will be found.

TOPICS FOR FURTHER INVESTIGATION. An up-to-date and comprehensive history of military and martial law is lacking and would be of value. Apart from this, however, the subject has been well worked over and it is not easy to suggest fruitful topics for further research. Records of military cases before the Court of the Constable and Marshal are scanty, doubtless because of the fact that much of the work occurred during campaigns overseas, but research in the Public Record Office might bring to light material which would repay study. The development of the functions and responsibilities of the judge advocate could be studied in more detail than by Stuart-Smith (78) by reference to the original records of proceedings since the seventeenth century. Military and naval punishments are also an interesting field of study; there is some account of them in many of the books already cited, notably in Grose (45) and Walton (86), and although Scott-Cleaver's *Under the Lash* (74) is a popular treatment of the subject rather than a serious work of scholarship, it provides information as to corporal punishment which would suggest lines for more scholarly investigation and treatment. The history of martial law could be studied from the standpoint of the contrast between British and United States practice; Clode II (31) enters into this its supplements (60). There is scope for detailed study of the development of the concept of war crimes and crimes against humanity and of the trials of war criminals. This would involve consideration of what are the limits of belligerent and prisoner of war status—does it extend, for example, to the numerous varieties of partisans—and such topics as the extent to which accused persons can rely upon the defence of superior orders. There is already a considerable literature, both of reports of cases and of juristic study, on these topics, but strictly they constitute a branch of international law and therefore lie outside the scope of this chapter.

The present writer knows of work on military law being done at the present time in King's College in the University of London (Mr. G. D. Kinley), the University of Sussex (Colonel G. I. A. D. Draper) and the University of Oxford.

BIBLIOGRAPHY

USEFUL LIBRARIES

1. *Ministry of Defence Library (Central and Army).*
2. *Naval Library.*
3. *Public Record Office Library.*
4. *British Museum Library.*
5. *Judge Advocate General's Library.*
6. *Middle Temple Library.*

BIBLIOGRAPHICAL VOLUMES

(The Indexes in the Public Record Office Library mentioned below are not listed here.)

7. Albion. *Naval and Maritime History: an annotated bibliography.* (Manson Institute of American Maritime History and the Manson Historical Association, Mystic, Connecticut, 3rd edit. 1963.)
8. Cockle. *Bibliography of English Military Books to 1642.* (London 1900.)
9. Davies. *Bibliography of British History, Stuart Period.* (Oxford 1928.) Section 2 contains title "Discipline," and Section 3 contains titles "Administration and Policy" and "Maritime Law."
10. Pollard and Redgrave. *Short Title Catalogue.* (London, the Bibliographical Society 1950). An annotated list of all books printed in England up to 1640, stating where copies can be found; many are in American libraries and some have been microfilmed. A number are of military legal interest.
11. *Thomasson Tracts,* a Catalogue of the Pamphlets, Books, Newspapers and Mss. as to the Civil War, the Commonwealth and the Restoration, collected by G. T. Thomasson 1640–1661 (London, 2 vols. 1908). The collection itself is in the British Museum Library; see (81). In Vol. 2 of the catalogue there is an index with titles such as "Marshal's Court."
12. *Annual Survey of Commonwealth Law,* ed. H. W. R. Wade and Miss B. Lillywhite (London, Butterworths). 1st volume covering 1965 appeared late in 1966. This publication is more than bibliographical in content; it contains references to current legal literature

including articles in periodicals. Prominence chiefly given to material from outside the United Kingdom.

ORIGINAL RECORDS

Most of the original documents, including court-martial proceedings, court-martial books, and order books, are in the Public Record Office Library (3), to which they have been transferred from the War Office, the Admiralty, the Judge Advocate General's Office, etc. Consult the specialist catalogues, e.g. *Guide to the War Office and other military records in the P.R.O.* vol. 53 of P.R.O. lists and indexes (1931), brought up to date by *Guide to the Contents of the P.R.O.,* vol. 2, title "War Office" (1963); there are sub-headings such as "Courts-martial," "Judge Advocate General," "Law, military" and "Punishment." Some papers of military interest are however classified under the headings "State Paper Office," "Home Office" and "Colonial Office." Some modern records are still in the custody of the Ministry of Defence and the Judge Advocate General; the Librarian to the former and the registrar to the latter will advise students as to how access can be arranged: see (1) and (5).

PRINTED SOURCES OTHER THAN PERIODICALS AND TEXT-BOOKS

13. *Acts of Parliament.* These were printed up to 1865 in the Statutes at Large. Since then they have been printed both by H.M.S.O. and as part of the Law Reports. Subordinate legislation (e.g., Rules of Procedure) is issued by H.M.S.O.
14. *Articles of War.* Most of the ancient codes are translated in Grose (45) who states where the originals can be found. The Ministry of Defence Library has original Articles from the 17th century; so also the Naval Library: (1) and (2).
15. *Commissions.* Some of these are in Rymer (71), Walton (86) and Clode I (30) below.
16. *Court-martial proceedings (printed).* Considerable collections of these, printed as books or pamphlets, are in the Ministry of Defence Library (1) and the Naval Library (2).
17. *Reports of Royal Commissions, Committees of Inquiry, etc.* These are in the Ministry of Defence and Naval Libraries (1) and (2) and the Judge Advocate General's Library (5) has a few of them.
    a) *Royal Commission on Corporal Punishment in the Army and Navy 1835–1836.*
    b) *Royal Commission on Courts-Martial and Punishments for Military Offences 1868–1869* (H.M.S.O. 21421 and 21421 (2)).
    c) *Select Committee on the Mutiny Acts 1878* (H.M.S.O.).
    d) *Committee of Inquiry into Military Courts-Martial* (the Darling Committee) 1919 (H.M.S.O. Cmd. 428 of 1919).
    e) *Committee of Inquiry into Army and Air Force Courts-*

Martial (the Oliver Committee) 1938 (H.M.S.O. Cmd. 6200 of 1938).

f) *Report of Inter-Departmental Committee to consider the Report of the Oliver Committee* (the McGeagh Committee) 1939 (H.M.S.O.).

g) *Committee of Inquiry into Army and Air Force Courts-Martial* (the Lewis Committee) 1946 (W.O. Paper 29542 of 1948).

h) *Report of Inter-Departmental Committee to consider the Report of the Lewis Committee* (the Napier Committee) 1948 (W.O. Paper No. 30678 of 1948).

i) *House of Commons Select Committee on the Army and Air Force Acts;* 4 Reports, with Evidence (H. C. Papers Nos. 244 and 331 of 1952, 289 of 1953 and 223 of 1954).

j) *Committee of Inquiry into the Administration of Justice under the Naval Discipline Acts,* 1st and 2nd Reports (the Pilcher Committee) H.M.S.O. Cmd. 7384 of 1948.

PERIODICALS

18. *Military Law and Law of War Review,* ed. Bosly, being the Journal of the International Society for Military Law and the Law of War (Palais de Justice, Brussels). This appears twice a year and articles are printed in English, French and sometimes in other languages. Historical articles are not infrequent: see, e.g. the Spring 1968 issue.

19. *Journal of the Society for Army Historical Research,* from 1921: Complete set in Ministry of Defence Library. See indexes to vols. 1–12, 13–38, and each subsequent volume. The following articles are of interest:

   Articles of War, in vols. 4 and 5.
   Courts-Martial, in vols. 3, 4, 6, 7, 8.
   Military Discipline 1264, in vol. 8.
   Material for Military History in the Reports of the Historical Mss. Commission, in vol. 21.
   Punishments, numerous articles.

20. *Law Quarterly Review,* ed. A. L. Goodhart (London, Stevens and Sons). Has occasionally had an article on military or martial law: e.g. (47) first appeared in the L.Q.R. And the issue for October 1969 contains an article by Stuart Smith entitled "Military Law: Its History, Administration and Practice."

21. *Cambridge Law Journal* (Cambridge). The same comment applies as to the *L.Q.R.*

22. *English Historical Review* (London). Again the same comment applies.

23. *Transactions of the Royal Historical Society* (London). Again the same comment applies.

PRINTED BOOKS (with known locations of copies in London):

24. *Abridgment of the English Military Discipline* (London, 1686). See Appendix on Articles of War (Ministry of Defence Library).

25. *Admiralty Memorandum on Naval Courts-Martial Procedure* (London, H.M.S.O. 1958.) Contains a short historical introduction. (Naval Library.)

26. Adye. *Treatise on Courts-Martial* (4th edit., London, 1796). Adye was Judge Advocate for the Army in North America (Ministry of Defence Library).

27. *Black Book of the Admiralty* (fifteenth century): reproduced in Nicholas (No. 62 below); see also No. 83 below. (Naval Library).

28. Blackburn, Mr. Justice. *Charge to the Grand Jury in R. v. Eyre* (London 1868). (Middle Temple Library.)

29. Brook. *English Naval Forces 1199–1272* (undated). (Naval Library).

30. Clode. *Military Forces of the Crown* (2 vols., London, 1868–9). (Ministry of Defence and Judge Advocate General's Libraries).

31. Clode. *Military and Martial Law* (London, 1872). (Ministry of Defence and Judge Advocate General's Libraries).

32. Cockburn, Chief Justice. *Charge to the Grand Jury in R. v. Nelson and Brand* (London, 1867). (Middle Temple Library).

33. Clowes. *History of the Royal Navy* (7 vols., London, 1897–1903). (Naval Library).

34. Cruickshank. *Elizabeth's Army* (2nd edit., Oxford, 1966). See Chapter 10 on Discipline (Ministry of Defence Library).

35. D'Aguiler. *Courts-Martial* (ed. by Endle, Dublin, 1850). (Ministry of Defence Library).

36. *Descriptions of Courts-Martial and Articles of War in several European Countries to 1586 and a Bibliography 1532–1746* (18th century, in ms.). (Public Record Office, W. O. Records 93/6).

37. Dicey. *Law of the Constitution* (1st edit. London, 1885; many subsequent editions). (In all legal libraries).

38. Digges. *Stratioticos* (London, 1579; 2nd edit. 1590). Has a section on military laws. 2nd edit. contains Leicester's "Articles of War for the Low Countries." (S.T.C. 6848).

39. Finlason. *Treatise upon Martial Law* (London, 1866). (Ministry of Defence Library).

40. Finlason. *Commentaries upon Martial Law* (London 1867). Deals with the cases arising from the Jamaica rebellion of 1865; see Nos. 28 and 32 above). (Ministry of Defence Library and Judge Advocate General's Library).

41. Firth. *Cromwell's Army*. London: University Paperbacks, 1962. See Chapter 12 on Discipline. (Ministry of Defence Library).

42. Firth and Rait. *Acts and Ordinances of the Interregnum 1642–1660* (3 vols., H.M.S.O., London, 1911).

43. Gardiner. *The Royal Oak Courts-Martial* (London, 1965). (Naval Library).

44. Garrard and Hitchcock. *Arte of Warre* (London, 1591). (S.T.C. 11625).

45. Grose. *Military Antiquities* (2 vols., London, 1788). Vol. 2 contains the material on law and military discipline. (Ministry of Defence Library).
46. Hannay. *Naval Courts-Martial* (London, 1915). (Naval Library).
47. Holdsworth. *Essays on Law and History* (ed. Goodhart, Oxford 1946). The first essay is on Martial Law Historically Considered. (Middle Temple Library).
48. Holdsworth. *History of English Law,* vol. 1 (7th Edition, London, 1956). Contains material on the Court of the Constable and Marshal, the Court of Admiralty, the Laws of Oleron, and the Black Book of the Admiralty. (In all legal libraries.)
49. Hough. *Precedents in Military Law and the Practice of Courts-Martial* (London, 1855). (This and several similar books by Hough are in the Ministry of Defence Library).
50. Keen. *The Laws of War in the Late Middle Ages* (London, 1965). Concerned with the laws of arms which governed disputes arising out of war, such as ransom and spoil, and not with military discipline. Contains a useful bibliography.
51. Kennedy. *Proceedings of General Courts-Martial* (Bombay, 1824). (Ministry of Defence Library).
52. Leicester. *Brief Report of the Military Service in the Low Countries* (London, 1587). (S.T.C. 7285).
53. Lewis. *The Navy of Britain* (London, 1948). See Part 5. (Naval Library).
54. McArthur. *Naval and Military Courts-Martial* (2 vols., 3rd edit., London, 1806). (Naval Library).
55. Maltby. *Treatise on Courts-Martial* (Boston, 1813). Gives the U. S. Articles of War (Ministry of Defence Library).
56. *Manual of Air Force Law* (1st edit. H.M.S.O., London, 1921; 4th edit. 1964 in 3 vols.). (Judge Advocate General's and most legal libraries.)
57. *Manual of Military Law* (1st edit. H.M.S.O., London, 1884; 11th edit. containing Part I only. 1965). (In most legal libraries.)
58. *Manual of Military Law Part II* (Issued in sections, H.M.S.O., London, 1953 onwards). (Ministry of Defence and Judge Advocate General's Libraries). There is also a Part III to the Manual (1958) which deals with International Law.
59. Markham. *Five Decades of Epistles of Warre* (London, 1622). See III 7 and 8. (Ministry of Defence Library).
60. *N.A.T.O. Status of Forces Agreement* (H.M.S.O., London, Cmd. 9363, 1955) and Supplementary Agreement on Forces stationed in the Federal Republic of Germany (H.M.S.O., London, Cmnd. 852, 1959).
61. Nicholas. *History of the Battle of Agincourt* (London, 1827). See Appendix VIII as to Articles of War for the Campaign, from the originals in the Library of the College of Heralds and in the British Museum. (Ministry of Defence Library).
62. Nicholas. *History of the Royal Navy* (2 vols., London, 1847). See

Volume I Chapter 4, Volume II Chapter 3, and Appendices 3 and 4 as to legal and disciplinary matters, including the *Black Book of the Admiralty*. (Naval Library).

63. Oman. *Wellington's Army*. (New York and London, 1915). Chapter 14 deals with punishments. (Ministry of Defence Library).

64. Oppenheim. *History of the Administration of the Royal Navy* (London, 1896; reprinted 1961). (Naval Library).

65. *Parliamentary History of England up to 1661* (in many volumes, 2nd edit., London, 1762). Sometimes cited as "Old Parliamentary History." Detailed accounts of the proceedings (Ministry of Defence Library).

66. *Parliamentary Papers* (1815 onwards). Reports and returns made to Parliament from time to time: e.g., returns from regiments as to cases of flogging, and individual notorious cases. (Ministry of Defence Library).

67. Phillips. *Discourses of the Offices of Lord High Steward Constable and Marshal of England, as well Judicial as Historical* (17th century, in ms.). Deals with the Court of the Constable and Marshal, and records cases. (Public Record Office, W.O. Records 93/5).

68. Rich. *Pathway to Military Practice* (London, 1587). Deals with discipline and Articles of War (S.T.C. 20995).

69. Robinson. *The British Fleet* (2nd edit., London, 1896). Part II deals with administration, including discipline. (Naval Library).

70. Rushworth. *Historical Collections* (8 vols., London, 1721 onwards). Records of Parliamentary proceedings 1618–1648. (Ministry of Defence Library).

71. Rymer. *Foedera* (20 vols., London, 1704–1735; Abridgment in English by Hardy, 2 vols., London 1869–1873). Reproductions of ancient documents, e.g., Commission to a Commander-in-Chief. (Middle Temple Library).

72. *Sackville, The Trial of Lord George*. (London, 1760). (Ministry of Defence Library).

73. Scott. *Excellence of the British Military Code* (London, 1811). Deals with recent cases (Ministry of Defence Library).

74. Scott-Cleaver. *Under the Lash: a history of corporal punishment in the British armed forces*. (London, 1954). A popular work, but contains useful references to sources. (Ministry of Defence Library).

75. Simes. *The Regulator: principles of military life, including courts-martial and duties of the Judge Advocate* (London, 1780). (Ministry of Defence Library).

76. Simmons. *Courts-Martial* (London, 1830; 6th edit. 1873). The direct forerunner of the Manual of Military Law. (Ministry of Defence Library).

77. Speed. *History of Great Britain* (2nd edit., London, 1623). Cited in Grose (No. 45 above) and elsewhere. (Ministry of Defence Library).

77a. Squibb. *The High Court of Chivalry*. London: Oxford University Press, 1959. (Ministry of Defence Library.)

78. Stuart-Smith. *Without Partiality Favour or Affection* (Brussels, 1963,

reprinted from the Review of Military Law and the Law of War). An account of the history and functions of the judge advocate. (Judge Advocate General's Library).

79. Styward. *Pathway to Martial Discipline* (London, 1581–1585). Includes a treatment of the duties of officers and military discipline. (S.T.C. 23413–4–5).

80. Sutcliffe. *Practice Proceedings and Laws of Armes* (London, 1593). Chapter 21 contains a code of laws for an army, and describes the duties of the Judge Marshal and others. (Ministry of Defence Library.)

81. *Thomasson Tracts*: Pamphlets, newspapers and mss. as to the civil war and the Commonwealth 1640–1661. (British Museum Library). (See also No. 11 above).

82. Thring. *Criminal Law of the Navy.* (London, 1861: 2nd edit. 1877). (Naval Library).

83. Twiss. *The Black Book of the Admiralty* (4 volumes, London, 1871–1876). An elaborate edition of the Black Book, with extensive commentaries. (British Museum Library).

84. Turner. *Pallas Armata: military essays on the art of war* (London, 1683). Describes Articles of War and the functions of the various kinds of courts-martial and their officials; an extensive section deals with punishments. (Ministry of Defence Library).

85. Tytler. *Military Law and the Practice of Courts-Martial* (London, 1st edit. 1799). (Ministry of Defence Library).

86. Walton. *History of the British Standing Army 1660–1700.* (London, 1894). Valuable for the large number of documents reproduced from contemporary records. (Ministry of Defence Library).

87. Wiener, Frederick Bernays. *Civilians under Military Justice: the British practice since 1689, especially in North America.* Chicago: University of Chicago Press, 1967.